TWENTIETH-CENTURY EUROPEAN HISTORY

WM. LAIRD KLEINE-AHLBRANDT
Purdue University

WEST PUBLISHING COMPANY

Saint Paul   New York   Los Angeles   San Francisco

Copyediting by Patricia Lewis

Text design by John Rokusek/Rokusek Design

Cover design by Pollock Design Group

Composition by Parkwood Composition

Art by Alice Thiede at Carto-Graphics

Index by Sandi Schroeder at Schroeder Indexing Services

Cover image by Ferdinand Leger, *The Game of Cards*. Collection: State Museum, Kröller-Müller, Otterlo, The Netherlands.

Production, prepress, printing, and binding by West Publishing Company

West's commitment to the environment

In 1906, West Publishing Company began recycling materials left over from the production of books. This began a tradition of efficient and responsible use of resources. Today, up to 95 percent of our legal books and 70 percent of our college texts are printed on recycled, acid-free stock. West also recycles nearly 22 million pounds of scrap paper annually—the equivalent of 181,717 trees. Since the 1960s, West has devised ways to capture and recycle waste inks, solvents, oils, and vapors created in the printing process. We also recycle plastics of all kinds, wood, glass, corrugated cardboard, and batteries, and have eliminated the use of styrofoam book packaging. We at West are proud of the longevity and the scope of our commitment to our environment.

Photo credits follow the index.

00 99 98 97 96 95 94 93   8 7 6 5 4 3 2 1 0

Library of Congress Cataloging-in-Publication Data

Kleine-Ahlbrandt, W. Laird (William Laird)
    Twentieth-century European history / W. Laird Kleine-Ahlbrandt.
        p.   cm.
    Includes index.
    ISBN 0-314-00006-2
    1. Europe—History—20th century.   I. Title.
    D424.K53   1992
    940.5—dc20
                                                    92-4517
                                                    CIP

In loving memory of my parents

Ernst Henry Louis Kleine, 1896–1968

and

Emma Louise Mithoefer, 1897–1987

That even the weariest river
Winds somewhere safe to sea.

CONTENTS

PREFACE

I first went to Europe on the *Liberté*, an oceanliner that the French had received as war reparations from the Germans. It crossed the Atlantic in eight days. I saw the outline of the continent through a blue-gray fog early on the morning of our landing and it made me think of the millions of Europeans who had looked back at that shoreline as they departed for America. One of the emigrés was my grandfather, who left to escape service in the Prussian army. His decision to dodge the draft proved to be a wise one, but later it seems that he had forgotten his reasons for leaving, since he incessantly bragged about how great things were in the old country.

At least three-quarters of American citizens can claim European ancestry. However, direct family ties are only part of the picture. Eurocentrism is not simply a matter of family, but of historical influence as well. Few Americans have been unaffected by what Europeans thought, what they created, how they cooked their food, constructed their buildings, ran their factories, spoke their languages, cured their sick, worshipped their God, and planned their future. How and against whom Europeans went to war also profoundly affected the world. Twice in the twentieth century European rivalries triggered world conflicts so suicidal and wasteful that eventual ruin and eclipse seemed certain. On the other hand, European history is also a story of endless recuperation. Positively and negatively, no other continent has had such a persistent, pervasive impact on the world, especially during our century.

Researching and trying to explain the main forces and themes in modern European history would have been infinitely more difficult had I not had the advice and support of others. I would like to sincerely thank those who have given me the benefit of their specialized knowledge and expertise:

L. Margaret Barnett	University of Southern Mississippi
Jon Bridgman	University of Washington
Robert Cole	Utah State University
Lawrence E. Daxton	University of Southern Colorado
Charles F. Delzell	Vanderbilt University
Gordon D. Drummond	University of Oklahoma
Keith Eubank	Queens College
Cornelius Gispen	University of Mississippi
Hans Heilbronner	University of New Hampshire
David W. Hendon	Baylor University
William Hoisington	University of Illinois at Chicago
J. Kim Munholland	University of Minnesota
Edward Homze	University of Nebraska
Dan L. LeMahieu	Lake Forest College
Stanley G. Payne	University of Wisconsin at Madison
Howard M. Sachar	George Washington University
Jose M. Sanchez	Saint Louis University
Marshall S. Shatz	University of Massachusetts at Boston

Donald E. Shepardson   University of Northern Iowa
Donald Schilling   Denison University
Wolfgang T. Schlauch   Eastern Illinois University
Hans A. Schmitt   University of Virginia
Joanne Schneider   Rhode Island College
Gerard Silberstein   University of Kentucky
Judith F. Stone   Western Michigan University
George Strong   College of William and Mary
James F. Tent   University of Alabama at Birmingham
John B. Wilson   DePauw University

My gratitude also extends to those colleagues at Purdue who read parts of the manuscript and made recommendations, which I eagerly followed: William Buffington, the post-Stalinist Soviet Union; Randy Roberts, the impact of sports in society; Lois Magner, the development of medicine; Gunther Rothenberg, military affairs; Donald Paarlberg, the agricultural practices of the Common Market; Robert McDaniel, Near Eastern affairs; Richard Haywood, Soviet affairs; Joseph Haberer, the Holocaust; and Gordon Mork, the Nazi period. Special thanks as well to Stéphanie Kleine-Ahlbrandt for help on the social policy of the Treaty of Rome, Marc Cornu on French society, and Sheila Hégy Swanson on feminism and cultural affairs. In matters of women's rights and writing style, Sheila never met a passive voice she didn't dislike. I would also like to gratefully acknowledge those who have provided me with secretarial and other technical assistance: Judy McHenry, Julie Mántica, Cornelia Bodde, Eleanor Gurns, and Joyce Good.

I scarcely can find enough praise for the staff at West Educational Publishing. I would especially like to thank Mary Schiller, my first project editor; Diane Colwyn, the developmental editor; and Laura Evans, a very patient and understanding production editor. I appreciate the maps created by Alice Thiede. Above all I would like to extend my great appreciation to Robert Jucha, who oversaw the entire project. Bob's interest, support, and friendship were invaluable. Lastly, I would like to pay tribute to Maurice Baumont, member of the *Institut de France* and my professor at the University of Geneva. Baumont's *La faillite de la paix* is still a classic of historical synthesis.

Wm. Laird Kleine-Ahlbrandt

PART ONE

THE COLLAPSE OF THE OLD ORDER, 1914–1919

CHAPTER 1

THE GREAT WAR, 1914–1916

Now, God be thanked Who has matched us with His hour,
And caught our youth, and wakened us from sleeping,
With hand made sure, clear eye, and sharpened power,
To turn, as swimmers into cleanness leaping,
Glad from a world grown old and cold and weary,
Leave the sick hearts that honour could not move,
And half-men, and their dirty songs and dreary,
And all the little emptiness of love![1]

PREFACE   While their governments prepared for war, many Europeans believed that war had become obsolete, that the use of military force was so nonproductive it was no longer a viable means of resolving disputes. Such blissful assumptions vanished in the crisis of 1914, however. No state that participated in the orgy of exaltation that became World War I believed that it was acting out of any other motive than self-defense. Yet none of those Europeans who shouted so freely "on to Berlin," "on to Paris," or any other appropriate slogan had the slightest idea of the nature of modern war. Few could imagine how it would affect their economic, political, and social systems or their individual lives and attitudes. In the first two and a half years of the conflict, they began to find out. To stay in the war, much less defeat the common enemy, the nations of Europe had to undergo a massive transformation, changing the relationships that had heretofore existed between governments and their citizens. God might still march on the side of the strongest battalions, but now that side also had to have the biggest factories and the firmest commitment to fight to the finish.

Nationalism, a potent force since the French Revolution, reached its height in the twentieth century. Touching all classes and intellects, it prompted nations to push their power to more suicidal lengths than ever before. The call of nationalism outweighed any loyalty to class or family. Nationalism generated the cold enthusiasm needed to fight a war of many years. It bound people together in one historical experience and mission, infusing them with a special sense of destiny, spirit, and dreadful energy.

THE MUTUAL BUTCHERY OF CIVILIZED NATIONS

The Drift toward War

A Europe of Armed Camps. The Germans wanted to preserve the advantageous position they had achieved after their impressive victory over the French in the Franco-Prussian War of 1870–1871. In the Treaty of Frankfurt, they demanded that France hand over most of Lorraine and practically all of Alsace. Otto von Bismarck, the German chancellor, was convinced that this buffer along the Rhine was necessary to protect his country against a future French attack. But taking the sacred soil of an enemy only made a war of revenge more likely. Bismarck, therefore, resorted to diplomacy to deprive France of allies and eventually succeeded in linking Germany to most of the major powers of Europe. The Dual Alliance with Austria (1879) was expanded to a Triple Alliance by including Italy (1882). Germany also established ties with Russia in the League of the Three Emperors (1873) and the Reinsurance Treaty (1887). Over time, however, only the alliance with Austria would prove durable. Even before he retired in 1890, Bismarck realized that his alliance system had encouraged the very danger it was designed to prevent.

The French could no longer be isolated. Recovering from the 1870 defeat, France successfully lured Russia away from its association with Berlin. The Franco-Russian Alliance of 1894 marked an important realignment in European politics. Each country promised to support the other if either were attacked by any country of the Triple Alliance. Furthermore, if any Triple Alliance member were to mobilize, France and Russia would also mobilize and move their forces as close to the enemy frontiers as possible. This provision made mobilization tantamount to a declaration of war. As relations between Russia and Austria were particularly strained in the Balkans, any crisis there could trigger a clash between France and Germany.

In 1904, the French alliance with Russia was followed by the Entente Cordiale with Great Britain. The British subsequently decided to resolve their differences with Russia. The Anglo-Russian Entente, signed in 1907, was not a formal alliance, but it became as politically significant as the agreement with France. The Triple Entente and the Triple Alliance thus divided Europe into two great power blocs. Such commitments did not in themselves cause World War I, but they did make containing the war more difficult.

The British decision to abandon "splendid isolation" and seek an association with a continental power was prompted by Germany's intention to create a navy to match its already impressive army. This new interest in naval affairs was part of a larger policy called *Weltpolitik*, or the intention to extend German power throughout the world. In this goal, the Germans were influenced by the doctrine of Captain Alfred Thayer Mahan of the American Naval War College, who argued that control of the seas with big capital ships was decisive in determining the outcome of war. Kaiser Wilhelm II even ordered that Mahan's *The Influence of Seapower on History* be translated into German and placed in every ship's wardroom. Specifically, the Germans hoped to claim their "place in the sun" at British expense.

The British moved to meet the German naval threat. In 1902, they signed an agreement with Japan that enabled them to reduce their naval strength in the Far East. Two years later, on 8 April 1904, they concluded the Entente Cordiale, which resolved their differences with France throughout the world. As a result, they were able to bring more of their widely dispersed naval squadrons back to home waters. The British also began to construct a superbattleship, the H.M.S. *Dreadnought*, which boasted a top speed of twenty-one knots and ten twelve-inch guns with a range of 14,000 yards. By rushing this ship to completion in 1905, the British hoped to send a warning to the Germans. The Germans, however, responded by building their own navy of dreadnoughts. Soon, other naval powers were also augmenting their flotillas. The arms race did not stop with navies. The growing militarism led to a general expansion of armies and weapons. Even smaller countries felt compelled to build appropriate war machines.

In 1908, a crisis broke out in the Balkans, prompted by the Austrian annexation of Bosnia. This challenge to the current balance of power poisoned relations between Austria and Russia and between Austria and Serbia, which also had designs on the territory. Although alarmed by Austria's aggressive policy, the Germans believed they had no choice but to support their ally unconditionally. This interpretation of Germany's obligations under the Dual Alliance was fateful. By supporting Austria in the Balkan adventure, Berlin weakened its control over events in Eastern Europe and destroyed the defensive character of the agreement. The Germans had turned the Dual Alliance into an instrument of Weltpolitik. In 1909, the Austrian chief of staff, Baron Franz Conrad von Hötzendorf asked his German counterpart, Count Helmuth von Moltke, what military support Austria could count on during a future crisis. Conrad von Hötzendorf specifically asked what Germany would do in the event that Austria attacked Serbia, Russia went to war with Austria, and France supported Russia. Moltke replied that Russian mobilization would mean German mobilization, German mobilization would mean French mobilization, and French mobilization would mean general war. Present-day Europe, Moltke added, was so intertwined with mutual agreements, ententes, and alliances that scarcely any of the Great Powers could draw its sword without creating an obligation for all European powers to attack some other European power. Moltke also made it clear that, in such a war, Germany would hurl the main body of its forces against France.

The German military commitment to Austria was now clear: the war would begin with an Austrian attack on Serbia and lead inevitably to the German invasion of France. But the Germans hoped to avoid fighting a long war because they feared that prolonged hostilities would raise the specter of revolution and endanger their social and political system. The German High Command, therefore, had developed a military strategy that the planners unrealistically believed could win a war with a single, predetermined maneuver. This scheme, prepared under the direction of Count Alfred von Schlieffen, called for the initial blow to be directed against France: in a vast wheeling movement, the German army would proceed through Luxembourg, Belgium, and the Dutch province of Limburg toward the plains of northern France. Schlieffen had calculated everything in minute detail and expected his army to advance with the crispness of troops on a drill field. Four weeks after mobilization, the Germans would control Artois and Picardy; two weeks later, they would have circled Paris and pushed the French army back to the Vosges Mountains where it would be crushed between the two mighty jaws of the German right and left wings. With France out of the way, defeating Russia would not be difficult. The planners realized that violating Belgian neutrality could lead to the intervention of Britain, but they believed that the German attack would proceed so quickly that even if the British managed to send an expeditionary force to help the French, it would have no effect on the outcome.

French military planning was influenced by a belief that *"Victoire c'est la volonté"* (Victory is the will to conquer). The psychology of the maximal offensive (*attaque à l'outrance*) became the spirit of Plan XVII, the French High Command's operational directive for a concerted drive into Lorraine and Alsace. This offensive would begin immediately after war with Germany was declared. Military thinkers, like Ferdinand Foch, a professor in the French War College, appreciated the importance of firepower and superior weaponry, but such realism frequently got lost in discussions about how to develop a proper esprit de corps.

On 20 May 1914, Moltke told Gottlieb von Jagow, the secretary of state for foreign affairs, that in two to three years Germany's enemies would have such military power that "he did not know how he could deal with it." He suggested that "there was no alternative but to fight a preventative war so as to beat the enemy while we could still emerge fairly well from the struggle." German policy, Moltke concluded, should "be geared to bringing about an early war."[2] Von Jagow was not opposed on principle to preventative war, but he questioned the timing. He did not believe the kaiser would fight unless "forced to do so by our enemies." The act that would catalyze this sense of urgency came sooner than expected.

A Friendly Visit to Sarajevo. Archduke Franz Ferdinand visited the Bosnian city of Sarajevo on 28 June 1914. It was Saint Vitus Day, a day the Serbs had celebrated as a national holiday since 1389. The official presence of the heir to the Austrian throne on such alien territory at that time was provocative, but the stubborn archduke insisted that his official military inspection tour take place as planned. He based his decision in part on a desire to see his wife Sophie accorded the respect he considered proper. Although a countess, Sophie Chotek was not of royal birth, and the Viennese court regarded her as a commoner. Franz Ferdinand had wed her morganatically, an arrangement that would prevent their children from acceding to the throne. In Bosnia, however, as the wife of the inspector-general, she would be treated with esteem. To ward off trouble, Franz Ferdinand wore a gold necklace containing seven religious medals. His wife brought with her an appropriate assortment of saintly relics.

The imperial couple arrived in town at mid-morning and proceeded to the city hall in a six-car motorcade. As the cars passed along the Quai Appel, somebody tossed a hand grenade at the visitors. The bomb hit the folded roof of the archduke's touring car, bounced into the street, and exploded under the following car, wounding two officers of the royal cortege and some spectators on the sidewalk. Unscathed, Franz Ferdinand arrived at the town hall in a rage and interrupted the lord mayor's welcoming speech: "Herr Burgermeister, what is the good of your speeches? I come to Sarajevo on a friendly visit and somebody throws a bomb at me. This is outrageous."[3] But the archduke quickly regained his composure and afterwards even quipped that the would-be assassin would probably be decorated with the Austrian order of merit. Franz Ferdinand realized that even his own people did not like him.

The attack forced some modifications in the day's schedule, but no one informed the chauffeurs of the two lead cars who turned into the Franz Josef Strasse toward the center of town instead of returning to the station along the Quai Appel. The driver of the archduke's car instinctively followed but, told of his error, stopped and was preparing to back up when a gunman stepped from the crowd

Franz-Ferdinand and his wife Sophie leave the Sarajevo City Hall for their last ride. On their way to the local hospital to visit the victims of an earlier bomb attack they were both shot dead by Gavrilo Princip.

and fired point-blank at the royal couple. The bullets struck the duchess on the right side and the archduke in the neck, severing his jugular vein. Within half an hour, both husband and wife were dead.

The assassin was a nineteen-year-old Bosnian student named Gavrilo Princip, who hoped that Franz Ferdinand's death would hasten the day of freedom for the Bosnian people. He had also intended to kill General Potiorek, the military governor of Bosnia, but had missed, hitting the duchess instead. Princip was one of six terrorists who had come to Sarajevo to kill the archduke. The conspirators' goals were not much different from those of a whole host of other anti-Austrian, pro-Serbian groups, the most notorious of which was *Ujedinjenje ili Smrt* (Freedom or Death), an organization headed by the chief of Serbian military intelligence, Colonel Dragutin Dimitrijević (nicknamed Apis, after the Egyptian bull god, because of his great physical strength). Freedom or Death had been organized in 1911 in the aftermath of the Austrian annexation of Bosnia. To further its purpose of unifying all Serbs through revolutionary action, it not only conducted its own activities in all territories inhabited by Serbs, but also helped other groups with similar aims. Thus, it became associated with Princip's Young Bosnians, supplying them with guns and bombs and helping them cross frontiers. Although Apis and Princip agreed on the basic goal of national liberation for the South Slavs, they differed considerably on what sort of political and social system should eventually follow.

Freedom or Death wanted the unification of all South Slavs under a greater Serbia, following the example of Prussia's creation of a Greater Germany. But the Young Bosnians favored only a loose South Slav federation. Whereas Princip wanted to kill the archduke for "the common good," Apis wanted him assassinated to strengthen his own political position in Serbia. In particular, he wanted to oust the Radical government of his mortal enemy Nikola Pašić. Pašić gave Freedom or Death its popular name the "Black Hand" because he viewed its members "as praetorians who were threatening the whole political system of Serbia."[4] When he had been informed that Apis's group had helped armed men cross into Bosnia, he ordered increased surveillance at the frontiers. Apis did not expect the assassination attempt at Sarajevo to succeed. Indeed, in light of his strained relations with the Serbian government, he had actually tried to convince Princip to call the whole thing off. Princip would have none of it. In the final analysis, therefore, the murder was Princip's responsibility.

Few mourned Franz Ferdinand. Considering he was heir presumptive to the Austrian throne, the funeral was modest and somewhat shabby.[5] Emperor Franz Josef had wished it so; he had never forgiven his nephew for choosing a mate of inferior rank. When informed of the assassination, Franz Josef remarked: "A higher power has restored that order I could unfortunately not maintain." There even were rumors that the archduke's enemies in Vienna had deliberately sent him to his death. Other rumors whispered of the complicity of the Magyars, or the Germans, or the Russians, or the Bolsheviks, or the Freemasons, or the Serbs. It really made little difference. The archduke's death provided the perfect excuse Austria needed for another bold move in the Balkans.

The day after the archduke's death, Baron Franz Conrad von Hötzendorf, the chief of the General Staff, told Count Leopold Berchtold, the Austro-Hungarian foreign minister, that the army should be immediately mobilized against Serbia. Conrad von Hötzendorf knew that such action was tantamount to a declaration of war, but he also recognized that any attack on Serbia was impossible unless Germany would provide protection against intervention by Russia. Berchtold was also eager to settle accounts with Serbia but feared that both the emperor and the prime minister of Hungary did not share his fervor. Nor did the German ambassador in Vienna, Count Heinrich von Tschirschky, who counseled moderation and restraint. Everything therefore depended on the attitude in Berlin.

Kaiser Wilhelm thirsted for action. On the margin of the diplomatic note from Vienna, he penciled "Let Tschirschky be good enough to drop this nonsense! The Serbs must be disposed of, *and* that right soon!"[6] Moreover, the German monarch had the unconditional support of his generals, many of whom felt that Germany would never be better prepared for hostilities. At Potsdam, on 5 July, the kaiser received a personal letter from Franz Josef who was under the influence of the Viennese war party. The Austrian emperor put full blame for the archduke's assassination on the Serbian government. Writing that his country could be secure in Eastern Europe only if Serbia were "eliminated as a political factor in the Balkans," he demanded retaliation against the criminal agitation in Belgrade.[7] The kaiser replied that the Austrians could count on Germany's full support "even should war between Austria-Hungary and Russia be unavoidable" and urged that Austria's action against Serbia "must not be delayed."[8]

The July Crisis. Wilhelm's promise of unconditional support (the so-called blank check) was adrenaline for the war hawks. The moderates in the Berlin government and foreign office also flocked to support their Supreme War Lord. But the Austrians were in no hurry. They slowly began to draft an ultimatum to Serbia that could serve as the basis for a declaration of war. In the meantime, life went on as usual. Emperor Franz Josef left Vienna to take the waters at Bad Ischl. General Conrad von Hötzendorf and the Austro-Hungarian minister of war, Alexander von Krobatin, also left on vacation. Kaiser Wilhelm was on a visit to Scandinavia. Army Quartermaster Erich von Falkenhayn, Secretary of State for the Navy Alfred von Tirpitz, and Colonel-General Moltke were away from Berlin as well. Gottlieb von Jagow, the secretary of state for foreign affairs, was on his honeymoon. Public statements were monitored to avoid rousing any suspicions. Chancellor Theobald Bethmann Hollweg ordered the Berlin press to suspend all anti-French polemics.

The Austrians needed all the time they could get. The dual nature of the Austro-Hungarian monarchy potentially doubled the time necessary to make decisions especially when these governments were not of one mind, as was the case now. Moreover, the multinational army was ill-prepared for rapid mobilization. The Hungarian premier, Count Istvan Tisza, did not fully agree to war until 14 July, and even Conrad von Hötzendorf himself had second thoughts. He said that Austria should not mobilize if it would risk fighting Italy as well as Serbia and Russia.[9] The Austrians kept the German government fully informed as they carefully drafted their ultimatum to Serbia.[10] Wilhelm was growing skittish. At the bottom of a dispatch from Vienna, he penned the words of Frederick the Great before the invasion of Silesia: "I am against all councils of war and conferences, since the more timid party always has the upper hand."[11] The Germans feared that unless they kept pressuring their ally into a solution by force, the Austrians might resolve the affair by negotiations. Bethmann Hollweg believed that any failure by Austria to force a showdown in the Balkans would lead to its elimination as a great power. War with Serbia was Austria's last chance of political rehabilitation.[12] The Germans felt they had an obligation to preserve Austria-Hungary from decline, even though the Dual Monarchy's character and internal politics made such a decline inevitable. Thus, rightly or wrongly, the Germans were convinced that a policy of force was necessary for their own security. But they had greater ambitions than maintaining the status quo. For all its bluster and bellicosity, the policy of Weltpolitik had been a failure. It had actually led to the strengthening of the very entente it was supposed to weaken (the Triple Entente of Britain, France, and Russia). A stunning coup in the Balkans would bring Bulgaria and Turkey into the Triple Alliance, strengthen German ties with Romania and Greece, and eliminate Russian influence from the area. Serbia would be isolated, and the Central Powers would have broken the vise of encirclement. Wishful thinking hardly added up to a coherent policy, but the leaders of Germany, propelled by their strong sense of moral superiority and national self-righteousness, did not feel they needed more concrete aims.

The Austrian Ultimatum. The Serbian government received Austria's demands on 23 July, immediately after the French president Raymond Poincaré and head of the government René Premier Viviani left St. Petersburg. The French leaders had been in the Russian capital for three days on a state visit, and the Austrians deliberately waited until they left "in order not to facilitate an agreement between the Dual Alliance Powers on any possible counter-action."[13] The ultimatum, written in French, listed a series of specific demands dealing with the elimination of all anti-Austrian agitation from the Serbian kingdom. Vienna demanded compliance within 48 hours—by 6 P.M. on 25 July.[14] The Entente powers received copies of the ultimatum about the same time as Serbia. Shortly afterwards, they received Germany's declaration of its official support for Austria, accompanied by a warning that "the intervention of any other Power would as a result of the various alliance obligations, bring about inestimable consequences."[15] The British, French, and Russians generally agreed that Austria was entitled to some sort of compensation[16] and tried to have the ultimatum's deadline extended so mediations could begin.

The Serbs' reply was conciliatory. They could hardly do otherwise, since none of the Entente partners, not even the Russians, was then offering much support, and the Serbs were frankly in no condition, either militarily or politically, to stand up to Austria alone. Belgrade specifically rejected only one of the demands—that Austrian officials be allowed to participate in the proceedings against the persons involved in the Sarajevo plot. They agreed to the others with slight qualification, but this was enough for Austria to charge noncompliance.[17] But the Austrians would have found any answer unacceptable, since the ultimatum was only a feint. They recalled their ambassador from Belgrade and severed diplomatic relations with Serbia. Even before they received the Serbian reply, they had already begun mobilization, anticipating its completion by 12 August, the day they would formally declare war.

The Entente powers stepped up their efforts to mediate the crisis. On 26 July, British foreign secretary, Sir Edward Grey, proposed an international conference between Britain, France, Italy, and Germany, the countries best able to cool the rising tensions. The Germans opposed the conference, fearing they would be outvoted as had happened at the conference at Algeciras, but they tried to give the impression that they were willing to restrain the Austrians. (The Germans were playing for British neutrality in case the Austro-Serbian conflict should become generalized. They would accept a European war, but feared a world war.) The Berlin government never held a full discussion of the alternatives, nor seriously considered the risks. There had been no cabinet meetings. The weak-willed kaiser and certain of his top advisers controlled all decision making. In this atmosphere, wishful thinking passed for logical analysis. The conflict could have been avoided had the Germans so desired.[18] Indeed, the kaiser himself was no longer spoiling for a showdown with the British and Russians.[19] In fact, his earlier bellicosity had been replaced by a lack of resolve. On 27 July, suspecting that Bethmann Hollweg did not keep him fully informed, Wilhelm cut short his Scandinavian jaunt and returned home. He became "persuaded that on the whole the wishes of the Danubian Monarchy are met . . . and thereby *all reason for war* falls to the ground [emphasis in original]."[20] He favored allowing Austria to occupy a part of Serbia, say, Belgrade, as a guarantee that the Serbs would keep their promises.

The kaiser's generals and ministers did not take their sovereign's about-face seriously, however. Chancellor Bethmann Hollweg and Jagow chose not to inform the Austrians that the kaiser now believed all reason for war was gone; without consulting Wilhelm, they pressured Austria into declaring war two weeks earlier than Vienna believed desirable. Consequently, the Austrians declared war on Serbia at 11 A.M. on 28 July. Bethmann Hollweg appeared more concerned with avoiding personal blame for having started a war than in avoiding war. On the one hand, he was trying to keep the war localized; on the other, he was maneuvering to put Germany in the best possible position should that fail. He did not want to give the Austrians the impression that the German government wished to hold them back.[21] He feared that a lack of encouragement for them to attack Serbia would lead to a dissolution of the Dual Alliance.

Had Germany de-escalated the crisis, Austria would have emerged with an impressive diplomatic victory, and the Dual Alliance would have been strengthened accordingly. Wilhelm II thought such gains sufficient, but his civilian and military chiefs did not; they desired the complete humiliation of Russia and the consequent disruption of the Franco-Russian alliance. If these goals could be achieved without a general war, so much the better. If they could not, then the Germans would put all the blame for the enlargement of hostilities on Russia, because if Russia were made to seem the aggressor, the neutrality of Great Britain could be ensured.

The Lamps Go Out. As soon as the Russians heard that Austria had declared war on Serbia, they ordered partial mobilization, putting their forces in the Odessa,

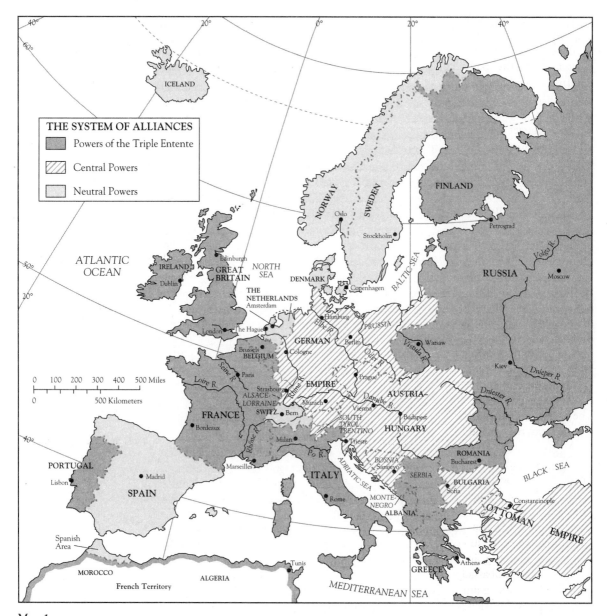

Map 1

Kiev, Moscow, and Kazan military districts on a war footing. All planning, however, had been for general mobilization, an indication of how committed many
Russians, especially those in the military, were to war. Tsar Nicholas changed the
order, only to rescind it again, after receiving a plea for moderation from Wilhelm
II. But Chief of Staff Moltke feared that Russian partial mobilization would still
put Austria-Hungary in a desperate position, forcing Germany to mobilize to give
it support. On 30 July, Moltke, without authorization from the civilian government, urged Vienna to mobilize against Russia. He already suspected that the
Russians had again ordered total mobilization, which would trigger the Franco-
Russian alliance and begin "the mutual butchery of the civilized nations of Europe."[22] The German military leaders alleged that France was preparing to attack
through Belgium along the Meuse. Though he had welcomed a war between Aus-

tria and Serbia as the best way to crush pan-Slav agitation, which threatened the existence of Austria and therefore Germany's vital interests, Chancellor Bethmann Hollweg viewed this escalation of the conflict with considerable fear. Russian mobilization and the likelihood of British intervention had pushed events beyond his control. His advice to Berchtold on 30 July to accept British mediation came too late. Although the chancellor's brinkmanship had been prompted more by a desire to reaffirm German prestige than to embark on a policy of expansionism, his motives no longer mattered. His provocative handling of the July crisis had turned policy decisions over to the military, which was counting the hours for the inevitable implementation of the Schlieffen Plan.[23]

On 1 August, Premier Viviani told German Ambassador Wilhelm von Schoen that, "France will have regard to her own interests." Schoen mulled this over for a few moments and replied, "I confess that my question is rather ingenuous. But, after all, have you not got a treaty of alliance?" "Exactly," Viviani answered.[24] At 3:30 that afternoon, the French cabinet decided to order general mobilization with General Joseph Joffre arguing convincingly that, if France delayed, it would be outstripped by German mobilization and find itself in a dangerous state of inferiority. Although the French ruling circles were not utterly opposed to war, they did not think that mobilization would automatically bring it about. A state of war, they believed, could only exist after a formal declaration. Besides, French mobilization plans did not automatically involve the invasion of another country as did the German. Also on 1 August, Friedrich von Pourtalès, the German ambassador in St. Petersburg, informed Sergei Sazonov, the Russian foreign minister, that a state of war existed between their two countries.[25] The Germans did not declare war on France until two days later. Ever the dilettante in affairs of state, the kaiser had signed the mobilization order telling the generals that they would rue the day they made him do it.

Meantime, the German army had begun the invasion of neutral Luxembourg, the first step in the direct implementation of the Schlieffen Plan, and had demanded that the Belgians allow free passage through their country. The Belgians refused and, on 4 August, a little past eight in the morning, the Germans crossed the Belgian frontier at Gemmerich. The invasion, they explained to the British, was "compelled by the duty of self-preservation."[26] The British government warned Germany to stop its invasion of Belgium by midnight or face a declaration of war. Bethmann Hollweg, in a state of considerable agitation, expressed astonishment to the British ambassador, Sir Edward Goschen, that "just for a scrap of paper, Great Britain was going to make war on a kindred nation who desired nothing better than to be friends with her."[27] British propagandists soon had great sport with the phrase "just for a scrap of paper." But the most apt words came from the usually colorless Sir Edward Grey. On the eve of the German invasion of Belgium, as he stood at a window in Whitehall watching the streetlights being lit below as dusk settled over London, he turned to his companion and said, "The lamps are going out all over Europe; we shall not see them lit again in our lifetime."[28] The Germans were not so pessimistic. Their willingness for a policy of force had stemmed from two contradictory assumptions: one group, including the kaiser and the leadership at the foreign office, believed that an Austro-Serbian war could be localized because none of the members of the Triple Entente could risk hostilities. Russia, they argued, was weak militarily and in constant need of money; France was too occupied with its domestic problems; and Britain feared both the loss of its continental markets and the danger of revolt in the empire, especially in Ireland. The other group, the generals and their allies, felt that whether the war was localized was unimportant since Germany had superior military force and infallible strategy. In any case the quicker the war could begin the better, because it would be over within several months, and Germany would gain her rightful place in the sun. Such vain hopes lay at the heart of the actions of Germany's leaders during the July crisis and prevented them from finding a more sensible solution.[29]

In the declining hours of peace, after the mobilization of Russia, an alarmed Hermann Müller, a leader of the German Socialist party, hastened to Paris to see if he could induce the French Socialists to join with their German counterparts in refusing to vote war credits. He could not. Müller was not even able to count on support from his own constituents at home. In fact, all the leading Socialist parties of Europe dutifully chose to support their own governments in the hour of crisis, dramatically repudiating the resolutions of the Second Workers' International, adopted at Stuttgart in 1907, to fight the outbreak of war by calling a general strike. The Socialist parties had further promised that, if war did occur despite everything, they would use it to rouse the people and hasten the end of capitalist class rule. During the July crisis, the great French Socialist leader Jean Jaurès called for a war against the war, but a nationalist fanatic's bullet silenced him the day before his country mobilized. Few followed his example. Socialist leaders suspected that similar entreaties would have been drowned in a surge of nationalistic hysteria. War had suddenly become fashionable, even essential, for the common good and national salvation. The pathetic death of the ideals of the Second International gave dramatic evidence that socialists would always be nationalists first, and that international working-class solidarity was just a pretty myth.

Opening Guns

The Schlieffen Plan in Action. The German regiments that crossed the Belgian frontier on 4 August 1914 were part of a total striking force of a million and a half troops—deployed in seven and a half armies—stretching from northern Belgium through Lorraine, along the Vosges Mountains to the borders of Switzerland. It was the greatest array of military might that the world had ever seen, surpassing its closest competitor, the Grand Army with which Napoleon had invaded Russia in 1812, by two and a half times.

Within a fortnight, the Germans had smashed the forts of Liège and Namur on the river Meuse and pushed the small, poorly trained and ill-equipped Belgian army back through Brussels to the defensive perimeter of Antwerp. The Germans entered the capital city on 20 August, marching through with "the pertinacity of a steamroller."[30] Nothing lay between them and the frontiers of France save an unimpressive contingent of the British Expeditionary Army at Mons. The Tommies clashed with the Germans on 23 August, standing their ground briefly until, outnumbered two to one, they were forced to withdraw. This was the first time that the British had fought in western Europe since Waterloo. The retreat so rattled the British commander, Sir John French, that he contemplated pulling his men out of the fighting and having them fall back on the Atlantic port of Le Havre.

The previous week, the Germans had also blunted a two-pronged French attack, one coming across the Lorraine frontier south of Metz, the other striking northward into the Ardennes. General Joseph Joffre, the French commander-in-chief, had erroneously believed that the Germans would strike through southern Belgium and Lorraine, not north of Namur as they had done. He also had failed to see that the Germans were using their reserves to increase their frontline strength; conse-

German troops enter Brussels on 20 August 1914. They goose-step across Place Rogier. "Like a river of steel [the army] flowed, gray and ghostlike," observed American journalist Richard Harding Davis.

quently, in many places where he had assumed local superiority, he was actually outnumbered. Plan XVII was in shambles. Pushed back to his original lines, Joffre had to redeploy his forces westward to meet the real threat on the plains of Flanders.

Moltke was confident he had won a decisive victory. The Allied armies were in retreat all along the line, and his own forces were approaching the river Somme. But Moltke was still at his headquarters in Koblenz. And communications were dreadful: telephones kept breaking down, the few radio transmitters were overused, messages had to be kept brief to the point of distortion, and delays in coding and decoding seemed endless. In fact, Moltke was in no position to know the true battle situation and had already lost operational control of his overextended army. He was not as disturbed about this as he should have been. He had patterned himself after his great uncle who had defeated the French from headquarters using the telegraph to keep informed. Although the elder Moltke's armchair generalship lost him control of parts of the battlefield, his failings were covered up and did not prove fatal. In 1914 the younger Moltke was not so lucky. On 27 August, still believing victory was near, he abandoned the Schlieffen Plan's emphasis on the strength of the right wing, which had already been weakened by transfer of troops to the Russian front and to Alsace-Lorraine to protect against a French attack, and ordered his commanders to attack all along the line to push the enemy back to the gates of Paris.

On 30 August, the commander of the First Army, General Alexander von Kluck, further altered the Schlieffen Plan by attacking eastward so as to bypass Paris on the north. Kluck felt he had no other choice if he were to maintain contact with the Second Army marching on his left, but by doing so he exposed his own right flank to attack. The elated commander of the Paris military district, General Joseph Galliéni, urged Joffre to attack before the Germans realized the danger threatening them. Logistics were crucial. The French army, unlike the German, had lateral railway lines along its line of march, making the transfer of troops and supplies through Paris from one sector to another a relatively simple matter. For the Germans it was more difficult. Their advancing armies constantly outdistanced the ability of the support services to keep up with the requisite supplies. Thanks to the enormous effort of the motor transport, the advance proceeded as far as it did, but ultimately it would have petered out.[31]

On 5 September, the French Sixth Army advanced from its base at Amiens to attack the exposed German flank. Kluck turned to meet the threat. In doing so, he created a gap of twenty-one miles between his forces and those of the Second Army on his left, allowing the British to interpose themselves between the two armies. Fearing envelopment, the Germans, on 9 September, withdrew to more defensible positions north of the river Aisne. After more than a month of continuous marching, the German soldiers were exhausted. The old modes of transportation proved inadequate to sustain a maneuver of this dimension. The vaunted Battle of the Marne proved to be a maneuver to avoid a battle.

In the east, the circumstance of war also led to the abandonment of the original plan, but with more spectacular results. The Russians mounted an offensive faster than the Germans had anticipated. Fulfilling a commitment to the French, the Russians had begun their advance within fifteen days after mobilization. On 17 August, the Vilna Army under General Pavel Rennenkampf moved west to invade East Prussia and engage the German Eighth Army. Three days later, the Warsaw Army, commanded by General Alexander Samsonov, started an advance from the south intending to pounce on the enemy's rear.

Abandoning plans to remain on the defensive in the east, Moltke transferred General Erich Ludendorff to the Eastern Front to organize an offensive. Ludendorff was to serve as the chief of staff for the titular commander General Paul von

Map 2

THE WESTERN FRONT

- **·····** Farthest German advance, September 1914
- **– – –** Winter: 1914–1918
- ──── German offensive, March–July 1918
- ──── Armistice Line
- **◄** German advances, Spring–Summer 1918
- **➤** Allied advances, Spring–Autumn 1918

Hindenburg, a retired officer whose noble ancestry was more impressive than his recent military experience.[32] On 25 August, Moltke also sent east six army corps, two from the critical right wing; this decision deprived his forces in France of the strength of almost an entire army and resulted in dangerous gaps between units.

Ludendorff, following a plan prepared by Colonel Max Hoffmann, first attacked the Warsaw Army on 26 August and, after three days of bitter fighting, cut it to pieces, killing 30,000 enemy soldiers and capturing another 92,000 along with 600 guns and herds of horses. Samsonov, separated from the main body of his army, shot himself through the head in despair. The Germans next turned on Rennenkampf and, in the Battle of the Masurian Lakes, pushed the hapless Russians back across the frontier with a loss of another 100,000 casualties. The Germans jubilantly called their twin victories the "Battle of Tannenberg" after a defeat the Slavs had inflicted on the Teutonic Knights five hundred years before.

Although the Schlieffen Plan had failed strategically—neither France nor Russia was knocked out of the war—it nevertheless was a remarkably successful military operation. In the east, the Russians would never again seriously threaten Prussia. In France, the Germans occupied the northern crescent; this area, which contained the bulk of the country's heavy industry, produced 20 percent of the country's grain, 40 percent of its coal, 90 percent of its iron ore, and 80 percent of its steel.

The Deadlock. Behind their defenses on the river Aisne, the Germans repelled all attempts to dislodge them. But nothing less than total victory would have been sufficient to protect Moltke, who was already cracking under the strain of command. Erich von Falkenhayn replaced him. The new commander continued the war of movement by trying to outflank his enemies on their left. The British and French retaliated with the same tactics. By October, both sides had reached the sea and could maneuver no further. They concentrated their efforts on fortifying their lines, which stretched across France southeast on a diagonal to the Vosges, then turned 45 degrees south to the Swiss border—a 500-mile front of trenches, sutured with barbed wire and nested with machine guns, that hardly moved more than ten miles in either direction for the next three years.

The Russians, although badly shaken during the first four months of war, still possessed a formidable army. At the end of September, they managed to offset their loss in East Prussia with a success in Galicia where they inflicted 300,000 casualties on the Austrian army and threatened to invade Silesia through Krakow. Only the arrival of four German corps from the Western Front checked their advance.

The Habsburg Empire had had a bad year. It had done poorly against Russia and even worse against its arch-rival Serbia. The Austrians had boasted they could defeat "this nation of pig-breeders" within two weeks. Instead, after three offensives, not one fighting unit remained on Serbian soil. Over half of their 400,000-man striking force was either dead, wounded, or captured. On 2 December, they had seized the enemy capital of Belgrade, but had lost it in less than a week. Only the exhaustion of the Serbs spared them further humiliation. At the end of 1914, the battle lines in the east had become stabilized. An 800-mile front extended north to south, from the Prussian marshes to the Carpathians.

Although most military commanders considered Europe the most important theater of the war, fighting did extend around the world. Japan declared war on Germany on 23 August 1914 and immediately began to collect the enemy's eastern possessions: the Marshall Islands, the Carolines, and the Shantung Peninsula. The British Dominions also saw action. New Zealand occupied Samoa, Australia forced the German garrison on New Guinea to surrender, and South Africa launched an attack into Southwest Africa. Elsewhere in Africa, the British and French seized Togoland and the Cameroons. But the splendid defense organized by the local German commander Paul von Lettow-Vorbeck frustrated a British attempt to capture East Africa with Indian troops. The Ottoman Empire joined the Central Powers at the end of October, while Britain sent troops to Mesopotamia.

On 9 September 1914, when confidence in immediate victory was especially strong, Chancellor Bethmann Hollweg issued a series of concrete war aims. These called for the complete economic and political reorganization of Europe. Germany intended to dominate Central Europe, France, Belgium, Holland, and Denmark and perhaps Italy, Sweden, and Norway. All Russian and British influence would be excluded from these areas. A permanently crippled France would become an economic vassal of Germany, while the German military would decide whether to demand the "cession of Belfort and western slopes of the Vosges," and the "cession of [a] coastal strip from Dunkirk to Boulogne." Belgium "must allow us to occupy any militarily important ports, must place her coast at our disposal in military respects, must become economically a German province." And Luxembourg "will become a German federal state" and, like the Netherlands, will be "internally dependent on the Reich." Furthermore in Africa, "a continuous Central African Colonial Empire" must be created.[33]

Already before the war, Germans had talked of establishing a Third Force in Central and Eastern Europe free from Russian, British, and American influence. All political parties, except for the Socialists, became committed to this expansionism.[34] Whether the rationalization was national security, the need to protect the monarchial system against political and social subversion, or the overblown optimism of a country that believed it was on the threshold of a great victory, these war aims were the most striking example of lust for European empire since the days of Napoleon Bonaparte.

A Year of Lost Opportunities

Neutrality in Favor of the Entente. On 4 August 1914, President Woodrow Wilson officially admonished Americans to remain neutral in both thought and deed—a declaration willingly accepted as the magic formula for nonparticipation and the continuation of normal trade and commerce. The president spared no effort to make people believe this was true. But whether Americans recognized it or not, the real question was when, and under what circumstances, they would participate.

From the outset, the British were determined to bring the United States into the war. Britain cut Germany's transatlantic cables to the United States and, in September 1914, created a Ministry of Information to present a systematically one-sided view of the war. Eventually, 500 permanent officials plus another 10,000 assistants staffed this special propaganda service. Using *Who's Who*, it compiled a 250,000-name mailing list and sent out fabrications, which had been used first at home, but now were suitably reworked for the American market. The British propagandists concocted stories about the Huns who cut off people's hands, gave poisoned candy to children, raped nuns in convents, and crucified enemy soldiers. The generally pro-British American press ran many of these items without change. Almost overnight the image of the kaiser as an upstanding grandson of Queen

Austro-Hungarian defenses on the Eastern Front, winter 1914–1915. The photo is obviously posed, but notice the absence of machine guns, barbed wire, and steel helmets—all necessary furnishings of later trench warfare. Also note the dangerously close proximity of the second to the first line of trenches.

Victoria was transformed into an image of Satan. In many cases, the propaganda pitch was superfluous. Many members of the Wilson administration were already pro-British. For example, the American ambassador in London, Walter Hines Page, was so pro-British that the British government would ask his advice on how to word its dispatches to Washington.

From the beginning, American neutrality was a sham, dictated by Wilson's love of Britain and by economics. Severe business recession marked the first two years of the Wilson administration. In 1914, there were 18,280 business failures, the highest yet recorded. Unemployment rose to 15 percent, affecting almost 6 million workers. Many factories were working at 60 percent capacity.[35] American recovery soon became dependent on European war orders, particularly British orders for munitions. The longer the stalemate lasted, the better for profits.

Though the British blockade constantly interfered with American shipping, David Lloyd George had little fear that Wilson's pro forma protests would lead to any sort of retaliation. He wrote: "The Country which is determined to remain neutral must be prepared to pocket its pride and put up with repeated irritations and infringements of its interests by the belligerents on both sides; compensating itself for these annoyances by the enhanced profits of its war-time trade."[36]

Had Wilson desired to make the British stop violating American neutral rights, he had only to threaten an embargo on exports. But he never considered taking that step. Wilson was committed to an Entente victory, although initially he did not favor direct participation. The Germans, however, could hardly permit the United States to put its entire productive capacity at the disposal of their enemies. On 4 February 1915, Berlin declared the whole area around the British Isles a war zone and warned the United States that its ships might be attacked, since the British continually used the flags of neutrals. The Germans suggested that the American government warn its citizens not to travel or send their goods on belligerent ships.

Wilson replied that he would hold Germany "strictly accountable" for the destruction of any American vessel or the killing of any Americans on the high seas. Wilson also sent a note to Britain telling it to stop using the American flag. Nevertheless, his position that the lives of Americans were sacrosanct, even if they sailed on the armed weapons carriers of Germany's enemies, was clearly provocative. But the Entente could not sit idly by waiting for Washington to leave off fence-sitting and intervene.

Attack Is the Better Part of Valor. The French were committed to the offensive by an understandable determination to push the invader off their country's soil. Joffre was confident the conflict could be decided in 1915 by returning to a war of maneuver. He had no experience with trench warfare—which heretofore the French had associated with the siege tactics developed by Vauban during the reign of Louis XIV—but had every reason to hope that a breakthrough could be achieved if enough guns and men could be assembled in one sector. When the British attacked the Germans in March 1915 near Neuve Chapelle, they had actually pushed through into open country. But inadequate reserves and hesitant leadership prevented them from fully exploiting their success. Joffre hoped to avoid these errors. His strategy was simple. He would sever the huge salient of the German lines with a dual thrust from Artois: one eastward, the other northward into Champagne.

He spent the first part of the year on preliminary thrusts, preparing for the big push in September and October. For all their efforts, however, the French did little more than dent the German lines. The losses were enormous. In the great autumn offensive, the British suffered 50,000 casualties, the French 190,000, and the Germans 140,000. Though the Allies were dying at a higher rate than their adversaries, Joffre believed victory would inevitably be theirs because the Allies had potentially more manpower than their adversaries. "I am nibbling at them," he boasted. Not all Allied commanders agreed with Joffre and Sir John French that the war had to be fought and won mainly on the Western Front. The first lord of the admiralty, Winston Churchill, and his first sea lord, John Fisher, proposed an expedition to capture the Gallipoli Peninsula. Success here, they argued, would lead to the capture of Istanbul and open a passage into the Black Sea. Then, perhaps, Russia could be supplied with sufficient armaments to enable it to relieve the pressure on the Allied armies in France.

The operation began on 19 February with a naval bombardment, which silenced the forts guarding the entrance into the straits. But failure to clear the waterway of mines led to the destruction of three battleships on 18 March, and damage to three more. The fleet commander, Rear-Admiral John de Robeck, could not wait to transfer the combat initiative to the army. On 25 April, a force of British, Australian, and French troops landed at several places on the Gallipoli Peninsula. But the troops were soon pinned down by Turkish artillery perched on the hills above the beaches. Unable to advance, they dug trenches and awaited reinforcements. But the additional levies proved insufficient to offset the Turkish advantage. A plan to cut behind the Turkish lines with a landing at Suvla Bay on 6 August also failed and prompted some to suggest the whole project should be disbanded. On 5 September, the entry of Bulgaria into the war on the side of the Central Powers presented an additional hazard.

As the weather grew colder and the likelihood of Allied success became bleaker, the British government finally gave up. Ironically, getting the troops back in the boats proved to be the most successful part of the operation. The soldiers were removed in two batches—on the nights of 19–20 December 1915 and 8–9 January 1916—without a single death. However, the venture had already cost over 200,000 lives in battle and from disease. The expedition's failure had important political repercussions. Churchill and Fisher resigned, and the reputations of Prime Minister Asquith and Minister of War Horatio Kitchener suffered irreparable damage.

Yet the Dardanelles campaign remained one of the most brilliant strategic conceptions of the entire war. Its failure had important consequences: it helped seal the fate of Russia, frustrated the formation of a great Balkan alliance against Germany, and allowed the Turks to roam freely over their empire, threatening the Suez Canal and the oil fields of Persia. The Allies eventually had to send over a million troops to the Middle East to protect these interests.

Italy Enters the War. Italy at first refused to honor its obligation to fight alongside the Central Powers, claiming that it had not been consulted about Austrian intentions to make territorial changes in the Balkans. Neutrality was popular. Aside from a handful of nationalists and monarchists and the commercial and colonial interests—which were badly divided among themselves—most of the Italian people genuinely wanted to stay out. The Socialists, with the largest bloc of seats in parliament, remained wedded to the antiwar position of the Second International and actively opposed intervention. The former Liberal prime minister, Giovanni Giolitti, saw no need to become involved since he believed that all of Italy's territorial claims would be granted as its reward for neutrality. A majority of his fellow legislators seemed to agree.

But Prime Minister Antonio Salandra implied that Italian participation could be negotiated. On 18 October 1914, he said that the government action would be influenced by "sacred egotism," meaning that Italy wanted the Austrian territory south of the Alps, plus an enhanced position along the Dalmatian coast and in the Adriatic. Foreign Minister Sidney Sonnino explained that Austria's weakening of Serbia necessitated strengthening Italy's strategic defenses. The Germans were willing to accommodate the Italians, and they tried to negotiate a deal that also included economic concessions and colonial territory from the British and French empires. But the Austrians were reluctant to part with national territory, and the discussions reached an impasse.

The British and the French were inclined to be more generous, especially on the eve of their Dardanelles expedition. In the secret Treaty of London, signed on 26 April, they gave Italy essentially all its demands: the Trentino, the South Tyrol, and the entire Istrian Peninsula to the outskirts of Fiume, including the offshore islands and the city and surrounding hinterland of Valona. Italy would also acquire the twelve Dodecanese islands in the Eastern Mediterranean and receive a share of the Ottoman Empire in the Turkish province of Adalia. A promise of "equitable" compensation recognized Italy's right to colonial spoils. The Allies would subsidize the cost of Italian armament and exclude the pope—whom the Italians believed was pro-Austrian—from participation in the peace settlement. It was quite a package. Italy declared war on Austria-Hungary on 23 May. But not until 27 August 1916 did this include Germany. Bringing Italy into the war was a great success for Entente diplomacy, but one that future British and French statesmen would have reason to regret.

A Position of Strength. By February 1915 the British Admiralty operated a network of naval monitoring stations that could receive almost every German naval signal along the English and Irish coasts. Therefore, on 5 May 1915, the British knew that the Cunard ocean liner *Lusitania*, headed toward the waters south of Kinsale Head, was going into an area where the German submarine *U20* lurked. The *Lusitania*, ostensibly a passenger ship, was really an auxiliary naval cruiser, outfitted for 12 six-inch guns. Its cargo was almost entirely contraband, including 1,248 cases of three-inch shells, 4,927 boxes of cartridges, and ten and a half tons of explosives. The Germans knew the ship was not what it pretended to be, and their Washington embassy even ran a warning in New York newspapers before the ship sailed, telling Americans not to travel on it.

As the *Lusitania* headed into Irish waters, it received the general warning issued to all ships in the area advising them to avoid headlands and steer a mid-channel course. When the Admiralty first detected submarine activity there, it made no attempt to divert the *Lusitania* around the north coast of Ireland. It also made no effort to provide the ship with an escort although patrol boats were stationed in nearby Queenstown harbor. The *Lusitania's* captain, perhaps counting on the ship's ability to outrun any submarine, continued on course toward Liverpool making no effort to zigzag. At 2:10 P.M. on 7 May, the *U20* shot one torpedo into the bow of the *Lusitania*, igniting the steamship's lethal cargo, which created a second blast that sent the boat to the bottom. The ship took just eighteen minutes to sink. One hundred and thirty-nine American passengers went down with her.

President Wilson reacted with predictable rage. He dismissed German allegations that the *Lusitania* was really a vessel of war, then declared that the point was irrelevant anyway. "The sinking of passenger ships involves principles of humanity which throws into the background any special circumstances of detail that may be thought to affect the cases," he declared, adding that his government was "contending for nothing less high and sacred than the rights of humanity."[37] But much to the disappointment of the British, Wilson was still unwilling to let his sense of indignation boil over into a declaration of war. At the time, it was doubtful whether he could have coaxed Congress to do so or could have rallied the country. Many Americans were outraged, but not enough to fight Germany. The Germans though were taking no chances. They were in no position to risk American military intervention. At the time of the *Lusitania* sinking, they had only about twenty-eight operational U-boats, hardly enough to be decisive. Besides, over 85 percent of their kills were being achieved according to the rules of cruiser warfare.[38] Thus, the military advantage of U-boats did not appear to compensate for the political risks, and Germany suspended unrestricted submarine warfare. In September 1915, Wilson told his special foreign affairs adviser, "Colonel" Edward House, that "he had never been sure that [the United States] ought not to take part in the conflict and, if it seemed evident that Germany and her militaristic ideas were to win, the obligation upon us was greater than ever."[39]

Despite their setback on the diplomatic front, the Germans and Austrians had reason for optimism. The British and French offensives had been thwarted in Flanders and Champagne. The Russians, punished in Galicia and pushed out of the Carpathians, had retreated 200 miles across the Dniester and Bug rivers into the Ukraine. The Germans had attacked the huge salient around the city of Warsaw and almost trapped the main Russian army; the German campaign ended with a sweep into Belorussia where they captured the provincial capital of Vilna on 19 September. By year's end, the Austrians had obliterated Serbia, conquered Montenegro, and captured most of Albania. Courland, Lithuania, and Poland were overrun, and the battle lines straightened from the Gulf of Riga to the frontier of Romania. Tens of thousands of Russians lay dead. Three-quarters of a million were prisoners. Falkenhayn had good reason to be proud, but he recognized that the war would not be over until a great triumph was achieved on the battlefields of France.

ORGANIZING THE WAR OF ATTRITION

Mobilization of National Resources

Preparation for Total War. The flight of the French government to Bordeaux on 2 September 1914 took place amid considerable panic and confusion and seemed to indicate that the civilians had lost their nerve. There were riots at the railway stations. The highways were clogged as people loaded down with personal belongings fled toward Fontainebleau, Orléans, and Versailles. The government burned all sensitive documents that could not be removed by trucks.

Under pressure from President Raymond Poincaré, Premier René Viviani had created a "Sacred Union" government with representatives from practically all of the major political parties. However, this government did not return to Paris until December, long after the danger to the capital had passed. Parliament reconvened on 22 December, after a recess of three and a half months, and as its first act voted unanimously to suspend elections for the duration of the war and declared that it would sit permanently. General Joffre viewed the return of the politicians with misgivings. He had grown accustomed to directing the war in their absence. Believing that he had saved the country from defeat, he did not understand why his freedom from their interference should not continue indefinitely.

In Britain, Prime Minister Herbert Asquith saw little reason to follow the French example and create a national union government by adding representatives of the Labour and Conservative parties. Instead, he chose to rule through a special executive committee, about one-third the normal size of the cabinet. Strategic thinking was still Napoleonic. Britain would blockade the enemy, be the arsenal of the Allies, and dispatch a volunteer expeditionary force to help out on the battlefield. During the early weeks of the conflict, however, Parliament passed the Defense of the Realm Act, which suspended civil liberties and imposed special controls on commerce, business, and information. The act gave the state the authority to outlaw strikes and, if necessary, order a factory owner to switch to needed war production. Lord Kitchener, the minister of war, hesitated to develop new sources of supply for weapons production, fearing that shells not manufactured by the state factories might prove unreliable. Yet, in fairness, Kitchener had done much to build the foundations for an eventual increase in supply. When the war began, he was almost the only soldier or politician to warn that Britain should prepare for a long and costly war against the Central Powers. Kitchener beat back an attempt by Parliament to establish a special committee to investigate his operations, but in March 1915, the Home Office counterattacked with a study showing that much of the country's industrial potential still remained unused. The same month, Parliament extended the Defense of the Realm Act to give the government authority to seize any factory it considered necessary for the war effort.

The kaiser's army did not march to battle; it rode on a railway system that had been planned down to the design of the gold buttons on the conductors' uniforms. Once war began, the entire network automatically came under the direct control of the High Command. The generals were interested in raising great armies and navies, not organizing labor, supplies, and material. They therefore had no similar plan to mobilize civilians. Germany, though, was particularly vulnerable to blockade. It lacked petroleum, nitrates, cotton, and copper and was incapable of feeding its population from domestic production. Some feared that the troops might not be home before the leaves fell.

Rhineland industrialist Walther Rathenau estimated that present supplies of strategic materials would last only a few months. Shortly after the war began, he went to see the head of the General War Department, Colonel Heinrich Scheüch, to find out what could be done to avert German strangulation. Scheüch arranged for Rathenau to meet directly with his superior, War Minister von Falkenhayn; as a result of their conversation, Rathenau became head of a newly created Department of War Raw Materials.

The character of German industry lent itself to central direction. Large enterprises were frequently grouped into cartels that normally regulated production and trade, monopolized markets and services, and set prices. These combines were especially strong in the coal, steel, chemical, textile, and construction industries. The state not only encouraged their development and gave them official protection, but was itself an entrepreneur in the fields of forestry, agriculture, and mining. The core of the new agency's control lay in its authority to sequester any materials it thought vital for the war effort. If these could not be obtained on the German market, from neutrals, or in the occupied areas, the Raw Materials Department had the power to provide substitutes. The department created an entire nitrate industry, using the nitrogen fixation process of Fritz Haber and Robert Bosch, and produced synthetic ammonia, synthetic cotton, and *ersatz* (substitute) machine belting, made from the hair women were told to save from their daily combings. At the end of 1915, impressed with the success of his *Kriegssozialismus* (war socialism), Rathenau claimed that the British blockade had failed. Nothing goes beyond these boundaries unless it be the cannonball hurled by our artillery, he boasted

In France, the famous *levée en masse* of the French Revolution had inaugurated the concept of total mobilization. The military possessed the authority to commandeer all available men and material during a period of hostility, but few leaders had appreciated the amount of organization and coordination necessary to keep the country at war. When the war began, the French had a fairly modern rifle, the Lebel, and an effective light cannon, the 75-mm rapid-firing field gun. But there were serious shortages in almost everything else, especially machine guns, heavy artillery, telephones, radio sets, and airplanes. Munitions were in short supply. In August 1914, when Joffre demanded 75,000 rounds a day for the 75s, the state arsenals were able to manufacture only 36,000 shells of all calibers. The French, relying on the superior purchasing power of the state to boost production, formed a special committee of industrialists to ensure that the military orders would be filled. They bribed entrepreneurs with interest-free loans that guaranteed huge profits. France was also increasingly obliged to rely upon war supplies from the United States that it acquired on credit.

The Russians developed no such relationship between the army and the civilian government. Contradictory orders flowed from military headquarters, the Foreign Office, the Ministry of War, and the Ministry of the Interior. The Russian Artillery Department was independent of the War Ministry, which itself had no effective liaison with the Supreme Command. The wartime blockade interrupted supplies from abroad. Russian industry was highly inefficient and found it difficult to expand to meet the demands of modern war. Scarcities were widespread. During the 1890s, Russia had led the world in rates of increase in iron production, pig iron smelting, and coal mining. Most of the financing for such development, as well as many of the technical skills, had come from abroad, however, principally from Britain, France, and Germany. Russia was still deficient in machine tools and precision instruments.

Poor logistics compounded shortages in military equipment. Soldiers in reserve detachments had to obtain their rifles from the casualties of the first wave. Anticipating a short war, the Russians began hostilities with only enough ammunition for three months. Their factories could only satisfy one-third of the demand for artillery shells. Clothes were in short supply, as were bandages, and the production of boots fell behind need by 20 million pairs a year. In the Carpathians, some soldiers fought barefooted.

Conscripted Societies. French generals and politicians took tremendous pride in the smoothness and rapidity of their military mobilization. The army increased from a normal peacetime force of 900,000 men to over 4 million. So many skilled and semiskilled workers were drafted that an instant civilian labor shortage developed. As a result, thousands of small businesses and industries closed, throwing many out of work. The Ministry of Labor therefore allowed women and children to be employed in previously forbidden jobs, and ruled that men henceforth could be required to work twelve hours a day. But not until the Dalbiez Law of 30 June 1915, which released about a half a million workers from the service to return to the factories, did the situation substantially improve.

Britain alone of the major European powers began the war with no military conscription. During the first year and a half, about 3 million men volunteered for military service. But with casualties running around 150,000 a month, continued reliance on patriotic fervor to fill the missing ranks became impossible. The National Registration Act of 1915 showed that there were at least 2 million men still available for military service. Before opting for a draft, the British government first tried to shame men into uniform—"What did you do in the war, Daddy?" asked one of the posters. The Labour party, however, felt that, before the government started to conscript bodies, it should conscript wealth. Bertrand Russell believed it a deep disgrace for the nation to have to admit that its citizens had to be forced to fight for freedom. And Lord Hugh Cecil observed, "There is nothing fine in killing, but there *is* something in being killed and conscription would take that away." Finally though, on 6 January 1916, Parliament adopted the compulsory military service bill, providing for full conscription of all physically fit married and unmarried men between the ages of eighteen and forty-one.

In Germany, the enactment of the Patriotic States Service Law on 5 December 1916 bound every German, aged seventeen to sixty, who was not already in the military to civilian war service. The War Department determined numbers and categories through its regional committees. Anybody who failed to heed a summons could be imprisoned for one year and fined 10,000 marks. Strikes were forbidden, and special arbitration boards were established to deal with grievances over wages and working conditions. The boards' decisions had the force of law. An Imperial Food Administration had the power to regulate the consumption, distribution, importation, rationing, production, and pricing of foodstuffs. Food substitutes were found. Bread, for example, was baked from turnips and potatoes, while coffee was fabricated from a blend of roasted barley, rye, and chicory, flavored with ground-up figs.

All governments exerted tight control over information. The French censorship law prohibited newspapers from printing any information that might give comfort to the enemy and harm the spirit of the army and people. Interpreted liberally, this meant no unauthorized news of French defeats—no matter how true—and no criticism of the conduct of the war. The government replaced the free flow of information with a steady stream of bowdlerized and distorted communiqués. But, of course, no amount of government censorship could conceal the tremendous casualties. Too many families were directly affected, and for Parisians it was a simple matter to visit the railway stations, particularly the Gare du Nord or the Gare de l'Est, and count the number of hospital trains arriving with the wounded. The war also brought price controls, food rationing, and the black market. Money depreciated as much as 40 percent with a resultant fall in the standard of living. The Paris economy profited by an increased population of soldiers, workers, and foreigners. Music halls and bistros stayed open, but the city was hardly bright and gay. Streetlights were turned off, and sugar was in chronic short supply. The opera stayed open, but people could not wear evening clothes to the performances.

The German War Office also established tight controls on information, keeping people so ignorant about the progress of the war that later many Germans could easily believe that they had been defeated because of a stab in the back from revolutionaries and traitors at home. German newspapers were even prohibited from making any references to the fact that there was censorship.

The British established a special Press Bureau to accredit war correspondents and regulate their dispatches, even the reports of foreign correspondents. Unless people managed to get information directly from the soldiers, they had little actual knowledge of conditions at the front. Yet criticism could not be completely stifled. On 21 May 1915, the *Daily Mail* took War Minister Kitchener to task for failing to provide enough shells for British artillery. The attack came at a time when the faltering Gallipoli expedition had already undermined confidence in the government. The Conservatives renewed their demand that they be given a share in running the war, and Asquith could no longer refuse. On 25 May, he created a coalition government with a Ministry of Munitions to control wartime production and mobilization. David Lloyd George, one of Asquith's most ardent critics, became its head.

The new minister proceeded to regulate "all private importation and the distribution of materials to non-munition as well as to munition trades, thereby virtually bringing all the industries using materials which entered into production of munitions under the control of the department."[40] The ministry also organized the domestic labor force. Lloyd George deplored Asquith's lack of drive and initiative and accused him of making decisions only when they were forced upon him: "He never surveyed the needs of the country and devised means for supplying them."[41] In June 1916, Lloyd George became minister of war. As much as possible, he wanted to relieve Asquith of the responsibility of coordinating and leading the war effort. Lloyd George had the support of the Conservative party ministers who feared that unless the government showed more energy and vigor Britain might be defeated. They were prepared to back Lloyd George in creating a special War Committee of three to four members to assume day-to-day direction of the war.[42] Asquith could remain as a figurehead. Asquith did not reject the plan out of hand; but after some soul-searching—his nerve already weakened by declining health and grief over the death of his eldest son, Raymond, killed in battle the previous September—he decided to resign. Perhaps he hoped that Lloyd George would fail and the country would have him back. It did not happen. Lloyd George became prime minister on 7 December 1916 at the age of fifty-three.

Tsar Nicholas was also incapable of effective leadership, but he was difficult to replace without bringing the whole tsarist system into question. The sovereign often sought mystical solutions to problems. After the disastrous retreat on the Galician and Polish front in 1915, he dismissed the commander-in-chief, Grand Duke Nicholas, and took personal charge himself. He left Petrograd for the *Stavka* (Supreme Army Headquarters) at Mogilev, believing that his divine presence would inspire victory. He left the home government in the hands of his wife, Alexandra, who was under the dangerous influence of Grigory Rasputin. This self-ordained holy man had found favor in the royal household a decade earlier because of his special powers of healing. Tsarevitch Alexei, the heir to the throne, was a hemophiliac and even under the most protected of circumstances was subject to painful seizures, which were certainly exacerbated by the highly neurotic atmosphere in which he lived. Rasputin possessed the ability to pacify Alexei during these attacks, and Alexandra felt him to be indispensable. The monk also put his hypnotic talents to work on the society ladies of St. Petersburg, and his debauchery became so flagrant that the tsar ordered his exile. But Alexandra prevailed upon her husband to bring Rasputin back to Petrograd. Protected by royal favor, Rasputin began meddling in affairs of state. If Nicholas was concerned, he did not show it and, shortly after taking up his new responsibilities, wrote his wife with characteristic fatalism: "But God's will be fulfilled—I feel so calm—a sort of feeling after the Holy Communion!" He ended the letter, also characteristically, with "God bless you, my beloved treasure, my Ray of Sunshine."[43] After twenty-one years of marriage, the tsar was obviously still in love with his wife.

Profile: David Lloyd George (1863–1945)

In the company of previous British prime ministers, David Lloyd George was a rank outsider. He was a Baptist,[44] a Welshman, and the son of a family of modest means. He was born in Manchester, England, but spent practically all of his early life in Wales. When David was a year and a half old, his father, William George, an acting headmaster of a religious school, died, leaving his widow to bring up three children. The mother, Elizabeth, took her family back to her home village of Llanystumdwy in north Wales to live with her bachelor brother Richard and her mother. Richard Lloyd, a shoemaker and co-pastor of a Disciples of Christ church in nearby Criccieth, became David's foster father. Richard Lloyd was a deeply religious man and a Welsh nationalist, and his views influenced young David. Most of the land and woods surrounding Llanystumdwy was owned by Anglicized Welsh squires whom David deeply resented. This was evident even in his childhood, when he sometimes conducted raids on the large estates to savage the squires' chickens. Although at times Lloyd George the politician implied he had had an impoverished youth, the family was fairly well off by contemporary rural standards. Nevertheless, he viewed society as divided between the property owners, who were also members of the Anglican church and elite clubs, on the one hand, and the independent, nonconformist small producers, who were often the landlords' victims, on the other. The future prime minister's social conscience was motivated more by hatred of the affluence and privileges of those above him than from any identification with the poor working classes.[45] Nevertheless, he had a strong moral conviction that those who destroy other people's lives must be held accountable.

At fifteen, Lloyd George began the study of law in a solicitor's office. He practiced law until he was twenty-seven, when he became the Liberal candidate for Parliament from the local Carnarvon Boroughs seat. He won by 18 votes out of 3,908 cast, defeating the Conservative Hugh Ellis Nanney, the owner of an estate on which Lloyd George had poached as a boy. Lloyd George held the same seat without interruption for over half a century, a record matched by no other prime minister. In Commons, he attacked the Conservatives while pressing for the rights of his fellow Welsh. But soon he found larger issues: first, denouncing the war against the Boers in South Africa and then defending free trade against attempted Tory protectionism.

When the Liberals won the election in 1905, he accepted the post of president of the Board of Trade, but three years later he advanced to chancellor of the exchequer. This office put Lloyd George in a position to work for the kind of social security program he thought the nation owed its people. In 1910, he presented his "People's Budget" to Parliament. In it he proposed financing a radical program of social reform through higher income taxes and death duties and increased property taxes on the large estates. In defense of his program, he said: "There are many in this country blessed by Providence with great wealth, and if there are amongst them men who grudge out of their riches a fair contribution towards the less fortunate of their fellow countrymen they are very shabby rich men."[46] Some suspected that Lloyd George deliberately put the land tax into the budget to bait the House of Lords into rejecting it so he could create a political crisis to strip the Lords of their power to veto legislation. If so, the ruse worked. The Lords did reject the People's Budget, and in the ensuing crisis their power was indeed reduced. In 1911, Lloyd George presented Parliament with his most significant social welfare program to date. The National Insurance Bill, which became law at the end of the year, contained a comprehensive package of health and unemployment insurance modeled on the German welfare legislation of the 1880s. It was the ancestor of the National Health Service that would surface after World War II and confirmed Lloyd George's reputation as a great reformer.

When war broke out in 1914, Lloyd George applied the same energy to mobilizing the defenses of the country. Britain's successful economic mobilization was largely due to his efforts, as were the policy of arming merchant ships and the establishment of the destroyer-protected convoy system. Although his departure from the Treasury to the new post of minister of munitions initially seemed a demotion, the new position became a stepping-stone toward the prime ministry. Lloyd George believed that the War Office was too fossilized to appreciate the nature of modern war. He would give the generals what he thought they should have, not what they thought they needed. He dismissed Kitchener's idea that there should be four machine guns to a battalion as woefully inadequate. "Take Kitchener's maximum," he said, "square it; multiply that result by two; and when you are in sight of that, double it again for good luck."[47] Lloyd George also pushed for the manufacture of bigger and more effective artillery, like the rapid-firing Stokes mortar, which Lloyd George supposedly financed with the 20,000 pounds sterling "donated" by an Indian maharajah. Whether true or not, the story seemed believable considering the energetic, frequently flamboyant means Lloyd George employed to achieve his ends.

His egocentric style of leadership did not prove beneficial to the unity of the Liberal party, however. Lloyd George split the Liberal party between a faction loyal to himself and another loyal to former leader Herbert Asquith. The division became permanent and marked the decline of the Liberals as a major political force. But Lloyd George himself seemed to sweep all before him. Most of the British people applauded his determination to fight "to a knockout." To this he added a tremendous organizational ability, a great physical charm, a powerful intellect, and "the great political gift of knowing what was going on in other people's minds."[48] He infused in the British people a new will to fight, a not inconsiderable task considering the lateness of the hour.

Women and the Cause. With so many thousands of men serving away from home, women were the great labor reserve of the warring nations. No mobilization could have succeeded without bringing them into the work force. Yet, ironically, the war's immediate effect on women already working—that is, on lower-class women—was unemployment. Many of these women were employed in businesses, such as dressmaking, clothing goods, and other luxury industries, that were no longer needed in an economy organized to supply soldiers. In Germany, Karl Helfferich, the secretary of state for interior affairs, refused to extend compulsory labor laws to include women because he discovered that would only worsen the problem of oversupply. The situation was only temporary, however.

The Germans organized a *Frauendienst* (women's service) and established work rooms in major cities where women could sew cartridge belts, uniforms, and sheets for hospitals. The War Office also established a special Female Labor Section to direct the procurement of women for war work. The official song of the German National Women's Service proclaimed that women loved serving "the Fatherland" by "cooking, sewing, and nursing."[49] French women were encouraged to knit socks, mittens, and scarves for the good of the men at the front. But they also were given a whole host of jobs traditionally performed by men: ploughing, repairing airplanes, blacksmithing, and postal work. In fact, women were soon working in all branches of agriculture, industry, and public service. In Great Britain, women eventually comprised 60 percent of all those employed in the armaments industry where many worked a twelve-hour day seven days a week. At the end of the war, women were doing all sorts of jobs that formerly only men were considered capable of performing: plumbers, steamfitters, police officers, and undertakers. But women were usually excluded from positions of authority and, despite the government's attempt to ensure equal pay scales, were compensated at lower rates. The "munitionettes," for example, earned only about half of what men received. In Russia, the legal profession still remained closed to women, and obstacles persisted in many middle-class occupations. Positions in industry were wide open, however. The percentage of women in the Petrograd industrial labor force rose from 25.3 percent in 1913 to 33.3 percent in 1917, and from 39.4 percent to 48.7 percent in the Moscow area. It became normal to see female conductors on streetcars and trains.[50]

Britain was most advanced in creating special women's auxiliaries of the armed services. Those who joined the Women's Army Auxiliary Corps were mostly employed as secretaries and as kitchen help, but they had their own khaki uniforms, slept in dormitories, and performed drills. The Air Force and the Navy had similar units. Russia had women's battalions that were used mostly to help maintain order in the cities. Feminist organizations saw these formations as proof that women were at last participating in the active defense of the country. Some even proposed that women be drafted.

In most countries, however, the true female warriors were the nurses. Working in a hospital or a clinic had always been considered a proper job for women; now it became a desperate necessity. Many of those who participated came from the privileged classes, including members of the British, German, and Russian royal families. One of the most famous heroines of the war, Edith Cavell, was a nurse. She worked with the Red Cross in German-occupied Belgium tending to British, German, and Belgian soldiers, but she was court-martialed and shot for having

British "munitionettes" load artillery shells. Female labor in industry was essential for fighting a modern war, but women were not paid as much as men and they did not become supervisors. Here their male bosses stand around watching them work.

helped Allied soldiers escape. Her execution produced a howl of indignation. The British erected a statue to her memory near Trafalgar Square in London. As the war progressed, nurses were routinely mentioned in dispatches for their bravery. Nurses served on all the fronts, and their work including driving ambulances and nursing near the front lines was dangerous and sometimes fatal.

War brought a certain leveling between the sexes, at least in terms of what women were capable of doing and in certain dangerous activities that could lead to death. No longer did people debate whether a certain kind of work could be performed by women since it already was. At the same time, the fear that women might keep their wartime jobs prompted the British trade unions to ask the government to promise that the old practices of industry would be restored once the war was over. Unions in other countries did not display the same anxiety, at least not so officially.

War service accomplished for women what years of suffragist agitation had failed to do: it removed all the arguments against giving them the right to vote. The new Russian government enfranchised women in 1917; a year later the British allowed all women over thirty to vote; German women could vote beginning in 1919. Between 1918 and 1919, Austria, Sweden, Luxembourg, and the Netherlands all opened up their political systems to female participation. Belgium gave the vote only to women who had been imprisoned by the Germans, war widows who had not remarried, and mothers whose sons had been killed. Even with these restrictions, Belgian women were better off than their counterparts in France and Italy where women remained disfranchised.

Despite its importance for women, World War I did not become the watershed that many women's groups hoped it would. Voting rights did not end sex prejudice. The war did bring certain social changes, however. Not the least important was the transformation in the way women dressed. It was not practical for working women to corset themselves and spend hours creating complex hairdos. Shorter skirts, bobbed hair, and looser clothes gave women freedom of movement. During the war, women also took to wearing makeup, a practice heretofore associated with prostitutes. Women also became accustomed to going out unchaperoned. For this new status, they often paid dearly. They worked long hours in poor working conditions for less than men made. Getting the vote was supposed to open a new era in the history of women, but many years passed before nations made a serious effort to end economic discrimination against them.

Efforts to Break the Stalemate

The Deadlock Continued. The longer the conflict dragged on, the tighter the Germans felt the noose of the British blockade. Although units from the German High Seas Fleet might prowl the North Sea, their ships were unable to break out into the Atlantic. Should they try, the numerically superior British fleet could seal the English Channel and the waters off Scotland and systematically hunt them down. The Germans therefore kept their High Seas Fleet protected behind mine fields and the batteries on the island of Helgoland. It harassed adversaries through occasional coastal raids and unrestricted submarine attacks on merchant shipping. In May 1915, fear of provoking American intervention led the Germans to suspend the U-boat attacks, but the new aggressive commander of the High Seas Fleet, Vice-Admiral Reinhard Scheer, was not content to tread water. Scheer believed he could weaken the British blockade with a carefully planned confrontation in open seas, specifically, an engagement in which the Germans had local superiority. Scheer wanted to lure the British battle cruiser squadrons stationed at Rosyth into a trap.

Sir John Jellicoe, the commander of the British Grand Fleet, was also thirsting for a chance to bring his dreadnoughts into action. But he could not afford to be as daring as Scheer. A loss for the Germans would simply return them to the defensive strategy they already practiced, but any setback to the Grand Fleet could endanger Britain's island security. Nevertheless, Jellicoe awaited an opportunity to do battle. On 30 May 1916, his cryptographers intercepted and decoded Scheer's order to the High Seas Fleet to rendezvous in the roadsteads outside the port of Wilhelmshaven. Though Jellicoe knew nothing of the Germans' intentions, he immediately ordered his own units to sea, actually getting them ready for action before the enemy fleet had left port—an indication of his organizational ability.

The Germans sortied in two sections, with the smaller contingent of battle cruisers, commanded by Vice-Admiral Franz Hipper, steaming forth first. On the afternoon of 31 May, they clashed with a scouting flotilla of British battle cruisers, commanded by Sir David Beatty. Hipper managed to sink two British ships before retreating as he tried to draw Beatty into the clutches of Scheer. The British did not suspect that the main body of the German High Seas Fleet was still in position until the pursuing Beatty saw the low silhouettes of the enemy's main forces on the horizon. He at once headed northward, hoping to lead the Germans toward Jellicoe.

The two navies met just before dusk.[51] Jellicoe maneuvered his fleet brilliantly and managed to cross the German fleet's "T," bringing the full power of his broadsides to bear on enemy ships, under the circumstances defended only by their forward guns. Scheer ordered a complete about-turn, retreating successfully behind a dense smoke screen, but leaving the British interposed between himself and his path back home. At night, the two battle fleets lost contact with one another. Early the next morning, Scheer managed to cross astern of Jellicoe's flagship and escape into safe waters. The battle was over.

The Germans claimed victory. Though numerically outnumbered, they had inflicted the greater damage.[52] Strategically though, the British had won the day. They had forced the enemy back to port and reinforced the blockade. Thus, the Battle of Jutland proved indecisive, a maritime equivalent of the stalemate on land. The check to his ambitions convinced Scheer that future action by the High Seas Fleet was hopeless, and he again advocated unrestricted submarine warfare despite its political hazards. General Falkenhayn, however, proposed to win the war on land.

The generals believed that the key to victory lay in destroying the French army's will to resist—this could be done without a breakthrough. Then, with France out of the war and Russia already collapsing, Britain would have to sue for peace. The German commander reasoned that the Germans could bleed the French army white if they could force the French to fight for an important enough sector. Falkenhayn suggested that either Belfort or Verdun, both of which were fortified cities with historical and strategic importance, would be a suitable target. He finally chose Verdun where an inviting salient into German lines offered the German gunners a better opportunity for killing the French defenders.

The battle began on 21 February 1916 with a murderous 1,200-gun bombardment that lasted from daybreak until four in the afternoon. When the guns fell silent, the German assault troops, attacking along an eight-mile front, easily pushed through the surprised French and captured the important fort of Douaumont within five days. The French would have been smart to retreat, but Falkenhayn's estimation of Verdun's psychological importance proved correct. The French decided to defend the city to the death and entrusted the job to General Henri Philippe Pétain. The French took tremendous losses, but stood fast and, by May, had destroyed the momentum of the German attack. At that point, the battle degenerated into a straight war of attrition, with both sides killing each other in equal proportion. Because of the commitment of egos and national pride to this engagement, the battle quickly assumed a dynamic of its own. By trumpeting the capture of Douaumont, Falkenhayn committed himself to a defense of the outpost come what may. The French were fiercely determined to succeed in its recapture, and their skilled use of artillery devastated the Germans.

The German attack at Verdun forced the Allies to abandon their plans for a joint offensive on the Somme, which became primarily a British show. The French, who regarded the Somme offensive as more necessary to relieve pressure on Verdun than to deliver the decisive blow to end the war, reduced their participation from forty-two to five divisions.

The British began with a week-long artillery barrage that chewed the ground into a pockmarked obstacle course and obliterated the German outposts and front trenches, but left the main body of defenders untouched in their meticulously constructed dugouts, some as deep as forty feet underground. When the bombardment lifted on 1 July, all possible resistance seemed to have been blown apart, and the British advanced almost nonchalantly in formations learned on the parade ground—six feet separating each man across the line, a hundred yards between each assault wave, and each soldier carrying a minimum backpack of sixty-six pounds. The Highland Regiments marched into battle behind their pipers. Meanwhile the Germans had scrambled up their steep tunnel-like shafts, pulling their machine guns with them, and were ready for action. On the first day of the infantry attack, they massacred 20,000 British soldiers and wounded another 40,000—a daily record.

Despite mounting losses, the British maintained the attack. Several times they seemed close to a breakthrough, but always the offensive lost its impetus. General Sir Douglas Haig, impressed by "the fighting power of the British race," persevered. "Our losses in July's fighting totalled about 120,000 more than they would have been had we not attacked," he wrote. "They can not be regarded as sufficient to justify any anxiety as to our ability to continue the offensive."[53] Only when the November rains made the battlefield a swamp did he change his mind. The battle relieved some pressure on Verdun, although the German attack there had already failed and had also been called off the same month. Nothing of strategic value had been gained. Neither the German army nor the French had fully recovered from this sausage grinder when the war was over.

The War in the East. Although a breakthrough failed to materialize in Flanders in 1916, one did occur on the Eastern Front. The Russians had slowly patched themselves together after the disaster of the previous year. They had largely overcome their frontline deficiencies of rifles and machine guns and, taking advantage of the winter's lull in the fighting, had trained new recruits and restored morale. But always the British and French were eager to profit from any Russian strengths, and they tried to push the Stavka into an immediate offensive to draw German troops away from the Western Front. The newly appointed commander of the southwest sector, General Alexei Brusilov, agreed, but he insisted that such an offensive begin with a diversionary thrust against the Austrians and Hungarians in Galicia.

The attack did not quite go according to plan. The major thrust against the Germans in the north failed to materialize, and the preliminary stroke against the Austrians became the principal effort. But, on 4 June, the first day of the attack, Brusilov's troops broke through the Austrian lines and within four days had captured the enemy headquarters located at Lutsk, forcing Archduke Josef Ferdinand to cancel the celebration of his birthday. Brusilov was confident that the Allies could achieve victory by the end of the year. But the Germans quickly moved to reinforce the Austrians. They suspended their offensive at Verdun, transferring thirty-five divisions from France to the east. The Austrians likewise had to draw troops away from the Italian front where they were on the verge of reaching a decision. The Eastern Front was again stabilized. The Brusilov attack helped keep the Entente alive at the cost of a Russian breakdown. The Austrians were also spent and, had they not received German help, would probably have been forced to sue for peace. As it was, the Russian collapse came first.

The Brusilov offensive convinced the government in Bucharest that the time to enter the war was near. Both the Allies and the Central Powers had tried to buy Romanian intervention. The Germans and Austrians promised them 17,000 square miles of Russian land, but the British and French were higher bidders with 50,000 square miles of Austro-Hungarian territory. The withdrawal of Austrian troops from Romania's western frontier in the summer of 1916 induced Prime Minister Ion Brătianu to seal the bargain. The secret Treaty of Bucharest, concluded on 17 August, promised Romania enough territory to double its prewar size, including the whole of the Banat, the area of Bukovina south of the Dniester, and most of Transylvania. The British, in the midst of their offensive on the Somme, were anxious to conclude the deal as fast as possible and also agreed to accord Romania the "same rights as her Allies" at the forthcoming peace conference in

A Mark I before Thiepval on the Somme in September 1916. This version of the tank was the first to see combat in the British army. It is armed with two six-pound canons. The girders on top if covered with wire mesh protect the "land battleship" against grenades; the rear wheels assist in steering.

exchange for a pledge that Romania would conclude "no separate or general peace except jointly and simultaneously with her Allies."[54]

Romania declared war on Austria-Hungary on 27 August and immediately tried to conquer Transylvania. Brătianu foresaw an easy victory, especially since he specifically did not extend his country's state of war to Germany. But the Germans had no intention of allowing their ally to collapse; as soon as they had blunted the Russian attack in the north, they mounted an assault on Romania. They quickly overran three-fourths of the country, capturing Bucharest on 6 December. Romanian belligerency had proved to be a windfall. The Germans could exploit most of the country's resources, especially its valuable wheat lands and oil fields. The fall of Romania also forced the Russians to extend their front to the Black Sea, tying up an estimated one-fourth of their forces to protect themselves from the threat of invasion. Romanian participation had done much to refute the commonly held belief that a country was better as an ally than as a neutral.

POSTSCRIPT   In putting their economies on a wartime footing, the warring nations sacrificed the predominantly laissez-faire systems under which they had lived for the past half-century. This was especially true of the pioneering efforts made by Walther Rathenau. His "war socialism" pointed the way to vastly increased state power that, even with demobilization, would remain a permanent feature of all postwar societies.

In military terms, the year 1916 remained one of the bloodiest of the war. The ill-fated Brusilov offensive, which had begun with such promise, had cost the Russians about a million men. The sequel would be the fall of the tsarist system. The Somme cost the Germans half a million casualties, the British 419,654, and the French 204,253. At Verdun, the combined losses of the French and Germans ran as high as 420,000 killed with another 800,000 gassed or wounded. Over 150,000 bodies were never identified. Neither engagement fulfilled the expectations of its sponsors who had hoped to bring an early end to the war.

Wars speed invention, although they are often given too much credit for being its source. The battlefield does make innovative use of technology. At Verdun, the Germans first introduced the flamethrower as an assault weapon and employed the phosgene gas artillery shell, a tremendous improvement over the wind-carried chlorine asphyxiants they used initially. At Verdun, the French perfected the technique of the creeping barrage and proved that a major fighting force could be supplied entirely by road transport, a single, unpaved secondary road that twisted southward over the Lorraine hills toward Bar-le-Duc. At the Somme, modern warfare changed dramatically with the first appearance of the tank, conceived as an antidote for the machine gun. Haig could not wait to use the new machine. In August 1916, with less than sixty delivered and in commission, he threw them into battle in a local operation. In doing so, he disregarded the advice of the tank's inventor, Colonel Ernest Swinton, that they only be deployed massively along a narrow front. But Haig would have done anything to redeem his offensive. Later, Lloyd George wrote bitterly, "So, the great secret was sold for the battering ruin of a little hamlet on the Somme, which was not worth capturing."[55] Proper use of this new weapon would have to wait until the following year.

In both battle areas today, reminders of the great struggle are everywhere: rusting barbed wire, caved-in parapets, and wide craters. Signs inform visitors that a village once stood on this spot and warn that this is still an area of unexploded shells. Parts of the battlefields are neatly preserved and maintained, but with trenches too clean and drained of water. Much land has never been reclaimed, and on some of this grows a particularly vicious nettle that prevents more agreeable vegetation from returning. Numerous military cemeteries and memorials dot the landscape, none more poignant than the cracked marble commemoration plaque cemented to one of the lichen-covered walls of Verdun's Fort Vaux: "To my son, since your eyes have shut, mine have never stopped crying."

ENDNOTES

1. *The Collected Poems of Rupert Brooke* (New York: Dodd, Mead, 1946), 101.
2. Quoted in Fritz Fischer, *War of Illusions* (New York: Norton, 1975), 402.
3. Vladimir Dedijer, *The Road to Sarajevo* (New York: Simon and Schuster, 1966), 13.
4. Ibid., 381.
5. See the account of Hertha Pauli, *The Secret of Sarajevo* (London: Collins, 1966), 290–95.
6. Immanuel Geiss, ed., *July 1914* (New York: Norton, 1974), 65.
7. Luigi Albertini, *The Origins of the War of 1914*, vol. 2 (London: Oxford University Press, 1953), 134.
8. Geiss, *July 1914*, 77.

9. Conrad had not always been so cautious. On the evening of the archduke's assassination, he had written his future wife that it did not matter that a war on two fronts—against Serbia and Russia—would be a hopeless struggle: "it must be because such an ancient monarchy and such an ancient army cannot perish ingloriously." Gunther Rothenberg, *The Army of Francis Joseph* (Lafayette, Ind.: Purdue University Press, 1976), 177.

10. On one occasion, Count Berchtold expressed anxiety about what might happen if the Serbs actually agreed to all its terms. The kaiser replied that Vienna should then demand the cession of Serbian territory, specifically, the famous Sanjak of Novi Pazar "to prevent the union of Serbia and Montenegro and the gaining of the sea coast by the Serbians." Geiss, *July 1914*, 107–8.

11. Ibid., 108.

12. Ibid., 122–23.

13. Ibid., 127. As it was, the Austrians almost slipped up. The German foreign secretary, Gottlieb von Jagow, correctly figured out the hour of Poincaré's departure in local time; otherwise the note would have been presented an hour too soon.

14. Specifically, the ultimatum required that Serbia (1) abolish all anti-Austrian publications; (2) immediately dissolve all anti-Austrian societies and organizations; (3 and 4) purge from its schools, military, and civil service all those guilty of anti-Austrian propaganda; (5) accept the collaboration of the Austro-Hungarian government in destroying anti-Austrian subversive organizations; (6) begin, with Austrian participation, judicial proceedings against those involved in the Sarajevo affair; (7) immediately arrest certain specified suspects; (8) stop the participation of Serbian officials in the illegal arms traffic across the frontiers; (9) suppress the anti-Austrian utterances of many Serbian high officials; and (10) keep the Austrian government informed of the steps taken to implement these measures. The full text is printed in *British Documents on the Origins of the War*, vol. 11, 364–66.

15. Ibid., 150.

16. The Russian foreign minister, Sergei Sazonov, told the German ambassador, Count Friedrich von Pourtalès, "There must be a way of giving Serbia her deserved lesson while sparing her sovereignty." Ibid., 242.

17. The full text with the Austrian reaction is printed in *British Documents on the Origins of the War*, 11 (London: His Majesty's Stationery Office, 1926), 367–71.

18. Soon after the Austrians severed diplomatic relations with Serbia, Russian foreign minister, Sergei Sazonov, begged the German ambassador, Count Friedrich von Pourtalès, to suggest a way peace might be preserved. On the spur of the moment, Pourtalès replied that this might be done if Austria could be induced to modify its demands to allow complete Serbian acceptance. Sasonov immediately made such a proposal, insisting that discussions to work out the details should begin at once. But Berlin opposed mediation. Von Jagow took the Russian proposal, edited it to remove any language that might give the Austrians an excuse to back down, and passed it along to Vienna without comment, an action that urged rejection.

19. Geiss, *July 1914*, 186.

20. Albertini, *Origins of the War*, 2: 468.

21. Ibid., 260.

22. Geiss, *July 1914*, 283.

23. See Konrad H. Jarausch, "The Illusion of Limited War, Bethmann Hollweg's Calculated Risk, July 1914," *Central European History* 2 (1969): 48–76.

24. René Viviani, *Réponse au Kaiser* (Paris: J. Ferenczi, 1923), 204–5.

25. The Austro-Hungarians waited until 6 August to issue their own declaration.

26. Geiss, *July 1914*, 355.

27. *British Documents*, 11: 351.

28. Viscount Grey, *Twenty Five Years*, vol. 2 (London: Hodder and Stoughton, 1925), 20.

29. Chronology and nationality influenced later discussions of who was responsible for

starting the war. Many of the early histories, surfacing in the victorious countries after the war, placed the blame squarely on Germany and accused it of deliberately planning the war to dominate Europe. The Germans, saddled with official war guilt, naturally disagreed. As the passions of the war receded, interwar historians became more balanced in their judgments. Many, while not exonerating Germany from responsibility, emphasized the faults of others. Some criticized the European state system itself, in particular, its extreme nationalism, militarism, and imperialism. Did not France and Russia also welcome the outbreak of hostilities as a means of improving their positions? There was obviously enough blame to go around. After World War II, the debate took on new energy, particularly among German historians. Two main theses emerged: (1) Germany did in fact desire a continental war to establish its hegemony in Europe; and (2) Germany desired to protect Austria from dissolution by encouraging a war with Serbia, but this could not be localized after the mobilization of Russia triggered the Schlieffen Plan. Recent historical inquiry has added more dimensions and complexities to the arguments. Details of decision making by leading participants are recreated in the climate and hidden pressures of the events they determined. While not denying individual responsibility, recent accounts have downgraded evil purpose to incompetence, stupidity, and miscalculation. For articles on the controversy, see the following collections: H. W. Koch, *The Origins of the First World War: Great Power Rivalry and German War Aims* (New York: Macmillan, 1990); and Dwight E. Lee, *The Outbreak of the First World War: Causes and Responsibilities* (Lexington, Mass.: D. C. Heath, 1975).

30. From an eyewitness account by the American journalist Richard Harding Davis in Louis L. Snyder and Richard Morris, eds., *A Treasury of Great Reporting* (New York: Simon and Schuster, 1949), 313–15.

31. Martin van Creveld, *Supplying War: Logistics from Wallenstein to Patton* (London: Cambridge University Press, 1977), 138–40.

32. Hindenburg had seen service in the war against Austria in 1866 and the Franco-Prussian War in 1870; he had also been on the General Staff. He was considered to be familiar with the area of the Eastern Front.

33. Fritz Fischer, *Germany's Aims in the First World War* (New York: Norton, 1967), 104.

34. These parties included the Reichstag wartime majority—a coalition of National Liberals, Centrists, and conservatives. They were joined by the powerful lobbies of big business, the Pan-German League, and, most importantly, the Supreme Command.

35. In 1913–1914 mercury production dropped 18.1 percent, pig iron was off 24.7 percent, steel tumbled by 13.9 percent, and iron ore slid by 33.4 percent. *Statistical Abstract of the United States, 1919* (Washington, D.C.: U.S. Government Printing Office, 1920), 785, 787, 788, 805.

36. David Lloyd George, *War Memoirs*, vol. 2 (London: Nicholson and Watson, 1933), 656, 662.

37. Charles Seymour, *The Intimate Papers of Colonel House*, vol. 2 (Boston: Houghton Mifflin, 1926), 2.

38. Under these rules, the U-boat would surface. The passengers on board the condemned ship would be allowed to leave in lifeboats. Then the submarine would sink the vessel with a deck gun. In the case of neutrals, this happened only if the ship carried contraband.

39. Seymour, *The Intimate Papers of Colonel House*, 84.

40. Ibid., 566.

41. Ibid., 1007.

42. Cameron Hazelhurst, "The Conspiracy Myth," in Martin Gilbert, ed., *Lloyd George* (Englewood Cliffs, N.J.: Prentice-Hall, 1968), 148–57.

43. *The Letters of the Tsar to the Tsaritsa, 1914–1917* (Hattiesburg, Miss.: Academic International, 1970), 70–72.

44. Technically, Lloyd George was a member of the Disciples of Christ, or Campbell-ites, a breakaway Baptist sect that based its faith on the New Testament, baptism by total immersion, and weekly communion. Welsh nonconformism—that is, opposition to Anglicanism—provided a strong cement for political action. Lloyd George often read the scriptures before the congregation in his uncle's church, Penymaes Chapel. Although in later life he became an agnostic, he always retained many of the moral and social values of his religious upbringing.

45. Don M. Cregier, *Bounder from Wales: Lloyd George's Career before the First World War* (Columbia, Mo.: University of Missouri Press, 1976), 8.

46. Gilbert, *Lloyd George*, 36.

47. Lloyd George, *War Memoirs*, 2: 605.

48. Interview with Sir Harold Nicolson, *Observer*, 11 December 1961, 10.

49. Bonnie S. Anderson and Judith P. Zinsser, *A History of Their Own*, vol. 2 (New York: Harper and Row, 1988), 198.

50. Linda H. Edmondson, *Feminism in Russia, 1900–17* (Stanford, Calif.: Stanford University Press, 1984), 162.

51. The German ships were better designed with more advanced armament, but the British outnumbered them in all categories: 28 to 22 battleships, 17 to 5 battle cruisers, 26 to 11 light cruisers, and 78 to 61 destroyers.

52. The British lost three battle cruisers, the same number of armored cruisers, and eight destroyers for a total of 111,980 tons of shipping and 6,000 deaths. In turn, they managed to sink one enemy dreadnought, one battle cruiser, four light cruisers, and five destroyers for a total tonnage of 62,233 and 2,500 men killed.

53. *The Private Papers of Douglas Haig* (London: Eyre and Spottiswoode, 1952), 157–58.

54. Harold Temperley, ed., *A History of the Peace Conference of Paris*, vol. 4 (London: Henry Frowde, 1921), 516–17.

55. Lloyd George, *War Memoirs*, 2: 646.

CHAPTER 2

PROTEST AND REVOLUTION, 1917–1918

PREFACE   The Europeans expected a brisk and merry war; they got a long and bloody war. By 1917 war had become a way of life. The conflict was so gigantic and so paradoxical that many people had difficulty placing their thoughts in perspective. Though many still hoped for an eventual breakthrough, others had serious doubts that would ever occur. They favored a peace without victory. But the strong leaders who now assumed the levers of government gave a fight to the finish their highest priority. They appeared to believe that a proper display of will and energy would bring that about.

The war ruined lives, distorted economies, perverted cultures, and now began to topple governments. As the war dragged on, generals everywhere assumed greater influence and control, but only in Germany did they actually change the process of governance. Effective organization was essential to keep in the fight, but the Russian empire failed to mobilize its strength effectively and became the first of the great empires to collapse. Before it made peace the following year, its government would change twice. Things also looked bleak for Britain and France. The battles of Verdun and the Somme had left wounds that had yet to heal; the year 1917 brought both countries new disasters.

The entry of the United States on the side of the Allies offered hope for eventual victory if the Americans could arrive in sufficient strength before the Germans could carry the day. At first, the Americans had been willing to let the Europeans fight it out among themselves. Protected by vast oceans, the Americans enjoyed absolute political domination in their own hemisphere and saw little reason to become involved. They had played little part in creating or maintaining the European balance of power, had no territorial ambitions, and did not believe their security would be jeopardized no matter which side won. Woodrow Wilson, however, wanted in for various moralistic reasons. His aims made little difference to the Entente, which desperately welcomed help from any quarter.

The Americans made a commitment to make the world safe for democracy, but their idealism did not go unchallenged. From Petrograd, as St. Petersburg was renamed in 1914, the messianic Communists called for world revolution, sowing the seeds of an East-West confrontation that would become one of the great themes of European history for most of the remaining years of the twentieth century. The techniques of propaganda and subversion learned and practiced in World War I would become front-line weapons in this confrontation. In 1917 and 1918, slogans passed for programs, and the factors that would become the basis for political developments after the war were now part of the arsenal to counter weariness, pacifism, mutiny, and defeatism.

THE STRAIN OF WAR

War and Artistic Creativity

The Mood of Dada. Switzerland was an island of neutrality amid the sound of the guns and became a logical place of refuge for pacifists and conscientious objectors. Shortly after the beginning of hostilities, German poet Hugo Ball fled Munich for Zurich where, in 1915, he and his companion, Emmy Hennings, ran a bar on the Spiegelgasse in the old section of the city. The Café Voltaire soon became a rendezvous for other emigré writers and artists who were searching for their own ideals. Jean Arp, an Alsatian who had avoided military service by convincing the German authorities that he was mentally deranged, wrote, "In Zurich, losing interest in the slaughter houses of the world war, we turned to the Fine Arts. While the thunder of the batteries rumbled in the distance, we pasted, we recited, we versified, we sang with all our soul. We searched for an elementary art that would, we thought, save mankind from the furious folly of these times. We aspired to a new order that might restore the balance between heaven and hell."[1]

Arp and his associates believed in the permanence of nothing and made a cult of instability and revolt. They wanted to shock the world out of its spiritual lethargy and to destroy the deceptions of reason. They called the new movement *Dada*, a word chosen characteristically at random from a French dictionary—it meant a hobby horse, but really stood for nothing at all. "I hereby declare that on February 8, 1916, Tristan Tzara discovered the word DADA," Arp stated. "This took place at the Café Terrasse in Zurich, and I wore a brioche in my left nostril. I am convinced that this word has no importance and that only imbeciles and Spanish professors can be interested in dates."[2] The Dada spirit flowed from a self-professed distrust of unity and, in the words of Arp, from a need to give the Venus de Milo an enema. The world was mad, but the Dadas were convinced that the inmates were on the other side of the asylum wall and affirmed their own sanity in a series of manifestations, happenings, and creations. The grand Dada *metteur en scène* was

Marcel Duchamp's "Nude Descending a Staircase, No. 2" (1912) was a personal reevaluation of art that prompted other explorations into abstraction and fantasy. Duchamp's idiosyncratic iconoclasm led him naturally into the realm of Dada.

usually Tristan Tzara, a young poet who was born Sami Rosenstock in Bucharest and wore a monocle. His famous Sabbaths at the Voltaire were total theater. One after another, the performers would take the stage to shout poems, hiccup, bark, or dance. Somebody might play an invisible violin, while another would beat time on wooden crates or boxes. Tzara once proclaimed a desire to *"pisser en couleurs diverses."* Sometimes there was yodeling or perhaps a *poème simultané* performed by twenty people who recited the text out of time with each other. The spectators responded with cat calls, laughter, and cries of "rubbish." Dada audiences, unlike Switzerland, had no policy of neutrality. Dadas meant their behavior to be outrageous and became past masters in the art of annoying people, but their buffoonery also became ritualized and trite and hardly produced the kind of significant communication the movement professed to give. Most of the Dadas really hoped to be taken seriously. They were avant-garde with a vengeance, but their belief that it was important to be ahead of the game automatically assumed that the game was worth playing.

Consequently, a distinct Dada style could develop in the plastic arts only with difficulty, if indeed at all. Technically, it grew out of a variety of schools ranging from futurism to cubism to abstraction. Psychologically though, it owed most to the attitude of Marcel Duchamp who believed that anything was art if the artist said that it was. To illustrate his point, Duchamp invented the anti-art object, the ready-made, which was an article of current manufacture to which, with little or no modification, he signed his name. He created instant sculpture from an ordinary snow shovel, which he titled "In Advance of the Broken Arm," or an unadorned bottle rack, called simply "Bottle Rack." But his greatest coup occurred in New York in 1917 when he signed a urinal with the name R. Mutt and entered it in the first New York *Salon des Independants*. The jury criticized the plagiarism as immoral and vulgar and refused it a place in the show. Duchamp answered the Philistines by claiming that his "Fountain" was no more immoral than a bathtub; he maintained that the charge that it was a simple piece of plumbing was absurd since the "only works of art America has given are her plumbing and her bridges." It was inconsequential that Mr. Mutt made the object with his own hands because "He CHOSE it. He took an ordinary article of life, placed it so that its useful significance disappeared under the new title and point of view—created a new thought for that object."[3] Two years later, Duchamp made his point again, in a new medium. He drew a pointed head and upturned moustache on a reproduction of the Mona Lisa and signed his name. He entitled the work L.H.O.O.Q., which became an obscenity when pronounced phonetically in French.[4]

Like Duchamp, most of the Dadas were constantly seeking new artistic techniques and materials. Francis Picabia made a portrait collage with matchsticks, hairpins, zippers, and coins. Alberto Giacometti created kinetic art by rearranging the painted parts of a large clock. Jean Arp made reliefs of sawed pieces of wood and glued scraps of randomly dropped torn paper on cardboard. Man Ray created aerographs with a spray gun and invented the Rayograph by arranging objects on sensitized paper. Max Ernst, Hanna Höch, and Karl Schwitters all cut up medical catalogs, magazine advertisements, prints, postcards, letters, and photographs and pasted them together in various collages.

After the war, Zurich Dada spread through the main art centers of Europe and became particularly strong in Berlin and Paris. However, the movement was already in decline. Avant-garde artists were searching for a creative synthesis stronger than one that reveled in the insanity of organized society. Dada had made its point, but in doing so, it had become as negativistic and inane as the war out of which it developed.

The Poetry of Death and Anger. Poets were no less enthusiastic for war than the rest of their countrymen. Some were even more so. Charles Péguy, a French humanitarian socialist, believed that, outside of Christian martyrdom, no death was as beautiful as death on the battlefield in a just cause: "Happy are those who die in a righteous war,"[5] he wrote. Péguy died in the First Battle of the Marne, fighting a war that fulfilled his specifications; his death came early enough for him to maintain his idealism intact. But modernist Guillaume Apollinaire was so self-absorbed that he approached combat as part of that total experience by which his personality would encompass the world:

Don't cry then over the horrors of war
Before it we had only the surface
Of the earth and the seas
After it we have the gorges
The depths and the lofty heights

Afterwards, Afterwards
We will take all the joys
Of conquerors who take their ease.[6]

Such sentiment, no matter how brilliantly expressed, was fundamentally superficial.

The accusation could not be leveled against the Austrian Georg Trakl who had no infantile illusions about the nature of war. "Oh the hopeless melancholy / Of an army; a shining helmet / Fell with a clank from purpled faces," he wrote.[7] Trakl served as a medical corpsman and was profoundly depressed by the sight of wounded men. After the Battle of Grodek, his friends had to stop him from killing himself. His last poem, called "Grodek," was one of his finest:

At evening the autumn woods ring
With the weapons of death, while the golden fields
And the blue lakes are cast over with
The darkening sun; the night envelops
The dying warriors and the savage moans
From their crushed mouths.[8]

Trakl's poetry was a singular phenomenon among writers in the German language. Although Stefan George, a German contemporary, might write of the metallic clatter of tramping armies and ask "Is this the last Roar of the gods over this country?"[9] he was only giving metaphorical expression to a classical poetical vision, not reacting to the realities of the current slaughter.

The war filled Italian poet Giuseppe Ungaretti with aversion, but because explicit description offended his aesthetic sense, his verse was less graphic than Trakl's. Instead, Ungaretti's service on the Isonzo front became a backdrop for personal reveries about human and spiritual identity. Ungaretti made no references to the enemy, and his relationship with his own country was part of his general relationship to all mankind. Men were as alone on the battlefield as they were elsewhere. Ungaretti saw war only in terms of death, but made few direct references to the fighting. Even when he did, he preferred to convey his feelings more by the sound of the words than by their apparent meaning:

The air is riddled
like a lace
from the shots
of men
withdrawn
in the trenches
like snails in their shells.[10]

Ungaretti retained his humanity only by restraining his emotions toward the immediate horrors of war.

Among all the belligerents only the British came close to developing a school of war poetry. Whereas the important poets of other countries reacted to the struggle individually, the British exhibited a creative collectivity. Their early poems displayed an alarming light-headedness. Rupert Brooke, who like Péguy never had to adjust his euphoria to the grim nature of modern war, reveled in the hour of combat, thanking God for this opportunity to purify the world of its sick hearts and dirty songs and "all the little emptiness of love." Brooke, a socially advantaged, rugger-playing undergraduate who had majored in classics at Cambridge, likened the war to a surgical operation that would result in a healthier patient. He prepared to meet death as a friend, calling those slain "the rich Dead." "There's none of these so lonely and poor of old / But dying, has made us rarer gifts than gold."[11] The poet never saw combat, dying en route to the Dardanelles from malaria. Like many romantic poets, he had prematurely celebrated his own end, but patriotically:

> If I should die, think only this of me:
> That there's some corner of a foreign field
> That is forever England.[12]

Once stripped of their naïveté, British poets had no patience with ambiguities or the perfection of poetical techniques. Most of these new writers came from the junior officers' ranks where casualties were the highest and the realization of the banality of death the strongest. Before the Battle of Loos, in which he died, Captain Charles Sorley wrote:

> When you see millions of the mouthless dead
> Across your dreams in pale battalions go,
> Say not soft things as other men have said . . .
> Say only this, 'They are dead' . . . .[13]

Sorley prefigured an entire movement. When Robert Graves met Siegfried Sassoon on the Béthune-la-bassée sector at the end of 1915, he showed him some drafts from his forthcoming book of poems *Over the Brazier*. Sassoon frowned and said that "war should not be written about in such a realistic way." He then showed Graves some of his poems, one of which began:

> Return to greet me, colours that were my joy
> Not in the woeful crimson of men slain,
> But shining as a garden; come with the streaming
> Banners of dawn and sundown after rain.

Sassoon had not yet been in the trenches, and Graves told him "he would soon change his style."[14] Graves was right. After the Battle of the Somme, Sassoon wrote:

> When I'm asleep dreaming and lulled and warm,
> They come, the homeless ones, the noiseless dead. . . .
> They whisper to my heart; their thoughts are mine.[15]

Though reminiscent of Sorley, Sassoon's poetry was much more ferocious and included some of the most graphic descriptions in any literature: "The place was rotten with dead. . . . Bulged clotted heads slept in the plastering slime."[16] Relating how life in the trenches drove an optimistic youth to suicide, Sassoon lashed out bitterly:

> You smug-faced crowds with kindling eye
> Who cheer when soldier lads march by,
> Sneak home and pray you'll never know
> The hell where youth and laughter go.[17]

British war poetry, if it said nothing else, affirmed that modern war offered no glory and no victory. Wilfred Owen, who was killed two weeks before the Armistice, asked:

> What passing bells for these who die as cattle?
>   —Only the monstrous anger of the guns.
>   Only the stuttering rifles' rapid rattle
> Can patter out their hasty orisons.

Owen became a pacifist—"Suffer dishonour and disgrace, but never resort to arms. Be bullied, be outraged; but do not kill."[18]—but he still continued to serve at the front because he felt that by doing so his protests against the war would carry greater force. But there were others who had no desire to come to any terms with a situation so completely absurd.

Most people were not likely to recite the poetry of Sassoon or Owen. They preferred the more patriotic verses with glorious and uplifting themes. The French even dredged up some of the early poetry of Victor Hugo, written during his exuberantly royalist days in which he celebrated the glory of dying for one's country. In Britain, one of the most anthologized poems was Lucy Whitmell's "Christ in Flanders," which restated the comfortable assumption that there were no atheists in the trenches: "We never thought about You much in England— / But now that we are far away from England— / We have no doubts, we know that You are here."[19] In Germany, poets like Rudolf Alexander Schröder produced the popular stuff: "Steel and iron shall lie shattered beneath your strength; / For you I will live—will die. / Germany! Germany!"[20] Later generations would find such chauvinistic utterances either embarrassing or funny.

The Culture of Flag Waving. The output of protest was minuscule compared to the production of official art. Propaganda, often best conveyed through graphic images, was an intimate part of the mobilization of societies and the power of their war message. With the constriction of the private art market, many artists turned their talents to war work to earn a living. Governments wanted to immortalize various aspects of the conflict with appropriate paintings and sculpture. Older, established artists naturally had the best chance to get these important commissions. Their younger, less prominent colleagues had to take what was left. A host of special agencies and military services awarded most of the contracts. For the most part, they used art to stimulate patriotism, sacrifice, and hatred for a specific purpose—to raise money for the Third War Loan, to help Belgian relief, to raise enlistments for the Navy, to collect women's hair, or to induce people to eat fish instead of meat.

The poster was the most effective medium. All countries embraced this form of advertisement with special delight, none more so than the United States. In

A triumphant Marianne, holding the French flag and brandishing her sword, shouts "For the Flag! For Victory!" Posters were without peer in projecting a simple visual image to exhort people to action, in this case to get the French to subscribe to a new war loan.

less than two years, the Americans printed twenty million copies of around 2,500 posters, more than all the other belligerents combined.[21] Poster art became the true art of the people. It was dramatic and did not have to be studied to be appreciated. But posters also had a sinister side, for through them the state was trying to control the hearts and minds of its citizens. Yet ironically, no record revealed the spirit of that period better, except perhaps music.

Everybody knew "Keep The Home-Fires Burning," the haunting ballad that ended with the promise "There's a silver lining Through the dark cloud shining. Turn the dark cloud inside out, Till the boys come Home."[22] Many songs were less bleary-eyed and expressed more aggressive hopes. The Belgians were going to put the kibosh on the kaiser, the Germans were going to sail against England, and the British were going to pack up their troubles in their old kit bag and smile, smile, smile. The longer the war lasted, however, the less such songs appealed to the soldiers themselves. Sassoon reacted furiously to cheap theatrical entertainment:

I'd like to see a Tank come down the stalls
Lurching to rag-time tunes, or 'Home, Sweet Home,'
And there'd be no more jokes in Music-halls
To mock the riddled corpses round Bapaume.[23]

One of the most popular antiwar songs was "I Didn't Raise My Boy to Be a Soldier": "I brought him up to be my pride and joy. Who dares to place a musket on his shoulder, To shoot some other mother's darling boy?"[24] But British soldiers preferred to make up their own caustic verses to old hymns and music hall tunes. They sang "When this bloody war is over" to the tune of "What a Friend We Have in Jesus," or "Forward Joe Soap's army, marching without fear, with our old commander safely in the rear" to the tune of "Onward, Christian Soldiers." The *poilu* found solace in the more gloomy "Chanson de Craonne": "Good-bye life, good-bye love, good-bye to all women. It's finished forever with this cruel war. It's on the heights of Craonne that one lays down his life. For we are all doomed, we are those sacrificed."[25]

The entry of the United States revived the uncritical gusto of earlier days. American songwriters more than made up for their country's Johnny-come-lately status, grinding out ditties like "Just like Washington Crossed the Delaware, General Pershing Will Cross the Rhine," "We're Going Over the Top and We'll Be Marching Thro' Berlin in the Morning," "When Yankee Doodle Marches through Berlin, There'll Be a Hot Time in the U.S.A.," and "It's a Long Way to Berlin but We'll Get There." Some songs expressed anxiety about the dangers of French civilization: "How 'Ya Gonna Keep 'em down on the Farm after They've Seen Paree?" and "You'll Have to Put Him to Sleep with the Marseillaise and Wake Him up with a Ooo-La-La." The lyrics of this last song warned American girls that the French women "have no loveless days and every kiss is chock full of pep." The most famous of all the American songs was George M. Cohan's "Over There," which immediately appeared in a French version. The French and British found out that the Americans would indeed arrive, and they would not go home "till it's over over there."[26] They badly needed such reassurance.

The Reorganization of Governments

The Fall of Nicholas II. In Russia, the tsarist government was disintegrating rapidly. The capricious Rasputin used his influence with the tsaritza to rearrange the ministry to suit himself, making any comprehensive policy impossible. He replaced the pro-English foreign minister, Sergei Sazonov, with Boris Stürmer who was known to be sympathetic to Germany. Stürmer was also premier and during his nine months in office gave no central direction to the affairs of state; to avoid criticism, he evaded the Duma as much as possible. After he was implicated in several financial scandals, mounting opposition finally brought about his resignation. His replacement, Aleksandr Trepov, tried to clean house. He even offered Rasputin a bribe of 200,000 rubles in cash if he would quit politics and return to Siberia. Rasputin told the tsaritza, thereby enhancing his reputation as incorruptible. The tsar had once protested that so many changes in government made his head spin, but he refused to heed the warnings that Rasputin's presence threatened his dynasty. At the end of 1916, every party in the Duma combined in opposition to the ministry. Already a plot was in motion to kill Rasputin; the date set was the night of 16 December after the closing session of the Duma.

The plotters came from the highest levels of society. The main instigator was Grand Duke Dimitri Pavlovich, a favorite nephew of the tsar. He had convinced the nominal leader Prince Feliks Yusupov, son of the richest woman in Russia and husband of a niece of the tsar, and Yusupov in turn had contacted Vladimir Purishkevich, the leader of the reactionary faction in the Duma, and two other participants. The conspirators invited Rasputin to Yusupov's town house and gave him some almond and chocolate pastries and Madeira laced with potassium cyanide. When the poison failed, Yusupov shot him with a revolver. Even then Rasputin was not dead and tried to escape. More shots finished the job, and the weighted body was dumped into the nearby icy Moika Canal where it was fished out two days later. Rasputin was only symptomatic of a diseased system, and his disappearance removed the last great excuse for the tsar's incapacity to govern Russia, exposing him as hollow symbol, who inspired more disgust than loyalty. The monk's death taught Nicholas nothing. The assassins had hoped Nicholas would come to his senses and accept the leadership of the Duma; instead he became more reactionary. Isolated in eighteenth-century baroque splendor at the palace of Tsarskoye Selo, fifteen miles south of Petrograd, where he had returned for the Christmas holidays, the tsar found it difficult to take the warnings of impending revolution seriously.

Meanwhile the war had lost its popularity. Each campaign had resulted in huge casualties with no apparent gains. After three years of war, 1.3 million Russians had been killed, while another 3.9 million were taken prisoner. An unprofessional mob had replaced the old army. Self-inflicted wounds were frequent and wholesale desertions commonplace. Yet, ironically, it was not so much the senseless fighting that made the soldiers mutinous as the breakdown of the food and support services on which they depended. Russian soldiers did not like war, but they wanted to remain patriotic. Now, feeling the government had abandoned them, they returned from the front, many flocking to the larger cities where they spread discontent and defeatism. During the first six weeks of 1917, 750,000 workers went on strike, more than in the entire preceding year. The writer Maksim Gorky found it difficult to determine the direction the mass discontent would go, but feared it would lead to anarchism.

Despite the urgency of the situation, the tsar continued to govern with a cabal left over from the time of Rasputin. Premier Prince Nikolai Golitzyn, approaching senility, could not control his subordinates. The minister of the interior, Aleksandr Protopopov, periodically consulted the dead Rasputin for guidance and spent a great deal of his time at the royal palace paying court to the tsaritza. The minister of war, General Mikhail Beliaeff, shocked the French and British representatives of the Supreme Command with his ignorance of military affairs. On 7 January, at a New Year's reception at the Winter Palace, Duma President Mikhail Rodzyanko begged the tsar to dismiss the cabinet and appoint one that would have the confidence of the nation. He warned that the monarch could no longer take the loyalty of his subjects for granted: "do not compel the people to choose between you and the good of the country. So far, the ideas of the Tsar and the Motherland were indissoluble, but lately they have begun to be separated."[27] Earlier General Brusilov had stated, "If I had to choose between the Emperor and Russia, I follow Russia."[28] Like him, many army commanders feared an approaching revolution, and some even welcomed a coup d'état.

The regime reacted to the current discontent by strengthening the forces of authority. Large quantities of automatic weapons, which should have been sent to the front, were distributed to the Petrograd police. The heavy artillery that the

French had delivered the previous year for use against the Germans remained at Tsarskoye Selo. The government placed the Petrograd military under its direct command. These measures reassured the tsar, and he warned that he would order the Duma dissolved unless criticism from its members ceased. Nicholas personally appointed General Sergei Khabalov to maintain order and, on 8 March, left to return to the Stavka at Mogilev. The tsar was happy to return to Supreme Headquarters: "My brain is resting here," he wrote, "no Ministers, no troublesome questions demanding thought." He told his wife he even had some time on his hands and had decided to "take up dominoes again."[29]

Back in Petrograd, people formed all-night queues in front of bakeries and grocery stores. Below-zero temperatures and an exceptionally heavy snowfall during the last week of February brought the city's public transportation system to a standstill. But despite the weather, the main streets were crowded with discontented citizens. On Thursday, 8 March 1917, those protesting the bread shortages were joined by demonstrations from a Socialist Woman's Day march and by groups of idle workers locked out of the Putilov armament factory because of a wage dispute. The police made little attempt to interfere. Few people were aware that a great change was imminent. Popular excitement increased the following morning, when the Red Flag appeared and demonstrators sang the "Marseillaise," while others shouted "Down with the war" or "Down with the autocracy." Troops were sent into working-class districts. In some cases the soldiers fired on the crowd; in others, they either hesitated or refused. As the crowds moved about the streets— the principal avenue in Petrograd, the Nevsky Prospect, was a solid mass of marchers—the soldiers and workers gradually began to coalesce. On the third day of the demonstration, the normal life of the city could no longer continue. The tsar disdainfully commanded his military deputy, General Khabalov, to end the turmoil within twenty-four hours.

By Sunday, 11 March, order appeared to have been restored. But this was merely the calm before the storm. During the next twenty-four hours the discipline of the Petrograd garrison evaporated. Out of a force of 150,000 men, Khabalov could only form a special detachment of 1,000, but when he used this unit for riot duty, it broke apart and disappeared into the crowd. The situation was chaotic. A subaltern of the mutinous Volynsky Regiment, fleeing after he had killed his captain, confessed that he did not know whether an hour later he would be a national hero or hanged. Rodzyanko telegraphed the tsar that the situation could yet be saved by making concessions. Nicholas remarked to one of his aides, "This fat Rodzyanko has written me some nonsense, to which I will not even reply." He ordered the Duma dissolved, but the deputies refused to obey. They stayed in their assembly hall, the Tauride Palace—built by Prince Potemkin, the lover of Catherine II—and created a special Provisional Committee to restore authority.

Thousands of people looked to the Duma for leadership. They flocked to the Tauride Palace, blocked the entrances, jammed the stairwells, and roamed the corridors. The authority of the Russian monarchy had collapsed, and nobody could restore order. The revolution had occurred almost exclusively in Petrograd. Less than two hundred had died. On 12 March, various left-wing members of the Duma met with labor representatives and rebel troop leaders in the Tauride Palace to form a provisional executive committee for a Soviet of Workers' and Soldiers' Deputies. The inspiration for this organization came from the St. Petersburg Soviet of Workers' Deputies, which had been formed in 1905 to direct the activities of the strikers. Starting as a coordinating group, it had grown into a formal representative body of the leading workers' organizations and socialist parties with its own executive committee. It was resuscitated in this form in 1917 with an executive committee that consisted exclusively of intellectuals representing the socialist parties. The meetings of its general assembly were more boisterous and disorganized.

At first, neither the Soviet nor the Provisional Government exercised any real control. The Soviet, like the Duma, claimed to be the real representative of the workers and soldiers, but it lacked constitutional authority. Its leaders were reluctant to provoke a direct confrontation and assume power on their own. They therefore decided to defend the interests of the proletariat by acting as watchdogs. Actually, the rapid collapse of the monarchy had caught the revolutionaries off guard. The trade union movement was disorganized. Its leaders were better trained in conspiracy than administration. The Soviet's ranks were made up of workers and soldiers with more spirit than ability.

In Petrograd, crowds, intoxicated with the prospect of creating a new Russia, burned police stations, tore imperial emblems from government buildings, and broke into stores and wineshops. Hungry, impatient factory workers demanded shorter hours and better living conditions; when these were not immediately forthcoming, they seized the factories. In the countryside, peasants were more concerned with expropriating the land than freedom of speech. They wanted land and refused to make any more compensation payments. The pressure by minorities for national autonomy also increased. The Poles, Georgians, Armenians, Finns, Letts, and Ukrainians, who had all traditionally resented Great Russian domination, sought independence under their own native leaders.

Nicholas tried to return home from army headquarters on 13 March, but orders from Petrograd diverted the imperial train to Pskov. From here the tsar telegraphed Rodzyanko of his willingness to make certain concessions, but he was too late. The politicians and the generals had decided that nothing could save the situation but the monarch's abdication. On the afternoon of 15 March, the formal document was placed before Nicholas. Impassively, Nicholas signed, abdicating first in favor of his son and then, when he was reminded that the boy's hemophilia was incurable, changing it in favor of his brother, Grand Duke Mikhail. But the crown of the Romanovs was no longer much of a prize, and Mikhail refused to accept it unless it was offered by an assembly of the people. The tsar's abdication hardly calmed the tensions of the Petrograd mob and had little effect on the fortunes of the soldiers at the front. The revolution was a revolution of defeatism, fanned by hunger; it was a protest against the ineptitude of a regime that had proved incapable of organizing the country for a war that no longer seemed to make much sense.

The Central Powers Change Leaders. By 1916, the German War Office had assumed almost total control over the economic life of the nation. General Wilhelm Gröner had compulsory authority over civilian labor; he was responsible for the procurement of raw materials and industrial productivity; he oversaw the newly created synthetics industry; and he directed foreign and domestic trade operations. The War Raw Materials Board, the Munitions Board, and the War Food Office were all under his supervision. Chancellor Bethmann Hollweg did not believe that the interests of the civilians should take precedence over the generals because, if a problem should arise, the kaiser had the power to make the final decision. However, Wilhelm invariably sided with his army commanders. In August 1916, after the French recaptured the fort of Douaumont, he followed their advice and replaced Erich Falkenhayn with Marshal Paul von Hindenburg and General Erich

The war lords of Imperial Germany gather for a strategy session. Paul von Hindenburg briefs his royal master Wilhelm II while First Quartermaster-general Erich Ludendorff attentively looks on. But by 1917 Ludendorff had become the real master of Germany. The obviously posed picture appears to have been taken at à hunting lodge rather than military headquarters. The three are hardly dressed for work.

Ludendorff, who were to share responsibility for military operations. The ruthless Ludendorff, as always, remained the real power in the tandem; to avoid any implication that he was second in command, he gave himself the title First Quartermaster-General. Ludendorff was totally committed to fighting the war to the finish.

Chancellor Bethmann Hollweg, once one of his country's most determined annexationists, had concluded that Germany could no longer win a decisive victory. He wanted to end the conflict by negotiations, even if this meant that Germany had to return to its pre-war frontiers. Others agreed. Certain Reichstag deputies, particularly the Social Democrats, were trying to pass a resolution that would commit Germany to a peace of understanding and permanent reconciliation of peoples without "forced territorial acquisitions and political, economic, or financial oppressions." But such a vaguely worded resolution could expect no support from the military or from the country at large, since most of the German people were still convinced of a German victory.

Any talk of reconciliation made the military leaders nervous, especially since the longer the war continued, the more Germany's traditional social system appeared to be threatened. Already many of the younger Junker officers had been killed and were being replaced by men with less impressive pedigrees. Certain Reichstag deputies had begun to discuss plans to strip Prussia of its favored political position. Ludendorff faulted the chancellor for failing to curb the agitation and resolved to get rid of him. The opportunity came with the Supreme Command's decision to resume unrestricted submarine warfare, which the chancellor feared would lead to the entry of the United States into the war. But Hindenburg argued that the war would be won before any American support could become decisive. The kaiser, eager to teach Wilson a lesson, supported his military chiefs. Bethmann Hollweg knew his days were numbered. On 27 February 1917, he addressed the Reichstag, promising constitutional reform after the war. The military chiefs told the kaiser that the chancellor's continued presence in office was deleterious to success, and Hindenburg and Ludendorff threatened to resign. The kaiser was indignant, but bowing to their pressure, he dumped Bethmann Hollweg. The army promptly replaced him with Dr. Georg Michaelis, but when this chancellor outlived his usefulness, the Supreme Command dismissed him as well. Michaelis's problem was that he had failed to control the Reichstag; specifically, he had failed to prevent the adoption, on 17 July 1917, of the Social Democrats' peace resolution, which passed with the support of the Progressive and Center parties. The Supreme Command then installed another puppet, Count Georg von Hertling.

In addition to their problems at home, the German generals were concerned about the growing war weariness of their oldest ally, Austria. For sixty-eight years, Emperor Franz Josef had ruled over his multinational empire like a beleaguered parent with a family of quarreling children. He had no solutions or long-range plans, but simply hoped to make it from one day to the next with his powers intact. His longevity was one of the regime's greatest assets, conveying an image of permanence that seemed to offer concrete evidence of the Habsburg dynasty's proud boast of eternal life written on its coat of arms. Even more than two years of war had not seemed to jeopardize the unity of the empire seriously. The government had imposed a tight censorship on the press, prohibited political assemblies, and suspended civil rights. Parliament was adjourned for an indefinite period. Still, the bureaucracy—heavily German and Hungarian at the top, but more supranational at the lower levels—was generally loyal to the dynasty, as was the army. What the absence of a glorious national historical tradition failed to provide, the fear of the consequences of disintegration did. Aristocrats dreaded social revolution. National minorities feared subjugation by outside powers. Industrialists foresaw economic chaos. Difficult as the present might be, it was preferable to an uncertain future even though confidence in the prospect of victory had been shattered. On 21 November 1916, Franz Josef died in his sleep at the age of eighty-six. For three days, he lay in state at Schönbrun Palace while thousands of subjects filed by his catafalque. Then his body was taken to the royal pantheon at the church of the Capuchins.

The new monarch Karl I (Karl IV of Hungary), Franz Josef's grand nephew, feared that a continuation of the war could destroy the unity of his heterogeneous kingdom. He was not disloyal to the Dual Alliance, but unlike his predecessor he had no desire to fight a war to the finish as an obedient junior partner of Germany. Therefore the central aim of his regime became his desire to end the fighting through negotiation. It was a difficult time. The German determination to resume unrestricted submarine warfare and to retain certain captured territory had virtually doomed the possibility of obtaining a peace with no annexations and no indemnities. Moreover, the Austrians themselves might have difficulty agreeing to the terms of the secret Treaty of London whose provisions had been leaked to them; it was also doubtful whether the leaders of the dominant national groups, the Austro-Germans and the Magyars, were prepared to agree to a separate peace.

Nevertheless, in the spring of 1917, Karl used his brother-in-law, Prince Sixtus, an officer in the Belgian Army, to send out feelers to the French president Raymond Poincaré. The French were suspicious, but were willing to listen, especially since Karl promised in a letter to support their claims to Alsace-Lorraine. The exchanges were brought to a sudden end, however, when Count Ottokar Czernin, the Austro-Hungarian foreign minister, alluded to their existence. This prompted Georges Clemenceau to publish the entire correspondence in April 1918. Karl denied everything and tried unsuccessfully to reassure the Germans of his loyalty, but henceforth they regarded him as a man who could not be trusted.

The Allies took a similar position and, shortly after the Sixtus affair, began recognizing the national councils of the empire's Slavic and Latin populations as agencies of their peoples, thereby accelerating the empire's decay. When parliament was allowed to reassemble in May 1917 after a three-year prohibition, the Slavic delegates left little doubt that they no longer remained loyal to the empire. Under Karl, the imperial government began to move toward recognizing local autonomy, but the Germans felt these steps went too far, while the Slavs denounced them as too vague and noncommittal. The empire's problems were more than political. The national debt stood at 70 billion crowns. Mounting government deficits were covered by printing more money. Industrial resources were heavily strained, and people were starving in many parts of the country. In Hungary the food situation was far better than in Austria, but the Hungarians chose to keep their supplies for themselves. Given such lack of internal unity and responsibility, the Austro-Hungarian Empire was clearly an anachronism. It had failed to solve its ethnic problems, to reform its society, or to modernize its economy. It had entered the war to try to prevent the very dissolution that was now occurring. The empire simply ran out of time. The demands of the conflict aggravated problems that might have been solvable in times of peace.

Politicians and Generals in the Entente. In Britain, Lloyd George gave most of the important posts in his government, formed 6 December 1916, to Conservatives. He established a special inner cabinet to make major decisions unfettered by normal politics. To this he added a "garden suburb," a group of experts who provided him with advice outside regular government channels. But despite the enormous power he exercised, Lloyd George was never able to get rid of Sir Douglas Haig, the army commander whom he personally blamed for the great casualties suffered on the Western Front. Differences in their backgrounds heightened the tensions between the two. Haig was an Anglicized Scot with a lust for a noble title. His close ties to all the right people helped him consolidate his command. Lloyd George first tried to reduce Haig's power by working out a special organizational arrangement with French Premier Aristide Briand. The British army commander would henceforth receive his orders from a specially created chief-of-staff operating out of French headquarters. The proposal was sprung on Haig at the Calais Conference at the end of February 1917 and so disgusted him that he said he would rather "be tried by Court Martial than betray the Army by agreeing to its being placed under the French."[30] The chief of the General Staff, Sir Henry Robertson, proposed that they both resign. Instead, the British army served under the French commander-in-chief, Robert Nivelle, only for the forthcoming spring offensive. Afterwards the situation continued as before. Haig kept George V secretly informed of the whole affair and offered to lay down his command if the king thought it best. But the British monarch reaffirmed his confidence in Haig and assured the general that he, George V, would "do his utmost to protect Haig's interests."[31]

In the meantime, the French general Joseph Joffre was having difficulty with the parliamentarians, especially those eligible for military service who had deferments for as long as the National Assembly remained in session. Since the National Assembly stayed in permanent session, they could decide for themselves how much time they would devote to government business and how much time they would spend in the army. This convenient arrangement put them beyond the reach of the conventional military authorities. In short, the delegates could come to the front and return to Paris when they chose; once back in Paris, they might decide to deal with the very misconduct and grievances that they had investigated at the front.

Continuous parliamentary pressure maintained the authority of the Sacred Union over the generals. The Ministry of War alone received some three hundred interpellations daily. After the failure of the attacks in Artois and Champagne in 1915 and the reverses at Verdun the following spring, the demands for account-ability increased. Both the Senate and the Chamber of Deputies created secret committees—eight were eventually established—to investigate military operations, and frequently the evidence of incompetence they heard was rather discouraging. One senator said that he often came away from these sessions "with a sad and startling feeling of doubt in the prospects for our victory."[32] At a secret session, on 16 June 1916, a soldier-delegate, André Maginot, charged the High Command with failure to provide Verdun with adequate defenses. (The destruction of the forts at Liège had made Joffre doubt the value of permanent fortifications, and he had removed Verdun's heavy guns.) That accusation soon translated into demands for Joffre's dismissal. Premier Aristide Briand tried to make it as painless as possible. On 3 December, he invited Joffre to resign as commander of the Armies of Northern France, while keeping the title of general-in-chief of the French Army, the first step in removing him from command altogether. The government pro-moted Joffre to the dignity of marshal, made him chief technical adviser to the government, gave him his own office at the Invalides, and forgot about him. Joffre's disgrace had no popular repercussions.

The public was more concerned with bread and butter issues: prices that rose much faster than wages; shortages of sugar, meat, and coal; and the inequity of demanding that the working classes sacrifice for victory without exacting compa-rable deprivations from the employers and capitalists. Most workers' organizations favored a "peace without indemnities and without annexations" based on the "self-determination of peoples." Some of the more radical unions advocated transform-ing the war into a class struggle against capitalism. But most French people also favored fighting until the Germans were pushed out of their country and were willing to support men who could get the job done.

General Robert Nivelle, whose use of the creeping barrage at Verdun wrongly enhanced his reputation and led to his replacement of Joffre as commander-in-chief, was convinced that the situation on the Western Front in the spring of 1917 was never better for a breakthrough. He intended to employ massive artillery and violent infantry assaults to break the great enemy wedge at Noyon in Picardy. Before the offensive could begin, however, the Germans removed the salient with a strategic withdrawal from one thousand square miles of French territory, willfully destroying everything of value in the abandoned areas. Ludendorff had decided to remain on the defensive in France until his submarine campaign showed positive results. Minister of War Paul Painlevé assumed that the evacuation would auto-matically force Nivelle to change his mind. But Nivelle informed him that the plan would go forth with only minor alteration, and he dismissed the likelihood of German reinforcements from the Eastern Front, saying, "I do not fear numbers. The greater the numbers, the greater the victory."[33] Nivelle even threatened to resign, confident that the government would not dare replace a newly appointed commander without giving him a chance to prove himself.

The Italians wanted to become a great power on the cheap, and they had made few serious preparations for entering the war. The head of the Italian army, General Luigi Cadorna, had no field command experience, his career having been shaped largely by staff work. He had, however, written a training manual that was widely used. Cadorna resented taking advice from anyone, including the battle-experienced commanders of Italy's allies. He also hated politicians. Little legislative control could be exerted over his actions for the simple reason that the Italian parliament had virtually ceased to exercise its authority during the war; instead, government decisions were enacted by decree. In this state of affairs, Cadorna managed to have his own nominee, General Vittorio Zupelli, made war minister.

Italy had three wartime premiers, none of whom was a real leader. Antonio Salandra, who took the country into the war unprepared, had gambled that the fighting would be over in three months. After a year of war, he had done little to strengthen the country's defenses or its will to fight. His successor Paolo Boselli, who replaced him in June 1916, was at seventy-eight the oldest deputy in parliament. Boselli was chosen because many feared that a younger man might exert too much control. His cabinet included right-wing Catholics, radicals, and reformist socialists. The idea of national union was good, but in practice it led to more squabbling and indecisive action. The lack of military success also led to defeatism and protest. In a bread riot in Turin in the summer of 1917, at least forty-one people died. Pope Benedict XV called for a peace without annexations. In October 1917, the ineffectual Boselli gave way to Vittorio Orlando who, although not a great improvement over his predecessors, had the advantage of being in office when the Central Powers went down to defeat. All in all, the war had cruelly exploited the patriotism of the Italian people and left the country impoverished and facing revolution and tyranny.

The Russian Revolution

The Competition for Power. Liberal Constitutional Democrats (Kadets) led by ineffectual Prince Georgi Lvov dominated the first cabinet of the Provisional Government that had been organized after proper consultation with the members of the Executive Committee of the Petrograd Soviet. The only person with direct ties to the two bodies was Alexander Kerensky who was minister of justice in the Provisional Government and vice-chairman of the Soviet Executive Committee. Kerensky completely overshadowed the bland Lvov. The Soviet did not demand that the Provisional Government nationalize industry, distribute lands to the peasantry, or immediately end the war. Instead, the Soviet pressed for political amnesty; advocated freedom of speech, press, and association; and agreed that "strict military discipline" should be preserved in the army. It left the question of whether a republic or a limited monarchy should be established to a future constituent assembly. The dual system of authority was copied throughout Russia. In Tsaritsyn (later Stalingrad, now Volgograd), the Soviet actually pushed aside the regular civilian authorities, but most other cities followed the example of Petrograd. Eager to demonstrate a break with the past, the Provisional Government scrupulously avoided spilling blood and, on 25 March, abolished the death penalty. The government's guarantee of freedom of expression established civil liberties for the first time in Russian history. The Provisional Government also proclaimed equality before the law and abolished all restrictions on religious and national minorities.

But Russia's new leaders were also eager to seize the spoils of victory and favored a continuation of the war. They wanted to strengthen their country's position in Poland and in the Ottoman Empire, but claimed that they did not want to increase Russia's "external power at the expense of other nations." Later, when the cabinet included more socialists, the stated goal became a "peace without annexations, without indemnities . . . on the basis of self-determination of peoples." But the

Forces of the provisional government fire on a group of protesters during the July Days of 1917. The Bolsheviks re-created this action on Petrograd's Nevsky Prospekt for propaganda purposes and claimed that photos taken then were photos of the actual event.

socialists were trying to have it both ways, since many of them also favored a continuation of the war against Germany. The March Revolution had not resulted from war weariness, but from a desire to create an effective government to defeat the Germans. Continuing the war was universally popular.

The Petrograd Soviet attracted a cross section of socialist parties from moderate to extreme; they were divided by strong doctrinal positions and disagreements on tactics. All Russian socialists wanted to create a more just society and to change human nature, but the similarities stopped there. The radicals were largely divided between the Socialist Revolutionaries and the Social Democrats, both of which formed just before the turn of the century. The Socialist Revolutionary party was committed to terrorism, including assassinations of public officials to provoke the masses into revolt. They made their appeal primarily, but not exclusively, to the peasants. They aimed to abolish private property and transfer control over the land to the village communes. The Socialist Revolutionaries had the support of most of the peasantry, but did not neglect the industrial workers whose support they also deemed necessary for revolution. They believed that urban and village workers were the real creators of wealth and were therefore bound together in opposition to the parasitical ruling classes.

The Social Democratic party rejected terrorism. It had an almost exclusively urban, industrial working-class constituency and viewed the peasantry with great contempt. Class was defined in terms of relationship to the means of production. Since 1912, the Social Democrats had been divided into two factions: the Mensheviks, who still called themselves the Social Democratic party, and the Bolsheviks, who took the name Russian Social Democratic Labor party. A clash of personalities and party organization occasioned the division. The Bolsheviks demanded that their followers give unquestioning obedience to the party central committee, while the Mensheviks allowed all party members to share democratically in the decision-making process. But the two also differed significantly on revolutionary tactics. The Mensheviks wanted the bourgeois democratic revolution to run its course before carrying out their own socialist revolution. Until then, they intended to cooperate with non-Marxist groups in governing Russia. The Bolsheviks, on the other hand, wanted to replace the Romanovs immediately with a dictatorship of the proletariat and carry out the destruction of capitalism.

The Soviet, run by its executive committee, the Ispolkom, was initially under the control of the Mensheviks. Their leader Nikolai Chkheidze became chairman; the vice-chairman, Kerensky, was a Socialist Revolutionary. The Ispolkom acted as if its decisions had the force of law. On 14 April, it issued "Order No. 1," which was intended to remove the threat of counterrevolution by tsarist army officers. The order called on the army to observe "the strictest military discipline"; it allowed soldiers to participate in elections to the Soviet and to army committees. When the order was broadcast to the troops at the front, it was wrongly interpreted as recognizing the soldiers' right to elect their own officers, causing the already weakened authority of military commanders to deteriorate further.

The Return of Lenin. The Bolsheviks had made little contribution to the March Revolution, and many of their leaders only returned after the general political amnesty. Their first manifesto, issued on 12 March, called for land to the people, the eight-hour day, and a constituent assembly elected by universal suffrage and secret ballot. They did not demand an end to the war. Lev Kamenev explained that the slogan "Down with the War" was a device to pressure the Provisional Government "to make an effort to persuade all the countries at war to open negotiations about the ways of stopping the world war." Until then, the soldiers would remain at their battle stations. But Kamenev was only a stand-in for the real head of the party, Vladimir Lenin, who had been living in Switzerland since the beginning of the war.

Lenin returned home because the Germans, hoping to take Russia out of the war, arranged his passage through their country in a sealed railway carriage, then allowed him to cross by boat to Sweden and from there to Finland. The Germans also subsidized the Bolsheviks with secret funds. A demonstration of anti-German socialists marred Lenin's leave-taking at the Zurich station. They shouted, "Spies! German spies! Look how happy they are—going home at the kaiser's expense!" However, Lenin accepted German aid without any sense of obligation.

Lenin believed that the imperialists had concocted the war in order to increase their power over the proletariat. He attacked the treachery of the socialists who had supported the very governments they should have tried to overthrow. He believed that the masses would have risen in a general strike to prevent the outbreak of the war had not opportunistic leaders betrayed them. Lenin proposed a new Workers' International to mobilize the proletariat for an assault on capitalist and imperialist governments. With his arrival at Petrograd's Finland station on 16 April 1917, the Bolsheviks' real struggle for power began. Lenin insisted that cooperation with the Provisional Government cease, and that the Soviets be used as organs of insurrection. He defined his position in the "April Theses," delivered in two speeches, in which he declared that the March Revolution had only started a process that would transform the world war into a class war and end with the victory of the proletariat. His program included "the establishment of a Soviet rather than a parliamentary republic; the abolition of the existing police, army and bureaucracy; the confiscation of all private lands; the immediate merger of all banks under Soviet control; the establishment of Soviet control of production and distribution of goods; [and] the rebuilding of the Socialist International along revolutionary lines."[34]

Most other Marxists viewed Lenin's program with hostility. They believed the call for an immediate revolution was premature; they also suspected that the Bolsheviks wanted to establish a new, militant International only to create their own dictatorship. Lenin even had difficulty convincing certain members of his own executive that the April Theses should be accepted as a program of action. Furthermore, many Bolsheviks did not oppose the continuation of the war, which they believed still had the support of most Russians.

Efforts at Stability. No effective policy could exist without a certain measure of coercion, but the members of the Provisional Government found it difficult to assert their authority. The tsarist police force had been disbanded and, as yet, had no replacement. The Soviet controlled the troops of the Petrograd garrison. A purge of the army officer corps had left whole units without adequate leadership. Furthermore, the cabinet itself lacked unity and will. Minister of War Alexander Kerensky hoped to increase popular support for the government by creating a new revolutionary spirit in the army. He had General Alexei Brusilov appointed commander-in-chief and sent a series of political commissars to the various units of the army to act as a liaison between the soldiers' committees and the government. Kerensky also began planning for a new campaign against the Germans.

The "Kerensky offensive" began on 29 June. The advance continued for two weeks, but took a tremendous toll in Russian lives. The German counterattack, which began on 19 July, pushed the Russians back with relative ease. With great difficulty, the Russian army commanders managed to keep the retreat from becoming a rout. Desertions increased, and whole regiments refused to fight. The troops of the Eleventh Army lynched their officers and went on a rampage of looting and arson.

Certain radical Bolsheviks believed the time was right to seize power in Petrograd. However, most of the members of the Central Committee felt that such an uprising would be premature, since the Petrograd Soviet still supported the government. But the extremists had their way and a revolt began on 15 July. Fearing the movement might succeed without them, the Bolshevik leaders decided to assume command, but were unable to mobilize any significant power to overthrow the government. Troops loyal to the Provisional Government entered the city and quickly restored order. The Bolsheviks were branded as German agents, and the Provisional Government ordered the arrest of their leaders. Lenin fled to Finland. On 6 August, a cabinet reshuffle, preceded by the mass resignation of the Kadets, made Kerensky prime minister and virtual dictator of the Provisional Government. His cabinet still received the support of the Petrograd Soviet, but Kerensky lacked the widespread support and the personality necessary to pursue a determined policy. He replaced Brusilov with General Lavr Kornilov, who tightened military discipline, and agreed to restore the death penalty in the army. Wanting to free the Provisional Government from its dependence on the Soviet, Kornilov demanded that Kerensky execute civilians who were guilty of sedition and place limits on freedom of expression, particularly the right to propagandize. When the Germans captured Riga on 3 September, Kornilov obliged the government to grant him direct control of the Petrograd garrison.

Kerensky, however, was now convinced that Kornilov wanted to take over the government and had him dismissed. But Kornilov refused to go and ordered his troops to march on Petrograd. The Soviet Executive Committee established a Military Revolutionary Committee, which included the Bolsheviks, and organized the resistance. Agents of the Soviet helped to undermine the loyalty of Kornilov's

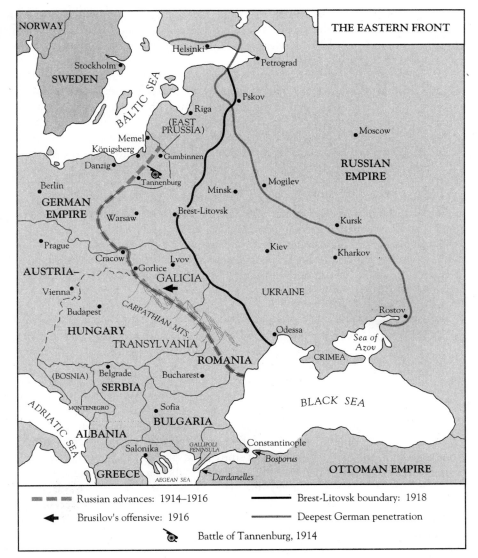

Map 3

THE EASTERN FRONT

Russian advances: 1914–1916

Brusilov's offensive: 1916

Brest-Litovsk boundary: 1918

Deepest German penetration

Battle of Tannenburg, 1914

own units, which refused to participate in an attack on the civilian government. The attempted coup fizzled.

Kerensky became commander-in-chief, but his authority remained weak. No increase in popularity among the representatives of "revolutionary democracy" offset his declining support from the officer corps and the liberal political parties. Furthermore, the Kornilov affair had rehabilitated the Bolsheviks who now had assembled their own military forces, including the Kronstadt naval detachments. On 19 September, the Petrograd Soviet elected Leon Trotsky, a former Menshevik and now a close associate of Lenin, as president; thus, the Bolsheviks had succeeded in establishing control. Lenin was still in exile in Finland.

The Bolshevik Coup d'État. The Petrograd Soviet refused to support Kerensky's coalition government and established a special Military Revolutionary Committee, headed by Trotsky, to control the local army garrison. Lenin returned secretly to the capital on 22 October and the following day managed to convince most of the eleven members of the Central Committee that the time had come for an armed uprising. The next two weeks were spent in active, but hardly secret preparations.

The final blow fell on 7 November. (Under the Russian Julian calender, this was 25 October.) Lenin directed the takeover from his headquarters in the Smolny Institute, a former convent school where the daughters of the tsarist nobility were educated. Trotsky mobilized the local regiments and the Red Guards of the factory workers. The Bolshevik forces occupied strategic buildings throughout the city, mostly without any resistance, posted pickets, and by evening attacked the Winter Palace, most of whose defenders had left at the first rifle shot. Shortly after nine o'clock, the attackers entered the building and arrested the members of the Provisional Government, marching them off to the fortress of St. Peter and St. Paul. In the meantime, Kerensky had escaped, leaving Petrograd disguised as a Serbian officer in a staff car of the American embassy. On his way out of town, he was frequently recognized and even saluted by detachments of troops loyal to the Bolsheviks. His subsequent attempts to organize a force to regain power failed, and he left Russia forever, eventually settling in the United States. Lenin hailed the beginning of the world revolution.

THE MISERY OF VICTORY

The Agony of the Allies

The Entry of the United States. Across the Atlantic, Wilson continued to strengthen his commitment to the Allies, while presuming to judge how Germany should fight the war against its enemies. He talked peace, but emphasized preparedness. In March 1916, he squashed the Gore-McLemore resolution to prohibit Americans from traveling on belligerent ships. That November he won reelection on the lackluster slogan "He kept us out of war." At the beginning of the following year, however, with a new four-year mandate, he began to enumerate war aims. In a speech before the Senate on 22 January 1917, he talked of the necessity of establishing "a peace that will win the approval of mankind," a peace based on "an equality of rights" and on "the principle that governments derive all their just powers from the consent of the governed, and that no right anywhere exists to hand peoples about from sovereignty to sovereignty as if they were property."[35] Wilson also endorsed freedom of the seas, disarmament, and collective security. With these vague, impressionistic "principles of mankind," Wilson committed the United States to a role in peace making that could *only* be attained if the nation participated directly in the war. He thus clearly separated himself from his previously announced policy and indeed from a majority of his own people. He already had his excuse for entry.

Earlier that month, the Germans had again committed themselves to unrestricted submarine warfare, although they knew that this might provoke American intervention. Germany could not afford the continuation of the military stalemate. The Allied blockade had caused severe shortages of food and other materials, and the Battle of Verdun had seriously drained its resources. Therefore the prospect of defeat from tolerating the United States putting its productive capacity at the disposal of the Entente began to outweigh the risks of American entry into the war. The kaiser, in one of his most famous bits of marginalia, wrote, "If Wilson

wants war, let him make it and let him have it." Ludendorff and Hindenburg
figured that if their fleet of 120 submarines could sink at least 600,000 tons of
shipping a month, they could knock Britain out of the war in half a year; the
largest proportion of their intended kill would come from the United States.

The campaign got off to a good start. In February and March 1917, 570,000
tons were sent to the bottom. "The continuation of this rate of loss," wrote a
British official, "would have brought disaster upon all the Allied campaigns and
might well have involved an unconditional surrender."[36] But the attacks had less
effect on American merchant shipping. From 3 August 1914 to 5 April 1917,
enemy torpedoes sunk only six ships for a combined tonnage of 25,988—another
thirteen ships were sunk by mines and gunfire—and took sixty-seven lives.[37] Nevertheless, the German announcement of unrestricted submarine warfare was a red
flag to Wilson, and on 3 February 1917, he severed diplomatic relations with
Berlin.

A further pretext for Wilson's move toward war came with the publication, on
1 March, of the Zimmermann telegram whose message the Americans felt directly
threatened their national security. The telegram, concocted by the German secretary for foreign affairs, Artur von Zimmermann, offered the government of Mexico the return of the "lost territories" from the Mexican War of 1846–1848 if it
attacked the United States in the event of war between the United States and
Germany. These territories included Texas, New Mexico, and Arizona. The Germans hoped to cash in on the strained relations between the United States and
Mexico due to the recent intervention of the United States in Mexican affairs.
The British had intercepted and decoded the transmission, however, and held on
to it until they judged the time right for its release.[38] American outrage was predictable—all the more so as the Germans made no effort to lie their way out of
the affair. Apparently, the American public believed it was all right for Wilson to
enumerate war aims when his country was at peace, but heinous when Germany
did so in the event war should occur. Across the country, newspaper headlines
spoke of a German invasion plot. Many Americans had little interest in European
affairs, but were outraged by Germany's crude attempt to draw Mexico into the
conflict. Neutrality against Germany was about to end.

Since the outbreak of the war in Europe, the United States had been committed
economically and moralistically to an Entente victory. Wilson determined this
could only be accomplished by direct American participation. Although the president did not think in terms of a balance of power—and therefore did not fear
that German hegemony on the European continent would threaten his country's
national security—he did believe that a German triumph would shatter his plans
for creating a new world order. Thus, his posture of neutrality remained viable
only if Germany did not appear to be capable of winning. On 2 April 1917, Wilson
delivered his war message, the greatest ideological invocation since the French
Revolution. "The world," he intoned, "must be made safe for democracy." Four
days later, the Congress gave Wilson what he wanted. The vote was 82 to 6 in
the Senate and 373 to 50 in the House. The United States was at war. With the
Russian Revolution conveniently eliminating tsarist despotism, the Americans
could now truly wave the banners in a fight for "Democracy against Autocracy."

The French Mutiny. Nivelle's attack in Champagne went forth on the sleet-
punished Monday morning of 16 April. Most of the first wave, advancing over the
muddy terrain, never made it to the German wire. Nivelle insisted they try again,
blaming his subordinates for their lack of nerve. The effort continued another

fortnight before it broke down completely on the artillery-infested heights of Craonne and the Chemin des Dames. The casualties had been no higher nor the mistakes any greater than in previous offensives. But the age of heroic blunders was out of fashion: in battalion after battalion, regiment after regiment, the troops refused to participate in further assaults.

The strike began on 29 April, when the Second Battalion of the Eighteenth Regiment, which had lost two-thirds of its men during the recent assault, refused to return to the line. The arrest and execution of the suspected ringleaders quickly ended the revolt. But the matter did not end there. It became a movement and spread, engulfing whole divisions. Then the problem became entirely different: how to arrest hundreds of soldiers and how to determine which were dependable and which were unreliable. In six weeks, 110 units, mostly in the Chemin des Dames sector, were affected. Over two-thirds of 151 recorded instances of mutiny were officially considered "grave." The war minister reported that by June there were only two divisions that were "absolutely and completely reliable" between Paris and the battlefront. As the revolt continued, it became touched by social revolution. Soldiers everywhere were affected by antiwar propaganda inspired by the example of the Russian Revolution. Two Russian brigades serving with the French forces were the most affected and helped to influence the French in nearby camps. Mutineers sang the "Internationale" and waved the red flag of revolution, and some tried to commandeer trains for Paris to petition the government to end the war. Regiments established soviets and elected their own leaders. There were riots, assaults on officers, and episodes of arson. The government and many generals thought they were facing a concerted, planned rebellion. Nothing could have been further from the truth. The strike was largely spontaneous, fueled by desperation, fatigue, and a sense of betrayal. The troops felt their lives were being squandered in senseless attacks. They also had deep-seated grievances against the miserable food and medical services and the absence of regular leave. Many had been in the line a year without permission to go home. The soldiers loathed army staff officers who never got their boots muddy.

The mutiny was part of a wider protest against the war. In May 1917, civilian discontent also reached its peak. One hundred thousand workers in all industries quit work. In Paris and in other large cities, there was considerable disorder. Workers paraded around town flying red flags, and shouted, "Down with the war." The militant metal workers' union, which had increased its membership from less than 10,000 to over 200,000 during the war, called for international working-class solidarity against "the war of conquest." People felt that nations like individuals were mortal.

On 16 May, General Henri-Philippe Pétain, the "savior of Verdun," replaced Nivelle. The new commander moved swiftly to restore morale by removing the major sources of discontent. In a heretofore almost unheard of practice, he made frequent visits to frontline units to address the men, discussing with them his future plans, asking them for their advice, and listening to their grievances. Pétain directed that cooking lessons be given to regimental chefs, began granting regular leave—one week's leave for every four months in the line—and awarded more decorations to sergeants and privates.

At the same time, special military courts-martial tried the mutiny's ringleaders. According to official accounts, 412 were condemned to death, of whom 23 were executed. The figure is questionably low. Many were frequently shot without formal trial or condemned for crimes not listed as mutiny. Over 23,000 men were sentenced to various terms of penal servitude or deprived of their civil rights. On 5

June, Pétain ordered his officers to take all necessary action to restore order, granting them broad powers with the words: "The Commander-in-Chief will protect with his authority all those who display vigor and energy in suppression."[39] Since reliable figures were lacking, the wildest rumors persisted. Disloyal units were supposedly marched into isolated sections of the front and blasted apart by artillery. General Haig said he was told that 30,000 rebels "had to be dealt with."[40] The army handled the mutiny with such discretion and speed that the Germans did not find out until later that whole sections of the enemy's front lines had been undefended. But the French army was never the same again. Pétain acknowledged this when he promised the men that there would be no more costly bloodlettings but only limited offensives using a minimum number of men supported by massive amounts of artillery. "We must wait for the Americans and the tanks," he said.

Passchendaele and Caporetto. During a ceremony at the tomb of Lafayette in the summer of 1917, the American commander, General John Pershing, pledged that his soldiers would "vanquish for the liberty of the world." But previous investigations of the situation at the front had convinced him that there was not much hope for victory that year. The French army, convalescing after the recent carnage and resultant mutiny in Champagne, was being reorganized. The British, having assumed the main role on the Western Front, were in somewhat better shape, but were in no condition to engage in any serious offensive action.

But General Haig thought differently. He planned to cut the enemy lines in Flanders and push northward to capture the channel coast. Admiral John Jellicoe's pessimistic assessment on 20 June 1917 partially dictated the strategy. Jellicoe reported "that owing to the great shortage of shipping due to German submarines, it would be impossible for Great Britain to continue the war in 1918."[41] The capture of the Belgian ports would diminish the danger from U-boats. More importantly, Haig believed that Germany was six months shy of total exhaustion and that "now was the favorable moment for pressing her."[42] Earlier Haig had planned his attack to help support a Russian offensive, but the situation had radically changed. The failure of the Kerensky offensive had effectively taken Russia out of the war. The changed circumstances only increased Haig's determination to gain a great triumph for the British army, which now bore the major brunt of the fighting.

The resultant Battle of Passchendaele lasted from the end of July to the beginning of November. The British fought in a mud porridge that was often so thick that men drowned in the rain-filled shellcraters, while the wounded and dying were sucked out of sight, and field guns were swallowed up. The British advanced their lines seven miles at a cost of 244,879 casualties. Lloyd George, who had opposed the offensive from the start, was furious and resolved to prevent Haig from ever attempting any more of these bloodlettings. The prime minister resolved to keep Haig so short of troops that another such attack would be impossible—a remarkable decision insofar as it might endanger the security of the British armies in France. But Haig's continued support in high places allowed him to weather this crisis, and he continued in command. He eventually received an earldom, but his military reputation had perished, like the lives of his men, in the ooze of Flanders. The defeat at Passchendaele was ironically followed by one of the most dramatic incidents of the war.

On 20 November, an armada of 381 British tanks lumbered toward the German lines near Cambrai. There had been no preliminary artillery bombardment to announce the assault, and the Germans were caught by surprise. The force quickly broke through the three belts of enemy wire and advanced five miles almost to open countryside. The next day victory bells rang out in London to hail the success while Ludendorff contemplated a general retreat. Lack of infantry reserves to exploit the attack killed the initial momentum, however, and within ten days a German counterattack slammed the door shut. What had begun as an attempt to restore British prestige by a *coup de théatre* ended with the resumption of the stalemate. But the advance had provided a glimpse of how tank weaponry would change the future of warfare.

The final phase of the Battle of Passchendaele coincided with the rout of the Italians at Caporetto. For the past two years, the Austrians and the Italians had been battling along their common frontier in the Isonzo River valley south of the Julian and Carnic Alps. The eleven battles fought here between May 1915 and October 1917 resulted in the deaths of over 115,000 Italians and 90,000 Austrians without a significant exchange of territory. The Austrians, exhausted by their battles with the Russians, doubted they could endure further losses and turned to Germany for help. The kaiser was only too pleased to get back at "faithless Italy." Ludendorff, fearing the collapse of the Austro-Hungarian Empire, delayed his Moldavian offensive against Russia and sent six German divisions to the Isonzo theater to reinforce the nine Austrian divisions already there. The Germans planned to outflank the enemy army and head for the plains to the south. They chose the Alpine market town of Caporetto as the point of their attack. Caporetto heretofore had been a quiet sector well to the north of the previous fighting.

The battle began with a five-hour barrage of gas shells and heavy artillery. The attackers then quickly punched a fifteen-mile hole in the Italian lines. From 24 October to 12 November, the Austro-German advance relentlessly drove the Italians back to the banks of the flood-swollen Piave River in headlong retreat. The attackers moved so fast they outdistanced their supplies. The Second Italian Army of 600,000 men practically ceased to exist, suffering 305,000 casualties, 270,000 of which were due to desertion and deliberate surrender. Italian prisoners shouted encouragement to their captors: "Long live Austria" and "On to Rome." The retreat from Caporetto was the greatest military defeat in modern Italian history.

General Armando Diaz replaced Luigi Cadorna as commander-in-chief. But the High Command needed further scapegoats. Blaming the reverse on seditious propaganda and the cowardly behavior of the troops, it sent special disciplinary squads into the retreat area to round up, court-martial, and shoot all officers who had been separated from their units. The war, which had been sold to the Italian people as a war of redemption and national regeneration, had little support among an army whose fighting spirit had been broken in costly, fruitless battles. Only the failure of the Austrians and Germans to take advantage of the rout saved Italy from total disaster. The Allies, fearful that their ally might be knocked out of the war, hastily sent six French and five British divisions and some American units to the Italian front. With their help the weary Italians were able to hold their position. During the following months, the Italian army regrouped and retrained. The generals analyzed the mistakes of the past and developed new tactics for an assault the following year.

Clemenceau Takes Charge. On 17 November 1917, Georges Clemenceau, aged seventy-six, became head of the French government. The new premier rapidly transformed his ministry into a tribunal dictatorship. He saw few practical differences among pacifists, defeatists, and traitors. In his view, they all opposed military victory, and their activities had to cease. Even parliamentary immunity offered no protection. The high court of the Senate condemned Louis Malvy to exile for treasonous contacts with the enemy. Malvy had failed to suppress antipatriotic propaganda when he was minister of the interior. The same court also sentenced would-be peace negotiator Joseph Caillaux to prison. Hard-core traitors were rounded up, court-martialed, and shot. This was the fate of the Germans' payoff man, the international crook Paul Bolo-Pasha, and the editor of the *Bonnet Rouge*, Émile Duval, who ran his paper with German subsidies. Clemenceau also reorganized the Army High Command. Despite Ferdinand Foch's Jesuit associations and insubordinate behavior, Clemenceau was convinced that he was the best available commander and had him appointed commander-in-chief. Even in the dark days of June 1918, when parliamentarians were demanding Foch be replaced, Clemenceau offered to resign rather than accede to their wishes. The premier realized that ultimate victory was possible only if he could show that the French, though wasted by three years of war, could still respond like their ancestors to a Jacobin call to arms.

But his cynicism and ruthless energy concealed a streak of sentimentality and splendid sensitivity. On one of his trips to the battlefields, he watched as thousands of French soldiers marched past on their way to the front lines from which they knew many would never return. They were carrying bunches of wildflowers that they threw at him, shouting, "Vive la France! Vive la France!" Clemenceau reached down and picked up a small bouquet of violets, which he kept, long after he had left public life, preserved in a shell case in his study. After he died, in accordance with his last testament, they were buried with him.

Profile: Georges Benjamin Clemenceau (1841–1929)

The new French war leader had been born three generations before, in 1841, in the small town of Mouilleron-en-Pareds in the Vendée, a region from which, he said, he got his instinct for independence, stubbornness, and combativeness. His character was also strongly influenced by his father, a physician who had been a republican during the monarchy of Louis-Philippe and was a notorious free-thinker, who believed that the main political problem of France was how to ensure that all citizens enjoyed the rights they had won during the Revolution. Clemenceau went to Paris to study medicine when he was nineteen. It was the height of the gaslight glory of the Second Empire, and he immediately became involved in political activities that resulted in his being sentenced to a month in prison. He eventually got his degree and for a time practiced medicine, but he preferred politics and, in February 1871, became a deputy to the National Assembly. In the debate at Bordeaux over the terms of peace with Prussia, he became one of the original signers of the protest opposing the cession of Alsace-Lorraine.

After the establishment of the Third Republic, Clemenceau continued to serve in parliament where he identified with the political left and its radical causes. He favored the destruction of the economic power of the vested interests and the elimination of the political influence of the Roman Catholic church. He opposed imperialism because he believed that such foreign adventures would bring France into conflict with Great Britain and divert the nation's attention away from the real aim of foreign policy: the vindication of French rights vis-à-vis Germany. Clemenceau had a genius for destructive criticism and was reputedly responsible for the downfall of at least eighteen ministries. From this reputation arose his nickname "the tiger," then considered pejorative.

During the divisive Dreyfus affair, Clemenceau became one of the most persistent advocates for a new trial. He published Émile Zola's open letter *J'accuse* (I accuse) in his newspaper *Aurore* (Dawn). The success of the Dreyfusards in their attack on the monarchists, clergy, and army confirmed the radicals in power for the next two decades. Clemenceau won election to the Senate in April 1903 and three years later formed his first ministry (October 1906–July 1909). In power, his policies were quite different from those he had advocated while in opposition. He had no hesitancy about using the full resources of the state to break a wave of violent strikes that swept the country. As labor became more militant, he became more repressive. In foreign affairs, he devoted his efforts to strengthening the French alliance system by having a new clause written into the Franco-Russian Treaty that provided for immediate and simultaneous mobilization in the event of German mobilization. He tried to get the British to develop a national army for immediate deployment on the continent in case of hostilities. When he was accused of neglecting the modernization of the navy, he resigned and resumed his role as critic. Not until the dark days of 1917 did he get another chance to form a cabinet.

In his view, the first step in the continuing struggle to ensure French security was winning the war. This, he believed, could only come about if Germany were permanently weakened, both economically and politically. Accordingly, he favored depriving Germany of control over all its territory on the Left Bank of the Rhine, where several client states would be created. He also believed that military and moral revenge must go together. The German defeat would achieve the first, the peace conference would achieve the second. But unifying France was more important than retribution. Clemenceau had not fought the scourge of Teutonic barbarism only to have his country torn apart by class warfare. Clemenceau knew, however, that France was fighting a coalition war and that the prospects of achieving all its aims were unlikely.

Russia Leaves the War. Events on the Eastern Front moved to the pace of the Russian Revolution. Immediately upon seizing power in Petrograd, Lenin proposed an armistice. But when he received no reply from the other Allied governments, he unilaterally repudiated Russia's commitment not to make a separate peace and opened direct negotiations with Berlin.

On 17 December 1917, the Germans agreed to suspend hostilities on the Eastern Front for three months. Five days later, they met with the Russians at Brest-Litovsk to negotiate a peace treaty. The Bolsheviks wanted a peace with no annexations or indemnities, based on the self-determination of all peoples. But the German Supreme Command intended to keep all the land Germany currently occupied. When asked why he wanted the eastern border states, Marshal Hindenburg explained, "I need them for the maneuvering of my left wing in the next war."[43]

The Bolsheviks realized that militarily they were in no position to stand up to the Germans, so they played for time, hoping the start of the world revolution or a successful Allied offensive on the Western Front would save them. The Germans became impatient. On 18 January 1918, General Max Hoffmann spread before the Bolsheviks a large staff map that indicated in blue crayon the future Russo-German frontier. Germany would get most of Poland, all of Lithuania, Courland, and western Latvia. The southern boundary would be settled by direct German discussions with Ukrainian nationalists. These harsh terms divided the Bolshevik leaders. One faction, led by Nicolai Bukharin and Karl Radek, wanted to break off negotiations and immediately begin organizing a revolutionary war. Leon Trotsky proposed that they simply declare an end to the war and demobilize without signing any peace. Lenin believed that, no matter what the conditions or circumstances, peace had to be made at once in order to save the Bolshevik revolution. But nine out of sixteen members on the Central Committee accepted Trotsky's formula "neither peace, nor war." Trotsky's announcement that Russia would demobilize its army and unilaterally declare the war over prompted Ludendorff to order a general advance to annex even more territory, including Lithuania and Estonia. Ludendorff also wanted to occupy the Ukraine to ensure that Germany could obtain sufficient grain to continue the war in the west. As the German army approached Petrograd, Lenin pleaded with the Central Committee to accept the enemy's terms. Though accused of compromising with the imperialists, he stood firm and ultimately won out.

Under the Treaty of Brest-Litovsk, signed on 3 March 1918, Russia lost 1,265,000 square miles, about 25 percent of the old tsarist empire, including Poland, Estonia, Latvia, Lithuania, and parts of White Russia, which were left to German disposition. Also lost were the trans-Caucasian districts of Ardahan, Kars, and Batum—these were assigned to Turkey—and Finland, Georgia, and the Ukraine, which were recognized as independent but were really German satellites.[44] The lost territories contained 62 million people—one-third of Russia's population—plus 33 percent of its croplands, 26 percent of its railways, 75 percent of its iron and coal, and almost all of its oil fields. The treaty prohibited nationalization of German property in the rest of Russia and forbade Bolshevik agitation or propaganda against the German government. Many Bolsheviks believed that Russia would regain all its losses with the advent of the great world revolution, but when somebody asked Lenin about this, he replied, "We shall see the World Revolution but meanwhile it is just a very good fairy-tale; a very pretty fairy-tale."[45]

Shortly after dictating peace to Russia, the Germans did the same with Romania. The terms of the Treaty of Bucharest of 7 May 1918 were as severe as those of Brest-Litovsk. The Romanians were compelled to reduce their army to the size of a domestic police force and to give up control of their coastline along the Black Sea by handing over the province of Dobrudja. They also surrendered control of their economy to the Central Powers who would monopolize Romania's entire agricultural output for the next nine years, control its oil production for thirty years, and obtain leases on certain Danube ports for forty years.

With Romania's capitulation, Germany had pacified the entire Eastern Front from the Baltic to the Black Sea. But Ludendorff had no faith in the permanence of any treaty unless it was backed by military force. He kept about one million troops in the East, particularly in the Ukraine, to ensure that Germany could control the region's economic resources; these troops might have tipped the balance on the Western Front.

The Allied War Aims

Secret Treaties. While the Germans had been able to put their war aims into practice with the treaties of Brest-Litovsk and Bucharest, the British and French could do little beyond making promises and public pronouncements. They had committed themselves to the political restoration of Belgium, Serbia, and Montenegro; the liberation of the occupied territories in France (including Alsace-

Lorraine), Russia, and Romania; and the payment of reparations by Germany. But nothing as comprehensive as Bethmann Hollweg's September Program had been formulated. When Wilson, in December 1916, requested that the belligerents detail their war aims, the British and French replied that they desired a reorganized and stable Europe based "on respect for nationalities and on the right to full security and liberty of economic development." They said that above all they desired to "ensure peace on the principles of liberty and justice, and upon the inviolable fidelity to international engagements by which the Government of the United States have ever been inspired."[46] And, in vague generalities mixed with specifics, they demanded "the restitution of provinces formerly torn from the allies by force or against the wish of their inhabitants; the liberation of the Italians, as also of the Slavs, Rumanes, and Czecho-Slovaks from foreign domination; the setting free of the populations subject to the bloody tyranny of the Turks."[47]

The British and French did not, of course, tell all. They did not mention their promises of additional territory to Italy and Romania as payment for joining the war, nor did they tell of their extensive plans for partitioning the Ottoman Empire. Turkish entry into the war had made it mandatory for the British, French, and Russians to come to some sort of an understanding to harmonize their aims. Their first attempt came with the "Constantinople Agreement," which had been concluded on 18 March 1915 in time for the landing on the Gallipoli Peninsula. In obvious anticipation of the expedition's success, the accord awarded the Turkish capital to Russia and recognized the special rights of Britain and France in Asiatic Turkey, to be delineated in a future accord.

The British, by allowing the Russians to annex Constantinople (later renamed Istanbul) and the straits, sacrificed a policy for which they had persistently fought during the nineteenth century, but one for which they would be compensated. Their position in both India and Egypt already gave them a commanding political advantage in the Middle East. And as soon as the war began, they launched an offensive against the Turks in Mesopotamia, reinforced their position at Suez, and contacted powerful native leaders of the Arabian Peninsula—including Emir Hussein of Mecca, the sheik of Kuwait, and Ibn Saud—promising liberation for their people if the Arabs would participate in the war against the Turks. The French feared that Britain's paternalistic association with the Arabs might enable it to obtain territory that they wanted for themselves, and they therefore pressed the British to formulate a definite commitment.

In the Sykes-Picot Agreement of 16 May 1916, France obtained a zone of influence in Syria, extending from the coast to the upper Tigris River valley and including the mineral-rich district of Mosul, and was accorded administrative control of the adjacent area of Cilicia. The British received southern Mesopotamia and a broad sphere of interest in northern Arabia where they could construct one or several Arab states. Russia would annex the large district of Erzurum in eastern Anatolia, including southern Kurdistan.

The Treaty of London cut Italy in for a share of the spoils, including possession of the Dodecanese Islands. Another agreement, that of St. Jean de Maurenne of 17 April 1917, accorded Italy territorial concessions in the western Turkish provinces adjacent to the Aegean Sea.

These secret agreements were intended to provide the basis upon which the Allies would conclude peace with the Ottoman Empire. But not until the United States had actually entered the war did the British government, through Foreign Secretary Arthur Balfour, inform President Wilson about the existence of all these secret arrangements, as well as those with Italy and Romania, and furnish him with official copies.[48] Lloyd George anticipated that the Americans would soon present him with specific demands of their own, especially since many of the arrangements had been modified by changing circumstances. Wilson though seemed reluctant to discuss any of these treaties, much less demand their abrogation. He appeared more intent on setting a proper moral tone than on criticizing the clandestine diplomacy of his associates. The matter was therefore left in the air, at least until 22 November 1917, when secret diplomacy became potentially embarrassing with the announcement by Leon Trotsky, the people's commissar of foreign affairs, that the Bolshevik government was going to publish the texts of all the treaties that the Allies had made during the war.

The notification came the day after the Bolsheviks had made a third unsuccessful attempt to arrange an armistice ending the war. First appearing in *Izvestia* and *Pravda* and immediately thereafter in Western papers, like the *New York Evening Post* and the *Manchester Guardian*, here were the texts of the agreements the Allies had concluded with the Italians and the Romanians, the plans to partition Turkey, and the understanding over the future frontiers of Germany. Secret diplomacy, Trotsky explained sanctimoniously, was a means by which the capitalists deceived and enslaved the workers. Its abolition was "the first essential of an honorable, popular, and really democratic foreign policy."[49]

The Self-Determination of Peoples. The Communist government's revelations convinced Lloyd George that some sort of reply had to be made to convince people, especially the Americans, that Britain did not continue the war "merely to gain a vindictive or looting triumph."[50] He therefore prepared a restatement of war aims that he presented on 5 January 1918 to the Trade Union Conference. Lloyd George demanded a peace of reason and justice and claimed that any territorial settlement must be based on the principle of government with the consent of the governed. Britain's aims, he said, included the restoration of occupied territories; the return of Alsace-Lorraine; the creation of an independent Poland; the satisfaction of the "legitimate claims" of Italy and the "legitimate aspirations" of Romania; the recognition of "separate national conditions" for Arabia, Armenia, Mesopotamia, Syria, and Palestine; and the placing of the native inhabitants of Germany's colonies "under the control of an administration acceptable to themselves." The prime minister denied that he sought the dissolution of the Austro-Hungarian Empire, but insisted upon the application of the right of self-determination. He concluded by endorsing "the creation of some international organization to limit the burden of armaments and diminish the probability of war."[51]

Wilson also felt the need to take the high ground. On 8 January 1918, he proclaimed his famous Fourteen Points before the Congress. Of these, he considered the first five, which laid down his goals for a peaceful world, to be the most important. The president advocated an end to secret diplomacy by calling for "open covenants of peace openly arrived at." He endorsed "absolute freedom of navigation upon the seas outside territorial waters alike in peace and war." He said that he wanted to remove "so far as possible . . . all economic barriers" and to establish "an equality of trade conditions among all the nations consenting to the peace and associating themselves for its maintenance." He pushed for guarantees "that national armaments will be reduced to the lowest point consistent with domestic safety." And he declared himself in favor of the principle of self-determination of peoples or, as he put it, of "a free, open-minded, and absolutely impartial adjustment of all colonial claims based upon a strict observance of the principle that . . . the interests of the populations concerned must have equal weight with the equitable claims of the Government whose title is to be determined." None of these were new, since all had been uttered previously in speeches, especially his "Peace without Victory" address a year earlier.

Points Six to Thirteen were more concrete but also added nothing new. Basically, they reiterated the territorial aims of the Entente: the evacuation of Russian territory; the evacuation and restoration of Belgium; the liberation and restoration of French territory, including Alsace-Lorraine; the readjustment of the frontiers of Italy "along clearly recognizable lines of nationality"; and autonomous development for the peoples of the Austro-Hungarian Empire. In addition, Romania, Serbia, and Montenegro were to be evacuated and restored; the subject peoples of the Ottoman Empire were to be allowed to determine their own development; and an independent Polish state was to be erected and assured "a free and secure access to the sea." Point Fourteen called for the establishment of a general association of nations "for the purpose of affording mutual guarantees of political independence and territorial integrity of great and small states alike."[52] With the exception of the first five and the last article, which related to Wilson's determination to change the conduct and basic nature of international relations, none of the points could be considered reasons for his having taken the United States into the war. Lloyd George lumped them together when he commented, "We never formally accepted them, and they constituted no part of the official policy of the Alliance."[53]

The Last Quarter-Hour. Despite a reputation for precision and clarity, the French made no public statement of aims comparable to that delivered by Lloyd George or Wilson. French leaders had emphasized the necessity for reparations, and they demanded the reacquisition of Alsace-Lorraine, but even in his great war speech of 8 March 1918, Clemenceau did not provide much clarification beyond that. "My foreign policy and my domestic policy are one," he said. "I make war. I keep making war . . . I continue to make war, and I will continue to make war until the last quarter-hour, because it is we who will have the last quarter-hour."[54] Clemenceau also spoke of "a democratic peace," one that will "silence Prussian militarism." The French knew what this meant.

The French wanted to dismantle Germany, to destroy German political and economic predominance forever by taking away as much territory and resources as possible, beginning with the entire Rhineland. Some of the territory, like the Saar, would go to France, and some of it to Belgium. A special police force would garrison the rest to make sure the area could never again serve as a route of invasion. France also wanted to remove from Germany one of the great economic supports for aggression—its coal. In the east, the more German territory that could be given to the new Poland the better, especially since the collapse of Russia made political support from that sector dubious. The French also demanded protection against German commerce; and they wanted a rightful share of the world's raw materials. They intended to take away all of Germany's overseas empire, although they had not yet committed themselves to keeping any of it for themselves. But they also realized that to keep Germany in its place, the wartime coalition must be preserved, even if this entailed making some concessions. Clemenceau therefore accepted most of Wilson's points in principle, although like the British he refused to elevate them to the status of war aims.

The Last Campaigns

The Ludendorff Offensive. The end of the war against Russia enabled Germany to achieve superiority of numbers in France. In the spring of 1918, Ludendorff had 192 divisions there, 20 more than his opponents. He felt he had to exploit this advantage before the arrival of American reinforcements could cheat him of victory—by March 1918, the United States had sent about 300,000 troops overseas—and he planned a series of three attacks to bulldoze his way through the Allied lines. In March, three German armies advanced along a sixty-mile front in the Cambrai–St. Quentin sector and succeeded in pushing the British back fourteen miles, putting the German heavy artillery within range of Paris. The following month, the Germans sledgehammered their way past Armentières and rolled across the Lys River, punching a huge salient in the British front. In May, their attack between Rheims and Soissons broke through the Franco-British positions and swept all the way to the Marne.

The sudden return to mobility after three years of stalemate was due in part to new tactics that had been pioneered by General Oskar von Hutier. In the first wave, "storm troopers" attacked in dispersed, small units with stick-bombs, light machine guns, and flamethrowers. They would punch through the forward positions, evading strong points to strike at the communication centers and artillery positions. After them came the second and third waves in mopping up operations. In those areas where the fog was thickest, the "expanding torrent" approach of these assault troops was quite spectacular. All World War II armies adapted these tactics, which are still useful to this day.

With Ludendorff relentlessly smashing their defenses, the Allies, for the first time since the war began, achieved a unified command. Previously, the military leaders favored the creation of real central authority only insofar as it could increase their own control. A Supreme War Council of politicians and generals had been formed at the end of 1917, but it concentrated mostly on questions of logistics. Strategy and tactics still remained the prerogatives of the national commanders. Squabbling was constant. Early in 1918, the French and British were deadlocked over the establishment of a common reserve army to be commanded by

The state of the art in big guns. The Krupp munitions works in Essen turned out one of these weapons every forty-five minutes near the end of the war. Such guns, originally built for the navy, were used for long-range interdiction of supply lines and rear-area shelling of troops and ammunition dumps. Shells from longer-barreled guns hit Paris during the Ludendorff offensive.

General Foch. Haig refused to cooperate, so Foch appealed directly to the Supreme War Council. Clemenceau supported Haig, and Lloyd George refused to intervene. During the Ludendorff offensive, however, Haig changed his mind because he feared that without command unity the French might fall back on Paris leaving his army to face the enemy alone. On 23 March, at the Inter-Allied Conference at Doullens, Foch received the authority "to coordinate the action of the Allied Armies on the Western front."[55] Later, on 14 May, Foch officially became the commander-in-chief of the Allied armies in France, a title that sounded more impressive than it was. Foch likened himself to the conductor of an orchestra, "Say, if you like that I beat time well." He could cajole, propose, convince, threaten, arrange, beg, persuade, blame, blackmail, and charm, but not force. A good case in point was his relationship with the United States.

The Americans were supposed to send over all units as soon as they were trained without waiting to form complete divisions. Foch was anxious to use them any-where he felt necessary, but the American commander, General John Pershing, was determined to establish his own independent army and would only allow his men to fill gaps as he saw fit. Even in the summer of 1918, when the American forces achieved autonomy, Pershing felt he was not answerable to any other com-mander for their use. In August, he told Haig that he might have to "withdraw the five American Divisions which [were] training with British Divisions." Haig replied that "he had done everything to equip and help these units of the Amer-ican Army" and now he could not even count on them to help him attack the Germans at the end of September.[56] Haig of all people should have been sensitive to the necessity for Pershing's insistence on such control even though the First American Army could not yet stand alone. (It contained four French divisions and was supplied almost entirely with French and British artillery. Its training was taken from the experience of the Allies.) Pershing knew that the piecemeal com-mitment of American troops would reduce his country's contribution to that of a spare parts department, considerably endangering troop morale apart from any political risks. As if to set the Allied commanders' minds at rest as to the American resolve to fight, General Tasker Bliss, Pershing's representative on the Supreme War Council, remarked, "We've come over here to get ourselves killed; if you want to use us what are you waiting for?"[57]

But even before the Americans put their first soldier in France, they had made an essential contribution. The Allies could not have lasted without their economic assistance. And in 1917, the American navy was important in helping the British win the war against the submarines. Although the Americans had no decisive effect on the tide of battle during their first year of participation, their troop strength was adequate by June 1918 to permit the Allies to counterattack.

Foch Strikes Back. Foch first planned a series of small, limited offensives to cap-ture the lateral railroad line that connected Amiens with Paris. Neither he nor the chief of the British General Staff, Sir Harry Wilson, believed that victory could be achieved before the next year. However, while Foch was still organizing his operation, Ludendorff attacked once more. The German offensive began on 15 July, but soon degenerated into a series of local actions without clear results. Ludendorff regarded the setback as temporary. The French riposted on 18 July and, from then on, had the Germans constantly on the defensive. The day 18 July became a turning point.

After a series of successful preparatory offensives in August and early September, Foch ordered an all-out assault from the Meuse to the North Sea. "Everybody is to attack as soon as they can, as strong as they can, for as long as they can," he ordered, secure in the knowledge that Wilson had promised to have 100 American divisions in France by July 1919. By September 1918, 1,200,000 American troops were already there, although only three double-sized divisions had seen combat. Although the American First Army was inept at its first engagement at St. Mihiel in September, its performance improved considerably in the Argonne-Meuse a few weeks later and earned the respect of the Germans. During the last months of the war, the British bore the brunt of the fighting despite the American contribution. But American potential clinched the victory since Ludendorff could draw on no comparable supply of troops. He had already mobilized the 1919 class of conscripts of 300,000. His offensive had failed, and early in August he concluded that the war must be ended. His army was demoralized: "Whole bodies of our men had surrendered to single troopers, or isolated squadrons. . . . The officers in many places had lost their influence and allowed themselves to be swept along with the rest."[58] Ludendorff felt that the Germans could defend the Western Front long enough to negotiate a suitable peace, but his calculations were outstripped by events.

On 15 September, an Allied army, marching north from its base in Salonika, chopped the Bulgarian army in two and forced Bulgaria out of the war. The Bulgarian Armistice opened the Danube valley to invasion. At the same time, the British broke the Turkish front in Palestine and rapidly advanced on Damascus. Ludendorff doubted whether the Germans could defend themselves on the Western Front while "establishing in Serbia and Rumania a new flank protection for Austria-Hungary . . . [and maintaining] communications with the Rumanian oil-fields."[59] Losing his nerve, he pushed for an armistice, thereby destroying the army's credibility to continue to defend the nation. On 29 September, the day British troops reached the Hindenburg line, the Supreme Command decided to ask the civilian government to contact Woodrow Wilson for a peace based on the Fourteen Points. Prince Max of Baden, a liberal, replaced the army's puppet chancellor. The kaiser signed a proclamation for the establishment of representative government, the first since the founding of the Reich in 1871.

Meanwhile, Ludendorff began to have second thoughts. He wondered if the German people could be aroused to renew the fight if the armistice terms they received were too harsh, and despite his doubts, he admonished the government not to "accept anything that makes it impossible to renew hostilities."[60] Ludendorff reasserted his authority, believing he was "still the head of a mighty army,"[61] and stalled for time to strengthen his hand. But Wilson had no intention of leaving the Germans in a position to resume hostilities. He had replied to Germany's petition by saying that Germany could have an armistice only if it were prepared to evacuate all the foreign territory it occupied in Western Europe. Then, on 23 October, Wilson notified Germany that unless the German government rid itself of its "military masters" and "monarchical aristocrats," the United States "must demand, not peace negotiations but surrender." Ludendorff advised fighting, but his display of determination owed more to a crass attempt to blame the civilians for Germany's defeat than to any sense of military reality.

Methodically, the Allies forced the German army back toward the Rhine. The fighting on the Western Front in 1918 showed to what extent the war had again become a war of movement. It was the Allies' turn to attack, and to help their offensive maintain its momentum, they employed the lessons learned at Cambrai the previous year. To the tank assault, they added air power in a combined operation, conceived by American Captain Billy Mitchell, that would be a hallmark of war a generation later.

Meanwhile the Dual Monarchy was breaking apart in great pieces. Ever since the beginning of the year, when a series of strikes swept the nation, the Habsburg regime had to rely almost exclusively on the army to maintain order, and until the last months of the war, it remained substantially loyal, with the notable exception of various Czech units that deserted to the Russians. There were no serious revolts in the provinces, no doubt because the death penalty for sedition discouraged independence movements from precipitous action. However, the inevitability of defeat changed all that. The failure of Ludendorff's last offensive prompted Emperor Karl to renounce the Dual Monarchy in favor of a federal monarchy in a desperate attempt to save his dynasty, and to promise the cession of Austria's Polish territory to a new independent state. His manifesto, dated 16 October 1918, informed Austria's nationalities that they could form their own diets to carry out the reform. However, the manifesto did not apply to Hungary and, in any case, came too late to have any influence. The Allies ignored it.

Thomas Masaryk, the head of the Czech National Council, dismissed Austrian promises as insincere and stemming only from weakness. On 28 October, the council proclaimed the birth of the Czechoslovak Republic at Prague. A day later in Zagreb, the National Council of Southern Slavs also announced their independence. On 31 October, the Hungarian government in Budapest pronounced the end of its association with Vienna. The following month, in Italy a British-Italian army advanced across the Piave. Several Austro-Hungarian regiments refused to fight, and the general retreat became a stampede. The Italians, avid to redeem themselves after the disaster the previous year, hailed this unopposed advance as a great victory.

Turkey surrendered on 31 October, and the next day, the Hungarians established an independent government. On 3 November 1918 when an armistice was signed, large chunks of the old empire were already occupied by Italian, French, Serbian, Polish, and Romanian troops. On 11 November, one hour after the cease-fire on the Western Front, Emperor Karl signed a statement, pledging not to stand in the way of the independent political development of the empire's nationalities. This was not an abdication, but recognition of an accomplished fact.

The Germans also had no desire to continue the war. Ludendorff resigned under pressure on 27 October. Four days later, the cabinet decided, on its own authority, to secure the abdication of Wilhelm II. On 3 November, a mutiny broke out in the German fleet at Kiel, when Admiral Scheer, anxious to salvage the honor of the German navy, gave the order to put to sea for a final suicidal battle against the British. The sailors, already demoralized by bad food and cruel leadership, seized control of the ships. Their protest, fanned by revolutionary propaganda, spread into Hamburg, Bremen, and Lübeck and the inland cities of Hanover, Brunswick, and Cologne. The German government ordered the railroad lines cut to prevent the sailors from descending on Berlin. At the same time, other disturbances unconnected with the mutiny occurred elsewhere. The independent socialists organized a mammoth demonstration in Munich to demand the abolition of the monarchy and the establishment of a Workers and Soldiers Soviet. In Berlin, on the morning of 9 November, the workers laid down their tools and flooded into the streets. Max of Baden immediately announced the abdication of the Hohenzollerns, and the socialist leader, Philip Scheidemann, proclaimed the German Republic. The kaiser was not in Berlin, but at military headquarters in Belgium. When his generals told him he no longer had the support of the army, he fled to Holland.

Concluding an Armistice. Wilson might have been content to conclude an armistice on the basis of the Fourteen Points; he even hesitated to inform the Allies he was exchanging notes with Germany. But, before concluding such an agreement, he had to satisfy the reservations of the Allies. At the end of October, the Allied leaders and Wilson's representative Colonel House met in Paris for discussions. Clemenceau and Lloyd George questioned what the American president meant by his proscription of secret diplomacy. Did this mean that he wanted to forbid secret negotiations? House said that was not intended. He only meant secret treaties. The point was approved.

The British prime minister rejected Point Two out of hand: "We will never accept that an ambiguous clause on the freedom of the seas be inserted in a treaty of peace with Germany." Articles Three, Four, and Five did not present too many problems because they contained deliberate qualifications. Economic barriers, for example, would be removed only "so far as possible." Both the French and British leaders demanded more precision on the definition of reparations. The word "restored," which appeared in Articles Seven and Eight, was much too vague, and they proposed that it be understood to mean that "compensation will be made by Germany for all damages done to the civilian populations of the Allies and their property by the aggression of Germany by land, by sea, and from the air." The Italian representative, Orlando, protested Article Nine, which he said ran counter to what his government felt it deserved as spoils.

On the battlefield, Foch continued the attack in Flanders, along the Aisne, and in the Marne valley in preparation for a thrust into Lorraine and an invasion of Bavaria. But, on 6 November, he received a wireless message from German Supreme Headquarters asking him to name a place for the conclusion of a cease-fire. He chose a railroad car from his train stationed near Rethondes in the forest of Compiègne. The meeting took place at nine o'clock on the morning of 8 November. The head of the German delegation was Matthias Erzberger, one of the most outspoken annexationists in the Reichstag. Foch received him with contempt. He coldly asked the purpose of the visit, and only when the Germans asked specifically for a cession of hostilities, did he deign to inform them "of the conditions subject to which it can be obtained."[62]

The principal paragraphs were read: The Germans would evacuate all conquered territory, including Alsace-Lorraine; they would withdraw all military forces from the Rhineland and from within a twenty-mile radius of the bridgeheads of Mainz, Coblenz, and Cologne; they would surrender the bulk of their cannons, machine guns, and warplanes; they would deliver all their submarines; they would sail their High Seas fleet to British ports for internment; they would renounce the Treaty of Brest-Litovsk; and they would promise to pay reparations. Until a definitive treaty of peace was signed, the Allies intended to continue the wartime blockade of Germany. The Armistice was signed on Monday, 11 November, at ten past five in the morning, and took effect at 11:00 A.M. that same day. By its terms Germany became a power vacuum.

Within two weeks after the signing of the Armistice, the Germans evacuated all the occupied territories. Hindenburg was determined to bring the troops home in good order and, as soon as they entered Germany, had the soldiers form into formal columns according to the district in which each lived. The units of the Imperial Guard entered Berlin on 11 December. The men of the infantry were tired and thin, but their uniforms were clean and their boots and equipment were polished. The cavalry rode on well-groomed horses and rode upright in their saddles, lances in hand. The officers were all wearing the Iron Cross. The band played "Deutschland uber Alles," as the soldiers marched down the Unter den Linden. The previous spring, houses along this avenue had carried signs offering to rent windows to watch the victory parade. But even for defeat, the spectators turned out by the thousands. They leaned from the balconies, waved from the windows and rooftops, and gathered along the line of march, shouting and cheering as the tightly ranked veterans filed past wearing oak leaves on their helmets and garlands on their guns. At the Brandenburg Gate, crowned with its famous quadriga of triumph, Friedrich Ebert greeted them as those whom "no enemy had defeated on the battlefield." Indeed how could such a force have surrendered when their flags flew so high? The Allies also celebrated the end of the war with parades, concluding the conflict as it had begun. Between these celebrations lay nine million corpses.

POSTSCRIPT   According to a French expression, everything ends with song. So did the war end with singing, dancing in the streets, and heavy drinking. In the midst of the celebrations, it was easy to overlook the damage that had been done to the social and political fabric of Europe. It was too early—and too disturbing—to assess the consequences soberly. The greater the destruction, the greater seemed the hope for the future. The euphoria did not last long and with its decline came a more pessimistic assessment of the meaning of all that human and material destruction. All the European participants came out of the conflict demonstrably poorer. It would take five to ten years before their economies would recover their prewar productive levels. The best-customer relationship between Germany and Britain was gone. The economic unity of the Danube valley lay in ruins, the trade between Russia and the West was suspended. The fear of the spread of Bolshevism and of a resurgent Germany prevented the reintegration of these countries into European affairs. The collapse of empires prolonged and rekindled ethnic hatreds, diverting energies away from the pressing problems of reconstruction and the building of new national loyalties through harmonization of effort.

Although teaching old dogs new tricks was difficult in the political arena, the practice of war was a different matter. To be sure, there were those, like the French, who believed that trench warfare proved the value of permanent fortifications—all the more so because such a defensive strategy seemed the best way of preventing the horrendous losses suffered in trying to achieve a breakthrough. But others learned different lessons. The new tactics of infiltration and increased mechanization pointed the way to a new kind of warfare. This was especially true in the use of air power, which had developed from reconnaissance to interdiction to tactical troop and armor support to strategic bombing. Germany's introduction of the twin-engined Gotha early in 1917 changed the future of warfare. The ability of this long-range heavy aircraft to strike at London prompted the British to create a new fighting service, the Royal Air Corps. According to a special report, prepared under the supervision of Jan Christian Smuts and laid before the cabinet in August 1917, the only effective answer to this weapon was a counter air offensive. The damage done by such bombers was minuscule compared to the destruction caused by the ground war, but air power would determine the course of future war, and strategic bombing, as General Smuts concluded, would be the essential element of that struggle. When bombers carried the fight to the enemies' home front, civilians were often as exposed to danger as those on the front lines. But the mobilization of peoples had already blurred the distinction between combatants and noncombatants. In war there was no time for politesse. Almost anyone was fair game.

The war had shaken the respect that people had for traditional institutions while it expanded the power of the state. Many aspects of mobilization remained after the war. In a sense, Russia under the Communists never demobilized. But everywhere people expected governments to manage their lives as never before. Yet many of those who might have shared in this process wanted nothing to do with affairs of state. Soldiers returning home having paid for the mistakes of their elders wanted no part of politics. These dropouts became the true "lost generation." In many countries, the older generation remained in power and tried unsuccessfully to apply the lessons they learned before the war to the new, often insurmountable problems of the present.

ENDNOTES

1. Lucy Lippard, ed., *Dadas on Art* (Englewood Cliffs, N.J.: Prentice-Hall, 1971), 23–24.
2. Ibid., 22.
3. Marcel Jean regarded the work as the most profound and original "that has ever been achieved in the field of plastic expression; an anti-picture, or rather non-picture; and therefore a masterpiece of the Dada spirit." Marcel Jean, *The History of Surrealist Painting* (New York: Grove, 1960), 36.
4. *"Elle a chaud au cul."* Duchamp is best known for his cubo-futuristic painting *Nude Descending a Staircase*, but of all his creations he spent the greatest amount of time (from 1915 to 1923) on his *Great Glass*, "The Bride Stripped Bare by her Bachelors, Even," a large freestanding glass construction that looked not unlike a huge American-style double-paned window (9′11″ × 5′7″). Duchamp applied the design on the surfaces of the upper and lower portions in paint, tinfoil, and lead wire, expressing a mechanistic relationship between the bride and her bachelors by motors, clockwork machinery, and magnetos. The work illustrated the dichotomy between the world of repetition (male) and the world of imagination (female), which posed a problem of reconciliation. Duchamp offered no solutions; rather he called the bride an "apparition of an appearance." (Jean, *History of Surrealist Painting*, 108, 112) Duchamp left the work unfinished, and, aside from producing a few more ready-mades, he subsequently transferred his creative energy into mastering the game of chess.
5. *"Heureux ceux qui sont mort dans une juste guerre."*

6. "Ne pleurez donc pas sur les horreurs de la guerre / Avant elle nous n'avons que la surface / De la terre et des mers / Après elle nous avons les abîmes." Guillaume Apollinaire, *Calligrammes* (Paris: Gallimard, 1925), 91.

7. "O grollende Schwermut / Des Heers; ein strahlender Helm / Sank klirrend von purpurner Stirne." Georg Trakl, *Dichtungen und Briefe* (Salzburg: Ottomüller, 1969), 161.

8. "Am Abend tönen die herbstlichen Wälder / Von tödlichen Waffen, die goldnen Ebenen / Und blauen Seen, darüber die Sonne / Düstrer hinrollt; unfängt die Nacht / Sterbende Krieger, die wilde Klage / Ihrer zerbrochen Münder." Ibid., 167.

9. ". . . Ist das der lezte / Aufruhr der gotter uber diesem land?" Stefan George, *Werke* (Munich: Helmut Küpper, 1958), 361.

10. "L'aria è crivellata / come una trina / dalle schioppettate / degli uomini / ritratti / nelle trincee / come le lumache nel loro quiscio." Giuseppe Ungaretti, *Allegria* (Milan: Arnoldo Mondadori, 1963), 61.

11. *Collected Poems of Rupert Brooke* (New York: Dodd, Mead, 1946), 103.

12. Ibid., 105.

13. George Clarke, *A Treasury of War Poetry* (London: Hodder and Stroughton, 1917), 370–71.

14. Robert Graves, *Goodbye to All That* (London: Cassell, 1929), 146.

15. Siegfried Sassoon, *Collected Poems* (London: Faber, 1956), 85. By permission of George Sassoon.

16. Ibid., 68.

17. Ibid., 78.

18. C. Day Lewis, ed., *The Collected Poems of Wilfred Owen* (London: Chatto and Windus, 1963), 108.

19. Catherine W. Reilly, *Scars upon My Heart: Woman's Poetry and Verse of the First World War* (London: Virago Books, 1981), 127.

20. A. J. P. Taylor, ed., *History of the 20th Century*, vol. 20 (London: BPC Publishing, 1969), 33.

21. Walton Rawls, *Wake Up, America: World War I and the American Poster* (New York: Abbeville Press, 1988), 12.

22. Words by Lena Guilbert Ford; music by Ivor Novello (London: Ascherberg, Hopwood and Crew, Ltd., 1914).

23. Sassoon, *Collected Poems*, 21.

24. Words by Alfred Bryan, music by Al Piantadosi (London: Ascherberg, Hopwood and Crew, Ltd., 1915).

25. "Adieu la vie, adieu l'amour, / Adieu toutes les femmes. / C'est bien fini, c'est pour toujours / De cette guerre infâme. / C'est à Croanne, sur le plateau / Qu'on doit laisser sa peau; / Car nous sommes tous condamnés, / Nous sommes les sacrifiés." André Gauthier, *Les chansons de notre histoire* (Paris: Pierre Waleffe, 1967), 190–91.

26. New York: Leo Feist, Inc, 1917.

27. Michael Rodzyanko, *The Reign of Rasputin* (London: Philpot, 1928), 253–54.

28. Ibid., 245.

29. *The Letters of the Tsar to the Tsaritsa, 1914–1917* (Hattiesburg, Miss.: Academic International, 1970), 313.

30. Douglas Haig, *The Private Papers of Douglas Haig, 1914–1919* (London: Eyre and Spottiswoode, 1952), 201.

31. Ibid., 206

32. Georges Bonnefous, *Histoire Politique de la Troisième République*, vol. 2 (Paris: Presses Universitaires, 1957), 128.

33. Sir Edward Spears, *Prelude to Victory* (London: Cape, 1930), 338.

34. *The Bolshevik Revolution: Documents and Materials* (Stanford: Stanford University Press, 1934), 7.

35. Donald Day, ed., *Woodrow Wilson's Own Story* (Boston: Little, Brown, 1952), 128–29.

36. J. Arthur Salter, *Inter-Allied Shipping Control: An Experiment in International Administration* (New York: Oxford University Press, 1920), 122.

37. By contrast Norway, during the same period, lost about one million tons of shipping. *Statistical Abstract of the United States* (Washington, D.C.: U.S. Government Printing Office, 1919), 199, 266.

38. By special arrangement with the United States, the Germans used the American diplomatic cable from Berlin to Washington. Early in the war the British had established a code-breaking operation whose efforts paid off with the deciphering of the Zimmermann telegram. To preserve the secret of their success, they pretended that they had gotten a copy of the document directly from agents in Mexico City.

39. *Les armées françaises dans la grande guerre*, Series V, vol. 2 (Paris: Imprimerie Nationale, 1925), 197.

40. Haig, *Private Papers*, 265.

41. Ibid., 240.

42. Ibid., 240.

43. John Wheeler-Bennett, *Brest-Litovsk: The Forgotten Peace* (London: Macmillan, 1963), 109.

44. On 9 February 1918, the Germans had already concluded peace with the Ukrainian nationalists, separating the entire region from the Russian empire and making it economically dependent on the Reich.

45. Wheeler-Bennett, *Brest-Litovsk*, 260.

46. H. W. V. Temperly, ed., *A History of the Peace Conference of Paris*, vol. 1 (London: Oxford University Press, 1920), 428–29.

47. Ibid., 428.

48. W. B. Fowler, *British American Relations 1917–1918* (Princeton: Princeton University Press, 1969), 28–29.

49. *The Bolshevik Revolution*, 243–44.

50. David Lloyd George, *War Memoirs*, vol. 5 (London: I. N. Cholson and Watson, 1936), 2484.

51. Ibid., 2526–7.

52. Temperly, *A History of the Peace Conference*, 1:433–35.

53. Lloyd George, *War Memoirs*, 5: 2489.

54. *Journal Officiel, Chambre*, 8 March 1918, 857–59.

55. Ferdinand Foch, *Mémoires pour servir à l'histoire de la guerre de 1914–1918* (Paris: Plon, 1931), 264.

56. Haig, *Private Papers*, 323.

57. Barrie Pitt, *1918: The Last Act* (New York: Norton, 1962), 113.

58. *Ludendorff's Own Story*, vol. 2 (New York: Harper, 1919), 331.

59. Ibid., 371–72.

60. Ibid., 415.

61. Ibid., 424.

62. Foch, *Mémoires*, 469.

CHAPTER 3

PEACEMAKING AT PARIS, 1919–1920

PREFACE Not for a hundred years—not since the Congress of Vienna in 1814—had there been anything even remotely like it. The Paris Conference hosted the delegates of thirty-two countries along with their hordes of advisers, experts, clerks, and stenographers. The contingents of smaller powers sometimes included sixty people. The British came over with four hundred; the Americans brought a whole boatload; and the French had the resources of their entire governmental bureaucracy. The peacemakers came to settle the problems of a sick and torn Europe. Where the Congress of Vienna had restored legitimate monarchs to their thrones and suppressed nationalism, the Paris Conference encouraged new sovereign states and new national identities. Formerly, a state had the right to self-determination if it could prove its claim by force, but now such questions were decided by experts in boundary commissions, acting under the pressure of the major powers and the lobbying of the lesser ones. Thus, the field was ripe for controversy.

The collapse of the Central Powers had created a vast power vacuum in Eastern Europe where new national units squabbled among themselves. The power of Germany and Russia was temporarily in eclipse. Both these defeated states had not been invited to the conference and took no direct part in its negotiations. But many of the smaller states that did come were similarly excluded from major decisions. The British, the French, and the Americans dominated the conference. French premier Georges Clemenceau justified control by the Great Powers by reminding the delegates of the smaller powers that "on the day when the war ceased, the Allies had 12,000,000 men fighting on various fronts." This, he said, entitled them to greater consideration. "We might perhaps have been selfish enough to consult only each other. It was our right."[1]

The results of the deliberations confirmed this attitude. The Paris settlements reflected the political concerns of the Big Three—the concentration on the problem of Germany and the creation of a League of Nations. Woodrow Wilson tried to emphasize the universal nature of peacemaking. He wanted to create a new world order that would ensure future peace, but his idealistic goals had little attraction to statesmen used to thinking in balance of power terms. Clemenceau said that the Fourteen Points could hardly "be taken as a point of departure because they are the principles of public right which may inspire the [peace] negotiations, but which do not possess the concrete character indispensable for approaching the precise regulations of concrete stipulations."[2]

Both Lloyd George and Clemenceau were more directly influenced by their public's expectations about peace than was Wilson with his fixed term of office. Lloyd George and Clemenceau had come to the peace conference backed by impressive votes of confidence, but both men presided over coalitions and could very easily have fallen from power if they found themselves at variance with the general will of their electorate. In this sense, they were victims of their wartime rhetoric. Neither of them viewed idealism as something that could be negotiated. The British and French had fought the war for survival, but having pretended to have joined hands under the loftier banners of democratic principles, they found it difficult to return openly to business as usual. Wilson seemed sincere about his dream to have the New World redress the balance of the old.

DIFFICULTIES OF PEACEMAKING, JANUARY–FEBRUARY 1919

Great Power Domination

Ideology and Realism. A flotilla of nine battleships, two crusiers, and twenty-six destroyers escorted the ocean liner *George Washington* into Brest harbor on 13 December 1918. Woodrow Wilson had arrived in France. The next day in Paris, he and President Raymond Poincaré rode up the length of the Champs Elysées from the Place de la Concorde to the Arc de Triomphe, passing under a huge banner emblazoned "Honor to Wilson the Just" that stretched across the entire width of the boulevard. Two million enthusiastic, curious people were on hand to cheer him on his way. The American president's international popularity had reached a phenomenal level. Ideology had not made a serious appearance as a war aim until 1917 when the rhetoric of Wilson and Lenin vied for world attention. But Communist Russia was currently torn apart by civil war; and even though the drive for world revolution continued, Lenin was too preoccupied with fighting to preserve his regime and the unity of his country to present a serious challenge to Wilson's authority and prestige. People were intensely optimistic about the president's ability to bring a new morality to international affairs. They believed that through collective security his League of Nations could guarantee nations against attack, forever ending the power politics practiced in days of old. Wilson claimed that the League would solve all disputes among nations peacefully and would make men drunk with the spirit of self-sacrifice.

Wilson could safely denounce secret diplomacy and stand forth as a champion of the rights of others. None of this could affect the security of the United States unless the new world order entailed the destruction of the sovereignty of the nation-state. Despite Wilson's rhetoric, there did not seem much danger of this happening. The Americans would continue to exercise hegemony in their own hemisphere and hold the balance of power in Europe and Asia. Wilsonianism endorsed the sovereign equality of states, but allowed intervention against those who threatened the good of civilization. Europeans feared this contradiction was a device by which the United States could promote its own national interests under the guise of moral superiority.

Lloyd George was in a fairly strong position. The kaiser's once proud High Seas Fleet no longer threatened his country. All the important capital ships had been rounded up and were headed for internment in the Orkneys in Scotland under British escort. Lloyd George's idea of a proper settlement was one that would restore his country to its position of leadership and enhance the security of the British Empire. He wanted the cooperation of the United States in maintaining European security. Germany must be allowed to recover enough to aid the British economic recovery by paying for the destruction it caused during the war. Lloyd George said he wanted a just peace, not a vindictive peace, but he also demanded a stern peace. "The occasion demands it. The crime demands it. But its severity must be designed, not to gratify vengeance, but to vindicate justice," he told Parliament.[3] Lloyd George also wanted to avoid making any political commitments to France. Clemenceau was not the least bit interested in the new world order Wilson proposed. "Mr. Wilson has lived in a world that has been fairly safe for democracy," he said, "I have lived in a world where it was good form to shoot a Democrat."[4] Clemenceau had seen the Germans invade his country twice—in 1870 and 1914. For him, security was everything.

Once Wilson had arrived, the peace conference had been expected to begin by the middle of December, but for one reason or another—the British elections, the French celebrations, the flu epidemic—the date was postponed, and the first plenary session did not take place until 18 January 1919, a date deliberately chosen to coincide with Bismarck's declaration of the German Empire in 1871 in the Hall of Mirrors at Versailles. In their passion to humiliate Germany, the French wanted to avenge as many historical insults as possible. The conference machinery evolved from the wartime high command: the Supreme War Council became, with the addition of Japan, the Supreme Peace Council, or the Council of Ten, each of the major powers having two delegates apiece. Wilson was no more eager than Lloyd George or Clemenceau to give any of the smaller states a significant voice in running the conference. The Great Powers assured themselves control of the fifty-two advisory committees, which were established to handle specific economic, territorial, financial, and military questions, by installing two delegates apiece on each committee, whereas they gave smaller states only five seats altogether on each committee. All the states had equal representation on the Plenary Council, but that body met only six times before the treaty with Germany was signed. Clemenceau, who chaired its gatherings, left no doubt that the lesser powers were there merely to endorse the decisions of the Great Powers without debate. "Adopté," he would say, banging down his gavel and passing quickly to the next item.

Lloyd George did not want to tie his hands with any set order of business. The French wanted each topic discussed systematically, beginning with the treaty with Germany. The League of Nations could come last. Wilson was opposed. He wanted the League discussed first. After all, he had made American participation in the conference contingent on the League being accepted as an integral part of the settlement. He further insisted that the League receive top priority on the conference's agenda, because, if it were discussed last, it might not be discussed at all. In Wilson's view, the responsibilities of this new organization would extend far beyond peacekeeping. He wanted it to require all new states to guarantee equal treatment to their racial minorities and to set world standards for working conditions, including the eight-hour workday.[5] He also wanted the League to establish mandates for the former German and Turkish colonial empires to prevent these territories from being routinely parceled out among the European and Commonwealth powers. Since the Great Powers could not agree on their priorities, the conference developed an agenda as it went along with the less important problems being discussed simultaneously with the more important.

Profile: (Thomas) Woodrow Wilson (1856–1924)

When Woodrow Wilson was one year old, his family moved from Staunton, Virginia, to Augusta, Georgia, where he lived throughout the Civil War. The war made a great impression on him and later influenced his determination to create an organization to guarantee peace and cooperation. He came from a religious background. His father, Joseph Ruggles Wilson, was a Presbyterian minister and theologian; his mother, Janet, was the daughter of a Presbyterian minister, Thomas Woodrow, who was pastor of a church in Carlisle, England, before he migrated to the United States in 1836. In 1919, as president, Woodrow Wilson had the privilege of preaching a sermon from his grandfather's old pulpit. It was one of the high points of his life.

In 1874, Wilson entered college, first at Davidson College in South Carolina and then, the following year, at the College of New Jersey (later Princeton University) where he participated in literary activities and in debates. In 1883, he entered Johns Hopkins University and, three years later, received his Ph.D. in government and history. Over the next decade and a half, he held a variety of academic positions: at Bryn Mawr College, Wesleyan University in Connecticut, and Princeton University where, in 1902, he became president. At Princeton, Wilson devoted himself to reshaping undergraduate education and worked to institute a preceptorial system whereby students and professors would live together in quadrangles to engage in common scholarly pursuits. But the plan was opposed by the trustees and never adopted. Wilson also failed to gain control of the graduate school. These blows to his self-esteem prompted him to turn to state politics as compensation. In 1910, he became the Democratic governor of New Jersey. In his campaign, he had promised to change the current election system by instituting direct primaries, to break up trusts, and to wipe out corruption. His reputation for reform soon brought him national attention, and in 1912, "forward looking" Democrats nominated him for president of the United States at the party convention in Baltimore. Wilson won on the forty-sixth ballot against Speaker of the House Champ Clark, the favorite of the old party regulars.

In the national election, Wilson ran against a badly divided Republican party, which was split between the candidacies of William Howard Taft and Theodore Roosevelt. Wilson received 42 percent of the popular vote, one million votes less than the combined strength of his opponents, but he captured 435 out of 531 votes in the Electoral College. The Democrats also managed to win control of both houses of Congress. Once inaugurated, Wilson was determined to carry out his campaign promises. He won the adoption of a federal income tax, created the Federal Reserve Board to regulate the nation's currency, and secured the enactment of the Clayton Anti-Trust Act, which strengthened labor's right to strike.

Wilson's confidence that he knew what was best for people also provided a justification for him to meddle in the affairs of other countries when he found a suitable rationale for doing so. For example, because of the complicity of General Victoriano Huerta in the murder of President Francisco Madero of Mexico, Wilson refused to recognize Huerta as president, telling the Congress that there could be no peace between the United States and Mexico until the dictator was eliminated. Wilson tried to bring about Huerta's downfall by clamping an embargo on the shipment of arms to Mexico and actively supporting Huerta's opponents. He used the pretext of the arrest of some marines at Tampico to order the occupation of Veracruz pending the collection of reparations. The pressure was sufficient to produce Huerta's resignation. Wilson also established a virtual protectorate over Haiti in 1915 and, the following year, instituted U.S. military government over Santo Domingo. He explained that he was preparing these states for self-government and dismissed taunts that he was acting as an imperialistic bully.

Wilson's great opportunity to arrange the affairs of nations came with World War I. But his chance to create a new world order was possible only because his country had helped defeat the Central Powers on the battlefield. In 1918 before leaving for Europe, he had told the American people that although the Armistice had given them everything for which they had fought, that was no longer enough. He said that it was his "duty to assist by example, by sober, friendly counsel, and by material aid in the establishment of just democracy throughout the world."[6] The president had never mentioned this as one of his war aims, although on 11 February 1918 he had said, "What we are striving for is a new international order based on broad and universal principles of right and justice—no mere peace of shreds and patches."[7] The president was convinced that he alone among the Allied leaders represented the true will of the people. He therefore felt it made no difference that the Democratic party had lost its majority in both the Senate and the House of Representatives in the recent November elections. Wilson said he expected to put the Republicans "in a position to realize their full responsibility"[8] and unwisely refused to make his peace delegation bipartisan.

The Colonial Settlement. The first issue on which the peace conference was able to reach agreement was the disposition of Germany's overseas empire, all of which had been conquered and occupied during the war. New Zealand held Samoa; South Africa possessed German Southwest Africa; Japan had seized the German concessions in China; Australia controlled New Guinea; and Britain had taken German East Africa and had divided Togoland and the Cameroon with France. None of the beneficiaries were eager to follow Wilson's exhortation to surrender control of these territories to a League of Nations. William Hughes, the prime minister of Australia, flatly informed the president that his country would annex the territories it had conquered. Wilson was incensed. "Mister Hughes," he replied gravely, "am I to understand that if the whole civilized world asks Australia to agree to a mandate in respect to these islands, Australia is prepared still to defy the appeal of the whole civilized world?" "That's about the size of it, President Wilson," Hughes snapped.[9]

The president wanted to postpone the colonial settlement until the establishment of a League of Nations would put him in a better position to get his way. To break the impasse over ownership, Jan Smuts of South Africa proposed establishing three kinds of mandates based on the level of maturity of their respective peoples. Category A, the highest, was reserved for territories whose peoples had reached a stage of development just shy of complete independence, category B included territories that were still subject to general outside supervision; and the lowest level, category C, was used for territories whose native peoples were judged so primitive that their affairs could best be administered as an integral part of the mandatory state.[10] Under this compromise, Britain got the lion's share: practically all of German East Africa, part of Togoland and the Cameroon; the territories of Palestine and Iraq in the old Ottoman Empire, and the Pacific island of Nauru. France came next, acquiring three-fourths of Togoland, almost the entire Cameroon, and a protectorate over Syria. Belgium, after protesting its initial exclusion from the African partition, took home Ruanda and Urundi in the northwestern part of East Africa, while Portugal received, as a similar sop, the district of Kioga. The Union of South Africa obtained German Southwest Africa; Australia kept New Guinea and picked up all the German islands south of the equator except Western Samoa, which went to New Zealand. Japan collected the islands north of the equator—the Carolines, Marianas, and Marshalls—and the old German sphere of influence on China's Shantung Peninsula.[11] In deference to Wilson, the mandates were not officially confirmed until three months later, after the League Covenant was completed.

In February 1919, the Pan-African Congress, organized by the black American writer William Edward (W. E. B.) Du Bois, had reservations concerning mandates. Clemenceau gave the congress permission to meet in Paris because he did not want to appear ungrateful for the service black African troops had rendered France during the war. The French government made available the ballroom of the Grand Hotel. The fifty-seven black delegates, mostly from the United States, drafted a petition asking the peace conference to recognize the rights of African natives to participate in their own governance "as fast as their development permits." They also called for international laws to protect the rights of the natives, prevent exploitation, eliminate slavery, and guarantee high-quality education. But Clemenceau felt no obligation to have these goals implemented. Without a powerful sponsor, the congress found that it could only score rhetorical points.

Italy also had little influence. Premier Vittorio Orlando said that he "would readily accept whatever principles might be adopted, provided they were equitably applied and also provided [his country] could participate in the work of civilization."[12] But Italy had never directly been promised any of Germany's empire,[13] and in fact it got none, a slight that resulted in the Italians having no vested interest in the overall colonial settlement.

The distribution of the imperial spoils was handled as a modern version of the white man's burden. Wilson, never happy with compromises, was displeased; he sensed that in applying his concept for mandates, the imperialists had succeeded in outmaneuvering him. His mistake was his refusal to demand mandates for the United States. Had he done so he could have disposed of them anyway he chose. Instead, he confined himself to deploring the actions of his allies who, he must have known, looked upon the League as a device through which they could project power.

The Russian Question

The Uninvited. Lloyd George seemed to favor inviting the Communist government in Russia to the Paris Conference. He maintained that foreign policy should not be determined by likes and dislikes. However, he ran into a stone wall of opposition from ministers within his own government and from the French government. The peace conference spent as much time on the Russian question as it did on any other. When the Council of Ten first discussed Russia on 16 January, Lloyd George explained that it was never actually his intent to offer the Communists a seat at the peace table. He claimed that he had only wanted to facilitate the arrangement of a truce between the warring factions of the civil war by having their representatives come to Paris "to explain their position and receive from the Allies, if possible, some suggestions for the accommodation of their differences."[14] He did not like the policy of isolating Russia (an early containment policy known as the *cordon sanitaire*) or promoting the overthrow of the Bolsheviks by cutting off vital supplies. He opposed escalating intervention. "Was anyone of the Western Allies prepared to send a million men into Russia?" he asked.[15] But the British cabinet had already secretly recognized Admiral Aleksandr Kolchak as the de facto head of Russia,[16] even though Kolchak had no chance of surviving without massive Allied aid. Lloyd George thought it time to admit that the hard-line policy against the Bolsheviks had failed.

The Bolsheviks were eager to remove the Allied forces from their country and wanted to begin negotiations. They offered to settle foreign debts and protect foreign property as an inducement. They also appeared willing to suspend subversive propaganda in foreign countries, grant amnesty to political prisoners, and recognize the self-determination of the Finnish, Polish, and Ukrainian peoples.[17]

Wilson was encouraged. He proposed that a meeting be held on one of the Princes Islands in the Sea of Marmara south of Constantinople.[18] He said he was prepared to recognize the Communist regime "without reservation" and to promise that the Allies would not make any attempt to overthrow it. He maintained that the Allies wanted only to promote peace and "happy co-operative relations" between the Russian people and the other peoples of the world.[19] But Wilson extended the invitation to almost any Russian with the price of a ticket to Turkey.[20] He alone seems to have believed success was possible.

Mutual Suspicions. Wilson's proposal to meet for discussions did not strike the suspicious Bolsheviks as genuine. They even had difficulty establishing the invitation's authenticity, since it was printed in the newspaper, not delivered through official channels. Small wonder that Leon Trotsky dismissed Wilson's offer as another of his "anemic professorial utopias."[21] Lenin feared the offer was a prelude for new Allied aggressions in Siberia and southern Russia and ordered the Red Army to capture Rostov, Chelyabinsk, and Omsk as soon as possible. This action reinforced Clemenceau's belief that the Bolsheviks were just trying to set a trap. Clemenceau was in favor of continuing the policy of intervention. He believed that as long as the Bolsheviks remained in power, French investors would have little chance of recovering the capital investments they had lost with the Bolshevik nationalizations. He also knew that the Bolshevik government, which had signed the shameful Treaty of Brest-Litovsk, did not favor reconstructing the prewar alliance against Germany. Despite the vital role Russia had played in the war, in his view, the separate peace the Bolsheviks had signed with Germany had negated any secret wartime promises the Allies had made to Russia, including control of the straits into the Black Sea, complete restoration of the prewar frontiers (including the Baltic states, Finland, Bessarabia, and Poland), reparations, and a sphere of interest in the Near East.

The Allies were worried about keeping Communism from spreading into Eastern Europe. The French insisted that this be accomplished with a joint Allied force, but the British and French interventionists tended to dismiss the enormity of the task of containing Russia. They misjudged the strength of the Bolsheviks and had great difficulty understanding the character of the Russian people. Some seemed to think that the appearance of a few Allied regiments would cause the Communists to run in panic. In addition, the Americans had no desire to make a long-range military commitment to Europe. Considering the brutal nature of the Russian civil war, only a total victory by the Bolsheviks or their opponents seemed possible as the foundation for some sort of solution.

The League of Nations

The Covenant. Wilson felt particularly honored to be named the president of the commission entrusted with the task of drafting the constitution of a new world organization. Wilson had come to Paris to do more than negotiate treaties and, in accepting the responsibility, he said he intended to establish a process whereby "the actions of the nations in the interest of peace and justice must be permanent."[22] Clemenceau listened to the speech with his eyes closed. He had heard it all before. His idea of creating an international council of Great Powers to enforce the peace was dramatically different from Wilson's League "with governmental functions to interfere in internal affairs, with trustees in various places sending reports to—he did not know whom."[23] Clemenceau wanted an international military force led by French generals. He was willing to consider the salvation of mankind only if that involved protecting his country against Germany—in other words, if the League were to be a continuation of the wartime alliance under a new guise.

So that his work on the League Covenant would not interfere with the daily business of the conference, Wilson scheduled meetings after hours in the late afternoon and at night. Although the organization that emerged from these deliberations failed to satisfy Clemenceau's hope for a new Holy Alliance, it did preserve the primacy of the Great Powers through their permanent seats on the League Council, the organization's powerful executive body.[24] As a sop, the lesser states were given four nonpermanent seats. The Council had the chief responsibility to deal "with any matter within the sphere of action of the League or affecting the peace of the world," to formulate policy, and to recommend sufficient action to protect the integrity of the Covenant. The Council would also supervise the system of mandates and handle the policy of disarmament. It had the authority to expel any member state for violating the Covenant.

All member states received equal representation in the Assembly, the League's legislature. This body was intended to be a sort of forum for world peace, but it had no authority to initiate action. In time though, as the Great Powers became reluctant to use the Council to resolve disputes, the Assembly did play a more active role by passing resolutions. A Secretariat was established to arrange meetings, keep records, and furnish stenographic and research services. Article 6 simply said that the Secretariat would comprise "a Secretary-General and such secretaries and staff as may be required," but the provision cleared the way for the creation of a gigantic international civil service with hundreds of directors, advisers, chiefs of section, and counselors—cadres from forty different nations who enjoyed special diplomatic status and freedom from national taxation. The Secretariat was divided into sections with specialized duties: Political, Economic and Financial, Communications and Transit, Mandates, Disarmament, Health, Opium Traffic, and Minorities and Administrative. This vast bureaucracy gave the Great Powers ample opportunities to increase their influence. Their citizens filled many key positions, including the important post of secretary-general who had great authority over the entire League machinery.[25] In the event of a dispute, the secretary-general would, on request, call the Council into session. He made "all necessary arrangements for a full investigation and consideration" of all unresolved disputes likely to lead to active conflict.[26]

Collective Security. Wilson viewed the League as a means of preventing war through compulsory arbitration; Clemenceau saw it as an instrument to preserve the peace settlement; Lloyd George thought it should be primarily a diplomatic agency through which treaties could be revised and boundary changes made. Reconciliation of these differences depended on the interpretation of two key articles of the Covenant: Articles 10 and 19. Article 10 pledged League members "to respect and preserve as against external aggression the territorial integrity and existing political independence of all Members of the League. In case of any such aggression or in case of any threat or danger of such aggression, the Council shall advise upon the means by which this obligation shall be fulfilled." In the event any war or threat of war should be considered a matter of official concern, "the League shall take any action that may be deemed wise and effectual to safeguard the peace of nations." According to Article 19, "The Assembly may from time to time advise the reconsideration of Members of the League of treaties which have become inapplicable, and the consideration of international conditions whose continuance might endanger the peace of the world."[27] Enforcement was a difficult proposition. As Professor William Rappard contemporaneously observed, "The League is in reality governed, not from its seat [in Geneva], but from and by the ministries and parliaments of the member states of the League."[28]

The Covenant did not require compulsory arbitration, nor did it outlaw war. It only tried to make it more difficult. League members agreed to submit all serious disputes among themselves to arbitration or judicial settlement and, in no case, to resort to war "until three months after the award by the arbitrators" or on the specific recommendation of the Council.[29] If a League member should undertake military action in violation of the Covenant, that state would be considered guilty of committing war against all the other members. These would immediately sever all trade and financial relations with the offending state. The Council would then recommend what military forces the members of the League should contribute to protect the Covenant. Military sanctions were not automatic, however.

Thus, although the League provided elaborate penalties against aggressors, it failed to establish appropriate enforcement machinery. Military sanctions were not mandatory, and even economic sanctions depended on the willingness of members to enforce them. In other words, each state had to satisfy itself that an act of aggression had taken place before collective sanctions could be applied. As long as the leading European nations cooperated, the League might be used to great effect, but it could also become a cover for doing nothing. Consequently, the League provided no *new* effective way of preserving world peace, least of all of protecting French security.

Wilson tried to assure Clemenceau: "When danger comes, we too will come and we will help you, but you must trust us." Wilson added: "We must all depend on our mutual good faith."[30] Clemenceau thought this was nonsense. He continued to argue in favor of a military league.

FORMULATING THE GERMAN TREATY, MARCH–JUNE 1919

Disagreement among the Allies

The Rhineland Controversy. Wilson was due to leave the conference for the United States on 15 February to wind up the current session of Congress, and he wanted to return home triumphantly bearing a completed draft of the League Covenant. But Clemenceau, intent on getting a league of victors, did not allow the vote on the League Covenant to take place until two days before Wilson was scheduled to depart.[31] With Wilson out of the way, Clemenceau focused his attention on completing the treaty with Germany. Even an anarchist's attempt on his life only slowed him down temporarily.[32] He convalesced ten days, seated in an armchair, because it was too painful for him to lie down. In this position he tried to work out the main provisions of the treaty with Colonel Edward House, Wilson's chief adviser, before the president returned. The most important French war aim was the separation of the Rhineland from Germany. The French regarded the Germans as a perpetually warlike people who had to be deprived of this territory to discourage future aggression. But Clemenceau's demand for the establishment of a separate Rhenish republic received no support from Lloyd George who waited until Wilson returned before proposing a compromise solution.

The Rhineland would not be separated from Germany, but it would be demilitarized and, together with a zone fifty kilometers deep along the eastern bank, would be placed under direct Allied occupation for fifteen years. Thus, in order for the Germans to invade France, they would have to cross this stretch of territory before the French could destroy the bridges, a difficult proposition. If the Germans fulfilled all their obligations under the treaty, Allied forces would leave the northern sector centered on Cologne after five years; the middle area around Koblenz after ten years; and the southern district around Mainz after the full fifteen years, or even earlier. However, any violation of the treaty by Germany could halt the process or provoke immediate reoccupation. Clemenceau also obtained a Treaty of Guarantee in which Britain and the United States promised to come to France's aid in the event of German aggression against France. Wilson must have suspected he would not get this treaty through the U.S. Senate, but his promise cleared the way for settling the Rhineland dispute. Clemenceau knew he could not convince Wilson and Lloyd George to give France such a durable position of strength in the Rhineland. He also knew that no nation as strong as Germany could be held down forever. France had bought time, but eventually it would have to reconcile itself to the restoration of German power as it had done with other past enemies. "The conqueror," Clemenceau once remarked, "is a prisoner to her conquest; that is the revenge of conquered nations."[33]

The Saar Dispute. The French premier hoped that by compromising over the Rhineland he would be in a better position to acquire the coal-rich Saarland, a territory that the French demanded both as compensation for Germany's wartime destruction of the mines of northern France and for the area's postwar reconstruction. The Saar dispute proved to be the bitterest of the conference. The extent to which this relatively minor issue dominated the proceedings, even threatening a breakdown, showed how strongly the security concerns of France dominated the conference. In a sense, the Saar dispute was another chapter in the continuing story of how to adjust to the unification of Germany. Clemenceau claimed that if

France did not get the Saar valley, he would not sign the peace treaty. "The history of the United States is glorious, but short," Clemenceau said sarcastically. "We have our conception of history which cannot be exactly the same as yours."[34] The complete cession of the territory, he maintained, would make an eventual German attack against France less likely, and would satisfy France's determination to return to its ancient frontiers.[35] It would help satisfy French claims for reparations. The output from Saarland mines—over 17 million tons in 1913–1914—would increase French annual coal production by 50 percent, effectively complementing the nearby iron and steel industries in the Forbach-Faulquemont-Carling area of north-eastern France. But Wilson and Lloyd George refused to allow the creation of a new issue that could permanently poison relations between France and Germany. Clemenceau had to compromise again. France would receive control of the Saar's mineral resources for fifteen years. During that time the region would be under the political administration of the League of Nations. A plebiscite would be held in 1935 when the Saarlanders could choose either to join France, return to Germany, or become an independent state.[36]

The dispute raged on for weeks and so unnerved Wilson that he considered going home. On 3 April, he was suddenly taken ill, ran a high fever, had coughing fits, and suffered from diarrhea, vomiting, and insomnia. His personal physician, Cary T. Grayson, diagnosed the illness as influenza, which, some say, then attacked his brain. However, a blood clot in his brain, a cerebral vascular occlusion popularly called a "little stroke," more probably caused the president's illness.[37] This stroke, as distinct from the big stroke that he suffered in September 1920, did not result in paralysis and loss of speech, but it nevertheless produced a profound change in his personality, causing him to fluctuate between euphoria and paranoia, issue contradictory orders, fatigue easily, and have difficulty grasping essentials. As a man of increasingly diminished capacity, Wilson was less able to withstand the pressures of Clemenceau.

Would We Go to War for Danzig? The Big Three also had difficulty setting Germany's frontiers with Poland. The Allies favored creating a viable Polish state with free and secure access to the sea, but they disagreed on how this should be accomplished. The French wanted to reconstruct as much of pre-1772 Poland as possible. Poland would be France's new ally in the east, insurance against the spread of Bolshevism and a resurgent Germany. But Wilson and Lloyd George were opposed to including great numbers of non-Polish minorities in the new state, fearing this would sow the needs of future conflict. (Wilson's American-Polish constituents, however, gave him a good domestic political reason for supporting Polish claims beyond what was reasonable on the grounds of self-determination.) The experts assigned to study the situation recommended establishing a corridor through east Prussia down the Vistula River valley, giving Poland the port of Danzig and large parts of Poznan, Silesia, and western Galicia.

The proposal seemed reasonable, but Lloyd George objected strongly to the Danzig award. He felt that Polish acquisition of this Hanseatic League town with its predominantly German population would invite revisionism. He said that no article should be put into the treaty that the Allies were not prepared to go to war to defend. "France would fight tomorrow to defend Alsace, if that were in dispute. But would we wage war for Danzig?"[38] His counsel prevailed.

Danzig became a free city under the supervision of the League of Nations. Its people could direct their own local affairs, but the area would be under Polish customs. Poland also received the right to develop the city's docks and wharfs and to regulate traffic on the Vistula. The arrangement satisfied hardly anyone. It poisoned relations between Germany and Poland almost as effectively as if Danzig had been given to Poland outright.

Arms Limitations. The Allies had less trouble imposing limits on the German armed forces. The new army would have only 100,000 troops, all of them volunteers serving a minimum enlistment of twelve years for the ranks and twenty-five years for officers. This prevented the Germans from training a large army through annual recruitment.[39] Germany was also forbidden to have heavy artillery and could possess only 288 pieces of light artillery. Nor could Germany build armored ships larger than 10,000 tons. It could have no submarines or air force; it could build no new fortifications, manufacture no poison gas, and construct no high-power telegraph stations. Finally, Germany was required to pay the costs of the Allied Control Commission and the army of occupation. This included everything from the upkeep of men and animals to paying for lodging and billeting, allowances, salaries, and wages.

Reparations. Contrary to popular belief, Clemenceau was not initially a hard-liner on the subject of reparations.[40] He was willing to adjust the French demands to the degree of financial aid France would receive from its allies. The less France had to depend on German resources for its recovery, the more moderate could be its demands for reparations. But the British and the Americans were not eager to assume new financial obligations. They were in the process of dismantling wartime controls, thereby weakening the power of the state to supervise reconstruction, and they had their own domestic worries. Moreover, underwriting the recovery of France would require a major change in the thrust of American foreign policy. France therefore was left with reparations as the chief means through which it could obtain the necessary capital and goods for regaining its national strength. Even so, Clemenceau wanted to keep the time period for payment to an absolute minimum to avoid a costly policy of enforcement. Accordingly, he was willing to set a relatively low figure, an amount that could be mobilized, say, through the sale of bonds on the American market—an ingenious plan for receiving indirect American aid. The French would get their money at the outset, when their need was greatest, and they would not have to worry about collection. If the Germans defaulted, the American bondholders, not the French government, would be left with worthless paper.

However, the Allies first had to agree on how much Germany should pay. The French set a minimum of 124 billion marks and a maximum of 188 billion marks. The Americans had a minimum of 100 billion and a maximum of 140 billion.[41] Left to themselves they could have reached an agreement, but the British refused to compromise and held out for 220 billion marks. It therefore became impossible to establish any concrete figure for inclusion in the treaty. Lloyd George knew that large reparations were popular with the British public. Such sums also gave him a strong position from which he could later negotiate concessions. The French, having failed to get the economic aid from their allies they thought necessary for recovery, increasingly followed the British cue and demanded heavy reparations from Germany to cover all civilian property damages. Lloyd George, seeing that this scheme would give the French the largest slice, insisted on the inclusion of Allied war pensions, thereby more than doubling Germany's financial obligation. Clemenceau readily agreed. The more Germany paid, the greater the chance of committing Britain to enforcing the treaty.

The Big Three left the establishment of Germany's final debt to a reparations commission with powers as yet undefined. This arrangement had the advantage of defusing the issue and obscuring it from public scrutiny, while allowing all options to be kept open until the Allies decided how much Germany should pay. In the meantime, they inserted a special clause in the treaty underlining Germany's duty to fulfill its obligations. Article 231 made the Germans assume all responsibility "for causing all the loss and damage to which the Allied and Associated Governments and their nationals have been subjected as a consequence of the war imposed upon them by the aggression of Germany and her Allies."[42] The war guilt clause did not specifically state that Germany *alone* was culpable, but its implication was clear. Clemenceau, who usually did not equate morality with political wisdom, left no doubt about his own interpretation: "It is only possible to conceive of such an obligation if its origin and cause is the responsibility of the author of the damage."[43] This strong moral justification for spoils of war—in part, public relations—did more to inflame the Germans than any other single article in the treaty.

The Dictated Peace

The Fontainebleau Memorandum. On 25 March, Lloyd George laid a paper before the Council of Four, arguing against a harsh peace. The new British policy position resulted from a weekend brainstorming session in the Hotel France et Angleterre at Fontainebleau. The prime minister warned that, if Germany felt "she has been unjustly treated in the peace of 1919 she will find means of exacting retribution from her conquerors." He insisted that the maintenance of peace would "depend on there being no causes of exasperation constantly stirring up the spirit of patriotism, of justice or of fair play."[44] He expressed fear that the Germans might throw in their lot with Bolsheviks and place their vast power and organizational genius at the Communists' disposal. Should the Communists seize power in Germany then, Lloyd George argued, "all Eastern Europe will be swept into the orbit of the Bolshevik revolution and within a year we may witness the spectacle of nearly one hundred million people organized into a vast red army under German instructors and German generals equipped with German cannons and German machine guns and prepared for a renewal of the attack on Western Europe."

The "Fontainebleau memorandum" has often been cited as evidence of the prime minister's commitment to a peace of moderation. But this was only partially true. Lloyd George was thinking primarily of territorial adjustment. Although he said that reparations ought "to disappear if possible with the generation which made the war," he still believed Germany should be required to make large redemption payments. He accepted that French security should be guaranteed by Britain and the United States, pending the establishment of the League.[45] The memorandum made Lloyd George seem more liberal than he in fact was. Clemenceau had no difficulty in deflating him, suggesting that Lloyd George might show his commitment to his new benevolence by renouncing reparations for Great Britain. But the premier was alarmed at this new development and insisted that "we must not compromise the result of our victory."[46] Clemenceau argued that the greatest danger was a peace of moderation that could only lead to great dissatisfaction and provoke the same revolutionary forces at home that the Allies were trying to contain abroad.

The Controversy over Ratification. The peace process seemed endless, even though the Council of Ten was streamlined to a Council of Four.[47] Japan was gone; Italy remained, but with little influence. The chief role of the Big Three remained unchanged. In the middle of April, Lloyd George, who was under attack at home for sacrificing British interests to Wilson, pushed to invite the Germans to come to Paris as soon as possible to receive the treaty, something he thought would give him ammunition to answer his critics. Both Clemenceau and Wilson agreed. Wilson was anxious to return home as soon as possible. Clemenceau feared that further delays could contribute to Allied weakness because of the ongoing pace of demobilization. The final draft was assembled with such haste and confusion that the official British rapporteur said, "apart from the members of the Drafting Committee, no one in the Conference, not even the Council of Three nor their Secretary, myself, had the slightest idea of its size, shape or total contents up to the eve of its presentation to the Germans."[48]

The German delegation, headed by Foreign Minister Count Ulrich von Brockdorff-Rantzau and containing 180 experts, arrived in France at the end of the month. The French quartered them at the Hotel des Reservoirs in Versailles, the same establishment where the Germans had lodged the French commission suing for peace from Bismarck in 1871. A barbed-wire fence surrounded the hotel. The French, making every effort to be inhospitable, dumped the Germans' luggage in the hotel courtyard, telling them to find their own rooms and carry it up themselves. For more than a week of cold and rainy weather, the Germans were bottled up in this hostelry with no central heat. Finally, Brockdorff was summoned to receive the treaty, on 7 May, in a special ceremony at the Trianon Palace in the park of the Chateau of Versailles. The Allies gave him a single copy of the document and told him to make comments only in writing—in either French or English. He was given fifteen days to reply.

The Germans had come with the intention of negotiating the treaty's contents, but it was plain that they would not get the chance. They believed that they would not be forced to accept anything inconsistent with Wilson's Fourteen Points. They did not consider that they had surrendered unconditionally. Since the kaiser's government had disappeared and Germany was a democracy—moreover a democracy that was protecting the West against the spread of Communism—they felt that Germany would be treated with consideration.

The text was some 80,000 words long and contained 440 separate articles. By its terms Germany emerged a weaker and smaller power, losing some 27,443 square miles of European territory with a population of 6.4 million people.[49] Germany also forfeited its entire overseas empire without receiving any compensation. Also surrendered without compensation were all the public property in the areas ceded to Belgium and all the public and *private* property in the territories given to France. When the document was translated, sent to Berlin, and published, the outrage was predictable. Chancellor Philipp Scheidemann called the terms "unacceptable" and assured the National Assembly that Germany would not sign it without significant changes. The only sour note in this litany of denunciation was sounded by the independent socialist leader, Hugo Haase, who, although also condemning the treaty, remarked that those who had favored the Treaty of Brest-Litovsk with the Russians were not in a very good position to demand justice from the Allies.

Meanwhile the German delegates at the Hotel des Reservoirs worked diligently to produce a reply before the expiration of the deadline, which had been extended a week. Instead of concentrating on the treaty's main inequities, they tried to protect their right to revision by submitting objections to all sections of the treaty that did not conform to Wilson's Fourteen Points. The process, parcelled out among teams of experts, lacked coordination; and the Allies got the impression that the Germans were going to contest every single article for whatever reason.

The signing of the Treaty of Versailles at the Hall of Mirrors on 28 June 1919. Georges Clemenceau, the presiding officer, invites the German plenipotentiaries to come forth and put their names to the document.

Fearing the Germans might refuse to sign altogether, on 16 June, the Big Three discussed the possibility of taking military action. Clemenceau maintained that nothing short of a march on Berlin would be necessary to force German compliance. If this were not done, he said, the Germans would think "us weakened and only able to take milder action."[50] Wilson and Lloyd George wanted to know if the Allied armies were capable of such an effort. Foch recommended an invasion of Baden, Württemberg, and Bavaria. The British and Americans were not eager to engage in military action. They feared the threat of Bolshevism more than they did German militarism. Lloyd George did not want to take any action that might induce Germany to put its "vast organizing power at the disposal of the revolutionary fanatics."[51] The Fontainebleau memorandum indicated he was already in favor of conciliation. Nevertheless, the Allies decided to remain resolute and authorized Foch to prepare contingency plans.

On 16 June, the Supreme Council rejected all the German protests and counterproposals, save for allowing plebiscites to be held in certain lands originally earmarked for Poland, and threatened to end the Armistice if the treaty were not signed within five days. Brockdorff-Rantzau resigned his post and returned to Berlin. The German cabinet fell, and a new one was formed. The treaty was submitted to the National Assembly whose president, Konstantin Fehrenbach, swore that the legislators would rather die like Roman senators than submit to such disgrace. But the final vote showed a different mood: 237 favored ratification, 138 were opposed, and 5 abstained. Germany was in no condition to mount any resistance. Furthermore, signing the treaty was the only way the Germans could get the Allies to lift the blockade and allow Germany open access to world markets.[52] The National Assembly's approval came just three hours before the Allies were expected to move their troops into unoccupied Germany.

The signing of the treaty with Germany took place on 28 June 1919 in the great Hall of Mirrors at the Chateau of Versailles. It was the fifth anniversary of the assassination of Archduke Franz Ferdinand at Sarajevo. Here in 1871, the victorious German states had proclaimed the creation of their new Kaiserreich. Now the French had avenged the insult.

This was the last meeting of the Big Three. Wilson returned to Washington, where, on 10 July, he reported to the Senate on the peace negotiations and requested ratification of the treaty with Germany. Wilson had left Paris in the private train of President Poincaré, but without the cheers that had greeted his arrival. Lloyd George also departed soon after the signing. He arrived at Victoria Station that same evening to be officially met by King George V. The prime minister would not have the problems of the American president in winning approval of his handiwork; he already had the votes to get the treaty through the House of Commons. Nevertheless he knew he would be attacked for being too soft on Germany, although ironically he believed that he had been too hard. Soon the controversy over the treaty would be crowded off the front pages by other time-consuming problems: labor unrest, Irish independence, economic recovery, and the loss of imperial prestige. Only Clemenceau remained in Paris to participate in the negotiations on the treaties with Germany's allies. Although he was in his seventy-eighth year, he had no intention of stepping down. The "creation continues," he said. But the following January, he resigned the premiership after his candidacy for president of the republic was rejected. Until then, however, he devoted all his energies to the peace conference and was therefore on hand when Austria signed its treaty.

THE TREATIES WITH GERMANY'S ALLIES, SEPTEMBER 1919–AUGUST 1920

Disposition of the Dual Monarchy

Contradictory Claims. The Allies had not desired the dismemberment of the Austro-Hungarian Empire, which they viewed as a force for stability in Eastern Europe. Clemenceau, in particular, was willing to treat the Habsburg monarchy with leniency because, despite its former adherence to the Dual Alliance, it could offer a counterbalance to Germany. When asked to justify this position in view of that state's role in starting the war, he replied that Austria had not invaded France. The British and the Americans hoped that the empire might be reconstituted as a federal union of Danubian nationalities. But the Allies had become prisoners of their own rhetoric.

In April 1918, representatives of the Czech, Slavic, Polish, and Romanian national groups had come together in Rome to proclaim their common desire to destroy the Habsburg monarchy and to assert their right to self-determination. The British and French accepted the inevitable and, shortly after the Rome meeting, recognized the Czech-Slovak Council as the de facto government of a new state. Several months later, Wilson followed suit. The rights of other national groups were recognized in turn. Subsequently, Wilson dismissed the Habsburg monarchy's offer to negotiate a peace on the basis of the Fourteen Points by replying that the United States had already recognized the right of the empire's separate nationalities to decide their own fate.

The Allies were still faced with the difficult task of drawing a map to accommodate the conflicting claims of these various groups. The Poles and the Czechs both wanted Teschen; the Italians and the Slavs claimed the Dalmatian coast; the Romanians and the Serbs were rivals for the Banat; the Austrians and Hungarians

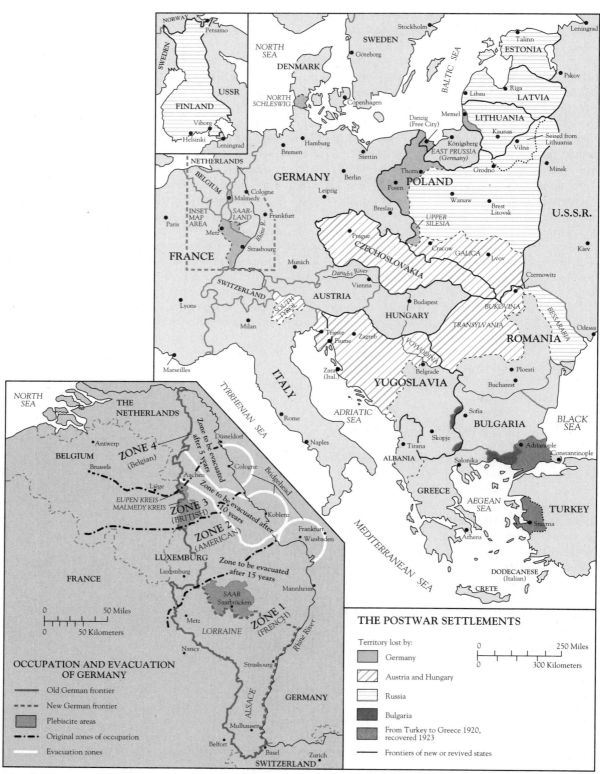

THE POSTWAR SETTLEMENTS

Territory lost by:

- Germany
- Austria and Hungary
- Russia
- Bulgaria
- From Turkey to Greece 1920, recovered 1923
- Frontiers of new or revived states

0   250 Miles
0   300 Kilometers

OCCUPATION AND EVACUATION OF GERMANY

- Old German frontier
- New German frontier
- Plebiscite areas
- Original zones of occupation
- Evacuation zones

0   50 Miles
0   50 Kilometers

Map 4

contested the area of the Burgenland; the Hungarians and the Romanians claimed Transylvania; and the Yugoslavs and the Austrians both coveted the Klagenfurt basin. The Allies turned these matters over to their boundary experts. The chief of the Austro-Hungarian commission, Charles Seymour, explained that the territorial commissions operated on the basis of ethnicity with the burden of proof always resting with those who wanted to depart from this principle. However, national claims frequently gave way to the imperatives of security, economic viability, and the interests of the Great Powers. Moreover, given the chaotic distribution of peoples, there were few clear-cut ethnic frontiers. Cities populated by one ethnic group often depended on agricultural areas settled by another. Historical frontiers, railways, and canals usually did not follow natural frontiers.

The claims written into the secret wartime treaties provided another complication. The Italians, for example, concentrated their attention on getting the lands of the Austro-Hungarian Empire that the Treaty of London had promised them in 1915. Specifically, the Italians wanted the Brenner frontier and sizable chunks of the Dalmatian coast. But Lloyd George and Clemenceau were no longer eager to hand over all this territory to the Italians and looked for an excuse to renege on their earlier commitment. They hoped that Wilson, who had not been party to the London agreement, would denounce its provisions so they could start with a clean slate. Wilson, however, appeared to have committed himself to some of the treaty's provisions. For example, he promised to allow Italy to annex the South Tyrol with its quarter of a million German-speaking Austrians. In doing so, he seriously compromised his doctrine of nationalities and forfeited an opportunity to invalidate a secret treaty. The president admitted he had made this promise through "insufficient study."[53] The Italians were encouraged to seek even more. They wanted the Adriatic port of Fiume, apparently ripe for the taking following the collapse of the Habsburg empire. But Fiume, peopled largely by Croatians, was to become part of the new kingdom of the Serbs, Croats, and Slovenes, later called Yugoslavia.

Lloyd George thought the Italians could be bought off with some other piece of territory, possibly in the Adriatic, but the Italians refused to budge. Wilson decided to resolve the impasse by appealing to the Italian people to abandon their claims to the city. Orlando and Foreign Minister Sidney Sonnino were outraged and quit the conference in protest, returning home to a tumultuous welcome. Sonnino charged that Wilson had lost his virginity over the German settlement and was trying to get it back over Fiume at Italian expense. Wilson's name was removed from all the streets named in his honor, and his pictures were torn down. Rallies were held throughout the country demanding annexation by force. The nationalists' slogan became L'Italia fara da se! (Italy will do it alone.)

The Big Three did not consider the satisfaction of Italian claims to be a top priority. In fact, they condescended toward their wartime ally as if Italy were a small child whose fussing was not to be taken very seriously. They felt that the Italians had little room for complaint since they had received substantially all they had been promised for joining the war. Besides, the collapse of the Austro-Hungarian Empire should satisfy the Italians. By treating the Italians as greedy and mean-spirited and responding to their demands with annoyance and contempt, the Allies encouraged a monumental resentment that contributed to the growth of Italian nationalist forces committed to revising any treaty.

The Treaty of St. Germain. The republic of Austria was the weakest state to stagger from the wreckage of the Dual Monarchy. Nevertheless the Allies did not regard it as a new entity and held it accountable for the acts and obligations of the old Habsburg empire, including the responsibility to pay reparations for the damage caused during the war. The Treaty of St. Germain, signed on 11 September 1919, was highly punitive. It reduced Austria to an almost exclusively German territory of 33,000 square miles, excluding many Germans who had been in the old empire. Italy took the South Tyrol, with its 250,000 Germans; Czechoslovakia obtained the 3 million Germans of the Sudetenland; and Hungary received the predominantly German-speaking area of the Burgenland. The treaty reduced the Austrian army to a long-service volunteer force, limited to 30,000 men and organized in units no larger than regiments. It limited armaments and forbade the construction of an air force. The treaty also reduced Austria's navy to three patrol boats on the Danube, ordering the rest to be surrendered to the Allies. The Reparations Commission was to fix the final amount of reparations, but the Austrians would make payments in kind in the meantime. They were to hand over to the Italians, Yugoslavs, and Romanians a specified number of cows, horses, and sheep, as well as the bulk of their merchant fleet. The Treaty of St. Germain also listed certain works of art that were to be given back to their former owners; some of these items, such as the crown jewels of the Medicis and the gold cup of King Ladislas IV of Poland, had been acquired as far back as the eighteenth century. In direct response to a French demand, Austria was perpetually denied the right to incorporate with Germany.

The Austrians protested the peace, using arguments similar to those advanced by the Germans. They claimed that the country's former rulers had started the war and that the country was now a democracy and should be treated with leniency. Moreover, they wanted the principle of self-determination to be honored by holding plebiscites in all the disputed territories. The Allies did allow a vote to be held in the Klagenfurt basin and as a result restored the Burgenland to Austria. But most of the other Austrian objections were brushed aside. Making changes in Austria's favor was too unpopular with Austria's neighbors. The Hungarians held on to the Burgenland's principal city of Sopron (Öldenburg) and never gave it up. Austria and Yugoslavia almost came to blows when Yugoslavia tried to seize the southern province of Carinthia and threatened to advance into Styria. The once proud Austrian state, which had decided the destinies of Europe, was now a lonely beggar, reduced to fighting over scraps. It entered the postwar world as an indigent.

The Hungarian Seesaw. The Magyars had tried to preserve the integrity of the lands of the Crown of St. Stephen by blaming Austria for starting the war. Shortly before the end of hostilities, the government in Budapest issued a declaration of independence and, like every other ethnic secessionist group, established a National Council. Its leader, Mihály Károlyi, seemed an ideal man to gain the confidence and friendship of the Allies. Károlyi was a liberal aristocrat, a humanitarian pacifist, and an advocate of the democratic ideals of Wilson. To emphasize his country's complete independence, he insisted on a separate armistice. The ploy did not work. The Allies consented to a separate armistice, but sent General Franchet d'Esperey to Budapest to carry it out. Franchet was not inclined toward generosity. He boasted he had only to give the word to unleash the Czechs, Slovaks, Romanians, and Yugoslavs "and you are destroyed." Hungary was forced to agree to armistice terms that left it defenseless.

On 16 November 1918, the Hungarians proclaimed their country a republic, and Károlyi became its first president. Unfortunately, Károlyi showed no more skill in handling the new state's internal problems than he had in befriending the Entente. People ignored his program to reconcile the nationalities and his plan to reform agriculture. After four months in office, he had achieved no lasting success in either domestic or foreign policy. The continuing disorder encouraged the Romanians to invade Transylvania. In January 1919, they advanced their armies to the Tisza River. Károlyi protested in vain. When it became clear that the Allies were going to assign the territory to Romania, Károlyi resigned. Many Hungarians now looked to the parties of the left for action. The Socialist party clamored for a Red parliament, and began organizing the demobilized soldiers into soviets. It formed an alliance with the Communists to get help from the Bolsheviks to drive the Romanians out of Transylvania. On 22 March 1919, a Socialist-Communist government under Alexander Garbai replaced Károlyi. However, the Communist leader, Béla Kun, who took the post of commissar of foreign affairs, exercised the real power.

Kun lost no time in forcing the Socialists to resign and then set out to create a regime like that established by Lenin.[54] He nationalized the entire work force, except street vendors; confiscated private property; expropriated the large landed estates, which he organized into collective farms; renounced the country's foreign debt; and created special revolutionary tribunals. He also reorganized the Hungarian army and, on 28 March, declared war on Czechoslovakia, where he proceeded to reconquer Slovakia and establish a Soviet Republic. The Allies in Paris were so alarmed that they threatened to take action unless the Hungarians withdrew their troops from Czechoslovakia. But Kun ignored the order and pressed the attack. He hoped to join forces with the Red Army, but Lenin, involved in his own civil war, could offer him no assistance.

The Hungarian forces soon became badly overextended. Taking advantage of this weakness, the Romanians, with French support, mounted a major assault. At the end of July 1919, they forced the Hungarians back to the gates of Budapest. The Social Democrats again saw their chance to assert their authority, and they forced Kun and his cabinet to resign. Most fled to Vienna. On 4 August, the Romanian army entered the Hungarian capital, where they remained for three months. When they finally left, on 14 November, they took with them all the booty they could carry. Budapest was in shambles.

Miklós Horthy, the former chief of the Austro-Hungarian navy, now emerged as Hungary's leader. The admiral wanted to restore the power and territory of the old Hungary, goals not unlike those of his predecessor. Socially and politically, however, he was much different, being a throwback to the former ruling class. Communists, Socialists, and liberals were all alike to him. His conservatism made him acceptable to the Allies, but did not seem to influence them when the time came to conclude peace.

The Treaty of Trianon. Considering the political confusion that had prevailed in Hungary since the end of the war, the delay in formulating a treaty was understandable. Preliminary terms appeared at the end of 1919, but it took another six months to complete the process. Under the treaty, Hungary lost more than 70 percent of its former territory and 63 percent of its old population. The treaty awarded Transylvania to Romania, Slovakia and Ruthenia to Czechoslovakia, Croatia and Slavonia to Yugoslavia, and the Burgenland to Austria. The new state was ethnically more homogeneous than before, but almost 3.5 million Magyars were living under alien rule. The Allies were more concerned with the geographical viability and territorial demands of the successor states than with Hungarian self-determination.

Nevertheless, because France was still looking for eventual allies among the new states of Eastern Europe, it paid Hungarian revisionism some deference. According to the treaty, if any dispute over the new frontiers revealed a lack of justice contrary to the general interest, the Council of the League of Nations would resolve the matter. Even though none of the other defeated countries received this promise, the Hungarians were not satisfied, believing that it did not go far enough.

The official signing took place on 4 June 1920 in the pink marble Trianon Palace built by Louis XIV to escape from the rigors of court etiquette at Versailles. As the Hungarian delegates approached the horseshoe-shaped table to sign the treaty before the representatives of the Allied powers, one observer was struck by their resemblance to the downtrodden burghers of Calais who during the Hundred Years' War were forced to present themselves to their conquerors with nooses around their necks.

Treaty Making with the Bulgarians and the Turks

The Treaty of Neuilly. The Allies signed the treaty of peace with Bulgaria in a dismal city hall in a suburb of Paris. The drab surroundings mirrored the lowly status that the Bulgarians had once occupied as a German ally. Bulgaria, formerly one of the largest states in Eastern Europe, next to Turkey, was one of the most persistent disturbers of the peace in the Balkans and got what it deserved.[55] The Allies were determined that the Bulgarians would not have another chance to disrupt the status quo. They intended to deprive them of a sufficient amount of territory to make future trouble impossible.

The peace treaty, signed on 27 November 1919, required Bulgaria to renounce its claims to all the territory it had occupied during the war and to cede to Yugoslavia certain lands (mostly populated by Bulgarians) along its western border to straighten out the frontier. Furthermore, it would surrender western Thrace and its territories along the Adriatic Sea to Greece. The Bulgarian army would be limited in size to a 20,000 all-volunteer force. Finally, the Bulgarians would make certain deliveries of coal, livestock, railroad equipment, and other payments in kind to Yugoslavia, Romania, and Greece; it would also pay 2.25 billion gold francs (about $450 million) to the Allied powers. The reparations were to be paid over a period of thirty-seven years.

The Bulgarians had believed that their change of government at the end of the war would get them a more moderate peace. The warlike King Ferdinand had been forced to abdicate in favor of his son, Boris III, and the Agrarian party leader, Alexander Stambolisky headed the current government. Stambolisky had gone to prison in 1915 for supporting the Allied cause. The Bulgarians were so bitter at the instrument they were forced to sign that they rejected an offer to guarantee them access to the Aegean. They felt acceptance would jeopardize their rights to complete revision. Although they were too weak to contest the settlement, the Bulgarians made the reacquisition of lost territory their prime foreign policy objective.

The Treaty of Sèvres. Allied troops occupied Constantinople during the first week of December 1918. The French commander, Franchet d'Esperey, entered the city at the head of his men in the style of an Islamic conqueror—mounted on a white charger, riding without reins. The British and French anchored their warships off the Golden Horn and stationed soldiers in a special "neutral zone" that they had traced east of the straits, from the upper Aegean to the Black Sea. They took under their "protection" the Ottoman ruler, Mehemed VI, whose feeble and tottering government could only wait helplessly for the Allies to decide its fate. The Allies seemed in no hurry. The secret treaties to partition the Ottoman Empire had been arranged during a period of great political tension, volatility, and military uncertainty. The Russian revolution, and the subsequent Bolshevik denunciation of the tsarist treaties, put the future of Constantinople again in dispute. The British victories in the Mesopotamian valley subjected the Sykes-Picot Agreement to change. Once again, everything seemed to be in contention.

The British had occupied the oil-rich district of Mosul, promised in 1916 to France. As the British began to exploit its resources, they were willing to allow the French no more than 25 percent. The French, who had counted on getting it all, were furious. At the San Remo Conference in April 1920, Premier Alexandre Millerand bitterly reminded Lloyd George that during the war the two nations had signed an agreement giving France the entire area. When Millerand demanded that the agreement be respected, the British prime minister bluntly replied that the situation had changed since he had made the arrangement with Briand. France had not cooperated in the conquest of Mesopotamia, despite British urging. Instead, Briand had contented "himself with making speeches. Great Britain had not conquered these territories by means of speeches."[56] Lloyd George might have won the argument, but the dispute, surfacing in another form, continued to divide the two allies.

More than a year and a half passed before the peace settlement was ready for signature. The ceremony took place in a less-than-majestic exposition room of the National Porcelain Factory at Sèvres on 20 October 1920. The Allies stripped the Ottoman Empire of all its possessions outside the Anatolian Peninsula, cutting its size from 613,000 to 175,000 square miles and its population from 20 to 8 million people. The former Arab-speaking provinces were divided into foreign spheres of interest: Syria and Mesopotamia, supposedly independent, were placed under the supervisory authority of France and Britain. Palestine became a mandate of Britain. The Greeks received western Thrace, almost to the suburbs of Constantinople, and eight Turkish islands in the upper Aegean. The Italians got the islands of the Dodecanese.

Practically all the western and southern portions of Turkey became areas of special interest: the Greeks were awarded the territory of Smyrna; the Italians received the province of Konya; and the French the area of Cilicia. Turkey agreed to recognize Armenia as a free and independent state, accepting a frontier the president of the United States would eventually set. Lloyd George and Clemenceau had once contemplated turning Constantinople and the straits into a League of Nations mandate, but neither trusted the other with its administration; since the United States refused to take on the responsibility, they felt it best not to deprive Turkey of the area after all. But the straits were internationalized, and the adjacent areas demilitarized. The delegates of Sultan Mehemed VI signed without hesitation, but the government they represented no longer spoke for the country. A new nationalistic government was being formed in the interior under the leadership of Mustapha Kemal, the hero of Gallipoli. Eventually, this force would force a revision of the treaty just signed.

POSTSCRIPT   World War I had been fought primarily against Germany. The peace that ended it was primarily against Germany. Although it had been humiliated, Germany still remained potentially the strongest nation in Europe, and, in time, its demands could not go ignored. The first great German protest against the peace treaty had occurred before the treaty was even signed. On 21 June, the skeleton crews left on board the German navy vessels interned in the harbor at Scapa Flow in Scotland simultaneously opened their ships' sea cocks, scuttling ten battleships, six battle cruisers, six light cruisers, and fifty destroyers, the bulk of the High Seas fleet that had seen action at Jutland. Clemenceau suspected the British had engineered the sinkings to avoid giving France its share of the naval spoils.

The Versailles settlement was rich in provisions that were not conducive to its longevity: the Eastern settlement, the military occupation of German territory, the clauses on reparations, and the provocative and politically disastrous "war guilt clause." Before signing the Armistice, the Germans had promised to make proper restitution. But they had never intended this obligation to imply that they were assuming responsibility for having started the war, nor for causing the damage done by their allies. Worse yet, the reparations policy rested on the contradiction that even though the Germans would be reluctant to pay, they would, at the same time, be willing to carry out their obligations in good faith.[57]

The Austro-Hungarian Empire had collapsed under the weight of the defeat and its own restive minorities. The settlement left Austria economically vulnerable, landlocked, poor in natural resources, cut off from its traditional markets, and surrounded by hostile neighbors. The capital city of Vienna was close to the country's eastern frontier and contained almost one-third of the state's entire population: 2 million out of 6.5 million people. The departure of the Habsburgs produced an identity crisis. The western province of Vorarlberg petitioned for inclusion in the Swiss confederation. The Austrian provisional National Assembly passed a resolution endorsing unification with Germany. The Allies permitted neither; they had specifically prohibited union (Anschluss) with Germany in the Paris peace treaties[58] and dismissed the argument that this would fulfill the Austrian right to self-determination.

The peace settlement had been equally unkind to the other defeated states. All emerged reduced in territory but with more homogeneous populations than before. Ironically, ethnic problems became a major concern of the new or enlarged beneficiary states. Despite their platitudes about the right of self-determination, the leaders of the Great Powers had ignored the national claims of the defeated states whenever it served their interest to put strategic, historical, or economic considerations first. The absence of Communist Russia at Paris made a peace settlement possible with only part of Europe. Russia had lost Finland, the Baltic states of Latvia, Lithuania, and Estonia, Bessarabia, and its possessions in Poland. It was certain to be revisionist no matter what its government.

The Paris settlement satisfied most of Wilson's Fourteen Points, especially the territorial aims. Considering the qualifications, the ideological points were also largely fulfilled, with the exception of Article 2 on freedom of the seas. Also honored were most of the promises contained in the secret Allied treaties (barring those made with Russia). In this respect, the peace conference was an Allied success. But permanent peace often depends on the flexibility of a settlement—its ability to change and accommodate to new conditions—and on the character of its application. The constant disagreements between Britain and France over enforcement and the absence of the United States as a balance did not produce the best atmosphere for constructive change that could have strengthened the Paris settlement. Revisionism was too often regarded as an attempt to destroy the foundations of the whole settlement. France, in particular, wanted to preserve the status quo 1919 at all costs, and this preoccupation became the main goal of its foreign policy for the next decade.

The Americans once again refused to exercise a role in Europe commensurate with their strength. They stayed aloof from politics, but continued to play a powerful, often contradictory, economic role. They determined to collect the war debts the Allies owed them, while encouraging private enterprise to make huge investments in the recovery of Europe. In the absence of the Americans, the French and British dominated the League of Nations. These countries could not understand the Americans' fear that they could be committed to preserving anything against their will. But even had the United States taken an active role in Geneva, the organization would still have become an instrument of Great Power politics. Despite Wilson's hope for a new diplomacy, the Great Powers used the League to perpetuate their domination over the smaller nations just as they had done so effectively at the peace conference. Even Wilson himself did not really want his League to become a superstate, but rather an instrument through which the peace-loving nations, such as the United States, could exercise authority throughout the world. Whether it was his intention or not, he conceded the use of the organization to the Great Powers when it served their purposes. In this respect, he was reinforcing, not diminishing, national sovereignty. Moreover, by insisting that the League become an integral part of the treaty with Germany, Wilson directly associated the organization with preserving the peace settlement. However, the League would display its greatest initiative in nonpolitical matters, such as the control of malaria, leprosy, and tuberculosis or the drafting of model labor legislation—areas in which the vital interests of the Great Powers were not involved.

World War I destroyed the traditional European balance of power. This could not have been reconstructed at Paris, even had the desire existed. Soon Germany and Russia would rearm and revive their economic and political strength, presenting the other states of Europe with the old dilemma of how to maintain an equilibrium that would guarantee their security against German and Russian power. Would a conciliatory peace have been more successful? The temptation is to answer automatically in the affirmative. Certainly, many historical examples can be found to support such a position. But consider the settlement that ended the Napoleonic wars: in 1814, the Quadruple Alliance gave France a treaty that imposed no indemnity and let it keep the revolutionary conquests of Savoy and the Saar. Yet, this gesture of moderation did not prevent the return of Napoleon and the Hundred Days. After Waterloo, the Allies were understandably more punitive: they pushed France back to the frontiers of 1789, made the French return captured works of art, imposed an indemnity of 700 million francs, and forced the country to support a 150,000-man foreign army of occupation for five years. The second Peace of Paris proved more durable than the first.

But perhaps a better question would be, Was a conciliatory peace possible? It must be remembered that a punitive peace was not something concocted by the Allied leaders. It was a popular movement. According to Lloyd George, the main outlines of the settlement with Germany were not defined in the hour of victory, but "when the issue was still in doubt, when the nations saw ahead nothing but the prospect of the complete dissipation of their hard earned treasure and the still darker outlook of the death or mutilation of myriads of their picked men in the flower of their youth."[59] He might have added that the massive propaganda campaigns the Allies directed against Germany during the war had created the monster of hate that now began to steer affairs of state. For France, the issue from first to last was security. Its current prominence was due to the simultaneous defeat of the three great empires that had been its adversaries through the ages. The Austrian empire would never rise again, but Germany and Russia might once again become important antagonists, perhaps even in alliance with each other, and France might be left to face them alone. France, Clemenceau insisted, had to have the security on land that Britain had on the seas. "I have not decided how this will be accomplished," he admitted. "I beg you to understand my feelings, as I am trying to understand yours. America is far away, protected by an ocean. Britain could not be reached even by Napoleon himself. You are, both of you are, sheltered, we are not."[60] As Lloyd George correctly surmised, Clemenceau's determination to separate Germans from Germany was driven by his desire to offset the falling French birth rate. He feared that, despite the victory, "Germany would have a population nearly twice as large as France."[61]

The Paris settlement tells us much about the nature of modern war. The statesmen in 1919 could not develop—and were not allowed to develop— the sort of detachment that might have made a peace of moderation a possibility. Even an unregenerate German-hater like Clemenceau had less room to maneuver than he liked. War had become a clash of popular wills. It had developed a sense of mission not found in Europe since the days of the wars of religion. And this mobilized fury of nations could not easily be staunched once the conflict no longer raged.

ENDNOTES

1. At the Plenary Session on 25 January 1919. U.S. State Department, *Foreign Relations of the United States: The Paris Peace Conference, 1919*, vol. 3 (Washington, D.C.: U.S. Government Printing Office, 1943), 196–97.
2. Ibid., 1: 353.
3. Great Britain, *Hansard's Parliamentary Debates*, 16 April 1919.
4. Stephen Bonsal, *Unfinished Business* (New York: Doubleday, Doran, 1944), 68.
5. Charles Seymour, *The Intimate Papers of Colonel House*, vol. 4 (Boston: Houghton Mifflin, 1928), 285.
6. Ibid., 580.
7. *Messages and Papers of the Presidents*, vol. 18 (New York: Bureau of National Literature, n.d.), 8449.
8. Ray Stannard Baker, *Woodrow Wilson, Life and Letters*, vol. 7 (New York: Doubleday, Doran, 1939), 591.
9. David Lloyd George, *The Truth about the Peace Treaties*, vol. 1 (London: Victor Gollancz, 1938), 195.
10. Smuts put certain communities formerly belonging to the Turkish empire into the first category; the next level contained the peoples of central Africa; and in the last category were such terrritories as Southwest Africa—which Smuts wanted assigned his own country—and certain islands in the South Pacific.
11. China refused to recognize this award and refused to sign the peace treaty. However, Japan restored the leased territories to China in 1922.
12. Lloyd George, *Peace Treaties*, 1: 767.
13. The Treaty of London (1915) had specified that if Britain and France were to increase their colonial territories in Africa at the expense of Germany, "Italy may claim some equitable compensation, particularly as regards the settlement in her favor of the questions relative to the frontiers of the Italian colonies of Eritrea, Somaliland, and Libya and the neighboring colonies belonging to France and Great Britain." *Command Papers*, cmd 671, misc. no. 7 (London: H. M. Stationery Office, 1920).
14. U.S. State Department, *The Paris Peace Conference*, 3: 581.
15. Ibid., 582.
16. J. F. N. Bradley, *Allied Intervention in Russia* (London: Weidenfeld & Nicolson, 1968), 113.
17. U.S. State Department, *The Paris Peace Conference*, 3: 643–45.
18. The city did not become known by its present name of Istanbul until 1930.

19. U.S. State Department, *The Paris Conference*, 3: 676–77.

20. That is to "every organized group that is now exercising or attempting to exercise, political authority or military control anywhere in Siberia, or within the boundaries of European Russia as they stood before the war just concluded (except Finland)." Ibid., 677.

21. Leon Trotsky, *My Life* (New York: Pathfinder Press, 1970), 360.

22. U.S. State Department, *The Paris Peace Conference*, 3: 180.

23. Ibid., 768.

24. Never would all the Great Powers be members at the same time. The five original permanent members were designated to be the United States, Britain, France, Italy, and Japan. Of these the United States never joined, Japan dropped out in 1933, and Italy quit in 1937. Germany was a member from 1926 to 1933, and the Soviet Union from 1934 to 1939. Only France and Britain were in the League from beginning to end.

25. During the active life of the League, the position was held by two career diplomats: one British, the other French. Respectively, they were James Eric Drummond (1919–1933) and Joseph Avenol (1933–1940).

26. U.S. State Department, *The Paris Peace Conference*, 3: 116.

27. League of Nations, *Ten Years of World Co-operation* (Geneva: Secretariat of the League of Nations, 1930), 417–30.

28. William E. Rappard, *International Relations from Geneva* (New Haven: Yale University Press, 1925), 161.

29. U.S. State Department, *The Paris Peace Conference*, 3: 115–16.

30. David Hunter Miller, *The Drafting of the Covenant*, vol. 2 (New York: G. P. Putnam's Sons, 1928), 297.

31. The president was away from Paris from 15 February to 14 March 1919.

32. This episode occurred on 19 February, four days after Wilson had left. Clemenceau was coming out of his apartment on the Rue Franklin to go to a conference at the Hotel Crillon, when Emile Cottin shot at him seven times. Only one bullet found its target, hitting the premier near his spine. Clemenceau dismissed the assassination attempt as an accident and said that the gunman should be punished only for his "careless use of a dangerous weapon and for poor marksmanship." Bonsal, *Unfinished Business*, 67.

33. Georges Clemenceau, *Grandeur and Misery of Victory* (New York: Harcourt Brace, 1930), 200.

34. Paul Mantoux, *Les Délibérations du Conseil des Quatres*, vol. 1 (Paris: Centre National de la Recherche Scientifique, 1955), 71.

35. The Saar had been part of France from 1792 to 1815.

36. When the plebiscite was held on 13 January 1935, 90 percent of the electorate voted for reunion with the Reich.

37. The April attack resulted in a "lesion in the right cerebral hemisphere extending to include deeper structures in the limbic-reticular system." Edwin A. Weinstein, "Woodrow Wilson's Neurological Illness," *Journal of American History* (1970): 342.

38. Mantoux, *Les Délibérations*, 1: 112.

39. Ferdinand Foch had argued against the long service concept. He felt that the more frequent the turnover of manpower, the less effective would be the training and the weaker the leadership. Quoting Marshal Thomas Bugeaud, the first military governor of Algeria, he said that "it would be better to have an army of sheep commanded by a lion than a number of lions commanded by an ass." U.S. State Department, *The Paris Peace Conference*, 4: 217.

40. This question was handled by the Supreme Economic Council, chaired by France's Etienne Clémentel. It first met on 5 February 1918 as the Economic Drafting Committee and assumed its permanent name three days later.

41. Mark Trachtenberg, *Reparation in World Politics: France and European Economic Diplomacy, 1916–1923* (New York: Columbia University Press, 1980), 63.

42. Harold W. Temperly, *A History of the Peace Conference of Paris*, vol. 3 (London: H. Frowde, 1924), 214.

43. Alma Luchau, *The German Delegation at the Paris Peace Conference* (New York: Howard Fertig, 1971), 254.

44. Lloyd George, *Peace Treaties*, 1: 405.

45. Ibid., 411.

46. Mantoux, *Les Délibérations*, 1: 44–45. Clemenceau's written answer, containing many of the same points, can be found in André Tardieu, *La Paix* (Paris: Payot, 1921), 139–42, and in Lloyd George, *Peace Treaties*, 1: 416–20.

47. By dropping the Japanese delegates, who were really only interested in Asian affairs, and also the foreign ministers.

48. Lord Hankey, *The Supreme Control at the Paris Peace Conference, 1919* (London: Allen and Unwin, 1963), 134.

49. The territories given to Poland contained 18,000 square miles and about 4 million people; the northern part of Schleswig, returned to Denmark after a plebiscite, included 1,500 square miles with 166,000 people; the districts of Eupen, Malmédy, and Moresnet, given to Belgium as reparations, comprised 399 square miles with 60,000 people; Memel had 1,000 square miles and 141,000 people; Danzig, 738 square miles and a population of 330,000; the territory ceded to Czechoslovakia, 122 square miles with a population of 166,000; and Alsace-Lorraine, reacquired by France, 5,605 square miles with 1.8 million people. *The Statesman's Year Book 1924*, 935–36.

50. U.S. State Department, *The Paris Peace Conference*, 6: 549.

51. Lloyd George, *Peace Treaties*, 1: 408.

52. The wartime blockade was still in effect, although some food supplies were allowed through.

53. Seymour, *The Intimate Papers of Colonel House*, 435.

54. The Russians had captured Kun in 1916; after their coup, the Bolsheviks gave him special instruction in revolutionary tactics to help him establish a People's Republic in Hungary. Lenin had been impressed by the similarities between tsarist Russia and Hungary—the persistence of feudal influences, the presence of large landed estates, and the dependence of the economy on foreign capital. Kun founded the Hungarian Communist party in December 1918 and began to agitate against the Károlyi government. He was arrested the following February after a particularly violent demonstration and was still in prison when the Social Democrats released him to form a new government.

55. Bulgaria's expansionist lust came from its sense of having been betrayed in July 1878 by the Congress of Berlin, which, in modifying the Treaty of San Stefano, considerably reduced the state's size. Some of this territory, particularly in Macedonia and the frontage on the Aegean, was regained in the war against Turkey in 1912, but the following year in the Second Balkan War, the humiliating Treaty of Bucharest awarded a large chunk of Bulgarian territory in the northeast to Romania and let Greece and Serbia keep the parts of Macedonia they were currently occupying. Although Bulgaria did not join the war in 1914, the prospect of satisfying its imperial ambitions through an alliance with the Central Powers was too strong for it to remain neutral. Germany was not at all hesitant in recognizing Bulgaria's territorial claims. And, on 11 October 1915, two days after the fall of Belgrade to an Austro-Germany army, Bulgarian troops invaded Serbia.

56. *Documents on British Foreign Policy*, 1st Series, VIII, 10.

57. There were also more unconventional articles. The British had inserted a demand for "the skull of the Sultan, Mkwawa, which was removed from the Protectorate of

German East Africa and taken to Germany." Temperly, *A History of the Peace Conference of Paris*, 3: 233–34. "I never imagined that I would meet this black ghost in the park of the Trianon," remarked an astonished German delegate, Walter Simons. Luchau, *German Delegation*, 120.

58. The Versailles treaty made Germany respect the inalienable independence of Austria; the St. Germain treaty required Austria "to abstain from any act which might directly or indirectly by any means whatever compromise her independence."

59. Lloyd George, *Peace Treaties*, 1: 22–23.

60. Mantoux, *Les Déliberations*, 1: 44–45.

61. Lloyd George, *Peace Treaties*, 1: 402.

PART TWO

THE FERVOR OF
REVOLUTION, 1919–1929

CHAPTER 4

THE RUINS OF EMPIRES

PREFACE   The Romanovs, the Hohenzollerns, and the Habsburgs had strutted the stage for hundreds of years. They had been on hand for the big events in times of rejoicing and times of misery, in times of peace and times of conflict. They had attended to the great affairs of state, helping to create the leagues, pacts, and alliances that had affected the fate of their peoples. Their births, marriages, and deaths were signposts of European history. Now they all were gone, never to return. For each dynasty, their country's defeat had been their defeat.

The Romanovs went first. Nicholas II, the most autocratic of Europe's rulers, had abdicated even while the battle raged. His presence proved an embarrassment to the new Provisional Government, which first confined him to the royal residence of Tsarskoye Selo. In August 1917, he and his family and some personal servants were moved to Tobolsk on the western Siberian plain. After the Bolsheviks seized power, they were transferred again. In May 1918, they went to Ekaterinburg (today Sverdlovsk). Here on 17 July 1918, they were all killed—the tsar, his wife, four daughters, a son, and four servants, eleven in all. A squad of executioners raked them with pistol fire. The royal couple died instantly, most of the rest after several volleys. Those still alive, including the daughter Anastasia, were finished off with bayonets and rifle butts. The bodies, wrapped in blankets and stacked in a truck, were driven ten miles northwest of town to an abandoned iron ore mine where they were hacked apart, burned, and dissolved in sulfuric acid. The remains were dumped down one of the disused pits or scattered from a moving truck.

Kaiser Wilhelm could have saved his cousin had he demanded that the tsar and his family be given to him as part of the Brest-Litovsk settlement. He did not because he feared an adverse reaction from the German Social Democrats, the very people who were demanding his abdication and an end to the war. Wilhelm was prepared to fight on, but on the morning of

9 November 1918, his generals confronted him at Supreme Army head-quarters in Spa, Belgium. The defeat, he was told, had destroyed the country's traditional respect for the monarchy. The generals claimed that the army could no longer be trusted to ensure the sovereign's personal safety. When the kaiser replied that he would put himself at the head of loyal units and restore order, General Wilhelm Gröner stated flatly that the army would not follow him. But what of the soldiers' oath to the colors and to their Supreme War Lord? the kaiser insisted. "Oath to the colors? War Lord?" Gröner repeated. "Today these are only words." Wilhelm became dramatic: "If only a few of my gentlemen remain loyal to me, I shall fight to the end, even if we are all killed."[1] But no one shared his desire to seek death on the battlefield. On 10 November, Wilhelm fled north to the Dutch border into exile. The new Social Democratic government in Berlin announced his abdication.[2]

Karl I, the last ruler of the Austro-Hungarian Empire, could not bring himself to abdicate his rights to the throne. "This crown is a responsibility given to me by God and I cannot renounce it," he insisted.[3] His family had been sovereigns since the thirteenth century. Shortly after midday on 11 November 1918, he signed a proclamation, removing himself from "all participation in the affairs of state"; then he moved out of the Schönbrun Palace and left for Eckartsau, a family hunting lodge, northeast of Vienna near the Czech and Hungarian frontiers. For the next five months, he lived there with his family and forty or more servants and hangers-on. Finally, he left for Switzerland. Although an exile, Karl was determined not to pass into oblivion and watched closely for an opportunity to regain his throne.

The new republics that had replaced the emperors had to build new standards of unity. They had to restructure their economies, adjust to new frontiers, and protect their people from civil war and starvation. The task was not going to be easy.

THE ESTABLISHMENT OF THE SOVIET UNION

War Communism

No Revolution without Shooting. The use of terror came easy to the Bolsheviks. They already had a siege mentality and believed that error had no rights. Their attempts to silence the opposition began the minute they occupied the Winter Palace. But the ship of state that they presumed to guide was a wreck. To bolster their position, they first received temporary authority from a Congress of Soviets to rule provisionally for a month pending the convocation of a constituent assembly. Lenin, though, did not intend to hand over authority to anyone. The great revolution had given him at last a chance to start laying the foundations of the one-party state. Terror was absolutely essential for this to be accomplished. When the Congress of Soviets voted to abolish the death penalty, Lenin was furious. "How can we accomplish a revolution without shooting?" he demanded. For

Lenin, the revolution meant class war, and class war meant people would be shot. Terror was necessary not only to enable the Bolsheviks to hold on to power, but also to promote the solidarity of the masses. Lenin favored capital punishment for entire social categories: "Not a single revolutionary government can dispense with the death penalty for the exploiters," he intoned.[4] The civil rights the Provisional Government so cherished would be scrapped, and all political opposition would be silenced by bullets.

At a meeting of the Central Executive on 14 December 1917, Leon Trotsky promised that soon "terror will assume very violent forms after the example of the great French revolutionaries. The guillotine will be ready for our enemies and not merely the jail."[5] On 20 December 1917, the Bolshevik regime institutionalized terror by creating the All-Russian Extraordinary Commission to Fight Counter-Revolution, Sabotage, and Speculation (known as the Cheka from its Russian initials). The Cheka received the authority to destroy summarily "counter-revolutionaries, spies, speculators, looters, hooligans, saboteurs, and other parasites."[6] Lenin believed that the Bolshevik revolution could not be legitimized without blood.[7] Henceforth, the Chekisty, under their chieftain Feliks Dzerzhinsky, acted as policemen, judges, jailers, and avenging angels of death, surpassing the old tsarist security service, the Okhrana, in both cruelty and efficiency. Idealists, who had joined the organization at the outset, either left in disgust or became completely brutalized. So many of the most corrupt and criminal elements of society were attracted to the Cheka's routine business of torture and extermination that even Dzerzhinsky complained, "Only saints or scoundrels can serve in the [secret police], but now the saints are running away from me and I am left with the scoundrels."[8] Not all the scoundrels were in the ranks.

Lenin chose to keep the Communist party and the state as separate entities, but with joint leadership that controlled the levers of power in both. The leaders in the party central committee also held all the ministerial posts in the government, thereby ensuring that the government would enact party decisions through the bureaucracy. The security police stood by to enforce the party's will. The arrangement made a good deal of practical sense. The Bolsheviks did not have enough followers to fill all the government posts and therefore had to rely on those who were already there. Furthermore, if any policy went wrong, the Bolsheviks could always blame the government. This arrangement became a model for most of the left- and right-wing one-party dictatorships that were to follow.[9] Non-Bolsheviks did not welcome the single-party framework, but it was a faithful reflection of the ideals for which Lenin had fought throughout his entire adult life.

Profile: Vladimir Ilyich Lenin (1870–1924)

Lenin displayed true political genius in holding onto and enlarging the power for which he had conspired all his adult life. But unlike the masses over whom he ruled, and in whose name he presumed to speak, he began life in relative ease and comfort.

Vladimir Ilyich Ulyanov—the name "Lenin" was adopted later as a cryptonym—was born in 1870 in the provincial capital of Simbirsk where his father was the chief inspector of schools, a position that was the civilian equivalent of a major-general in the military and carried with it the title of "excellency." The execution of his elder brother Alexander in 1887 significantly marked Lenin's adolescence. Alexander had been convicted of trying to assassinate Tsar Alexander III. From that moment on, Lenin dedicated himself to revolution, although he was

more influenced at this point by the ideals of populism than by Marxism. Despite the cloud of suspicion overhanging his family, Lenin was admitted to Kazan University later in 1887. Several months later, however, he was expelled for participating in a student demonstration. He returned home and studied for his law examination on his own, passing it in 1891.

In 1893, he went to live in St. Petersburg where he worked as a lawyer. This was a period when the revolutionary ideas of Marx had great attraction for the Russian intelligentsia, and in 1894 Lenin joined an underground cell of a social democratic circle, one of many in the St. Petersburg area and other Russian cities. But in 1895 he and some other independents established their own group, the Petersburg Union of Struggle for the Liberation of the Working Class, to try to unite all of these disparate groups so they could agitate more effectively among the workers. In December, Lenin and most of his associates were arrested and sent to prison and then into exile in Siberia.

During the three years he spent in a Siberian village, Lenin refined his ideas, creating his own version of Marxist ideology. Released from Siberia in 1900, he left Russia and for the next seventeen years lived in various Western European cities—Zurich, London, Paris (where his bicycle was stolen), Munich, and Geneva—studying, writing, contacting other exiles, and joining in their intrigues and acrimonious doctrinal disputes.

In 1902, he published a primer on revolutionary strategy entitled *What Is to Be Done?* in which he advocated the creation of a professional party elite to act as the vanguard of the revolution. Lenin believed that the only thing the workers could create spontaneously was trade unionism. Professional revolutionary leaders must therefore establish the party line and inculcate the masses with a proper social democratic consciousness. This elite, a strict hierarchy with absolute command vested in the party's central committee, had to organize its activities in the strictest secrecy. Lenin's five long-winded postulates of essential revolutionary organization can be reduced to a single rule: The greater the discipline and organization of the professional revolutionary leaders, the greater will be the movement's mass support and the greater its chances of success.[10]

His authoritarianism found little favor among other Russian revolutionaries who had been more influenced by Western European social democracy; many of them favored a broad proletarian party with membership open to all who agreed to support its program. Unlike Lenin, they believed that revolution was the responsibility of an entire class and feared that too much reliance on elitism would foster a one-man dictatorship.

In 1903 at the "Second" Social Democratic Party Congress, which met in Brussels, and then London, Lenin pressed for the adoption of a resolution defining party membership in accordance with his definition in *What Is to Be Done?* Instead, a resolution of Iuly Martov favoring a broad party not restricted to professional revolutionaries passed by 28 votes to 23. However, Lenin refused to give up. In the subsequent election of members to the party's central organs, taken after various members had left, Lenin won 22 votes to 20 with 2 abstentions. The victory gave him temporary control of the party paper, *Iskra* ("The Spark"). But more significantly, it enabled him henceforth to declare that his faction was the party of the majority, the Bolsheviks (from the Russian word *bolshe*, more), and that those who advocated a broad proletarian party were the Mensheviks (from *menshe*, fewer). This attitude hardly reflected the true desires of the Russian Social Democrats, most of whom favored the more open-minded "Mensheviks" who already controlled most of the local party committees, but it was a brilliant propaganda coup.

The leader of the rival Socialist Revolutionary party, Viktor Chernov, would describe Lenin as a man who "possesses a devotion to the revolutionary cause which permeates his entire being. But to him the revolution is embodied in his person . . . he possesses an outstanding mind, but it is a mind that embraces things not with three dimensions; it is a *mind of one dimension*, a unilinear mind [emphasis in original]."[11] Trotsky, then a Menshevik, called him a "despot and a terrorist" and said that should Lenin ever take power "the leonine head of Marx would be the first to fall under the guillotine." Lenin even lost control over his own Bolshevik faction for a time when the Central Committee expelled him for obstructionism early in 1905. But he hastily formed his own rival subgroup as a device for reasserting control.

In the turbulent year of 1905, Lenin profited by a general amnesty and returned to Russia. He arrived in St. Petersburg in November, in time for the downfall of the local workers' Soviet. Although he had taken little direct part in the antitsarist protest, he was impressed with the potential of using the Soviet as a means for revolutionary action. Nevertheless, when he returned into exile, he despaired that he would ever live to see the overthrow of the tsarist regime. His wife, Nadezhda Krupskaya, told how people wilted the longer they remained outside Russia: "The petty worries of emigrant life, the daily cares and struggles to make a living got them down."[12]

In 1912, Lenin broke with all the other revolutionary groups and established his own Social Democratic Labor party with a handpicked Central Committee of "party-minded" Bolsheviks like Alexei Rykov, Gregori Zinoviev, and Lev Kamenev. Lenin formed political associations with the religious scruples of a medieval saint, anathematizing those who did not accept his own vision of revolutionary truth. He adapted Marxism to his own purposes, using *Das Kapital* and the *Communist Manifesto* to justify positions he had already taken. In his work *State and Revolution*, written in 1917 when he was in exile in Finland, Lenin accepted the Marxist thesis that a political structure depends upon the relationship of the class structure to the means of production; capitalism and democracy are therefore mutually exclusive because any system in which the minority owns the property is a dictatorship of the bourgeoisie. The socialist revolution would establish the dictatorship of the proletariat with "the majority of the wage slaves" overthrowing "the minority of exploiters." Once exploitation has been removed, the state can "wither away" and society will apply the formula "From each according to his ability, to each according to his needs."

In power, Lenin proved less utopian: "We leave the question of length of time, on the concrete forms of the withering away, quite open, because *no material is available* to enable us to answer these questions [emphasis in original]." He was equally pragmatic about the timing for beginning the revolution. Many of his followers were arguing, as good Marxists, that socialism could not be established unless a country had passed through an appropriate bourgeois-capitalist phase—a state that backward Russia had obviously not achieved. But Lenin declared that since the tsarist system had been imperialist, and since imperialism was the last stage before the revolution, it was unnecessary to wait for the growth of an industrial economy and power could be seized immediately.

Lenin may have been sincere in his desire to improve the conditions of the Russian people, but his appalling lack of respect for the rights of the individual and his constant mechanical references to the obligation of the masses to subordinate their narrow interests to the higher wisdom of the party elite showed that he viewed the proletariat primarily as an abstraction that needed to be ruled by force. The great Russian writer, Maksim Gorky, said that Lenin had "no pity for the mass of the people," that workers were to him what "minerals are to the metallurgist."

Lenin rarely set foot in a factory except to make a speech; he assumed he already had the workers' support. No matter how many touching anecdotes are told about his love of children or concern for old peasant women, he was a fanatically self-righteous bourgeois who subordinated most human values to the attainment of power. In a sense, he followed a long line of Russian intellectuals, who traditionally had been messianic, their longing for a new order energized by their country's intolerable conditions and their own hatreds and personal despair.

The Command Society. The Provisional Government had promised elections for a national legislature to give Russia a new constitution. The Bolsheviks had been very vocal in their support of this aim, but that was before they had seized power. Nevertheless, they felt they had to hold the promised elections, which then took place on 25 November 1917. From their standpoint, the results were disastrous. The Bolshevik candidates received only 9.8 million out of 41.7 million votes cast, giving them 275 of the 707 seats. Even in Petrograd, the Bolsheviks received less than half (45 percent) of the vote. The Socialist Revolutionaries with 370 seats emerged with a clear majority.

When the Constituent Assembly met on 18 January 1918 in the Tauride Palace, it rejected the Bolshevik nominee for chairman, Yakov Sverdlov, and elected instead the Socialist Revolutionary leader, Viktor Chernov. Furthermore, it refused to surrender its mandate to the Council of People's Commissars, through which the Bolsheviks directed the affairs of state. The Bolsheviks and their allies stomped out of the Tauride Palace. The next morning, a squad of Lithuanian soldiers closed down the assembly by force. The first, feeble experiment in Russian democracy was over. The act of dissolution prompted no organized protest. Most of the people were exhausted from the war and tired of the political chaos of the preceding year. They had little understanding of the democratic process and appeared willing to support any government that would bring stability and restore order.

Lenin was much impressed by Walther Rathenau's War Socialism, which had mobilized the German economy for war. However, Lenin intended to carry the practice much further—to extend it to the entire economy not just that part related to the prosecution of the war. The policy, later known as War Communism, coincided with the period of the civil war and foreign intervention, but had its own dynamic and rationale. It began with the expropriation of real estate, taking farm property away from nonpeasant owners and suspending commerce in urban real estate. These measures were followed by a prohibition on the sale, purchase, or leasing of all industrial and commercial enterprises. Another decree outlawed inheritance. The Bolsheviks intended to bring the entire economy under the control of the state by nationalizing the means of production, ending all private commerce, inaugurating an official barter system to replace money, and introducing compulsory labor for all able-bodied male adults.[13] In many cases the practice fell far short of the intentions, but the primary aim was clear: to eliminate the political independence of the people by depriving them of all productive wealth and control over their own labor. None of these measures was really necessary to fight the civil war and get rid of foreign intervention.

Between 1918 and 1920, the Bolsheviks made the grain trade and foreign trade state monopolies and established that land was to be shared on the basis of need. They instituted civil marriage and recognized divorce by mutual consent. The power of the Russian Orthodox church was destroyed as the Bolsheviks ended its control of education and confiscated its wealth. All tsarist debts were repudiated. The Bolsheviks also revamped the judicial system—the tsarist system actually had a reputation of being one of the most liberal and impartial branches of that government—and asserted control over the trade union movement, making labor leaders agents of the state responsible for controlling the working class. They mobilized a "Food Army" of 45,000 men and forcibly confiscated grain from the peasants. Those who did not cooperate were deemed enemies of the people and were liable to a minimum sentence of ten years in prison. When the Bolsheviks tried to incite class war in the villages by turning the poor peasants against those who were somewhat better off, the peasants declined to cooperate. They refused to plant crops they knew would be confiscated and produced little more than enough for their own use. As supplies of food dwindled, urban areas were threatened with starvation. The Bolsheviks' policy of labor conscription further aroused discontent and opposition; under this policy, workers were liable for transfer from one locality to another, or to another trade. The scarcity of supplies and equipment coupled with the lack of incentives and food shortages in the cities prompted many workers to return to the farms. From 1917 to 1920, urban centers lost one-third of their labor force; in Petrograd and Moscow, the work force fell by as much as 50 percent. The economic goals of War Communism were to raise productivity, but in fact the opposite occurred. All sectors—both agricultural and urban—participated in the decline. By 1920, productivity had fallen to one-sixth of what it had been before 1917 and, had the trend continued, might well have ceased altogether. Trade continued only in the illegal private sector, and if the Bolsheviks had enforced the prohibitions against it, there would have been no trade at all.

At the beginning of 1918, no organized force existed that was strong enough to challenge the Bolshevik government. Ending the war with Germany removed one large source of danger, but others equally formidable soon arose. On 6 March 1918, Lenin changed the name of the party from the Russian Social Democratic Workers' party, commonly known as the Bolshevik party, to the Communist party. The change was more than symbolic. To Lenin it conveyed the obligation to return to its more militant traditions, to carry the torch of the revolution from Russia to the world.[14] On 12 March, the Communists moved their capital from Petrograd to Moscow. The latter was a safer city than exposed, revolutionary Petrograd and was much better for consolidating a regime from which most of the world, including the Western powers, withheld recognition. By this time, the Allies had withdrawn their ambassadors and were represented, if at all, by lower-level diplomatic officers, many of whom refused to take up residence in the new capital.

Allied Intervention and the Civil War. Following the signing of the Treaty of Brest-Litovsk, the Allies sent a small detachment of British marines and French and American naval units to Murmansk. In May, they extended the intervention to include Archangel. At about the same time, they landed troops at Vladivostok where the Japanese had already maintained a significant presence since December 1917. The Allies claimed that they were intervening to prevent the stores of military supplies, given to the previous government, from falling into the hands of the Germans. In fact, the Communists had already removed most of these supplies. But the Allies, encouraged by their desire to replace the Communist regime with one that would bring Russia back into the war against Germany, continued to send more troops.

A further spur to intervention was the heroic attempt of the Czech brigade to leave Russia and fight on the Western Front. The Provisional Government had formed the Czech prisoners of war into an armed legion of about 40,000 men to fight the Austrians. But when the Bolsheviks came to power, they could not wait to be rid of them and tried to arrange their evacuation to Vladivostok where they would embark on Allied ships. On 14 May 1918, at Chelyabinsk in the Urals, a trainload of these soldiers, heading east over the Trans-Siberian Railway, clashed with a group of pro-Communist volunteers. Trotsky, the people's commissar for war, ordered the Czech legion disarmed, but the task proved too great for the local Red Guards. As the legion moved eastward, one city after another, from Penza, west of the Volga, to Omsk, 1,200 miles distant, fell under their control. By July 1918, the Czechs controlled most of the Trans-Siberian Railway from the Urals to Vladivostok. Communist authority often collapsed after they appeared at the local train station.

July also marked the final break between the Socialist Revolutionaries and the Bolsheviks/Communists. The Socialist Revolutionaries had opposed the Brest-Litovsk peace and advocated a resumption of the war against Germany and had also denounced the Communist repression of the peasantry. They tried to seize power in Moscow; and when that failed, they shot the new German ambassador, Count Wilhelm von Mirbach, in the hope of provoking a German attack. All the other non-Communist parties, including the Mensheviks, Kadets, Popular Social-ists, monarchists, and independent national minority groups, were similarly dedi-cated to overthrowing the Communist regime. They established a whole series of anti-Communist administrations throughout eastern Russia. The mounting oppo-sition encouraged the Allies to send additional troops to Vladivostok to support the Czechs and the anti-Communist governments in an effort to re-create the Eastern Front as a first step toward Russian liberation.

The Allied War Council said the action was necessary "to prevent the unlim-ited military and economic domination of Russia by Germany in her own inter-ests."[15] At the same time, France and Great Britain prepared to occupy key ports on the Black Sea: the French were to control Odessa, the British to land a force at Batumi near the Turkish border. The two powers had concluded a military convention making the Ukraine a French sphere of operations and the Transcau-casus a British sphere. Both powers agreed to supply the anti-Communist armies with military aid.[16]

In September 1918, the representatives of many of the anti-Communist gov-ernments met at Ufa, in the Urals, to establish an All-Russian Provisional Gov-ernment as trustee for a future constituent assembly. But the organization had no fixed area of jurisdiction, lacked significant support from local inhabitants, and had difficulty recruiting a proper army. Internal squabbling was constant. Within two months, a rightist government, led by Admiral Aleksandr Kolchak, former com-mander of the Black Sea fleet, replaced it. Kolchak got rid of the socialists and began preparing for an attack against Moscow. The British, French, and Americans welcomed the change as their best chance to overthrow the Communists and reestablish constitutional government.

However, the end of the war in Europe prompted the Allies to reevaluate their entire policy of intervention. The soldiers, having survived the conflict, were un-derstandably hesitant about risking their lives anew. Certain leaders, like Winston Churchill and Georges Clemenceau, were eager to continue intervention to crush Bolshevism, but others, including Wilson and Lloyd George, were anxious to find a peaceful solution so they could concentrate on reconstruction at home. Besides, Allied aid to various White (anti-Communist) forces, concentrated mostly in the coastal areas, had not produced impressive results. Many local anti-Communist forces lacked proper organization, unity, and discipline. Their leaders found it hard to change their image as representatives of the old regime. In areas that fell to their control, the former landlords were often allowed to take back their old estates. Moreover, the White forces often imposed a terror as savage as that of the Communists. Each White "government" had its own version of the Cheka that indiscriminately slaughtered all those suspected of opposition, including prisoners of war and those who refused to join their armies. Relying on such men seemed as stupid as building houses on sand. As the costs, hazards, and doubts increased, the Communist army grew steadily stronger.

The defeat of Germany enabled the Communists to move their armies into those territories lost by the Treaty of Brest-Litovsk. From this position, they were able to strike westward toward the Baltic and southward into the Ukraine. In short order, they overran Latvia, occupying Riga, and advanced on Odessa. When the civil war began, the only effective forces upon which the Communists could rely were badly trained units of the Red Guards, plus the remnants of the decaying Imperial Army, a smattering of volunteers, and various local partisan bands. From this motley assortment, they had forged a formidable fighting force, the Red Army, whose framework Trotsky had created the previous March using professionals from the old tsarist army. He supervised their performance with political commissars attached to each company-sized unit, who acted as spies, propagandists, and military strategists; for insurance, he held the families of the officers and soldiers hostage. He encouraged success in battle with such directives as "if any unit retreats voluntarily, first the commissar shall be shot, then the commander." All men between eighteen and forty years of age were liable for conscription. The army grew steadily and, by December 1918, numbered 800,000 men. Two years later, it reached nearly 3 million. Still, many men either failed to report for service or later deserted, and the combat-ready troops in the regular army were only a fraction of its total numbers. Much of the significant fighting was therefore done by partisan units.

Throughout 1919 and 1920, the Communists fought at least four main enemy armies. But initially their main attack was directed against the White armies in the East. In June 1919, they took Ufa and pushed across the Urals toward Chelyabinsk. In November, they decisively defeated Kolchak and drove him from his capital at Omsk. In January 1920, the retreating Czechs handed Kolchak over to the Communist Political Center at Irkutsk where he was shot. The Communists had similar success in southern Russia where they blunted a White offensive in the Ukraine, driving the army, led by General Anton Denikin, out of Kiev, and, by December 1919, back into the Crimea.

Meanwhile, the Allies had abandoned Archangel on 30 September 1919 and evacuated Murmansk on 12 October. The anti-Communist puppet government, kept alive by the presence of Allied soldiers, quickly collapsed, and the territories almost immediately fell to the Red Army. In April 1920, a new front was opened when the Poles invaded the Ukraine in an effort to restore their former eighteenth-century frontiers. Within two weeks, they had captured Kiev. A vigorous Communist counterattack checked their advance and, by August, had pushed them all the way back to the outskirts of Warsaw. The Russo-Polish war allowed the White forces in the south, reorganized under a new commander, Baron Piotr Wrangel, to advance again into the Ukraine. By this time, the Poles had recovered from their earlier setback and were forcing the Red Army into White Russia. But in October the Soviets signed an armistice with the Poles, freeing the Communist forces for a successful counterattack against Wrangel.

With the collapse of the White Army's southern front, the British and French prepared to close up shop altogether. The British left first, followed by the French whose last act was the evacuation of Wrangel's disheveled army to Constantinople. Only Japanese troops remained in the area around Vladivostok. These foreigners remained on Russian soil until 25 October 1922, but they hardly constituted a threat to the Communist regime.

All in all, the foreign intervention had been a confused policy of cross-purposes. It was ill-conceived from the start and failed to receive public support. The kind of aid that would have made success possible was not forthcoming, nor, considering the political realities of the times, would it have been. Furthermore, a country torn by the fanaticism of revolution hardly offered a propitious opportunity for political success. Unless an intervening country was willing to match the determination of its adversaries, its efforts were doomed from the start. The Communists were fighting for their very existence—a fact that they used to their advantage in further consolidating their hold over the country. The Communist state emerged from the civil war more unified than before the war began, but with a ruined economy, a death toll in the millions, and a leadership that virulently hated the West.

The Era of the New Economic Policy

A Ban on Factions. The Communists had triumphed over a numerically stronger foe, but their victory did not come about by accident. They owed their success to their determination and the superior leadership of men like Lenin and Trotsky. They had made the most of their interior lines of communication and had proved to be the better propagandists, convincing the Russian people that they were the true defenders of social progress and national independence and further justifying their establishment of a command society. However, contrary to the belief that the use of terror was a political necessity, the Red atrocities often horrified people and made victory more difficult. It was the same with the Whites who had the further handicap of lack of organization and unity. Their lingering attachment to tsarism and reliance on the help of foreigners hopelessly compromised their cause.

Russia had been at war almost continually since August 1914. War Communism, instituted shortly after the November coup, had failed; it had contributed to the near-defeat of the Communists and had hardly brought about the new society it intended. The Bolsheviks claimed it had been forced on them by circumstances beyond their control.[17] In fact, the policy had been inaugurated in spite of the civil war not because of it. The country was now territorially smaller. It had lost its border provinces of Finland, Latvia, Lithuania, Estonia, Poland, Bessarabia, and parts of Georgia. The world revolution, which many Communists had believed inevitable, had failed to materialize. The regime was alone, isolated from the rest of Europe, which it continued to view with intense distrust and hatred. The feeling was mutual.

The Communists had nationalized industry and trade, but the Supreme Council of National Economy was incapable of effective management. Only the illegal continuation of private enterprise kept the system from total paralysis. The forced requisition of grain and the compulsory labor service had ruined incentive and resulted in a dramatic decline in the production of goods and services. The regime's inability to satisfy its citizens' minimum needs contributed to the growth of a black market and encouraged stealing, looting, and the concealment and reduction of output. Between 1920 and 1922, an estimated 9 million people died, either directly from starvation or from malnutrition and disease in the worst famine in Russia's history. Distress was particularly acute in the drought-ridden Ukraine where twenty-one of fifty provinces experienced peasant revolts. Conditions were equally bad in the cities. The barter system that had been established between town and country broke down, and workers increasingly went without necessities. The Communists made sure that those who did not work got little food. A workcard, showing that a certain assigned amount of work had been finished, entitled the bearer to a given quantity of bread. Nonworkers received a token daily ration of only one-sixteenth of a pound.

Strikes and demonstrations became more frequent and turned increasingly anti-Communist. Although many party leaders were convinced that the answer to the prevailing confusion and anarchy lay in greater centralization and stricter control, Lenin had to acknowledge that the policy of War Communism, as an attempt to transform the old economic system into a socialist economy, was a failure. The most serious example of anti-Communist discontent was the mutiny of the sailors at Kronstadt in March 1921. The sailors demanded civil liberties for all workers and peasants, free trade unions and political parties, and elections to a new Soviet by secret ballot. They accused the Communists of creating for the workers "an ever present fear of being dragged into the torture chambers of the Cheka, which exceed by many times in its horrors the gendarmerie administration of the Tzarist regime."[18] Trotsky mercilessly crushed the rebellion with loyal troops. But the shock effect of the uprising was sufficient to confirm the necessity for a new policy.

The Tenth Party Congress, which opened on 8 March 1921, while the Kronstadt revolt was still going on, strengthened party unity, confirming the doctrine of rigorous centralism. For those Communists who believed in interparty democracy, the battle had already been lost. Just as the government had become a facade for party rule, the party itself was becoming window dressing for rule by Lenin. Lenin wanted the party to speak as one voice. Two years before, he had created two smaller groups within the party Central Committee: the five-man Politburo and the Organization Bureau. This measure consolidated his control and ensured that all local Communist parties throughout the nation would be controlled by, and not deviate from, the policy set in Moscow. The creation of the inner circle was the first step toward the cult of leadership.[19] The Tenth Party Congress continued the process. Henceforth any opposition, no matter how loyal or well-intentioned, was automatically regarded as counterrevolutionary. The Central Committee assumed greater power to enforce discipline "including all measures of party punishment up to expulsion," a resolution intended to impose stringent uniformity on the structure of party organizations. It therefore reinforced the basis of the totalitarian system that had been a major objective of the policy of War Communism.

At this point, the Communists began to attack their former allies. Lenin had no desire to come to terms with any other socialists, even those among the Mensheviks and Social Revolutionaries who had supported him during the civil war. In 1922, many of their leaders were put on trial; some escaped with their lives only through the intervention of European socialist parties. Unquestionably, the principal driving force behind the extinction of these revolutionaries was Lenin himself. Where he could have chosen reconciliation and cooperation, he once again preferred blood. Lenin dismissed those who advocated moderation as "lunatics." He believed the crackdown was a necessary adjunct to the creation of a rigidly centralized party, but the purge was also a foretaste of what the following decade would offer, when the purge would affect all levels of Soviet society. The ban on factions was also immensely important for the future of the Communist party itself, giving the leadership carte blanche to attack any part of the membership as they saw fit.

A Calculated Reintroduction of Free Trade. While the Tenth Party Congress was remarkable for its affirmation of political orthodoxy, it was more liberal in economics. Lenin stressed the necessity of making economic concessions to save political power: "we must say plainly that the peasantry is not content with the form of relationship we have established with it, that it does not want this form of relationship, and that it will not go on living this way."

Lenin proposed a New Economic Policy (NEP)—a reintroduction of capitalism into the economy and a relaxation of economic controls to safeguard internal political stability. A tax in kind would replace the forceful requisitioning of grain, and the peasants would be allowed to dispose of their surpluses on the open market. The peasants would also be permitted to lease land and hire labor. Private trade would be legalized, and small industry—sectors utilizing no more than 15 percent of the total labor force—would be denationalized and returned to the private sector. The larger enterprises would remain under direct state control, but would be encouraged to adopt more businesslike practices and reduce bureaucratic inefficiency; they would operate within a general market economy, a system not unlike monopoly capitalism, but with the state deciding where the profits should be spent.

To appease the workers, a new labor code established the eight-hour day, prohibited child labor, and guaranteed an annual two-week holiday with pay. Trade unions, though, were still considered agents of the state with the responsibility of regulating the labor force, recruiting personnel for industry, engaging in factory inspections, and helping set production norms. Although they might defend the workers against bureaucratic abuse, the unions had no rights of collective bargaining. Wage scales were based on ability, not need. This economic liberalization, with some sops thrown to the workers to win their cooperation, proved transitional and was only a prelude to the tight central control that would be imposed under new, even more authoritarian leaders.

A Struggle for Succession

The Death of Lenin. In May 1922, Lenin suffered a stroke, which limited his political activity; a second attack followed ten months later, removing him from practical leadership altogether. Paralyzed, without the ability to write or speak, he was unable to prevent a power struggle within the party.

The most famous man in the party next to Lenin was Leon Trotsky, who had served as chairman of the Petrograd Soviet, as leader of the Military Revolutionary Committee, and as chief of the Red Army. He was also a powerful demagogue and a brilliant writer. Lenin considered him to be "the most able man on the present Central Committee," but also one who was "prone to excessive self-confidence and to excessive involvement with the purely administrative aspect of affairs."[20] Trotsky's obvious rival, Joseph Stalin, was almost unknown outside the party, and compared to other leaders, his role in the November Revolution had been negligible. Stalin, though, was a skillful empire builder and had transformed his post of Secretary-General of the Party Central Committee, to which he was named in April 1922, from a position of administrative coordination into a platform for personal power. Being a member of the Party Organization Bureau (Orgburo) allowed him to control party appointments at the lower and intermediate echelons and gave him the opportunity to insinuate his own men into positions of responsibility.

Lenin doubted whether Stalin would be able to use the power he had acquired "with sufficient caution"; he felt him to be "too rude" and recommended that he be replaced as Secretary-General by someone who was "more tolerant, more loyal, more polite, and more attentive to the comrades, with less capriciousness, etc."[21] Lenin's assessments of his two colleagues, which were written after his first stroke, had no effect on subsequent events, although they were generally known among the party's elite.

A Change of Direction. Stalin gradually isolated Trotsky within the party and formed alliances with Trotsky's enemies to have him condemned for factionalism and "petty-bourgeois deviation." When Lenin died on 21 January 1924, Stalin's campaign to assume leadership of the party was already well advanced. He stepped up his attack against Trotsky, removing the latter's supporters from positions of authority. Stalin and Trotsky stood on opposite sides of the ideological fence when it came to the issue of world revolution. Trotsky was a strong internationalist who believed that socialism at home was impossible without the triumph of the class struggle in other countries; Stalin favored concentrating on strengthening socialism in Russia before promoting socialist revolutions abroad. On this issue, Stalin had the support of many fellow Communists, a factor that facilitated his campaign to isolate his rival. In January 1925, Trotsky lost his position as commissar of war; in October 1926, he lost his seat on the Politburo; one year later, he was expelled from the Central Committee. In November 1927, he was thrown out of the party; and in 1929, he left the country altogether.[22] With Trotsky out of the way, Stalin concentrated on ridding the party entirely of its old guard. In doing so, he appealed to a general desire of party members to concentrate on building Communism at home rather than continuing to dream of world revolution.

The constitution of 1924 reaffirmed the formation of the Union of Soviet Socialist Republics, composed of four member units—the Russian, Ukrainian, Belorussian, and Transcaucasian republics.[23] The central government exercised exclusive jurisdiction over foreign affairs, the military, foreign trade, and communications. Reserve powers—all powers not delegated to the federal republic—were left to the four union republics. However, since the highly centralized Communist party dominated all government agencies and espoused a single policy, the system was only federal and independent in theory. The members of the Politburo of the Communist party controlled both the government's executive Council of People's Commissars and the legislative Presidium. The constitution made the secret police a principal agency of the government. Theoretically, the legislature, the All-Union Congress of Soviets, elected by all "productive" workers over the age of eighteen, was the most important governing body, but power did not flow from bottom to top. In actuality, the situation was quite the reverse. The leaders of the Communist party determined the members, the agenda, and the leaders of all so-called elected assemblies. The All-Union Congress of Soviets met only to hear reports and ratify the party's decisions.[24]

THE UNION OF SOVIET SOCIALIST
REPUBLICS
1922–1936

0   200   400 Miles

0   500 Kilometers

CENTRAL
ASIAN
REPUBLICS

ARCTIC
OCEAN

Petsamo

Murmansk

CASPIAN SEA

ARAL
SEA

Tselinograd

Omsk

Karaganda

Lake Balkhash

TURKMEN
SSR

UZBEK
SSR

Tashkent

Frunze

Alma Ata

Ashkhabad

IRAN

Bukhara

KIRGIZ
SSR

CHINA

Dusanbe

TADZHIK
SSR

0   600 miles

AFGHANISTAN

0   600 km

Arkhangel'sk

Northern Dvina River

FINLAND
Independent 1918

Petrozavodsk

LAKE
ONEGA

Sukhana River

RUSSIAN

Turku

Helsinki

Viipuri

LAKE
LADOGA

Leningrad

Novgorod

Vologda

Vyatka

Perm

URAL MTS.

Sverdlovsk

BALTIC SEA

Talinn

ESTONIA

Tartu

Riga

Pskov

Tver

Yaroslavl

Kostroma

Volga River

S.F.S.

Kazan

Ufa

Memel

LATVIA

Dvinsk

LITHUANIA

Kovno

Gdansk

EAST
PRUSSIA

Vilna

Minsk

Smolensk

Moscow

Ulyanovsk

Belostok

Warsaw

Brest

BELORUSSIA
S.S. REPUBLIC

REPUBLIC

Kubyshev

Orenburg

POLAND

Chernigov

Lvov

CZECHOSLOVAKIA

Kiev

Poltava

Kharkov

Don River

Stalingrad

KAZAKH
REPUBLIC

UKRAINIAN
REPUBLIC

Ekaterinoslav

BESSARABIA

MOLDAVIA

Dnieper River

Rostov

Volga River

Astrakhan

Kishinev

Odessa

ROMANIA

CRIMEA

SEA OF
AZOV

Krasnodar

TRANSCAUCASIAN S.F.S.R.

BLACK SEA

Simferopol

CAUCASUS MTS.

CASPIAN
SEA

GEORGIA

Batum

Tiflis

TURKMEN
REPUBLIC

Latvia, Lithuania and Estonia, Independent 1918

Poland, Independent 1918

Vilna Region, ceded to Lithuania by Russia
and seized by Poland, 1920

Bessarabia, seized by Romania, 1918

Russian Boundary, 1921–1938

Russian borders in Poland, Lithuania, and S.W. Russia
(N.E. Galician frontier), 1914

Curzon Line

Other international boundaries after the
Versailles Settlements

Boundaries of Republics comprising the U.S.S.R.

Boundaries of Autonomous Republics and Provinces

Ardahan

ARMENIA

Baku

Kars

Yerevan

Area ceded to Turkey, 1921

AZERBAIJAN

Map 5

GERMANY AND THE FOUNDATION OF THE WEIMAR REPUBLIC

Establishing a New Legitimacy

Red Week in Berlin. The political revolution that followed Germany's defeat was not accompanied by any great intellectual movement and, except for the end of the monarchy, led to no significant social change. The imperial bureaucracy remained virtually intact. The army, though reduced, guarded its old prerogatives. The political parties continued with the same leaders and the same philosophies. The dictated peace of Versailles made it easy for them to romanticize the old regime and more difficult to accept the new. Philosopher Oswald Spengler called the revolution of 1918 the most stupid and cowardly revolution in world history. But Spengler's view was not universal. Despite their lack of experience in modern representative government and their attachment to the old monarchy, most Germans wanted to reform their governmental institutions, and, considering the great numbers who voted for the Social Democratic party before the war, they also wanted significant social changes. The elections of 1919 and the beliefs of Chancellor Friedrich Ebert, a Social Democrat, confirmed this desire.

Ebert was more interested in restoring peace and stability than he was in carrying out a political vendetta. He wanted to create a national constituent assembly at the earliest opportunity to decide the future form of government. He had a great faith in the good sense of the German people to develop a regime of social justice and democracy. In the meantime, he worked hard to maintain order. But it was obvious that many groups from the extreme right and left would not accept a democratic government in any form. Even before a new constitution could be produced, an attempt was made to take over the state.

Moderate socialists controlled Ebert's provisional executive, the Council of People's Representatives, but this government also received support from other groups that favored parliamentary democracy and relied on the strength of the organized labor movement. The army leaders had reservations, but appeared willing to accept any government, short of a Communist regime, that would maintain the integrity of the professional officer corps and restore stability and unity. Most workers wanted to change society, but not destroy it. They might enjoy inflammatory rhetoric, but they disliked chaos and had little stomach for a reign of terror. They therefore deplored the rise in many German cities of various soldiers' and workers' councils that the radical Marxists hoped to use as a means for overthrowing the provisional government. These Marxists, who called themselves Spartacists after the gladiator Spartacus who led a slave revolt against Rome in 73 B.C., believed history was on their side. They held that the downfall of the monarchy had begun the "Kerensky" phase of the German revolution, which would continue through various stages until it climaxed with their own inevitable success. The organization's leaders, Karl Liebknecht and Rosa Luxemburg, had reservations about taking action at this time, but they were outvoted by those hungry for immediate action. Liebknecht and Luxemburg had impeccable revolutionary credentials; their hesitation was tactical, not ideological. They wanted to wait until they had built up more mass support. Before the war they had been among the most outspoken advocates for revolutionary action in the Socialist party. They had both opposed the war, but when it came, they wanted to turn it into a class struggle.

On the morning of 6 January 1919, the Spartacists occupied important buildings in Berlin. Ebert took refuge in the chancellery and refused to go home for fear that he would be arrested. Minister of Defense Gustav Noske established temporary

Red Week in Berlin, January 1919. Berlin police, assisted by men of the Freikorps (wearing World War I headgear) mount guard behind a barricade of overturned barrels that contain drum-rolls of newspaper stock. The density of the paper was more than sufficient to stop bullets.

headquarters in a girls' boarding school in the district of Dahlem and recruited a paramilitary force of World War I army veterans to crush the uprising. Order was restored with considerable ferocity. Noske employed troops who hated the workers. By 13 January, the government was again in control of the capital, but the situation had not returned to normal. On 15 January, units of the volunteer *Freikorps* (Freecorps) pulled Liebknecht and Luxemburg out of hiding. The two were beaten senseless; Liebknecht was shot "trying to escape," and he and his companion, both still unconscious, were thrown into the Landwehr Canal. The participation of the political right in smashing the Spartacist revolt created a permanent breach between the moderate and radical sections of the German working class. The Communists ultimately would join the Right in destroying the democratic republic rather than join with the socialists in its defense. For their part, the majority Social Democrats did not appreciate the grave dangers to the republic from an alliance with monarchist soldiers and officers.

Constitution Making. The Spartacist revolt was put down in time for national elections, on 19 January 1919, to choose an assembly to draft a new constitution. No party received a majority of the 423 available seats. Ebert's Social Democrats received 165, the second-ranking Catholic Center party won 91, while the liberal German Democratic party, heir to the middle-of-the-road Progressive party, came in third with 75. These three moderate parties together enjoyed an absolute majority and, as the Weimar coalition, were to remain a force in German politics throughout most of the next decade. The rightist Nationalist and People's parties marshalled only 63 seats combined. If the elections were not a clear-cut victory for any one group, they at least showed that the Germans had no immediate desire to return to the monarchy.

On 6 February, the day the constituent assembly first convened, the Spartacists staged protest strikes in Berlin, Hamburg, Munich, and Dresden. But the legislature's deliberations were being held far away from the political turmoil of the large cities in the small Thuringian town of Weimar, famous for its literary associations with Goethe and Schiller. A defensive perimeter, manned by 7,000 soldiers, protected the town. In this atmosphere of enforced calm, the representatives produced a document that made Germany a federal republic, based upon the sovereignty of the people.

Eighteen individual states, or *Länder*, were to exercise control over education, religious affairs, the courts, and local government. The central government had authority over foreign affairs, customs, coinage, social legislation, health, and the armed forces. The legislature was divided into a Lower House, the *Reichstag*, with one deputy for every 60,000 Germans, and an Upper House, the *Reichsrat*, which represented the states. The Reichsrat could veto legislation, but the *Reichstag* could override it by a two-thirds vote. The chancellor, the head of the government, and his cabinet exercised executive power. The ministry was responsible to the legislature. But the chief of state, the Reichspräsident, also had important prerogatives. Elected for a term of seven years, he chose the chancellor, subject to the approval of the legislature. In case of deadlock, he could dissolve the Reichstag and appeal directly to the electorate. Under Article 48, he had the authority to rule by decree in times of emergency, providing his orders were countersigned by an appropriate minister.[25]

An important shortcoming of the new republic lay in its proportional representation system of voting, which, in giving the greatest possible weight to each vote, favored the growth of splinter groups at the expense of a large stable parliamentary majority. Germany was divided into thirty-five electoral districts, in which the voters cast ballots for party lists rather than individual candidates. The number of votes each list received determined the number of Reichstag seats it would be allotted. These seats would then be assigned by the party bosses. The system therefore resulted in the election of candidates more valued for their loyalty and subservience than for their originality and independence and undermined any sense of personal identification the voters might have with their own local deputies.

Moreover, the constitution antagonized the official bureaucracy, which was already heavily monarchist in sympathy, by its abolition of the old orders and dignities: chief among these was the coveted title of *Geheimrat* (state's councilor)— *Frau Geheimrat* for wives. This was an important mistake in a country that had seen a waiter's title evolve from *Kellner* to *Ober Kellner* (head waiter) to simply *Ober* and finally *Herr Ober* (mister head). The choice of colors for the state flag also provoked considerable dissatisfaction. Some had wanted to keep the black, white, and red of the Second Reich, while others insisted on the black, red, and gold of the 1848 Frankfurt Assembly. It was finally decided to adopt black, red, and gold for the state flag and black, white, and red (with a black, red, and gold insert in the upper corner) for the merchant marine, but nationalist and antirepublican groups never accepted the compromise.

The creators of the Weimar constitution assumed that Germans would ultimately become converts to democracy. But the new system was born into a cruel world. The republic was the heir to defeat, and the French policy of strict accountability made the Versailles humiliation worse. The Weimar leaders were lackluster politicians who failed miserably to dramatize the institutions they served. During this initial phase of the Weimar Republic, it had the good fortune to be directed by politicians who had the temperament and desire to try to make democracy work. But as the more conservative parties regrouped, the influence of these men began to decline.

Threats from the Right. The government's success in smashing the Spartacists was largely due to the support it received from the Freikorps, volunteer units of army veterans who had little sympathy for the democratic system they had been called upon to protect. Soldiers, given the important position that they had once occupied in German society, regarded demobilization with a special horror and sought ways to avoid its bitter consequences. Many therefore were eager to enlist in the special police forces that were being raised to keep order in the cities and along the frontiers.

The first of these units was formed in Berlin during the second week of December 1918, roughly a month before the Communist uprising, by General Ludwig von Märcker, the former commander of the 214th Infantry Division. The group, supported with funds from the Supreme Command, was composed of handpicked men from the old army who were known for their fighting ability and iron discipline. Similar units soon sprang up elsewhere. Finding volunteers was not difficult, but in the absence of centralized direction, the character of the groups varied considerably, usually according to the personality of their leaders. Märcker ran his corps with the discipline and esprit of the old imperial army, but units thrown together by more junior officers displayed a high degree of political adventurism and lack of moderation. Many future Nazi leaders, including Martin Bormann, Kurt Daluege, Hans Frank, Reinhard Heydrich, Victor Lutze, and Rudolf Hess, were Freikorps fighters. The old military establishment helped the Freikorps with money and equipment, but those trained in the imperial service were not very enthusiastic about rubbing shoulders with petty bourgeois extremists who reveled in the unpredictable and sleazy business of street fighting.

Freikorps units might contain anywhere from 200 to 1,500 men. The Third Naval Brigade, organized by Admiral Wilfried von Löwenfeld, had as many as 8,000. Recruiting posters were everywhere. Noske ran ads in the newspapers, urging individual commanders to organize their own detachments. To bring this vast number of men—estimated at 400,000—under closer supervision of the government, he created a special central *Reichsführer*. But this scheme had little practical effect. Some Freikorps units, like the Anti-Bolshevik League formed by wealthy industrialists, became independent of official subsidies by receiving money from private sources. Despite these concerns, the government did not feel that it could do without the Freikorps as long as the Spartacists remained a danger. In addition, Bavaria was on the verge of civil war.

The situation in Bavaria had been chaotic ever since the Armistice. A socialist republic, under Kurt Eisner, had replaced the Wittelsbach dynasty. Eisner called for the establishment of a "United States of Germany" with a completely socialized economic structure. But few Bavarians were interested in keeping him in office. In the elections for the Bavarian Diet in January 1919, his party received only two percent of the vote and three seats in the Landtag. On 21 February 1919, while Eisner was on his way to the parliament to offer his resignation, a counter-revolutionary student shot him dead.

The moderate socialists, led by Johannes Hoffmann, took charge. This government lasted only until 7 April, when it was ousted by a group of radicals who proclaimed the establishment of a Bavarian Republic of Soviets. The putschists' chieftain, Ernst Toller, believed that regeneration of the human soul could be found only in free art. He opened the university to everybody over eighteen years of age regardless of their qualifications, suppressed the study of history as the "enemy of civilization," and urged all citizens to educate themselves according to their own beliefs. His foreign minister, Franz Lipp, declared war on Switzerland for failing to lend Bavaria railroad engines and complained to Lenin that, when Hoffmann had fled the government, he had taken with him the keys to the foreign office toilet. This regime lasted about a week. The continuing political and economic bedlam of postwar Munich brought forth, on 13 April, a Communist dictatorship, which, encouraged by the presence of a similar regime in Hungary, represented neither the German Spartacists, nor the Russian Communists. But like its predecessors, the Munich Commune found it difficult to keep itself in power. It tried unsuccessfully to build up its own defense force with enticements of high wages and free prostitutes.

Meanwhile Johannes Hoffmann called on Gustav Noske for assistance in reestablishing the legitimate government. The defense minister responded by sending 30,000 Freikorps troops who accomplished the task with considerable brutality. The Communists were overthrown during the first twenty-four hours, but for almost a week afterwards, until 6 May, the freebooters swaggered through the streets of Munich, shooting people on any pretext. So many corpses littered the streets that the bodies presented a health hazard.

The moderate socialists again took charge on May 13. Munich was in shambles. The episode had shown the difficulty of controlling the Freikorps, which, in the six months since their birth, had undergone a significant transformation. They were no longer content to maintain order or smash "Bolsheviks," but increasingly considered their goal to be the destruction of democratic republican government. The Freikorpsmen talked freely of a coup d'état and might have succeeded had their leaders been able to establish a unified command. The longer they procrastinated, however, the less likely their success seemed.

At the beginning of 1920, the Allied Control Commission demanded that all paramilitary forces in Germany be disbanded. The Weimar government, given a good excuse to eliminate a dangerous adversary, ordered the dissolution of the Freikorps, beginning, on 10 February, with the brigade organized by Hermann Ehrhardt, a former naval Lt. Commander. But the head of the First Army District in Berlin, Senior Reichswehr Commander, General Walther von Luttwitz, refused to disband the troops and encouraged Ehrhardt to march on Berlin. At 7:00 A.M. on 12 March, the brigade marched through the Brandenburg Gate into the German capital. By noon the troops had occupied the major public buildings and were masters of the city. Dr. Wolfgang Kapp, an East Prussian bureaucrat and a founder of the ultra-nationalist Fatherland party, assumed political direction of the movement. He proclaimed himself chancellor, but had no program. He had spent too much time figuring out how to take power and not enough considering what to do if he succeeded. He ordered a few people arrested and issued several proclamations, one suspending examinations at the University of Berlin, another confiscating the supplies of matzo flour for the forthcoming Passover.

Most Berliners viewed the Kapp Putsch with contempt, and the bureaucrats refused to follow his orders. When Kapp tried to obtain money from the Reichsbank, the officials refused to honor his signature because it was not validated with the proper stamp. Meanwhile, the government had fled to Dresden. Before he left, Defense Minister Noske ordered the Reichswehr to protect the republic. Only Major-General Walther Reinhardt, the commander-in-chief, agreed. The others at supreme headquarters declared their neutrality. Chief of staff, Colonel-General Hans von Seeckt, flatly stated, "[German] soldiers do not fire on each other." Seeckt wanted to preserve the interests of the army above all else. He therefore went home, leaving the destruction of Kapp's government to others.

Almost as soon as Berlin fell to the freebooters, the Social Democratic party called a general strike. During the next four days, as long as Kapp remained in the chancellery, the city was virtually closed down. There were no public services, newspapers, garbage collections, communications, streetcars, or electricity. It was perhaps the most significant demonstration of working-class solidarity in the history of Germany. On 17 March, Kapp, unable to restore the normal functions of the city, "resigned" and fled to Sweden. Most of his lieutenants went into hiding. As the Berliners with obvious relief watched the Ehrhardt Brigade march out of the city, one of the Freikorps officers, in a parting act of savagery, had his men shoot point-blank into the crowd.

Problems of Consolidation

The Independence of the Military. The government returned badly shaken, but instead of carrying out a vigorous purge of the army and bureaucracy to get rid of the obviously disloyal, it reacted with weakness and pusillanimity. Noske resigned. The loyal General Reinhardt followed. General Seeckt, the very commander who had so categorically refused to perform his constitutional duty, took his place.

Consequently, the Reichswehr was never republicanized and continued to hold fast to its antidemocratic monarchist traditions. It continued to be led by former officers of the imperial army with the bulk of its troops recruited from the conservative peasantry. Seeckt was a monarchist, but since no party specifically made the restoration of the Hohenzollerns part of its political goals, the chances of a restoration seemed remote. He therefore was inclined to tolerate the Weimar Republic as long as it served his purpose in preserving the German Reich and the strength of the army. He would allow Reichswehr units to be used against leftist revolutionaries, like the Spartacists; and he even supported the government's policy of disbanding the Freikorps because those units were a major source of competition. But Seeckt like many Germans was violently opposed to the Versailles settlement and devoted the rest of his career to violating its military clauses.

He reconstituted the General Staff, forbidden by Article 160, as the *Truppenamt* of the Defense Ministry; and he established war academies and staff training institutes, forbidden by Articles 176 and 177, under the cover of special courses in military history and general culture in German universities. Article 160 of the treaty limited the number of officers to 4,000, but did not restrict the ranks of noncommissioned officers. Sergeants therefore became junior officers and consistently made up about half of the enlisted ranks the Versailles treaty allowed. Only those with the rank of private and corporal were really sergeants. The Reichswehr also had it own reserve army, the so-called Black Reichswehr, which matched the regular formations of the army unit for unit. There were also crypto-military groups attached to the Ministry of Interior, like the *Sicherheitspolizei* (security police) detachments, which were recruited from imperial army officers and noncommissioned officers with known monarchist sympathies, and the *Einwohnerwehr*, a sort of home guard that received periodic military training. Both organizations were provided with guns and ammunition that were kept in storage in secret depots.

Seeckt also circumvented the Versailles treaty's restrictions on the size and production of armaments by organizing a special secret weaponry and mobilization division, which gathered supplies sufficient to support a German army ten times larger than the current one. This work was camouflaged through the production of nonmilitary articles that could rapidly be converted into instruments of war: heavy agricultural tractors could serve as the basis for future tanks; civilian cargo planes could be transformed into tomorrow's bombers; and research into industrial chemicals could be reoriented toward weaponry. The development of rockets, unmentioned in the Treaty of Versailles, became top priority. In addition, the

German army established a series of holding companies in foreign countries for the production of ships, guns, submarines, and airplanes.

No sooner had the Treaty of Versailles been signed than contacts with Communist Russia were established to begin trade relations. Seeckt established a special secret unit within the Reichswehr to handle cooperation with the Soviet General Staff and was already prepared for action when Lenin turned to the Germans for assistance in reorganizing the Red Army in 1921. In exchange, the Germans received training and industrial facilities. The Germans furthered their aircraft technology in Russian factories, helping to build prototypes that benefited the development of fighter aircraft in both countries.

A Worthless Currency. While the French blamed all their economic troubles on the unwillingness of the Germans to pay reparations, the Germans blamed their problems on the French for making them pay too much. The situation was certainly complicated by reparations. Purchasing hard currency to make payments weakened the German mark and stimulated a rise in domestic prices, thereby raising the costs of reconstruction. However, the amount Germany paid the Allies in reparations was totally offset by foreign investment in the German economy.[26] The Germans could only blame themselves for their financial mess. The country had financed the war on credit. Until 1916, the state relied mainly on the sale of war bonds to raise additional revenue, but when this device proved insufficient, the treasury simply began to print more money. Patriotism and war socialism were able to maintain stability only until the end of the war. Germany had experienced little direct war damage, but certain industries, like textiles, potash, and iron and steel (those connected with Alsace-Lorraine), had been greatly disrupted. The country's overseas investments were gone, and its gold reserves were completely exhausted.

The Reichsbank simply continued the mad practice of printing more bank notes to meet its obligations. It kept over 2,000 printing presses and 300 paper mills working overtime to meet its demands. Direct taxes remained low (about 25 percent of expenditures), while credit was expanded, largely in the form of low interest loans to businesses and large indemnities paid to the owners of factories in the lost territories. German business leaders and industrialists loved this policy of cheap money. For them, it was a wonderful means of liquidating old debts and expanding their empires. They borrowed huge sums of money and used it to buy companies that were less creditworthy. They accumulated generous reserves of hard currency by refusing to repatriate money earned from exports, but paid their domestic obligations—mortgages, taxes, and wages—in inflated paper currency. The value of the mark declined rapidly. It had been about 4 to the dollar in 1914 and 8.9 at the end of the war; but by 1921, it had climbed to 200, and in October 1922, it stood at 4,500 to the dollar. The resultant inflation was a social disaster; it ruined white-collar workers, small business owners, bureaucrats, and everyone living on fixed incomes. It proletarianized and degraded the middle class. Prices rose faster than wages, and Germans consumed less food: 25 percent fewer potatoes than before the war, 33 percent less meat, and only 50 percent as much beer. It took an average worker two days to earn enough to buy a pound of butter, one day to purchase the same amount of margarine, and four and a half months for a suit of clothes.

The crisis also created a new class of speculators and profiteers. For example, Hugo Stinnes, who came from a prosperous family of Rhineland industrialists and merchants, used the inflation to build one of the largest European conglomerates.

At its height, it included iron and steel manufacturing, coal mining, shipping, insurance, banking, railroads, film making, hotels, paper mills, newspapers, oil wells, and refineries. Stinnes also had political ambitions: he was a Reichstag delegate from the Volkspartei and participated in the 1920 Spa Conference, where he was best remembered for the remark, "I rise in order to be able to look the enemy delegates in the eyes." He detested the Weimar Republic, which he blamed for the very inflation for which he was partly responsible.

In January 1923, the French occupied the Ruhr on the pretext that the Weimar Republic had defaulted in its payments of lumber and telegraph poles.[27] "We are going to look for coal, that's all," Premier Raymond Poincaré promised the Chamber of Deputies. The action almost tore Germany apart. Berlin proclaimed a policy of passive resistance and endeavored to support the unemployed with new issues of paper money. German production of steel and pig iron immediately declined by 80 percent. The mark, already almost worthless, lost more of its value.

When the invasion began, the mark stood at 7,000 to the dollar; six months later, it had fallen to 1 million, and the worst was still to come. The rate changed so rapidly that workers were paid every day around noon so they could rush out in a mad frenzy during their lunch period to spend their wages before the mark declined further. A loaf of bread in Berlin that cost 3,465 marks in July cost 201 billion marks in November. Painters Karl Schwitters and Laszlo Moholy-Nagy, without money to buy paint and canvas, began to construct collages out of Reichsbank notes. There were scattered uprisings and disturbances throughout the country, accompanied by pressure from separatist movements in Bavaria, Thuringia, Saxony, and the Rhineland.

The Beer Hall Putsch. The push for separatism in Bavaria came from the rightist administration of Commissioner Gustav von Kahr. In Saxony and Thuringia, it was associated with leftist "popular front" governments, while in the Rhineland the French sponsored the separatist movement. On 26 September, the new government of Gustav Stresemann had President Ebert declare a state of emergency, giving the army broad powers to restore order. The Reichswehr chieftain Seeckt had no difficulty responding to Stresemann's orders to turn the leftists out of the Saxon and Thuringian governments, but he hesitated to act against the Bavarian right.

In Munich, on the evening of 8 November, Commissioner Kahr presided over a gathering of separatists and monarchists in the Burgerbraukeller on the Rosenheimerstrasse. The meeting was presumably called to announce the secession of Bavaria from the federal union. At any rate, this was what Adolf Hitler, the leader of a small extreme right-wing group, the National Socialist German Workers party, believed. But Hitler had greater ambitions than furthering Bavarian separatism: he wanted to overthrow the Weimar Republic.

Kahr was no more than twenty minutes into his speech on the moral justification of dictatorship, when suddenly Hitler jumped on a chair and shot a revolver at the ceiling. Nazis appeared everywhere, armed with pistols and hand grenades. Hitler took charge and offered to include Kahr and his associates in the national government he was forming with General Erich Ludendorff as commander of the new National Army.

The next day, the Nazis attempted to rally the people of Munich with a march on the Bavarian War Ministry. But a police cordon at the Feldherrnhalle opened fire, killing fourteen of the demonstrators. Four policemen also died, and many on both sides were wounded. Hitler escaped by ducking down a side street. But General Ludendorff continued to walk through the police lines, and nobody made any attempt to stop him. He was arrested later, but acquitted after a brief trial. Hitler was not so fortunate. He was also apprehended, but not being as illustrious as Ludendorff, he along with three of his associates was convicted and sentenced to five years in prison with the possibility of parole after six months.

Considering the seriousness of his offense, Hitler was treated with leniency. The incident gave him a national reputation, but at the time it hardly seemed to be a triumph. The authority of the central government rose, while the Nazi party was in disarray. The Bavarian separatists would never again constitute a serious threat. The personal authority of Seeckt also declined. As the political crisis passed, Berlin returned its attention to the monetary crisis.

The Return of Stability. On 15 November 1923, the government issued a new currency, the Rentenmark, backed by a national "mortgage" on agricultural land and industrial property. In fact, this was largely a ploy to return confidence to the currency. A new exchange rate was established: 4.2 trillion of the old marks for one of the new. Wiping out a dozen zeros returned the currency to its prewar exchange rate. The illusion of stability was further fostered by issuing the bills on good-quality rag paper that, unlike the flimsy inflation currency, had printing on both sides and was watermarked.

The government made every effort to make its new financial scheme viable. Hjalmar Schacht became special commissioner for national currency to control the printing of bank notes and to suppress all the unofficial currencies that various local governments and corporations had issued during the crisis. When this was done, Schacht felt it was essential to back the currency with something more substantial than mortgages. In October 1924, with the ballast of a $200 million loan from abroad, Schacht was able to issue the Reichsmark, which was pegged to gold. The new currency became completely convertible and laid the groundwork for a sound financial system that formed the basis for a new period of growth and prosperity. Unfortunately, political stability proved to be another matter.

In the elections of 1920, the Social Democrats lost their majority in the Reichstag and never regained it. For most of the decade, Germany was ruled by middle-class parties, many of whose members were hardly friends of democracy. The Catholic Center party, which garnered more cabinet posts than any other party, was a disparate blend of left-wing democrats and rock-hard conservatives. The left wing could cooperate comfortably with the Social Democrats, while the other preferred to associate with antirepublican monarchists, such as the German People's party, one of whose great leaders, Gustav Stresemann, grew to accept the republic as the best possible solution under the circumstances. Other members of the party never trusted him, however. Even more implacably antirepublican was the Nationalist party. This group had strong associations with powerful industrialists and former leaders of the imperial regime, all of whom hated democracy. The Nationalists often had ties with the outwardly revolutionary National Socialists, who played the democratic game to gain power to establish a one-party state. On the other side of the barricades, but blood brothers of a sort, were the Communists. The *Komministische Partei Deutschlands* affiliated with Lenin's Third International and remained a willing tool of the Soviet Union. The Communists consistently pursued a course calculated to cause the downfall of the Weimar Republic even if that meant voting with the rightists and militarists who desired the same thing.[28]

Between 1920 and 1933, the Weimar Republic experienced eight general elections and twenty-one changes of government. But so enormous were its political problems and so intense were the personal and ideological rivalries of its politicians that finding solutions to its economic and social problems was often shoved onto the back burner. Frequently, however, the crises became so acute they could not be ignored. During this period, Germany went through two major depressions. The second proved fatal. Many saw this as entirely proper since they believed the Germans had never really been fit to govern themselves.

THE BREAKUP OF THE AUSTRO-HUNGARIAN EMPIRE

The Austrian Republic

A Weak Self-Image. The Austrian constitution, promulgated in 1920, was a compromise between a unitary system of government, with a strong national assembly, and a Swiss-type federalism, with an upper house—the Federal Council—elected by the provinces. The leftist Social Democrats favored the former system, while the conservative Christian Socialists advocated the latter. The result was a bicameral legislature with the government ministry primarily responsible to the lower house, or National Council, which had almost complete control over legislation. The upper house could only delay the implementation of law with a suspensive veto. The chancellor exercised executive power through the Council of Ministers; the office of president was almost entirely ceremonial.

A sharp rise in unemployment and increasing economic instability marked the early years of the republic. The new state's poor trade relations with the other states of Eastern Europe deprived it of timber, coal, oil, agricultural products, and mineral supplies, which it had formerly obtained from Bohemia, Transylvania, Poland, and Hungary. The new Austria had 30 percent of the Habsburg Empire's industrial plant, but only 1 percent of its coal reserves. The result was a drastic decline in the production of iron and steel and electrical energy, which had to be rationed. Railroads had only enough power to carry essential goods. On certain days there was no current at all.

Government expenses skyrocketed, driven up by unemployment payments and the general costs of recovery. The currency—the crown *(krone)*—which had lost 80 percent of its value during the war, declined even further. The state met expenses by watering its money, causing inflation. The monthly food bill for an average family rose from 2,500 crowns in 1919 to twice that amount the following year and to 300,000 crowns by 1922. Speculation and food hoarding were rampant. Trade unions demanded constant salary adjustments to keep wages in step with prices. The rapid depreciation of the currency made it difficult for Austria to secure the foreign exchange it needed to buy essential raw materials.

A Loss of Sovereignty. In August 1922, with the crown worth less than two percent of its prewar value in gold, Austria appealed to the Allied powers for a loan of $70 million. The Allies referred the matter to the League of Nations. Lloyd George explained that the taxpayers of the Allied countries were already bearing a heavy financial burden and could not subsidize Austria unless the League could formulate a program that would guarantee "substantial improvement" in Austrian finances and would help attract money from private sources.

The rightist Christian Socialist government of Monsignor Ignaz Seipel said it would place Austria under Italian protection in exchange for financial assistance. The threat worked. France, in particular, did not want to see an increase of Italian influence in Eastern Europe. Consequently, on 4 October, a series of protocols was signed between Austria and Britain, Italy, France, and Czechoslovakia—the countries the League Council appointed to deal with the Austrian problem—conferring on Austria a loan of 50 million crowns.

Henceforth a special League high commissioner was to direct Austrian finances. The commissioner was to supervise all important transactions, including the raising and deposition of loans and the issuance of paper money. He would also manage the security account—collected from customs and tobacco monopoly receipts—for repaying the loan. The Austrian government was also obliged to carry out a program of economic reform, ensuring the profitability of the state commercial enterprises. This involved increasing fares on the railroads and drastically reducing the number of employees on the state payroll.[29]

Foreign stewardship reduced Austria's inflation and stabilized the national currency in a new monetary unit, the schilling. By June 1926, with recovery assured, Austria again took charge of its own economic affairs. However, this temporary loss of sovereignty had compounded the prevailing political confusion and division.

The Politics of Irreconcilability. The Social Democrats were Marxist and their goals were revolutionary, but they devoted their energy to the establishment of democratic constitutional government rather than to the nationalization of the means of production. The party chief, Karl Renner, was a moderate and a pragmatist who avoided enacting radical programs because he feared they might contribute to the distress of the proletariat. Even Otto Bauer, the chief of the party's revolutionary left wing, favored gradualism. Socialist strength was almost exclusively concentrated in the industrial centers, especially Vienna—"Red Vienna"— where the party controlled two-thirds of the seats in the City Council. In parliament it had about 50 percent of the delegates. Its organizational strength was rooted in the free, noncompany, trade unions. Its philosophy was as universalistic as that of the medieval church, and it provided its constituents with a broad list of appropriate services.

The party ran the *Kinderfreunde* (children's friends), which were elementary schools with libraries and special day care and instructional centers. Here the sons and daughters of the workers were instructed in the basic tenets of socialism; the curriculum was anticlerical and anticapitalist to be sure, but was also heavy on social obligations and cooperation. The Kinderfreunde also sponsored the Red Falcon youth movement for girls and boys between the ages of ten and fourteen. The Falcons took an oath pledging loyalty and fraternity to the working class and participated in a wide range of party-sponsored activities, such as helping at workers' festivals, distributing party circulars, assisting party charities, and helping the poor. But they also had a full range of less didactic, more strictly youth-centered activities ranging from athletics to culture and crafts—the full complement that would be found in any decent scouting movement.

For the adults, the activities included a people's theater, choral clubs, a stamp collectors' guild, an Esperanto league, a mushroom growers' interest group, an anti-Catholic Federation of Freethinkers, the Association for Biblical Socialism, the Union of Religious Socialists, and the Flame Crematory Society. In 1923, the Social Democrats founded the *Republikanischer Schutzbund* (Republican Defense Alliance), a party army committed to protecting the republic against its class enemies.

The Catholic conservatives drew their support mostly from the peasantry, the lower middle classes, owners of small businesses, and white-collar workers. The party's leaders came from the older ruling elites: former army officers, industrialists, financiers, landowners, aristocrats, and the hierarchy of the Roman Catholic church. The Christian Social party professed a belief in democracy but had no tolerance for any but its own increasingly theological point of view. The Roman Catholic bishops, in their pastoral letter of December 1925, threatened the Social Democrats with a quotation from Matthew 18:6: "Whoever destroys the faith of one of the little ones and blights his eternal salvation deserves that a millstone be hanged about his neck and that he be drowned in the depth of the sea."

The industrialists, fearing the strength of the working class, threw their weight behind a vigorous policy of repression. Antidemocratic organizations, like the *Alpine Montan Gesellschaft* (Alps Mountain Group), subsidized and encouraged extreme right-wing paramilitary organizations. The most important of these was the *Heimwehr* (Home Guard), which was originally formed to maintain the security of the border areas, for example, protecting Styria and Carinthia against incursions from Yugoslavia. But the Heimwehr, like the German paramilitary forces, began to intervene in domestic affairs.

Heimwehr units, often acting with official sanction, smashed workers' demonstrations and broke up strikes. Some of its leaders were even involved in a scheme to create a separate Roman Catholic state under the Wittelsbach dynasty that would include southern Germany and western Austria. Even with the general recovery, the Heimwehr still continued to exert a powerful influence on the course of Austrian politics.

The Hungarian Republic

A Kingdom without a King. Miklós Horthy favored the eventual restoration of the Hungarian monarchy, although he considered it impractical at the present time and had himself proclaimed regent. Thus he enjoyed most of the powers of a crowned sovereign except the right to create noble titles and appoint church officials. He was also supreme war lord of the armed forces. He could not be deposed without his own consent and could convoke, adjourn, and dissolve the parliament at his pleasure.

Although required to rule "in agreement" with the legislature—he supposedly had only a suspensive veto over legislation—the regent chose the minister-president without any thought to whether the parliament agreed with his appointment. Horthy regarded his power as a sacred trust, but just how loyal he was to the House of Habsburg became clear when Karl tried to regain his throne. The deposed monarch made two attempts to return to Hungary and have himself proclaimed sovereign. He assumed that his mere presence on Hungarian soil would be sufficient to ensure his success. The first attempt came in March 1921, the second the following October. Both times he had the tacit support of the French government, both times he made it to Budapest, and both times he failed to rally the support of the people. And both times Horthy refused to step aside and let Karl take his place. The second time Karl tried to win him over by creating Horthy a duke. After the last bid, the pretender was handed over to the British who exiled him to the Madeira Islands. He never returned.[30]

The Political Machine. During his first decade as regent, Horthy exercised his power judiciously. He did not interfere with the day-to-day business of government and never used his suspensive veto over legislation. During that time, the normal business of government was in the hands of a minister-president, Count István

Bethlen, who organized his cabinet in the interests of the propertied conservative classes. Bethlen's system was undemocratic and authoritarian, but not totalitarian. Opposition parties were tolerated, although the official Party of Unity was the only political organization through which one could hope to exercise power and influence. Elections served as a tool through which the ruling party could purge its disloyal and insubordinate members.

Still a certain amount of free choice was tolerated. The party had no official position on free trade or protectionism, it expressed no preference for agricultural interests as opposed to urban interests, and it did not take a firm stand on the question of free enterprise versus public corporatism. As minister-president and party leader, Bethlen promoted harmony between the legislature, the bureaucracy, and the politicians. The foreign and domestic policy of the Bethlen government was built on a profound contradiction, however. The supreme goal of all Hungarians was to recover the lands the Treaty of the Trianon had taken from them. But revisionism could only be achieved if Hungary were to become economically strong. To become economically strong, Hungary needed help from abroad, especially from the Allies. But the Allies would not tolerate changing the peace treaties. There was a further contradiction insofar as no government could continue in office without the support of the traditional ruling and conservative classes— the landlords, professional classes, businessmen, industrialists, bankers, and the upper echelons of the bureaucracy. Revisionism was not in their best economic interests.

By playing the part of a moderate, Bethlen succeeded in negotiating an international loan in March 1924. The arrangement—signed with Britain, France, Italy, and the nations of the Little Entente—was formulated, as in the case of Austria, under the auspices of the League of Nations and also involved League control of the national budget. Hungary, in exchange, pledged to respect the Trianon treaty and to continue paying reparations, which never, in fact, were paid.

The credits—250 million crowns worth—encouraged loans from private sources. A new Hungarian monetary unit, the *pengö*, appeared and swiftly became one of Europe's most stable currencies. In 1924, the budget was balanced, and for the next six years, receipts exceeded expenses. Much of the capital was invested in industry, and between 1921 and 1928, the work force grew from 137,000 to 236,000. During the same period, foreign trade doubled.

Hungary still dreamed of revisionism, however, and searched for allies who would support its claims. It tried to weaken its neighbors by arousing discontent among their minorities—the Magyars in Romania, the Slovaks and Ruthenians in Czechoslovakia, and the Croats in Yugoslavia. The temporary absence of Germany and Russia from Eastern European affairs brought Hungary into alliance with Italy, based upon their mutual dislike of the new state unifying the south Slavs, the Kingdom of the Serbs, Croats, and Slovenes. In April 1927, they signed a Treaty of Friendship and Cooperation, which they followed with a secret military convention. But being weak and restricted by treaty to only 35,000 troops, Hungary had difficulty being taken seriously as a military power.

POSTSCRIPT   The Soviet Union recovered from the war without much help from abroad. Its new leaders were often inexperienced and inefficient, having better political credentials than economic expertise. Nevertheless, by 1928, productivity had generally reached its prewar levels. The quality of goods, however, was poor and the cost in human terms extremely high. The new rulers professed faith in progress and in the ideals of social justice and democracy. But they also believed that their virtue and enlightenment, which rested on the general will of the proletariat, gave them the right to direct the affairs of state. Beginning in the last two decades of the nineteenth century, Russia had undergone considerable industrialization and therefore had a significant amount of industry and a large restive proletariat by 1917, but it was still predominantly a country of peasants, who wanted to own their own property—a decidedly bourgeois ideal. Since the urban working class was a minority, the Communists could be said to be exercising power in the name of a class that had yet to develop. This made it all the more difficult for them to apply the Marxist doctrine of the industrial revolution to the backward rural areas of the country.

The Bolsheviks had come to power as a result of a successful political intrigue, not as a result of historical inevitability. From the downfall of the tsar in March 1917, the pendulum had swung gradually to the left and froze at its farthest point. Under its new masters, the old Russia continued, albeit in a different and much more effectively autocratic form. The upheaval led to the liquidation of the former society, particularly in terms of the power associated with landholding, and prepared the way for the unhampered development of industry.

Germany, already the most industrialized country in Europe, should by Communist theory have been the first country to have experienced a people's revolution. Yet, by the latter part of the 1920s, most Germans seemed quite content to accept the present economic system, especially since, despite certain inequities, it seemed best able to ensure their prosperity. Productivity was the highest it had ever been,[31] and with confirmed free access to the world's money markets, the Germans had no difficulty getting capital from abroad to modernize their industries and utilities and refurbish their cities. So much money flowed into the country in the six years after the appearance of the Reichsmark that the Germans paid no reparations from their own resources.[32] The prevailing arrangement seemed as triangular as the old colonial rum trade—the United States loaned money to Germany; Germany paid reparations to Britain and France; and these two countries then paid war debts to the United States, which loaned the money to Germany.

Industrialists were quick to adopt American methods of mass production and scientific management, appreciably increasing efficiency and the productivity of individual workers. For example, by 1929 over three-fourths of all coal mining was done by machines (compared to only one-fifth in Britain); and the annual output per worker increased from 175 to 315 tons between 1925 and 1929. The whole industry was organized in a gigantic cartel, the *Rheinisch Westfalischer Kohlensyndicat*, which controlled prices and assigned each member company a specific share of the total market.

The number of cartels increased considerably during the Weimar Republic, rising by 1926 to almost 2,500. One of the largest and most diversified was I. G. Farben, which employed over 300,000 workers and completely dominated the chemical industry. The trust directed the manufacture of dyes, pharmaceuticals, acids, paints, lubricating oils, plastics, and motion picture film. It also controlled the production of synthetic nitrates. In addition, it had licensing, production, and marketing agreements with Imperial Chemical Industries of Great Britain, Royal Dutch Shell, Du Pont de Nemours, and Standard Oil of New Jersey. I. G. Farben also cooperated with the Reichswehr in the secret rearmament of Germany and had its own intelligence service.

In the period from 1926 to 1929, Germany was second only to the United States in percentage of world industrial production.[33] But even though the country enjoyed a higher standard of living than at any other time in its history, an economic gulf—greater than that in Great Britain—existed between its upper and lower classes. Furthermore, large elements of the population were still opponents of democracy.

The presidential election of 1925 brought seventy-seven-year-old Field Marshall Paul von Hindenburg into office. The enemies of the republic hailed this as a triumph of nationalism and militarism while others felt that his victory indicated the old regime had at last accepted the new. These hypotheses would soon be tested when Germany's period of economic prosperity came to an end.

Within half a decade, the dangers of civil war in Germany and Russia had passed, and the unity of those states was again reaffirmed and strengthened. Despite territorial losses, these two countries had emerged from the war with the bulk of their national resources intact, a privileged position the two successor states of the Austro-Hungarian Empire hardly enjoyed. The new Austria and the new Hungary had to adjust to an entirely different set of political and economic circumstances and could not depend on reviving previous patterns of loyalty and cooperation. The problems of adjustment were enormous, and in frustration the Austrian and Hungarian peoples turned against themselves, displaying a hatred that they had previously reserved for their enemies abroad.

The Austrians had difficulty living at peace with themselves. Class violence always lurked just below the surface. In July 1927, the streets of Vienna became a bloody battlefield following the acquittal of three nationalists, one a member of the rightist Front Fighters, charged with the killing of two members of the working class.[34] The day after the publication of the verdict, hordes of enraged workers poured into Vienna's Inner City, their numbers eventually swelling to about a quarter of a million. Both the regular civilian police and the Social Democratic party leaders, who had decided against mass action, were caught completely off guard. The demonstrators ransacked the beautiful palace of justice, scattered public documents, and then set them on fire. Soon the building itself was engulfed in flames. Other buildings were also put to the torch, including the offices of the Christian Social newspaper, the *State News (Reichspost)*. Socialist leaders, unable to control their own rank and file, met with Chancellor Seipel and tried to induce him to agree to a coalition. Seipel refused.

The government hastily deputized a force of 600 men, armed them with rifles, and ordered them to bring the situation under control, whatever the cost. Soon everybody in the streets became a target. For three hours the troops fired into the crowds, killing 85 people and wounding 1,057 others. Many of the casualties were onlookers who had come from the suburbs to see the excitement. The socialists rejected plans to arm the workers for a counterblow, but called for a twenty-four-hour general strike. They also urged their followers to quit the Roman Catholic church. Seipel, who was determined not to relax until the Schutzbund had been disarmed and the power of the socialists destroyed, concluded an alliance with the Heimwehr.

By the time Seipel left office in the spring of 1929, he had created a terrible legacy. His country was now divided into two irreconcilable camps. From the Christian Social point of view, the issue was between those who believed in the forces of Christianity and those who believed in atheistic socialism. Not since the June Days in the French revolution of 1848 had history seen a clearer example of class warfare. In 1930, the leaders of a rejuvenated Heimwehr adopted the Korneuburger program, which was committed to the destruction of parliamentary democracy and to the creation of a fascist state, by force if necessary. The Christian Social party also shared these goals. Thus, those who desired Austria's salvation prepared its damnation.

The Hungarian workers were not as well organized as their Austrian counterparts and did not resolve their differences in the streets; nevertheless their hatred was strong. Even in the best of times, an estimated two-thirds of the peasants lived a marginal existence. Large estates were not broken up. The government enacted an elementary social insurance scheme for factory workers, but did nothing comparable for those who worked on the farms. One journalist called Hungary a nation of three million beggars.

Continued economic prosperity was dependent on factors over which the state had no control. As long as Hungary could rely on a steady supply of foreign capital, it remained fairly prosperous and maintained a positive balance in its international payments. But despite its industrial progress, Hungary remained primarily an agricultural country. Farm commodities comprised 80 percent of its exports. It therefore was very sensitive to world market prices, particularly the price of wheat. Any significant decline in the value of these commodities immediately affected the purchasing power of the Hungarian people and the resources of the state. Hungarian recovery might be impressive if one did not look too closely—it was like a facade of brightly painted stucco behind which prowled ruin, misery, and eventual foreign domination.

ENDNOTES

1. Joachim von Kürenberg, *The Kaiser* (New York: Simon and Schuster, 1955), 371.
2. The ex-kaiser lived the next twenty-three years of his life in relative ease and peace. He purchased a large house in the village of Doorn, where he surrounded himself with the bulk of his personal possessions, which the new government generously allowed to follow him into exile. These included the snuffboxes used by Frederick the Great, the family photographs and portraits, several porcelain chandeliers, library books, some tapestries, the office desk with its famous riding-saddle seat, and his beloved dachshunds.
3. Gordon Brooke-Shepherd, *The Last Habsburg* (New York: Waybright and Talley, 1968), 210.
4. Robert Conquest, "The Human Cost of Soviet Communism," Senate Judiciary Committee Document, 91st Congress (Washington, D.C.: U.S. Government Printing Office, 1970), 7.
5. J. Bunyan and H. H. Fisher, *The Bolshevik Revolution, 1917–1918: Documents and Materials* (Stanford: Stanford University Press, 1934), 362.
6. Announcement in *Pravda* on 23 February 1918, Conquest, "Human Cost," 8.
7. Among the most famous victims of this early terror were the former tsar and his family, killed, as Trotsky made clear, on the authority of Lenin as part of a larger effort that would include tens of thousands of others.
8. Isaac Deutscher, *The Prophet Unarmed* (London: Oxford University Press, 1959), 109. Dzerzhinsky stayed in office until his death in 1926. To honor his services, the regime erected a gigantic statue of him at Moscow in the square before the Lubyanka prison in whose cellars so many enemies of the state were eliminated. Few other regimes had so ostentatiously immortalized their hangmen.
9. Richard Pipes, *The Russian Revolution* (New York: Alfred A. Knopf, 1990), 506–9.
10. V. I. Lenin, *What Is to Be Done?* (Moscow: Progress Publishers, 1969), 121.
11. *Russian Provisional Government Documents*, vol. 3 (Palo Alto: Stanford University Press, 1961), 1207.
12. Nadezhda Krupskaia, *Memories of Lenin (1893–1917)* (London: Lawrence and Wishart, 1942), 200.
13. Pipes, *Russian Revolution*, 673.
14. Adam B. Ulam, *The Bolsheviks: The Intellectual and Political History of the Triumph of Communism in Russia* (New York: Collier Books, 1965), 407.
15. James Bunyan, ed., *Intervention, Civil War, and Communism in Russia, April–December 1918: Documents and Materials* (New York: Octagon Books, 1976), 106–8.
16. The Bolsheviks regarded this Anglo-French agreement, signed on 23 December 1917, as irrefutable proof of the Allies' desire to partition Russia. J. F. N. Bradley, *Civil War in Russia, 1917–1920* (New York: St. Martin's Press, 1975), 69–70.
17. Pipes, *Russian Revolution*, 671–72.
18. Conquest, "Human Cost," 11.
19. Ulam, *The Bolsheviks*, 459–60.
20. *The Trotsky Papers, 1917–1922* (The Hague: Mouton, 1917), 793. The so-called Lenin's Testament came from Lenin's notes written on 24 December 1922 and 4

January 1923. They were not intended for publication.

21. Ibid., 793–94.

22. Trotsky eventually settled in Mexico City, where he continued to attack Stalin, calling him a power-mad mediocrity who had betrayed the revolution. In August 1940, while Trotsky was working on the final draft of his biography of Stalin, a Stalinist agent smashed his head with an ice ax. His death struggles splashed the pages of the manuscript with blood.

23. To a great extent, the U.S.S.R. based its principal administrative subdivisions on nationality, with its most numerous ethnic groups accorded the status of a Union Republic. The Soviet Union came into existence in 1922 with the creation of the first four Soviet republics: the Russian Soviet Federated Socialist Republic, the Ukrainian Soviet Socialist Republic, the Belorussian Soviet Socialist Republic, and the Transcaucasian Socialist Soviet Federated Republic. In 1936, the Transcaucasian Republic was split into the Armenian Soviet Socialist Republic, the Azerbaijan Soviet Socialist Republic, and the Georgian Soviet Socialist Republic. By then, the Central Asian republics also existed: the Turkmen Soviet Socialist Republic and the Uzbek Soviet Socialist Republic (1925); the Tadzhik Soviet Socialist Republic (1929); and the Kirgiz Soviet Socialist Republic and the Kazakh Soviet Socialist Republic (1936). Nearly all of the U.S.S.R. republics contained additional subdivisions, called "autonomous republics," to further accommodate the union's multinational character. However, the vaunted independence of these governmental units was largely fictitious.

24. Care must be taken not to confuse the Central Committee of the Communist party, whose ruling group was the Politburo, with the government's All-Union Central Executive Committee, which emanated from the Congress of Soviets. The government cabinet called the Council of People's Commissars, later known as the Council of Ministers, handled executive affairs; the Presidium dealt with legislative matters.

25. During the next fourteen years, Article 48 was used more than 250 times, mostly to enact the pet projects of special-interest groups who could not get their schemes passed any other way.

26. Between 1919 and 1924, Germany paid about $6 billion in reparations.

27. The Ruhr episode is discussed in more detail in chapter 6, pages 178–179.

28. Koppel S. Pinson, *Modern Germany: Its History and Civilization* (New York: Macmillan, 1966), 411–21.

29. The committee discovered, for example, that Vienna had more civil servants in 1922 than it had before the war when the city was the head of a vast empire of over 50 million people.

30. Karl lived at Funchal isolated from any semblance of the world he had known. He died on 1 April 1922 of viral pneumonia at the age of thirty-five. His queen, Zita, was only twenty-nine. He left her with eight children, the oldest of whom, Crown Prince Otto, was only ten.

31. Based on an index in which productivity in 1913 is equal to 100, productivity in 1920 was 61; in 1922, it was 86; and in 1928, it had risen to 102.

32. From 1924 to 1931, Germany paid $2,000,600,000 in reparations but received over $6 billion in loans.

33. The United States was responsible for 42.4 percent of world industrial output; Germany for 11.6 percent; Britain, 9.4 percent; France, 6.6 percent; Russia, 4.3 percent; and Italy, 3.3 percent.

34. The incident had occurred six months earlier in the small Burgenland village of Schattendorf when some Front Fighters clashed with members of the socialist Shutzbund. A crippled war veteran and a child were killed, apparently by a Front Fighter and two sons of a local tavern owner. After most of the brawling had ceased, the three began to fire indiscriminately from a window on the crowds in the street.

CHAPTER 5

CRISIS IN THE DEMOCRATIC ORDER

PREFACE   The great parade held in Paris on Bastille Day, 14 July 1919, just over two weeks after the signing of the Treaty of Versailles, was by all accounts the greatest and most impressive of the Allied victory celebrations. People lined the sidewalks along the route of march from the Porte Maillot, the Place de l'Étoile, Rue Royale, and the Grand Boulevards to the Place de la République many hours in advance; some had spent the previous night sitting on the curbstones passing the time by singing, playing cards, and handing around bottles of wine. One old lady climbed onto a ten-foot ledge at the Ministry of Marine and stayed there during the whole parade; others found vantage points in trees and on monuments. The prefect of police tried to discourage apartment owners from renting their balconies by warning them that they were financially liable for any mishaps. One balcony did give way, injuring eighteen people. So dense was the crowd that some people with tickets in the stands found it impossible to get to their seats.

But lest the festivities encourage forgetfulness, even for one day, the place of honor in the parade was given to one thousand severely wounded soldiers, representing all the French departments, branches of service, and, judging from the civilian clothes that many wore, all levels of society. They were the first to pass under the Arc de Triomphe, preceding even Foch on his white charger, and they were the first to come down the Champs Élysées to the Rond Point where Clemenceau and Poincaré stood.

The men of the column made no effort to keep formation or walk in step—indeed, it was impossible for many of them to do so. They shuffled along as best they could with their bandages, dark glasses, and plaster casts: some were blind, others were maimed; some walked with the help of crutches, canes, or artificial legs; some were led by a companion; and some were pushed like babies in perambulators.

France had called up 7.5 million men, more than half its entire active male population. Over one-fifth of these—1,384,300—had died; another 3 million had been wounded, and as many as a third of these were invalids. No other belligerent had either mobilized or lost a greater proportion of its manpower. The peasantry suffered the most casualties, but the liberal professions suffered as well—one-half of all the teachers drafted had been killed. Thirty percent of those between the ages of twenty and thirty never returned, many having no known graves. The body of the Unknown Soldier in the tomb in front of the Arc de Triomphe was only one of 250,000 similarly unidentified dead.

The war had demolished 20,000 factories, 1,200 churches, 5,000 bridges, 3,200 miles of railroad tracks, and 32,000 miles of roads. In Aisne, the worst hit department, 814 out of 841 cities had been devastated. Only 14 out of 16,000 houses in Rheims escaped damage. Seven percent of *all* French property was in ruins with 250,000 buildings completely destroyed and another 500,000 partially demolished. The war had pockmarked the battle zones with shell holes, scarred them with trenches, crisscrossed them with barbed wire, and made whole areas unfit for habitation or cultivation. It had laid waste 8,000 square miles of agricultural land and 1,875 square miles of forest. Such staggering losses proved the truth of the old adage that the people who win wars are those who win the fewest battles.

By comparison, the material damage in Britain was slight. There the fighting had threatened few civilians directly. Isolation from the path of destruction explained the greater enthusiasm the British people maintained throughout the war, despite mounting pacifism and war weariness. It also explained their greater capacity to forgive the Germans once the hostilities ceased. Unlike the French, the British people had suffered relatively few deprivations. German submarines destroyed almost eight million tons of shipping, but imports fell by only five percent, hardly enough to affect the caloric intake of the population. People grumbled when the government weakened their beer, but rationing and government controls on commodities caused little strain. If anything, they reinforced national solidarity—"after all, it's the least we can do for the war"—and fostered a confidence that led to the disappearance of food queues. There were shortages of meat and temporary scarcities of cheese, but bread, tea, and jam were almost always available. Few people believed that the war had caused more than a temporary halt in the inevitable march toward prosperity. But no longer could the British be accused of letting their allies do most of the fighting: 750,000 soldiers—over 12 percent of those mobilized—would never return. And British society had experienced a profound shock. The year after the Armistice was marked by labor unrest, a rebellion in Ireland, and an influenza epidemic that claimed the lives of 150,000 people in England and Wales alone.

In Italy, the end of hostilities squelched the wartime economic expansion; industries went bankrupt, and unemployment climbed to over two million. The public debt, which in 1914 was 15 million lire, now stood at 50 million. Current taxation was inadequate to pay expenses, and the government met its obligation by increasing the amount of money in circulation. The value of the lira fell from 5 to the dollar (set in 1914) to 30 to the dollar by 1921. Of the 5,758,277 men that Italy had mobilized, 670,000 had been killed and another million wounded. The war cost twice as much as the expenses for running the state during the entire period from 1861 to 1913.

Inflation pauperized the country and undermined middle-class security. Strikes, riots, and lawless disorder sharply increased. Even though Italy had received some 9,000 square miles of territory promised by the Treaty of London, Italians felt cheated. The *vittoria mutilata*, the lost peace, was a convenient issue to take their minds off domestic problems. It was also an issue that was symptomatic of the unpopularity of the prevailing democratic institutions, which many Italians considered unresponsive to their needs.

In the Great War, something more than people had died, and more than property had been destroyed. The victorious French, British, and Italians now knew their nations were not immortal. Their power had been eroded. Social tensions that had been papered over during the fighting surfaced once again and threatened the countries' basic political and social structures. Fear that they would now be asked to share power with the working classes—or, worse, relinquish it altogether—made the old elites dig in their heels. Britain and France managed to adjust to the new forces without endangering their democratic systems. This was not the case in Italy where the absence of a firm democratic tradition coupled with the inability of the political parties to agree on a responsible program of reconstruction brought widespread discontent with the parliamentary system and a search for radical alternatives.

ITALY AND THE TRIUMPH OF FASCISM

The Death of the Parliamentary System

The Growth of Authoritarianism. On 10 September 1919, two days after the signing of the Treaty of St. Germain with Austria, the aviator-poet Gabriele D'Annunzio led a mixed force of adventurers, *arditi* (storm troopers) and other war veterans, and nationalists into the Adriatic port of Fiume. The fifty-six-year-old warrior, his literary and amorous image on the wane, found the new role of *commandante* to his liking. He ruled whimsically, harangued the crowds in the oratorical style of ancient Rome, and drafted his own constitution, proclaiming the "Regency of the Carnaro" as a commonwealth of "true citizens." The legislature would include nine autonomous corporations of manual and intellectual labor and a tenth "consecrated to the unknown genius, to the apparition of the very new man." The executive consisted of seven directors with power to appoint a dictator. D'Annunzio's escapade gave a certain lift to postwar Italian politics, although it officially embarrassed the Italian government. Many politicians were secretly sympathetic and envious. D'Annunzio ignored all warnings to leave and became even more mercurial. One of his followers wrote that D'Annunzio's vision passed the frontiers of the Adriatic: "He dreams of noble crusades everywhere, wherever there are rebels in the world."[1]

Finally, in December 1920, fifteen months after the affair had begun, the Italian government dispatched the warship *Andrea Doria* to Fiume. D'Annunzio proclaimed that he would stand fast: "Fiume or Death." But when the ship fired a few token rounds, D'Annunzio changed his mind and fled the city on 5 January 1921. The *condottiere* had not solved the question of Fiume, but the Italians admired his panache, and, with the authority of the government badly shaken, his example proved contagious.

Postwar discontent initially benefited the parties of the left. In the elections of 1919 (the first in six years), the Socialists tripled their representation to control the largest block of seats (156) in the parliament. The second largest party with 100 seats was the recently formed *Partito popolare italiano* (Italian Popular party), the first mass-based Catholic party in Italian politics. Together these two parties possessed just over half the total of 508 delegates. In a coalition, they could have given Italy the governmental stability necessary to strengthen the parliamentary system. Many of their programs were similar: both believed in democratic, secular reform, the right to unionize, women's suffrage, and a foreign policy based on the League of Nations. The Popular party, however, according to its priest-founder, Don Luigi Sturzo, was committed to weakening the Socialists through a workers' movement "inspired by the ethics of Christianity."[2] And the Socialists advocated eliminating the Catholic church completely from politics and bringing about fundamental change in the existing social order. Neither the Socialist party nor the Popular party could form a government by itself, but each was able to frustrate the other's efforts to do so. Between 1919 and 1922, Italy had five governments, none of which lasted long enough to undertake a serious program of recovery. Inflation and civil disorder went unchecked. And no sooner was the D'Annunzio affair concluded than a series of strikes shook the country.

In September 1920, workers seized control of the factories. The government preferred to wait until the situation cooled, but property owners and conservatives, deploring the official inactivity, began looking for extralegal ways to guarantee their own security. The General Confederation of Industry, for example, recruited a private army. The specter of Communism terrified the Italian middle and upper classes, and they turned for salvation to antidemocratic political associations that promised to keep the lower classes caged.

Toward the March on Rome. In March 1919, Benito Mussolini organized the first *fascio di combattimento* (Fascist fighting unit) in Milan. His followers, who wore black shirts as a party uniform, were Socialist dissidents, war veterans, and syndicalists drawn together by their discontent with the status quo and their desire for revolt. The unstructured nature of the organization and its ill-defined program encouraged the establishment of similar cells in other Italian cities and towns. Initially, however, the Fascists had very little political influence. In the November 1919 national elections, they ran candidates only in Milan where their popular support was greatest. Their program called for the imposition of a capital levy on war profits, the expropriation of church property, worker participation in the management of factories, and the annexation of Fiume. No Fascists were elected. In their home territory, they received only 4,795 votes, whereas the Socialists, with whom Mussolini was in direct competition for working-class support, swept the election with a total of 170,000 votes.

Mussolini promptly purged his program of all its proletarian cant and concentrated more narrowly on gaining bourgeoisie support. He tried to appear more respectable, shaving his beard regularly and taking to wearing spats. But not until he was able to prove his real value to the middle class were the Blackshirts able to emerge from their relative obscurity and make a play for national power. The opportunity came with the wave of strikes that swept the country in the winter of 1920–1921.

The Italian economy had difficulty in making the adjustment from war to peace. Allied subsidies stopped, agricultural and industrial prices became inflated, and old-fashioned production techniques led to a decline in demand for Italian goods, especially on the international markets. These enormous problems resulted in widespread unrest as workers seized control of the factories and peasants occupied the great estates. Both demanded greater participation in the political and economic life of the nation. The industrialists and landowners were terrified, and many believed the emerging Fascist movement might be a means of protecting their position. During 1921 the number of *fasci* cells increased from 70 to 830 with a combined membership of a quarter of a million men.

In the national elections of May 1921, Prime Minister Giovanni Giolitti increased the threat to Italian democracy by tacitly allowing Fascist candidates to run for parliament in a common list with other nationalist parties. He believed that the weak parliamentary government could be reinvigorated by such an infusion. Giolitti's initiative helped to elect thirty-two Fascists, giving them seven percent of the seats in the lower chamber. Mussolini became a deputy from Milan, but he seldom attended the sessions, preferring to stay near his home base to better control the growth of his disparate movement. In November, the fasci officially became the *Partito nazionale fascista* (Fascist party).

Fascism was essentially opportunistic and contained many contradictions. Its supporters were a strange mixture of nationalists and neutralists, republicans and monarchists, syndicalists and industrialists, moderates and extremists, Catholics and atheists. They comprised a wide range of occupational groups from landowners and capitalists to peasants, students, shopkeepers, and bureaucrats, but all were attracted to the movement by its spirit of revolt and change and its promise to right wrongs and destroy enemies. Much of Fascism's strength lay in its lower-middle-class constituency whose members saw it as a means of pushing aside the traditional ruling classes and participating in the social and political life of the nation. Mussolini thus had a dilemma: he had to satisfy the desires and longings of the masses while convincing the ruling classes that he would protect the traditional social structure and the sacred right of property.

Mussolini used his party army of *squadristi* to attack Socialist meetings, beat party followers, and destroy their property. In certain areas—notably in the Romagna, Emilia, and parts of Tuscany and Lombardy—these Blackshirts, through the neutrality or collusion of government officials, acted as the de facto government. In 1922, Fascist thugs broke up the May Day celebrations. In Milan, they burned down the office of the Socialist paper *Avanti (Forward)*, Mussolini's old paper. In October, local Fascists occupied the cities of Trento and Bolzano in the Trentino. The government did nothing. Its failure to act convinced Mussolini that the time was ripe for a violent seizure of power.

On 27 October, Fascist gangs occupied police stations, communications centers, and arsenals throughout the provinces, while a force of 25,000 began a march on Rome. Many bands failed to reach their assigned gathering points, and those that did were badly armed and poorly disciplined, but the government panicked. Despite the fact that the ragtag Fascist units were no match for the 12,000 regular army troops entrusted with the capital's security, Premier Luigi Facta hesitated to order the immediate arrest of the Fascist leaders. When his order to the commander of the Roman garrison, General Umberto Pugilese, for martial law failed to win the signature of King Victor Emmanuel III,[3] Facta resigned in protest, and negotiations began with the Fascists. Mussolini demanded the prime ministry. Immobilized with fear, the king consented, thereby ensuring the Fascists the victory they would have had difficulty getting any other way. On the night of 29 October, Mussolini took a sleeping car to Rome. The next morning, a handful of his lieutenants met him at the station, and together they made their way to the palace, where the king entrusted them with the formation of a new government.

The transition of power was peaceful, and most Italians had no idea what had taken place until afterwards. It was hardly the violent revolution that the Fascists preached. In order to create the proper impression that the Fascists had seized power from the streets, Mussolini had the Blackshirt army stage a demonstration the day after his investiture. Party photographers filmed the scene for posterity.

Profile: Benito Mussolini (1883–1945)

When he became premier in 1922, Benito Mussolini was thirty-nine years old, the youngest person to hold that office in the history of modern Italy. He was born on 25 July 1883 in the commune of Predappio in the Romagna, an agricultural region southeast of Bologna known for its hard-working peasants, its piety, and its radical politics. His father was a blacksmith, a Socialist, and a freethinker. He named his son after the Mexican revolutionary Benito Juarez. Mussolini's mother, however, was a devout Catholic and insisted that he attend the local parochial school run by the Society of St. Francis de Sales. Benito loathed the constant surveillance and strict discipline and was expelled after a year for stabbing a fellow student. He transferred to a state normal school, from which he graduated in 1901 with a teaching diploma. But he was able to obtain only substitute teaching positions, and in July 1902, he left Italy to try his luck in Switzerland. For the next two years, he moved from canton to canton—Tessin, Bern, Vaud, Geneva—working at odd jobs: construction worker, clerk, errand boy, and journalist for a Socialist paper. Having a falsified passport got him thrown out of Geneva; the police of Lausanne arrested him for vagrancy.[4] Mussolini's early humiliations confirmed his hatred for the bourgeoisie and reinforced his belief in authoritarianism.

In 1903, he was sentenced to a year in prison in absentia for failing to report for military service. But the following year, profiting from a general amnesty on the occasion of the birth of the king's son, he returned to Italy to enter the army. He served from January 1905 to September 1906 and afterwards taught French. Soon, however, he became a professional organizer for the Socialists in Forlì, where he also edited the weekly newspaper *La lotta di classe* (*The Class Struggle*). He associated himself with the party's revolutionary wing. In 1911, agitation against the Italo-Turkish War over Tripoli earned him five months in prison. However, he emerged from the experience with his reputation enhanced. The party rewarded him at its congress in Reggio in July 1912 with a position on the Central Committee and the editorship of *Avanti*, the leading Italian Socialist newspaper headquartered in Milan. Mussolini's belief in revolutionary action had wide appeal with the party's young radicals and intellectuals.

When World War I began, he first endorsed the Socialist position of absolute neutrality but, fearing that this would lead to political isolation and weakness, soon became a rabid interventionist. The shift led to his dismissal as editor of *Avanti* and to his subsequent expulsion from the Socialist party. However, subsidies from wealthy industrialists and the French government, both of which were interested in bringing Italy into the war on the side of the Allies, enabled him to found his own newspaper *Il Popolo d'Italia (The People of Italy)* on 15 November 1914.

In August 1915, Mussolini was drafted into the army. On 16 December 1915, while he was home on leave, he married Rachele Guidi, the woman he had been living with for the past six years and by whom he already had a daughter and a son. This union would produce two more boys and another girl. He served in the army until February 1917, when he was discharged because of wounds he received from the explosion of a badly loaded shell during mortar practice. After his release from the hospital, he returned to his newspaper in Milan, boasting of his life under fire and insisting that war veterans had the right to govern Italy. He glorified combat and violence, but philosophically he remained a dilettante and an opportunist. Mussolini had acquired enough Marxism to enable him to hold his own in the general discussions of the Socialist party meetings, but his knowledge was essentially superficial. After his break with socialism, he dropped his leftist references and began quoting conservatives and aggressive nationalists. He was determined to impose his will on Italy and would use any means to do so.

From Government to Regime. Mussolini's first government was a coalition, in which his party shared power with the Liberal, Conservative, and Catholic parties. But the Fascists controlled the most important ministries: Foreign Affairs, Justice, Finance, and the Interior, which ran the national police. At its November session, the Chamber of Deputies voted overwhelmingly (306 votes to 130) to grant Mussolini full powers to legislate by decree for the next twelve months. This practice had been fairly common during the war, but Mussolini used the opportunity to consolidate his position. While posing as a defender of the constitution, he divided and weakened his opposition. He stuffed prefectures, police headquarters, and state agencies with party members. He fused various other nationalist parties into his movement to broaden its base. And he had the Chamber of Deputies pass a new election law under which the party securing the most votes in a national election (as long as it received 25 percent of all votes cast) would receive two-thirds of the 535 seats in the lower house.

In the elections of April 1924, the Fascist national ticket captured 65 percent of the popular vote and 374 seats in the Chamber of Deputies. Although the Fascists controlled the election machinery and ran their campaign with considerable violence, their triumph could not be explained by threats and beatings alone. Mussolini was genuinely popular. The conservative classes saw him as the means of preserving their traditional power. But a great many poorer Italians, particularly in the agricultural regions of central and southern Italy, also enthusiastically and willingly supported him. The 1924 electoral victory put an end to parliamentary government as it had existed since the unification of modern Italy. But the opposition parties, though seriously weakened, were not yet destroyed.

On 30 May 1924, Giacomo Matteotti, the political secretary of the moderate United Socialist party, denounced the Fascists in a two-hour speech in the Chamber of Deputies, accusing them of fraud, treachery, and brutality. He declared that the recent elections had no validity, and he moved that new ones be held.[5] Mussolini, who was present at the time, turned to his press officer and said, "After such a speech, that man shouldn't be allowed to walk around."[6]

Ten days later, as Matteotti was walking to parliament along the Tiber, five men attacked him and shoved him into a waiting car. He was never seen alive again. The Liberals, Popolare, and Socialists refused to believe Mussolini's protestations that he had nothing to do with Matteotti's disappearance. After adopting a resolution that they would not participate in parliamentary life until justice was done, they marched from the chamber in protest. Mussolini now was faced with one of the most serious challenges to his authority since coming to power.

But the so-called Aventine Secession—named after Gaius Gracchus's last stand on the Aventine Hill in 121 B.C.—soon lost its fire and cohesion. Mussolini appeased some of his opponents by reshuffling his government to incorporate a few critics. He made some conciliatory speeches, claiming that the revolutionary phase of Fascism was over. The secessionists hoped Victor Emmanuel would demand Mussolini's resignation, but the king feared that doing so would turn over power to the Socialists. The situation was not helped by Pope Pius XI, who admonished the Popular party against forming any coalition with the Socialists by declaring he would not tolerate "cooperation in evil" even for the "purpose of public benefit."[7] But the real, though highly understandable, failings were those of the Aventines themselves who were not prepared to go any farther than moral outrage. These people were professionals, businessmen, and labor organizers, who were used to the give and take of negotiation and service and were ill-suited psychologically to present a significant challenge to the ruling powers. The criticism of Mussolini gradually declined. The crisis had passed.[8]

Mussolini developed an ulcer during the crisis but otherwise emerged unscathed. He lashed out at his parliamentary opposition with renewed vigor, specifically accusing the Aventines of sedition and moving to deprive them of their parliamentary seats.[9] The antidemocratic attack extended to all non-Fascist political parties and organizations. Mussolini took the title of Duce—the Head of the Government—and assumed complete control of legislative initiative.

Italy was beginning to recover from the postwar depression when Mussolini came to power. At first, the regime did little more than make a few financial reforms to please the business community: it abolished price and rent controls, stopped subsidizing cooperatives, and shelved agricultural reform. The telephone system and the match industry were returned to private enterprise. In 1925, for the first time since the war, the government balanced the budget, and the lira strengthened on international money markets.

In the aftermath of the Matteotti affair, as the regime became more secure the drift toward greater political and economic control accelerated. In January 1926, Mussolini obtained unrestrained authority to issue decrees with the force of law. This assumption of power began what Mussolini called his "Napoleonic Year," which concluded with the eradication of the last vestiges of the legal anti-Fascist opposition. On 5 November, all political parties, save the Fascist party, were dissolved. Four days later a Special Tribunal for the Defense of the State was created to handle political crimes. Anti-Fascist crimes were made retroactive, and the tribunal's sentences were not subject to appeal.

A law of December 1928 made the Fascist Grand Council the chief organ of the state with power to decide the succession to the throne, to regulate the composition and functions of parliament, and to determine the organization of labor unions. It could also, when necessary, choose Mussolini's successor. With this law, all local party self-rule was abolished. Next the regime disarmed the Blackshirts and gave their repressive functions to the police. Deprived of their reason for being, the Blackshirts lost their militancy and turned to enjoying the fruits of their success.[10] The Fascist government made the prefects the direct representatives of its power, subject to the orders of the Ministry of the Interior.

Fascist Policies

Born of the Need for Action. During his first three years in power, Mussolini had governed in coalition with the traditional ruling parties. Since the Fascists made no attempt to change the social system, their attack on democracy was not particularly alarming; indeed, it was accepted as a necessary step in reducing the power and pretensions of the lower-middle and working classes. Even after 1925, when the Fascists embarked on building a new regime, the conservatives still did not find accommodation particularly painful: many adjusted simply by symbolically draping themselves in black shirts and continuing as before. However, Mussolini had no intention of becoming the tool of the old establishment. He had not made a revolution to pour old wine into new bottles. The Duce wanted the Fascist party to become an organization of mass control and also the means through which the Italian people could participate in a new national experience. He wanted his ideology to transform crowds and create a new secular religion.

The Duce was the first to admit that Fascist doctrine had not been worked out ahead of time but was "born of the need for action and was itself from the beginning practical rather than theoretical."[11] Mussolini glorified the ethical state that established its own morality and forced all citizens to obey its will. The state, he said, was an absolute—only within the state can anything exist or have value; it "is a spiritual and moral fact in itself." Mussolini rejected the Marxist materialist interpretation of history, maintaining that actions were influenced not by economics, but by "holiness and heroism." He claimed that Fascism, based on the general will of individuals, removed from them "useless and harmful liberties while preserving those which are essential." Mussolini's glorification of the power of the state found popular expression in countless slogans that were plastered on billboards, painted on public buildings, chiseled on monuments, printed in the state-controlled press, and hung in classrooms across Italy: "He who has steel has bread!" "Nothing is ever won in history without bloodshed!" "A minute on the battlefield is worth a lifetime of peace!" "War is to the man what childbearing is to a woman!" The entire doctrine might be summed up in the regime's two most famous slogans: *"Credere! Ubbidire! Combattere!"* (Believe! Obey! Fight!) and *"Mussolini ha sempre ragione"* (Mussolini is always right). The latter reflected the Fascist emphasis on the cult of the leader.

The flexible nature of Fascist doctrine was admirably suited to the needs of a multifarious party. Since Fascism lacked a complicated dialectic or an obsession with racial purity,[12] the interpretation of Fascist scripture depended upon the definitions a person gave to a series of abstractions—morality, heroism, tradition. A favorite theme was that through mobilization the inertia of the masses could be transformed into a vibrant national spirit. Life was a constant struggle in which the individual could only be enriched through collective action, just as a soldier was magnified in an army battalion. Fascism repudiated the basic tenet of the Western liberal tradition: that a state of peace was intrinsically desirable. "Only war," Mussolini said, "takes human energy to its highest tension and puts the stamp of nobility upon the peoples who have the courage to meet it. All other trials are substitutes, which never really put men into the position where they have to make the great decision—the alternative of life or death."[13] Mussolini infused this idea of combat into all his programs.

The Corporate State. Mussolini's campaign to make Italy economically self-sufficient—a necessity if it was to pursue a forceful foreign policy—began in 1925 with the *battaglia del grano* (battle of wheat). This policy of autarky met with initial success. By increasing the number of productive agricultural units, the Fascist planners were able to boost crop yields, doubling the domestic production of cereals. They accomplished this by encouraging the intensive cultivation of current crop-lands and by bringing new areas under cultivation, especially through land reclamation. One of the greatest such projects was the draining of the Pontine marshes southwest of Rome for planting wheat. Roads were constructed, and the new cities of Pontinia and Sabaudia were built. The project was one of the regime's proudest achievements, but most of the benefits went to large landowners. Italy still remained dependent on foreign supplies of grain.

Italy had none of the basic natural resources—oil, coal, iron ore, or strategic minerals—necessary for self-sufficiency. The law of comparative advantage could not be disregarded in favor of a new system of national priorities without a steep cost. Benefits achieved through autarky soon reached the point of diminishing returns, as each new goal became more costly than the preceding one. For example, the Italian people soon paid 50 percent more for domestic wheat than the price on the world market, a significant factor in the standard of living of the lower class whose staple diet was bread and pasta. The concentration on growing wheat also undermined livestock production. The conversion of pasture lands to grain fields made fodder dearer, increasing the price of meat and also raising its price above that of foreign imports. Taking productive factors away from the cultivation of fruits and vegetables not only made them more expensive for the Italian consumer, but also damaged foreign exchange, because these products with their early growing season had an absolute advantage in northern European markets. Furthermore, the regime's efforts to reevaluate the lira upward for purposes of prestige made exports less competitive, thereby further damaging foreign trade.

Mussolini touted the rural way of life as superior to the life-style of the decadent cities, but the profits of wheat production went to the big producers, not to the individual peasants. This added to the disparity of wealth in a country where the gulf between rich and poor was already significant. The Fascists also imposed restrictions on emigration from the countryside to the cities, in effect tying the peasants to the soil.

At its most utopian, Fascism pretended to harmonize capitalism and socialism, joining capital and labor together in a self-governing corporation to decide questions of mutual interest amicably and establish economic policy for the whole society. Mussolini set out his vision of the corporate state in the "Law for the Judicial Regulation of Labor Disputes," adopted on 3 April 1926. The legislation recognized one organization of workers and employers for each industry. These syndicates were to regulate conditions of labor, establish wages, set norms of productivity, and resolve disputes. Strikes and lockouts were illegal. The law paved the way for the establishment of a Ministry of Corporations to regulate the nation's major economic activities through a National Council of Corporations. Eventually, twenty-two corporations were established, each with its own council of workers and employers; the sectors represented included agriculture, manufacturing, commerce, transportation, the hotel business, the arts and professions, insurance, entertainment, and credit. Each corporate council sent delegates to the National Council of Corporations to make general policy, but the legislative apparatus was a fraud.

Mussolini had no intention of letting the working class make real decisions. The corporations exercised no authority, and the decisions of the National Council were merely advisory. The Fascist government appointed all the officials of the National Council and suppressed all manifestations of workers' independence. Moreover, the state established the Institute of Industrial Reconstruction as a holding company for state-run enterprises. It functioned without any reference to the Ministry of Corporations, as indeed did those who ran the whole policy of autarky. Mussolini professed neutrality between labor and capital but constantly favored the industrialists. Nevertheless, corporatism remained an important theoretical component of Fascist ideology. Ugo Spirito, one of its leading exponents, even argued that the logical end of corporatism was corporate ownership of the means of production. The establishment of such a third force between capitalism and socialism never went beyond the bounds of wishful thinking, however.

Church and State

Toward a Solution of the Roman Question. Relations between the Vatican and the kingdom of Italy had been clouded ever since 1870, when the church lost secular control of Rome. Pope Pius IX created the "Roman question" by refusing to recognize the Italian kingdom, declaring in 1874 that it was inadvisable *(non-expedit)* for Catholics to run for office or even vote. Not until 1904 did Pope Pius X allow Catholics to participate in elections, and then he did so in order to defeat Socialist candidates. Only at the end of World War I did Pope Benedict XV completely lift the proscription, permitting the organization of the Popular party. Benedict favored reconciliation with parliamentary democracy and began negotiations to end the prevailing uncertainty over the Vatican's legal status. But there had been no real progress at the time of his death in 1922.

His successor, Pius XI, considered such an agreement to be vital to his policy of reinforcing Catholicism in Italy and increasing the spiritual and financial importance of the church throughout the world. The triumph of Fascism did not discourage him. When he had been archbishop of Milan, he had come to view the squadristi as defenders of law and order and had even allowed them to bring their flags and emblems into the great cathedral. The only difficulty was that Mussolini was an atheist and had previously boasted of his disbelief in saints, apostles, and salvation. Since he had assumed power, however, he had become more moderate. He allowed public school classrooms to display a crucifix and proclaimed that the basic aim of elementary education was to teach Christian doctrine in accordance with the Catholic faith. Above all, Mussolini presented himself to the pontiff as the man who had saved Italy from Communism. The tactic paid off.

Pius helped destroy the influence of the Popular party by withdrawing Vatican support. The pontiff feared that a party of Catholics would alienate Mussolini and prevent a complete solution to the Roman question. He also wanted the papal-controlled *Azione cattolica italiana* (Catholic Action movement) to be the only secular organization representing the social and economic interests of the church and wanted it to speak for the church on political issues. When Popolare leader Luigi Sturzo refused to sanction an alliance with the Fascists, the Fascists branded

him an enemy of the state. The Vatican added that he was "creating embarrass-
ments to the Church."[14] Obligingly, Sturzo resigned his post as political secretary.
But his life was in danger, he became increasingly isolated, and on 25 October
1924, he fled to London. The papal secretary of state, Cardinal Pietro Gasparri,
helped arrange his departure. The Popular party declined rapidly and within two
years it had disappeared.

The Lateran Treaties. In August 1926, the Fascist state and the Vatican began
negotiations, and after two and a half years of hard bargaining, they reached an
agreement. The settlement included a conciliation treaty, a financial convention,
and a concordat. The purpose of the accord, as stated in the preamble, was to
assure the Holy See a permanent de facto and de jure position "which shall guarantee absolute independence for the fulfillment of its exalted mission in the world"
in exchange for which the Holy See would "consider as finally and irrevocably
settled the Roman Question which arose in 1870 because of the annexation of
Rome to the kingdom of Italy."[15] This meant that the church recognized Rome
as the capital of the kingdom of Italy with the house of Savoy as the reigning
dynasty, and that the pope renounced all former territorial claims.

For his part, Mussolini accepted "the Catholic Apostolic Roman religion [as]
the only State religion" and recognized the full sovereignty of the Holy See over
Vatican City. The Duce wanted to limit the temporal sovereignty of the church
as much as possible—he did not want to offer the Vatican any more than had
previous governments—but he agreed to construct a railway station within the
Vatican and provide the state direct "connection with other States by means of
telegraph, telephone, wireless, broadcasting, and postal services." Ecclesiastical
property and salaries were exempt from the payment of taxes or customs duties.
To compensate the church for its lost territory, the Fascist government offered to
pay the Vatican a lump sum of 750 million lire ($39,472,500) in cash and another
one billion lire in five percent negotiable Italian state bonds. The Holy See became
one of the largest single holders of Fascist securities and therefore had a direct
material interest in the stability of the Fascist regime.

But from the standpoint of the church, the heart of the settlement lay in the
concordat in which the government assured the free exercise of Roman Catholicism and promised to protect the church's religious prerogatives with the forces of
secular authority. The concordat granted the church special privileges in a wide
range of state activities: the state accepted the canon law of marriage as valid for
Catholics; it agreed that religious education, which was currently given in the
public elementary schools, would be extended to secondary schools; and for the
most part, it excused ecclesiastics and members of religious orders from military
service and jury duty. In case of arrest, clerics were to receive special treatment.

In exchange for this new status, the Vatican consented to clear all its appointments for archbishop and bishop with the Italian government "in order to be
assured that the latter has no objections of a political nature to this nomination."
It also agreed to remain politically neutral: in international affairs, the Vatican
would not participate in the conferences of rival states "except in the event of
such parties making a mutual appeal to the pacific mission of the Holy See"; in
domestic affairs, it would prohibit "any Italian ecclesiastics and members of religious orders [from] joining, or working in, any political party." Prior to taking possession of their sees, bishops had to take an oath of allegiance to the state in which
they promised to "enter into no agreement, nor attend any council, which may
be prejudicial to the interests of the Italian State or to public order." They also

agreed to do their "utmost to prevent any evil which might threaten it." This last clause in essence obliged bishops to become active agents for the preservation of the Fascist system.

The treaty made Italy a confessional state, destroying the liberalistic religious reforms of the nineteenth century. In exchange, Pius XI obtained the promise of the Italian state to help him enforce his authority over the clergy. For example, Article 5 forbade ecclesiastics from holding government employment or any public employment without the specific permission of the Vatican and stated that "no priest who is apostate or under censure may take up or continue in a post as a teacher, or an office or employment in which he will come in direct contact with the public." Another victory for the papacy was the right of Catholic Action to exercise its functions "under the immediate direction of the hierarchy of the Church, for the diffusion and practice of Catholic principles." Catholic Action became the only non-Fascist organization allowed to exist—an important concession from a regime that pretended to be totalitarian.

The official signing took place on 11 February 1929 in the sober and elegant Apostolic Palace of the Lateran in Rome. Cardinal Gasparri signed for the Vatican, Mussolini for Italy. The pope had blessed the gold pen that the churchman used, and Gasparri formally presented it to the Duce as a souvenir of the occasion. The concordat recognized the eleventh of February as a national holiday. The broad avenue from the Castel San Angelo to the piazza of Saint Peter's became the *Via della Conciliazione* (Avenue of Reconciliation); and Pius XI praised Mussolini as a man that "Providence has given Us to meet, a man who has not the preoccupations of the Liberal School." Pius characterized the agreement as the best solution possible, one that has "given back God to Italy and Italy to God." Mussolini was also highly pleased; he boasted of a victory for the state. He had succeeded where all the democratic governments of the past had failed; he had obtained for his dictatorship the official blessing of the Roman church. In the plebiscite after the signing of the Lateran pact, priests and bishops urged their parishioners to turn out in large numbers to support the Fascist regime. The Lateran accords also gave Mussolini much needed international prestige at a time when democratic nations were beginning to look at Fascism with horror.

The Vatican concludes the Concordat with Fascist Italy. Cardinal Pietro Gasparri signs for the church in Rome's Lateran Palace on 11 February 1929. The Duce, dressed in full diplomatic regalia and seated at Gasparri's right, will sign next.

GREAT BRITAIN TRIES BUSINESS AS USUAL

Irish Independence

A Bitter Heritage. The "Khaki Election" of 14 December 1918 was a huge personal triumph for Lloyd George. The problems of peace demanded a new mandate, but in scheduling elections immediately after the end of the war, the prime minister deliberately hoped to capitalize on his immense popularity. Since the last elections of 1910, a new franchise law had given all women over the age of thirty the right to vote and had established universal suffrage for all men over twenty-one, thereby adding eight million new voters to the rolls.

Lloyd George organized his campaign with caution. He continued the wartime coalition, trying to garner as much support as possible from the Liberal party, but most of his strength came from the Conservatives (Unionists) headed by Andrew Bonar Law. The 106 Liberals who remained loyal to former prime minister Herbert Asquith were denied the coalition's official letter of endorsement,[16] and they joined the Labour party in opposition. Lloyd George adapted his campaign rhetoric to fit the chauvinistic temper of the electorate. He promised to make Britain a "fit country for heroes to live in." He pledged to bring the kaiser and other war criminals to trial and said he would make Germany pay to the "uttermost farthing." The strategy worked. The elections gave the coalition about two-thirds of the seats in Parliament (342 Conservatives and 136 Liberals supporting Lloyd George). Asquith's faction was practically exterminated: only 27 managed to win seats; all the former ministers, including Asquith himself, were defeated. Labour with 59 seats, an increase of 20, became the chief opposition party.

Middle-aged, middle-class businessmen set the tone of the new Parliament. Younger men who had done the actual fighting in the war were conspicuously absent. They returned from the war with little passion for politics and with an intense skepticism about the permanence of traditional institutions. The new Parliament assembled without 73 of its Irish delegates. The Republican nationalists of the *Sinn Fein* (Ourselves Alone) movement had received 70 percent of the total vote, capturing every seat outside Ulster except those of the University of Dublin. The Irish nationalists, not counting the 36 still in jail, assembled at Mansion House in Dublin to proclaim Irish independence and organize their own national assembly, the Dail Eireann. The breach between Ireland and England was irreparable.

In September 1914, the British Parliament had approved a Home Rule measure, then immediately suspended its enactment for the duration of the war. On Easter Sunday, 23 April 1916, Irish extremists of the ultranationalist wing of the Irish Republican Brotherhood and the separatist Sinn Fein seized the Dublin Post Office and proclaimed an Irish Republic. The rebellion had active support from only about 2,000, it was badly organized, and the Irish people failed to answer the call to arms. It was all over in less than a week and might have been forgotten had not Sir John Maxwell, the military commander of Dublin, ordered the execution of fifteen of the rebel leaders. Most Irish reacted to the executions with horror.[17] The atrocity achieved the goal of the rising's leaders: it aroused Ireland to rebellion.

In 1918, the newly proclaimed Irish Republic reinforced its claim to sovereignty by sending a delegation to Paris to petition the peace conference for recognition of the Irish right of self-determination. Eamon de Valera, the president of the renegade republic who was saved from execution in 1916 because he was born in

New York and had an American mother, went on a fund-raising campaign to the United States and returned with a "loan" of $5 million. At home the Dail raised $2 million, a sum that was augmented by bank holdups and post office and payroll robberies. The new government organized its own Irish Republican Army (IRA) under a newly constituted Ministry for Defense. Armed with rifles and ammunition that they smuggled in or captured in attacks against police barracks, the IRA began guerrilla operations against the British.

The rebels sought to make all normal government impossible. They ostracized and sometimes killed any Irish who worked for the British. They so demoralized the policemen of the Royal Irish Constabulary—a well-armed, paramilitary force living in barracks scattered throughout Ireland—that resignations occurred in great numbers and no new Irish recruits took their place. Any person suspected of serving the British was treated as a potential traitor. In December 1919, the IRA tried to assassinate the new Irish governor-general, Lord French (Sir John French), one-time commander of the British armies in France during World War I.

The British matched terror with terror. They replenished the Royal Irish Constabulary with British war veterans. Wearing khaki uniforms, black belts, and dark green garrison caps, these "Black and Tans" embarked on a course of terrible repression. In one of their raids, they burned several blocks of the city of Cork, including its city hall, free library, and most of the main business district.

During these months of terror and violence, the British Parliament worked to complete Home Rule legislation. On 20 December 1920, it passed a bill, recognizing the division of the country into Southern Ireland with 26 counties and Northern Ireland, or Ulster, with 6 counties; each part was to have its own parliament. A General Council of Ireland would work to promote the eventual unification of the country, but Ireland would remain part of the United Kingdom.[18] The proposed settlement was not enough.

The Irish Free State. The Irish nationalists demanded the complete independence of a unified Ireland. In the first elections held under the new legislation, the Sinn Fein won every one of the 128 seats in Southern Ireland, except the 4 of Trinity College of the University of Dublin. In the North, however, the Unionists led the way with 40 seats to the Sinn Fein's 12.

The British people were sick of the Irish war. No longer sure they knew what was best for others, they wanted to stop the fighting and withdraw the troops. Lloyd George also wanted out. He called for a truce and then issued an open invitation to the Sinn Fein leaders to begin negotiations for an eventual treaty. The government prepared to grant Ireland dominion status, with Ulster free to choose for itself. The Sinn Fein, though, continued to demand a united Ireland. Lloyd George promised that if Ireland would join the Commonwealth, he would not insist on a separate status for Ulster.

The Articles of Agreement for a Treaty, signed in London on 6 December 1921, recognized Ireland, or rather the Irish Free State, as a British dominion. On the Ulster question, the treaty established that if the North did not choose to join the South, the Council of Ireland, provided for in the 1920 act, would continue in existence and a boundary commission would establish the boundaries in accordance with economics, geography, and the precepts of self-determination. During the negotiations, Lloyd George craftily assured the Irish delegates that the ultimate boundaries of Ulster would be drawn so narrowly that its existence as an independent entity would be impossible and it would have to join the South to survive.

The British Parliament ratified the treaty without serious opposition, but the Dail vote was much closer—64 in favor to 57 against. Arthur Griffith, the country's new president and a founder of the Sinn Fein, appealed for unity, but the radicals refused to be placated. Turning the hatred they once reserved for the British against their former comrades, they began a civil war that became one of the bloodiest episodes in Irish history. In two years, from 1922 to 1923, more Irish killed each other than had died in the previous six-year struggle against Britain. Whereas the British had executed 77 Irish rebels, the new government of Ireland sent five times as many before the firing squads.[19] The Irish settlement was also the beginning of the end for the British Empire, which had been at its height in 1920, when Britain controlled more overseas territory than ever before in its history. The loss of Ireland was a wound that proved mortal.

The Politics of Reconstruction

Working-Class Discontent. The unstable economic conditions that followed the war increased working-class discontent. Leftist activism reinforced Tory fears that a Labour party government would inaugurate an era of sexual profligacy, republicanism, and Bolshevism. But nothing could have been further from the truth. Labour was puritanical, monarchist, and vehemently anti-Communist. It was primarily interested in bread and butter issues. In May 1920, the Labour party, the Independent Labour party, and the trade unions sent a joint delegation to the Soviet Union to find out whether Soviet democracy and British democracy were in any way compatible. They concluded that they were not.

Not all protest was economic. In May 1920, the militant dockers refused to coal the *Jolly Roger* to prevent it from leaving for Poland because they suspected that the British government was sending arms to the Poles for use in the war against the Russians. At the end of the summer, when the cabinet considered direct intervention on the Polish side to save Warsaw from attack, the Labour party organized protest demonstrations and warned the government that any attempt to implement such a policy would immediately be met with a general strike. Lloyd George took no further action, and the recovery of the Polish army at the Vistula, on 14 August, ended the crisis. But Labour had forestalled government action with a direct political challenge.

As a foretaste of future trouble, the coal miners began to campaign for the nationalization of the coal industry. They hoped that this would help protect their jobs, which were being threatened by cutbacks in production due to a resumption of competition from European coal fields. In October, they stopped work for a week. The government enacted the Emergency Powers Act, which restored the state's authority under the wartime Defense of the Realm Act to issue Orders in Council to maintain the nation's fundamental economic and social services.

The miners continued their agitation, demanding that profits be pooled in a national fund, that wages be standardized, and that the state provide extended subsidies. The government rejected the proposals. In April 1921, the miners called on the railway workers and the transport workers to join them in a general strike. The government, fearing civil war, recruited a special defense force that turned Kensington Gardens in central London into a military encampment. The miners downed their tools, but the other unions refused to join them. Most of the labor movement was nonrevolutionary, and its leaders were reluctant to give the government an excuse to carry out a policy of repression. In 1921, the Labour party rebuffed an attempt by the newly formed British Communist party to join its ranks—Lenin had urged the British Communists to support Labour "as a rope supports a man who is hanged"—and refused all association with the Third International.

The resolution of the Irish Question was Lloyd George's last great performance. Tories professed to be shocked at the giveaway, and many younger members of the party wanted to end the coalition because they felt it was frustrating their careers. Lloyd George had no current success to silence his critics. The increased labor agitation and concern about his foreign policy, which had almost provoked a war with Turkey,[20] made the prime minister particularly vulnerable. Moreover, his lavish dispensation of peerages and knighthoods to party favorites had prompted Parliament to establish a special committee of investigation.

At a meeting in the Carlton Club on 19 October 1922, Stanley Baldwin successfully persuaded the assembled Tory members of Parliament that Lloyd George would ruin the unity of the Conservative party in the same way he had smashed the unity of the Liberal party. Deprived of Tory support, Lloyd George resigned. Bonar Law replaced him as prime minister and called for new elections. Campaigning on a slogan of "tranquility and stability" in the November elections, the Conservatives captured 347 seats for a clear majority of 87. Bonar Law did not have long to enjoy the triumph, however; he resigned the following May after finding out he had throat cancer. Stanley Baldwin, the chancellor of the exchequer, took his place. Baldwin remained the leader of the party for the next decade and a half. He was a good party manager, but distrusted clever men.

Baldwin thought that the best way to fight unemployment was through a tariff to protect British industry from foreign competition. However, since Britain had traditionally favored free trade, such a dramatic change in policy required a new mandate from the electorate. Therefore, less than six months after becoming prime minister, he found himself calling for new elections. But in the polling on 6 December 1923, the Conservatives lost the majority they had won the previous year, and in January 1924, the Labour party formed a government for the first time in its history.[21]

The First Labour Government. Many Conservatives cringed at the prospect of a Labour party government, but Baldwin looked upon it as an opportunity to reunify and consolidate his own forces. Since Labour was obviously not going to disappear (during the war union membership had almost doubled, from 4,189,000 in 1913 to 8,081,000 in 1919), when would there be a better chance to have it learn the responsibility of government? That Labour had to count on the votes from the Liberals to stay in office meant that there would be no social experimentation.

The new cabinet, headed by James Ramsay MacDonald, was almost the antithesis of a revolutionary body. Most of the parliamentary leaders had come from the middle and upper-middle classes; only five of the twenty cabinet members were trade unionists. Many of the middle-class intellectuals who provided the party with its brains had joined with the conviction that socialism was applied Christianity. The Labourites strenuously avoided Marxian phraseology and dogma. The Labour party program favored the right to work and the establishment of an extensive program of social security. It advocated a minimum wage law, progressive taxation, and the nationalization of the railroads, the coal mines, electrical power, communications, transport, and the manufacture and sale of alcoholic beverages. The party believed in the peaceful and evolutionary transformation of society, which meant achieving socialism through parliamentary means and paying compensation to the owners of nationalized industries. In the Labourites' view, socialism should reorganize society to benefit the individual.[22]

Prime Minister MacDonald tried to restrain the party radicals while pursuing a policy that would not alienate the Liberals upon whom he relied for support.

During his nine months in office, he was almost constantly on the defensive. The Labour government managed to reduce duties on sugar, tea, coffee, and cocoa and to increase the subsidy to builders of municipal housing for lower-income groups. But its most notable, and controversial, achievement came in foreign affairs.

On 1 February 1924, the British government officially recognized the Soviet Union. MacDonald began negotiations to settle the British claims for confiscated property and to establish normal commercial relations; he hoped to stimulate British industry and reduce unemployment by opening up the great Russian market. The policy produced two agreements: a commercial treaty that granted the Soviet Union most-favored-nation trading privileges and a general treaty that provided for a settlement of outstanding claims. MacDonald tried to tempt the Communists into paying compensation by promising the Soviets a developmental loan. The Conservatives promptly accused the Labour government of selling out British interests. When the Liberals joined in, MacDonald resigned without waiting for a motion of censure. General elections were scheduled at once—the third time in less than two years that the British people had been asked to choose a new Parliament.

On 25 October 1924, less than a week before polling time, the lackadaisical campaign suddenly picked up steam with the appearance of an article in the *Times* entitled "Soviet Plot, Red Propaganda in Britain. Revolution urged by Zinoviev. Foreign Office 'Bombshell.'" According to the report, the head of the Comintern, Gregori Zinoviev, had sent a letter to the British Communist party urging it to support the Russian treaty as a means "to extend and develop the propaganda of ideas of Leninism in England." The letter was a forgery, but enough people believed in its authenticity to sweep the Conservative party back into office.[23] The Tories would have won without the fear of Bolshevism, but Baldwin had a strong mandate to work toward the domestic harmony that he believed so essential for the stability of British society.

The Tory Era

Baldwin Returns to Power. Baldwin was chiefly interested in domestic politics. He especially wanted to preserve Britain's traditional institutions against socialist erosion and believed that the Conservative party was the best instrument for bridging the gap between the classes. Exuding common sense and middle-class moderation, he projected the image of a kindly country gentleman, an unflappable pipe smoker and lover of animals, who would not be carried away by revolutionary theories and harebrained schemes.

But 1924 was not an advantageous time to take power. The postwar boom was dead. Over 10 percent of the British work force was idle. Unemployment in the coal mines and the cotton mills was many times greater than the national average. One problem was that international demand for British exports had declined. The European market was disrupted. France would not buy British coal as long as it could get it from Germany in reparations. Moreover, Britain had sacrificed many of its world investments to pay for the war and now found that the United States and Japan had taken away its customers. Everywhere Britain was faced with high tariffs and import quotas. Another problem was that its industrial plant was obsolete. The loss of markets was particularly acute in the old staple industries of cotton textiles, shipbuilding, and iron and steel. The output of cotton declined after the war by 30 percent. The decline was worse in shipbuilding, an industry plagued by outmoded techniques and by the reluctance of the shipyard owners to convert from coal to diesel propulsion. The iron and steel industry was also grossly inefficient. The multiplicity of small productive units, the lack of integration, and the absence of large-scale capital investment made British products too expensive to compete successfully in the world market.

The British tried to regain their prosperity by returning to the liberal economy of former times. All controls that the government had exercised over the economy during the war had been rapidly abolished, but no planning for the reorganization and reconstruction of industry had followed. The Tories believed a return to free-market capitalism would solve Britain's economic problems. They feared budgetary deficits and inflationary policies and desired a sound monetary system based on gold, but few Conservatives had any conception of the fundamental changes caused by the war.

Compared to the wild inflation of continental European currencies, the British pound had changed very little. Before the war it had a value of $4.86. In 1920, it fell briefly to $3.40, but three years later it had climbed back to $4.70. It generally fluctuated between $4.30 and $4.50. Because the pound was a world currency, any decision affecting its status had international consequences. British leaders realized they had the double responsibility of promoting world economic stability as well as national recovery. On 28 April 1925, Chancellor of the Exchequer Winston Churchill, spurred by the Bank of England's director Montague Norman, announced that the pound would be pegged at its prewar gold standard. Churchill argued that this would help stabilize prices and wages and inspire general confidence in British currency. The policy would also make Britain's trade position more secure and contribute to international monetary cooperation.

However, Britain's most famous economist, John Maynard Keynes, warned that this policy would overvalue the pound by 10 percent, forcing a deflation of domestic prices that would lead to a reduction of salaries and wages. Industry, he argued, would be hurt by credit restrictions and expensive money. Keynes advocated curing unemployment and promoting recovery through a policy of monetary inflation, not one of stability. Keynes's prediction proved true. Exports became too expensive and continued to decline. But the monetary policy was not the only reason for Britain's sluggish recovery.

The country's real problems lay in the inefficiency and obsolescence of its industrial establishment. Without an energetic competitive spirit to push recovery, it was doubtful any policy could have worked. Foreign sales fell, but Britain managed to maintain its balance of payments because of its favorable terms of trade—Britain paid relatively less for its imports and received more for its exports. In addition, the shipping business, the sale of insurance, and commissions from brokerage and banking fees brought in income.

Since the beginning of the Conservative's deflationary policy, every labor union was on the alert for layoffs and wage cuts. The Labour leadership remained calm, but the rank and file were becoming increasingly restive. One month after the return to the gold standard, the mine owners announced that they would abrogate the previous year's contract and pay minimum wages for increased hours. The miners, fearing their real wages would be reduced as much as 48 percent, felt the owners should "sweat out," that is, use the profits they had made during the war, to pay for their bad management after the war. Baldwin favored wage cuts to allow industry to recover, but feared such a position would lead to a strike; therefore he favored a temporary government subsidy to maintain wage levels. The prime minister appointed a Royal Commission of Inquiry.

The General Strike. The commission, under the chairmanship of Sir Herbert Samuel, deliberated nearly five months. In March 1926, it recommended that the efficiency of the mines be improved through merging or abolishing the less profitable operations. It proposed the nationalization of coal royalties and the granting of state subsidies for research and development. It also advocated improving labor relations by establishing various housing and profit-sharing schemes. But in order to allow the new program to start up, the miners would have to accept a temporary wage reduction.

Neither side was pleased. The mine owners approved only the pay cuts; the miners endorsed everything but the pay cuts. The miners believed that the government had put more emphasis on the necessity of their making sacrifices than on the reorganization of the coal industry. By the middle of April, the negotiations were hopelessly deadlocked. The miners, shouting their slogan "not a penny off the pay, not a minute on the day," stopped working on 30 April 1926. When attempts to get them to return to work failed, the government declared a state of emergency on 4 May. The Trade Union Congress (TUC) called on the other key unions to suspend work as well. The response was immediate.

The railway workers, the printers, the dockers, the transporters, the construction workers, and the workers in the chemical, metallurgical, electrical power, and gas industries all walked out. Hardly any trains ran, public transportation stopped, newspapers did not appear. Business activity was seriously curtailed, and the nation was paralyzed. The strike was highly popular among the working-class rank and file. The workers' feelings were intense, but they acted with commendable restraint, even perhaps with accustomed servility. The strike involved millions of men, but there was very little public violence. For many, the strike almost came as a welcome relief from their dull routine. The weather was magnificent. Journalists, who had arrived from abroad to cover the great British revolution, were disappointed to find striking workers playing soccer with the custodians of public order.

The government had anticipated trouble and therefore was in a much better position than the strikers to ride out the ordeal. Already a half year before, the government had started to stockpile coal. It had reactivated the wartime emergency road transport scheme and, under the authority of the Emergency Powers Act of 1920, had forced various organizations to maintain essential supplies and services. As soon as the strike began, army equipment and personnel began supplying towns with food; sailors stoked furnaces to provide electricity; and special constables were in place to help maintain order. Volunteers maintained other vital services. Winston Churchill had the time of his life publishing the government daily, the *British Gazette*. The TUC brought forth its own creation, the *British Worker*.

The government maintained that the workers were challenging the supremacy of Parliament and the sovereignty of the state: the strike was therefore constitutionally illegal. The TUC protested that the strike was only economic and had nothing to do with the constitution. But the Labour leaders were cautious; faced with the superior organizational power of the government, they saw no sense in prolonging a hopeless situation. Therefore, taking advantage of a personal initiative by Sir Herbert Samuel who promised no wage cuts until the miners were assured a program leading to efficiency, the TUC decided to end the General Strike. It had lasted nine days. The announcement came at noon on 12 May. All returned to work except the miners, who did not end their strike until the following December, after suffering terrible deprivations.

London "bobbies" push a stalled food truck during the General Strike in May 1926. The vehicle, its engine disabled by strikers, was destined for London's King's Cross station. It had been marked "food only" to deter such sabotage.

By calling off the General Strike, the TUC no doubt spared the country considerable violence and saved the unions from a wave of repression. The government remained the master of the situation, but the strike was a setback for Baldwin's program of social harmony. The trade unions were divided and bitter, while the property owners wanted revenge. In response, Parliament passed the Trade Disputes and Trade Union Act in 1927, which outlawed general strikes and most sympathetic strikes. The law prohibited organizations of state employees from affiliating with the TUC; restricted the right to picket; and forbade political contributions to the Labour party unless the workers gave written notice of their desire to contribute. The legislation was hardly ever used. The provision against strikes was ignored, but remained on the books as a symbolic affront to the trade unions until a Labour government repealed it in 1946.

In time, the General Strike entered the folklore of the labor movement as a confrontation of capitalists and proletarians—the forces of reaction versus those of progress. But the responses of the union leaders were more down to earth. They realized they had allowed themselves to be drawn into an adventure for which they were hardly prepared. They had used a syndicalist technique of revolution, when the desire to overthrow the state was furthest from their minds. "Never again" was their reaction. The labor movement had not changed its ideals, but in the future, the end would have to be justified by the means, and those means would have to be parliamentary.

FRANCE AND THE STRUGGLE FOR STABILITY

A Fitful Recovery

Obstacles to Change. The French had had their fill of *élan vital* and panache and, like the British, chose colorless and unimaginative leaders after the war. In November 1919, the *Bloc national républicain* won a majority of the seats in the Chamber of Deputies. The bloc was an alliance of conservatives, many with very little previous political experience, who were largely practicing Roman Catholics and army veterans. The Nationalist victory seemed to epitomize a desire to return to the good old days before the war. Over half of the old deputies lost their seats. So many of the Nationalists wore their light-colored army uniforms to the opening session of the new assembly that it became known as the chamber of the blue horizon. The National Bloc spoke mainly for the upper-middle class. It opposed state monopolies, but not private cartels. It denounced the progressive income tax, but not protective tariffs. It was antisocialist, antilabor, antidemocratic, and, of course, anti-Communist. It professed loyalty to existing institutions, but desired a constitutional revision that would give more power to the executive.

Although more than half of the French population lived in cities, the representation in parliament was still largely weighted toward the countryside, and rural legislators were not interested in the problems of the urban working class. They hardly bothered to understand the concerns of their own constituents. Most of these politicians, who professed to speak for the peasants, were landlords or members of the professional classes, not practicing farmers. They expected the tillers of the fields to accept their lowly fate with resignation. Labor unions in the countryside were practically unknown; those in the cities seemed subversive. The National Bloc wanted to prevent any working-class party, no matter how reform minded, from getting power.

In 1919 and 1920, there were 3,858 strikes,[24] the most serious being the railroad strike of May 1920, which touched off a mass protest that involved the miners, dockers, merchant seamen, metal workers, and construction and electrical workers. But the government brought the protest rapidly under control. It arrested the militants and used the army to run the trains and maintain other public services. The authorities harassed the workers and threatened to dissolve the *Confédération générale du travail* (General Confederation of Labor), the main trade union. It made no difference that the workers had serious grievances about their standard of living, which had slipped by 15 percent during the war. Few employers could understand that paying higher wages would stimulate production and ultimately increase profits. The trade unions did not have the organizational clout to force concessions. Union membership had jumped during the war by more than 50 percent, but still only about one-sixth of the industrial proletariat was unionized.[25] After the failure of the 1920 strikes, union membership dropped by 75 percent. The parochial character of French industry with its widely dispersed, small production units and the large influx of foreign labor also helped to undermine the strength of the unions. The foreign workers were willing to work for less than the French workers and threatened to replace them in the event of a labor dispute.[26] Union leaders found it impossible to integrate the foreigners into the structure of their local unions.

Syndicalist leaders were often better at heaping recriminations on each other than on the capitalists. The great controversy over whether to affiliate with the newly formed Communist International further split the working-class movement. At the Congress of Tours in 1920, the Socialist party's revolutionary wing clashed with its constitutional wing. The party's radicals pushed through a resolution—by 3,247 votes to 1,938—to join the Comintern and change the party's name to the Communist party. The moderates, led by Léon Blum, quit the party in protest, abandoning its assets, including the newspaper, *L'Humanité*, to the revolutionaries. Blum's group then reorganized itself under the party's old name *Section française de l'internationale ouvrière* (French Branch of the Working-Class International) and began the process of rebuilding. Socialist deputies still refused to participate in government ministries, a decision that denied them direct influence over legislation. The Communists constantly denounced the Socialists as "Social Fascists" and welcomed increased working-class misery as the best means to hasten the revolution.

The Politics of Inflation. Before 1914, the French franc was one of the world's most stable currencies, but the war dramatically increased government expenditures while boosting the amount of money in circulation; in 1919, when the French abandoned currency controls, the value of the franc immediately plunged. In March 1919, it stood at 5.5 to the dollar, but during the following year, it slipped in value by an additional two-thirds. The government precipitated the decline by printing 18 billion francs worth of new bank notes, independent of any corresponding increase in goods and services.

The resultant inflation was disastrous for those on fixed incomes. Prices rose faster than wages. In the cities, the cost of living was three and a half times its 1914 level. The inflation was caused by a blend of cowardice, ignorance, and design. The French government prepared its budgets using a multiple system of bookkeeping. It maintained an ordinary budget for current expenses, which were paid from taxes and revenues. With 19 billion francs in receipts and 13 billion in expenses, this budget had a comfortable surplus. A second budget for reconstruction costs and war pensions had a deficit of 29 billion, however, making the combined total a negative 23 billion. This was not cause for alarm, however, because everybody expected German reparations payments to cover the discrepancy. After all, most deputies, whatever their disagreement over tactics, were committed to making Germany pay full reparations. The French government could have obtained the income necessary to meet its obligations through taxation; but raising taxes would require new legislation, which could then be blamed on specific politicians. Furthermore, taxation was unpopular because it took money away from people before they had a chance to spend it, whereas inflation increased the state's share of the national product more anonymously—no individuals could be blamed—and less dramatically. Since the government had the power to create money, it could always obtain the goods and services it needed. Inflation allowed private spending to continue, although people got less for what they spent. The process could always be explained as a phenomenon of nature, as inevitable as death and, well, taxes.

A general rise in prices was not just the consequence of inflation; it was the essence of the government's policy. To finance reconstruction, the French government had to compete with the private sector for goods and services that would otherwise be used for other purposes. Therefore, to ensure that sufficient resources would be directed to repairing war damages, the government intentionally drove up prices by increasing the amount of money in circulation. Since the state could print new money faster than the private sector could earn it, the government priorities always prevailed. During the interwar period, the amount of currency in circulation always increased faster than industrial growth, particularly after 1924, when borrowing had reached its limit.

The French government added to its income by having financial institutions create additional supplies of "bank money" specifically for reconstruction. The government relied heavily on advances from the Bank of France and created a special joint stock company, the *Crédit national,* which the public treasury capitalized with appropriations from taxes and from government securities. For example, the treasury still issued short-term treasury bonds, which in the form of National Defense Bonds had been a principal way of raising revenue during the war. The National Credit was used to idemnify the war losses of private citizens. The government also encouraged a series of other credit establishments; the Agricultural Credit Fund, the Maritime Credit Bank, the Credit for Artisans, the National Bank for Foreign Trade, and the *banques populaires*, which dealt with small businesses. Thus, although the National Bloc was theoretically opposed to statism, government participation in the economic life of the nation gradually increased. Immediately after the war, there had been a reaction against wartime economic controls, but soon political and economic circumstances and pressure from special interests brought a drift back to government regulation.

Reconstruction and payment of war pensions were only part of the problem; another drain on the country's resources was the military establishment. France had the largest standing army in Europe and participated in a variety of military adventures—intervention in Russia, pacification of Syria, participation in the Russo-Polish war, operations against the Berber tribesmen in Morocco, and, of course, enforcement of the Treaty of Versailles in Germany. The National Bloc had further weakened the franc by adding some 150 billion francs to the public debt. By sending troops into the Ruhr in 1923 to collect reparations, it deprived the public treasury of payments worth about 1.5 billion gold marks, a shortfall the government tried to make up through borrowing. In January 1924, however, the National Credit failed, shocking the National Bloc and indicating that its days in office were numbered.

The Pendulum Swings Back

The Cartel of the Left. By 1924, French production had regained its prewar level, and over the next five years, it grew steadily. The general industrial index climbed by 60 percent. Iron ore and steel production both doubled, and the chemical, electric, rayon, aluminum, and automobile industries made similar gains. In 1913, there were 90,000 private cars in France; in 1930, there were over a million. In only five years, the coal mines of the north and the Pas de Calais returned to their prewar production levels. By 1924, two-thirds of the buildings destroyed by the war had been rebuilt, and almost all the roads were repaired. A year later agriculture was back to normal. The recovery of the large enterprises was aided by inflation—they received higher prices for their goods and reduced their labor costs by paying their workers in inflated currency.

A leftist coalition, the *Cartel des gauches*, won the elections of May 1924. The main strength of the group came from the Radical and Socialist parties. The Radicals had become more conservative since their earlier days, but they still believed, at least officially, in state control of private monopolies, public exploitation of natural resources, and a welfare program that called for public housing, improved working conditions, and the institution of social insurance. The leader of the Radicals, Edouard Herriot, longtime mayor of Lyons, belonged to that generation of politicians who believed problems could be solved by making eloquent speeches. Herriot worked to improve relations with Great Britain and achieve reconciliation with Germany. He opposed using military force to exact payment of reparations. But like many of his colleagues, he little understood economic and financial affairs and was unable to do much about inflation.

The Cartel of the Left was too committed to the practices of the past to welcome reform. Direct taxes remained low and were levied mostly on the appearance of wealth. The *quatres vieilles* (the four oldies), which dated from the time of the

Directory, were still in effect: a tax on land; a tax on the rentable value of property, even if it was not rented; a tax on commerce and the professions; and a tax on *portes et fenêtres* (doors and windows), an imposition that explains why older French dwellings often had small apertures. In 1912, a tax on securities was added, and during the war, a tax on income was imposed, with the highest rate set at two percent. Since these direct taxes produced only limited revenues, much of the state income came from a whole series of indirect taxes on food and staple goods, which put a greater burden on the poorer classes and, of course, kept the government short of funds. The Socialists favored a massive reorganization of the tax structure and a capital levy on the great fortunes, but they lacked the votes to get it passed. Nevertheless, the wealthy, who feared for their fortunes, usually maintained extensive investments abroad. Switzerland came into its own as a place to stash wealth. Without exchange controls to protect the currency, governments had to rely on the confidence and good faith of the wealthy—a reliance that usually proved futile.

The Cartel of the Left tried unsuccessfully to continue the borrowing policy of the past. Public confidence in short-term treasury bonds was so badly shaken that demands for reimbursement exceeded new subscriptions. During the Cartel's two years in power (May 1924–July 1926), it changed finance ministers seven times. At the same time, the amount of money in circulation rose by 12 billion francs (about 35 percent), and drafts from the Bank of France increased from 21 billion to 37.5 billion francs. The government proposed a series of new taxes—a turnover tax, a 14 percent tax on capital holdings and real estate, a retroactive hike in the income tax, an increase in the tax on tobacco, and a tax on financial transactions. These failed to pass the National Assembly. The Cartel then tried to persuade the United States to link the payment of war debts with reparations. The Americans refused. Next the Cartel asked for special powers that would enable it to balance the budget and stabilize the franc by decree. The assembly refused. The budget crisis grew so bad that the Cartel proposed selling part of the public domain to the highest bidder. As the franc lost two-thirds of its value (from 18 to 50 to the dollar), all confidence in the Cartel evaporated.

The Poincaré Miracle. On 22 July 1926, Raymond Poincaré responded to President Gaston Doumergue's summons to form a National Union government to save the franc. The new premier quickly obtained emergency powers from the assembly to enact a broad program of financial reform. Poincaré was the unanimous choice of those who feared that the Cartel of the Left pandered too much to the working class. The conservatives hoped for a return to the good old days when workers and peasants knew their place.

Poincaré lived up to expectations. He made no attempts to carry out social reform. He increased indirect taxes, rather than property taxes, and made minor economies in government by reducing the number of subprefectures and district courts. He curtailed the issuance of short-term treasury bonds, established a special fund to redeem the public debt, and raised the interest rate to 7.5 percent to lure back capital that had found refuge abroad. He officially devalued the franc by 80 percent from its 1914 level to correspond with the free-market price; then he returned France to the gold standard. The reforms were hardly radical, but they had a marked psychological impact. Poincaré's seriousness of purpose—his law and order image—was almost sufficient by itself to reestablish confidence in the government.

Financial stability returned, but the French never regained the faith they once had in their money. No amount of financial reform could restore the human and material resources lost in the war. Debts remained and still had to be paid. The Poincaré devaluation reduced the public debt by four-fifths and created a windfall for big borrowers, who could liquidate their obligations with cheap money. Hardest hit were the lower classes, especially those who had laboriously saved money for their retirement and now faced an old age of penury and semistarvation. The solid currency that they had entrusted to banks and invested in bonds and insurance annuities had lost most of its value. Saving was no longer a virtue; only those in debt seemed to benefit. Money was best spent as fast as it was made. Speculators took advantage of the situation to make fortunes. Small business owners demanded special tax benefits and protection from competition. The bourgeoisie, obsessed with finding a hedge against the rise in the cost of living, tried to maintain its position through subsidies, immunities, grants, and favors. Industries defended themselves by negotiating marketing agreements and forming pressure groups.

The inheritance records of 1933 showed that France was still a country of great fortunes. Less than half a percent of the people inherited 29 percent of the reported wealth, and 13.4 percent received 47.8 percent while the remaining 86.2 percent got the rest. People of modest circumstances did not export their money or invest in property, art, or stocks as a hedge against inflation. They hoarded gold, primarily coins, giving France the largest private gold reserves in Europe.

Yet, in spite of its economic backwardness, France had seemingly survived the convulsions that shook other less fortunate societies. As a people, the French seemed to have discovered the art of living at peace with themselves. Nevertheless, the apparent social harmony was an illusion that covered up an intense bitterness and class hatred that would in time lead to the collapse of the Third Republic.

POSTSCRIPT   Although Italy lacked a democratic tradition and had severe handicaps—mass illiteracy and economic instability—the end of parliamentary government was more a case of suicide than death by natural causes. Badly shaken by the insurmountable problems stemming from the war, Italian democracy succumbed because Liberal politicians, the monarchy, the industrialists, and the Catholic church all helped Mussolini consolidate his power when alternatives were still possible. These groups believed Mussolini would help them preserve their privileges against the lower-middle and working classes who wanted a greater role in running the affairs of state. Ironically, the lower classes also saw in the Duce the means to gain influence; Fascism with its mass theatrics provided them with a significance long denied them by a government indifferent to their needs. The Fascists were able to bridge the gap between right and left, urban and rural, upper classes and proletarians. Such a political transformation had never been achieved before.

Mussolini's regime had no vast concentration camps or slave labor camps. It harassed its enemies, beat them up, imprisoned them, took away their jobs, and exiled them to mountain villages or islands, but it did not routinely exterminate them. The Italian dictatorship was venal and insincere, rather than serious and fanatic. The people even retained a certain sense of humor: *Question:* How can you test the strength of a new bridge? *Answer:* Fill a truck with Fascist officials. If the bridge stands, it is a good bridge; if it collapses, it is a better bridge. Still, Fascism was hardly a laughing matter and it cost Italy dearly.

Despite certain social benefits—accident and old-age insurance, maternity subsidies, recreational opportunities, and tuberculosis clinics—the well-being of the working class actually declined. The Fascists scrapped the eight-hour day, abandoned minimum wages, and allowed child labor to increase. Real wages gradually fell until they were substantially lower than they had been prior to the war. In rural areas, agricultural workers worked longer for less pay. Superficial land reform was implemented. According to the Fascist census of 1930, less than 1 percent of the farm population owned 42 percent of the land while 87 percent held only 13 percent. As many as 300,000 to 400,000 Italians still lived in earth and stick hovels or in caves, and many more crowded into slum tenements, where they sometimes lived ten to a room. The regime was vulgar and brutal and an economic and political disaster. But for most of its life it had, tragically, the support of a majority of Italians.

In no other major European country did a belief in the democratic system remain as strong as in Britain. But the Conservatives, who ran the government for most of the 1920s, did little to solve the basic problems out of which the General Strike developed. Baldwin had no viable program to restore health to Britain's sick industries or to handle the corollary problem of unemployment. What energy the Tory government displayed was, in the main, produced by its minister of health, Neville Chamberlain, who between 1925 and 1929 managed to obtain an increase in pensions for widows, orphans, and the aged; reorganize poor relief; ease the burden of the local authorities with direct government subsidies; spend public monies for the construction of new housing; and extend unemployment benefits.

Baldwin's lack of leadership was much criticized, but many people became accustomed to his lethargy and lack of imagination. To his credit, Baldwin managed to prevent the diehards in his party from further humiliating the working class in the aftermath of the General Strike. His attitude that in the end everything would come up right helped heal society's wounds. The British, however, never managed to recover from World War I and create the sound economy upon which the survival of their world leadership depended.

Economic disorder was a permanent feature of French postwar society; it shook the stability of the French middle class and undermined established traditions. It broke down the extended family, killed the marriage dowry, and loosened respect for constitutionalism. However, democratic institutions were sufficiently strong to deny widespread support to those who advocated destroying the republic. The strong parliamentary system prevented the establishment of a dictatorship, but also discouraged the exercise of positive leadership. It was commonly assumed that any system that had survived the test of the Great War was fundamentally sound and needed no changes. Indeed, many French longed to return to society as it had been before the war. Yet everything around them attested to this period's extinction.

The evidence was in the obituaries. Dead were the great politicians and generals: Theophile Delcassé, the Entente Cordial's creator; René Viviani, the first leader of the Great War and the head of the Sacred Union government; and Georges Clemenceau, the last war leader. Viviani died in 1925, the Tiger's turn came four years later. He was eighty-eight. Gone also were those who had commanded the nation's armies: Manoury of the Marne, Mangan of Verdun, Nivelle of the Chemin des Dames, Sarrail of Salonika, and Generalissimo Foch himself, who died the same year as his great adversary, Clemenceau. Also dead was Empress Eugénie, the widow of Napoleon III; she died in England at the age of ninety-four, having lived in exile for half a century. The French government officially boycotted her funeral, which was held in England and attended by King George and Queen Mary. Not so famous, but every bit as compelling and influential was Professor Émile Coué. He died in 1926. Coué preached the curative power of autosuggestion. His clinic in Nancy became a pilgrimage center for people throughout the world. The master's formula was simple: repeat constantly, "Every day in every way, I'm getting better and better." It was not strong enough to guarantee immortality. Coué was sixty-nine when he stopped worrying about thinking positively. He departed the year French recovery from the war seemed assured. It was as good a time as any to die.

ENDNOTES

1. Carlo Sforza, *Contemporary Italy* (New York: E. P. Dutton, 1944), 29.
2. Luigi Sturzo, *Italy and Fascism* (London: Faber and Gwyer, 1926), 97.
3. The monarch, who was vacationing at the time near Pisa, was terrified that if the Fascists brought off their coup, they would give his throne to his cousin, the duke of Aosta, a devotee of Mussolini. Since Italy was a constitutional monarchy, the king's approval should have been pro forma.
4. In 1923, when Mussolini returned to Geneva as head of the Italian government to attend an international conference, he recalled the experience to the local chief of police. Mussolini even remembered the precise bridge under which the arrest was made. The policeman, without changing his expression, replied, "That's life, *Monsieur le président.*"
5. The speech is reprinted in Frances Keen, ed., *Neither Liberty Nor Bread* (New York: Harper, 1940), 45–57.
6. Harry Fornari, *Mussolini's Gadfly: Roberto Farniacci* (Nashville: Vanderbilt University Press, 1971), 81.

7.   *Survey of International Affairs, 1929* (London: Oxford University Press), 442–43.

8.   Matteotti's death had been accomplished by members of a special enforcement squad within the Fascist party, led by the party's administrative secretary, Giovanni Marinelli, but there is no doubt that it was carried out with Mussolini's approval.

9.   The intensity of Mussolini's campaign was in part prompted by the necessity to head off a revolt by party hard-liners, many of them provincial squadristi who feared that if Mussolini became a moderate, he would throw them to the dogs.

10. Mussolini had pulled the teeth of the radicals within his own party, especially the unruly local party bosses and their violent squadristi, by the simple expedient of bureaucratizing the party formations and giving the activists government jobs. Thus, potential troublemakers were socialized within the state administration.

11. In an article that appeared over his name in the *Enciclopedia italiana di scienze, lettere ed arti*, vol. 14 (1932). The essay was actually written by Giovanni Gentile, the encyclopedia's general editor. An English translation is available in "The Political and Social Doctrine of Fascism," *International Conciliation*, no. 306 (New York: Carnegie Foundation, 1935), 5–17.

12. Later, under the influence of Hitler, anti-Semitic legislation was introduced.

13. *Enciclopedia italiana*, vol. 14: 849.

14. Richard Webster, *The Cross and the Fasces* (Stanford: Stanford University Press, 1960), 83.

15. The treaty is printed in *Documents on International Affairs 1929* (London: Oxford University Press, 1930), 216–41.

16. Lloyd George determined this on the basis of a vote held in Parliament the previous May. Asquith had introduced a motion calling for the establishment of a select committee to investigate the circumstances surrounding Lloyd George's recent firing of the chief of military operations, General Maurice. The prime minister viewed the matter as a vote of confidence and vowed to ruin all who voted for the motion.

17. George Bernard Shaw claimed, "The shot Irishmen will now take their places beside Emmet and the Manchester martyrs in Ireland, and beside the heroes of Poland and Serbia and Belgium in Europe; and nothing in Heaven or Earth can prevent it." *Daily News*, 20 May 1916, quoted in Dorothy Macardle, *The Irish Republic* (Dublin: Irish Press, 1951), 187.

18. Under this arrangement, the likelihood of unification was remote. The strongly Protestant and Unionist Ulster would resist, by force if necessary, any attempt at incorporation with the rest of the country.

19. In the following years, the Irish moved toward the complete separation from Britain for which the Republican extremists had fought. De Valera became prime minister in 1932 and proceeded to legislate the independence he had not achieved through force of arms ten years earlier. The 1937 constitution made no mention of the British Commonwealth. The Irish Free State became Eire; a presidency replaced the post of governor-general. During World War II, de Valera, holding good to an earlier threat that he would never support Britain while Ireland remained divided, proclaimed Irish neutrality. In 1949, Eire became the Republic of Ireland.

20. See the Chanak crisis in Chapter 6.

21. With 257 seats the Conservatives still had the largest number of representatives. The Liberals elected 158, an increase of 41 from their 1922 totals. But the greatest gain was shown by Labour, which added 50 seats to its previous parliamentary delegation of 142. The Conservatives did not have sufficient strength to govern on their own and had no desire to form another coalition with the Liberals. Labour therefore took office with the conditional support, but not the participation, of the Liberals.

22. The 1918 party manifesto pledged: "To secure for the producers by hand and by brain the full fruits of their industry, and the most equitable distribution thereof that may be possible, upon the basis of the common ownership of the means of production and the best obtainable system of popular administration and con-

trol of each industry and service." *Report of the 17th Annual Conference of the Labour Party* (London: British Labour Party, 1918), 140.

23. The Tories received 415 seats in the Commons—a majority of 211 seats. Labour was reduced to 152 seats, and the Liberals to only 42. Many people who might have voted Liberal were frightened into playing it safe by voting for the Conservatives.

24. Brian R. Mitchell, *European Historical Statistics, 1750–1970* (New York: Columbia University Press, 1975), 174.

25. Union membership was 941,000 in 1913, and 1,473,000 in 1919.

26. By 1931, immigrants made up about 7 percent of the entire French work force. The percentages were actually higher in the service industries, in agriculture, and in mining where, by 1927, foreign labor accounted for 42 percent of all the jobs. Most of the immigrants came from Italy (30 percent) and Poland (19 percent), the rest chiefly from the Balkans, Algeria, and Spain.

CHAPTER 6

THE SHATTERED EQUILIBRIUM, 1919–1929

PREFACE   The interests of the Great Powers were too divergent to allow the continuation of the wartime alliance after the common enemy had been defeated. The American Senate felt no obligation to ratify the Treaty of Versailles as it was presented by President Wilson. Most of the senators, no matter what party, were in favor of ratification, but not as the treaty stood. Many were concerned, often unreasonably, that acceptance of Article 10 of the League Covenant would endanger the national sovereignty of the United States. The special Treaty of Guarantee, which had made it easier for the French to compromise over the Rhineland, was not even reported out of committee.

The British government had little desire to compensate for the omissions of the American legislature, and it used the Senate's refusal to guarantee French security as an excuse not to live up to its part of the bargain. The British did not really appreciate the fear their ally had of a resurgent Germany, especially France's determination to protect its eastern frontier against another attack. The Germans had not blown up British bridges, wiped out their villages, poisoned their wells, cut down their trees, or flooded their mines. The British could afford to demobilize their army because a nonexistent German war fleet could not threaten the security of the island kingdom. But what the British referred to pejoratively as "the French hegemony of Europe" was hardly a return to a Bonapartist past. French policy was essentially defensive. It sought no acquisition of territory, but merely wanted to preserve the peace settlement as written.

The French found it inconceivable that any nation would be a party to an agreement without intending to enforce it. Yet among the Great Powers, they seemed alone in this belief. Still worse, in France's view, was the failure to partition Germany. The French had also failed to obtain a treaty of guarantee. They had failed to convert the League of Nations into a league of victors. They were assured that security was collective, but that was no security. France might have been the most glorious of victors, but the final triumph owed more to American intervention, for which France was not responsible, than to Gallic strength of arms. Their victory was Pyrrhic and the recuperative power of Germany was vast.

For centuries the English had viewed France, not Germany, as the traditional enemy. The war had spared British farmlands and cities, and there seemed little profit in nursing hatred now that the threat of Junker militarism had ended. Rather than viewing German recovery as a threat, the British welcomed it as the means by which they could regain their chief continental market and reduce unemployment. German industriousness was much admired. Lloyd George was sensitive to how the passage of time affected the policies of nations: "The impression, the deep impression, made upon the human heart by four years of unexampled slaughter will disappear with the hearts upon which it has been marked by the terrible sword of the great war. The maintenance of peace will then depend upon there being no causes of exasperation constantly stirring up the spirit of patriotism, of justice or of fair play."[1] The British took the Treaty of Versailles as a point of departure for accommodation and change. They criticized it from the moment it was published, with the attacks coming from a broad cross section of the public without regard to party affiliation, social class, or occupation. The treaty was blamed for everything that was wrong with European politics. Many people singled out Woodrow Wilson for particular scorn. Harold Nicolson, a member of the Foreign Office delegation, wrote, "We came to Paris confident that the new order was about to be established; we left it convinced that the new order had merely fouled the old. We arrived as fervent apprentices in the school of President Wilson: we left as renegades."[2] Others had no illusions to destroy.

The most influential and devastating denunciation was John Maynard Keynes's *The Economic Consequences of the Peace*, which appeared at the end of 1919. This work, which sold an initial 140,000 copies and was eventually translated into eleven languages, provided the ammunition for much subsequent criticism. To Keynes, the treaty was a massive economic blunder; he devoted over one-third of the book to reparations:

> The policy of reducing Germany to servitude for a generation, of degrading the lives of millions of human beings, and of depriving a whole nation of happiness should be abhorrent and detestable. . . . Some preach it in the name of Justice. In the great events of man's history, in the unwinding of the complex fates of nations Justice is not so simple. And if it were, nations are not authorized, by religion or by national morals, to visit on the children of their enemies the misdoings of parents or of rulers.[3]

Criticism of the Treaty of Versailles went further in Britain than in any other Allied country. It both encouraged the Germans in their revisionism and heightened the insecurity of the French, especially in light of their increasingly strained relations with the British. Britain seemed to be the only country that sought to re-create a real balance of power, but even its aspirations were justifiably suspect. With all the other countries, however, there could be no doubt of their intentions. The French wanted to maintain the position of power they held at the end of the war; the Soviets sought to destroy all established societies; the Italians wanted more territory and influence than they had achieved at Paris; and the Germans prepared for the reassertion of national power.

MAINTAINING A STATUS QUO

The Versailles Settlement under Attack

The Victors Disagree. The British and French began squabbling over enforcement even before the Versailles treaty was signed. The French wanted to arrest important German war leaders and hold a series of war crimes trials. They presented a list of 334 names, including those of Hindenburg and Ludendorff. The British list was shorter and restricted to those guilty of specific atrocities; Lloyd George was utterly opposed to demanding the arrest of men whom the Germans considered national heroes. He feared that no German government could possibly comply and that insistence would only jeopardize the entire treaty. But the French were adamant. To break the deadlock, Lloyd George leaked the disagreement to the press. Premier Alexandre Millerand was furious, not only because he was violently opposed to any policy of leniency toward Germany—believing that would only encourage Germany to avoid complying with the entire treaty—but also because he wanted to maintain the fiction of a common Allied front. He therefore was forced to let Lloyd George have his way, giving the prime minister his first victory for conciliation. No war crimes trials were held. But Anglo-French disagreements could not be papered over indefinitely.

The French were particularly worried about Germany's procrastination in fulfilling the treaty's disarmament provisions; their concern was exacerbated by the tremendous growth of the Freikorps, the German paramilitary units, whose numbers were impossible to measure. Only the sudden collapse of the Kapp Putsch prevented France from sending troops into Germany early in March 1920. But no sooner had the Weimar government survived one armed threat than it was faced with another: on 19 March 1920, a "Red Army" of Spartacists staged an uprising in the Ruhr to seize the coal and steel industry. Since the Ruhr was within the demilitarized zone outlined in the Versailles treaty, the German government appealed to the Allied powers for permission to dispatch units of the Reichswehr to suppress the revolt.[4] The British, eager to see the Communist threat stamped out, willingly agreed. But the French were more hesitant, believing the affair was a ploy to further weaken the Versailles treaty. The French viewed all German officials in the occupied zones as Prussian propagandists who were purposely there to spread discord. Marshal Foch recommended that if the Ruhr situation were so serious that an army was required, the Allied governments themselves should send in troops to restore order. The British refused, believing that the French wanted to use this opportunity to further humiliate Germany and possibly sever the Rhineland from its authority.

While the Allies debated the matter, the situation in the Ruhr became increasingly critical. The undisciplined Red Army began to terrorize the civilian population. The Spartacists let the supplies of coal dwindle, confiscated private property, and looted banks. On 3 April 1920, the German government finally sent the Reichswehr into the Ruhr to restore peace. The French retaliated by occupying Frankfurt, Darmstadt, Hanau, Bad Homburg, and Dieburg, charging Germany with treaty violation. British Foreign Secretary George Curzon denounced the French action as incompatible with the mutual understanding and common action upon which the stability of the alliance and the security of Europe both depended. The French offered no apologies, but did offer to consult with the British in the future before taking action. However, the damage had been done.

The British tendency to go easy on Germany continued to reflect their deep concern about the Bolshevik threat that had colored the negotiations at Paris. The French, while not discounting the potential for Communist aggression, did not feel the danger took precedence over their tough policy toward Germany. They always believed that the Germans took advantage of the Red menace to revise the peace treaties and had little respect for the British for not seeing through this deceit.

The French Seek Allies. France had the largest standing army in Europe, but was still hungry for allies. It had to begin building a security system from scratch. Effective alliances were best formed with other great powers. However, with the United States withdrawn into isolation, Russia racked by civil war and revolution, Italy plagued by domestic unrest, and Great Britain committed to making changes in the peace settlement, France had no choice but to seek alliances among the smaller states.

On 7 September 1920, France concluded a military alliance with Belgium—the signatories promised a common response to any German mobilization and pledged to coordinate the defense of their eastern frontiers. This meant that France could use Belgium as a battleground to meet a German attack or as a staging area for an offensive into the lower Rhineland, thereby fighting a war on another nation's soil. In Belgium the pact touched off a debate between those who believed that such an alliance was necessary for the nation's security and those who feared that it would provoke the very attack it was intended to prevent. The disagreement was frequently ethnic: the Flemish were against the treaty, the Walloons in favor. This unsettled question of national security made the French connection the more tenuous.

The following year, in February 1921, the French concluded an alliance with Poland. This arrangement, however, could hardly compensate for the loss of Russia as an ally, though Poland did oppose revision of the Treaty of Versailles, and both countries agreed on containing Communist Russia. France had already routinely supported Polish interests at the Paris Peace Conference and, in 1920, had provided the new state with military advice and assistance, enabling it to push the Red Army back into White Russia.

The treaty maintained this cooperation, providing for political, economic, and military cooperation and for continued diplomatic support. It specified that the partners would take joint action in the event "either or both" should be attacked. An accompanying secret military convention explained that this meant mutual

Map 6

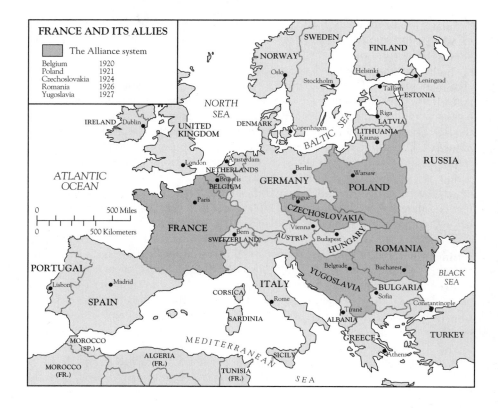

FRANCE AND ITS ALLIES

The Alliance system

Belgium	1920
Poland	1921
Czechoslovakia	1924
Romania	1926
Yugoslavia	1927

aid in the case of German aggression. However, in the event of a war with the Soviet Union, France only promised to keep the Germans in check and help Poland maintain open lines of communication. In short, the French had not promised to protect Poland's eastern boundaries, nor had they even committed themselves to send any soldiers to fight on Polish soil. The Poles agreed to build a peacetime army with thirty infantry divisions organized on the model of the French army. Although many French statesmen viewed the alliance as essential for French security, others feared that Poland was too exposed and too distant geographically to be much of an asset. Marshal Foch contemptuously dismissed the Polish army leaders as amateurs, although this did not prevent him from accepting the black steel mace of a Polish field marshal.

The French also pressed their search for allies among the states of the defunct Austro-Hungarian Empire, where two possibilities were apparent: The French could either promote some sort of federal union of states with Hungary as the pivotal power (perhaps with a Habsburg restoration), or they could form an alliance with the three newly created and enlarged states of Czechoslovakia, Romania, and Yugoslavia. Both policies had advocates, and for a while, the French pursued both simultaneously. In the spring of 1920, the Quai d'Orsay, the French Foreign Office, suggested to Hungary that it might obtain a realignment of the Trianon frontiers if it were to grant special concessions to French banking and business interests. Rumors of this initiative prompted Czechoslovakia and Yugoslavia, who were already alarmed about Hungarian revisionism, to begin negotiating an alliance with each other; on 14 August 1920, they pledged to maintain the integrity of the Trianon treaty and to come to each other's aid in the event of an "unprovoked attack on the part of Hungary." The following April, Czechoslovakia signed a similar agreement with Romania, and in June 1921, Romania signed one with Yugoslavia. The Romanian-Yugoslav treaty of June 1921 also included a provision against Bulgarian revision of the Treaty of Neuilly.

The first test for the Czech-Romanian-Yugoslav alliance, known as the Little Entente, came in October 1921 with the second attempt of the Habsburg pretender, Karl I, to regain the Crown of St. Stephen. The Entente considered the ex-king's presence in Hungary a casus belli and mobilized their armies. The Hungarian government immediately forced the pretender to leave and agreed to respect the territorial and military clauses of the Treaty of the Trianon. France had not actively promoted the formation of the Little Entente, but its display of unity prompted France to seek its members as allies—a diplomatic process that continued for most of the remaining years of the decade.

Reparations

Getting Germany to Pay. Whether the payments were called reparations, indemnities, or spoils, the right to extract payment from Germany was conditioned by the determination and strength of the victors and the resources and willingness of the vanquished. Contrary to the desire of the United States, the Paris Peace Conference did not set any definitive figure. The United States was the only country to make any attempt to survey the damage systematically. Both Britain and France felt these matters were potentially too divisive to be discussed at Paris and preferred to have the Reparations Commission handle the question. The Germans had already recognized their obligation to pay compensation for direct material loss, and they requested that the total amount be set before the treaty was signed. They strongly protested being held accountable for pensions and separation allowances.

Meanwhile, until the Reparations Commission made its report, the Allies demanded that the Germans hand over $5 billion in gold (or an equivalent), pay the costs of occupation, and accord most-favored-nation treatment to the Allies for five years without reciprocity. The Germans were reluctant to comply and made only token payments in kind: ships, dye stuffs, coal, and livestock. It was not long before the Supreme Council charged them with default and demanded an explanation.

At the conference at Spa in July 1920, the Germans did not prove overly cooperative. They wanted to postpone the reduction of their army. And they showed scant willingness to meet the French demand for increased coal deliveries, claiming that they had more than met the initial $5 billion amount. Unable to coax payment by negotiations, the Allies threatened military sanctions and forced Germany to sign two protocols: one for the reduction of the Reichswehr, the other for the monthly delivery of coal.

But German intransigence continued. In 1921, when they failed to accept the Allied schedule of reparations payments, the military occupation was extended (on March 8) to Düsseldorf, Ruhrort, and Duisburg. A special tax was imposed on German exports into Allied countries, and a customs barrier sealed off the occupied area of the Rhineland from the rest of Germany. Germany protested to the League of Nations, but the Reparations Commission held Germany in default by $3 billion. The commission allocated most of the reparations Germany had paid to occupation costs, leaving its indebtedness virtually unchanged.

In April 1921, the Reparations Commission established Germany's total obligation at 132 billion gold marks ($33 billion). As was subsequently decided, this would be payable in fixed yearly amounts of two billion marks and a variable annual amount equal to 26 percent of the value of German exports. Germany was required to pledge the revenues from its customs duties, its special tax funds, and a 25 percent levy on exports as security. When the commission concluded that Germany had paid its total debt, reparations would finally end. The arrangement resembled Hercules' match with the turtle: no matter how hard Germany ran, it could never win.

Lloyd George realized that the French leaders were under tremendous pressure to make Germany pay, but he feared that the use of military force would be self-defeating, costing more than the amount of reparations received. The French disagreed. Since their goals were essentially political, they did not view treaty enforcement as an exercise in cost-benefit analysis. This immediately put them at odds with the British who were anxious "to get on with business" and blamed the increase in their unemployment on the French desire for strict enforcement of the treaty.

Lloyd George told Premier Briand, "France must satisfy Great Britain in regard to the purpose in view, and that there was no intention to exercise force in order to bully or trample on Germany or to kick it when it was down. Force must only be used for some purpose which British public opinion would regard as reasonable, just and practicable, and which would commend itself to reasonable men as fair and practicable without offending a great people or keeping it in servitude for forty or fifty years."[5]

On 10 May 1921, the Germans formed a government that accepted the Allied demands and met the first payment with a loan from abroad. However, the necessity of buying foreign currency steadily weakened the exchange value of the mark, and the absence of a proper fiscal policy prevented the German government from accumulating budgetary surpluses with which to make additional payments.

Means of Enforcement. Lloyd George preferred to handle treaty enforcement and German violations through ad hoc conferences, which would give him an opportunity to achieve German rehabilitation within the context of overall European reconstruction. As the only one of the Big Three still in office, he felt a special responsibility for winning the peace. Before his resignation in October 1922, the Allies held twenty-two international conferences. He attended most of them. But he felt that American absence made his efforts at conciliation more difficult. He had expected the United States to be a moderating influence on France. Indeed, the whole settlement had been drafted with the assumption that the Americans would be active partners in helping carry it out. Lloyd George had particularly counted on their cooperation on questions concerning reparations. European reconstruction suffered a serious blow when the most industrially advanced state in the world failed to assume responsibilities commensurate with its power.

In December 1921, when Germany asked for a moratorium on its payment of reparations, the British prime minister suggested that the question be presented at a forthcoming conference on European reconstruction and security scheduled to be held at Cannes on the French Riviera during the second week of January 1922. Lloyd George hoped this meeting would produce substantial results for his policy of conciliation. To obtain French cooperation, he was prepared to guarantee unconditionally that Britain would come to their aid in the event of an unprovoked attack by Germany.

However, the British offer gave France little it did not already have. In fact, it may even have amounted to something less because such assistance would undoubtedly have been forthcoming without a treaty. In any case, the French believed that Britain was not willing to fight to preserve the demilitarization of the Rhineland once the foreign troops were withdrawn. Premier Briand insisted on a specific commitment with a technical convention for direct military cooperation. Even this was not good enough for the French ultranationalists who feared that any agreement with Great Britain could jeopardize the policy of integral treaty enforcement.

The suspicion that Briand was playing Lloyd George's game of appeasement led President Millerand to summon the premier to Paris. Rather than weather the storm, Briand chose to resign. His place was taken by Raymond Poincaré, a tactical hard-liner who was not opposed to using reparations as a device to keep Germany weak. Faced by such intransigence, the Cannes Conference ended in failure.

The End of the Entente

Poincaré's Dilemma. Despite Poincaré's obstructionism, Lloyd George forged ahead with plans for European reconstruction. Several months later, the largest international gathering since the war took place at Genoa, Italy, from 10 April to 19 May 1922.[6] Poincaré refused to attend and warned that he would withdraw the French representatives if any concessions were made to Germany. While the conference was in session, he made a speech in his hometown of Bar-le-Duc in which he threatened to invade the Ruhr should Germany fail to meet its next reparations installment.[7] Thus, the conference was already under a cloud when the biggest bombshell was dropped.

On 16 April at nearby Rapallo, the two outcast states, Germany and the Soviet Union, signed a treaty in which they renounced reparations, agreed to a resumption of diplomatic relations, and agreed to an increase in trade. The Soviets promised to compensate Germany for the private property they had nationalized. Both parties denied the treaty had any secret military clauses, and indeed in a sense they told the truth, since the secret military agreements already existed. The French felt that the pact posed a dangerous challenge to their system of alliances in Eastern Europe; they accused the Germans of deceit and insisted the Allies had the right to void any clauses in the Russo-German agreement that ran counter to existing treaties. The atmosphere at Genoa grew extremely bitter and any chance for an agreement evaporated.

The failure of the conference was a personal defeat for Lloyd George and a resultant benefit for Poincaré's policy of sanctions. Yet Poincaré was not eager to send troops into Germany despite the pressure he was getting from the nationalists to do so. He feared the adverse effect that such a step would have on relations with Great Britain, whose cooperation he still believed was necessary to obtain German compliance with the treaty. In addition, he did not want to put an additional strain on French finances.

But Poincaré clearly had to so something if he wanted to remain head of the government. Further, to guarantee French recovery, he would have to get reparations, raise taxes, or obtain foreign loans. But these were not free choices because it was unlikely that the Chamber of Deputies would approve more taxes or consent to more borrowing unless coercive measures were applied to Germany. Poincaré was trapped: unless he obtained reparations, he would have to resort to a policy of force. He did not need to be reminded that Germany would be better able to pay reparations if it were allowed to build up significant surpluses in its balance of payments. But Germany's increased economic activity and industrial efficiency would make it more powerful than before. Poincaré saw nothing contradictory about keeping Germany economically weak and demanding reparations at the same time. Somebody had to pay reparations, the question was who. Poincaré saw nothing wrong in this being the Germans. He would have preferred that this be accomplished without sending French troops into the Ruhr, but his options were limited. In November 1922, his cabinet ordered the French army to be ready for action should the Germans be held in default again.

Although Germany was meeting its cash payments, albeit on the reduced basis the Reparations Commission allowed, it failed to make certain payments in kind—specifically, 23,560 cubic meters of lumber out of a required 55,000 cubic meters and 141,648 telephone poles out of the necessary 200,000. On 26 December 1922, Poincaré requested that the Reparations Commission find Germany in default of timber deliveries. The Germans explained that the shortages were due to the refusal of contractors to accept inflated marks. They promised to rectify the situation by making future payments in gold.

All of Germany's options for making the payments had drawbacks. To make the payments in gold or hard currency, Germany would have to sell its products on the world market—an activity that could dislocate international markets and lead to dumping. Borrowing money could inflate Germany's currency, making its products cheaper and giving it a trade advantage. And paying compensation in services would result in undesirable competition. The French rejected Germany's offer to send its skilled labor directly into the devastated zones of northern France because of the threat to the French construction industry. Another option was to make payments in kind, but these were insufficient for French needs. Before the war, most of Germany's exports were manufactured goods, while raw materials comprised two-thirds of its total imports. Its greatest raw material export was coal, but this amounted to only seven percent of total exports.

The French were in no mood for excuses. Over the opposition of the British, they enlisted the support of Italy and Belgium to have Germany declared in default, the fourth time that the Reparations Commission had so ruled. As they had done in the past, the British tried to resolve the crisis by negotiations. They proposed that reparations be reduced to fifty billion marks ($12.5 billion), which would be used to help offset the war debt Britain owed to the United States. But France wanted reparations to repair its damaged areas and refused to be sidetracked until this was accomplished. The talks broke down after two days. Poincaré was prepared to accept the inevitable. Psychologically, it was an easy decision. He detested the Germans so much that he believed they were capable of deliberately wrecking their credit and currency in order to violate the Treaty of Versailles.

The Ruhr Occupation. On 11 January 1923, French and Belgian troops entered the Ruhr. The Germans answered with a policy of passive resistance and refused to pay reparations as long as the invaders remained. The French therefore had to content themselves with the raw materials, supplies, and customs duties that they managed to expropriate or collect on their own. Poincaré refused to consider any mediation until the German government ended its policy of passive resistance and became more cooperative. He doubted the British would ever understand the German mentality. Before any policy could succeed, he thought that the Germans must first realize that they were the ones who had lost the war.

The occupation had its effect. From the middle of June 1923 to the middle of September, the German mark tumbled in value from 100,000 to 100 million to the dollar. The resultant economic chaos and distress fanned the flames of civil war and contributed to the growth of political extremism. Finally, on 26 September 1923, in the face of mounting confusion and skyrocketing unemployment, the

German government abandoned passive resistance and agreed to look for ways to satisfy the French demands. Poincaré had scored a great political victory. But the French were at a crossroads: they could allow a stable regime to develop in Germany, or they could encourage further collapse and confusion. The French, apart from some extreme nationalists, were not in favor of a long occupation, especially since the costs of the venture were rapidly becoming prohibitive, further dramatizing that France could not afford to enforce the Versailles settlement by itself. Poincaré therefore agreed to follow a British initiative to end the crisis.

Prime Minister Stanley Baldwin urged that the reparations question be studied by neutral experts. Two committees were established: one, chaired by the American Charles G. Dawes, was to investigate German domestic finances; the other, chaired by Britain's Reginald McKenna, dealt with the flight of German capital abroad. Meanwhile Poincaré engaged in his own talks with German industrialists. He demanded they give him special pledges in exchange for permission to resume normal production. According to the mining industry contract, signed 23 November, France consented to release confiscated stocks of iron and steel amounting to 30 to 40 percent of the Ruhr coal and coke output. The British feared that the French scheme would lead to an international coal cartel that would shut Britain out of the continental market entirely. The French made similar agreements concerning the sale and export of paper, leather, wine, textiles, and chemicals. In each case, the French helped themselves to more reparations than the schedule of payments allowed.

The French also encouraged Rhenish separatist movements. In December 1923, they permitted the formation of the "Autonomous Government of the Palatinate" and allowed the Rhineland High Commission to register its decrees. The British were alarmed. Their investigations revealed that an "overwhelming mass" of the local population were opposed to this government, which could never have come into existence without French support and would immediately be driven out if French support were withdrawn. They made a strong protest, but the problem was solved for them on 9 January 1924, when the entire five-man directorate of the Autonomous Palatinate Government was assassinated in the dining room of a hotel in Speyer. The murderers boated back across the Rhine and were never caught. The incident prodded Poincaré to end the whole venture and reconcile himself to the decisions of the committees of experts.

The Dawes Plan. On 9 April 1924, after three months' work, the Dawes Commission revealed its plan, the essence of which was to adjust reparations to Germany's capacity to pay. The experts recognized that the reconstruction of Germany was part of the overall reconstruction of Europe and felt that, before Germany could meet its treaty payments, it first had to have a stable currency and a balanced budget. The commission therefore proposed the organization of a new bank under the general supervision of an international board of directors, buttressed with a loan of $200 million to help Germany build up necessary gold reserves. Payments would be secured with specific revenues from taxes, railway bonds, and industrial debentures and would be geared to an index of prosperity. They would resume with an initial annual amount of $250 million, rising over the next four years to $625 million. This amount could either be increased or lowered depending on German prosperity. In addition, the Dawes Commission insisted that foreign troops be evacuated from the Ruhr to enable Germany to regain its economic integrity.

Many aspects of the plan were not new, including the proposed creation of a new Reichsbank, which was an improved version of the already established Rentenbank; the pledge of state revenues to secure payment; and the use of an index of prosperity. A clever innovation though was a scheme to allow Germany to pay its debts directly in German marks—the transfer of this money being the responsibility of the Allies. This device gave the Allies a direct financial stake in the stability of the German mark.

The Dawes Plan was presented as a complete package so the French had to either accept it or reject it. They agreed. The national elections of May 1924 ended the current tenure of Poincaré and brought into power the more conciliatory government of Edouard Herriot. On 18 August, two days after German acceptance, French and Belgian troops began leaving the Ruhr. The evacuation continued by stages until, three months later to the day, it was completed. Then the Dawes Plan was in full operation.

A New Security Arrangement

Convergence of Interests. The occupation of the Ruhr was the last time the French attempted to enforce the Treaty of Versailles with military might, and at first, their efforts appeared to have been successful. Germany began to pay reparations on schedule—by 1930 the total reached almost $2 billion—but the Ruhr episode added to the French feeling of isolation.

In January 1924, the French had signed a treaty with Czechoslovakia, adding to the pacts already concluded with Belgium and Poland. But the arrangement with Prague was less binding than the French had wanted. The two countries had only pledged to coordinate their foreign policies in case another power attacked them. The French occupation of the Ruhr alarmed Czech president Edvard Beneš, prompting him to direct his country's foreign policy more toward the collective security of the League of Nations. Furthermore, he did not share the French hatred of Germany. Thus, France had yet to achieve the security guarantees it had been promised at the Paris Conference; nor had it found a suitable alternative.

Austen Chamberlain, the British foreign secretary, had talked about concluding some sort of a defensive arrangement with France, but most of the members of the British cabinet were opposed. Nevertheless, the French were still hopeful that a treaty would be forthcoming. They had other prospects as well. The German Foreign Office had attracted the attention of the British and French by offering to develop a nonaggression pact among the Rhineland powers. This led to a series of meetings during the first half of 1925 that discussed the possibility of concluding a general European security pact. The French insisted on the inviolability of the Treaty of Versailles. They also wanted any agreement to be accompanied by German entrance into the League of Nations and by some sort of general guarantee. Aristide Briand, who had returned to the French Foreign Office in April 1925, still wanted the British to guarantee the Eastern European frontiers, but was not optimistic they would do so. At this point, however, he was ready to consider any agreement that could temper the forces of German revisionism.

Gustav Stresemann, the German foreign minister (until his death in 1929), realized that in order to achieve revision of the Treaty of Versailles, the Germans would have to make concessions. At the very least, they would have to make a convincing pretense of cooperation. Open resistance to the Treaty of Versailles was self-defeating. If any proof were needed, there was the recent French refusal to evacuate the first of the occupied zones of the Rhineland, scheduled for January 1925, because the Germans continued to violate the treaty's disarmament provisions. At a minimum, the Germans knew they had to accept the permanent demilitarization of the Rhineland and to make an effort to pay reparations. In exchange, they wanted the question of war guilt settled; the complete evacuation of all foreign troops from the Rhineland; and protection against another French invasion. But in their hidden agenda they wanted to get back most of their lost national territory, especially that ceded to Poland. The best way for the Germans to regain their sovereignty was by demonstrating that they were prepared to honor their obligations. Stresemann was suspicious of any policy of reconciliation, but did not intend to make any moves that might endanger the Soviet connection and its tangible military benefits. He favored the continuation of secret rearmament and the maximum use of economic strength. He also believed that German recovery should be accelerated through foreign loans from the United States—another reason for not acting like a troublemaker—from whom Germany was currently receiving more money than it was paying out in reparations. He knew he had to convince the British and French that he did not want to upset the balance of power and that his intentions were honorable. A contemporary cartoon showed Stresemann proclaiming, "We have no more territorial claims. . . . The borders of 1914 are perfectly adequate for us."[8] Stresemann liked it so much that he saved a copy. The German quest for national honor and independence, coupled with the French desire for a guarantee treaty and the British policy of appeasement, led to the signing of the Treaty of Locarno the following October.

The Locarno Agreement. The atmosphere at Locarno was relaxed, the weather was magnificent, the scenery splendid. Wordsworth had called this Swiss city "fair Locarno . . . embowered in walnut slopes and citron isles." The discussions among Stresemann, Briand, and Chamberlain were conducted with remarkable cordiality and seriousness of purpose. Because eight months had already been spent in painstaking preparation and exploration, the delegates arrived with many of the major details already decided, and the final agreement was concluded in less than a week. The result was a collection of eight treaties of guarantee and arbitration.

The principal instrument, signed by Germany, Belgium, France, Great Britain, and Italy, recognized the inviolability of the German-Belgian and German-French frontiers and guaranteed the demilitarization of the Rhineland as established in

The last session of the Locarno conference, 16 October 1926. Mussolini arrived just in time to participate and to have his picture taken with the other delegates at the Palais de Justice. He is seated in the back row, fourth from the left. Gustav Stresemann is in front of and to the right of Mussolini. Austen Chamberlain sits in the back row wearing a monocle and Aristide Briand is at the extreme right, holding a cigarette.

the Treaty of Versailles. The signatories pledged to commit no aggression against each other. In the event of "flagrant violations" by one of the contracting parties, the others undertook to come immediately to the aid of the party against whom such an unprovoked act of aggression had been directed—particularly if the demilitarized Rhineland were invaded or if armed forces were assembled there.[9] Germany signed arbitration conventions with France and Belgium, but no guarantees were made for Germany's eastern boundaries. Instead, Germany simply promised that any revision would be accomplished through peaceful means and, to this effect, signed treaties of arbitration with Poland and Czechoslovakia. France bolstered the arrangement with special guarantee treaties to its two allies: it reiterated its obligations to the Poles and augmented its agreement with Czechoslovakia by agreeing to come to its aid in the event of an unprovoked attack. This pledge still did not contain specific military obligations, however.

German assurances that revisionism would only be achieved through peaceful negotiations did not eliminate existing anxieties. The Polish foreign minister, Count Skrzynski, remarked that a security pact that did not include a guarantee of the eastern frontiers was like "having a house which contained beautiful tapestries and taking precautions for them alone, abandoning all the objects accumulated in the neighboring rooms to the danger of fire."[10]

For Austen Chamberlain, the Locarno accord was the line of demarcation between the years of war and the years of peace; he viewed it as one of his proudest achievements. Well he might. He had accomplished his goal of restoring friendly relations with France, enabling Britain to exercise a moderating influence over French policy to prevent repetition of the Ruhr occupation. He had limited commitments to the Rhineland and the Western European countries in which Britain already had a vital interest. He had seemingly vindicated Britain's efforts to reconcile the rivalries of France and Germany and had prepared for the establishment of a true European balance of power. The "Locarno spirit" became a stock phrase of the time.

Locarno was not really a substitute for an Anglo-American treaty of guarantee, however. It contained no enforcement provisions against possible violations by Germany, the country most interested in revisionism. Furthermore, before a country would commit its forces to defend the treaty's provisions, it first had to satisfy itself that a "flagrant" violation worthy of immediate action had occurred. Britain proved to be more concerned with holding France in check than with preventing German rearmament.

In purely power terms, France still maintained its security by the strength of its army. The territorial issues had not been put to rest. In not guaranteeing the eastern frontiers, the treaty effectively acknowledged their impermanence; and the Franco-Polish alliance was correspondingly that much weaker. Furthermore, was it realistic to expect that the Germans with their determination to wipe out the Versailles diktat would not do so by force should the opportunity arise? For such a diplomatic victory, Germany was gladly willing to recognize the demilitarization of the Rhineland and to promise to continue paying reparations.

Locarno provided a base for future concessions to Germany. It did not solve the disagreement between France and Britain over how strong Germany should be allowed to become before it would be considered a threat to their vital interests. France might take comfort that Germany, in promising to enter the League of Nations, was recognizing the status quo, but the Germans interpreted their membership differently.

At Locarno, however, both France and Britain negotiated from a position of strength and did so in an atmosphere remarkably free of threats and talk of surrender. Appeasement in 1925 flowed from a realization that it was better to try to domesticate Germany from a position of power than to wait until the advantage had shifted to the Germans. Only later would appeasement become a policy of weakness determined by the demands of the aggressors.

The men who signed the agreement had no illusions about the Locarno spirit. They had been negotiating for the better part of a year and had made every effort to resolve differences and set realistic goals. They recognized the futility of trying to guarantee the eastern boundaries. The agreement sprang primarily from a desire to liquidate the tensions of World War I and was based on the assumption that Germany's goals were not unlimited and were therefore negotiable. If anyone believed the myth that a new age of peace had been established at Locarno, they were doomed to be disillusioned. Britain and France disagreed over treaty enforcement in almost every area. These differences facilitated revisionism, especially in the Middle East, where the traditional Anglo-French rivalry was heightened by new nationalist forces emerging from the collapse of the old Ottoman Empire.

OTHER FORCES OF REVISIONISM

Establishing a Balance in the Eastern Mediterranean

The Turkish Revolution. In the interior of Anatolia, a dissident nationalist government had been established at Angora—later to become Ankara—under the leadership of the hero of Gallipoli, Mustapha Kemal. His program, known as the National Pact, demanded full sovereignty for Turkey over Anatolia, over the area on both sides of the straits into the Black Sea, and over eastern Thrace. Kemal created his own Grand National Assembly, had himself elected president, and, helped by the unpopularity of the harsh terms of peace, began a national war of liberation to destroy the foreign spheres of influence and give Turkey a new system of government. His greatest obstacle in achieving these goals seemed to be the British prime minister.

Unlike many of his principal associates, Lloyd George was convinced that the coming power in the Eastern Mediterranean was Greece, not Turkey; accordingly, he vigorously supported Greek ambitions in the Aegean. In 1919, he had endorsed Greece's acquisition of the Vilayet of Smyrna, and then its occupation of the whole of eastern Thrace. Faced with the prospect of enforcing the Treaty of Sèvres without adequate British military strength, he willingly turned for help to the Greek army.

On 22 June 1920, the Greeks crossed the demarcation line in Asia Minor and marched north from Smyrna to destroy the Kemalist forces in Anatolia. Their advance was practically unopposed; and after a 250-mile trek, they captured the city of Bursa on 9 July. By the following year, Kemal, with the help of his chief lieutenant, Ismet, had succeeded in creating a disciplined fighting force that held back the Greeks in a series of defensive engagements. Kemal then turned east to destroy the army of the Armenian nationalists[11] and shake the overextended French loose from Cilicia. The victorious Kemalist army convinced the French that the Turkish nationalists were the real power in Anatolia. Consequently, with no love lost for the British, the French began negotiations with Kemal in June 1921, reaching an agreement four months later—during which time Kemal had beaten the Greek army in the Battle of Sakarya.

In the agreement, the French abandoned all their claims to Cilicia in exchange for certain economic concessions. These included the right to control sections of the Baghdad railway and, in a separate enclosure, the right to exploit mineral resources in the Karshut valley. Further concessions were promised. The treaty gave Kemal all he demanded. In addition, to show that they were deadly serious about cementing an alliance with his government, the French gave his army large stocks of guns, ammunition, and supplies, strengthening it for a decisive offensive against the Greeks.

The French had pretended that their representative in Angora, Henri Franklin-Bouillon, was empowered only to discuss questions pertaining to French prisoners of war and the protection of minorities in Cilicia, and had promised that no agreement would be made without specific prior consultation with London. But they had not only signed an agreement that recognized the Kemal regime as the official government of Turkey, they had violated their wartime agreement not to conclude a separate peace with any enemy power. France clearly considered the Treaty of Sèvres moribund.

In Paris in March 1922, the Allies approved a limited revision of the Treaty of Sèvres, allowing the whole of Smyrna and the Asiatic side of the straits to return to Turkish sovereignty. They also promised to repartition eastern Thrace in Turkey's favor and agreed to an early evacuation of foreign troops from Constantinople and Asia Minor, except from the northern coast of the Sea of Marmara. The Greek and Kemal governments accepted the new provisions in principle only: the Greeks were concerned about the fate of the Greek minorities who remained in the evacuated areas, and the Turks refused to stop fighting until the Greek army had withdrawn from the country.

But events moved too quickly for the discussions of diplomats. On 26 August, Kemal counterattacked. Four days later, the Greek army was routed at Dumlupinar and fled in confusion to the coast. The Turks entered the port of Smyrna a week later. It was undefended, the last remnants of the Greek army having already sailed away. The road to Constantinople lay open, and Kemal boasted that he would be there in a week. But to accomplish this, he would first have to cross the Neutral Zone and pass along the southern shore of the Dardanelles at Chanak where units of the British army were stationed.

A New Treaty. Kemal had nothing to gain by attacking the British—especially since the British had air superiority, and the land approaches to the British positions were under the big guns of the Royal Navy dreadnoughts prowling in the Sea of Marmara. The Turkish leader intended only to make a respectable show of strength to force further revisions of the Treaty of Sèvres. Lloyd George though believed the likelihood of war genuine enough and appealed to the Dominions for help.[12]

Meanwhile Lord Curzon tried to restore a common Franco-British front. He told French premier Poincaré, at a meeting in Paris in September, that the British were determined to defend the Neutral Zone from violation, and, that to do so, they had reinforced their position at Chanak and Constantinople with additional troops and naval units because "Gallipoli was a sacred and Imperial interest of the British Empire."[13] Poincaré turned a deaf ear. He had already ordered the French contingent at Chanak withdrawn, and responded to Curzon's urgent plea for unity by saying that he believed it impossible for the Allies to defend their position against "a nation of fanatics flushed with victory." He recommended that the Ankara government be given the lands they demanded in their National Pact.

Curzon retorted that the French refusal to defend their responsibilities in the Neutral Zone in time of danger meant that "so far as Asia was concerned, the *Entente* had ceased to exist, and that the French were leaving Great Britain to bear the brunt of the defense of the Asiatic shores of the Straits."[14] Poincaré replied flatly that the French parliament would never sanction a war with Turkey or "expose French troops to being shot by Turkish soldiers."[15] Curzon could hardly contain himself. When he left the meeting, he was fuming and blurted out to the British ambassador, Lord Hardinge, "I can't bear that horrid little man."

Lloyd George refused to panic and the British held their ground alone. The prime minister convinced the Turks to promise to respect the Neutral Zone and to wait for a peace conference ruling before trying to occupy any more territory. But his decision to stand firm not only heightened the Anglo-French division, it led to his own downfall. Facing down the terrible Turk might secretly have appealed to the imperial instincts of the Tories; and, had the prime minister been anyone other than Lloyd George, they might have given the policy their full public support. But instead they became convinced that the crisis at Chanak proved how dangerous, irresponsible, reckless, and untrustworthy the prime minister was. They resolved to give him no further support.

The peace conference opened at Lausanne on 20 November 1922 and was dominated from the outset by Lord Curzon, a man determined to restore British prestige in the Middle East. A draft treaty, ready by February of the following year, recognized the unrestricted sovereignty of Turkey over Constantinople and eastern Thrace, including the straits. It guaranteed freedom of navigation for all commercial shipping and military shipping in time of peace or Turkish neutrality.[16]

Although the Turks had largely secured the aims of their National Pact, they were still suspicious of British intentions and especially of Lord Curzon who was already proclaiming victory for his side. Consequently, the Turks refused to sign and insisted on complete independence from all financial, economic, and commercial restrictions. Curzon therefore went home without an agreement, regarding the Turks with contempt. When he learned that Ismet Pasha, the chief Turkish negotiator, had tried to telephone him before his departure, Curzon smirked, "Like a true Turk he thought that he could still catch me before I turned the corner of the street in order to have a final transaction over the price of the carpet."[17]

Curzon probably suspected he had been bested. He was also bitter about the lack of support he had received from France and claimed that he stood by his colleagues to the end, "choosing to return without a Treaty sooner than sacrifice the cause of allied unity to which I had pledged my faith." He had resisted Ismet Pasha's attempt to conclude a separate treaty with Britain. "Had France adopted a similar attitude instead of deserting us at a critical juncture the result might have been very different."[18]

The conference resumed on 24 April and dragged on for three more months. Neither side desired war, but Kemal's political survival depended on achieving his goals, and he was less hesitant about beginning hostilities than were the British, especially after Lloyd George's forced resignation. In the second stage of the negotiations, Kemal got virtually his entire program: Turkey was released from paying any reparations, the special tax-exempt status of foreign economic holdings ended, and a separate Turkish-Greek accord provided for a compulsory exchange of populations. The treaty was signed in the *grande salle* of the University of Lausanne on 24 July 1923. It marked the first time a defeated power had successfully achieved treaty revision.

Soviet Foreign Relations

Bolshevik Diplomacy. The forces of revisionism were strong among all the defeated states. Germany and Turkey managed to better their positions by taking advantage of the disagreement of the British and French over treaty enforcement. But the Russians were operating under a different set of circumstances: as an Entente power in World War I, Russia was not an enemy state. However, its current revolutionary government earned it the open, universal hostility and distrust of its former allies who made no attempt to satisfy any Communist demands. Such frontiers as could be established at the Paris Conference were drawn at Russia's expense.

Isolated without normal diplomatic contacts, the Bolsheviks remained pariahs. They were not disturbed. In fact, they denied that any non-Communist nations had a right to exist and made little effort to reestablish normal relations with others. Their idea of legitimate government had something in common with the early Christians who believed that heretics had no rights; in the Communist view, this principle applied to states that were by nature impure or, as in the case of capitalist states, were racist, exploitative, warlike, and imperialist.

Soviet diplomacy began at Brest-Litovsk. As the train bringing the Bolshevik peacemakers pulled into the station, Karl Radek leaned out a window and threw revolutionary leaflets to the German soldiers lining the tracks. The Communists had come to propagandize as well as negotiate. They believed that the world revolution was imminent, and if they could gain time—at least until the beginning of the proletarian uprising in Germany—defeat would turn to victory. Leon Trotsky, the leader of the Bolshevik delegation, had great faith in the power of his words. He insisted that the talks be held publicly so he could score debating points. Trotsky was a master of the personal attack, the moral and political invective, and the non sequitur. His tactics so infuriated General Max von Hoffmann, the representative of the German High Command, that Hoffmann observed sarcastically that the Russian delegation talked as if it represented the victor who had occupied Germany. "I want to point out that the facts are just reversed," Hoffmann snapped.

The resourceful Bolsheviks also took advantage of one of the conditions of the Armistice, which included the right of fraternization—provided there were present at any one time not "more than twenty-five unarmed persons from each side."[19] They had also tried to propagandize the German troops in the Ukraine. In addition, they sent emissaries to all the prison camps in Russia and Siberia to organize Communist cells among the German and Austrian soldiers. These efforts at subversion continued unabated even after the signing of the treaty. Ludendorff claimed that the morale of his eastern divisions was so undermined that he could no longer rely upon them to be an effective fighting force.

The Brest-Litovsk treaty made Germany the first great power to recognize the Bolshevik regime and open formal diplomatic relations. But the Communists who arrived in Berlin to establish the first embassy were no ordinary diplomats. Adolf Joffe, the ambassador, was an agent provocateur who came to organize an uprising against the government to which he was accredited. He gave subsidies to socialist newspapers, bribed government officials, distributed antigovernment propaganda, advised German Marxists on the tactics of subversion, and purchased arms and supplies for them.

The Germans finally had enough. Early in November 1918 (less than a week before the Armistice), the imperial government declared Joffe and his staff personae non grata and closed the Russian embassy. Official diplomatic relations would not be resumed between the two nations until four years later.

An End of Isolation. Trotsky believed the need for a diplomatic service was only temporary. "I will issue a few revolutionary pamphlets and then close up shop," he supposedly remarked. In any case, he thought the main purpose of diplomacy was to disseminate propaganda and subversion to hasten the world revolution. Under his direction, the old tsarist diplomatic service disappeared in favor of a team of ideologues. Trotsky opposed the conclusion of the Treaty of Brest-Litovsk and resigned as foreign commissar to head the more important People's Commissariat of War.

His successor, Georgi Chicherin, did not believe that the rest of the world would soon follow the Bolshevik path toward the new utopia and began to create a more conventional foreign office committed to more or less normal diplomatic practices. Lenin saw no conflict in allowing Chicherin to seek formal political, economic, and cultural relations with other states, while, at the same time, seeking to undermine those states by revolutionary action. Chicherin was perfect for the traditional role. He was schooled in the old ways, a veteran diplomat who had joined the Bolshevik party only after the November coup. He remained commissar of foreign affairs until 1930. One of his first moves was to reestablish ties with Germany. In May 1921, he concluded a commercial agreement that provided for an increased exchange of goods and services with special emphasis on military needs. The following year, he boldly and publicly proclaimed the existence of the Russo-German entente by negotiating the famous Rapallo Agreement, signed 17 February 1922. The accord increased the bargaining positions of the signatories, eroded the Anglo-French monopoly on continental politics, and moved Europe back toward a balance of power. Chicherin gave diplomatic support to Berlin during the French invasion of the Ruhr, while the Communist International mobilized the German Communist party for insurrection. To Lenin, who embodied a combination of Marxist and Russian patterns of thought, such a schizoid approach was perfectly proper. It did not unleash a revolution either in Germany or elsewhere, but it did help protect the Communist state against the West. Remarkably, German and Russian relations remained relatively friendly throughout the years of the Weimar Republic, even though the Soviets were constantly worried that Germany might establish closer ties with the West at their expense.

On 26 April 1926, the two countries signed the Treaty of Berlin, a treaty of reassurance to remove any misunderstandings over Germany's commitments under the Locarno Pact. Germany guaranteed that its rapprochement with the West, including its candidacy for the League of Nations, would not entail participation in any unfriendly political, economic, or financial act against Russia. The validity of the Rapallo Agreement was affirmed. Both partners promised not to join hostile coalitions against the other, either in peace or in war, and pledged to remain neutral in the event of a third-party attack. Stresemann pledged that Germany would not be bound by League sanctions directed against the Soviet Union.

The treaty revealed the Soviet Union's complete distrust of the League of Nations. Maksim Litvinov, Chicherin's associate and successor, called the organization a "diplomatic bourse, where the strong Powers arrange their business and conduct their mutual accounts behind the back, and at the expense of, the small and weak nations." Securing Germany's reservation to the League Covenant was quite a diplomatic coup.

The Communists also sought to establish regular relations with other countries. The British Labour government extended *de jure* recognition in February 1924 and negotiated a particularly promising commercial agreement. But fear of Communist tactics of subversion—culminating in the Red scare over the Zinoviev letter—led the wary Conservatives to break off diplomatic relations and denounce all existing treaties. By 1925, however, every major state, except the United States, had diplomatic ties with the Soviet Union.[20] The Russian market was seen as the answer to the economic woes of countries that were still trying to recover from the war.

Lenin's death in January 1924 marked the decline of the influence of the old revolutionary generation. Josef Stalin, the new strongman, had never lived outside Russia and spoke no foreign languages. He was more interested in dividing Russia's enemies and avoiding war with stronger states than in world revolution. His policy was "Socialism in One Country," which became a means of controlling the party's left-wing internationalists. It is often believed that this concept was Stalin's original contribution to Marxism-Leninism. In fact, it came from Lenin himself. After the seizure of power, Lenin's moves became less and less ideological and more attuned to the expedients of maintaining his authority in Russia. But none of this would matter unless Russia could become strong enough to withstand any attack from the outside.

In the last half of the 1920s, when the Soviet Union seemed in no danger of being attacked, Stalin pursued a low-key and surprisingly conciliatory foreign policy. Soviet diplomats participated actively in various international conferences. They negotiated treaties with their neighbors for the collective renunciation of war—the so-called Litvinov Protocol, which was eventually ratified by Poland, Estonia, Latvia, Romania, Turkey, Lithuania, Persia, and the free city of Danzig. The Soviet Union also concluded a series of bilateral nonaggression treaties with Poland, the Baltic states, Finland, and France.

But no amount of diplomacy could make the Soviets acceptable members of the world community of nations. Communist diplomats were notorious for their bad manners and the great delight with which they attacked the alleged decadence and wickedness of everybody else. Although the West moved toward closer relations with the Soviets, it still continued to view them as a world apart.

The Communist International. A major obstacle to any significant normalization of relations between the Bolshevik regime and the rest of the world was the ominous presence of the Communist International (Comintern), an organization created in 1919 to further the cause of world revolution—a goal that seemingly contradicted the Soviet Union's desire to regulate its affairs with the capitalist states through diplomacy. The Soviets, however, never believed a conflict existed. The Comintern was always intimately related to the basic task of foreign affairs, which was protecting the security of the homeland. From the outset, therefore, the Comintern's first duty was to protect the revolution in Russia by enlisting the support of foreign Communist parties. The resolution of the Second Comintern Congress (July–August 1920) made clear the relationship of these parties to Moscow: each national party was expected to purge all stray elements from its ranks and communicate with other national Communist parties only through the central organization. No previous International had tried to control its members so thoroughly.

Such extreme authoritarianism was hardly suited to the federalized character of Marxism and split the socialist movement into two warring camps, with those who owed allegiance to the Comintern becoming virtual Russian agents who were willing to accept Russian concepts of world revolution. At the Second Comintern Congress, chieftain Gregori Zinoviev proclaimed that it was "not only permissible but even obligatory to intervene in the affairs of the [member] parties." And, indeed, intervention became constant, involving all aspects of party affairs: organization, finance, propaganda, and tactics.

Lenin had placed his highest hopes for a successful revolution on Germany, the birthplace of Karl Marx and the homeland of the largest and best organized socialist movement in Western Europe. But the Social Democratic majority were moderate socialists, who were more nationalistic than revolutionary and were attached to constitutional democratic government. The Spartacists and the Communist regime of Bavaria had failed to hold onto power. Nevertheless, Leon Trotsky, the most convinced advocate of permanent revolution, continued to push for greater commitment to the German revolutionary struggle.

In 1923, the Comintern, taking advantage of the economic collapse accompanying the passive resistance to the French occupation of the Ruhr, planned an uprising and began supplying the German Communists with lavish amounts of money and weapons. However, unlike the situation in Petrograd in 1917, the German forces of order stayed loyal to the government, and the would-be revolution was easily crushed.

A little over a year later, the Comintern tried to effect a coup d'état in Estonia where it planned to seize control of the government and proclaim the establishment of an Estonian Soviet Republic, which would then petition to be incorporated into the Soviet Union. The revolt began on 1 December 1924, with the occupation of strategic positions inside the chief port of Tallinn. But the Estonian government immediately established martial law and gave the army special powers to smash the revolt and bring the conspirators, who were mostly Russian, to trial. The Estonian attack had repercussions in nearby Latvia and Finland where wholesale roundups of Communists took place.

The German and Estonian experiences effectively ended the efforts to try to capture power by direct action. Stalin had reservations about such tactics anyway and took full advantage of the failure to further denigrate his political enemies. He directed that henceforth the Comintern should concentrate on the infiltration of other working-class parties. But no matter what tactics it used, the Comintern had little success. In Eastern Europe, Communist activity was badly organized and easily controlled. In Yugoslavia and Czechoslovakia, multinationalism and geographic regionalism frustrated effective development. In Austria, the Socialist party had too strong a monopoly on working-class loyalties. In Poland, Romania, and Finland, any movement associated with Russia was anathema. Communism achieved a temporary success in Hungary, but this resulted from a nationalistic drive for treaty revision rather than any proletarian sympathy for the creation of a new system. In Germany, the Communists' steadfast refusal to support any constitutional government eventually helped the extreme right destroy the Weimar Republic. Still, the myth of world revolution gave the Comintern its ideological legitimacy, and its lack of success ironically made it more powerful, since the national Communist parties became increasingly dependent on the Soviet Union.

The Russian experience shaped Comintern policy and was difficult to export for the obvious reason that internationalism was always a fraud, having no independent life outside the self-serving needs of the Soviet Union. The Comintern became a service agency for the protection of Russian Communism and a cemetery for revolutionaries. Its activities were motivated less by a concern for human welfare than by traditional Russian imperialism. Revolutions in other countries were only good insofar as they increased the power of the Soviet Union. If it were to the advantage of the Soviet Union to promote the growth and stability of capitalism, the Comintern would pursue this goal, no matter what the ideological considerations. In any case, the Communists believed that foreign policy was ultimately determined by objective considerations. Therefore, in the end, the capitalist countries would always come to terms with the Soviet Union. The capitalists would do so because they needed to counteract the rivalries that existed among themselves, because their working classes demanded it, or because they needed trade advantages.

The Pursuit of Western Technology. No matter how convinced the Soviets were that the capitalists would eventually pursue the Russian market, the Soviets obviously needed Western assistance more than the West needed the additional profits. To the Soviets, foreign trade was a political act, and they always insisted that their economic experts be treated with the same respect and courtesy as their embassy and consular officials. The power of a monolithic state gave the Soviet negotiators certain advantages denied those from market economy countries. To induce more favorable terms, the Soviets could threaten embargoes, resort to dumping, or cut off trade.

The economic power of the United States had a special attraction for the Soviets, and they negotiated trade agreements with some of the biggest American corporations: Standard Oil of New York, General Electric Company, General Motors, International Harvester, Du Pont de Nemours, and Radio Corporation of America. *Amtorg*, the official Soviet trading corporation, made its largest deal with Henry Ford, signed 31 May 1929, for the construction of an automobile factory at Nizhni Novgorod (Gorky) to produce 100,000 cars annually. Ford agreed to send engineers to Russia to build the plant, to supply the patents for the construction of the cars, and to train Russian engineers and mechanics. The Soviets agreed to pay all costs plus a 15 percent profit and to buy $30 million worth of supplies directly from Ford. The Amtorg-Ford agreement was one of thirty such pacts signed that year. American capitalists found that doing business with the Communists was not so bad after all. They could rejoice in the guaranteed profits and even envy a system that had freed itself from the annoyances of such practices as collective bargaining. And the Communists discovered that they could easily profit from Western industrial expertise without being contaminated by Western ideas.

Disarmament

The Washington Conference. The great nations had become accustomed to large military establishments that served as tangible expressions of their prestige and sovereignty as well as providing security. Especially after having fought a war of survival, the Allies were reluctant to consider any limitations on the military, despite the lip service paid to disarmament. Nevertheless, within four years after the Armistice, an agreement was achieved in the limited area of naval tonnage. Success here was due mainly to the initiative of the United States, which in 1921 invited the world's major naval powers—Great Britain, France, Italy, and Japan (and others with interests in the Far East, including China, Portugal, Belgium, and the Netherlands)—to Washington for a security conference.

On 12 November 1921, the first day of the conference, Secretary of State Charles Evans Hughes proposed that the naval powers adopt a ten-year moratorium on the building of capital ships (those over 10,000 tons) and proceed to a wholesale destruction of other older warships to achieve proportional strength in overall tonnage. Britain and the United States would be limited to a capital-ship tonnage of roughly 500,000, Japan to 300,000, and Italy and France to 175,000 apiece. The scheme, if realized, would commit the United States to far greater reductions than the others—a point of strength for the American bargaining position—although in making such sacrifices in naval hardware, the United States was hardly endangering its own security, which was then still close to absolute.

Such a radical move to disarm was feasible because of the restricted nature of the scheme, the ease of verification—capital ships were difficult to conceal—the rather small number of states with world navies, and the ability of the United States to build a fleet beyond the reach of everybody else if no agreement was reached. It also was successful because certain political problems in the Pacific had been solved. In this regard, the United States, Great Britain, France, and Japan signed the four-power Pacific Treaty in which they guaranteed each other's possessions in the Far East and pledged to consult each other should their rights be threatened. When ratified, this agreement would supersede the Anglo-Japanese Treaty of 1902, which had been made obsolete by the collapse of German and Russian power. All the participants at the conference also signed a nine-power agreement that safeguarded the territorial and administrative integrity of China. These arrangements also enabled the United States to maintain Far Eastern security through a nine-power regional system, buttressed with a four-power commitment to defend the balance of power. The realization that Japan was willing to accept the status quo had enabled Hughes to put his major emphasis on disarmament.

The Naval Armaments Treaty, signed on 6 February 1922, contained most of the provisions advocated by Hughes in his opening address: the ten-year ban on building capital ships, a ratio of capital tonnage among the chief naval powers of 5–5–3–1.75–1.75, and limitations on the tonnage and the size of guns for replacement ships. The treaty contained a list of the capital ships that the five powers would scrap, and it established a ban on building any new fortifications and naval bases in the Pacific.[21] At French insistence, however, no limits were placed on the construction of ships of less than 10,000 tons, i.e., light cruisers and destroyers, and no limits were placed on the construction of submarines or on aircraft carriers. Regarding aircraft carriers, the conference maintained the same ratio as for battleships with Britain and the United States entitled to a maximum of 135,000 tons. Since no nation currently had that much, the conference had actually approved an increase in this category of naval weapons.

The achievements at Washington were a logical consequence of the desire to avoid another costly naval race. The conference achieved a decade of stability in the Far East and encouraged further attempts at disarmament. In 1927, discussions to extend the limitation on tonnage to warships of less than 10,000 tons ended in deadlock. But three years later at the London Naval Conference, Britain, Japan, and the United States (without the participation or concurrence of Italy and France) finally reached an agreement. The British and Americans allowed themselves fifty light cruisers each, and the Japanese were permitted thirty-five (70 percent of the British and American allotments, an increase of 10 percent over what they had been allowed in capital ships). These levels would remain in effect as long as the international situation stayed the same.

In another direction, the British tried to apply the Washington Conference formulas to ground forces. A plan, sponsored by Viscount Esher, a permanent member of the Committee of Imperial Defense, counted armies in units of 30,000 troops. Under Esher's scheme, France had a ratio of 6, Italy and Poland 4, and Great Britain 3. How various units within this framework would be weighted was somewhat vague, but Esher hoped his suggestions would form the basis for serious League discussion. However, this became impossible. While Britain might believe in direct arms reductions, France felt that no steps could be taken toward disarmament unless questions of security were discussed first. Since the French felt particularly vulnerable to German industrial might, they did not view the limitation of weaponry as an end in itself. And besides, since Germany was already disarmed, what could it offer in return?

The Role of the League. Article 8 of the League of Nations Covenant entrusted the Council with the task of formulating disarmament proposals, but the Assembly, at its first meeting, established its own agency, the Temporary Mixed Commission, to draft plans and present them to the Council. No problem that came before the Geneva organization was as persistent, nor provided such a clear indication of the organization's nature as the question of disarmament. It was the best example of the tremendous hope for a better world that many people had after the war. True, the efforts do not seem to add up to much today, but the dedication was genuine. So were the long hours, the endless negotiations, the eyestrain that developed from reading too many documents, and the loss of sleep. None of this was faked, and it showed the great determination that many had to build a world free from the pain of war. From 1920 to 1933, disarmament was discussed in every session of the Assembly.

The recognition that no disarmament could begin before a reduction of international tensions was at the heart of the Mixed Commission's proposal to strengthen collective security. Every signatory promised to give immediate assistance to all other signatories in the event of attack. According to the draft treaty, the League Council would have the authority to specify what each country should contribute, but only states that had reduced their armaments would be eligible for help. The scheme received a mixed response. France and Italy were favorable, but Britain objected that the plan would reduce its security by increasing its commitments. Nevertheless, the search for some sort of agreement continued.

In 1924, the Assembly brought forth the Geneva Protocol, which linked disarmament and arbitration. Every signatory was asked to pledge to submit all major disputes to the World Court or to bring them before the Council. Any state that refused and resorted to force in violation of its pledge would be branded the aggressor, and all other signatories would automatically aid the state that had been attacked. Briand, in pledging French support for the protocol, hailed it as a "land mark in the annals of mankind." The League overwhelmingly endorsed the plan and opened it for signature. But the enthusiasm in Geneva did not extend to the home governments. In Britain, the newly elected ministry of Stanley Baldwin came out in opposition because, like previous governments, it did not want to accept anything that might involve Britain in guaranteeing the territorial settlements of Eastern Europe.

In 1925, the League Assembly began planning for a general conference on arms reduction. The Council appointed a special preparatory commission, even including representatives from the United States and the Soviet Union. Over the next five years, the commission extensively studied disarmament from its military, geographic, industrial, and demographic aspects. It discussed what forms reduction might take, tried to distinguish between offensive and defensive weapons, and considered regional differences and limitations. It even tried to coordinate and allow for national disagreements and rivalries.

The long-awaited Conference for Reduction and Limitation of Armaments finally met in February 1932 and remained in session until June 1934. But the delegates from fifty-seven countries did not seriously discuss the proposals that had taken five years to prepare. Differing national interests were irreconcilable. Germany insisted on equality in armaments. France first wanted a scheme of supervision. Japan, which had resumed its expansionist policies, was ignoring the naval limitations imposed by the Washington and London treaties. Italy was also beginning an arms buildup. The League of Nations disarmament efforts ended in failure.

This was hardly surprising. Any scheme that sought to limit or reduce armaments in accordance with an overall international plan struck at the heart of national sovereignty—above all else, modern states jealously guarded the right to determine their own military needs. The question of disarmament would not have been so widely discussed had not the League given it special consideration, but by and large the time spent was wasted effort. Still, for most of its first decade of existence, the League commanded enormous respect.

A Fair Amount of Tranquillity

The Persistence of Revisionism. The first evacuations from the Rhineland—the northern occupied zone—began in December 1925, almost a year behind schedule. But by the end of the following January, the last contingents of British troops had pulled out of Cologne, and the French had left Bonn. Despite private doubts and crossed fingers, the Locarno spirit appeared to flourish.

But a month before the agreement had been signed, Stresemann, in a letter to the former crown prince, described the forthcoming treaty as the means to drive a wedge between the British and French in order to create new opportunities for German power in Eastern Europe. He stated that Germany's goals went beyond ending the Allied occupation and bringing about a favorable solution of the problem of reparations. The aim of his foreign policy was the readjustment of the eastern frontiers, specifically, the reincorporation of Danzig, the Polish Corridor, and the lands of Upper Silesia. Stresemann further advocated union with Austria and, although recognizing it was out of the question for the time being, the reacquisition of Alsace-Lorraine. In short, he wanted the Reich restored to its 1914 frontiers.

Stresemann had skillfully exploited the differences between the British and French, but much was yet to be done, and he continued to play the role of responsible statesman, constantly affirming his willingness to honor Germany's obligations and commitments. On 8 September 1926, the country entered the League of Nations and received a permanent seat on the Council. The tactic paid off. The evacuation of foreign troops from the Rhineland continued on schedule. In February 1927, the Allied Control Commission was disbanded, even though its final report acknowledged that "Germany had never disarmed, had never had the intention of disarming, and for seven years had done everything in its power to deceive and 'counter-control' the Commission appointed to control its disarmament."[22]

In September 1927, in a speech dedicating the war memorial to the victory at Tannenberg, Reichspräsident Paul von Hindenburg repudiated the war guilt clause of the Versailles treaty. Still, the rebuilding of German military power did not particularly alarm the British. In their view, it posed no threat to the prevailing European equilibrium, since it was mostly defensive and within the limits of parity. Besides, a strong Germany was necessary to contain Bolshevik Russia.

The French were full of doubts but they followed the British lead, continuing to do so throughout most of the next decade. Briand had tried to steer a middle course between the Poincarists, who demanded unilateral enforcement of the treaty, and the Socialists, who were inclined toward pacifism. He realized that the position of power France had enjoyed after World War I could not last with full German recovery.

The French army was no longer the same fighting force as before. The Great War had been followed by massive resignations from the ranks of the professional officers. Inflation and low pay made a military career less attractive. In 1923, mandatory military service dropped to eighteen months, the second reduction in as many years, and there was talk of reducing it further. France had other military commitments besides those along the Rhine, specifically, in North Africa and Syria. Briand felt that the best guarantee for the continuation of Germany's policy of fulfillment was to help Stresemann maintain his position against the extreme right-wing antidemocratic opposition. Briand hoped that the remaining differences between the two countries would eventually be resolved once the Franco-German rapprochement was given a chance to work. He therefore tended to be somewhat indulgent of violations of the Versailles treaty's military clauses.

The conversation that took place between Briand and Stresemann, on 17 September 1927, over lunch at Thoiry—a village outside Geneva in the foothills of the Juras—was concerned chiefly with German rearmament. Briand was almost a suppliant, virtually begging the German foreign minister to control the German military. "I have a feeling," he said, "that the Reichswehr is doing all manner of things of which you have no knowledge. I don't consider that too tragic. The military is the same everywhere. But our policy must not suffer for it."[23] Briand wanted Stresemann's help in silencing his persistent critics in the French government. But all Briand's efforts to reconcile the Germans to a less prominent position than they had enjoyed prior to the war ultimately failed.

The Kellogg-Briand Peace Pact. A surrogate of sorts appeared in August 1928 in the form of a pact proclaiming a universal repudiation of aggressive war. Briand had first expressed the idea in a speech commemorating the tenth anniversary of the American entry into the war. He was primarily interested in developing closer ties with the United States, but Frank Kellogg, Calvin Coolidge's secretary of state, thought he could get off the hook by expanding a Franco-American entente into a nonenforceable scheme to outlaw war. Kellogg had no faith that such a declaration would accomplish anything substantial, but peace groups were pestering him and he wanted to placate them. The French were leery that a broad declaration could undermine their treaty system without further guaranteeing security. However, Kellogg's proposal, in the form it was presented, seemed harmless enough. Besides, no nation wanted to have people believe it actually *favored* war. Kellogg, against French objections, offered the pact to any nation that cared to sign. Indeed, every sovereign independent state in the world did so. And why not? Nations were left free to fight defensive wars and were constrained by no sanctions, other than that dubiously effective force known as world public opinion.

The Young Plan. Meanwhile, the Germans continued to make reparations payments under the Dawes Plan, while working to achieve the complete withdrawal of foreign troops. They still violated the Treaty of Versailles, especially its military clauses, but no more so than usual.

In February 1929, a committee of experts under the chairmanship of the American Owen D. Young met in Paris to work out a definitive settlement of reparations. The Young Plan replaced the Reparations Commission and the Reichsbank supervisory committee, established by the Dawes Plan to handle German annuities, with a Bank of International Settlements, established at Basel. And, for the first time, a final date was established. All reparations would end in 1988!

Between 1929 and 1931, payments were to be reduced from $625 to $425 million; then they would steadily climb, reaching the maximum payment of $600 million in 1965; from there they would gradually recede to $225 million the year of the last payment. Capitalized, the value of the entire amount was currently $9.25 billion, a rather significant reduction from the $33 billion the Reparations Commission set in 1921. The Young Plan tried to relieve the Germans of the stigma of having their economic affairs controlled by foreigners. The experts were proud that they had produced a scheme free from political passions. "This is the way wise business functions, and as businessmen we have taken that method here," Young remarked at the signing ceremonies on 7 June 1929.

But this could not change the fact that the whole policy of reparations was a national humiliation. After a decade, Germans had forgotten the destruction they had caused and saw the payments as punishment, not restitution. The Allies hoped to commercialize part of the reparations payments to make vast sums of capital available for international economic growth and development. However, politics could not be ignored. Stresemann made it clear that Germany's acceptance of the Young Plan would be conditional on the complete evacuation of Allied troops from the Rhineland. Briand agreed, but insisted the priorities be reversed. The result was the same. The Young Plan did not provide for Germany to pay occupation costs. In September, the withdrawal of Allied troops from the two remaining zones began. By June 1930, five years ahead of schedule, no foreign soldiers remained on German soil.

POSTSCRIPT   Over the nearly ten years in which it was treated as a second-rate power, Germany had regained its freedom of action and was once again acknowledged to be a great European power. The Young Plan of 1929 was the last hurrah for reparations. Even if the present generation of German leaders had been sincere in living up to its part of the bargain, to believe that successive generations of Germans would feel an obligation to continue payments for sixty years was wishful thinking. With no foreign troops on German soil and no chance of another invasion of the Ruhr, the Young Plan was difficult to enforce.

The Russians were as determined as the Germans to reestablish their old frontiers, but their current weakness prevented them from doing so. For the time being, they practiced a policy of cooperation and detente. Ultimately, though, the power vacuum that existed in Central Europe would draw them like a powerful magnet. As with the Germans, the fundamental question became, when and in what respect would the Russians decide to play a greater role in that region?

After Locarno, French policy became more defensive, resulting in 1930 in the beginning of the Maginot Line, a supertrench of reinforced concrete blockhouses, bunkers, and pillboxes across their vulnerable northern and eastern frontiers.[24] The French also continued to collect allies. They signed a mutual defense treaty with Romania in January 1926 and one with Yugoslavia in November 1927. The signatories committed themselves to maintaining the status quo in Eastern and Western Europe, pledging to back their obligations with armed force in the event of unprovoked aggression. However, these latest pacts contained no firm military clauses, meaning that the obligations rested on good intentions.

The system was hardly a powerful force in international affairs. French military assistance to the countries of the Little Entente was insignificant, which was not surprising in view of the absence of military conventions. But economic exchanges were also not impressive, enabling Germany to reassert its traditional economic and political domination over the area. With the possible exception of the Polish treaty, it is difficult to believe that France took its alliance system seriously. It reflected the political circumstances of Europe after World War I. Though five treaties with five smaller states hardly carried the political clout of one alliance with a Great Power, France had apparently made the best of a bad situation. Even without counting the resources of France, on paper the Eastern states more than matched Germany in population, and their territory was two and a quarter times greater.

But aside from a fear of Hungarian irredentism, the partners of the Little Entente lacked a common enemy. Romania, fattened with the former Russian territory of Bessarabia, feared an attack from the Soviet Union; Yugoslavia, having experienced the occupation of Fiume, was worried over further Italian claims in Dalmatia; and Czechoslovakia was anxious about a revival of Pan-Germanism and its effect on its own German minority. Furthermore, no member of the alliance system had any significant economic relations with another. The French gave the system a certain cement, but France was primarily concerned with defending the Treaty of Versailles, next to which the treaties of the Trianon and St. Germain were of secondary importance. Even had the French alliance system possessed sufficient determination, it lacked the strength to bridle the collective revisionism of Germany, Italy, Soviet Russia, Hungary, and Bulgaria. Thus, the French system could be no more than a temporarily beneficial arrangement, pending an association with a major power.

The permanent feature of European diplomacy during the 1920s was the great difference that existed between Britain and France over how to enforce the peace. None of the arrangements they made with their former enemies came without an argument. The absence of Anglo-French accord encouraged revisionism, indecision, and weakness, faults that would become worse in the next decade. Many believed that the best guarantee of postwar political security lay in the preservation of Anglo-French unity. Allied disunity sometimes could produce lasting benefits, however. The Treaty of Lausanne, made possible because of Allied *disunity*, ironically proved to be the most stable and durable of the peace settlements.

At the end of the twenties, tension among the states of Europe was lower than it had been for a century; the new decade seemed to be ushering in a period almost as tranquil as the one that had followed the Treaty of Vienna in 1815. The diplomacy of states settled back into traditional nineteenth-century patterns. But the statesmen, particularly those in the Western democracies, little understood the new realities of the postwar world, especially the interrelationship between economics and politics and the violent forces of revisionism and expansionism that would dominate the affairs of European nations in the decade to follow. Nations became concerned primarily with domestic problems: the British with the repercussions of the General Strike, the French with their struggle to stabilize the franc, the Germans with the rationalization of their industry, the Russians with their Five-Year Plans, and the Italians with getting the trains to run on time. The Great War, it seemed, had truly been laid to rest.

If Paris had been the worst place to have a peace conference, Geneva seemed ideal for the League of Nations. Lacking the fast pace and the filth and slums of European capitals, the Swiss city appeared as an urban counterpart to the optimism that accompanied the League's birth. On clear days there was an uninterrupted view of the Alps, the Juras, and the Salèves from the quays along the yet unpolluted waters of the lake. The meticulously cared-for parks were splendid, and here normally short-lived poplars grew to dignified, patriarchal old age. The "Geneva spirit" of internationalism prompted a swarm of specialized institutions and multinational agencies to establish their headquarters in the city. Such rapid growth put a tremendous strain on the city's resources, but the magnificent ambiance offset any discomfort. The Assembly usually held its annual meeting in September when the weather was superb. But later, in the winter, the cold wind of the *Bise* blew down the lake. The sun hid behind a layer of leaden clouds—sometimes for as long as three weeks—the suicide rate went up, and spring came very, very late.

ENDNOTES

1. David Lloyd George, *Memoirs of the Peace Conference*, vol. 1 (New Haven: Yale University Press, 1939), 267.
2. Harold Nicolson, *Peacemaking 1919* (New York: Grosset and Dunlap, 1965), 187.
3. John Maynard Keynes, *The Economic Consequences of the Peace* (New York: Harcourt, Brace and Rowe, 1920), 225.
4. By special dispensation, Germany had been given the right to garrison as many as 17,000 troops in the Ruhr until April 1920, and the present request was really for reinforcements.
5. *British Foreign Policy Documents*, 1st series, vol. 15, 465.
6. Represented at the conference were the British Dominions plus twenty-nine European states, including Germany and, for the first time, Russia.
7. The French army had already prepared a contingency plan to this effect.
8. Hans W. Gatzke, *Stresemann and the Rearmament of Germany* (Baltimore: Johns Hopkins University Press, 1954), 114.

9. *Survey of International Affairs, 1925*, vol. 2 (London: Oxford University Press, 1926), 442.
10. Ibid., 29.
11. Kemal's success against the Armenians led to the signing of a treaty with the Soviet Union, on 16 March 1921, which restored the frontier that Turkey had before 1878.
12. *British Foreign Policy Documents*, 1st series, 18:41 (London: Her Majesty's Stationery Office, 1972).
13. Only Australia and New Zealand responded positively to Lloyd George's call for help.
14. *British Foreign Policy Documents*, 1st series, 18:52.
15. Ibid., 53
16. In addition, demilitarized zones would be established along the Bosporus and the Dardanelles and the Greco-Turkish frontiers. The problem of the oil-rich territory of Mosul would be left to a separate conference.
17. *British Foreign Policy Documents*, 1st series, 18:506.
18. Ibid., 506–7.
19. John Wheeler-Bennett, *Brest-Litovsk: The Forgotten Peace, March 1918* (London: Macmillan, 1963), 93.
20. The United States finally extended recognition in 1933.
21. The ban would not apply to islands adjacent to the continental bases of the signatories, including the Hawaiian Islands. The prohibition would be in effect until 1936 unless a formal two-year notice were given to terminate it.
22. Wheeler-Bennett, *Brest-Litovsk*, 185.
23. Gatzke, *Stresemann*, 58.
24. The line's 225 miles of fortifications were completed by World War II. The French intended to funnel a German attack through Holland and Belgium and left the northern stretch along the Belgian border unfortified. They hoped the Germans would repeat their mistake of 1914.

PART THREE

THE MARCH
OF THE DICTATORS,
1929–1939

CHAPTER 7

THE GREAT DEPRESSION

PREFACE   World War I destroyed a free enterprise system that was more honored in the breach than in the observance. A network of special protections, subsidies, and monopolistic practices along with an enormous concentration of wealth in the hands of relatively few people weakened social stability and contributed to unrest and discontent in all the major European countries. Commentators disagreed as to whether the war had staved off a potential revolution or postponed needed social legislation. According to one scenario, Europe was headed for major social and political upheavals when the war intervened and delayed the explosion. According to the other, Europe, despite its problems, was making strides toward democracy and economic well-being before the war. If the war had not come, many of the tensions would have been resolved through legislation.

All could agree that the conflict had left Europe a nightmare of insecurities. Many countries had become beggars, unable to survive without handouts from abroad. Even the more independent nations were mired in inflation and recession. Tariffs had risen; restrictive quotas, exchange controls, cartels, and marketing agreements flourished. Statesmen had learned that success in war depended on the ability to survive a blockade as much as on military triumph on the battlefield. Governments, therefore, sought to strengthen, develop, and protect the industries that had assured them victory. Most major countries subsidized chemical research; all promoted aviation. The new mercantilism, stimulated by the disappearance of prewar international monetary unity, led to a decline in export income, put pressure on foreign exchange reserves, and weakened the value of national currencies. By the middle of the 1920s, most countries seemed to have put their houses in order, halting the depreciation of the currency, restoring the gold standard, and returning industrial productivity to prewar levels.

Still, protectionism remained and prevented the free flow of goods and services. Many nations hoped that free and healthy commerce would gradually develop between states through the application of the most-favored-nation principle. But they were reluctant to sign treaties to that effect, and preferred to attack the protectionism of others rather than accept responsibility themselves. The apparently successful recovery of Europe in the latter part of the decade seemed to prove the wisdom of the old adage: if it ain't broke, don't fix it.

During the twenties, a series of developments transformed economic institutions in many countries. Industry became more dependent on special markets and was increasingly organized into discriminatory cartels and holding companies. The regulation of markets through price fixing and marketing agreements became standard. Trade unions protected their members by inflexible commitments to high wage scales. Tension had always existed between workers and employers, but as power became concentrated in the trade unions and manufacturers' organizations, governments increasingly had to play the role of arbiters. The wartime expansion of the factory system accelerated the transformation of large numbers of agricultural workers into urban wage earners, more dependent than ever before on public and social services. But these services were expensive. Constant economic expansion became essential to finance high fixed governmental expenditures, particularly on welfare, reconstruction, and war pensions. When taxes were insufficient, governments covered their deficits by borrowing or by inflating their currencies.

Industry was capable of producing more goods, but it demanded comparatively fewer primary products in order to do so. Higher efficiency, improved techniques, and processing refinements reduced the need for certain raw materials and, at the same time, helped to increase their supply. World prices for some goods fell drastically. For example, the development of the cord tire and the use of reclaimed rubber contributed to a serious oversupply of crude rubber despite the expansion of the automobile industry. The increased demand for rubber sheet during the war had led growers in the Dutch East Indies to compete directly with major suppliers in Malaysia and Ceylon. The boom collapsed with the sudden end of military spending, and the price per pound fell below the cost of production. The British tried to restore the market by limiting production, but they were unable to get the planters of Java and Sumatra to cooperate. American manufacturers, who consumed two-thirds of the world's supply, found that they could practically set their own price. Consequently, rubber fell on the London market from a high of 3 shillings 2.5 pence per pound in 1925 to 8.7 pence by the end of 1928. It dropped below 4 pence per pound three years later. Similarly, the increased use of oil hurt the coal industry, the development of synthetics hurt the cotton industry, the use of artificial nitrogen practically ruined the economy of Chile (which depended heavily on nitrates), and the increase in silver production from improved smelting of base metal caused the devaluation of the Chinese currency and affected the prosperity of Mexico.

The overextended wartime production in world agriculture caused a general price collapse. When the Canadian government developed its own wheat pool, the Europeans began importing more grain from Argentina. Other countries tried to maintain prices by destroying their agricultural surpluses. The Greek government destroyed the excess supply of currants. The Brazilians set fire to tons of coffee beans or used them in the roadbeds of highways. The price collapse meant that Europeans could buy more commodities for less money, but it also meant that the primary producing countries were realizing less revenue from the sale of their products and were therefore able to buy fewer European exports. The unfavorable terms of trade prompted countries like India, Japan, and Australia to accelerate their own industrial development and protect their domestic markets with high tariffs. Nobody could prevent the depression in agriculture and raw materials from upsetting the traditional balance of payments and causing a marked decrease in world trade.

On 5 September 1929, Aristide Briand celebrated the tenth anniversary of the League of Nations with a grandiloquent speech on the need for European unity: "I think that among peoples constituting geographical groups like the peoples of Europe, there should be some kind of federal bond; it should be possible for them to get into touch at any time to confer about their interests, to agree on joint resolutions and to establish among themselves a bond of solidarity which will enable them, if need be, to meet any grave emergency that may arise." This association would be "primarily economic, for that is the most urgent aspect of the question," but "political and social ties could also be established without affecting the sovereignty of any of the nations belonging." Briand's proposal was vague, and European states were not slow to figure out its implications. Germany worried that such a European federation would be prejudicial to the revision of its eastern frontiers. Italy regarded it as a device for the expansion of Bolshevism, and Great Britain feared the federation's particularism would undermine ties with the Commonwealth.

European economic collaboration seemed unable to go beyond a fight over tariff reduction. Indeed, a majority of European states actually raised their tariffs. The glittering generalities of Briand on the Geneva podium did not lead to a softening of his own country's protectionism. The French refused to consider reducing tariffs unless they had first reinforced protection.[1] The barriers to international trade were only part of a problem that included the depression in world agriculture and the chaos in international exchange and finance. Nevertheless, despite these problems, in the last half of the decade, world production and world trade continued to expand, and prices remained stable. Politicians and economists assumed that the old days of boom and bust were over and that if the national currencies remained stable, progress would continue indefinitely. That optimism persisted until the crash of 1929 shocked the leaders and nations and contributed to the rise of a virulent nationalism that would once more turn Europe in the direction of war.

THE UNITED STATES AND THE EUROPEAN RECOVERY

Foreign Loans and Foreign Policy

Creditors and Debtors. Herbert Hoover, the U.S. secretary of commerce through most of the 1920s, was a convinced advocate of independent, nongovernmental internationalism. To facilitate business activity, he established offices abroad that supplied him with extensive economic and political information. These data were the basis for constant discussions between Hoover and Secretaries of State Charles Evan Hughes and Frank B. Kellogg.[2] Hoover believed his new commercial nuncios were as vital to the formulation of American foreign policy as traditional diplomats.

Hoover opposed governmental foreign aid. He felt that economic development and prosperity had to come from private enterprise. He set idealistic goals for business: "American business needs a lifting purpose greater than the struggle of materialism. It lies in the higher pitch of economic life, in a finer regard for the rights of others, a stronger devotion to obligations of citizenship that will assure an improved leadership in every community and in the nation."[3] Hoover's faith that voluntary cooperation would generate domestic prosperity and promote world peace did not prevent him from helping the process by granting tax credits for investments abroad. He promised that companies that merged their foreign trade operations would be free from antitrust suits. His research service supplied them with the latest intelligence on foreign markets. He pushed the expansion of the merchant marine and persuaded American banks to establish branch offices abroad. He did all this despite his belief that the United States could "reestablish its material prosperity and comfort without European trade."[4]

Hoover apparently saw nothing contradictory about Americans expanding their commercial contacts abroad while maintaining protectionism at home. In his view, the "American system" should combine high tariffs with the virtual independence of the United States from foreign markets—a sort of American version of autarky. Accordingly, Americans should import less and raise their consumption of domestic production from its current 90 to 97 percent.

The cheap money policy of the Federal Reserve and the generally higher rates of interest abroad lured American investors into lending money to Europe on a vast scale. Between 1923 and 1930, private investments abroad more than tripled, going from one-sixth of the world's total to almost one-third, or from $1.3 billion to $4.5 billion.[5] Profits kept pace: from 1925 to 1929, net earnings on short- and long-term private investment went from $355 million to $565 million. During the same period, American firms significantly expanded their overseas operations, usually by producing the same things that the parent company manufactured at home.

Operating factories inside foreign countries was additional insurance. It removed the possibility that sales might be lost through tariffs and import quotas. Indeed, the subsidiaries, being proximate to European raw materials and without heavy transportation costs, held a decided competitive edge.

Underwriting European industry helped to correct the imbalance on the current account between the American creditor state and its European debtors.[6] To avoid the danger that such lending might undermine the objectives of American foreign policy, in March 1922 the White House issued a directive that all loan proposals should be submitted to the State Department for an opinion as to their political desirability. State would then pass them over to the Commerce Department for an economic opinion. Both opinions would only be advisory, however. In a letter to Hughes, Hoover warned that unless this capital were used for "reproductive purposes," there would be "little hope of economic recovery." Using American capital to subsidize unbalanced budgets or to support armies would be destructive expenditures. "The most pertinent fact with regard to Europe today," he observed pessimistically, "is that the whole political and economic life is enveloped in an atmosphere of war and not of peace. Restrictions on loans made from the United States to reproductive purposes will at least give the tendency to render impossible that form of statesmanship which would maintain such an atmosphere."[7]

On this score, at least, he and Hughes could agree. The secretary of state was not above using economic weapons as a means of political coercion. He threatened to cut back on American investments in France if Briand did not accept the American proposals at the Washington Naval Conference. Hughes feared that if the Europeans continued to build battleships, they would be less able to pay their war debts and more likely to force the United States to spend money in a naval race that the Americans wanted to avoid.

The Recipients. The top four European countries receiving American investment money were, in order, Britain, Germany, France, and Italy. Most of this money was invested in industries traditionally regarded as the safest: electrical goods, machine tools, and metal products. Other investments ran the gamut from automobiles to typewriters, record players, and milling machines and even Spanish cork, Madeira lace, and French gloves. (One sector that did not benefit was the liquor industry. The United States still had a constitutional amendment outlawing intoxicating beverages, and the Republican administration wanted Americans to avoid promoting the consumption of alcohol.) Such extensive American involvement in European business could hardly be called a policy of isolationism. As a result, changes in American interest rates came to have a more profound effect on relations between nations than embassies filled with diplomats. In 1927, the peak year of American investing abroad, over $1.5 billion of foreign securities were sold on the American market; 40 percent of these transactions were for Europe alone.

The French were delighted to get American credits at last. Their failure to obtain American loans immediately after the war was at least partially responsible for their demanding large reparations payments from Germany. Most of the money they received was in direct investments. The British did even better. They attracted about one-third of all American investments in Europe. Not far behind came the Germans. In many ways, American investment in the German economy was the most remarkable and, as it proved, the most hazardous.

German large-scale borrowing began with the offering of the first international loan under the Dawes Plan in October 1924. The American quota of the $200 million offering was $110 million. From then until July 1929, the Germans floated 161 stock and bond issues on the American market, totaling nearly $1.25 billion.[8] In 1926, 23 percent of all American foreign security loans went to Germany with the biggest customers being the German central government and the individual federal states. Bavaria floated three bond issues for a total of $43 million, Prussia received $42 million, and the district of Hamburg $15 million. German cities ran up a total of $132 million, the leader being Berlin with $29 million; next came Frankfurt-am-Main with $9 million, followed by Munich, Cologne, and Württemberg, with over $8 million each. These municipalities often used these funds for huge, prestigious public works projects—civic centers, sports complexes, and parks. Although German urban renewal was certainly not an American foreign policy objective, it might as well have been.

Money was also extended to public utility companies like the Stetten Public Utilities Company, the Oberfalz Electric Power Company, the Rhine-Ruhr Water Service Union, and the Hamburg Elevated, Underground, and Street Railway Company. There were loans to public and private banking and credit companies and loans to Germany's industrial giants: the Krupp Iron Works, the August Thyssen Steel Works, and the United Steel Works. Money became available for railway and steamship companies, a cable company, a motion picture studio, a department store, and the Leipzig Trade Fair Corporation. Real estate developers in Berlin, needing money to build houses, went to the New York market. Silesian land-owners, wanting funds to improve their farms, went to the New York market. The Roman Catholic church of Bavaria, desiring to promote certain of its welfare projects, went to the New York market. Catholics from other regions of Germany and Protestants also went to the New York market.[9] The flow of so much American wealth to Germany was a great delight to Gustav Stresemann who promoted economic recovery as a means of increasing Germany's political leverage.

The Germans took full advantage of this "foreign aid" to rationalize and modernize their industries, thereby creating the power upon which future demands for revision of the Versailles treaty would be based. Stresemann even considered arranging some sort of a loan to France to facilitate a revision of the war debt the French owed the United States.[10] For this favor, the Germans would naturally press for revision of the Dawes Plan and the removal of all foreign troops from the Rhineland. However, the import of so much capital also had dangers: the threat of inflation and the possibility that German interest rates would be manipulated by the American government. The Germans might become more independent in Europe but at the expense of surrendering some of their sovereignty to the United States. On 12 November 1926, the Weimar government's Advisory Board on Foreign Loans endeavored to tighten control over the borrowing of the federal states and the municipalities by imposing a 10 percent tax on income from all foreign securities. Initially, the measure had some effect and led to a decline of borrowing. In 1928, however, the volume of German securities issued in the United States surged forward again. But in October 1929, the New York Stock Exchange plunged precipitously; the crash caused a severe retraction of investment capital in Europe and helped plunge Germany into depression and political chaos.

The Trouble on Wall Street

Tight Money. Since the beginning of the 1920s, the price of leading common stocks on the New York exchange had more than quadrupled. These high prices were borne aloft by a collective belief that the bull market had found the secret of immortality and a profound, unprecedented (and misplaced) faith in the infallibility of American business. Those who contradicted the American businessman's confidence in the future economic growth of the country risked being called unpatriotic, intimations of doom and gloom being perceived as alien to the American character. The superabundance of investment capital encouraged entrepreneurs to expand their businesses with the expectation that the market would cheerfully be able to absorb all new production. Andrew Mellon, the secretary of the treasury, assured the country that the system was fundamentally sound even though stock values were above any acknowledged reasonable relationship to earnings. Occasional downturns in the index were explained as "seasonal corrections." The strong performance of such pacesetting industries as housing and construction and automobile production blinded people to the sick agricultural sector. The federal government took a hands-off attitude. It made no serious attempt to impose restraint on the foreign securities market and opposed all action to introduce the mildest sort of regulations into the stock market. Secretary of the Treasury Mellon was a firm believer in the "trickle down" effect in economics. He preached that the success of American business was due to the lightness of its tax burden and the absence of regulation. The resultant growth would ultimately engulf the whole community in prosperity. Mellon's policies of rapid accumulation of wealth and investment helped to swell the bubble that was about to burst. As long as the prices on the stock market were going up, few complained.

In July 1929, industrial production dropped slightly, but then recovered and continued to rise. The decline in stock values persisted, however, and in October, the securities index took a steep nosedive. Leading shares tumbled. Marginal traders, unable to produce the extra cash to protect their loans, were forced to sell.[11] Yet even at this late hour, some financial experts were saying that the price of stocks had not yet caught up with their real value. On 24 October 1929, confidence revived when the heads of some of New York's biggest banks—the Chase, Morgan's, Guaranty Trust, Bankers Trust, and National City Bank—agreed to come to the support of the market. Prices remained steady for several days. Then came 29 October, "Black Tuesday," the worst day in the history of the New York stock market. A record-setting 23.5 million shares changed hands on the New York Stock and Curb Exchanges. Before it was over, $18 billion on paper had disappeared. Worse was to follow. Over the next few days, another $40 billion disappeared—a sum equivalent to the entire cost of the United States' participation in World War I. During the first week of November, coincidental with the publication of the song "Happy Days Are Here Again," the market started to recover. By the following April, it had struggled back, from an index low of 145 to 171. This was the last gasp of the dying patient. In June 1932, the index hit bottom at 34, with blue chip stocks pacing the descent: U.S. Steel fell from a 1929 high of $261\frac{3}{4}$ to a 1931 low of 36, Eastman Kodak dropped from $264\frac{3}{4}$ to 77, and Westinghouse toppled from $298\frac{5}{8}$ to $22\frac{1}{2}$.

A Crisis of Liquidity. The American stock market crash was a critical factor in causing a great worldwide depression. The Wall Street boom had repatriated a large share of the investment capital that had formerly been loaned to Europe to assist recovery. Foreign securities, freely quoted on the New York market, were in ferocious competition with American common stocks. The bond market was abandoned because investors were reluctant to tie up money in securities that paid fixed rates of interest. Reconstruction loans, issued as bonds, were dumped back on the market.

When the New York market began to slide, the flow of money to the United States increased. New foreign security issues on the New York market dropped to zero. And American short-term credit, upon which many European governments relied to maintain their budgetary equilibrium, almost disappeared. The international situation did not cause the crash, but the effect of the crash on the rest of the world was overpowering. The sudden contraction of American demand and the repatriation of money forced down prices and created a monumental shortage of capital. Hoover and his advisers believed that periodic downswings in the business cycle were not only inevitable but necessary, and they refused to use the authority of the government to temper the crisis. Mellon advocated meeting the depression through retrenchment. The Federal Reserve made some effort to curb speculation and continued its tight money policy. And the Republican-dominated Congress further limited foreign competition by passing the highest schedule of tariffs in the history of the United States: the Hawley-Smoot Act of 1930.

Between 1929 and 1932, American trade declined by two-thirds. In 1931, the government at last tried to spur economic activity through public works and subsidies to industry and agriculture. The funds were inadequate and had little effect: unemployment reached 14 million, the index of industrial production fell by more than 50 percent, and payrolls dropped by two-thirds. The already unbalanced international economic structure heightened the impact the collapse of the American economy had on the rest of the world. The inflationary way in which most belligerents had financed the war helped to create monetary instability. War debts and reparations, used by France as a means of political coercion, had subverted normal financial and commercial relations. The fall of world prices prompted greater protectionism and seriously undermined international cooperation and specialization. In eastern Europe, virulent national rivalries had already thwarted stability. Every state actively feared or was engaged in a running dispute with at least one of its neighbors. Each successor state had enormous problems with its own minorities. Most of the area was agrarian, backward, and economically weak, and practically all the states there had lapsed into repressive dictatorships. It was a perfect environment for catching the American virus.

THE RECESSION HITS EUROPE

The Infection Spreads

The Collapse of the Kreditanstalt. It took more than a year for the full effects of the American stock market crash to hit Europe. It first affected one of the weakest and most artificial of the eastern countries, Austria. Austrian leaders had tried to avert the impending crisis by attempting to form a customs union with Germany—a move first proposed soon after the war. In March 1931, the two countries agreed to abolish all bilateral tariffs and arrange complete commercial assimilation. The French objected as they had done previously. They feared the political repercussions of such an arrangement. They remembered the Prussian Zollverein, which had formed the framework for the eventual unification of Germany, and were particularly suspicious because the proposed Austro-German customs union came on the heels of the final evacuation of French troops from the Rhineland. Great Britain, Italy, and the countries of the Little Entente were also opposed. In May, the matter was referred to the Permanent Court of International

Justice in The Hague to determine whether such a union was contrary to the treaties of Versailles and St. Germain.

Meanwhile on 12 May 1931, Austria's largest bank, the *Kreditanstalt*, declared that it was unable to meet its obligations. The announcement caused financial panic throughout Central Europe. The Austrian government and the Rothschilds, who had founded the bank in 1855, struggled to restore solvency. In June, the British treasury loaned the Kreditanstalt 150 million Austrian shillings (about $20 million), enough to guarantee the bank's foreign debts. But confidence could not be restored, and the crisis spread.

A wave of selling hit the German investment market, which was already weakened by anxiety over the success of extremist parties in the national elections. Foreign banks (mainly American, Dutch, and Swiss) began to repatriate their short-term capital. Desperately, the Germans tried to protect the value of their currency by cashing gold and foreign exchange reserves. During the first three weeks of June, they saw over one billion marks (about $250 million) worth disappear. They raised the discount rate from five to seven percent, but this only heightened fears about the collapse the German government was trying to prevent. On 20 June, following a two-day spree in which the Reichsbank lost 150 million marks, President Hoover, acting on an appeal from Hindenburg, suggested a moratorium on all interallied war debts and on the payment of reparations. European governments discussed the proposal while the situation deteriorated further. The French government, supported by the Socialists, accepted the moratorium in principle, but many parliamentarians were opposed because they feared that a debt holiday would lead to the complete abandonment of reparations. The American president's proposal struck them as particularly unfair and selfish. France would receive no payments for a year, while the Americans still expected war debts to be paid. The French stood to lose 2 billion francs and wanted compensation for such a sacrifice.

The French also felt ill-treated by the British. Montague Norman, the governor of the Bank of England, had begged them not to redeem their holdings of British securities to keep from worsening the crisis. However, on 24 September 1931, when the British decided to let their currency float on the open market, the pound immediately fell in value, causing the French portfolio to incur heavy losses. French exports were also hurt the following year when the British slapped a 20 percent duty on foreign manufactured goods.[12]

Germany quickly exhausted a $200 million loan advanced through the Bank for International Credits. By July, the panic touched private banking. On 13 July, the prestigious Darmstadt and National Bank (the Danat) closed its doors. The failure was linked to calamitous stock market speculations of the North German Wool Exchange, one of the nation's largest textile firms. The Danat, its principal creditor, was left with worthless paper. The Dresdner Bank, the Commerz Bank, and the Deutsche Bank, which also had a financial stake in the Wool Exchange, were likewise affected. The situation sparked a general run on the banks. The government was able to stave off complete disaster only by establishing control over foreign exchange, closing the stock market, and rationing bank payments. The Finance Ministry raised the discount rate to an astronomical 15 percent, which stabilized things until August, when the moratorium agreement was finally approved. Any relief, though, had to come from abroad. The British had experience in such things and were willing to help, but they no longer had the means.

The British Abandon the Gold Standard. Great Britain was a leading market for short-term capital movements and was second only to the United States as the world's leading creditor nation. Nevertheless, the British had had difficulty sustaining a real postwar recovery. The depression of certain basic industries, like cotton textiles, shipbuilding, and, of course, coal, contributed to the high rate of unemployment. Foreign trade was down because of the decision taken in 1925 to return the pound to the prewar gold standard. This overvaluation of the currency made many British goods too expensive. Not everyone was affected, however, because the price of raw materials was relatively low in comparison with manufactured goods. Consequently, industries dependent on such imports were shielded from the worst effects of the gold policy, but the low cost of raw materials limited the buying power of foreign countries that once had been good customers for British exports. Thus, this "scissors" effect cushioned Britain but at the same time made an effective recovery more difficult.

The British, like the Americans, were reluctant to impose regulations on their booming securities market. Such permissiveness led to eventual abuse that helped to shake the confidence of investors at what turned out to be a crucial time. The most famous fraud of the late twenties was the stock manipulation capers of Clarence Charles Hatry. The presiding judge at Hatry's trial called the scheme the most appalling that "ever disfigured the commercial reputation of the country." Hatry, taking advantage of easy credit, had created a gigantic conglomerate that included department stores, home finance corporations, and vending machine companies. He used these companies as security to mobilize the eight million pounds necessary to purchase the entire capital, debentures, and obligations of the United Steel Companies, Ltd. He then "borrowed" more, using forged securities and duplicated shares of stock as collateral. When the decline of the stock market in the summer of 1929 prompted Hatry's creditors to demand additional guarantees, the confidence man admitted certain irregularities and tried unsuccessfully to stall for time. On 20 September 1929, trading was suspended in six of Hatry's companies. An official investigation revealed that Hatry had bilked investors of 13,750,000 pounds (roughly $67 million). The con-man was sentenced to fourteen years in prison. Many believed the punishment was excessive, since most of Hatry's victims had been banks, brokerage houses, financial institutions, and wealthy investors, all of whom should have known better and would certainly have little difficulty covering their losses. Some even said that it was a shame to put a man like that behind bars when his talents could be used to help the government make money.

The Bank of England tried to attract foreign capital and restore confidence by raising the discount rate from 5.5 to 6.5 percent. In particular, the governors wanted to maintain the level of lending from the United States. They insisted on keeping the London money market open, even though other countries were adopting exchange controls. But the effects of the Wall Street crash and the subsequent crises in Austria and Germany were too great for the British to continue business as usual. Foreign investors began cashing in their sterling accounts and selling their British securities. They demanded that the Bank of England reimburse them in gold. During the last two weeks of July 1931, the Bank of England lost $10 million worth of gold daily. At the same time, new orders for British goods continued to slide. Even a $225 million advance from the Bank of France and the American Federal Reserve could not reverse the trend. The British requested further credits. The French and Americans refused, demanding that the British first balance their budget. With their room to maneuver restricted, British leaders hastily formed a new national union government composed of Conservatives and members of the Labour party loyal to leader Ramsay MacDonald. The national government proposed to balance the budget by cutting the salaries of civil servants

(10 percent for teachers, 5 percent for police officers), slashing allowances by 10 percent, and increasing taxes. The new government, headed by MacDonald, then obtained a loan of 80 million pounds from the New York Federal Reserve and the Bank of Paris.

Money still continued to flow out of Britain in great quantities. The austerity program failed to restore confidence, and the new foreign credit was almost gone within two weeks. On 21 September 1931, Britain finally abandoned the gold standard. Most other countries followed suit if they had not done so before. John Maynard Keynes, who had been a long-time critic of Britain's monetary policy—especially Churchill's overevaluation of the pound—felt the abandonment of gold was the first step toward recovery. Many feared the action would have immense psychological consequences, however. Arnold Toynbee wrote that "the members of this great and ancient and hitherto triumphant society were asking themselves whether the secular process of Western life and growth might conceivably be coming to an end in their day."[13] In fact, most people scarcely noticed the difference.

There was more concern over the proposal to enact protective tariffs. Many politicians and businessmen still considered the principles of free trade sacrosanct. The British Labour party flatly opposed a tariff. The Liberal party was split over the issue. The Conservatives were in favor, but they recognized that the question was too serious to be resolved without a new mandate from the electorate and, in October 1931, called for new elections. Prime Minister MacDonald campaigned for a doctor's mandate, a free hand to cure economic problems as the government saw fit. The coalition government had no real program, but then neither did the opposition. The British people hoped for the best and voted overwhelmingly for Conservative candidates who captured 472 seats. The opposition won 31 percent of the popular vote but less than 10 percent of the seats in Commons. MacDonald remained prime minister until his retirement in 1935; but his faction was weak, and the Conservative leader Stanley Baldwin exercised the real power. Baldwin had presided over the lackluster Tory administration in the last half of the twenties. His victory signaled a return to past attitudes, not new solutions. Baldwin had no disposition for strong action or for any experimentation.

The government let the pound float downward, and it reversed Britain's traditional free trade policy by imposing high tariffs on imports. The devaluation of the pound had a deflationary effect on other currencies and added to the confusion in the world economy. However, as the prices of British goods dropped in foreign countries, trade picked up. Eventually retaliation, particularly from the United States, again slowed it down. In the 1930s, the British economy became more parochial. Its expansion came largely from the domestic market. Consumption increased as real wages began to outstrip prices and the cost of living remained steady. The British depression bottomed out in 1932, marking a starting point for recovery. Progress continued throughout the rest of the decade, but this was due less to a dynamic economy than to increased government spending on weapons of war. The British were generally reluctant to throw money at the depression especially if that caused budgetary deficits, but putting money into national defense was a permissible exception. Rearmament reduced unemployment. The results seemed to prove what economist Keynes had advocated in *The General Theory of Employment, Interest and Money*: spending was good for recovery.

Profile: The New Economics of John Maynard Keynes (1883–1946)

When *The General Theory of Employment, Interest and Money* appeared in 1936, a 15 percent rate of unemployment plagued Britain. About two million workers were affected. The stability and well-being of prewar days seemed gone forever, and past economic beliefs and assumptions began dying as well. To those who believed that all economic problems would ultimately be solved by the free, unfettered operation of the forces of the marketplace, Keynes replied that "ultimately we shall all be dead." Keynes had once accepted the classical views on supply and demand that he had learned at Cambridge where he had been a student of Alfred Marshall, the great laissez-faire economist.[14] Keynes now explained the causes of the depression and unemployment differently.

His general theory maintained that output could not increase unless demand were deliberately strengthened. Keynes wrote that while wage cuts might temporarily benefit a particular business, such cuts were disastrous for economic recovery in the long run: less money reduced demand and less demand reduced production. Adherents of laissez-faire capitalism believed that the normal situation was one of fluctuation between full employment and widespread unemployment,[15] and that production would increase until an equilibrium had been achieved at full employment. But Keynes argued that the level of output and the rate of employment were determined by total consumption and investment. If the entire labor force was not needed to achieve a balance, there would be unemployment. Indeed, it was unavoidable because the amount of goods and services that a community purchased was influenced primarily by income. People were disposed "to increase their consumption as their income increases, but not as much as the increase in their income." An increase in a propensity to consume was the key to recovery and to heightened business activity. Anticipated profits determined investment, which, in turn, was based on the level of business activity and the cost of borrowing money.[16] The central bank determined monetary supply and interest rates.

Therefore, if a government wanted full employment, it should take active steps to promote more investment. A cheap money policy would stimulate private investment and raise the level of aggregate demand. At the same time, the government should also promote growth through increased expenditures on public works. Any activity was better than nothing. "If the Treasury," Keynes wrote, "were to fill old bottles with banknotes, bury them at suitable depths in disused coal mines which are then filled up to the surface with town rubbish, and leave it to private enterprise on well-tried principles of *laissez-faire* to dig the notes up again, ... there need be no more unemployment and, with the help of the repercussions, the real income of the community, and its capital wealth also, would probably become a good deal greater than it actually is."[17] Keynes drew an analogy between such activity and gold mining, which societies found completely proper although it added "nothing whatever to the real wealth of the world."

Keynesian theory disturbed traditional assumptions and seemed to run contrary to the entire Protestant ethic, which preached saving, not spending. Keynes was pessimistic about the government taking his ideas seriously. He said that practical men who believed themselves free from intellectual influences were usually the slaves of some dead economist. "Mad men in authority, who hear voices in the air, are distilling their frenzy from some academic scribbles of a few years back. I am sure that power of vested interests is vastly exaggerated compared with the gradual encroachment of ideas. . . . [For ultimately], it is ideas, not vested interests, which are dangerous for good or evil."[18] Keynes seemed to be proved correct when the British government embarked on a program of rearmament. This was the level of spending Keynes had advocated, but, as he had written bitterly, wars "have been the only form of large-scale loan expenditure which statesmen have thought justifiable."

However, if spending (adding money to the economy) was a way to ease the depression, then taxation (taking money away from the economy) was a way of easing inflation. The formula was not automatically successful in practice. Inflation and depression did not always prove to be countervailing forces. They sometimes went hand in hand as the "stagflation" eras of the 1970s and 1980s would show. Still Keynesian thought has provided the rationale for the central government management of most modern European currencies, from the Bank of England to the Bank of France to the Deutschesbank. Almost everywhere, it has been considered bad politics to leave a nation's financial system at the mercy of free enterprise.

The German Depression. Though the Young Plan was still technically operative, it now had no chance of being fulfilled. From 1924 to 1930, Germany borrowed about $240 million annually, making it easy to pay reparations and the interest on debts.[19] The money also allowed an increase in gold reserves and provided adequate capital to finance business recovery. Such an abundance of money disposed municipal governments to finance extravagant public works and induced entrepreneurs to overcapitalize their businesses in anticipation of increased volumes of sales. Loans, frequently borrowed at short-term rates, were made available to industry at long-term rates. But in 1929, foreign borrowing began to dry up and within two years disappeared almost entirely.

Furthermore, Germany found no demand for its exports, and creditors refused reimbursement in anything but hard currency. Deprived of foreign loans, and unable to earn money through exports, Germany could no longer pay reparations, which had previously been taken out of the increased revenues from industrial taxes. Between 1928 and 1932, German national income declined from 75 billion to 45 billion marks; the volume of industrial production dropped 46 percent and the output of capital goods by 65 percent. In two years, unemployment rose from 1.3 million to 3 million workers. At the same time, increased welfare payments to those out of work, coupled with decreasing revenues from taxes, put an intolerable strain on public finances. The government coalition of Social Democrats, Catholic Centrists, Liberal Democrats, and People's party conservatives (with constituents ranging from the labor unions on the left to industrial managers on the right) could not agree on a program to restore stability to the national finances.

The unemployment insurance fund became insolvent. The workers wanted the employers to increase the benefits that the employers wanted to reduce. Chancellor Hermann Müller, a Social Democrat, tried to negotiate a compromise. He proposed to cut expenses and raise everybody's contribution from 3.5 to 3.75 percent. The scheme was rejected by Müller's own party, and the chancellor resigned. The crisis over 0.25 percent developed into a major disaster for the democratic system.

Müller's successor, Heinrich Brüning, tried to get economic aid from France. The French were afraid of a resurgence of extreme German nationalism. They were especially alarmed at the recent electoral success of rightist parties in the Rhineland, following the evacuation of Allied troops, and at the German navy's construction of "pocket battleships." French premier Pierre Laval would not consider giving Germany economic aid unless he first got a moratorium against further revision of the Treaty of Versailles. Brüning told Laval such a commitment would lead to his downfall. Laval replied that he would also be overthrown if he made the loan without such guarantees. Brüning said despairingly, "It will always be the same drama between [France and Germany]. We will never make the same gesture nor utter at the same time the same words."[20]

Losing their jobs traumatized the German workers. Hoards of beggars clogged the city streets, men stood around on street corners, factories were idle, and shops pulled down their shutters. For the second time within a decade, the nation had suffered a major economic collapse. The middle and lower-middle classes were especially affected. They viewed proletarianization as the worst possible humiliation and were willing to trade political freedom for economic security with little hesitation. The increased efficiency of German industry, which had supplied so much of the country's prosperity, was the source of increased misery. Rationalization of industry had contributed to increased unemployment even before the crash and thereby helped to strengthen extremist political parties. Not surprisingly, the support for such parties increased in a direct ratio to unemployment.[21]

The misfortune of the Germans was that they were unable to agree on a series of institutions that would remain through thick and thin. While historically the French had had an equally impressive history of contempt for democracy, they had long ago made their peace with the Third Republic as the government that divided them least.

French Protectionism. France had been able to withstand the initial effects of the world depression with relative ease. Isolated behind a wall of protectionism with a domestic market cushioned by a series of cartel arrangements and by a recent devaluation of the franc, France could almost rejoice at its good fortune.

A run on the Darmstadt and National Bank has the Berlin police holding off worried depositors. The bank collapsed in July 1931. Such closings took a heavy toll on the liquid resources of the middle class, which seems to make up the majority of this crowd.

Furthermore, the government of André Tardieu (1929–1932) was in the midst of a great program of national refurbishment: public works programs, improvement of the infrastructure, and social security legislation. Tardieu wanted an effective two-party system with a strong executive in the manner of Britain and the United States. The politicians and the voters, however, failed to respond to his plans for political reform. And so did the economy.

In the second half of 1931, a definite downswing occurred, occasioned by a serious restriction in sales abroad and a perilous drop in tourism, which affected thousands of people in the hotel and transportation industries and in the manufacture and sale of luxury goods. The resultant cutbacks and loss of foreign exchange heightened political tensions and revealed more than ever the essential inefficiency of many sectors of the French economy.

No area was more backward than agriculture.[22] France had some of the best farmland in the world—it was the only European country capable of feeding its own people—but popular consumption of many basic commodities including milk, sugar, meat, fruits, and vegetables was significantly inferior to that of Germany, Belgium, Great Britain, and Scandinavia. Many French farms were badly equipped and poorly organized and were only marginally productive. Since the war, the purchasing power of the French peasants had steadily declined. Although politicians acknowledged the legitimate grievances of their rural constituents from time to time, they made little effort to satisfy their needs. Politically, they could get away with such behavior because the peasants were more poorly organized than the urban workers. Only larger producers carried enough weight to command special attention. Therefore, in 1931, the government focused its efforts mostly on providing protection to the two main "electoral crops," wine and wheat.

The French wine producers had traditionally received a high degree of protection against foreign competition, even getting increased duties on tea, which was regarded as a competitive beverage. However, the slackening of world demand brought on by the depression, which happened to correspond with a series of bumper crops, dropped the price of wine below its cost of production. The government tried to offset the loss by regulating planting and marketing and subsidizing an uprooting of vines. It ordered the distillation of wine into industrial alcohol, which it sold at a loss (at taxpayers' expense) to producers of motor fuel. The wine growers tried to boost consumption through advertising. They touted their product as "the strength and joy of the world" and denounced the "pernicious campaign that blames it for the damages of alcoholism." They extolled wine as a national treasure. Despite all these efforts, the price of wine still continued to fall. Over the next five years, foreign sales dropped by 68 percent.[23] A similar situation prevailed in the wheat market. The amount produced remained fairly steady, but prices collapsed. In 1935, the General Association of Wheat Growers declared that they had hit their lowest level since the French Revolution. The government established controls over acreage and began purchasing surplus output, but these protective measures failed to stabilize prices. In pandering to such special interests, the government failed to promote the general well-being of the economy. The French paid for such short-sightedness with a sluggish recovery and increased social tension which would lead to increased exasperation with the institutions of the Third Republic.

International Solutions

The End of War Debts and Reparations. The decline of world trade and the prevailing anarchy in European finances mandated a readjustment of international debts. At the end of 1931, a special advisory committee of the International Bank of Settlements declared that Germany was too weak to be able to resume paying reparations after the moratorium expired on 30 June 1932. The crisis had destroyed the will to collect, and even the French were becoming resigned to abolition. In July 1932, the Reparations Conference at Lausanne agreed to liquidate Germany's entire obligation in a final payment of three billion marks. The British, French, Belgians, and Italians made their ratification conditional upon a satisfactory settlement of war debts. Even now the United States was no more disposed to recognize the interrelationship of reparations and war debts than it had been ten years earlier. Members of Congress, government officials, and community leaders found it popular to accuse the Europeans of using the crisis as an excuse to cheat on their debts.

The new Democratic president, Franklin Roosevelt, who was inaugurated in January 1933, was similarly reluctant to consider cancellation of war debts. He was willing to negotiate and invited the British to Washington for discussions. The atmosphere was cordial, but the Americans pointed out that until a final solution could be reached, they still expected to receive their semiannual debt installments on schedule. Britain consented to pay a token amount, $10 million, and Roosevelt eased the burden somewhat by allowing the sum to be acquitted in silver at the rate of 50 cents an ounce—a considerable savings since Britain bought the necessary 20 million ounces from the government of India at the world price of 30 cents an ounce. The British were unable to reach any final settlement. They made another token payment in December 1933, though not in silver. Four months later, the U.S. Congress demanded integral reimbursement, and Britain stopped all payments. Those countries that had not already defaulted followed suit. Only Finland, whose obligation was a minuscule part of the overall Russian debt, continued to meet its annuities much to the enduring respect of the Americans.

The Value of Cooperation. The British thought the international crisis required more than a piecemeal approach, and largely through their efforts, a World Economic Conference met in London, at the South Kensington Geological Museum, in June 1933. Sixty-six states sent a total of 168 official delegates, making it the largest international gathering since the Paris Peace Conference, and the most ambitious attempt to solve the depression. George V personally gave the speech of welcome, speaking of the "new recognition of the interdependence of nations and of the value of collaboration." The king hoped that this "new consciousness of common interests" would be put to the "service of mankind."[24] His words were well enough received and touched off a staggering amount of similar optimistic rhetoric.

The delegates generally agreed that a financial equilibrium should be regained as soon as possible, and that this could best be assured by a return to the gold standard. The French, for example, were even willing to allow some of their own copious gold reserves be used to further the process. They particularly wanted to help stabilize the pound to restore Britain's ability to grant short-term loans to Eastern Europe, where French political interests were strong. Even before the conference began, Edouard Daladier remarked to MacDonald that the presence of German paramilitary units in the Rhineland "did not exactly facilitate the regulation of economic questions."[25] The French premier predicted that if events continued to develop that way, the conference would have little chance of success. The French sadly realized that economic stabilization was impossible without political stabilization.

The British were eager to become the world's banker again, but they thought that the return to a satisfactory international monetary standard was conditional on several factors: a proper settlement of the war debts problem, a general reduction of tariffs, and a substantial increase in world prices. Everybody had different priorities, however. Much time was therefore wasted on trying to agree to an agenda. The delegates also could not decide whether to accept the most-favored-nation principle or to reduce customs through bilateral and multilateral agreements. Understandably, the conference could only reach a consensus on secondary matters—like the scheme to impose special restrictions on the sales of wheat and silver.

After one week of deliberations, Senator Key Pittman, the deputy-leader of the American delegation, presented a resolution for the reestablishment of a gold standard for international exchange. The United States had gone off gold in April 1933, and the new Democratic administration was deliberately fostering inflation: it was allowing the value of the dollar to decline in order to encourage an increase in prices and wages and a decline in interest rates to stimulate business activity. Secretary of State Cordell Hull, the head of the American delegation in London, was at a complete loss as to how he could build negotiations around such unpredictable financial experimentation. Hull was also hampered in his efforts to negotiate a mutual reduction of tariffs, which he considered to be as important as the achievement of equilibrium in exchange. In that spirit, he advised that the elimination of tariffs and other restrictions and obstructions was essential to the stabilization of currencies. Yet the administration dragged its feet in introducing the proper legislation. It was doubtful whether Roosevelt himself had yet made up his mind which course to follow. Only after Hull had reached a preliminary understanding with the British and French on currency stabilization did Roosevelt send the bad news that he would continue to allow the dollar to fluctuate.

A Hatchet Job. Roosevelt sent Raymond Moley to London to brief the American delegation. On 22 June, Hull finally admitted that Washington found "measures of temporary stabilization would be untimely." The announcement shocked the conference. Prime Minister Ramsay MacDonald remarked with classic understatement, "during this week we have had a little setback." Moley apparently did not want to be regarded as the villain, and he joined the U.S. delegation in trying to find a compromise that could serve until American finances became more settled. The resultant position paper advocated international monetary stability and endorsed efforts to limit speculation. It allowed countries to reestablish a general international gold standard "when the time comes." However, even this innocuous declaration struck Roosevelt as excessive. On board his yacht at Campobello, he delivered the coup de grace: he said it would be a world tragedy if the great conference of nations should "allow itself to be diverted by the proposal of a purely artificial and temporary experiment affecting the monetary exchange of a few nations only."[26]

The American president's cable plunged the conference into a fatal coma. The patient died on 27 July. Roosevelt was blamed for its death. Clearly, no world currency stabilization could have been achieved without fixing an exchange ratio between the pound and the dollar. Roosevelt was interested solely in the recovery of the United States and refused to consider any curtailing of his options. He in turn blamed the demise of the conference on the failure of the Europeans to solve the fundamental causes of the depression, whatever that meant. It was obvious that most European states were no more convinced internationalists than the American president. All found it more convenient to point the finger elsewhere than admit their own failings. The depression made nations more self-absorbed than usual. Under the circumstances, it was difficult to convince leaders that by being a bit less selfish they might undertake policies that were mutually advantageous. The settlement that ended World War I did not encourage such thinking, and statesmen reacted in the only way they knew—by relying on solutions of the past. Roosevelt, though, seemed eager to try anything. His own inclination was to spend his way out of the depression any way he saw fit. As a practical politician, he realized that his constituency was not the world. His Wilsonian instincts would rise to the surface later.

POSTSCRIPT   European countries owed the United States more than $10 billion for their collective wartime purchases of weapons and supplies.[27] Since most of this money had been spent in the United States and had contributed to American industrial development, the expectation was that Washington would write off the debts as part of the cost of fighting the war. The Americans demanded full reimbursement. They were well within their rights to do so, but to foster the kind of prosperity that would have made such repayment possible, they would have had to be willing to actively promote the stabilization of international exchange and to allow the Europeans to earn money through sales on the American markets. Instead, the Americans raised their tariffs, obliging debtors to sell their goods elsewhere. American entrepreneurs, insulated from dependence on international commerce by a vast domestic market, conducted their foreign financial transactions as an extension of their own domestic requirements.

Many Americans were bitter about their failure to make the world safe for democracy. They still viewed European politicians as Old World retrogrades who delighted in rehashing old disputes and conflicts. That the United States remained aloof from the political affairs of Europe as much as possible was deemed wise policy. President Warren G. Harding once boasted to a *New York Times* reporter, "I don't know anything about this European stuff." And his similarly inclined successor, Calvin Coolidge, said about the Locarno Pact, "I don't know any way that America could cooperate in that. It seems to be that it is almost entirely a European political subject in which we can't take any very helpful part."[28] But Coolidge was determined to get the Europeans to pay their war debts. Any hint of cancellation brought his simmering anti-Europeanism to a boil. The chief executive had never been to Europe—he had never even been outside the country except to Montreal on his honeymoon and later to Cuba on a two-day visit—and he judged everything by his own parochial standards.

Secretaries of State Charles Evans Hughes and Frank Kellogg did not consider themselves isolationists, but after the war the United States had reduced its political commitments to Europe. The refusal to become involved in guaranteeing European security clearly did not extend to commercial activity, however. This preoccupation with economics came from a determined desire to foster the interests of American business, as well as from a belief that peace could be promoted through private investment and an increased exchange of goods and services. During the 1920s, the Department of Commerce was under the direction of men who strongly believed in world peace through world trade. Such privatized foreign policy put the American government at a disadvantage when it needed to act more officially. Nevertheless, it remained reluctant to make any long-lasting commitments, let alone offer political guarantees. Admittedly, American isolationism was not as complete as it is often represented, but the United States government seemed willing to come to the aid of Europeans only in times of crisis. The Dawes and Young Plans were good indications of how Americans liked to operate. They preferred subjecting political problems to technical solutions. The approach was admirable and proved effective, but continuing success could only be assured by long-range involvement. World War I and the Great Depression clearly showed how interrelated American and European economic and security interests were. Yet during the 1930s, the Americans again let Europeans try to sort out their differences and problems among themselves. After World War II, this mistake would not be repeated.

ENDNOTES

1. *Survey of International Affairs, 1930* (London: Oxford University Press, 1931), 493.
2. Herbert Hoover, *Memoirs: The Cabinet and the Presidency, 1920–1933* (New York: Macmillan, 1952), 177.
3. Melvyn P. Leffler, *The Elusive Quest: America's Pursuit of European Stability and French Security, 1919–1933* (Chapel Hill: University of North Carolina Press, 1979), 172.
4. Ibid., 81.
5. U.S. Department of Commerce, *Balance of International Payments of the United States, 1926–1933* (Washington, D.C.: U.S. Government Printing Office, 1927–33).
6. U.S. Department of Commerce, *American Underwriting of Foreign Securities* (Washington, D.C.: U.S. Government Printing Office, 1928–31).
7. Hoover, *Memoirs*, 87.
8. Commerce Department, *American Underwriting of Foreign Securities* (1928, 1931).
9. See especially Commerce Department, *American Underwriting of German Securities* (1929).
10. French Foreign Ministry Archives: *MAE*. Série Z, vol. 400, 198.
11. Permissive legislation allowed purchasers of stock to borrow up to four-fifths the price of their investment. At the end of 1928, such outstanding stock loans totaled nearly $6.5 billion.
12. While French imports remained fairly constant, exports steadily declined. In 1933, they earned only 21 billion francs, compared to 38 billion four years earlier. From 1931 to 1933, France had an average deficit of 10.6 billion francs in its balance of payments. Textiles were hit especially hard, and the market for luxury items, like leather goods and jewelry, practically disappeared. The whole price structure was undermined. From a high of 660 (1913 = 100), the wholesale index fell to 442 by the end of 1931, continuing downward to 322 in July 1935.
13. *Survey of International Affairs, 1931,* 1.
14. The most important biography of Keynes is the one written by his former student

and colleague: Roy Harrod, *The Life of John Maynard Keynes* (New York: Macmillan, 1951).

15. A lengthy explanation of the Keynesian Revolution can be found in Dudley Dillard, *The Economics of John Maynard Keynes: The Theory of a Monetary Economy* (Englewood Cliffs, N.J.: Prentice-Hall, 1958).

16. John Maynard Keynes, *The General Theory of Employment, Interest and Money* (New York: Harcourt Brace, 1935).

17. Ibid., 129.

18. Ibid., 383–84.

19. Until the depression, Germany paid 22,891,000,000 gold marks in reparations. Of this, France received less than half, or 9,585,000,000 gold marks, barely enough to cover one-third of its reconstruction costs.

20. *International Herald Tribune*, 11 April 1970.

21. For example, in 1928, when registered unemployment was 1.3 million, the Nazis had 24 seats in the Reichstag. In 1930, when it was 3 million, they had 107 seats. In July 1932, with 6 million out of work, they received 230 seats.

22. About 62 percent of the French people still lived in cities with fewer than 10,000 people.

23. Brian R. Mitchell, *European Historical Statistics, 1750–1970* (New York: Columbia University Press, 1975), 349.

24. *Survey of International Affairs, 1933*, 45.

25. *Documents Diplomatique Françaises*, lère série, vol. 2, 778.

26. Ibid., 63.

27. To be exact, $7,077,144,750 lent during the war, another $3,273,364,324.70 after the Armistice. The interest initially was 5 percent per annum ($4^{1}/_4$ percent bonds plus $^3/_4$ percent service charge).

28. Howard H. Quint and Robert H. Ferrell, eds., *The Talkative President: The Off the Record Press Conferences of Calvin Coolidge* (Amherst: University of Massachusetts Press, 1964), 206.

CHAPTER 8

NATIONAL SOCIALIST GERMANY

PREFACE   The inability to ensure economic security and political stability soured German support for democracy. The constant squabbling of more than thirty political parties led many Germans to long for the good old prewar days of authority and order. The traditional elites—the army and naval officers, the upper-level civil servants, the judges, the clergy, the industrialists, the university professors—all treated the republic with contempt throughout its brief, turbulent life. The republic, an orphan of defeat, had been born into a cruel world. It was so tainted with bastardy that no official celebrations marked its anniversaries. The German people saved their parades and fireworks for 18 January, the day that Bismarck had founded the Second Reich in 1871. And each year, on 28 June, they hung out black bunting to mourn the signing of the Treaty of Versailles. Thus, they nurtured their myths and hatreds.

Germans took no pride in their democracy, which to them meant indecision, pusillanimity, and national humiliation. The German path to glory had been built, as Bismarck recognized, on blood and iron, not representative assemblies. The Wilhelmian period showed that free institutions were not necessary for prosperity and security. To Germany, the great theme of the modern age was the intensification of the power of the community over the individual, not that of the individual over the government. The mobilization achieved during World War I was a triumph of this spirit, just as the defeat was its undoing. The Germans had been psychologically devastated; now, presented with new and unwelcome burdens, they turned to those who promised a return to past greatness.

The growth of the National Socialist movement was part of this search, but the party itself remained on the fringe of the antidemocratic movement until it was able to profit from the chaos of the Great Depression. Then, the Germans, threatened with the loss of their livelihood for the second time in less than ten years, turned on the Weimar Republic with savage hatred. In the elections of 1930 and 1932, the Nazis received more popular votes from a wider range of people, classes, and districts than any other party in the history of the Weimar Republic.[1] Large sections of the middle and lower-middle classes and the peasantry completely abandoned democracy and became converts to Nazism.[2] Women voted for the Nazis in almost equal numbers as the men. German society in the 1920s was quite traditional, despite the women's movement associated with such large cities as Berlin. Therefore much of the support that Hitler received from women came precisely because of his blatant antifeminism.[3]

The Nazi system exuberantly exploited the widespread frustration with the new democratic system. Hitler was a consummate demagogue who was able to convince people that his party had viable solutions to pressing problems and that he had a positive program for national regeneration. He successfully presented the Nazi party as the true heir of Frederick the Great and Bismarck. Hitler knew the prejudices of his constituents and became an active expression of their general will. He spoke openly of his willingness to curtail civil liberties. But by then, to many Germans, democracy did not seem as important as adequate food and heat.

Hitler appealed to the sympathies of people from both the political Right and Left by synthesizing the two great movements of modern times: nationalism and socialism. He did not direct his appeal to one class or to one part of society. In taking a position above the class structure, he was akin to Mussolini who also was able to unite many disparate groups in one mass movement committed to the cause of rebirth and greatness. Both men also exploited the political circumstances at hand, coming to power when their respective democratic systems were about to collapse. But their success was not inevitable. Both had organized their movements to take advantage of the prevailing crises, but neither could have had a chance to rule without the support of the traditional ruling classes which saw in Hitler and Mussolini a means to preserve their own prerogatives. But although Hitler and Mussolini used the old ruling classes to gain power, neither intended to let these groups rule. Once the dictators seized the reins of power, they surrendered them to no one and proceeded to drive the state toward their own destinations.

THE POLICY OF COORDINATION

The Fall of German Democracy

The End of the Weimar Republic. On 28 March 1930, President Hindenburg asked centrist leader Heinrich Brüning to form a new government to replace the republican coalition headed by Hermann Müller. Brüning, a leader of the right wing of his party, was the personal choice of General Kurt von Schleicher, the

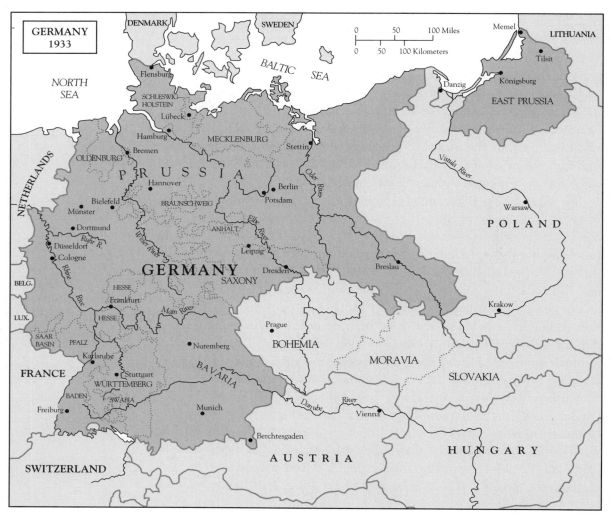

Map 7

head of the political department of the Reichswehr. Schleicher was a friend of the Rhenish-Westphalian industrialists whose opposition to democracy was well known. Schleicher saw Müller's fall as an occasion to break the power of the Social Democratic party, which he and his friends loathed for its constant opposition to German rearmament.[4] The new government represented only a rightist minority in the Reichstag, but could rely on the personal backing of Hindenburg, who was prepared to buttress its authority with the threat of dissolution and the use of emergency powers under Article 48 of the Weimar Constitution.

Brüning's government pretended to be above special interests, but it was intimately concerned with the welfare of the Junker landowners. Ostensibly, its agricultural policy aimed at protecting all German farmers against the collapse of world food prices, but the special subsidies for refinancing agricultural debts and the new tariffs against foreign competition particularly favored the inefficient estates of East Prussia. The eastern aid program *(Osthilfe)* established a special pro-tective tariff on rye, which enabled the Junker farmers to charge the consumers of *schwarzbrot* and pumpernickel twice the world market price.

The government's financial program was deflationary: Brüning proposed cutting government expenditures and increasing taxes. He intended to dock 2.5 percent from the wages of government officials as national assistance *(Reichshilfe)* to reduce unemployment payments. He enacted his budget by decree.

The September elections gave the political extremes an opportunity to dem-onstrate their power.[5] Although the democratic parties still held a majority, normal parliamentary government had virtually ceased to exist. Brüning routinely used the emergency powers under Article 48. His program to cut social security expenditures backed the Social Democrats to the wall. They feared the disastrous consequences of overthrowing the government and watched in horror while the entire program for which they had fought since the birth of the republic was reduced to tatters. But the Communists were delighted, and the Nazis flourished.

Brüning's spartan measures only exacerbated the political crisis. He cut costs, reduced wages, curtailed social services, and introduced price controls, hoping to outlast the depression. The remnants of the old Weimar coalition were reluctant to overturn his emergency decrees for fear of worsening the crisis. The president's willingness to support Brüning still provided a measure of stability, but Hinden-burg's term of office was due to expire in the spring of 1932. Brüning felt that only Hindenburg had the mass appeal sufficient to preserve the republic and per-suaded him to run again to save Germany from civil war.

The election of 1932 was bitterly contested. The National Socialists carried out a vicious smear campaign against Hindenburg. Nazi leader Adolf Hitler staged huge public rallies, sometimes giving three major speeches a day. The results of the 13 March polling gave Hindenburg a plurality of the votes, but not the absolute majority he needed for election.[6] In the runoff election, held on 10 April, Hin-denburg won sufficiently, but not impressively.[7] The presidential elections had revealed that a great many Germans were disgusted with their democratic system. Brüning returned to the chancellery, but with diminished authority. When he proposed a new land resettlement scheme for eastern Prussia in May 1932, he encountered the universal opposition of the large landowners who protested di-rectly to Hindenburg that such expropriation would take away the ancestral land of some of Prussia's oldest and most distinguished families and would undermine the will of the farmer to defend the soil against foreign invaders. They convinced the feeble old marshal that Brüning had been responsible for tarnishing his repu-tation in the recent election. On 29 May, Hindenburg announced his intention to reconstitute the cabinet. Brüning resigned.

A Back Room Intrigue. During its last eight months, the Weimar Republic was run by a coalition of antidemocratic aristocrats, who acted in the interests of the traditional ruling class. On 1 June 1932, Franz von Papen, a former member of the Catholic Center party who had recently joined forces with the Nationalists, replaced Heinrich Brüning as chancellor and formed a cabinet "of independent men"; four of its members were barons, another was a count, and practically all had served in socially respectable regiments, like the Potsdam Guards or the Pom-eranian Dragoons. No German government since the war had had less experience and received less support from the parties in the Reichstag. This hardly mattered, for Papen's goal was to destroy German democracy once and for all and to replace it with an authoritarian government. His first major act was to smash the Social Democrat–controlled government in Prussia.[8]

Acting on the pretext that the Social Democrats had failed to guarantee public order, he used his emergency powers to oust their leaders from office and, on 20 July, appointed a Reich commissioner in their place. The Social Democrats protested, but had no significant allies who could help them counter the action. The Nazis had heavily infiltrated the police, and the labor unions were too divided to call a general strike. In fact, the Communists rejoiced at Papen's coup, seeing it as the beginning of a general collapse that they thought would bring them to power. This was not the first time the Communists had actively worked against the republic. In 1925, they had gratuitously helped to split the working-class vote, thereby ensuring the election of Hindenburg. In 1930, they combined with the Nazis to attack the Social Democrats, the only major party that was genuinely interested in preserving German democracy.

Papen tried to increase his popular support and set new elections for 31 July. But the strategy backfired. Adolf Hitler fought a furious campaign and managed to capture 230 of the 608 seats in the Reichstag—his was the largest party delegation. The Nazi popular vote, combined with the total votes for all the antidemocratic parties of both the Right and the Left, showed that more Germans had voted against the Weimar Republic than had voted for it.[9] The two antidemocratic parties, the Nazis and the Communists, controlled 52 percent of the seats in parliament.

The Nazis were the most virulent manifestation of a larger antidemocratic movement that included the Communists, the Nationalists, and a sizable group of Catholic Centrists. The traditional monarchist opposition to democracy had been replaced by a more savage threat manifested in the countless right-wing organizations that followed the breakup of the Freikorps movement. The largest, and most dangerous, of the older veterans' organizations was the *Stahlhelm* (Steel Helmet), which issued a "declaration of hate" against the Weimar Republic in 1928. From time to time, the Stahlhelm formed alliances with the Nazi party and the Nationalist party. Alfred Huguenberg, the leader of the Nationalists, helped form the antidemocratic cabal that helped Hitler become chancellor. But many "ordinary" Germans also never accepted the legitimacy of the Weimar Republic. The republic had failed badly to dramatize the importance of free institutions and to embody national honor. Regional animosities and the mounting forces of separatism also enabled the Nazis to lay claim to the heritage of Bismarck.

While the political situation remained more confused than ever, the economy did experience some improvement. The recession hit bottom in August 1932. According to the official statistics, unemployment peaked at 6,192,000, but this figure was probably understated by about 15 to 20 percent, and vast numbers of workers could find only part-time employment. Threatened by the loss of their livelihood, disgusted with the cowardice of the Weimar regime, large sections of the middle class and the peasantry, who had tolerated the republic during its period of prosperity, were willing converts to Nazism. Many of those who supported Hitler did not regard him as the embodiment of destructive nihilism, no matter how fanatical his oratory or his street tactics. They viewed him chiefly as a forceful spokesman for moral and national regeneration. Hitler concentrated on uniting other like-minded political groups under his leadership and on seeking financial and political support from powerful interest groups, like the Rhineland industrialists. He had left no doubt about his intention to establish a one-party state. There was nothing unconstitutional about such a goal. The Weimar Constitution contained no articles forbidding the destruction of the democratic republican system, providing the job was done legally. The constitution also made no mention of political parties and gave them no specific protection.[10]

Papen reacted by trying to entice Hitler into joining his ministry by offering him the post of vice-chancellor. He believed that the Nazi party "could be neutralized" by being saddled "with its full share of public responsibility."[11] But Hitler refused to serve in a cabinet he could not control. Parliamentary government of any sort became impossible, and Papen again dissolved the chamber and called for new elections. In the voting of 6 November, the Nazis lost some strength, but still had the largest delegation, while the Communists managed modest gains. Lacking the strength to form a viable government, Papen resigned. His place was taken by General Kurt von Schleicher, the army's political expert and an intimate of President Hindenburg.

Schleicher, who heretofore had been playing politics behind the scenes, had been the architect of the policy of negotiating with the Nazis to get their support for a presidential government. But as chancellor he had no more luck than Papen in these negotiations. The Nazis still refused to cooperate, and Schleicher's attempt to form a "labor axis" government with the Catholic Center party and the Social Democrats failed because the Social Democrats had difficulty believing in Schleicher's good faith. Schleicher also came up empty-handed when he tried to split the Nazi party by bringing Gregor Strasser, the leader of the party's left wing, into his cabinet. Strasser left the Nazi party under a cloud. At the end of January 1933, Schleicher confessed that he had failed to neutralize the Nazis or form a viable parliamentary coalition, and he requested that President Hindenburg grant him special powers to establish an emergency dictatorship. Hindenburg refused and Schleicher resigned.

The stage was set for Papen's scheme to control the Nazis by taking them into an alliance with the traditional Right. Papen touted Hitler as the man who could save Germany from Bolshevism and civil war, and, on 30 January, Hindenburg appointed Hitler head of the government.[12] Since Hitler did not have the necessary majority, he became head of a presidential cabinet like his three predecessors. This meant he could stay in office as long as he managed to avoid a vote of no confidence. Hindenburg was not particularly enthusiastic about this political upstart, but Hitler seemed the candidate most likely to garner the necessary support for a conservative cabinet, thereby ending the use of Article 48 and returning to normal constitutional government. He had the parliamentary strength and mass support that Papen and others like him lacked. Papen, who became vice-chancellor, believed that his special relationship with Hindenburg would make him the real head of the government. He was confident Hitler could be controlled and even boasted to one of his aides that in two months Hitler would be pushed into a corner so hard that he would be squealing. But Hitler was the sort of political leader they little understood. Whereas the conservatives merely wanted to destroy the power of the Left and curb democracy, Hitler wanted to effect a fundamental restructuring of the relationship between the individual and the state, in much the same way as he had already organized the Nazi party itself.

Profile: Adolf Hitler (1889–1945)

The last chancellor of the Weimar Republic was born on 20 April 1889 in the small, provincial Austrian border town of Braunau on the river Inn. His father, Alois Hitler, was a minor customs official of the Habsburg civil service. His mother

was Klara Pölzl, a domestic servant, who was also her husband's niece-in-law and was twenty-three years his junior. (It is not known whether they were in any way blood relatives.) She was Alois's third wife, and Adolf was the third child of their marriage. Alois was demanding and tyrannical, obsequious to the outside world, but frequently violent at home, often beating his wife and children and kicking the dog. He was also stingy but did provide for his family's creature comforts. Alois had been born out of wedlock, and until he was legitimized in 1876, thirteen years before his son's birth, he had gone by his mother's family name of Schicklgruber. Although the future dictator was sometimes derisively referred to by this matronymic, his legal name was always Hitler.[13]

Intimidated by his father, Adolf became extraordinarily close to his mother. All his life he carried her picture with him. When he became chancellor, he always kept a portrait of her hanging over his bed in his official residences. Yet his strong attachment was not without hostility, prompted in part by her docility in not standing up to her husband. Adolf began his formal education in 1895, the year of his father's retirement. He started well enough, but by his twelfth year, when the family moved to Linz, his performance began to decline. His father's death in 1903 came as a relief; he remembered the years immediately following as the happiest of his life. Freed of this parental authority, he assumed the role of a gentleman dandy, deliberately undermining his father's plans to have him prepare for the life of a civil servant. His studies continued to flag, and in 1905, at the age of sixteen, he abandoned school altogether, probably at official insistence.

For the next two years, Hitler hung around Linz, dabbling in the arts. He haphazardly wrote poetry and dreamed about achieving the architectural transformation of Linz—his enthusiasm for construction would later develop into a mania. He displayed the aptitude of a decent Sunday painter, but was incapable of the discipline necessary to develop his talents. He reacted to an unappreciative society by withdrawing and brooding about his destiny in the manner of a nineteenth-century romantic. He lacked any capacity for self-criticism and seemed unlikely to pursue any course of action long enough to succeed. As long as he remained in the provinces, his moody, aristocratic pose had some success, but all this changed when he moved to Vienna in 1907 during his eighteenth year.

Life in the Austrian capital was more cosmopolitan, but also more lonely and frustrating. Hitler applied to the Viennese Academy of Fine Arts but was rejected. He tried again a year later and was turned down a second time. Between the two examinations, he had characteristically done nothing to improve his chances. As usual, he blamed his failure on others. Without a secondary school diploma and with no vocational training, Hitler had to rely on his orphan's pension and a small inheritance to keep from falling to the lowest level of proletarian existence. Although he was never destitute, he later exaggerated his poverty, claiming that he had never had enough to eat: "Hunger was then my faithful bodyguard; he never left me for a moment and partook of all I had, share and share alike."[14] Hitler included this typical revelation of the misery of his early life in an explanation to the Austrian authorities of why he had failed to register for military service. From 1910 to 1913, Hitler performed various odd jobs: beating carpets, serving as a red cap at the railroad station, and painting small watercolors for sale at fairs and beer halls. He hated his frugal life and, in frustration, denounced the Habsburgs, the Roman Catholic clergy, the Social Democrats, and, especially, the Jews whom he believed were masterminding a worldwide conspiracy to subjugate the Teutonic or, as he called it, the Aryan race.

The Führer's anti-Semitism developed from the small town provincial milieu in which he was raised. In such a conservative society, Jews were regarded as outsiders and, although tolerated, were considered an affront to Christianity because of their role in the crucifixion of Christ. But Hitler's antipathy went much farther and became bound up with his feelings of inadequacy and his search for personal identity. To him Jews became a satanic presence on which he projected the faults of society.[15] He blamed them for pornography, prostitution, psychiatry, treason, incest, Marxism, decadence in art, disease, economic exploitation, and the collapse of society. "Once," he wrote, " as I was strolling through the Inner City, I suddenly encountered an apparition in a black caftan and black hair locks. Is this a Jew? was my first thought. For to be sure, they had not looked like that in Linz. I observed the man furtively and cautiously, but the longer I stared at this foreign face, scrutinizing feature for feature, the more my first question assumed a new form: Is this a German?"[16] For Hitler, mere difference became a rationale for removal.

Hitler moved to Munich in 1913. His life-style here was hardly better than in Vienna, but he rejoiced at living in a "truly" German city. He claimed that he had been revolted by Vienna's conglomeration of races: "this whole mixture of Czechs, Poles, Hungarians, Ruthenians, Serbs, and Croats, and everywhere, the eternal mushroom of humanity—Jews and more Jews." The city had seemed to him "the embodiment of racial desecration."[17]

Hitler probably would have finished his days a total nonentity had it not been for World War I. He volunteered for a Bavarian regiment and was sent to the Western Front as a dispatch runner. There he participated in such battles as Ypres, the Somme, Arras, and Passchendaele and was promoted to lance corporal.[18] He received the Iron Cross second and first class—an unusual recognition of bravery for an enlisted man in the imperial army. In October 1918, he was temporarily blinded in a British gas attack and was still in a military hospital when the Armistice was signed. War had been his great adventure, an experience that had given his life a sense of purpose—"a release from the painful feelings of my youth." He wrote that he had thanked Heaven for granting him the good fortune "of being permitted to live at this time."[19] When he heard the news of the defeat, he threw himself on his bunk, buried his head in his pillow, and cried. It was, he said, only the second time in his life he had shed tears, the first occasion being his mother's funeral.

Unwilling to believe that Germany had been defeated on the battlefield, he zealously endorsed the nationalistic myth that held that domestic traitors—the Social Democrats, Communists, and Jews—had stabbed the army in the back. These "November criminals" were synonymous with everything Hitler despised: democracy, international cooperation, and peace. With demobilization, he found employment in the political department of the District Military Command, which, in early autumn 1919, assigned him the task of investigating the German Workers' party. Like countless other political groups, this recently formed political organization had grown out of the prevailing political chaos and discontent. Hitler became a member of the party's central committee and ultimately its leader. Within a decade he would build this small collection of malcontents into Germany's mightiest party. In the critical early days, he was helped by Captain Ernst Röhm, a District Command staff officer, who swelled the party's ranks with army veterans who were used to create the nucleus of a party army, the Storm Troops (*Sturmabteilung* or the SA), known as the Brownshirts from their uniforms.

Hitler had a genius for demagoguery. He appealed to racists and nationalists by demanding the destruction of the Treaty of Versailles, the unification of all Germans into one state, and the disfranchisement of the Jews. He convinced other like-minded political groups to accept his leadership and solicited financial and political support from powerful interest groups. However, wealthy patrons were scarce in those days. The Nazi party's anticapitalist program scared many industrialists. Therefore, the party had to rely principally on its own general membership, which paid dues and bought tickets to its functions. The rank and file also paid for their own uniforms, flags, and insignia and purchased the official pamphlets and propaganda leaflets.[20] To strengthen its general appeal, the party changed its name to the *Nationalsozialistische Deutsche Arbeiterpartei* or NSDAP (National Socialist German Workers' party).

The failure to seize power in Munich on 9 November 1923 (in the so-called Beer Hall Putsch) and the subsequent trial for treason brought Hitler national attention. His denunciation of the Weimar Republic in court was widely and sympathetically reported in the conservative German press. Although he was convicted, his sentence was fairly light: five years in the castle-prison of Landsberg. Hitler later bragged that his incarceration gave him "the chance of deepening various notions for which I then had only an instinctive feeling." He also "acquired that fearless faith, that optimism, that confidence in our destiny, which nothing could shake thereafter." His confinement was not onerous. He was allowed to decorate his cell with Nazi party flags and paraphernalia, set his own bedtime, and have his breakfast brought to him by other prisoners assigned to him as servants. Admirers sent him so many gifts of food that his cell resembled a delicatessen. At Landsberg, he dictated his memoirs *Mein Kampf (My Struggle)* to his personal secretary Rudolf Hess.[21] He was released after serving less than nine months of his sentence and immediately resumed his political activities in Munich.

Hitler first had to concentrate on gathering up the pieces of the party and bringing it under his absolute control. He recognized that times had changed; it was futile to try to overthrow the Weimar government by direct force. Accordingly, over the next five years, he consolidated the strength of the party to enable him to capture power legally. The Nazis formed the so-called People's Bloc *(Völkish Bloc)* with other similar factions, but their electoral success was not impressive. In the May 1924 elections, they won thirty-two seats in the Reichstag, but their representation slipped to fourteen seats seven months later. This was the most they held until the Great Depression. By that time, thanks to Hitler, the party, supported by a powerful ideology, was much better organized and united than before. Therefore when the opportunity came, the Nazis were well prepared to persuade people that they really did have simple solutions to complicated problems.[22]

The Leadership Principle. "Only what Adolf Hitler, our Führer commands, allows, or does not allow is our conscience" was the basic article of faith of National Socialism.[23] Never before had the Germans been presented with the proposition that the personal intuition of the head of their government should surpass the sovereign will of the state; never before had constitutional legitimacy rested upon the personal intuition of a Führer. These features made Hitler's regime unique among contemporary dictatorships, but akin in some respects to the divine right monarchies of the past. The regime's political leaders were annually required to reaffirm their devotion to this doctrine of leadership *(Führerprinzip)*: "I pledge eternal allegiance to Adolf Hitler. I pledge unconditional obedience to him and the Führers appointed by him."[24] Hitler became the incarnation of the spirit of the German people. "One people! One state! One leader!" *(Ein Volk! Ein Reich! Ein Führer!)* was the Nazi counterpart to "Liberty! Equality! Fraternity!" The emphasis was on the role of the leader and his rule over the racially pure community (*Volksgemeinschaft*).

In the speech Hitler gave before the Munich court on 27 March 1924, after his attempted seizure of power, he said that the state was "a 'volkic' organism" whose purpose was "to provide the people with its food-supply and with the position of power in the world which is its due." Germany, surrounded by rivals, "can maintain itself only when it places a power-policy (*Machtpolitik*) ruthlessly in the foreground."[25] These principles, which had already been adopted by the Nazi party, were to be imposed on the nation.

The Elimination of the Opposition. The Nazis were part of a coalition government. Although they had the two important posts of chancellor (Hitler) and minister of the interior (Wilhelm Frick),[26] the other positions were held by non-Nazi conservatives who shared the Nazis' animosity toward democracy. The Nazis wanted a one-party state, however, and were not content to share power. To this end, Hitler developed a two-tier strategy. He planned to craft an electoral triumph that would give the Nazis a majority of the seats in the Reichstag, ensuring his hold on the chancellorship; then he would persuade the other political parties to support the passage of a special enabling law that would give him the power to rule by decree. Both schemes succeeded brilliantly.

Hitler began by affecting a great reverence for tradition and legality. In his first proclamation, on 1 February 1933, he pledged to restore Germany's "unity of will and spirit" on the foundations of church and family. "In place of turbulent instincts, the government will once again make national discipline our guide. In doing so, it will consider with great care all institutions which are the guarantors of the strength and power of our nation." But he carefully avoided any attempt to form a majority out of the present Reichstag and induced Hindenburg to call for new elections.

The ensuing campaign was extremely hard-fought and brutal. The Brownshirts were called into action and harassed and beat the Nazis' political opponents. They destroyed Communist party headquarters, suppressed hostile newspapers, and bullied people into donating money. On 20 February, Hitler told a group of twenty-five prominent Ruhr industrialists that dictatorship was the only way to protect the national interest. "Private enterprise," he said, "cannot be maintained in the age of democracy; it is conceivable only if the people have a sound idea of authority and personality."[27] He held out the threat of a Bolshevik revolution.

A week later, Hitler's fortunes were boosted when the Reichstag building was set ablaze. A mentally unstable Dutch Communist, Marinus van der Lubbe, actually committed the act. Yet, so neatly did the arson fit in with Hitler's warnings that Germany was on the brink of revolution, that the Nazis themselves were suspected of having done it.[28] In any case, the Nazis were not slow to exploit the fire to their own advantage. Hitler denounced it as part of a Communist plot to take over the state, and on 28 February, he convinced President Hindenburg to sign a decree "For the Protection of the People and the State." The decree suspended constitutional guarantees of due process, including the right to habeas corpus and the right of appeal. The police were given wide powers to arrest and detain suspects, search and seize property, and censor anti-Nazi literature. The decree also granted the central government the authority to coerce the state governments (*Länder*). Hitler used the decree to crack down on the Communist party and to round up Social Democratic leaders and silence their press. He justified these measures as being necessary to maintain law and order. With this decree, Hitler had taken the first step toward the establishment of his one-party state.

In the elections of 5 March, the Nazis received 45 percent of the seats in the Reichstag. This was shy of the absolute majority they craved, but with an additional 8 percent from the Nationalists, Hitler had sufficient strength to form a majority government. Now he was in a good position to carry out the next phase of his plan: the passage of a special law giving him the authority to legislate by decree. Laws giving the government the right to enact emergency legislation did not originate with the Nazis. The practice had already been established during the Weimar era, when, for example, it was used to adopt special economic measures during the inflation of 1923. Hitler made it clear that he would seek similar powers when he became chancellor. He also implied that passage of such a measure would bring an end to the power of the Reichstag.

By continuing to play on the fears of the Nationalists, the Centrists, and the delegates from other middle-class parties that Germany was on the brink of civil war, Hitler managed to corral the necessary support for an enabling law that transferred the powers of the legislature to the Nazi cabinet. On 23 March at Berlin's Kroll Opera House, the *Gesetz zur Behebung der Not von Volk und Reich* (Law for Terminating the Distress of the People and Nation) was approved by 444 of the 538 deputies present, 49 more than were necessary for passage. The 94 Social Democrats voted unanimously against the law, the only party to do so. (The Communists who had won 13 percent of the seats were barred from participation.) By giving Hitler what he wanted, the other non-Nazi parties showed the extent to which they thought the destruction of the democratic system was a reasonable price to pay for national solidarity.

The enabling law gave Hitler the power to legislate on his own authority for the next four years and even empowered him to effect constitutional change. Technically, the Weimar Republic continued to exist, but all of its laws, including those protecting the rights of citizens, were subject to new interpretation. Hitler promised that he would use his new powers only insofar as they were "essential for carrying out vitally necessary measures."[29] But he soon showed what this meant by putting an end to party government.

The suppression of the Communists was followed by the elimination of the Social Democrats and then by the destruction of the trade union movement. On 2 May, the official Nazi Labor Front, under Robert Ley, officially took charge of the entire administrative apparatus, real estate, and treasury of the Social Democratic party. The workers were reorganized into the Labor Front, which abolished collective bargaining, regulated working conditions, and strived to imbue its members with a proper National Socialist spirit. Next it was the turn of Hitler's erstwhile allies. They were persuaded to agree to their own dissolution. The Nationalists, the German State party, the Bavarian Peoples party and the Centrists all expressed "full agreement with the Chancellor" that the multiparty system was obsolete. On 14 July 1933, the NSDAP officially became the only political party of the state.

The complete nazification of German society and its institutions proceeded with ease. The state's federal structure disappeared. Nazi governors (*Reichsstatthalters*) took charge, reducing the state governments to powerless administrative units. The national civil service was cleansed of "undesirables." Hitler also began a campaign to bring the Christian churches into line and to destroy the independence of the German army. He waged war on the Jews. He nazified the educational system, established norms in art and culture, militarized the youth, and relegated women to the status of second-class citizens.

Most Germans were co-opted to serve the needs of the regime in some way. This policy of *Gleichschaltung* (coordination or leveling) was one of the regime's most striking features. At its most elemental, it involved the ludicrous requirement of giving the Nazi salute and repeating "Heil Hitler." In its other incarnations, it conferred economic advantages; for example, all the profits made by countless firms, many quite modest in size, in turning out badges, awards, and activity pins. There was some sort of propaganda badge for every occasion; some simply commemorated *Reichsparteitag* (Party Day), *Deutsches Jugendfest* (German Youth Festival), and *Tag des Deutschen Handwerks* (Day of German Crafts), while others trumpeted Nazi triumphs like the annexation of Austria and the Sudetenland and the ground breaking for the new Volkswagen plant. On the badge for the latter, the sprocket wheel enclosing a swastika is larger than the representation of a car. These "tinnies" were usually stamped in thin aluminum. They not only profited the seller and the manufacturer, but also made every German aware of what regime was in power. Gleichschaltung also included one of history's greatest dress-up parades. All party, and many state, organizations had uniforms, often with an appropriate dagger for special occasions. The weapon of the German Red Cross, for example, was a broad-bladed short sword with a saw-toothed back and a square point designed to do double duty as a symbol of the organization and a tool of the trade, presumably for removing plaster splints. In solidifying his hold over the government and the free will of the German people, Hitler encountered little serious opposition. As it happened, he had more to fear from renegade elements within his own party.

The Order of the Death's Head

The Night of the Long Knives. Hitler's Storm Troopers, or the SA, had been the frontline strength in his march to power. With their brown shirts, Sam Brown belts, booted leggings, flags, badges, and daggers, they had acted as bodyguards, security forces, public demonstrators, fund raisers, and shills. Although organized along military lines, this private army was not really a paramilitary organization.

Ernst Röhm, the chief of the SA, and Heinrich Himmler, head of the SS, inspect a company of Storm Troops in August 1933. Röhm's desire to turn his street fighters into a Nazi People's Army led to his murder the following June in the Night of the Long Knives in which Himmler played a major role.

It was used mainly for propaganda purposes, for controlling the streets and spreading terror in the hearts of enemies. Its ranks were initially packed with war veterans and Freikorps volunteers, but it increasingly became a haven for young toughs who had a penchant for intolerance and violence. Hitler became head of the SA in 1930, but asked his old Munich commander, Ernst Röhm, to return from Bolivia to become its chief of staff.

Once Hitler became chancellor, the SA went on a wild binge, holding boisterous celebrations and flaunting its power in parades and street violence. Röhm had his own stubborn idea of how these street fighters should be rewarded. He proposed fusing the 3 million members of the SA with the regular professional army (*Reichswehr*), creating a National Socialist People's Army over which he would preside as minister of defense. He also advocated carrying out a second revolution to bring about fundamental economic and social change. All of this alarmed the other Nazi overlords, who were also concerned by Röhm's ostentatious display of his homosexuality. They knew that a policy to level classes would find little favor with their conservative allies, whose support was still essential to keep Hitler in power. They feared that the German people were becoming alienated not only from the SA, but from the entire Nazi regime. Most importantly, the professional army had yet to be brought under Hitler's control; it still owed allegiance to Hindenburg who could dismiss the chancellor and turn over power to someone else, perhaps a Hohenzollern regent. The generals would have fought to the death against any SA-Reichswehr amalgamation. With Hindenburg near death, Hitler wanted the blessings of the Army High Command to merge the offices of president and chancellor. He therefore had to affirm the Reichswehr's right to be the sole military authority in Germany, and this meant that the power of the SA must be smashed. Hitler was reluctant to act against his old comrades, but was finally stirred into action when he was informed that if he could not control the situation, Hindenburg would declare martial law and hand over executive power to the army.

For the task of destroying the SA, Hitler used the *Gestapo* (Secret State Police) and his elite security guard (the *Schutzstaffel* or SS), commanded by Heinrich Himmler. On 30 June 1934, and for the next three days, special SS detachments rounded up the SA chieftains, murdering most of those captured. Karl Ernst, the head of the Berlin SA, who was on his honeymoon when captured, was so surprised and confused that when he was shoved against the wall at Berlin's Lichterfelde barracks, he shouted "Heil Hitler." Röhm was pulled out of bed in the Bavarian lakeside resort of Wiessee and hauled into Stadelheim prison in Munich where he was shot in his cell. Hitler had been extremely reluctant to give the order for the execution. Among the other eighty-one known victims were some who had nothing to do with the events at hand. Former chancellor Kurt von Schleicher and Gustav von Kahr, the man who had helped crush the 1923 Beer Hall Putsch, were shot in their homes. Gregor Strasser, one of the founders of the Nazi party but now estranged from Hitler, was killed with a bullet to the back of his head. Dr. Willi Schmid, a music critic of a Munich daily, was gunned down because he was mistaken for a local SA leader named Willi Schmidt. His widow later received an apology, and her husband's body was returned with instructions not to open the coffin.

Hitler explained—and had allowed himself to be convinced—that the "Night of the Long Knives" was necessary to prevent the SA from seizing power. In a limited sense this was true, especially for the Reichswehr generals who were highly pleased at being rid of a dangerous rival. Major-General Erwin von Witzleben rejoiced when he heard the news of the executions. "What a pity. I ought to have been there," was his only regret. When Hindenburg died on 2 August 1934, the army leaders recognized Hitler as their supreme commander, pledging "to give him unconditional obedience" and, if necessary, uphold this oath with their lives. Henceforth, all soldiers would be required to take the same oath.

But if the High Command imagined that the destruction of Röhm and his lieutenants would result in the affirmation of their independence, they were wrong. Their victory was hollow. The events of 30 June ended the struggle between the Nazi party's nationalists and proletarians[30] but also elevated the SS to independent status within the Nazi party. The SS eventually became the most powerful instrument of the state. Henceforth, the Reichswehr would have to contend with the overweening ambitions of SS overlord Himmler.

Himmler's Empire. The SS began in 1925 as a special unit of the SA charged with protecting Hitler. It had replaced an earlier unit, the *Stosstrupp* (shock troop), which had been disbanded after the abortive 1923 putsch. Himmler became its head in 1929 and enlarged the scope of its activities. When the Nazis took power, however, he received no national office, only the post of police-president of Munich.[31] Nevertheless he made the most of it. He took charge of the Bavarian political police and created the first SS concentration camp on the outskirts of Munich at Dachau. He then organized the first Nazi Chancery Guard, the *Leibstandarte—SS Adolf Hitler*; using the guard as a model, he established a series of special protective detachments and political action squads throughout Germany. Next, Himmler gradually established control over the political police in most of the other Länder, including the Prussian *Geheime Staatspolizei* and the Gestapo, which had originally been headed by Hermann Göring.

Himmler patterned the SS after the Order of Teutonic Knights and the Society of Jesus. Brigadeführer Walter Schellenberg, head of the SS Foreign Intelligence Service, said that Himmler intended his position "to be the counterpart of the Jesuits' General of the Order," and that the whole leadership structure was adopted from Himmler's studies "of the hierarchic order of the Catholic Church."[32] Himmler was passionately attached to ceremony and form. With a highly romantic view of German history, he chose as his hero King Henry the Fowler, the tenth-century duke of Saxony and king of Germany who appears as a character in Wagner's opera *Lohengrin*. In 1937, Himmler had his hero's bones transferred to Quedlingburg Cathedral where he would come every year on the anniversary of the ruler's death for spiritual communion. Himmler claimed that the king gave him advice, and he eventually regarded himself as the monarch's reincarnation.

Himmler's fascination with death and medieval mysticism knew few limits. The SS emblem was a silver death's head, its initials stylized as flashes of lightning. The dagger worn by officers, a replica of a medieval knight's dagger, had *"Meine Ehre Heisst Treue"* (My Honor Is Loyalty) etched along the blade. Himmler had his own Camelot in the Westphalian castle of Wewelsburg near Paderborn, where the order's disciples—the twelve *Obergruppenführer* of the major divisions—would gather every year. Each member had "his own armchair with an engraved silver name plate, and each had to devote himself to a ritual of spiritual exercises aimed mainly at mental concentration."[33] The castle had a specially built keep in whose crypt a knight's coat of arms would be ceremoniously burned after his death. Himmler had his own concentration/work camp near the castle and intended to transform the entire area by destroying the surrounding village and constructing a gigantic leadership center on the site to train the future masters of Europe. Grand Master Heinrich hoped to form an SS state out of the old middle kingdom of the Burgundian dukes. In this territory, stretching from the Swiss Vaud to the Flemish plains, he would rule as an independent sovereign, part mystic, part brute.

Himmler was obsessed with abstractions like racial purity, destiny, and sacrifice. As the professed guardian of National Socialism, Himmler assumed that he and the SS had the right to influence every important activity of the state. In 1936, he became chief of the German police with control of the regular criminal police and the national uniformed gendarmerie. He incorporated the Gestapo as a state organization under the *Sicherheitsdienst* (SS Security Service or SD). By 1937, his rulings had the status of official decrees.

After the Night of the Long Knives, Hitler allowed the SS to form three militarized regiments for "special internal political tasks." Himmler therefore combined the *Leibstandarte* (bodyguard) detachment with his *Politische Bereitschaften* (political action units) to form the *Verfügungstruppe*, the first SS army, which became a permanent state formation. When World War II began, the organization grew to division size and became the nucleus of the SS army, the *Waffen-SS*.

At one time Himmler had tried to make a living raising poultry on a farm near Munich; now he was master of the German police, exercised wide authority in ideological and racial policy, and had staked out a considerable claim over military affairs. World War II eventually would give him the opportunity to extend his power over most of Europe. But his own sense of inferiority allowed him no higher ambition than first servant of the Führer whom he worshiped with the same zeal as his Saxon heroes.

REGULATION AND REPRESSION

The Campaign against the Jews

The Nuremberg Laws. The Nazi government was a profusion of rival fiefdoms and confused jurisdictions. The Führer's will was absolute, but that will had to be interpreted and implemented by men who were frequently in fierce competition with each other. Hitler's beliefs acted as a stimulus to their activities, but that did not lessen the rivalries. This was especially true in Jewish affairs, the area to which Hitler was most deeply committed and where the struggle for control the most intense. Hitler believed that the main conflict of history was racial, although he acknowledged that he did not see the Jews in this light until he arrived in Vienna. Following his initial encounter with a Hassidic Jew, he bought his first anti-Semitic pamphlet; and what had begun as curiosity and revulsion soon developed into an obsession.

Hitler rationalized his prejudice by cloaking it in a pseudoscientific mantle. He saw the organic forces of humanity locked in a ceaseless struggle with the inorganic forces of nature. Good, he believed, could only triumph if a superior race—the Aryans—could construct a culture powerful enough to preserve civilization against its mortal enemies. As the purest Aryans, the Germans had the ultimate responsibility of leadership, but they could only be effective if a supreme warrior would bind them together in a gigantic synthesis of blood and soil and end the threat of Jewish biological and spiritual pollution. Long before Hitler came to power, he was talking of the necessity of cleansing society of its "Jewish corruption."

Several months after Hitler became chancellor, the first anti-Jewish terror began with attacks against individuals and property. On 1 April 1933, a national boycott was proclaimed against Jewish businesses. This measure was followed by a series of decrees (*Reichsgesetzblatt*) that denied Jews the right to hold public office and civil service positions and restricted their employment in newspapers and broadcasting. Jews were also excluded from farming and ousted from jobs in high schools, universities, film studios, and symphony orchestras. The citizenship of naturalized Jews was annulled. The next year, Jews were banned from stock exchanges and brokerage houses.

A great deal of vigilante action accompanied these measures, with local rowdies acting on their own or under the authority of local party or SA leaders. However, most Nazi officials, even the crude Boycott Director Julius Streicher, opposed independent action, preferring to handle the "Jewish problem" within a proper legal framework. While appropriate measures were being prepared, the terror subsided. This pause encouraged many Jews to believe that they could withstand Nazi persecution just as their ancestors had survived previous persecutions. Some of those who had fled Germany even returned home.

In 1935, the onslaught began again with the Nuremberg laws "For the Protection of German Blood and Honor." Jews were forbidden from marriage or sexual intercourse with persons of German or related blood. They were prohibited from employing German females under the age of forty-five in their households. They could not fly the German flag and were excluded from German citizenship and relegated to the status of subjects.

Measurement for Semitism. Despite all the Nazi rhetoric about distinctive racial characteristics, the regime based its documentation of Jewishness on religious records. Hence, a Jew was a person who by such "proof" had at least three Jewish grandparents or a person who claimed membership in the Jewish community and had two Jewish grandparents. A person who had two Jewish grandparents who did not follow the Jewish religion (that is, lacked evidence of belonging to a Jewish community or was a convert to another religion) was considered a half-Jew (*Mischlinge*) of the first degree; a person with one Jewish grandparent was a *Mischlinge* of the second degree. "Half-Jews" were non-Germans; they were forbidden from joining the civil service or the party, serving in the army above the enlisted ranks, or marrying Germans without official permission, but they suffered less discrimination than "full-Jews," against whom the regime turned with special loathing.

In 1936, a law denied full-Jews the right to vote. Two years later, a decree forbade them to practice law and medicine. Next, they were denied access to theaters, movie houses, cabarets, public concerts, lecture halls, museums, streetcars, trams, buses, public bathhouses, amusement centers, beaches, and pools. Entire towns, usually vacation centers such as ski resorts and spas, were placed off-limits. Cities barred them from certain sidewalks and districts. For example, in Berlin they were forbidden access to the center of town and to many of the capital's important streets and thoroughfares. Violation was punishable by six weeks in jail. Jews were also barred from attending universities, and their driver's licenses were revoked. In addition, they were excluded from participation in business and commerce and often had difficulty purchasing food and drugs and receiving proper medical attention.

The policy of denigration was overwhelmingly successful, but it was not considered a permanent solution. Heinrich Himmler, always on the alert for any opportunity to increase his own power, proposed that Germany get rid of its Jews by having the SS ship them off to Palestine. He established contacts with German and Palestinian Zionist organizations that were working for the same goal. The reluctance of German Jews to change their conceptions about their nationality complicated the task. The Jews had been among the most enthusiastic supporters of German unification; their contributions to Germany's cultural life were remarkable, and they were intensely patriotic. Of the 100,000 Jews who served in World War I, 80,000 fought in frontline units; 35,000 of these were decorated for bravery and 12,000 were killed in action. But to Hitler they would always be slackers: "Nearly every clerk was a Jew and every Jew a clerk." He could "not help but compare them with their rare representatives at the front."[34] Hitler liked to dwell on the Jews' involvement with the Communist party.

The SS next tried to carry out its goals by force. At the beginning of 1938, a Reich Central Office for Jewish Emigration was established in Berlin to bring direct pressure on Jews to leave the country. The first victims of this policy of forced deportation were foreign Jews. For example, 17,000 Polish Jews living in Germany were rounded up, transported to the east in boxcars, and dumped across the frontier. But Britain's restrictions on immigration to Palestine and the unwillingness of many countries to open their frontiers to such large numbers of aliens frustrated the SS scheme for handling German Jews in a similar manner.

Crystal Night. In Germany, Jewish affairs became so important that everybody wanted to assume responsibility for their direction. Josef Goebbels, the minister of propaganda and district party boss (*Gauleiter*) of Berlin, deeply resented SS interference in an area he considered his own. In November 1938, he made an open bid for control. The assassination in Paris of Ernst vom Rath, third secretary of the German embassy, provided the occasion. The killer was Herschel Grynszpan, an exiled Polish Jew who wanted to avenge the deportation of his father in the recent SS roundup. No sooner had Goebbels heard the news of Rath's death than he ordered party and SA leaders throughout Germany to carry out an organized persecution. This pogrom had the approval of Hitler, who was with Goebbels in Munich commemorating the fifteenth anniversary of the Beer Hall Putsch. When the Führer heard the news of vom Rath's assassination, he commented that the "SA should be allowed to have a fling."[35] The general strategy for such an activity had already been formulated.

Operation *Kristallnacht* began in the late hours of 9 November and lasted throughout the following day. Synagogues were burned or dynamited, Jewish businesses plundered, and people savagely attacked. In Berlin, mobs of demonstrators were let loose in the Jewish quarters to smash, loot, and maim at will. The seven large synagogues in the capital were torched while the police routinely diverted traffic away from the affected areas. Scenes like these were repeated in Leipzig, Stuttgart, Freiburg, Heidelberg, Karlsruhe, and Frankfurt—in fact, in most of Germany's major cities. In the health resort of Baden-Baden, the pogrom did not begin until after seven in the morning so as not to disturb the sleep of the late season hotel guests in town to take the cure.

Hitler did not want to become directly involved and left Goebbels in charge. Himmler, informed only after the demonstrations were underway, was infuriated at Goebbels's power play and took steps to turn it to his advantage. The SS went into action to prevent looting and damage to German life and property while, at the same time, taking wealthy Jews into "protective custody."[36] Himmler's strategy paid off. Crystal Night dramatized the danger of resorting to mob action and convinced Hitler that the Jewish problem had to be handled in a systematic manner; he assigned the task to the SS.

Additional anti-Semitic legislation was soon passed. The insurance money owed to the Jews as a result of the damage was paid directly to the state. Some 20,000

Jews, between the ages of sixteen and eighty, were arrested and put into concentration camps, primarily Dachau, Buchenwald, and Sachsenhausen. As a final insult, the entire Jewish community was fined one billion marks for having provoked the German people. Perhaps as many as 2,500 men, women, and children died as a result of the action, including several hundred prisoners who expired in the camps. The other prisoners were released in batches over the next six months, often after being forced to turn over money or property to the state.

The violence toward the Jews was inexcusable by any standards. The Nazis tried to concoct a rationale by claiming that the Jews posed a real economic and political threat to the security of the state. Germany, in fact, had relatively few Jews—only about half a million in 1933.[37] Berlin, the only city with an appreciable concentration, had a community of 170,000; Frankfurt-am-Main was next with 29,000. The Jewish danger was solely in the mind of Hitler. He believed that everything he had written or said in his speeches and conversations about the need to rid the world of Jews was literally true, and he felt he had a special destiny to fulfill this task. Rarely in history has the personal antipathy of one man had such an alarming effect on the values of government, but, of course, one man could not prevail alone. Anti-Semitism was not just a German phenomenon. Hitler had encountered it in Vienna, Austria, but it existed in all the nations of Europe, although to a lesser extent in Western Europe, where assimilation was more advanced than in the ghetto-ridden atmosphere of Eastern Europe. There persecution of the Jews rather than integration tended to be the norm.[38] Hitler established this most virulent form of anti-Semitism as official national policy and took it to its murderous conclusion in the "Final Solution."

National Socialism and Christianity

The Concordat with Rome. In a speech Hitler delivered in Stuttgart two weeks after he became chancellor, he said that his government was dedicated to filling the entire German culture "once more with a Christian spirit."[39] What he considered attractive in Christianity however, was not found in its gospels or the sayings of Jesus, not even the Beatitudes. Instead, Hitler admired Christianity's ability to inspire, unify, and control the masses. He retained a grudging respect for the Roman Catholic church in whose faith he had been raised, but he did not believe that an individual could be both a German and a Christian. The regime intended to replace traditional religion with an official state tribalism, which according to Alfred Rosenberg, the party cultural minister, meant "the full expansion of the organic forces of the peoples of Nordic race." Hitler thought he could build this new cult on the pagan beliefs and values that still existed among the peasantry; in his view, Christianity was only a veneer that could be stripped off to allow the true people's religion to emerge. But such an overt campaign against religion was politically dangerous especially in the early days of his chancellorship. He therefore embarked on another tack.

Shortly after coming to power, he established contact with the Vatican to work for the conclusion of an agreement that would enable him to regulate religious affairs. The Roman Catholic church had already been engaged in similar talks with the Weimar regime and did not want them to go to waste.[40] Thus Hitler was able to conclude a concordat in a very short time. It was signed in Rome on 8 July 1933. Monsignor Eugenio Pacelli (later Pope Pius XII) officiated for the Vatican, Franz von Papen for Germany. This agreement guaranteed the Catholic church the right to appoint ecclesiastics to the German dioceses without interference, to maintain its own youth organizations, to provide religious instruction for its youth, and to have its property safeguarded. In exchange, the Vatican pledged to dissuade the German clergy from political activities. Pope Pius XI was primarily interested in the fate of Roman Catholicism and believed that this agreement ensured that the church could continue its primary mission of saving souls.

But the Roman Catholic church could no longer resolve church-state differences to its advantage by working things out on paper. Pius strengthened the Nazi regime at a critical time. By making it acceptable for Roman Catholics to serve Hitler, he helped the Center party support the enabling law. Moreover, once the Führer's power became more secure, he began to violate the agreement. He suppressed Catholic youth movements, leaving only the Hitler Youth. Church publications were banned, Roman Catholic schools were forced to close, and thousands of priests were arrested as common criminals. The Nazis explained that such measures had only been taken against "political Roman Catholicism" and assured the Vatican of their good faith. Nevertheless, Pius XI felt compelled to speak out. In his encyclical "With Burning Sorrow" (*Mit brennender Sorge*), issued on 14 March 1937, the pontiff deplored the campaign and criticized the regime for not living up to its treaty obligations. In doing so, the Holy See came the closest it ever did to condemning the Nazi system, but it was not the intention of Pius to call for resistance against Hitler. He did consider denouncing the concordat, but never did.

Controlling the Protestants. Hitler's antipathy for Roman Catholics was exceeded only by his disgust for Protestants whom he dismissed as insignificant, submissive little people, lacking the power of the church of Rome. Hitler appointed the pro-Nazi Reichswehr chaplain Ludwig Müller as his personal representative for Protestant affairs, giving him authority to create a unified Reich church. Since many of the larger Protestant congregations, like the Prussian Lutheran church, were proudly authoritarian and had a long record of subservience to the state, the Nazis were encouraged to believe that they would have little difficulty bringing the thirty or so denominations under their effective control. In July 1933, provincial church leaders were assembled to write a constitution for the unified church. But instead of electing Müller as first bishop, the pastors chose the more moderate Friedrich von Bodelschwing. Hitler nullified the results, forced the clerics to accept Müller, and threatened to take away the pulpits of those who disobeyed.

At the end of 1933, however, the rebels formed their own breakaway Confessional church (*Bekennende Kirche*). Some of the protesters, led by Pastor Martin Niemöller, went further and denounced the Nazis' anti-Christian tendencies. In May 1936, they sent Hitler a memorandum in which they deplored the regime's anti-Semitism, the abuses of the Gestapo, the concentration camps, the oppression of individual conscience, and the attacks on religion. The regime struck back. The following year it arrested the leaders of the Confessional church, a powerful example that encouraged widespread compliance from practically all the Protestant congregations. Most pastors apparently found the example of Martin Luther's submission to the princes more relevant than his defiance of the emperor.

The Nazis organized their own state "religious" festivals to take the place of church holidays. Mass demonstrations became a form of secular communion. The Nazi extravaganzas began on 30 January with the observance of the "Day of the Seizure of Power." In March came the "Day of the Commemoration of the Heroes." Hitler's birthday was celebrated in April, while May featured the "Day of National Labor." September offered two events: the Nazi Harvest Festival and the Nuremberg party rally. The year ended on 9 November with the commemoration of the Munich Beer Hall Putsch. Hitler took his functions as spiritual leader of Germany very seriously. The most sacred relic of the Nazis was the "Blood Flag," reputedly dipped in the wounds of those who had fallen in the 1923 putsch. At the November ceremony, the Führer himself consecrated all new banners by touching them with this holy treasure.

Economic Development

Industrial Planning. The Nazi social and economic program, set out in the party's original twenty-five points, put public interest over private interest and proposed a broad series of reforms. It called for the end of profiteering and usury, the care of the elderly, the abolition of unearned income, and profit-sharing plans for workers in large-scale industry. The program also favored comprehensive land reform, including the protection of the peasantry and the confiscation, without compensation, of real estate for community purposes. Other provisions called for the confiscation of war profits, the nationalization of trusts, and the abolition of interest on mortgages. In addition, the program declared that "the Roman Law, which serves the materialistic world order, shall be replaced by a German common law."[41] It also advocated ending the economic power of the Jews and extending German living space into Eastern Europe.

Hitler's socialism should not be taken too literally. In concept, it had more in common with Mussolini's corporate state than with any incarnation of Marxism. Hitler believed that Germany's industrial development and political development were inseparable. Although he did not intend to nationalize German industry, it would be tightly regulated. His goal was to make the country economically self-sufficient, an aim that many other countries shared in the depression years. Hitler, however, felt that German self-sufficiency depended on gaining additional national territory—enough to enable Germany to defend itself against any possible hostile military coalition. But the first step toward autarky entailed organizing the resources the country already possessed. The regime therefore needed the support and cooperation of the business community and could not afford to wage war against it. Conveniently, most of the party's socialistic goals had already been shelved even before Hitler became chancellor. Many in the party still believed in them, however, which was one of the reasons for Hitler's confrontation with the old SA.

The most immediate problem was how to end unemployment. Fortunately, Germany had already begun to recover from the depression. To maintain this momentum, the Nazis embarked on an extensive program of direct public expenditure for the construction of *Autobahns* (superhighways), canals, railroads, and public buildings. These projects were supplemented by financial assistance to the private sector in the form of subsidies and tax privileges. But many of the jobs created at this time did little to boost productivity since a sizable number of the new employees were given government jobs for which there was little need. Genuine recovery had to wait until the industries on which Germany had traditionally relied for its strength and power—machine tools, steel rolling equipment, chemicals, and synthetics—had begun to increase production through a rearmament program.

Preparing for War. In September 1936, at the Nuremberg party rally, Hitler announced a new Four-Year Plan. Its goals were twofold: the German economy was to be made self-sufficient, and the country was to be readied for war. Hermann Göring was named commissioner-general and given sweeping powers "to issue directions to all the highest offices of the state and the party."[42] Policy and central planning agencies were established, and a series of supervisory working committees (Food Supply, Labor Supply, Foreign Exchange, Raw Materials and Synthetics) were created to intervene in specific areas of the economy and enforce the official decrees. Göring also appointed ad hoc commissions to handle particular problems. But the instrumentalities of the Four-Year Plan usually operated through organizations already existent in the various ministries (Agriculture, Labor, and Economics). As a result, central planning often became a victim of personal power rivalries.

For example, Göring, who was supposed to provide central direction, was clearly partial to building up the strength of the air force, which he served in his dual capacity as commander-in-chief and minister of aviation. In 1937, in the face of a steel shortage, he ensured that his priorities would be met by creating his own factory, the "Hermann Göring" Reichswerke, a move that brought him into conflict with Hjalmar Schacht, the minister of economics. Hitler was already growing tired of Schacht's constant complaints and used the opportunity to strip him of his ministerial functions. Göring then assumed Schacht's functions himself, running the Finance Ministry as an agency of the Four-Year Plan. In January 1938, Göring relinquished the Finance Ministry to Walter Funk.

In addition to the jurisdictional confusion, the plan encountered other problems. The individual enterprises were frequently reluctant to obey the official plans. Supervision was inadequate to assure that raw material allocations were being used for the purposes intended. In addition, priorities were often not very well established, and manufacturers could decide for themselves which orders they would fill first. Thus, the official organization of the German economy was hardly totalitarian. It frequently lacked unified control, possessed no master plan, and had little central administrative machinery. Since Germany was already a major industrial power with a business class favorably disposed toward the regime, tight central control was not essential. The state could control the nation's resources without removing them from private ownership. After 1936, rearmament fueled all industrial development. By 1939, Germany was producing far more aluminum than any other country; its steel industry was second only to that of the United States; it had dramatically expanded its synthetic oil and rubber industries; and it had stockpiled enough raw materials to carry it through a war of twelve months. Still, this was a far cry from preparation for total war. Military expenditures increased, but private consumption also rose as the regime continued to encourage private spending. Even at a time when his foreign policy was becoming more aggressive, Hitler feared that any request for sacrifice on the part of the German people would result in a decline in his own popularity.

Regimentation of the Workers. The abolition of class distinctions seemed a logical goal for a system that took as its motto "one race, one state, and one leader." Furthermore, Hitler's skid row experiences had left him with hatred for the privileged classes, and he constantly referred to them in terms of derision. He preferred the company of his lower-middle-class cronies and spurned those who might be, or might consider themselves to be, socially superior. However, such prejudices did not prevent Hitler from appeasing the conservatives. He was extremely reluctant to make any changes in the country's traditional class structure and refused to consider nationalizing the means of production on the grounds that free enterprise was more efficient and flexible—and less dangerous politically—than a bureaucratically run industry.

The Nazi party was drawn largely from the middle and lower-middle classes—small businessmen, artisans, white-collar workers, and civil servants—who had scant sympathy for the proletariat whose ranks had traditionally supported the Social Democratic and Communist parties. The regime's difficult task was to reconcile the workers with the other classes of the nation without changing society's basic hierarchies. To do this, it was necessary to create the illusion of a classless society in which everyone would contribute to the common good. Hitler presented himself as an honest broker who would join together the different strata of society. In practice, this meant that the capitalists would be allowed considerable latitude, while the workers would be subject to control. The Nazi ideology of the classless society (*Volksgemeinschaft*) hardly entailed shared sacrifice.

Nevertheless, Hitler constantly reminded the workers of his humble origins, claiming that he too came from the common folk—"I myself was a laboring man for years in the building trade and had to earn my own bread."[43] His descriptions in *Mein Kampf* of how poor and underfed he was in those days in Vienna were no more than fairy tales to endear himself to the masses.[44] These experiences, he claimed, made him determined to serve the German people to the best of his ability. "Honor work and respect the worker," one of his mottoes proclaimed. Propaganda aside, few German leaders had so clearly identified themselves with the work ethics of the masses or so praised them for their loyalty, constancy, and stability.

The regime dramatized its official concern for the inherent equality of all Germans with a variety of programs and awards. After 1935, there was compulsory *Arbeitsdienst* (Labor Service) in which eighteen-year-old youths served for six months in special camps where they learned the value of manual labor. The female counterpart was the League of German Maidens with its obligatory Land Jahr, a year's stint on the farms where they worked in the house and in the fields. The *Blut und Boden* (Blood and Soil) campaign extolled the farmers as the source of national strength, elevating them to a new level of social respectability. The word *"Bauer"* became an honored title. It suggested more than "peasant"; it implied that one had a mystical relationship with the land. The Day of National Labor on 1 May was the greatest Nazi celebration in terms of overall participation. Through it all, the Führer presented himself as a leader who had renounced normal creature comforts, denying himself even a private life, to work for the welfare of his people. But behind each of these programs lurked exploitation. The Hereditary Farm Law, designed to protect the integrity of the family farm by preventing it from being taken away from the family for debt, also had the effect of binding the farmers to the soil.[45] And the cost of farm supplies more than offset the state's mandated rise in farm prices.

By 1936, the regime had succeeded in restoring full employment (helped by the regime's building program and by rearmament), but the ensuing scarcity of labor did not result in a rise in wages. A wage freeze, instituted shortly after the Nazis came to power, continued throughout the rest of the 1930s. As a result, hourly wages rose very little. Nevertheless, the affinity of workers for the Third Reich remained high, attesting to the regime's success in convincing the working class that they were playing an important role in restoring national glory, albeit under the domination of others.

POSTSCRIPT   Prior to World War II, most Germans were more aware of the Nazi regime's positive achievements than they were of its scorn for conventional values. Had Hitler died in 1938, perhaps the Germans might have regarded him as one of their leading statesmen. Unemployment, which had affected one-third of the work force at the height of the depression, was practically gone. Public works and services helped mask the regime's abuses and seemed symbolic of each German's right to prosperity in the commonwealth. Many Germans did not find the regime particularly oppressive or fanatical, nor did they believe it had come to power illegally. One of the common misconceptions is that Hitler overthrew the Weimar Republic. Constitutionally, in fact, the Weimar Republic continued to exist. A back room intrigue of conservatives who thought they could make him their cat's paw gave Hitler his chance to become chancellor, but his destruction of German democracy was accomplished quite lawfully by turning the power of the government against the state. According to the Weimar Constitution, the president had the authority to appoint as chancellor whomever he liked as long as that person could win the confidence of the Reichstag. This Hitler managed to achieve. The enabling act, the main legal underpinning of his dictatorship, had originally been enacted for four years. Hitler took care to extend it in 1937 after its original life had expired. It was renewed twice more in 1939 and 1942.

Germany, unlike the Soviet Union, was never cut off from the rest of the world. The regime had its black list of a few thousand people who were not permitted to travel abroad, but aside from the limitations imposed by currency restrictions, Germans could generally go where they pleased. In turn, foreign tourists were encouraged to visit Germany, and they continued to do so in great numbers. *Deutschland* was still as quaint as before, but behind its pretty facade lurked the terror of the secret police and the concentration camps.

The Gestapo possessed the authority to take anyone it wished into preventive custody, a prerogative that was used liberally in the early days of the regime. The Gestapo had informers in practically every city block and district. Parents had to watch what they said at home for fear their children would report them. Even on vacation cruises, agents spied on their fellow travelers, writing reports about their behavior and noting whether they were late for breakfast or guilty of currency violations. But most people considered such impositions a small price to pay for a new society. Many foreigners also seemed to ignore the repressive aspects.

Former British prime minister Lloyd George, certainly no friend of dictatorship, saw in the Nazi leadership a drive and vision lacking at home. Returning from a trip to Germany in 1936, he praised Hitler's accomplishments in ending unemployment and improving the health of German youth. Lloyd George said that Hitler inspired a new confidence in his people: "He is a born leader of men. A magnetic, dynamic personality with a single-minded purpose. . . . The old trust him. The young idolize him."

Lloyd George remarked that he found everywhere a hostility to Bolshevism coupled "with a genuine admiration for the British people."[46]

Hitler impressed people with his talk about the progress that could come through hard work, but by progress he meant improving the strength of the nation rather than the lot of the individual. In fact, traditional class relationships changed little under the Third Reich. The old economic elite maintained its position. The aristocracy continued to dominate high posts in the armed forces. The foreign service continued to be staffed by conservative career diplomats. Even the Nazi party, originally the greatest single force for advancement regardless of background, courted members from the established upper class. The SS emerged as a new leadership elite, but Himmler actively recruited from among the old aristocracy and from the educated middle class—many joined for career reasons, not because they believed in SS ideology.

The regime's only real standard of equality was the duty of all Germans to submit equally to the will of the Führer. Improvements in public welfare or steps toward a classless society were useful only if they reinforced or extended Hitler's and the regime's political power. The supreme irony of the National Socialist system lay in its assumption that the German racial community, the master race, was fit to fulfill its destiny as a race of people which had been deprived of its freedom. However, the Nazi regime was never as all-powerful as its leaders pretended. Its hierarchy consisted of a series of Byzantine elites, all jealously guarding their own prerogatives and nurturing their rivalries and hatreds. Nor did Hitler wish it otherwise. As a people's emperor, he presided over his unruly vassals, confident that they would give him unquestioning loyalty, out of both emotional commitment and a desire for personal advantage. He often found it necessary to come to terms with various pre-Nazi power structures: the army, the churches, and the industrial interests. Such constant accommodation attenuated the tyranny of National Socialism and directed its force upon the most exposed and helpless—the Jews, the Communists, and the dissident intellectuals. If a German were of the proper racial type and remained apolitical, life under the Nazis could be pleasant, prosperous, and secure—providing one did not look too closely at the political environment or too far into the future.

ENDNOTES

1. In the September 1930 elections, the Nazis received 6.4 million votes, or 18.3 percent of the total; in July 1932, they won 13.75 million votes, or 37.4 percent of the total.
2. See Richard F. Hamilton, *Who Voted for Hitler* (Princeton, N.J.: Princeton University Press, 1982) and Thomas Childers, *The Nazi Voter* (Chapel Hill: University of North Carolina Press, 1983).

3. In the Weimar national elections, women were given gray ballots; the men received white, making it easy to determine gender.

4. For example, in 1928 the Social Democrats had tried to halt the construction of armored cruisers, or rather pocket battleships, which were being built to the tonnage restrictions imposed by the Treaty of Versailles. This supercruiser was designed to outrun any ship it could not outgun, and outgun most ships it could outrun.

5. The Social Democrats still remained the largest party, but the extreme right National Socialists increased their strength tenfold, the German Nationalists gained 41 seats, and the Communists won 77 seats, an increase of 23.

6. Hindenburg received 18.6 million votes, or 49.6 percent; Hitler received 11.3 million (30.4 percent); Ernst Thälmann, the Communist candidate, had 4.9 million (13.2 percent); and Theodor Düsterberg, the leader of the antidemocratic war veterans organization *Stahlhelm*, trailed with 2.5 million (6.8 percent).

7. Hindenburg received 19.3 million, or 53 percent; Hitler, 13.4 million (36.8 percent); and Thälmann, the Communist, 3.7 million (10.2 percent).

8. Prussia was the largest of the states, comprising 60 percent of Germany's area.

9. For example, the Nationalists had 37 deputies and the Communists had 89.

10. This omission was not unique to the Weimar Constitution. The United States Constitution, for example, also does not mention political parties or forbid the destruction of the democratic system.

11. Franz von Papen, *Memoirs* (New York: E. P. Dutton, 1953), 251.

12. Hitler did not officially become a German citizen until 25 February 1932 when he was made a *Regierungsrat*, state counsellor, by the Nationalist-Nazi coalition government of Brunswick. Since Hitler had no intention of fulfilling the duties of the post, it might have been argued that the naturalization the position conferred was not valid, but nobody was prepared to press the point.

13. For portraits of Hitler's parents, see Robert G. L. Waite, *The Psychopathic God Adolf Hitler* (New York: Basic Books, 1977), 152–66.

14. Adolf Hitler, *Mein Kampf* (Boston: Houghton Mifflin, 1962), 21–22.

15. In attempting to explain his irrational hatred, some writers have focused on Hitler's relationship with his mother, specifically, the fantasies and guilt he felt about Oedipal fulfillment. (Waite, *Psychological God*, 424). Another line of investigation concerns the trauma Hitler had felt over the death of Klara Hitler. During her final illness with breast cancer, she was treated by a Jewish doctor. It has been suggested that Hitler viewed this man as a substitute father, "the brutal attacker who had finally mutilated and killed his beloved mother." (Ibid., 218).

16. Hitler, *Mein Kampf*, 56.

17. Ibid., 123.

18. The American army has no comparable rank, but it would be about the equivalent of a private first class.

19. Hitler, *Mein Kampf*, 161.

20. Large donations from big business were apparently few and far between; the capitalists, aside from a few individuals like steel magnate Fritz Thyssen, preferred to invest their money in the more traditional nationalist parties. Many others, like Gustav Krupp, were cool to the Nazis until the Nazis took power. Then they did an about-face. See Henry Ashby Turner, *German Big Business and the Rise of Hitler* (New York: Oxford University Press, 1985).

21. *Mein Kampf* first appeared in the autumn of 1925 and had a limited first-year sale of 9,473 copies. Hitler's publisher, Max Amann, had hoped for an exciting account of the author's political adventures, but got instead a repetitious catalog of personal antipathies.

22. See Karl Dietrich Bracher, *Adolf Hitler* (Bern: Schere Verlag, 1964); Joachim C. Fest, *Hitler* (New York: Harcourt Brace Jovanovich, 1974); and Charles B. Flood, *Hitler: The Path to Power* (Boston: Houghton Mifflin, 1989).

23. Enunciated by Robert Ley, the head of the party's political organization. *Nazi Con-*

spiracy and Aggression, vol. 1 (Washington, D.C.: Government Printing Office, 1947), 193.

24. Ibid., 193.
25. Adolf Hitler, *My New Order* (New York: Reynal and Hitchcock, 1941), 82.
26. In addition, Hermann Göring, the current president of the Reichstag and a minister without portfolio, was minister of interior for Prussia.
27. *Nazi Conspiracy and Aggression*, 1:353.
28. It was said that the arson had been arranged by Hermann Göring and that a special squad of Berlin storm troopers entered the Reichstag through a tunnel leading from the building across the street in which Göring had his office as Reichstag president. Van der Lubbe's trial lasted from September to December 1933. The accused insisted that he was solely responsible and was condemned to death and beheaded—in a traditional medieval manner, facing upwards. The Communists who were tried with him were acquitted for lack of evidence.
29. Norman H. Baynes, ed., *The Speeches of Adolf Hitler*, vol. 1 (London: Oxford University Press, 1942), 420–21.
30. The SA under its new chief of staff, Viktor Lutze, degenerated into a social club for elbow-benders and Jew-baiters. They dressed up and paraded around on official occasions.
31. The central government did not yet exercise police power, which was still in the hands of the sixteen Länder.
32. Walter Schellenberg, *The Labyrinth* (New York: Harper, 1956), 15.
33. Ibid., 15.
34. Ibid., 193.
35. Rita Thalmann and Emmanuel Feinermann, *Crystal Night* (New York: Holocaust Library, 1974), 58.
36. An SS survey of the damage reported the destruction of 815 shops and 171 residences; the burning of 267 synagogues, of which 76 were completely ruined; and the murder of 36 Jews and severe injury to 36 others.
37. In 1933, Germany had 499,682 religious Jews. There were another 40,000 nonreligious Jews with three or four Jewish grandparents. (The Nazis considered these fullblood Jews.) The number of those with two or one Jewish grandparent was unknown in 1933, but six years later their numbers were given as 52,005 and 32,669, respectively.
38. Sebastian Haffner, *The Meaning of Hitler* (Cambridge, Mass.: Harvard University Press, 1983), 9.
39. Baynes, *The Speeches of Adolf Hitler*, 1:370.
40. Stewart Stehlin, *Weimar and the Vatican* (Princeton, N.J.: Princeton University Press, 1983), Chapter 7.
41. Gottfried Feder, *Hitler's Official Program and Its Fundamental Ideas* (New York: Howard Fertig, 1971), 40–41.
42. *Nazi Conspiracy and Aggression*, 7:465.
43. In a speech at the First Congress of German Workers on 10 May 1933. Baynes, *The Speeches of Adolf Hitler*, 1:862.
44. Franz Jetzinger, *Hitler's Youth* (Westport, Conn.: Greenwood Press, 1976), 109.
45. The law applied to farms of less than 125 hectares that were capable of supporting a farm family.
46. Martin Gilbert, ed., *Lloyd George* (Englewood Cliffs, N.J.: Prentice-Hall, 1968), 77.

CHAPTER 9

STALINIST RUSSIA

PREFACE   All nations have holy treasures that symbolize some grand moment in the country's history. For some, the treasure is a jeweled crown, a sacred stone, an icon, or a historic throne; for others, it is a constitutional document; and for others, a battle flag or the bloodstained clothing of martyred heroes. Whatever the treasure, it is usually kept on display where it can inspire the populace. When Lenin died, he became the Soviet regime's greatest relic. After his brain was removed for analysis,[1] the rest of his remains were embalmed, packaged in a sarcophagus covered by plate glass, and put on view in a wooden structure near the Kremlin. The cult of Lenin had begun. His body became the country's greatest attraction, far surpassing the pilgrimage to the monastery of the caves at Kiev in tsarist times. Viewing his remains was a means of affirming the legitimacy of the Communist state.[2]

A reddish porphyry and gray granite boxlike mausoleum soon replaced the original, temporary wooden tomb. On the roof of the new structure was a reviewing stand from which dignitaries could watch the parades and demonstrations held in Red Square. The Communists discontinued the Russian Orthodox church's traffic in religious relics, icons, and medals, but encouraged the production and sale of all manner of mementos of the late Communist savior, including various campaign-type buttons that reproduced his baby picture. The city of Petrograd was renamed Leningrad in his honor, and the Order of Lenin was created as the nation's highest service award. Lenin's writings, akin to holy writ, appeared in endless pamphlets, anthologies, and editions. More statues were erected in his honor than had been erected to any other man in modern history. Almost every place that Lenin had ever stayed or lived either sported a commemorative plaque or became a museum. Children were told that nothing was more noble than to follow Lenin's way, to dedicate themselves to the cause to which he had devoted his life. But now that cause was in the hands of his successor, Josef Stalin.

Stalin inherited an established dictatorship in which there was neither respect for civil liberties nor toleration for any views except those officially endorsed by the state. Stalin would carry out a change of direction without modifying the basic character of that dictatorship. Under his leadership, a new class of revolutionaries, less intellectual and idealistic than their predecessors, became increasingly powerful. By 1930, all those who had served on the Politburo, the chief policy-making body of the Communist party, during Lenin's time had been replaced except Stalin himself.[3] Stalin chose his henchmen on the basis of personal loyalty.[4] This new power elite, more devoted to routine organization than to dialectics, would preside over one of the most far-reaching transformations of a society in modern times. The basis of property ownership would be altered, including the peasants' relation to the land, and a new industrial establishment would be built under the aegis of strict state supervision, planning, and control. In the process, Stalin spared his people none of the horrors of the industrial revolution already experienced by the more advanced countries of the West. His legacy was a strong, awesome, modern state, but one marked by cruelty, murder, and fear. Hardly a family escaped untouched.

THE CONTROL OF THE ECONOMY

Collectivization in Agriculture

War against the Countryside. The Communist leaders were predominantly city dwellers with an urban mentality. But the Soviet Union was basically rural and agricultural. In 1928, 75 percent of all its people were still engaged in working the land. Wooden ploughs, strip farming, natural manure, and the three-field system of crop rotation were all in current use. The Moscow party leaders resented the country's dependence on such medieval agrarian methods and the backward mentality that went with them. Lenin had promised land to the peasants when he wanted their support, but he detested their lower-middle-class sense of property and their personal identity with the soil. Stalin turned this antipathy into open warfare in a continuing campaign aimed at enslaving the peasantry.

The New Economic Policy (NEP), which had been adopted in 1921, had left the peasants relatively free from state interference. Although the regime had officially nationalized the land in November 1917, private ownership of farm enterprises persisted and had become an important source of surplus food for the economy. The NEP period added to the prestige and power of the more enterprising and efficient peasants who were able to lease land and hire labor, thereby increasing their holdings and prosperity. By Western standards, these village entrepreneurs, or *kulaks*, were men of modest means, but in their own milieu they constituted an elite. They were also an active source of resistance to any schemes that threatened their independence. The regime was not powerful enough to force these

A collective farm in the Central Volga district loads wheat to send to the regional granary. This kolkhoz had a work force of 1,500 and covered an area of 25,000 hectares. By touting such abundance the Communists hoped to show the success of their agricultural policy. Yet by 1933, deaths from starvation in that same region could be counted in the millions.

landholders to produce against their will. When it attempted to increase their taxes, they fought back by limiting production and refusing to sell grain at the official price. Thus, the regime had a double problem. It wanted to enforce political orthodoxy and obedience on the countryside by eliminating class differences, but it also wanted to improve agricultural productivity. By 1928, the agrarian sector had yet to equal, let alone surpass, the levels of productivity reached in 1913 (28,000 metric tons of wheat in 1913 versus 22,000 in 1928, for example). Stalin, believing it politically dangerous to continue to depend on the output of the leased agricultural holdings, established *sovkhozes*, large state-owned farms operated like factories by government administrative specialists. Workers were hired for specific functions, with their production going exclusively to the state. These units, which were supplied with tractors imported from abroad, were expected to develop new farming techniques that would set an example for all peasants. But the sovkhozes had little impact and led to no significant increase in overall productivity.

In addition to the state farms, Stalin tried to create larger, more efficient agricultural units by promoting the formation of collectivized associations of peasants, or *kolkhozes*, in which the land was theoretically owned by the local community, not the state, and could neither be alienated nor sold. Initially, collective farm membership was voluntary. The state added more land to the original acreage in an effort to induce the peasants to become members. But by October 1929, only about four percent of the 25.5 million peasant families had joined, and most of these were only in loose arrangements that provided for common cultivation. The Stalinists began to impose sterner measures: executions, arrests, and deportations. An estimated 5 million people were sentenced to penal servitude. The state incited class warfare in the villages, encouraging poorer peasants to inform against their slightly better-off neighbors who might be withholding grain. Within six months, despite an increase in peasant hostility and protests, the number of "officially" collectivized households had increased to 58 percent, or 14,264,000 families.

The Communist leaders now had two choices—the proverbial carrot or the stick. They could encourage the peasants to supply the country's needs by letting prices rise and offering the peasants rewards, such as more consumer goods, or they could attempt to crush the opposition by force. By this time, however, Stalin had found that giving the state the power to make decisions on production was preferable to having it determined by the peasants and the price structure. He feared peasant capitalism and had no desire to slow down his crash program for the development of heavy industry by producing consumer goods. Stalin intended to make the peasants bear the full cost of industrialization and therefore expanded the program of collectivization, a decision that entailed the eradication of the kulaks. The peasants resisted, slaughtering their livestock and refusing to work the common fields. The regime reacted to this resistance with renewed determination to crush these adversaries once and for all. The campaign escalated as it went along. In the process, over a million peasant families were despoiled, driven into exile, or sent to forced labor camps. But the destruction of so many human resources, accompanied by the peasants' wholesale slaughter of livestock and the chaotic disruption of the harvest due to forced expropriation of grain, did nothing to help productivity. Stalin had little choice but to ease up.

In March 1930, he proclaimed the party was "dizzy from success" and characteristically blamed others for his failures—specifically, the provincial leadership that had carried out his orders. He appeared as a moderate, denouncing the use of force and brutality to bring the peasants into collectives. Encouraged by this apparently conciliatory attitude, the peasants withdrew from the collective farms in droves until fewer than 6 million households remained. Stalin had not abandoned the collectivization drive, however. He had simply decided to modify its tactics and now offered the peasants inducements: tax benefits, credit allowances, and special machinery for collectives. The offensive resumed after a brief breathing space, and the number of collectivized households soon reached and exceeded its previous level. By 1940, all but three percent of the peasants were in collective farms.

Profile: Josef Stalin (1879–1953)

The new Communist overlord, then named Josef Vissarionovich Dzhugashvili, was born on 21 December 1879 in Gori, a small town fifty miles northwest of Tiflis in the transcaucasian province of Georgia. He was the son of a cobbler and a washerwoman and was, therefore, one of the few Bolshevik leaders who actually came from the working classes. His home was a one-room brick hovel. Stalin's father was an abusive drunk who beat his wife and his son, no doubt leading his son to accept erratic and irrational brutality as proper behavior. The father expected his son to earn his living as a factory worker, but, thanks to his mother, Josef received a formal education. He first attended the local parish school, where he was judged an excellent student, and later the theological seminary in Tiflis where he began studies for the priesthood—a clerical career being a potential avenue for social betterment. Through his schooling, he became fluent in Russian, although he always spoke it with a Georgian accent. He also lost his religious faith. His daughter, Svetlana Alliluyeva, claimed that the parochial schools determined her father's character for the rest of his life: "From his experiences at the seminary, he had come to the conclusion that men were intolerant, coarse, deceiving their flocks in order to hold them in obedience; that they intrigued, lied, and as a rule possessed numerous faults and very few virtues."[5] On the eve of his graduation, he was expelled for his subversive political opinions, which then were a blend of Marxism and Georgian (anti-Russian) nationalism.

In 1901, Stalin became a member of the underground Social Democratic Committee, one of the most extreme of the various revolutionary factions, and eventually he developed a strong admiration for Lenin whose aggressive tenet that the great questions in the life of a nation can be settled only by force was clearly in tune with Stalin's own nature. Lenin's idea of a tight-knit revolutionary party also satisfied Stalin's search for personal identity in a community of the elect. Stalin's hatred of, and revolt against, the prevailing tsarist autocracy was an amplification of the resistance to authority he had felt first against his father and then against the punitive nature of his church schooling. Marxism, and specifically the Leninist strain of Marxism, legitimized his rebellion and resentment, turning it into a noble struggle by the downtrodden against their oppressors. Even before he had met Lenin at a Bolshevik congress at Tammersfors, Finland, in December 1905, Stalin had translated the writings of his "mountain eagle" from Russian into Georgian. He continued to maintain contact with Lenin through correspondence and meetings at other party conventions in Stockholm, London, Cracow, and Vienna. Yet, even while working for the Bolsheviks, Stalin occasionally served as a part-time informer for the *okhrana*, the tsarist secret police, denouncing comrades whom he regarded as possible rivals or against whom he wanted to take revenge.[6]

Stalin joined the Bolshevik wing of the Russian Social Democratic movement because he saw in Lenin an opportunity to fulfill his psychological needs and ambitions. It was his chance to become an apostle of the masses, to lead them to victory. He not only endorsed Lenin's ideology, but also adopted Lenin's Great Russian nationality, rejecting his own Georgian identity. In the process, he became strongly anti-Semitic, an antipathy that would eventually grow into an obsession. Stalin's struggle to develop a new persona, his passion to fight on the winning side, and his hero worship eventually paid off. Lenin rewarded his devotion by making him a member of the Bolshevik Central Committee and promoting him to editorship of *Pravda*, the party newssheet. The new assignment, which came in 1912, offered Stalin a change of pace in a career that had included robbing banks— a favorite means of revolutionary fund raising—and organizing oil workers in Baku. Stalin (he began using this cryptonym, meaning "man of steel," at this time) tried to prove himself equal to the task by writing, under Lenin's guidance, a justification for the self-determination of oppressed nationalities, entitled *Marxism and the National Problem*. In 1913, he was arrested and exiled to northern Siberia. The experience was not new. He had been banished on five previous occasions and had escaped each time. This time, however, he was out of circulation until the March Revolution of 1917, when he returned to Petrograd to become one of the inner circle of party policymakers.

Stalin always seemed out of place among the other more middle-class Bolshevik leaders who resented his arrogant pride and cruelty as well as his extremism and lack of sociability. After the November coup, he received the minor post of commissar of nationalities. But he was determined to prove himself by cold-bloodedly purging the indigenous Communist leadership in his native Georgia. He did this with such savagery that even the normally hard-hearted Lenin was alarmed.[7] Stalin held the nationalities post until 1923, but in the meantime he picked up a more important responsibility, the Commissariat of Workers-Peasant Inspection. This position enabled him, under the cover of fighting corruption and inefficiency, to push his influence directly into the Soviet bureaucracy. His appointment as secretary-general of the party in 1922 also allowed him to increase his authority as he turned what had been intended as a routine administrative position into one of real power in the Communist party. He was consequently in a good position to profit when Lenin was virtually incapacitated by a stroke. In the last year of his life, Lenin could do nothing more than dictate a few letters expressing his disapprobation at Stalin's usurpation of power.

After Lenin's death, Stalin systematically rid himself of the prominent old Bolsheviks. He first isolated Trotsky by forming an alliance with Gregori Zinoviev and Lev Kamenev in a "troika" against the leftist opposition. Then in 1925 he formed an alliance with the party moderates—Mikhail Tomsky, Alexei Rykov, and Nikolai Bukharin—against a so-called leftist coalition of Kamenev and Zinoviev who had joined Trotsky. When Stalin had pushed the leftists out of the way, he turned against his former allies and by 1928 was indisputably in command of the party. But merely neutralizing the power of his rivals was not sufficient. These former associates of Lenin were unwilling to give him unquestioned obedience; they would never idolize the dictator and would remain his enemies no matter how diminished their power. Stalin wanted deification and, for that reason, automatically viewed all adversaries—real or imagined—as personal enemies to be callously liquidated.[8]

Stalin knew that he had to give the appearance of continuing Lenin's policies in order to take full advantage of the reverence in which his predecessor was held. He therefore presented his decisions in Leninist terms even when he was actually departing from the theories of the past. Often it was a simple matter of choosing which facet to emphasize. For example, Lenin had preached that the development of Communism in the Soviet Union was contingent on the success of revolution in the rest of Europe, because only with substantial assistance from more industrialized Communist nations could Russia be saved from its backwardness. Yet Lenin also believed in developing Communist strength at home, no matter what happened abroad. Stalin tried to field his way between these two positions. In a series of lectures, given in April 1924 at Moscow's Sverdlov University, he first said that the efforts of a single country "particularly of such a peasant country as Russia" were inadequate to achieve the final victory of socialism. The organization of socialist production also depended on "the efforts of the proletariat of several advanced countries."[9] But even as the words were spoken, Stalin knew it was unlikely that any other European governments would follow Russia's lead. He therefore soon began to declare that the Soviet Union *could* develop socialism by itself. The victory of socialism in one country, Stalin explained, "means the possibility of solving the contradictions between the workers and the peasants with the aid of the internal forces of our country; it means the possibility of the proletariat's seizing power and using that power for the construction of complete socialist society in our country, with the sympathy and the support of the workers of other countries, but without the preliminary victory of the proletarian revolution in other countries."[10] He had the official text of his Sverdlov lectures changed to conform to the new line.[11]

Stalin continued to dabble in world revolution while advocating that the Soviet Union should become the arsenal of the international working class. He further quoted Lenin to show that war with the capitalist nations was inevitable and that, until the final victory of Communism, there could be no relaxation of the authority of the state whose power he had developed into a cult. Such an interpretation was popular with the party bosses and technocrats who wanted to concentrate on affairs at home rather than tilting at windmills abroad. Even before it became hazardous for one's health to budge from the official line, these politicians saw in Stalin's leadership a practical and realistic approach to the Communist transformation of Russia from a backward agrarian nation into a modern industrial giant.

A Second Revolution. The drive for collectivization in the Soviet Union produced a fundamental change in the relationship of the peasants to the land, destroying a way of life that had existed for centuries. In this respect it was much more irreversible than the political revolution of 1917 to which it compares in significance. The policy also caused the greatest human-made peacetime famine in modern times. The Soviet authorities supplied food to the urban areas by ruthlessly confiscating grain and leaving the peasants to starve. In 1933, the novelist Arthur Koestler saw the ravages of this policy in the Ukraine: "Hordes of families in rags begging at the railway stations, the women lifting up to the compartment window their starving brats which—with drumstick limbs, big cadaverous heads and puffed bellies—looked like embryos out of alcohol bottles; the old men with frost-bitten toes sticking out of torn slippers. I was told that these were kulaks who had resisted the collectivization of the land . . . they were enemies of the people, who preferred begging to work."[12] The term "kulak" had become purely propagandistic—it was applied to any peasant whom the Stalinist regime chose to crush. During the height of the political famine, which claimed the lives of between 7 million and 14 million people, largely in the Ukraine and the northern Caucasus region, Stalin continued to earn investment capital by selling grain abroad, almost two million tons during 1932–1933. Because of this, many foreigners had difficulty believing that Soviet people were actually dying of starvation.

The Communist bosses demanded that the collectives supply the state a specified amount of food (usually around 40 percent of total production) at below-market prices. These deliveries were to be made no matter what the weather, the results of the harvest, or the cost. As a sop, the state allowed each peasant household a small family plot. Because the peasants could often earn twice as much money from working these gardens as from their collective farm wages, they tried to spend as much time as possible on their own plots, avoiding the "official" work. Naturally, pressure to enlarge these holdings was strong. Most of the specialty foods in the Soviet Union came from these parcels.

The state established norms for crop production, livestock breeding, mechanization, irrigation works, and antidrought measures. Farm organization, like the general organization of the state, followed the familiar hierarchical pyramid: the party and government officials were at the top, followed by specialists and brigadiers for special services; then came the skilled workers, and finally the common laborers. Control was ensured by the secret police with their spies and informers and through such devices as the Machine Tractor Stations. The tractor stations had a monopoly on farm machinery and charged the collective farms from 45 to 51 percent of their crop for use of the equipment.

The stations were outposts of the state in the countryside and were usually staffed by imported party operatives who, in addition to their economic responsibilities, engaged in agitation and propaganda and, of course, political surveillance. The stations' share of farm produce, together with the portion already claimed by the state, meant that only about 15 percent of the annual production actually remained with the collective farms. Some farms had a larger economic base, but most were underprivileged. Despite the increased use of mechanized equipment, overall agricultural production was barely adequate to keep pace with the expanding population. During the first two five-year plans, the cultivated area increased by about one-fifth, with certain industrial crops such as sugar beets, cotton, and sunflower seeds developing more rapidly. However, the production of grain, the most important food crop, rose very little, if at all. Between 1928 and 1933, gross agricultural output actually declined.[13] It later recovered, but by 1937 it was only eight percent greater than it had been a decade before. The result was probably much worse as official Soviet production statistics were often inflated.

The collectivization of agriculture was launched to ensure state control over food distribution and achieved some success at that goal, but there was to be no significant improvement in productivity. The agricultural sector often fell behind the level of output necessary to maintain minimum nutritional standards for the industrial proletariat; when the discrepancy became significant, the regime forced the peasants to sell the grain they needed for fodder and even for their food. Moreover, the collectivization campaign had caught the rural Communist party members completely off guard, and they spent a great deal of effort trying to adjust to its demands. In the process, they lost the support of their constituents while failing to win the approval of their superiors. Moscow continued to regard agrarian functionaries with suspicion—even contempt—and expended considerable effort to increase the rural party officials' political awareness and improve their organization. Nevertheless, Moscow failed to convert the rural party to the new policy.[14] Many rural party officials, seeing the harsh consequences of forced appropriation of food at firsthand, detested the policy. Although their opposition was seldom overt, many orders coming from the central government were ignored or carried out perfunctorily.

To the Stalinist regime, acting contrary to party policies was tantamount to treason even though it was in the best interests of the local population. The general purge of 1933–1934 ostensibly was conducted to rid the party of inefficient and incompetent officials, but it was mostly directed at the ideologically unreliable. Those purged included officials who had failed to reach goals, and the purge did not consider the reasonableness of the goals or whether the officials had made efforts to achieve them. Stalin accepted no blame for the peasants' suffering and was completely indifferent to their misery. When some officials tried to bring the starvation in the countryside to his attention, he accused them of deliberately telling lies in order to frighten him.

Emphasis on Heavy Industry

A Five-Year Plan. State planning was not invented by the Communists, nor was it new to Russia. The tsars had pushed the development of state industry and maintained vast landed estates worked by government serfs. Never before, however, had the entire economic life of a nation been subject to such regulation and control. The First Five-Year Plan, inaugurated in 1928, sought to convert a backward agrarian economy into a centrally organized industrial giant as rapidly as possible; in the process, all vestiges of private enterprise were to be completely eradicated. This colossal task was entrusted to *Gosudarstvennaia Planovaia Komissia* (State Planning Commission or Gosplan), which was composed of party leaders and economic experts operating under the direct supervision of the chief administrative and executive body of the Soviet Union, the *Sovnarkom*. This body issued decrees with the force of law. The Gosplan established basic production quotas and goals and each year prepared a detailed report to govern development for the following twelve months. The first plan took two years to prepare and filled six volumes, including revisions. Soviet economic planning was approximate in that it set both maximum and minimum goals, which could be altered when economic or political circumstances changed. Stalin admitted that no economic plan could take into account all the possibilities that were hidden in the "depths of our society" and that were revealed only in the course of work. In sharp contrast to a market economy, where individual enterprises would be free to establish their own priorities within an existing legal framework, the Gosplan tried to establish central collective norms. Any failure to fulfill these quotas was considered a political offense, even though no amount of expert planning could encompass all the economic activities of 147 million people living in a territory covering 8 million square miles. In fact, detailed plans generally were prepared only for those activities that the state considered particularly important; but even these plans were essentially predictions.

The 1928 Five-Year Plan earmarked 64.5 million rubles for overall industrial expansion, about two and a half times more than was invested during the entire Leninist period. More than half of this amount was allotted to the expansion of large-scale enterprise, which was to be increased by 179 percent compared to 135.9 percent for the economy as a whole. Labor productivity was expected to rise 110 percent overall and was to be accompanied by significant cost reductions: 35 percent in industrial production, 50 percent in construction, and 30 percent in fuel consumption. The 1928 plan singled out fifty industries for specific development.

The Soviet Union had to raise most of its investment capital from its own meager resources. The Communist repudiation of the old tsarist debts had made it difficult to secure foreign loans and credit. Since comparatively little hard currency was obtained through the sale of manufactured products, industrial expansion had to be financed by tightly regulating domestic consumption and reinvesting most capital surpluses. As a result, the standard of living of the average Soviet citizen remained at the subsistence level. Overall, the Soviet share of world trade remained smaller than in prewar days. In 1932, it was only 2.44 percent, about the same amount as Switzerland. Stalin believed that capitalist society would eventually collapse under the weight of its own contradictions, but until that happened, he could see no reason why the Soviets should not normalize relations with the capitalist nations and strengthen the Communist system by expanding trade with them.

In practice, however, this was difficult. The Soviet economy was not capable of producing the quantity, quality, and variety of goods that were commercially attractive to Western consumers. Therefore, the Soviets had to earn the capital necessary to finance their purchases abroad by concentrating on readily marketable raw materials and commodities such as gold, furs, timber, oil, and wheat, which they sold for less than the world market price—not counting the human cost to the Russian people.[15] When the revenues from these commodities proved insufficient, the Soviets began to sell works of art from their state collections.

With Politburo approval, the Commissariat of Foreign Trade, presided over by its chief Anastas Mikoyan, arranged the "great sale" to various foreign art dealers and collectors. One of these collectors, the Armenian financier Calouste Gulbenkian, bought several loads from the Hermitage, Russia's most famous national museum.[16] With his treasures safely stowed in his town house in Paris,[17] the tycoon presumptuously advised the sellers, "You know that I have always held the opinion that the objects which have been in your museums for many years should not be sold. Not only do they represent a national heritage, but they are also a great source of culture and a cause of pride for the nation. . . . If you stand in need of foreign credit, you can do whatever you wish, but you are in fact making use of such credit and at the same time you are doing something which can do nothing but harm."[18]

The Soviets did not listen. They continued selling. In 1930, Andrew Mellon, the U.S. secretary of the treasury, bought $6,654,053 worth of paintings.[19] His purchases amounted to roughly one-third of all Soviet exports to the United States for that year. The Soviets liked doing business with Mellon: he not only had a ready supply of cash and settled up immediately with a certified banker's check, but he also was willing to go easy on enforcing laws against Soviet dumping of timber and manganese on the American market.[20] Mellon eventually donated his entire collection to the American people, housing it in the National Gallery of Art in Washington, D.C. He thereby gained a sort of immortality. The Soviets, by contrast, were able to buy more tractors.

Regimentation of the Industrial Work Force. The leaders of the Soviet Union developed trade unions to be "schools of Communism"; their primary tasks were to disseminate technical knowledge, stimulate production, and promote working-class reliability, not engage in collective bargaining. Workers were encouraged to organize special labor shock troops (*udarniki*) to inspire others with their high achievement. Factories would challenge each other in "Socialist competition." To push the workers into goals higher than those set by the current five-year plan, a special movement was launched in 1935 in the person of a Donets miner named Alexei Stakhanov. According to the official claim, this worker-hero exceeded his quota by 14.5 times, cutting 102 tons of coal (instead of 7) out of the vein during his 5-hour 45-minute shift. The regime held up this titanic, most likely bogus, achievement as a goal for other industries. Special teams of Stakhanovites traveled around the country, participating in staged events. They would go into a factory or mine and break all previous production records. As planned, this new record would result in increased quotas for the regular workers, whose resentment can be imagined. Workers who markedly increased their productivity could expect to receive higher wages, better living conditions, and special honors and recognition, including honorary membership in the party, the title "Hero of Socialist Toil," and perhaps even the Order of Lenin.

Wage scales were calculated on the basis of skills, aptitudes, and levels of productivity, not egalitarianism. The earlier socialist goal of "from each according to his ability, to each according to his need" remained an empty ideal without practical value. Rewards were now apportioned "to each according to his work." Stalin attacked wage equalization as "leftist" and urged higher compensation for the positions the regime considered of higher priority. The state, he said, could not tolerate a situation where a rolling-mill hand in a steel plant earned no more than a broom handler. The practice of paying by piecework was widely utilized and, by 1935, had become the standard for three-fourths of the labor force. This method of compensation was generally regarded as reactionary by Western trade unions, except by the Communist unions, especially those in France, which suddenly found the practice acceptable. The authority to determine wages was completely removed from the direct influence of the workers and was vested in the Council of People's Commissars, which used wage schedules as an important tool of economic planning. Higher salaries were offered in industries and geographical areas where development was particularly desired. State administrative personnel were the best paid, followed by workers in banking, construction, transport, large-scale manufacturing, education, medical services, agriculture, and restaurants.

During the 1930s, adults normally worked a seven-hour day, six days a week. In 1940, this was increased to an eight-hour day. The Soviet people were told that a forty-eight-hour week was still the shortest in the world despite the increase. But such assurances did little to improve per capita output. Frequently, the regime had to rely on threats and coercion. Absenteeism was heavily penalized by suspension from work for as much as six months, a punishment that entailed the loss of ration cards and living quarters. Rule infractions, delinquency (such as being more than twenty minutes late for work without a valid excuse), insubordination, malingering, and hooliganism might be punished with a reduction of wages, compulsory extra labor, or prison sentences. Plant managers were under great pressure to fulfill their quotas and possessed wide discretionary powers for enforcing discipline.

Economic Results and Human Costs. The First Five-Year Plan was officially completed in a little over four years, success being calculated by the increase in the monetary value of output—a rather unreliable standard considering that the planners set the monetary values themselves. Even on this basis, many industries fell short of their goals. Where the plan had envisaged an output of 106 million metric tons of grain, only 70 million metric tons were produced. Metallurgy, wool, and textiles were off the mark by one-third. Machinery and electrical equipment, however, surpassed their goals by five percent. By ignoring temporary reductions in German, French, and British output due to the depression, the planners were able to boast that the Soviet Union was second only to the United States in world steel production in 1932. Although it was difficult to assess how much of this output was achieved because of a deliberate disregard for quality, that such an increase could take place at a time when production in the rest of the world was falling seemed a remarkable achievement.

The Second Five-Year Plan immediately followed the first and was also completed early: in four and a quarter years between 1933 and 1937. But its goals were more modest, as a result of an ongoing battle between party radicals and moderates who disagreed dramatically over the tactics and speed necessary for building Communism. The Seventeenth Party Congress (26 January–10 February 1934), meeting to confirm the plan, saw a floor fight between Vyacheslav Molotov, the chairman of the Council of People's Commissars (prime minister), and Sergo Ordzhonikdze, the commissar for heavy industry, over how fast the economy should grow. Molotov pushed for higher targets, while Ordzhonikdze thought more modest rates were more realistic. He argued that the emphasis on increased quantity and speed would result in poor-quality goods. The confrontation was a continuation of a dispute that had arisen during the preliminary drafting of the Second Five-Year Plan three years earlier. Stalin, who previously had favored accelerating the pace of industrialization, this time sided with the moderates in reducing the annual targets from 22 percent to 16.5 percent. The plan concentrated on improving the quality of goods and the efficiency of labor. Production again increased, but not as much as planned—even the reduced goals were too high. Miners dug 128 million tons of coal instead of 152.2 million, and mill workers produced 3.5 billion meters of cotton textiles instead of a projected 5 billion. Nevertheless, this was four times as much coal and twice as many textiles as Russia produced before World War I.

Stalin's support of the moderates proved to be only a tactic, however, as revealed by his strong support of the Stakhanov movement, which was once again being used to raise work quotas. Stalin hailed these shock workers as part of a genuine revolutionary movement that challenged the unimaginative standards and leadership of the administrators of Soviet enterprises, most of whom had apparently accepted the argument that a slower rate of growth was preferable to a more radical one. In a speech in November 1935, Stalin asked ominously, "Will we really lack the courage to smash the conservatism of certain of our engineers and technicians, to smash the old traditions and standards and allow free scope to the new forces of the working class?"[21] The Third Five-Year Plan, begun in 1938 but interrupted by the war, returned to the practices of the first plan in setting high goals and concentrating on heavy industry, but it stressed the development of new areas: the lower Volga, the Urals, and Central Asia. By 1940, the Soviet Union was second in world production of oil, third in steel, and fourth in coal.

SELECTED INDUSTRIAL OUTPUT IN THE SOVIET UNION, 1928–1938 (in 1,000 Metric Tons)

	Coal	Petroleum	Iron Ore	Crude Steel	Sulfuric Acid
1928	36,510	11,625	6,133	4,251	211
1933	76,333	21,489	14,455	6,889	627
1938	133,263	30,186	26,585	18,057	1,544

Source: Brian R. Mitchell, *European Historical Statistics, 1750–1970* (New York: Columbia University Press, 1975), 368, 373, 389, 401, 462.

As a device to achieve rapid industrialization, the five-year plans were highly successful. But even though the quantity of goods increased, individual output was not impressive, Stakhanovism nothwithstanding, and quality was often abominable. Furthermore, the Communist regime had done very little to improve the people's general standard of living. An expansion of social services offset this somewhat, but often the benefits from disability payments, old-age pensions, maternity subsidies, and paid vacations varied considerably, according to length and fidelity of employment and political reliability. Expenditures on public welfare increased from 107 million rubles in 1928 to 1.3 billion a decade later. The state provided medical services, rest homes, and sanatoria and established rehabilitation centers for delinquents. It provided monthly disability and old-age pensions of 25 to 50 rubles for recipients without dependents, 25 to 75 rubles for those with two or more dependents, 35 rubles a month for dependents of deceased workers, and between 7.5 and 22.5 rubles for veterans of World War I (Law of 28 December 1938). But since the average monthly wage was 287 rubles, the state subsidies were not overly generous.

In 1930, the regime abolished unemployment insurance on the ground that unemployment no longer existed. Indeed, throughout the 1930s, the number of jobs did exceed the supply of workers. The industrial work force increased from 11.5 million in 1928 to 31.5 million in 1940, with most of the new workers coming from the countryside. By 1938, all workers had to carry "labor books," showing their complete employment record. They could not be hired without this record; nor could they change jobs without permission. In 1939, Prime Minister Molotov announced that the Soviet Union had successfully eliminated the "causes of exploitation of man by man" and that "the socialist society of the U.S.S.R. consists now of two classes friendly to one another—the workers and the peasants." From 1940 to 1956, all workers were officially frozen in their jobs. Even the ultimate protest against work, living the life of a tramp, was illegal and punishable by "collective labor." Molotov maintained that anything done in the name of the people could not be contrary to the will of the people; furthermore, exploitation could not exist because the means of production belonged to the people, and the owners could not exploit themselves.

A SYSTEM OF TERROR

Clearing Away the Debris of the Past

The Attack on Organized Religion. The Leninist regime had separated the church from the state, but not the state from the church. The right to disseminate antireligious propaganda was guaranteed, but not the right to proselytize. People could form religious congregations, but could not worship wherever they chose. Churches that were not used for something else (turned into museums of revolutionary history and atheism, clubhouses, warehouses, factories, movie houses, or granaries) might continue as houses of worship, at least until the authorities decided otherwise.

After the revolution, the strength of organized religion inevitably declined because of the close association between the once all-powerful Russian Orthodox church and the discredited tsarist regime. Yet millions of the faithful still remained members, and during the era of the New Economic Policy, people started returning to the churches. The primate of the ecclesiastical province of Moscow, Metropolitan Tikhon, was elected patriarch of Moscow in November 1917, thereby restoring a position that had been abolished by Peter the Great in 1721. Tikhon fought the confiscation of church property, a stance that landed him in jail in 1922. He was released a couple of years later, only after he promised not to engage in further political activities. Other church leaders, however, felt that the survival of the Russian Orthodox church depended not on confrontation, but on a willingness to cooperate with the new order. When Tikhon died in 1925, his designated successor, Metropolitan Sergius, openly proclaimed the Holy Synod's loyalty to the state. "The founding of the Soviet government has appeared to many to be some sort of misunderstanding," he said, but instead the revolution was "the work of God's providence, unswervingly leading every nation toward its predestined goal."[22] Sergius's submission was in the best tradition of Russian Orthodoxy and, under the circumstances, was highly expedient, but it was not enough to satisfy Stalin.

On 8 April 1929, the state ordered all religious societies and groups of believers to register with the authorities and submit to a complete audit of their finances, including the amount of assessments and voluntary contributions. Churches were forbidden to engage in charitable activities or to organize "special meetings for children, youths, and women for prayer purposes and generally biblical, literary, needlework, and other meetings for the teaching of religion."[23] Except for the last rites and burials, religious ceremonies could take place only in designated areas. The state gradually intensified its attack on the religious "survivals of the feudal and capitalist past," mounting a particularly concentrated offensive in the schools. It frequently ordered churches and synagogues closed under the pretext that the buildings were structurally unsafe. It officially sponsored the League of Militant Atheists, whose agitators denounced priests to the secret police and encouraged the destruction of many church buildings. The league, headed by Yemelyan Yaroslavsky, a leading proponent of Stalinist doctrine, published its own journal, *The Godless.* The secret police rounded up priests and sent them to concentration camps where many died from overwork and exhaustion.

Church affiliation was not in itself illegal; but the regime, regarding all religion as a tool of the exploiting class, had the secret police maintain routine dossiers on communicants and believers. By its own standards, though, the regime treated religion with relative moderation. Stalin had it within his power to eradicate the Russian Orthodox church completely, but he nevertheless permitted its survival. Perhaps, as an ex-seminary student, he realized the impossibility of destroying people's faith in revealed religion. Toward other adversaries, he was not so generous.

The Secret Police Apparatus. The growth of a secret police force was already well advanced by the time Stalin became supreme leader. In the early years, the party had fought for the rights of the peasants and the workers, yet the regime could no longer count on the unfailing loyalty of these groups—if indeed it could ever have done so. In the first real democratic election in Russia's history (the Constituent Assembly election in 1918), the Bolsheviks had been so badly out-voted that Lenin saw no recourse but to suppress the assembly and establish a Bolshevik dictatorship that regarded individual liberty and personal freedom as outgrowths of a bourgeois system it was committed to destroy. Lenin explained that real freedom of assembly could not exist in a building that was owned by capitalists. Obviously, a leader capable of such arguments could justify anything, even the enslavement of the workers in the name of liberation. In this atmosphere, the spectacular growth of the state political administration was not surprising.

Ironically, as the regime became more secure, its official enemies became more numerous. The first secret police organization, the Cheka, had confined its attacks to the former ruling classes: the nobility, upper bourgeoisie, church officials, large landowners, and, during the civil war, the non-Bolshevik Marxists and those suspected of giving aid and comfort to the White armies. Even in February 1922, when the Cheka became part of the *Gosudartvennoe Politicheskoe Upravlenie* (State Political Administration Division or GPU), it still concentrated on the extermination of counterrevolutionaries: Mensheviks, Social Revolutionaries, anarchists, and other non-Communist factions. In 1924, with the formal creation of the Soviet Union, the GPU became the *Obedinenoe Gosudartvennoe Politicheskoe Upravlenie* (All-Union State Political Administration or OGPU), a department of the People's Commissariat for the Interior. Feliks Dzerzhinsky was the perennial secret police chief until his death in 1926 when he was succeeded by Vyacheslav Menzhinsky.

With the rise of Stalin, the responsibilities of the secret police increased profoundly. They infiltrated the armed forces and the bureaucracy, spied on foreign embassies and émigré groups, and conducted foreign espionage, including the direct assassination of traitors. With the five-year plans came the new classification of social and economic criminals; these were the intellectuals, the private traders, the kulaks, the peasants who opposed collectivization, and the workers who failed to produce. This group also included workers who could serve as scapegoats for the mistakes of their bosses and writers who failed to adhere to the party line.

In March 1928, a group of Russian technicians in the Donets Coal Basin were charged with conspiracy and espionage for failing to meet their production quotas. In 1930, forty-eight technicians in the food industry were shot after being convicted of plotting to destroy the food supplies of the working class. The same year, eight prominent engineers were accused of conspiring with the French General Staff to sabotage Soviet industry. A literary witch-hunt began with an attack on the neorealist novelist Yevgeni Zamyatin for criticizing the growth of totalitarianism; in 1931, the author was forced into exile.

In June 1934, Stalin reorganized the secret police into the *Narodnyi Kommissariat Vnutrennykh Del* (People's Commissariat of Internal Affairs or NKVD) under

Genrikh Yagoda. The bureau's scope was increased by giving it control of the gendarmerie, the militia, the administration of highways, and the records of vital statistics. The new organization was also responsible for the penal system and all places of detention, including the forced labor or concentration camps (as many as 200 were in existence, scattered throughout the country). Officially, these camps were reeducation centers where lawbreakers were given a chance to become socially useful citizens. However, the secret police mercilessly exploited the prisoners, many of whom were confined for only minor political offenses or for none at all.

The system encompassed much more than the concentration camps proper (the largest of these were mostly located in the remote timber and mining areas of the northern and eastern Soviet Union). Forced labor included those "prisoners" who were compelled to work in specific areas of the country, those who were ordered to accept only certain jobs, and those who were required to work longer hours and receive less pay as penalties for lateness or absenteeism. Forced labor also included workers in the camps near industrial cities where inmates participated in special projects, such as digging the Moscow subway system or constructing hydroelectric stations.

One of the largest such work projects was the Belamor Canal, linking the lakes of Karelia north of Leningrad; this was a brainchild of Stalin who wanted to make it possible for Soviet ships to travel directly from the Baltic Sea to the Arctic Ocean. He himself selected the 168-mile route of this human-made waterway. The GPU, lacking the money to buy heavy equipment from abroad, had the work done by hand with a technology from the eighteenth century. Stones were broken with sledgehammers, cliff faces pulled apart with crowbars, rubble cleared away on wooden sledges, and piledrivers run by human treadmills. Work continued nonstop throughout the winter, but the prisoners had no protective clothing. They pulled cables into place with blood gushing from their hands. Those who tried to escape were shot. Food was distributed according to output, thereby ensuring the death of the weak and the ill. The dead were then tossed into shallow ditches to be eaten by carrion crows. The canal opened in August 1933 with Stalin in atten-

Grandiose projects like the opulent Moscow subway system helped to mask the Stalinist regime's ugliness. The stations in the city's central urban area were decorated with mosaics, marble-faced pillars, ceramic tiles, designer light fixtures (even crystal chandeliers), gold trim, and other lavish appointments worthy of a tsarist palace.

dance. But the despot reportedly was not pleased. The canal did not serve its purpose: it was too shallow and too narrow and was frozen almost half the year. In the five years of its construction, 60,000 prisoners had perished. The survivors, who had expected to be freed when the canal was completed, were cheated; some were retained to maintain the canal, the rest were transferred to other projects. As this illustrates, forced labor was a key part of the Soviet economy.

The "State Plan of Development of the National Economy of the USSR for 1941," a copy of which was captured by the Nazis during World War II, revealed the extent of the economic activity directed by the secret police. That year the Gosplan allotted the secret police just under 7 billion rubles, about 12 percent of total capital investment. The NKVD was responsible for 17 percent of all production in the construction industry (which employed about 1,172,000 prisoners), about 12 percent in the lumber industry, and slightly smaller percentages in the coal and oil industries. The files did not reveal figures on armaments, nor on gold mining, which was already a secret police monopoly.

In its heyday, the forced labor system had a population of between 7 and 14 million prisoners. The work was mostly manual labor, with each prisoner forced to fulfill a certain quota to earn enough food to sustain his or her life, usually a pound of bread and one nutritionally inferior meal a day. Those who fell short of their assigned work quota were given a basic daily allowance of ten ounces of bread on which they gradually starved. Mortality was high, especially among intellectuals, office workers, and professionals who were not used to strenuous physical labor. Political prisoners, regarded by camp authorities as the lowest form of life, were constantly exposed to the brutality of the common criminals, who often served as foremen and overseers.

Though individuals were supposedly not arrested for the purpose of working in forced labor camps, the NKVD had a vested interest in maintaining a high prison population, and as the protector of state security, it had no difficulty obtaining all the workers it needed. Slave labor did contribute to the economic development of backward and inaccessible areas, particularly northern Siberia, but the results could hardly be justified in economic, let alone human, terms.

The regime's extensive reliance on the secret police stemmed in large part from the low regard and mistrust that Stalin had for the Communist party itself. It is not certain precisely when Stalin lost confidence in the party, but by the Seventeenth Party Congress in 1934, he clearly had done so. By that time, many of the older members had become unhappy with Stalin's leadership. They feared his arbitrary use of power, disliked his practice of blaming them for his own failures, and resented his tendency to favor his entourage of handpicked toadies over them. At the 1934 conclave, 292 delegates cast negative votes against his election to the Party Central Committee by deliberately scratching out his name. The protest was indicative of their displeasure, but it was also futile, since balloting by closed slate automatically assured Stalin's election. But the strategy was to replace Stalin as general-secretary with the chief of the Leningrad organization, Sergei Kirov. Apprised of the tactic, Stalin had his trusted henchman Lazar Kaganovitch destroy 289 of the offending ballots, thereby leaving him with the same number of negative votes as Kirov had received. Stalin thus remained the acknowledged ruler of the Soviet Union, but many in the party no longer viewed him as an infallible demigod. Although Kirov had earlier told the Leningrad committee he would not accept the post of general-secretary if elected, he feared his days were numbered. As he left the meeting, he remarked to a colleague that his head was now on the block.

In addition to such manifest signs of opposition, Stalin had other reasons to mistrust the party. For one thing, many party members were incompetent, tainted by corruption, or characterized by inertia, sloth, and lack of education, both practical and ideological. Moreover, the radicals and the moderates engaged in endless squabbles, divided by personality conflicts, rivalries, and vested interests. These interminable disputes compromised effective action and undermined loyalty to the Stalinist "general line." In addition, the provincial party secretaries had become too independent and devoted their energies to protecting themselves and their jobs against outside pressures. Although there had been periodic purges of parasites and incompetents, the party's record of reforming itself was not impressive. One attempted housecleaning, in 1933, had revealed deplorable chaos in the party records and in membership accountability—many nonmembers had managed to obtain party cards and were taking advantage of the special privileges. All these were signs of a serious breakdown of party discipline.[24] It is small wonder then that Stalin turned to the more reliable secret police to create the totalitarian system he desired.

Terror Is the Order of the Day

The Death of Kirov. On 1 December 1934, Leonid Nikolayev came to the headquarters of the Leningrad Soviet, located in the neoclassical Smolny Institute, the former aristocratic girls' school from which Lenin had directed the November Revolution, with the express purpose of killing local party boss Sergei Kirov. Nikolayev showed a pass and was allowed inside. He made his way up to the third floor and stationed himself near Kirov's office; when Kirov came down the corridor, he shot him in the back of the head. The assassin, upon apprehension by Kirov's associates, protested, "they made me a promise, they made me a promise." Nikolayev, a party member since 1920, had acted out of personal desperation and general hatred of party bureaucrats whom he believed had treated him contemptuously and unjustly, but he had been the dupe of others. The path of responsibility leads to I. V. Zaporozhets, the deputy chief of the Leningrad secret police, who arranged[25] for Nikolayev to assassinate Kirov under instructions of the head of the Soviet secret police, Genrikh Yagoda, who would not have dared carry out such a deed without the direct approval of Stalin.[26] Stalin feared Kirov as a potential successor, but his complicity in the murder or in the three previous attempts to assassinate Kirov is still debated.[27]

Whether Kirov had been assassinated at his instigation or not, Stalin was ready to take advantage of the murder to expand the terror campaign he had begun with the attacks on the peasantry during the drive for collectivization. Through terror, he believed he could establish supreme control over the levers of power. He issued a special decree, ordering that all terrorists be executed immediately after sentencing, and came to Leningrad to take personal charge of the Nikolayev investigation. The first victims of the new law were hundreds of suspected counterrevolutionaries who were not connected with Kirov's death but who were unfortunate enough to be in jail at the time. (Ultimately, Nikolayev himself fell victim to the decree as did his family and associates.)

The preliminary investigation of Kirov's murder was conducted inefficiently, revealing an absence of careful planning similar to the inauguration of the First Five-Year Plan. Its direction became clear on 16 December, however, when Gregori Zinoviev, Lev Kamenev, and sixteen of their associates were arrested for maintaining a "Moscow Center" of opposition through which they had allegedly encouraged the recent Leningrad terrorism by "ideological" means. These "conspirators" were tried in secret and sentenced (on 16 January 1936) to five to ten years in prison. In fact, none was ever released. This was the first time that Stalin had brought open criminal charges against members of the Communist party. Next came a general roundup of all the Zinoviev "oppositionists" and more secret trials. After this general housecleaning—the Leningrad organization was almost completely changed and put under Stalin's trusted henchman, Andrei Zhdanov—the terror momentarily subsided. Stalin exercised a great deal of caution, while continuing to increase his hold over the party through careful appointments and consolidation of the secret police.[28] The publication in July 1936 of a new constitution seemed to mark the beginning of a period of moderation, however.

The Constitution of 1936. The framing of a new constitution for the Soviet state had been underway for several years. According to the regime, socialist ownership of industry, collectivization, and the need to further democratize the electoral system had made a new constitution necessary. The previous constitution of 1924 had merely set out the formal framework of the state without describing the structures of power in detail. In this respect, the new instrument was unique in that it recognized the existence of the Communist party, conferring on it the power to nominate candidates for election to public offices. Furthermore, the Soviet people were guaranteed "freedom of speech, freedom of the press, freedom of assembly, including the holding of mass meetings; [and] freedom of street processions and demonstration." They were assured "inviolability of the person, inviolability of the homes [and] privacy of correspondence."[29] Thus, on paper, at least, Soviet citizens had the same basic civil liberties as citizens of the Western democracies—and such an explicit enumeration of rights was no doubt intended to convince the rest of the world that the Soviet system was really democratic.

However, these rights could only be exercised in "conformity with the interests of the working people, and in order to strengthen the Socialist system."[30] This qualifier, as interpreted by Stalin, meant that the state had absolute power to decide what was in conformity with the interests of the working people or the socialist system. Thus, virtually any activity could be declared illegal. Article 58–1 of the Soviet criminal code defined as counterrevolutionary any act that aimed "at the overthrow, subversion, or weakening of the power of the workers and peasants . . . [and] at the subversion or weakening of the external security of the USSR or of the fundamental economic political and national conquests realized by the Proletarian Revolution." The judiciary was accorded the right to convict people of offenses that were not explicitly prohibited by law: "If a socially dangerous act is not directly foreseen by the present Code, the reasons and limits of responsibility for such an act are determined by analogy to those articles of the Code which foresee offenses of a similar type." Guilt by analogy was reminiscent of the practices of the Inquisition. Like all other officials, Soviet judges were creatures of the executive branch. As such, they were expected to cooperate in carrying out Stalinist policies. Even the most important of their functions—the power to issue arrest warrants—was shared with, and in many cases monopolized by, the procurator-general, who had the authority to supervise the activities of every official, organization, and individual in the Soviet Union.

Andrei Vyshinsky, one of the leading architects of Stalinist legal science, held this important position from 1935 to 1940. In the convoluted style of Communist legalese, he said it was his duty "to ferret out every single crime for punishment while carrying on, in association with the organs of the People's Commissariat of the Interior and the courts, a decisive struggle with all the remnants of the Trotsky-Bukharin bandit gangs, with hirelings of Fascist reconnaissance, with spies and diversionists, with pillagers of socialist property, and with robbers, thieves and hooligans—in a word with all species of criminality."[31]

The bulk of counterrevolutionary crimes were handled by special three-man commissions, or *troikas*, which were part of a special board of the Interior Department. This arrangement, one of the main instrumentalities of the Stalinist terror, enabled NKVD judges to circumvent normal criminal procedure and dispose of cases, often within minutes and in secret.

The Show Trials. Stalinist justice, however, is more commonly associated with the three spectacular public trials held between 1936 and 1939—trials that were actually carefully rehearsed stage plays with Vyshinsky acting as director. These trials were designed to put the country on an emergency footing to protect it against its enemies at home and abroad. To obtain the proper effects, the secret police had put in many months of hard work, fabricating evidence and preparing witnesses.

The first great trial of Trotsky's associates opened on 19 August 1936 in the hall of the Trade Union House, formerly the ballroom of the tsarist Nobles Club. The stars of the proceeding were the same men who had been tried seven months earlier: the "Moscow Center" conspirators, headed by Zinoviev and Kamenev. Prior to the trial, they had been carefully coached to confess to the assassination of Kirov and to having organized a plot to murder Stalin. Zinoviev and Kamenev were promised that their lives and the lives of their families would be spared if they cooperated. The audience included some thirty foreign journalists and diplomats and 150 Soviet stooges carefully coached by the NKVD to start a commotion should any embarrassing departure from the script occur. The precaution proved unnecessary. All the accused recited their lines well. They admitted their guilt and said they deserved whatever fate awaited them. Kamenev concluded his final speech by addressing his two sons through the court: "No matter what my sentence will be, I in advance consider it just. Don't look back. Go forward. Together with the Soviet people, follow Stalin." On the edge of the grave, this former Bolshevik was still capable of practicing politics. But it did him no good. Twenty-four hours after being sentenced to death, he and the other accused were dead: shot in the back of the head in the cellars of the Lubyanka prison. The dead men's families then were arrested and disappeared. For good measure, Stalin ordered Yagoda to execute five thousand other "oppositionists" currently in custody.

A second great trial followed in January 1937. Its seventeen defendants, tried on charges similar to those at the first trial, included the journalist Karl Radek and Gregori Sokolnikov, a former people's commissar of finance and delegate to the Brest-Litovsk peace talks. Both had been close associates of Lenin. Thirteen of the accused received death sentences; the other four, including Radek and Sokolnikov, were sentenced to prison, but were never heard from again.

The terror continued and gained new momentum under its new secret police chief, Nikolai Yezhov. Yagoda, who had been replaced by Yezhov shortly after the first trial, was now under arrest for fomenting counterrevolution.[32] Yagoda was removed, it was said, because he knew too much. But Stalin had better reasons. Few of the current party leaders were interested in continuing the purge, apparently including Yagoda. But Stalin was not ready to quit. What appeared to be periods of moderation were simply times of gestation.

Stalin himself prepared the indictments for the third great show trial, which began on 2 March 1938, and watched the proceedings from a special curtained box above the court. Stalin, who in the course of his workday had to make decisions on a host of other matters, seemed obsessed by these macabre proceedings. He pored over dossiers, passed sentences on those he knew, and enjoyed hearing anecdotes about the final hours of the condemned. Aside from his obvious delight in seeing men die, Stalin was establishing himself more firmly in power through the systematic elimination of anyone who could possibly present a challenge to his authority. The political strength of totalitarian regimes depends heavily on their ability to inspire fear. What better way to do so than by democratizing death. If everyone can be killed and no one is safe, people will think of little else but their survival and how they can better serve their masters.

The third trial featured twenty-one highly placed defendants, headed by Alexei Rykov, a former people's commissar of internal affairs, Yagoda, and the star of the proceedings, Nikolai Bukharin. Bukharin was a leading party theorist who with Lenin had prepared the Communist program adopted in 1919. Lenin called him the "darling of the party." Although Bukharin had sided with Stalin and helped him consolidate his power, Stalin feared Bukharin's influence and had him stripped of all his party positions. However, Bukharin remained a member of the Central Committee and had helped draft Stalin's constitution of 1936. Now, charged with capital crimes, he grandiloquently pleaded guilty to "the sum total of crimes committed by the counterrevolutionary organization irrespective of whether or not I knew of, whether or not I took a direct part in any particular act." The second part of the statement obviously made the first part absurd, which was Bukharin's strategy.

Bukharin knew he was doomed. He had been interrogated continuously for three months and had agreed to testify publicly only after the prosecution had threatened the lives of his wife and newborn son. He testified to protect his family, but he also wanted to indict Stalinism for future generations of Communists. "The confession of the accused is a medieval principle of jurisprudence,"[33] he said. Bukharin's ideological heresy involved his continued advocacy of policies no longer considered orthodox, specifically his support of the NEP and his denunciation of the forced collectivization of the peasantry. His crimes of treason and espionage were, of course, pure fabrications. Stalin wanted to rid himself of Bukharin because Bukharin's past prominence affronted Stalin's current legitimacy. But Bukharin's heroic efforts to preserve his dignity on the edge of the grave did not make him a tragic hero. He was not a victim of a remorseless fate, but was consumed by the very system that he had helped create. His reward was a bullet in the back of his head in a cellar of the Lubyanka prison.[34] Yagoda, also condemned to death, begged forgiveness before being shot.[35]

A Society Based on Fear. Every important city in the Soviet Union had its killing center, usually a part of the secret police headquarters, to which the hapless victims would be taken for interrogation and execution. Throughout the land there were mass graves for Stalin extended the terror into every aspect of Soviet society. It cut a huge swath through the party ranks. From 1934 to 1939, 1.25 million members, out of a previous membership of 2.8 million, were liquidated. Almost the entire old Leninist leadership disappeared. Of the 71 members of the Central Committee at the Seventeenth Party Congress, the gathering that had proved so unreliable, only 16 were present at the Eighteenth Party Congress five years later; most of those absent had been shot, only 4 died from presumably natural causes.

Of the 68 former candidate members, all but 5 had vanished. At the Eighteenth Party Congress (10–21 March 1939), all but 59 of the nearly 2,000 delegates were new. Of the 1,966 participants at the 1934 meeting, about 60 percent (1,108) had been liquidated on trumped-up charges of treason or sabotage.

In the armed forces, the terror took practically all the famous commanders of the civil war, including three out of five Soviet marshals: Mikhail Tukhachevsky, deputy people's commissar of defense and founder of the modern Soviet army; Vasili Blyukher, commander of the Far Eastern army; and Alexei Yegorov, chief of the General Staff. All but one of the army commanders were also shot, plus all the corps commanders, almost all the division and brigade commanders, about half the regimental commanders, and thousands of lower ranking officers. The navy lost nineteen of twenty-five senior admirals. The deliberate massacre of such military talent reinforced Adolf Hitler's convictions that a war against the Soviet Union was winnable.

The terror affected millions of others. Victims bred victims. The wives of those put to death usually were sentenced to eight years in prison. All children over twelve years old were subject to arrest. A veterinarian was charged with being a spy because he had treated the pets of foreign diplomats; his son was also arrested. A film actor who had portrayed the part of a tsarist official too convincingly in a movie was sent to a forced labor camp. An engineer was convicted of espionage because an uncle living in Poland had sent him some shoes. A Ukrainian peasant who had earlier been falsely charged and released was again taken into custody because his earlier arrest made him suspect.

Whole categories of people were fair game: those associated with organized religion, former landowners, non-Communist socialists, and any conceivable oppositionists, including the moderates who had argued for a slower pace of industrialization. Anybody who failed to achieve his or her production quota was an automatic suspect. The assistant director of the Moscow zoo was sent to a forced labor camp because 16 percent of his monkeys died of tuberculosis. Anyone involved in an industrial accident was automatically in trouble. Tractors that broke down, trains that did not run on time, or crops that did not grow were obviously the result of conspiracies. Peasants who had been dragooned into the urban labor force and made mistakes through lack of experience and training were branded as "wreckers" and "saboteurs" and were either shot or sent to the camps. The answer to failed production quotas was to send in more bureaucrats and police agents to heighten the terror. The overall result was the disappearance of practically all economic initiative in a broad mass of workers.

Certainly, the regime had been successful at mobilizing the work force and setting national goals, especially in the heroic early days of the five-year plans. Spectacular gains were achieved in high-priority areas, but the economy developed unevenly, especially in the agrarian and consumer goods sectors. The regime's unrelenting opposition to anything less than ironclad control forced the lower-level managers to operate strictly by the book. As a result, the economy was locked into a dogmatic rigidity that frustrated future growth. Although Stalin had not freed people from the exploitation associated with capitalism, many, despite their misery, still had faith in his leadership and were reluctant to blame him for the terror, which they believed was carried out without his knowledge. They found it hard to accept that to him power was more important than their well-being. But adulation and ideological commitment would only take the Soviet economy so far. No matter what their willingness to sacrifice, people wanted something more tangible than the satisfaction of working diligently for a receding utopia. In time, the supplies of labor necessary to feed an expanding industry began to dry up. Consequently, the regime relied more on the economic activities of the NKVD. The great outburst of mass arrests in 1937 was prompted in part by this search for new sources of cheap labor. Those sent to the camps received no financial remuneration or welfare benefits; they often worked twelve hours a day and were kept in a state of semistarvation with more food offered as an incentive to produce.[36]

The families of some of Stalin's top advisers also felt the effects of the terror—no doubt, this was one of Stalin's ways of encouraging his ministers to greater efforts. The wife of Vyacheslav Molotov, the chairman of the Council of People's Commissars, and the wife of Mikhail Kalinin, chairman of the Presidium, were sent to work camps. The brother of Lazar Kaganovich, the deputy prime minister, was shot. Many victims were denounced by those who wanted to settle old scores or hoped to get an enemy's job, apartment, or spouse. Informers received a portion of the wealth of those arrested. In this atmosphere, since all the victims were innocent, everyone was guilty and everyone was vulnerable. Death sentences were carried out on children as young as twelve.

Not counting the earlier deaths from the famine, the Stalinist terror claimed the lives of at least 7 million people, either shot or victims of forced labor camps. The NKVD had its own quotas. The Sverdlovsk office was once assigned the task of killing 15,000 "enemies of the people." About 19 million people were arrested.[37] Most of the victims were men in the prime of life, between the ages of thirty and fifty-five. The terror began with the peasantry and continued with everyone else. In the Kuropaty Forest, near the city of Minsk, the NKVD killed between 100,000 and 250,000 innocent peasants. Every day between 1937 and 1941, vans loaded with ordinary men and women arrived at the site where deep pits had been dug. Two by two, the people were led to the edge, shot in the back of the head, and pushed in until the pit was full. Most graves contained between 150 and 250 persons depending on the weather—fewer victims could be accommodated in the winter because of their heavy clothing. Some graves thirty feet across held as many as 1,000 persons. Kuropaty Forest has over 1,000 graves. It is not the only such site in the Soviet Union.

The psychological effect of the terror was profound. The journalist Louis Fischer wrote that:

> [The] Moscow trials and confessions were merely the sensational, highly-silhouetted shape of an everyday Soviet phenomenon, and it is only against the background of this phenomenon that the confessions can be understood. Millions of Soviet citizens live lies every day to save their lives and their jobs. They make false confessions day in and day out. They write lies, speak lies. They lie to one another and know it. They lie to themselves and get accustomed to it. They lose their illusions and succumb to the sole cynical goal of self-preservation until a better day. The assassination of character and the annihilation of personality is the dictatorship's chief weapon which it never forgets.[38]

Yet surprisingly Stalin did not lack for admirers in the democratic West. Some sympathizers were simply fooled—unwilling to believe that such a pretentiously positive and humane ideology could have a murderous, dark side. Others, when faced with a Hitler, thought Stalin's sins were trivial by comparison. Still others simply turned a blind eye to what was happening. Many believe that those in the last category are hardest to forgive.

On 21 August 1938, Yezhov was demoted to people's commissar of water transport, and his duties as chief of the NKVD were assumed by Lavrenti Beria, a thorough degenerate whose bodyguards would abduct women he selected and bring them to his house on Moscow's Malaya Nikitinskaya Street where he would rape them. Yezhov vanished without a trace, and the town hyphenated in his honor, Yezhovo-Cherkessk, lost its prefix. Most of his colleagues and goons perished with him. The great terror was approaching its end, yet the practice of drawing up lists of innocent people for preventive eradication continued. Stalin routinely signed list after list, day after day. Yet, by 1939, the purges had served their purpose. Stalin's power was unassailable.

POSTSCRIPT   Many survivors of the terror had difficulty explaining why they had been spared. Future party general-secretary Nikita Khrushchev often asked himself that question and arrived at an explanation that revealed his uncertainty:

> The fact that I am truly devoted to the party has always been beyond doubt. But those comrades who perished were also devoted to the party, and they, too, contributed to the struggle for Stalin's General Line. Why did I escape the fate which they suffered? I think part of the answer is that Nadya's [Stalin's wife] reports about me helped to determine Stalin's attitude toward me. I call it my lottery ticket. I drew a lucky lottery ticket when it happened that Stalin observed my activities through Nadezhda Sergeyevna. It was because of her that Stalin trusted me.[39]

Perhaps Khrushchev was right.

Stalin justified the massacre doctrinally by claiming it was necessary to strengthen the Marxist-Leninist system. He advanced the "theory" that the class struggle becomes more intense as the opponents of Communism become weaker. But his motives were much more personal and paranoid, and the political effects were profound. Stalin had carried out a political coup. He had replaced the Communist party with the NKVD as the principal organ of state power. By completely liquidating the old Communist leadership, he had cleared the way for a new group of younger *apparatchiki*. Uncompromised by the doctrinal and political feuds of the 1920s and early 1930s, they were ready to accept him as absolute dictator.

The price was awesome. Stalin had destroyed the country's most industrious class of peasants, its best factory managers and technicians, the cream of its armed forces, and the Communist party's founding fathers. Although the decline in industrial production during the Third Five-Year Plan can be ascribed in part to the diversion of the country's resources to rearmament, much was also due to the wholesale liquidation of technical and economic planners. Between 1938 and 1941, for example, almost the whole staff of the Gosplan was eliminated, the transportation industry was deprived of many qualified specialists, and other enterprises lost most of their engineers and executives. The result was a serious shortage of qualified managers.[40] The contradictions inherent in building a modern economy under a system so wasteful of its top talent ensured that Russia would again become backward. Stalin, however, was pleased. He praised his new managerial class as "the flesh and blood of our people." This class, he said, "has never known the yoke of exploitation [and] hates exploiters, and . . . is ready to serve the peoples of the USSR faithfully and devotedly. I think that the rise of this new, socialist intelligentsia of the people is one of the most important results of the cultural revolutions in our country."[41]

This group provided the pool of leadership that would direct the destinies of the country for the next half century. To facilitate the admission of these new leaders to the party, the Eighteenth Party Congress in 1939 required candidates merely to accept the Communist program, not master its principles. The program emphasized loyalty and readiness to defend the party line. This new Soviet upper class received all kinds of preferential treatment. These managers enjoyed personal incomes many times that of the average worker. They received special consideration in living quarters, often maintained second houses in the countryside, and had the right to shop in state discount stores that stocked goods unavailable to the rest of the population. A plethora of old-fashioned titles enhanced the authority of the new leadership class, complete with the restoration of tsarist-style military, diplomatic, and bureaucratic ranks.

In 1948, for example, the Ministry of Communications established nine special titles, four of which were subdivided into classes: state director-general; state director; state director of the first, second, and third class; director, director of the first, second, and third class; senior inspector; inspector; inspector of the first, second, and third class; and junior inspector of the first, second and third class. Each category in the civil service had its own quasi-military uniform, complete with badges of rank that were worn on distinctive hard-board epaulettes. According to Article 183 of the Criminal Code, anyone caught wearing a civilian rank or decoration to which he or she was not entitled could be punished by three months of correctional labor or a fine of 300 rubles.

As the ranks indicated, the upper class was far from monolithic. Significant differences existed between, say, the high party officials, armed forces commanders, upper-echelon scientists, and favored creative artists at the top and the petty bureaucrats at the bottom. The working class exhibited comparable divisions ranging from the Stakhanovites who were able to command wages equal to those of the general intelligentsia down to the manual laborers living at subsistence level. Obviously, in the land of the dictatorship of the proletariat, those who worked with their hands did not enjoy a great advantage. At the same time, those the regime favored were also in a sense the most vulnerable, at least as long as Stalin was alive.

They performed their functions with constant fear that the slightest transgression or mistake could cost them their position, their freedom, or their life. There was no alternative to being employed by the state, and in order to survive, one had to become an expert in political nuance and sycophancy.

Stalin, like a latter-day Caligula, was worshiped as a god during his own lifetime. Even Hitler, for all his personal absolutism, was never regarded as such an embodiment of the national genius. In the Soviet Union, all progress was attributed to Stalin's inspiration: "Without the victorious Socialist Great October Revolution, without Lenin and Stalin, without the Soviet State, without the guiding role of our glorious Bolshevik Party, the Leninist-Stalinist Party, there would have not occurred the great achievements in our national sciences and physiology. . . . This is why we glorify the name of the great Stalin and are able to make progress by being inspired by the Stalinist era by the direct influence of the Great Stalinist ideas."[42] This eulogy was included in an article entitled "The Clinical Psychological Trend in the Soviet Neuropathology"; its author, Professor Traschenko, was obviously a man who took no chances. The article, however, reveals less about the writer than about the pathological nature of the system under which he and his fellow citizens lived. Almost every Soviet citizen lost family members or friends; their senseless deaths created in the survivors a sense of resentment against the Communist system that contributed to the system's eventual demise and loosened the very cement that held the Soviet Union together.

ENDNOTES

1. As many as 34,000 slices were made from the right hemisphere of the cerebrum (the side unaffected by the strokes) and turned over to a special institute for the study of Lenin's brain established in Moscow in 1925. The Soviets wanted to analyze Lenin's genius scientifically. Stefan T. Possony, *Lenin: The Compulsive Revolutionary* (Chicago: Henry Regnery Company, 1964), 363. The institute also obtained the brains of other important Soviets: party leaders, writers, scientists, etc. Stalin's is also in the collection. The last brain to be catalogued was that of Andrei Sakharov in December 1989.

2. A visit to Lenin's mausoleum was a carefully stage-managed event. Numerous guards kept the crowds moving past at such a constant rate that it was impossible to take more than a brief look at Lenin's hands and face, visible under artfully arranged spotlights. The Soviets claimed that the dead leader's lifelike appearance was due to an innovative, revolutionary process in the art of embalming that was a closely guarded secret. Some uncharitably suggested that what was on display came from the waxworks. Ibid., 374–75.

3. The Political Bureau (Politburo) first appeared in October 1917, but had no policy-making functions until March 1919, when it was given permanent status within the Communist party. After 1934, Stalin deprived it of most of its power, abolishing it in 1952 and replacing it with the Presidium of the Central Committee. After Stalin's death in 1953, this organization regained much of its lost power.

4. Of his nine leading associates, all except three came from the lower middle class, and only two had had careers outside the party bureaucracy.

5. Svetlana Alliluyeva, *Only One Year Later* (London: Hutchinson, 1969), 355.

6. Robert C. Tucker, *Stalin as Revolutionary: A Study in History and Personality* (New York: W. W. Norton, 1973), 108–14.

7. Ibid., 239–91.

8. See Gustav Bychowski, "Joseph V. Stalin: Paranoia and the Dictatorship of the Proletariat" in *The Psychoanalytic Interpretation of History*, edited by Benjamin B. Wolman (New York: Basic Books, 1971), 115–47.

9. Joseph Stalin, *Problems of Leninism* (New York: International Publishers, 1924), 61.

10. Ibid., 65.

11. Joseph Stalin, *Foundations of Leninism* (New York: International Publishers, 1939), 46. For example, the passage just quoted became: "Therefore, the revolution in the victorious country must regard itself not as a self-sufficient entity but as a means of hastening the victory of the proletariat in other countries." The Fourteenth Communist Party Congress of March 1925 overwhelmingly endorsed the "socialism in one country" doctrine.

12. Richard Crossman, ed., *The God That Failed* (New York: Harper and Brothers, 1949), 60. See also Robert Conquest, *The Harvest of Sorrow: Soviet Collectivization and the Terror-Famine* (New York: Oxford University Press, 1986), 225–59.

13. Using the index of productivity in 1928 as 100, then in 1929, it equaled 98; in 1930, it was 94.4; in 1931, it was 92; in 1932, it was 86; and in 1933, it was 81.5. Roy A. Medvedev, *Let History Judge* (New York: Knopf, 1972), 90.

14. Daniel Thorniley, *The Rise and Fall of the Rural Communist Party, 1927–39* (New York: St. Martin's Press, 1988), 6–22.

15. Paul Haensel, *The Economic Policy of Soviet Russia* (London: P. S. King, 1930), 152–53.

16. Gulbenkian initially purchased a quantity of eighteenth-century French silver, a Louis XVI writing table, two paintings by Hubert Robert, and the world-famous *Annunciation* by Flemish master Dirk Bouts. Later, he obtained three Rembrandts (*Portrait of Titus, Pallas Athena*, and *Portrait of an Old Man*), a Rubens (*Portrait of Helene Fourment*), a Watteau (*Le Mezzetin*), a Gerard Ter Borch (*The Music Lesson*), and Nicolas Lancret's *Les Baigneuses (The Bathers)*, plus more French silver. The first two Rembrandts eventually went to the Rijksmuseum; the Watteau, Lancret, and Ter Borch ended up in the Metropolitan Museum in New York; the rest are in the Gulbenkian Museum in Lisbon. Robert C. Williams, *Russian Art and American Money, 1900–1940* (Cambridge, Mass: Harvard University Press, 1980).

17. See Maurice Rheims, *The Glorious Obsession* (London: Souvenir Press, 1975), 59–74.

18. Williams, *Russian Art*, 162.

19. Mellon obtained five Rembrandts, four Van Dykes, two Franz Hals, two Raphaels (one the stunning *Alba Madonna*), plus individual masterpieces by Rubens, Titian, Botticelli, Veronese, Chardin, Perugino, Van Eyck, and Velasquez. Ibid., 173.

20. Ibid., 169.

21. J. Arch Getty, *Origins of the Great Purges: The Soviet Communist Party Reconsidered, 1933–1938* (Cambridge: Cambridge University Press, 1985), 130.

22. William Fletcher, *A Study in Survival: The Church in Russia, 1927–1943* (New York: Macmillan, 1965), 29–30.

23. *International Conciliation Documents* (New York: Carnegie Endowment for World Peace, 1930), 305–6.

24. Getty, *Origins of the Great Purges*, 48–57.

25. For the past four months, Nikolayev had been trained for his task by the NKVD, which even provided him with target practice. Several days before the assassination, Nikolayev had tried to enter the Smolny, armed with a loaded Nagan revolver, but an alert guard stopped him, found the gun, and had him arrested. Shortly after-

wards, however, Nicolayev was released and his pistol returned. On the fatal day, the guards who were usually stationed at all the floors were gone, and Kirov's personal bodyguard was detained outside the building by agents of the secret police.

26. See Robert Conquest, *Stalin and the Kirov Murder* (New York: Oxford University Press, 1989).

27. Although some maintain that Stalin's involvement has not been proved (Getty, *Origins of the Great Purges*, 207–10), many believe otherwise, including Robert Conquest, Roy Medvedev, Adam Ulam, and Robert Tucker. Furthermore, Olga Shatunovskaya, a member of the special commission established in 1957 to investigate the crime, testified in an interview that the evidence was incontrovertible. But the full report of the investigation has yet to be made public as Secretary-General Nikita Khrushchev, who sponsored the inquiry, called the findings too explosive. Jonathan Lewis, producer and author, *Stalin*, Part 2—Thames Television (Copyright Boston: WGBN Educational Foundation, 1990).

28. Leonard Schapiro, *The Communist Party of the Soviet Union* (New York: Random House, 1971), 407.

29. *Constitution (Fundamental Law) of the Union of Soviet Socialist Republics* (Moscow: Progress Publishers, 1937), Articles 125, 127, 128.

30. Ibid., Article 125.

31. W. W. Kulski, *The Soviet Regime* (Syracuse: Syracuse University Press, 1954), 215.

32. He was charged with liquidating Kirov, murdering former Security Chief Vyacheslav Menzhinsky, poisoning the author Maxim Gorky, and working with foreign agents for the destruction of the Soviet system.

33. Kulski, *The Soviet Regime*, 400–401.

34. Moreover, Bukharin had failed to save his wife, Anna, who was arrested and spent over twenty years in prison. She did not see her son for practically the entire time.

35. A former Comintern official pictured Yagoda as sitting "in one of those cells in the Moscow prison of the [NKVD], which he himself had built, reading the regulation which he had signed, awaiting an examination, a judgement, an execution, the rites of which he knows by heart—understand at last what he has done, what he had become, what those like him have made of the Revolution." Victor Serge, *From Lenin to Stalin* (New York: Nomad Press, 1973), 130.

36. Stanislaw Swianiewicz, "The Main Features of Soviet Forced Labor" in William L. Blackwell, ed., *Russian Economic Development from Peter the Great to Stalin* (New York: Franklin Watts, 1974), 279–91.

37. Christopher Andrew and Oleg Gordievsky, *The KGB: The Inside Story* (New York: HarperCollins, 1990), 139–40. See also Robert Conquest, *The Great Terror* (New York: Macmillan, 1968), 525–35.

38. Louis Fischer, *Men and Politics* (New York: Harper and Row, 1966), 528–29.

39. Nikita Khrushchev, *Khrushchev Remembers* (Boston: Little, Brown, 1970), 44.

40. Raymond Hutchings, *Soviet Economic Development* (New York: New York University Press, 1982), 64–65.

41. Josef Stalin, *Report on the Work of the Central Committee to the XVIII Congress of the Communist Party of the Soviet Union* (Moscow: Foreign Languages Publishing House, 1939), 31.

42. Kulski, *The Soviet Regime*, 59.

CHAPTER 10

DEMOCRACY UNDER STRESS

PREFACE "I have lived in a world where it was considered good form to shoot a democrat," Clemenceau recalled in an interview during the Paris Peace Conference. Such sport no longer seemed to be in fashion in France, but it had not fallen out of favor elsewhere. Only countries with firm democratic traditions, like France, Britain, and some of the smaller western and northern European states, had the determination to turn their backs on those who believed that the proper way to run a country was by smashing heads. The democratic states, therefore, rejected fascist solutions and tried to find other ways to protect the fabric of their society. In these democratic states, the traditional ruling classes had to make their peace with working-class parties if the system were to work and survive. They had to make changes in order for things to stay the same. In Britain, the cooperation of the Conservative party with leaders of the Labour party in forming the National Government was a good example of this effort. It was also smart politics. The cooperation fractionalized the Conservatives' habitual opponents and helped guarantee Conservative political dominance for the remainder of the decade.

Similarly, in France, the bourgeois Radical party joined forces in a government with the Socialists despite the Radicals' antipathy for state welfare and leftist schemes of nationalization. A perceived need to defend the Third Republic against its extremist enemies overcame the unnaturalness of this alliance. The Radicals managed to maintain their party's integrity and preserve their own careers as politicians by presenting state commitment to the well-being of the workers in such a bland way that it did not offend the middle class. In both Britain and France, the defensive strategy proved beneficial for preserving the status quo.

Although initially the desire to return to the laissez-faire practices of old was strong, in most of the democratic countries of Western Europe the interwar period saw a change in attitude toward the role of the state in the lives of its people. Yet not until the Great Depression destroyed the illusion that it was possible to turn back the clock was this increased reliance on government accepted as a means for solving problems and transforming society. However, the leaders of the democracies were still reluctant to mobilize their nations and return to the kind of *dirigisme* that had existed during the war. Certain extremist groups had fewer reservations and pushed for the establishment of command societies, following the examples of the Soviet Union and Italy. But the bulk of the masses refused to follow them. Traditional working class parties, like the British Labour party and the French Socialist party, remained essentially cautious and nonrevolutionary.[1] Still, a larger role for government seemed inevitable. Many intellectuals thought there was something dreadfully wrong with a system that did not make an active commitment to workers' rights and social welfare. The French Popular Front of 1936 did try to implement such a program, but had only modest success. The Scandinavian countries, which had been neutral during the war, went much farther than other countries. Norway, Sweden, and Denmark all had socialist governments that used the direct power of government to promote the prosperity and well-being of their citizens. Their success showed that economic planning could be instituted without abandoning democracy.

GREAT BRITAIN MUDDLES THROUGH

A Lack of Solutions

A Return to Protectionism. The National Government had been formed in August 1931 ostensibly to save the value of the British currency, but actually in an urgent attempt to lift the country out of the depression. In the October elections, it won 556 of 615 seats in the Commons (more than 90 percent), although it received only two-thirds of the popular vote. The National Government hoped that its protectionist policy would allow it to negotiate favorable trade agreements with other protectionist countries and thereby would promote recovery in the badly depressed export industries.[2] The policy achieved few positive results.[3] Without a general program of industrial modernization, the economy remained sluggish and unemployment stayed high. In 1932, unemployment peaked at 22.5 percent of the work force, just under 3 million persons.[4] The Labour opposition criticized the National Government's failures, but put forth no positive proposals of its own.[5] Party chief Clement Attlee and trade union boss Ernest Bevin generally acted with moderation and restraint. Their efforts were not appreciated by the party's left-wing intellectuals. People like Harold Laski and Stafford Cripps wanted to create socialism through political upheaval. John Strachey, leader of the extreme Independent Labour party (ILP), openly advocated a Marxist revolution. The ILP leaders believed that the depression stemmed directly from capitalist greed and mismanagement. In their view, class warfare between the exploiters and the exploited was inevitable, and foreign relations were a simplistic struggle between the peace-loving peoples and the imperialist warmongers. The ILP tried to increase its political clout by promoting the formation of a common front with all leftist parties.

In 1934, it joined with the Communist party to create the Anti-Fascist Action Committee.

Labour categorically refused to have anything to do with the arrangement. When the British Communist party sought to conclude a political alliance, the Labour party executive not only refused, but made it clear that it would not tolerate any support for a Popular Front from the general membership. Those who persisted were dismissed from the party. In fact, the Communist party (whose membership approached 16,000 by 1938) had scant success proselytizing among the British workers. The many popular demonstrations it helped to organize, mostly concerned with the threat of Fascism abroad, brought the party no lasting benefits. The rise of Hitler and the outbreak of the Spanish Civil War probably had more impact on the radicalism of intellectuals than did the economic situation at home. Sacrificing the constitution to save the world from Fascism seemed a small price to pay. To the ILP the Labour party was a group of muddle-headed moderates with no backbone for the class war. George Landsbury, the Labour party leader from 1931 to 1935, was even a pacifist.

The radicals formed their own associations. In 1936, Laski, Strachey, and publisher Victor Gollancz launched the Left Book Club. Within a year membership climbed to 50,000. If the intellectuals could not take to the streets, they could at least be assured of receiving a leftist point of view on every issue. Those hungry for direct action joined the International Brigades to fight for the Republic in Spain. In time, though, many of those who had embraced radicalism found their way back into the Labour party where they moderated their call for revolution into a commitment to work for the establishment of a society that would provide employment and social security for all citizens.

Extremism on the Right. During the 1930s, radicalism on the political right constituted a more clear and present danger. Sir Oswald Mosley founded the British Union of Fascists (BUF). A visit to Italy in 1932 convinced him that Mussolini represented the wave of the future.[6] Mosley had been in political limbo since 1930 when the Labour party expelled him for insubordination. He had proposed retraining and relocation for workers caught in dying industries like shipbuilding. But timid leaders like MacDonald were not ready for such imaginative schemes and insisted on party discipline much to Mosley's frustration. Mosley responded by calling for the creation of a one-party state with a syndicalist House of Commons in which the members would represent economic units rather than geographical areas. Mosley said he intended to come to power constitutionally, but claimed that he was prepared to save Britain by force from those who would seek to destroy it by force. The BUF used the Roman salute and adopted black shirts and black tunics with silver fasces emblems. Its membership, drawn largely from lower-class youth, increased rapidly but was not very stable. Perhaps as many as 100,000 passed through at some time, although certainly no more than 6,000 paid dues at any one time.

In April 1934, 10,000 people attended a boisterous BUF rally in London's Albert Hall. Two months later at the Olympia, the crowd was even larger and more unruly. In fact, the Olympia conclave turned into one of the bloodiest indoor political meetings in modern British history. BUF members pounced on and brutally assaulted all hecklers. Mosley defended such tactics, saying they were necessary to guarantee freedom of speech against the Jews who were provoking him.

As Mosley's movement became more violent and more anti-Semitic, it lost many of its respectable conservative supporters, including press tycoon Lord Roth-

British Fascists greet Sir Oswald Mosley, their leader. Flashing the Nazi salute, these blackshirted youths prepare to show their strength in London's poor East End district in October 1936. However, counter-demonstrations forced them to cut their march short.

ermere whose editorials had once touted the Blackshirts as a force of salvation from the "inertia and indecision" of the National Government. Mosley entered no candidates in the 1935 elections; he claimed that the large number of voter abstentions proved that the future was with Fascism. But the BUF, plagued by money problems, personal quarrels, and poor organization, was already on the wane. Following a BUF demonstration in London's East End in October 1936, the government enacted a special Public Order Bill that prohibited the wearing of political uniforms and the use of party standards at outdoor meetings. The police were given the authority to prohibit demonstrations that might lead to civil disorder. The movement continued to decline in the latter part of the decade, numbering less than 1,000 by 1939. When war began with Germany in 1939, many of the BUF leaders, including Mosley, were arrested and put into prison.

This threat from the Right would seem less important later than it did at the time. Although the government was in no serious danger, the very existence of the BUF was an implicit criticism of the inept leadership of both the Conservative and Labour parties. Extremism appealed to those directly affected by the country's failure to recover from the war. By 1934, the BUF had 180 local branches, mostly in the poorer areas of London and northern industrial cities such as Manchester, Liverpool, Leeds, and Birmingham, where unemployment and discontent were high and where brutality and intolerance were not always directed toward political ends. Although the crisis passed, class attitudes and class resentment remained and continued to influence British politics.

The Direction of the National Government

Persistent Unemployment. With the general collapse of world trade, many British industries continued to perform badly, especially the heavy industries in the east Midlands, south Wales, and Scotland. In these so-called dismal areas, which depended on exports, industries such as shipbuilding, steel, and textiles never really recovered. Britain continued to be a leading producer of coal, second to Germany in Europe, but throughout the 1930s it produced consistently less than it had in 1929. The most persistent domestic problem continued to be unemployment, which in this decade never fell below 1.4 million, or 11 percent of the labor force; usually, it hovered above the 2 million mark, or between 16 and 22 percent.[7] The rate varied throughout the country. In the London area, it stayed around 14 percent, while in Wales it reached 36 percent. In some depressed areas, it went over 60 percent. To make matters worse, most young people left school at age fourteen, thereby providing a steady stream of cheap unskilled labor that was easily replaceable when the age cohort reached adulthood and began to demand higher wages. Furthermore, the overall population of Great Britain increased at the end of the decade due to the fall off in emigration and the influx of refugees.

The Conservative-dominated government reacted to unemployment with a certain amount of resignation; it assumed that 15 percent of the people would always be unemployed. The Tories convinced themselves that people were out of work because they refused to accept lower wages; they castigated the trade unions for frustrating such reductions. Insisting that the economy would recover and return to full employment on its own, the Conservatives adamantly refused to combat unemployment by increasing public expenditures. Indeed, the Tories argued that going into debt would undermine business confidence and really *delay* the recovery. In their view, using the limited supply of investment income for public works such as roads and housing would actually increase unemployment by depriving more productive industries of the capital they needed to expand. Accordingly, the Conservatives first attempted to promote recovery by reducing expenditures and balancing the budget.

In contrast to the Conservatives, Lloyd George advocated more government planning. Insisting that classical remedies were no longer sufficient to solve the present crisis, he urged the government to create a special statutory council to survey the country's economic resources and provide long-range guidance for economic growth and development. He rejected the conventional economic wisdom that said that the problem would eventually cure itself; according to this scenario, unemployment would produce cheaper labor, which in turn would lead to lower production costs and to increased investment and employment. Lloyd George did not believe that the "iron law" of the marketplace would automatically solve the problem.

Despite such urgings, the Conservatives still shied away from a managed economy. Nevertheless, they did not oppose all state intervention in the free market. Indeed, government intervention in economic affairs became more and more prevalent during the 1930s—and more and more acceptable. Among other things, the central government began to assume some of the social security obligations that had previously been left to the local authorities. In 1934, Parliament passed the Unemployment Insurance Act, which established the government's obligation to look after those who had lost their jobs. In addition, the Exchequer adopted a cheap money policy to stimulate investment. (The bank, or discount, rate would ultimately be brought down to two percent.) The protectionist tariff policy, another form of intervention in the economy, was supposed to protect the home markets.

Despite these measures, unemployment remained a permanent fixture of British society in the 1920s and 1930s. Yet the pattern of British recovery was not much different from that of most other industrial countries. From 1931 to 1937, the country's indexes of industrial production increased more than 30 percent. Domestic industries, which generally did better than in the previous decade, registered most of the gain. The electrical appliance industry boomed, as did chemicals and synthetic fabrics. The number of private motor cars increased to 390,000 units by 1937—over twice as many as had been produced in 1929, the peak year of the 1920s. Due to the increased output and better distribution of electric power, industrial plants no longer had to be located near the coal-producing regions of the north and west. Much of the new industrial expansion took place in the south of England, in the traditional garden suburbs near London that were closer to the markets the new products were intended to serve. Given the high rate of unemployment, entrepreneurs could find labor anywhere they chose to establish their businesses. The dismal depressed areas of the Midlands held small attraction for them.

An improved housing industry stimulated the expansion. With interest rates fairly low, more people found home ownership as affordable as renting. The government's cheap money policy enabled private contractors to obtain adequate financing with no difficulty. With improvements to the London transport system, bedroom communities sprang up around the ever-growing metropolitan area, the supply of new units comfortably keeping pace with the demand. Such private initiative allowed the government to concentrate on slum clearance.

From Baldwin to Chamberlain. Ramsay MacDonald retired in June 1935, and Stanley Baldwin again took over as prime minister. In the national elections the following November, Baldwin ran on a "trust me" platform almost identical to the one he had used in 1924. The tactic worked so successfully that the coalition government returned with a vast majority of 267 seats, 90 percent of these being held by Tories. The elections produced no real change in leadership or policy. This Commons would sit for the next ten years, until the end of World War II. Baldwin's own temperament reflected the National Government's antipathy for strong action. Baldwin believed that if the need for a particular policy were great enough, the people would insist on that policy. This attitude could serve as an excuse for doing as little as possible. At the same time, Baldwin was committed to promoting social harmony by avoiding confrontation. Thanks to him the turbulent days of the depression when strident Communists matched epithets with truculent Fascists passed as peacefully as they did.[8] In 1936, he put his talents of moderation and conciliation to work in the abdication crisis.

King George V died five minutes before midnight, on 20 January 1936, in the twenty-sixth year of his reign. Few monarchs, aside from Queen Victoria, were more sincerely mourned. The Silver Jubilee of his reign had been commemorated the previous year with a celebration of love and devotion that had no parallel in modern times. When George lay dying, crowds of people pressed against the gates of Buckingham Palace waiting for the latest medical bulletins, while others sat by their radio sets listening to the BBC announcer solemnly repeat, "The King's life is moving peacefully toward its close." George had been in considerable agony, and his doctor hastened his end with a fatal injection. The king's successor was his eldest son, David, who took the title of Edward VIII. The new king was a bachelor.

British newspapers avoided gossip about the royal family, and, therefore, not until the end of the year did the public become aware that their king was seriously involved with a twice-divorced American socialite, Mrs. Wallis Warfield Simpson. Baldwin, sensing trouble, had tried to hustle the lady out of the country. Edward flatly informed him that he intended to marry her, even if that meant losing his crown. A British monarch's choice of consort was hardly his own business, however. The king was expected to embody the highest moral values of the country, and marriage to a divorcee, even morganatically, was out of the question.[9] Even the Dominion governments were inflexibly opposed to such a match. Edward, as he certainly knew, had only two choices: he could renounce Mrs. Simpson and "return to duty," or he could abdicate. He abdicated. Before he left the country for a self-imposed exile, he explained in a radio address that he found it impossible to carry the heavy burden of responsibility and to discharge his kingly duties without the help and support of the woman he loved.

Throughout the crisis, Baldwin played a cautious game. He took action only when it became unavoidable, after the press had broken its silence on 3 December 1936. Even then, only after the affair had been settled did he take Parliament into his confidence (on 10 December 1936). The Commons subsequently passed the official Act of Abdication by 403 votes to 5. The abdication crisis was the most famous episode in the modern history of the British monarchy. Edward was a flawed specimen at best; his replacement by his more responsible brother Albert, who became George VI, greatly improved the prestige of the monarchy. Baldwin had handled the affair masterfully. Some called it his finest performance. It was also one of his last.

At the end of May 1937, a fortnight after George VI was crowned king, Baldwin resigned. He was seventy years old and had been complaining of exhaustion for some time. Neville Chamberlain succeeded him.[10] The new prime minister had entered Parliament at the end of World War I. Until he became chancellor of the Exchequer in 1931, he had lived in the political shadow of his more famous half-brother, Austen. In the 1924–1929 government, he sponsored a bill to provide government pensions for widows and orphans and presided over the transformation of county poor relief into national public assistance. Chamberlain believed that the government should help those who help themselves, but his action, although modest, helped to further the development of a welfare state.

In the 1931 government, in which he ran the Exchequer, he guided the adoption of the protective tariff and steered the Unemployment Insurance Act of 1934 through Parliament. A tireless worker and a competent, if unpopular, administrator, he increasingly dominated the cabinet. He therefore became the logical man to succeed Baldwin. Chamberlain's political style was quite different from his predecessor's, however. Fellow Tory Leopold Amery wrote:

> Baldwin, as Prime Minister, was content to assume that his colleagues were competently discharging their duties. Chamberlain soon showed them that he was not merely Chairman in Cabinet, but a general manager who wished to know what his department managers were doing, to discuss their problems with them and to keep them up to the work. What is more, he knew his own mind and saw to it that he had his way. An autocrat with all the courage of his convictions, right or wrong.[11]

FRANCE'S HOUSE DIVIDED

A Society in Discord

A Stagnant Economy. France had been able to withstand the initial effects of the world depression with comparative ease. Isolated behind a wall of protectionism with cartel arrangements and a cheaper franc cushioning the domestic market, the

French could almost rejoice at their good fortune. However, the postwar high for industrial production had already been reached in 1930. Over the next five years, it plunged downward, dropping by almost 30 percent. At the same time, unemployment, which had been virtually nonexistent at the end of 1929, increased by a factor of 35, from 13,000 in 1930 to 464,000 in 1935.[12] These statistics did not include those who were working fewer hours or the thousands of foreign laborers who were sent back to their home countries, nor did the figures include unemployed women who were still considered housewives although they had worked outside the home. But foreigners and women did not have the right to vote and could be properly discounted. Many first-generation city dwellers returned to the family farms to await better times, but these were mostly unskilled workers. The steel and building industries and many small and medium-sized firms were particularly hard hit. The employers took advantage of the helplessness of the workers in the face of unemployment to attack the unions and tried to have social insurance and family allowances abolished. Thanks to a series of financial scandals in 1930 and 1931, complex political issues were transformed into a simple struggle between the rich and the poor, the little people versus the ruling classes. Yet the workers, aside from those who were Communist, remained faithful to the institutions of the Third Republic and never seriously challenged its right to govern. This was not the case with the political Right where an array of militant political action groups, bound together by a common ultranationalist, militarist, and staunch Roman Catholicism, already existed.

The depression had not hit these groups as hard as it had many other French, but they were prepared to take advantage of the situation to overthrow the constitution. Although they admired Mussolini for having put the working classes in their place, many of the "established" groups did not feel that they needed to build up a similar mass following to save the country.

The Leagues. One of the oldest of these superconservative, authoritarian groups was the *Action française* (French Action), founded before World War I by Charles Maurras who wanted to free the country from the corrupting influences of medieval Germanic mysticism. The Action Française joined the antidemocratic and anti-Semitic coalition in the famous Dreyfus affair. Although monarchies were generally out of fashion, Maurras's group advocated a Bourbon-Orleanist restoration as part of its program to return France to its pure Greco-Roman heritage. In 1926, however, Maurras's books and pamphlets were placed on the papal Index of Forbidden Books. Pope Pius XI condemned the Action Française for "atheism, paganism, and amoralism," thereby prompting the pretender to the French throne, the count of Paris, to formally disassociate himself from the movement. Nevertheless, the Action Française, although crippled, remained popular with many French conservatives because it opposed both centralism and popular sovereignty. Maurras responded to his opponents by using his prewar youth group, the *Camelots du roi* (Hawkers of the King),[13] as special shock troops to carry the struggle into the streets. The Camelots adopted Mussolini's tactics of beating people up in public, especially targeting Socialists and Communists.

Other groups similarly rejected the current democratic system, but did not repudiate republicanism. Among these were the *Jeunesses patriotes* (Young Patriots), formed in 1924 by the wealthy champagne manufacturer, Pierre Taittinger, in the aftermath of the electoral victory of the Cartel of the Left. Taittinger's association, like its forerunner the League of Patriots founded in 1882 by the vitriolic Paul Déroulède, wanted a strong presidential system and an emasculated legislature. The example of Benito Mussolini also strongly influenced the Young Patriots and other rightist leagues, like the *Solidarité française* (French Solidarity), which was heavily subsidized by the perfume and talcum powder tycoon René Coty. French Solidarity adopted a Fascist-type uniform of blue shirt, black beret, and jack boots and fought under the slogan "France for the French"—a clear warning to all Jews, Socialists, Communists, Freemasons, and leftists. In the same spirit, the members of Marcel Bucard's *Francisme* (Frenchness) wore blue shirts and spouted slogans extolling order, authority, and racial purity, i.e., anti-Semitism. The radical *Jeunesses paysannes* (Young Peasants) of Henri Dorgères wore green shirts and adopted as their motto "Believe, Obey, Serve." Although all these groups bore more than a passing resemblance to Italian Fascism and German Nazism, none really fit those categories. The French organizations were more committed to destroying liberalism and vilifying parliamentarianism than they were in mobilizing the masses to create a one-party state or changing the capitalist system. The small size of the organizations also limited their effectiveness. Their mutual suspicions made unity impossible, and their elitism made large memberships difficult to recruit.

The *Croix de feu* (Cross of Fire), founded in 1928 by Colonel François de la Rocque as a combat veterans' organization, built up one of the largest popular followings. In 1931, membership was open to any "patriot" who wanted to purge the government of objectionable elements. In its heyday, the Cross of Fire claimed a membership of several hundred thousand. The number was exaggerated and, even if true, was not terribly impressive. Nevertheless, properly mobilized in conjunction with the other Paris-based leagues, the Cross of Fire was capable of doing considerable mischief. Only a spark was necessary to bring it into action.

The Stavisky Affair and the Riots of February 1934. In January 1934, the extensive financial swindles of Serge Alexander Stavisky suddenly became public. Stavisky, a naturalized Russian Jew, had a record of arrests dating back two decades. However, thanks to certain political connections and occasional service as a police informer, he never served much time. In 1926, he was jailed for swindling a stockbroker out of 7.5 million francs. He was soon released on provisional liberty and managed to get his trial postponed nineteen times, all the while continuing his frauds, each more ambitious than its predecessor. In 1932, with the cooperation of the mayor of Bayonne, who was also a Radical party deputy, Stavisky issued bonds in the amount of 200 million francs through the Bayonne credit bank, using fake jewelry as collateral. Supported by recommendations from the minister of labor, Albert Dalimier, Stavisky managed to sell these securities to various insurance companies and semipublic institutions and, with the proceeds, acquired a string of Bayonne pawnshops. He used these assets to float more bonds. A default in loan payments, however, led to a warrant being issued for his arrest on 29 December 1933. By that time, Stavisky had already gone into hiding.

The case soon drew public attention and outrage. Premier Camille Chautemps was suspected of complicity because his brother had at one time been Stavisky's attorney and his brother-in-law was currently the public prosecutor for the tribunal of the Seine, which on previous occasions had given Stavisky special consideration. To many, Stavisky's career epitomized the filth and rot in the system the enemies of the republic sought to exploit. For them, the Third Republic deserved their most pejorative epithet, *la gueuse* (the whore).

On 8 January 1934, the police located Stavisky in a chalet near Chamonix. As they closed in, he committed suicide. Many people, however, believed that Stavisky had been killed on orders from the government because he knew too much. The satirical weekly review *Canard enchaînè* wrote, "Stavisky commits suicide with a pistol he had fired at him at point blank range."[14] Various arrests followed, including two journalists and two Radical deputies: one of the deputies was Joseph Garat, the mayor of Bayonne; the other was Gaston Bonnaure, Stavisky's lawyer who had been paid off with half a million francs. The Radical party eventually expelled six of its deputies for associations with Stavisky, but was never able to cleanse itself of the mud with which it had been splattered.

Indignation gave rise to action. On 10 January, the Camelots du Roi demonstrated before the Chamber of Deputies. The next day, reinforced by units of the Young Patriots, they protested in the Latin Quarter. Throughout the next two weeks, sporadic outbursts of violence rocked Paris almost every night. The right-wing Paris prefect of police, Jean Chiappe, took a hands-off attitude toward the demonstrators, thereby encouraging them to continue their activities. On 27 January, Premier Chautemps resigned although he still had a majority in the parliament. The president of the republic, Albert Lebrun, felt that the gravity of the situation justified the formation of a government of national union, and he called upon his predecessor, Gaston Doumergue, to undertake the task. Doumergue declined because of his age, and Edouard Daladier tried to form a new cabinet. To obtain the cooperation of the Socialists, Daladier dismissed Chiappe, an act that provoked further rioting.

On 6 February, as Daladier presented his government to the chamber for confirmation, the leagues mobilized in the Place de la Concorde, across the Seine River from the parliament building. The demonstrators made several attempts to cross the river, but the police had erected a barricade on the Concorde Bridge and were prepared to defend it. Fighting continued throughout the evening. When it was over, sixteen demonstrators and one policeman lay dead with another two thousand or so wounded. Many of the less seriously injured did not seek medical attention and therefore did not appear in the official count. Daladier declared that he would not let himself be intimidated by threats from the streets, but he resigned almost at once. He too had had a parliamentary majority. Once again Lebrun asked Doumergue to try to form a government. This time Doumergue agreed. Although his ministry was little different from the one it replaced, the change seemed to satisfy the rioters, and peace once again returned to the streets of Paris.

As many as 40,000 people had been involved in the demonstrations. Fortunately, the leagues, despite their revolutionary oratory, lacked the coordination, strength, and professional fanaticism necessary to overthrow the Third Republic. The most they could accomplish was the resignation of two governments. Apart from a minority of extremists, the leagues had no stomach for revolution. They were populated with war veterans who shied away from destroying a system that had saved France from German imperialism. And the demonstrators themselves, many of whom were under the age of thirty, appeared more interested in scaring the deputies than in killing them. The protesters made their point and, for the most part, left the streets before midnight, just in time to catch the last subway home. By not taking the protest farther, the active political Right lost momentum. Anti-Communism remained its strongest source of unity, but such negativism proved insufficient to ensure success. The leaders of the Right had pretensions of saving the country from spiritual decadence, but their romantic intellectualizing did not capture the popular mood. The French could accept the cult of energy, but not the cult of the leader—at least not as proposed by such groups. The working classes saw the leagues as the agents of capitalism, while the middle classes were still deriving too many benefits from the system in its current form to be drawn into such a perilous escapade. Although some extreme factions never gave up, they did not have another opportunity to topple the government until the defeat by Nazi Germany in 1940.[15]

The Left Comes to Power

The Formation of the Popular Front. The riots of February 1934 were confined almost exclusively to Paris, but they enabled Doumergue to obtain authority to enact legislation by decree to combat the emergency. His proposals were meager. He attempted to reduce the budget deficit while supporting the current value of the franc to assuage the business community's fears that devaluation would lead to the destruction of capitalism. As a result, the price of exports remained too high for profitable trade. When other countries were beginning to recover, France was still trapped in the depression. Doumergue believed that political and economic recovery depended on the creation of a stronger executive. Speaking on the radio, he proposed that the head of the government be given the power to dissolve the Chamber of Deputies after a vote of no confidence. The deputies were outraged at the prospect of facing new elections and hounded him from office. He had lasted only nine months.

The events of February convinced the Socialists and Communists that a genuine attempt had been made to overthrow the democratic government, and they began working toward a political alliance. Jacques Doriot, the Communist mayor of the Paris suburb of Saint Denis, proposed a broad anti-Fascist vigilance committee. However, the Central Committee of the Communist party was not yet prepared to organize a united front and regarded Doriot's initiative as an attempt to discredit the leadership of Secretary-General Maurice Thorez. Prevailing Comintern policy prohibited a Communist alliance with the French Socialist party. Moscow violently attacked Doriot and accused him of favoring the united front

The leaders of the Popular Front celebrate Bastille Day, 14 July 1936, at the Place de la Nation. French premier Léon Blum, the Socialist leader, stands next to Communist party chief Maurice Thorez. The man on Thorez's left is Roger Salengro, the minister of the Interior, whose suicide became symbolic of the divisive nature of French politics in the late 1930s.

in order to split the party. Shortly afterwards though, Stalin, alarmed by the threat of Nazism, eased his prohibition against seeking alliances with other leftist parties. This new policy prompted the French Communists to sign an agreement with the Socialists, on 27 July 1934, to prepare common action "to mobilize the entire working population against the Fascist organizations in order to disarm and destroy them." During the next year, the alliance was enlarged to include the Radicals.

On 14 July 1935, at a Bastille Day rally in the Parisian suburb of Montrouge, the Triple Alliance proclaimed the Popular Front publicly. The three parties took an oath to preserve the republic from Fascism and "to defend the democratic liberties conquered by the people of France, to give to the workers bread, to the young people work, and the world a great human peace." The Socialists pushed a program of social welfare; the more conservative Radicals concentrated on warning against the growing threats to international peace. The Communists, who wanted to attract as much support as possible for the anti-Fascist coalition, also favored keeping the economic program vague. They preferred the old makeshift practice of solving crises with special decrees.

The First Socialist Government. In January 1936, the Radicals, Socialists, and Communists openly reaffirmed the oath they had taken the previous July in preparation for the parliamentary elections scheduled for the following April. The campaign, fought in the shadow of Hitler's remilitarization of the Rhineland, was extremely bitter. The French electorate did not change its fundamental voting habits. Through a shift of about half a million votes, the Popular Front received a slight majority, with the Socialists becoming the largest party in the chamber. The Radicals dropped to second place while the Communists came next. The latter refused to join the government, but promised to support its program in parliament. The three main parties of the coalition together controlled a substantial majority of the 614 seats in the chamber.[16] In the cabinet the Socialists held thirteen posts, the Radicals eighteen.[17]

The new head of the government, Socialist leader Léon Blum, was a scholarly looking, middle-class intellectual who hoped to transform French society through existing institutions without a social revolution. Blum feared that the workers might confuse a parliamentary exercise of power with the Marxist goal of the conquest of power that would lead to the dictatorship of the proletariat. However, a great wave of strikes hit the nation even before the government was officially installed. In the Paris region, the workers staged sit-down strikes that affected the metallurgical, aviation, and automobile industries, the building trades, transportation, the newspapers, slaughterhouses, and large department stores. The workers were more preoccupied with bread and butter issues than revolution, however, and the atmosphere remained calm. The workers respected the property they now occupied. At the Galleries Lafayette department store, for example, the salesclerks slept on the floor rather than risk dirtying the new bedding. In factories with a mixed labor force, women were not allowed to spend the night. Strong alcohol was forbidden. In some places, like the Renault factory, workers danced.

Despite the peaceful nature of the strikes, Blum was apprehensive and felt he had no time to lose. On 7 June, the day after he officially took power, he met with the leaders of the *Confédération générale du travail* (General Confederation of Labor or CGT) and the employers of the General Confederation of French Production at his office at the Matignon Palace, the official Paris residence of the head of the government. Although these organizations did not represent every trade union or private industrial group, the agreement they reached was generally accepted. The agreement increased salaries from 7 to 15 percent; recognized the right of workers to organize and engage in collective bargaining; and guaranteed the right of the unions to appoint shop stewards (in every plant employing more than ten workers) and to present grievances on salaries, working conditions, hygiene, and safety. Blum assured the trade union boss, Léon Jouhaux, that he would sponsor bills instituting the forty-hour week, annual paid vacations, and a legal framework for collective bargaining. These promises would all be kept.

The Popular Front celebrated the Matignon accords with a massive demonstration on 14 July at the Place de la Bastille with the tricolor and the Red flag flying side by side. This great manifestation of the solidarity of the Popular Front was also its last. As soon as the threat of violence disappeared, the employers saw no reason to honor the agreement. Class hatred resurfaced. The middle classes detested annual paid vacations for workers because the working-class vacationers flocked to the beaches and picnic grounds that had formerly been the exclusive preserve of the middle class. The reactionary press turned nasty. It charged that Blum, because of his Jewish origins, was seeking to provoke a war of revenge with Nazi Germany. It accused Pierre Cot, the minister of air, of giving Russia the plans to a top secret aerial cannon. Minister of Interior Roger Salengro had to endure the slander that he had deserted to the Germans in the last war. Salengro was so depressed by these false charges that he committed suicide. Enemies of the Popular Front shouted slogans like "Better a Hitler than a Blum."

A Continuing Crisis. Léon Blum had made a serious effort to enact legislation that would make his country a more just place in which to live. His agenda for reform was hardly revolutionary, but to be effective, it would have to be based on prosperity. And the Popular Front proved a sad failure at revitalizing the economy. Production remained below the 1930 level; the supply of goods could not satisfy the rise in demand stimulated by recent salary increases. Consequently, the cost of living rose. The export of capital, prompted by the July strikes, accelerated, and the value of the franc declined. On 28 July, the Finance Ministry devalued the franc by 30 percent. But, without a vigorous recovery program, this cheap money policy had little effect. In September 1936, Blum repudiated an earlier campaign promise. He suspended the convertibility of the franc and placed an embargo on the export of gold.

The task of reviving the economy was certainly too formidable to be accomplished in a short time. Two contradictory imperatives influenced the Popular Front's monetary policy: one was to maintain a balanced budget, the other was to increase government spending by providing more social services. The Finance Ministry was chronically short of funds. In 1936, expenses surpassed receipts by 16.9 billion francs; the following year the deficit rose to 21 billion and in 1938 to 27.7 billion. With the decline of revenues from taxes and National Treasury Bonds, the government became more and more dependent on loans from private banking. Blum feared this would lead to blackmail by the financial interests, whom he accused of sabotaging his reforms by sending money abroad rather than investing it in domestic enterprises. In July 1936, he had nationalized the Bank of France with a new statute, abolishing the old general directorate of large private stockholders (the so-called 200 families who dated to the time of Napoleon) in favor of a new, state-appointed regency council. Two months later, he extended public control into the armaments industry by establishing a special state agency to oversee the manufacture and distribution of war matériels.

The Radicals became alarmed. They had never felt comfortable with the Socialists whom they feared might try to carry mild reforms to alarming lengths. But without the Radical votes, the Socialists could not remain in power. At the beginning of 1937, the Radicals forced Blum to announce a "temporary" halt in his program of nationalization. The action provoked a new wave of strikes. In Paris, even the workers on the Palais de Chaillot, the French pavilion for the 1937 World Exposition, refused to maintain their work schedules. Meanwhile, the Communists began denouncing Blum for being soft on Fascism because the government seemed to repress the demonstrations of the workers and not those of the rightist organizations. In June, Blum tried to convince the National Assembly to grant him special powers so he could enact his economic program by decree—he wanted a capital levy, further nationalizations, and state control of foreign exchange. The chamber gave conditional consent, but the conservative-dominated Senate refused. Blum resigned without waiting for a formal vote of no confidence. The Radicals took over the government, giving less than half of the portfolios to the Socialists. During the following year, the cabinet was reshuffled three more times—Blum even returned for a brief twenty-five days—but the period of reform associated with the Popular Front was over. The Radicals, who opposed state intervention in the economy, wanted to revive confidence in the government so the members of the business community would repatriate their money. Accordingly, the Radicals proposed lowering business taxes and abandoning some of the previously enacted reforms including the forty-hour week.

The scheme provoked an immediate, dramatic response from labor. In November 1938, the General Confederation of Labor called for a general strike. The government called out the army. Troops drove the workers out of the factories, and the authorities requisitioned all public services and suspended striking government employees. When the crisis abated, the General Confederation lay wounded, and the old class hatreds continued with renewed bitterness. French industrial output was about seven percent less than it had been in 1913.[18] One reason for the decline was that the country's industrial plant had become increasingly obsolete, and the owners had no incentive to modernize because they were protected from foreign competition. The workers also opposed modernization because it might deprive them of their jobs.

In the closing days of the 1930s, production deficiencies increasingly threatened national security as Nazi Germany outperformed France in most major industrial categories. In 1938, Germany produced 8 times as much coal as France, twice as much pig iron, 3.6 times as much crude steel, 4 times as much aluminum, 7.6 times as much crude petroleum, 78 percent more sulfuric acid, and 2.6 times as much electric power.[19] France retained an edge in iron ore production, but the home market underutilized this resource. France sent 15.5 million of its 33.1 million metric tons of ore abroad, while Germany added to its domestic supplies of 11.1 million metric tons by importing 20.6 million metric tons.[20] But, superficially at least, the French did not appear overly pessimistic or distraught. Things had been good in the past, perhaps they would get better in the future. Only the present was annoying.

THE LESSER DEMOCRATIC POWERS

The Eastern Exception: Czechoslovakia

Until Czechoslovakia fell victim to Nazi aggression, it, alone among all the states of Eastern Europe, remained true to the democratic institutions inspired by France and the United States. President Tomáš Masaryk had managed to guide the country's destinies for a decade and a half, but the world depression deeply marked his last years in office, making the maintenance of political stability increasingly difficult. Czechoslovakia's viability depended on its ability to sell abroad. But, from 1929 to 1933, exports fell by almost 70 percent, while unemployment rose by a factor of 17.5, from 42,000 to 738,000. Almost one-fourth of the country's families had no wage earner. The economic slump was less severe in Bohemia and Moravia than in Slovakia and the German-speaking Sudetenland, a mountainous region circling the country to the west, where ethnic hatred was never far from the surface.[21]

The Sudeten Germans accused the Prague government of willfully prolonging their misery by withholding the aid necessary for their recovery. Extreme nationalist parties, quiescent during the 1920s, increased in strength. The radical National Socialist Workers party, one of the most bitter enemies of the new Czechoslovak state, gained control of the German nationalist movement and expanded its contacts with Hitler, inviting Nazi dignitaries like propaganda chief Josef Goebbels and youth leader Baldur von Schirach to speak at party rallies in Prague. In 1931, the Czechoslovak government retaliated by banning the wearing of party uniforms and forbidding visits of foreign Nazi party officials. The following year, the government disbanded the National Socialist party's youth clubs and sports leagues and arrested some of its leaders on charges of treason. When Hitler became chancellor in Germany, the Prague government outlawed all pan-German parties, an action that the Sudeten German leaders had anticipated.

The Sudeten German National Socialist Workers party had already begun to reconstitute itself into a new organization, less overtly Nazi and less openly separatist. This *Sudetendeutsche Partei* (Sudenten German party), led by Konrad Henlein, the former director of the ultranationalist Gymnastics Union, publicly favored the creation of Czech-German unity within the existing state. But privately, Henlein continued the party's association with Hitler, who gave it direct financial support through the German Foreign Office to the tune of 180,000 marks a year. The Czechoslovak government, initially unaware of Henlein's strong connections with a foreign power, allowed the party to operate quite openly. Such toleration enabled the Sudeten German party to capture two-thirds of the German ethnic vote in the elections of 1935; it emerged with forty-four seats in the national parliament, second only to the Social Democrats. The victory brought shudders to the leaders of non-German parties; and when Masaryk resigned in 1935, they showed a rare example of unity by unanimously endorsing his old associate Edvard Beneš as president. Even with such widespread confidence, Beneš soon found he had little room to maneuver. The reason was that the "Sudeten problem" was only one element in a multitude of ethnic difficulties faced by the new state. Each of the other "national" minorities—Poles, Ruthenians, Hungarians, Jews[22]—had its own concept of what the state should be, and all were different from the state established after World War I. Since all these groups were relatively weak, however, they had little chance of bringing about change. The prospects of the more numerous Slovaks were more promising. Over a decade of union with the Czechs had not eradicated the Slovaks' feelings of alienation nor their desire for autonomy.

Initially, the Slovak deputies in the National Assembly had accepted the Czech idea of a strong central government. They wanted protection against the Hungarians and against Communism; and, relatively inexperienced in government, even welcomed Czech administrators to teach them how to run their affairs. As stability returned, however, and the Slovaks began to develop their own leaders, they increasingly resented taking orders from Prague. A further complication arose because the Slovak Protestant minority tended to be more Czechophile than the Slovak Catholic majority.[23] Slovak administrators who worked with the Czechs therefore tended to be largely Protestant and also anticlerical. In contrast, the Slovak Catholics had no tradition of separation of church and state. Historically, many of their principal leaders were priests.

In 1922, the Slovak Populist party, led by Father Andrej Hlinka, introduced a proposal for autonomy in the National Assembly. The bill failed to pass. Eight years later, the party tried again, but that bill was also voted down, though by a narrower margin. The Great Depression took a terrible toll on Slovakia where about one-third of the people had no regular income. As in the Sudetenland, the increased misery had serious political repercussions. Violence increased as did resentment against the Czechs and demands for Slovak autonomy. In December 1932, Hlinka vowed to defend the Slovak nation even at the expense of the republic, a fateful expansion of his program. Heretofore the party had always said it was trying to find a solution within the framework of the Czechoslovak state. A new "Autonomist Bloc," composed of the Slovak Populists, the Polish party in Silesia, and the Ruthenian Autonomist Agrarian Union, appeared in the National Assembly. The Sudeten German party and the Hungarian National party remained unaffiliated but supportive.

President Beneš began negotiations with the Slovak separatists, but steadfastly refused to consider changing the unitary nature of the state. The Slovak Populists, however, refused to give up. When Hlinka died in August 1938, he was replaced by the leader of the party's radical right wing, Monsignor Jozef Tiso. Tiso, who looked upon Mussolini's Fascist state as his ideal, ultimately presided over the establishment of a Slovak republic. Permission for that was to come from Berlin, not Prague.

The Social Democracies of the North: Sweden, Norway, and Denmark

The Scandinavian monarchies had been neutral during World War I, but they all suffered its effects, particularly in a loss of trade and the deprivation brought about by the Allied blockade. Their feeling of isolation along with the real effects of hunger and malnutrition promoted a sense of unity, which led to the conclusion of friendship agreements in 1917. These pacts facilitated the exchange of goods, especially Danish farm produce, Norwegian nitrates, and Swedish industrial products. Common democratic traditions also drew the countries together, and these traditions were steadily reinforced at the expense of royal prerogatives. After the war, Denmark and Sweden adopted full universal suffrage, which Norwegian citizens had enjoyed since 1913. At the same time, all three countries strengthened the authority of the lower houses of their legislatures. The influence of leftist parties continued to grow throughout the 1920s. Social Democratic ministries presided in all three countries by the middle of the 1930s.[24]

The Scandinavian socialists believed in using the powers of government to advance the welfare of their peoples. Although growth of the industrial urban areas had weakened the rural base of conservatism, the socialists did not want to change the basic economic structure.[25] They, therefore, did not seek to nationalize the means of production, preferring to cooperate with private industry to create the necessary wealth to improve the general standard of living. The success of the Social Democratic parties was often due less to their own strengths than to the disarray in the ranks of the opposition. The conservative parties could offer little more than preserving the status quo and extolling the virtues of king and country, slogans that had little appeal to a blue-collar, mostly unionized labor force.[26] Consequently, the socialists gained in strength, dragging the conservatives with them. In time, collective bargaining lost its class warfare overtones.

The world depression hit Scandinavia particularly hard. Throughout the thirties, unemployment was generally higher than in Britain and France. In Sweden, it went as high as 23.7 percent and never fell to less than 10 percent; in Denmark, it stayed between 13.7 percent and 31.7 percent; and in Norway, the worst hit, it hovered between 16.2 percent and 33.4 percent. The Social Democrats blamed the slump on the failings of capitalism, but they still endeavored to reform, rather than destroy, the capitalist system. They tried to show that human misery was not an inevitable by-product of capitalist society. In doing so, they were disregarding two of the tenets of Marxism: the increasing misery inherent in capitalist society and the necessity for class warfare. The Social Democrats claimed that progress was possible without a dictatorship of the proletariat and without violence and insisted that it could occur within the framework of a free market. They intended to provide the people with a broad safety net of welfare measures—guaranteed health care, family maintenance allowances, unemployment insurance, and disability insurance—paid for by progressive taxation. Scandinavian social and economic policies helped limit the impact of the depression and created a stable environment for recovery. In this atmosphere, antidemocratic extremist groups became irrelevant. They declined into tiny fringe groups with only token representation in the parliaments.

During the thirties, the indexes of industrial production rebounded in all three countries. Denmark's climbed by 60 percent, Norway's by 78 percent, and Sweden's by 86 percent.[27] At the same time, the cost of living remained relatively steady, rising only between one and two percent a year. Those on the margins of society enjoyed a greater degree of government protection and care and received a greater range of public benefits than the poorer classes in other capitalist countries. Nevertheless, despite the moves toward a more egalitarian society, significant differences still existed between the well-to-do and the poorer classes.

The Scandinavian countries preferred to protect society by spending money on welfare rather than on big armies. In external affairs, they tried to remain outside the conflicts preoccupying the rest of Europe, placing their faith in the collective security of the League of Nations. They also worked hard to promote regional solidarity. Only Sweden, prompted by an age-old fear of the Russians, maintained a significant military deterrence. The Swedes had a thriving armaments industry that produced high-quality small arms and guns of heavier caliber, bomber and reconnaissance aircraft, and battleships for coastal defense and torpedo boats. Much of this output was exported. The Danes had a smaller armaments industry— their Madsen machine and submachine guns were world famous—but during the thirties they virtually disbanded their armed forces. During the same period, the Norwegians followed suit, becoming less and less capable of self-defense. Many Scandinavians cherished the hope that their more powerful neighbors would respect their independence as had been done in 1914.

The Low Countries: Belgium and the Netherlands

The Dutch had succeeded in staying neutral throughout World War I. The Belgians, whose lands were inconveniently included in the operation of the Schlieffen Plan, were not so lucky. Until the German invasion, the Belgians had not demonstrated any particular affinity for the Entente, their relationship with Germany being very amicable as befit their interests as a small power. Before 1914, Germany was Belgium's major trading partner. Similarly, the Dutch had also been favorably disposed toward Germany. Although the war presented a threat to their independence, they steadfastly adhered to their policy of neutrality despite Allied efforts to bring them into the war—the Allies treated the Dutch with hostility when they refused. In contrast, the Belgians, who had been such conspicuous victims, came out of the war as heroes. This high regard brought them few advantages, however.[28]

Both Belgium and the Netherlands were constitutional monarchies with sovereigns responsible to the will of the people as expressed through representative institutions. In fact, though, both monarchs had extensive prerogatives, the most important being the right to form a new government after an election or the fall of a cabinet. During these interim periods, the crown became the center of political activity and could be a real force, given the often confused nature of the multiparty systems. Both monarchs were deemed inviolate and were not responsible for the measures a cabinet adopted in their names.[29] Of the two, the Belgian king had more opportunity to exercise his personal authority. As commander-in-chief of the armed forces, he could assume personal command of the army, and he traditionally played a major role in shaping the country's foreign policy.[30] The historical reverence accorded the institution of the monarchy in Belgium resulted in a politically docile people. The multiplicity of factions further heightened the sovereign's influence.

In the Netherlands, the sheer number of national parties with comprehensive programs and distinct ideologies was enormous. In 1933, for example, fifty-four parties ran candidates in the national elections. Usually, however, some combination of the five most important parties formed a coalition. The situation was similar in Belgium, although the total number of parties was smaller and the ideological divisions were less acute. The extension of the suffrage at the end of the nineteenth century presented the traditional conservative, or liberal, parties with a challenge from the socialists who advocated the abolition of class distinctions and a redistribution of wealth. These leftist parties wanted to use the power of the government, not private enterprise, to solve the nation's problems. In general, Belgian socialists were less doctrinally rigid than their Dutch counterparts, a flexibility that accounted for their inclusion in most of the interwar governments. The Dutch socialists were more interested in revolutionary theorizing than pragmatism. They did not participate in a cabinet until August 1939. In addition to strong socialist and liberal parties, both countries had confessional parties, a religious feature almost unique in European affairs and a significant political presence.

In both countries, the strength of the religious parties provided much of the stability usually associated with the political center. The confessional parties wanted to preserve a Christian society within a democratic framework by halting secularization and the growth of state power. In practice, this meant that the various groups strived to create and preserve their own organizational structures within the life of the nation. They wanted their own schools, trade unions, cultural clubs, and radio stations. In the Netherlands, the groups were divided between Catholics and Protestants. In Belgium, the main religious party was exclusively Catholic, its support coming mainly from the Flemish-speaking parts of the country. (The French-speaking Walloons were generally more anticlerical.) The presence of special-interest religious parties added to the other divisions in Belgian and Dutch political life, but the impassioned speeches of the religious leaders did not lead to any violent confrontation. The major political groupings preferred to cooperate quietly with each other to make the parliamentary system work. Consequently, in the interwar years the representatives of religious groups participated in all the cabinets in both the Netherlands and Belgium. In Belgium, the prime minister was usually a practicing Catholic. These parties wanted to protect the prerogatives of their respective religions rather than bring about any great change in the economy or society. They were therefore great defenders of the status quo. However, such conservatism did not please everyone. In Belgium, young Catholics who venerated the cult of authority were attracted by an extreme right movement known as the Rexists.

The Rexist movement was born at the Catholic University of Louvain in 1923 when a group of students organized a political action group called the *Ligue de jeunesse nouvelle* (New Youth League). The league advocated restoring order and authority to the state, a goal reflected in the new name of their organization *Ligue pour restoration de l'ordre et de l'authorité dans l'état*. The league followed the example of the Action Française in France until the pope denounced the latter organization for paganism. Léon Degrelle was one of the early members of the league. In 1930, Degrelle became the head of the Christus-Rex Catholic publishing house, sponsored in part by the Catholic Association of Belgian Youth. Degrelle, then only twenty-four, began building an empire that included a network of religious weeklies, all propounding his beliefs that Belgium needed to be reformed along corporate—that is, Mussolinian—lines. He formed the Rex party and ran candidates in the May 1936 elections. With astounding success, his forces managed to win over 11 percent of the popular vote, earning them thirty-three seats in the parliament (twenty-one in the lower house, eight in the Senate). Degrelle had not stood for election himself, but his call for national regeneration had reached a sympathetic audience.

The Rexists had been extremely energetic in attacking the corruption of the prevailing party system. They proved to be less effective in the day-to-day business of government. Denouncing others led to headlines but not to constructive programs. Besides, the Rexists were poorly organized, and their rowdy behavior in the legislature, as well as in the streets, alarmed many people, including the hierarchy of the Roman Catholic church. Rexist party meetings frequently provoked such violence that the government had to proclaim martial law. Degrelle talked about making heads roll and developed ties with Mussolini from whom he received money. In April 1937, Degrelle tried to win a seat in parliament in a by-election. The current prime minister, Paul van Zeeland, head of the Catholic party, met the challenge head on and ran against him. The primate of Belgium, Cardinal Joseph van Roey, archbishop of Brussels, joined the fray by urging Catholics to vote against Degrelle. Van Roey openly condemned Rexist doctrine and tactics. Van Zeeland swept the contest with a 76 percent majority, sending the Rexists into decline. By 1939, they had only four representatives in parliament, one of these being Degrelle himself who finally found a "safe seat." With the war and a little help from its Nazi friends, however, the organization managed to stage a comeback.

The passing of the Rexist threat coincided with the recovery of the country from the depths of the depression. The recovery produced an interesting phenomenon. Unlike the situation in Germany, the Belgian electorate did not vote heavily for extremist parties when the economy was at its worst (in 1932), but waited until the recovery was already advanced. The same pattern was apparent in the Netherlands, with many Dutch voting for an authoritarian movement of national regeneration in 1935 when the worse was over. In that year, the Dutch National

Socialist party scored its greatest success by winning eight percent of the popular vote in the elections for the Provincial States (upper house of parliament). Two years later, however, in the voting for the Second, or lower, Chamber, its support fell by half. By then, production had again reached the levels set at the end of the previous decade. Thus, both countries flirted with extremism but were unwilling to go ahead with the marriage; nevertheless, during World War II, Dutch and Belgian extremism contributed to the extension of Nazi tyranny.

POSTSCRIPT   The late thirties were not unlike those years before World War I when social change had been greatly anticipated. In Britain, the National Government could have used the power of the state to end the current economic malaise, but Chamberlain turned his primary attention to foreign affairs. The British people did not criticize him for this; they were willing to postpone the new society in exchange for peace. In the end, they had to wait for both. In France, the Socialist party finally had a chance to form a government in 1936, ending a dogged, self-imposed exile from participation in "bourgeois" cabinets dating back thirty years. The Socialists underwent a revival under Léon Blum; nevertheless, they were still unable to gain the political power they had assumed would naturally be theirs once the ballot box was opened to all people. This, plus a certain middle-class conservatism, prevented them from taking bold new initiatives.

After World War I, political leaders thought the key to their nation's prosperity lay in a rapid return to the practices of the past. The war upon which both France and Britain blamed all of their current economic problems had shown the difficulty of recovery without the direct participation of the state. After 1931, whether they consciously realized it or not, British and French leaders thought less in terms of the way things had been done and more in terms of finding solutions to satisfy an age yet to come. Government planning, although carried out with a certain amount of confusion, was questioned less and less and formed the basis upon which the societies of both countries would be structured after World War II. The existence of Fascism in both countries was more a manifestation of discontent with the current ineffectual leadership than a serious challenge to the constitutional order, even though the movements' zealots were no friends of democracy. Proto-Fascist movements were a European-wide phenomenon. Even stuffy Switzerland witnessed as much as 40 percent of its German-speaking electorate voting for brands of the radical right during Fascism's heyday.

The Scandinavians did not undergo such prolonged soul-searching. Socialist parties took control of the levers of power and proceeded confidently to engineer the transformation of society, producing a certain amount of state ownership of services and a significant extension of welfare. The Scandinavian socialists expanded the regulatory powers of government to prevent economic recession and raise the standard of living. They had no desire to use this authority to destroy capitalism and could cooperate with most of the other constitutional parties. Like Britain and France, all the smaller democracies rejected Fascism, but they could only watch hopelessly as it became more powerful internationally. They took refuge in neutrality, hoping that this would protect their independence. The Czechs tried a different approach by seeking alliances; they nevertheless remained equally vulnerable.

The French and British also indulged in a large amount of wishful think-ing. A popular song of the period told the tale of a vacationing noble-woman who telephones her butler, James, to find out how things are at home. James begins by telling her of the death of her favorite horse and finishes by telling her that she has lost everything she has, including her husband. After each item, in this gradual cascade of horrors, he reassuringly adds: "But aside from that, Madame Marchioness, Everything's going all right, everything's all right."[31] Many would have liked to believe as much.

ENDNOTES

1. The official name of the French Socialist party was the *Section française de l'interna-tionale ouvrière* (French section of the worker's international or SFIO).

2. Tariffs were imposed on all imports except certain raw materials and products from the Dominions.

3. A crucial test came at the Imperial Economic Conference, which convened in Ot-tawa from 21 July to 20 August 1932. The Dominions were hesitant to abandon protectionism for a dubious preference on the British market, and the final agree-ment was lopsided. Britain continued to grant imperial preference; the Dominions kept tariffs with the United Kingdom the same, but raised them against other countries.

4. Brian R. Mitchell, *European Historical Statistics, 1750–1970* (New York: Columbia University Press, 1975), 171.

5. Those Labourites who had refused to be associated with MacDonald's coalition held less than 10 percent of the seats in Parliament following the October 1931 elections.

6. See Colin Cross, *The Fascists in Britain* (New York: St. Martin's Press, 1963) and Richard Thurlow, *Fascism in Britain, 1918–1985* (New York: Blackwell, 1987).

7. Mitchell, *European Historical Statistics*, 171.

8. John Campbell, "Stanley Baldwin" in John P. Mackintosh, ed., *British Prime Minis-ters in the Twentieth Century* (New York: St. Martin's Press, 1977), 188–216.

9. There was another complication that had nothing to do with the divorce business. Sir Robert Vansittart, the permanent head of the British Foreign Office and the un-official chief of MI-6, the British Secret Service, was convinced that Wallis Simp-son had leaked British state documents in the possession of the king to the Ger-mans. Charles Higham, *The Duchess of Windsor: The Secret Life* (New York: McGraw-Hill, 1988), 152–55.

10. The authorized biography of Chamberlain is Keith Feiling, *The Life of Neville Cham-berlain* (London: Macmillan, 1946).

11. Leopold Amery, *My Political Life*, vol. 3 (London: Hutchinson, 1955), 225.

12. Ibid., 169.

13. The Hawkers derived their name from the "hawkers" who peddled royalist newspapers on street corners.

14. An official investigation a year later concluded that Stavisky had indeed shot himself, but that the police had refused to call medical assistance, allowing him to bleed slowly to death.

15. A secret organization known as *La cagoule* (The Hood), which claimed it was saving the republic from a Communist takeover, made an unsuccessful attempt to overthrow the government in November 1937. Philippe Bourdrel, *La Cagoule* (Paris: Albin Michel, 1970), 251–312.

16. The Socialists had 146 seats (an increase of 49); the Radicals had 115, a decline of 43; and the Communists had 72, a significant increase from 10.

17. André Nouschi and Maurice Agulhon, *La France de 1914 à 1940* (Paris: Fernand Nathan, 1974), 76–82.

18. Mitchell, *European Historical Statistics*, 356.

19. Ibid., 365–66, 372, 395, 401, 405, 462, 481.

20. Ibid., 389, 425.

21. See Joseph Rothschild, *East Central Europe between the Two World Wars* (Seattle: University of Washington Press, 1974).

22. The 1921 census recognized a separate Jewish nationality that persons of Jewish faith could embrace if they desired. Only 180,000 of the 354,000 Jews living in Czechoslovakia chose to do so.

23. Victor S. Mamety and Radomir Liza, *A History of the Czechoslovak Republic, 1918–1948* (Princeton, N.J.: Princeton University Press, 1973), 77–78.

24. See Francis G. Castles, *The Social Democratic Image of Society* (London: Routledge and Kegan Paul, 1978).

25. Eric S. Einhorn and John Logue, *Modern Welfare States: Politics and Policies in Social Democratic Scandinavia* (New York: Praeger, 1989), 12–15.

26. Neil Elder, Alastair Thomas, and David Arter, *The Consensual Democracies? The Government and Politics of the Scandinavian States* (Oxford: Martin Robinson, 1982), 17–21.

27. Mitchell, *European Historical Statistics*, 356–57.

28. See Gordon L. Weil, *The Benelux Nations: The Politics of Small-Country Democracies* (New York: Holt, Rinehart and Winston, 1970); and Vernon Mallinson, *Belgium* (New York: Praeger, 1970).

29. In the Netherlands, Wilhelmina reigned from 1890 to 1948; in Belgium, Albert I reigned from 1909 to 1934 and Leopold III from 1934 to 1951.

30. See E. H. Kossmann, *The Low Countries, 1780–1940* (Oxford: Clarendon Press, 1978).

31. André Gauthier, *Les chansons de notre histoire* (Paris: Pierre Waleffe, 1967), 198.

CHAPTER 11

REPRESSION AND REACTION IN THE LESSER POWERS

PREFACE   In most European countries, the love affair with democracy proved to be a mere infatuation, a relationship that hardly lasted past the first encounter. Woodrow Wilson had been a powerful suitor, but Benito Mussolini proved a more enticing one. In retrospect, it was not so surprising. Many states lacked the stability upon which successful free institutions could be built. Authoritarianism seemed the perfect remedy for social disorder, economic malaise, and political upheaval. Most of the states that were trying democracy for the first time lacked any modern experience of statehood. Even in Spain, which had a representative constitutional monarchy and a long tradition of unity, the ties to the feudal past with all its separatism and regionalization were difficult to shake. Most of the Eastern European peoples had learned the art of government by serving under the tutelage of imperial masters, and their sense of purpose was built more on xenophobia than on a larger idea of community. Considering the amount of disaffection and mutual hostility among their mixed populations and ethnic minorities, achieving a sense of national identity was difficult, if not impossible. Liberal solutions were never very popular, and minority problems, as often as not, were handled by force. Authoritarianism was so ingrained that few could envision government by any other means.

Liberal institutions failed in Spain because the Spanish people could not live at peace with themselves. They preferred fighting each other to working together to develop their natural wealth. Spain had achieved unity earlier than most other European states, but nowhere was localism, and the wish for separatism, so strong. The country's inability to adjust to a new set of political and economic circumstances in the nineteenth and twentieth centuries had made it, with the exception of Portugal, the most backward country of Western Europe. As the Spanish monarchy lost its traditional status as a symbol of national unity and authority, the army rose to an unprecedented position of power. Movements for local autonomy sprang up among the Catalans, Basques, and Galicians. Praetorianism and separatism were symptoms of the fundamental disagreement of Spaniards over their basic governmental structure. Spanish generals dreamed of saving their country by taking over its government.

The countries of Eastern Europe had never had the opportunity to develop a national identity, let alone solve their fundamental economic and social problems and alleviate class antagonisms. These states, lacking the minerals and industry of Spain, were still primarily agrarian. In the Great Depression, the lowering of world prices for foodstuffs had a disastrous effect on national income. To make the agricultural sector competitive and efficient, even in more prosperous times, would have required a capital investment far beyond the means available. Eastern Europe was "peasant Europe" with 75 percent of its combined population of 300 million existing as they had for centuries. The industrial proletariat and middle class were numerically small, but politically important.

Democratic institutions could not hope to solve in a few years the problems of centuries. Indeed, they seemed to open the gates to radicalism and revolution. Dictatorships of the right offered protection against chaos and promised to encourage the growth of a national spirit. Fascism went a step farther; it pretended to point the way to a complete social regeneration that would cure malaise and stagnation. But most of the strong men of Spain and Eastern Europe were more interested in protecting the traditional institutions of the church, monarchy, aristocracy, and army against social upheaval than they were in creating a brave new world. They lacked Fascism's strong sense of political unity as well as its large base of popular support.[1] They relied on courtiers, upper-middle-class professionals, land-owners, and military officers—a social grouping hardly well equipped to solve the nation's social problems and diminish its ethnic hatreds. Most of these countries had restive minorities hungry for greater independence. The absence of respect for the rights of others produced the chaos, terrorism, and butchery around which the political life of their nations turned.

THE RISE AND FALL OF THE SECOND SPANISH REPUBLIC

The End of the Monarchy

The Rule of General Primo de Rivera. World War I contributed to a rapid expansion of Spanish trade with Britain and France and a subsequent rise in the size of the urban proletariat. The boom did not last. With the end of hostilities, foreign demand for Spanish products declined, leaving the workers with falling wages and widespread unemployment. In Barcelona, the anarchist-dominated National Confederation of Work organized a series of protest strikes; employers countered by forming special protection societies complete with hired gunmen. During 1920 and 1921, class warfare and political terrorism caused the death of at least 139 people. The inability of the government to ensure order brought the army directly into politics—not a new phenomenon in Spanish history—and it crushed the strike by force of arms. The army's successful restoration of order at home was offset by its failure overseas.

In June 1921, at Anual in the central Riff of northern Morocco, an army of Berbers, led by Abd el-Krim, annihilated half the effective command of General Fernandez Silvestre's 18,000-man army. Following a further victory at Mount Arrui, Abd el-Krim became the undisputed master of central Spanish Morocco. The defeat provoked a huge outcry back home. The Spanish army, for all its bellicose pretensions, had proved worthless as a fighting force. An investigation revealed that corruption, mismanagement, and incompetence were widespread. Certain army officers were accused of embezzlement and cowardice, and King Alfonso XIII was suspected of complicity. The uproar prompted Miguel Primo de Rivera, the captain-general of Catalonia, to seize power on 13 September 1923. Primo purportedly did so to maintain public order and give his country "unity, honesty, and a sense of purpose."[2] The king betrayed his oath to the constitution by approving the takeover.

Primo found the exercise of power rewarding. He had originally promised to step aside after ninety days, but this time limit stretched on into the next decade. The dictator's greatest success came when he ended the Moroccan crisis by assuming personal command of the army. By 1927, he had managed to pacify the entire region, but needed considerable help from the French in the process.[3] Primo also stimulated Spain's economic growth. He built more modern roadways and improved the railway system, pushed electrification into rural areas, and stimulated business through increased government spending. Throughout the rest of the 1920s, Spanish productivity grew by more than 30 percent. It was killed by the world depression, but Primo was in trouble politically even before the full impact of the collapse was felt.

Although a great admirer of Mussolini, Primo failed to build up a mass following or to institutionalize his dictatorship. In fact, he successively managed to antagonize most of the important elements of society. Professors, intellectuals, and students protested the censorship and interference in the universities. Separatists denounced the general's endorsement of Castilian centrism. Financial interests were enraged at his irresponsible banking and investment policies. The liberal and professional middle classes resented being treated with contempt. To make things worse, none of Primo's grandiose schemes to transform the Spanish economy survived the slump of 1929. Primo could ignore most of this criticism as long as he retained the support of the army, but eventually this was no longer certain. Artillery officers revolted when Primo changed their system of promotion, and their discontent spread throughout the army. Primo addressed a letter to all the garrisons in Spain saying he would resign if his fellow officers declared against him. They did, and their vote of no confidence pushed the king to request the dictator's resignation. Primo left office on 28 January 1930 and went immediately into exile. He died shortly afterward in Paris in a small hotel on the Rue du Bac.

A New Constitution. Primo's resignation came too late to spare Alfonso XIII blame for the general's dictatorship. In the elections of April 1931, all the major cities and provincial capitals voted for republican candidates. In the trade union strongholds of Madrid and Barcelona, demands for an end to the monarchy were heard. Support for the monarchy came only from the rural areas, where the regime still controlled the election process. The king, realizing he had few defenders, left in a motor car for France. He claimed he had saved his country from "a fratricidal civil war." Given his lack of popularity, he assumed too much.

After his departure, the Liberals and Socialists organized a provisional government with Niceto Alcalá Zamora as president. Elections held on 28 June 1931 for a new National Constituent Assembly gave power to a Center-Left coalition of Socialists, Radicals, and Catalonian and Galician regionalists. The new constitution created a secular democratic state. It promised to protect labor, provide social security, reform the agricultural sector, and grant local autonomy to the country's regional minorities.[4]

The Second Republic came into existence at a difficult time.[5] The world demand for Spanish commodities, including iron ore, copper, mercury, olive oil, flax, tobacco, wine, and oranges, had declined. Between 1930 and 1932, sales fell by almost two-thirds (from 2.3 million to 742,000 pesetas). Only a few goods, like textiles, maintained their usual levels of production. Falling prices caused landowners and industrialists to cut wages and reduce their labor force. To balance the budget and help meet its obligations, the government floated a series of bonds and imposed new property and excise taxes. In an effort to alleviate unemployment, it instituted public works, such as the construction of a subway to link the three railway stations of Madrid. It also planned to modernize Spanish agriculture, but lacked sufficient capital to do so. All major political groups, including the conservatives, recognized the backwardness of Spanish agriculture, but they strongly disagreed on the steps needed to improve it.[6]

The Second Republic faced other problems as well. The new constitution was vehemently anticlerical. It recognized civil marriage and divorce (dissolution of marriage by mutual consent or for just cause), mandated the secularization of education, and promised an end to all state and municipal aid to the church and its institutions. Certain religious orders, including the Jesuits, were dissolved. Others were prohibited from participating in "industry, commerce or teaching." Their right to hold property was limited, and their wealth became subject to taxation or nationalization. These moves distressed many progressive Catholics, who had originally supported the Republic; now they were outspokenly hostile and bitter.

Nevertheless, from 1931 to 1933, most of the constitution's religious articles became law. On 10 May 1933, the Law of Religious Confessions and Congregations decreed an end to all Catholic primary and secondary education within six months. The Republic embarked on a national program of school building, but the dissolution of the Catholic schools left a vacuum that obviously could not be filled at once. Many reformers, however, felt that no instruction was preferable to Catholic instruction. Meanwhile the Spanish bishops openly defied the law by forbidding Roman Catholics to accept state education and by continuing the parochial school system. They had the support of most of the middle and upper classes who believed that the preservation of Catholic instruction was necessary for political order and social stability. Conservatives and moderates deplored the permissiveness of the government toward leftist civil disobedience. Although much of the Spanish working class was committed to evolutionary change, a significant element was highly militant. Here, traditional Spanish anarchism with its commitment to "propaganda by deed"[7] blended with radical Marxist socialism. The desire for revolution was strong among the rank and file in the trade unions.

In 1933, the ruling coalition fell apart when the republicans refused to accept more Socialist legislation. The president dismissed Prime Minister Manuel Azana in September and dissolved the Cortes, the Spanish national parliament. New elections were set for the coming November.

The Clash of the Extremes

A Drift to the Right. The national election of 1933 was a referendum on all the reform legislation enacted over the past two years. The campaign lasted six weeks and marked the official reentry into politics of the antidemocratic Right. The monarchists were still split between the Carlists and the Alphonsists, two branches of the royal family. And the recently organized Fascist party, the *Falange Española*, led by José Antonio Primo de Rivera, the late dictator's son, as yet had no large following. None of these groups had much success at the polls. The conservatives gave most of their support to the Confederation of the Autonomous Right (*Confederación Española de Derechas Autónomas* or *CEDA*), whose parties scored an impressive triumph and emerged with the most seats in the legislature.[8] The CEDA appeared willing to tolerate the Republic as long as it protected traditional social and economic privileges and upheld the authority of the Catholic church. It was determined to see that the Law of Congregations would never be put into effect. The CEDA's chief, José Mariá Gil Robles, advocated the Christian Socialism expounded by Pope Leo XIII in his encyclical *Rerum Novarum*.[9]

Despite the strength of the CEDA, President Alcalá Zamora refused to entrust the government to Gil Robles because he believed that Gil Robles and his followers were insincere in their support of the Republic. Alcalá Zamora therefore called upon the Radical leader, Alejandro Lerroux, to form a cabinet. Lerroux filled all the principal cabinet posts with members of his own party. Nevertheless, the power of the CEDA could not be ignored forever. Within the year, three of its representatives had joined the government.

The Socialists and their Radical allies used this as a pretext for action. Fearing the inclusion of conservatives in the cabinet would lead to the abandonment of earlier reforms, trade union chief Largo Caballero and other militant labor leaders organized the Workers' Alliance to carry out a nationwide protest campaign. In October 1934, uprisings occurred in Madrid, Catalonia, the Basque provinces, and the Asturias.[10] The government in Catalonia, the *Generalitat*, refused to recognize the central government's authority over land reform. The Socialist party became increasingly radical; many of its leaders believed that if the party could not come to power legally, then it was acceptable to do so by revolution. The 1934 revolts had little cohesion and practically no coordination, however. The government restored order quickly in all areas except the Asturias. There the workers wanted more than a simple blood sacrifice.

The Revolt in the Asturias. The Asturias region, isolated in northern Spain between the Cantabrian Mountains and the Bay of Biscay, contained some of the country's richest mineral deposits, but wealth from its coal, iron, zinc, and copper fields and its deposits of mercury, manganese, and vanadium brought little benefit to the local inhabitants, a group of almost pure Celts. The Asturians lived in a series of relatively small mining communities, spread out along the mountain valleys down the Aller and Nalon rivers west of the provincial capital of Oviedo. The depression hit the region particularly hard. Between 1930 and 1934, Spain's annual output of coal fell by almost one-fifth, with prices tumbling even farther.

The Asturians had an extremely close-knit society, intensely parochial and deeply imbued with class consciousness. Their labor unions gave them the protection and sense of purpose that the hazardous and unsanitary circumstances of their work failed to provide. Here, unlike the rest of the country, the various working-class groups experienced a common sense of mission. Sectarian squabbles among Socialists, Anarchists, and Communists were laid aside as various local village committees cooperated in the Workers' Alliance under the slogan "Working-class brothers, unite."

On the night of 4 October 1934, in conjunction with the revolts in Madrid and Barcelona, Asturian revolutionary committees responded to the formation of the new conservative government by calling for a general strike. The next day, a force of two hundred miners took control of the town of Mieres, touching off a revolt that soon spread over the entire province. Thirty thousand armed workers, outnumbering the government forces by at least ten to one, occupied every important city, including eventually the provincial capital of Oviedo, and demanded their own autonomous people's republic.

The Asturian revolt was isolated from the events elsewhere in Spain, however. With the rapid restoration of order in Castile and Catalonia, the authorities in Madrid were able to concentrate their forces. The Lerroux government was reluctant to order regular army troops to fight their fellow Spaniards and sent instead the elite units of the Foreign Legion and the regiments of the North African Moors. The counterattack began on 10 October. After a week and a half of bloody fighting, the workers' revolt was smashed. In a final act of desperation, the workers wantonly destroyed any property that symbolized the establishment: churches, police barracks, and government buildings. Meanwhile, the victors treated the Asturias as a conquered nation; they instituted a systematic reign of terror, compounding the horror of the butchery that occurred during the actual fighting with judicial murder. According to the modest figures the Ministry of Interior released later, the October rebellions cost the lives of 1,335 Spaniards and left 2,951 wounded. Most of these casualties occurred in the Asturias. The revolt had raised the specter of class warfare over Spain, preventing any prospect of reconciliation between the Left and the Right.

Spain was being torn apart by its extremes. The revolts of 1934 had showed the low esteem that large sections of the Left had for constitutional niceties. Now that the revolts had been put down, the Right turned against the reforms of the past with renewed energy. It halted the redistribution of agricultural land, refused to enforce welfare legislation, and scorned public education. The Catholic church continued to operate its schools with the state paying the wages of clergy who did not belong to religious orders. The right-wing government became increasingly reactionary. It stripped the regulatory and arbitration commissions of their progressive chairmen, suspended the statute of autonomy for Catalonia, and instituted press censorship. Minister of War Gil Robles wanted to revitalize the army and protect it against leftist influence, arousing suspicions that he and other CEDA leaders were plotting to turn the Republic into a clerical, corporate state. On the other side, the Right was convinced that the Left was intent on establishing a people's republic, and it ordered a general roundup of suspected revolutionaries. The size of the *Guardia civil*, the natural predator of the working class, was increased. Many conservatives now believed that the only force capable of bringing an end to the public disorder and halting the course of Communist revolution was the army.

Army Intervention. The Republic's founding fathers had tried to eliminate military influence from government affairs. They had renounced war as an instrument of national policy and had suppressed the politically influential post of captain-general. They had also repealed the Law of Jurisdictions, which gave the army the right to court-martial "slanderous" civilians. And they had begun to discharge superfluous officers, allowing all those who refused to take an oath of allegiance to the new constitution to retire on full pay. However, ministries changed so often that the army was never really brought under the control of the civilian government.

In September 1935, the Lerroux cabinet—the twenty-sixth since the Republic had been founded four and a half years before—fell because of a financial scandal. Since President Alcalá Zamora could find no suitable replacement, he dissolved the Cortes on 4 January 1936 and called for new elections the following month. The principal parties of the Right—the Agrarians, the Confederation of the Right, the Monarchists, and the Carlists—formed a National Front to present a common list of candidates at the polls. The Left did likewise, bringing together the Republican Left, the Social Democrats, the Catalan Separatist Left, and the Communists into a Popular Front.

The balloting took place on 16 February 1936 almost without incident—only three men were reportedly shot—and resulted in a narrow victory for the Popular Front.[11] The electorate had rejected the leadership of the Right without giving firm support to the Left. Azana again became the head of the government and, in one of his first official acts, pardoned all those who had been arrested in the aftermath of the October 1934 rebellion. He then lifted the suspension of Catalan autonomy and once more pushed for agrarian reform. Although Azana appealed to the Spanish to remain calm, scarcely a day went by without beatings, arson, or murder. Extremists on both sides committed outrages. While Largo Caballero traveled around the country advocating a dictatorship of the proletariat, the army readied itself for action.

Military plotting against the Republic had begun almost as soon as the constitution had been adopted in 1931. Army leaders, keen to preserve national unity, were fearful of any situation that suggested the disintegration of the Spanish nation. The victory of the Popular Front, and the acts of violence that followed, prompted the generals to discuss dates for a *pronunciamento*. The rebellion's architect was General Emilio Mola Vidal, the commander of the Pamplona military district. Mola wanted to purge the country of Socialists, Freemasons, Anarchists, and Communists. He believed that once the military had restored order, power would be returned to the conservatives, with the army retaining control only of the Ministry of the Interior. He wanted to preserve legitimate reforms, including the separation of church and state, and did not favor a restoration of the monarchy. Mola established contact with a broad spectrum of rightist politicians—the Carlist pretender; the monarchist leader, Calvo Sotelo; the leader of the rightist CEDA, Gil Robles; and the founder of the Falange, José Antonio Primo de Rivera. Nevertheless, Mola intended that the forthcoming takeover would be primarily a military show.

Although officers had talked revolt, Mola found that many were reluctant to commit themselves and that the only units that could be counted on with absolute certitude were those stationed in Morocco. He managed to get one of the key figures, Francisco Franco, to join the rebellion, but only in June. The doubts of many other fence sitters were not resolved until 12 July 1936, when Calvo Sotelo was murdered by leftist members of the security police in retaliation for the shooting of one of their officers by Falangist gunmen. The conspirators now scheduled the uprising for the night of 15 July. Spain, as it had done so many times in its past, was about to drown its problems in blood.[12]

THE STRONG MEN OF EASTERN EUROPE

The Danubian Dictatorships

The Regency of Hungary. Hungary discarded its democracy in 1920, the first Eastern European country to do so. The Hungarians hardly missed it. Regent Miklós Horthy began his rule with a "White Terror" that was famous throughout Europe for its brutality. Its victims were not only the Communists of Béla Kun, but all those whom the new masters did not like: Socialists, farm laborers, city workers, and Jews. Admiral Horthy and his National Union party controlled both houses of parliament, which had become little more than a private club for wealthy landowners. Together they built a semifeudal political system that continued to govern in a semifeudal political way. The National Union party was not so much a party as a collection of individuals who were useful to the regime. Parliament continued to exist, but only as a blind for the dictatorship. Horthy's paternalism was atypical of Eastern European dictators. He liked to believe that he came from a class—the landowning gentry—that truly represented all that was best in Hungarian life, and he insisted that greatness had been thrust upon him and that he had never acquired a thirst for power.[13]

In 1921, Horthy chose Count Isteván Bethlen as his prime minister.[14] Bethlen operated in the interests of the historic ruling classes. Although his contempt for the proletariat was enormous, he allowed the Social Democrats to organize trade unions as long as their activities did not extend outside the cities. The Horthy regime intended to maintain full control over the countryside where the great landowners held sway. In those areas, all voting was done publicly for maximum control. The Horthy machine turned Hungary into a paradise of voter apathy and stage-managed elections. The representatives of the opposition parties obtained seats in parliament mostly through the sufferance of the regime rather than through fair election results. The old vested interests held sway in the Upper House. They included members of the Habsburg nobility, high church officials, representatives of rural and municipal councils, university administrators, and leaders of agriculture and industry plus forty-four others personally appointed by the regent. Because of its traditional, conservative character, the Upper House became an opponent of the more extreme, revolutionary forces of the Right. It also became an opponent of anti-Semitism. The chief rabbi and other Jewish notables sat in the Upper House.

The prosperity that Hungary experienced in the 1920s came to an end with the Great Depression. The resultant misery boosted the fortunes of the radical Right. In 1932, under pressure from younger members of the National Union party, who blamed Bethlen for the lack of success at revising the Treaty of the Trianon and detested his toleration of the Jews, Horthy appointed Gyula Gömbös prime minister. Gömbös was a great admirer of Mussolini and had ambitions of becoming Hungary's duce. He looked for support to a whole array of patriotic societies, which were advocating a Hungarian national revival based upon Christianity and racial purity. Gömbös had once been one of their number, but his ambitions were now

**THE DICTATORSHIPS OF EASTERN EUROPE
1919–1939**

Map 8

FINLAND

0 ——— 300 miles

0 ——— 300 km

SWEDEN

DENMARK

BALTIC SEA

**ESTONIA
1934**
Tallinn
Tartu

Riga
**LATVIA
1934**

Memel
LITHUANIA   **1936**
Kaunas
Vilna

Duna River

EAST
PRUSSIA

U.S.S.R.

GERMANY

Oder River

Vistula River

Posnan
Warsaw
Lodz
**POLAND
1926**

Dnieper River

Krakow
Lvov

Niemen River

CZECHOSLOVAKIA

Danube River

Dniester River

Inn River
Salzburg
Vienna
**AUSTRIA
1934**

Budapest
**HUNGARY
1920**

Drava River
Zagreb
Szeged

Sava River

Kishinev

**ROMANIA
1938**

Ploesti
Bucharest

ADRIATIC SEA

Sarajevo
Belgrade

Danube River

ITALY

**YUGOSLAVIA
1929**

Sofia
Varna
Burgas

BLACK
SEA

TYRRHENIAN
SEA

ALBANIA

**BULGARIA
1919**

**GREECE
1936**

AEGEAN
SEA

TURKEY

restrained by the very system he wanted to exploit for his own advantage. He could not abolish parliament or indeed rise above the post to which he had been appointed. He hardly had the makings of a popular demagogue and was leery of any political factions that appealed to the country's lower classes. He came down especially hard on the Agrarian party of Tibor Eckhardt, who was preaching land reform on behalf of the country's three million tenant farmers. Gömbös talked about economic and political reform but in fact accomplished very little except to strengthen the authority of the state, which he bolstered with his mystical, romantic notions of Hungarian nationalism.[15]

In the elections of 11 April 1935, the candidates of the opposition outpolled the official government party by over 100,000 votes out of the 2 million cast. However, because of gerrymandering and fraud, they received only 50 seats in the Lower House. Gömbös saw to it that the National Union party received 166 seats and that the government offices reflected his choices. He died in 1936 before he had an opportunity to develop this strength into a personal political base, but his legacy of political bossism was dangerous enough. In addition he committed Hungary to a German-Italian orientation in foreign affairs—a fatal combination.

Kalaman Daranyi succeeded him at a time when Hungarian National Socialism was posing an increasing threat. This extremist party appealed to the disadvantaged lower classes and to the resentful half a million ethnic Germans who lived in the northern part of the country. The strength of the movement prompted the government to improve its own position by seeking alliances with the moderate Left, which was also alarmed at the rise of Adolf Hitler and his totalitarianism.

One of the most powerful radical right-wing groups was the Arrow Cross movement of Ferenc Szálasi, who claimed that he had been divinely ordained to redeem the Magyar people.[16] He believed that a Hungary under his leadership could develop a truly Christian moral order and become the supreme power in Europe's Carpathian Basin. The Jews would have no place in this state; Szálasi considered them a pestilence and wanted them expelled from Hungary. He would allow them to take some of their property with them, however. This "generosity" made Szálasi a moderate within his faction, which included many who favored a more extreme policy including extermination. Szálasi was also a strong antifeminist, believing that a woman's place was in the home. In marked contrast to Hungary's aristocratic rulers, however, he apparently had a genuine concern for the welfare of the lower classes. Under the Arrow Cross, the nation would be a working nation comprised of peasants and industrial workers. Intellectuals would guide the affairs of state under Szálasi's direction.[17]

By the summer of 1937, the Arrow Cross had a membership of 20,000. Szálasi toured the country building up further support. Some of the party's lieutenants won election to parliament in a by-election. As a section of the Budapest press endorsed the program of the Arrow Cross, rumors circulated that Szálasi was planning a coup. Horthy had had enough. The regent replaced Daranyi with Béla Imrédy and ordered a crackdown. In February 1938, the police arrested Szálasi and three score of his associates. But even with their leader in prison, the popularity of the Arrow Cross continued to grow. In the May 1939 elections, it received 750,000 out of 3 million votes cast, finding its greatest support in working-class districts. The government continued its offensive. It tried to steal the radical Right's thunder by promising economic reforms and limiting the participation of Jews in business and the professions. At the same time, Horthy continued to maintain good relations with Germany whose help he needed to achieve Hungary's revisionist aims.

Almost all Hungarians still wanted the restoration of the historic lands of the Crown of St. Stephen that had been lost at the end of World War I. Part of Szálasi's popularity stemmed from the emphasis he put on regaining these possessions to create a unified Carpatho-Danubian Great Fatherland that would include parts of Yugoslavia and Romania. Horthy's aims were more modest, but he still would need outside help to achieve them. Throwing in his lot with Hitler was a dangerous gamble. It not only sidetracked the government's efforts to solve pressing social and economic problems, but also risked transforming the Hungarians from German allies into German vassals.[18]

The Austrian Fatherland Front. The Austrians also had difficulty establishing their national sovereignty. Their country was small, it had an exposed geographical position, and it was weakened by religious, ideological, economic, and social divisions. Only the Social Democrats and some liberals had supported the 1920 democratic constitution. The conservative Christian Social party, which in the early years of the Republic had grudgingly tolerated the country's representative institutions, had become increasingly attracted to authoritarianism, especially so as it seemed the best way to crush the power of the Social Democrats. The Catholics had never even adjusted to the liberal, secular trends of the nineteenth century.

The Great Depression heightened existing tensions. The proposed customs union with Germany was another sign of the nation's underlying uncertainty about its own future. The issue of *Anschluss*, or union with Germany, continued to be one of the nation's most complicated and politically divisive issues. Immediately after World War I, a majority of Austrians had favored Anschluss, but many of those who initially supported it developed second thoughts. Many had come to associate their northern neighbor with a revival of Prussian militarism. Staunch Roman Catholics feared the pernicious influence of German Protestantism. The Social Democrats were of two minds. Certain party leaders thought union with Germany would lead to a decline in their own importance, while others welcomed integration with Germany's strong Social Democratic movement. Cutting across all groups and classes, however, was a basic nineteenth-century pan-Germanism. This continued to thrive even after, or because of, the rise of Hitler.

Following the failure of the Kreditanstalt, Austria's central bank, the government enacted a drastic program of austerity. This did little good, and in desperation Austria turned again to the League of Nations for help in regulating its accounts. In May 1932, the new Christian Socialist government of Engelbert Dollfuss managed to secure a loan of 300 million shillings. In exchange, Austria had to promise not to form any economic or political association with Germany for the next twenty years. The pledge raised a storm of protest and gave the Social Democrats further ammunition with which to attack the Christian Social party. The Social Democrats had the largest number of deputies in the Austrian parliament, but they steadfastly refused to participate in any national union government and worked instead to keep Dollfuss from getting a viable majority.

When Hitler became chancellor of Germany in January 1933, the *Grossdeutsch* deputies in the Austrian assembly (those representatives who favored union with Germany) withdrew their support from Dollfuss's coalition, bringing parliamentary life to a standstill. President Wilhelm Miklas then authorized Dollfuss to rule by decree. Dollfuss disbanded the *Schutzbund*, the Social Democratic party's paramilitary army, curtailed freedom of the press, and forbade political parades and assemblies. When the Austrian Nazis defied the ban and staged a rally on 29 March, he called forth the police and had the demonstrators arrested. Relations with Germany consequently deteriorated, and Dollfuss turned to Mussolini for support.

The death of Austrian democracy delighted the Duce. He had much in common with the principles of the rightist *Heimwehr* (Home Guard), which was working to turn Austria into a one-party, corporate state.[19] The Heimwehr's Korneuburg Oath could have been written in Rome. It denounced the Marxist class struggle, the liberal capitalistic economic order, and democracy. The Heimwehr wanted to establish a national leadership government that would consist of "leading members of the large corporations and of the ablest most trustworthy men in our own class movement."[20] Above all, the Heimwehr wanted to destroy the Austrian Social Democratic party.

When Dollfuss visited Rome at Eastertime in 1933, Mussolini encouraged him to turn Austria into a true one-party state. Pius XI gave Dollfuss slightly different advice. Playing on Dollfuss's mystical, fervent faith in Catholicism, Pius told him to establish the corporate political system that the pontiff had described in his recent encyclical, *Quadragesimo Anno*. Dollfuss took the pope's advice to heart, and shortly after he returned home, he founded the Fatherland Front in cooperation with the Heimwehr. In June, he suppressed the Austrian Nazi party; eight months later, on 11 February 1934, his government decreed the abolition of all political parties save the Fatherland Front. The Social Democrats answered with a general strike. Dollfuss then proclaimed martial law and, with help from Heimwehr units, proceeded to crush the Social Democrats by force. The government used artillery to shell the great blocks of workers' apartments in the Viennese suburbs of Ottakring, Döbling, and Florisdorf. The municipal Social Democratic government had taxed wealthy property owners to build these structures, the largest of which was the famed Karl Marx Hof. (Once the buildings were erected, though, the workers complained about their shoddy construction.) They looked like fortresses, but were hardly meant to withstand a military attack. The buildings soon collapsed in rubble. Fighting continued for another three days and ended with the utter defeat of the Social Democrats.[21] The burial of Austrian democracy followed quickly. Dollfuss announced his intent to govern according to the corporatism of Pius's *Quadragesimo Anno*.

On 1 May, a new, highly authoritarian constitution replaced the original constitution adopted in 1920. The leaders of the Fatherland Front now ruled Austria through the bureaucracy and the police. The chief of the Heimwehr, Prince Rüdiger von Starhemberg, became vice-chancellor. In crushing the Social Democrats, Dollfuss had further weakened his country's independence, opening the door wider for National Socialism.

Hitler reacted to the ban of the Austrian Nazi party by creating the Austrian Legion. He stationed this force in Bavaria near the Austrian frontier and directed it to train with units of the SS and SA. The Austrian government had removed a powerful source of opposition to German intervention when it destroyed the Social Democratic party. Only the Austrian Catholic church now seemed to stand in the Führer's way. Hitler had little regard for Austrian nationalism; he dismissed

The aftermath of the attack on Socialist party headquarters in Vienna. Fatherland Front and Heimwehr forces used machine guns and light artillery to reduce the building to shambles in February 1934. The destruction is physical evidence of the death of Austrian democracy.

the Heimwehr since many of its followers were already pro-Nazi. By the beginning of July, the Austrian Nazis operating outside the country were ready for action. Their leader Theodor Habicht planned to have a special SS unit composed of Austrian war veterans topple the government by kidnapping Dollfuss and his entire cabinet. In a parallel action, they would seize the Viennese radio transmitter and the telephone exchange. A new National Socialist government would then take power and immediately petition Hitler for incorporation into the Reich. The plotters assured the Führer that the putsch would be supported by units from the regular Austrian army. Hitler, seeing a cheap way to achieve his goals, gave his approval and told the conspirators they could count on his support.

One hour past noon on 25 July 1934, 154 members of SS Standarte 89, disguised in Austrian uniforms, entered the courtyard of the Austrian chancellery in trucks. They easily overpowered the guards and entered the building. The government had been warned, however, and most of the ministers had already fled. Only three were captured, including Chancellor Dollfuss. In the ensuing melee, he was shot twice, one of the bullets entering his neck. The putschists dragged the wounded man to a nearby sofa, covered him with a piece of canvas, and let him slowly bleed to death. They even refused Dollfuss the last rites of the Roman Catholic church. Meanwhile, units of the Austrian army and some from the Heimwehr surrounded the chancellery and crushed the revolt. Nazi disturbances outside the capital—in Styria, Carinthia, and the Tyrol—were also put down. Within three days, the Austrian government was again in control of the situation. Hitler pulled in his horns, not the least because he feared Mussolini would intervene to prevent the expansion of German power by keeping Austria independent.

With Dollfuss dead, Vice-chancellor Starhemberg moved to take control of the government. But President Miklas, wary of the growing power of the Heimwehr, chose the relatively unknown minister of education, Kurt von Schuschnigg, instead and made Starhemberg head of the Fatherland Front. The arrangement added to the precariousness of the chancellor's position. In October 1935, Schuschnigg ordered the Heimwehr disbanded and removed its ministers from the government. He then proclaimed himself führer of the Fatherland Front, which he tried to expand into a national coalition, including even token remnants of the Social Democratic party. Schuschnigg tried to preserve Austrian independence, but the country lacked the strength and unity to prevent it from being drawn increasingly within the German orbit.[22]

The Polish Overlords

Domination by Pilsudski. The Poles had no democratic tradition, but they were not prepared to scrap parliamentary institutions entirely. The legislature continued to meet; its members could even criticize the government, but it had no power to change the nature of the regime. Marshal Josef Pilsudski, who had seized power in a coup d'état in May 1926, ran the state with a mixture of military authoritarianism and big city machine politics. Pilsudski hoped to strengthen Poland through dictatorship, but despite his determination and prestige, he never succeeded in mobilizing the mass support necessary to create real national unity. His semi-autocratic system gave Poland a measure of cohesion, but his relations with parliament became increasingly strained, especially during the depression years from 1929 to 1933. Industrial production fell by 37 percent; foreign trade revenue was down by 72 percent; and government income declined by 38 percent.

Six parties from the Center and the Left formed an alliance to try to force Pilsudski's resignation. The marshal responded by ordering the dissolution of parliament and the arrest of many opposition leaders. Then, through intimidation and direct manipulation of the electoral process, he engineered a resounding victory in the November 1930 elections, producing a legislature of guaranteed subservience. The regime now became more severely authoritarian. Pilsudski, suffering from poor health, depended more than ever on a small group of old military associates—the so-called colonels. These men looked forward to the day when they would govern without Pilsudski. They favored total abolition of the 1920 constitution in favor of a more structured oligarchy, a change that would, in fact, be accomplished in April 1935, just three weeks before Pilsudski's death.

The Rule of the Colonels. Under this new constitution, the president had increased authority to legislate by decree and to control parliament through the direct appointment of senators. Pilsudski's old position of inspector-general was still the most important position in the government and was now occupied by Marshal Edward Rydz-Smigly. Rydz-Smigly, favoring the creation of a true Fascist Polish state, furthered the establishment of a National Unity party as the only legal political party in the nation. Pilsudski had died at an opportune time for his reputation. His successors, lacking his charisma, now had to cope with all the problems that the old marshal had failed to solve. Despite more civilian participation in the affairs of state, the military still continued to set policy.[23]

Nevertheless, the opposition, though weakened, was not yet eliminated, and with the return of a certain amount of economic stability, it tried to reestablish its strength through direct action. In 1936, a wave of protest strikes swept the country. Twice as many work days were lost as in the previous year. The Agrarian and Socialist parties, denied representation in the national parliament by the new electoral law, concentrated their attention on the municipal level. During the fall of 1938, they managed to capture most of the available seats in the city council elections. Their dramatic victory deterred Rydz-Smigly and his gang from establishing tighter control over the country. But this bitter confrontation between those who desired the restoration of the democratic constitution of 1920 and those who favored dictatorship was a game that could have no winners. It sapped the nation's strength and diverted attention during the time of its greatest danger.[24]

Royal Autocracy

The Yugoslavian Monarch Takes Charge. The palace putsch of King Alexander in 1929, which had suspended parliament and outlawed all political parties, increased the friction already existent among the country's three main ethnic groups.[25] Alexander confirmed and extended the political primacy of the Serbs at the expense of the Slovenes and the Croats. He smothered protest with arrest and imprisonment, while proclaiming that he intended to create a new nation through the fusion of all its peoples. But Yugoslavian nationalism was a myth. Each ethnic group was unwilling to give up its own identity in favor of some vague, possibly insincere concept of nationhood. Alexander had no faith in democratic institutions and genuinely believed that he was acting out of the deepest concern for the unity of his country and the future of his dynasty. He wanted to build a new national unity, improve the well-being of his people, and defend society against Communism. But his policy failed. The well-organized Croats answered repression with violence. They hated the Serbs with a primeval passion and felt they had been freer under the Hungarians. In 1934, the leading Croat terrorist organization, the Ustashi (Ustaše), assassinated Alexander in Marseilles while he was on a state visit to France. The crime was so horrible that, for a time, people rallied to the monarchy, but the spirit of cooperation did not last long.

A regency under Alexander's brother, Paul, was established in favor of Alexander's eleven-year-old son.[26] Paul tried to appease the Croats, but Vladko Maček, leader of the Croatian Peasant party, formed an alliance with the Serbian Liberal party and demanded a democratic, federal constitution. Following their success in the 1938 elections, the opposition forced the resignation of Prime Minister Milan Stojadinović and his cabinet. Maček then lobbied for Croatian home rule and threatened to seek the help of Nazi Germany to obtain complete independence if his demands were not granted immediately. Alarmed, the new government of Dragiša Cvetković created an autonomous Croatia and, at the same time, promised to reestablish democratic government throughout the kingdom. The breakdown of international order soon overshadowed constitutional reform. A barter agreement tied Yugoslavia to Germany economically, but the arrangement was not popular. The opposition favored a revitalization of the Little Entente, the alliance with Czechoslovakia and Romania, and a strong association with France. These counsels were lost on Prince Paul and his advisers who continued to move their country closer to Hitler.

King Carol and the Romanian Iron Guard. The Yugoslav example of monarchical dictatorship was contagious. In 1925, the heir to the Romanian throne Prince Carol had renounced his rights of succession, left his wife, and gone to live in France with his fiery mistress, Magda Lupescu. When Carol's father, King Ferdinand, died in 1927, a regency council was created in favor of Carol's six-year-old son Michael. Meanwhile, Carol was becoming bored with life abroad. In 1930, with the permission of Premier Julius Maniu, the leader of the National Peasant party, he returned home. Maniu hoped that Carol, who enjoyed a certain popularity among the Romanian people, would add ballast to his government, which was being battered by the growing economic recession.

Carol, backed with support from the army, soon proved more than Maniu could handle. The premier, already in poor health, resigned when Carol refused to honor his promise to give up his mistress and return to his wife. But Maniu's real reason was Carol's constant attempts to divide and conquer by inciting the main parties against each other so he could form his own party. Cabinets and ministers were circulated in and out of office with the rapidity of a revolving door. During the 1930s, Romania had eighteen different premiers; governments changed at the rate of over two a year. Carol ruled parliament through a regent's party, established with royal supporters in the Liberal and National Peasant parties. His administration was dictatorial and anti-Semitic.

Romania was experiencing the growth of an authoritarian movement of another sort in the Fascist Iron Guard. This organization had developed out of the Legion of the Archangel Michael, founded in 1927 by Corneliu Codreanu. Codreanu believed in "righteous violence" to bring honesty and discipline to the nation.[27] The main source of Iron Guard strength came from white-collar workers and university students. The group, under Nazi urging, directed its attention to increasing its following among the ranks of the urban and rural working classes. The Iron Guard's program was rather vague. It wanted to replace the present society with a new order based on honesty, responsibility, and industry. In short, it espoused goals that boy scouts swear to uphold, but laced them with a cult of violence and hatred of the Jews. Soon the Iron Guard amassed enough strength in parliament to prevent the formation of a workable coalition government; at the end of 1937, it provoked the dissolution of the legislature and forced new elections.

In February 1938, however, before these elections could be held, Carol proclaimed himself the sole source of executive and legislative power. On 8 June, parliament named him king in place of his son. King Carol promulgated a new constitution, making Romania a corporate state.[28] The king's National Renaissance Front became the only recognized political party. Codreanu called upon his followers to submit to the new royal order, but Carol took no chances and ordered Codreanu and his lieutenants arrested. In November, following an illegal Iron Guard demonstration, the prisoners were all strangled in their cells. The government claimed that Codreanu and his associates had been shot while trying to escape. The Iron Guard plotted revenge. In September 1939, it tried to seize power, assassinating Premier Armand Calinescu in the attempt. In reprisal, the government ordered the summary execution of hundreds of Iron Guard prisoners.

Carol's attempt to establish his own brand of authoritarianism independent of Nazi influence was a losing battle. On September 1940, under pressure from Berlin, he was forced to abdicate in favor of his son who became King Michael. But the real power was exercised by the Iron Guard leader General Ion Antonescu, who had been appointed premier with dictatorial powers. Antonescu turned Romania into a National Legionary State and an ally of Germany.

The Baltic States

The Origins of Independence. The sovereign independence of Lithuania, Latvia, and Estonia was brief. Success with democratic government was even briefer. The chances that they would retain either one had not been good. These states, which form a geographical unit along the Soviet Union's northwestern frontier, had been ruled by foreigners since the Middle Ages—Danes, Germans, Poles, and Swedes. In the eighteenth century, all three states became part of the Russian empire—Latvia in 1710, Estonia in 1721, and Lithuania in 1795. They remained there until the twentieth century.

During World War I, control of the area passed to the Germans who occupied Lithuania in March 1915. Gradually, they extended their military control northward until by February 1918 the entire territory was in their hands. The Germans separated the Baltic states from the Russian empire both politically and economically, posing as liberators although that was not their intention. Kaiser Wilhelm II recognized the "sovereignty" of Lithuania in March 1918, even though the country still remained part of the *Ober-Ost Verwaltung,* the general authority responsible for carrying out German policy in the Baltic provinces.[29] Under the terms of the Treaty of Brest-Litovsk and its addenda, the Bolsheviks renounced all claims to the area. Berlin had not yet decided on the Baltics' eventual political fate, but had no desire to allow them to determine their own destiny.

Germany's defeat in November 1918 and the subsequent Soviet renunciation of the Treaty of Brest-Litovsk led to a new period of struggle. The Bolsheviks wanted to re-annex the states and were prepared to crush all demands for self-determination by force. Leon Trotsky viewed the reconquest as an essential step in the march toward world revolution.[30] However, the Lithuanians, Latvians, and Estonians were no more enthusiastic about being reincorporated into Russia than they had been about being part of a Greater Germany. Local communities organized volunteer defense forces, and the provisional governments began forming national armies. Partisan forces sprang up. Many of these were able to equip themselves from arms and supplies left by the retreating Germans. Surprisingly, these ragtag forces, combined with troops that had seen military service under the tsars, were able to prevent the Red Army from taking possession of the Baltic territories. Resistance increased when the inhabitants in the areas the Bolsheviks had temporarily "liberated" had an opportunity to experience a Red Terror. The British, French, and Americans were not enthusiastic about intervening themselves, but they wanted to weaken the Bolshevik regime and briefly tolerated the continued presence of German troops in the Baltic. The Allies did not have much control over what was happening on the Soviet frontier, however, since a peace settlement there depended on how those people resolved their own differences.

Lenin had to worry about ending a civil war in the rest of the Soviet empire and was prepared to come to terms with the Baltic peoples so that he could concentrate on the remainder of the country. He also wanted to deny the area to the White Army, which might use it as a base for an attack on Petrograd. In a series of treaties signed during 1920, the Soviets recognized the independence of all three Baltic states.[31] They renounced all tsarist debts and indemnities and promised to sign trade agreements with preferential tariffs. In return, the Baltic states all pledged to allow no foreign armies to establish military bases or conduct political activities on their territories.[32] (The Soviets also obtained the right to build a free port at Tallinn, Estonia.) Had the Soviets succeeded in defeating Poland in the 1920 war, the independence of Lithuania, and subsequently that of Latvia and Estonia, might well have disappeared despite the recognition of independence.[33] Failing this, however, the Bolsheviks had at least kept the Baltic states out of the hands of their enemies.

A Search for Identity. The Baltic states drafted remarkably similar constitutions. Each established a republican, parliamentary system with a single-chamber legislature and a weak executive. Voting was by universal suffrage through secret ballot and proportional representation. All the Baltic states were multiracial in population,[34] and their economies were largely dependent on agriculture. Sixty percent of the people of Estonia, 66 percent of the Latvians, and 75 percent of the Lithuanians engaged in farming. Nevertheless, the states differed in some respects. The Lithuanians were predominantly Roman Catholic, whereas the Latvians and Estonians were mostly Lutheran.[35] They also had different languages, and their competition in foreign trade kept them from establishing close economic ties with each other.

The Baltic states emerged from the war period with their economies in recession and their administrations in turmoil. They had little experience in self-government, a common problem in Eastern Europe. Their sense of national identity was weak. For them, self-determination had meant trying to gain home rule rather than seeking independence. The first priority of their governments was to satisfy the land hunger of their people since a majority of the farming population had none at all. Much of the land had been farmed in great estates owned by a foreign upper class: Germans, Poles, and Russians. These latifundia had to be broken up for social and political reasons. All three states passed expropriation bills, taking the land with little or no compensation. (Only Lithuania paid some compensation, but only to non-Russian owners.) Such confiscation was the most revolutionary example of land reform outside the Soviet Union. The policy altered the social character of the countryside by creating a class of small landowners, but the change did not guarantee prosperity. Destroying the large estates proved easier than making the new units productive. Initially, the farm sector suffered a decline in income.

Latvia and Estonia tried to increase their national income by building up their industrial base and improving trade with the West. Exports to the Soviet Union declined while those to Britain and Germany increased. Estonia's largest manufacturing industry was textiles, while Latvia's specialty was metal products. In 1930, 17.4 percent of the Estonian work force was employed in urban industry compared to 13.5 percent in Latvia and 6 percent in Lithuania.[36] Agricultural products, therefore, continued to be the Baltics' largest export product. Consequently, the continuing prosperity of all three countries was remarkably sensitive to the prices of these commodities on the world market. During the 1920s, their income rose steadily, but this suddenly ended with the world depression. The precipitous fall in agricultural prices caused great distress in rural areas. Banks collapsed, foreign credits disappeared, and unemployment increased. The democratic systems slipped into dictatorship.

The Authoritarian Solution. Baltic politics were marked by a multiplicity of parties, weak executive governments, and rapid ministerial turnover. Between 1919 and 1933, Estonia had twenty-one governments, an average of one every eight months. This, coupled with the worsening economic situation, led to demands that the constitution be altered to create an authoritarian presidential system.[37] Attempts to accomplish this by referendum in August 1932 and June 1933 failed to win the necessary votes. However, right-wing groups, influenced by the examples of Mussolini and Hitler, persisted. In October 1933, another attempt succeeded. This scheme had the active support of the Association of Estonian Freedom Fighters. This one-time veterans' group had developed under the leadership of Artur Sirk into a Fascist-style paramilitary organization. Sirk organized his followers into companies and sections and dressed them in gray-green shirts with black and white armbands. The party emblem was a hand clasping a dagger. The new constitution created a president with full executive powers, including the ability to dissolve parliament and rule by decree.

In 1934, the campaign to elect the first president became so violent that, on 12 March, the current prime minister, Konstantin Päts, assumed emergency powers and disbanded the Freedom Fighters as a threat to the security of the state. Indeed, there was reason to believe that Sirk was planning a coup d'état. Päts suspended the presidential election, dissolved parliament, and ran the country by decree. He then drafted a new constitution and, in 1938, had himself installed as Estonia's first president. The constitution guaranteed freedom of expression, but allowed that freedom to be restricted "in defense of the security of the State, of public order, morality and the good name of the citizen." Päts believed that the current international situation was too ominous to allow the Estonian people to exercise the civil liberties laid out in the constitution.[38] Supported by the army, he pushed Estonia toward a one-party state. His government limited freedom of speech, censored the press, and curtailed the activities of the unions. The regime was authoritarian, but not tyrannical. Liberties were restricted, but some dissent was tolerated.

In Latvia, the effects of the world depression and the growth of authoritarianism throughout Eastern Europe and in Germany strongly influenced the growth of antiparliamentarian movements. As in Estonia, demands arose from both the Right and the Left to increase the power of the executive. Various Fascist groups called for the persecution of the Jews and the other national minorities; they also wanted a planned economy. Some admired Hitler; others were anti-German. One of the latter was the ultranationalist Thunder Cross organization whose members wore gray shirts and black berets and shouted Fascist slogans. Thunder Cross members hated Jews and democratic politicians. Premier Karlis Ulmanis, taking his cue from recent events in Estonia, assumed emergency powers under the pretext of preventing a Communist takeover. On 16 March 1934, he suspended parliament, limited political activity, and ordered the arrest of the leaders of the Thunder Cross organization. Most of the other political parties were proscribed as well. Ulmanis ruled the country through a special directorate. In 1936, he further consolidated his authoritarian rule by fusing the position of president with that of premier. As in Estonia, the Latvian leaders believed that it was necessary to destroy democracy in order to save it. Practically no protest was raised by the Latvian people.

Lithuania's path to dictatorship was paved with rural distress and unemployment. Popular discontent led to the growth of authoritarian political movements, ranging from Fascist militias to veterans' organizations. On February 1934, the government passed a law for the protection of the state and nation.[39] This led to increased unrest, which prompted a government crackdown on all political parties except that of the ruling Nationalists. In February 1936, a new constitution enhanced the powers of the presidency. Antanas Smetona, who had held the office since 1926, assumed the title of leader of the people and turned Lithuania into a one-party state. Thus, the Baltic states proved no exception to the Eastern European rule. Yet the dictatorships that emerged there were not known for their brutality, nor were they firmly entrenched. In time, the states might well have found their way back to democratic liberties.

POSTSCRIPT   Democracy had disappeared in Hungary almost as fast as it had been installed. It faded soon afterward in Poland and was gone by the end of the 1920s in Yugoslavia. In the following decade, Austria, Estonia, Latvia, Bulgaria, Greece, Lithuania, and Romania all joined the march to dictatorship—a clean sweep across Eastern Europe (with the exception of Czechoslovakia), encompassing ten countries, almost 100 million people, and an area of 730,000 square miles, three and a half times the size of France and four times the size of Germany.

Yet whatever the government, little appeared to have changed. Eastern Europe was primarily agricultural, and the life of the average peasant went on much as before. In many areas, the peasants wore rags, had no money to buy shoes, and lived in primitive hovels with no modern amenities. Five or six persons might share a bed while livestock were tethered in the same room. Meat was eaten rarely, the staple diet being mostly rye bread, maize, or polenta—food that was usually sufficient to keep people alive but hardly in good health. Overwork weakened their bodies and made them more susceptible to disease.

Eastern Europe had not experienced the same massive migration from the farms to the cities that had occurred in the more advanced states of the West. The area remained essentially rural. More than three-fourths of the people in Romania, Yugoslavia, and Bulgaria earned their living from agriculture. In Poland, the farm population numbered more than 60 percent; in Hungary, it was over half; and in the Baltic states, roughly two-thirds. Only in Czechoslovakia had a real industrial society developed.

Although agriculture was pervasive, the yield per acre remained relatively low. Land reforms had been carried out in most of the newly emergent successor states, but family holdings averaged less than 12.5 acres—hardly sufficient for basic sustenance.[40] Nor had Eastern European peasants acquired the technical knowledge to maximize the yields of their fields, which were usually planted in grains and cereals, products whose prices dropped sharply during the Great Depression. For example, between 1929 and 1933, agricultural income declined over 50 percent in Hungary and over 40 percent in Romania.

The loss of so much income in an already backward economy made the fall in the standard of living especially severe. Tourists often viewed the Eastern European peoples as smiling peasants in brilliantly colored costumes cavorting to the music of quaint tunes played on ancient wooden instruments. In reality, most of the peasants in this part of Europe danced to a different tune—one of misery, boredom, and drudgery. Scant wonder that they had little time or patience for representative institutions. The new democratic order inaugurated by the Paris Peace Conference was a luxury many felt they could not afford. The question was not democracy versus dictatorship, but rather what form dictatorship would take. The choice was between a traditional type of authoritarianism and the more revolutionary sort that had been established in Italy and Germany. The allure of the radical Right lay in its promise of social progress and national purpose, although these goals were frequently to be achieved at the expense of the rights of minorities. The older, more aristocratic autocracies promised less, but asked less in return. Their reactionary nature often made them less cruel by default. If democracy in this part of Europe was highly fragile, so was national independence. These states enjoyed sovereignty on borrowed time. It was impossible for such small states to insulate themselves from the problems of the rest of Europe. Had they had more time, they might have found some solutions for their internal problems. But their freedom was possible only as long as they had no powerful, predatory neighbors. That was hardly the case.

ENDNOTES

1. For an appreciation of the diverse character of European Fascism, see Henry A. Turner, ed., *Reappraisals of Fascism* (New York: New Viewpoints, 1975). There are also informative essays in Walter Laqueur, ed., *Fascism: A Reader's Guide* (Berkeley: University of California Press, 1976); and Stuart Woolf, ed., *Fascism in Europe* (London: Methuen, 1981). Individual countries are covered in Stein Larsen, *Who Were the Fascists?* (Irvington-on-Hudson, N.Y.: Columbia University Press, 1980).

2. Compare Shlomo Ben-Ami, *Fascism from Above: The Dictatorship of Primo de Rivera, 1923–1930* (New York: Clarendon Press, 1983) and James H. Rial, *Revolution from Above: The Primo de Rivera Dictatorship in Spain, 1923–1930* (Fairfax, Va.: George Mason University Press, 1986).

3. When the Berber leader, Abd el-Krim, moved his base of operations into French Morocco, Paris sent down Marshal Pétain, in July 1925, to crush the revolt once and for all. By May 1926, Krim had surrendered and the Riff tribesmen under his command soon abandoned all resistance. Krim was exiled to the island of Réunion where he became something of a romantic hero. The Riff revolt inspired Sigmund Romberg's Broadway musical *The Desert Song* with its lyrics "Blue heaven and you and I, and sand kissing a moonlit sky . . . ."

4. For the squabbling of political parties and factions that typified the Second Republic's history, see Paul Preston, *The Coming of the Spanish Civil War: Reform, Reaction and Revolution in the Second Republic 1931–1936* (New York: Methuen, 1978).

5. A radical majority in the Spanish national assembly proclaimed the First Republic on 12 February 1873 following the abdication of King Amadeo I. It lasted until 31 December 1874 when it was overthrown by a military coup that proclaimed Alfonso XII king. Alfonso XII was the father of Alfonso XIII who vacated the throne in 1931.

6. Stanley G. Payne, *A History of Spain and Portugal*, vol. 2 (Madison: University of Wisconsin Press, 1973), 633–34.

7. Gerald Brenan, *The Spanish Labyrinth: An Account of the Social and Political Background of the Civil War* (Cambridge: Cambridge University Press, 1950), 131–66.

8. The representation of the Socialists was cut in half, while that of the Radicals barely managed to stay the same.

9. The pontiff's instruction, issued 15 May 1891, was prompted by his fear of the growing power of socialism. He reaffirmed the natural right to private property, but argued that the poor and helpless have a special claim to protection. "The richer class have many ways of shielding themselves, and stand less in need of help from the State; whereas those who are badly off have no resources of their own to fall back upon, and must chiefly depend upon the assistance of the State." Anne Fremantle, ed., *The Papal Encyclicals* (New York: Mentor, 1956), 183–84.

10. Stanley G. Payne, *The Spanish Revolution* (New York: Norton, 1970), 130–56.

11. The Popular Front parties won 256 seats in the Cortes compared to 143 for the parties of the National Front. In the popular vote, the sides were more evenly balanced, with the Popular Front receiving 4,176,156 votes and the National Front 3,783,601. In addition, the Basque nationalists, who threw in their lot with the Popular Front, had garnered 130,000 votes, and the Center parties, including the Radicals, won 681,047 votes.

12. Raymond Carr, *Spain, 1810–1939* (London: Oxford University Press, 1966); Gabriel Jackson, *The Spanish Republic and the Civil War, 1931–1939* (Princeton: Princeton University Press, 1965); and Payne, *The Spanish Revolution.*

13. Owen Rutter, *Regent of Hungary: The Authorized Life of Admiral Nicholas Horthy* (London: Rich and Cowan, 1938), 338–45.

14. Joseph Rothschild, *East Central Europe between the Two World Wars* (Seattle: University of Washington Press, 1974), 158–71.

15. Nicolas Nagy-Talavera, *The Green Shirts and the Others: A History of Fascism in Hungary and Rumania* (Stanford: Hoover Institution Press, 1970), 561–62.

16. István Deák, "Hungary," in Hans Rogger and Eugen Weber, *The European Right: A Historical Profile* (Berkeley: University of California Press, 1966), 388–91.

17. Nagy-Talavera, *The Green Shirts*, 114–120.

18. Paul Ignotus, *Hungary* (New York: Praeger, 1972), 185–92.

19. C. Earl Edmondson, *The Heimwehr and Austrian Politics, 1918–1936* (Athens: University of Georgia Press, 1978), 97–101.

20. Ludwig Jedlicka, "The Austrian Heimwehr," in *International Fascism, 1920–1945*

(New York: Harper and Row, 1966), 139.

21. Karl R. Stadler, *Austria* (New York: Praeger, 1971), 128–32, 147–48.

22. Elizabeth Barker, *Austria, 1918–1972* (Coral Gables: University of Miami Press, 1973), 97–112.

23. Jerzy J. Wiatr, *The Soldier and the Nation: The Role of the Military in Polish Politics, 1918–1985* (Boulder: Westview Press, 1988), 72–74.

24. Hans Roos, *A History of Modern Poland: From the Foundation of the State in the First World War to the Present Day* (New York: Knopf, 1966), 143–58.

25. Rothschild, *East Central Europe*, 237–40.

26. Ibid., 258–60.

27. Nagy-Talavera, *The Green Shirts*, 279–82.

28. Ibid., 284–96.

29. Alfred Erich Senn, *The Emergence of Modern Lithuania* (New York: Columbia University Press, 1959), 33.

30. Georg von Rauch, *The Baltic States: The Years of Independence, Estonia, Latvia, Lithuania, 1917–1940* (Berkeley: University of California Press, 1974), 49–52.

31. The Treaty of Tartu signed 2 February 1920 with Estonia, the Treaty of Moscow signed 9 May 1920 with Lithuania, and the Treaty of Riga signed 1 August 1920 with Latvia.

32. Rauch, *The Baltic States*, 72–75.

33. Senn, *The Emergence of Lithuania*, 220.

34. The largest ethnic minorities in Estonia and Latvia were the Russians with 8.2 and 7.8 percent of the population, respectively; in Lithuania the Jewish minority with 7.6 percent of the total population was the largest.

35. Hugh Seton-Watson, *Eastern Europe between the Wars, 1918–1941* (New York: Harper and Row, 1962), 75–120.

36. Rauch, *The Baltic States*, 124.

37. Emanuel Nodel, *Estonia: Nation on the Anvil* (New York: Bookman Associates, 1963), 172–75.

38. J. Hampden Jackson, *Estonia* (Westport, Conn.: Greenwood Press, 1979), 211.

39. Rauch, *The Baltic States*, 162.

40. Seton-Watson, *Eastern Europe*, 75–120.

PART FOUR

EUROPEAN CULTURE AND SOCIETY BETWEEN THE WARS

CHAPTER 12

AVANT-GARDE, OLD GUARD

PREFACE   World War I affected artists' lives and changed their views of society, but the fundamental vision that molded their creativity had been formed prior to 1914. Indeed, almost every work of modern art owed a debt to Paul Cézanne, who believed that a picture existed by itself, independent of any need for rational or realistic justification. According to Cézanne, the final artistic determinant was the artist himself who gave images shape, form, and color according to individual inspiration. Cézanne broke up his landscapes into their geometric components, thereby foreshadowing cubism. Cézanne's disciples also rejected the traditional lessons taught by their classical masters and thereby created an enduring revolution in the world of art.

Modern art broke with the Renaissance laws of perspective. The aim of traditional art had been to reproduce the visual world as it existed, to give an objective vision of beings and things. But once modern physics had broken down matter into its atomic components, appearances could no longer be accepted as reality. "Everything was soft, uncertain, vacillating," wrote abstract artist Wassili Kandinsky.[1] Therefore the personal truth of the artist was the only reality. "There is nothing real outside of us," Albert Gleizes and Jean Metzinger remarked, "there is nothing real except the coincidence of a feeling and an individual mental direction. We are not likely to doubt the existence of the objects that impress our senses. But we cannot be certain about the images they make appear in our mind."[2] These artists were writing about cubism, but they defined modern art.

Although the creators of modern art were not necessarily prompted by the chaos and decline of order in their societies, the increasing instability did play its part. World War I certainly reinforced and contributed to this new frame of reference. A certain fundamental belief in permanence, which had sustained earlier generations, disappeared, and many despaired that it would never return. In this atmosphere, the modern art movements that had been largely scorned before the war, in many cases because they were unfamiliar and lacked significant patronage, began to gain acceptance.

Yet the trauma of the war could just as easily lead artists to reassert older values. The conflict managed at the same time to produce a deliberately provocative movement such as dada and to reinforce the more established movements of futurism, expressionism, abstractionism, and cubism. It also led to a classical revival. The need to protest against fragmentation and the desire to return to tradition proved just as strong as the urge to pursue modernism. Moreover, representational art had a greater appeal among the population at large. Individual artists reacted in various ways. Some who had been in the forefront of the modern movement reverted completely to previous styles, seeking a safe haven from political and artistic confusion. Others, torn by multiple desires, continued both modes of expression; often their art reflected their own contradictions and indecision.

In any case, the classical revival was tailor-made for the official art of repressive regimes. Mussolini, Stalin, and Hitler all preferred traditional representational art and encouraged its production. The association of art with dictatorship did not automatically lead to inferior art, any more than the association of art with modernity produced something worthwhile. No matter how revolutionary or conservative its creators, or how enlightened or odious its patrons, the art of this period—like the art of any period—is best judged on its own merits.

ART IS ANYTHING YOU CAN GET AWAY WITH

The Surrealist Synthesis

"The World Is Blue like an Orange." In 1924, André Breton described surrealism as "Pure psychic automatism by which one is proposed to express, by either speech, by writing, or in any other way, the real process of thought." Breton, a medical student interested in Freudian psychoanalysis, said that "surrealism rests on the belief in the superiority of certain forms of previously neglected associations, in the omnipotence of dreams, in the disinterested play of thought. It leads to the definitive ruin of all other psychic mechanisms and takes their place in solving the main problems of life."[3] The poet Guillaume Apollinaire had actually coined the word "surrealism" before the war in program notes that he had written for an Erik Satie ballet, but had not defined the term. Breton's definition officially founded a movement that aimed at changing the world by freeing the individual from traditional social and cultural restraints. In this respect, the surrealist movement distinguished itself from dada, which had no such cosmic illusions. Moreover, surrealism's intellectual pedigree seemed loftier. Breton maintained that Sigmund Freud's techniques of psychoanalysis showed him the means of discovering the fundamental realities of life through the liberation of the human subconscious.

Surrealism wanted to create a new reality, to amplify life in order to revolutionize it. It therefore made an express break with dadaism and its anarchic lunacy.

The surrealists did not intend only to paint their vision, they intended to live it. To this end, they sought experience uncorrupted by the society in which they lived. "The means was simple enough: merely buy a Sunday ticket at a suburban railway station and shunt for hours and hours on all tracks of a landscape of desolation, on a journey whose end is never fixed in advance."[4] By encouraging words to flow directly from the subconscious, surrealists tried to achieve the same spontaneity and adventure in their writing. René Crevel advised authors to eliminate all rational control of expression by putting themselves into a hypnotic trance. The use of this technique produced a lot of nonsense. But it also, on occasion, stimulated some beautiful, enigmatic poetry like the verse of Robert Desnos:

> At the post office of yesterday you will cable
> that we are quite dead with the swallows
> Sad postman, postman with a coffin under your arm
> go and take my letter to the flowers with a sudden jerk[5]

Chance and the Subconscious. The surrealists went from dreams to chance. They invented a new type of literary creativity: *le cadavre exquis*. A sheet of folded paper would be passed from one player to another. Each person, without seeing what had been written previously, would add in turn a subject, an adjective, a verb, and so forth until a sentence emerged. The first product of this technique gave the genre its name: *Le cadavre—exquis—boira—le vin—nouveau* (The exquisite corpse will drink the new wine). Chance was also touted in politics. André Breton, in his Second Manifesto—written five years after the first—said, "the simplest of surrealist acts consists in walking through the streets, a revolver in each fist, and shooting haphazardly and as often as one can into the crowd." Despite such anarchistic bluster, the surrealists were hardly men of action, even though many became tremendously infatuated with the dynamics of the Bolshevik revolution.

In Western Europe, many intellectuals automatically identified with the political Left. In 1925, a group of French poets and critics, outraged by their country's involvement in the Riff war in Morocco, formed an alliance with the Communist party. But the surrealists had difficulty confining their individualism within the narrow bounds of party discipline. Breton wanted to plot grand revolutionary strategy, not, as he was required to do, draft a technical report on the Italian gas industry for an audience of Parisian workers. The party bosses had scant patience with these political dilettantes whose sense of commitment to the class struggle was so detached. Louis Aragon, who for a time put his pen at the service of the Soviet Union, once wrote that the Russian Revolution "measured by the yardstick of ideas . . . is nothing more than a trivial ministerial crisis."[6]

Most of the movement's original fire had cooled by the 1930s. By that time, in a sense, the surrealists were preaching to the converted. They were bourgeois haters when bourgeois hating was passé. They were wordsmiths with no political influence. They talked of transforming society but had no rapport with the masses. And their techniques for liberating themselves from traditional restraints were too contrived to be spontaneous. Indeed, if—as Carl Jung showed—the conscious always held the key to the subconscious, then complete liberation from present reality could never be achieved. Therefore, self-professed surrealism became more a gimmick than a technique of perceiving the "concrete face of the infinite." Although surrealist authors and poets did not place great emphasis on the visual or dramatic arts, the movement achieved its greatest permanence in those fields—in the theater of the absurd, in the cinema, and especially in art.

Shortly after the appearance of Breton's manifesto, the surrealist school of painting quickly established itself as one of the most significant movements of twentieth-century art. Fortunately, surrealism inspired several truly great artists. Although the center of its activity was Paris, many of the movement's most famous artists were non-French: Salvador Dali, whose *Persistence of Memory* gave the world the limp watch, was born in Spain, as was Joan Miró. René Magritte and Paul Delvaux were Belgian. Max Ernst was German, and Roberto Matta Chilean. Surrealist painting, the art of the fantastic, held all the fascination and dread of discovering what made a noise in an empty room. Some artists, like Dali, Delvaux, and Magritte, remained faithful to traditional concepts of perspective and conventional oil techniques; others were more revolutionary and abstract.

Max Ernst tried to carry automatic writing into the field of art with his technique of *frottage*, explaining, "I took a series of drawings from the floorboards by covering them at random with sheets of paper which I rubbed with a soft pencil. When gazing attentively at these drawings, I was surprised at the sudden intensification of my visionary facilities and at the hallucinatory succession of contradictory images being superimposed on each other." Ernst also experimented with different materials—the veins of leaves, the texture of sack cloth, or thread unrolled from a spool. Gordon Onslow Ford invented *coulage* by pouring paint in great swirls of color on his canvas. Wolfgang Paalen used a candle flame to make random burns and scorch marks, giving the world *fumage*. André Masson, finding all mechanical devices impeded his "psychic impulses," took to smearing paint and glue on a canvas with his hands, then pouring on sand.

Many surrealist painters had the satisfaction of outliving their critics and seeing their works regarded as a fountainhead of modern visual artistry. Sadly, the only tumult their work really produced was the rush of well-heeled bidders hurrying to snap up their tableaux at art auctions.

The Silver Age of the Weimar Republic

The Bauhaus. For all its political and economic shortcomings, the Weimar period remains one of the most remarkable decades of cultural creativity in modern European history. Once Germany was liberated from the ponderous academic standards of the Second Reich, new life flowed into styles previously in official disfavor. Many of the Weimar Republic's leaders, particularly the Social Democrats, saw in the works of Emile Nolde, Ernst Ludwig Kirchner, Otto Müller, and Karl Schmidt-Rottluff a common concern for society and compassion for humanity. In the Weimar Republic, artistic expression seldom strayed very far from political commitment, usually to the Left. Expressionist artists were frequently given responsible positions in state museums, professorships in art institutes, and official commissions. Schmidt-Rottluff was asked to redesign the state emblem, the imperial eagle. The tremendous demand for expressionist paintings spurred the production of expressionist drawings and graphics. Printmaking underwent such a renaissance that artists like Ernst Barlach and Käthe Kollwitz were able to establish major reputations working almost exclusively in that medium.

The Weimar Republic also established a distinctive style in modern architecture. In 1919, it commissioned Walter Gropius to reorganize the former Grand Ducal School of Applied Arts and the Academy of Arts in the city of Weimar. Gropius had sweeping ambitions. He wanted to create a pilot school of interna-

Walter Gropius's Bauhaus in Dessau, Germany, was remarkable for its extreme functionalism. Its flat roof and uncluttered walls give it a lightness in which space expands along its vertical and horizontal planes.

tional design to teach "the common citizenship of all forms of creative work and their logical interdependence upon one another." He conceived architecture as rigidly functional "whose inner logic [was] radiant and naked, unencumbered by lying facades and trickeries." His *Bauhaus* (Building Institute) style emphasized volume rather than mass. It eliminated the outside wall as the main weight-bearing element in favor of steel inside girders, which supported a concrete slab roof and floors. Through this device, the building, enclosed in a curtain of framed glass windows, could be increased in size almost indefinitely—an ideal design for factories and standardized housing.

In Germany, Gropius's most important achievement was the construction of the new Bauhaus building in Dessau, where he had moved his school in 1925. He designed the structure as a series of interconnecting rectangular and cube-shaped buildings, each with a reinforced concrete skeleton, enclosed by a glass curtain. The unit was revolutionary in its conception of space. Siegfried Gideon wrote, "there is the hovering, vertical grouping of planes which satisfies our feeling for a relational space, and there is the extensive transparency that permits interior and exterior to be seen simultaneously."[7] Bauhaus design went beyond simply constructing buildings, however. It purported to be a thoroughly integrated style, involving the design of coffee cups, furniture, stained glass windows, knives and forks, and kitchen utensils. The Bauhaus aim here, as in architecture, was to break down the artificial barriers that existed between art and science, creating a single unity. The ideal, conceived before World War I but with its first flowering in Weimar, caught on slowly. In time, its clean, functional approach to architecture and design became the major standard for the twentieth century. With Ludwig Mies van der Rohe, who fled Hitler's Germany in 1937, the style came to Chicago. Mies became a professor at the Illinois Institute of Technology and designed many important glass and steel structures in Chicago and other American cities.[8]

Tradition and Innovation in Music. The Weimar period was also a time of tremendous musical creativity. Berlin became the home of many of the world's most illustrious performers (Rudolf Serkin, Vladimir Horowitz, Gregor Piatigorsky), conductors (Bruno Walter, Otto Klemperer, Wilhelm Furtwängler), and composers (Ferruccio Busoni, Arnold Schönberg). The Berlin Philharmonic had a reputation of being one of the best symphonies in the world, and the city hosted three famous opera houses: the State, the Municipal, and the Kroll. While repertoires generally remained traditional, the works of modern composers were not neglected.

Alban Berg's *Wozzeck*, refused performance elsewhere, premiered at the State Opera on 14 December 1925. The plot of the opera about a solider who kills his mistress and then commits suicide came from a nineteenth-century play. It still had the power to disturb modern audiences. Paul Zschorlich, critic of the *Deutsche Zeitung*, wrote, "I felt that I was not leaving a public place, dedicated to the arts, but a public insane asylum, on the stage, in the orchestra, in the audience—only lunatics. . . . [Berg] is a musical mountebank, a composer dangerous to the public welfare."[9] Part of the difficulty lay in Berg's atonal score, which, like the music of his teacher Arnold Schönberg, ignored conventional harmonic relationships and gave all twelve tones of the chromatic scale equal importance and independence. To audiences used to hearing easily remembered waltzes, themes, and arias, the music was cacophonous and inane. Yet seldom had music been used to better dramatic effect.

The opera's final scene is hard to forget: Wozzeck's illegitimate son is playing with some other children, when one of them tells the boy that his mother is dead. All the other children run off to look at her body, which is lying by the edge of a nearby pool. Alone and not yet understanding what has happened, the little boy hesitates, then slowly rides off on his hobby horse to join the others, leaving an empty stage.

Expressionism's Second Generation. Postwar artists seemed to thrive on the period's decadence and neuroses. They also believed they had a responsibility for healing the German spirit and producing a new society. Directly affected by World War I, the young avant-garde artists rallied behind the socialist cause in the 1918 uprising. Artists like Gert Wolheim, Conrad Felixmüller, Otto Dix, and George Grosz adopted the bright, often garish, colors and the distorted, strident perspectives and forms of the earlier generation of expressionists (with a mixture of cubism and futurism). Thematically, they were more political than their predecessors and maintained that art could help build a peaceful and just society. Disciples of this belief formed groups in most of the country's larger cities: Berlin, Dresden, Bielefeld, Cologne, Hanover, Kiel, Magdeburg, and Munich. The most famous of these artists' associations, the *Novembergruppe*, founded in Berlin at the end of 1918, called on avant-garde artists to work for the moral regeneration of Germany. "We feel young, free, and pure," its manifesto boldly proclaimed.[10] Because the group believed that it had a special duty to gather together all significant artistic talent and "dedicate it to the collective well-being of the nation," it sponsored exhibitions and encouraged the publication of periodicals that included writers, architects, and composers along with pictorial artists. However, unity was often alien to artistic expression. One organization, one manifesto, one vision could not contain the talents of all the revolutionary artists, and the Novembergruppe soon splintered. Rival groups were formed; similar organizations operated under other leaders; and individual artists often preferred to work apart from all groups.

Berlin's most corrosive artist, George Grosz, was a member of the Novembergruppe for a brief time, but did most of his work outside its confines in accordance with his own personal vision. He had a special desire to portray the horror and violence of war and the pervasive corruption of Weimar society. Grosz adopted a new, more realistic style, which came to be known as the new objectivity (*Neue Sachlichkeit*). In 1923, Grosz published *Ecce Homo*, a collection of lithographs depicting his vision of postwar German society. The authorities protested, found Grosz guilty of "corrupting the inborn sense of shame and virtue incarnate in the German people,"[11] and fined him six thousand marks. The court also ordered two dozen of the book's most salacious plates confiscated. The artist remarked, "my drawings expressed my despair, hate and disillusionment. I had utter contempt for mankind in general. I drew drunkards; public men; men with clenched fists cursing at the moon; men who had murdered women, sitting on their coffins playing *skat*, while within the coffins would be seen their bloody victims. I drew wine drinkers, beer drinkers, Schnapps drinkers. . . . I drew a cross-section of a tenement house: through one window could be seen a man attacking his wife with a broom; through another two people making love; from a third hung a suicide with his body covered by swarming flies."[12] Although Grosz's professed loss of faith in humanity seemed to clash with his Marxism, he directed his barbs at stereotypical class enemies. *Ecce Homo* attacked the German middle and upper classes: the celluloid-collared bureaucrats; the callous profiteers; the rapacious speculators; and the overfed, cigar-smoking, smug supernationalists. Grosz drew them as squalid, sexually obsessed creatures surrounded by prostitutes. This pessimistic vision has come to be identified with the squalor of Berlin during the Weimar Republic. It is a one-sided interpretation, at best a first impression. Nevertheless, it is the view that has proved the most durable.

By the second half of the 1920s, the revolutionary dreams that had preoccupied many artists foundered on a harsher reality. Society seemed incapable of change. The working classes with whom many artists intellectually identified scorned their attempts to make contact and viewed their art with an egregious lack of comprehension. As the Weimar Republic became more bourgeois, the artists came to realize that their paintings, woodcuts, and posters might reflect their own visions and desires but would change few minds, let alone blaze a trail toward a new society.[13]

The Cinema

Didactics and Commercialism.   General Erich Ludendorff was not much of a movie buff. However, he did appreciate the political importance of the new technological iconography; and, in 1916, shortly after becoming supreme quartermaster general, he set about reorganizing his country's film industry. Through his initiative, the main film studios merged into a government-controlled consortium, Universal Film Associates (*Universum Film Actiengesellschaft*), or UFA, which Ludendorff hoped would produce more effective propaganda. The general wanted the German side of the story told in the neutral countries of Latin America and in Switzerland, Holland, and Denmark. UFA, bolstered enormously by subsidies from the public treasury, was able to improve the quality of its films, increase its production, and expand the dissemination of its product. By the end of the war, when the military dictatorship finally collapsed, the German film industry had become one of the strongest in the world and appeared to be the only one capable of competing seriously with the American movie industry.

By 1919, ownership of UFA passed to the Deutsche Bank whose directors, although no great fans of artistic freedom, were nevertheless willing to accord studio managers considerable leeway as long as they increased corporate profits.

As long as the films made money, the studios apparently could produce what they liked. In the early days of Weimar—at least until May 1920 when the Reichstag passed a law on movie censorship—the German blue movie enjoyed a gilded age. Films sallied forth with such alluring titles as *Hyenas of Lust*, *From the Brink of the Swamp*, *The Maiden and the Men*, and *From a Man's Maidenhood* (a "flicker" about homosexuality). Occasionally, one of these creations actually attained a certain artistic respectability. For example, *Vow of Chastity* (a tale of a libidinous priest) featured the novel technique of crosscutting, showing scenes of the cleric in flagrante delicto interspersed with scenes of his congregation praying for his soul.

Richard Oswald, who had learned his craft directing wartime training films, including one about the evil effects of syphilis, a venture for which he cleverly got the endorsement of the Society for Combating Venereal Disease, became one of the most successful practitioners of celluloid pornography. With public demand for his talents running high, he built an entire career around his less than socially redeeming creations.

The costume drama also enjoyed great popular success. *Madame Dubarry* combined boudoir romance with history, interspersing revolutionary violence with bed-hopping. In the last reel, the heroine, whose immoral goings-on have apparently led to the fall of the ancien régime, is led to the guillotine while a bloodthirsty mob demonstrates its approval with shouts and clenched fists. The film's director, Ernst Lubitsch, said that he endeavored to produce the same nuance in crowd movements that he had in the more intimate scenes. His artistry, however, eluded many Germans who enjoyed the film on a more primitive level. German audiences appreciated *Madame Dubarry* because it associated sexual decadence with their hated former enemy, France. French authorities denounced the film as a smear and a distortion; naturally, the denunciation boosted attendance. Other historical extravaganzas that also enjoyed notable success included: *Danton*, another grandiose misrepresentation of the dynamics of the French Revolution; *Anne Boleyn*, an excuse for showing the sexual appetites of King Henry VIII; and the intentionally ultranationalist *Fredericus Rex*, which appeared in 1923, the same year as the French invasion of the Ruhr.

Innovation and Creativity. The cinema was obviously not an exclusively German medium. The filmmakers of Hollywood had a tremendous and sustained impact on every aspect of the cinematic art in all countries, including the Soviet Union. The movies bridged high and low culture. In Germany, the output not only reflected the age's commercialism and new permissiveness, but was accorded the traditional respect with which the Germans had always viewed creative artists. Before the war, the most prestigious field for directors and actors was the legitimate theater. However, the film industry's endorsement by the state helped to dissipate such prejudice. At the same time, serious critics were able to appreciate the medium's capacity to create new levels of expression and philosophical vision and to make use of styles of expression found in the other visual arts.

In February 1920, during the same week as the beginning of the Kapp Putsch, Robert Wiene's *Das Cabinet des Dr. Caligari* (*The Office of Dr. Caligari*) premiered in Berlin. The film tells a gruesome tale of a sinister mountebank who hypnotizes his medium, Cesare, and programs him to kill his enemies.[14] Caligari represents the insanity of unlimited power, and his medium is the common man, which the authoritarian state trains to do its killing. Expressionistic sets further dramatize the film's sinister treatment of murder and terror. Material objects are handled subjectively, with stark black shadows painted across geometrically irregular streets, win-

In Robert Wiene's "The Cabinet of Dr. Caligari" (1920) Cesare carries a victim across sinister rooftops.

dows striped like arrows or kites, and rooftops running in zigzags among leaning chimneys. Wiene's forboding and ominous atmosphere heightens primitive sensations and experiences in his outward projection of psychological events.[15]

Power and madness, as well as the macabre and the supernatural, were frequent subjects of the art film. Two years after the release of *Caligari* came *Nosferatu*, the first movie version of Bram Stoker's novel *Dracula*, directed by Friedrich Wilhelm Murnau. A person has only to look at Count Orlok's pointed ears, bad teeth, and mandarin-style fingernails to know he is up to no good. He is the un-dead serial killer, and he brings death wherever he goes. The ending is upbeat: the count/vampire stays out past his bedtime and conveniently dissolves in the rays of the morning sun. Fritz Lang's *Dr. Mabuse, der Spieler* (*Doctor Mabuse, the Gambler*) was more in tune with the daily life of the times. The film depicts the career of a master criminal who heads a gang of counterfeiters, thieves, and murderers. Although Mabuse is eventually apprehended, his kind of depravity, terror, and chaos plainly will never end. Lang meant the film to be a comment on German postwar society in which evil existed everywhere without localization or control.

Directors like Murnau and Lang became famous for their ability to sustain dramatic intensity through the creation of atmosphere and contrast within shots. They excelled at selecting camera angles and camera movements that added emotional weight to their characters and settings. Their best works became classics, setting a standard of excellence for succeeding generations of German filmmakers. The expressionist vogue in German filmmaking lasted only a short time and even in its heyday constituted only a small part of total production. As the Weimar Republic achieved a certain amount of stability and acceptance, the cinema of the fantastic and unreal gave way to more conventional subjects that reflected people's immediate circumstances or their romantic ideals—the way they hoped life might be.

Matinee idol Walter Slezak recalled that such dramas fell into three types.[16] In the *Innocent boy seduced by the worldly-wise vamp films,* the boy's father finds out, buys off the vamp, and becomes her lover himself, but *only* to show his son what a worthless woman she is. In the *War hero films,* a young naval officer, son of a great war hero, is regarded as a coward because he does not believe in self-sacrifice and death for the Fatherland. He falls in love with a nurse, but when she rejects him, he gets mad; and the next time he goes to sea, he dies, after committing all sorts of brave deeds that earn him a hero's burial wrapped in an imperial flag. When the nurse hears the tragic news, she bursts into tears but still reveals her pride. In the *Student films*, the scion of a wealthy and prominent family goes off to the university where he falls in love with the daughter of his landlady who is neither prominent nor wealthy. His family finds out and tries to break up the romance. The son contemplates suicide, but a kindly professor dissuades him. He decides to marry the girl anyway, his family forgives him, and the movie ends with the singing of "Gaudeamus Igitur." This genre became the most popular of all.

To Serve the Interests of the Proletariat. In the Soviet Union, where everything had to serve a strict political purpose, frivolous themes were considered counter-revolutionary. Boy-meets-girl was not as important as boy-meets-tractor. Lenin immediately saw the vast potential for political propaganda in the Soviet motion picture industry, and in 1919 he decreed its nationalization. He supposedly wanted to bring the American director David Ward Griffith, best known for the epic *Birth of a Nation*, to Russia to take charge of production.

The Soviet film industry was in sad condition. Its equipment was antiquated, there was hardly any film, and about the only movies produced were some agricultural/revolutionary pieces, one-reelers heavily larded with praise for the wisdom of the Bolsheviks. Soviet film directors were allowed to practice their craft only insofar as they pleased the regime. As a result, most of them became artistic hacks. A few talented cinematographers, however, freed from having to worry about box office receipts, took the opportunity to concentrate on technical experimentation. Whatever international reputation the Soviet film industry achieved came largely from a handful of able directors including Vsevolod Pudovkin, Aleksandr Dovzhenko, and, the most famous of the group, Sergei Eisenstein, whose *Battleship Potemkin* was one of the best films, albeit propaganda films, of all time.

This work, made to commemorate the revolution of 1905, was intended to symbolize the determination of the Russian working class to achieve freedom through revolution. Eisenstein carefully organized his shots to portray particular social and political conditions. A close-up of maggots crawling around in a sailor's

The film "Battleship Potemkin" (1925) shows the forces of tsarism crushing a popular demonstration on the great steps of Odessa. No such incident actually took place, but director Sergei Eisenstein liked the setting and made it seem that it had.

meat depicted "the inhuman conditions in which the whole mass of exploited classes . . . lived."[17] Similarly, the characters were meant to be types, rather than specific individuals. Eisenstein searched until he found people who possessed the greatest number of traits he wanted to represent. In an Odessa hotel, he found a furnace keeper, whose appearance he deemed just right for the part of the ship's surgeon. Eisenstein dressed the man in a tsarist uniform and gave him a pince-nez on a thin gold chain. The prop helped symbolize the character's "physical and mental shortsightedness," and Eisenstein hoped that whenever it appeared on the screen, it would force the viewer to reconstruct the whole picture from one of its elements. The use of this device—often overworked today—became a trademark of Eisenstein's cinematography.

Techniques of the New Art Form. Eisenstein is even better known for his development and use of montage; that is, the careful editing and arrangement of shots within sequences to, as he put it, "evoke in the perceptions and feelings of the spectator the most complete image of the theme itself." The technique supposedly arose from the necessity of working with unexposed celluloid only a few frames in length. In linking together a whole series of different shots for maximum psychological impact, however, Eisenstein often seemed just as motivated by the demands of political ideology.

While filming his version of the Bolshevik coup in *Ten Days That Shook the World*, he noticed a large clock in the Winter Palace with a main dial surrounded by a series of smaller dials that simultaneously told the time in the other cities of the world. Eisenstein decided to use this clock for a special montage effect that would:

> drive home especially forcefully the historic moment of victory and establishment of Soviet power . . . we repeated the hour of the fall of the Provisional Government, dependent on the main dial in Petrograd time, throughout the whole series of subsidiary dials recording the time in London, Paris, New York, Shanghai. Thus this hour, unique in history and the destiny of peoples, emerged through all the multitudinous variety of local readings of time, as though uniting and fusing all peoples in the perception of the moment of victory.

The rotation of the surrounding smaller dials dramatized the same concept. They revolved ever faster, making "a plastic fusion of all the different separate indices of time in the sensation of one single historic hour."[18]

The Soviets recognized Eisenstein's importance as a pioneer in the development of modern cinematography after the premier of *Battleship Potemkin* in Berlin. German critics were lavish with praise that continued when the film opened in other Western cities. World fame did not make the director's work any easier, however. The government suspended his next film, on the collectivization of agriculture, and denounced as formalistic his film on the Bolshevik revolution. Between 1927 and 1928, the official Communist censors suppressed half of the 135 films that were produced, causing the motion picture industry to degenerate until it produced only propagandistic sermons. Eisenstein completed fewer and fewer films. Those he did make, notably *Alexander Nevsky* and *Ivan the Terrible*, revealed flashes of his earlier brilliance, but were overly contrived, suffered from technological imperfections, and contained more clichés than second-rate Hollywood westerns. His films became increasingly difficult to enjoy.

The most prolific and famous artist of his time, Pablo Ruiz Picasso was born on 25 October 1881 in Málaga, Spain. He first learned to draw from his father, José Ruiz Blasco, an art teacher, painter, and curator of the local museum, who saw that his son was well grounded in the classical style of art, especially the traditional laws of proportion and harmony of color. Pablo became so formidable a draftsman that Don José abandoned his own painting and gave his son all of his materials when Pablo was thirteen years old.

In 1895, the family moved to Barcelona where Pablo enrolled at the local School of Fine Arts. He stayed there two years before moving on to the more prestigious Royal Academy of San Fernando at Madrid. Pablo's developing personal style and growing professional confidence put him increasingly at odds with the strictures of art taught by his hidebound professors. He quit the Madrid academy to return to Barcelona, which was then in the throes of a modernist revolution, just the sort of atmosphere to stimulate experimentation and independence. But Pablo still felt constricted, and he persuaded his father to give him the money to go to London. On the journey, he stopped off in Paris, which so impressed him that he decided to go no farther. Henceforth, during the most creative periods of his life, the French capital would be his home. At this time, he adopted his mother's maiden name as his own, Picasso being less common than Ruiz. The change also dramatically symbolized the break that he made with the academic and, for him, stultifying artistic values of his father.

This initial association with Paris, and with it a prolonged exposure to the works of Degas, Gauguin, and Toulouse-Lautrec, led Picasso to modify his artistic style. He eliminated bright colors from his palette, began painting in monochromatic blue, and substituted flatter, more solid surfaces for his carefully modeled figures. Picasso, though, could not remain faithful to any one style for long. By 1904, his mood had changed; he abandoned cold colors in favor of warmer, more romantic tones. He also found new subject matter, painting circus performers instead of the downtrodden and the poor. But just as the Blue Period had passed, so did the Rose Period. His new paintings became more classically ponderous, perhaps even naïve, in their reflection of prehistoric art. The twenty-four-year-old Picasso had apparently found a style that he could exploit for years to come. Yet, he was on the threshold of a sudden change in direction that would lay the foundations of modern art.

During the last half of the nineteenth century, French artists had discovered new ways of expression in which they depicted light through color and distorted perspective to transform shape and form. These innovations strongly influenced Picasso, but until 1906, he had yet to go beyond them. In that year, however, he began working on a canvas that would break completely with the traditional spatial organization of the past. In *Les demoiselles d'Avignon* (*The Young Ladies of Avignon*), painted on a canvas nearly eight feet square, he showed the distorted anatomy of five nude women in a jarring assembly of disorderly facets, triangular and rectangular wedges, and other confusing geometric shapes. Two of the figures are wearing hideous African-like masks. The eyes of the other three are on different levels, and their noses jut out like pieces of architecture. The painting has no rational focus of attention; the viewer is forced to look everywhere as if at pieces of broken glass. *Demoiselles* is now recognized as the first truly modern painting of the twentieth century. However, when Picasso showed the painting to his friends—none of whom were exactly reactionaries when it came to accepting new ideas—the

Picasso's "Les Demoiselles d'Avignon" (1907) reflects the artist's explorations of African and Spanish art, with more than a passing reference to the art of Henri Matisse and Paul Cézanne. The eclectic geometry of its composition and distortion of its perspective helped set Picasso's creative direction for much of the remainder of his life.

reaction was almost universally negative. As a result, Picasso rolled up the canvas and refused to exhibit it publicly, thereby preventing it from having a direct influence on the course of the modern movement. Nevertheless, the painting had firmly established Picasso's artistic direction; it marked his great adieu to the past.

In embarking on this hazardous artistic journey, Picasso had had a guide in the mature works of Cézanne, which had also distorted shapes and contours and broken down images into an infinite series of individual geometric perceptions. Picasso and his close collaborator Georges Braque, who had been heading in the same direction, invented cubism. They broke down their figures into a series of flat tonal planes that in succeeding pictures became progressively more abstract. Their palette was reduced to only a few colors. So close was Picasso's association with Braque that it was often difficult to tell which painter painted which canvas. The partnership ended, however, with the outbreak of World War I and Braque's departure for military service.

Despite these advances, Picasso did not completely abandon realistic portraiture; the academic realism of his youth persisted into the modernist synthesis of his early adulthood. Many of his more traditional figure paintings reflect his interest in sculpture; frequently the subjects were inspired by classical mythology. Sometimes, he would alternate, doing a portrait first in one style and then in another. He reintroduced perspective depth into his cubist paintings, making their figures less abstract yet more fantastic, a characteristic that pointed in yet another direction.

Picasso's ensuing productivity is almost impossible to classify neatly. Throughout the interwar years, he continued to distort human anatomy, reemploying a technique he had developed in his early cubist days. This entailed rearranging pictorial features so that one part of the anatomy is seen simultaneously from many angles at once—front, back, and side. *Guernica* (1937), his most famous painting of this period, shows this technique as well as his preoccupation with violence. The masterpiece, nearly twelve by twenty-six feet, was finished as a commemorative protest of the German bombing of that Basque city during the Spanish Civil War.[19] *Guernica* was a universal statement of human anguish expressed through cubist and expressionist techniques. The terror of the people and animals was depicted through exaggeration and distortion, through the overlapping planes and absence of modeling. Picasso displayed the painting at the Spanish Pavilion of the 1937 International Exposition in Paris where it became the center of attention and controversy.

By this time, Picasso had become sufficiently famous that anything he did became noteworthy: his numerous affairs with women, his membership in the Communist party, his friendships with writers and movie stars, his work habits, and tastes in food. Dora Maar, his mistress during the *Guernica* period, said that during Picasso's postcubist days, the woman he loved influenced his style, as did the place he lived, his circle of friends, and even his dog. Western society, which so highly prized artistic diversity and innovation, revered Picasso as the quintessential genius. A master in every medium he put his mind to—painting, sculpture, graphics, ceramics—he, more than any other single artist of his age, altered the way people approached, viewed, and accepted art. Constantly moving from one style to another, he destroyed forever the hold that Renaissance concepts of pictorial space held over artists, especially their devotion to the canon that flat images on a canvas are given dimension and perspective through diminution in size and change in colorist atmosphere. Picasso broke his figures into fragments, split them into geometric shapes, and had them occupy diverse planes, ignoring any rational relationship they had to their environment. He made his images exist independently of nature, giving them no unifying point of view and no fixed perspective. He even made them completely abstract. By forging a new tradition, Picasso revealed a more profound reality. He recognized that the human eye was highly selective and often glanced at objects haphazardly; it focused on bits and pieces, highlighting certain planes and aspects and divorcing the particular from the totality, independent of any natural arrangement of shapes, lines, and colors.

Picasso transcended the times in which he lived. His talent remained fresh and vibrant throughout his entire professional life of over sixty years. And his creations, despite their great diversity, possessed a unity based on the strength of his own remarkable personality and vast talent for regeneration. He died on 8 April 1973 in Mougins, France.

ART IN THE TOTALITARIAN AGE

The New Rome

A Tendency to Overbuild. Official Fascist art was largely derivative. Mussolini eagerly grabbed anything that would enhance his glory, especially if it could be used to help his regime evoke the cultural splendor of ancient Rome. The official results, demonstrated primarily in grandiose building projects, were often sterile and vulgar. On the outskirts of Rome, Mussolini pushed the construction of his own forum, the *Foro Mussolini*, a gigantic sports complex. Its centerpiece was the great stadium decorated with sixty marble statues of· nude athletes, including a mountain climber and a skier, and a sixty-foot obelisk with the word DUX chiseled on its base. The regime also built showcase superhighways, new civic centers, party headquarters, bridges, and dams. Its pride and joy—its secular temples and cathedrals—were its railroad stations. Most major cities had to have one. In Rome, the Fascists built a great neoclassical terminal; its severe lines and massive proportions had all the charm of a modern mausoleum. In Milan, the mood was more traditional: a huge Corinthian-columned monstrosity, cluttered with flocks of stone Fascist eagles that still perch impassively on the cornices.

Mussolini also embarked on a program to restore Italy's antiquities. In October 1934, he inaugurated a clearance project for the area near the mausoleum of Augustus. This involved demolishing the dwellings that had been built against the tomb and creating a vast open area on the banks of the Tiber. "The millenial monuments of our history must loom gigantic in their necessary solitude," he said.[20] The mausoleum of Augustus carried special meaning because it enabled Mussolini to associate his regime with the splendor of Rome's imperial past.[21] He wanted the project finished in time for the two-thousand-year anniversary of the emperor's birth.

Under Mussolini's regime, special academies administered cultural patronage and awarded commissions to those who worked in the approved style. Although the regime ostracized nonconformists, it made little effort to persecute them. Such toleration, which would be unusual in a truly totalitarian system, could, in part, be attributed to Fascism's association with futurism, an art movement already well established before Mussolini came to power.

Futurism. The first futurist call to arms had appeared on the front page of *Le Figaro*, on 20 February 1909, over the name of Filippo Tommaso Marinetti, an Italian ultranationalist born in Egypt. Marinetti demanded that Italy be liberated from its gangrene of professors, archaeologists, tourist guides, and antique dealers. He denounced the dead hand of the past, which hung over Italian life: "the daily haunting of museums, of libraries, and of academies is for the artists what the prolonged tutelage of parents is to intelligent youths who are wild with talent and ambitious determination." He declared "that the splendor of the world is enriched by a new beauty: the beauty of speed. A racing car with its hood adorned with tubes like snakes with explosive breath . . . a roaring automobile appearing to brace machine gun bullets, is more beautiful than the *Winged-Victory of Samothrace*." We wish, wrote Marinetti in his manifesto, "to glorify war—the world's only hygiene—militarism, patriotism, the destructive goals of the Anarchists, the beautiful Thoughts worth death, and the scorn for women. . . . We sing of the great crowds aroused by work, pleasure, and revolt."[22]

Marinetti's passionate glorification of the filth, noise, and frenzy of the machine age came from a slick distillation of the elitism of Nietzsche, the emotional vitalism of Bergson, and the flamboyant anarchism of Italy. It soon found common ground with Fascism with which it had much in common. Both movements had developed out of the same turbulent milieu of prewar Milan, both attacked bourgeois conformity and intellectualism, and both extolled revolt and brute force. The futurist manifesto declared that "art can be nothing but violence, cruelty and injustice."

Such a crass doctrine would hardly seem attractive to sensitive artists. Yet, within a year, a group of Italy's most promising painters—Umberto Boccioni, Carlo

Umberto Boccioni's "Unique Forms of Continuity in Space" (1913) demonstrates the dynamics of two-dimensional movement. Boccioni, the only sculptor among the futurists, tried to capture the machine age in the figure's swirling, spiraling path through space.

Carrà, Luigi Russolo, Giacomo Balla, and Gino Severini—had responded to the call. In their own technical manifesto, they complained that traditional art was too static and isolated from the viewer. They maintained that futurist artists should paint dynamic sensation and motion: "An outline is never stationary before us, but it appears and disappears endlessly. Given the persistence of the image on the retina, objects in movement multiply, and change form rapidly like quick vibrations in moving space. Therefore a running horse does not have four hooves but twenty and their movements are triangular."[23]

A Manifesto in Practice. The futurists recognized two kinds of motion: internal and outward. Each object had a centripetal force that conveyed its internal mass and possessed a rhythmic relationship with other objects, and with space itself. The choice of proper colors became crucial: "brown tints have never coursed beneath our skin; one should realize that yellow shines from our skin, that red flashed there, and that green, blue, and violet dance there with a thousand voluptuous and caressing charms." Although they had produced a manifesto, the five artists had yet to complete a futurist painting. All of them had already developed distinctive styles of their own, which, although they denounced all forms of imitation, revealed their absorption with the linear values of the cubists, the colors of the postimpressionists (in Italy known as divisionists), and the emotional subjectivism of the expressionists.

The first exhibition of their works in Milan, on 30 April 1911, showed the futurists' commitment to depicting motion, smells, and sounds. Although the show was not an enormous success, over the next five years, futurism enjoyed a golden age. Before its decline, it produced a profusion of masterpieces. Carlo Carrà explained that futurist paintings embodied the "sounds, noises and smells of theatres, music halls, movie houses, bordellos, railroad stations, ports, garages, clinics, [and] factories." Sounds and noises and odors, he explained, could be concave or convex, triangular, elliptical, oblong, conical, spherical, or spiral in shape. Colors were determined by location: "In stations, factories, garages and hangars, in the mechanical and sports world, sounds, noises and smells are almost always red; in restaurants, cafes and saloons they are silver, yellow and violet. While the sounds, noises, and smells of women are green, sky blue and violet."[24]

In *Dog on a Leash*, Giacomo Balla, the oldest of the original five, represented motion—a woman walking her dog—as a series of superimposed photographic stills. And he united motion and atmosphere in *Swifts: Paths of Movement + Dynamic Sequences* and *Mercury Passing before the Sun as Seen through a Telescope*. Balla's more talented pupil, Gino Severini, developed an abstract rhythmic style, or "dynamic hieroglyph," to express his highly personalized vision. With flashes of silver and green, his painting *Dances* = Sea + Vase of Flowers associated the moving sea with the image of a brightly spangled dancer and with "the vision of a grand bouquet of flowers." Severini used the same technique of combining relationships and impressions on his better known, more representative canvas *Dynamic Hieroglyphic of the Bal Tabarin*. Umberto Boccioni, one of the most talented members of the group, synthesized sound and sight in *The Noise of the Street Penetrates the House* and *The City Rises*, certainly one of the greatest paintings of the twentieth century. Boccioni carried the new doctrine into sculpture with his *Unique Forms of Continuity in Space*, which captured the inner tensions of a standing figure cutting its way through space. His death after a fall from a horse in 1916 deprived futurism of its dynamic center.[25]

A Dubious Association. Marinetti, more than anyone else, provided the tangible link between futurism and Fascism. He always remained a political gadfly. On Mussolini's fortieth birthday in 1923, Marinetti saluted the Duce's marvelous futuristic temperament: "Bent over his desk on large elbows, his arms as alert as levers, he threatens to leap across his papers at any pest or enemy. . . . His will splits the crowd like a swift antisubmarine boat, an exploding torpedo. Rash but sure because his elastic good sense has accurately judged the distance."[26]

Mussolini enjoyed being associated with one of the greatest art movements of modern times. Yet, despite all of Marinetti's efforts, the Duce never made futurism the official style of his regime. Like most dictators, he preferred works of art immediately accessible to the masses and favored those that displayed a strong dose of realism as if the reiteration and enlargement of basic forms could best express grandeur. The Duce saw little need to persecute nonconformists, however; he thought art could best be controlled through the distribution of favors and positions. Many major Italian artists were anti-Fascists, but they never dared criticize the regime publicly, an act usually punished with internal exile. Many who refused to adhere to the declamatory style of the regime were accused of being Bolsheviks or other disagreeable forms of lowlifes and were officially ostracized. But the dissidents were not prohibited from painting.

Modern Art and the Bolshevik Revolution

Culture for the Proletariat. Since the eighteenth century, Russia's rulers had tried to create an official art style. The St. Petersburg Academy of Fine Arts, established in 1757, became the center of artistic pedagogy, the chief arbiter of tastes, and the principal source of cultural patronage. The institution fostered works of art that aimed at immortalizing the tsarist system and the great men who served it. During most of the nineteenth century, Russian art languished in an official straitjacket. Deprived of independent sources of patronage such as those that appeared in the growing acquisitive middle class of Western Europe, painters were forced to conform or risk starvation. Yet despite the heavy, restrictive presence of the state, rebels existed. A movement of Itinerants (*peredvzhniki*) detached themselves from the academy and often satirized the existing social order and dramatized the suffering of the poor. Yet Itinerant painters such as Vasili Perov and Ilya Repin still paid careful attention to classical norms of composition. Their work became an important forerunner of Soviet art.

While the avant-garde movements of Munich, Vienna, and Paris pointed the way to a new creativity, Russian artists were understandably reluctant to follow the call. Yet they were on the threshold of a great age of innovation and experimentation. In the last days of tsarism, Russian art was a mass of antagonistic, often independent, nerve centers, representing different traditions, purposes, and styles. Some artists searched for their roots in Russian folk art. Others, frustrated by the confines of nationalistic formalism, associated themselves with artistic movements in Western Europe. The cry of "art for art's sake" coexisted with the belief in art for the sake of the nation or the proletariat. Traditionalism began to erode, leading to a frenzied search for new artistic forms based on a highly personal view of life.

Some artists believed the Communist regime would allow them the freedom to create whatever they wanted. Lenin once remarked that "art belongs to the people. Its roots should be deeply implanted in the very thick of the labouring masses. It should be understood and loved by those masses. It must unite and elevate their feelings, thoughts, and will. It must stir to activity and develop the art instincts within them."[27] He did not emphasize control, and during its early years, the Bolshevik regime devoted its attention to the more important matter of basic survival. Lenin believed that being revolutionary in political and economic affairs was temporarily sufficient.

Lenin had conventional bourgeois tastes and neither understood nor enjoyed schools of modern art such as expressionism, futurism, and cubism. According to one of his associates, he "never made guiding principles out of his aesthetical likes and dislikes,"[28] but the associate was mistaken. What Lenin gave with one hand, he could take away with the other. Once he remarked that "every artist, and everyone who considers himself such, has the right to create freely, to follow this ideal regardless of everything. But, then, we are communists, and ought not to stand idly by and give chaos free rein to develop. We should steer this process according to a worked-out plan and must shape its results."[29]

To this end, in 1920, he affirmed party control over the proletarian cultural and educational organizations (*Prolekult*), seeing to it that these groups were placed under the direction of the People's Commissariat of Education. Obviously, bureaucrats and party officials would preside over the reform of Russian society through a new working-class art movement. Until such control materialized, Russian artists enjoyed a period of relative independence in which they had an opportunity to develop their talents and individual styles as they had rarely had before.

Suprematism and Constructivism. One of the most important Russian artists of the modern period was Kazimir Malevich who, before World War I, had completely abandoned all representational art in favor of his own style of "pure nonobjectivity," which he called suprematism. "I have transformed myself into the nullity of forms and pulled myself out of the circle of things, out of the circle-horizon in which the artist and forms of nature are linked," he wrote.[30] He achieved this by blending pure geometric shapes on an indefinite background. Malevich believed that the end of artistic creation lay in the complete domination of the forms of nature, and he painted works with such self-explanatory titles as *Black Trapezium and Red Square* and *Yellow Quadrilateral on White*. His *White Square on White*, which eliminated all color, pushed the de-objectivization of art to an extreme. Malevich believed he had discovered the absolute reality of form. He had no more worlds left to conquer; his abstract art could develop no farther. Since his works were little appreciated by his Communist masters, he spent the last fifteen years of his life teaching.

Other Russians were also moving in the direction of completely nonobjective art. Wassili Kandinsky could claim to have created the first abstract work of art with a watercolor he painted in 1910. A Muscovite by birth, he spent most of the period between 1896 and 1914 in Munich where he first achieved his artistic notion, the "principle of interior necessity." Kandinsky was actually a more abstract artist than Malevich whose nonobjective squares and rectangles were still recognizably geometric shapes. Kandinsky's blotches and squiggly lines contained nothing identifiable. When he returned to Russia at the outbreak of World War I, he fell under the decisive influence of suprematism.

Russian avant-garde artists hailed the overthrow of tsarism as the prelude to a new order, which they believed they had helped bring about. In 1920, Malevich wrote that "Cubism and Futurism were the revolutionary forces in art foreshadowing the revolution in political and economic life in 1917." While the Bolshevik regime struggled against its counterrevolutionary foes, the artists busily organized huge supportive propaganda displays. In October 1920, for example, Nathan Altman staged a reenactment of the storming of the Winter Palace. These artists believed that their talents were indispensable in reorganizing society.

Intent on creating a Bolshevik style of art, El Lissitzky prepared a collection of agitational-instructional material that toured the country in special trains. He brought suprematism into the graphic arts with such posters as his famous *Beat the Whites with the Red Wedge*; and he created a new three-dimensional medium, the "Proun," as an interchange between painting and architecture. He remained confident that his geometric functionalism would serve as the supreme inspiration for the society of the future: "if communism which set human labor on the throne and suprematism which raised aloft the square pennant of creativity now march forward together then in the further stages of development it is communism which will have to remain behind because suprematism . . . will liberate all those engaged in creative activity and make the world into a true model of perfection."[31] In 1921, Lissitzky became head of the faculty of architecture at the recently created Vkhutemas Academy in Moscow.

Another member of the academy faculty was the founder of constructivism, Vladimir Tatlin. Tatlin carried the ideas of the supremacists into sculpture and architecture. He had a particular reverence for the spiral, which he regarded as the form that best characterized the spirit of the modern age. In 1919, the Bolshevik government commissioned Tatlin to build a memorial to the Third International. Tatlin conceived a gigantic structure a quarter of a mile in height, consisting of three huge revolving tubelike spirals that were telescoped within one another. The uppermost cylinder, leaning on its asymmetrical axis, would make one complete rotation every twenty-four hours, the middle portion would do the same every month, while the main base, which contained offices and conference halls would turn once a year. The structure would be constructed of glass and steel, be floodlit at night, and contain special equipment for projecting revolutionary slogans on the low-hanging clouds in the Moscow sky. Tatlin made a wood and wire model of his vision, but unfortunately the Communist regime had neither the material resources nor the sense of humor to carry the project further.

Countless other constructivist schemes, many of which were egregiously impractical, shared a similar fate. The regime was more concerned with building factories. Extensive use of glass did not seem very appropriate for cold Russian winters, and the designs were often monotonous and uninspired. Constructivists either built houses resembling matchboxes—caricatures of modern simplicity with abysmal architectural lines—or drew up plans for bizarre structures like Tatlin's Third International monument and his glider, a nonfunctional airship reminiscent of a praying mantis. The most famous constructivist edifice that was actually built—and one that was fairly restrained for the genre—was Lenin's tomb.

The Bolsheviks tried to coordinate artistic creativity through a special Department of Fine Arts that was part of the People's Commissariat of Education. Anatoli Lunacharsky supervised the operation. Lunacharsky was a man of wide erudition—he wrote literary criticism, philosophical treatises, and plays—who tended to sympathize with modernistic trends in art and literature. He invited Isadora Duncan to the Soviet Union to teach Russian children modern dance and encouraged the theatrical experiments of Konstantin Stanislavsky and Vsevoslod Meyerhold. Such diverse talents as Marc Chagall and Malevich obtained teaching positions with his help. He also encouraged the development of Soviet cinematography.

The comparatively free cultural atmosphere of the 1920s was too much for the artists to bear. They split into factions as dogmatic as those of the prerevolutionary Marxists. Some groups attacked "easel art" and "pure art," arguing that the artist should be a social engineer who transformed labor into art. Others claimed art was an ideal means of shaping people's vision of the world. The functionalists, who ultimately controlled the Prolekult, had no misgiving about showing their adversaries the errors of their ways. For example, when Malevich joined the staff of the Vitebsk School of Art, he lost no time in ousting Marc Chagall as director because he regarded Chagall's art as hopelessly reactionary.

The squabbling did not last long because the regime was becoming decidedly cool to art "too removed from the people." Lunacharsky began losing his earlier tolerance. The reason was not hard to fathom. Lenin had already begun tightening the screws. The official Association of Revolutionary Painters, established in February 1922, endorsed realism as the art form best suited to the proletariat. It emphasized the themes of labor, the Revolution, and economic progress.

Artists who could not conform to the new line went into exile. Chagall left for Paris; Kandinsky returned to Germany; and the constructivist Anton Pevsner went to France, while his brother Naum Gabo went to the United States. (This cultural exodus also carried over into the fields of music and ballet.) The harassment of artists by artists paled beside the persecution meted out by the state. Stalin felt that art was too important to be left to the artists, and by the end of the twenties, he had targeted artistic creativity for increased regimentation.

Socialist Realism. The uneasy alliance between the Russian avant-garde and the Communist system collapsed entirely in 1932. All artistic groups that lacked state approval were abolished. The Communist party created special unions of writers, composers, and artists and proceeded to bring the entire artistic life of the country under totalitarian control. At the writers' first All-Union Congress, held in 1934 in Moscow, Stalin's spokesman, Andrei Zhdanov, defined the regime's goals in the doctrine of socialist realism: "You must know life to be able to depict it truthfully in artistic creations, to depict neither 'scholastically,' nor lifelessly, nor simply as 'objective reality,' but rather as reality in its revolutionary development. The truthfulness and historical exactitude of the artistic image must be linked with the task of ideological transformation, of the education of the working people in the spirit of socialism."[32] Zhdanov charged the writers, and by extension all creative artists, to choose their themes from "the lives of men and women workers and collective farmers, Party and state workers, engineers, Komsomols, Pioneers." *Partiynost* (party character), or clear identification with the proletarian cause, meant, above all, a proper choice of subject matter. Writers were shown little mercy. Of the 700 delegates at the writers' congress in 1934, only about 50 were alive two decades later—a decline that cannot be explained by either the war or age alone.

In the visual arts, the Bolsheviks ordered the artists to depict the themes of the Revolution and to concentrate on social and technological progress and the greatness of Stalinist leadership. The best—least dangerous—art was theatrical, didactic, and representational, but not realistic. The last requirement meant that shapes and forms should be recognizable, but that the artist should show things the way they should be—or the way the regime wanted them to be—not the way they actually were. Stalin demanded that art make an impact on the masses. Since "modern art" alienated the spectator, it was counterrevolutionary. But Stalinist paintings were so propagandistic, the West found it difficult to accept them as true art. All in all, the Soviet regime killed artistic development and experimentation, making its art false and dull. In form, the art resembled the academic art of the nineteenth century, the art that the bourgeoisie, the very people the regime anathematized, had adored. Yet, within these limitations, the Soviet masters produced many works that compare in technical mastery and composition with the best figurative art of any age. Although these artists were not permitted to move toward a creative future in a direction dictated by their own spirit, at least they did a remarkable job of re-creating the past.

On 17 January 1936, Josef Stalin went to see a performance of Ivan Dzerzhinsky's new opera *And Quiet Flows the Don*. Vyacheslav Molotov, the chairman of the people's commissars, and Andrei Bubnov, the commissar of education, accompanied him. The Soviet dictator had no real love of music. He disclosed the reason for his official presence at an interview with the young composer during intermission. According to *Pravda*, Stalin told Dzerzhinsky that the time was ripe to create a school of classical Soviet opera that would be "emotionally inspiring" and make wide use of the "melodic inflections of folk music . . . [and] all the latest devices of musical techniques, but [in an idiom] close to the masses, clear and accessible."[33]

Perhaps by intention, Dzerzhinsky's opera had anticipated Stalin's wishes. It was based on Mikhail Sholokhov's book of the same name about the Russian civil war, but the original characters had been stripped of their complexity in favor of Communist stereotypes. Futhermore, Dzerzhinsky had loaded the work with hummable tunes and ended it with a triumphal chorus—"From Border to Border"—that demonstrated revolutionary fervor at its most intense. The opera immediately secured an honored place in the Soviet repertoire. Other composers drew the necessary conclusions, and soon a flood of similar works poured forth, monopolizing new operatic productions. Not all composers were willing to follow suit, however.

Not long after Stalin heard Dzerzhinsky's opera, he attended a performance of Dimitri Shostakovich's *Lady Macbeth at Mtsensk District*. This time the Communist boss was not amused, and he left the theater in the middle of the performance. About a week later, his reaction appeared in a *Pravda* editorial entitled "Chaos instead of Music." The article said: "From the very first moment the audience is deafened by a purposely harsh and discordant stream of sounds. Fragments of melody, the rudiments of a musical phrase are drowned, torn to pieces, and disappear in a rumbling, grating, screeching din. It is difficult enough to follow such music; to remember it is impossible." In the critic's view, the plot was utterly lacking in quality: "Everyone in the opera, both merchants and the people, are presented in the guise of a beast . . . . and 'love' in its most vulgar form is daubed all over the opera. The merchant's double bed is the central part on the stage. On it all the 'problems' are solved. In the same crude naturalistic style a death from poisoning and a flogging are practically shown on the very stage." The *Pravda* review, a critique of more than the music, contained the following warning: "We are given Leftist chaos instead of natural human music. The power that music has of seizing the imagination of the masses is sacrificed to strained, petty bourgeois, formalistic effects and pretensions to originality by means of cheap eccentricity. It is a silly game that may end very badly."[34] Shostakovich had intended his opera to be the first part of a tetralogy about the emancipation of Russian women. The cycle was never completed. Shostakovich took the hint and, henceforth, devoted most of his energy to composing symphonic music; for inspiration, he returned to the romantic musical idiom of the nineteenth century.

Considering Russia's musical heritage, it was natural that the campaign to end the freedom of Soviet composers should begin in the opera house. "Opera has always served as a forum for public opinion," the Soviet critic Lyudmilla Polyakova wrote. "If we take, for instance, music in the 19th Century, we will see that it was indeed to opera that great composers who held progressive views turned to expound before the large masses of listeners their lofty ideas of humanism, to call on the people to fight for justice and happiness."[35] Whether this opinion was true or not, the Soviet leaders accepted it. They also believed that a great culture could only flourish in a country where socialism had triumphed. Bourgeois culture had nothing more to offer, they maintained. Its great works had been created when capitalism first triumphed over feudalism. That time was long past and would never return. Zhdanov described bourgeois culture as a decadent "riot of mysticism, religious mania and pornography."[36]

Yet when the Bolsheviks came to power, the anticipated flood of masterpieces failed to materialize. The first true Soviet opera, *For Red Petrograd* (about the Bolsheviks' defense of the city in 1919 against the White Army of Yudenich), folded after a dozen performances. Other attempts to turn the Revolution into grand opera also flopped. Consequently, the standard repertoire, even of such progressive companies as Leningrad's Malyi Opera Theater, depended heavily on the works of Puccini, Mozart, Verdi, Gounod, Bizet, and the Russian masters, which were performed in traditional versions.[37]

Stalin generally spared the lives of his composers—perhaps he did not find musical tonality as threatening as words—but he greatly restricted their artistic expression. The composers played it safe, writing orthodox music with ingratiating melodies. Dzerzhinsky led the way in composing operas filled with popular songs that the audience could hum as it left the theater. In the decade after 1936, he wrote seven of these compositions. None of them, like most of the other operas of the period, found a permanent place in the repertoire. Soviet academician Boris Asafiev, writing later in a safer era, dismissed these operas as rhythmically monotonous and dramatically dull. He mocked their constant use of marches and their rousing finales in which heroic emotions were reduced to clichés. "Melody, the powerful means of emotional expression and characterization, was substituted by strophic and fragmentary modern street ditties, akin to limerick and sentimental romance," he complained. Asafiev also charged that the preoccupation of these operas with realism brought about the "degeneration of the aria as an expression of passionate depth of feeling."[38]

But then opera composition was a very risky business. The composers tried to meet the demands of the Stalinist censors by glorifying the class conflict and the heroic struggle of the Soviet people and including a proper balance of social and political conflict. Still the official imperatives were confusing, and many composers therefore avoided contemporary themes. Konstantin Dankevich wrote *Bogdan Khmelnitzky* about the seventeenth-century Ukrainian Cossack hero who led a successful revolt against the Poles. Nevertheless, official critics blasted the opera for its lack of unity and weak music drama. *Pravda* said the work failed to emphasize that the Ukrainian people were not fighting the Polish people—they were fighting the Polish *feudal class*. The audience, therefore, could not clearly understand why the Ukrainians desired to unite with the Russians. Dankevich confessed the work had ideological shortcomings and revised it to conform to official desires. Only then did the regime restore him to favor.

The apparatus of cultural control was firmly fixed by the end of the 1930s. The Moscow-based Union of Soviet Composers, under the overall control of the Ministry of Culture, regulated all Soviet music through branches located in all the major cities and republics. Membership, which was limited to composers and musicologists, was supposedly voluntary. However, any artists with aspirations of reaching an audience larger than their own families and friends had to join. The regime demanded quantity as well as orthodoxy and applied the same production standards to composers as were imposed on the rest of Communist society. Composers were expected to provide appropriate music for great state occasions, like the celebration of the anniversary of the Revolution, the opening of a party congress, or Stalin's birthday. In return, they received one of the highest standards of living in the Soviet Union. Shostakovich reportedly earned about $10,000 per symphony, $25,000 for each of his six Stalin prizes, and extensive royalties from the performances and recordings of his works. Like other composers, he also received free secretarial and copying services, travel allowances, and subsidized vacations. In Moscow the composers lived in their own apartment complex—with concert hall, library, restaurant, and private lounges—whose living units had been built with specially designed windows that provided ventilation and filtered out noise. Any deviation from the principles of socialist realism could bring it all to an end, however. To keep the composers orthodox, the Composers' Union sponsored a special group therapy conference to discourage transgressions. (The regime had subjected Shostakovich to one of these sessions for corporate self-criticism after the condemnation of his opera *Lady Macbeth*.) The conference lasted three full days and was so well attended that the Moscow hotel where it was held could not accommodate all the participants. A frenzy of mutual denunciation and repentance marked the sessions. Shostakovich testified that there could be no music without ideology. The conference was an elaborately staged ritual in which the composers bore public witness to their faith. An individual might be damned alone, but could only be saved with others. Stalin, it should be remembered, had been educated at the Tiflis theological seminary.

National Socialist Taste

The House of German Art. Hitler believed he was the cultural and spiritual leader of his people as well as their political messiah. As such, he believed he had a duty to purge the art world of those unclean elements that had a "disintegrating influence" on the life of the German people. In March 1933, a five-point program appeared, entitled "What German artists expect from the New Government." What the artists expected, whether they knew it or not, or wanted it or not, was the removal and destruction of all Bolshevik and "cosmopolitan" art from German museums and the dismantling of all offensive sculpture from public squares and parks. They also "demanded" the removal of all gallery directors, museum curators, and public officials whose waste of public funds constituted a sin against the nation. Alfred Rosenberg, a bit of a political lightweight, became the director of the Office for the Supervision of the Cultural and Ideological Education and Training of the Nazi Party. Josef Goebbels, however, had greater access to Hitler and soon pushed him out of the way. Goebbels could easily adapt his own artistic tastes to conform to those of the Führer. In November 1933, Goebbels created the *Reichskammer der bildenden Kunst* (State Board of the Visual Arts), the controlling agency for the nation's cultural activities, to which all artists possessing the necessary reliability or suitability were forced to belong. Within five years, the organization's members included 10,500 painters and 3,200 sculptors. Less reliable individuals, including many of Germany's most famous modern artists, were stripped of their citizenship, fired from their professorships at art schools, specifically prohibited from exercising their talents, and driven into exile.

Hitler replaced the multifaceted German art scene with one official style and selected Munich, the city where his party had been born, as the site of its temple. The great museum for Nazi-approved art, the *Haus der Kunst* (House of German Art), opened on 18 July 1937 with an exhibition of 884 works of art, all of them highly realistic. Hitler had helped make the final selection from the 15,000 submissions and boasted at the exhibition's inauguration that he had ended the nation's artistic pollution and lunacy. Many mediocre artists had gained admission by successfully depicting the regime's favorite themes: militarism, rural domesticity, maternity, and service to the party and nation.

Not all the artists included in the exhibition could be dismissed as hacks. Arno Breker, one of the National Socialism's most famous sculptors, had already established himself before Hitler came to power. During the twenties, Breker had lived in Paris where he worked in the abstract style and associated with actors and avant-garde artists. By the time he returned to Germany in 1934, his style had changed and become more figurative. Intellect more than politics prompted this development. Certain sculptors, including the French masters Emile-Antoine Bourdelle

The Nazis displayed Max Beckmann's expressionist masterpiece "Christ and the Woman Taken in Adultery" prominently in the first room of the 1937 Degenerate Art exhibition. The authorities found the forgiveness of an adulteress insulting to the National Socialist family ideal. On the opening day of the exhibition, Beckmann and his wife left Germany, never to return.

and Aristide Maillol, who were interested in turning realism into idealism, had begun a scholarly reinvestigation of Greek art. Breker, in turn, was influenced by Maillol, his friend and teacher. Due to this interest in realism, Breker was a good catch for the Nazis, and under their patronage, his artistic production and importance soared. He is probably best remembered for the two huge nude sword-bearing warriors that stood outside the entrance of the Reichs Chancellery. These works seemed to embody the essence of the Nazi spirit in art. Yet any attempt to divorce Breker from his origins and from the revival of realism in early twentieth-century art is doomed to failure. Breker, like other artists who worked for the Nazi regime, continued to pursue styles he had previously developed. Many others, of course, were forced to change—for reasons of personal security. Nevertheless, the fact remains that the Nazis did not create a new art; rather they suppressed the kinds of art they did not like and tolerated only those that they did. As a result, art of the Nazi era tended to be uniform in style and restricted in theme; its reiteration of Teutonic superiority became boring and eventually pernicious because the art was identified with a brutal regime.

The Nazis called any art they did not like degenerate whether they disliked it for political, racial, or artistic reasons. Therefore, anything a Communist did was degenerate; anything a Jew did was degenerate; anything that called attention to the horrors of war was degenerate; and anything that satirized the military, attacked capitalism, or lampooned the glorification of the nation was degenerate. Anything unclear, ambiguous, or abstract, anything that had broken lines, or looked distorted, crude, or garish was degenerate. Thus, all of the schools of modern art—cubism, expressionism, abstractionism, dadaism, and futurism—were degenerate. Hitler himself loved the salon art of his youth—the art of the Wilhemian era around the turn of the century—and viewed almost anything less realistic than this as degenerate. On his orders, the full force of the state was turned against the "moral degenerates," and their works were confiscated and often destroyed.[39]

On 19 July 1937, the day after the opening of the exhibition of "German" art at the Haus der Kunst, a special exposition of degenerate art opened at Munich's Municipal Archaeological Institute.[40] The authorities selected works by 120 artists from the plunder of the leading public galleries and museums (including 16,000 avant-garde works) and exhibited them in an unorganized way to stimulate ridicule.[41] As if that were not sufficient, derogatory comments took the place of explanations. The catalog combined attack and vituperation, complete with many quotations from Hitler's speeches.[42] Attendance was huge. Almost three million attended the four-month exhibition and its subsequent four-year tour of Austria and Germany. The aura of evil probably boosted attendance, but then most of the works displayed were indeed masterpieces.

Unlike many National Socialist structures, the Haus der Kunst building survived the war better than the reputation of the art it once held. As the State Gallery of Modern Art (*Staatsgalerie Moderner Kunst*), it still functions as an art museum and houses a respectable collection of modern art from impressionism to German expressionism, the school Hitler particularly hated.

The Style of Empire. Paul Ludwig Troost, the architect of the Haus der Kunst, designed a structure in the Spartan neo-empire style he had developed before 1914 in association with the Bauhaus architects such as Walter Gropius and Peter Behrens. While Hitler's taste tended more to the heavy baroque of the late nineteenth century—he adored the gaudy Paris and Vienna opera houses—he recognized the importance of this more modern monumental style of classicism. Hitler, a would-be architect, took a keen interest in every detail of the art museum's construction, including the choice of colors for the fabrics covering the walls. The Führer had a passion for architecture and wanted buildings that would reflect his power and mastery and would "transmit his time and its spirit to posterity." He considered architecture the best medium for communicating the glory of his regime to future generations. National Socialist architectural works should speak, like the buildings of the Roman Empire, "to the conscience of a future Germany centuries from now."[43] Troost would help him achieve this immortality. But Troost died in 1934, even before he had finished his Munich creation, and his mantle passed to the twenty-eight-year-old Albert Speer.

Speer's first important commission was to build permanent stone bleachers on Zeppelin Field in Nuremberg where the Nazi party held its yearly rallies. Speer, finding inspiration in the ancient world's Pergamum altar,[44] designed a structure 80 feet high and 1,300 feet long, "a mighty flight of stairs topped and enclosed by a long colonnade, flanked on both sides by stone abutments."[45] This monumental, classical edifice was just the sort of thing Hitler considered suitable for transmitting his spirit to posterity. Speer's future was assured. After seeing Speer's design of the reviewing stand, Hitler entrusted him with planning the whole party rally area. Speer conceived this as an integrated whole, encompassing the field for military exercises, the congress hall for Hitler's speeches, and a vast stadium to hold 400,000 people.

Leni Riefenstahl's film "Triumph of the Will" (1935) was the cinematographic equivalent of Hitler's deification through monumental architecture. Hitler, flanked by Himmler and SA chief Viktor Lutze, walks toward the huge rectangular tribune constructed in Nuremberg's Luitpold Arena. This architectural stage was intended to enhance the Führer's image as the savior of his people.

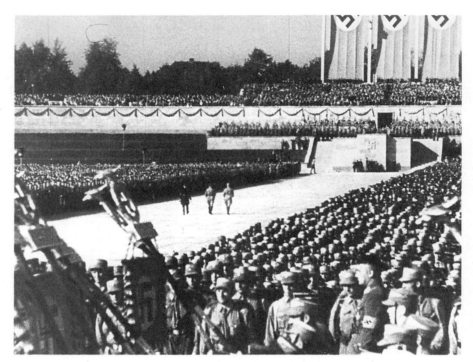

But such a stage, though adequate for a leader of the Nazi party, did not do justice to a leader who wanted to make his mark on history. Hitler's world stage was Berlin. In late January 1938, he commissioned Speer to build a new Reichs Chancellery. The old one he dismissed as "fit for a soap company."[46] Speer obliged with a long rectangular structure with a line of double columns across the facade; they stood in front of a grand gallery 480 feet long, twice as long as the Hall of Mirrors at Versailles. Hitler was impressed. The building was finished in less than a year and was ready for occupancy on 9 January 1939. This edifice was to be only part of the total redesign of the central part of Berlin.

Many other great buildings were planned as well: the ministries of Interior, Transportation, Justice, Economics, Food, and eventually the Colonies were to have new homes, which would flank a grand boulevard. The plans also called for two movie houses—one for important premieres, one for the masses—a new opera house, a hotel, a concert hall, and three other theaters. At one end of the broad avenue an arch of triumph would rise 386 feet, more than twice as tall as the arch Napoleon had built in Paris; it was to be 550 feet wide by 390 feet deep. At the other end of the boulevard would be a great domed hall, modeled after the Pantheon in Rome, but with a diameter almost six times as large; its dome would rise to a height of 726 feet. Other Nazi buildings had already been built in downtown Berlin, including the Propaganda Ministry, the Air Ministry, a soldiers' hall, two railroad stations, a town hall, a war academy, police headquarters, and the offices of the High Command of the Navy. All were inspired by the empire style that Napoleon I had thought a fit expression of his regime's grandeur and his personal genius. It was an architecture that transcended and dwarfed human beings. Although most European nations have at some time evidenced similar preferences for classicism, the Nazi conception outshone all others in extravagance. The buildings, replete with Doric columns marching across their marble and limestone facades, showed a mania for gold leaf; in the words of Speer, they were "the show palaces of Oriental despots."[47]

POSTSCRIPT   Art is action. In a sense, it is aggression, albeit moral and spiritual. It involves a struggle for survival. Art movements exemplify humanity's turmoil as much as wars and revolutions. Yet, major cultural changes happen infrequently—usually not more than once a century. Many possibilities and ramifications must be explored and exhausted before a new vision is ready to take the place of the old; the process is necessarily a lengthy one.

The decade and a half before World War I saw the emergence of a staggering array of different schools and techniques: cubism, expressionism, futurism, constructivism, suprematism, and abstractionism, all of which have profoundly influenced artistic creativity ever since. The emergence of such a profusion of themes, variations, and syntheses in such a short time was practically unique in the history of Western art. Largely as a result of this abundance, the decade of the 1920s, for all its energy and talent, was more preoccupied with developing these earlier concepts than with beginning new ones. With so much confusion, a lessening of artistic standards appeared inevitable, especially because many new wave artists believed that they also had a mission to change society; their self-righteousness often produced more discussion about art than art. In the process, a lot of trash masqueraded as magnificence.

In most of Europe, art freed itself from its traditional moorings. This collapse of former standards, accompanied by the end of official patronage, became a source of both liberation and damnation. Art became more exciting and energetic. Success and worth, however, were frequently a matter of proper labeling and packaging, with masterpieces acclaimed by hype and mass approval. Art was anything one said it was. Artistic freedom, however, like academic freedom, was a fairly recent concept. Historically, artists had been expected to conform, to work for those in power, extolling their virtues. Since the Renaissance, many of the greatest talents had been servants of the state, an employment that they had accepted not out of fear, but out of the conviction that this was the best way to achieve their personal and artistic goals.

Even in the modern age, not everyone accepted the idea of artists as individualists who were free to do their own thing. Authoritarian regimes exercised a degree of control almost without precedent. In such societies, artists were not intended to be antagonistic to society; they were not allowed to experiment; they were not expected to challenge the way the political leaders thought the people should think. The regimes ordered their artists to return to the realistic styles that the modern art movement so emphatically repudiated. This absence of artistic freedom might be deplorable, but it would be wrong to assume that artistic creativity could thrive only in a free society. Some eras of great cultural achievement, such as the age of Augustus, the Renaissance, and the France of Louis XIV, were periods of political authoritarianism in which the duty of the artist was to glorify the secular rulers. Lenin had praised the state's cultural monopoly as a force of liberation: "In society based on private property the artist produces for the market, needs customers. Our revolution freed artists from the yoke of these extremely prosaic conditions. It turned the state into their defender and client, providing them with orders. Every artist, and everyone who considers himself such, has the right to create freely, to follow his ideal regardless of everything." At the time, Lenin had more important priorities than establishing artistic conformity. When the occasion allowed, most dictators found the challenge irresistible. Indeed, both Hitler and Mussolini believed themselves experts in artistic taste and automatically patronized those artists with whom they identified. Like Stalin, they carried the system of patronage into dictation of form and content. This desire for regimentation produced in many cases a class of technically competent hacks who would have agreed with the Soviet author Alexei Tolstoy who remarked cynically: "I am an ordinary mortal who wants to live . . . I don't give a damn; I'll write whatever is wanted. If [Stalin] wants Ivan the Terrible and Rasputin rehabilitated and turned into learned Marxists, I don't care."

For all societies and systems, however, the age when an artist could shock the public was over. Revolutionary techniques had become less revolutionary. As to subject matter, no artist could exceed the confusion, hell, and brutality of modern war or the infinite capacity for destruction and horror of organized intolerance.

ENDNOTES

1. Jean-Louis Ferrier, ed., *Art of Our Century: The Chronicle of Western Art, 1900 to the Present* (New York: Prentice-Hall, 1988), 7.
2. Ibid., 133.
3. André Breton, *Manifeste du surrealism* (Paris: Jean-Jacques Pauvent, 1962), 40.
4. Maurice Nadeau, *The History of Surrealism* (New York: Macmillan, 1965), 98.
5. "*A la poste d'hier tu télégraphieras que nous sommes bien mortes avec les hirondelles / Facteur triste facteur un cercueil sous ton bras / va-t-en porter ma lettre aux fleurs à tire d'elle.*" André Lagarde et Laurent Michard, *XXe Siècle, Les Grands Auteurs Français* (Paris: Bordas, 1965), 348.
6. Robert Short, "The Politics of Surrealism, 1920–36" in Walter Laqueur and George Mosse, eds., *The Left-Wing Intellectuals between the Wars, 1919–1939* (New York: Harper & Row, 1966), 6.
7. Siegfried Gideon, *Space, Time and Architecture* (Cambridge, Mass.: Harvard University Press, 1965), 48.
8. In Chicago, he built the Lake Shore Apartments (1950) and the post office. In New York, he designed the famous Lever Brothers Building (1952), whose glass fa-

cade reflected the images of the surrounding buildings, providing a constantly changing series of images. He followed this with the Seagram Building (1958), a thirty-nine-story masterpiece of the international style. A structure of bronze ribs emphasized its verticality.

9. Otto Friedrich, *Before the Deluge* (New York: Harper & Row, 1972), 183.

10. Stephanie Barron, ed., *German Expressionism, 1915–1925: The Second Generation* (Munich: Los Angeles County Museum of Art/Prestel-Verlage, 1988), 13.

11. Jane Clapp, *Art Censorship* (Metuchen, N.J.: Scarecrow Press, 1972), 212.

12. George Grosz, *A Little Yes and a Big No* (New York: Dial Press, 1946), 146–47.

13. A good discussion of the cultural milieu of this period, although it is heavily Marxist in interpretation, is Bärbel Schrader and Jürgern Schebera, *The "Golden" Twenties: Art and Literature in the Weimar Republic* (New Haven: Yale University Press, 1988).

14. Cesare was played by Conrad Veidt, who later, as Major Strasser, was dispatched by Humphrey Bogart in the closing reel of *Casablanca*.

15. See Siegfried Kracauer, *From Caligari to Hitler* (New York: Farrar, Straus, and Cudahy, 1949), 71.

16. Walter Slezak, *What Time's the Next Swan?* (Garden City, N.Y.: Doubleday, 1962), 132–34.

17. Sergei Eisenstein, *Notes of a Film Director* (London: Lawrence and Wishart, 1959), 29.

18. Sergei Eisenstein, *The Film Scene* (New York: Harcourt Brace, 1942), 22.

19. Many of the images used in the finished painting had been worked out prior to the event and therefore could not have been inspired by it.

20. Spiro Kostof, "The Emperor and the Duce: The Planning of Piazzale Augusto Imperatore in Rome," in Henry A. Million and Linda Nochlin, *Art and Architecture in the Service of Politics* (Cambridge, Mass.: MIT Press, 1978), 279.

21. According to Spiro Kostof, the completed project was unimpressive and failed to serve its political purpose of enhancing Mussolini's authority. "The Duce yields to the emperor and is lost. The piazzale, in the end, remains a collossal mistake." Ibid., 322.

22. Quoted in José Pierre, *Le Futurisme et le Dadaisme* (Lausanne: Editions Recontre, 1967), 98–99. Marinetti, a minor symbolist and novelist, published his manifesto first in French to gain the widest possible audience.

23. Ibid., 101.

24. Ibid., 105.

25. Esther Coen, "The Violent Urge towards Modernity: Futurism and the International Avant-Garde" in Emily Braun, *Italian Art in the 20th Century: Painting and Sculpture, 1900–1988* (Munich: Prestel-Verlag, 1989), 49–56.

26. Filippo Marinetti, *Selected Writings* (New York: Farrar, Straus, and Giroux, 1971), 159.

27. Clara Zetkin, "My Recollections of Lenin" in Vladimir Lenin, *On Culture and Cultural Revolution* (Moscow: Progress Publishers, 1970).

28. Antoly Lunacharsky, "Lenin and the Arts" in Lenin, *On Culture and Cultural Revolution*, 247.

29. Zetkin, "My Recollections of Lenin," 232.

30. Camilla Gray, *The Great Experiment* (New York: Abrams, 1962), 207.

31. Sophie Lissitzky-Kuppers, *El Lissitzky* (London: Thames and Hudson, 1968), 330.

32. A. A. Zhdanov, *On Literature, Music, and Philosophy* (London: Lawrence and Wishart, 1950), 13.

33. Boris Schwarz, *Music and Musical Life in Soviet Russia* (New York: Norton, 1972), 144.

34. Kurt London, *The Seven Soviet Arts* (London: Faber and Faber, 1937), 72–73.

35. Lyudmilla Polyakova, *Soviet Music* (Moscow: Foreign Languages Publishing House, n.d.), 99.

36. Zhdanov, *On Literature*, 13.
37. Some of the classics were updated, however. *Tosca* was moved from Rome in 1800 to Paris in 1871; under its new title *The Fight for the Commune*, it became a struggle of the proletariat against capitalist exploitation. Meyerbeer's *Les Huguenots* was changed into *The Decembrists*, a story about the 1825 revolt against Nicholas I. *Carmen* was modernized into *Carmencita and the Soldier*, a drama about factory workers; and in the new *Traviata*, Violetta became an actress driven to suicide by an oppressive bourgeois society. *Rienzi*, *Don Giovanni*, and *A Life for the Tsar* were also presented in new versions. Such proletarianization did not prove lastingly popular, however, and was actually discouraged during the Stalinist period.
38. Polyakova, *Soviet Music*, 108.
39. Albert Speer, *Inside the Third Reich* (New York: Macmillan, 1970), 44.
40. Henry Grosshans, *Hitler and the Artists* (New York: Holmes and Meier, 1983), 95–116.
41. Those represented constituted a who's who of the masters of modern art, including Paul Gauguin, Pablo Picasso, Paul Klee, Emile Nolde, Otto Dix, Max Ernst, Ernst Barlach, Erich Heckel, and Karl Schmidt-Rottluff.
42. In 1991 Stephanie Barron, curator of twentieth-century art at the Los Angeles County Museum of Art, organized a reconstruction of the "Degenerate Art" exposition, managing to reassemble over 150 works of art of the 680 in the original show. The catalog of this second exposition is a masterpiece of artistic scholarship. Stephanie Barron et al., *"Degenerate Art," The Fate of the Avant-Garde in Nazi Germany* (Los Angeles: Los Angeles County Museum of Art, 1991).
43. Speer, *Inside the Third Reich*, 55, 56.
44. In the Wilhelmine era, the remains of the building had been brought from Anatolia and reassembled in a Berlin museum bearing the monument's name.
45. Speer, *Inside the Third Reich*, 55.
46. Ibid., 102.
47. Ibid., 159.

CHAPTER 13

THE CHANGING SOCIETY

PREFACE   No generalization can do justice to the complex society of twentieth-century Europe. Life-styles ranged from medieval rural to progressive urban. Beliefs encompassed everything from paganism to scientific determinism. The practice of medicine spanned faith healing and miracle drugs. During the 1920s and 1930s, Europeans tried to regain the stability they had lost in the Great War. Great differences still existed between countries and regions, but common problems created common themes: the fluctuations between inflation and depression, the displacement of populations, the concentration of resources in the cities, and the new status of women. In solving their problems, the democracies seemed lackluster next to the dictatorships, which forged ahead with new techniques for changing the old world into a brave new world. Everywhere, however, the role of government increased. People who had once been accustomed to fending for themselves now expected protection, almost from the cradle to the grave. The notion of laissez-faire had apparently gone the way of the dodo.

The traditional leadership of the old aristocracy also ended. A title might earn one a place at the winter cotillion or in the inner circle at the racetrack, but noble lineage no longer guaranteed ascendency in government or business where the "old boy" network of the upper-middle class continued to hold sway. Eastern Europe had become a "graveyard" for ruling princes—often quite literally, as in Soviet Russia. Where they still existed, aristocrats continued to enjoy undeserved reputations as trendsetters, but they were forced to share the stage with movie stars, inflation millionaires, and avant-garde artists. The aristocracy retained some of its former importance in rural areas, but even here declining revenues from land and the migration of rural dwellers to the cities doomed its old way of life. More and more, the owners of stately homes and chateaux had to depend on the entrance fees they charged tourists to keep their roofs from leaking.

The middle class changed much less, but it also was preoccupied with maintaining its position. In the face of inflation and increased taxation, more of its offspring were looking for money-making careers, including its daughters who, during the war, had already assumed jobs that once had been considered a male monopoly. Although suffragist agitation and demands for protective legislation were temporarily suspended during the war, the increased demand for labor speeded up migration from farms to cities, where working conditions were more regulated and working hours were generally shorter and better compensated. The war also led to a decline in private domestic service, as educated women found respectable jobs in public administration and social service.

Urbanization continued after the war with hardly a break in its momentum. The growing populations of the cities were made possible by many factors: a revolution in agriculture, which created the necessary surplus food; improvements in medicine, which controlled diseases that had lurked in crowded urban areas; and advances in technology, which facilitated transportation and provided the necessary heat and electricity. People also flocked to the cities because jobs were available there and because urban life was deemed less boring and more prosperous than life in the country. A new leisure industry developed to provide mass entertainment and preserve the illusion that urban life was filled with adventure, success, and excitement, not routine and misery.

PROGRESS AND STABILIZATION

Health and Leisure

The Great "Spanish" Flu Pandemic. Preventing the spread of typhus among the millions of men massed in the trenches of northern France was one of the great accomplishments of modern applied science. Because military medicine focuses on prevention and maintenance, it has frequently been responsible for important advances in disease control. The discovery of the role of the mosquito in the spread of yellow fever prompted American army doctor Walter Reed to achieve its eradication. The knowledge that lice are involved in the transmission of typhus, discovered in the decade before the war, led to an intensive program of immunization and delousing that kept the trenches in France fairly safe from the disease. Only on the Eastern Front, where the military authorities were less committed, did typhus take a significant toll. As in previous wars, however, the number of casualties from disease in World War I continued to exceed those received in battle— by nearly 100 percent. Most of these casualties were caused by water-transmitted diseases, such as cholera, typhoid, and dysentery—all preventable by chlorination of the water supply.

There proved to be no protection against the airborne "Spanish" flu virus that appeared in the war's closing months, however. The virus surfaced first in the United States in March 1918.[1] Since the American medical authorities did not consider influenza a reportable disease, they did not take the initial outbreak seriously. However, the flu moved rapidly, particularly at army bases where congested conditions facilitated its spread. Infected soldiers carried the flu to Europe, where it appeared in April at an army camp near Bordeaux, France. The disease then passed from army to army. At the end of the month, it hit the British Expeditionary Force. In May, it infected the French army and jumped across no-man's-land to strike the Germans, who called it "Flanders Fever." It also hastened down to Spain and then to Italy. By June, the flu had arrived in England, Wales, Germany, and the Scandinavian countries. In the next four months, it circled the globe, cutting a particularly broad path of devastation in Africa, India, and China. Only a small number of those infected died, but a high proportion of the dead were young adults.[2] In this respect, the Spanish flu differed from other strains that had wreaked their greatest havoc among the very young and the old. The illness began with an ache and cough, and in its last stage, it attacked the lungs, filling them with a thin, bloody froth. A victim who reached this stage almost always died, often within forty-eight hours after experiencing the first symptoms. The Spanish flu came in three waves, each more deadly than its predecessor, before it ran its course. By the spring of 1919, it had killed 27 million people, more than the total who died on the battlefields.

Although research into infectious diseases had been in progress since the end of the nineteenth century, the worldwide character of the pestilence gave the research a new urgency. It also demonstrated the necessity of dealing with infectious diseases along multinational lines. Here, too, some steps had been taken before the war. In 1910, the Europeans had established an International Office of Public Hygiene in Paris to monitor the spread of major diseases such as smallpox, cholera, yellow fever, malaria, and typhus, scourges that were being eliminated from their countries. This work continued after the war through the Health Section of the League of Nations. Public health also became a high priority at home.

In the 1920s, European countries probably spent more money on research on influenza and other infectious diseases than at any other time in their history. A new social medicine appeared that was less exclusively bacteriological and more microbiological. Until then, successes in bacteriology had overshadowed or obstructed progress in virology. Although specific animal and plant viral diseases had been closely monitored for the past thirty years, many researchers still expected to find that unusual, or extremely small, bacteria were responsible for virtually all infectious diseases. During World War I, the discovery of viruses that attack bacteria helped encourage new channels of research, and the flu pandemic concentrated attention on airborne diseases that heretofore had been inadequately understood. Only in the 1930s did doctors appreciate that viruses were qualitatively different pathological entities. In 1933, the virus that had caused so much destruction in 1918 and 1919 was at last identified, allowing research on a vaccine to proceed. At the same time, researchers were unlocking the mysteries in patterns of dissemination, including how disease could be transmitted by supposedly uninfected people. The "healthy carrier" had been an important agent in the spread of the flu, typhoid, hepatitis, and cholera.

The new emphasis on preventive medicine led to a dramatic improvement in the general health of European peoples. Public health education became an integral part of medical training as national leaders increasingly recognized that the health of the worker, no less than that of the soldier at the front, affected the fortunes of the country, including its productivity and its ability to recover from the war. Certain countries openly acknowledged their obligation to provide their citizens with proper health care. Communist Russia established the first nationalized health service in July 1918. But putting the obligation on paper could not obliterate the fact that Russia was 150 years behind the rest of the civilized world in providing health care for its people.[3] In time when the other European countries, especially those in Western Europe, instituted socialized medicine, they not only began at a higher level than the Communists had, but they also managed to exceed them in quality of service. The interwar years also saw new developments in nutritional science. Eating a "balanced diet" was easier than it had been because of improved refrigeration, which allowed the urban markets to have continued access to fresh fruits and vegetables. New techniques for slowing the spoilage of pasteurized milk similarly helped distribution and promoted its consumption by children, thereby helping to reduce infant mortality.

A Reduction of Infant Mortality. One of the immediate benefits of increased attention to public health was a drop in the rate of infant mortality, which declined steadily in practically all European countries. The one exception was Greece, but even here, children were more likely to survive their first year than children in most Eastern European countries, which had the worst records in Europe.[4] Not surprisingly, the countries with the most advanced public health programs had the lowest infant mortality rates: the Netherlands and Norway (45 deaths per 1,000 during the first year), Switzerland (48), and Sweden (50). Among the major powers, the Soviet Union had the highest infant mortality, and that rate most likely increased during the political famines of the Stalinist period.[5] The precise rates are unknown because the Soviets not only refused to provide statistics that might prove embarrassing, they also changed the names of diseases to cover up the fact that they existed. Under Stalin, typhus could no longer be called typhus. It became "disease form No. 2."[6] In other European countries, however, the average infant mortality continued to drop. Between 1929 and 1938 it declined from 127 to 97 in Italy, from 123 to 70 in France, from 131 to 60 in Germany, and from 80 to 53 in England and Wales.

Larger families tended to be normal in peasant families where the fear of having another mouth to feed was counterbalanced by the expectation that children could contribute to the economic well-being of the family. However, better health and improved social security made a large family no longer necessary to ensure the continuation of the family line or to support the parents in old age. Governments were now providing old-age insurance. Advances in contraception made it easier for families to have fewer children, and the craving for a higher standard of living made doing so more desirable. Children were consumer goods—the more a family produced the less money it had available for other purchases. The fewer siblings, the more attention and benefits each could potentially receive. Somewhat ironically, parental responsibilities increased as the number of offspring declined because parents were expected to do more for their children. In working-class families, for example, successful parenting no longer meant that the parents received a material reward from their children's labor; it meant that they had helped their children to get a good start in life.[7]

Since the end of the nineteenth century, in most European countries the family had declined across classes as an important productive unit and as the transmitter of farm or business property. The family was no longer the principal social organization. Now children were expected to establish lives of their own, separate from their parents. Daughters no longer remained at home as care givers. Like sons, they would grow up and leave the nest. All children would get jobs and leave the parents to fend for themselves. Yet the family was hardly on the brink of collapse.

Its diminished economic role did not lead to a similar reduction in its psychological and social roles and in defining people's relations to each other.

Recreation. A life marked by diversions had always seemed the exclusive prerogative of the upper classes. Their pleasure in riding to the hounds and attending balls, regattas, and sporting events had contributed to the image of the wealthy and privileged as a class that danced. In contrast, the middle class was expected to work hard, make money, get ahead, and take life seriously. It had no time to relax. Although the working class might have liked to enjoy itself more, its role was to work, keep the wheels turning, and stay on the job—for long hours. It could not be allowed to waste time. Workers had one day off—Sunday, when they were expected to go to church. During the nineteenth century, the work day had been reduced several times, but a forty-hour week seemed positively utopian. The Second International boldly advocated the forty-eight-hour week (8 hours a day × 6),[8] but employers feared that this would sound the death knell for the traditional work ethic. Worse yet, what would workers do with all that spare time? Were not idle hands the devil's tools? The war forced people to rethink their positions. What had once appeared impossible now became a reality. Workers, whose unions had deliberately postponed agitating for better conditions until after the war, felt they had something coming. The Bolsheviks proclaimed the right of workers to the forty-hour week—a right that was rescinded under Stalin. Nevertheless, the Soviet announcement challenged the democracies to do the same. Western workers not only wanted the forty-hour week, they also wanted guaranteed annual vacations with pay.

With more time off the job, workers gave serious consideration to play. "In the morning, in the evening, ain't we got fun. / Not much money, oh but, honey, ain't we got fun?" went the lyrics of a popular song.[9] The commercial entertainment industry, which had existed in all major urban centers before the war, became more important. The movies gradually replaced the music hall. Spectator sports became big business. People identified with their favorite soccer or rugby teams with a passion that approached hysteria. Fans wore their team's colors and sometimes defended its honor with violence. Seaside resorts undertook new construction, modernizing the amusements on the boardwalks and piers that had proved so popular during the late Victorian age. Railroads enticed travelers with special weekend excursion fares, cheap family rates to Windsor Park, Fontainebleau, the *Hermannsdenkmal*, or Hadrian's villa. Many activities were less costly and more mundane: taking walks, bicycling, betting on the national lottery, sitting in cafés, or drinking in pubs. In France, the state established special holiday camps, *colonies des vacances*, to give all schoolchildren the opportunity to go to the mountains or the beach, places many had never been. Many people simply stayed home and listened to the radio. Dictatorships were not slow to realize the importance of this form of entertainment, but took steps to ensure that people heard only what the regime wanted them to hear. Even in democracies the governments became involved, if only to decide how to allocate on-air programming.[10]

In Britain, the Wireless Telegraphy Act of 1904 gave control of the airwaves to the British Post Office, which awarded the Marconi Company, a manufacturer of wireless equipment, the first license to begin broadcasting. The first transmission on 14 February 1922 reflected the company's desire to make this venture a financial success by deliberately catering to the tastes of the hoi polloi. The government soon stepped in, deciding that such an important enterprise should not be immersed in commercialism and banality. On 18 October 1922, it created the British Broadcasting Corporation (BBC), granting it an exclusive monopoly over transmissions. John Reith, the company's first general manager, thought that using radio purely for entertainment would insult the character and intelligence of the people. The BBC, therefore, provided a balanced program of news, information, music, educational materials, speeches, weather reports, and theatrical entertainment. In short, it gave the people what it thought they should have, not what they necessarily wanted. A special user's fee, not advertisements, provided the BBC's main financial support. A board of governors appointed by the Crown ran the corporation, subject to the authority of the postmaster general who reported to the cabinet; this organization was duplicated in other public corporations created after World War II.

Radio broadcasting grew extremely rapidly. By 1931, stations or power relays covered the entire United Kingdom. The BBC also began to experiment with television. In July 1930, it made its first transmission with Luigi Pirandello's play, *The Man with a Flower in His Mouth*. Two years later, it established the first formal television studio. The original charter of the BBC included the principle of political impartiality. This mandate was generally honored except during the General Strike when a clear bias appeared. The French also tried to appear neutral. Often they managed this by having their state-run networks concentrate on cultural programming, thereby avoiding topics that were politically, morally, or socially sensitive. By refusing to pander to lowbrow tastes, these operations spared their public much of the banality, triviality, and vulgarity that was so characteristic of American broadcasting. But then the Americans had found that a little trash was just the sort of thing that heightened interest.

While the democracies did not try to dictate what sort of leisure activities their citizens should enjoy, Europe's strongmen thought differently. The Soviet Union attempted to control most social activities under a single hierarchical command, but delegated some authority to factories, cooperatives, and various occupational organizations. Resources were scarce and often had to be stretched to the limit. By 1939, the Communist authorities had established only 3,000 movie houses. They managed to build up a film audience by putting portable projectors in villages, factories, schools, libraries, and other public buildings. Trade unions sponsored inexpensive vacations to resorts, including those on the Black Sea. Space was limited and was often allocated on the basis of favoritism. Important people had their own dachas in the countryside. The regime's leaders romped in special compounds with their own exclusive recreational facilities: tennis courts, swimming pools, and hiking paths. Lesser people had to make do with public parks, museums, and visits to memorials to the Revolution. The Communist regime also made a concerted effort to furnish its people with a variety of other diversions, including mass displays and pageants, excursions, circuses, and sporting events.

In the first years after the Revolution, competitive sports were considered remnants of the decadent, bourgeois past and fell victim to the revolutionary physical culture movement. The regime put on a whole range of proletarian games, vast spectacles with an ideological content. Six thousand people participated in a production called "Indians, British, and Reds," which was held in the summer of 1924 in Moscow's Sparrow Hills. Its purpose was to demonstrate that Communism promoted sports as a means of encouraging harmony among nations, whereas the British pursued them as a means of conquering the world. The game ended with the Indians and the Reds attacking and defeating the British, after which the victors celebrated the inauguration of a new Communist world.[11] Such theatrics soon fell into disfavor, however.

Good old-fashioned bourgeois competition returned, now touted as a means of inspiring pride in the Soviet Union and support for the Communist party. In April 1930, the regime established the All-Union Physical Culture Council to act as a ministry of sport and oversee and direct all organized sport. The council promoted all manner of competitive sports, especially those with special mass appeal. It encouraged leagues, championships, and the building of stadiums and other facilities; it also created sports' heroes. These athletes took their place with other Stakhanovites as the regime's darlings. They received special privileges and put on demonstrations to promote solidarity and inspire the workers to work hard to transform backward Russia into a world power.[12]

One of the most successful state-run leisure programs was established by the Nazis. Ostensibly created to reward the workers for their labor, it actually served as a means of control to ensure good behavior. The German Labor Front promoted *Kraft durch Freude* (Strength through Joy), a program that included a whole series of inexpensive leisure activities ranging from gymnastic courses and museum and factory tours to short excursions and Mediterranean cruises. Strength through Joy sold tickets to other sports and activities, from chess to mountain climbing. It operated resort hotels, ran a fleet of ships, and had its own ninety-musician symphony orchestra. The activities, financed by compulsory Labor Front dues, were highly regimented in the Teutonic tradition. Even so, the general response to Strength through Joy was favorable. During its first years of operation, from 1934 to 1937, participation in its activities rose from 2 to 9.5 million people, many of whom filled scrapbooks with photos of their excursions. But these outings were also occasions for more ominous activities. In January 1938, a Gestapo spy, accompanying a Strength through Joy excursion to Spain, reported to his superiors that sixty revelers arrived late at the passport office and were violating currency restrictions. Moreover, he said, one of the passengers had failed to stand rigidly at attention when the national anthem was sung. The spy identified the nonchalant culprit by name, including his place of residence and date of birth.

In Italy as well, leisure activities came under Fascist regulation. The *Dopolavoro* (After Work) program, like Germany's Strength through Joy, arranged cheap vacations and other recreational activities for the workers. Mussolini's regime also expanded children's physical education programs and built and enlarged sporting facilities throughout the country to encourage sports among older people. Middle-aged Achille Starace, who had been appointed Fascist party secretary in 1931, tried to set an example by showing off his athleticism at sporting meets. In one of his best routines, he dived through a burning hoop. Mussolini put primary emphasis, however, on co-opting the two big-time sports of bicycling and football (soccer), which passed from local club and private control to national control. The official Directorate of Football was a large bureaucracy with regional branches, run by a horde of administrators and officials. The directorate licensed referees and players and organized the competitions and tournaments. Large stadiums, built in the major cities, became showpieces for sporting spectaculars designed to glorify Fascism. Even the country's Olympic Games Committee was taken over by Fascists. In boxing, Primo Carnera, the six-and-a-half-foot "Ambling Alp," became a national hero when he knocked out Jack Sharkey to become the world heavyweight champion in 1933. No one seemed to care that gangsters had bankrolled this former carpenter's pugilistic career, and that his title-winning bout, like his previous victories, was somewhat questionable.[13] Supposedly, an uppercut caught Sharkey who cleverly managed to fall forward on his face. Mussolini was admitting to more than he realized when he called boxing an essentially Fascist method of self-expression.

On the Move

Modern Transportation. World War I did wonders for the development of the internal combustion engine. In most countries, the total miles of railroad track did not change significantly. The basic system had been largely in place before the war, but the amount of passenger travel increased.[14] A more dramatic change was the development of commercial aviation, an industry that did not exist before the war. In 1920, French airports processed 73,000 passengers; by 1939, the number had risen to 600 million. In Germany, passenger traffic went from 4 million to 114 million in the same two decades. In Italy, it climbed from 8 million in 1926 to 246 million in 1939; in Great Britain, from 4.3 million in 1925 to over 90 million by 1939. Although passenger fares were still a long way from the billions who would travel by air after World War II, air travel was no longer a mode of transport only for the rich and adventurous. People's perceptions of distance and mobility were changing and so were their expectations.

Although the Europeans trailed the Americans in private car ownership—in 1921 one in 14 Americans owned a car while only one in 168 in Britain did—they clearly did not intend to be left behind. Production of military vehicles had given the Europeans the technical skills to develop an automobile industry, although the unstable economic conditions after the war did not favor the growth of such large-capitalization industries. Nevertheless the French, Germans, British, and Italians pressed ahead.[15] By adopting American assembly line techniques, they were able to move away from producing exclusively for the rich who wanted cars of *grande marque*. In 1919, André Citroën formed a company to produce cars for the growing middle-class market. His first car, the Model A, was the first European car to be mass produced; the car was turned out at the rate of 100 a day, rising to 500 a day in 1926, its last year of production. All the other major European companies followed suit with their own lines of bourgeois cars, while at the same time they worked to develop cheaper and cheaper models. The Austin Seven of 1922 was a four-cylinder runabout, seating two adults and selling for 165 pounds. The English called it the "bed pan." It helped save the company from financial difficulties. The Morris Minor cost 125 pounds when it appeared at the end of the 1920s. In the early 1930s, the German government decided it was time more people were motorized, and it induced Ferdinand Porsche to undertake the production of "a car for all." The first Volkswagen prototype appeared in 1932. At least thirty other preproduction models would be built. The Nazis liked the concept so much that they constructed a factory for its production near Wolfsburg with special housing for the workers nearby. In 1937, the government initiated a scheme that put the purchase of a Volkswagen within the reach of the average consumer. It set up a savings plan whereby anyone could reserve one of the new people's cars by paying five marks a month. As an added inducement, the government abolished the motor-vehicle tax. Within a short time, the plan had 170,000 subscribers, but hardly any of the promised "Beetles" were actually delivered.[16] The Italians, not to be outdone by the Germans, had their own version of the Volkswagen called the *Topolino* (Little Mouse). Built as a two-seater, it appeared in June 1936, had a 13-horsepower engine, and featured optional front and back bumpers. It became a significant part of Italy's total automobile production.

During the 1930s, Germany produced 275,000 cars annually; the Italians turned out 61,000, the French 182,000, and the British 390,000. All these additional cars on the public highways and streets produced enormous congestion. European thoroughfares had been built for the horse and carriage, and many cities still had streets wide enough only for pedestrians. Modernization came slowly. Among the first modern highway systems were the *autobahns* built in Nazi Germany, but these roadways were constructed primarily to move troops rapidly. Everywhere the number of motor cars exceeded the facilities necessary to provide them service. The number of filling stations was insufficient, and gasoline was often dispensed from buses or trucks pulled up on the side of the road. In time, these makeshift arrangements were replaced by something more permanent, but all too often these new garages were thrown up with little attention paid to their appearance. Moreover, burning insufficiently refined fuels in inefficient engines created pollution. In London, the "pea-soup" fog, which was already oppressive due to the soot from soft coal emitted by thousands of chimneys, was made worse by malodorous gas fumes, whose toxicity presented an increased danger for those with respiratory ailments. Yet the desire to live in urban areas did not cease.

Migration to the Cities. Cities held the key to economic advancement and cultural excitement. "How 'ya gonna keep 'em down on the farm, after they've seen Paree?" asked a post-World War I American song.[17] In the metropolis, the opportunities for self-enrichment seemed limitless. While the country offered only boredom, backwardness, and stagnation, the city, with its variety and drama, offered liberation. Urban populations grew faster than the European population as a whole.[18] Cities of more than 100,000 showed the greatest gains. All of Europe's capitals increased significantly. In less than twenty years, the population of Moscow almost tripled to slightly over 4 million; Rome's population grew by 67 percent to 1.1 million; and London jumped 16 percent to over 8.7 million. Berlin increased 14 percent to 4.3 million.[19] The burgeoning populations increased the demand for housing and better sanitation and put pressure on parks, stores, and public services. Low-cost housing even pushed into the suburbs; these were areas on the outskirts of the cities, which lacked municipal centers and had nothing to tie them together except their bedroom community status. For example, Paris lost 77,000 people and was now down to 2.8 million, but added population in the working-class suburbs more than offset this loss. These were the so-called red suburbs, which consistently voted Communist: Saint-Denis, Courbevoie, Nanterre, Ivry, and Puteaux. They ringed Paris like a noose and were connected to it by public transportation.

Although cities offered many exciting opportunities, not everyone could take advantage of them. For many urban dwellers, the reality of urban life was far from pleasant. Insufficient social services, crowding, and dingy working-class neighborhoods unchanged since the nineteenth century all contributed to the drabness and squalor of much of urban life. "As you walk through the industrial towns you lose yourself in labyrinths of little brick houses blackened by smoke, festering in planless chaos round miry alleys and little cindered yards where there are stinking dustbins and lines of grimy washing and half-ruinous w.c's," wrote George Orwell in a book about life in England's industrial Midlands.[20] The author had been commissioned by Victor Gollancz, the left-wing book publisher, to write a book about unemployment and poverty in the depressed areas of Lancashire and Yorkshire. Orwell's account, although didactic, was nevertheless a powerful description of the miserable conditions that still dogged the lives of the British lower classes. The number of British living in poverty had been reduced over the past several decades,[21] but almost 20 percent still did not eat a diet the British Medical Association judged adequate. Orwell saw proof of this on their faces. Watching the crowd in Trafalgar Square on the day of King George V's funeral, he observed the Londoner's "puny limbs [and] sickly faces. . . . hardly a well-built man or a decent-looking woman, and not a fresh complexion anywhere." These people were for the most part "the shopkeeper-commercial-traveller type, with a sprinkling of the well-to-do."[22]

Psychological costs, indifference, and lack of concern accompanied physical deprivation. Between the wars, the city was too often a place where lives became as disposable as cheap consumer goods. In this respect, little had changed since the nineteenth century. When Jean Jaurès, the future leader of the French Socialist party, first arrived in Paris from the provinces in 1878, the city's lack of humanity and the lonely desperation of its men and women horrified him. His first impression stayed with him, and many years later he recalled: "I saw thousands upon thousands of people, passing each other without the slightest sign of recognition, each completely isolated from the rest. And I asked myself how could they accept it, how such an unjust social order could endure."[23]

Compartmentalization, rootlessness, and a lack of a sense of community were all too often the sad components of urban life. It was difficult to determine if the workers were much better off than they were before the war. Certainly, real wages had not changed much. In Britain, industrial wages dropped one-third during the 1920s and fell another 5 percent during the 1930s. A corresponding decline in the cost of living matched the losses, however. In Germany, a similar fall in the cost of living also offset wages. In Italy, industrial wages rose by 28 percent in the 1920s, but the cost of living rose by 65 percent. In the 1930s, wages fell 15 percent while the cost of living declined 25 percent. Only the French workers' position improved. In France, wages consistently rose more than the cost of living, especially in the 1930s when they climbed by 61 percent, while the cost of living went up just 15 percent.[24]

On the positive side, the increased willingness of governments to take measures to improve the welfare of their people helped change the belief that poverty was inevitable, if not necessary. This new attitude came from a sense of obligation to those who had made so many sacrifices in the war and also from a fear that the example of the Bolshevik revolution might be contagious. Most political parties at least gave lip service to the need to work for social improvement. The major right-wing dictatorships, helped into power by conservative fears, offered socialist programs aimed at the regeneration of the nation through the transformation of society. Even before they became dictatorships, Germany, Italy, Austria, Poland, and Bulgaria all had compulsory unemployment insurance schemes. Britain began its social insurance coverage before the war. France had to wait until the legislation of the Popular Front. Few now doubted that the government had a primary obligation to ensure people a basic standard of living. The great thinkers of the eighteenth-century enlightenment had assumed that the task of government was to protect the people against political injustice; now this concept had been successfully extended to economics. The Keynesian revolution advanced the proposition that government should act directly to cure unemployment and depression by stimulating production and expanding consumption.

Immigrants and Refugees. The Lausanne Convention, signed in January 1923, provided for the compulsory exchange of populations between Greece and Turkey. Even before the accord was signed, the evacuations had already begun. Ernest Hemingway, then correspondent for the *Toronto Star*, watched the exodus of Christians from eastern Thrace. "Twenty miles of carts drawn by cows, bullocks and muddy-flanked water buffalo, with exhausted staggering men, women, and children, blankets over their heads, walking blindly along in the rain beside their worldly goods. ... A husband spreads a blanket over a woman in labor in one of the carts to keep off the driving rain. She is the only person making a sound. Her little daughter looks at her in horror and begins to cry. And the procession keeps moving."[25] Those who managed to leave were the lucky ones. The victorious Kemalist armies determined to rid the country of foreigners had already massacred many Greeks living in Anatolia. Only half of the 2 million Greeks living in Turkey in 1914 were left to be evacuated in 1922–1923. In all, over 1.25 million Greeks and 356,000 Turks would be exchanged. The transfer, the biggest to date in history, hit Greece especially hard. The new arrivals were stashed everywhere, mostly in urban areas. In Athens, they were housed in schools, railway stations, churches, warehouses, theaters, and movie houses, more than doubling the city's population. Municipal services were overwhelmed, disease and malnutrition rose, and mortality rates soared. The added burden on public services almost brought the society to the point of collapse.[26]

The Greek refugee problem, though one of the most severe, was all too common. Many Western European cities now had thousands of these unwelcome guests. The disintegration of the large empires and the patchwork of smaller states they had engendered had exposed millions of peoples to the full fury of hunger, political repression, and war. Each area had pockets and regions of alien peoples surrounded by larger ethnic groups who looked upon these minorities as mortal enemies, fit only for extermination or banishment. During the civil war in Russia, many of the displaced fled to other parts of the country—into the Ukraine or down to the Crimea or into the Don or Kuban regions. Many went to Finland or into the Baltic provinces, others fled to Poland. In 1920, the Ukrainian nationalist army of Simon Petlyura sought asylum in western Galicia. The defeated White Army of Peter Wrangel sailed from the Crimea to Constantinople (later Istanbul); the soldiers took their dependents with them, 130,000 refugees in all. Such numbers completely swamped the city's resources and led to outbreaks of cholera, smallpox, and typhus. Many of the survivors were then evacuated, under League of Nations auspices, to other locations, including Greece, Yugoslavia, Bulgaria, and North Africa.

The political changes established at the Paris Conference uprooted thousands of Eastern European peoples. Ethnic Germans left the Polish Corridor, the Baltic states, and Russia. Magyars fled from the areas lost to Czechoslovakia, Romania, and Yugoslavia. They tried to enter Hungary, but that country, finding itself unable to handle the influx of 250,000 newcomers, closed its frontiers, stranding thousands in squalid border towns. Jews experienced the greatest dislocation. Centuries-old attitudes singled them out for persecution and deportation. In the aftermath of the collapse of the Austro-Hungarian Empire, anti-Jewish riots and demonstrations occurred everywhere. In Hungary, pogroms broke out in 50 towns after the downfall of Béla Kun, and the new government of Miklós Horthy passed a sweeping anti-Jewish law, prompting the Jews to flee to countries they hoped would be more tolerant. In Russia and the Ukraine, almost half of the Jewish population was left homeless by the civil war. All over Eastern Europe, Jews flocked to countries that would take them—Romania, Poland, Germany, Czechoslovakia, Austria, Belgium, Holland, France, and the United States. Nowhere were they welcome. Poland and Austria began deportations. So did the Bavarians and the Romanians. International and Jewish relief organizations tried to find countries to which they could be sent. Some left for South America or the British Dominions, others went to

Palestine. In 1924, the United States tightened its restrictions against all immigration. Many Jews, with no place to go, remained where they were—unwelcome and stateless, with no prospects of leading a normal life or changing their stateless status.

Political exiles also became a permanent fixture of European society between the wars.[27] Former aristocrats, tsarist army officers, clerics, and members of rival political parties fled Communist Russia until the mid-1920s when Stalin closed the frontiers. Members of anti-Fascist political parties, journalists, intellectuals, and other opponents of Mussolini's regime left Italy. Most of the approximately 10,000 refugees went to France. When Hitler came to power in 1933, Germans started to leave Germany—first Jews, then others, including scientists, artists, and political dissidents. The victory of Francisco Franco in Spain in 1939 created still more refugees; 450,000 supporters of the Loyalist government rushed to the French border trying to get out before the frontier was closed.

Each dictatorship had its victims and produced its exiles. The most famous comprised a veritable who's who of the political, cultural, and intellectual talents of the age. Even when the host countries were favorably disposed, the influx of all these people came at a bad time—when the hosts were recovering either from the war or from the depression. France proved to be the most important sanctuary, receiving between 200,000 and 300,000 refugees in the interwar years before the Spanish Republican influx. France had a tradition of being a country of refuge. In addition, its willingness to accept so many foreigners was facilitated by the great losses it had suffered in World War I.[28] Another 3 million foreigners came legally to France to find jobs, many thousands more were undoubtedly there illegally. Altogether, perhaps as much as 10 percent of the French population was composed of foreigners, a cause for some alarm. During the 1930s, the liberal policy changed, as the French, fearing a potential alien fifth column, adopted a policy of denationalization. Some foreigners were expelled, others' work permits were not renewed, and procedures for entering the country were tightened.

Refugees formed their own urban subcultures. Each large European city had foreign districts where the aliens congregated; they maintained their own social hierarchies, joined their own associations, patronized their own stores and restaurants, read their own newspapers, and attended their own churches. The foreigners often continued their old political disputes, sometimes with violence, and longed for the day when they could return home. Many held low-paying industrial or service jobs, which kept them in the working class and frustrated their assimilation. Thus, they remained easy to identify. Many refugees who had not managed to leave the European continent were living on borrowed time. When the Nazis swept over most of Europe, extermination of Germany's racial and political enemies was high on their list of priorities.

A WOMAN'S PLACE

Greater Emancipation

Devices to Save Labor. After the war, women received the right to vote in Great Britain, Germany, Russia, the successor states of the Austro-Hungarian Empire, the Baltic states, and Sweden. They were not enfranchised in Italy or in France, although they came close in the latter.[29] During the war, women had entered the labor force in increasing numbers, supposedly as custodians for the jobs of men.

Women's right to vote was recognized in many European countries after World War I. But for this woman, voting for the first time in a British postwar election, it probably changed her life very little as the male power structure remained firmly entrenched.

For many women, there was no going back. Many worked out of economic necessity and because the death of millions of men in battle had reduced their chances for marriage. All the warring countries had a great surplus of women between the prime childbearing years of eighteen to thirty-eight.[30] The percentage of working women therefore remained fairly constant despite the high unemployment in many countries.[31] No doubt, the inferior wages paid to women and the fact that many of their jobs were in the necessary service sector reduced their vulnerability to layoffs. Women's increased financial importance and independence created the potential for them to participate more actively in decisions affecting their welfare. However, their lack of political experience often kept them from using their position to advantage. Women were harder to organize, and their demands usually received lower priorities than those of men. Women had been raised to be passive and to think of themselves primarily as homemakers. On the jobs, they were frequently under the supervision of male bosses who saw no reason why they should treat women equally, especially when that would mean paying them wages commensurate with those of their male counterparts.

The period saw a shift in the kinds of work women were doing. Fewer worked in textile plants, while more found jobs in the chemical, auto, metallurgical, and electrical industries. Increased mechanization meant that muscle power was no longer as important as before. The creation of new opportunities in manufacturing did not lead to a comparable increase in women's status, however. They obtained many jobs only because the jobs were inferior to those given to men. Often women and men worked separately, in different parts of the same factory or in different industries. This segregation in the workplace usually led to the exclusion of women from labor unions; as a result, women's wages remained low. Even when women worked the same jobs as men, they usually were paid less money.[32] The cycle was hard to break.

More women worked in "white-collar jobs" than in manufacturing. They held positions as secretaries, receptionists, and stenographers and assumed many jobs in the service sector including retail sales, communications, transport, and social work. They also retained their lead in nursing, a traditional occupation for women, and shared teaching responsibilities with men in primary and, to a lesser extent, secondary education.

Because of the inflation of the 1920s, many women who might once have dropped out of the work force when they got married continued to work to help make ends meet. But having to work both at home and in the marketplace imposed additional burdens, especially on working-class women who were expected to do both jobs well without any additional compensation or increase in prestige. Many labor-saving devices appeared that purported to revolutionize and simplify home-making. Electric heaters, cookers, toasters, and kettles became readily available. Electric sewing machines and electric sweepers also appeared. The electric mixer made its debut in 1920, followed by the washing machine, the hair dryer, and, in 1926, the refrigerator. The contention that these appliances saved labor was largely fictitious, however, especially in lower-class homes where such devices were not as commonplace as in middle-class residences. Moreover, women who had formerly sent out their dirty laundry—a common practice even in poorer homes—were now expected to wash it themselves. Women who once would have had maids were now supposed to do the housework alone. Electricity became intimately associated with woman's liberation; it was also a source of added responsibilities and drudgery.

Changing Morality. The presence of so many women in the work force led to the gradual loosening of family restraints. Now men and women had far more opportunities to meet informally than before. Courtship patterns became less rigid and less ritualized; parental consent was no longer as essential for marriage, which now was more likely to be arranged on the basis of the mutual attraction of the individuals than on how the alliance would affect the family as a whole. The disappearance of the dowry meant that parents had less control over their daughter's choice of a mate. Women, living independently in an urban environment, also became more vulnerable. They went to pubs, movies, and concerts without escorts. "Bright young things" puffed cigarettes, plastered themselves with makeup, guzzled cocktails, and frequented nightclubs where they danced the recent American crazes like the charleston, the black bottom, and the heebie-jeebies. The utilitarian demands of their employment and the need to function with ease in an urban environment dictated that they dress more comfortably. They abandoned corsets, shortened their skirts and bobbed their hair. Clothes began to be made of more durable fabrics. The 1920s saw the introduction of rayon, a synthetic of British invention. It was followed in 1938 by nylon, first manufactured by Du Pont. Nylon was not only more crease-resistant than rayon, it could be used in the production of other goods, including toothbrushes and other utensils. In 1939, the first nylon stockings appeared.

Extended social contacts led to changing attitudes toward sex. Whether this inevitably meant an increase in promiscuity is not certain, but advertisers seemed to assume that was the case. The "sex sell" had even been used on World War I posters to titillate men into joining the armed forces. Now advertisements used it to get people to buy everything from soap powder to automobiles to cigarettes. Plays and movies reinforced the idea that sexual relationships between unmarried adults were prevalent and desirable. Premarital sex, if it did not suddenly increase, at least seemed more socially acceptable. The use of contraceptive devices became widespread. Couples freed from the fear and responsibility of pregnancy could enjoy sex as they did other forms of recreation. The advice that Queen Victoria reputedly gave her daughter—"close your eyes and think of England"—seemed worth repeating only as a joke. Yet, the idea that a woman's place was in the home had not died out and in some societies was made official policy.

Women and the Dictators

Fascists and the Battle of the Births. Mussolini believed that a woman's primary responsibility was to make babies. He bestowed upon the most prolific mother in each district honorary membership in the Fascist party. This was part of his drive to increase the Italian population, a policy known as the "Battle of the Births." In an overpopulated country feeling the effects of the restrictions that the United States imposed on immigration, a program to increase the Italian birthrate seemed the height of folly. Yet Mussolini was convinced that an index of a nation's virility was its capacity to produce babies or, more specifically, future soldiers. He therefore outlawed all information about birth control and forbade the sale of contraceptives. He imposed a tax on bachelors, practically doubling their financial obligations, and paid subsidies to couples with large families. A National Program for the Protection of Mothers and Infants provided monies to improve infant health care. Mussolini hoped to increase the Italian population from 40 million to 60 million within a generation.

In pushing his policy, Mussolini abandoned the promise he had made before coming to power to give women the right to vote.[33] Nevertheless, women did not lose any political rights under Mussolini since they had not been enfranchised and had not participated actively in politics before he came to power. The conservative ideal of women as mothers and wives, restricted to the home and subject to the authority of the male head of the household, was prevalent in Italy prior to Mussolini, at least in middle- and upper-class families where the pressure to work was not strong. The traditional exclusion of women from any decision-making or managerial responsibilities outside the home had the full support of the Roman Catholic church. In 1891 in the encyclical *Rerum Novarum* (The Condition of Labor), Pope Leo XIII wrote that a woman was by nature fitted for housework, an occupation "which is best adapted at once to preserve her modesty, and to promote the bringing up of children and the well-being of the family."[34]

Mussolini wanted women to continue this subservience. He also wanted their active help in strengthening Fascism. To this end he allowed them to participate in various party organizations, like the *Fasci Femminili*. But such activism would bring them out of the home, thereby making them less than ideal homemakers. To offset this loss, Mussolini undertook to bolster men's rights over their families. A husband could now enforce his authority with corporal punishment; he could use the police to pursue a runaway wife, and he could directly and personally punish faithlessness. A 1932 law exempted a man from punishment for killing an adulterous wife, mother, or sister, the act being considered "a crime of honor." Failing that, a woman who cheated on her husband could be imprisoned for up to two years. On the other hand, a man who had extramarital affairs was rarely punished. Nor, for that matter, were rapists ever brought to justice, since all the rapist had to do was to show that his victim had a bad reputation or had provoked him by seductive behavior—a comparatively easy thing to do.[35] Perhaps granting men dictatorial powers over their families was intended to compensate them for the loss of political freedom.

The women had no such compensation. In addition to having no political liberties and being under the authority of men at home, they also had to endure discrimination and denigration in the work force. Already women were being paid about a third less than the men for comparable work. In 1927, the Fascist regime reduced that to half. The regime also gave men better health, accident, and unemployment insurance and longer vacations. Despite the drive to put women back in the home, one-third of the labor force throughout the Fascist period was female. An increasingly militarized economy simply could not get along without this supply of cheap labor, especially in offices, hospitals and clinics, and factories. Very few women rose to managerial positions, however, despite the fact that more women were attending universities than ever before and were aspiring to such positions.

The Duce's macho image reinforced the conservative antifeminist attitudes of the past. Mussolini insisted that the regime give an impression of youth and virility. He shaved his head to disguise his natural baldness and habitually displayed his own family of five children, but prevented any mention of the fact that he was a grandfather. He projected an aggressive sexuality. Unlike the many sexually puritanical dictators who clutter up the pages of twentieth-century history, Mussolini was one of the greatest womanizers of his age. His associates tried to convince him to be more discrete about his extramarital affairs, fearing that in staunchly Roman Catholic Italy such conduct would affront traditional Christian morality and cost him public support. But the Duce's belief that women were objects for the enjoyment of men actually added to his popularity. Party photographers reinforced his machismo by snapping him in all sorts of strenuous activities: fencing with sabers, riding horses or cutting wheat amid the peasants with sweat pouring from his bare chest. In the early days, Mussolini liked to drive around the Villa Borghese in his Alfa Romeo with a lion cub next to him on the front seat. Women knew that the way to the Duce's heart was often through his sex organs. Oftentimes, he would dispatch attractive petitioners on the floor of his office at the Palazzo Venezia. Clara Petacci, who later became his mistress, recalled that the first time he "did not even take off his boots."[36]

Emancipation Soviet Style. In patriarchal tsarist Russia, women had little opportunity to improve their status through legitimate protest and agitation. Some daughters of the upper classes found compensation in study abroad; others joined socialist parties that proclaimed women's equality as one of their goals. A few Russian women became well-known terrorists. The Bolshevik party was a male-dominated organization, but with the November Revolution, women's emancipation suddenly seemed to be possible. Lenin had committed himself to women's liberation, calling housework "barbarously unproductive, petty, nerve-wracking, stultifying and crushing drudgery."[37] His stand was politically astute. Women activists were a prime source of support for the Bolshevik cause, agitating, demonstrating, and organizing factory workers.

Even though Lenin's associates did not appear to be as committed as he was to women's rights—the upper echelons of the party had a complete dearth of women—the Bolshevik state guaranteed women complete legal equality with men. Constitutionally, the law was the most progressive such legislation in Europe. Soviet women had equal status in marriage, including the right to divorce their husbands, to inherit and own property, and to keep their own name. They also had equal rights in litigation. Abortion was legalized and wage discrimination was forbidden. The Woman's Department of the Communist party (*Zhenotdel*) worked to transform these paper promises into reality. It spent much of its effort on education, trying to bring the message of women's liberation to the more backward areas of the country. One of its leaders, Alexandra Kollontai, believed that women would gain the dignity and respect they deserved only if they became economically independent and had their own income. Such emancipation, she believed, was contingent on the establishment of state-run child care centers to take care of the offspring. But changing the practices and attitudes of a masculine-dominated society was difficult no matter how sincere the leadership. Rural backwardness, the traditional inferiority accorded women by the Russian Orthodox and Islamic faiths, illiteracy, poverty, cynicism, conservatism, and suspicion by women themselves all made achievement of the ideal impossible. Regulations excluding women from heavy work were often disregarded. Women living with men without marriage received little financial or legal protection. Women were often laid off work before men. Sexual exploitation continued and indeed became worse as the creation of a new proletarian morality denied its existence. Above all, the Communist leadership, which continued to be dominated by men, had more important things to do than cater to women.

Nevertheless, during the Stalinist period, significant advances did take place.[38] Stalin was not known for his commitment to women's liberation, but his mission to transform Soviet Russia into an industrial colossus could not be achieved without the participation of females. Therefore, during the 1930s, women received opportunities they had never enjoyed before. They were sent to school to learn skills previously possessed only by men. They became veterinarians, engineers, lawyers, and doctors. (Undoubtedly, the low pay scale and low social status of doctors in the Soviet Union were related to the fact that many were women without much formal training.) Women became a significant, indispensable part of the skilled labor force. The percentage of women in the work force increased from 28 to 38 percent between 1928 and 1938. By the end of the decade, 40 percent of the country's technicians were women.

Article 122 of the Stalinist Constitution of 1936 boldly stated that women were accorded "all rights on an equal footing with men in all spheres of economic, government, cultural, political, and other social activity."[39] Women paid dearly for these words. Wives who held jobs—employment was essential to supplement the family income—also were expected to be full-time homemakers. They were supposed to shop, cook, clean the house, and take care of the family. Russian men still viewed women as inferiors who should stay at home raising children, and the Stalinist regime, despite its official constitutional stance, seemed to agree. It stiffened the divorce laws, outlawed abortion, and made birth control devices increasingly more difficult to obtain. Women who produced large numbers of babies received awards reminiscent of those handed out to soldiers: women with five children received a Medal of Motherhood–Second Class; those with six children, a Medal of Motherhood–First Class; those with seven children, an Order of Maternal Glory–Third Class; those with eight children, an Order of Maternal Glory–Second Class; those with nine children, an Order of Maternal Glory–First Class; and those with ten children, an Order of the Mother-Heroine.

Women in the Fatherland. The ideal of a male-dominated society was not Hitler's alone. Many Germans had looked in alarm at the breakdown of their paternalistic society and blamed its decline on the permissiveness of the Weimar Republic. Although Hitler idealized and romanticized women, he was a complete misogynist who relegated women to the lowest level of the master race. He believed that both the masses and women were ruled by passion and longed to submit to masculine authority.

Women, being a part of the masses, were subject to a double inferiority. They had to submit to the will of the supreme ruler and to the will of men. A man could serve the state in various capacities. A woman's capacity to serve was officially restricted. Her primary function was to be a wife and mother. Although a woman might work as a teacher, nurse, or social worker, or perform farm labor, or hold a job in the service sector, her work could never be as important as her basic obligation to increase and preserve the German race. Under no circumstances would she be allowed to participate in politics, a calling for which she was intellectually and emotionally unsuited. Women also were not allowed in the armed services, the cadres of the civil service, or the justice department. They could not become lawyers and were discouraged from becoming doctors and university teachers.

Putting women back in the home sent a powerful message to women and men alike. Point 21 of the Nazi program called for the protection of mothers. Traditional family values had a great appeal in all societies, but the Nazis pretended to give them more than lip service. The Women's League (*Frauenschaft*) of the Nazi party was in the forefront of the campaign to take women out of the labor force and return them to their supposed natural habitat. The league sponsored various outreach programs that provided prenatal instruction and child care; it ran home economics courses for schoolgirls; and it provided guidance in the formation and maintenance of proper womanly attitudes. It also made special marriage loans that were reduced if the couple had children. If a couple had at least four children, the loan would be canceled. In addition to putting women in their place, the regime strengthened the role of the husband as head of the household. Under a reaffirmed Wilhelmine legal code, a man could prevent his wife from holding a job outside the home. The property she brought with her into the marriage and any income from that property came under his control. Even if the couple divorced, the husband could continue to make all the decisions about the children's education and religion.

Despite these efforts, the regime did not significantly decrease the number of women in the work force. Women were crucial for the success of the rearmament program. In recognition of this dependency, the Women's League established a special branch to increase the morale of the more than five million women working outside the home in businesses, factories, and on the farms. While the employment of women increased, the Nazis mandated that female wages not exceed 70 percent of that paid to men for the same kind of work. Moreover, women were usually relegated to all sorts of menial jobs, many of which involved hard manual labor.[40]

Despite these measures, women seemed to enjoy life in Nazi Germany—at least that was what the regime would have had one believe. The pictures are still disturbing: women in near hysterics in the Führer's presence. Hitler's photographer, Heinrich Hoffmann, must have worked very hard to get such choice shots of adulation. This strange phenomenon was not altogether contrived. Like men, women found much to admire in Hitler. They liked his determination to protect the family, to restore social stability, and to improve health services. Even before Hitler had come to power, many women had questioned whether the feminists had not missed the point by concentrating too much on equality. Women, after all, had a special nature and special needs.[41] Similar questions were being asked in the other European countries, all of which had male-dominated political systems.

But the cheers belied the disappointment and disillusionment. Women of the Third Reich protested when they were expelled from positions of responsibility in the labor force. They were angered when the regime dissolved their religious organizations. They refused to follow Nazi eugenics concerning decisions on child-bearing. They found the Lebensborn program, which elevated unmarried mothers to the level of heroines, a violation of the Nazi promise to protect home and hearth.

Still, many women did cheer—and loudly. Hitler appealed to almost everyone's fantasies. He was not the rugged, he-man type, but he did not lack sexual attraction. Everybody talked about Hitler's hypnotic eyes. He came across as gallant, caring, visionary, romantic, gracious, and a good provider for his people. He was able to project these qualities in public and used this talent to evoke an appreciative response. Any second thoughts or resistance from his audience are not apparent in the faces of those caught on film. But out of range of Hitler's mesmeric stare, women had ample opportunity to grieve silently about their enforced subservience.

POSTSCRIPT   After the war, the European people wanted to return to normal—well, not exactly normal. Actually, they wanted something a bit better than the "normal" life they had had before the war. Now that the fighting was over, business as usual seemed a bit macabre. The "war to end all wars" was over in time for Christmas—"Peace Christmas" it was called—and people were in a mood to shop, and stores were in a mood to have them shop, and shopping editors were in a mood to give advice on where to shop. The shopping editor of one of London's most important journals had just checked out Carter's, on the corner of New Cavendish and Great Portland Streets, and was full of praise for their gadgets to ease the suffering of the wounded and the sick. "Invalid chairs, self-propelling chairs, tricycle-chairs that go along famously by arm-work, bed tables, reading-stands adjusted by a touch, spinal carriages for those who must for a time lie flat, adjustable couches and reclining chairs, useful and practical bed-tables, bath-chairs and invalid carriages, are in endless variety. They are for outdoor or indoor use."[42] The list was another indication that "normal" was being redefined.

The Armistice was followed by economic chaos, war, revolution, labor unrest, political confusion, and plague—not exactly an auspicious foundation upon which to reconstruct society. Not all of the developments were negative, however. The private car industry began slowly when recovery from the war sapped much of people's discretionary income, but it grew to become the economic miracle of the age. Other achievements could also be cited. The health of Europeans was generally better. Literature and the arts experienced a remarkable flowering. And, despite mixed results, women did take on new importance.

During the interwar period, women achieved several victories but some of them were Pyrrhic. Many of their gains possessed a darker side as well. In going from the home to the factory or office, women often exchanged one form of drudgery for another. Sometimes it was not an even exchange as they now had to work at two jobs instead of one. In the process, they became sex objects and had to contend with a backlash of antifeminism and stereotyping that condemned many of them to menial jobs. Often their advances came as a result of the most crass form of economic determinism: since women were needed, some consideration had to be given to their well-being and their desires. Yet getting a foot on the economic ladder was essential if women were to make further gains. Equal pay for equal work was still in the future. Yet despite these problems, only in the dictatorships was there a demonstrable march backwards. Nazi Germany and Fascist Italy enacted discriminatory legislation aimed specifically at keeping women subservient. At the same time, these states continued to exploit women's labor and betray their generosity. Nevertheless, by the end of the 1930s, in Europe as a whole, women had established a base in politics and the economy from which they could launch the drive for more important advances in the future.

ENDNOTES

1. The "Spanish" flu did not originate in Spain, but received its name because most of the world found out about the cases in that country before they learned about cases in countries where wartime censorship prevented the release of such information.
2. Alfred W. Crosby, *Epidemic and Peace, 1918* (Westport, Conn.: Greenwood Press, 1976), 37–44.
3. William A. Knaus, *Inside Russian Medicine: An American Doctor's First-Hand Report* (Boston: Beacon Press, 1981), 77.
4. Romania suffered 182 infant deaths per 1,000 during the first year; Hungary, 152; Bulgaria, 147; Poland and Portugal, 139; Yugoslavia, 134; Czechoslovakia, 130; and Greece, 115. These figures were calculated by averaging the yearly annual figures between 1929 and 1938. Brian R. Mitchell, *European Historical Statistics, 1750–1970* (New York: Columbia University Press, 1975), 130–31.
5. In the 1920s, 178 Soviet children per 1,000 died in their first year. After 1928, the Communist government refused to release statistics.
6. Knaus, *Inside Russian Medicine*, 83.
7. Louise A. Tilly and Joan W. Scott, *Women, Work, and Family* (New York: Holt, Rinehart and Winston, 1978), 211–12.
8. In France in 1848, the state regulated the conditions of work for the first time in its history. The work day was reduced one hour: from 11 to 10 hours in Paris, and from 12 to 11 hours in the provinces, six days a week. However, this law found little favor with employers and was not enforced.
9. Song by Richard Whitney (New York: Remich, 1921), featured in the musical revue *Satires of 1920*, but popularized in vaudeville by Ruth Royce.
10. The technical problems, namely, the allocation of the airwaves, were more easily solved. In 1906, twenty-seven countries signed a convention allocating airwaves for messages between ships and to shore. This led to the International Telecommunica-

tions Union, which allocated frequencies, adjusted priorities, and coordinated its work with the national regulatory systems.

11. James Riordan, *Sport in Soviet Society: Development of Sport and Physical Education in Russia and the USSR* (Cambridge: Cambridge University Press, 1980), 101–3.

12. Ibid., 120–52.

13. The regime prohibited the publication of any pictures of Carnera on the mat. But this courtesy did not prevent Maxie Baer from flooring Carnera the following year to take away the title.

14. In 1920, France reported 500 million passenger fares were sold; a decade later, fares had risen to 790 million. In Italy, the passenger traffic increased from 112.8 million to 125.8 million; in Russia, from 143 to 558 million; in Poland from 67 million to 154 million. Yet fewer British were taking the train: 1,579,000 in 1930 versus 844,300,000 in 1920. Mitchell, *European Historical Statistics*, 608–10.

15. Marco Ruiz, et al., *One Hundred Years of the Automobile, 1886–1986* (New York: Gallery Books, 1985), 46–71.

16. Thus, the "shareholders" were left with worthless chits. After the war, however, the reemergent Volkswagen factory honored a portion of the money paid during the Nazi period by allowing would-be buyers a deduction on the price of a new car. If a person no longer wanted to buy a Volkswagen, the option could be sold on the open market.

17. Music by Walter Donaldson; words by Sam M. Lewis and Joe Young (New York: Waterson, Berlin and Snyder, 1919).

18. Between 1925 and 1935, the German population increased by 10 percent to 69.5 million; between 1921 and 1936, the Italian population increased by 13 percent to 42.9 million; between 1921 and 1931, the British population increased by 5 percent to 44.8 million people; between 1921 and 1936 the French population was up 6 percent to 41.2 million; and between 1926 and 1939, the Soviet population was up 16 percent to 170.5 million. Mitchell, *European Historical Statistics*, 20–24. Although the French birthrate had gone up in the twenties, it dropped during the following decade leaving fewer French at the end of the decade than at the beginning. Naturally, this *dénatalization* alarmed French demographers who blamed it on everything from the supposed liberation of women to an increase in homosexuality to a pernicious use of the bidet.

19. Mitchell, *European Historical Statistics*, 76–78.

20. George Orwell, *The Road to Wigan Pier* (New York: Harcourt Brace Jovanovich, 1958), 51.

21. In 1889, for example, 30 percent of the population of London lived in poverty; while in 1929 the number was a bit less than 10 percent.

22. Orwell, *The Road to Wigan Pier*, 97.

23. Harvey Goldberg, *The Life of Jean Jaurès* (Madison: University of Wisconsin Press, 1962), 17.

24. Mitchell, *European Historical Statistics*, 186–87, 745–46.

25. Ernest Hemingway, *By-Line Ernest Hemingway* (New York: Scribner's Sons, 1967), 51.

26. Michael R. Marrus, *The Unwanted: European Refugees in the Twentieth Century* (New York: Oxford University Press, 1985), 97–106.

27. Ibid., 122–35.

28. Donald R. Taft and Richard Robbins, *International Migrations: The Immigrant in the Modern World* (New York: Ronald Press, 1955), 187–90.

29. The bill passed the Chamber of Deputies, but was defeated in the more conservative Senate.

30. In Italy, women outnumbered men by almost 9 percent; in Russia, by 13 percent; in Great Britain and Germany, by 17 percent; and in France, by 20 percent. Mitchell, *European Historical Statistics*, 36, 37, 47, 52–53.

31. In Germany, the employment rate was about 35 percent; in Britain, about 29 per-

cent; in Italy, 28 percent; and in France, 36 percent.

32.   Laura Levine Frader, "Women in the Industrial Capitalist Economy" in Renate Bridenthal, Claudia Koonz, and Susan Stuard, eds., *Becoming Visible: Women in European History* (Boston: Houghton Mifflin, 1987), 321–22.

33.   Claudia Koonz, "The Fascist Solution to the Woman Question in Italy and Germany" in *Becoming Visible*, 504–5.

34.   Anne Fremantel, ed., *The Social Teachings of the Church* (New York: The New American Library, 1963), 45. *Pacem in Terris* (Peace on Earth) issued by Pope John XXIII took notice of the greater participation of women in public life, but underscored the obligation to provide them with working conditions "in accordance with their requirements and their duties as wives and mothers." Ibid., 281.

35.   Koonz, "The Fascist Solution," 508–9.

36.   Paolo Monelli, *Mussolini* (New York: Vanguard, 1954), 32.

37.   Vladimir Lenin, *The Emancipation of Women* (Moscow: International Publishers, 1972), 61–62.

38.   Richard Stites, "Women and the Revolutionary Process in Russia" in *Becoming Visible*, 451–71.

39.   The article continues: "The possibility of exercising these rights is ensured by women being accorded the same rights as men to work, payment for work, rest and leisure, social insurance and education, and also by state protection of the interests of mother and child, state aid to mothers of large families and to unmarried mothers, maternity leave with full pay, and the provision of a wide network of maternity homes, nurseries and kindergartens." *Constitution (Fundamental Law) of the Union of Soviet Socialist Republics* (Moscow: Progress Publishers, 1969), 100–101.

40.   See Claudia Koonz, *Mothers in the Fatherland: Women, the Family, and Nazi Politics* (New York: St. Martin's Press, 1987).

41.   Koonz, "The Fascist Solution," 519.

42.   *Illustrated London News*, 7 December 1918, 764.

PART FIVE

THE SECOND WORLD WAR

CHAPTER 14

THE TWILIGHT YEARS OF PEACE, 1933–1939

PREFACE   Hermann Göring was a difficult man to upstage. On 10 June 1934, in his official capacity as *Reichsjägermeister* (Chief Huntsman of the State), he played host to members of the diplomatic corps at Karinhall, his recently completed forest retreat an hour's drive north of Berlin. The baronial estate, made ready for occupancy in a short ten months, had been constructed with state funds as a ministerial residence with no expense being spared. Göring had been intimately involved in all aspects of its planning, even down to the design of the door handles. Göring greeted his guests at the entrance of the property, his ample figure costumed in a nifty flying suit, a large horn-handled deer knife stuck in the black leather belt, and took them on a personal tour. He first escorted them to a bison enclosure to watch a bull service four cows. (The demonstration was a flop because the bull was not in the mood.) He next led them to a vast marsh where he delivered a lecture on the splendors of bird life. Then, getting back into his car, he raced ahead to the fortress-like lodge for a quick change of clothes. When the others arrived, he emerged wearing a green leather jerkin, white flannel suit, duck trousers, and tennis shoes. The sightseeing continued with a room-by-room inspection of the premises, the highlight being the great hall with a huge oak tree growing up through the ceiling like the tree in the first act of Wagner's *Die Walküre*. Dinner was served on the flagstone terrace behind the house. Afterwards, there was a stroll to the mausoleum, a huge rectangular block of red granite; beneath it was a crypt that held a pewter double casket, half of which contained the body of Göring's late wife for whom the estate was named. The other half of this Göring-designed, metal sarcophagus was intended to hold the hunt master's remains when the time came. The tomb's vault had walls six feet thick, Göring remarked reassuringly.

British ambassador Sir Eric Phipps, one of the guests, was appalled at Göring's pompous bragging. He showed us "his toys," Phipps reported, "like a big, fat, spoilt child: his primeval woods, his bison and birds, his shooting-box and lake and bathing beach, his blond 'private' secretary [i.e., Emmy Sonnemann, Göring's companion, later wife], his wife's mausoleum and swans and sarsen stones, all mere toys to satisfy his varying moods, and all, or nearly all, as he was careful to explain, Germanic." Also, Phipps reflected, "there were other toys, less innocent, though winged, and these might some day be launched in their murderous mission in the same child-like spirit and with the same childlike glee."[1]

The British ambassador in Berlin had not been the first to sound an alarm about German intentions. Even before Hitler had come to power, Sir Robert Vansittart, the permanent undersecretary of the British Foreign Office, predicted that at the earliest opportunity Germany would take a dramatic step to change the status quo in Europe by annexing Austria and by revising its current frontiers with Poland.[2] Vansittart feared little would be done to prevent this from happening. The British, he felt, had lost their capacity for self-preservation.[3] The judgment was made in desperation. Vansittart realized Britain was no longer a first-class power. Nevertheless, the British felt they were in a better position than the French to maintain the diplomatic initiative. During the 1920s, they had been foremost in trying to secure German cooperation in maintaining the European equilibrium. They judged this policy a success and saw no reason to abandon it with Hitler in power.

The British leaders anticipated that the Nazi regime would become more moderate as it became more secure. They blamed the Treaty of Versailles for much German discontent and did not find it alarming that Hitler should advocate further revision, nor were they surprised that Germany might seek other territorial rectifications. It seemed only plausible that Hitler would wish to regain the independence the Paris settlement had denied Germany and that he would want to restore the country to its 1914 frontiers. Hitler claimed that the principle of self-determination established at the Paris Peace Conference gave the German peoples the right to live together in a Greater Germany. However, he was less explicit—publicly at least—about his desire for *Lebensraum* (living space). Yet his plan to seize the eastern border states, the Ukraine, and western Russia to create a vast empire for the survival and growth of the Aryan race had already been set forth in his book *Mein Kampf*.[4] Such ambitions were hardly traditional German foreign policy goals. In the context of the nationalist hysteria against the Versailles system, however, they appeared a permissible exaggeration, the campaign rhetoric of a relatively unsuccessful politician hankering after votes. Thus, the European democracies dismissed Hitler's declaration of his aims as hyperbole and never considered that it might be a literal blueprint for aggression. Hitler, however, had meant every word, and he was determined to achieve his goals, come what may.

THE DEATH OF VERSAILLES

Hitler's Early Diplomacy

Success in Warsaw. In one of his first speeches after becoming chancellor, Hitler warned that unless the other Great Powers were willing to carry out the disarmament measures to which they were bound, "Germany had a moral obligation to achieve military equality."[5] He was kicking in an open door because Germany's rights to equality had already been recognized at the Disarmament Conference in 1932. What Hitler really wanted was the license to manufacture as many weapons as he chose. On 14 October, he announced that Germany would withdraw from the Disarmament Conference and pull out of the League of Nations. The Germans, he insisted, could not tolerate having less rights than other peoples.

Hitler attacked the Versailles treaty's territorial clauses, especially the frontier with Poland, which he claimed "had been drawn in such a way . . . that a peaceful coexistence of the two nations was practically inconceivable."[6] But any alteration of the border seemed unlikely at present. The Poles had an army of 250,000 men, outnumbering, on paper at least, the military power of Germany. Furthermore, Poland had based its entire security system on an association with France.

France, however, no longer had the strength to protect Poland against German and Soviet revisionism. Moreover, the French no longer seemed to have the will to do so. The Locarno Pact raised suspicions that France might even agree to a revision of the Treaty of Versailles at Polish expense. The construction of the extensive fortifications known as the Maginot Line was a sign that the French were thinking only of their own protection without considering Poland. Furthermore, the French had made little effort to help Poland weather the world depression; and much to the chagrin of the Polish dictator, Marshal Józef Pilsudski, they had done little to improve the weaponry of the Polish army.

Pilsudski concluded that his country must follow a more independent and aggressive course in foreign policy if it was to win the respect it deserved and obtain the security it needed. In 1932, his government signed a nonaggression treaty with the Soviet Union; and the following year, he demanded, and received, a promise from Hitler not to interfere with Polish rights in Danzig. Then, most dramatic of all, on 26 January 1934, Pilsudski concluded a ten-year nonaggession pact with Germany. The commitment was, in fact, only a simple declaration that the two parties agreed to settle all their disputes through direct negotiations. The pact also affirmed respect for the Kellogg-Briand Peace Pact of 1928. An economic convention, signed subsequently, opened Germany to Polish exports, and both countries raised their diplomatic missions to the level of embassies. The pact contained nothing that affected Poland's agreements with other nations.

The French, however, were concerned. They suspected the nonaggression pact contained secret clauses that seriously impaired their eastern security system. They attempted to counter the pact by reinforcing their relations with Poland. Foreign Minister Louis Barthou visited Warsaw on 22 April, but Pilsudski was not very cooperative. The Polish leader refused to become involved in a scheme that would permit the Soviet Union—in a sort of Eastern Locarno—to move Red Army troops through Poland in a time of crisis. He also refused to guarantee the borders of Czechoslovakia, because Poland had claims on certain Czech territory. All in all, Pilsudski did not think the French were very serious about helping Poland, and he refused to be shaken loose from his new association with Germany.[7] Barthou was outraged at the rebuff, and, in September, during a League of Nations diplomatic luncheon at Geneva, he cut the Poles down to size. When Polish foreign minister Józef Beck lobbied for Poland's increased participation on League committees, Barthou remarked sarcastically: "And then there are the great powers"— pause—"and Poland. Poland we all know, because we have been told so, is a great power"—pause—"a very, very great power."[8]

The nonaggression pact also damaged the German policy of cooperation with the Soviet Union that had been in existence since the 1922 Treaty of Rapallo. Stalin was sufficiently alarmed to propose that the Germans and Soviets jointly guarantee the independence of the Baltic states, but Hitler refused. Hitler also rejected the arguments of Rudolf Nadolny, his ambassador in Moscow, who warned him that Germany was risking encirclement. Poland, Nadolny wrote, will "not provide us with the necessary flank protection in the East. Our entire international position is therefore to a not inconsiderable degree dependent on the character of our relations with the Soviet Union."[9] Nadolny resigned from the foreign service "because of political differences."

Failure in Vienna. Hitler believed that the union of his Austrian homeland with Germany was "a task to be furthered with every means our lives long."[10] As soon as he became chancellor, he began a policy of harassment and intimidation to bring it about. He encouraged the Austrian Nazis, a section of the German party, to demonstrate against their government; he imposed a 1,000 mark tax on all Germans visiting Austria in an effort to weaken the Austrian economy; and he began denouncing the Austrian government for frustrating the desire of its people to be incorporated into a greater German Reich.

On 19 June 1933, Engelbert Dollfuss, the Austrian chancellor, ordered the Austrian Nazi party dissolved. In retaliation, the Germans formed the Austrian Legion, training its soldiers with units of the SS and the SA in encampments near the Bavarian-Austrian frontier. The force soon numbered 6,000 men. Austria solicited protection from Mussolini; and, on 18 March 1934, the two nations signed the Rome Protocols, which underscored the Duce's desire to maintain Austrian independence. Hitler was disturbed and arranged a personal meeting with Mussolini. The two dictators met for the first time in Venice on 15 June 1934. The Führer, dressed in mufti, crumpled raincoat, and grey fedora, looked insignificant next to the Duce in full Fascist party regalia. Mussolini opposed the incorporation of Austria into Germany, but Hitler received a contrary impression. Part of the misunderstanding came from Mussolini's eagerness to show off his command of the German language by insisting that the meeting be conducted without an interpreter. Hitler returned home encouraged. He approved a plan to kidnap Dollfuss and his entire cabinet, thereby creating an instant power vacuum that would bring a National Socialist government to power. The government would then petition Germany for incorporation into the Reich.

The attempted takeover took place on 25 July 1934. Hitler was attending a performance of *Das Rheingold* in Bayreuth, and the news was flashed to him in his box at the Festival Hall. Adjutants rushed back and forth from a telephone in a nearby anteroom to get the latest developments. The news was not good. Hitler became so excited that his nostrils flared out until "they stretched almost to his ears."[11] But afterwards, he tried to remove any suspicion that he had anything to do with the coup by appearing in town for a postopera snack. He and his entourage sat in a local restaurant "eating liver dumplings."[12] The Führer "denounced the rashness and stupidity of the Austrian Nazi party for having involved him in such an appalling situation."[13] Mussolini issued a communiqué stating that "in view of possible complications," he had ordered army and air force units "towards Brenner and Carinthia frontier districts . . . sufficient for dealing with any eventuality."[14] It was a bluff. The Italian Ministry of War had made the announcement "for political motives," to take advantage of "slight variations" in the movements of troops already on training exercises in the Alpine area.

The attempt to seize power in Vienna was Hitler's first great blunder. He lamented that Mussolini had deliberately foiled his attempt to destroy Austria, and even years later, he called it "the one political mistake of [Mussolini's] life."[15] The fiasco had no effect on Hitler's position in Germany, however, and international reaction was fairly mild. Nevertheless, Hitler felt humiliated and vowed to succeed the next time.

Mussolini's Lust for Empire

Traditional Imperialism. In 1929, Mussolini took up residence at the Palazzo Venezia, a fortresslike structure occupying a whole city block at the foot of the Capitoline Hill. The Duce installed his office on the second floor in the *Sala del mappomondo*, a two-story room as large as a tennis court, where everything emphasized the ruler's power, including a heavy baroque desk and chair and a gigantic map stand placed near a massive Renaissance fireplace at the far corner of the room. Twenty yards of marble-tiled floor separated Mussolini's desk from the carved double portal that admitted official visitors. In the center of the outside wall, French doors led onto a stone balcony that overlooked the Piazza Venezia. This great square could be packed at will with enthusiastic Italians, eager to chant their leader's name and listen to his bellicose harangues.

Yet the grandiose setting did not seem to change the Duce's desire to live within the prevailing European equilibrium. Fascist foreign policy, despite occasional outbursts of pugnacity, had been fairly restrained. Italy's signature on the Locarno Pact in 1925 made it one of the principal guarantors of European security, and Mussolini explained that Fascist imperialism was not so much "expressed in territorial or military terms as in terms of morality and the spirit," that is, "without the need for conquering a single square yard of territory."[16] After the failure of the Vienna coup, the Duce acted as if he had personally prevented Anschluss. "Perhaps the Great Powers will recognize the German danger," he remarked. "It may be possible to organize a great coalition against Germany. I cannot always be the one to march to the Brenner. Others must show some interest in Austria and the Danube Basin."[17] Even as he spoke, his mind was elsewhere.

Disappointed with his lack of success in Europe, he decided to make his influence felt in Africa. There was nothing singularly Fascist about a policy of colonial expansion, nor anything particularly surprising about Mussolini's choice of Ethiopia as a target. In 1896, Italy had attempted to annex Ethiopia, but had lost half of its 20,000-man army in the attempt. At Adowa alone, the Ethiopians slaughtered a force of 6,000, leaving only a few castrated survivors to report the disaster. The Italians withdrew back into Eritrea. This marked the first time a European country had been defeated in an attempt to establish an African colony. Nevertheless, the Italian ruling class remained imperialistic and continued to covet Ethiopia with the idea of eventually avenging Adowa.

In 1906, Italy signed an agreement with France and Britain in which the entire western half of Ethiopia, from Eritrea to Somaliland, was acknowledged as an Italian sphere of interest. The three signatories did not, of course, bother to consult the Ethiopians. Italy did not push its claims, but continued to view the country with special proprietary concern. In 1923, it sponsored Ethiopia's membership into the League of Nations; five years later, it concluded a twenty-year treaty of friend-ship with the Ethiopians, promising to take no action prejudicial to Ethiopia's independence. In 1930, Mussolini gave the new Ethiopian emperor, Haile Selassie, a tank as a coronation present and arranged to have him invested with Italy's highest decoration, the Order of the Annunciation, which gave him the privilege of addressing the king of Italy as cousin. Yet, at the same time, contingency plans were being readied for an invasion should that be considered unavoidable. But before any action could be taken, Mussolini had to cover his bases in Europe.

Italy had deeply resented France's failure to compensate it with colonial territory as promised under the 1915 Treaty of London. But, on 7 January 1934, the matter was apparently laid to rest when Mussolini accepted the discharge of the French obligations with only token tribute.[18] In exchange, the pro-Fascist French foreign minister Pierre Laval secretly assured Mussolini that he could have a free hand in Ethiopia, and that France would offer no opposition should Italy decide to add that country to its colonial empire. Laval was not endorsing armed conquest— the use of Italian military power in Africa would have weakened the value of Italy as a deterrent to Germany in Europe—but Mussolini would not have agreed to such an easy satisfaction of his colonial claims had he assumed that the French really cared about the fate of Ethiopia. Concerning Europe, the French and Italians promised to promote the independence of Austria through the conclusion of a general nonintervention pact among all "particularly interested states," and they agreed to consult on a mutual course of action should Hitler again threaten Anschluss, or should he embark on a crash program of rearmament. Thus, Mussolini's ambitions for an African empire were inextricably bound to France's desire for Italian cooperation in maintaining the status quo in Europe. Considering the Duce's desire to be active and decisive on all fronts at once, France was playing a risky game.

Mussolini had further ambitions in Eastern Europe. He wanted to subvert Yugoslavia, a French ally, and to this end he supported Croatian separatism. Croatian terrorists, known as the Ustashi, came to Italy for training and carried Italian passports. On 9 November 1934, a Macedonian agent with links to this group succeeded in assassinating the Yugoslav king, Alexander I, in Marseilles. The monarch was on an official visit to France. French foreign minister Louis Barthou was not a target, but one of the bullets hit him and he slowly bled to death. In retrospect, the death of Barthou was a disaster. The foreign minister was not fooled by Hitler's seeming moderation and was prepared to devote French foreign policy to keeping him in check. Barthou's continued presence in the French government might have stiffened his country's resolve before it proved too late. Without him, the French continued their efforts to maintain a European equilibrium, but they increasingly looked to London for direction.

The Walwal Incident and the Stresa Conference. On 23 November 1934, an Anglo-Ethiopian boundary commission, surveying the grazing land in the south-eastern corner of Ethiopia, arrived at the waterhole of Walwal. Existing maps showed the site to be some sixty miles inside the Ethiopian border; but when the commission arrived, a force of Italian-led native troops was in occupation. The commander of the force refused the new arrivals permission to camp. The British commissioners withdrew to avoid trouble; their Ethiopian escort remained behind. The situation grew extremely tense and on 5 December finally exploded into fighting. The Italians called for air support and forced the Ethiopians to retreat. Mussolini played the injured party. He demanded that Ethiopia apologize and pay a heavy indemnity. He disregarded Emperor Haile Selassie's request for arbitration under the friendship treaty, although he said later that he was prepared to negotiate a peaceful solution. Mussolini intended to use the incident as a pretext to destroy Ethiopia's independence. He would become the avenger of the defeat at Adowa thirty-eight years before. He thought this feat might be accomplished without much effort. Ethiopia was a heterogeneous collection of tribes speaking seventy languages and two hundred dialects. If he sowed enough internal dissension, the country might fall without Italy firing a shot. Mussolini could afford to take his time, but he wanted the matter "settled no later than 1936."[19]

Ethiopia appealed to the League of Nations, but the Geneva organization was only as powerful as the Great Powers decided it should be, and they preferred to solve problems through normal diplomatic channels. The British and French wanted to deal with Mussolini directly. From 11 to 13 April 1935, they met at Stresa. The discussion between the respective heads of government and foreign ministers took place in the resplendent seventeenth-century Palazzo Borromeo on the Isola Bella, a setting that proved more impressive than the results of the talks. The French tried to get an agreement on European cooperation. Foreign Minister Pierre Laval insisted that the time for "moral sanctions was long past," and predicted that Germany would continue to violate its treaty obligations. He proposed that the Council of the League of Nations be made an agency for enforcing treaties of international peace and security.[20]

The British refused to enter any new agreements.[21] Prime Minister Ramsay MacDonald insisted that the independence and integrity of Austria were still an object of British policy, but he reiterated that his government wanted "to be in the position of a state that blessed and approved without being committed further."[22] MacDonald threw Ethiopia to the wolves. He told Mussolini that Britain remained a loyal partner in the League, but made it clear that the League's moral authority extended only to Europe.[23]

The conference's closing declaration sounded formidable, but a "Stresa Front" never emerged. The three nations declared they were in "complete agreement in opposing, by all possible means, any unilateral repudiation of treaties which may endanger the peace of Europe," and they promised to "act in close and cordial collaboration for this purpose."[24] They favored strengthening collective security. The British seemed more eager than usual to disassociate themselves from Eastern Europe. They were confident that they could play the role of mediator with Germany, and they avoided taking any strong position against treaty revisionism. Mussolini was so preoccupied with his Ethiopian escapade that he had time for little else.

The Conquest of Ethiopia. The Italians had assembled an expeditionary army of 250,000 men in Eritrea and Somaliland, on the frontiers of Ethiopia. Such a force could hardly be expected to return home without a victory. On 2 October 1935, Mussolini finally took the plunge. Certain of success, he broadcast his call to arms—"Italy of Vittorio Veneto and of the Revolution, to your feet! To your feet!" The next day, Italian troops surged across the Mareb River into Ethiopia to fight an army that was in no condition to wage a modern war. The Ethiopians had scant experience with the airplane or the tank, and they had little knowledge of

ITALY AND ITS EMPIRE

Italian Empire – 1939

SPAIN, 1936

Map 9

guerrilla warfare. Their chiefs seemed more concerned with what their men should wear into battle—lion skins—than with machine gun deployment. The Italians possessed enough firepower to withstand any direct enemy assault.

Commander-in-Chief Emilio de Bono, one of Mussolini's political cronies, showed little skill in the offensive use of artillery, tanks, and aircraft. The Duce grew impatient at his slow progress. He promoted de Bono to the dignity of marshal and replaced him with the more savvy General Pietro Badoglio.

Four days after the start of the invasion, the League Council condemned Italy for aggression. On 11 October, in the Assembly fifty states voted to impose sanctions. As no state was anxious to adopt any measures that might lead to war, military sanctions were not considered, however, and economic sanctions were only to be applied by the individual states and were not made sufficiently inclusive. For example, the League adopted a prohibition on the export of arms and strategic materials to Italy but did not recommend an embargo on oil or recommend closing the Suez Canal, the most important "weapon" of all. Mussolini had threatened reprisals against nations that voted for either. In the general elections of 1935, Stanley Baldwin promised that collective security would remain the cornerstone of British foreign policy. The British, though, were not prepared to give the League unconditional support. They only wanted to use the organization as a prod to induce Mussolini to settle the affair through direct negotiations. At the same time, the Foreign Office was looking for ways to buy Mussolini off.

Foreign Secretary Sir Samuel Hoare met Pierre Laval in Paris on 7 and 8 December. The two agreed to allow Mussolini to acquire more than half of Ethiopia's territory: about 60,000 square miles in the north and southeast with the whole southern part of the country, 160,000 square miles, being reserved for Italy as a zone of economic expansion. Laval insisted the award to Italy be as generous as possible, and several times during the course of the conversations, he telephoned Mussolini directly to ensure his approval. Before the Hoare-Laval agreement could be officially presented to Mussolini, it was leaked to the press. Public disclosure set off such a furor in Britain that Baldwin quickly withdrew his support. He saddled Hoare with all the blame and forced him to resign, replacing him with Anthony Eden, whom the British people perceived as a strong supporter of the League. Still, for all practical purposes, the League of Nations was dead, and the fate of Ethiopia was sealed.

The Italian army entered the Ethiopian capital of Addis Ababa in May 1936. Mussolini's popularity among his own people soared. The invasion had cost the Italians a mere 2,000 men compared with 275,000 of their Ethiopian adversaries. Pope Pius XI was enthusiastic about the prospect of bringing the nominally Christian Ethiopians under papal authority. The conquest dramatically confirmed the fundamental Fascist faith in the mystique of war and violence. Mussolini's aviator son Vittorio believed "it to be the real duty of every man to take part in at least one war" and boasted of his prowess. "I dropped one aerial torpedo right in the center [of some tribesmen], and the group opened up just like a flowering rose. It was most entertaining."[25]

The End of Locarno

Unfinished Business. On 16 March 1935, Hitler formally denounced the arms limitation clauses of the Versailles treaty and proclaimed his intention to build a peacetime army of thirty-six divisions (about 550,000 troops). As a pretext, the Führer cited the French decision to increase the period of their national military service from one to two years.[26] Hitler's announcement was not unexpected, nor was it as dramatic as it appeared. While officially the increase would put German troop strength at five times what the Treaty of Versailles allowed, the German army had never been reduced to the limits specified in the treaty. The British and French were well aware that the real strength of the Reichswehr was between 300,000 and 400,000 troops, with the paramilitary police troops adding perhaps a third more. Nor was it a secret that the German generals were laying the foundations for a large expansion of the army pending favorable circumstances.[27] Therefore, the reaction to Hitler's announcement was mild. Even the Poles, the people who had the most immediate fear of German rearmament, made no fuss. To do so would be an open acknowledgment that they had no faith in the non-aggression treaty they had signed with Germany. Nevertheless, Hitler was careful to make the announcement after the Saarland had formally been returned to the Reich in accordance with the Treaty of Versailles.[28]

The British had already decided to seek a bilateral agreement with Hitler on naval arms limitation, which in effect constituted official acquiescence in Hitler's denunciation of the arms clauses. The Anglo-German Treaty, signed on 18 June 1935, permitted Germany to build a surface fleet equal to 35 percent, and a submarine force equal to 45 percent, of British tonnage. The British reasoned that since Germany was going to build a modern navy anyway, it would do no harm to get an agreement to limit its size.[29] The British had no guarantee that Hitler would keep his word, but they believed it would take at least a decade before a rebuilt German navy could constitute a serious threat.[30] The British were not so naïve as to expect the Germans to accept second-class status perpetually, but they hoped that any changes in the status quo could be accomplished slowly through proper negotiation. The Locarno Pact had been based on the artificial condition of German disarmament.

Hitler made it clear that previous agreements would not limit Germany's freedom of action. He even boasted that the rest of Europe would soon rely on Germany to protect it against Bolshevism.[31] Rearmament, he claimed, was not a matter for negotiation, but an absolute necessity. In a speech on 21 May 1935, Hitler renounced war as an instrument of national policy, agreeing to "uphold and fulfill all obligations arising out of the Locarno Treaty, so long as the other partners are on their side ready to stand by that pact."[32] The qualification was important because Hitler had already ordered that the remilitarization of the Rhineland be carried out "by lightning surprise."[33]

The Remilitarization of the Rhineland. The French government had received ample warning of Hitler's intentions from its diplomats abroad (the consuls in Dusseldorf and Cologne, the ambassador in Bern, and the military attaché in Berlin) but had prepared no effective countermeasures. The minister of war, General Louis Maurin, admitted "that the mission of the French Army was conceived entirely in terms of the defensive, that it had nothing in preparation and was still less ready for use in a military intervention."[34] The General Staff left the matter to the politicians.

The destruction of the Treaty of Locarno presented greater risks to Germany than those it had encountered in revising the Treaty of Versailles. The Locarno accords allowed any of the parties to take immediate action if the frontier were crossed or if armed forces assembled in the demilitarized zone.[35] Furthermore, each signatory pledged to aid the state against which such violation was directed. On 27 February, however, the French Council of Ministers decided to take no unilateral action should Germany enter the demilitarized zone; instead, France would consult with the British, Belgian, and Italian governments "with the object of finding a common course of action to enforce the Covenant of the League of Nations and the Locarno agreements."[36] The last attempt to enforce the Treaty of Versailles militarily had been the French occupation of the Ruhr. The Treaty of Locarno had made a repetition of this 1923 action unlikely, but Hitler had even less to worry about than he supposed.[37]

On the morning of 7 March, three battalions of German infantry crossed into the Rhineland, fanning out in the directions of Trier, Aachen, and Saarbrücken. Later in the day, four divisions of the *Landespolizei* (Home Guard) were mobilized. The total force of less than 12,000 was hardly adequate to withstand a determined French riposte. Hitler believed there would be no intervention; to help make sure, he had planned the remilitarization for a Saturday, when many British and French leaders would be out of town for the weekend. The French cabinet was currently a caretaker government pending the spring elections. It debated furiously for several days, but ruled out independent action against Germany. A few ministers, like Pierre Flandin, Joseph Paul Boncour, and Georges Mandel, urged retaliation, but they received no support either from their civilian colleagues or from the military chiefs, who strenuously opposed any action. The French generals believed that the German army would prove stronger than the French army in all-out war. Accordingly, they were prepared to guarantee the security of their troops only along the Maginot line, and they opposed general mobilization without firm support from the British. But the British saw no reason to suppose, as Foreign Secretary Anthony Eden said, "that the present German action implies a threat of hostilities."[38] They gave no indication that they would have backed a French move against Germany. At a meeting of the Locarno powers in London on 12 March, Eden said that his government agreed to allow the League Council to discuss the matter, but "he carefully avoided commenting in any way on the inference that could be drawn from such acquiescence."[39]

The remilitarization of the Rhineland presented the British and French with their first real opportunity to check Hitler's ambitions, but they chose not to do so. In their view, German occupation of German territory was not a significant threat to the balance of power. Britain and France still assumed they had sufficient power to protect themselves and believed the existence of that power would be sufficient to deter the German leader from aggression. They guessed wrong. Hitler was only impressed by the determination to *use* military power, not by the mere existence of hardware and battalions of soldiers.

The French had already realized that a demilitarized Rhineland could not guarantee their country against attack; to protect themselves, they had constructed a gigantic supertrench along their eastern and northern border. One of the project's staunchest advocates, Chief of Staff Maxim Weygand, touted the value of permanent fortifications because they would force Germany to acquire an almost impossible margin of superiority before it could wage war victoriously against France.[40] Marshal Ferdinand Foch, however, Weygand's onetime superior, had attacked the whole concept when Marshal Philippe Pétain first presented it to the Supreme War Council in 1922. Foch believed that building such permanent fortifications would lead to the strategic demoralization of the French army. Foch's death in 1929 left the field to the project's advocates, and the National Assembly voted the necessary funds with a large majority.

The Maginot Line consisted of a series of reinforced concrete bunkers and blockhouses connected by tunnels.[41] The bunkers were carefully positioned to cover the middle ground with powerful cross fire. The line began near Basel and stretched north along the Rhine to above Strasbourg, then it turned west to Longwy at the Belgian frontier. It was never completed to the coast because Belgium objected. Presumably, Belgium would fill in the gap with its own system. In addition, the cost of construction was enormous, and extending the line to the coast would have preempted funds that depression-ridden France could use else-where. The Maginot strategy seemed to rule out direct military assistance to France's Eastern European allies. Paul Reynaud asked, "Is it, by any chance, that we have abandoned our policy of giving assistance? It is because we conceive assistance as flowing towards, and not from us?"[42] Reynaud advocated that France create several special armored divisions for swift offensive action. He was ignored.

Hitler was understandably jubilant at having destroyed the French security fron-tier established after World War I. He was firmly convinced of the superiority of his own intuition over the professional opinions of his conservative generals. Even much later, he continued to boast that his "unshakable obstinacy and . . . amazing aplomb" had saved Germany from disaster. "Anybody other than myself . . . would have lost his nerve."[43]

A Crucial Meeting at the Reichs Chancellery. Yet, for all his conceit about firmness of will, Hitler was a natural procrastinator. He filled his days with trivia until decisions on important matters could no longer be delayed; then he would burst into a flurry of activity and "spend a few days of intensive work giving shape to his solutions [only to relapse] again into his idleness."[44] The Führer was afraid that he would die before his life's work was accomplished. He constantly com-plained of pains and insomnia. His personal physician, Theodore Morell, diagnosed his complaints as "complete exhaustion of the intestinal flora [due to] the over-burdening of his nervous system" and treated him with capsules of bacteria from Bulgarian peasants and injections from animal testicles. Morell was never able to cure his patient's morbidity. "I always counted on having time to realize my plans," Hitler lamented. "I must carry them out myself. None of my successors will have the force to. I must carry out my aims as long as I can hold up, for my health is growing worse all the time."[45] Hitler's method of work made the formulation of schedules and timetables difficult.

In a memorandum of August 1936, Hitler specified that the army had to be operational and the economy fit for war within four years. "The final solution lies in extending the space of our people and/or the sources of its raw materials and food stuffs." He made no attempt to be more specific, adding vaguely, "it is the task of the political leadership one day to solve this problem."[46] One evening in 1936 at his Obersalzberg retreat, as he sat looking out a window at the gathering dusk, he told his court architect Albert Speer that there were two possibilities: "To win through with all plans, or to fail. If I win, I shall be one of the greatest men in history. If I fail, I shall be condemned, despised and damned."[47]

The following year, on 5 November 1937, in the more formal surroundings of the Reichs Chancellery, before an audience consisting of the combined military high command and the head of the foreign office,[48] Hitler revealed that "it was his unalterable resolve to solve Germany's problem of space at the latest by 1943–45."[49] He explained that within six to eight years German power would reach its peak. Afterwards "our relative strength would decrease in relation to the rearma-ment which would by then have been carried out by the rest of the world." Ger-many could perhaps act earlier—should France be crippled by civil strife or should the present tensions in the Mediterranean lead to war—but its first objective in any event "must be to overthrow Czechoslovakia and Austria simultaneously in order to remove the threat to our flank in any possible operation against the West." Hitler believed that Britain and France "had already tacitly written off the Czechs and were reconciled to the fact that this question would be cleared up in due course by Germany." He spoke for more than four hours and with characteristic melodrama enjoined his audience to regard his exposition "in the event of his death, as his last will and testament."[50]

No one doubted the Führer meant what he said. Colonel-General Werner von Fritsch feared German military power would be insufficient to overcome the French and Czech fortifications and was so alarmed over the prospect of an immediate conflict that he thought he had better cancel his regular leave, due to begin in five days. When Marshal Werner von Blomberg returned to his office, he immediately began drafting the necessary plans. On 7 December 1937, he issued a directive making the implementation of Hitler's objectives dependent on achieving "complete preparedness for war in all fields, then the military conditions will have been created for carrying out an offensive war against Czechoslovakia, so that the solution of the German problem of living space can be carried to a victorious end even if one or the other of the Great Powers intervenes against us."[51]

The chancellery meeting and the war minister's subsequent communication did not reveal any new departures in National Socialist policy. The atmosphere was still infused with the Führer's overriding belief in pan-Germanism and Lebensraum. But Hitler had considerably narrowed his immediate objectives. In view of his remarks, Göring felt that the time had come to end Germany's intervention in the Spanish Civil War.

THE ROAD TO WAR

The Spanish Civil War

The Revolt of the Generals. The final, long agony of the Spanish Second Republic began on the afternoon of 17 July 1936 with an uprising of the army garrison in the port of Ceuta, Spanish Morocco. The ringleader General Emilio Mola had planned for a simultaneous seizure of power in all the army commands, except Barcelona and Madrid where initial success was believed unlikely. These cities would be captured as soon as matters were under control elsewhere. The insurgents succeeded in North Africa and seized control of Seville, Córdoba, Zaragoza, Burgos, Valladolid, and Salamanca in Spain. By the end of the month, they had occupied Navarre, León, Galicia, most of old Castile, large chunks of Aragon, and bits and pieces of Andalucía—altogether about one-third of the national territory of Spain. The rebels had as yet no clear hierarchy. General José Sanjurjo, who was expected to take charge, died when the plane that was to bring him from his Lisbon exile to Burgos crashed on takeoff.[52] General Manuel Goded, another contender, was arrested as he landed in Barcelona to direct the revolt in Catalonia and was later shot. The field narrowed down to General Emilio Mola, who commanded in the north, and General Francisco Franco, who had assumed leadership in Spanish Morocco. Franco was of little importance unless his North African detachments could be transported across the Strait of Gibraltar. (A map of Spain appears on page 379.) Since most of the Spanish navy and air force were loyal to the Madrid government, Franco turned to Hitler and Mussolini for assistance.

The two dictators were eager to help, and by the end of September, German and Italian aerial transport had ferried over half of the Moroccan army to the Spanish mainland. Franco, whose earlier caution about joining the revolt had earned him the nickname of "Miss Canary Islands of 1936," became the most important insurgent army commander in the field. Half of the estimated 60,000-man rebel force was under his personal direction, and his was clearly the best

Generals Francisco Franco and Emilio Mola go to church. Franco was not known for his devotion to religion before the civil war began.

trained and equipped half. Consequently, on 28 September, he was officially rec-ognized as "Chief of the Government of the Spanish State" with control over both military and civilian affairs.

In changing from an ad hoc military conspiracy into a permanent government, the Nationalist regime became more authoritarian. Generals held all the important posts except foreign affairs. Franco wanted to enlarge this strictly military dicta-torship into a national political movement that would include the political parties and factions of the antidemocratic Right. In April 1937, he announced the cre-ation of the *Falange española tradicionalista* (Spanish Phalanx) as the regime's unique political organization.[53] However, the state remained completely under military direction. Even in local government, the commander of the regional army district had the last word. In the Nationalist zone, the reforms instituted by the Republic, including the secularization of education and the redistribution of land, were either halted or reversed. The Nationalists regarded the proletariat as their enemy and punished all strikes with death. Although previously their leaders had never been famous for piety, the military revolt became a crusade to defend Cath-olic Spain. Many Nationalist generals had once been anticlerical and had wanted to maintain the separation of church and state. Now they insisted that members of the church hierarchy be present at all of their official functions and ceremonies.

The Republic Fights Back. The July Rebellion caught the Republican leaders off guard. The government still held most of the country—the principal cities of Madrid, Barcelona, Valencia, and Bilbao—and the greater part of Spanish industry and the state gold reserves remained in its hands. The army had disintegrated however, and had to be rebuilt from the ground up. The new force was formed around civilians who had had military training—ex-conscripts and members of the Civil Guard, the Assault Guards, and other leftist paramilitary organizations—but these were hardly the equivalent of the disciplined units that formed the nucleus of the Nationalist Army. Political organization was equally confused. Republican Spain became divided into three semi-independent federated areas: Catalonia, the Basque provinces, and the Madrid district, with each local government assuming primary responsibility for its own war effort. The left-wing socialist general trade union, the UGT (*Union General del Trabajadores*), exercised executive power in Madrid. It, rather than the normal city government, was responsible for the food supply and the maintenance of essential services. The UGT similarly controlled other towns throughout New Castile, La Mancha, and parts of Estremadura. The Anti-Fascist Militias Committee ran Barcelona. This organization included representatives from the Anarchist Federation, the FAI (*Federacion Anarquista Iberica*), and the syndicalist National Confederation of Work, the CNT (*Confederacion Nacional del Trabajo*). While Madrid delayed carrying out the great social revolution, Barcelona went straight ahead. Banks, factories, hotels, and stores were expropriated and placed under the control of workers' committees. Authority in Bilbao was in the hands of the Basque nationalists. In Valencia, the CNT was the strongest ruling group; Andaluciá was controlled by the Anarchists. The local town councils or trade unions also shared power. Many of these were more interested in social revolution than mobilization. Lack of central control encouraged many self-appointed terrorists to indulge in an orgy of church burning and indiscriminate liquidation of class enemies.

The Spanish Civil War gave the Communists the opportunity to become the major political force they never had been before. They participated in the Madrid government—the first Communists to enter a European government since the regime of Béla Kun—and they controlled the popular army. They attached political commissars to every army unit to ensure the loyalty of the commanding officers and to supervise the political education of the troops. The Soviet secret police administered the entire operation through their embassy. Still, the Communists were reluctant to take over final direction of the government until a Republican victory.

The Fiction of Nonintervention. When the war began, the Republic tried to buy weapons from France and did, in fact, obtain some shipments of arms and ammunition. Léon Blum feared that any significant commitment to the Madrid government would lead to the downfall of his own government—the Socialists favored giving aid, the Radicals did not—and would thereby endanger his entire program of social reform. The British were more concerned about the grave international consequences that could arise if France aided the Loyalists, especially since Italy and Germany had intervened. The British therefore strongly supported a French proposal for a general undertaking to forbid the sale of arms to both sides. Most of the other European states, including Germany, Italy, and the Soviet Union, endorsed the nonintervention agreement. They established a Nonintervention Committee in London to handle violations and keep the discredited League of Nations from discussing the war.[54]

The policy of nonintervention was a sham. Italy sent the largest quantity of aid to Franco. The Duce wanted to establish another Fascist state in southern Europe as part of his policy to supplant British strategic influence in the Mediterranean.[55] At the beginning of the war, Italian troops occupied Majorca. Entire army divisions were transported to Spain to fight alongside Nationalist units. In addition, Mussolini deployed his fleet of submarines to prey on ships that supplied the Loyalists. He also hoped that a Nationalist victory would force France to divide its forces. Lastly, he viewed participation in the Spanish war as necessary to maintain the dynamics of his own power. "When the war in Spain is over," he remarked, "I shall find something else; the Italian character has to be formed through fighting." At the peak in mid-1937, Italy had as many as 50,000 troops in Spain, although the overall number of those who served there was higher.

Hitler used the war to divert attention from his ambitions in Central Europe. He hoped to embroil France and Britain in a conflict with Italy and did not want Franco to achieve an early victory. Spain provided the German military with an opportunity "to blood its weapons," in particular, to test its aircraft and tanks. Most German aid therefore came in equipment, technical assistance, and special forces. German advisers were dispatched to Nationalist military schools and helped to train over 50,000 officers. The Luftwaffe's Kondor Legion provided the Nationalists with air power; the German pilots were constantly rotated to give all of them combat experience. Military targets were selected with ruthless efficiency.

On 26 April 1937, a fleet of Heinkel 111 and Junker 52 bombers pounded Guernica, the sacred city of the Basques. The town was twenty miles behind the lines and on the chosen day was filled with people from the surrounding area doing their weekly marketing. Although casualties were surprisingly light, the whole center of the town was wiped out. Guernica had not been selected for its military importance; rather, as Göring later admitted, it was a testing ground for the technique of saturation bombing. The raid was also intended to terrorize the Basques into surrender. Once the Nationalists occupied the Basque provinces, Hitler anticipated receiving a monopoly of Spanish iron ore production, which was essential for his rearmament program.

The Republic, denied help from the British and the French, turned to the Soviet Union for assistance. Stalin handled his Spanish commitment cautiously. His aid was never as plentiful, nor as consistent, as that of the Germans and Italians, but it was sufficient to keep the Republic alive. Soviet supplies and advisers helped save Madrid in 1936. Soviet tanks and airplanes helped stop the Nationalists at Jarama and rout the Italians at Guadalajara in 1937. Stalin wanted to keep the war going as long as possible to absorb the attention and sap the energy of the Germans, but he had no desire to go to war over Spain. He never gave the Loyalists enough to win, but at crucial moments he gave them enough to prevent them from losing. The Soviets sent no troops as such, only advisers. There were never more than 500 advisers at a given time, and they almost never participated in active combat.

Through the Comintern, the Soviets recruited a surrogate army in the International Brigades; these were units of various nationalities, but mostly French, German, Austrian, Italian, American, and British (in order of importance). Each of the national Communist parties was instructed to recruit an assigned quota of volunteers. About 60 percent of those who served were already Communists, another 20 percent became Communists while in Spain. Some were lured by a sense of adventure, others by a sense of mission. Among the volunteers were intellectuals, writers, and disillusioned pacifists. Many believed that they had come to Spain to fight for democracy against the forces of Fascism. "I go forward," one of them said, "confident that I shall try to do my duty against the enemies of progress, and that whatever comes, the strength of the workers will overcome all opposition in Spain and the rest of the world."[56] They made their first appearance during the successful defense of Madrid in the fall of 1936 and continued to fight throughout most of the war; they played a role in some of the important battles, usually as shock troops. Their casualties were so high that the Comintern discouraged the further recruitment of party members, preferring that new volunteers be non-Communists. Their martyrdom would increase party prestige, but not reduce its strength for the coming power struggle back home. Altogether, approximately 40,000 *Internationales* served.

The Policy of Simmering. In view of the constant violations, it is difficult to believe that anyone really expected nonintervention to be more than "a theoretical guardian of a fictitious neutrality,"[57] as French historian Maurice Baumont described it. Atrocities like Guernica inflamed public opinion in Britain and France, but aroused no general demand for direct involvement. Both Britain and France feared that abandoning nonintervention would lead to war. Stanley Baldwin explained, "if there are some leaks in a dam it may at any rate keep the water out for the time being, and you may stop the leaks. It is a very different thing from sweeping away that dam altogether." Unlike the French Socialists, the British Conservatives had no great sympathy for the Spanish Republic, which they believed was controlled by the Communists. The British were in some respects captives of their past. Their intervention in Spain during the Napoleonic era had not been a happy one and had soured them on the prospect of doing it again. Their more recent intervention in Russia after World War I had further reinforced their belief that becoming involved in the civil wars of other nations was futile.

The Spanish Civil War has been called the first battle of World War II. Certainly, it aroused the passions of many people. Some saw it as a struggle between the forces of atheism and the armies of Christ, while others believed it was a struggle of freedom against tyranny. Describing the conflict in such terms made it understandable to millions, although the passions, sympathy, and horror that it engendered were insufficient to carry the struggle beyond the boundaries of Spain. The British chose to contain the war. They believed—the sacrifice or distress of the Spanish people aside—that a Nationalist victory was the best means of preserving Spanish independence. They reasoned correctly that Franco would not allow his country to become either a German or an Italian puppet.[58] The French, for their part, were too divided to support either side. They had a real fear of civil war at home. But whatever their reasons, the inaction of the democracies helped to forge the axis between Hitler and Mussolini. The dictators looked with contempt on the ineffectual democracies that were obviously too weak to stand in their way. Hitler, in particular, reasoned that if the British and French would go to such lengths to avoid the threat of war over Spain where their strategic interests were strong, they could not be expected to take bold action against German expansion in Central Europe.

The Golden Age of Appeasement

Austria Becomes a German Province. After the failure to grab Austria in 1934, Hitler decided that Anschluss could best be achieved if it became "the exclusive concern of those whose function it is to conduct foreign policy."[59] Coordination (*Gleichshaltung*) would replace muggings and assassination. Austria would be annexed after it had been peacefully drawn into the German sphere of influence. Hitler no longer feared Italy might stand in his way. The Duce was so bogged down in his foreign adventures, first Ethiopia, now Spain, that he no longer had the will or the power to guarantee Austrian independence.[60] On 11 July 1936, Germany forced Austria to recognize that it was part of the "German cultural orbit" and should now conduct "its foreign policy in the light of the peaceful endeavors of the German Government's foreign policy."[61] The Austrian economy was tied to the German economy. Austrian Chancellor Kurt von Schuschnigg feared that serious protest would only give Hitler a pretext to ask for more. Austria had no treaties with a major power, but was vulnerable for other reasons as well.

The Austrian army with its old imperial code of loyalty would probably have supported the government in an emergency, but Hitler's low opinion of the country's national spirit was largely justified. Schuschnigg was a poor national leader: aloof, dictatorial, and partisan, he was the head of a party, the Fatherland Front, which had suppressed the Social Democrats, the one group whose strength could have formed the basis of an anti-Nazi coalition. Furthermore, the Austrian people were more anti-Italian than anti-German, and many actually welcomed Anschluss. Schuschnigg weakly tried to play for time, hoping that some sort of guarantee of his country's independence could be arranged. In the meantime, he tried to strengthen his hand by cracking down on Nazi operations at home.

On 25 January 1938, the police raided the Austrian Nazi party headquarters on Vienna's Teinfalstrasse, confiscating all sorts of incriminating material, including a scheme, unknown to Hitler, to provoke German intervention by assassinating the German ambassador, Franz von Papen, and blaming the murder on the Austrian monarchists. When the Führer found out, he was furious. He sacked the head of the Austrian Nazis, Josef Leopold, and took personal charge of Austrian affairs. Next, he arranged a personal meeting with Schuschnigg.

The two government chiefs met at the Berghof, Hitler's retreat in the Bavarian Alps, on 12 February, 1938. Three generals in full-dress uniforms standing beside Hitler created a proper mood of intimidation. One of these was the newly appointed head of the General Staff, Wilhelm Keitel.[62] Hitler had recently brought the Army High Command under his direct personal control. He had purged its old leadership and reorganized the General Staff by creating a new body, the *Oberkommando der Wehrmacht* (Supreme Command of the Armed Forces or OKW), and had become his own war minister.

When Schuschnigg tried to make small talk to relieve the tension, Hitler snapped that Schuschnigg had not been brought there to discuss the weather. Hitler then demanded that Austria prepare itself for complete economic integration with Germany. He also wanted the Austrian Nazi party legalized and an amnesty granted to all party members now in jail. He insisted that the local Nazi leader, Artur Seyss-Inquart, be appointed minister of interior and warned that if these terms were not approved within three days, the German army would attack.

Schuschnigg agreed to implement Hitler's demands, but when he arrived back in Vienna, he tried a desperate gamble. On 9 March, he announced that he would

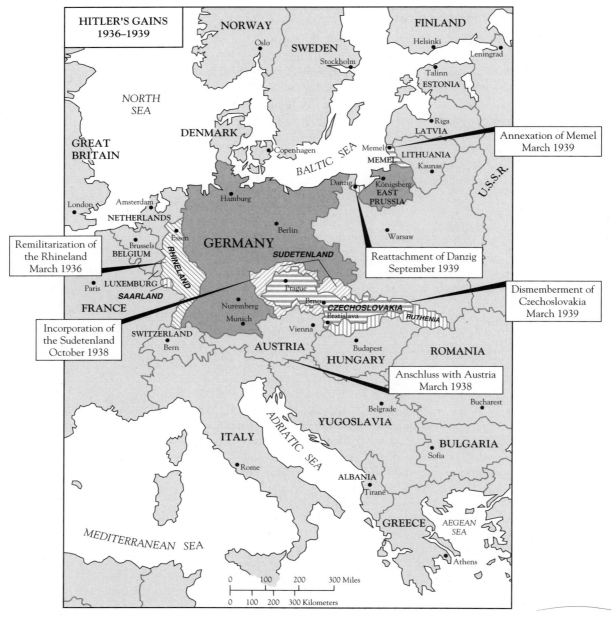

HITLER'S GAINS 1936–1939

Annexation of Memel
March 1939

Reattachment of Danzig
September 1939

Dismemberment of
Czechoslovakia
March 1939

Remilitarization of
the Rhineland
March 1936

Incorporation of
the Sudetenland
October 1938

Anschluss with Austria
March 1938

Map 10

let the Austrian people decide their own fate: to vote yes or no on whether they favored a free and independent Austria. They were not asked to vote specifically on Anschluss although a no vote implied it. Schuschnigg had no assurance that a majority of the Austrian people would vote for independence. Anschluss was very popular, even among members of his own party. Realizing this, the chancellor appealed to the Austrian workers for support, never mind that his party had smashed their trade unions and disbanded the Social Democratic party. Nevertheless, the Social Democratic leaders responded to his call to help defend the country's independence. In exchange, they asked for the restoration of their political privileges. Schuschnigg agreed, but now it was too late.

A surprised Hitler was not about to risk a referendum no matter how favorable the outcome. He warned Schuschnigg that unless the vote was canceled, Germany would have to intervene. Schuschnigg backed down, but that was not enough. Hitler wanted him out. From Berlin, Hermann Göring instructed the Austrian Nazis to see that the Austrians replaced Schuschnigg with Seyss-Inquart. President Wilhelm Miklas at first refused, then capitulated. With the appointment of a Nazi as chancellor, Austria's fate was sealed. It was possibly the only time in history that a country was conquered by telephone. Hitler ordered the German army to advance into Austria. Mussolini, with the best possible grace, wished Hitler well, and the Wehrmacht crossed the Austrian border at daybreak on 12 March.

The invasion of Austria was the German army's largest operation since World War I. Most of the soldiers had had no practice and were unfamiliar with their new equipment. They followed a plan improvised from one originally intended to prevent a Habsburg restoration. Logistics were so poor that the motorized columns advancing on Vienna were instructed to refuel at Austrian filling stations. The commander of the Second Panzer Division used a tourist map to chart his route. General Alfred Jodl, the chief of operations, confessed that 70 percent of the German tanks and trucks broke down during the operation. The afternoon of day one, Hitler arrived in Linz, the village of his youth. He had originally planned to keep Austria a separate, satellite state; but, as he maintained later, the great enthusiasm of the Austrian people for Anschluss convinced him to decree that Austria should become a province of the Reich. This, he said, was the fulfillment of the Wilsonian principle of self-determination. Britain and France, as Hitler had surmised, were not prepared to go beyond protests.

The Czechoslovak Crisis. The German takeover of Austria significantly altered the European balance of power. Germany became much stronger geopolitically, gaining a common frontier with Italy, Yugoslavia, and Hungary. With control of most of the Upper Danube, Germany now had direct access to Czechoslovakia's central plateau, the key to controlling the entire country. Hitler boasted that the German army had outflanked Czechoslovakia's western mountain defenses, trapping Czechoslovakia in a pincers.[63] Czechoslovakia, though, seemed a more difficult target than Austria. It had a good army and a defensive system that was reputedly comparable to the Maginot Line. It had treaties with both France and the Soviet Union. However, the French reliance on defensive fortifications had led the Soviets to question the value of French military assistance against German aggression.[64] When the Soviets signed a treaty of mutual guarantee with Czechoslovakia on 16 May 1936, they cleverly made its operation contingent on the French *first* living up to their own commitment to defend the Czechs against aggression. Nevertheless, Hitler recognized that the subjugation of Czechoslovakia would involve more careful planning than his slapdash operation against Austria.

Czechoslovakia had one exploitable weakness. Specifically, the 3.25 million Sudeten Germans in the mountains of northwestern Bohemia wanted to join the Reich and had organized themselves into the *Sudetendeutsche Partei*. On 28 March 1938, Hitler appointed their leader Konrad Henlein *Statthalter* (vice-regent) and told him that "he intended to settle the Sudeten-German problem in the not-too-distant future."[65] Hitler then instructed Henlein to advance claims that would lead to "freedom for the Sudeten Germans,"[66] but would not involve the German government. Hitler cautioned Henlein to have the Sudeten Germans "observe calm and discipline, and avoid imprudent behavior."[67]

On 20 May, the Czechs, spurred by rumors that German army units were being concentrated in Saxony across their northwestern border, ordered the partial mobilization of their army. The action drew international support. The British warned Germany that an attack on Czechoslovakia would lead to a European war. The French reaffirmed their treaty obligations. But France was inclined to follow the lead of the British, and the British had never been willing to act as a guarantor of Eastern Europe. Prime Minister Neville Chamberlain regarded the affair as a conflict between 7 million Czechs and their national minorities, complicated by possible German intervention. He had no desire to fight a war to keep Hitler from annexing the area. The Committee on Imperial Defense had already judged Czechoslovakia to be indefensible. Chamberlain feared that the situation could lead to a general European conflict if it were not properly handled. Therefore, in August, he sent Lord Walter Runciman to Prague to induce President Edvard Beneš to recognize a special corporate status for the Sudeten Germans. Beneš thought the scheme was "utterly absurd, for it would establish for one section of the population a totalitarian system within the democratic Czechoslovak Republic,"[68] but he nevertheless agreed. He correctly predicted that the Sudeten German party would not accept it.

After the humiliating May crisis, Hitler had ordered the Wehrmacht to prepare itself for action against Czechoslovakia at the beginning of October. In the meantime, he kept the crisis alive with threats and subversion. On 12 September, in his closing speech at the Nazi Party Congress at Nuremberg, he denounced the Czechs for oppressing the Sudeten Germans and pledged "that if these tortured creatures can of themselves find no justice and no help they will get both from us." Several hours later, an armed revolt, supplied with smuggled German weapons, broke out in the Sudetenland. The Czechs restored order, and Henlein fled to Germany and broadcast over German radio, "we want to return to the Reich."[69]

Meanwhile, the British prime minister had decided to see what he could do to resolve the crisis in a face-to-face meeting with Hitler. Chamberlain believed he could find out what the Führer wanted and within reason see that he was satisfied. Chamberlain had been a businessman before he entered politics, and this was the way businessmen solved their disputes.

Chamberlain's Personal Diplomacy. Chamberlain's initial meeting with Hitler took place at the Berghof, near Berchtesgaden, on 15 September.[70] The discussion lasted three hours. Hitler demanded that the Sudetenland with its 3.25 million Germans be "returned" to the Reich. He promised that this was the last major demand he would make on Europe. He reminded Chamberlain that the Germans had not concocted self-determination; that was the creation of the Allies who had wanted to establish a moral basis for the Treaty of Versailles. Hitler confessed that he could not understand why the British and French would go to war over an issue in which they had absolutely no direct national interest. The meeting reaffirmed Chamberlain's conviction that he was on the right track. He was impressed with the Nazi leader's power and determination, and he was convinced that Hitler's objectives "were strictly limited."[71] The French were not so sure. Premier Edouard Daladier feared that "Germany's real aim was the disintegration of Czechoslovakia and the realization of pan-German ideals through a march to the East."[72] But Daladier was determined to avoid war, and he agreed to allow the Germans to annex those areas of Czechoslovakia the Sudeten Germans inhabited. The Czechs also fell in line. Without the support of the British and the French, they felt they had to surrender the Sudetenland in the hope of preserving the independence of the rest of their country.

On 22 September, Hitler and Chamberlain met again, this time at Bad Godesberg, near Bonn. Chamberlain was in high spirits. He hoped to put the crisis
to rest. Hitler abruptly destroyed his illusions. The Sudetenland, Hitler said, was
no longer enough. There was the question of Czechoslovakia's other minorities—
the Poles, Hungarians, and Slovaks. Obviously, "peace could not be established in
Central Europe until the claims of all these nationalities had been settled."[73] Furthermore, the areas Germany claimed must be occupied immediately before any
plebiscite was held. Hitler thrust a map of Bohemia at Chamberlain. The areas he
wanted for Germany were circled in red. He had warned the Czech government
that if it did not surrender these territories by 1 October, Germany would take
them by force. Chamberlain was no longer smiling. He promised to transmit these
new terms to the French, Czech, and British governments, but he was not sure
they would be accepted.

The Czechs ordered general mobilization and seemed determined to resist.
France appeared resigned to honor its treaty of assistance. Chamberlain was de-
spondent. He could not understand why Hitler, having been granted the substance
of his demands, would fight over a question of procedure. In a radio speech to the
nation on 27 September, he lamented: "How horrible, fantastic, incredible it is
that we should be digging trenches and tying on gas masks here because of a quarrel
in a far away country between people of whom we know nothing."[74] Most of his
listeners no doubt agreed. On 28 September, Chamberlain accepted a proposal—
made by Mussolini at Chamberlain's request—to resolve the Sudeten problem
through Four-Power negotiations; Chamberlain, Daladier, and Mussolini would
meet with Hitler at Munich, the birthplace of the Nazi movement.

The Munich Agreement. The conference, held on 29–30 September, was anti-
climactic. Chamberlain and Daladier had not bothered to confer ahead of time,
and neither had prepared an agenda. They accepted an agenda Mussolini proposed
as the basis for discussions. It had really come from the German Foreign Office.
German demands, already accepted earlier at Berchtesgaden, were confirmed during the first hour of the meeting, and the rest of the time was spent working out
the details, though not without considerable tension. Chamberlain, for example,
questioned how the Czechoslovaks would be paid for the public property they lost,
and he asked if the Czechs evicted from the Sudetenland could take their livestock
with them. Hitler snapped that he should not waste valuable time with trivialities.
The agreement was signed just before 2 A.M. on 30 September, and a copy was
immediately transmitted to the waiting Czechoslovak representatives. They had
been periodically briefed throughout the conference, but had not been allowed to
participate in the discussions. They had prepared themselves for the worst.

The Czechoslovaks despondently returned to Prague to place the document
before their government. But it was clear that if it were rejected, Czechoslovakia
would be left to face Germany alone. The Munich agreement was a stunning
reminder that the nations that had helped to create Czechoslovakia at Paris in
1919 could once again decide its fate. Like jackals, Czechoslovakia's other neighbors came in for the kill. Poland demanded, and received, the district of Teschen.
The Hungarians, with German support, grabbed the long sliver of territory along
Czechoslovakia's southern frontier—and its more than a million inhabitants—that
had been taken from them in 1919. And Slovakia, which already had local autonomy, upped the stakes by demanding complete separation. Ruthenia became a
National Socialist satellite.

The final decision whether to fight for the sovereignty of their country lay with
the Czechoslovaks themselves, and they chose not to do so. Considering their

Mussolini greets Chamberlain at a reception during the Munich conference, while Reichsmarshal Göring keeps a firm eye on the food. The Duce is flanked (left to right) by his foreign minister Count Galeazzo Ciano and French premier Edouard Daladier. Paul Schmidt, Hitler's interpreter, stands behind Ciano and at the extreme right is the French ambassador to Berlin, André François-Poncet.

relative weakness and diplomatic isolation, the decision was understandable. The Czechs believed the fight for independence would be too costly. Had they decided otherwise, they could have availed themselves of certain military assets that were not negligible. They had a strong series of fortifications along the western frontier,[75] a modern air force,[76] and an army composed of forty-five reputedly well-trained, efficient divisions. Had the Germans overrun Moravia, the broken and mountainous terrain of Bohemia and Slovakia would have restricted the mobility of their troops and impeded the progress of their tanks. Consequently, the Germans would have required a greater advantage in men and matériel than is usually necessary for an attacking force. Still, few peoples have been faced with such a dramatic choice as the Czechoslovaks. Their decision to surrender the Sudetenland was not based on military considerations alone. Czechoslovakia was too divided and its birth had been too painless for it to have developed a vital commitment to its own survival such as Switzerland had developed over the centuries. The Czechs, who monopolized most of the important positions in the central government, had failed to create a genuine Czechoslovak nationalism. Their surrender to the Nazi demands undoubtedly saved much bloodshed; but by ceding to a mortal enemy the territory that contained their most important defense network, the Czechs prepared the way for the eventual dismemberment of the entire state and the servitude of its people.

Had the Czechs made a stand, there is no evidence to suggest that France and Britain would have helped them. France had no more desire to fulfill its treaty obligations to Czechoslovakia, than it had had to defend the Treaty of Locarno during the Rhineland crisis. A declaration of war was no guarantee of assistance. An offensive against Germany was the furthest thing from the minds of the French generals (as they would prove a year later when war did begin). Nothing less than a total French commitment could have stirred the British to action. And nothing would have moved Stalin except a direct attack on the Soviet Union. Britain would have watched the destruction of Czechoslovakia with a bad conscience perhaps, but would have felt no compunction to intervene.

Chamberlain was proud of his success at Munich and hoped it would lead to some sort of agreement on the limitation of armaments. But he admitted that "it would be madness for the country to stop rearming until we were convinced that other countries would act in the same way." Chamberlain did not sign the Munich

Agreement to gain time for the British to prepare for war; he believed he had bought his country "peace in our time." The only person to resign from the British government in protest was First Lord of the Admiralty Duff Cooper, who believed there could be no peace in Europe as long as Britain refused to stand up to Nazi Germany. Winston Churchill, then only a member of Parliament, attacked Chamberlain for sacrificing traditional British security: "The whole equilibrium of Europe has been deranged, and . . . terrible words have for the first time been pronounced against the Western Democracies: 'Thou art weighed in the balance and found wanting.' "[77] Still, Churchill recognized appeasement was popular with the British people and wrote that it was to Chamberlain's credit that he did not "yield to temptations and pressures to seek a general election on the morrow of Munich."[78]

King George VI led the way in praising Chamberlain. In his message to the nation on Sunday, 2 October, the monarch gave thanks to "the Almighty for His mercy in sparing us the horrors of war" and called the efforts of the prime minister in the cause of peace "magnificent." These sentiments were echoed in the popular press. The London *Times* said, "No conqueror retiring from a victory on the battlefield has come adorned with nobler laurels." The *Daily Express* reported incorrectly that Chamberlain would soon be made a Knight of the Garter. A *Mass Observation* poll showed that 54 percent of the electorate supported the Munich Agreement—not unanimous, but certainly substantial. In France, *Paris-Soir* began a national subscription to buy the British prime minister a summer home in the Dordogne and, in less than a week, received pledges for 500,000 francs. Daladier, when he returned from Munich, was surprised to be welcomed almost as a hero. The leading advocate of appeasement in Daladier's cabinet, Foreign Minister Georges Bonnet, greeted him at Le Bourget airport in Paris with the traditional kiss on both cheeks. The premier refused to be carried away. He knew the Munich accord was a strategic disaster—the coup de grace of the French postwar security system.

Profile: The Balance of the Great Powers in 1938

In 1919, Marshal Foch wrote a memorandum to the French government in which he said that future peace could be assured only if Germany were reduced in population and deprived of national territory, especially of the land along the Rhine.[79] He said that it was not sufficient to change governments. The German people would still remain bellicose. Foch warned that Germany's basic credo was "might makes right." He feared that a republic might be even more menacing than the old monarchy because it would achieve greater unity and, humiliated by defeat, would develop a more intense spirit and sense of purpose.

The 1919 settlement had reduced the German nation by about 28,000 square miles. The demilitarization of the Rhineland had made the German frontier with France less menacing. Two decades later, these scant advantages were gone. The Saarland had been reacquired, the Rhineland had been remilitarized, and Austria and the Sudetenland had been annexed. Germany had added over 10,000 square miles and more than 10 million people to its prewar size and was larger and more populous than at any time in its history.[80] More alarming yet was the normal increase in the German population. Since Hitler came to power, it had risen by 477,000 people annually, while the French population had gone up a scant 4,000 a year.[81] Small wonder that demographers concerned with analyzing the statistics of national power could only wonder when the next shoe would drop. Even had

TABLE 1: RESOURCES AND PRODUCTIVITY

	France	Germany	Great Britain	Italy	Soviet Union	United States
Population (*millions*)	42	76.4	45	43.6	166	123
Area (*thousands of square miles*)	213	225	89	120	8,096	2,974
Steel production (*thousands of metric tons*)	6,137	22,656	10,565	2,323	18,057	34,882 (1939)
Sulfuric acid production (*thousands of metric tons*)	1,272	2,272	960	1,076	1,544	5,147
Electrical energy (*millions of kilowatt-hours*)	20.8	55.33	33.77	15.43	39.37	116,681

TABLE 2: COMPARATIVE MILITARY STRENGTH

	France	Germany	Great Britain	Italy	Soviet Union	United States
Army (*thousands of personnel*)	491	720	159.4	260	1,214	185.5
Navy (*thousands of personnel*)	77.4	46.6	112	74.6	23.6	137.4
Battleships and battlecruisers (*pre-1914*)	7(4)	5(0)	15(12)	4(all)	3(all)	15(6)
Cruisers	19	12	61	22	6	33
Destroyers	59	30	168	56	23	206
Submarines	77	36	54	105	134	89
Aircraft carriers	1	0	7	0	0	5
First-line aircraft	1,630	5,040	1,750	2,500	1,920	1,600

there been no militant nationalist movement guiding its destinies, Germany would have played a major role in Europe's future. Only when German strength was balanced with that of the other powers did it seem manageable (see Table 1). In statistical terms, there seemed sufficient deterrence.[82]

Britain was too weak to continue acting as the "holder," the makeweight, of the balance of power, but it avoided forging an alliance with France to do the job collectively. The only countries with the necessary geographical detachment to take the place of the British were the Soviet Union and the United States. Neither had the desire. The Soviets were not interested in preserving the status quo. They had territorial claims against Finland, the Baltic states, Poland, Romania, and Turkey. The United States consistently refused to participate actively in the affairs of Europe. As Vansittart wrote bitterly at the beginning of the decade, the United States "neither lives, nor desires to live, in touch with reality so long as filmland is open to her, and she has a good spell of illusions still ahead."[83] Indeed, Chamberlain neither wanted, nor apparently thought it necessary that the United States, let alone the Soviet Union, become involved. The affairs at Munich were conducted without the participation of either. It was the last important European conference to hold that distinction.

An assessment of military strength showed that Germany was better prepared to begin hostilities in 1938 than were Britain, France, and the Soviet Union (see Table 2). Only the forces of the Soviet Union were numerically superior to Germany's, but due to the Stalin purges, the Red Army was in disarray, and many questioned its effectiveness. In contrast, there were few doubts about the quality of the German military; it was the product of a highly motivated people and had been achieved by the mobilization of an entire society, including the economy, the educational system, and labor and youth organizations. From the British point of view, the most chilling aspect of the German armaments program was the development of the Luftwaffe, whose bomber fleets operating from bases in the Rhineland could strike targets across the English Channel. What was worse, since the American General William Mitchell proved conclusively in the 1920s that bombers could indeed sink battleships, the Royal Navy was no longer a primary shield against invasion.

Estimating overall air force size was difficult. The British service had a listed strength of 83,000 men, the French had 62,495 men, and the Italians 38,262. The Luftwaffe was assumed to be larger than the British Royal Air Force (RAF), but Hitler constantly exaggerated its size for maximum political effect.[84] After Munich, Britain concentrated on increasing the strength of the RAF. By April 1939, the first-line strength of the Metropolitan Air Force was 1,750 aircraft, organized into 157 regular squadrons. By the middle of the year, the production of war planes had climbed to over 600 a month, compared to 200 a month in 1938. The fighter squadrons of the RAF were thereby increased fivefold and equipped with Hurricanes and Spitfires. Britain completed its projected radar system, quadrupled its production of antiaircraft guns, and reorganized its civil defense. The improvement in army and naval strength was less marked, but British overall military strength had increased by a larger percentage than the German military had increased. French gains, however, were comparatively insignificant.

One of Britain's most valuable military assets did not appear in the conventional charts. Sometime during the summer of 1938, thanks to the Polish secret service, the British were able to lay their hands on the principal cryptograph of the German armed forces, the Enigma machine. Over the next two years, British experts developed an electronic computer that would enable them to intercept and decode the German Supreme Command messages to its army, navy, and air force field headquarters and units. This unique source of intelligence, code-named Ultra, was used under operational conditions for the first time during the Battle of France in May and June 1940. The rapidity of the German Blitzkrieg allowed little time to take advantage of the information obtained. During the aerial Battle of Britain, however, Ultra was absolutely essential to Britain's success, an advantage that continued in other engagements throughout the war.[85]

Hitler Maintains the Initiative

The Aftermath of Munich. The Munich Agreement cost Czechoslovakia 40 percent of its heavy chemical industry, 55 percent of its bituminous coal reserves, 63 percent of its paper production, 68 percent of its copper, 97 percent of its lignite, and all of its graphite and zinc. Still, Hitler was dissatisfied. He felt that he had wrongfully been persuaded to solve the crisis peacefully. "It was a moment of weakness. There was Chamberlain's pleading, there were the fears of the German people, there were the doubts of my generals. I gave way. But no longer. I return to my original plan."[86] The Führer was convinced that he had wide latitude to redraw the map of Eastern Europe without fear of French or British intervention. In March 1939, the Germans smashed the Munich Agreement by occupying the rest of Bohemia and establishing a protectorate over Slovakia and Ruthenia. Chamberlain was dismayed at Hitler's unreliability, but not angry enough to abandon his policy of appeasement. This latest Nazi aggression, however, put him under considerable pressure to broaden his cabinet, perhaps by taking in Winston Churchill, to emphasize the seriousness with which the British viewed the situation. Instead, the prime minister chose to quiet his critics with a speech. At Birmingham on 17 March, he denounced Hitler for breaking his word. "Is this the last attack upon a small state or is it to be followed by another?" he asked. "Is this in fact a step in the direction of an attempt to dominate the world by force?"[87] He warned that Britain would resist such a challenge to the limits of its power.

Tough talk did not impress Hitler. Two days later, he boarded the pocket battleship *Deutschland*[88] and sailed into the Baltic in the direction of Lithuania. The Baltic at that time of year was very rough, and Hitler was violently seasick for the entire voyage. On 23 March, he landed at Memel and, in the style of a Spanish conquistador, reclaimed it as part of the Reich. Foreign Minister Joachim von Ribbentrop had already made the necessary arrangements for an appropriate transfer of sovereignty in Berlin. The Lithuanian government was given the usual Hobson's chance: either peacefully accede to the Nazi demands or have the territory taken by force. Hitler entered the city to the shouts of the German-speaking population. Memeland was the last chunk of territory he would acquire without war.

Like any good German nationalist, Hitler found the Polish Corridor and the loss of Danzig intolerable. On 24 October 1938, he had promised Poland he would respect the eastern frontiers if Germany were given Danzig and an access strip across the Polish Corridor. The offer was made just to throw Poland off guard. Józef Beck, the Polish Foreign Minister, was no fool. He suspected the Führer's real intentions, but feared jeopardizing his country's independence by turning to the Western democracies for help. Considering the performance of Britain and France at Munich, Beck feared they would force him to make concessions to Hitler.

Beck hoped to create a third force in Central Europe through an alliance with the other smaller states, but Romania was the only country with which Poland was on good terms. Beck, therefore, determined to stand up to Hitler alone. After all, the Czechs had gotten nowhere with their policy of capitulation. Then help seemed to appear from an unexpected quarter.

On 29 March, Ian Colvin, the Berlin correspondent of the *News Chronicle*, told Lord Halifax that "he was convinced Hitler would attack Poland very shortly unless it was made quite certain that we would then attack him."[89] This prompted Chamberlain, with French approval, to unilaterally guarantee the independence of Poland.[90] Britain apparently had ended its hands-off policy toward eastern Europe. But things were not so simple. Chamberlain hoped that the move would improve his chances for negotiating a peaceful settlement with Germany. Hitler believed that the British guarantee of Poland was meant only for domestic consumption, that it was Chamberlain's way of neutralizing his opposition. "The campaign of antagonism against Germany," Hitler remarked, "was organized by Churchill on the orders of his Jewish paymasters, and with the collaboration of Eden, Vansittart and company . . . any and every nation which fails to eliminate the Jews in its midst will sooner or later finish by being itself devoured by them."[91] On 3 April 1939, he ordered a plan for the invasion of Poland (Operation White) to begin at the earliest on 1 September if Poland had not surrendered the territory Germany demanded. Later that same month, Hitler denounced the nonaggression treaty.

On 22 May, he concluded the Pact of Steel with Mussolini. In this treaty, Italy and Germany pledged to come to each other's aid in *any* eventual war—even if such involvement was "against the wishes and hopes of the High Contracting Parties."[92] Mussolini emphasized that Italy would not be prepared for hostilities before 1942. Nevertheless, in signing the treaty, he surrendered to Germany the sovereign right of his nation to decide when to go to war. The Duce was convinced that the salvation of Fascism lay in an alliance with Germany. Hitler believed that an attack on Poland should begin at the first suitable opportunity. He thought this could quite possibly lead to a life and death struggle with Britain and France that could last from ten to fifteen years. First, however, he had to strike a bargain with the Soviet Union.

The Nazi-Soviet Nonaggression Pact. In May 1939, Maksim Litvinov entered the Foreign Ministry, and discovered that Vyacheslav Molotov, the chairman of the Council of People's Commissars (prime minister) had replaced him. The next day, an announcement said that Litvinov had resigned because of ill health. The ouster signaled the end of the Soviet Union's flirtation with collective security and its return, at least temporarily, to a policy of neutrality. Litvinov had been symbolic of the Soviet Union's attempt to organize a European coalition against Germany. Furthermore he was a Jew. With the rise of the "Hitlerites," Stalin had sought closer contact with the Western democracies and had advocated the formation of Popular Fronts with bourgeois and socialist parties to fight the growth of Fascism. The Munich Agreement convinced him that the British and French were plotting to turn Hitler eastward. Their policy, he said, "reveals an eagerness, a desire, not to hinder the aggressors in their nefarious work."[93] Stalin declared that the Soviet Union would not be drawn into a conflict by "warmongers who are accustomed to have others pull the chestnuts out of the fire for them."[94] Beneath his words was a deep-seated fear that Germany would attack. The Soviet armed forces were in shambles following the great purges, and Stalin resorted to diplomacy to neutralize the threat. He encouraged the Germans to believe that he would conclude an alliance with Britain and France; at the same time, he encouraged the British and French to believe that he would come to terms with Hitler. From April until August 1939, Stalin carried on negotiations with both the British and the Germans simultaneously.

Stalin proposed the British sign a sweeping three-power guarantee to render "all manner of assistance, including that of a military nature, to Eastern Europe states situated between Baltic and Black Seas and bordering on U.S.S.R., in case of aggression against these states."[95] He demanded that a group of eight states—Estonia, Latvia, Lithuania, Poland, Romania, Turkey, Greece, and Belgium—be guaranteed against "an internal coup d'état or a reversal of policy in the interests of the aggressor."[96] In other words, under the guise of protecting itself against "indirect aggression," the Soviet Union could occupy those countries any time it wished. In effect, the Soviets were asking the British to recognize the legality of Soviet expansion. Stalin did not give his plan much chance of success. He believed that the chances of Maginot-minded France or isolationist Britain providing direct military assistance to Eastern Europe were remote. He feared that the British would repeat their Munich strategy and make another deal with Hitler, leaving the Soviet Union to face German aggression alone.[97] On 17 August, he broke off these negotiations. By then he had already decided to conclude an agreement with Hitler.

Ribbentrop, the Nazi foreign minister, arrived in Moscow on 23 August to clinch the deal. He and Stalin found they had much in common. Ribbentrop dismissed Britain "as a weak country that wanted to let others fight for her presumptuous claim to world domination." Stalin agreed and replied that if Britain dominated the world in spite of its weakness, it "was due to the stupidity of the other countries that always let themselves be bluffed."[98] At the end of the session, Stalin drank a toast to the health of the Führer and to a new era of German-Soviet relations. An agreement was signed later that day. This Nazi-Soviet pact was similar to other nonaggression treaties, with two important exceptions. First, it contained no clause permitting one of the signatories to denounce the treaty should war be declared against a third party—thus, Germany could attack Poland without jeopardizing the agreement. Second, a secret additional protocol carved up Eastern Europe into German and Soviet spheres of influence. Poland was partitioned with a dividing line that ran through the middle of the country along the Narev, Vistula, and San rivers; future political developments were to determine "whether the interests of both parties make the maintenance of an independent Polish state appear desirable."[99] The Germans also accorded the Soviets a free hand in determining the fate of Finland, Estonia, Latvia, and the Romanian territory of Bessarabia.

Stalin had supposedly signed the pact to gain time to prepare the Soviet Union for an inevitable clash with Germany. Yet, if this was the case, he took little advantage of the breathing space he had won. Few new fortifications were built. Military units were not redeployed for such a defense, leaving the Soviet army in the west woefully unprepared for an eventual invasion. More likely, the Soviet dictator had discounted the likelihood of a German attack and had signed the pact with the Nazis to avoid war altogether. He believed that he had outsmarted Hitler and turned him westward. The treaty almost totally satisfied the Soviet Union's revisionist aims dating from World War I.[100] Moreover, Stalin went to extra lengths to appease Hitler. He was especially careful to deliver Soviet raw materials to Germany. And to prove his good faith, he handed over to the Gestapo those German Communists who had sought asylum in the Soviet Union.

Stalin believed that Chamberlain and Daladier had deliberately and consistently helped Hitler realize his aims because they wanted to embroil him in a war with the Soviet Union that would exhaust both countries. In rejecting any alliance against Nazi aggression, the British and French were in effect trying to isolate the Soviet Union, leaving it to face German aggression alone.

The Invasion of Poland. The nonaggression treaty gave Germany carte blanche to invade Poland. Hitler wanted the fighting to be localized. He believed that Chamberlain was trying to wiggle out of his commitments to Poland. On 23 August—the same day the pact was concluded with Stalin—he wrote to the prime minister, saying that "Germany was prepared to settle the questions of Danzig and of the Corridor by the method of negotiation on the basis of a proposal of truly unparalleled magnanimity."[101] Unlike the Czechs, the Poles had decided to fight against the dismemberment of their country. Hitler hoped that Chamberlain would pressure Beck the same way the prime minister had pressured Beneš.

Chamberlain was still determined to find a solution short of war and continued diplomatic exchanges with Germany. The pope made an appeal for peace. Mussolini, fearing that the invasion of Poland would lead to a war for which he was unprepared, tried to resolve the crisis with a repeat of his Munich performance. But Hitler was only interested in military action. On Friday, 1 September, at 4:45 in the morning, Wehrmacht Panzer units rolled across the Polish frontier.

The British and French governments cried that Germany had plunged the world into war and begged the pope to express his profound grief. Pius refused to do so on the grounds that the suggestion involved a "specific intervention in international politics."[102] Italy proclaimed its neutrality. Chamberlain suggested an international conference. He promised the Germans that the situation could return to what it had been before the invasion if they would withdraw. British public opinion was overwhelmingly against further appeasement. The prime minister's delay in delivering an ultimatum to Hitler was roundly denounced in the House of Commons. Even Conservatives, who had previously supported Chamberlain, joined in. Reluctantly, Chamberlain accepted the inevitable. He gave Hitler until eleven o'clock on 3 September to withdraw his troops from Poland. When no reply was received, Britain declared war. The French were more generous. They set a deadline six hours later.

POSTSCRIPT   Britain had never promised to guarantee the inviolability of the eastern peace treaties. Its policy was based on maintaining the security of Western Europe only. Chamberlain assumed that appeasing Hitler was a small price to pay to avoid the outbreak of hostilities. He based his assessment on several dangerous assumptions: he thought Hitler was reasonable, that his ultimate goals were definable, and that his ambitions could be satisfied without destroying the balance of power. His belief that Hitler had limited objectives was obviously way off the mark, but national leaders like Hitler have been fairly rare in modern Western history. People with such unlimited ambitions lack conventional political wisdom and are therefore immune to any normal stimuli. A successful policy of deterrence is based on the assumption that an opponent will act with a certain amount of restraint and reason.

Hitler was one of the most literal men of his age. He firmly believed that he was destined to accomplish his dreams. Yet foreign leaders with whom he came in contact did not find him that outlandish. In his meetings with them, he was hardly the screaming madman he had been reported to be. With his subordinates, he often created scenes for effect, not because he had lost control. Most of the time, however, he seemed mature and sensible. When he talked to foreigners about his desire for peace, he could be very convincing. In 1933, he said that Germany had "no other wish than to guide the rivalries of the peoples of Europe once more to those spheres in which they had given to humanity in the noblest of mutual rivalries those supreme gifts to civilization, of culture, of art which today enrich and beautify the picture of the world."[103] This was one of his favorite themes, and it worked particularly well on people like Chamberlain who wanted to hear it. Hitler conducted foreign affairs intuitively, but soon degenerated into self-delusion. Even while pressing the attack against Poland, he continued to assume that the fighting would not lead to general hostilities, that his victory would be so rapid and impressive the West would think twice before taking him on. He had assured State Secretary Ernst Weizsäcker, "in two months, Poland will be finished; then we shall have a great peace conference with the Western Powers."[104]

In the years after the Munich conference, appeasement became synonymous with diplomatic failure, but the motives behind the practice were honorable. A policy of conciliation can adjust national ambitions and rivalries, compensate for changes in the international power structure, and serve to maintain an equilibrium. Revisionism is not bad in itself. Changing circumstances need not lead to the destruction of international harmony. Appeasement had worked well in the 1920s, and the British saw no reason why it should not continue to do so. However, the appeasement Chamberlain practiced was no longer a policy of strength initiated by victors. It was a policy of weakness determined by the demands of the aggressors. Times had changed. The League of Nations was ineffective, France was defeatist, Mussolini was drawing closer to Hitler, and British rearmament had barely begun.

The pacifist tendencies of the British voters made rearmament politically risky. In 1936, when Colonel Hastings Ismay, the deputy-secretary of the Imperial Defense Committee, proposed additional expenditures for anti-aircraft artillery, Neville Chamberlain, then the chancellor of the exchequer, replied "that he was prepared to agree to the additional guns now proposed, but that he sincerely hoped that the last word had been spoken and there would be no further demands."[105] The British still could not conceive of rearmament as a preparation of war. The British leaders were slow to recognize that past techniques were no longer valid. Chamberlain was convinced that he could avert a European conflict. After all, a lack of communication among nations did contribute to the outbreak of World War I.

ENDNOTES

1. *Documents of British Foreign Policy*, series 2, vol. 6, 751.
2. Vansittart also feared the intentions of Fascist Italy. Mussolini, he said, hoped to fill the vacuum left by the collapse of the Austro-Hungarian Empire in the Balkans and would move to supplant the power of France and Britain in the Mediterranean. Mussolini would most likely turn to Germany for support and therein lay the beginning of the next war.
3. *Documents of British Foreign Policy*, series 1a, vol. 7, 834–52.
4. A complete English translation of the book appeared only in 1939. *Mein Kampf* (New York: Reynal and Hitchcock, 1939).
5. Norman H. Baynes, ed., *The Speeches of Adolf Hitler*, vol. 2, (London: Oxford University Press, 1942), 1057.
6. *Documents of German Foreign Policy*, series C, vol. 1, 366.
7. When Barthou visited the capitals of the Little Entente (Prague, April 26–27; Bucharest, June 20–23; and Belgrade, June 24–26), he discovered that only the Czechs took the German menace seriously. The Romanians and Yugoslavs felt they had more to gain, particularly in improved commercial relations, from a policy of friendship with Germany than from a grand alliance against it. Besides, they had other preoccupations. Just as Poland nursed deep grievances against Czechoslovakia, Romania stood guard against Hungarian expansionism, and Yugoslavia feared Italian expansion in the Adriatic.
8. Anthony Eden, *Facing the Dictators* (Boston: Houghton Mifflin, 1962), 105.
9. *Documents of British Foreign Policy*, series C, vol. 2, 861–62.
10. Hitler, *Mein Kampf*, 3.
11. Friedelind Wagner, *Heritage of Fire* (New York: Harper, 1945), 109.
12. Ibid., 124. Dumplings, *Ja*, but liver most assuredly, *Nein!* Hitler was a vegetarian.
13. Franz von Papen, *Memoirs* (New York: E. P. Dutton, 1953), 339.
14. *Documents of British Foreign Policy*, 2d series, vol. 6, 871.
15. Hitler, *Secret Conversations*, translated by Norman Cameron and R. H. Stevens (New York: Farrar, Straus and Young, 1953), 338.
16. "The Political and Social Doctrine of Fascism," *International Conciliation Documents* (New York: Carnegie Foundation, 1935), 16.
17. Ernest Rudiger Starhemberg, *Between Hitler and Mussolini* (New York: Harper, 1942), 167.
18. France ceded to Italian Libya 44,000 square miles of arid, uninhabited desert from Equatorial Africa, gave 13.5 miles of additional coastline to Eritrea plus a tiny offshore island, and allowed Italy to purchase seven percent of the shares in the French-owned Djibouti–Addis Ababa railroad.
19. Emilio DeBono, *Anno XIII: The Conquest of an Empire* (London: Cresset Press, 1937), 13.
20. *Documents of British Foreign Policy*, 2d series, vol. 12, 879.
21. Ibid., 883.
22. Ibid., 888.
23. Ibid., 863.
24. Royal Institute of International Affairs, *Documents on International Affairs, 1935*, vol. 1, 82.
25. Vittorio Mussolini, *Flight over the Amba Mountains*, quoted in A. J. Barker, *The Civilizing Mission* (New York: Deal Press, 1968), 234–35.
26. The French were merely trying to offset their low birthrate during the years of World War I.
27. *Documents of British Foreign Policy*, 2d series, vol. 1, 603.
28. The plebiscite, conducted under the supervision of the League of Nations, had

been held on 13 January 1935. Ninety percent of the population voted to return to Germany in preference to union with France or remaining under the administration of the League. The official date of reincorporation was 1 March.

29. In 1935, the second pocket battleship *Admiral Scheer* was launched, and a third, *Graf Spee*, was nearing completion. Also under construction were the 26,000-ton battlecruisers *Scharnhorst* and *Gneisenau*.

30. The Royal Navy still received the lion's share of military budgetary appropriations, over half of the 1934 total. By contrast, the Royal Air Force received only enough to add four new squadrons, raising the number of first-line aircraft from 850 to 890—a situation that caused Winston Churchill to comment, "I dread the day when the means of threatening the heart of the British Empire should pass into the hands of the present rulers of Germany." Winston S. Churchill, *The Gathering Storm* (Boston: Houghton Mifflin, 1948), 112.

31. *Documents of British Foreign Policy*, 2d series, vol. 1, 708, 727.

32. Baynes, ed., *Speeches of Hitler*, 1241.

33. *Nazi Conspiracy and Aggression*, vol. 6 (Washington, D.C.: U.S. Government Printing Office, 1946), 951–52.

34. Pierre-Etienne Flandin, *Politique française, 1919–1940* (Paris: Les éditions nouvelles, 1947), 195–96.

35. Arnold Wolfers, *Britain and France between the Wars: Conflicting Strategies of Peace Since Versailles* (New York: Harcourt, Brace, 1940), 45–46.

36. *Documents diplomatiques français*, 2ème série, vol. 1, 339.

37. The pretext he used was the signing of a Franco-Soviet treaty due for ratification by the Chamber of Deputies in early March 1936. The agreement was fairly mild. The signatories pledged to respond to an unprovoked attack on the other only *after* the League of Nations had failed to agree on a course of action. No time limit was placed on the deliberations of the Council. The treaty, in an obvious reference to the Treaty of Locarno, was not intended to contravene any previously assumed commitments toward other states. The arrangement gave France a perfect excuse to do nothing.

38. On 9 March 1936; *Hansard Parliamentary Debates*, 309, 5th series, 1812.

39. *Documents diplomatiques français*, 2ème série, vol. 1, 541.

40. *Documents of British Foreign Policy*, 2d series, vol. 6, 684.

41. The line was named after the Minister of War André Maginot, a wounded veteran of Verdun. On 4 January 1930, the government of André Tardieu promulgated the law that furnished credits for its construction.

42. Paul Reynaud, *In the Thick of the Fight* (New York: Simon & Schuster, 1956), 107.

43. Hitler, *Secret Conversations*, 211.

44. Albert Speer, *Inside the Third Reich* (New York: Macmillan, 1970), 131.

45. Ibid., 105–6.

46. Ibid., 857.

47. Ibid., 101.

48. Field-Marshal Werner von Blomberg, minister of war and commander-in-chief of the armed forces; Colonel-General Freiherr Werner von Fritsch, commander of the army; Admiral Erich Raeder, commander of the navy; Colonel-General Hermann Göring, commander of the Luftwaffe, and Freiherr Konstantin von Neurath, foreign minister. Colonel Friedrich Hossbach was the rapporteur.

49. *Documents of German Foreign Policy*, series D, vol. 1, 43–45.

50. Ibid., 29.

51. *Documents of German Foreign Policy*, series D, vol. 7, 635–36.

52. Sanjurjo died a victim of his own vanity—not sabotage as suspected. His plane was overloaded with heavy trunks full of uniforms that he intended to wear as Spain's new chief of state.

53. The Falange party adopted the national syndicalism of José-Antonio Primo de Rivera, but without his commitment to work for social justice.

54. William Laird Kleine-Ahlbrandt, *The Policy of Simmering: A Study of British Policy*

during the Spanish Civil War, 1936–1939 (The Hague: Martinus Nijhoff, 1962) 23–36.

55. For Britain, the Mediterranean was not just a shortcut, but an essential artery; it was the outer defense perimeter of the Home Fleet. It connected Britain with three-fourths of the land in its Empire-Commonwealth. Through it went one-fifth of British imports.

56. Quoted in Kleine-Ahlbrandt, *The Policy of Simmering*, 107.

57. Maurice Baumont, *La faillité de la paix*, vol. 2 (Paris: Presses Universitaires, 1960), 714.

58. Kleine-Ahlbrandt, *The Policy of Simmering*, 140–44.

59. *Documents of German Foreign Policy*, series C, vol. 3, 342.

60. However, the Italian foreign minister, Count Galeazzo Ciano, feared the dangerous implications for Italian security of Anschluss, which would bring Germany's 70 million people to Italy's northern frontier. Ciano wanted to keep his options open for a deal with the British.

61. *Documents of German Foreign Policy*, series D, vol. 1, 280.

62. Keitel later admitted: "We generals played no part in the conferences and had no inkling of either the objectives or the aims of the talks until Schuschnigg's departure: we were fearfully bored." *The Memoirs of Field-Marshal Keitel* (New York: Stein and Day, 1966), 57.

63. Speer, *Inside the Third Reich*, 109.

64. Marshal Mikhail Tukhachevsky wrote that the French army "with its twenty divisions, its hastily assembled units, and slow rate of expansion by stages under mobilization, [was] already incapable of active opposition to Germany." Jane Degras, ed., *Soviet Documents on Foreign Policy* (London: Oxford University Press, 1953), 125.

65. *Documents of German Foreign Policy*, series D, vol. 2, 198.

66. Ibid., 204.

67. Ibid., 204–5.

68. Ibid., 178.

69. Royal Institute of International Affairs, *Survey of International Affairs*, 1938, vol. 2, 261.

70. The airplane that flew Chamberlain to his historic meeting with Hitler was a twin-engine Lockheed Electra. Some people found it upsetting that no suitable British aircraft was available and feared that this would convince Germans that Britain had no good aircraft designers. Cf. *Flight*, September 22, 1938 (London: Flight Publishing Co., 1938), vol. 34, 250.

71. Ian Colvin, *The Chamberlain Cabinet* (New York: Taplinger, 1971), 155.

72. *Documents of British Foreign Policy*, 3d series, vol. 2, 384.

73. *Documents of German Foreign Policy*, series D, vol. 2, 874.

74. *Documents on International Affairs*, 1935, 2:270.

75. Jonathan Zorach points out their weakness in "Czechoslovakia's Fortifications," *Militargeschichtliche mittellungen* (1976), 2, 81–94. Nevertheless Hitler was impressed. Upon taking possession, the German military conducted a test bombardment and discovered that their own guns were ineffective. "Given a resolute defense, taking them would have been very difficult and would have cost us a great many lives," Hitler said. "Now we have obtained them without loss of blood. One thing is certain: I shall never again permit the Czechs to build a new defense line. What a marvelous starting position we have now. We are over the mountains and already in the valleys of Bohemia." Speer, *Inside the Third Reich*, 111.

76. By the time of the Munich crisis, the standard fighter of the Czechoslovak Air Force was the Avia B 534, a highly maneuverable biplane, the finest of its type in Europe. During the Zurich Air Show in 1937, it came in second in all important contests, closely behind the Messerschmitt Bf 109. With its four Mk 30 machine guns, it could have put up a strong defense against the Luftwaffe squadrons. In all, 445 of the 534s were built. These were captured by Germany, when it occupied

the rest of Bohemia and Moravia in March 1939. Many were given to the Nazi satellite, the Slovak Republic, and were used against the Soviet Air Force in World War II.

77.   Churchill, *The Gathering Storm*, 329.
78.   Ibid., 330.
79.   MAE, Pichon Papers, vol. 7 (1919), 7.
80.   Austria had a population of 6.7 million and an area of 32,000 square miles; the Sudetenland had a population of 3.5 million people and an area of 10,800 square miles. In 1914, Germany had 209,000 square miles and 65 million people.
81.   *The Statesman's Year Book 1939* (New York: St. Martin's Press), 895, 976.
82.   Paul Kennedy, *The Rise and Fall of the Great Powers: Economic Change and Military Conflict from 1500 to 2000* (New York: Random House, 1987), 303–10.
83.   *Documents of British Foreign Policy*, series 1a, vol. 7, 849.
84.   The U.S. Air Force was split between the Army and the Navy. The Army budget for 1938 allocated 15.5 percent to its air arm, the Navy allocated 7.8 percent. In the aftermath of the Munich accord (September 1938), President Franklin D. Roosevelt proposed a massive buildup in air power to a minimum frontline strength of 10,000 planes.
85.   Statistics in this profile were taken from the following sources: *Statesman's Year Book* (1914, 1924, 1938, and 1939); *Statistical Abstract of the United States* (Washington, D.C.: U.S. Government Printing Office, 1941); *Statistical History of the United States from Colonial Times to the Present* (Washington, D.C.: U.S. Government Printing Office, 1980); Mark Skinner Watson, *Chief of Staff: Pre-War Plans and Preparations* (Washington, D.C.: Department of the Army, 1950); and Brian R. Mitchell, *European Historical Statistics, 1750–1970* (New York: Columbia University Press, 1975).
86.   Leonard Mosley, *On Borrowed Time* (New York: Random House, 1969), 98.
87.   Neville Chamberlain, *In Search of Peace* (New York: G.P. Putnam, 1939), 275.
88.   After the start of World War II, Hitler rechristened the *Deutschland Lützow* to avoid national embarrassment should the ship bearing the country's name be sunk.
89.   Colvin, *The Chamberlain Cabinet*, 194.
90.   On 31 March, Chamberlain announced in Parliament that "in the event of any action which clearly threatened Polish independence and which the Polish Government accordingly considered it vital to resist with their armed forces, His Majesty's Government would feel themselves bound at once to lend the Polish Government all support in their power." Ibid., 180.
91.   Hitler, *Secret Conversations*, 551.
92.   *Documents of German Foreign Policy*, series D, vol. 6, 562.
93.   "Stalin's Report to the Eighteenth Congress of the C.P.S.U." (10 March 1939) in Degras, Soviet Documents, 3:319.
94.   Ibid., 322.
95.   *Documents of British Foreign Policy*, 3d series, vol. 5, 228.
96.   Ibid., vol. 6, 251.
97.   Ibid., 641.
98.   *Documents of German Foreign Policy*, series D, vol. 7, 227.
99.   Ibid., 246–47.
100. A future Soviet premier, Nikita Khrushchev, wrote that from a territorial point of view the reacquisition of the western Ukraine from Poland gave the Soviet Union "practically nothing except what we were legally entitled to." *Khrushchev Remembers* (Boston: Little, Brown, 1970), 139.
101. *Documents of German Foreign Policy*, series D, vol. 7, 217.
102. *Documents of British Foreign Policy*, 3d series, vol. 7, 495.
103. Baynes, ed., *Speeches of Hitler*, 1098.
104. Ernst Weizsäcker, *Memoirs* (London: Gollanz, 1951), 208.
105. Lord Ismay, *Memoirs* (New York: Viking, 1960), 80.

CHAPTER 15

EUROPE UNDER THE AXIS

PREFACE   No cheering crowds greeted the outbreak of war in September 1939. Even in Germany, where the leadership's desire for combat was strongest, the people did not respond with a comparable sense of exhilaration. Hitler, sensing this lack of enthusiasm, left for the Polish front after bidding his henchmen a terse farewell at the chancellery. "Obviously Goebbels could have provided a cheering crowd of any size," observed Albert Speer, "but [Hitler] apparently was not in the mood to do it."[1] Hitler's attitude toward the beginning of the war seemed to mirror his reckless attitude toward politics: "All my life I have played for 'all or nothing,' " he explained to Hermann Göring.

The declaration of war on Poland had not been intended to provoke hostilities with the British and the French. German military preparations were as yet incomplete. Fortunately for Hitler, Germany's adversaries were even less prepared. Thus, the fighting was initially restricted to the partition of Poland, an apparent example of traditional German expansionism. Indeed, once this goal was achieved, Hitler tried to make peace with Britain and France, claiming there was no longer any reason for them to continue the state of war. He even held out the prospect of re-creating Poland—in a smaller version. The British and French refused.

However, from the very beginning, it was clear that this conflict was not going to remain limited. The fighting in Europe had implications for the rest of the world. The subsequent defeat of France and the attempted invasion of Britain gave Japan an opportunity to advance its plans for conquest in the Far East, putting it on a collision course with the United States. At that point, the European war became the Second World War.

For Hitler, the invasion of the Soviet Union was the centerpiece of his foreign policy. The east was the prime area for the expansion of the German racial community. In *Mein Kampf,* he had talked about the struggle for ethnic, ideological, and economic mastery reaching its climax on the plains of Russia and the Ukraine. There the great clash of Russian and German power, the main theme of European history since the eighteenth century, would be at its most ferocious. The Germans did not intend to lose. They planned to exterminate these inferior peoples and replace them with the master race. But there their dreams would be dashed. Out of their defeat came the shape of Europe for the next fifty years.

THE EUROPEAN WAR, 1939–1941

The Partition of Eastern Europe

The Destruction of Poland. Once the war began, Hitler became totally absorbed by military affairs. He raised his banner in the old Polish Corridor and visited the front every day. Success followed success. Poland had no defensible frontiers. Its western plains bulged along a 350-mile boundary from east Prussia to Czechoslovakia. The German spearheads gouged deep holes in this salient from north and south, then thrust rapidly eastward to trap the main Polish army west of Warsaw. Within three days, the Germans had secured the Polish Corridor and pushed their divisions fifty miles across the southern plains. By 8 September, they had reached the outskirts of the Polish capital, where the badly bruised divisions of the Polish army intended to make a stand. The Germans looked at the forthcoming battle of Warsaw as a mopping-up operation. The Luftwaffe had destroyed most of the Polish air force on the ground and, with air supremacy assured, would concentrate on hitting enemy troop movements and supply lines, creating openings for the onrushing Panzer and infantry divisions. With armor massed for maximum fire-power, the Germans used their dive-bombers as mobile artillery, constantly shepherding the attack along the lines of least resistance, exploiting enemy weakness, and allowing the confused Poles no time to recover.

On 10 September, Marshal Edward Smigly-Rydz ordered the Polish army to retreat, but the Germans had already closed the trap west of the Vistula. Very few Polish army units managed to escape to participate in the battle of Warsaw. The attack on the city was primarily a display of German air power—the largest show of its kind to date. Luftwaffe chief Hermann Göring had grandstands built outside the city and invited dignitaries to watch Warsaw being pounded to rubble. The pyrotechnics were superb, especially during the final sortie, on 25 September, when the bombers hit the city with one million pounds of high explosives and nearly 150,000 pounds of incendiaries; airmen shoveled them out of the Junker 52s side hatches. Smoke from the stricken city was so thick that the planes had to suspend operations. The artillery took over. Two days later, Warsaw surrendered.

Göring ordered one more sortie to record the victory on film. The result was Hans Bertram's documentary *Feuertaufe (Baptism of Fire)*. The movie shows close-ups of young Stuka pilots, smiling as they turn Warsaw into a city of "ruined and burned-out houses, starving and grieving people . . . a dead city."[2] Hitler, determined to deprive the Poles of their political and cultural center, did not intend for anything to be rebuilt.

Throughout the entire Polish campaign, the Germans received cooperation from the Soviet Union. As soon as the invasion began, Luftwaffe Chief of Staff Hans Jeschonnek requested that the broadcasting station at Minsk provide radio directional guidance for the German pilots by sending out "a special call sign

THE MARCH OF THE AXIS
1939–1940

- Axis powers
- Under Axis control
- Allied powers
- Soviet annexations
- Neutral powers
- Vichy France

Map 11

between its programs, and introduce the name 'Minsk' in its transmissions."[3] The Soviet government omitted the code sign "to avoid attracting attention" but agreed to introduce "as often as possible" the word "Minsk." The Soviets also extended the station's normal broadcasting time by two hours. The Germans were so confident they would triumph in a few short weeks that they became concerned that they might become involved in military action against the Polish forces in the Soviet sphere of influence (the territories assigned to the Soviets under the Nazi-Soviet Pact of August 1939) unless the Soviets quickly took action.[4]

Stalin had not intended to act so soon. He wanted to wait to avoid being branded an aggressor. The speed of the Blitzkrieg, however, made him fear that if he delayed too long, the war would be over and Germany might conclude an armistice to his disadvantage. Therefore, on 17 September, the Soviets moved their armies into eastern Poland. They argued that the "Polish state had disintegrated and no longer existed. [Therefore] all agreements concluded with Poland were void." They also claimed they had "to intervene to protect [their] Ukrainian and White Russian brothers." The Soviets previously had not expressed much interest in Poland's minorities, but now their welfare seemed as good a justification as any.[5] The Soviet attack caught the already demoralized Polish army completely off guard, and it offered little resistance. The war was over by the end of the month.

Soviet Expansion in the Baltic. With the conquest of eastern Poland, Stalin became concerned about the status of Lithuania, which the 1939 agreement had placed in the German sphere of influence. Stalin wanted to strengthen Russian security in the Baltic region, and he now proposed that the Germans waive their claims to Lithuania in exchange for more Polish territory, specifically "all the Province of Lubin and that portion of the Province of Warsaw which extended to the Bug [river]."[6] Hitler agreed.

On 27 September, Joachim Ribbentrop came to Moscow to finalize the deal. The Nazi foreign minister was impressed by Soviet cordiality. He said later that he had felt "as if I were among old party comrades of ours, *Mein Führer!*"[7] Stalin was in such a charitable mood that he took a map and circled an area along the border of the Russian zone, "which he presented to Ribbentrop as a vast hunting preserve." Göring was miffed. He insisted that Stalin's largesse was not a gift to Ribbentrop personally but "a grant to the German Reich and consequently to himself as Reichs-Master of the Hunt."[8]

On 28 September, the same day on which Stalin and Ribbentrop signed the secret protocol, the Soviets concluded a mutual assistance pact with Estonia. A week later, they signed one with Latvia, and five days after that, one with Lithuania. All three treaties gave the Soviets the right to garrison armed forces in these countries along the Baltic. The Soviets wanted Finland to conclude a similar arrangement, but the Finns refused. Stalin then insisted that they make specific cessions of territory: the islands commanding the approaches to Leningrad, the Hangö naval base at the mouth of the Gulf of Finland, much of the Karelian isthmus surrounding Lake Ladoga, and part of Lapland in the Arctic. When the Finns rejected practically all these demands, the Soviets staged a series of border incidents and, on 30 November, attacked Finland, invading in five main thrusts along the entire length of their common frontier.

The League of Nations promptly branded the Soviet Union the aggressor and took away its membership rights. The British and French talked of intervention, but provided little real assistance. Finland put up an impressive defense, but this nation with a population of less than four million, could hardly hold off a power with over fifty times as many people. The Soviet attackers quickly cut through the Finnish fortifications on the Karelian isthmus, forcing the Finns to sue for peace. By this time, however, the Soviet price had gone up. Stalin now wanted the *entire* Karelian isthmus with all of Lake Ladoga and every important island in the Gulf of Finland—in all, over 25,000 miles of territory containing 11 percent of Finland's industrial and agricultural resources.

The conditions, according to General Karl Gustav von Mannerheim, commander-in-chief of the Finnish army, were a crushing blow to Finland's strategic situation: "The new frontier left the country open to attack [and] . . . deprived us of security and freedom of action in foreign affairs."[9] In fact, the Finns were lucky. Stalin had originally wanted to install a puppet Communist government in Helsinki, and only when faced with the prospect of more stubborn Finnish resistance did he decide it would be more trouble than it was worth. The Treaty of Moscow, signed on 12 March 1940, gave the Soviets sufficient strategic advantages without upsetting the status quo between the Soviet Union and Nazi Germany. Hitler had been remarkably cooperative and indulgent, even at a risk to his relations with Mussolini who was pushing for a more active anti-Communist foreign policy. Finland remained the only entity Russia lost during World War I that Stalin did not ultimately recover.

Stalin now turned his attention in other directions. In June 1940, he demanded that Romania hand back the old province of Bessarabia (plus for good measure, northern Bukovina, which had once been part of the Austrian Empire). The following month, he formally reincorporated Latvia, Lithuania, and Estonia into the Soviet Union.

The Phony War

Maginot Mentality. While the Germans and Russians were partitioning northeastern Europe, the French sat in their Maginot Line fortifications, waiting for the Germans to make the next move. The Germans were glad the French had not been more aggressive. They had stationed second-class troops, which were incapable of withstanding heavy-caliber shelling, in their western fortifications along the Siegfried Line.[10] The eighty-five fully armed French divisions were superior to the German forces they faced across the frontier, but the French were not inclined to spill their blood to help rescue the Poles. The war itself was not very popular. The government had declared war by decree without even taking a vote in the National Assembly. The deputies might not have supported a declaration of war against Germany.[11]

According to the military convention signed with Poland in May 1939, France had promised to attack Germany in force fifteen days after mobilization. However, the head of the French army, General Maurice Gamelin, agreed only to send nine divisions into the Saar. They crossed the frontier on 8 September, advanced a few miles, spent several weeks skirmishing, and then withdrew. The general staff had thought better of it and decided to wait for the British Expeditionary Force, thus "saving French blood." Their attitude, wrote General André Beaufre, "was based upon a conscious lack of enthusiasm which found its beginnings in the slaughter of 1914–18. It was deep-seated in the minds of the veterans of the Great War who were now in command."[12] Such inactivity proved deleterious for troop morale. Boredom increased and so did alcoholism.

The government in Paris had its own frustrations. Leaders of the main political parties refused to abandon their personal hatreds and failed to construct a coalition of national union, as had been done in 1914. In March 1940, a vote of no confidence overturned the government of Edouard Daladier. At issue was his failure to take a firmer stand against the Soviet invasion of Finland, not the mishandling of the war against Germany. Paul Reynaud, who replaced Daladier on 21 March,

THE SECOND WORLD WAR

was confirmed in office by a margin of only one vote! The new premier was more dynamic than his predecessor, but he was a political maverick, who was handicapped by the lack of a solid party following. He therefore had to include Daladier in his cabinet because Daladier's Radical Socialist party was the largest in the assembly. Daladier took the important post of minister of national defense and war, and the two men settled down to bicker and snip at each other to the detriment of effective leadership. For all his drive and energy, Reynaud departed very little from the policy of his predecessor. He also failed to create a government of national union.

British Restraint. During the 1930s, the British had neglected their army, which was in no condition to fight any major battles. Small wonder that the British believed their "contribution to the defense of the West should consist mainly of the naval and air forces."[13] By October 1939, they had sent four divisions to the continent (with another half dozen due six months later), but these were not sufficient to blunt a serious German assault. When Prime Minister Neville Chamberlain came to France in December, he asked General Bernard Montgomery rhetorically, "I don't think the Germans have any intention of attacking us. Do you?"[14]

The Royal Navy was in better shape. It enjoyed a tremendous numerical superiority over the enemy fleet[15] and, without firing a shot, immediately cut Germany off from all overseas communications. The Germans, not daring to risk a sea battle, found a surrogate in raiding commercial shipping. Their pocket battleships *Admiral Graf Spee* and *Deutschland* were already loose in the Atlantic. The *Deutschland* returned home in November after a disappointing cruise, but the *Graf Spee* continued operating in the south Atlantic, sinking over 50,000 tons of shipping before a hunting party of British cruisers cornered it west of the mouth of the Rio de la Plata. The British succeeded in damaging the battleship, forcing it to seek repairs in Montevideo harbor 300 miles away. After three days, Uruguay ordered the *Graf Spee* to leave. The ship headed out into Rio de la Plata estuary, where, on 17 December, its crew scuttled it. The British hailed the event as a great victory. The crews of the pursuing ships were brought to London and given a hero's welcome, but the celebration hardly compensated for the lackluster leadership of the Chamberlain cabinet.

Those who had run the country's affairs for the past decade remained in office. The opposition parties did not have enough confidence in the present cabinet to join it in a national coalition. The Liberals and Labour agreed only to suspend general elections for the duration of the war. They also declared an electoral truce; that is, they would not enter a candidate in a by-election if a member of another party held the seat.

Meanwhile, the government slowly implemented prewar emergency plans. It established special ministries for shipping, information, economic warfare (blockade operations), and food. Under a program of civilian defense adopted in 1935, the British began constructing air-raid warning systems and bomb shelters. During the invasion of Poland, the country was divided into several evacuation zones for the transfer of people. A million and a half people voluntarily left London, most of them juveniles who were moved out of the city by school classes. The government also ordered the distribution of gas masks, imposed blackouts in the large cities, closed movie theaters, and began to ration various foodstuffs. The controls were applied with the utmost confusion. The Treasury doled out money so stingily that the new wartime departments could not recruit the staff necessary to carry out their functions. Anyway all this effort seemed wasted when the German attack did not come as expected.

The young Conservative members of Parliament feared Chamberlain would never mobilize the country for action. Indeed, the prime minister was convinced that the best attitude toward the war was one of restraint. He favored the imposition of a blockade against Germany. Recalling that economic warfare had caused shortages of food and strategic materials and hastened the collapse of Imperial Germany,[16] he had great expectations that sanctions would be successful and wanted to give them time to work. Chamberlain hoped the war would end with the collapse of the German home front, and he did not want to do anything to alienate the German people. He quipped that Hitler had missed the bus.

British reluctance to begin military operations was also due to a fear of repeating the bloodletting of World War I. Accordingly, Britain felt its way slowly. It tried to surround Germany with as many neutrals as possible. It also continued to appease Mussolini. Only after 1 March 1940, did the British treat German coal shipments to Italy as contraband. Bomber Command planned no raids on German industrial targets. Instead, the Royal Air Force flew some "truth" missions in which planes dumped millions of propaganda leaflets on Germany to convince the people that they could not win the war. When Leopold Amery, a strong Tory critic of appeasement, suggested that incendiary bombs be dropped on German forests, Sir Kingsley Wood, the air minister, was shocked at the idea of destroying private property.

The reluctance to begin operations against Germany did not dampen the British desire to aid Finland against the Soviet Union, however. The Chamberlain government permitted a recruiting office to open in London to sign up volunteers; and it provided several scores of aircraft as direct aid.

The Norway Debate. In March 1940, the British Supreme War Council proposed to interrupt Swedish iron ore shipments to Germany by mining Norwegian coastal waters. It also wanted to land British troops at Narvik, the Norwegian port that handled one-third of all Swedish ore shipments. The Germans were apprised of British intentions, and no sooner had the mine-laying operation begun than the Germans, on 9 April 1940, seized the Norwegian capital of Oslo in a lightning coup and began occupying the North Sea ports. At the same time, they invaded Denmark. Göring insisted on "the use of the Danish airfields in Jutland" to shorten "the flight from Germany to Norway."[17]

The British tried to forestall German control over Norway by landing troops at strategic points along Norway's central and northern coast. The attempt failed miserably. Members of Parliament demanded an explanation.

The Commons debated the question on 8 May.[18] The result was one of the most dramatic and important divisions of the house in modern parliamentary history. Lack of confidence in Chamberlain's handling of the war had risen significantly, and the debate, which began on normal party lines as a discussion of the failure of the Norway venture, soon developed into a general indictment of the Chamberlain ministry. The prime minister was confident the two hundred members who usually supported his actions would be sufficient to block any challenge to his leadership. He had already banished any Tory who showed the least amount of independence to the back benches. Leopold Amery helped spearhead the attack, denouncing the government for its lack of vision and absence of daring. To great effect, he quoted Oliver Cromwell's famous prorogation of the Long Parliament:

"You have sat here too long for any good you have been doing. Depart, I say, and let us have done with you. In the name of God go."

The next day, Chamberlain appealed to party discipline rather than logic by calling on his "friends in the House" to give him support. Lloyd George, in one of the last great speeches of his parliamentary career, replied that it was not a question of friendship but of competent leadership, and he called on the prime minister to contribute to the war effort by surrendering the seals of his office. Chamberlain survived a vote of confidence by 281 votes to 200, but his majority had dwindled disastrously. Thirty-three Conservatives, mostly the younger back-benchers who were nearly all in uniform, had joined the opposition, and another sixty-five had abstained. From the opposition benches, the chant now arose: "Go! Go! Go!"[19] Chamberlain hoped to remain in office by creating a coalition government, but the Labour party viewed him as the archenemy and refused to join. Chamberlain therefore submitted his resignation to the king and advised that he send for Winston Churchill.[20]

Ironically, the disastrous Narvik expedition—and, in fact, the whole scheme to violate Norwegian neutrality—had been Churchill's pet project. During the Norway debate, he had assumed complete responsibility for everything he had done as first lord of the admiralty. Lloyd George came to his rescue. He replied that Churchill should not let himself be used as an "air raid shelter to keep the splinters from hitting his colleagues."

On 10 May, the day Germany invaded Belgium and Holland, Churchill went to Buckingham Palace. King George VI joked that he did not suppose Churchill knew why he was summoned and then asked him to form a government. After the war, when Churchill was no longer in power, he wrote bitterly:

> Thus, then, on the night of the tenth of May, at the outset of this mighty battle, I acquired the chief power in the State, which henceforth I wielded in ever-growing measure for five years and three months of world war, at the end of which time, all our enemies having surrendered unconditionally or being about to do so, I was immediately dismissed by the British electorate from all further conduct of their affairs.[21]

Profile: Winston Spencer Churchill (1874–1965)

Churchill hastily assembled his cabinet. He met with the leaders of the three parties, obtained their promises of support, and filled the most important posts in his government. He went to bed at 3:00 A.M. with the feeling that he was "walking with Destiny, and that all [his] past life had been but as preparation for this hour and for this trial."[22] Considering his political experience and his illustrious family connections, such sentiments did not appear unreasonable.

Winston Spencer Churchill's father was Lord Randolph Churchill, the third son of the seventh duke of Marlborough. In 1886, Lord Randolph had served as chancellor of the exchequer in the second ministry of Lord Salisbury. Winston's mother, Jennie Jerome, was the daughter of an American millionaire, Leonard Jerome, who had been a founder of the New York Academy of Music. In later years, Churchill would make much of his American ancestry. In a speech to the U.S. Congress in 1941, he remarked that if his father had been an American and his mother British instead of vice versa, he "might have got here on my own."[23] However, for an Englishman, having a grandfather who was a duke and the proprietor of Blenheim Palace, one of the country's most famous stately homes, was

quite adequate. Churchill was born at Blenheim on 30 November 1874, when his party-loving mother went into premature labor during a ball. Jennie Jerome found socializing more to her taste than raising children. Consequently, Nanny Everest played a larger role in shaping Winston's unusual character than his aloof parents. Winston regarded her as his "dearest and most intimate friend."[24]

With his strong sense of romance and destiny, Churchill developed a burning ambition to rival—even exceed—the glory of the founder of his line, John Churchill, whose victories against France at the beginning of the eighteenth century made his reputation and fortune. His first try at politics came in 1896 when he ran as a Conservative candidate in a by-election in the manufacturing district of Oldham. He lost. Another try five years later was a triumph. By then, Churchill had become a national celebrity thanks to a daring escape he made from a South African detention camp when he was covering the Boer War as a civilian correspondent.

He took his seat in 1901, the year Queen Victoria died. From the start he was a political maverick. He found the Conservative party imperious and complacent and seemingly little inclined to do anything about the growing poverty of the masses and the sad state of the British navy. He toured the country calling for a significant increase in funding. As a result of his efforts, money was taken from the army and earmarked for the improvement of ships. Churchill also found himself at odds with Conservative leadership over its abandonment of free trade in favor of protectionism. He failed to make many converts.

Feeling that he was being blocked for promotion, in May 1904, he quit the Conservative party and joined the Liberals, finding a seat in a by-election. Churchill's upper-crust associates considered him a class traitor, but the timing of his defection was fortuitous. Lloyd George, the most dynamic force in the Liberal ranks, immediately took him under his wing. With the Liberal victory in the election of 1906, Churchill obtained his first government post as under secretary of state for colonies. Two years later, he became a full member of the cabinet as president of the Board of Trade. He was only thirty-four.

From 1908 until his retirement in 1964, Churchill was never out of the Commons save for two years, 1922–1924. Under the Liberals, his rise was steady.[25] Along the way, he acquired many enemies, people who resented his brashness, did not appreciate his frankness, or were humiliated by his sharp tongue. "There, but for the grace of God, goes God," he once said of a political opponent. And of another: "He's the sort of person who gives pederasty a bad name." In attacking opponents, he seldom pulled his punches. He remained a Liberal for twenty years, lambasting the Tories with great vigor. With the disintegration of the Liberal party after World War I, he made his peace with the Conservatives and rejoined the party. He now began attacking Labour. After the Conservative victory in 1924, he became chancellor of the exchequer. Changing party allegiances did not make him any more charitable toward his new associates. He continued to take on anyone he thought stood in his way.

Churchill always identified with the interests of the particular ministry he happened to be serving. When he was first lord of the admiralty before World War I, he fought for an increase in naval budgets. As chancellor of the exchequer, he fought to have the naval budget slashed. John Davidson, the head of the Admiralty at the time and the object of Churchill's attacks, wrote that "Churchill was hell-bent on economy at the expense of the fighting services." In a very real sense, he was "the architect of the delays in rearmament against which he chafed in the 1930s."[26] Over the course of his long career, Churchill seems to have been at odds with practically everybody at one time or another.

When he left the Exchequer in 1929, he would not have another post for the next ten years. He feared that his career had fizzled and that, like his father, he would go down in history as someone who had failed to fulfill his early promise. However, his decade in the political wilderness gave him the opportunity to become identified again with the great cause of British security. He constantly attacked the leadership of his own party for letting the country's defense falter. His ability to go to the heart of a matter proved a great asset during a time of crisis, and when war broke out again, his reentry into the government was, appropriately, as first lord of the admiralty.

He was the only logical choice to replace Chamberlain as prime minister. Few of his colleagues doubted that he was the most able and experienced politician on the scene and the man most likely to lead them to victory. Supreme command gave him supreme self-confidence. Few leaders had so little self-doubt. His only acknowledged peer was Lloyd George for whom he had immense respect.[27] Churchill admired Lloyd George's inexhaustible mental agility, his ability to regard each day as a new beginning, and his "peculiar power of drawing from misfortune itself the means of future success."[28] Clearly, Churchill applied these same qualities to himself.

The Fall of France

The Manstein Plan. On 9 October 1940, shortly after the conquest of Poland, Hitler ordered the Wehrmacht to formulate plans "for an attacking operation on the northern wing of the Western Front through the areas of Luxembourg, Belgium and Holland."[29] Several days before the offensive was scheduled to begin on 12 November, Hitler called the operation off. He blamed bad weather. A new date was set, but it too was canceled. In all there were to be fourteen postponements. The usual excuse was the weather, but there were more substantial reasons, like the invasion of Norway, which proved to be an unfortunate distraction. The western offensive, as originally conceived, was to be a straight drive through Belgium to the English Channel. It would secure a territorial base in Holland, Belgium, and northern France "for conducting a promising air and sea war against England and as a protective zone for the vital Ruhr area."[30] As with the Schlieffen Plan, the German army's main strength would be concentrated in its right wing, with the center and left wing relegated to essentially defensive roles.

General Erich von Manstein, chief of staff of Army Group Center, found the plan too obvious. He proposed shifting the attack's main weight from the right to the center, "launching a *surprise attack through the Ardennes*—where the enemy would certainly not be expecting any armour because of the terrain—towards the lower Somme in order to cut off the enemy forces thrown into Belgium forward of that river . . . destroying the enemy's entire northern wing in Belgium preparatory to winning a final victory in France."[31] Hitler was receptive. The new scheme was bolder than the original plan, and he believed that an offensive that failed to achieve conclusive political results was inadequate. On 20 February, he ordered the Army Supreme Command to give the Manstein Plan operational detail.[32] The Luftwaffe had the task of ensuring that the offensive would maintain its momentum. Its first job was to neutralize the Dutch.

Just before dawn on 10 May, Junker 52s carrying 5,000 paratroopers headed toward south Holland. The airborne troops made descents all along the Rhine-

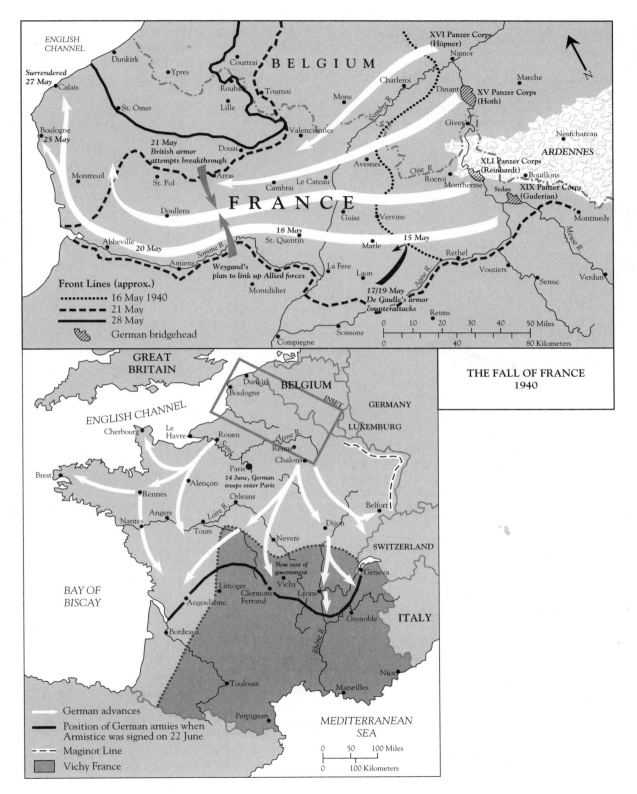

ENGLISH CHANNEL

Dunkirk
Ypres
Courtrai
B E L G I U M

XVI Panzer Corps
(Höpner)
Namor
Marche

*Surrendered
27 May* Calais

St. Omer
Roubaix
Tournai
Lille
Mons
Charleroi
Dinant
XV Panzer Corps
(Hoth)

Boulogne
25 May
Valenciennes
Givet
Neufchateau

*21 May
British armor
attempts breakthrough*
Douai
ARDENNES

Montreuil
Avesnes
Oise R.
XLI Panzer Corps
(Reinhardt)
Bouillons

St. Pol
Arras
F R A N C E
Rocroi
Montherme
Sedan
XIX Panzer Corps
(Guderian)

Doullens
Cambrai
Le Cateau
Guise
Vervins
Montmedy

Abbeville
20 May
Amiens
Somme R.
St. Quentin
18 May
Marle
15 May
Rethel
Vouziers
Senuc
Verdun

*Weygand's
plan to link up Allied forces*
La Fere
Laon
Aisne R.
Meuse R.

Front Lines (approx.)
Montdidier
*17/19 May
De Gaulle's armor
counterattacks*
Reims

· · · · · · 16 May 1940
- - - - - - 21 May
———— 28 May

Compiegne
Soissons

0 10 20 30 40 50 Miles
0   40   80 Kilometers

German bridgehead

**THE FALL OF FRANCE
1940**

GREAT
BRITAIN

Dunkirk
Boulogne
B E L G I U M
INSET
GERMANY

ENGLISH CHANNEL
LUXEMBURG

Cherbourg
Le Havre
Rouen
Seine
Aisne R.
Reims
Chalons

Brest
Paris
*14 June, German
troops enter Paris*

Rennes
Alençon
Orleans
Belfort

Nantes
Angers
Loire R.
Tours
Nevers
Dijon
SWITZERLAND

BAY OF
BISCAY
Limoges
*New seat of
government*
Vichy
Lyons
Geneva

Angoulième
Clermont
Ferrand
Grenoble
ITALY

Bordeaux
Rhône R.

Toulouse
Nice

Marseilles

→ German advances

——— Position of German armies when
Armistice was signed on 22 June

- · - · - Maginot Line

Vichy France

Perpignan
MEDITERRANEAN
SEA

0   50   100 Miles
0   100 Kilometers

Map 12

Meuse estuary, capturing intact the important bridges at Moerdijk, Dordrecht, and Rotterdam. The Dutch managed to defend the Hague against a landing, which was intended to capture the government, but the sensational German bombing of Rotterdam destroyed the Dutch will to resist. After only five days of war, the Dutch surrendered.

Belgium's fate was also decided in the early hours of the offensive. At the same time the Germans were making paratroop landings in Holland, they dispatched a glider-borne force of assault troops to seize the bridges of the Albert Canal (a waterway that connected the Meuse with the Scheldt) and dropped a small contingent of parachute-engineers on Eben Emael, an important fort that commanded the Meuse valley south of Maastricht. Securing their objectives, the Germans advanced their army to the Flemish plain.

The opening phase of the German offensive convinced the British and French that they were experiencing a reenactment of the Schlieffen Plan. The Allies intended to advance into Belgium as soon as hostilities began. The bulk of the French mobile forces would take up positions along the Dyle River, south of Antwerp, and along the Meuse River, from Namur to the French frontier. The confrontation would be a set piece. The French did not think a thrust through the hilly, heavily wooded Ardennes was probable. The area had only two secondary roads, which were hardly sufficient to support the movement of modern armor. Even if the Germans could reach the Meuse River, they could not cross it without heavy artillery, which would take five or six days to bring into action. This would be more than enough time for the French to reinforce the lightly equipped reserve units stationed in the area.

However, the Germans reached the north bank of the Meuse in two and a half days and smoothly captured the historic fortress of Sedan. The next day, on 13 May, the Germans were across the river, thanks to maximum support from the Luftwaffe—some 1,000 aircraft, including an entire corps of JU-87 Stukas, were used in place of the heavy artillery upon which the French had based their calculations. The Germans had outflanked the Maginot Line, and little now stood between their Panzers and the English Channel.

The attack moved easily across the World War I battlefields along the Aisne, Oise, and Somme. On 20 May, two German Panzer divisions seized Amiens and Abbeville on the lower Somme, cutting the Allied armies in two. "What proved fatal to the French," wrote Basil Liddell Hart, "was not, as is commonly imagined, their defensive attitude or Maginot Line complex, but the more offensive side of their plan. By pushing into Belgium with their left shoulder forward they played into the hands of their enemy, and wedged themselves in a trap—just as had happened with their near-fatal Plan XVII of 1914."[33] On 21 May, General Heinz Guderian turned the attack northward and, two days later, was besieging Calais on the Dover Straits. On the afternoon of 24 May, Hitler ordered his tanks to halt along the Aire–St. Omer Canal, some twenty miles shy of Dunkirk. The reduction of the Allied armies would be left to the Luftwaffe. It was a big mistake. Almost three weeks of ceaseless operations had exhausted the German pilots, and further hampered by inclement weather, they failed in their mission. On 26 May, Hitler ordered his Panzers to resume the advance.

In the meantime, the British had been able to strengthen the defensive perimeter around Dunkirk, and under a low cloud cover, they began to ferry their beleaguered troops across the English Channel. They loaded them on almost anything that could float, from small sailboats to cruisers. Dunkirk fell on 4 June. By then, 338,226 Allied soldiers (over two-thirds of them British, the rest mostly

French) had managed to escape. It was a remarkable achievement, but an evacuation, no matter how superb, was hardly victory. The French and British alliance was crumbling. The British had difficulty hiding their disgust for French weakness and incompetence. The French accused the British of caring about nothing but saving their own skins. Certainly, from the French perspective, the British had behaved selfishly. Nevertheless, the deliverance at Dunkirk deprived Hitler of an opportunity for annihilation. The British had fought and run away, but they lived to fight another day.[34] The French were not so lucky. They had to face the full force of the Third Reich war machine alone and could only try to make the best deal they could with their conquerors.

The Death of the Third Republic. As many as 800,000 French fled before the Germans. The late spring was warm, and the grain in the fields was beginning to ripen. Civilians poured onto the highways from the cities and villages, heading south. These refugees, many of them unused to travel, walked, bicycled, and hitched rides in tumbrels, trucks, or cars; they took along as many of their household possessions and family treasures as they could carry. The government had already fled, first to the Loire and then to Bordeaux, just as it had done in 1870 and 1914. Sensitive documents that could not be taken along were destroyed. Foreign office archives were dumped into the courtyard of the Quai d'Orsay and set on fire. Paris, declared an open city, fell to the Germans on 14 June without a struggle. Few believed the German advance could be stopped.

Paul Reynaud wanted to continue the fight from overseas, specifically from Algeria, but not many politicians and soldiers shared his determination. Even his mistress, the comtesse de Portes, was among the defeatists. Former premier Pierre Laval, embittered by his exclusion from power since 1936, was actively working to make the eighty-four-year-old Philippe Pétain, the current vice-president of the Council of Ministers, the leader of a new government, which he, Laval, would control. Pétain felt the best course of action lay in seeking an accommodation with Germany. Although French society had been weakened by the bitter clashes between the Right and the Left during the 1930s, the 1940 defeat was still primarily a military defeat. Many French, no matter what their politics, saw no reason to go on fighting once the outcome was inevitable.

Winston Churchill tried to strengthen Reynaud and keep France in the war by proposing the creation of a Franco-British union with joint ministries of defense, foreign affairs, and economic policies. The French and British parliaments would be merged, and, for the duration of hostilities, there would be "a single War Cabinet, and all the forces of Britain and France, whether on land, sea, or in the air, will be placed under its direction."[35] In France, however, the pressure for a peace with Germany was too strong to be checked. Reynaud resigned and was succeeded by Pétain, who immediately began negotiations for an armistice with Hitler.

Hitler was prepared to recognize the territorial integrity of France and to allow the French the fiction of an independent government. He wanted to forestall any French effort to continue the war from overseas. Germany, he decided, must occupy France's most valuable strategic areas—about 60 percent of the country, including the Channel and Atlantic coasts in their entirety and the prosperous industrial north and east, which included the Loire and Paris basins, the Flemish and Champagne lowlands, and Alsace. (The territory he sought was roughly the same as had been envisaged in Bethmann Hollweg's September Program in 1914.) France was to pay the maintenance costs of the German occupation. The French

The victorious German army marches through Paris in June 1940. Unlike the Imperial triumphal procession that followed the Franco-Prussian War in 1871, Hitler's soldiers skirted the Arc de Triomphe rather than passing under it. Ironically, the statuary group against the monument celebrates one of Napoleon's victories.

armed forces were to be demobilized, and its war fleet neutralized and placed under German supervision. French citizens were forbidden to fight against Germany "in the service of states with which Germany is still at war."[36] Those who disobeyed would be regarded as snipers and, if caught, executed. All German political refugees living in France or in its possessions were to be surrendered to the Nazi authorities on demand.

Hitler wanted to conclude the armistice as soon as possible so he could devote his full attention to the fight against Britain. He insisted that the French capitulation take place in the same railway carriage used for the German surrender twenty-two years before. Even the table and chairs were the same. Hitler chose for himself the exact chair once occupied by Generalissimo Foch. The armistice was signed on 22 June.

Five days later, Hitler toured Paris in the company of his architect, Albert Speer. The Führer especially wanted to visit the Opera House whose neobaroque eclecticism he particularly admired. He also saw the Eiffel Tower, the Arch of Triumph, the Panthéon, the tomb of Napoleon, and the Church of the Sacre Coeur. "It was the dream of my life to be permitted to see Paris," he said. "I cannot say how happy I am to have that dream fulfilled today." At one time he had considered having the French capital destroyed, but now, having defeated one of the world's strongest nations in less time than Bismarck took to humble the Austrian Empire three-quarters of a century before, he decided otherwise. "When we are finished in Berlin, Paris will only be a shadow. So why should we destroy it?"[37]

The Battle of Britain

Operation Sea Lion. Mussolini, who had entered the war against France on 10 June, now begged Hitler to let Italian ground and air forces participate in the conquest of Great Britain. Hitler refused and changed the subject with a complaint:

I have made to Britain so many offers of agreement, even of cooperation, and have been treated so shabbily that I am even now convinced that any new appeal to reason would meet with a similar rejection. For in that country at present it is not reason that rules, but probably the smallest portion of wisdom in history. I believe, however, that for this reason we must all the more put our struggle on the broadest possible basis and neglect nothing in any way likely to hurt this powerful adversary and help our cause.[38]

Hitler urged Mussolini to attack Egypt and the Suez Canal.

Hitler's plan to invade Britain—Operation Sea Lion—issued on 16 July 1940, envisaged a surprise amphibious assault on a broad front along the southeastern English coast from Ramsgate past the Isle of Wight. The success of such an operation depended on certain conditions: the sealing off of the Straits of Dover on both flanks and the defeat of the Royal Air Force (RAF) so "that it can no longer display any appreciable aggressive force."[39] Göring thought he could destroy the RAF in four weeks, and he ordered the Luftwaffe to concentrate its attacks against the British planes, ground organization, supply installations, and aircraft factories. On paper, the Germans possessed the most powerful air force in history. Göring was prepared to commit over 2,000 of its planes to the operation, including 929 fighters, two-thirds of which were the first-rate Messerschmitt 109s.[40] The British faced this armada with a frontline strength of 820 fighters, most of them modern Spitfires and Hurricanes.

The Luftwaffe, which had been developed primarily as a tactical strike force, had difficulty adjusting to its new assignment. The Messerschmitt 109 had an operational radius of 125 miles, giving it a combat effectiveness of less than half an hour. Its role was to clear the air of enemy fighters[41] and escort the twin-engine bombers and Stukas. The British grouped their Spitfire and Hurricane squadrons in the London area, the periphery of the Messerschmitt's range, thereby presenting the enemy with "a similar predicament to a dog on a chain who wants to attack the foe but cannot harm him, because of the limitation of the chain."[42] The defenders had another advantage. The fighting took place over British territory, and German pilots were almost always captured when they were forced to bail out, while a downed British flyer might quickly regain his base and participate in another sortie on the same day.

The Blitz. The Battle of Britain developed in stages: the first was essentially a clash between the Spitfires and Messerschmitts.[43] On 13 August, the day Göring designated *Adlertag* (Eagle Day), the German bombers came over in strength. In two days, the Germans flew 3,271 sorties, mostly against British airfields. Göring tried to maximize morale by having loudspeakers all over Germany and the occupied territories play incessantly "Bombing of England," a song written especially for the occasion. Overoptimism led to many miscalculations. Luftwaffe headquarters, for example, accepted uncritically the reports of its bomber pilots that air bases were out of action, when the bases were, in fact, only slightly damaged. And "one day according to the calculations in Berlin there were no more British fighters."[44] German intelligence on RAF replacement strength was also inaccurate. The Germans estimated that the British aircraft factories produced only 180 to 300 planes in August and September, when they actually turned out between 460 and 500. Such errors cost dearly, but the Germans seemed better able to sustain heavy losses than their adversaries. While British factories could usually make good the destroyed fighters, replacing experienced pilots was not so easy. Between 23 August

A Spitfire attacks a Dornier 17. The Spitfire has just made a rear pass at the slower-moving German bomber and is maneuvering for another strike. Dorniers without appropriate fighter protection were usually sitting ducks for the heavier-armed, more agile British interceptors.

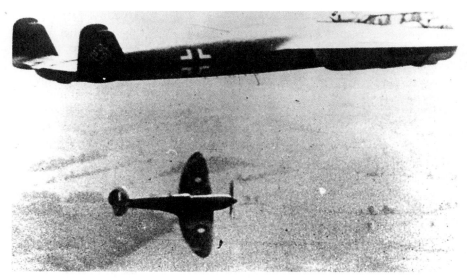

and 6 September, the British lost 103 airmen killed and another 128 seriously wounded, a quarter of their total strength. At this rate, Fighter Command would soon have had few combat flyers left. In addition, the sector air defense system, which directed the intercepts, was so badly damaged that Britain was close to losing control over it.

Just as Göring seemed close to achieving his objective, however, he turned the brunt of his attack against British cities. The reasons for this "foolish mistake"[45] are still debated. Apparently, Göring was convinced that the battle had been won. He was satisfied with the amount of destruction done to Britain's ground installations. (He had failed to appreciate the importance of the radar stations and allowed them to continue to function practically without interruption through the whole battle.) Furthermore, Hitler had reacted with fury to a series of nighttime raids Bomber Command made on Berlin. The first of these, on 25 August 1940, was in retaliation for a German raid on London, an attack that had actually been a mistake. The Germans now began to pound London beginning on 7 September. Göring calculated that the British would defend the city with everything they had and would throw the Hurricanes and Spitfires into a battle where they could be annihilated. Nothing of the sort happened. This new phase of the battle gave Fighter Command an opportunity to regain its strength. It rose again to the attack, destroying more enemy planes than the German factories were capable of producing. On 17 September, Hitler postponed the invasion of England indefinitely.

The Battle of Britain continued, but now the Luftwaffe shifted to nighttime operations and bombing missions against selected industrial and military targets. Attacks continued against London, Plymouth, Southampton, Liverpool, Manchester, Birmingham, Cardiff, Sheffield, Bristol, and Aberdeen. On 14 November, German bombers dropped one million pounds of bombs on the manufacturing town of Coventry in a ten-hour raid. The city was left in ruins. The Blitz took a terrible toll on British property, but the Germans were unable to force the British to their knees.

Did Hitler really intend to invade Britain? Much the same question was raised 135 years earlier about the intentions of Napoleon. Neither question may ever have a definitive answer. However, neither attempt could have succeeded.

Napoleon failed to win naval supremacy; Hitler failed to win air superiority. If Napoleon and Hitler were bluffing, British resistance destroyed the credibility of that bluff. In both cases, the British deprived their adversaries of easy victories and forced them to fight a long drawn-out war on more than one front.[46]

The Ultra Secret. In the House of Commons, Churchill paid tribute to the persistent bravery of the British airmen: "Never in the field of human conflict was so much owed by so many to so few."[47] But the battle was not decided by courage alone. In the Ultra system, the British had a device that helped them determine the direction and sometimes the targets of the German planes. With their special electronic computer attached to the principal cryptograph of the German armed forces, the Enigma machine, the British could intercept and decode messages that the German High Command sent to its army, navy, and air force units. Ultra picked up the details of Operation Sea Lion as soon as Göring delivered the plan to his air force generals. The British also obtained information on the vast preparations the Germans were making to assemble an invasion force. The British discovered, for example, that the German army had little idea of what a large amphibious operation really entailed. The Germans did not have enough barges to ferry over their troops, and only a few of those they assembled were self-propelled. Suitable engines were scarce, and in some cases they used airplane engines instead. "Signals became acrimonious and the whole picture began to show how very hastily the invasion arrangements had been put together."[48]

Ultra signals revealed that Göring intended to destroy the RAF by luring aloft as many British fighters as possible. The head of Fighter Command, Hugh Dowding, refused to take the bait and decided to meet each German sortie with a small number of fighters that would sow maximum destruction in the enemy formations. He was severely criticized by many of his colleagues for these tactics. However, many of the critics, who constantly urged Dowding to attack the Luftwaffe in strength, had no knowledge of Ultra. Dowding also received a picture of the enemy's intentions as well as information on German losses and the state of enemy morale. His success in preserving the RAF prevented the Germans from gaining the air superiority necessary to launch Operation Sea Lion.

Ultra had its limitations, however. It never provided complete details about Germany's military activities. One of the great myths that came out of the Blitz was that Ultra had warned the British of the impending attack on the city of Coventry five hours before it occurred on 14 November 1941. According to the story, Churchill, fearing that any special efforts to save the city and its citizens would compromise the secret, allowed the enemy attack to take place without attempting to mitigate its effect. In fact, Ultra never picked up a specific reference to Coventry. It did find out that there would be a raid of exceptional size, code-named Moonlight Sonata, but it was not clear when this would occur. All targets were in code. British intelligence assumed that the operation would take place on 15 November and that the principal target would be London.

Clearly, Ultra had to be supplemented with other intelligence. In the Battle of Britain, radar (radio detection and ranging) proved invaluable. The system developed out of a 1934 scheme sponsored by the Defense Ministry that hoped to knock enemy planes out of the air with radio waves. Nothing came of the death-ray machine, but the project did discover that radio energy could be used to measure aircraft distances. (Similar experiments were also underway in Germany, the Netherlands, France, and the United States, but the British were furthest advanced in radar's practical application.) By 1940, Britain had established a series of high-

and low-level transmitting and receiving stations along its coasts. Controllers were therefore able to detect major German formations and direct RAF interceptions. Radar installations, which were located on conspicuous heights, initially became the targets of Luftwaffe dive-bombers, but Göring falsely assumed that the main equipment was located underground and did not persist in the attacks.

Ultra proved most valuable in the war against submarines where it not only helped determine their whereabouts, but helped locate their supply ships as well.[49] The necessity of preventing the Germans from suspecting that their secret messages had been compromised was diffused by having an aerial patrol happen to make the "discovery" prior to taking military action. As in the Battle of Britain, radar also helped in locating enemy submarines, especially when they surfaced. To detect submerged submarines, there was sonar, a radar variant. Both systems robbed the U-boats of their invisibility.

Ultra was so valuable that compromising its integrity was an offense punishable by death. Its secrecy was so well guarded that the Germans never changed their code or their basic means of transmission. The existence of Ultra was publicly revealed thirty years after the end of the war. Until the wraps were taken off, British historian Peter Calvocoressi, who had worked on Ultra at Bletchley Park during the war, was at a loss as to how he should write a true account of the war. He decided to honor his promise of secrecy and wrote with the sad knowledge that his account was distorted by the omission of the Ultra ingredient.[50]

THE NAZIS IN TRIUMPH

Widening the Conflict

The Balkan Campaign and the Desert War. With the fall of France, the balance of naval and military forces in the Mediterranean became weighted in Italy's favor. Mussolini had some 300,000 troops in the Italian colony of Libya, sandwiched between the French in Tunisia and the British in Egypt. The fear that he might use these troops to cut the Suez Canal and threaten the oil resources of the Persian Gulf prompted Churchill to send 150 tanks to the Middle East at a time when Britain itself was being threatened by invasion.

Indeed, Hitler's refusal to allow Italian troops to participate in the invasion of Britain prompted the Duce to look elsewhere for conquest. In August 1940, his forces in Ethiopia invaded and captured British Somaliland. The following month, the divisions of Marshal Rodolfo Graziani, stationed in Libya, pushed eastward into Egypt. The Italians, outnumbering the British by six to one, moved easily to Sidi Barrani, about fifty miles from their starting point. There they stopped to regroup.

Mussolini wanted to be a decisive influence in the Balkans as well as in North Africa. At the end of October, Italian troops crossed the Albanian border into Greece. However, the campaign did not go as planned. Within a week, the Greeks counterattacked, throwing the Italians back across the frontier. By the third week of November, the Greeks had cleared their territory of the invaders. Moreover, on the night of 11–12 November, a British attack at Taranto, the main Italian naval base on the instep of the peninsula's boot, had resulted in the sinking of one battleship and had put two others out of commission, thereby shaking Italy's naval superiority in the Mediterranean.

German Mark III tanks in the Libyan desert move around Tobruk. The armor of the Afrika Korps outclassed that of its British counterparts in the early days of the desert war. During the first half of 1941, Rommel's legionnaires pushed the British forces back to the frontiers of Egypt, cutting off a Dominion garrison at Tobruk.

The British were also bankrupting the fortunes of Italy in Africa. On 8 December 1940, the British, under General Sir Archibald Wavell, opened a surprise offensive and began to push the Italians back across the desert. At the same time, starting in January 1941, a 30,000-man British army moved to dislodge the Italians from East Africa. In a little over three months, the British captured the Ethiopian capital of Addis Ababa. Throughout the rest of the year, they mopped up all enemy resistance in Somaliland, Ethiopia, and Eritrea. Though stunningly successful, the operation was never more than a sideshow to the real battles being fought in the northern desert.

Within two months, Wavell's forces had captured over 114,000 Italian prisoners and opened the road to Tripoli. The Duce, who previously had vehemently opposed the inclusion of German troops in Italy's theater of operations—he had rejected Hitler's offer to send German armored units to North Africa—now welcomed Wehrmacht units to help defend Tripolitania. The Germans hastily formed the Afrika Korps. In March 1941, this unit under Lieutenant-General Erwin Rommel had its first taste of combat in an offensive probe against the British positions around El Agheila in eastern Libya. Rommel found the British army much weaker than he had anticipated. Several weeks earlier, Churchill had withdrawn troops from Wavell's command to form the nucleus of a 50,000-man force to protect Greece against the Axis. Churchill knew that Britain alone could not challenge the Axis powers on the European continent, but he hoped that by supporting Greek independence he would gain the sympathy, and perhaps the eventual participation, of the United States. The Greeks feared that the aid would not be sufficient to deter further Axis aggression; nevertheless, in February 1941, they rejected a German offer of immunity from invasion in exchange for a promise of neutrality.

After the initial Italian defeats, the Germans had drafted plans for the invasion of Greece. Now, with the British threatening their southern flank, they advanced their plan, code-named Operation Marita. The Germans had already obtained transit rights to attack Greece through Hungary, Romania, and Bulgaria. These three countries had committed themselves to Hitler's New Order by signing the Tripartite Pact previously concluded by Germany, Italy, and Japan. Hitler also wanted the cooperation of Yugoslavia. He offered the Yugoslavs a nonaggression pact with a promise of the Greek territory of Salonika. The regency government of Prince Paul hesitated, but fearing a German attack, he signed the Tripartite Pact on 25 March 1941. The regent's action was popular among the pro-German Croatians, but not with the pro-Greek Serbs. On 27 March, a coup, led by Air Force General Bora Mirovic, ousted Paul's government and installed one headed by General Dusan Simovic. Hitler reacted angrily.

Without waiting to find out if the new government was really hostile, he ordered the conquest of Yugoslavia. The action would take place in conjunction with the attack on Greece. Hitler was determined to restore order in the Balkans, although he was also in the process of planning his massive attack on the Soviet Union. The Balkan campaign began, on 6 April, with the bombing of Belgrade. The attack lasted two days and leveled the center of the Yugoslav capital. While the attack continued, German ground forces advanced into Yugoslavia from the south across the Bulgarian frontier. Yugoslav resistance lasted only twelve days.

Meanwhile, on 7 April, the German army had moved into Greece. The port of Salonika fell on 8 April; the Greek forces in the rest of the country surrendered on 21 April. The British units fought on, but by the end of the month, those that had not surrendered or been killed escaped to Crete and Egypt. The German troops reached the Aegean.

In trying to protect Greece, the British had weakened their position in North Africa. In April 1941, the Afrika Korps was able to push the main British forces out of Libya back to the Egyptian frontier. At that point, however, Rommel's offensive ran out of steam. Now it was Hitler's turn to take forces out of Africa—in this case, to support his attack on the Soviet Union. Meanwhile the Germans had some unfinished business in the Mediterranean. In May, German paratroopers landed on the island of Crete. In ten days, the island was theirs. The operation did not delay the Soviet invasion since Hitler had set the date for Operation Barbarossa on 27 March after his victory on the Greek mainland.

In North Africa, the evacuation of German troops gave the British some breathing space, but they were in no position to take advantage of the enemy weakness. British tactics, organization, and equipment was not as good as the German. The British commanders were naturally reluctant to undertake any offensives until their situation improved. Churchill, however, was not sympathetic to their caution. The North African desert was the only place that the British and Commonwealth armies could engage the Germans at this time. Furthermore, Churchill was becoming fascinated with the person of Rommel. In his mind, the desert war began to assume a larger dimension than the mere defense of Egypt and the Suez Canal and the protection of Arabian oil. It had developed into a personal duel between the prime minister and the German commander. Churchill urged General Wavell to undertake an offensive against the "Desert Fox." Wavell felt his army was unprepared, but went ahead anyway. The attack failed. Churchill sacked Wavell and replaced him with General Sir Claude Auchinleck. He then proceeded to press Auchinleck for an offensive, but the general held off until

November. His attack was initially successful, but once again priorities elsewhere determined its fate. This time, the British High Command transferred troops from Africa for service against the Japanese in Burma and Malaysia.

Hitler, unlike Churchill, always considered the war in North Africa to be of secondary importance. His mind was on the great struggle between the Germans and the Slavs for control of the vast spaces of Russia. Even during General Staff discussions over Operation Sea Lion, Hitler insisted that the quicker Germany smashed Russia, the better. Such a victory would guarantee Germany mastery of Europe and ensure the success of the Thousand-Year Reich.

The Invasion of the Soviet Union. Hitler conceived the invasion of the Soviet Union as a gigantic pincers movement—one thrust through the Ukraine toward Kiev and down the Dnieper to Odessa, another attack across the northern plains toward Moscow.[51] With 180 German divisions, the German army could master the country in five months. In a conference at the Berghof, on 31 July 1940, Hitler ordered his generals to prepare to begin operations within ten months. Hitler chose to call the invasion "Barbarossa" in honor of Frederick I of Hohenstaufen, a leader of the Third Crusade, who according to legend was waiting in a Hartz Mountain grotto for a summons to lead Germania forth to victory. The invasion plan, as presented in its twelfth draft in December 1940, was to destroy the Soviet army in western Russia "by driving forward deep armoured wedges" to prevent "the retreat of units capable of combat into the vast mass of Russian territory" and then "to establish a cover against Asiatic Russia from the general line Volga-Archangel."[52] Preparations were to be complete by 15 May 1941.

But before the Germans could launch their attack, they became involved in the affairs of Yugoslavia, which set back their timetable. How important this was is still open to debate. The delay was only a matter of a few weeks; considering the vast scale of the operation, such a short time did not appear to be critical. When the Barbarossa directive was issued, the Germans had about 25 percent of their army in the east—a sizable increase over the 3 percent that were there when the Battle of Britain had started. By June 1941, the percentage had risen to 68 percent, or 123 of the Wehrmacht's 180 total divisions. Such a massive buildup was impossible to keep secret.

Indeed, on 20 March 1941, the chief of Soviet military intelligence, General Filipp Golikov, reported the essence of the Barbarossa Plan, naming the commanders of each army group and their military objectives. Nevertheless, the German explanation that they were in east Prussia and Poland to conduct maneuvers for the British invasion out of range of RAF bombers apparently convinced Stalin. The Soviet dictator did not believe that Hitler would fight a war on two fronts.

The Nazis carefully maintained normal diplomatic and economic contacts throughout the entire preparatory period. They were especially punctual in delivering machine tools that the Soviets had ordered under the terms of a current commercial agreement. On the very eve of the invasion, the atmosphere of normality was remarkable. On 22 June 1941, just three hours before dawn, when German troops were scheduled to cross the Soviet frontier, the chief of staff of the Fourth Army, General Gunther Blumentritt, recalled watching the international Berlin-Moscow express pass through Brest-Litovsk without incident.[53]

Early Victories. The Germans attacked the Soviet Union along a broad front—from the Black Sea to northern Finland. Their three million–man army had been victorious in every major campaign since the war began in September 1940. The

Soviets were stunned. The attack sent Stalin into a profound psychological depression, which brought him to the point of collapse. Vyacheslav Molotov had to inform the Soviet people of the invasion. For the next week and a half, Stalin saw few people and signed no directives. The leadership crisis increased the confusion and facilitated the task of the Germans. When he recovered, Stalin savagely turned on his own army leaders. Countless officers were charged with treason—that is, for having been defeated—and were executed. All soldiers who surrendered, no matter what the circumstances, were branded deserters, and they and their families were held criminally liable. Thousands of relatives of other prisoners of war experienced similar fates.

A new special division of State Security, called SMERSH (*Smert Shpionam*, "Death to the Spies"), was established to ensure Red Army morale. Its agents infiltrated military units to create the proper political and fighting spirit; retreating soldiers were often shot. This counterintelligence organization also eliminated suspected opponents of the regime among prisoners of war, refugees, and inhabitants of German-occupied territories, as well as among those who had lived, or were living, outside the Soviet Union. Such stern measures had little effect on the German offensive.

The invaders, divided into Army Groups North, Center, and South, moved eastward in three great parallel thrusts. As with the invasion of France, the *Schwerpunkt* (center of gravity) was the Center Army, commanded by Fedor von Bock and led by two Panzer groups, containing almost eight hundred tanks each. The attack was launched in the direction of Moscow, but Hitler had no desire to capture cities. The German armies had instructions to smash quickly through the Soviet defenses and entrap the main enemy forces before they had a chance to retreat. By mid-July, the Center Army had punched through the Soviet defenses as far as Smolensk, opening the road to Moscow, the same route Napoleon had used in 1812. Meanwhile Army Group North, under Field Marshal Wilhelm von Leeb, attacking from east Prussia, had penetrated about 300 miles into the Baltic states and was advancing toward Leningrad; and Field Marshal Gerd von Rundstedt's Army Group South had occupied most of the Ukraine west of the Dnieper and headed toward Kiev. The mood back at Hitler's headquarters was ecstatic. Never before had a country lost so much territory in such a short time without surrendering. But even with their armies in retreat everywhere, the Soviets continued to resist. They desperately tried to buy time with space and with lives.

Russia's backwardness and its inhospitable terrain helped the Soviet defenders. "It was appallingly difficult country for tank movement," wrote General Blumentritt, "great virgin forests, widespread swamps, terrible roads, and bridges not strong enough to bear the weight of tanks. . . . The great motor highway leading from the frontier to Moscow was unfinished. . . . Such country was bad enough for the tanks, but worse still for the transport accompanying them." Nearly all the German transport consisted of wheeled vehicles whose movements were restricted to the roads. Many Soviet highways were unpaved and, after an hour or two of rain, became impassable. "It was an extraordinary sight, with groups of tanks and transport strung out over a hundred-mile stretch, all stuck—until the sun came out and the ground dried."[54]

During the first part of August, Hitler gave priority to a drive into the Ukraine where his armies successfully overran the pocket of Soviet troops massed around Kiev. Hitler was confident that he could seal his triumph before the coming winter would make further offensives impossible, and he ordered a resumption of the drive toward Moscow. At the same time, he directed the offensive in the south to continue to sweep along the Black Sea coast to the gates of the Caucasus. Army Group North also continued its advance and by September began the encirclement of Leningrad. The German siege would last for the next three years.[55]

The combined objectives of the original German attack were becoming increasingly difficult to maintain. The German army was reaching a point of exhaustion. Nevertheless, Hitler was so confident that the war was nearing its end that he allowed German factories to cut back on their production of munitions, and he began planning the settlement of Germans in the occupied territories of the Soviet Union. The colonies would be architecturally uniform, conforming to blueprints provided by the Berlin-based special administration for "new cities." Hitler also planned to use Russian granite and marble to renovate the great cities of Germany: Berlin, Nuremberg, Munich, Hanover, Weimar, Bremen, Augsburg, and Linz, the town of his boyhood.

In the meantime, Stalin had established a State Defense Committee and given the Supreme Command of the Armed Forces authority to carry out the complete mobilization of the country. The fighting front was divided into three sectors: northwestern, western, and southwestern. The Soviets decided to fight for every square meter of terrain to slow down the German advance. They took horrible losses, especially in prisoners. In the defense of Smolensk, 300,000 Soviet troops were captured; in the defense of Kiev, another 500,000; in the south at Uman and in the retreat back to Kharkov, another 200,000. The Germans either shot most of these prisoners or allowed them to starve to death. Yet, despite their staggering losses, the Soviets were able to prevent the Germans from completing their campaign objectives. Hitler now ordered that the main attack be directed against Moscow in the hope that the capture of the capital would end Soviet resistance once and for all. The attack began on 2 October 1941, but was slowed by the autumn rains that turned the roadways to quagmires bogging down the German armor. This gave the Soviets time to stiffen their resistance, so that when the early frosts came and the Germans were again on the roll, the defenders had reinforced the approaches to the capital and were able to blunt the impact of the Nazi shock troops. At the same time, the Soviets attacked in the Leningrad and Rostov areas to prevent the Germans from beefing up their offensive against Moscow with troops from Army Groups North and South.

Finally, the weather came to the aid of the Soviets. The winter of 1941 was the worst in recent memory. The German invaders had never experienced such intense cold. Temperatures fell to 48 degrees below zero, solidifying motor oil, bursting engine blocks, freezing breath and bodily extremities, and addling thoughts. The Wehrmacht troops lacked proper winter clothing and suffered twice as many casualties from the cold as from battle. The soldiers called the Russian campaign medal the *Gefrierfleisch Orden*, the frozen meat award. Logistics became chaotic. Supplies of artillery shells fell short while trainloads of red wine arrived to help morale. "The anger of a unit which received a trainload of wine instead of the shells it urgently needed can be readily imagined," wrote General Blumentritt. "Even as wine such a cargo was frequently useless . . . it had often frozen in transit, burst its bottles and all that remained were chunks of red ice."[56] On 5 December, the Soviets counterattacked north and south of Moscow, trying to surround and destroy the enemy. The German generals believed their position was too exposed and prepared to withdraw to a safer winter line, but Hitler ordered them not to retreat. The Soviet counterattack lost its momentum, but it had saved Moscow. The Soviets were able to bring in new divisions and reinforcements to stabilize the front.[57]

Hitler concluded that "his principle of rigid defense must always and in all circumstances be correct and he applied it throughout the rest of the war."[58] Although he was the commander-in-chief of the German army, Hitler personally involved himself only with operations on the Eastern Front, where Germany now had three-quarters of its effective military strength.

Hitler's Europe

The National Socialist Preserve. The Nazis had a grand design that was politically very simple: The Germans would extend their racial community and force all peoples within it to accept Nazi values. The limits of this empire were vague, but Hitler believed he could rearrange the shape of Europe to his liking. Germany would be enlarged. It would regain the territories lost after World War I: Danzig, North Schleswig, St. Vith, Eupen, Malmédy, Alsace-Lorraine, and the areas lost to Poland. Germany would also annex Luxembourg, Norway, and Denmark; and, after a concentrated program of germanization, it would acquire the Baltic states, the Voivodeship of Bialystok, the Volga German districts, Baku and its oil-producing hinterland, and the Crimea. Some old states would be destroyed, some new ones created. The people of Flanders, for example, would have a new nation as would the Celts of Brittany. Whole cities would be obliterated, including Leningrad, which Hitler intended to "raze . . . to the ground and then hand over to the Finns."[59] Entire civilizations and races would be liquidated.

The habitat of the Germans and their subject peoples would not have set borders. People would be moved around according to the dictates of power. Hitler envisioned the Greater Germanic Estate, or *Grossraum*, as a sort of huge nature preserve for the convenience of the German people; it would be a gigantic territory, possibly stretching from the Atlantic Ocean to the Ural Mountains, a distance of almost 3,000 miles, and including five times the prewar expanse of Germany.

This vast territory would have a single integrated economy in which each area would function as part of the whole to serve the needs and requirements of the master race. The Nazis as yet had no blueprint for the administration of this empire. Hitler thought there would be adequate time for that once the war was over. In the meantime, a formidable control apparatus would ensure that the conquered areas would provide the human and material supplies necessary to ensure victory. Governance, though, differed significantly from one area to another.

The Danes were allowed to retain their normal civilian government, including the king and his cabinet. Relations between Germany and Denmark were conducted through normal diplomatic channels. This quasi sovereignty lasted until 1943 when the Germans dissolved the Danish parliament, disbanded its army, and put the king under house arrest. From then on, the SS ran the country. Nazi prefects already governed most of the other countries outside the Greater German Reich. Reichscommissioners ruled in Norway and the Netherlands. These men, who reported directly to Hitler, ruled by decree and had the power to suspend existing laws. They permitted the local administrative machinery to remain in place, but controlled it with specially appointed deputies, including chiefs of police. Only political parties and organizations of the National Socialist type were allowed.

A Reichsprotector governed in the supposedly autonomous regions of Bohemia and Moravia. The protector "advised" the local government and saw to it that his advice was followed. Most ministries were still staffed by Czechs, but some, like the Ministry of Justice, were run directly from Berlin. Northern France, Belgium, Serbia, and Greece had military governors. There the local administrations were allowed to function as before, subject, of course, to the review and control of the occupation authorities. In all of these areas, German control could appear almost invisible, at least to the average person who had no real contact with the upper echelons of power. The locals continued to operate the civil service, administer justice, and teach in the schools. The chance of a native actually receiving a direct order from a German was remote. The Germans kept watch but as unobtrusively as possible to disguise the extent to which they had established control.

No such subtlety was wasted on the territories of Eastern Europe. In Poland—that is, that part left after the German annexations—Governor-General Hans Frank ruled from his capital in Cracow with a bloody fist. He destroyed the local leadership, replacing the Polish administration with his own, and reduced the country to the level of a colony. Even the Poles' right to leisure was abolished, turning them into a race of slaves. The Ministry for the East, which ran the Baltic and Russian territories, was equally brutal. Its head, Alfred Rosenberg, exercised executive and legislative powers analogous to those exercised by Frank. All state property was transferred to the German state. A Reichscommissioner in Riga permitted the Baltic territories some degree of local administrative autonomy, but the Russian and Ukrainian portions were another matter. Erich Koch, Rosenberg's Reichscommissioner in Rovno, aimed at the total destruction of the region's political and national identity. Its economy would be transformed from industrial to pastoral, its people would be turned into workers of the Reich. In time, the denigration, deportation, and eventually extermination of these inhabitants would clear the area for German settlement.

In central Europe, Hitler tried to maintain good relations with Hungary and Bulgaria by enlarging their countries at the expense of their neighbors. For a time, they remained faithful allies, but once it became clear that Germany was losing the power to reward or threaten, their desire for collaboration began to weaken. Romania entered the German orbit out of fear of the Soviet Union. Slovakia, under Monsignor Tiso, was from the outset a German satellite, as was the Fascist state of Croatia.

The Germans had organized their war effort to win battles, not to exploit their victories. Believing that the war would be a short one, they had not made elaborate plans for economic mobilization or for the rapid expansion of production. Instead, they expected the German economy would simply convert as necessary. In foreign countries under direct German control, Göring ordered factories to produce materials of war. In other areas, the Germans tried to purchase what they needed, using whatever control they had over resources and the political system to accomplish their aims. In this way, they gradually co-opted the industrial production of much of Europe, often setting prices themselves because they were the principal purchasers.

In France, for example, the Germans deducted the cost of their "purchases" from their occupation and armistice expenses, amounts that were grossly inflated. The terms of the armistice required the French to pay a tribute of 300 million francs a day (later raised to 700 million), which enabled the Germans to obtain virtually any raw materials and industrial products they desired; in effect, they systematically looted the country. The French even paid for the costs of Nazi propaganda and for building the Atlantic wall, including the room and board of the German engineers and construction workers. The Germans met French protests with threats, but initially the French were too stunned by the defeat to offer much resistance.

The Vichy Regime. France was the only country to sign an armistice with the Germans. Faced with defeat, the French scrapped the governmental institutions that had existed for the past seven decades. The National Assembly held its last session on the afternoon of 10 July at Vichy in the white stucco Grand Casino. The fate of the Republic was already sealed. An overwhelming majority of senators and deputies (659 to 80 with 17 abstentions) gave Marshal Pétain the authority to create a new constitution.[60] The legislators seemed to desire a continuation of the representative system, but they endorsed a committee report, possessing the force of law, that gave Pétain complete executive and legislative power. On 11 July, he became head of the French state with "plenary governmental powers," including the authority to appoint and remove ministers and secretaries of state and the right to promulgate and execute laws. Neither these measures, nor any of the others that followed, were ever ratified by any authority other than Pétain himself. Nevertheless, they formed the main legal underpinnings of his personal dictatorship in unoccupied France.

Pétain ruled his fief from the Hôtel du Parc, in which were also located the offices of the vice-president of the Council and the minister of foreign affairs. The rest of Pétain's administration was scattered throughout the city in various other hotels. Many members of the conservative Catholic upper class regarded the Vichy regime as a golden opportunity to purify their national heritage and rid it of the influence of the Jews, Socialists, and Freemasons. They wanted to establish a new order of corporatism, domesticity, agrarianism, and religious conformity under the motto *Travail, Famille, Patrie* (Work, Family, Country). Pétain did not believe that the French needed democracy. Like a troop of soldiers, they needed to be led. He therefore favored the establishment of an authoritarian system in which the individual would be merged into one great organic whole.

The traditional French Right had no quarrel with this concept of government. Catholics wanted a return to clericalism; industrialists wanted to put the Socialists in their place; the members of the leagues and other right-wing groups wanted to destroy parliament; certain technocrats and civil servants wanted a more ordered society; and the peasants wanted a redress of their grievances. All saw in Vichy a positive force that would reverse decades of moral decline.

Vichy gave France its most repressive political system since the dictatorship of Napoleon III. A series of laws dissolved the trade unions, forbade seditious speech, and outlawed membership in unapproved organizations. The new rulers dismissed unreliable magistrates, councillors, bureaucrats, and military and civil personnel; excluded Jews from public employment and from the media; and lifted the citizenship of those who had fled the country between 10 May and 30 June 1940. In exchange for this repression, the government claimed it would give France a "new morality."[61] Among other things, Vichy tried to improve working conditions, reinforce the family, and combat alcoholism. In December 1940, the Vichy Ministry of Education restored religion to public schools. The following year, the state provided subsidies to parochial schools by giving money to the bishops for educational purposes. Religious orders that had been banned by the Law of Associations in 1901 were allowed again, and church property seized in 1905 was returned.

Initially, Pétain had the support of most Frenchmen, both at home and in the empire. Furthermore, he received the official recognition of a host of nonbelligerent states, including the Holy See, the Soviet Union, and the United States. The French people wanted to achieve a comfortable relationship with Nazi Germany, which directly occupied three-fifths of their country—all the territory in the northern half of the country and a strip of land 60 to 150 miles wide along the Atlantic coast down to the Spanish frontier. In August 1940, despite their promises to respect the territorial integrity of France, the Germans put Alsace and Lorraine under a special civilian government, making German the official language and beginning the expulsion of the inhabitants they believed were incapable of assimilation. In French-speaking Lorraine, where this policy hit the hardest, some 100,000 people who insisted on keeping their old citizenship were forced to leave within four months.

In occupied France, the Germans conducted an intensive policy of nazification and plundered the country's resources, taking over half of its annual income. In the south, the Vichy leaders considered themselves safe. They wanted to be left alone to liberate France from the decadence of the past. By paying the Germans protection money, they vainly hoped they could keep their country safe from the ravages of war. They were encouraged in these delusions by Hitler's plenipotentiary in Paris, Otto Abetz, who acted as an adviser to the Vichy government. His job was to prevent the growth of any undue independence and to ensure that Vichy continued to put its resources at the disposal of Germany. The politicians of the Vichy regime hardly ever proved a disappointment.

The SS Empire. Heinrich Himmler was not content to wait for the end of the war to create the New Order. Nor was he inclined to accept civilian or military government control of occupied Europe. He was determined to expand the German racial community, starting with German colonies in parts of Poland, the Baltic states, and the Soviet Union. In time these outposts would expand into permanent settlements. The natives would be gradually exterminated unless they possessed Teutonic features, in which case they might be integrated into the German racial community. In May 1940, Himmler produced "Some thoughts on the treatment of foreign population in the East" to give practical shape to Hitler's policy of Lebensraum. The plan proposed that the SS be given final authority to eliminate all the non-Teutonic races in Poland, beginning with the systematic extermination of the Polish ruling classes and the massive deportation of the Jews.

Himmler insinuated the SS into all the Reich's territories, mainly through his control of the police. This power play led to constant turf battles. In the Soviet Union, Himmler's henchmen tried to order the Reichscommissioners about. In the Netherlands, which was under "civilian" control, SS leaders obeyed only the directives they chose. In Poland, they used their control of the security services to challenge the authority of Hans Frank.

Himmler had obtained Hitler's permission to establish special *Einsatzgruppen* (strike forces) to carry out selected missions of extermination. Initially, five such groups were formed with four to six hundred commandos each. These units were ostensibly assigned to the armies in the field, but were, in fact, under the immediate authority of Reinhard Heydrich, who, since August 1939, headed the newly created *Reichssicherheitshauptamt* (State Security Head Office or RSHA). The RSHA was an omnibus organization that combined party and state agencies, including the *Sicherheitsdienst* (Security Service or SD), the Criminal Police, and the Gestapo. Through the Einsatzgruppen, SS political terror and murder came to all the conquered countries of Europe.

In Poland, the *Einsatzkommandos* systematically exterminated the country's leaders—priests, lawyers, government officials, and teachers. Less than a month after the campaign started, Heydrich boasted that at least 97 percent of the Polish upper classes had disappeared. The Russians were treated as badly. At the end of March 1941, Hitler told his senior military commanders that in the war against the Soviet

Union they could "dispense with all their outdated and traditional ideas about chivalry and the generally accepted rules of warfare." Soviet political commissars, whom he considered the backbone of the Stalinist system, were not to be treated as ordinary prisoners of war but were to be "shot down in the course of battle or executed out of hand."[62]

Himmler created his own army in the *Waffen-SS* (Fighting-SS). These units grew out of earlier armed detachments, but not until the war did Hitler allow them to grow to division strength.[63] Four SS divisions took part in the initial attack on the Soviet Union. Finding them inexperienced, but well equipped and reckless, the Wehrmacht commanders used the SS divisions as shock troops, but they suffered so many casualties that they had to be temporarily withdrawn from the battle for rest and reorganization. Himmler saw his soldiers as the vanguard of the new German warrior: tough, racially pure, and fearlessly loyal to the National Socialist doctrine.[64] They also won a reputation for their brutality. In some instances, they carried out exterminations alongside SS police units.

The size of the Waffen-SS doubled annually, reaching almost 600,000 near the end of the war. Himmler preempted recruitment for the regular army and also launched a massive campaign for recruits from foreign countries. The first drafts began in 1941 with levies from Norway, Denmark, and Belgium. To these were added Dutch, French, Balts, and Croatians. As the demands for more troops intensified, racial standards started to slip. Himmler claimed that Islam with its stress on courage was a practical religion for a soldier and allowed the formation of a Muslim SS division. There were also SS formations of Ukrainians, Serbs, Hungarians, Romanians, and Cossacks. Obviously, not all of these soldiers joined because they agreed with Nazi ideology. Racial hatred against other ethnic groups prompted some, others wanted to escape forced labor, some thought that they would be fighting for the freedom of their country, and some wanted to participate in the crusade against Bolshevism. Many members of the Waffen-SS were ordinary soldiers who had been indoctrinated with Nazi ideology. They added significantly to the growing influence of Himmler, who was the second most powerful man in Europe now that the plan to exterminate the Jews had become a reality. In the formulation and execution of the Final Solution, Himmler believed he had found the heroic purpose for which he had searched throughout his life.[65]

The Final Solution. By May 1941, Himmler had some 3,000 Einsatzkommandos ready for action; and in the six months following the invasion of the Soviet Union, they murdered about 300,000 Jews. Battalion commander Otto Ohlendorf described a typical operation:

> The unit selected for this task would enter a village or a city and order prominent Jewish citizens to call together all Jews for the purposes of resettlement. They were requested to hand over their valuables to the leader of the unit, and shortly before execution to surrender their outer clothing. The men, women and children were led to a place of execution which in most cases was located next to a deeply excavated antitank ditch. Then they were shot, kneeling or standing, and the corpses thrown into the ditch.[66]

The bodies were stacked on top of each other, like cords of wood, until the ditch was full enough to be covered over. In the spring of 1942, a gas van appeared into which the victims, usually women and children, were loaded under the pretext that they were being resettled. The doors were closed. Then the engines started, filling the compartment with carbon monoxide gas. After a quarter of an hour, usually all were dead. The corpses were then taken out and buried.

The architects of genocide, Heinrich Himmler and Reinhard Heydrich, used the Wahnsee Conference as a device to extend their power. By 1941, Himmler had become the strongest man in the Third Reich after Hitler.

In time, SS police chiefs, arriving with the regular occupation authorities, replaced the mobile Einsatzgruppen. These permanently based officials were responsible for most of the 900,000 Jews murdered in the Soviet Union. The executioners spoke of their task in euphemisms: "special treatment" or "special actions," "cleansing operations," "executive measures," "appropriate handling," "relocation," and the "final solution." The policy of the mass murder of European Jewry was planned rather than improvised. Although put in motion during the war, the decision to carry it out had been made before the conflict began. It therefore predated the attack on the Soviet Union, which may have affected its timing. The absence of concrete documentation has led some historians to relate it to the failure to take Moscow in 1941.

The previous summer, when a rapid victory still seemed likely, Himmler received word that Hitler wanted the Jews liquidated without exception.[67] This decision had probably been reached as early as 1938.[68] On 20 January 1942, it was revealed to a select gathering of senior state officials at a conference in the Central Security Office headquarters in the Berlin suburb of Wannsee. The meeting was the culmination of at least six months of planning; preparations had been underway since 31 July 1941, when Göring had ordered Reinhart Heydrich to submit an overall plan to carry out the "final solution of the Jewish question."[69] This was the first time that the words "final solution" were used to describe the mass murder of the Jews.

Heydrich now showed the Wannsee gathering a chart indicating which Jewish communities would be deported to the east and organized into labor battalions. Most of these people, he explained, could be expected to die naturally in the course of their work, but those who did not would be "handled accordingly." The meeting included some true ideological fanatics, like Lieutenant-Colonel Adolf Eichmann, but most of those in attendance were bureaucrats from one ministry or another who were there to tie everything neatly together according to official procedures. In this respect, the Wannsee conference was a huge SS triumph. The other departments of the Nazi power structure were willing to allow the SS to have ultimate responsibility for carrying out the policy.[70]

In Poland, the SS established six special killing centers at Treblinka, Sobibor, Maydanek, Belzec, Kulmhof, and Auschwitz, equipping them with gas chambers and crematoria that were capable of handling huge numbers of people on an assembly-line basis. The operation became so efficient that all the Jews in a boxcar could be unloaded after breakfast, gassed, and reduced to ashes before supper. Once, within a twenty-four-hour period at Auschwitz, over 9,000 people were gassed and their corpses burned. A standard procedure was followed. Commandant Rudolf Höss recalled:

> Jews selected for gassing were taken as quietly as possible to the crematoriums, the men being separated from the women. In the undressing rooms ... [they were told] that they were going to be bathed and deloused. ... After undressing, the Jews went into the gas chambers which were furnished with showers and water pipes and gave a realistic impression of a bath house. ... The door would now be quickly screwed up and the gas immediately discharged ... those who were standing nearest to the induction vents were killed at once. It can be said that about one third died straight away. The remainder staggered about and began to scream and struggle for air. The screaming, however, soon changed to the death rattle and in a few minutes all lay still. ... Those who screamed and those who were old or sick or weak, or the small children, died quicker than those who were healthy or young.[71]

Jews capable of strenuous work were spared until they were no longer useful. Thousands of prisoners were worked to death; others took their own lives.

Hitler was determined to eradicate as many Jews as he could, even those outside the areas of his immediate control. As the extent of German-occupied territory increased (for example, when the Germans occupied the rest of France in November 1942 and the area north of Rome in Italy in September 1943), so did the activities of the SS. Early in 1942, the German Foreign Office signed an agreement with the Slovak government for the deportation of its Jews. The Slovak government paid a fee of 500 reichsmarks per capita to cover costs. The Croatian government also allowed its Jews to be sent to their deaths in Germany. But Jews were not the only people on the Croatian hate list. Croatia had its own death camps that carried out exterminations of Gypsies and Orthodox Serbs.[72]

The German Foreign Office also tried to arrange for the deportation of the Jews in Germany's allies. The Hungarians refused. When the Germans invaded the country in 1944, however, the roundup began. It could not have been successful without the full cooperation of the Hungarian police. The Danes, though, did not cooperate. In fact, they hastily arranged to send their Jews out of the country to Sweden before the Gestapo could lay hands on them. The Jews of Bulgaria were also for the most part saved. There domestic opposition prevented the government from cooperating with Germany. In Romania, anti-Semitism was particularly nasty. The Germans induced the government to agree to a plan to deport all the Romanian Jews to their deaths, but the policy was not carried out. Apparently, the government was no longer convinced the Germans were going to win the war and decided to wait. Consequently, the only Romanian Jews who were killed came from those areas that had been ceded to the Soviet Union in 1940 and were now occupied by the Germans.

In one way or another, the Germans were responsible for the murder of at least 5 million Jews. Three million were murdered in the camps; another 1 million were killed by Einsatzgruppen, SS police, and the Wehrmacht; and some 700,000 perished in various ghetto operations.[73] Polish Jewry was hardest hit: 3 million men, women, and children, or 90 percent of the prewar population, died. The Soviet Union lost 900,000 or 28 percent of its Jews; Hungary 300,000, or 75 percent; Romania 270,000, or 34 percent; France and Italy 70,000, or 22 percent. Only 6,000 of 100,000 Dutch Jews survived. Before the war, 207,000 of Germany's 503,000 Jews had fled abroad; most of the remainder were exterminated.

Perhaps 50,000 Germans participated directly in the extermination process. But due to the tremendous logistical demands of such an operation, many more were indirectly involved. This mass murder was one of the most horrendous examples of barbarism in modern history. Ironically, as German chances for victory became more uncertain, Nazi savagery intensified. In April 1943, units of the Wehrmacht and the Waffen-SS were ordered to round up all Jews still in the Warsaw ghetto— some 60,000 of an original 400,000—and send them to extermination camps. But the Germans encountered such determined opposition that the three days allocated for the operation became four weeks. The task was completed only through the use of tanks, artillery, and flamethrowers. The assault commander, SS Brigadeführer Jurgen Stopp, was so proud of his accomplishment that he had his official seventy-five-page report typed on heavy bond and bound in leather.

Even in their retreat from the Soviet Union, the invaders still had time to continue their campaign of extermination. On 5 October 1943, at Dubro in the western Ukraine, Hermann Gräbe, a German business representative of a Solingen firm witnessed a mass execution, the kind that had by then become routine:

The people who had gotten off the trucks—men, women, and children of all ages—had to undress upon the orders of an SS man who carried a riding or dog whip. They had to put down their clothes in fixed places, sorted according to shoes, over and underclothing. I saw a pile of shoes of about 800 to 1,000 pairs, great piles of laundry and clothing. Without screaming or crying these people undressed, stood around by families, kissed each other, said farewells and waited for the nod of another SS man, who stood near the excavation, also with a whip in his hand. During the 15 minutes that I stood near the excavation I heard no complaint and no request for mercy. I watched a family of about 8 persons, a man and woman, both about 50 with their children of about 1, 8, and 10, and two grown-up daughters of about 20 to 24. An old woman with snow-white hair held the one-year-old child in her arms and sang for it, and tickled it. The child was squeaking from joy. The couple looked on with tears in their eyes. The father held the hand of a boy about 10 years old and spoke to him softly; the boy was fighting his tears. The father pointed toward the sky, fondled his hand, and seemed to explain something to him. At that moment the SS-man at the excavation called something to his comrades. The latter counted off about 20 persons and instructed them to walk behind the earth mound. Among them was the family which I had mentioned. I remember very well a girl, blackhaired and slender, passing near me; she pointed at herself and said, "23 years." I walked around the mound, and stood in front of a tremendous grave. Closely pressed together the people were lying on top of each other so that only their heads were visible. Several of the people shot still moved. Some lifted their arms and turned their heads to show that they were still alive. The excavation was already two-thirds full. I estimated that it contained about 1,000 people. I looked for the man who did the shooting. I saw an SS-man who sat at the rim of the narrow end of the excavation, his feet dangling into the excavation. On his knees he had a machine pistol and he was smoking a cigarette. The completely naked people descended a stairway which was dug into the clay of the excavation and slipped over the heads of the people lying there already to the place to which the SS-man directed them. They laid themselves in front of the dead or injured people, some touched tenderly those who were still alive and spoke to them in a low voice. Then I heard a number of shots. I looked into the excavation and saw how the bodies jerked or the heads rested already motionless on top of the bodies that lay before them.[74]

POSTSCRIPT   World War II was a war the British did not want and could not afford to fight. Yet, in contrast to the lethargic way they had protected their security during the 1930s, they rose to the challenge admirably. The Tories, despite their conceit of leadership, were ordinary men who overcame faults and weaknesses with difficulty. The Chamberlain government had been woefully outclassed by its adversaries, but its failure to prepare the country for war was not its fault alone. The British people also believed war could be avoided through proper diplomacy. Their island location gave them a sense of security. They were notoriously in favor of appeasement and strongly opposed to increased military expenditures. Once the war began, however, their resolution to stand fast in the face of adversity did much to atone for their past mistakes. But without their geographical isolation from the continent, they would have had no second chance.

The French had no English Channel to protect them against the German onslaught. Their defeat in 1940 was so complete that they were reluctant to use what trumps they had left: their fleet and their empire. The Vichy leaders were too absorbed with preserving a fictitious independence to want to go on fighting. Instead, they directed their efforts to destroying the libertarian and egalitarian influences that had grown in France since the 1789 Revolution. The Germans had little difficulty getting whatever they wanted. It was not French refusal to comply that prevented more French Jews from being delivered to the Germans or more French workers from being sent to work in German factories. Yet, despite its willingness to collaborate, France was spared none of the misery the other German-occupied countries of Western Europe experienced.

Throughout the first two years of the war, Hitler was unpunished and could enjoy his spoils with confidence. Blitzkrieg had carried Hitler's Panzers beyond Paris, into North Africa, and to within twenty miles of Moscow. The Germans had achieved almost absolute European hegemony. Those lands their army did not occupy were either docile neutrals, like Sweden and Switzerland; allies, like Romania, Bulgaria, and Italy; collaborators, like Vichy France; or were distinctly pro-Axis, like Spain. Hitler triumphantly proclaimed 1941 the "year of a great European new order," the supreme hour for the Greater German racial community.

The creation of a vast empire in Eastern Europe was Hitler's dream. He hoped that the shock of the German attack would lead to the political collapse of the Stalinist system, something akin to what had occurred with the Third Republic in France. The signs were encouraging. In many areas, particularly among the Soviet Union's dissident national minorities, the Germans were regarded as liberators. General Heinz Guderian said that in Belorussia "women came out from their villages onto the very battlefield bringing wooden plates of bread and butter and eggs."[75] But the Soviet Union was not France. The Soviets fought with a determination and desperation the Germans had encountered nowhere else, and their spirit proved decisive. By any ordinary logic, a nation that had sustained such losses should have collapsed within the first six months.

In contrast to the savage brutality with which the war was fought on the Russian front, the war in North Africa was almost gentlemanly. For the Germans, once the glorious days of mobility in Russia had ended, Africa was the only place the Wehrmacht could still practice the kind of warfare for which it had been trained. This was a war where very few civilians could get in the way, where a semblance of chivalry could still prevail. Out of this theater came one of the most memorable songs of the war, "Lili Marlene."[76] The British picked it up from German radio transmissions; translated into English, it became an instant favorite:

> *Outside the barracks, by the corner light,*
> *I'll always stand and wait for you by night.*
> *We will create a world for two,*
> *I'll wait for you, the whole night through*
> *For you Lili Marlene, for you Lili Marlene.*

Yet, the image of a brothers-in-arms war that this conjures up is more than destroyed by the horror of the Final Solution.

ENDNOTES

1. Albert Speer, *Inside the Third Reich* (New York: Macmillan, 1970), 167.
2. Walter Schellenberg, *The Labyrinth* (New York: Harper and Row, 1956), 47.
3. *Documents of German Foreign Policy*, series D, vol. 7, 480.
4. Ibid., 541.

5. Ibid., vol. 8, 77.
6. Ibid., 130.
7. Speer, *Inside the Third Reich*, 168.
8. Ibid., 168.
9. Karl Gustav von Mannerheim, *The Memoirs of Marshal Mannerheim* (London: Cassell, 1953), 388.
10. See Friedrich Wilhelm von Mellenthin, *Panzer Battles* (London: Cassell, 1955).
11. Pierre-Etienne Flandin, *Politique Française, 1919–1940* (Paris, 1947), 336.
12. André Beaufre, *1940: The Fall of France* (New York: Knopf, 1968), 163.
13. Bernard Law Montgomery, *The Memoirs of Field-Marshal Montgomery* (New York: World Publishing, 1958), 43.
14. Ibid., 51.
15. The British had 12 battleships, 3 battle cruisers, 64 heavy and light cruisers, 7 aircraft carriers, and 184 destroyers. The Germans possessed no battleships nor aircraft carriers; they had 2 battle cruisers, 3 pocket battleships, 8 heavy and light cruisers, and 22 destroyers.
16. Tom Shachtman, *The Phony War, 1939–1940* (New York: Harper and Row, 1982), 115–16.
17. Erich Raeder, *My Life* (New York: Arno, 1980), 309.
18. Shachtman, *The Phony War*, 187–90.
19. Dingle Foot, "When the Parliament Said 'Go,' " *The Observer*, 8 May 1960, 6, 10.
20. Chamberlain would have preferred his foreign secretary, Lord Halifax, to succeed him, but a prime minister who sat in the House of Lords was an impossibility. The last minister to have accomplished that was Lord Salisbury, whose third and last ministry lasted from 1895 to 1902.
21. Winston Churchill, *The Gathering Storm* (London: Cassell, 1948), 666–67.
22. Ibid., 667.
23. Winston Churchill, *Maxims and Reflections* (Boston: Houghton Mifflin, 1949), 34.
24. Ibid., 63.
25. Churchill held the positions of home secretary, 1910–1911; first lord of the admiralty, 1911–1915; minister of munitions, 1917; secretary of state for air and war, 1919–1921; and colonial secretary, 1921–1922.
26. Robert Rhodes James, *Memoirs of a Conservative: J. C. C. Davidson's Memoirs and Papers* (New York: Macmillan, 1969), 211–12.
27. Churchill also regarded Clemenceau as a peer. Clemenceau, he wrote, "embodied and expressed France. As much as any simple human being, miraculously magnified, can ever be a nation, he *was* France." Churchill, *Maxims and Reflections*, 69.
28. Winston S. Churchill, *The World Crisis, 1916–1918* (London: Odhams, 1927), 256–57.
29. *Documents of German Foreign Policy*, series D, vol. 8, 249.
30. Ibid., 249.
31. Erich von Manstein, *Lost Victories* (Chicago: Henry Regnery, 1958), 104.
32. Manstein would have no part in its execution. He had already been replaced, in January, as chief of staff of Army Group A and had been given command of a corps that had no assigned role in the forthcoming attack.
33. Basil Liddell Hart, *The German Generals Talk* (New York: William Morrow, 1948), 116.
34. Shachtman, *The Phony War*, 225–38.
35. Winston S. Churchill, *Their Finest Hour* (Boston: Houghton Mifflin, 1949), 208–9.
36. Ibid., 674.
37. Speer, *Inside the Third Reich*, 172.
38. Letter dated 13 July 1940, *Documents of German Foreign Policy*, series D, vol. 10, 211.
39. Ibid., 226.

40. These were supported by 875 high-level bombers, mainly Dornier 17s and Heinkel 111s and some Junker 88s, and 316 Stuka dive-bombers. The slow-moving Stukas proved so difficult to protect and were shot down in such great numbers that the Luftwaffe command soon withdrew them from the battle altogether. The whole battle fleet was organized in two air fleets (Luftflotten 2 and 3), operating in northern France and the Low Countries.

41. The Messerschmitt 109 and the Vickers Supermarine Spitfire were almost evenly matched: the German fighter was slightly faster; the Spitfire was more maneuverable.

42. Adolf Galland, *The First and the Last* (New York: Henry Holt, 1954), 25.

43. Len Deighton, *Fighter: The True Story of the Battle of Britain* (New York: Knopf, 1978), 3–33.

44. Galland, *The First and the Last*, 31.

45. Churchill, *Their Finest Hour*, 331.

46. Deighton, *Fighter*, 223–45.

47. Ibid., 340.

48. F. W. Winterbotham, *The Ultra Secret* (New York: Harper and Row, 1975), 43–44.

49. Wladyslaw Kozaczuk, *Enigma: How the German Machine Cipher Was Broken and How It Was Read by the Allies in World War Two* (Frederick, Md.: University Publications of America, 1985), 193–223.

50. Peter Calvocoressi et al., *Total War: Causes and Courses of the Second World War* (London: Allen Lane, 1972), xxiii–xxiv.

51. Bryan I. Fugate, *Operation Barbarossa: Strategy and Tactics on the Eastern Front, 1941* (Novato, Calif.: Presidio, 1984), 61–93.

52. Ibid., 900.

53. Seymour Freidin and William Richardson, eds., *The Fatal Decisions* (New York: William Sloan, 1956), 55.

54. Liddell Hart, *The German Generals Talk*, 178–79.

55. Harrison E. Salisbury, *The 900 Days: The Siege of Leningrad* (New York: Da Capo, 1969), 202–13.

56. Freidin and Richardson, *The Fatal Decisions*, 73–74.

57. John Erickson, *The Road to Stalingrad: Stalin's War with Germany* (London: Weidenfeld and Nicolson, 1975), 249–96.

58. Walter Warlimont, *Inside Hitler's Headquarters, 1939–45* (New York: Praeger, 1964), 223.

59. *Documents of German Foreign Policy*, series D, vol. 13, 152.

60. Maurice Duverger, *Constitutions et Documents Politiques* (Paris: Presses Universitaires, 1960), 115.

61. Robert O. Paxton, *Vichy France: Old Guard and New Order, 1940–1944* (New York: Norton, 1972), 136–68.

62. Wilhelm Keitel, *The Memoirs of Field-Marshal Keitel* (New York: Stein and Day, 1966), 135.

63. Heinz Höhne, *The Order of the Death's Head* (New York: Ballantine Books, 1977), 493–545.

64. Bernd Wegner, *The Waffen-SS: Organization: Ideology and Function* (Oxford: Basil Blackwell, 1990), 198–222.

65. See Peter Padfield, *Himmler* (New York: Holt, Rinehart and Winston, 1991).

66. *Nazi Conspiracy and Aggression*, vol. 5 (Washington, D.C.: U.S. Government Printing Office, 1946), 342.

67. Gerald Fleming, *Hitler and the Final Solution* (Berkeley: University of California Press, 1982), 47–48.

68. See Richard Breitman, *The Architect of Genocide: Himmler and Final Solution* (New York: Knopf, 1991).

69. Yehuda Bauer, *A History of the Holocaust* (New York: Franklin Watts, 1982), 201.

70.   Martin Gilbert, *The Holocaust: A History of the Jews of Europe during the Second World War* (New York: Holt, Rinehart and Winston, 1985), 280–93.

71.   Rudolf Höss, *Commandant of Auschwitz* (Cleveland: World Publishing, 1959), 222.

72.   Helen Fein, *Accounting for Genocide: National Responses and Jewish Victimization during the Holocaust* (New York: Free Press, 1979), 102–5.

73.   Raul Hilberg, *The Destruction of the European Jews* (New York: Holmes and Meier, 1985), 767. Bauer sets the total at 5,820,960, which is closer to the generally accepted figure of 6 million. See *A History of the Holocaust*, 335.

74.   *Nazi Conspiracy and Aggression*, 2: 268–69.

75.   Heinz Guderian, *Panzer Leader* (New York: Dutton, 1952), 193.

76.   Vor der Kaserne, vor dem grossen Tor / Steht eine Laterne, und steht sie noch davor. / Wenn sich die späten Nebel drehn, Bei der Laterne woll'n wir stehn / Wie einst Lili Marlene, Wie einst Lili Marlene.

CHAPTER 16

THE TRIUMPH OF
THE ALLIES

PREFACE   Churchill assessed the situation. With the entry of the United States into the war, "Hitler's fate was sealed. Mussolini's fate was sealed." The Japanese would be ground to powder. "All the rest was merely the proper application of overwhelming force."[1] Accordingly, following the example of Lloyd George in World War I, Churchill set out to bring the United States into the war. He feared, however, that his reputation for having a "reactionary Old-World outlook" would make the task more difficult. He also knew that the Americans would never fly war banners promising a restoration of the European balance of power. He therefore worked out a set of war aims that he hoped would appeal to the ideological sensitivities of President Roosevelt—"a British production cast in my own words" was how he phrased it.[2]

Churchill had discussed this program with Roosevelt at their 11 August 1941 meeting on board the American warship *Augusta* in Placentia Bay off the Newfoundland coast. Although these ideals were somewhat platitudinous, they became a fixture in the rhetoric of postwar international relations. Churchill's moral agenda called for the self-determination of peoples, the reduction of armaments, the guaranteeing of security through international organization, and the establishment of government with the consent of the governed. Churchill also proposed that the United States and Britain "strive to bring about a fair and equitable distribution of essential produce, not only within their territorial boundaries, but between the nations of the world."[3] Roosevelt liked what he heard and added a few principles of his own: "a peace to establish for all safety on the high seas and oceans" and "that all the nations of the world must be guided in spirit to the abandonment of the use of force." Both leaders advocated "improved labor standards, economic advancement, and social security" throughout the world, long-time goals of the British Labour party, which lobbied for their inclusion. Roosevelt insisted on a strong endorsement of the principles of international justice and civilization to avoid giving the impression that he was making any specific commitments to Great Britain. He hoped this "Atlantic Charter," which reflected his own Wilsonian idealism, would have a positive impact on American public opinion.

Considering that the United States was still technically neutral, Roosevelt's acceptance of the charter was a stunning diplomatic coup.[4] Churchill observed that the charter's reference to "final destruction of Nazi tyranny . . . amounted to a challenge which in ordinary times would have implied war-like action. Finally, not the least striking feature was the realism of the last paragraph, where there was a plain and bold ultimatum that after the war the United States would join with us in policing the world until the establishment of a better order."[5]

The two leaders sent a text of the agreement to the Soviet Union. Stalin, in due course, promised to carry out its provisions.[6] However, the Soviet dictator wanted to have his association with the British and Americans defined in a more formal treaty that would include a clear description of the political geography of Europe after the defeat of Germany. Specifically, Stalin wanted Austria to become independent; the Rhineland, and possibly Bavaria, to be separated from Germany as independent states or protectorates; East Prussia to be given to Poland; and the Sudetenland to be returned to Czechoslovakia. He also thought that Yugoslavia should receive territory from Italy and that Turkey should be given the Dodecanese Islands, parts of Bulgaria, and possibly northern Syria. Furthermore, he insisted that the boundaries of the Soviet Union should be extended to the frontiers delineated in the Non-Aggression Pact with Germany and to the 1941 frontier with Finland. In addition, the Soviets should receive the Baltic states (Latvia, Lithuania, and Estonia), Bessarabia, military bases in Romania, and the eastern half of Poland. Despite his endorsement of the Atlantic Charter, Stalin suspected that Roosevelt and Churchill were ganging up on him and that the agreement was "directed against the U.S.S.R."[7]

Churchill did not let gratuitous moral considerations stand in the way of practical politics. With or without British approval, the Soviet Union would take the territories it wanted once the war ended. Nevertheless, Churchill was reluctant to urge Roosevelt to recognize Stalin's demands, fearing he might appear to be an advocate for Soviet interests. The prime minister was also worried that Roosevelt might view the Far East, not Europe, as the primary theater of war. Churchill, therefore, followed Roosevelt's cue and accepted that such questions "could only be settled upon the termination of the war."[8]

THE GERMANS SURRENDER THE INITIATIVE

The Turning Point, 1942

The Axis Declares War on the United States. On 7 December 1941, 350 Japanese attack planes took off from a special carrier task force to bomb the American naval base at Pearl Harbor. It was Sunday morning. Most of the American Pacific Fleet was in port, including eight battleships moored east of Ford Island. The first wave of Japanese torpedo planes swept in so low that those on the ground could see the expressions on the pilots' faces. Then came the high-level bombers and dive-bombers. After ten minutes, the place was in shambles. The attacking force sunk four battleships, damaged four others, and disabled three light cruisers and three destroyers. At nearby Hickham and Wheeler fields, most of the American planes were pulverized before they had a chance to take off. The Japanese regarded the attack as a great success, marred only by the escape of the American aircraft carriers, which had been out at sea.

The United States declared war on Japan on 8 December 1941. Although the Americans had anticipated a war with Japan, the Pearl Harbor attack came as a complete surprise. Relations between the two countries had been gradually deteriorating. For the past decade, Japan had been on an imperial romp that started with the conquest of Manchuria in 1931. In 1937 Japan had invaded China. These successes had led to a bid to control the whole of Southeast Asia from India and Australia eastward to the Hawaiian Islands. After the fall of France in June 1940, the Tokyo war lords pressured the Vichy government to grant them military bases in Indochina and forced the British to close the Burma Road. On 27 September 1940, Japan agreed to transform the Anti-Comintern Pact with Italy and Germany into a military alliance. As a result, Japan agreed to respect the leadership of Germany and Italy in the establishment of the New Order in Europe in exchange for German and Italian recognition of a Japanese New Order in Greater East Asia. If any power not currently involved in the European war or in the Sino-Japanese conflict attacked any of the signatories, they would assist each other with all political, economic, and military means.[9] The unnamed power was clearly the United States.

At the same time Japanese torpedo planes were sinking the American battleships at Pearl Harbor, Japanese troops were landing on the Malay Peninsula to prepare for the invasion of the Philippines and Thailand. On 10 December, Japanese naval bombers eliminated British sea power in the southwest Pacific by sinking the battle cruiser *Repulse* and the recently commissioned battleship *Prince of Wales*. During the next six months, the Japanese conquered the Philippines, captured Malaysia and Singapore, and occupied much of the Dutch East Indies. Their attacks against the British and Americans brought together the wars of Europe and Asia.

Congress had initially declared war only on Japan, not on Germany and Italy. The European dictators declared war first. Hitler joyfully showed Wilhelm Keitel and Alfred Jodl the telegram with the news about the attack on Pearl Harbor, and on 11 December, he declared war on the United States. Mussolini declared war at the same time. These actions seemed the height of folly in that the Axis had yet to eliminate either British or Soviet resistance. Taking on yet another enemy appeared to be strategic lunacy. Neither dictator had done any planning for war against the United States, considering it unnecessary. Hitler, however, believed

Map 13

that he had already practiced too much restraint against the United States given that the Americans had stripped away their own veneer of neutrality with the Atlantic Charter. Declaring war, he thought, would give him an opportunity to retaliate against American shipping with his submarines. He would also help his Japanese ally by forcing the common enemy to fight a war on two fronts.[10] However, Hitler had underestimated the capacity of the United States for a rapid buildup. He believed that the Americans were already demoralized and economically weak, perhaps even on the verge of a social upheaval. He incorrectly calculated that the European war would be over before American participation could make any difference.

Retreat in the Desert. At the end of January 1942, Erwin Rommel had received enough reinforcements to go on the offensive again. By July 1942, he had pushed the enemy to El Alamein some sixty miles from Alexandria. There, General Sir Claude Auchinleck, the commander of the Middle East Land Forces, organized a spirited defense, forcing Rommel to fight the kind of static war the German commander deplored. Auchinleck, informed through Ultra that the German divisions were below half-strength and were short of fuel and supplies, successfully parried Rommel's attack in one of the most important engagements of the North African war. Even so, the success was not enough for Churchill who badly needed a more positive victory.

The prime minister was in political hot water. The Conservatives had lost heavily in the recent by-elections. To make matters worse, the Dominion governments felt they were being asked to carry an unfair share of the fighting. Sixty-five percent of the 23,000 defenders at Tobruk had been Australians, and Prime Minister John Curtin seemed ready to make his resentment public. Churchill pleaded that all "personal feelings be subordinated to an appearance of unity."[11] He came to Egypt in August 1942 and tried to pressure Auchinleck into an immediate offensive. When Auchinleck argued that the British army was not ready, Churchill replaced him with General Sir Harold Alexander. Alexander brought in Lt. General Sir Bernard Law Montgomery to command the Eighth Army, but Montgomery, like Auchinleck, refused to be pressured into premature action. He insisted on clear superiority before mounting an offensive. Time was on his side.

The Afrika Korps was growing short of manpower; all available reinforcements were now going to the Eastern Front. Whereas there were 180 German and 15 to 20 Romanian, Hungarian, and Italian divisions in Russia in September 1942, the desert armies had only 4 German and 8 Italian divisions. Furthermore, Rommel did not take the fighting power of the Italians seriously. His adjutant observed that the Italians "either do not come forward at all, or if they do, run at the first shot. If an Englishman so much as comes in sight, their hands go up."[12] Rommel believed that unless his army received massive supplies of food, ammunition, and gasoline, the North African war would soon be over. But, even if the supplies had been available, there was now no assurance that they could be delivered. From their base on the island of Malta, the British routinely destroyed 40 percent of German and Italian shipping between Sicily and Libya. The past summer, RAF bombers with a combat range of four hundred miles had managed to sink three-fourths of Axis shipping to Africa! Supplies to Rommel's army diminished "to an average total of 6,000 tons a month or approximately one-fifth of [its] normal requirements."[13] Through the Ultra intercepts, the British could pinpoint the location of almost every Axis convoy.

In the meantime, Montgomery's army had acquired an impressive superiority thanks to a massive flow of matériel from the United States. The new equipment included over 1,200 tanks, half of them the latest Grants and Shermans. They were more than a match for the 520 older-model machines of Rommel's army. The British also had twice as many antitank guns, twice as many field and medium-range guns, and twice as many men. In addition, they had complete air superiority. Overall, the British advantage was so significant that German defeat was inevitable. On 23 October 1942, the second battle of El Alamein began. It was a World War I confrontation fought with the technology of World War II: the Germans defended their lines with barbed wire and minefields, dugouts, and strong points; the British began with an artillery barrage followed by an infantry and tank attack. Montgomery's forces broke through on their second attempt. Although British losses were greater—the Germans destroyed more enemy tanks than they themselves possessed—the strength of the British reserves was too formidable for the Panzer Army to overcome. By 4 November 1942, the Germans were in full retreat. The victory gave the British what they wanted most: a major military triumph before the arrival of the Americans. It came none too soon.

On 8 November, four days after the breakthrough at El Alamein, American army units landed in Morocco, and an Anglo-American force went ashore in Algeria. The objective of Operation Torch was to capture Tunisia. In three days, French resistance ended. Admiral Jean François Darlan, the commander of the Vichy armed forces, happened to be in Algiers at the time of the invasion. He soon realized that further struggle was fruitless and gave the order for a cease-fire. He hesitated for several more days, however, before deciding to cooperate with the Allies. The delay allowed the Germans to send reinforcements to North Africa and set up a defensive line in the mountains west of the Tunisian Plain. At the same time, the Germans moved troops into Vichy France, conquering the rest of the country.

Montgomery delayed the pursuit of the defeated German army, allowing it to escape back through Libya to the Mareth Line, their fortified positions in southern Tunisia. Another six months would pass before all German resistance in North Africa finally ended. The desert war was the last great parade ground of the British Empire. It had a full panoply of forces including Sikhs, lancers, and highlanders; such an array would never again campaign side-by-side. Although the success of the North African campaign was important for ultimate Allied victory, the more important battles of 1942 took place in the Soviet Union. Here the Red Army was fighting a whole German field army, not just a corps.

The Surrender at Stalingrad. In 1942, the Germans were no longer able to maintain the three-pronged effort they had made the previous year. German casualties now approached a million men. Some generals advised withdrawal, even back to Poland. However, Hitler planned a new spring offensive to capture the Caucasus where 75 percent of the Soviet Union's petroleum reserves were located—more than enough to ensure operational independence for the German Panzers. Hitler conceived the assault in two stages: first, an attack eastward, annihilating the Soviet armies in the bend of the Don River; then, a push on Stalingrad on the Volga to prepare the way for the principal onslaught southward into the Caucasus. "The capture of Stalingrad," explained Field-Marshal Paul von Kleist, "was subsidiary to the main aim. It was only of importance as a convenient place in the bottleneck between the Don and the Volga, where we could block an attack on our flank by Russian forces coming from the east."[14] Initially, Stalingrad was no more than a name on a map.

The campaign began on 28 June 1942. It did not proceed according to plan, but at first this did not seem to matter. By August, German advance units had captured the oil fields at Maikop in the foothills of the western Caucasus Mountains. Two weeks later, they reached the Volga, just above Stalingrad, and had achieved most of their objectives. But Stalingrad had begun to exert a strange fascination on Hitler, and he ordered Sixth Army commander, Friedrich von

German prisoners at Stalingrad shuffle past the skeletons of ruined buildings, February 1943. Most of these men will not survive captivity. They are part of the remnants of the Sixth Army, which defended an encircled city for two-and-a-half months.

Paulus, to capture it. The Panzers closed in and, after a three-day Luftwaffe bombardment, were on the city's outskirts. Scored by hills and deep gullies, Stalingrad stretched twelve miles along the western bank of the Volga. Founded as Tsaritsyn at the end of the sixteenth century to protect the Don basin, it had remained a rather neglected district capital until 1925 when Stalin renamed it after himself to commemorate the role he purportedly played in the city's defense during the Civil War. Under his patronage, this Communist showpiece developed into a reinforced-concrete factory town with the largest heavy tractor plant in the Soviet Union; its population quadrupled.

Stalin also took a personal interest in the battle; he wanted "to regulate everything from Moscow" and carried centralized control to such an extreme that "he hamstrung his commanders and commissars at the front."[15] He refused to allow Stalingrad's civilians to flee because he believed Soviet soldiers would fight harder for a live city than a dead one. Soviet propaganda extolled Stalin's leadership and issued a host of official slogans: "Not one step back," "Fight to the death," and "Don't give up Stalingrad." In the famous "Oath of the Defenders of Stalingrad," the soldiers swore to fight to the end: "Under [Stalin's] leadership we shall win the great Battle of Stalingrad."[16]

In this struggle, success was measured by the number of buildings captured, not by thousands of square kilometers. Blitzkrieg expertise counted for little. After two months of bitter street fighting, the Germans captured most of the city, but they could not dislodge the 40,000 Soviet troops dug into the bluffs along the Volga. The main Soviet army, stationed on the other side of the river, ferried across reinforcements at night to replace the daily losses. The Soviet Supreme Command planned a counterstroke outside the city, a huge double envelopment north and south of the city against the German supply lines, which were protected mainly by Italians, Hungarians, and Romanians. These forces were incapable of matching the Soviets in either equipment or spirit. The counterattack began on 19 November 1942 with a strike from the north against the Romanian Third Army; then, on the next day came an attack from the south. Within four days, the pincers had cut through the Romanians and linked at Kalach, forty miles due west of Stalingrad. Kurt Zeitzler, the newly appointed chief of the German General Staff, advised that the Sixth Army should immediately attack westward before the Soviet army could consolidate its position.

Hitler refused. He was determined to stay on the Volga. "We must show firmness of character in misfortune," he said. "We must remember Frederick the Great."[17] He grandiloquently dubbed the city "Fortress Stalingrad" and planned to supply the beleaguered garrison by air pending the arrival of a relief force. Hermann Göring promised to fly in 500 tons of material a day, but the Luftwaffe managed to drop only 100 tons of supplies daily. In December 1942, an attempt to break the Soviet stranglehold failed thirty miles southwest of the city. At the end of the month, the supply of bread to the troops of the Stalingrad garrison dropped to slightly less than two ounces a day. Soldiers ate horses that had been frozen in the snow. On 8 January 1943, the Soviets called upon the Germans to surrender. They promised that soldiers could keep their uniforms and decorations and that high-ranking officers could keep their swords. Paulus asked the Führer to give him freedom of action, but Hitler ordered the army to "fight to the last man."[18] By 24 January, Paulus, who no longer had effective command of his troops, again requested permission to capitulate. Hitler again said no. On 31 January 1943, he promoted Paulus to field-marshal, knowing that no German officer of that rank had ever been taken alive. Paulus chose surrender to suicide, capitulating on the very day of his promotion. As it happened, 31 January was also the tenth anniversary of Hitler's appointment as chancellor.

The Battle of Stalingrad was costly for both sides. Between 19 November and 2 February, the Soviets lost a total of 32 divisions and 3 brigades, and another 16 divisions suffered casualties of 25 to 50 percent. The Germans paid an even higher price. In the whole Volga-Don-Stalingrad area, they lost as many as 1.5 million men. The Soviets took 90,000 soldiers of the Sixth Army prisoner, including a score of generals and 2,000 officers. Only 6,000 of those who surrendered at Stalingrad ever returned home. "History will pay the tribute due to those soldiers who thought only of their duty and who accomplished it to the last," wrote Zeitzler. The verdict of German novelist Theodor Plievier was more brutal: "Where fearless speech before thrones was the need of the hour, there had sounded the single heel-click of four-and-twenty generals; where the fury of hordes of soldiers should have battered down the walls of the general's quarters, there was nothing but bodily and spiritual decay and apathy and dying without even a curse on the lips."[19]

Josef Goebbels said the news of the heroic sacrifice at Stalingrad should be announced in sentences "as if engraved in bronze," written to "stir people's hearts for centuries to come"; the announcement would rank "with Caesar's addresses to his troops, Frederick the Great's appeal to his generals before the Battle of Leuthen, and Napoleon's appeals to his guards."[20] Although Goebbels insisted the event be "exploited psychologically for the strengthening of our people," no amount of skill with words could conceal the catastrophe. Hitler blamed Paulus and the other captured generals for the disaster and swore he would court-martial them all after the war. From his eastern headquarters at Rastenburg, where he now spent most of his time planning new offensives, he immediately decreed the creation of a new Sixth Army.

The battle marked the first major defeat of the vaunted Wehrmacht. The famous Sixth Army, the force that two and a half years before had marched triumphantly through the streets of Berlin after its victories in France, had now disappeared. There would be no more celebrations. Hitler, in his determination to hold on to Fortress Stalingrad, had not only sealed the fate of the Sixth Army, but had contributed to the eventual collapse of his whole Soviet front. Yet, had he not rejected the advice of his commanders to withdraw the German forces from the city to form a new defensive line further west, the disaster might have been even worse. The Soviets in Operation Saturn had planned to envelop the entire German Southern Front, beginning with an attack across the Don River west of Stalingrad and reaching all the way to the Black Sea. The tenacious German defense of Stalingrad tied up Soviet troops and unknowingly prevented the Soviets from carrying out this larger scheme that might have brought an earlier end to the war.

The Differing War Aims

The Second Front Controversy. Churchill tried to play to the Wilsonianism of Roosevelt while addressing the special concerns of Stalin. He feared that failure to satisfy Stalin on aims fundamental to Soviet security might prompt the Soviet dictator to make another arrangement with Hitler. Churchill wanted to reach an agreement while the Soviet Union was still heavily dependent on outside aid. Later, when the war was as good as won, Stalin would have the power to do what he pleased without considering Western desires. Churchill was willing to recognize the Soviet incorporation of the Baltic states, but he hesitated to do so without the consent of Washington. The Anglo-Russian treaty of alliance, signed in London on 26 May 1942, contained only vague promises "to preserve peace and resist aggression" and "to agree to work together in close and friendly collaboration after the reestablishment of peace for the organization of security and economic prosperity in Europe."[21] As long as the Soviet armies were on the defensive, Stalin appeared conciliatory. He saw no reason to provoke the West before he was ready to establish Soviet control over Eastern Europe. He wanted the Americans and British to invade France to draw "at least forty German divisions from the U.S.S.R."[22]

Roosevelt told Stalin that he hoped and expected to open a second front by the end of 1942. The American president wanted Stalin's cooperation in reorganizing postwar international relations. He believed that the balance of power system was no longer workable and should be replaced by a new international peacekeeping organization. Specifically, he wanted a new United Nations instead of a re-created League of Nations. In this world body, the major powers would "act as the policeman of the world."[23] They would disarm all other states and submit them to inspection. "If any nation menaced the peace, it would be blockaded and then if still recalcitrant, bombed," Roosevelt proposed candidly.[24]

The president also suspected Churchill might try to use the war to shore up the British Empire. Churchill knew that a cross-channel invasion was currently impractical. He first wanted to secure the Mediterranean to protect the oil of the Middle East and to prepare the way for an assault along Europe's southern flank. In 1942, the British did not have sufficient sea transportation to ferry the troops in North Africa back to Britain even had they desired to do so. Fearing that the Americans might send the bulk of their forces against Japan, Churchill wanted to commit the United States to an immediate operation against Germany. His answer to Stalin's request for a second front was Operation Torch, the invasion of Algeria and Morocco. That currently more British divisions than American were fighting the enemy added weight to his arguments, and Roosevelt agreed to attack in North Africa, thereby postponing the prospect of a cross-channel invasion of Europe. Churchill broke the news to Stalin when they met in Moscow in August 1942. Churchill later remembered, "I pondered on my mission to this sullen, sinister Bolshevik State that I had once tried so hard to strangle at its birth, and which, until Hitler appeared, I had regarded as the mortal foe of civilized freedom." Churchill reflected that telling Stalin there would be no second front that year would be "like carrying a lump of ice to the North Pole."[25] Stalin took the news badly. He accused the British of being afraid of the Germans: "Troops must be bloodied in battle. If you did not blood your troops you had no idea what their value was."[26]

Stalin was not convinced by Churchill's argument about securing Europe's southern flank. He feared the political implications of the Mediterranean strategy. An Anglo-American attack in the Balkans—a strike against Europe's soft under-belly according to Churchill—could bring the Western armies into direct contact with the Red Army. Stalin regarded the Balkans as a Soviet security zone. He also suspected that the British and Americans were delaying the invasion of France to let the Soviet army continue to bear the brunt of the German onslaught. For this reason he refused to make any commitment for close military cooperation and even rejected Churchill's offer to send British and American fighter squadrons to the Caucasus. Stalin thought the latter proposal was an attempt to occupy part of the Soviet Union. "At the most crucial phase of the fighting on the Soviet-German front," wrote Marshal Andrei Grechko echoing the official Stalinist line, "the Allies, being more concerned with weakening the Soviet Union than genu-inely assisting it, were conniving behind the back of the Soviet Government."[27] Stalin also refused to participate in the top-level discussions between Roosevelt and Churchill that were scheduled to take place the beginning of the following year in Morocco.

Grand Strategy and High Politics at Casablanca. Churchill had become accus-tomed to Soviet suspicions. He viewed the Anglo-American partnership as the cornerstone of the wartime alliance and was not terribly disappointed by Stalin's refusal to come to Casablanca. The talks opened on 12 January 1943 at the Anfa Hotel. (By coincidence the Warner Brothers' film classic *Casablanca* with Humphrey Bogart and Ingrid Bergman was released shortly before the meeting; "Rick's Place" became the code name for Roosevelt's headquarters.) Churchill proposed Sicily as the next target, that is, following the surrender of the Axis in North Africa. This invasion would set up the defeat of Italy and prepare for Allied penetration into Eastern Europe, possibly with an attack in the Upper Adriatic across into the Danube River valley. He did not want the cross-channel invasion to begin before 1944. Meanwhile, the air war against German cities would inten-sify, "with its inevitable results on German morale, and on industrial capacity and its effects in producing heavy casualties in her population and great misery by the destruction of their dwellings."[28]

Churchill got his way—the last time his views on strategy prevailed.[29] The most difficult problems at Casablanca were not military, however. Churchill was thinking of the political reconstruction of France, and he wanted to create a united French resistance government that would include all anti-German French forces.[30] This meant fusing the French Imperial Council, headed by General Henri Giraud, with the Free French movement of Charles de Gaulle. Giraud had become famous when he escaped from a German prison in April 1942 after two years' imprisonment. De Gaulle had already tried to persuade Giraud to form a common front to fight for the liberation of France, but did not want such a union to occur at the behest of the British and Americans. De Gaulle correctly suspected that the Allies, particularly the Americans, were trying to maneuver him into taking orders from Giraud.

In November 1942, following the invasion of Morocco and Algeria, the Allies had convinced Admiral Jean-François Darlan to change sides and ally with them against the Germans. Darlan could give orders to Vichy's proconsuls. When he was assassinated in December, the Allies began pinning their hopes on Giraud, who had earned a great reputation among conservative army officers. The Allies had managed to smuggle him out of France and hoped to groom him for a major role in the liberation of his country. In fact, Roosevelt viewed Giraud as a prime candidate for undoing the influence of de Gaulle. De Gaulle, who had been given no prior information about Operation Torch, was understandably suspicious of the Allied invitation to come to the Casablanca Conference. "If I must go to the Anfa [Casablanca] Conference to enter a race wearing the British colors while the Americans backed their own entry against me," he wrote, "the resulting comedy would be indecent, not to mention dangerous."[31] He refused to leave London.

Churchill knew de Gaulle would prove difficult. The prime minister had once quipped that he had many crosses to bear, but the heaviest was the Cross of Lorraine (the symbol of de Gaulle's movement). Yet Churchill could not hide his admiration of such an effective leader: "Here he was—a refugee, an exile from his country under sentence of death, in a position entirely dependent upon the good will of the British Government, and also now of the United States. Germans had conquered his country. He had no real foothold anywhere. Never mind; he defied all."[32] Roosevelt was not so generous. "Why doesn't De Gaulle go to war?" he asked Churchill. "Why doesn't he start North by West half West from Brazenville [sic]? It would take him a long time to get to the Oasis of Somewhere."[33] Nevertheless, Roosevelt was willing to give Churchill's proposition a chance and insisted that de Gaulle leave his London headquarters and join the discussions at Casablanca. Roosevelt did not know much about the politics of the French resistance, however:

> We delivered our bridegroom, General Giraud, who was most cooperative on the impending marriage, and I am sure was ready to go through with it on our terms. However, our friends could not produce the bride, the temperamental lady de Gaulle. She has got quite snooty about the whole idea and does not want to see either of us, and is showing no intention of getting into bed with Giraud.[34]

Only when Churchill threatened not to recognize de Gaulle as head of the Free French if he refused to come to Casablanca did de Gaulle reluctantly give in. Nevertheless, he never doubted that he, not Giraud, represented the general will of the French people. He had organized the resistance groups into a nationwide federation under his French National Committee (*Comité national français*), which he had established in 1941. Now this organization would provide the basis for the restoration of French greatness. At Casablanca he was willing to acknowledge that he and Giraud had reached an understanding on "unity of purpose and objective which augurs well for the future course of the common effort of the war."[35] However, this agreement did not mean that de Gaulle and Giraud were now co-leaders of the French National Committee. In fact, de Gaulle had rejected every Allied attempt to induce him to share political leadership.

Roosevelt seemed to assume otherwise. Eager to display the new spirit of co-operation between de Gaulle and Giraud, the president suggested that the two men be photographed shaking hands. When some photographers missed the scene the first time around, Roosevelt insisted the two generals do it again. De Gaulle hated it, but he need not have worried that the gesture would threaten his position. Giraud proved to be a better escapee than a politician. Within six months, de Gaulle had outmaneuvered him and become the undisputed head of the newly created French Committee of National Liberation (*Comité français de la libération nationale*). He soon styled himself "President of the French Government," leaving no doubt that he would determine his country's future destiny.[36]

Unconditional Surrender. At 12:15 on 24 January 1943, about a quarter of an hour after the de Gaulle–Giraud handshaking ceremony, Roosevelt and Churchill held a press conference for about fifty Allied journalists. Roosevelt, referring frequently to several sheets of notes that rested on his knees, began with a general discussion of the purpose of the Casablanca Conference, emphasizing that the Allies were resolved to maintain the initiative against the Axis. Then, almost in an aside, he said:

> We had a General called U. S. Grant. His name was Ulysses Simpson Grant, but in my, and the Prime Minister's, early days he was called "Unconditional Surrender" Grant. The elimination of German, Japanese and Italian war power means the unconditional surrender by Germany, Italy and Japan. That means a reasonable assurance of future world peace. It does not mean the destruction of the population of Germany, Italy, or Japan, but it does mean the destruction of the philosophies in those countries which are based on conquest and the subjugation of peoples.[37]

"Unconditional surrender" had been a frequent topic of conversation the previous week, and Churchill had helped write the notes on which Roosevelt's public statement was based. Nevertheless, the concept did not play as large a role in Churchill's thinking as it did in Roosevelt's; the president's Advisory Committee on Post-War Foreign Policy had first discussed it the previous May.

"Unconditional surrender" soon became the most popular slogan of the war. Although critics charged that it was responsible for needlessly prolonging the conflict, Roosevelt resisted all attempts to modify it, believing it was essential for the political reformation of Germany and was needed to prevent the growth of another stab-in-the-back legend. When he first uttered the words publicly, however, his chief concern was probably to allay Stalin's suspicions that the Western Allies might negotiate a separate peace with the Nazi regime; he also wanted to strike a new moral tone to silence recent criticism over his dealings with Vichy's leaders. Berlin viewed the doctrine as a sign of Allied disunity; Goebbels believed Roosevelt had to call for unconditional surrender in order to silence arguments in favor of an agreement with Germany. Hitler thought it of little consequence. In a proclamation of 30 January 1943, he said, "in this war there will be neither victors nor vanquished, but only survivors and annihilated." The Führer proclaimed that the Nazi war aim was the preservation of "the Germanic state of the German nation, as the eternal and equal home of all men and women of our nation—the National Socialist Greater Reich."[38]

In practice, the policy proved to be more flexible than it first seemed. Both the Italians and Japanese capitulated with conditions. Had the attempt on Hitler's life in 1944 succeeded, the circumstances of Germany's surrender might also have been different. Certainly, the Allies had no intention of negotiating as long as the Nazis remained in power, a fact that hardly needed the proclamation of a policy of unconditional surrender. The elimination of Hitler and the purging of Nazism from Germany had clearly become Allied war aims and were viewed as essential for the security of Europe after the war.

The most serious consequence of Roosevelt's pronouncement was its effect on Roosevelt himself. He apparently believed it was a war aim instead of a mere slogan and, as a result, postponed important political decisions until the end of the conflict. This was a fatal mistake. By its very nature, the war fought against the Nazis would lead inevitably to an eclipse of German power and would involve the occupying nations in a whole series of complicated arrangements and conflicts of interest. The American president's inability to foresee this and make adequate preparations was one of the great omissions of his wartime leadership.

Tightening the Noose, 1943

The Red Army Strikes West. After their victory at Stalingrad, the Soviets began a counteroffensive that pushed the Germans back to the battle lines of the previous summer. Within six weeks, they had liberated the Don River basin and reached the Dnieper River at Dnepropetrovsk. The effort left them badly overextended. The Germans forced them back across the Donets River with the greatest weight of armor yet committed to a battle, recapturing Kharkov, which they had lost the previous February. In the north, the Soviets partially lifted the siege of Leningrad. At the end of March, however, the fighting slowed down, beginning a three-month lull in which both sides regrouped their forces.

The Germans slowly marshaled an army of fifty divisions, one-third of them armored, totaling 900,000 men. Their objective was to reduce the huge salient that bulged around the city of Kursk between Kharkov and Orël. Hitler had decided that Operation Citadel should be the only major offensive of 1943. The German attack began on 5 July with a great pincers movement: the Ninth Army attacked the salient from Orël in the north; the Fourth Panzer Army advanced from Belgorod in the south.

The well-prepared Soviets had anticipated the move and, within five days, had brought the German offensive to a halt. The Germans desperately threw in the rest of their available armor and, on 12 July, squared off with the Soviets in the greatest tank battle of the war. The struggle involved 1,500 machines from both sides. The German crews were exhausted, and many of their tanks were in need of repairs; meanwhile the Soviet forces were fresh and their equipment undamaged. After eight hours of murderous fighting, the Soviets mastered the field. They had destroyed over half of the German armor before Hitler called off the attack. The initiative on the Eastern Front now passed to the Soviets. At Moscow, they had halted the Germans at the end of their offensive. At Stalingrad, they had smashed them during the height of the offensive. At Kursk, they stopped the offensive as soon as it had begun. The Soviets were now free to choose where to strike. By the spring of 1944, they had liberated most of the Ukraine.

The Collapse of Italy. On 10 July 1943, British and American troops landed on the southern coast of Sicily. The invasion came exactly two months after the final surrender of the Axis troops in Tunisia—a victory that had resulted in the capture of 300,000 battle-tested German troops. The Allies now had air and sea control of the Mediterranean.

Hitler attempted to strengthen the Italians' resolve. On 19 July, he conferred with Mussolini in a country house near Feltre, a village in the Dolomites between Venice and the Brenner Pass. Hitler did most of the talking, but avoided discussing the main purpose for his visit: the organization of a unified military command. Instead, he gave a lecture on raw materials and manpower. He promised "that a number of additional German formations would be sent to [Sicily] which would enable us ultimately to take the offensive."[39] The announcement came as a complete surprise to his own operations staff. Hitler left the meeting convinced that he had stiffened Mussolini's backbone and solidified the alliance. When Mussolini returned to Rome, however, he told the king that he hoped to dissolve the Axis by the middle of September. Mussolini's behavior at Feltre convinced many of his associates, including his generals, that he was incapable of leadership. On 24 July in a ten-hour session at the Palazzo Venezia, the Fascist Grand Council voted 19 to 7 to end Mussolini's personal dictatorship and give effective command of the armed forces to King Victor Emmanuel III. The next day, after an audience with the king, Mussolini was taken into custody. The Sicilian offensive was then in its fifteenth day; more than half of the island was now in Allied hands. The invasion of the mainland was only a matter of time.

Marshal Pietro Badoglio, the head of the new Italian government, wanted to end the war as quickly as possible. Nevertheless, he continued to assure Hitler that Italy would remain "loyal to its pledged word in defense of its military tradition" and would continue the war on Germany's side. Hitler knew he was lying: "We'll get everything ready to lay hands on . . . the whole crew," he said. "And then you watch them creep and crawl and in two or three days there'll be another *coup*."[40] Badoglio was indeed not to be trusted. He planned to surrender "unconditionally" to the Allies, provided Italy could join "in fighting the Germans."[41]

On 31 August, the Allies presented their terms to the Italian emissaries at an army camp near Palermo, Sicily. They demanded that Italy agree to the complete and indefinite Allied control of Italy and allow the Allies to occupy any territory they wished. The Allied authorities would control the administration, the judiciary, and the public services. They would regulate the currency, control foreign exchange, supervise foreign commercial transactions, and regulate trade and production.[42] The harsh peace did not seem to bother the Italian officials. "Are you strong enough to protect us from the Germans?" they asked. They insisted they would "not sign any agreement unless the Allies would guarantee to land some troops north of Rome."[43] The Allies, suspecting a stall, threatened to bomb Rome unless their terms were immediately accepted. The Italians signed the surrender document on 3 September 1943. On that day, the British Eighth Army crossed the straits of Messina to begin the invasion of the Italian mainland.

As soon as Hitler learned of the capitulation, he ordered the Italian army disarmed and Rome occupied. Field-Marshal Albert Kesselring, commander of the German armies in southern Italy, expected stiff opposition from the Italians and doubted he had enough troops to capture the capital. However, he soon discovered that the Italian army had virtually disintegrated, and the Germans took Rome with little resistance. Kesselring prepared the Gustav Line to halt the Allied advance southeast of Rome along the Garigliano River; he hoped to hold out until the new year if possible.[44]

Meanwhile, on 13 September, a group of German commandos landed gliders on the Gran Sasso in the Abruzzi Mountains and freed Mussolini from the mountaintop hotel where he had been held prisoner. They took the Duce to Rome. From there on Hitler's orders he was taken to Vienna and then to Rastenburg

where the Führer insisted that Mussolini again become head of an Italian government. Mussolini reluctantly accepted. His first official act as head of the Italian
Social Republic was to abolish the monarchy for failing to do its duty. "As for
traditions," the Duce claimed, "Italy has more republican traditions than it has
monarchical ones."[45] The new regime established its headquarters near Salò on
Lake Garda. Mussolini ruled at the pleasure of his German saviors who kept him
a virtual prisoner. The SS controlled all his communications and prevented his
return to Rome. The Duce likened his situation to the exile of Napoleon on the
island of Elba. The Germans also ran affairs elsewhere in Italy to suit themselves.
They arrested whomever they pleased, confiscated vital equipment and supplies,
and rounded up Italian men for work in the Fatherland. At Hitler's urging,
Mussolini ceded to Germany Trieste, Istria, and the South Tyrol, Italy's acquisitions from World War I. In November, a Fascist party congress in Verona ordered
the arrest and trial of all who had voted against Mussolini at the Fascist Grand
Council meeting the previous July. Those who were caught were executed.[46]

On 13 October 1943, the other Italian government, the "Kingdom of the
South," declared war on Germany. Marshal Badoglio now considered himself a co-
belligerent with the British and Americans in the war against Germany.[47] General
P. A. Mason MacFarlane, head of the Allied mission to the new government,
thought Badoglio was a second-rate "has-been." MacFarlane did not see how the
Italians could contribute anything to the Allied war effort. "The bloody bastards
tried for years to do us in, and now look at them," he muttered.[48] The Badoglio
government was hardly democratic. It banned the Fascist party, but prohibited all
other objectionable groups as well. The Allies, however, insisted on the restoration
of democracy.

The fighting continued, sparing the Italian people none of the horrors of war.
The Allies failed to capture Rome by the winter of 1943 as they had intended.
Instead they butted their heads against the German positions along the Gustav
Line. At Monte Cassino they encountered one of the strongest natural obstacles
in Italy. In January 1944, they tried to outflank the German positions with an
amphibious assault on the beaches at Anzio. Not until the following May was the
invasion force able to break out of its beachhead. Hitler tried desperately to hold
on to Italy as long as possible and kept more German troops there in proportion
to the Allied forces than in any other theater of operations.[49]

THE CIVILIANS AT WAR

Home Fronts

Nazi Forced Labor. Hitler was so completely absorbed in military affairs that he
had little time to run the rest of the country. Direct supervision of domestic affairs
passed into the hands of Martin Bormann, the shadowy "secretary to the Führer,"
who was obsessed with increasing his own power and prevented practically everybody from seeing Hitler. Consequently, the government ministries were increasingly left on their own; the bureaucrats had little incentive to consult each other
and defied outside efforts to coordinate their activities. Albert Speer, the "chief
representative for armament" and the only civilian minister who still had direct
access to the Führer, had his hands full trying to get their cooperation. Speer
found labor channeled to the wrong ends, inadequately organized, and inefficiently
used. A million workers were needed. Many factories operated only one shift. Speer

proposed consolidating production to get maximum use from equipment. He wanted to close down nonessential industries and, above all, to bring more women into the labor force.

Hitler had placed so much faith in Blitzkrieg that he had not believed total wartime mobilization would be needed. The Four-Year Plan, launched in 1936 to make Germany economically self-sufficient, was supposed to provide central direction for the economy, maintain an adequate supply of labor, and increase the output of armaments. The plan was only partially successful. In September 1942, Hitler put Speer in charge of armaments. The selection of his court architect was another example of Hitler's preference for the talented amateur over the expert, but this time he proved to have made a wise choice. Speer received no job description—Hitler still preferred to handle things as they came along—and constantly had to seek the Führer's support against all sorts of vested interests. Göring, Speer's nominal superior, fought his efforts to bring more German women into the labor force. Göring believed that women belonged in the home, bearing and caring for the children of the Fatherland. Speer not only got his way on this issue, but also received Hitler's permission to import 400,000 to 500,000 women from the eastern territories to help out in German households. Speer also accelerated the import of slave labor and foreign labor, a practice that had already begun with the conquest of Poland.

The Germans would seal off whole villages or districts of towns and cart off every able-bodied person to work in German factories. There they would be stuffed into overcrowded camps, often without proper sanitation or adequate food rations. A labor mobilization directive of 20 April 1942 required that the foreign workers be "fed, sheltered and treated in such a way as to exploit them to the highest possible extent at the lowest conceivable degree of expenditure."[50] Forty percent of these laborers worked directly in the manufacture of armaments and munitions; the rest worked in construction, mining, agriculture, and transportation. Try as he might, Speer never seemed to have enough workers. He insisted that political prisoners be put to work in the armaments industry and made lavish use of prisoners of war, mostly French and Soviets captured in the battles of 1940 and 1941. He also persuaded Hitler to change his mind about allowing the SS divisions in Russia to take no prisoners; instead all prisoners of war were to be spared and transferred to armaments production.[51] Under an arrangement between Speer and Heinrich Himmler, escaped prisoners of war who were caught by the SS were treated as convicts and sent to the factories. At the end of 1944, over 8 million foreign civilians were working in the Third Reich. Although some had come willingly, persuaded by promises of high pay, most had been coerced.

Procurement and transportation were the job of Fritz Sauckel, who since March 1942 had been the plenipotentiary general for the allocation of labor. After the Poles, Soviet civilians and Red Army prisoners of war were the first important source. Beginning in January 1943, however, the Germans actively conscripted young French workers as part of a new policy calling for the total mobilization of European labor. The new program began with a draft of all German males between the ages of fifteen and sixty-five and all females between the ages of seventeen and forty-five. On 16 February, the Vichy government of Pierre Laval established a similar draft for men, requiring them to work for two years in Germany. Recruiters called on French workers to save Europe from Bolshevism and promised them financial benefits. "An end to hard times. Papa earns money in Germany," one poster said.[52] Through such means, but mostly by force, the Reich obtained about 400,000 French workers during the first six months. But the supply was not steady: workers failed to report for service; many of those who refused joined the resistance. Thus, even in France, Sauckel was deprived of French labor. He plumbed other sources, however, increasing the supply of workers from Poland and, with the installation of the Salò Republic, from Italy.

When they arrived in Germany, foreign workers were grouped and treated according to their national origins. Workers from Eastern European countries were forced to wear special badges that proclaimed their racial inferiority. They paid a special tax and received few social security benefits. Prohibited from living in private houses, most were housed in temporary insalubrious labor camps near the factories; the food rations were poor and the medical attention practically nonexistent. Conditions were so bad that Speer tried to improve them; he had found that undernourished workers were less productive than better-fed workers. Even in death, the Eastern European workers received different treatment: they were buried in mass graves in special cemeteries. Conditions for the workers from Western European countries were somewhat better, but were still too poor to encourage productivity. The French, whom the Germans preferred to the Russians because they were more highly skilled, nevertheless had a reputation for doing shoddy work and sometimes even resorted to sabotage. The Dutch were considered to be the best; the Italians the worst.

Foreign workers made up 20 percent of the Reich's labor force and, despite their generally low productivity, did play an important role in the German war effort. After the defeat, Speer admitted that he had objected to the policy of bringing forced labor to Germany only "when the transport of foreign workers did great damage to me as far as the production in the occupied countries [was] concerned." When asked how such a practice could be justified on moral and legal grounds, he replied, "I cannot remember that, but I will think about it."[53] Still, he managed to make a favorable enough impression on his judges at the Nuremberg War Crimes Trial to be spared from execution.

The German People at War. The euphoria of seemingly easy victory and the apparently unlimited supply of foreign labor delayed the German people's total commitment to the war effort. Nazi propaganda continued to tout victory long after any such hope was gone. Speer complained that people's confidence in victory and their faith in Hitler's genius constantly hindered his efforts at economic mobilization. He wanted to follow in the footsteps of Walther Rathenau by increasing production through the exchange of technical expertise, a division of labor from plant to plant, and the promotion of greater standardization.[54] Speer called his version "industrial self-responsibility." He established special supervisory committees to allocate resources, regulate the production of all types of armament, and develop new weapons. With the cooperation of thousands of technicians, he succeeded in boosting armament production by almost 60 percent within six months of his appointment. After two and a half years, he had increased it over three times. Speer also received help from another quarter.

On 18 February 1943, two weeks after the fall of Stalingrad, Propaganda Minister Goebbels addressed a handpicked crowd of bureaucrats, party stalwarts, and members of the armed and professional services in Berlin's Sports Palace. In a performance that lasted over two hours, Goebbels gave one of the most remarkable speeches of his career. He declared that total war was the demand of the hour: "We must wage this war, which is a war for the survival of our nation, with the whole life of the nation." He said that Germany was facing a giant danger and that the country's effort to oppose that danger must be just as gigantic, that Germany's mission was to save European civilization from Bolshevism.[55] While assuring the members of his audience that this sacrifice would not permanently change Germany's social structure, he asked them if they were prepared to work sixteen hours a day. Would they encourage German women to commit themselves totally to the war? Would they approve of radical measures—even capital punishment—against all shirkers, defeatists, and racketeers no matter how high their station? The members of the audience roared their assent to each question. Then, Goebbels brought them to their feet with his frenzied delivery of the famous words from the war of liberation against Napoleon: "Now folk arise and storm break loose!" The propaganda minister intended not only to bolster popular morale and rekindle faith in the inevitability of victory, but also to target Nazi leaders who had not responded to the demands of the total war economy.

Hitler had always feared the effect that a general program of austerity might have on public opinion. When Speer slashed the production of consumer goods by 12 percent during 1942, the Führer protested that the cuts were too large. Hitler believed morale could be maintained by concessions, not sacrifice, and by setting a proper example. He himself loved frugality and dressed simply. He liked to invite photographers to the chancellery to show that on occasion he would eat a one-pot meal. Less publicized, however, were the activities of the 28,000 workers who were making additions to his various residences. In 1944, more concrete was used on the vast Führerbunker at Bad Charlottenbrunn than was allocated for the construction of air-raid shelters for Berlin's entire civilian population. Nor did the Nazi oligarchs commit themselves to total war. They were constantly obtaining special exceptions to allow them to complete one or another of their pet projects: the refurbishing of a castle, the building of a party forum, or the remodeling of another headquarters building. These party leaders were so committed to their sybaritic life-styles that even in the most critical periods of the war, they maintained their "big houses, hunting lodges, estates and palaces, many servants, a rich table, and a select wine cellar."[56] Goebbels became highly unpopular when he used his authority as gauleiter of Berlin to close the Ruhleben race course and dismantle it to build storage huts. He suspended football championships, forbade horseback riding in the Grunewald and the Tiergarten, and started to close Berlin's luxurious restaurants, including Horcher's, the capital's most famous gourmet establishment and a favorite eatery of Reichsmarshal Göring. When Göring ordered the restaurant to remain open, Goebbels had a special squad of SA toughs smash its windows. The tiff was resolved through compromise: Horcher's was closed to the public, but reopened as a private Luftwaffe club.

The war profoundly changed the life-style of the not-so-privileged, however. Speer insisted that all Germans who worked less than forty-eight hours a week be required to register for war work and that all women under the age of fifty be liable for conscription. The draft age for military service dropped to sixteen. In key industries, people worked ten hours a day, six days a week. Like a doctor working hard to prolong the life of a terminally ill patient, Speer complained, "Whereas Churchill promised his people only blood, sweat, and tears, all we heard during the various phases and various crises of the war was Hitler's slogan: 'The final victory is certain.' "[57] Goebbels continued his efforts to awaken the people to the dangers of a Bolshevik victory—"one hardly dares to imagine what would happen to Germany and Europe if this Asiatic-Jewish flood were to inundate our country and our continent."[58]

Meanwhile Allied bombers were reducing German cities to rubble. About 400,000 German civilians died in these attacks. Countless more were left homeless.

As the end drew near, the Nazis increased their terror against the people. Using the famous *Kuglerlass* or Bullet Decree, the police turned over dissidents to the Security Service for execution. The SS set up flying courts-martial, rounding up and executing those suspected of defeatism and desertion. Bodies swung from trees and twisted girders with placards pinned on their chests: "I hang here because I left my unit without permission," or "I betrayed the Führer." In Berlin, the SS went into subway stations, used as air-raid shelters against the Soviet shelling, and into cellars and dragged out and shot anyone they pleased.

The British Government Assumes Emergency Powers. The British mobilized reluctantly, but thoroughly. When war began, the only branch of the service that was prepared was the navy. At first, this seemed sufficient since the fighting was a long way off. Unlike 1914, the outbreak of war in 1939 saw no great rush to the colors. Conscription had been introduced in August, the first in a time of "peace." Those affected simply waited their turn. Parliament also passed an emergency powers bill, the equivalent of World War I's Defense of the Realm Act. Under its authority, the government closed down movie theaters and other places of entertainment, but within two weeks it allowed them to open again. More casualties came from motor accidents during the blackouts than from combat. Neville Chamberlain remained an appeaser at heart and hoped, even now, that Hitler would realize the error of his ways or fall victim to a coup. Nevertheless, the estimates were that the war could last as long as three years.

The government planned to have twenty divisions trained and equipped by the end of the first year and another thirty-five by the close of the second. The British expected great things from their blockade. Meanwhile the government encouraged the evacuation of all children from London. Adults moved out as well. By the end of September 1939, about 2.5 million people had changed residences. (Over the course of the entire war, 60 million people moved, more than the total population

Sleeping in the subway became a nightly routine for many Londoners. The station of Aldwych lay beneath the Strand, an area of central London hit particularly hard during the Blitz. Enduring such ordeals reinforced popular demand for a better society after the war.

of the British Isles. By 1945, bombs had destroyed or made inhabitable over half a million dwellings.) On 13 September, the government created six new ministries: War Production, Information, Food, Shipping, Economic Warfare, and Home Security. A campaign for the allocation of domestic food supplies began, but rationing was not formally adopted until 8 January 1940. "This is no time for ease and comfort," said Churchill in a speech at Manchester. "It's a time to dare and endure. That is why we are rationing ourselves, even while our resources are expanding. That is why we mean to regulate every ton that is carried across the sea and make sure that it is carried solely for the purpose of victory."[59] The British were not yet convinced of the necessity for such sacrifices, however; they felt more inconvenienced than patriotic.

The disaster at Dunkirk and the menace of the German U-boats shattered British complacency once and for all. They rapidly completed total mobilization for total war. By the time the Germans attacked France in May 1940, the government had assumed power over the country's entire economy, including the regulation of labor and the conditions of employment. Ernest Bevin, the minister of Labour and National Service, could compel factory owners to establish suitable welfare facilities and improve the status of the lower-paid workers. The government also began to prepare for the postwar society through the recently created Ministry of Reconstruction.

In June 1941, the Ministry of Reconstruction, under pressure from the Trade Union Congress, commissioned the Liberal leader Sir William Beveridge to head a special nonpartisan committee to survey British social services and make recommendations. The study took a year and a half to complete and received suggestions from the Labour Party Congress, which called for a comprehensive program of social security including a scheme of family allowances and a national health service. The long-awaited Beveridge Report, *Social Insurance and Allied Services,* which appeared on 1 December 1942, concentrated almost exclusively on Labour's demands. It contained a number of suggestions for improving the existent welfare system, but recommended the creation of a Ministry of Social Security to assume responsibility for social insurance and national assistance. The report proposed a considerable increase in welfare benefits and the extension of pensions to new classes of recipients, including housewives who would be covered by their husbands' contribution, suggestions that had been made in the past. Two major innovations were the extension of the social security system to all classes in society and the guarantee of a minimum level of subsistence. These were minimum demands; Beveridge saw his scheme as one aspect of a much larger welfare program that included "allowances for children up to the age of 15," "comprehensive health and rehabilitation services for prevention and cure of disease and restoration of capacity for work," and "the maintenance of mass employment."[60] Beveridge wanted his social insurance to be treated as part of a comprehensive policy of social progress, providing protection against society's Five Giant Evils: Want, Disease, Ignorance, Squalor, and Idleness. In less Victorian terminology, he wanted to guarantee each British subject proper health, proper education, proper housing, and a proper job.

The report was immediately elevated to the status of an Allied war aim. That the Atlantic Charter, which had appeared the previous August, contained only one small reference to social welfare made no difference. A majority of the British people supported the report enthusiastically. Churchill kept his hostility to himself. Indeed, the government even used the report to score propaganda points. The Ministry of Information, for example, referred to it in countering the claims of the

National Socialist and Communist regimes that they alone had managed to ensure the welfare of the masses. The report already had the endorsement of Labour, and it helped to convert many younger Conservatives to the concept of a welfare state. The British people now had a clearer idea of what they could expect from their modern industrialized society and the role government would play in ensuring their well-being. The Beveridge Report inspired a plethora of concrete government proposals about how its provisions should be implemented after the war.

The Great Patriotic War. After a six-month offensive, the Germans had overrun one-third of European Russia, an area containing two-thirds of Soviet industry. Initially, the Soviets did not put up a fierce resistance. The Great Purges had demoralized the country, and many Soviets saw German victory as a means of getting rid of Stalin and the Communist system. The Germans created the "Committee for the Liberation of the Peoples of Russia" to give expression to this sentiment; the committee was headed by General Andrei Vlasov, a captured defector who had previously distinguished himself in the defense of Kiev and Moscow. Even before Vlasov's betrayal, Stalin had realized that the Soviet people were not likely to fight to protect the Communist dialectic. At the anniversary celebration of the Bolshevik Revolution in November 1941, he had told the crowd on Red Square that the heroic figures of the country's past should be their inspiration: Aleksandr Nevsky, Dimitri Donskoi, Aleksandr Suvorov, and Mikhail Kutuzov. This appeal to traditional Russian nationalism made Marxist-Leninist purists squirm, but it had a tremendous effect on the morale of the people.[61]

The state also created its own contemporary heroes. It chose an eighteen-year-old Komsomol girl, Zoya Kosmodemianskaya, a member of the resistance who had been tortured and hanged by the Germans, to be a sort of latter-day Joan of Arc. A play written about her martyrdom included an important role for Stalin. In the final scene, this character announced the salvation of Moscow. The Soviet regime also mobilized artists, composers, and writers, the very intellectuals it had mauled during the Great Terror, and enjoined them to inspire new patriotism in the Soviet people. The response was overwhelming. The great Soviet novelist Ilya Ehrenburg turned to propaganda. On the eve of the battle of Stalingrad, he wrote a column for *Red Star*, the army newspaper:

> One can bear everything: the plague, and hunger and death. But one cannot bear the Germans. One cannot bear these fish-eyed oafs contemptuously snorting at everything Russian. . . . We cannot live as long as these grey-green slugs are alive. Today there are no books, today there are no stars in the sky, today there is only one thought: Kill the Germans. Kill them all and dig them into the earth. Then we can go to sleep. Then we can think again of life, and books, and girls, and happiness.[62]

Soviet composers were equally responsive. Dimitri Shostakovich began work on his great Seventh Symphony while in Leningrad. Evacuated to Kuybïshev, he completed the work in December 1941 and dedicated it to the besieged city. The symphony became a symbol of Soviet resistance against the German invaders. The war also gave impetus to Sergei Prokofiev's opera *War and Peace*. Originally conceived as an intimate work focusing on the personal drama of the main characters, it became an epic work centering on the sections of the Tolstoy novel that dealt with Napoleon's invasion. Prokofiev made the Russian people the opera's real hero "in their sufferings, wrath, courage, and victory over the invaders."[63] Prokofiev also wrote the film score for Sergei Eisenstein's film *Ivan the Terrible, Part I*. The movie, which premiered in 1945, took two years to complete. It praised Tsar Ivan IV who had unified Russia in the sixteenth century. That the portrayal of the monarch, a prototypical megalomaniac, was not altogether flattering showed to what extent the Stalinist regime had relaxed its ideological artistic standards or was, at least, less concerned about invidious comparisons.

The regime also made it easier for people to join the Communist party. During the war, its membership trebled from 2 to 6 million. At the same time, society became less mobile. The tremendous industrial expansion of the 1930s had created an open class system. Now the regime contributed to social stratification by becoming more exclusive in dispensing rewards and favors. It closed certain stores to all but favored members of society, established differential procedures for evacuating people from threatened areas, and granted certain military decorations, like the Order of Victory, only to high-ranking officers and civilians—state recognition was now as likely to result from a person's status as from service beyond the call of duty. Civilians had ranks, uniforms, titles, and insignia just like their military counterparts. The establishment of such a blatant hierarchy stratified society in a way unknown since the days of the tsars.[64] Furthermore, these benefits for the "upper classes" came at a time when the standard of living and the level of comfort were decreasing for most people. With the Nazis in control of the industrial heart of the country, the Soviet people had to work harder than before. They tirelessly transferred as many factories to the east as they could, carting away over 1,500 industrial enterprises during the first six months of the war. These plants were dismantled and reassembled in the Urals, Siberia, and Central Asiatic Republics. As many as 10 million people went with them. Workers arriving at eastern destinations frequently found no houses, fuel, electricity, or supplies. They lived in tents and worked out in the open.

During 1941, the Soviet gross national product fell by more than 50 percent. It recovered the next year, but only to prewar levels. All this was achieved through heroic effort. Officials had the power to order workers to work overtime, up to three hours a day. All holidays were abolished. Workers conscripted for war industries were assigned to the areas of the country where they were most needed and were not permitted to leave their jobs without permission. As labor was drained from the countryside, those who remained had to put forth a greater effort. Many of these were women and children who performed their tasks without machinery. Rationing created extra burdens. The local Soviets allocated fixed amounts of bread, sugar, barley, butter, meat, and soap. Shop windows tauntingly displayed cardboard pictures of hams, sausages, and cheese—items no longer available. Those who managed to get their hands on cigarettes could charge passersby two rubles a puff. Average consumption declined by 40 percent. Consumer goods as well as clothing were unavailable. People walked around in heavily patched dresses, suits, and coats. Almost every village had its used-clothes market.

Inside the besieged city of Leningrad, living conditions were infinitely worse than in other unoccupied areas of the Soviet Union. The Germans had invested the city from the south and the west; the Finns had reoccupied the land to the north that they had lost during the 1939 winter war.[65] Hitler intended to destroy Leningrad and all its inhabitants. By September 1941, his armies had cut all land routes into the city, and German artillery began to pound the city to rubble. The Luftwaffe joined in with aerial bombardments. The object was to break the will of the inhabitants and starve them into submission. The investiture lasted until January 1943. Provisions entered the city across Lake Ladoga by boat in the summer, by truck when the lake froze. This lifeline, within range of the German guns, was not adequate to keep the city supplied at its prewar level. The supply of rations fluctuated. The winters were especially hard. Often there was no fuel for apartments and offices. There was no electricity and little food. People did not have the energy to bury their dead. "You could enter almost any house and any apartment, walk through the frozen rooms and see the dead, lying on the floor, lying on the beds, or in chairs around the stove where the fire had long since died away."[66] People simply walked around the bodies that cluttered the streets and sidewalks. Leningrad's normal peacetime population fell by three-fourths. The siege killed a minimum of 1 million civilians and another 100,000 to 200,000 soldiers. About 1 million were evacuated. More people died in the siege of Leningrad than in any other city in any modern war.[67]

The Resistance

Set Europe Ablaze. The German attack came so fast and was so decisive that it stunned people into submission and resigned them to the New Order. At first there was little resistance. Keeping a job, supporting a family, maintaining the necessities of life were primary concerns. Until the Germans began to lose battles, protest was limited to small things. People might refuse to speak German or leave a room or a shop when a German came in. They might give a German soldier wrong directions or write provocative slogans on a wall. People listened to forbidden broadcasts, refused to report for work assignments, dispatched goods to the wrong addresses, and ignored regulations.

The Germans treated the people of Eastern Europe with great brutality. Any act of disobedience was punished by death. In Western Europe, however, the Germans tried to be nice, at least initially. They gave sweets to children, sponsored cultural exchanges, and held band concerts on Sunday afternoons, all the while impressing people with their invincibility. *"Deutschland Siegt Auf Allen Fronten"* (Germany conquers on all fronts) read a huge banner hung on the Eiffel Tower and on other Paris buildings and monuments. But even in the West, the rigors of German occupation soon became apparent: the identity cards, the curfews, the ration books, the elimination of private transport, the restrictions on travel, the censorship of mail, and, of course, the arrests and executions. People learned the meaning of the colors on German posters: yellow with black borders announced the death of spies, black and white borders the shooting of hostages, and red and black borders the execution of terrorists. Resistance became more serious and more dangerous. For every person engaged in anti-German activities, there were several willing informers. A French traitor denounced Jean Moulin, a resistance leader who had returned to France from England with orders from de Gaulle to unify the resistance. The Gestapo arrested Moulin in a suburb of Lyons and tortured him to death. Moulin had arrived in France in a British plane. In July 1940, the British had established the Special Operations Executive (SOE), to support and develop underground networks throughout occupied Europe. Churchill wanted to "set Europe ablaze." From its secret headquarters in London, the SOE helped train agents to gather information and commit sabotage and murder. In addition to Moulin, it transported Jan Kubis and Josef Gabcik back to Prague to assassinate Reinhart Heydrich, the protector of Bohemia. The secret agents threw a bomb at their quarry as he rode to work on the morning of 27 May 1942. The explosion blew the steel springs from the rear seat of Heydrich's Mercedes up into his body. The protector died in great agony eight days later.

The assassination prompted the SS to wage an all-out war against the Czech resistance. It singled out the village of Lidice for a special revenge. In a leisurely ten-hour massacre, the Germans shot all the men in the village over the age of sixteen, 172 in all. All the women were sent to the concentration camp at Ravensbrück. The children were dispersed to other camps; those with Nordic features were put up for adoption with German families. Lidice was then leveled. Soon this policy of punishing innocent civilians was applied throughout Europe, thereby removing any distinction between combatants and noncombatants. The Germans executed batches of hostages for every attack by the resistance. When the Americans entered the war, they established their own Office of Strategic Services (OSS), whose lavish operations rivaled those of the SOE.

In the movie *Casablanca,* the Germans want to arrest Victor Lazlo because he knows the names of all the European resistance leaders. In reality, of course, the resistance had no overall command. The resistance was an organization of sections and fragments, comprised of isolated cells. For obvious reasons, the names of many of its leaders were kept secret. Georges Bidault, Moulin's successor as head of the *Comité national de la résistance* (National Council of the Resistance or CNR), knew that too much centralization was incompatible with a secret and hunted existence. "When your liaison agents get arrested and your leaders move from house to house deliberately leaving no traces, each echelon must work independently and do what it thinks best, as well as jealously guard its freedom of action."[68]

Stalin exploited the Soviet resistance to rebuild his authority. He supported the partisan units operating behind German lines in the Soviet Union, mostly in the forests of White Russia where the German hold over the countryside was weakest. These forces eventually reached half a million men and women and, in the last days of the German retreat, controlled vast areas in western Russia. They performed a valuable service in liberating the country, but Stalin never really trusted them. After the war, he initiated a crackdown on their units to quash any possible opposition. Stalin also provided assistance to certain resistance movements in Eastern Europe, but his motives were less anti-German than pro-Soviet. He wanted to lay the groundwork for loyal postwar Communist regimes and therefore sponsored his own governments in exile. Eastern European resistance movements that were not under the Soviet thumb were treated with hostility. Thus, he failed to help the Polish Home Army during its uprising against the Germans in 1944.

The Polish Home Army in Warsaw, acting on instructions from the Polish government in exile in London, rose up in revolt on 1 August 1944. It was joined by some units of the Communist-led People's Army and an assortment of forces from other resistance groups. General Tadeusz Bor-Komorowski, the Home Army commander, realized the revolt could not succeed without Soviet help. Stalin, however, concentrated his attention on the Romanian front, leaving the Polish Home Army to fight on its own. Thus, the Germans had the field to themselves. SS units, comprised of turncoat Soviet prisoners, assorted Eastern European riffraff, and German convicts on probation, carried out the repression with great savagery. They burned prisoners alive with gasoline, impaled babies on bayonets, and hung women in rows from balconies.[69] In September, the Soviets made a half-hearted, unsuccessful attempt to penetrate the city with a force of Moscow Poles, but Stalin refused to allow American and British planes to use Soviet airfields to fly supplies to the insurgents. Bor-Komorowski finally had to surrender. Considering the circumstances, he received good terms from the local SS commander. General Erich von dem Bach-Zelewski, possibly thinking of how he might avoid war crimes charges after the war, promised to treat the defeated Polish soldiers as prisoners of

war. Hitler, however, ordered Warsaw to be leveled. In crushing the Warsaw rebellion, the Germans did the Soviets a favor, but the actions of both countries
were consistent with their previous policies. Both Stalin and Hitler wanted to
crush Polish independence. In 1939, they had partitioned the country. First Hitler
had taken it all; now it was Stalin's turn. His handling of the Warsaw uprising
was another sad chapter in the way powerful neighbors sought to handle the
"Polish Question."

With the retreat of the German armies, the resistance became more daring. Its
forces, now better armed, were ready to take the fight directly to the enemy. The
French resistance, for example, stationed 4,000 men under arms in the Vercors.
(The Vercors was an alpine plateau thirty miles long and ten miles wide between
Valence and Grenoble.) The threat posed by this army diverted German attention
and resources from the battlefields of Normandy and southern France, which the
Allies were planning to invade. The Germans attacked the redoubt on 19 July
1944 with two divisions of ground troops and airborne units of the SS. The Italians
also had a significant number of troops fighting behind the lines. At the end of
1944, 80,000 armed partisans were operating in northern Italy alone. Upon discovering that the son of one of his own associates was in the resistance, Mussolini
remarked that he would be doing the same thing if he were younger.[70]

In France and Italy, the Communists used the resistance to position themselves
for power after the war. As long as the Hitler-Stalin Pact of 1939 appeared to be
working, they had remained aloof, denouncing the war as Anglo-Saxon imperialism. Their position changed completely with the invasion of the Soviet Union.
Communists now threw themselves into the fight with great energy. Their unity
and determination were great assets in fighting the Germans, and their role in the
resistance gave them a new popularity.

The resistance also helped the French and Italians recover from the shame of
Fascism. Out of the resistance grew the demand for a new European society after
the war. In the closing days of the conflict, resistance forces frequently provided
the only order in regions from which the Germans had withdrawn. However, they
often used their power to carry out their own bloody reprisals against suspected
collaborators. Nevertheless, while the battle continued, they provided valuable
support for the Allied forces by harassing the fleeing German armies.

An Attempted Assassination. Hitler had spent a great deal of time warring
against his domestic adversaries. His idea of the nation was never all-encompassing,
only selectively ideological. The anti-Hitler resistance at home naturally took a
different form from that in the occupied countries. Given the success of the police
state and its indigenous character, organizing coherent resistance was difficult even
when the desire existed. An uprising of a few students at the University of Munich
in February 1943 was quickly and barbarically smashed. The members of the so-
called Kreisau Circle, a group of intellectual idealists who gathered at the estate
of Count Helmuth von Moltke (the great-great-nephew of the World War I commander) to discuss the social and spiritual regeneration of German society after
the war, were likewise arrested and executed. A more serious threat was posed by
those who made attempts on Hitler's life.

The prospect of German defeat, brought home by the debacle at Stalingrad,
convinced certain politicians and soldiers that the only way to save the Fatherland
from complete destruction was to assassinate the Führer. Some half dozen attempts
were made in 1943. A plan to blow up Hitler's plane came closest to success, but
the detonator of the bomb failed to fire. The following year another attempt was

made. This time the plot involved General Ludwig Beck, onetime head of the General Staff, and Karl Gördeler, the former mayor of Leipzig. The plotters also included General Friedrich Olbricht, currently chief of staff of the Home Army, and his deputy, Colonel Claus von Stauffenberg. After Hitler's death, they planned to begin negotiations with the Allies to end the war. On 20 July 1944, Stauffenberg managed to smuggle a bomb into a military briefing at Rastenburg. The force of the explosion destroyed the conference room, sending bodies hurtling through the air. Miraculously, Hitler survived.[71] Hitler believed his escape was providential—later he even claimed that the explosion had cured him of a tremor in his left leg—and he vowed a terrible revenge.

Stauffenberg and Olbricht were summarily shot. Beck committed suicide. Many others were implicated, including the families and friends of the accused. The infamous People's Court (*Volksgerichtshof*) sentenced others to death after summary trials. They were hanged in Plötzensee prison with piano wire attached to meat-hooks. Hitler later watched films of their death agonies. Arrests and executions continued into the following year. In all, the plot claimed about 5,000 victims. Most of these were executed; others committed, or were forced to commit, suicide. Field-Marshal Rommel, whose crime was possible knowledge, was given a choice: trial before a People's Court, with the understanding that his family would suffer serious consequences, or death by potassium cyanide, followed by a state funeral. Rommel chose to kill himself. His death was explained as a cerebral embolism, and he was buried with full military honors. Those who became involved in the plot of 20 July did so in order to save Germany from the consequences of Nazism. Most had had little difficulty serving Hitler in his days of glory, but changed their minds when faced with inevitable defeat, the invasion of the Soviet Union being its most dramatic proof. Soldiers could not easily reconcile acts of disloyalty against Hitler with their oath of personal allegiance to him. Did not the Führer embody the German nation? They rightly feared that the German people still had faith in Hitler and would regard his assassination as the ultimate treason. The habits of obedience were so strong that the political effects of the July plot were minimal. If anything, the regime was strengthened.

The newly appointed chief of the General Staff, Heinz Guderian, told his senior commanders that he expected them to be prototypical National-Socialist leaders who would cooperate to the fullest in helping indoctrinate their younger commanders in the beliefs of Adolf Hitler. Guderian explained his own opposition to the attempted assassination: "For myself I refuse to accept murder in any form. Our Christian religion forbids it in the clearest possible terms. I cannot therefore approve of the plan of assassination."[72]

THE FINAL ASSAULT

The Giant Pincers, 1944–1945

The Normandy Invasion. From his headquarters at Saint Germain-en-Laye, fifteen miles west of Paris, Field Marshal Gerd von Rundstedt tried to prepare against an impending Allied invasion. The commander-in-chief in the West was pessimistic. Many of the fifty divisions at his disposal were either newly formed training battalions, second-rate units of older men, or exhausted and under-strength Eastern Front divisions sent to France for rest and recuperation. Half of these were garrisoned in the bunkers of the Atlantic Wall, a series of fortified points spread along

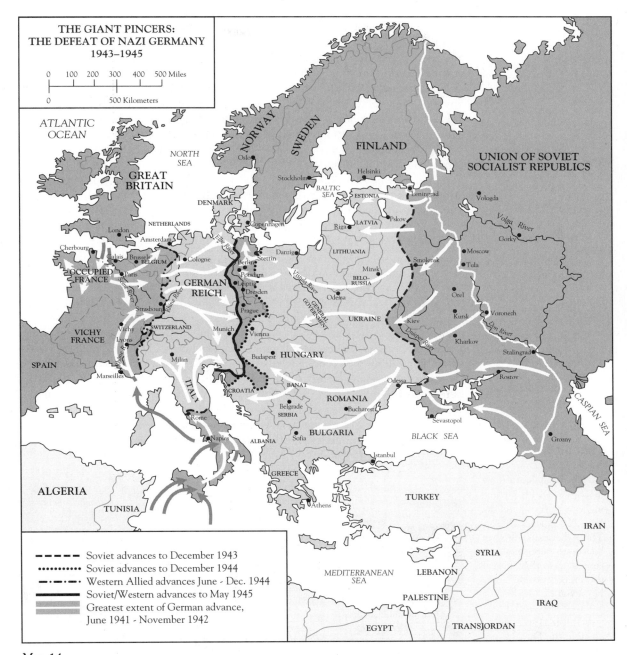

THE GIANT PINCERS:
THE DEFEAT OF NAZI GERMANY
1943–1945

0   100   200   300   400   500 Miles

0   500 Kilometers

- - - - - Soviet advances to December 1943
· · · · · · Soviet advances to December 1944
- · - · - · Western Allied advances June - Dec. 1944
Soviet/Western advances to May 1945
Greatest extent of German advance,
June 1941 - November 1942

Map 14

the northwestern coast from France to the Netherlands. The war in the Soviet
Union remained the main theater of operations and, as Rundstedt recognized,
would determine the eventual outcome of the war. The battle of France, he remarked, "could be, perhaps was being, lost on the Eastern Front before ever the
Anglo-Saxon armies set foot on the continent. The men, the guns and tanks which
would be needed to repel the probable invasion were being consumed in the vast
holocaust raging at the other end of Europe."[73] The Supreme Command answered

Rundstedt's request for reinforcements with a promise to send sixty battalions composed mostly of former Soviet prisoners of war, many of whom had "volunteered" for service to avoid starvation in German POW camps. The most heavily fortified section on Rundstedt's front was at the Pas de Calais, the narrowest point of the English Channel, which, he believed, was the most likely place for an invasion. But to cover his bets, he wanted to keep his reserves behind the lines for use when the point where the British and Americans would make their main effort became apparent. However, Marshal Rommel, the commander of the coastal divisions, believed that the Anglo-American invasion would come somewhere along the stretch of land from the Seine estuary westward through Normandy. Rommel, fearing that Allied air superiority would prevent rapid deployment of his troops, insisted on concentrating his forces in the immediate coastal area to destroy the attack on the beaches.

The Allies knew, from their Ultra intercepts, of this disagreement between Rundstedt and Rommel, and they took special pains to reinforce the belief that the invasion would fall near the Pas de Calais. They created a special paper army at the channel narrows along the Kentish coast under the "command" of General George Patton, the American commander who had led the invasion of Sicily, but was now temporarily in disgrace for having slapped a seemingly cowardly soldier. Since Patton had previously been the superior of General Omar Bradley, the commander of the American invasion army, the Americans hoped the Germans would assume Patton was still in overall command. Operation Overlord called for a series of landings along the Normandy coast to seal off the Cotentin peninsula and gain control of the valuable port of Cherbourg. The armies would then thrust eastward across the Falaise plain toward the flat country of the Paris basin in preparation for the final assault through Flanders and Lorraine into the Rhineland. The deception led Hitler to embrace the ideas of Rundstedt and keep four Panzer divisions in reserve near Paris under the direct command of Supreme Headquarters, thus

Parisians celebrate their deliverance with a parade in front of the Hotel de Ville, 30 August 1944. The Americans felt they had more important things to do than liberate the French capital. However, de Gaulle believed it essential to reestablish as soon as possible the French central government in its traditional seat of power.

depriving Rommel of control over the main armored force. Hitler thought that no invasion could succeed without the capture of a suitable supply port, and there were no such facilities along the Normandy beaches.

The Allied invasion began on 6 June. It did not face the full weight of the German armored reserve and soon established and began enlarging its beachhead. Ultra intercepts continued to reveal German intentions, and Allied air superiority made major enemy troop movements practically impossible except at night. Hitler continued to believe the invasion in Normandy was a feint in preparation for the main thrust at the Pas de Calais. Nevertheless, the Allies found progress inland rough going. The British bore the brunt of the German counterattacks, while the Americans built up their forces for a breakthrough. The Allies solved their supply problems by building an artificial harbor, "Mulberry," near Arromanches. Montgomery hoped the Allied breakout could be achieved within three weeks after the initial landings, but the attackers had little room to maneuver, and the Germans were able to block their path with a screen of tanks and antiaircraft guns. This gave the Germans time to prepare a strong defensive position behind the Seine, but Hitler refused to allow his divisions to withdraw, insisting that they stay put and fight it out. When the Allied breakout occurred at the end of July with the assistance of a massive air bombardment, the onrushing torrent succeeded in forcing the Germans to squander their manpower, thereby contributing to an earlier defeat in France.

Two days before the Allies stormed the beaches of Normandy, the American Fifth Army entered Rome. Many Italians hoped that the Allies would now complete the liberation of their country, but the offensive stopped with the British occupation of Florence on 12 August. For the next eight months, the battle lines stretched across Italy from Lucca to Rimini and remained virtually unchanged while the main Allied attack continued in France. On 15 August, the Allies landed on the Mediterranean coast and began to advance up the Rhone valley. Ten days later in the north, the American First Army cleared the path for the entry of the Second French Armored Division into Paris; then it advanced into Belgium, crossed Luxembourg, and pushed forward to the German frontier. At the same time, the British liberated Brussels and, on 4 September, entered the port of Antwerp.

The Soviets Strike at Will. In contrast to the 61 divisions they had committed to the defense of France and the Low Countries, the Germans had a combined strength of 228 divisions and 23 brigades in action on the Eastern Front. They hoped to remain on the defensive in the East while checking the attack in the West. The Soviets, though, allowed them no relief. The Red Army had more than 300 divisions and possessed good lateral communications between its fronts. The Soviets were thus able to attack wherever they wanted. They aimed their main blow at the German center in Belorussia and in the western Ukraine. First, however, on 10 June 1944, they attacked toward Leningrad, breaking the Finnish defenses along the Mannerheim Line in ten days and capturing the port of Viborg. They advanced to the 1940 Russo-Finnish frontier and forced the Helsinki government to accept an armistice. With their northern flank secured, they began the main offensive into Belorussia, "Operation Bagration," code-named after the tsarist general of the Napoleonic wars. With 118 infantry and 43 tank divisions, they attacked north of the Pripet Marshes along a 250-mile front. By the end of July, they had liberated Belorussia, most of Lithuania, part of Latvia, and practically all of Poland east of the Vistula. The Germans lost 25 divisions. At the end of

August, the Soviets also smashed the German and Romanian armies in the southern Ukraine, opening the lower Danube. Bulgaria demanded that all German troops be evacuated and began negotiations with the Allies for an armistice. In Bucharest, on 25 August, a coup overthrew the pro-German regime of Marshal Ion Antonescu. The new Romanian government then declared war on Germany. The Romanian oil fields around Ploesti fell to the Soviets on 30 August, creating a major fuel crisis in Germany. Although the Germans were manufacturing more Messerschmitts and Focke-Wulfs than ever before, they lacked the gasoline to put them in the air. At the end of September, according to Speer, one Krefeld fighter squadron had enough fuel to fly only one day out of three and then only on brief sorties with about half its planes.

The Soviet offensive in Poland temporarily reached its limits with the establishment of a small bridgehead across the Vistula at Sandomierz. After a month's lull, the Soviets were in a position to resume the advance in Poland; indeed, a strong offensive there might well have ended the war in a couple of months. For political reasons, though, Stalin preferred to shift the spearhead of his attack to the Danube. He feared that if Germany surrendered before the Soviets had established their military power in the Balkans, the Bulgarians, Romanians, and Hungarians would set up governments free from Communist influence. Furthermore, a direct thrust toward Berlin might have frightened the Germans into sending more troops to protect Prussia, the birthplace of so many of their generals. Therefore the Soviets did not resume their attack in the north until the end of the year. They swept all the way to the Oder River, into Silesia and Brandenburg. Their advanced units were now just forty miles from Berlin.

The Broad-Front Strategy. The Western Allies followed the plan of Supreme Commander Dwight D. Eisenhower, with all their armies attacking simultaneously along a broad front. Montgomery opposed this concept; he had proposed a sort of Schlieffen Plan in reverse: concentrate maximum strength on the left flank and make a powerful sweep through Belgium and into the Ruhr.[74] Eisenhower had rejected the single-thrust offensive as unworkable logistically. German garrisons still held the French ports of Dunkirk, Calais, Boulogne, and Le Havre, and enemy defenses covered Antwerp on the Scheldt estuary. Eisenhower saw that there was no immediate "possibility of maintaining a force in Germany capable of penetrating to its capital. There was still a considerable reserve in the middle of the enemy country and I knew that any pencil-like thrust into the heart of Germany such as [Montgomery] proposed would meet nothing but certain destruction."[75]

On 10 September, Eisenhower gave the British the task of cleaning up the Antwerp approaches. He also approved Montgomery's plan to extend the security of the Allied lines by gaining a bridgehead over the Rhine with an airborne attack in the region of Arnhem.[76] Montgomery hoped "Operation Market-Garden" would become "the spearhead of a major Allied movement on the Northern flank designed to isolate, and finally occupy the Ruhr."[77] Whatever its intention, the operation proved to be a disaster. The Second SS Panzer Corps, which happened to be in the area for rest and reorganization, cut the paratroopers apart as soon as they landed on 17 September. Eisenhower blamed the setback on bad weather, which prevented reinforcements from reaching the battle area. Montgomery believed the plan failed because Market-Garden had not been part of a direct drive into the Rhineland. "The trouble was," Montgomery wrote, "that Eisenhower wanted the Saar, the Frankfurt area, the Ruhr, Antwerp, and the line of the Rhine.... To get *all* these in one forward movement was impossible.... After Normandy our strategy became unstitched. There was no plan; and we moved by disconnected jerks ... we did not advance to the Rhine on a *broad* front; we advanced to the Rhine on several fronts, which were uncoordinated. And what was the German answer? A single and concentrated punch in the Ardennes, when we had become unbalanced and unduly extended."[78]

In the Ardennes, that wooded, hilly piece of real estate in Luxembourg and eastern Belgium, site of the glorious 1940 campaign that had knocked France out of the war, the Germans launched their final, great counterattack. The lull in Poland had given Hitler an opportunity to deploy a reserve force of twenty-eight divisions along a 75-mile front in the Eifel Mountains. The Führer hoped this army could advance across Belgium to Antwerp; he believed that depriving the Allies of their belief in victory would bring about an armistice. The Germans began their advance on the morning of 16 December 1944. Confronted by only four American divisions, they quickly punched a huge bulge in the enemy lines. The Germans had maintained radio silence prior to the attack, allowing no intercepts, and the overcast sky protected them from aerial surveillance. The attack caught the Allies completely off guard, but resistance soon stiffened. In the stubborn defense at Bastogne, the Americans forced the Germans into an unsuccessful, time-consuming siege. When the weather finally cleared, Allied air strikes slowed the Wehrmacht units to a halt. Within a week, American reinforcements sparked a counterattack, forcing the Germans again on the defensive. On 3 January 1945, the German High Command authorized a withdrawal, and the initiative passed back to the Allies.

The German position in Italy had also become precarious. The Allies controlled most of the peninsula south of Leghorn on the Ligurian Sea across to Ancona on the Adriatic, but they showed little inclination to push beyond. With the German collapse, the resistance became the de facto government in many places. After the American army liberated Bologna on 19 April 1945, partisan bands hunted down and shot enemies, Fascist or otherwise. Similar massacres occurred elsewhere. No sooner had the Wehrmacht left Milan than the National Liberation Front for Northern Italy warned that all Fascists guilty of "suppressing the constitutional guarantees, destroying popular liberties, creating the Fascist regime, compromising and betraying the fate of the country, and conducting it to the present catastrophe" were to be put to death. Lesser crimes were to be punished with "life imprisonment."[79] The National Liberation Front established special people's courts and war crime tribunals. Palmiro Togliatti, the secretary general of the Communist party and current vice-premier of Italy, demanded that the members of the Salò government be summarily executed, including Mussolini.

The Death of the Dictators, 1945

Crossing the Rhine. Even before the Allies fully recovered from the Battle of the Bulge, they were making plans for a major offensive into the Ruhr. The operation began on 8 February, with a drive east of Nijmegen into the Reichswald. In the next several weeks, the British and Americans occupied all the cities west of the Rhine in some of the bitterest fighting of the war. On 7 March 1945, a platoon of soldiers from the American First Army saved the Ludendorff railway bridge at

Remagen from demolition. In an attempt to seal off this bridgehead, the Germans weakened their defensive positions elsewhere. On 22 March, units of Patton's Third Army made an unopposed crossing between Mainz and Worms. A day later, further downstream near the Dutch frontier where the river is a quarter of a mile or more wide, Montgomery's Twenty-first Army Group also went over. The two branches of the Allied armies then swung round the Ruhr in a classic double envelopment, trapping 400,000 Germans in a pocket eighty miles wide. Ultra constantly informed the advancing armies of the weakness in the enemy's defense. Eisenhower decided to direct the next main thrust into central Germany, but Churchill thought the Allies should head straight for Berlin, a move he felt was necessary to crush the enemy's will to fight and vital for establishing the Anglo-American political position after the war.

Berlin was already lost to the Allies, however. While the Allies were still reeling from the Germans' blows in the Ardennes, the Soviets were preparing for their final assault. Had the Western Allies decided to aim their offensive at Berlin, they probably could not have arrived there before the Soviet army. At the beginning of April, the Red Army swarmed across the Oder River with more than seventy armored brigades, over twice as many troops as the nearest Allied army possessed. Stalin still feared that the British and Americans would make some sort of deal with the Germans to free the Wehrmacht to fight the Soviets. He believed that negotiations to this effect were taking place in Bern under the cover of arranging an armistice on the Italian front. He even implied that Roosevelt had allowed the Germans "to move three divisions from Northern Italy to the Soviet front."[80]

The Surrender of Germany. Even in the closing weeks of the war, many people still had faith in Hitler. "The Führer is still holding something in reserve that he'll play at the last moment," said a Westphalian farmer. "It's only a trap, his letting

The Germans sign the instrument of capitulation at Eisenhower's headquarters near Rheims, France, 7 May 1945. Eisenhower refused to attend and sent instead his chief of staff, Lt. General Walter Bedell Smith (in the middle of the group at the extreme right), and others of similar rank. The Allied representatives thus held lesser rank than the German delegation. The Germans were headed by Hitler's chief of operations, Colonel-General Alfred Gustaf Jodl (second from left).

the enemy come so far into our country."[81] To shore up public morale in a hopeless situation, Goebbels even resorted to tampering with the astrological charts, making horoscopes speak of "valleys of darkness which had to be passed through," "imminent surprises," and "happy outcomes."[82] As the end drew near, the Nazi overlords still engaged in conspiracy and intrigue. Himmler, realizing the war was lost, tried to arrange a separate peace with the Allies in the hope he could participate in the future government of Germany. (He eventually tried to escape, but was caught by the British and swallowed a cyanide capsule.) Göring, Hitler's heir-apparent, attempted to negotiate with Eisenhower. Bormann then prodded Hitler into denouncing both Göring and Himmler for defeatism and for bringing irreparable shame on the German people.

Hitler spent his last days in the cramped quarters of his bunker thirty feet below the old Weimar Republic chancellery in Berlin. He had recently turned fifty-six. Emaciated and ashen and suffering from an advanced stage of Parkinson's disease, he looked much older. His mood declined from optimism to despair. The Battle of Berlin was in its third week. When it began, he proclaimed: "If every soldier on the Eastern front does his duty in the days and weeks that lie ahead, the last assault of Asia will shatter, just as the breakthrough of our enemies in the West will, in spite of everything, fail in the end."[83] As fighting raged in the streets above, he accepted his fate to die like a tribal god in the flames of his ruined capital. The German masses had proved unworthy of his leadership. Those "who remain alive after the battles are over are . . . only inferior persons, since the best have fallen," he said. Yet in matters of death, as in everything else, he procrastinated. Not until 29 April did he dictate his last testament. In it he blamed the war on the Jews.[84] Earlier that day he had been informed that Mussolini had been shot by Italian partisans. It was one of the last messages to reach the bunker from the outside world.

Local partisans of Dongo had captured the Duce as he fled the country in a German motor caravan. His arrest immediately became known to Luigi Longo, Communist party boss of northern Italy. Longo ordered Walter Audisio ("Colonel Valerio") to arrange the Duce's execution. The next day Valerio went to Dongo and took Mussolini and the Duce's mistress, Clara Petacci, into personal custody. He had them driven about a mile out of town to a large stone gate in front of the Villa Belmonte where they were ordered out of the car. Valerio then cut them down at point-blank range with one continuous burst from a French machine pistol. Mussolini was hit nine times, but was still alive. Valerio dispatched him with a bullet to the heart. Mussolini's body and that of his companion, together with the cadavers of more than a dozen other members of Mussolini's entourage who were executed in the Dongo village square later that day, were trucked into Milan and dumped in the Pizzale Loreto. Mussolini, Clara, and one-time Fascist party secretary Achille Starace, who had just been killed, were hoisted by their feet to one of the exposed girders of a bombed-out filling station. The crowd became hysterical and began to mutilate the bodies. People spat, threw things, and beat the swinging cadavers with sticks. It was a macabre spectacle. In death Mussolini satisfied the same lust for excitement as he had in his vainglorious prime.[85]

Hitler was determined that he would not meet such a humiliating end.[86] On 30 April, just after three o'clock in the afternoon, he solemnly bade farewell to those still in the bunker. Then, accompanied by Eva Braun, whom he had married the previous day, he retired to his private quarters where he bit into a glass ampoule of cyanide. His wife delivered the *coup de grace* by shooting him in the right temple after which she also took poison.[87] Aides carried the two bodies into the chancellery garden and burned them in accordance with Hitler's wish. Shortly afterwards, a detachment from *Smersh*, the Soviet counterintelligence organization, discovered the charred remains and took them with other corpses to a surgical field hospital in the Berlin suburb of Buch for autopsy.[88] Dental records provided positive identification.[89]

Just before his suicide, Hitler had designated Admiral Karl Dönitz his successor and commander-in-chief of the armed forces. He made Goebbels the new chancellor and Bormann the head of the party. Now Hitler, Goebbels, and Bormann all were gone. At 10 P.M. on 1 May 1945, Radio Hamburg announced that Hitler had died "fighting against Bolshevism to his last breath." The remnants of power passed to Plön in Schleswig-Holstein where Dönitz had his headquarters. Dönitz tried to play for time. He had obtained a copy of the Allied plan to divide Germany into several occupation zones and wanted to fight the Soviets as long as possible to allow German civilians and soldiers to flee westward. He sent a delegation to General Montgomery proposing to surrender the German armies fighting in the East to the British because all the Russians were savages. Montgomery replied that "the Germans should have thought of all these things before they began the war, and particularly before they attacked the Russians in June 1941."[90] Eisenhower informed Dönitz that unless he surrendered immediately, the entire Allied front would be closed to prevent any more German refugees from entering the American zone. Dönitz surrendered. The instrument of capitulation was signed on 7 May in Eisenhower's headquarters at Rheims, France. The Dönitz government continued to meet at Flensburg until all the German armies in the field were disarmed. It assembled for the last time, on 23 May, in the saloon bar of the beached German passenger boat *Patria*. Then Dönitz and his ministers were summoned before the representatives of the Allied Control Commission and arrested as prisoners of war. The Third Reich ended just 987 years, 7 months, and 5 days short of its anticipated life span.

The End of the War against Japan. The war against Japan now became the major preoccupation of the Allied coalition. By the end of April 1945, Japan's position had become hopeless. American marines had reconquered most of the Philippines, secured Iwo Jima, and conquered most of Okinawa. The imperial fleet had practically ceased to exist. The Japanese concentrated most of their offensive power in massed attacks by *Kamikaze* suicide planes, flown directly from the home islands. The Japanese merchant navy at one million tons was 10 percent of its former size, one-third the shipping necessary to provide basic sustenance to the Japanese people who needed food imports to survive. The empire, upon which the Japanese war machine had depended for raw materials, had disappeared. By April no foreign fuel reached Japan. The Japanese formed a new government under the elderly Admiral Kantaro Suzuki to open negotiations with the Allies to end hostilities, but many military leaders still wanted to fight on. With the end of the war in Europe and the prospect of being faced with the full force of Allied military might, the Japanese government asked the Soviets to mediate a surrender to the British and Americans. Stalin advised Churchill and Truman to modify their demands for unconditional surrender to ease the way for capitulation. However, the Soviet dictator was not eager to end the conflict in the Far East before he had a chance to declare war on Japan and obtain the territory promised him at the Yalta Conference in February 1945. He therefore tried to delay the surrender by telling the Japanese government that its proposals were not definite enough.

The Americans had intercepted and decoded the Japanese government's messages to its ambassador in Moscow and were already aware of Japan's desire to end the war. Many American military leaders felt that Japanese capitulation would come only after the home islands were invaded with an incalculable loss of life. General George Marshall thought an invasion might cost half a million American lives. The Americans still regarded the Japanese army as formidable and feared 1.75 million men might be brought from China and Manchuria to defend the homeland. Bringing Japan to its knees might take until the end of 1946. On 16 July 1945, President Truman knew he had the means to force an immediate surrender. On that day he was informed that the test of an atomic bomb at Alamagordo, New Mexico, had been a complete success. Truman never doubted that this new weapon should be used as long as it was "dropped on a military target."[91] His military advisers selected four cities as possible targets: Hiroshima, Kokura, Niigata, and Nagasaki. General Carl Spaatz, the commander of the Strategic Air Force, received instructions to be ready to attack any one of these as soon after 3 August as weather and operational conditions permitted. Meanwhile, an Allied ultimatum ordered the Japanese to lay down their arms. The Tokyo government made no formal reply, but, on 28 July, broadcast that Japan would continue the war. Truman's order to Spaatz thereby remained in effect.

On 6 August, a B-29 dropped the first atomic bomb on Hiroshima. The weapon had the explosive force of 20,000 tons of TNT and completely obliterated the center of the city, killing 80,000 people, roughly one-fourth of the city's normal population. "If [the Japanese leaders] do not now accept our terms, they may expect a rain of ruin from the air, the like of which has never been seen on this earth," Truman vowed.[92] The Japanese were given three days to make up their minds, but no surrender came. That the Japanese government might be in such a state of shock that it would need more time to assess the impact of such a weapon was not considered. General Spaatz was ordered to prepare another strike. On 9 August, a second bomb dropped on Nagasaki. That same day, the Soviet Union declared war on Japan, and Soviet troops immediately crossed the frontier into Manchuria. Stalin had already specified 8 August as a likely date for beginning hostilities. By then he had mobilized over 1.5 million troops for that purpose. On the morning of 10 August, the Japanese government announced it was willing to surrender. The formal ceremony took place on 2 September, on board the American battleship *Missouri* anchored in Tokyo Bay. One of the flags the Americans flew that day was the ensign with thirty-one stars that Commodore Perry had displayed when he first landed in Japan ninety-two years before.

POSTSCRIPT   War is hell no matter where it is waged. However, the main struggle of World War II was on the Eastern Front where the Germans consistently kept at least three-quarters of their combat troop strength. They regarded other theaters of operations as subordinate. In North Africa, Rommel constantly overstated his losses in an effort to con-

vince the OKW to send him more supplies, but the tactic was seldom
successful. His army never grew beyond six divisions. The British, though,
viewed the desert war as vital to the preservation of their security. North
Africa provided them with the opportunity to fight the Germans before
they were strong enough to engage them anywhere else. The contest also
appealed to Winston Churchill's sense of the romantic. Even his generals
tended to exaggerate the contribution of the desert struggle to the German
defeat. Marshal Georgi Zhukov, for example, bristled when Field-Marshal
Montgomery later claimed that the Battle of El Alamein was as significant
as that of Stalingrad. Zhukov found no reasonable comparison. The El
Alamein operation, Zhukov remarked, "was carried out on an army scale,
while at Stalingrad the operation engaged a group of fronts and it had a
vast strategic importance. . . . It was an operation that actually marked a
radical turning-point in the war and insured the retreat of the German
forces from our country."[93] At El Alamein, Montgomery defeated a
German corps and then let it get away.

Few Soviet soldiers who had lived through the hell of the Nazi invasion
of their homeland had much sympathy for the sacrifices of the Americans
and British whose countries had escaped occupation. Understandably, they
tended to dismiss the contribution their allies had made to the defeat of
Hitler. They resented the fact that the Western Allies built their postwar
strength on the sacrifices of the Red Army. In return, the British and
Americans frequently slighted the Soviets. Such mutual underestimation
had serious consequences after the fighting ceased. The makeup of postwar
Europe would be determined by where the troops were when the fighting
stopped. Stalin would not invite the Allies to help determine the fate of
those countries that the Red Army had liberated, neither would the Western Allies invite Stalin to share in the governance of the areas they controlled: Italy, France, the Low Countries, and Japan. Both sides believed
that what was theirs was indeed theirs.

World War II was not only a war between nations, but also a war between peoples, a civil war between collaborators and resisters, between
ethnic and racial groups, between political enemies and class enemies.
States were not all-encompassing communities. The Nazis and Soviets
spent a great deal of time in battle with domestic adversaries. Hitler had
enemies in very high places. In the Soviet Union, separatist ambitions
persisted despite Stalin's attempt to stamp them out. Europe's multinational
states were extremely fragile.

Even before the rubble had been cleared away, people began to wonder
how the outcome would have differed if the war had been fought another
way. The decision to use the atomic bomb was the subject of considerable
controversy, often with moral and racial overtones. Liddell Hart wrote that
Hiroshima was destroyed merely to demonstrate the overwhelming power

of a new weapon. It "had done no more than hasten the moment of surrender."[94] The Americans did not think that was so bad. They believed that the Japanese might not have given up so easily without the bomb. Restraint, whatever its merits, had not been seriously considered. The risks were unacceptable. No state engaged in war had ever failed to use a new weapon if the advantages of use outweighed the disadvantages. Some suggested that Truman wanted to give the Soviets a practical demonstration of this awesome power to make them more cooperative in resolving the problems of Europe.[95] The question of whether he would have used it as willingly against the Germans as against the Japanese remains moot because the surrender in Europe took place before the bomb was operational. Nevertheless, causing additional casualties was not a major concern. More Germans died in the daylight precision bombing raids on German cities than in the blast at Hiroshima.

The world has been haunted by Truman's decision. It is fortunate that the use of the bomb has prompted such strong emotions. One of the most persistent safeguards against a future nuclear holocaust lay in the practical demonstration of the horror of this weapon. People sometimes adopt civilized behavior because they are frightened into restraint. The destruction of Hiroshima and Nagasaki certainly prevented a lot of romantic illusion about a world war of the future. Obviously, no future such conflict is winnable. World War II was a total war and total victory was its logical outcome. The essence of war is violence; the bomb showed just how violent it could be. Even in an age when governments talked about mutually assured destruction, its presence had a sobering effect.

Seldom has justice been better served than with the defeats of Nazi Germany, Fascist Italy, and Imperial Japan. Although a heavy price was paid in the destruction of property and the loss of life, those costs do not seem too high given what the world would have experienced had the Axis won. Benjamin Franklin's observation that there never has been a good war seems a relic of another age considering the evil that existed in the bellicose totalitarian systems of the twentieth century.

ENDNOTES

1. Winston S. Churchill, *The Grand Alliance* (Boston: Houghton Mifflin, 1950), 607.
2. Ibid., 434.
3. Ibid., 434.
4. It had been presented to him on 10 August 1941, the second day of the conference in Placentia Bay, Newfoundland. It was discussed the next day.
5. Churchill, *The Grand Alliance*, 444.
6. The exile governments of Belgium, Czechoslovakia, Greece, Luxembourg, the Netherlands, Norway, Poland, Yugoslavia, and France also agreed.

7. United States, Department of State, *Foreign Relations of the United States*, vol. 3 (Washington, D.C.: U.S. Government Printing Office, 1942), 502. Stalin revealed these goals to British Foreign Secretary Anthony Eden, when Eden visited Moscow in December 1941. Stalin assumed that on certain of these points, namely, the permanent incorporation of the Baltic states into the Soviet Union, no agreement with the West was necessary. He became terribly annoyed when Eden insisted that formal agreement on *all* matters was essential.

8. Ibid., 521.

9. *Documents of German Foreign Policy*, D, vol. 11, 204–5.

10. Peter Calvocoressi, Guy Wint, and John Pritchard, *Total War: The Causes and Courses of the Second World War* (New York: Pantheon Books, 1989), 224–29.

11. Churchill, *The Grand Alliance*, 415.

12. Erwin Rommel, *The Rommel Papers* (New York: Harcourt, Brace, 1953), 130.

13. Seymour K. Freidin and William Richardson, *The Fatal Decisions* (New York: Sloane, 1956), 101.

14. Basil Liddell Hart, *The German Generals Talk* (New York: Morrow, 1948), 199.

15. Nikita Khrushchev, *Khrushchev Remembers* (Boston: Little, Brown, 1970), 191.

16. Alexander Werth, *Russia at War, 1941–1945* (New York: Dutton, 1964), 490.

17. Freidin and Richardson, *The Fatal Decisions*, 151.

18. Walter Warlimont, *Inside Hitler's Headquarters, 1939–45* (New York: Praeger, 1964), 286.

19. Theodor Plivier, *Stalingrad: The Death of an Army* (London: Athenaeum, 1948), 331–32.

20. Ibid., 324.

21. *Foreign Relations of the United States*, vol. 3 (1942), 562.

22. Winston S. Churchill, *The Hinge of Fate* (Boston: Houghton Mifflin, 1950), 332.

23. *Foreign Relations of the United States*, vol. 3 (1942), 568.

24. Ibid., 568–69.

25. Churchill, *The Hinge of Fate*, 475.

26. Ibid., 479.

27. Marshal Andrei Grechko, *Battle for the Caucasus* (Moscow: Progress Publishers, 1971), 87.

28. Churchill, *The Hinge of Fate*, 587.

29. At the time of the Casablanca Conference, the Americans had only eight divisions in the European theater: one in England, one in Ireland, and six in the Mediterranean.

30. Churchill, *The Hinge of Fate*, 630.

31. Charles de Gaulle, *The War Memoirs of Charles de Gaulle: Unity, 1942–44* (New York: Simon and Schuster, 1959), 83.

32. Churchill, *The Hinge of Fate*, 682.

33. *Foreign Relations of the United States*, vol. 2 (1943), 24.

34. Ibid., vol. 2 (1942), 816.

35. Ibid., 822.

36. De Gaulle, *War Memoirs*, 129.

37. *Foreign Relations of the United States, Casablanca*, 727.

38. Joseph Goebbels, *The Secret Conferences of Dr. Goebbels* (New York: Dutton, 1970), 324–26.

39. Warlimont, *Inside Hitler's Headquarters*, 339.

40. Ibid., 347.

41. *Foreign Relations of the United States, Conferences at Washington and Quebec 1943*, 590.

42. Ibid., 1161–69.

43. Robert Murphy, *Diplomat among Warriors* (New York: Doubleday, 1964), 191.

44. Albert Kesselring, *Kesselring: A Soldier's Record* (New York: Morrow, 1954), 226.

45. Shepard B. Clough and Salvatore Saladino, *A History of Modern Italy* (New York: Columbia University Press, 1968), 521.

46. Only six were captured: Tullio Cianetti, Galeazzo Ciano, Emilio de Bono, Luciano Gottardi, Giovanni Marinelli, and Carlo Pareschi. Their trial began in Verona on 8 January 1944. All denied they were guilty of treason; most explained that by returning the command of the armed forces to the king, they hoped for a more vigorous prosecution of the war. Marinelli was so deaf that he thought the motion had actually come from Mussolini. All were sentenced to death. On 11 January, the condemned were taken to a rifle range in the Forte San Procolo, where they were bound astride collapsible chairs. With their backs as targets, they were shot by a firing squad. The first volley went wild, killing only two. The others had to be dispatched by coups de grace.

47. General Montgomery, the British commander, was confused. He did not see how such an attitude could be reconciled with "unconditional surrender," and he was even more amazed at the attitude of the commander-in-chief of the Italian Seventh Army, General M. Arizio, who thought that "since he was the senior Army General in Southern Italy, the [British] Eighth Army should therefore come under his command, as we were now Allies." Montgomery says he soon put the matter straight. Bernard Montgomery, *The Memoirs of Field-Marshal Montgomery* (New York: World Publishing Co., 1958), 180.

48. Murphy, *Diplomat among Warriors*, 197.

49. On 23 March 1944, a column of 156 SS police troops with motor vehicle escort was attacked on the narrow Via Rasella, in the neighborhood where Mussolini had once had an apartment. Twenty pounds of TNT gouged a hole in the shank of the column, immediately killing two dozen soldiers, scattering the dead and wounded up and down the street. The blast was so powerful that it tore large chunks of masonry from the facades of the surrounding buildings and knocked over a city bus a block away. The partisans responsible threw hand bombs before they made their escape. This attack was reported to Hitler at Rastenburg; in a rage, he demanded the demolition of an entire city district and the execution of thirty to fifty Italians for every dead German. The local Wehrmacht commander, Kesselring, reduced Hitler's number to ten Italian civilians for every German, and the Roman Gestapo prepared a list of 335 hostages—five more than necessary—that consisted mostly of Jews, Communists, and suspected saboteurs. These were loaded into trucks and driven outside the city to the Ardeatine Caves, where in batches of five, they were shot in the back of the head. Kesselring felt that "Partisan war was a complete violation of international law and contradicted every principle of clean soldierly fighting." Kesselring, *A Soldier's Record*, 227.

50. *Nazi Conspiracy and Aggression*, vol. 1 (Washington, D.C.: U.S. Government Printing Office, 1946), 898.

51. According to official tabulations, in January 1945, 1,873,000 prisoners of war were working in Germany as forced laborers; 245,000 were employed directly in the manufacture of armaments and munitions. This constituted a drop of 155,000 from the previous June. Ibid., 894.

52. Pierre Bourget and Charles Lacretelle, *Sur les Murs de Paris, 1940–1944* (Paris: Hachette, 1959), 125–30.

53. *Nazi Conspiracy and Aggression*, 6:448.

54. Albert Speer, *Inside the Third Reich* (New York: Macmillan, 1970), 208.

55. *New York Times*, 19 February 1943, 8.

56. Speer, *Inside the Third Reich*, 217.

57. Ibid., 214.

58. Joseph Goebbels, *The Goebbels Diaries, 1942–1943* (Garden City, N.Y.: Doubleday, 1948), 331.

59. Winston Churchill, *Blood, Sweat, and Tears* (New York: Putnam, 1941), 175–76.

60. *Social Insurance and Allied Services* (The Beveridge Report), 1942–1943, vol. 6, *Command Document* 6404.
61. Werth, *Russia at War*, 249.
62. Ibid., 414.
63. David Ewen, *Encyclopedia of the Opera* (New York: Hill and Wang, 1955), 540.
64. Alex Inkeles, *Social Change in Soviet Russia* (New York: Simon and Schuster, 1971), 156–60.
65. The Finns had no desire to do more than regain land they thought was rightfully theirs. They saw themselves as co-belligerents. Once they reached their old frontiers, they went on the defensive and refused to participate in operations against Leningrad.
66. Harrison Salisbury, *The 900 Days: The Siege of Leningrad* (New York: Harper and Row, 1969), 444.
67. Ibid., 513–17.
68. Georges Bidault, *Resistance* (New York: Praeger, 1967), 16–42.
69. Alan Clark, *Barbarossa: The Russian-German Conflict, 1941–1945* (New York: Morrow, 1965), 337.
70. Ivone Kirkpatrick, *Mussolini* (New York: Hawthorne, 1964), 648.
71. The explosive device was in a briefcase that was placed on the floor not far from where the Führer was standing. But, in the course of the briefing, the case was inadvertently moved to the other side of the heavy oak supports of the conference table, thus protecting Hitler from the direct force of the blast.
72. Heinz Guderian, *Panzer Leader* (New York: Dutton, 1952), 348.
73. Lieutenant General Bodo Zimmerman, "France 1944," in Freidin and Richardson, *The Fatal Decisions*, 200.
74. Montgomery objected to describing this as a "pencil-like thrust," as Eisenhower called it, since "a strong thrust by forty divisions can hardly be described as a 'narrow front,' it would represent a major *blow*." Montgomery, *Memoirs*, 256.
75. Dwight Eisenhower, *Crusade in Europe* (New York: Doubleday, 1948), 306.
76. Ibid., 307.
77. Montgomery, *Memoirs*, 265.
78. Ibid., 256–57.
79. Kirkpatrick, *Mussolini*, 664.
80. *Stalin's Correspondence with Roosevelt and Truman* (New York: Capricorn Books, 1965), 200.
81. Speer, *Inside the Third Reich*, 446.
82. Ibid., 411.
83. George Stein, ed., *Hitler* (Englewood Cliffs, N.J.: Prentice-Hall, 1968), 83.
84. Ibid., 84.
85. Mussolini was buried in a pauper's grave in Milan's Cimitero Maggiore. Twelve years later, the remains were allowed to be reinterred in the family vault at Predappio.
86. Neither had Mussolini, for that matter. The Duce swore he would kill himself rather than be taken prisoner and exhibited in New York's Madison Square Garden.
87. Robert Waite, "Hitler's Anti-Semitism," in Bruce Mazlish *Psychoanalysis and History* (New York: Universal Library, 1971).
88. The others were the Minister of Propaganda Josef Goebbels, Frau Goebbels, and their six children, aged four to twelve, who had been poisoned by their mother. Goebbels could not conceive of them being raised in any other system than National Socialism. Also found was Hitler's military aide, Major-General Hans Krebs. All were dead by cyanide.
89. Among other things, the autopsy revealed what the lyrics of that famous British wartime ditty (sung to the tune of "Colonel Bogey") had asserted all along: Hitler was a monorchid. For some unknown reason, Stalin never told his allies of the dis-

covery of Hitler's body, nor of the postmortem examination. The record was only made public a decade and a half after the Soviet dictator's death. Lev Bezymenski, *The Death of Adolf Hitler* (New York: Harcourt, Brace & World, 1968), 44–50.

90. Montgomery, *Memoirs*, 300.

91. Harry Truman, *Memoirs*, vol. 1 (Garden City, N.Y.: Doubleday, 1955), 420.

92. Ibid., 422.

93. Georgi Zhukov, *The Memoirs of Marshal Zhukov* (New York: Delacorte Press, 1971), 661.

94. Liddell Hart, *The German Generals Talk*, 698.

95. Martin J. Sherwin, *A World Destroyed: The Atomic Bomb and the Grand Alliance* (New York: Alfred A. Knopf, 1975), 199, 203.

THE WAR AGAINST THE JEWS

Defamation and Degradation. Hitler believed that he had a divine mission to wage a holy war against the Jews. His electoral triumph in March 1933, which put the Nazis and their nationalist allies in control of the Reichstag, gave him the power to begin a campaign of intimidation and denigration. The Nazi government first ordered a boycott (*Judenboykott*) against Jewish businesses, department stores, physicians, and lawyers. The "Central Committee for Deflecting Jewish Atrocity and Boycott Mongering," led by Julius Streicher, directed the ban and organized local action committees throughout Germany. Posters and graffiti warned people to stay away from Jewish establishments (photo 1). Oftentimes SA sentries mounted guard at the entrances of Jewish stores and doctors' offices to discourage patronage. The Nazis intended that this first outburst of official discrimination would help consolidate their regime and, at the same time, carry anti-Semitic theory into practice by preparing the way for the enactment of specific anti-Jewish legislation. Early laws prohibited Jews from government service and forbade them from practicing law and from attending the universities. The Nuremberg laws of 1935 provided a legal definition of Jewishness and deprived Jews of German citizenship, reducing their status to that of subjects.

A variety of government offices and party sections handled Jewish affairs, from ministries in Berlin to committees at local levels. Their activities included "research institutes," emigration departments, and press and information bureaus. The Nazis wanted to infuse the entire German population with a proper anti-Semitic spirit and to lay the groundwork for more extreme measures. Jewish affairs became a fertile ground for interparty rivalry. This administrative and bureaucratic confusion was clearly in evidence during the Night of the Broken Glass (*Khristalnacht*)

1 **The word "Jew" has been painted on several windows of one of Berlin's medium-sized department stores.** Other windows show the Star of David, a caricature, and the warning, "Jews get out." Although the general boycott lasted only several days, action continued against individual businesses, fostering a sentiment toward permanent boycott of the Jewish community.

2 **The burning of a Berlin synagogue.** The building was torched after the SA smashed its interior, the Torah scrolls perishing in the conflagration. The fire department refused to help put out the blaze due to a "shortage of manpower." However, fire trucks were sent to protect adjacent property which, in this photo, seems to be that of a Nazi party motor pool.

in November 1938. *Khristalnacht* advanced the terror campaign against the Jews—hundreds of synagogues burned, thousands of Jewish businesses were vandalized, and many Jews were beaten and sent to detention camps—but the affair lacked coordination and central direction (photo 2). In its aftermath, Hitler assigned responsibility for Jewish affairs exclusively to the SS and Heinrich Himmler.

Himmler appointed Reinhard Heydrich to head the Reich Central Office for Jewish Emigration. The agency directed its attention toward forcing Germany's half million Jews to leave the country. For example, the 10,000 Jews who were arrested and sent to Buchenwald after *Khristalnacht* were threatened with physical violence to convince them to emigrate. These harassment tactics produced some results; between 1933 and 1941, 260,000 Jews left Germany. However, many countries were reluctant to accept any more such refugees. The Jews that stayed were clearly in danger. In a speech he gave to the Reichstag on 30 January 1939, Hitler warned that the next European war would result in the eradication of all Jews.

Resettlement and Concentration. The defeat of Poland in September 1939 gave the Germans power over two million more Jews. In November, the Germans began herding the Jews into particular areas of cities that had large Jewish populations. The largest such settlement was the Jewish quarter (*Judische Wohnbeziek*) in Warsaw. A twelve-foot wall capped with barbed wire surrounded the ghetto's 400,000 people. Although many of these died from sickness and starvation, Jews brought in from the outside constantly replenished the losses. In July 1942, the Germans began rounding up residents of the Warsaw ghetto for transportation to Treblinka, where gassing facilities had just been constructed. The Germans told the Jews that they were being evacuated for resettlement. Historically, Jews had learned to live under persecution, and, therefore, few imagined that there could be a fate worse than life in the ghetto. Many saw the deportations as an opportunity for a new life and cooperated with the German authorities in carrying out the policy.

However, when the true nature of Nazi intentions became clear, cooperation turned to rebellion. Although the Warsaw Jews had no hope of prevailing against the organized might of the Third Reich, many resolved to die fighting rather than as lambs being led to the slaughter. In April 1943, they met a new deportation order with armed resistance. The Germans quickly mobilized a group of SS and German army units with Polish police and Ukrainian militia reinforcements. It was a desperate struggle and, despite the disparity in the resources of the adversaries, it lasted from 19 April until 16 May 1943. The Nazi commander, SS Brigadeführer Jürgen Stroop, finally broke Jewish resistance by burning down the ghetto block by block. Then his troops flushed out the survivors and marched them off for extermination (photo 3).

Forced Labor and Extermination. The Nazi state had no budget for the extermination of the Jews. The operation was paid for by the sale of confiscated Jewish property. Thus the victims financed their own destruction. The main "killing centers" were established in what had once been Poland. It built the largest of these facilities at Auschwitz-Birkenau, located west of Krakow. A decree of 12 October 1942 mandated that all the Jews of Germany be transferred there. Eventually, the complex became the focal point of a vast deportation network with railway lines stretching into all the occupied countries of Europe. Special trains arrived daily, sometimes several times a day, discharging their tightly-packed human cargos. The Reichsbahn, the state railroad agency, arranged all transportation through its Central European Travel Office. Its officials mobilized resources both inside and outside Germany, carrying out their jobs as if they were planning routine

3 **Waffen SS troops flush out a contingent of Jews from the burning Warsaw ghetto.** These terrified people, together with others rounded up in the operation, were taken to a collection point and then sent to Treblinka for extermination. During the final weeks of fighting, more than 56,000 Jews either perished in the fighting or were burned alive, shot on the spot, or sent to the gas chambers. For his service to the Fatherland, the leader of the operation, Jürgen Stroop, received the Iron Cross, First Class.

4 **An old woman and three small children, their bodies drenched with fatigue from their ordeal, trudge off to their deaths.** They have been told to carry only small packages as their heavier baggage will be delivered to them later. They will not have far to walk. The construction of an arrival platform at Birkenau brought the Jews almost to within the shadows of the crematoria chimneys.

excursion travel. The agency charged the SS a set rate for each person per kilometer traveled. Children under 4 went free; those under 10 were half fare. Consignments over 400 persons were also half fare. The SS saved money by automatically claiming that any shipment with more than 200 persons contained over 400. To further economize, the transports had no sanitary facilities and the prisoners received little food or water.

Camp guards drove the condemned from the boxcars and made them form two lines: men on the left, women and children on the right. Then they marched them to the end of the platform where SS officers separated those to die from those assigned to forced labor. In the first group were the non–able bodied, the old, the very young, and women with children. These people were immediately marched off to the gas chambers (photo 4). Their bodies were cremated that same day. The

5 **Buchenwald, established north of Weimar, was primarily a work camp for political prisoners.** Established in 1937, it became a relay station for thousands of Jews sent to the extermination camps of the east. In 1945, prisoners from other camps were moved here to keep them from being freed by the Allied armies. The Americans entered the camp on 11 April.

6 **When the British entered Bergen-Belsen, on 15 April 1945, they found thousands of unburied bodies littering the ground and crowding the barracks.** Many bodies were those of Jewish prisoners who had been moved there from other camps. Little care had been taken to house and feed them and protect them from disease. Over 18,000 had died from typhus in March 1945 alone. The camp was without food or water for five days before the British arrived. Almost one half of the 60,000 survivors died within several weeks of liberation.

others performed hard manual labor until they too became expendable and were sent to the gas chambers. Average life expectancy in the work camps was only a few months. Other extermination centers, like Treblinka, Sobibor, and Belzek, had no labor camps and no *Selektion,* but more people died at Auschwitz than anywhere else. The total was about 1,600,000 men, women, and children or more than one-fourth of all those who perished in the Holocaust. Tens of thousands of Gypsies and Soviet prisoners of war also died there.

In the summer of 1944, as the Soviet armies began their great offensive, the death camps started curtailing their killing operations. In November, Himmler ordered the gas chambers at Auschwitz dismantled and directed that the prison population be transferred to camps in Germany, like those at Dachau, Bergen-Belsen, and Buchenwald. Many prisoners died on the way from lack of food and water. Those who fell behind were shot. The "death marches" continued until Germany's surrender and took the lives of a quarter of a million people.

Although the SS maintained the strictest secrecy about the Final Solution, details about its operation gradually filtered out of Germany. Jewish exile groups learned of the gas chambers at Auschwitz and, in the spring of 1944, informed the British and American authorities of them, hoping to convince the two countries to bomb the camps' technical installations. However, their pleas went unanswered. Only at the end of the war did the grim details of the Final Solution become generally known, and the Allies made a great effort to find and punish the guilty. They captured many documents; the Germans had kept exact records. To these they added their own records. These included the photographs and movies taken when their armies liberated the camps. The pictures are unforgettable (photos 5 and 6). They show a dimension of human depravity which confounds justice and defies comprehension and forgiveness.

PART SIX

EUROPE IN THE AGE OF THE SUPERPOWERS, 1945–1960

CHAPTER 17

WAR AIMS AND POSTWAR RECONSTRUCTION, 1943–1948

PREFACE   The British and Americans and the Soviets came from different worlds with vastly different attitudes toward international politics. Just as Woodrow Wilson had minimized the security needs of the French in 1919, so Franklin D. Roosevelt a quarter of a century later also ignored crucial historical differences between his country and the Soviet Union. The United States was protected by two oceans and had traditionally viewed its security as absolute. Russia, as part of a great landmass, was surrounded by hostile neighbors with which it constantly competed for territory and power. The Communists did not need Marxist-Leninist doctrine to tell them that they occupied a precarious position in a hostile world. Stalin took his fears to the point of paranoia with his belief that the Western democracies were ganging up on him; yet, from the Soviet perspective, this seemed to be a safe assumption. In Russia, friendship was always a fragile straw upon which to base a policy. Thus, Stalin suspected that every decision the British and Americans made concerning the conduct of the war had a malevolent purpose. He refused to consider a combined command for fighting the war and put off meeting with Roosevelt until he believed he was in an advantageous position militarily; even then he selected a site for the conference that was close to the Soviet Union in territory occupied by the Red Army.

A dictator as brutal as Stalin was an affront to the very ideals Roosevelt espoused. Nevertheless, the American president was determined to win Stalin's confidence, even at the risk of chilled relations with Churchill. The task was impossible, however, and not just because of differences in background and attitude. As long as Roosevelt insisted on the right of self-determination of peoples, it was impossible to satisfy the Soviet demands for security. Moreover, Roosevelt could not even convince Stalin that the United States was wholeheartedly committed to the defeat of Nazi Germany. (Stalin believed only a cross-channel invasion of France could prove their determination.) Roosevelt, though, had high hopes that the global war would be followed by a global peace. Only the United States and the Soviet Union could guarantee this. Roosevelt's opportunity to discuss his great plans with Stalin came at Teheran in November 1943. This first summit conference of the three Allied powers set the stage for others to follow, but also showed the extent of the disagreement among the victors— differences that would determine the future shape and character of Europe.

THE END OF THE GRAND ALLIANCE

Negotiations at Teheran

Anglo-American Dissension. Britain wanted to fight the war as economically as possible, not out of stinginess but of necessity. Its efforts were truly heroic. Churchill knew that if his country suffered losses on the scale it had experienced in France during the last war, its position might be further weakened in the postwar world. For this reason, he refused to consider a cross-channel invasion until the Allied advantage was overwhelming. The British preferred to continue their efforts in the Mediterranean until the American buildup was so massive that there was no possibility of defeat. Only in August 1943 at Quebec did Roosevelt and Churchill finally agree to give priority to the invasion of France, setting a target date of 1 May 1944, a delay they knew carried risks. The Soviet victory at the Battle of Kursk in July 1943 had been so impressive that Churchill and Roosevelt thought the German defeat might come sooner than expected. The overthrow of Mussolini at the end of July showed how rapidly political circumstances could change. Therefore, the Americans presented a contingency plan, code-named "Rankin," calling for the immediate deployment of Anglo-American forces to the continent should suddenly German resistance end. In that event, Roosevelt was confident that the Allied armies could reach Berlin at the same time as the Soviets.

When the Teheran conference opened on 28 November 1943, the military situation was decidedly to the Soviet's advantage. The Red Army had an almost two-to-one superiority against the Germans. It had crossed the Dnieper the previous month and had liberated Kiev on 6 November. Meantime, the British and American advance in Italy was stalled along the Gustav line south of Rome, less than halfway up the peninsula. Nevertheless, the situation might change, and Stalin wanted an agreement on spheres of influence before Allied troops advanced farther north and closer to Central Europe. Stalin had chosen the capital city of Iran for the meeting because it was currently under joint Soviet-British protection, and because the Soviets controlled direct land communications to Moscow.[1] Roosevelt, however, protested that the remoteness of Teheran might prevent him from fulfilling his constitutional duty to sign or veto legislation within the required ten-day congressional limit.[2] Stalin replied that unless Teheran was chosen he could not attend, as he was obliged "to direct military operations day in and day out."[3] Roosevelt therefore gave way and worked out an arrangement whereby he would quit Teheran temporarily and fly to Tunis if a bill required his attention.

The foul mood of Churchill offset the high spirits and optimism of Roosevelt. When the prime minister arrived at the airport on 27 November 1943, his throat was so sore that he could speak only with difficulty. However, his cold was of small concern compared to the cold shoulder he felt Roosevelt was giving him. The two had not worked out a common conference strategy although they had flown to Teheran directly from Cairo, where they had just met with the Nationalist Chinese leader, Chiang Kai-shek.[4] Roosevelt had spent the whole time discussing the Far East situation and, at one point, had even suggested that Britain give up Hong Kong as a *"beau geste."* He avoided all private discussions with Churchill on the forthcoming conference and wasted enormous amounts of time posing for pictures. In fact, he was doing everything he could to avoid giving Stalin the impression that the Soviet Union would be faced by an Anglo-American front at Teheran. Churchill thought Roosevelt was "a charming country gentleman," but was appalled at his lack of professionalism.[5] Roosevelt was preoccupied with his grand plans for rearranging the affairs of the world. His great affection and personal friendship for Churchill did not erase his suspicion that the prime minister's foreign policy was geared toward the preservation and strengthening of Britain's imperial interests.

Once in Teheran, Roosevelt accepted Stalin's invitation to take up residence in a villa on the Soviet embassy grounds. Ostensibly, this housing solved the problems of security and discomfort due to Roosevelt's physical handicap, but it also gave Stalin an opportunity to disturb the current diplomatic equilibrium. When Roosevelt arrived, Stalin paid him a personal visit, setting a precedent for similar private meetings that were to continue throughout the conference.

Discussions on Strategy. The Americans and Soviets were in general agreement on how to fight the war. Churchill, though, keenly aware that the politics of postwar Europe would be determined by where the troops were when the fighting ceased, wanted to continue operations in the Mediterranean as part of a drive into Central Europe. He wanted to advance to Rome, push the Germans out of central Italy, and then launch an expedition across the Adriatic to help the Yugoslav partisans. He further believed that Turkey should be pressured into the war in order to "open up the Aegean Sea and assure an uninterrupted supply route to Russia into the Black Sea."[6] Turkish belligerency, Churchill said, would "undoubtedly have an effect on Rumania from whom peace feelers had already been received, and also from Hungary and might well start a landslide among the satellite states."[7] He wanted to exploit these opportunities even if it meant delaying the invasion of France. Churchill hoped this eastern strategy would limit Soviet influence in Eastern Europe at the end of the war.

Stalin opposed Churchill's scheme for that very reason, but, politics notwithstanding, the Soviet leader's arguments against the plan made sense militarily. He doubted the Turks would enter the war and questioned the wisdom of scattering Allied forces in various Mediterranean operations. Italy, he felt, was a poor place from which to launch an attack on Germany because the Alps constituted an almost insuperable barrier. He insisted that, after the capture of Rome, the Allied troops should be readied for an invasion of southern France to support the cross-channel attack in the north. "Russian experience," he remarked, "had shown that an attack from one direction was not effective and that the Soviet armies now launched an offensive from two sides at once which forced the enemy to move his reserve back and forth."[8] Roosevelt agreed, and the invasion of France, planned for spring 1944, was given top priority. The Soviets had wanted a second front in

1942, when the danger of Nazi victory was strong. Now they were to have it, two years later. Stalin believed the delay was deliberate to allow the West to profit from the further destruction of his country.

The British and Americans contemplated invading France with a combined force of thirty-five divisions, which in size were about the equivalent of fifty German divisions—an unimpressive army by Soviet standards. The Soviets currently had five million men fighting to Germany's three million. It was therefore romantic nonsense to believe that Churchill's southern strategy could have prevented a Soviet movement into Eastern Europe. As Churchill himself told Stalin, only two or three divisions were available for capturing the islands of the Aegean Sea and a scant "20 squadrons of fighters and several anti-aircraft regiments"[9] to send to aid Turkey, hardly a force capable of making any great impact. Had the British and Americans been capable of invading the Romanian and Hungarian plains in sufficient numbers to launch an attack up the Danube, had they been able to overcome the enormous problems posed by extended supply lines, they would still not have been able to prevent the eventual division of Europe between the Soviet Union and the democracies. An army as vast and powerful as the Soviet force would not have stood idly by while the British and Americans were butting their heads against mountainous defenses in unfamiliar terrain, possibly waiting for the military effort of their adversaries to collapse quickly as had occurred in the Balkan theater at the end of World War I. The Soviets most likely would have concentrated their efforts in eastern Prussia and Poland, striking across Germany to the Low Countries and dividing Europe north and south rather than east and west. Certainly, Stalin was protecting his country's right to a clear field in the Balkans, a traditional area of Russian interest, by insisting that the second front be opened in France, but his strategy also promoted the best interests of the Western powers. How lasting would have been any British and American guarantees in the Balkans, a part of Europe to which they had never before felt any particular obligation?

The British had always shied away from commitments in Eastern Europe; the Americans had difficulty accepting political responsibility for *any* part of Europe. George C. Marshall, the American chief of staff, dismissed Churchill's contention that Europe had a "soft underbelly." In the fall of 1943, he wrote: "Even though we were now firmly entrenched in North Africa to have attempted to force Germany from the South across the Alpine barrier was on the face of it impracticable. In Europe's innumerable wars no vigorously opposed crossing of the Alps had ever been successfully executed."[10] Any major Allied offensive in the Balkans would have given the Germans the welcome advantage of fighting all their major enemies on the same front.

The German Question. The problem of how to treat Germany proved even more ticklish. Faced with the persistent brutality of the Nazi regime, the three leaders assumed that the best way to guarantee a future free of German aggression was to break up the country into smaller units. Roosevelt proposed cutting up the country into seven parts: five would be self-governing areas; the other two would be placed under international control. Stalin wanted Germany dismembered to avoid a rebirth of militarism.[11] The Soviet dictator believed that the Germans would always follow men such as Hitler, an opinion that contained no little amount of irony considering his own brutal style of leadership.[12] Stalin insisted that the subjugation and control of Germany must last indefinitely. At a dinner at the Soviet embassy on 29 November, he said that effective control of Germany required the physical liquidation of between 50,000 and 100,000 German military leaders—a conservative number by Stalin's murderous standards. An angry Churchill declared that he would rather "be taken out into the garden here and now and be shot myself than sully my own and my country's honour by such infamy."[13] Whereupon he left the table and walked into the next room. Stalin followed him and, smiling broadly, tried to pass off the remark as a joke. Churchill believed that Stalin was serious.[14]

Churchill believed that wars were fought to restore balances of power. Germany, therefore, should not be defeated so badly as to allow the Soviet Union to rise in its place. Such an outcome to the war could only threaten the security of the rest of Europe, including Great Britain. The prime minister wanted a united, economically prosperous, democratic Germany, but agreed to settle for a three-way split. Churchill believed that a European equilibrium had to be ensured with the reconstruction of France as a strong nation, friendly to the West. Stalin wanted France kept weak as punishment for French collaboration with Germany. He believed that the whole French nation, particularly its leaders and upper classes, was rotten and that it did not deserve to play an important part in the immediate postwar world. Roosevelt seemed to agree. "Many years of honest labour would be necessary before France would be re-established. He said the first necessity for the French, not only for the Government but the people as well, was to become honest citizens."[15]

Stalin was full of other friendly advice. He suggested "that Great Britain and the United States install more suitable government in Spain and Portugal, since he was convinced that Franco was no friend."[16] He also encouraged the British to annex more land around Gibraltar.

On the Future of Poland. Britain and the United States were both committed to the reestablishment of a strong and independent Poland. However, the Soviet Union intended to determine that nation's future. Churchill recognized the irony of going to war to defend a state that lay outside the traditional British sphere of interest. Roosevelt had shed his previous reluctance to consider Soviet revisionism in Eastern Europe, but he did not want to appear as if he were participating in an arrangement that would jeopardize Poland's national independence. He explained that six or seven million Americans of Polish extraction dictated his attitude. As a practical man, he did not wish to lose their vote.

The West was not in a very strong position to establish Poland's future frontiers. Churchill had reconciled himself to this loss of influence and told Stalin that "he personally had no attachment to any specific frontier between Poland and the Soviet Union; [but] that he felt that the consideration of Soviet security on their western frontiers was a governing factor."[17] Stalin insisted that Poland's eastern frontiers would be those established by the 1939 German-Soviet Nonaggression Pact; he felt these were "just right."[18] He intended to compensate Poland with German territory, pushing the country's western boundary to the Oder River and into eastern Prussia. Furthermore, since it seemed unlikely that Stalin could be coaxed into recognizing the Polish government in exile in London, any future Polish government would exist only at Soviet sufferance. The same was true of the Baltic peoples. Stalin did not consider the future status of Latvia, Lithuania, and Estonia subject to negotiation: these states would be reincorporated automatically into the Soviet Union. When Churchill expressed a desire to see Finland remain independent, Stalin agreed, but insisted "they must pay half of the damage they had caused."[19]

The Four Policemen. Stalin's authority at Teheran flowed naturally from the power of his army, which was more than adequate to ensure Soviet domination of Eastern Europe. The negotiations helped him gauge Western intentions. He saw that the British and Americans had serious disagreements over the character of their future political commitments to Europe. Churchill wanted to prevent Great Power—that is, Soviet—domination of the continent. Roosevelt was preoccupied with creating a new world organization, which, as he explained on the first day of the conference, meant establishing sovereignty in a collective body such as the United Nations, "a concept which had never been developed in past history."[20] Roosevelt envisioned the basic power of this postwar organization in the hands of the "Four Policemen"; that is, the Soviet Union, the United States, Great Britain, and China—states with the strength to deal with any emergency and threat to peace. As policemen, they would have the right to threaten aggressive nations with "immediate bombardment and possible invasion."[21] When Roosevelt explained his personal commitment to worldwide organization, he gave the Soviets the impression that they need not fear the United States as a powerful rival in postwar European affairs. The Americans, in keeping with their past record in foreign wars, would initiate a disengagement as soon as victory was achieved. Roosevelt told Stalin that only in the most extreme case, such as the current crisis, would the Americans ever again contemplate sending troops to Europe. In a lesser crisis, he envisaged the "sending of American planes and ships," but "England and the Soviet Union would have to handle the land armies in the event of any future threat to peace."[22]

Stalin wanted to recover the territory lost by Russia at the end of World War I, and he wanted to establish a sphere of influence in Eastern Europe. Beyond this, his aims seemed dependent upon "what form of security organization would be developed after the war and how far the United States and British governments were prepared to go in implementing the police power of such an organization."[23] Although no final decisions were made at Teheran, the discussions revealed the fears and hopes of the participants, and the conference established the agenda for future meetings of the Big Three. Stalin was always more an opportunist than a rigid doctrinaire. In his determination to wield absolute power, he had made the Communist dialectic his servant. Thus, the future confrontation with his Western allies developed more from the practical concerns of projecting power than from an inevitable clash of contradictory ideologies. Stalin made it clear at Teheran that Soviet security would not be satisfied with anything less than the domination of Poland. Furthermore, he would set that country's new boundaries.

Roosevelt would have preferred a sovereign Poland, but he was not prepared to risk antagonizing Stalin and thereby losing Soviet cooperation after the war by insisting on freedom for the Poles. Roosevelt also set the strategy that would bring final victory in Europe by definitively agreeing on the two-pronged invasion of France from the west and the south—an operation Churchill had tried to delay as long as possible.[24]

The Conference at Yalta

Soviet Hegemony in Eastern Europe. By the late summer of 1944, the western Allies had liberated Paris and were across the Seine; meanwhile the Soviet army had reached the borders of prewar Poland and was driving into Romania. The German invaders had been successfully cleared from almost the entire country. Romania capitulated on 23 August; Bulgaria surrendered the following month.

At a reception in the Livadia Palace during the Yalta Conference, host President Franklin Roosevelt seems to be the only one paying attention to the toast being offered by Secretary of State Edward Stettinius. Josef Stalin and Winston Churchill on Roosevelt's right and left have their attention focused elsewhere, while Soviet Foreign Minister Vyacheslav, at the end of the table, peruses the menu. Many more toasts will be offered before this banquet is over.

Stalin knew that the Red Army would assure the Soviets control of Eastern Europe, but not until the war against Germany was as good as over did he consent to another summit meeting, this time at Yalta, the favorite summer residence of the last tsar. The Germans had evacuated the town the previous year and had left it in shambles. The Soviets worked hard to refurbish the place, completing the job just weeks before the conference opened on 4 February 1945. Every effort was made to ensure the comfort of the guests. A member of the British delegation casually remarked that the cocktails contained no lemon peels, and "the next day a lemon tree loaded with fruit was growing in the hall."[25] This courtesy made up in part for the bedbugs and toilets that did not flush. Stalin was friendly, charming, and confident. He had good reason to be.

While the British and the Americans were still recovering the ground they had lost during the Battle of the Bulge, the Red Army was forty miles from Berlin, a bit more than a day's march if unopposed. German resistance in Hungary had been crushed, and the road to Vienna lay open, with the Soviets in control of most of the territory of Eastern and Southeastern Europe. Stalin had largely decided what he wanted and was now determined to keep it. In December 1944, much to the dismay of the West, he had recognized his own creation, the Communist Lublin government, as the basis upon which he would construct the future political administration of Poland. He was also entrenching Communist leaders in positions of power in Bulgaria, Romania, and Hungary.

Churchill and Roosevelt wanted to prevent the communization of Poland, but with the Soviets already occupying most of the country, Churchill could only complain that Poland should be mistress of her house and captain of her soul. Roosevelt, by this time a very sick man with only a few months to live, again tried to coax Stalin into making a gesture by reminding him of the six or seven million Polish-Americans who formed part of the Democratic party's electorate. Stalin was not inclined to be generous. He insisted that the security of the Soviet Union depended upon a subservient Poland. He did agree to "add to the Provisional Polish (Lublin) Government some democratic leaders from Polish émigré circles . . . . and from inside Poland," a vague concession more than offset by maximum demands over Poland's future boundaries. Stalin had decided that Poland's western frontiers should be traced from the town of Stettin southward to and along the Oder River and then south along the Neisse River.[26] Since the hundreds of thousands of Germans who lived in this area would be cleared out, its separation from the Reich might cause permanent Polish-German hostility and allow the Soviet Union to assume the role of Poland's protector. The British and Americans realized this would be the likely outcome, but they could do little to prevent it. They saved face by deferring the question to an eventual postwar peace conference.

Although the Polish question was discussed at seven of the eight plenary sessions, the Western leaders had more important things on their minds. Churchill, still trying to get the Soviet Union's help in restoring a general European balance of power, lobbied for an occupation zone for France in Germany. Roosevelt pushed for amplification of the authority of the United Nations through which he hoped to re-create international order and extend American influence.[27] He also wanted China to be elevated to Great Power status, and he wanted the cooperation of the Soviet Union in the war against Japan.

As a result of the desperate, suicidal resistance by the Japanese on Okinawa and Iwo Jima, the Americans assumed that an invasion of the Japanese home islands would be necessary to end the war. General Leslie Groves, the head of the Manhattan Project to develop an atomic bomb, had judged that a bomb equivalent to ten thousand tons of TNT, enough power to wreck a large city, would be operational only by August 1945. Less than two weeks before the beginning of the Yalta Conference, the Joint Chiefs of Staff informed Roosevelt that "Russia's entry at as early a date as possible consistent with her ability to engage in offensive operations is necessary to provide maximum assistance to our Pacific operations."[28] Roosevelt was therefore prepared to offer the Soviets powerful inducements to fight the Japanese. Specifically, he promised the restoration of Russia's former rights "violated by the treacherous attack of Japan in 1904," including the southern half of Sakhalin Island, the lease of Port Arthur as a Soviet naval base, and the joint operation of the Chinese-Eastern and South-Manchurian Railroads. The Soviets would also get the Kurile Islands.[29] In exchange, Stalin agreed to attack Japan within ninety days after the end of the war in Europe, enough time for the Soviets to transfer their armies to Asia. He also pledged to conclude a pact of friendship and alliance with the National Government of China "in order to render assistance to China with its armed forces for the purposes of liberating China from the Japanese yoke."[30] The Americans assumed that China would emerge as a major East Asian power and wanted to promote the stability of the Nationalist government. They also believed that since the Soviet Union was a Far Eastern as well as a European power, it was better to offer the Soviets something and win their support for the status quo rather than risk making them perpetual antagonists.

How to Treat Germany. The major problem facing the Big Three continued to be the question of Germany. Roosevelt and Stalin were still disposed to treat the defeated with great severity. The American president had once advocated a plan, advanced by his secretary of the treasury Henry Morgenthau, that proposed to destroy Germany's industrial potential and return the country to a pastoral economy. Churchill had gone along, especially when (at the second Quebec Conference in September 1944) his acquiescense had produced an American commitment to lend Britain $6.5 billion after the war.

No sooner had he agreed than he began to have second thoughts. Roosevelt was also becoming somewhat less extreme. Both Secretary of State Cordell Hull and Secretary of War Henry Stimson thought the impoverishment of Germany would be disastrous for rebuilding a prosperous Europe. Although the stern approach had gradually lost favor, the attitudes that had inspired it nevertheless remained and helped prolong the discussions on dismembering Germany. At the session on 5 February, Stalin said he assumed that everybody was still in favor of partition and asked what this would involve. Would the Allies establish one German government, or would they set up separate governments for each of the various parts? Since Churchill was unwilling to go further than recognizing the principle of dismemberment, no agreement was possible. Therefore, the Allies recognized the likelihood of dismemberment only if that became necessary for future peace and security.

The Big Three confirmed the zones of occupation, which had been agreed upon in principle at the Moscow Conference of Foreign Ministers in October 1943. In February 1944, the foreign ministers set the future zone of Soviet occupation and agreed on the joint occupation of Berlin. These decisions were confirmed and further defined at Yalta. Under the plan, each of the three powers would occupy its own zone but would coordinate administration and control through a central commission consisting of the Supreme Commanders of the Three Powers. This would mean that roughly 40 percent of pre-1938 German territory (with 36 percent of the population) would be under Soviet control with the rest divided between Britain and the United States. Berlin was to be administered under the combined control of all three. Mainly through pressure from Churchill, Stalin agreed that France could have a zone of occupation and participate in the administration of postwar Germany, providing the French share came from the area allotted to the British and Americans. The inclusion of France marked a major change in attitude from the Teheran Conference where Stalin and Roosevelt had maintained that France would not be allowed to play a major role in European politics after the war. Only Churchill had put in a good word for the French, saying that he could not conceive of a civilized world without a flourishing and lively France. The inclusion of France in the occupation plan had positive and negative aspects. On the one hand, France, not being a party to the Yalta accords, did not feel bound by them; on the other hand, the Western powers had enlarged their stake in German affairs, especially their position in Berlin, a city completely surrounded by Soviet territory. French inclusion enhanced the legal independence of the city and increased the determination of the Western powers to hold on to their share during the Soviet blockade of 1948.[31]

Stalin demanded that Germany pay heavy reparations. He wanted certain industries, like machine tools, to be transferred to the Soviet Union; he wanted the rolling stock, plus yearly payments in kind for a decade. He also demanded a general reduction of German heavy industry by 80 percent and insisted that "in the interests of the orderly execution of the reparations plan and for the security of Europe there should be an Anglo-Soviet-American control over the German economy which would last beyond the period of the reparations payment."[32] Roosevelt favored giving the German people only enough to keep them from starvation, while Churchill warned that the exaggerated demands made on Germany after World War I eventually proved self-defeating. The question was not settled. The Allies declared Germany responsible for the losses it caused during the war and left it to the Reparations Commission to work out the details.

Lesser Issues. The British and Americans tried to obtain an agreement for the development of independent governments in Eastern Europe; they settled for a confirmation of the Atlantic Charter in the "Declaration of Liberated Europe," which promised that "the restoration of sovereign rights and self-government [would go] to those people who have been forcibly deprived of them by the aggressive nations."[33] Stalin showed a willingness to reach an agreement on the establishment of the United Nations, an area that he believed Roosevelt considered important largely to satisfy American popular opinion. Stalin emphasized that "he was prepared in concert with the United States and Great Britain to protect the rights of the small powers but that he would never agree to having any action of any of the Great Powers submitted to the judgment of the small powers."[34] The five permanent members of the United Nations Security Council (the Soviet Union, the United States, Britain, France, and China) had to agree unanimously on how to enforce the peace. None of them believed that a system of world security could really prevent aggression.

Stalin did not consider the Yalta agreements an inhibition on his freedom of action in Eastern Europe. His promise to allow free elections in Eastern Europe was not sincere. He once remarked to Marshal Georgi Zhukov: "Churchill wants the Soviet Union to border with a bourgeois Poland, alien to us, while we can not allow this to happen. We want to have, once and for all, a friendly Poland as our neighbor, and that is what the Polish people want too."[35] Stalin apparently believed Roosevelt's assurances that American troops would be gone from Europe within two years.[36] Therefore, once he had consolidated his hold in Eastern Europe, there would be nothing to prevent him from extending Soviet influence westward if he so desired.

SPHERES OF INFLUENCE

The Potsdam Conference

A Campaign of Stalinization. Shortly after the end of the Yalta Conference, Stalin dispatched Andrei Vyshinsky to Romania. Vyshinsky's job was to pressure King Michael into dismissing his present government, which the Soviets deemed terroristic and incompatible with the principles of a people's democracy, and replacing it with one totally controlled by Communists. The king gave way. In the new ministry, representatives of "bourgeois" parties held only two portfolios. Roosevelt charged that the Soviet action was incompatible with Stalin's promises at Yalta, which were embodied in the Declaration of Liberated Europe. But the protests changed nothing.

Stalin's heavy hand in Romanian politics was the prelude for a general purge of all non-Communists from the left-of-center coalition governments that had emerged elsewhere in Eastern Europe. When in March 1945 the West protested the arrest of certain non-Communist Polish underground leaders, Stalin defiantly replied:

> You evidently do not agree that the Soviet Union is entitled to seek in Poland a Government that would be friendly to it, that the Soviet Government can not agree to the existence in Poland of a Government hostile to it. I do not know whether a genuinely representative government has been

established in Greece, or whether the Belgian Government is a genuinely democratic one. The Soviet Union was not consulted when those governments were being formed, nor did it claim the right to interfere in these matters, because it realized how important Belgium and Greece are to the security of Great Britain.[37]

Stalin insisted that the arrests were necessary for military security.[38] The Czechs tried to head off similar Soviet pressure by voluntarily reorganizing their government to include Communists. This action did not dissuade Stalin from demanding Ruthenia. Historically, this territory had never been part of Russia, but Stalin wanted it because it would move the Soviet frontier across the Carpathian Mountains and create a common border with Hungary. Stalin also retained a piece of prewar Romanian territory that gave the Soviet Union part of the mouth of the Danube River; and he lopped off the northern part of East Prussia, which bordered on the Baltic and included the famous ice-free port of Königsberg. The Soviets claimed to be merely administering the area pending a German peace treaty, but the acquisition became permanent.

The British and Americans had been willing to recognize the Soviet Union as a paramount power in Eastern Europe, but they were horrified at Stalin's systematic extinction of the area's political independence. They hoped the example of Finland might provide a suitable alternative to tight control. Finland had recognized Soviet hegemony, yet retained its independence. The campaign of stalinization in Eastern Europe seemed to be motivated by more than a desire for security, and it only confirmed their suspicions that Stalin was developing bases from which he would project Soviet power westward. The Soviets also continued to pressure Turkey to cede the Transcaucasian areas that the Treaty of Brest-Litovsk had detached from Russia in 1918. They also demanded revision of the Montreux Convention to allow their warships free passage through the Istanbul Straits, and they wanted to establish a Soviet military and naval base on the Sea of Marmara, in effect blocking the passage of others from the Aegean to the Black Sea. Moreover, the international Communist movement, though not the Comintern, which had been dissolved in 1943 to appease the British and the Americans, was being reactivated and reorganized to prepare for a new era of revolutionary militancy.

The Soviets wanted to avoid any direct confrontation with the West, at least until they had established firm control over Eastern Europe. They therefore cooperated in the establishment of the United Nations and freely signed proclamations in favor of democratic liberties and national independence. Stalin had learned to count on what he regarded as Roosevelt's generous idealism. He was therefore greatly disturbed by news of the American war leader's death on 12 April 1945. Harry Truman, Roosevelt's successor, was an unknown quantity. He had little experience in foreign affairs, but intended to show that he could be firm and would make no concessions from basic principles or traditions in order to win Soviet favor.[39] Stalin, anxious to discover whether Truman contemplated any policy changes, had Foreign Minister Vyacheslav Molotov stop off in Washington on his way to the United Nations meeting at San Francisco. Molotov found that the new chief executive regarded the Polish question as the acid test of Soviet willingness to cooperate. Truman accused the Soviets of violating the Yalta accord, and when Molotov became evasive, the president became more forceful. "I have never been talked to like that in my life," protested Molotov. "Carry out your agreements and you won't get talked to like that," the president replied.[40]

The Strains of Diplomacy. The final defeat of Nazi Germany made another summit conference necessary. On 6 May, the day before the German surrender at Reims, Churchill proposed that one be held "in some unshattered town in Germany, if such can be found."[41] The prime minister was particularly delighted that President Truman, whom he had never met, intended to stand firmly on "our rightful interpretation of the Yalta Agreements," but the Americans' intention to pull their troops out of Europe deeply worried him. Churchill feared that if the outstanding differences between the West and the Soviet Union were not settled before this withdrawal occurred, there would be no satisfactory solution and very little chance of preventing a third world war.[42]

The conference finally got under way in Potsdam, near Berlin, on 17 July. Its meetings were held at the Cecilienhof Palace, the country estate of Crown Prince Wilhelm, the last Hohenzollern heir to the throne. The purpose of the meeting was to prepare for an eventual peace conference that would draft a treaty of peace with Germany. The task of drafting treaties of peace with Italy, Romania, Bulgaria, Hungary, and Finland was assigned to a special council of foreign ministers from the five major victorious governments: the United States, Britain, the Soviet Union, France, and China.[43] Truman hoped the Foreign Ministers Council would expedite the final peace, but with the heads of government so divided, the group's ability to propose solutions to problems was limited.

Stalin came to Potsdam to get the West to accept his new order in Eastern Europe. The British and Americans had officially rejected, but privately accepted, the Soviet presence there, but they disagreed over important details. Churchill protested the Soviet scheme to turn the parts of Germany that were to form Poland's western frontier over to Polish administration. He said this would admit the Poles as a fifth occupying power and "would undoubtedly mark a breakdown of the Conference."[44] Stalin claimed that these territories were practically all Polish because the local German population had fled before the Red Army had arrived.[45] Truman supported Churchill and asked if Germany were going to be given away piecemeal. But nothing was going to stop Stalin from carrying out the changes he thought necessary. All Germans in the lands east of the Oder-Neisse line were systematically being rounded up and expelled. The Poles did not want any repetition of the irredentist agitation that had followed World War I.

There were acrimonious exchanges over German reparations. The Soviets insisted they immediately be paid half of the $20 billion they claimed at Yalta. Churchill and Truman feared that such an amount would critically damage the German economy, contribute to revolution, civil disorder, and starvation, and force the West to subsidize the German standard of living. In short, Britain and the United States would bankroll Soviet reparations. Churchill knew that his country was in no condition to undertake such support, even had it desired to do so. He told Truman that Britain itself needed aid. In order to fight the war, he said, Britain "had spent more than half her foreign investments for the common cause when we were alone, and now emerged from the war with a great external debt of three thousand million pounds . . . . we should [therefore] have to ask for help to become a going concern again, and until we got our wheels turning properly we could be of little use to world security."[46] The Soviets also continued to demand official recognition of their Eastern European puppet regimes. The Americans countered by asking that the Soviets honor the Declaration of Liberated Europe. Stalin pushed for greater Soviet influence in Iran and Turkey; a share in

At Potsdam, two
newcomers to
international diplomacy,
Prime Minister Clement
Attlee and President
Harry Truman, stand
next to veteran
negotiator Josef Stalin,
who as usual is backed by
his faithful henchman
Molotov. Attlee defeated
Churchill in the British
general election and
replaced him halfway
through the conference.

the administration of Libya, the old Italian colony of Tripoli; and the annexation of the port of Königsberg. At a banquet in Churchill's honor on 23 July, he asked in the middle of the toasts, "If you find it impossible to give us a fortified position in the Marmara, could we not have a base at Dedeagatch [Alexandroúpolis]?"[47]

A Proposed Compromise. Midway through the conference, the British electorate replaced Churchill with Clement Attlee. The new prime minister, who arrived in Potsdam on 28 July, brought no change to British policy—he had been Churchill's deputy and needed no special briefing—but, lacking the prestige of his predecessor, he was not as forceful in pressing the Soviets. This opened the way for Truman, who was becoming impatient and wanted to conclude the negotiations as quickly as possible. The Americans proposed a compromise: they would agree to the Polish western boundary if the Soviets would give in on German reparations. Truman allowed the Poles to administer all the German territory east of the Oder-Neisse line, pending a final settlement at the peace conference, in exchange for Stalin's agreement to take most of his reparations from the Soviet zone.[48] The compromise was not an entirely happy one for either party. Reparation was the issue on which the Soviets had the greatest moral claim, but the one on which they received the least satisfaction; and by informally recognizing the Soviet frontiers for Poland, the Americans seemed to be sacrificing liberty for expediency.[49]

The exchange of promises was not significant in political terms; both reparations and Poland were lost causes. However, the compromise did allow agreement to be reached on a series of minor issues. There was to be no immediate reestablishment of a German central government, although the division of the country into zones was not intended to be permanent. (Had Stalin then considered politically separating the Soviet zone from the rest of Germany, it does not seem likely that he would have given so much valuable German territory to Poland.) Finance, transport, communications, foreign trade, and industry would be administered collectively, and the country would be treated as a single economic unit with common policies on industrial production, wages and prices, currency and banking, central taxation, and customs. But, despite these accords, the wartime alliance was finished. The Potsdam decisions were intended to be provisional pending final ne-gotiations at a peace conference. It was doubtful such a meeting would ever be held. Furthermore, the agreement was achieved without the participation of France. The Big Three had assumed that Charles de Gaulle would automatically give his assent. This was a mistake. De Gaulle did not feel bound by the decisions of any conference to which he had not been invited.

Great Power Rivalry

Efforts at Peacemaking. The two meetings of the Council of Foreign Ministers immediately after Potsdam, held in London in September 1945 and in Moscow in December 1945, produced little progress toward peacemaking and only reaf-firmed existing disagreements. When the Americans continued to push for free elections in Eastern Europe, the Soviets took their insistence as evidence of an unfriendly attitude, a charge the Americans staunchly denied. Yet establishing Western-style democracies was difficult in a region with such a strong authoritarian tradition. Only the Czechs had really succeeded. Moreover, the Soviets feared that allowing free elections would have resulted in the victory of anti-Soviet, anti-Communist leaders. The Soviets, therefore, assumed the Americans were only interested in weakening Soviet control so they could extend Western influence. The Soviets, with a certain amount of truth, pointed out that the United States wanted entry to the Soviet sphere of interest while excluding the Soviet Union from the Western sphere. The Soviets also feared the United States might threaten them with nuclear weapons. At the September meeting in London, when Molotov asked Secretary of State James Byrnes if he had an atomic bomb in his side pocket, Byrnes replied, "We carry our artillery in our hip pocket. If you don't cut out this stalling and let us get down to work, I am going to pull an atomic bomb out of my hip pocket and let you have it."[50] The remark did not actually reflect American nuclear diplomacy, but the sour-faced Molotov could hardly be expected to ap-preciate the American brand of humor.

The atmosphere was not nearly so tense at the December conference. Never-theless, the failure to reach any agreement over levels of German production and economic unity convinced Secretary of State Byrnes that the Soviets were eager to profit politically from the country's weakness. The Soviets did consent to broaden the Communist-dominated regimes in Bulgaria and Romania to include other anti-fascist parties. And they agreed to attend a general peace conference to be held in Paris the following year and to help prepare for the peaceful use of nuclear energy through a United Nations Atomic Energy Commission.

Truman thought such gestures meaningless. Yet, while he talked about con-fronting the Soviets with an iron fist, his administration was presiding over one of the most complete and rapid military demobilizations of modern times. In less than two years after Hitler's defeat, only two American, four British, and three French divisions were stationed in Western Europe, all uncoordinated by any ef-fective military alliance. The Soviets had also demobilized, though not as signifi-cantly. They had reduced the 500 divisions in existence at the time of Germany's surrender down to 175, concentrating 60 percent of these forces in the occupied countries of Europe and the proximate western border regions of the Soviet Union. In East Germany alone, the Soviets had 22 divisions, 18 of them armored. The cutback had actually resulted in a more efficient and better equipped force. More-over, as soon as hostilities ended, the Soviets launched a major arms modernization program, with emphasis on the development of a long-range air force and a first-class oceangoing navy. The Americans believed such military strength vastly exceeded what the Soviets needed for legitimate self-defense.

George Kennan, the American chargé d'affaires in Moscow, sounded the alarm about Soviet intentions when he called the Soviet Union:

> a political force committed fanatically to the belief that with the U.S. there can be no permanent *modus vivendi* that it is desirable and necessary that the internal harmony of our society be disrupted, our traditional way of life be destroyed, the international authority of our state be broken, if Soviet power is to be secure. This political force . . . . is borne along by deep and powerful currents of Russian nationalism. . . . For it, the vast fund of objective fact about human society is not, as with us, the measure against which outlook is constantly being tested and re-formed, but a grab bag from which individual items are selected arbitrarily and tendentiously to bolster an outlook already preconceived. . . . [But] Soviet power, unlike that of Hitlerite Germany, is neither schematic nor adventuristic. It does not work by fixed plans. It does not take unnecessary risks. [It is] impervious to [the] logic of reasons, [but] it is highly sensitive to [the] logic of force. For this reason it can easily withdraw—and usually does—when strong resistance is encountered at any point. Thus, if the adversary has sufficient force and makes clear his readiness to use it, he rarely has to do so.[51]

Kennan got support from a welcome quarter. Winston Churchill, in his famous speech at Fulton, Missouri (5 March 1946), said:

> Nobody knows what Soviet Russia and its Communist international organization intends to do in the immediate future, or what are the limits, if any, to their expansive and proselytizing tendencies. . . . From Stettin in the Baltic to Trieste in the Adriatic an iron curtain has descended across the continent. . . . The communist parties, which were very small in these eastern states of Europe, have been raised to pre-eminence and power beyond their numbers and are seeking everywhere to obtain totalitarian control.[52]

Stalin's attitude clearly was "I control what I conquer," but to belabor the point, the West was also unwilling to allow Soviet influence in its zones of occupation. Churchill, who was no longer prime minister, was unlikely to have made this speech without the approval of President Truman, who was in the audience.

Stalin took the words as conclusive evidence of an Anglo-American cabal. He described the speech as "an unfriendly act and an unwarranted attack on himself and the U.S.S.R. which, if it had been directed against the United States, would never have been permitted in Russia."[53] Stalin thought that Churchill was trying to instigate war against the Soviet Union with the participation of the United States, as had been done in 1919. In response, Soviet propaganda became more violently anti-American. American leaders were denounced for having abandoned Roosevelt's heritage and succumbed to "militarist, imperialist, and expansionist tendencies incompatible with international peace and security."[54] The United States was Fascism in another guise, "a manifestation of capitalist society in its imperialistic phase." The Soviets believed that both the United States and Great Britain were supporting Fascism to fight democracy and the Soviet Union. However, the United States was "much the greater menace since it emerged from the war as the strongest of capitalist countries."[55] In this tense atmosphere, the victors met to try to produce a peace settlement.

The Results of the Plenary Conference. Representatives of twenty-two states gathered in Paris in the Luxembourg Palace, on 29 July 1946, to draft peace treaties between the Allies and Italy, Bulgaria, Hungary, Romania, and Finland. The contrasts between this peace conference and the one that followed World War I were striking. The 1919 conference had moments of high drama and genuine accomplishment; the participants in 1946 were men of lesser stature—although South Africa's Jan Christian Smuts was present at both—and their deliberations seemed lackluster. Most of the preparatory work had been done the previous spring by experts who labored over the texts of the treaties, trying to produce drafts that would win final approval. Their efforts were far from conclusive. The Plenary Conference continued the work, deliberating for almost three months over a host of amendments. Even when the "final" texts were submitted to the Council of Foreign Ministers the second week of October, the deadlock continued. The representatives of the Great Powers decided to continue the discussions at a later date among themselves. Thus, the Plenary Conference ended without achieving its purpose. Georges Bidault, the French foreign minister and later premier, wrote, "When everyone got together, there were no results at all." Nor was anything accomplished when the four countries discussed things by themselves. Only "the tone changed slightly."[56] Bidault's judgment may have been too harsh. Although the council failed to reach an overall agreement on Central Europe, peace treaties were eventually worked out with the lesser enemy powers. Moreover, the Soviets were willing to permit the existence of a reasonably independent Finland.

The Council of Foreign Ministers finalized the treaties at sessions held at the Waldorf Astoria in New York (4 November–6 December). The signing ceremony took place in Paris on 10 February 1947 at the French Foreign Ministry in the Salle de l'Horloge, the same room where the plenary sessions of the Paris Conference negotiating the Treaty of Versailles in 1919 were held. Each of the five treaties contained an affirmation of the inviolability of human rights and fundamental freedoms as well as reparations clauses and disarmament provisions. Their territorial provisions were heavily influenced by former treaties, especially those negotiated at Paris in 1919–1920. The previous summer each of the enemy countries had an opportunity to make comments and observations on the draft treaties. They all sought to mitigate the terms, claiming that they were not the same nations they had been previously. Little of this special pleading had been effective.

Italy was shorn of all the territory it had annexed during the Fascist period and was deprived of its colonial possessions. Its losses included Rhodes and the Dodecanese, which went to Greece; most of the territory on the Dalmatian coast (the greater part of Venezia Giulia with Istria, Fiume, and the Adriatic islands), which went to Yugoslavia; and some small northwestern frontier areas, which went to France. The Italians also surrendered sovereignty over Ethiopia, Libya, Eritrea, and Italian Somaliland. Italy was allowed to keep the South Tyrol, and it managed—in 1954—to recover the city of Trieste, which the treaty originally created a free city under the protection of the Security Council of the United Nations.[57] The Italian armed forces were limited to 300,000 troops; and the country was required to pay a total of $360 million in reparations to the Soviet Union, Greece, Yugoslavia, Ethiopia, and Albania.

The other Axis states were also stripped of their ill-gotten gains. Romania was forced to give Bessarabia and northern Bukovina to the Soviet Union, surrender the Black Sea province of Dobruja to Bulgaria, and cede Transylvania to Hungary. In addition, Romania was required to pay the Soviets $300 million in reparations and limit the size of its armed forces to 138,000 troops. Hungary returned to the

GERMAN ZONES
OF OCCUPATION

SOVIET TERRITORIAL GAINS
1946

From Poland

From Finland

From Germany

From Czechoslovakia

From Romania

From Estonia, Lithuania,
and Latvia

POLISH TERRITORIAL GAINS
1946

From Germany

Soviet Republic Boundary

Iron Curtain

Map 15

frontiers of the Treaty of Trianon. Its armed forces were reduced to 70,000 men, and it was forced to pay an indemnity of $200 million to the Soviet Union and $100 million apiece to Czechoslovakia and Yugoslavia. Bulgaria lost the lands it had added as a result of its association with Nazi Germany but gained Dobruja from Romania. Finland did not get off so easily. In addition to the territories the Soviets had taken in March 1940 as a result of the Winter War (the Karelian isthmus, the strategic port of Vyborg, and the lands surrounding Lake Ladoga), the Finns lost the strategic northern area of Petsamo thereby cutting off direct Finnish access to the Arctic Ocean. (The Soviet Union now had a common frontier with Norway.) The Finnish armed forces were limited to 41,500 men, and Finland was forced to pay $300 million in reparations. Despite the severity of these terms, the Finns could consider themselves lucky that the Soviets had not chosen to control the whole country as they had done with Hungary, Romania, and Bulgaria.

Peacemaking after World War II was remarkable for the degree to which most of the former enemy states had become satellites or clients of the chief negotiators. Since the Soviet Union had by then established complete authority over Romania, Bulgaria, and Hungary, no formal peace settlement was really imperative. Regularizing the situation did offer certain advantages, however. The Soviets especially wanted to abolish the Allied Control Commissions that gave the Western powers an official presence in their satellites. Moreover, after the peace settlement, the American and British troops would leave Italy, allowing greater freedom of action for the Communist party. No similar provisions required the Soviets to withdraw their armies from Eastern Europe.

The Truman Doctrine

The Mediterranean Crises. The British had been the dominant power in the Mediterranean Sea since the eclipse of Turkish power a century earlier. Nevertheless, historically, the Soviets also had strong interests in the area. On 7 August 1946, the Soviets demanded that Turkey give them certain naval bases in the Dardanelles. Previously, the Soviets had tried to bully Turkey into returning the provinces of Kars and Ardahan lost by the Treaty of Brest-Litovsk. Washington viewed these moves as the beginning of a Soviet campaign to gain control of this vital waterway. On 15 August, Dean Acheson, under secretary of state, told Truman that if Stalin's claims against Turkey were not opposed, they "would be followed next by infiltration and domination of Greece . . . with the obvious consequences in the Middle East and the obvious threat to the line of communications of the British to India." Acheson thought this Soviet "trial balloon" should be strongly resisted even though it might lead to armed conflict. Truman was of a like mind.

The British no longer had the strength to protect Europe's southern flank, but were reluctant to disengage. In Whitehall, fear of a horrendous scenario took shape: Greece would go Communist, Turkey would follow suit, and the Soviet Union would gain control of the entire eastern Mediterranean. The policy that the British had laboriously shaped during the nineteenth century to contain Russian imperialism would be in ruins. The British hoped the Americans could be shocked into making long-range commitments, but until this new Soviet threat, the Americans had given little thought to making a major commitment in the Mediterranean.

Truman now ordered Acheson to canvass the secretaries of war and navy and the chiefs of staff for their views on whether "to take a firm attitude on the Russian *démarche* or whether we should do as we have in the past—protest, but ultimately give in."[58] The situation was tricky because the Americans had not yet developed a military capacity to back up a strong response. They had some warships in the Mediterranean, including the aircraft carrier *Franklin D. Roosevelt,* but a very large number of ships in the "active" fleet could not go to sea "because of lack of competent personnel." The air strength available in Europe was then 460 fighters, only 175 of which were first-line, and about 90 bombers.[59] Even if these bombers had all been operational, and if the United States had been able to arm each with an atomic bomb, there was little assurance they would reach their targets, given the strength of the Soviet air defenses. Yet, to prevent the Red Army from over-running Western Europe and depriving the Americans of their strike bases, the bombers would have had to knock out the Soviets in the first assault. Furthermore, if the Red Army had moved into Western Europe, would the United States have used its atomic weapons to try to stop the Soviets—that is, would the United States have bombed targets in Western Europe? It is impossible to say. Truman, for all his determination, was probably not prepared to go to such lengths to keep the Soviets from acquiring Turkish bases. Fortunately, the crisis never came to that. Stalin was more cautious than the Americans gave him credit for being. His main concern was, as usual, the strengthening of Stalinism at home. He had learned it was easier to make war on his own people than to risk one with foreigners. He had no desire to push the Turkish crisis to the point of confrontation.

The Allies were not so sure of the Soviet dictator's restraint. Ever since the withdrawal of German troops from Greece, beginning in September 1944, the British had been actively involved in preventing the Greek Communists, who had built up a powerful military force during the resistance, from taking power. Churchill apparently believed that Moscow was not interested in helping out its Greek Communist comrades. In December 1944, Stalin did nothing to prevent the British from putting down a local Communist insurrection in Athens. Soviet neutrality changed with the breakdown of the wartime alliance, however. In the fall of 1946, the Greek Communists made another bid for power, this time with help from Albania, Bulgaria, and Yugoslavia; undoubtedly, this assistance had Stalin's approval. The Communist guerrilla armies were particularly successful in the northern border areas close to these foreign sources of supply. Intervention in the Greek civil war put a tremendous strain on the resources of the British who were then in the midst of a major economic crisis. The London government realized that it must withdraw. On Friday, 21 February 1947, the British embassy in Washington informed the U.S. Department of State that as of the following 30 March, Britain would discontinue all aid and support to the governments of Greece and Turkey. The Americans had been expecting such a move, but did not anticipate it so soon. Coming in the wake of the Turkish affair, however, it had not caught them completely off guard.

To Support Free Peoples. President Truman quickly summoned leaders of both houses of Congress to the White House on 27 February 1947. Under Secretary of State Dean Acheson painted a grim picture. He said that the Soviet "corruption of Greece would infect Iran, and all to the East" and "would also carry infection to Africa through Asia Minor and Egypt, and to Europe through Italy and France." To hear him tell it, the United States had reached a great turning point in history: "The Soviet Union was playing one of the greatest gambles in history at minimal cost. It did not need to win all possibilities, even one or two offered immense gains. We and we alone were in a position to break up the play."[60] Acheson's appraisal of Soviet intentions and the aggressive nature of Communism became a basic American belief; this article of faith persisted for over a generation, giving U.S. foreign policy a monumental rigidity and simplicity. At the time, however, Truman feared that others did not share the same sense of danger. He particularly feared that Republican majorities in the House and Senate might refuse to appropriate the additional funds the United States needed to move into the power vacuum the British withdrawal from the Mediterranean had created.

On 11 March, he told a joint session of Congress that he intended "to support free peoples who are resisting attempted subjugation by armed minorities or by outside pressure." He said he believed the United States must help free peoples work out their own destinies by giving them massive economic and financial aid, beginning with $400 million for Turkey and Greece. He also wanted authority to send those countries civilian and military personnel to help them maintain internal stability and independence. Truman said he was determined to defend a system "based on the will of the majority . . . distinguished by free institutions, representative government, guarantees of individual liberty, freedom of speech and election and freedom from political oppression" against one "based upon the will of a minority forcibly imposed on the majority, . . . [relying] upon terror and oppression, a controlled press and radio, fixed elections and the suppression of personal freedoms."[61] In a more tangible way, his doctrine committed the United States to the protection and reconstruction of Western Europe. Many French and British critics of the "Truman Doctrine" were not convinced that the Soviet Union was a real threat to their security. They argued that the policy would ensure the permanent division of Europe. Some wanted to create a third force between the United States and the Soviet Union, even though such a federation could hardly become effective without the economic recovery that could only be achieved with assistance from the United States.

In Greece the new doctrine had its first dramatic success. American military aid started to arrive in August 1947, and shortly thereafter a joint Greek-American military command was formed. Although it would be another two years before all resistance ended, the Americans had already shown that they would not allow the Greek Communists to take power. The arrival of General James A. Van Fleet as effective commander of operations inaugurated a period of more aggressive field tactics that gradually cleared the Communist forces from one sector of the country after another. Finally, the closing of the Greek-Yugoslav border by Tito in July 1949 led the Communists to abandon their struggle altogether.[62] Their defeat marked the first time in the Cold War when a Communist army trying to seize power had been crushed by force of arms. The victory was a perfect tonic to convince the Americans that they were on the right road; it also provided an example to future Cold War planners who came to believe that American intervention would produce similar results in other situations.

INTERNATIONAL ECONOMIC AND POLITICAL ORDER

Creating International Monetary Stability

The Background. The same Cold War that had helped dash the hopes of the Atlantic Charter and had once again made Europe a dangerous place to live also contributed to a unification process that in time would determine the future course of European politics. While the Americans and the British contemplated Europe's political future, they were also engaged in discussions about postwar economic reconstruction. This emphasis on economic matters was in stark contrast to the almost total absence of such considerations during and at the end of World War I.

In the summer of 1941, British Treasury representative John Maynard Keynes came to Washington to arrange a Lend-Lease agreement with Secretary of the Treasury Henry Morgenthau. That subject was not the only one on Keyne's mind, however. He managed to broaden the negotiations into a discussion of the whole question of postwar economic recovery. He said that his country hoped to restore its foreign trade through a series of bilateral agreements that would induce other countries to buy British goods and thus would enable the British to avoid deficits in their balance of payments. The Americans were interested in the concept, but not the particulars. Keynes's trading scheme was too narrow; it also contained the seeds of discrimination against American products.[63] The Americans wanted to consider a system that established an equilibrium.

When Keynes returned home, he drafted his "Proposals for an International Currency Union" in which he advocated establishing a monetary system with fixed rates of exchange. He hoped this was closer to what the United States had in mind. The British had no economic resource that could balance the $30 billion they received in Lend-Lease aid. They were wary of being drawn into the American economic orbit, but hoped that an arrangement with the world's principal creditor nation would result in real benefits. Specifically, they wanted to ensure full employment at home and enhance the prestige of the pound as a world currency. They also desired to strengthen their economic and financial ties with the Commonwealth. The Americans needed little prompting. Roosevelt believed that his country had to exert a leading role in shaping the world's economic environment. This commitment to a new world order was the fundamental premise of the Atlantic Charter. It did not originate there, however.

Even before World War I, American leaders believed that the promotion of trade among nations was the best way to prevent war. In their view, the failure of the peace settlement in 1919 to create a proper economic foundation had led to the instability that prepared the ground for future conflict. Herbert C. Hoover, secretary of commerce from 1921 to 1928, hoped to stifle nationalistic rivalries and rebuild the shattered European economy through the extension of private investment. The administration tried to encourage American bankers to assume responsibility for stabilizing European currencies, while it brought order to foreign exchange by reconstructing the gold standard and resolving the issues of war debts and reparations. The Dawes and Young Plans were examples of this effort. Convertibility of national currencies would lead to the reestablishment of multilateral trade and check economic nationalism and discrimination against American goods. Cordell Hull, secretary of state from 1933 to 1944, believed that national rivalry was caused by economic discrimination and trade warfare, a view that implied that World War II had its roots in the economic chaos of the 1930s. This view was shared by Henry Morgenthau, secretary of the treasury, who thought that the currency disorders of the depression had contributed to unemployment and poverty and made people easy prey for demagogues and dictators. "Bewilderment and bitterness [became] the breeders of fascism and, finally, of war," he said.[64]

Americans not only wanted to make the world safe from exchange control and quotas, they also wanted to open markets to their products. Therefore, the planners of the Roosevelt administration were determined to construct an economic counterpart to the United Nations that would provide the foundation for recovery, reconstruction, prosperity, world peace, and the free flow of goods.

The Bretton Woods Arrangements. American leaders did not hesitate to use their country's economic power to achieve their ends. In that spirit they organized the Monetary and Financial Conference that opened, on 1 July 1944, at the Mount Washington Hotel in Bretton Woods, New Hampshire.[65] Forty-four states sent delegates, but the conclave was largely an Anglo-American show. Italy, Germany, and Japan had, of course, not been invited. France, currently under enemy occupation, participated only marginally. The Soviet Union, attending at the last minute, made no positive contribution. In these circumstances, it is difficult to see how the United States, the world's principal creditor nation, could have been prevented from achieving its goals.

Under Secretary of the Treasury Harry Dexter White proposed avoiding the competitive currency devaluations of the 1930s by establishing fixed rates of exchange that could not be substantially altered without the consent of the other parties. The Americans wanted to encourage multilateral trade by preventing restrictive controls on foreign exchange transactions; and they wanted an international stabilization fund, backed by gold and national currencies, that would extend credit to member states to alleviate foreign exchange difficulties caused by temporary fluctuations and speculation.[66] They also wanted to establish an international institution to facilitate the creation of credit for postwar reconstruction and development. This scheme of applied capitalism gave rise to the International Monetary Fund (IMF) and the International Bank for Reconstruction and Development (World Bank).

The member states created the IMF from their own currencies or stocks of gold, giving themselves drawing rights on the collective resources to cure temporary deficits in their balance of payments. The amount each subscribed was determined by taking into account national income, trade, gold reserves, and value of currency convertible into gold. The IMF was a gigantic insurance scheme in which countries paid premiums to protect themselves against disasters that could threaten the stability of their currencies. With this security, nations would no longer need to resort to protectionist measures like currency controls and could thereby maintain freedom of exchange. Economists and politicians did not forget that the rise of economic nationalism and the breakdown of international liquidity helped cause and deepen the Great Depression of the early 1930s.

The World Bank was established in like manner, its principal stockholders being the nations that subscribed a certain amount of capital and put up the credit for its basic operations. Backed by these funds, the bank could mobilize further capital by issuing bonds. The bank would also guarantee loans from other sources and would create a special reserve fund to encourage private investors to put their money into worthy ventures. Furthermore, it would investigate potential borrowers to make sure they could pay back their loans and would never guarantee an amount greater than its own capital and resources. The member states would proportionally share the risks of default. The bank, which would be run along conservative lines, expected profit from the ventures it financed. Morgenthau, in his closing address to the conference, tried to minimize American influence in the agreement by insisting that all countries had joined hands and worked in unity. The United States, he said, wanted to protect its own national interests, but he added that "the only enlightened form of national self-interest [lies] in international accord."[67] Considering the previous tendency of the United States to go it alone, commitment to a multilateral scheme to maintain financial security was a remarkable about-face.

Despite their denials, the Americans with their vast economic power dominated the two organizations established at Bretton Woods. The amount of money each country put into the system determined its share of operational control. The Americans contributed one-third of the total.[68] Washington became the headquarters of these organizations, and Americans monopolized the directorships, especially the presidency of the World Bank. The Soviets realized that they could hardly hold their own against such an American presence and refrained from membership.[69] They were not missed. The market-economy countries could not do business with a state that exercised such control over its economy, and the Soviets were unwilling to change the dictatorial, central-planning premises upon which their system was based. On balance, the Bretton Woods agreement was a success; it provided the basis for world trade and investment that helped sustain the postwar recovery for the next quarter of a century.

The European Economic Community

The Marshall Plan. Even before 1900, American leaders knew that their country's well-being depended on European economic prosperity. The failure of the Republican policies of the 1920s to ensure economic stability at home and abroad indicated that a different approach was required if the disappointing results of the past were to be avoided. With the increased threat of Stalinist expansion, the task was all the more urgent. Truman administration officials had hoped European currencies could be stabilized through the International Monetary Fund and that bilateral loans and relief provided through such agencies as the United Nations Relief and Rehabilitation Administration (UNRRA) would push Europe on the road to recovery.

The anticipated recovery did not take place, however. At the beginning of 1947, Europe was entering one of its bleakest peacetime periods with political turmoil mounting in France and Italy and the crisis brewing in the Mediterranean. Surveying the scene, American planners concluded that only a comprehensive plan for economic integration could assure European recovery and save Western Europe from the danger of Communism. An integrated approach had the added advantage of ensuring that Germany's recovery would be contained within a larger context and would therefore be less likely to threaten the security of its neighbors. Some officials in the administration also saw European integration as a way to reconcile the differences between East and West, preventing the permanent division of the continent into rival blocs; others, taking their cue from Kennan, despaired of ever doing business with the Soviets and believed the consolidation of Western Europe was the only solution compatible with the nation's strategic interests.[70] The stream of invective coming from Moscow gave credence to the arguments of the hard-liners. For example, the 1 May 1947 edition of *Pravda* contained a half-page article, signed by Ilya Ehrenburg, who likened Truman's March speech and Churchill's Iron Curtain speech to the speeches of Mussolini and Hitler. And "before Fulton and Washington," Ehrenburg said, "there were the Piazza Venezia balcony and Berlin Stadium."[71]

Following high-level discussions in Washington, the promotion of European economic integration became official American policy. Secretary of State George Marshall outlined this proposal in his commencement address at Harvard University on 5 June 1947. The speech, drafted by Marshall's special assistant, Charles E. Bohlen, proposed reviving Europe's economy "so as to permit the emergence of political and social conditions in which free institutions can exist." This, Marshall said, would be done through a continuing, coordinated program of massive American aid. He invited participation from "any government that is willing to assist in the task," provided it did not seek to perpetuate human misery for political profit. This meant that the scheme was open to Soviet participation, although few believed Stalin would actually agree to do so.

The Americans expected, in fact insisted, that the Europeans would advance concrete proposals for the plan's mechanics and cooperate substantially in its execution:

> It would be neither fitting nor efficacious for [the American] Government to undertake to draw up unilaterally a program designed to place Europe on its feet economically. This is the business of the Europeans. The initiative . . . must come from Europe. The role of [the United States] should consist of friendly aid in the drafting of a European program and of later support of such a program so far as it may be practical for us to do so. The program should be a joint one, agreed to by a number, if not all, European nations.[72]

What the Americans wanted beyond the cooperation of the Europeans in their own recovery was specific proposals about how the strengths and assets of one country could be made to complement those of another. In a sense, they wanted to apply David Riccardo's laws of comparative advantage to the whole continent. By insisting that the Europeans work together, the Americans contributed to the systematic destruction of trade and exchange barriers among Western European states and initiated a movement toward integration that proved well-nigh irreversible. The Marshall Plan was further hard evidence that the Americans were not going to shy away from involvement in European affairs as they had done after World War I and that they were seriously committed to promoting economic recovery, a task already begun in a different form at the conference at Bretton Woods. The Americans were not just being Santa Claus—they needed a revived Europe to counter the Stalinist menace. In the process, however, they contributed to the greatest period of European prosperity and cooperation in history.

Ernest Bevin, the British foreign secretary, saw in this proposal the opportunity to establish the close Anglo-American cooperation he thought necessary for economic recovery and protection against the rise of Soviet power (the latter would be accomplished through a British-led European security system). He immediately arranged a meeting with his French counterpart, Georges Bidault. On 17 June in Paris, the two agreed to create a European economic commission. They invited the Soviet foreign minister, Vyacheslav Molotov, to join their discussions, but the invitation was only a tactic. Bevin knew that despite Marshall's lofty gesture,[73] Washington never really intended the Soviet Union to be a recipient of American aid and that it would be only too delighted if he and Bidault were to act as hatchet men, thereby ensuring their countries a greater share of American largesse. Bidault played the invitation for its propaganda benefits. He maintained that the offer to the Soviets showed how serious the French and British were about achieving a genuine detente in Europe, and said that it would give the Soviets a chance to display their similar good intentions.[74] Privately, he worked with Bevin to maneuver the Soviets out of participation.

Molotov joined the other two in Paris on 27 June for tripartite discussions, but suspected he was walking into a trap. He apparently believed that the recovery scheme was a ruse to build up Western, especially German, power at Soviet expense and weaken Soviet control over Eastern Europe. Molotov participated in the discussions for only four days, during which he denounced the British and French for causing the division of Europe and dismissed Bevin and Bidault as lackeys of the United States. Being disagreeable was one of the few talents this subservient and generally incompetent foreign minister possessed. He was also adept at following Stalin's orders. Stalin refused to participate further in the talks and forbade all the Eastern European countries within his sphere of influence to do so as well. The Soviets wanted American aid, guaranteed in advance, with no strings attached. Any participation, they believed, would liberalize their economy and reduce the dependency of their satellites. Their country would be at the mercy of the American Congress, which would dole out further loans only to enhance capitalism. Such risks were unacceptable.

Molotov's departure simplified the task of Bevin and Bidault. They now invited the other European states to help create the machinery through which the American aid would be channeled.[75] There was a great deal of disagreement over the scope and objectives of the program with the conferees deciding that each member country would retain control of its domestic economy but would coordinate its other activities through the Committee on European Economic Cooperation (CEEC). They subsequently committed themselves to the mutual reduction of tariffs, a multilateral system of payments, and the free convertibility of currencies. The British and French steered the conference toward endorsement of their desire to establish a long-term program of industrial modernization. The British, however, were reluctant to see any scheme for European economic integration interfere with their Commonwealth trade, which at the time was twice as large as Britain's trade with the continent. The French wanted to make their country the focal point of an economically integrated Europe. To that end, they sought limits on German steel production. Other countries, though, believed a revived Germany would aid their own recovery and were suspicious of French efforts to restrict Germany's production.

Such national priorities made the Americans dubious that the Europeans could transcend their national sovereignties and make the kind of adjustments necessary to promote recovery and economic integration.[76] Nevertheless, the U.S. Congress adopted the Marshall Plan as official national policy and, on 3 April 1948, appropriated an initial $13 billion. Bidault, who saw in the plan the means to contain a revitalized Germany, loftily claimed that there had "never been a finer, more far-sighted gesture in history than the Marshall Plan."[77] Far-sighted perhaps, but hardly unselfish. The dollars would return to the United States as the devastated Europeans bought American products. The Americans wanted to remake the European economy in their own image; their goal was an economy integrated like their own without trade barriers and with the forces of the free market determining rational development.[78] European institutions would have to become more supranational and develop the ability to transcend sovereignties, quell nationalist rivalries, and promote cooperation among private corporations. The balancing act between government and private business would be delicate but necessary if the European countries were to achieve mutual economic growth. Through such growth, the old political and class rivalries of Europe would diminish, and out of this shrinking area of conflict, the new European order would emerge.

The planners of the Democratic party envisaged a new reformed capitalist system for Europe that they had only incompletely achieved at home. In such a system, the working classes would share the fruits of their labor more equitably, the public sector would be significantly expanded, and professionals from business, labor, and government would rationally discuss the best means to solve society's problems. Interdependence would resolve the old problems of how to contain an expanding Germany and how to guarantee French security; increased wealth would enable the Europeans to repel the Communist threat at home and rearm against it abroad. While American planners were not trying to bring about a united states of Europe in the political sense, they did hope that increased integration would make the Europeans strong enough to play a major role in the containment of world Communism, thereby supporting America's global strategic objectives.

The Soviet Response. As relations between the two superpowers became more rigid, Stalin prepared for new encounters with his capitalist enemies by carrying out a major reorganization of the Communist International. In September 1947, the Poles hosted a meeting in Silesia of the representatives of the Communist parties of Bulgaria, Czechoslovakia, France, Hungary, Italy, Poland, Romania, and Yugoslavia. The Soviet delegation was headed by Stalin's main spearbearer, Andrei Zhdanov, who in his keynote address dismissed the Marshall Plan as a scheme for the political subjugation of Western Europe. "American imperialism," he said, "is endeavoring, like a usurer, to take advantage of the postwar difficulties of the European countries ... to dictate to them extortionate terms for any assistance rendered. With an eye to the impending economic crisis, the United States is in a hurry to find new monopoly spheres of capital investment and markets for its goods. American economic 'assistance' pursues the broad aid of bringing Europe into bondage to American capital."[79]

Zhdanov believed the world was divided between the imperialists headquartered in Washington and the peacelovers based in Moscow. The "peacelovers" needed an organization through which they could maintain close ties with the European Communist parties outside the immediate satellite area. The answer was a refurbished international Communist movement, known as the Cominform (the Communist Information Bureau), an agency that would enlist "all anti-fascist and freedom loving elements in the struggle against the new American expansionist plans for the enslavement of Europe." In the struggle, the French and Italian Communist parties were accorded a special responsibility: "They must take up the standard in defense of the national independence and sovereignty of their countries."[80]

The Communists now took to the streets. Shortly after the formation of the Cominform, a series of strikes swept Western Europe. Their organizers hoped to kill the Marshall Plan and weaken Europe's ties with the United States, especially in France and Italy. Stalin apparently believed that the United States was itself on the brink of economic collapse. But, although Western Europe was still in a sorry state economically, political recovery was well under way, and by the end of the year, the Communist threat was successfully contained. The Communist parties were obviously not going to disappear, but parliamentary regimes, with their welfare states in place, were more securely entrenched than before. Failure to participate in the global economy developing in Western Europe helped condemn the Soviet Union and its satellites to economic backwardness and decline and led ultimately to the failure of the Communist system. Almost two generations would pass before that became evident, however; for the time being, Soviet power was real and serious enough.

The United Nations

The Charter. The Soviet-American confrontation stemmed from the same historic forces that had created, shaped, and conditioned earlier balance-of-power systems. For those who believed in the basic harmony of national interests and still had faith in collective security, the reality was harsh. On 26 June 1945, the fifty states that attended the San Francisco Conference resolved "to unite [their] strength to maintain international peace and security, and to ensure, by the acceptance of principles and the institution of methods, that armed force shall not be used, save in the common interest."[81] Poland was absent but was considered a charter member. The participants at the conference hoped the United Nations (UN) would succeed where the League of Nations had failed, but structurally the new organization for peace was remarkably like its predecessor.

It had a General Assembly, consisting of all member states, with the authority to discuss any questions related to "the maintenance of international peace and security"; in reality, its powers were largely consultative. There was an executive council, the Security Council, composed of five permanent members (France, Great Britain, the Soviet Union, the United States, and China) and six nonpermanent members elected for a term of two years. The League's Permanent Court of International Justice continued exactly as before, with only a slight change of name—the International Court of Justice. Both the League and the UN had secretariats, headed by a secretary-general, and various economic and social agencies.

The myth of sovereign equality was strong in both organizations, but the reality was less in the UN. All members of the UN agreed "to accept and carry out the decisions of the Security Council in accordance with the . . . Charter," but any of the Security Council's permanent members could block action by voting against any nonprocedural decision. The veto power, a recognition that the UN was incapable of effective operation without Great Power unanimity, was particularly opposed by the smaller powers who resented giving the Security Council's permanent members even more authority than they had enjoyed in the League.[82] Furthermore, Article 2, Section 7, forbade interference in matters that were essentially within a state's jurisdiction. The purpose of this clause was to provide special protection for nations with colonial possessions. Protection of a different sort was provided in Article 52, Section 1, which allowed "the existence of regional arrangements or agencies for dealing with such matters relating to the maintenance of international peace and security." Thus, all sorts of military alliances were perfectly legal, provided that "their activities are consistent with the Purposes and Principles of the United Nations." Nominally, of course, they all were.

Multilateral Problem Solving. The United Nations purported to be more than just a system of collective security. The League had left the final decision to apply sanctions against an aggressor to the individual states. Once sanctions were voted, however, the UN required each member to make a commitment in advance to "undertake to make available to the Security Council, on its call and in accordance with a special agreement or agreements, armed forces, assistance, and facilities, including rights of passage, necessary for the purpose of maintaining international peace and security." But the "agreement or agreements" needed to give this article (43) its teeth were never adopted; thus, in the long run, the UN was in no better position to enforce its decisions militarily than was the League.[83] Once again, the fault was not so much in the institutions of the organization but in the willingness to use them. When the major powers, especially the Soviet Union and the United States, agreed to cooperate, the original purposes of the organization could be achieved.

The failure of the UN to deal with international problems stemmed from the nature of the modern state system, especially as it confronted the political realities of the postwar world. The UN, like the League, had no independent sovereignty; it was simply one among many diplomatic devices, and exercised only the authority that the member states chose to confer upon it. Its agencies could be used for the peaceful settlement of disputes, but could also heighten the very tension they were supposed to dissipate. The speeches made in the Security Council or the General Assembly almost never influenced the actions of nations. In fact, UN speeches were usually carefully crafted monologues, intended primarily for propaganda. All permanent members of the Security Council favored the veto power as an ultimate safeguard, but only the Soviet Union used it as a normal diplomatic device to prevent consideration of any issue related to national security, no matter how distantly. Consequently, certain states, the United States among them, favored giving more power to the General Assembly, which reached decisions with a two-thirds majority of those present and voting. The Soviet Union, however, fought to keep supreme decision-making power in the Security Council.

The UN could be used as an agency for solving disputes when the United States and the Soviet Union were in agreement. This occurred over the question of Palestine and produced a resolution, calling for the establishment of two independent states, one Jewish, one Arab, to replace the British mandate. But the UN had no power to prevent the Arabs and Israelis from later fighting among themselves. The UN was sometimes used on problems related to the Cold War, but then usually as a forum for announcing decisions already made elsewhere. Thus, for example, a special UN commission was established to help bring an end to the civil war in Greece because the Soviet Union saw no further profit in supporting the cause of the Greek Communist guerrillas. The UN was also used during the Berlin crisis, when both sides accepted the invitation of the organization's secretary-general to begin informal discussions leading to the end of the blockade. By then, the success of the airlift had been established, and it was evident that the Western powers could not be forced out of the city, short of war. Thus, in these instances, the UN was only an instrumentality for putting the finishing touches on a settlement that would have come anyway.

Although many other issues, including the reunification of Korea, the Italian-Yugoslav dispute over Trieste, and the Soviet subversion of Czechoslovakia, were all brought to the UN's attention, the organization had no success in bringing about an accord. And only the temporary withdrawal of the Soviet representative from the Security Council made possible the UN's involvement in the Korean War in 1950.[84] Even here the real force behind the resolution to resist aggression was the United States, which would have committed its army in any case. The absence of the Soviet Union from the UN led to the passage, in November 1950, of the U.S.-sponsored "Uniting for Peace Resolution," which allowed the General Assembly to discuss, in emergency session, any important measure that had been vetoed in the Security Council. But this virtual revision of the Charter did not change the fact that the Great Powers still made the major political decisions outside the UN.

POSTSCRIPT   Allied diplomacy marched to the sound of battle and to the dreams of Wilsonian idealism. This blend of the real and the imaginary complicated the practical task of agreeing on the conduct of the war and building a firm structure for postwar Europe. Among the major questions to be decided were the boundaries of Eastern Europe, the nature of political and economic reconstruction, including the treatment of Germany, and the most difficult task of all, how to establish future security and harmony. The Americans were determined to avoid the cardinal mistake they had made after World War I when they refused to join the League. Roosevelt intended to work closely with a United Nations organization in conjunction with the Soviet Union to achieve the idealistic goals he first enumerated in the Atlantic Charter.

Until the Soviets open their archives, it is impossible to know whether Stalin's goals were clearer and better defined than those of Churchill and Roosevelt. His actions showed that he believed that Soviet security must be enhanced by creating "friendly" governments in those states bordering his country's western frontier. When he spoke of free and democratic development, his words had a special meaning. George Kennan, counselor of the American embassy in Moscow, affirmed:

> No one can stop Russia from doing the taking, if she is determined to go through with it. No one can force Russia to do the giving, if she is determined not to go through with it. In these circumstances, others may worry. The Kremlin chimes, never silent since those turbulent days when Lenin had them repaired and set in motion, now peal out the hours of night with a ring of self-assurance and of confidence in the future. And the sleep of those who lie within the Kremlin walls is sound and undisturbed.[85]

Stalin expected his allies to recognize that Eastern Europe was within the Soviet orbit and appeared willing to recognize that Britain and the United States were similarly free to arrange the affairs of Western Europe. Roosevelt was unwise to believe that he could gain Stalin's trust and work with him for a better world. Nor was Roosevelt on firm moral ground in his concept of collective security: his view of the Four Policemen obviously implied establishing the very spheres of influence he was to deride the Soviets for creating. The participation of the United States in both world wars was essential to prevent the destruction of the European balance of power. Whereas in 1914, and again in 1939, the United States had the capacity to be the holder of the balance, it preferred to leave the task to others, and even when forced into war, it hardly viewed its participation in terms of maintaining an equilibrium. A conscientious effort to counter Great Power domination of the European continent in times of peace was therefore something new.

In 1947, no country but the United States was capable of standing up to the Soviet Union. American leaders feared that their country's continued disengagement from Europe would result in an eventual Soviet takeover, but their interest went beyond the present crisis. The Americans had a concept of a peaceful Europe based on harmonization of national rivalries through economic integration. They believed that political problems were essentially technical problems and were consequently solvable. The greatness of the Marshall Plan lay in the way it managed to transcend the immediate political pressures and concerns to become a positive force for the stabilization and integration of Europe. However, the clash between the superpowers seemed to determine all action. Byrnes based his policy on the not preposterous assumption that the Soviets were prepared to bide their time until they developed local leaders who could make the communization of Western Europe a success. "By the threat of strikes and by encouraging discontent, they can in many states exert power without having responsibility."[86] Military occupation of the whole of Europe would have put an intolerable strain on Soviet resources, perhaps endangering Stalin's control at home. Then, too, for Stalin successful communization of such countries as Germany, France, and Britain was not without its dangers. Unless perfect Stalinist regimes could be installed and maintained, these states would compete with the Soviet Union for world Communist leadership. Nevertheless, the leaders in the Kremlin showed themselves willing to exploit any weakness they perceived in the Western camp. Even if the Soviets had no intent of using their massive position in Eastern Europe as a springboard for aggression against the West, the fact that they were there was a significant alteration of the European balance of power and was *ipso facto* threatening. Over time, however, the confrontation in Europe between the superpowers took on the comfortable predictability of a stalemate. Danger still lurked at the periphery where the two great spheres of influence had not become consolidated, but the superpowers had decided that whatever their differences and rivalries, these were not worth an all-out war. The longer the standoff continued, the more feeble became the conviction that any of their policies would lead to the creation of a brave new world, notwithstanding all the utopianism and chest puffing in which both indulged.

ENDNOTES

1. Iran had been invaded by British and Soviet forces in August 1941 to crush German influence and ensure a supply line to the Soviet Union. The occupation, following an arrangement worked out in 1907, gave the Soviets control of the north, the British control of the south, and put the capital under joint protection.
2. The president had suggested Cairo, Asmara in Eritrea, Ankara in Turkey, or some port in the eastern Mediterranean.
3. *Stalin's Correspondence with Churchill, Attlee, Roosevelt and Truman, 1941–45* (London: Lawrence & Wishart, 1958), 104.
4. Roosevelt, without informing Churchill, had also invited Vyacheslav Molotov to join the discussions. Molotov refused to attend because this might imply a commitment to the Nationalist Chinese.
5. Anthony Eden, *The Reckoning* (London: Cassell, 1965), 491.

6. United States, Department of State, *Conferences at Cairo and Teheran, 1943* (Washington, D.C.: U.S. Government Printing Office, 1961), 492.

7. Ibid., 493.

8. Ibid., 495.

9. Ibid., 494.

10. General Marshall's Report, *The Winning of the War in Europe and the Pacific* (War Department: Simon and Schuster, 1945), II.

11. *Conferences at Cairo and Teheran*, 602.

12. Stalin recalled that when he was in Leipzig in 1907, "200 German workers failed to appear at an important mass meeting because there was no controller at the station platform to punch their tickets which would permit them to leave the station." Ibid., 513. This was one of his favorite stories. See Milovan Djilas, *Conversations with Stalin* (New York: Harcourt, Brace and World, 1962).

13. Winston Churchill, *Closing the Ring* (Boston: Houghton Mifflin, 1951), 374.

14. Stalin had earlier suggested that Churchill nursed "a secret affection for Germany and desired to see a soft peace." *Conferences at Cairo and Teheran*, 533.

15. Ibid., 485.

16. Ibid., 554.

17. Ibid., 512.

18. Ibid., 595.

19. Ibid., 592.

20. Ibid., 511.

21. Ibid., 532.

22. Ibid., 531.

23. Ibid., 514.

24. On the importance of the neglected conference of Teheran, see Keith Eubank, *Summit at Teheran* (New York: William Morrow, 1985).

25. Winston S. Churchill, *Triumph and Tragedy* (Boston: Houghton, Mifflin, 1953), 347.

26. United States, Department of State, *The Conferences at Malta and Yalta, 1945* (Washington, D.C.: U.S. Government Printing Office, 1955), 716. Hereafter referred to as *Yalta Conference*.

27. The essential features of the United Nations had been adopted at the Dumbarton Oaks Conference, held from 21 August to 9 October 1944. It was not surprising that in scope and responsibilities the organization was a political agency of the superpowers.

28. *Yalta Conference*, 396.

29. This chain of thirty-six islands between Kamchatka and Hokkaido had been Russian during the eighteenth and most of the nineteenth centuries. The Japanese got them in 1875.

30. *Yalta Conference*, 984.

31. J. P. Nettl, *The Eastern Zone and Soviet Policy in Germany, 1945–1950* (New York: Farrar, Straus, and Giroux, 1977), 37–38.

32. *Yalta Conference*, 620.

33. Ibid., 972.

34. Ibid., 589.

35. Georgi Zhukov, *The Memoirs of Marshall Zhukov* (New York: Delacourte Press, 1971), 583.

36. The American president had repeated the assurance he had made at Teheran that Congress and the American people would support "any reasonable measures designed to safeguard the future peace, but he did not believe that this would extend to the maintenance of an appreciable American force in Europe." *Yalta Conference*, 617.

37. *Stalin's Correspondence*, 331.

38. Ibid., 348.

39. Harry S Truman, *Memoirs*, vol. 2, 71–72.

40. Ibid., 82.

41. United States, Department of State, *The Conference of Berlin (Potsdam) 1945*, vol. 1 (Washington, D.C.: U.S. Government Printing Office), 6. Hereafter cited as *Potsdam Conference*.

42. Ibid., 7.

43. These nations would only participate in the formulation of settlements if they had signed the respective terms of surrender. Thus, China could not participate in the decisions concerning the fate of Europe.

44. *Potsdam Conference*, 385.

45. At this point, Admiral William Leahy whispered to Truman. "Of course there are no Germans left. The Bolshies have killed them all." Truman, 369.

46. Churchill, *Triumph and Tragedy*, 631–32.

47. Ibid., 669.

48. Stalin renounced his rights to assets in defeated countries outside Bulgaria, Finland, Hungary, Romania, and eastern Austria and agreed to make no demands on the German gold that the other Allies had captured. He also abandoned his support of a scheme to internationalize the Ruhr.

49. Stalin helped to cushion the blow by promising that the Polish Provisional Government would hold "free and unfettered elections as soon as possible on the basis of universal suffrage and secret ballot in which all democratic and anti-Nazi parties shall have the right to take part and put forward candidates." *Potsdam Conference*, 2:1491.

50. In Lisle Rose, *After Yalta* (New York: Charles Scribner's Sons, 1973), 123–24.

51. Foreign Relations of the United States, 1946, VI, 706–7.

52. *New York Times*, 6 March 1946.

53. *Foreign Relations of the United States*, 1946, VI, 73–74.

54. Ibid., 768.

55. According to a 7 June 1946 attack delivered by Fedor Nesterovich Oleshchuk, the assistant-chief of the Agitation and Propaganda Administration of the Communist Party Central Committee. Ibid., 770.

56. Georges Bidault, *Resistance* (London: Weidenfeld and Nicolson, 1967), 127.

57. The "Free Territory of Trieste" had been divided into two zones, A and B. After much squabbling, the Trieste problem was solved in the agreement of 5 October 1954, which awarded zone A (the city proper) to the Italians and zone B (the hinterland) to the Yugoslavs.

58. Dean Acheson, *Present at the Creation; My Years in the State Department* (New York: Norton, 1969), 191.

59. Ibid., 196.

60. Ibid., 219.

61. *Department of State Bulletin*, 23 March 1947, 534–37.

62. Tito needed all his energy for his confrontation with Moscow. In addition, having a friendly non-Communist country on his southern frontier was infinitely preferable to a potentially hostile Communist one.

63. This caveat was subsequently incorporated into the Mutual Aid Agreement (of 23 February 1942) whose goal was "to promote mutually advantageous economic relations between [the United States and Britain] and the betterment of world-wide economic relations." (Article 7)

64. *Proceedings and Documents of United Nations Monetary and Financial Conference, Bretton Woods NH* (Washington, D.C.: Department of State, 1948), I, 71.

65. See: A. L. K. Acheson, J. F. Chant, and M. F. J. Prachowny, eds., *Bretton Woods Revisited* (Toronto: University of Toronto Press, 1972); Richard N. Gardner, *Sterling-Dollar Diplomacy: The Origins and the Prospects of Our International Economic Order* (New York: McGraw Hill, 1969); R. G. Hawtrey, *Bretton Woods, For Better or Worse* (London: Longmans, Green, 1946); Edward S. Mason and Robert E. Asher,

The World Bank since Bretton Woods (Washington, D.C.: Brookings Institution, 1973); Sidney Rolfe, *Gold and World Power: The Dollar, the Pound, and the Plans for Reform* (New York: Harper and Row, 1966); Armand Van Dormael, *Bretton Woods: Birth of a Monetary System* (New York: Holmes and Meier, 1978).

66. In 1942, Keynes had made a similar proposal when he advocated the establishment of a clearing union that would reinforce a state's currency through drawing rights on an international fund established by participating countries.

67. Van Dormael, *Bretton Woods*, 221–22.

68. The United States put up half of the original start-up capital, however.

69. They were joined by Liberia and New Zealand.

70. Michael J. Hogan, *The Marshall Plan: America, Britain, and the Reconstruction of Western Europe, 1947–1952* (Cambridge: Cambridge University Press, 1987), 29–45.

71. *Foreign Relations of the United States*, 1947, IV, 557.

72. *Department of State Bulletin*, 16 (1947), 1159–60.

73. The secretary of the navy, James Forrestal, described Marshall's objective as a tactic "to show to both the world and our country that every effort had been made on our part to secure [Soviet] cooperation so that we should have the support of public opinion in whatever policy we found it necessary to adopt thereafter." *The Forrestal Diaries*, ed. Walter Mills (New York: Viking, 1951), 192.

74. Bidault, *Resistance*, 150.

75. Sixteen nations attended: Austria, Belgium, Britain, Denmark, France, Greece, Iceland, Ireland, Italy, Luxembourg, the Netherlands, Norway, Portugal, Sweden, Switzerland, and Turkey. The Soviet Union vetoed participation by Bulgaria, Czechoslovakia, Hungary, Finland, Poland, and Romania.

76. Hogan, *The Marshall Plan*, 64–70.

77. Bidault, *Resistance*, 151.

78. Hogan, *The Marshall Plan*, 427–30.

79. *Documents on International Affairs, 1947–1948*, 127.

80. Ibid., 137.

81. The Charter of the UN can be found in *The United Nations in the Making: Basic Documents* (Boston: World Peace Foundation, 1947), 41–72.

82. The League Covenant had required any League Council decision to be unanimous, but any member who was a party to the dispute would *not* be allowed to vote.

83. Peace forces were created though from time to time to handle particular crises, but they never became permanent.

84. In 1990 and 1991, the United Nations was used to help forge the coalition that ended the aggression of Iraq against Kuwait. In that crisis, the Security Council could act because of the unanimity of the Great Powers.

85. *Foreign Relations of the United States*, 1944, IV, 909.

86. James F. Byrnes, *All in One Lifetime* (New York: Harper and Brothers, 1958), 294.

GERMANY BETWEEN EAST AND WEST

PREFACE   Stalin considered Germany the most important country in Europe. Its control would ensure Soviet security, its loss would make all other gains meaningless. In Germany were fought the first great battles of the Cold War. During the closing weeks of World War II, the British and American armies entered parts of Germany that had been marked for Soviet occupation: Thuringia, Saxony, and Mecklenburg. Churchill favored keeping them as bargaining chips for the forthcoming negotiations at Potsdam, but Stalin refused to allow any Allied control machinery to be established until all these territories had been handed over to his armies. Only then did he allow the French, British, and American military commissions to come to Berlin to establish a government in accordance with the Yalta agreement.

When the Allied commanders arrived in the German capital on 5 June 1945, the Soviets kept them waiting. Dwight D. Eisenhower and Bernard Montgomery were so annoyed that they threatened to leave. Hasty apologies ensued and within half an hour the ceremony took place. The agreement confirmed the Allied Control Commission, the division of Germany into four zones of occupation, and the establishment of a special Inter-Allied Governing Authority (the *Kommandatura*) to administer Greater Berlin jointly. The post of chief executive would rotate every three months among the four Allied commanders.

Marshal Georgi Zhukov hosted a reception after the official business. It featured speeches and toasts and a huge groaning board of Russian delicacies. The Red Army Chorus presented a short concert. The affair "developed into a sort of mutual congratulation society, Field-Marshal Montgomery recalled."[1] All of this warmth and bonhomie could not cover up the fundamental divisions and hostilities, however. Stalin had already refused to recognize the right of the Allies to use certain routes into Berlin. Had he specifically done so, the Allies probably would not have accepted them anyway. The Allies feared that accepting such routes might mean forfeiting rights over all others. Instead, they concluded a temporary agreement with Stalin. The Soviets allocated a main highway, a rail line, and two air corridors and agreed that these would be freed "from border search or control by customs or military authorities."[2] Only the agreement on air corridors was put in writing.[3]

Stalin believed that his wartime allies were planning to use the resources of Germany for future aggression against the Soviet Union. These suspicions also permeated the upper echelons of the Communist hierarchy. When Marshal Zhukov visited Eisenhower in the ruined city of Frankfurt five days after the ceremony in Berlin, he noticed that the I. G. Farben chemical factory, in which the American general had established his headquarters, was undamaged. He concluded "that Washington and London had given the Allied High Command special instructions" to save it from destruction, along with I. G. Farben's property in other parts of Germany.[4]

Germany's recent attempt to destroy the balance of power had cost it heavily. Approximately 4.2 million Germans, soldiers and civilians, had been killed; 6 million more had been wounded; and some 2 million were prisoners of war. Countless more were refugees who had either fled before the advance of the Soviets or had been expelled as undesirable aliens from the Eastern European countries. About 10 million of these sought refuge in western Germany, where they currently were living in special camps.[5] The desperate plight of the Germans elicited little sympathy. In the eyes of the Allies, the Germans had brought such misery to others that they deserved to suffer. Now was their time of reckoning. Germany should atone for its sins and must never be allowed to threaten the peace of Europe again. Furthermore, the Germans should make financial reparation for the damage they had caused.

But how could the Germans pay if they were not allowed to recover? Yet if they were allowed to recover, would they not once again become a threat? These questions, which had also arisen after World War I, would now be answered in the context of a military occupation. A properly supervised recovery would keep Germany from threatening European security and prevent the rebirth of German militarism. To make the occupation work, however, the occupiers had to cooperate with each other—all the more so, since much of Germany's food and raw materials lay in the Soviet zone, while the bulk of the country's industry was in the Western zones. From the Soviet point of view, the solution was simple. They would tighten their hold over East Germany while preparing the ground for the eventual socialization of the rest of the country. They were prepared to take advantage of every opportunity presented to them.

FOUR-POWER GOVERNANCE

The Occupation

Diverse Styles. The Joint Chiefs of Staff directive 1067 of April 1945 instructed the American occupation commander that "Germany's ruthless warfare and the fanatical Nazi resistance have destroyed the German economy and made chaos and suffering inevitable and that the Germans cannot escape responsibility for what they have brought upon themselves."[6] Consequently, no action would be taken "that would tend to support basic living standards in Germany on a higher level than that existing in any one of the neighboring united nations."[7] Many Americans had Old Testament notions of collective guilt and took special pains to make the Germans aware of the suffering they had caused. They bused many citizens of Munich out to Dachau to view, and in some cases to clean up, the rotting corpses. They also showed films of Nazi atrocities to German elementary and secondary schoolchildren and to entire populations of some towns.

The Soviets, officially at least, tried to distinguish between the Nazis and other Germans. Toward the end of the war, Stalin was careful to emphasize that the Soviet Union was fighting to liberate the German people from the Hitlerites. When the Soviets entered Berlin, they pasted up posters, proclaiming, "The Hitlers come and go but the German people, the German state remain." Even before all the rubble was cleared from the streets, the Soviets erected a gigantic statue honoring the Soviet soldiers who had saved the German people from oppression.

Soviet occupation was very harsh. The Soviets immediately widened the gauge of the German railways to correspond with their own and confiscated and shipped anything of value to the Soviet Union. Montgomery received reports that in the Soviet zone the Germans "were living like beasts on whatever they could get, and that starvation was already evident."[8] The Red Army continued to terrorize the population. Film actress Hildegard Knef remembered "hiding in a shed in a Berlin suburb listening to the screams of the women being raped by Russian soldiers in the house across the street."[9] Every female was fair game, regardless of age. German Communist leaders, returning from exile, wanted "to see that no excesses took place in relations between the German population and the Soviet troops,"[10] but they had no control over the Red Army, and the terror ran its course.

Meanwhile the French viewed their zone as a source of industrial booty, which they deemed reparations. Since a large section of the area was rural, they took what they could, even cutting down trees in the Black Forest. Because the Germans had invaded their country three times in as many generations, the French felt completely justified in exploiting their zone to the fullest. The French also had a political agenda. As after World War I, France wanted to separate the Rhineland and the Saar from Germany and even encouraged separatist movements in the regions it occupied.

Despite their animosity for Germans and their tendency to treat Germany almost as a colonial possession, British leaders, possibly more than the other Allies, were concerned with not repeating old mistakes. Montgomery felt it necessary to "give the German people hope for the future; they must be made to realize that they could reach a worthwhile future only by their own work. That meant fixing the level of industry so that there would be a decent standard of living with the minimum of unemployment. If this were not done the Germans would merely look to the past and be ready to follow any evil leader who might arise."[11] Montgomery might have added that many of his own subordinates were helping to make that possible by engaging in all kinds of unsavory activities from black marketeering to theft and sexual concubinage. "German women," recalled one British second lieutenant, "were really no more than a commodity on the black market"; if a woman ran out of things to trade, "she could always trade herself."[12] The American record was not much better.

The occupation powers abolished the main Nazi administrative unit of the *Gau* and reorganized Germany into a series of states (*Länder*), ranging in size from 156 square miles (Bremen) to 18,000 square miles (Lower Saxony), and from 500,000 people in Bremen to 12 million in North Rhine–Westphalia (Table 1). By restoring Germany's federal character, the Allies hoped to curb and dissipate the country's aggressive nationalism. The new Länder emerged out of the combination or division of former states. The British, for example, combined Hanover, Oldenburg, Brunswick, and Schaumburg-Lippe into Lower Saxony. The French put together parts of Baden and Württemberg to form the Rhine-Palatinate. Prussia disappeared completely. This shifting of boundaries broke down the old federalist pattern and formed new units that the occupiers hoped would in time develop their own loyalties and identities. Only Bavaria, whose former boundaries remained virtually unchanged, preserved its regional integrity.

TABLE 1   GERMANY IN 1946

	Size (Square Miles)	Population
British Zone		
(North Rhine–Westphalia, Lower Saxony, Schleswig-Holstein, Hamburg)	37,721	22,304,509
American Zone		
(Barvaria, Greater Hesse, Württemberg-Baden, Bremen)	41,490	17,254,945
French Zone		
(Württemberg-Hohenzollern, Rhine-Palatinate, Baden)	15,527	5,077,806
Soviet Zone		
(Brandenburg, Saxony, Mecklenburg-Vorpommern, Thuringia, Saxony-Anhalt)	41,380	17,313,734
Berlin	344	3,199,938
Total	136,462	65,150,932

Note: Square kilometers have been converted to square miles.

Source: Survey of International Affairs: Four-Power Control in Germany and Austria, 1945–1946 (London: Oxford University Press), 191.

The terms of the Potsdam agreement specified that Germany would be governed as an administrative whole, but Charles de Gaulle, who had not been party to the accord, did not feel bound by its provisions. According to Georges Bidault, the French foreign minister, de Gaulle wanted "to go back to the treaty of Westphalia."[13] He still advocated the dismemberment of Germany and a special status for the Rhineland and the Ruhr, policies that the other powers had by now abandoned. De Gaulle wanted to annex the Saar and opposed the establishment of any machinery of central government. At the end of October 1945, he effectively vetoed a proposal to formulate common directives for the whole of Germany. As a result, henceforth, each power assumed responsibility for setting policy in its own zone. De Gaulle's policies were guided by his fear that a revived Germany under Soviet domination would eventually invade France. He suspected that the Americans were not going to stay long in Europe. On 3 November 1945, he told the U.S. envoy in Paris, Jefferson Caffery, that France viewed Europe as "a matter of life and death," while for the United States, it was "one interesting question among many others." Nor did de Gaulle expect help from the British; they "lack courage and are worn out," he said.[14]

De Gaulle's intransigence caught the Soviet Union off guard. Stalin had decided that the continuation of four-power control was less dangerous than a divided Germany in which the capitalists enjoyed unrestricted domination over the largest, most industrialized part of the country. Under four-power control, the Soviets could veto any measure they did not like, since decisions had to be made unanimously. The only serious obstacle to the rise of Communist power in Europe was the United States, but the Soviet dictator had every reason to expect that the Americans would not continually involve themselves in European affairs. German central government would, therefore, inevitably fall under Soviet domination. Meanwhile he consolidated Soviet power in his own sphere.

The Nuremberg War Crimes Trial. A rare example of successful Allied cooperation was exhibited in the first of the great war crimes trials that began on 20 November 1945 in Nuremberg, the sacred city of National Socialism. If Stalin had had his way, there would have been no trials. He no doubt was serious when he told Roosevelt and Churchill at Yalta that he favored summarily shooting 50,000 of Germany's leaders. The Nuremberg trial, however, served a double purpose: first, it fulfilled the desire for retribution, and secondly, it established rules of international law for future generations, outlawing aggressive war and holding those persons who caused it personally responsible. On trial were twenty-four Nazi leaders and six Nazi organizations. The 25,000-word indictment listed three categories of crimes: crimes against peace, war crimes, and crimes against humanity. The defendants were specifically charged with preparing and waging a war of aggression; being responsible for the murder of civilians and prisoners of war; wantonly destroying and plundering property; and preparing the extermination, enslavement, and deportation of people for political, racial, and religious reasons. The defendants were also charged with conspiracy to commit those crimes, a concept consistent with Anglo-American jurisprudence, but alien to French, German, and Soviet law. Until now, military aggression and the violation of treaties had never been considered illegal. Crimes against humanity were only justiciable if one side was capable of enforcing its concept of guilt on the other. At Nuremberg, the entire indictment was held to be valid "whether or not [any of the crimes were] in violation of domestic law of the country where perpetrated."[15]

The great room of Nuremberg's neo-Gothic courthouse looked like an avant-garde theater; the defendants sat side by side in two long rows, as if they were waiting for the house lights to dim. A line of white-helmeted American soldiers stood guard at their backs. The prisoners were seated more or less in order of political importance. In the best location—first row, first seat—sat Hermann Göring, the most imposing of the defendants, and in the last seat of the second row was Hans Fritzsche, the radio broadcasting chief in the propaganda ministry. Fritzsche, a comparative unknown, was really there at Soviet insistence as a stand-in for his old boss, Josef Goebbels.[16] Not all the indicted were present: Ernst Kaltenbrunner, chief of the SS Security Service, was suffering from a cerebral hemorrhage and could not make the opening session; Robert Ley, boss of the Nazi Labor Front, hanged himself from a pipe in his cell a month before the trial began; Gustav Krupp von Bohlen, the armaments manufacturer, was excused because he was too senile; and Martin Bormann, once deputy führer, could not be found.[17]

The legal problems were daunting. The Americans and the British used English common law; the French, Roman law; and the Soviets, their own brand of positive class-struggle law. This divergence led to enormous problems about presumed innocence or guilt, obscured the rights of the defense, and clouded the rules of evidence. The gathering of evidence was no problem, however, as the American prosecutor, Justice Robert Jackson, declared in his opening statement: "We do not ask you to convict these men on the testimony of their foes. There is no count of the indictment that cannot be proved by books and records. The Germans were always meticulous record keepers, and these defendants had their share of the Teutonic passion of thoroughness in putting things on paper."[18] Altogether, the proceedings produced over 4 million words of evidence and testimony. Three hundred sworn statements were admitted, 240 witnesses were heard, and 5,330 documents were produced. More than 40,000 pounds of paper were used. Every spoken word was simultaneously translated into French, English, Russian, and German and was recorded.

The trial became a gigantic history lesson. It examined Hitler's rise to power, the Reichstag fire (which Göring denied he had anything to do with), the origins and development of the concentration camps, the destruction of the trade unions, the Night of the Long Knives, and the persecution of the Jews. It detailed the assassination of Austrian chancellor Englebert Dollfuss, the remilitarization of the Rhineland, the Anschluss, the Axis intervention in the Spanish Civil War, the extinction of Czechoslovakia, and the invasion of Poland. The prosecution introduced the Hossbach Memorandum of the chancellery meeting of 5 November 1937 as prima facie evidence of the Nazi premeditation of World War II. The document, according to U.S. associate trial counsel, Sidney Alderman, destroyed "any possible doubt about the well-laid plans of the Nazis in their crimes against peace." He read it into the record in its entirety. Most of the testimony on World War II concentrated on Nazi behavior behind the lines—the treatment of civilians in the occupied countries, especially the organized extermination of the Jews. The prosecution augmented the written evidence by showing atrocity films, which disturbed some defendants. "When I see such things I'm ashamed of being a German," General Wilhelm Keitel remarked. Göring had a different reaction: "They were reading my telephone conversations on the Austrian affair," he complained, "and everybody was laughing with me—and then they showed that awful film, and it just spoiled everything."[19]

Hans Frank, former Nazi overlord in Poland, now a recent convert to Roman Catholicism, enthusiastically confessed his sins and willingly gave the prosecution his incriminating thirty-eight-volume diary. "A thousand years will pass and the guilt of Germany will not pass away," he said with religious fervor. Another approach was taken by SS Obergruppenführer Ernst Kaltenbrunner who denied all personal complicity. He put the blame entirely on Hitler and Himmler. When evidence was introduced showing that he had killings staged in his honor, he insisted he had been responsible only for problems of civilian morale. "You Americans . . . seem to think that our whole R.S.H.A. [SS Security Service] was nothing but an organized gang of criminals," he told the prison psychologist, G. M. Gilbert. "I must say that impression does exist," Gilbert replied. "Then how can I defend myself against such prejudice?" Kaltenbrunner snapped.[20]

Had the Germans won the war, they might have charged the Americans with the bombing of Dresden, tried the Soviets for their invasion of Finland, and indicted the British for their commando raids. Such evidence about Allied and Soviet conduct was ruled inadmissible at Nuremberg, however. When Göring's lawyer tried to justify Germany's treatment of Russian prisoners by describing how the Soviets had treated Germans, he was cut short. The president of the court, Sir Geoffrey Lawrence, explained: "The question is how can you justify in a trial of the major war criminals of Germany evidence against Great Britain, or against the United States of America, or against the U.S.S.R. or against France? If you are going to try the actions of all these signatory powers, apart from other considerations, there would be no end to the trial at all."[21] Contradictions were thus inevitable.

For example, the Germans were charged with the invasion of Poland, but the secret clauses of the Nazi-Soviet Non-Aggression Treaty that made the invasion possible were not admissible. Yet the Germans were accused of violating that treaty when they attacked the Soviet Union. The defendants were also disadvantaged by being denied access to the documents from which the prosecution prepared its case. If the defendants requested a particular order or letter, the Allies would conduct a search, but in asking for the document, the defense would have disclosed its strategy. The defendants' lawyers could not travel without permission from the prosecution, and their witnesses were often treated as enemies and harassed. The Soviets, who were used to a different type of trial procedure, expected the accused to be docile and their lawyers to cooperate in establishing a predetermined verdict.

Despite fundamental disagreement between the prosecution and the defense over the validity of the trial, the defense was accorded a certain latitude to present its case, and sometimes did so with telling effect. For example, the Soviets had insisted, against the advice of the Americans and British, that the massacre in the Katyn Forest be blamed on the Germans. Dr. Otto Stahmer, the attorney of Hermann Göring, so skillfully discredited the Soviet evidence that the charge was removed from the indictment and all mention of Katyn was dropped from the trial. In the end, nobody was held responsible. The American prosecutor Robert Jackson, who had little experience in cross-examination, proved to be a poor choice. He was much better at setting a moral tone. In his closing address on 26 July 1946, he said: "The future will never have to ask, with misgiving, 'What could the Nazis have said in their favor?' History will know that whatever could be said, they were allowed to say. They have been given the kind of a trial which they, in the days of their pomp and power, never gave to any man."[22] Of the twenty-one defendants, the court sentenced only eleven—Göring, Streicher, Frick, Ribbentrop, Kaltenbrunner, Sauckel, Keitel, Jodl, Frank, Rosenberg, and Seyss-Inquart—to death. It acquitted three of the accused: Papen, Fritzsche, and Schacht. The others were sentenced to prison terms ranging from ten years to life.

The Nuremberg tribunal delivers its judgment. For the twenty-one accused, seated in the two rows on the right, there were eleven death sentences, seven prison sentences, and three acquittals. Chief defendant Göring, wearing his dove-colored Reichsmarshal's uniform devoid of insignia and decorations, knew that he could cheat the hangman with the poison that had been smuggled to him in his cell.

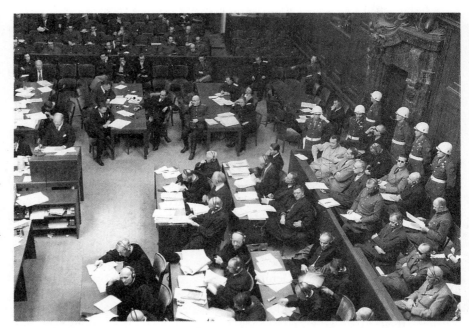

Only Göring cheated the executioner by taking a cyanide capsule. The reichs-marshal had bragged, "In fifty years there will be statues of Hermann Göring in Germany." Göring apparently thought the Germans possessed a faith in their leaders that would transcend the bitterness of defeat.

The trials left an ambiguous legacy. Some people questioned whether it was right to try defendants for crimes that were defined after the fact. Yet, the trials also ensured that World War II would not give rise to a "stab in the back" myth or a mystique about the greatness of the National Socialist period.

The Nuremberg tribunal continued in session—by the end of 1946, 447 more cases, involving 1,341 suspects, were ready for prosecution. Over the next four years, however, only 199 persons were actually put on trial. Thirty-six received death sentences, half of which were carried out. Nuremberg was not the only city to hold war crimes trials. The Americans also convened courts at Dachau, and trials were held in the other three occupation zones and indeed throughout Europe. The Soviets led the way in death and prison sentences—over 10,000 in the decade and a half following the war. The British, French, and American courts, and the German courts that followed them, sentenced about 10,555 persons; 200 of the judgments resulted in executions. All these trials were part of a general program of denazification, the essential purpose of which was reeducation.[23]

The Eastern Zone

The Rebirth of the Communist Party. The Soviets pretended to govern with restraint. On 10 June 1945, Marshal Zhukov proclaimed that the Germans were free to engage in social and political activity through the formation of "anti-fascist parties" dedicated to "the consolidation of the foundations of democracy and civil liberties"; such parties should also recognize the right of the workers "to unite in free trade unions and organizations to protect the interests and rights of all working people."[24] This directive was in keeping with the party line established earlier in which political activity in Germany could only be developed "initially in the context of a large scale comprehensive anti-Fascist movement under the title of the 'Bloc for Militant Democracy.' "[25]

On 12 June 1945, the German Communist party (*Kommunistische Partei Deutschlands* or *KPD*) was officially reestablished before a small audience of two hundred people in the Berlin city hall. The proclamation stated that "the method of imposing the Soviet system on Germany would be wrong, since this method does not correspond to present-day conditions of development in Germany." The German Communists took the view "that the overriding interests of the German people in their present-day situation prescribe a different method for Germany, namely the method of establishing democratic rights and liberties for the people."[26] The decree also recognized the "complete and unrestricted development of free commerce and private enterprise on the basis of private property." Nowhere was there any mention of Marx or Engels or socialism. This public endorsement of independent political activity (as long as it was anti-Fascist) was at odds with what Communist party officials had been taught and would have come as a surprise had it been taken seriously.

The basic strategy for the ultimate triumph of Communism had been worked out in Moscow before the end of the war. Even before the Red Army had ended all Nazi resistance, German Communist leaders had moved into key areas to take over the local administration under the supervision of the Soviet military authorities. Walter Ulbricht took charge in Berlin. He wanted everything to appear democratic on the surface and therefore advocated a broad coalition of all anti-Fascist parties. These, in addition to the KPD, included the Social Democratic party (SPD), the Christian Democratic Union (CDU), and the Liberal Democratic party of Germany (LDPD). The Soviet Military Administration was to handle affairs in East Germany, but the Communists did not want to appear too greedy for political power. They usually installed a well-known non-Communist as mayor, while retaining for themselves the key position of deputy mayor and other important posts in the municipal government. In Berlin, for example, they took charge of personnel, education, social welfare, finance, the post office and communications, and labor deployment.[27] From this powerful base, the Stalinists began quietly to tighten their control over East Germany and in the process gave up their earlier prohibition against seeking an alliance with the Social Democrats.

One-Party Government. Many Social Democrats had favored joining with the Communists to form a single party in which they would be the senior partners. They remembered how the Communist and Social Democratic split had contributed to the triumph of Hitler. However, their growing strength at the polls and the opposition of the West German Social Democrats to a union with the Communists had given them second thoughts. In the meantime, the Communists, alarmed at this new mood of independence, also had a change of heart.

In November 1945, Ulbricht called for an immediate union of the parties. He had witnessed the drift away from Communism in nearby Hungary and Austria and the gains made by the Social Democrats, at the expense of the Communists, in the local elections in West Germany and Berlin. Promising a German road to socialism, the KPD launched a massive recruitment campaign. It formed local KPD-SPD action committees and held meetings and conferences. The Soviet Military Administration did its part by banning Social Democratic meetings and arresting those who spoke out against unification. Finally, the Communists decided the time for persuasion was over and announced that fusion with the Social Democrats was an accomplished fact.

At the unification congress on 26 April, Wilhelm Pieck, the head of the Communists, and Otto Grotewohl, chief of the Social Democrats, officially proclaimed the establishment of the Socialist Unity party (*Sozialistische Einheitspartei Deutschlands* or *SED*) with a strict Marxist-Leninist program: "the transformation of the capitalist ownership of the means of production into social ownership and the transformation of capitalist production of goods into socialist production."[28] The SED claimed to represent the people and made a genuine attempt to appeal to the voters. It refused to accept the eastern boundary with Poland as final, and it promised to give former Nazis fair treatment. Such public relations ploys were part of Stalin's strategy of trying to influence political developments in the rest of Germany. However, the Americans, British, and French prohibited the SED from operating in their zones.

Even with considerable help from the Soviet authorities, who constantly harassed opposition party members and refused to place their candidates on the ballots, the SED failed to win a majority of the votes in the Kreis and Landtag elections of October 1946.[29] The party assumed control anyway. Within a year it had risen to two million members, more than all the other parties combined. Between 1946 and 1948, it expelled, degraded, falsely accused, or purged most of the leading Social Democrats.[30] Other political groups were turned into Communist auxiliaries or similarly eliminated. The establishment of one-party Stalinist rule in East Germany confirmed the country's division into two halves. Stalin severed all East Germany's ties with Western political parties and ended any hope that the country might take an independent road to socialism.

The Sectors of the West

The Development of Grass-Roots Democracy. In accordance with the Potsdam provisions on "the decentralization of the political structure and the development of local responsibility,[31] the British, Americans, and French each developed their own brand of German government. The British treated their zone as a sort of colony, one that was in transition from complete military control "to an eventual civilian organization in which there would be a German administration with British control at the top."[32] Thus, the British would use the army only in emergencies and would gradually allow the Germans to assume greater responsibilities. At the end of 1946, the British accorded the Länder the power to regulate their own industrial development, enact housing and town planning ordinances, and adopt measures concerning freedom of the press and association. Nevertheless, no measure the Länder legislatures passed could become law until the regional British commander countersigned it. The British also changed the traditional function of the town mayor. Previously, a *Bürgermeister* (mayor) had been both a city's chief executive and its chief legislator—as such, the mayors were frequently more responsible to the central government than to their own constituents. The British made the mayor head only of the town council and gave the executive functions to a professional city manager, the *Stadtdirector* (town clerk). By separating these functions, the British hoped to make the elected city council responsible for policy and show that the administrators were its servants, "dependent on its good will."[33]

The Americans also tried to inculcate democracy by extending popular participation to all levels of village, city, county, and state government. They allowed the people to ratify the constitutions drafted for Bavaria, Württemberg-Baden, and Hesse.[34] At the same time, however, the Americans never let the Germans forget who ultimately pulled the strings. General Lucius Clay ran things from his "capital" at Stuttgart, personally presiding over the monthly meeting of the minister-presidents of the various states. He used the occasion to charge them with specific responsibilities and to issue warnings. At the first meeting, he announced: "Since you will in fact develop the measures necessary for full cooperation between your units, it must be assumed that each of you individually will carry out what you have agreed to collectively. I wish to emphasize that, within United States policy, yours is the responsibility. We will not dictate to you except as you violate expressed policy."[35]

As for the French, General Pierre Koenig ruled from Baden-Baden like a king's viceroy. He thought it unfair that East Germany, but not the West, should be under a harsh rule. Consequently, he stubbornly refused to coordinate his policies with those of the British and Americans. His country's own economic problems virtually precluded it from supplying the Germans with any aid or providing much logistical support for its forces of occupation. The French tried to live off the land as much as possible, even to the extent of bringing over hordes of relatives to dwell with the soldiers in requisitioned quarters. To conserve rations, the French refused to accept refugees from other parts of Germany. They were interested in getting reparations, and they also wanted to annex the Saar, persisting in their demand long after it was plain that their cause was hopeless. The question of the Saar poisoned Franco-German relations for over a decade until the issue was finally resolved in 1957. Then, just as they had done in 1935, the Saarlanders voted overwhelmingly to become a permanent part of Germany. In one way, though, the French were less harsh than the other occupying powers. They seldom turned Germans out of their homes. They simply moved in on them, occupying the best rooms, sitting in the best chairs, and sometimes relegating the former occupants to the basement. Still, this was better than in the other zones where if a house or an apartment was needed, the inhabitants were simply ordered to leave.

Denazification. The Americans were optimistic that they could change the German national character and therefore pushed denazification harder than any of the other occupying powers. The Joint Chiefs of Staff directive 1067 determined to purge from public office and positions of importance all members of the Nazi party who were "more than normal participants in its activities, all active supporters of Nazism or militarism and all other persons hostile to Allied purposes."[36] These included officeholders, party activists, organizers, participants in Nazi unions, and those who had voluntarily given substantial support or assistance to the National Socialist cause. The Americans believed that everyone who joined the party before 1937 had done so out of commitment, not necessity. To identify the suspects, they prepared a personal questionnaire (*Fragebogen*) with 131 questions. Every German over the age of eighteen had to complete one. The process was carried out through local registration boards somewhat reminiscent of the U.S. Selective Service System. The Americans examined the answers and assigned the respondents to the appropriate classifications: major offender, offender, lesser offender, follower, or exonerated. The table of punishments for each category (except major war criminals who were placed in a special category) ranged from imprisonment to loss of property, and from exclusion from public office to prohibition from voting.

The Americans ordered the Germans to create a Special Ministry of Political Education and establish their own denazification courts under the supervision of the Public Safety Branch of the Military Government. In its heyday, the operation was massive, comprising 545 separate tribunals with a combined personnel of over 22,000 people. Thirteen million Germans were registered, 3 million of whom were charged, but only 930 received sentences. Denazification concentrated a tremendous amount of energy on an essentially negative task, which was never completely successful. Nazism had, after all, been an indigenous movement, and people had many reasons for joining—some out of ideological enthusiasm, others because it was a good way to advance their careers. Some were required to become members because they held positions of responsibility and trust and the party officials ordered all such people to belong. If all Nazi party members had been excluded from participation in the political and economic life of postwar Germany, the society would have ceased to function. General George Patton, briefly military governor of Bavaria, had no difficulty using Nazi civil servants to run his province, and he was not alone. The Americans also suspected that the Germans were not particularly keen to pursue their compatriots.

The Soviets were more tolerant of a person's past—if that person were willing to join the Socialist Unity party. After all, the psychology of totalitarianism was the same whether it was from the Left or the Right—a person could serve one just as well as the other. The British endorsed denazification, but compiled dossiers on only two million persons. The French believed all Germans were guilty anyway so they saw little to be gained in pursuing former Nazis unless they had committed specific crimes against the French.

The way the denazification policy was implemented aroused considerable dissatisfaction. Nevertheless, a great many former Nazis *were* removed from active public life, thereby creating opportunities for those who were less politically compromised. The purge was necessary to encourage the democratic elements, who had been terrorized during the Nazi period, to once again play an active role in the political life of their country. The Germans may have been critical of the policy, but the society in which they lived was better for being at least partially cleansed of its unwholesome elements. Had the Weimar Republic carried out a similar purge of the old imperial bureaucracy, its democracy might have had a better chance of survival.

Removing the unsavory elements was only part of the process of denazification. The Allies believed that if Nazism were to be eradicated, the demons of the past would have to be exorcised through reeducation.[37] To this end, the Americans, British, French, and Soviets all wanted to make profound changes in the schools, including purging them of National Socialist books and curricula, screening teachers for the proper moral and political qualities, and imposing a new educational policy on Germany. Their philosophies varied as did their techniques and their degree of success.

The Soviets, who did not have to worry about imbuing the Germans with a love of democracy, accomplished the most significant structural changes. But then they had more and longer opportunities than the Western powers. The Soviet Military Administration (after 1949 the Soviet High Commissioner) and the SED, the official political party, did not have to face competition. East German teachers had already been schooled in obedience. The centralized Nazi educational administration continued under another guise with those who believed in Marxist Leninism replacing those who followed the Führerprinzip. Politics aside, the Soviets did effect a significant and lasting social alteration. Whereas the German system had previously trained different social classes for different tasks, the Soviets abolished the special advantages of the middle and upper classes and created comprehensive, more egalitarian schools.

The three Western powers were primarily interested in inculcating the Germans with democracy. The French rivaled the Soviets in reformist zeal, although they had less practical effect. They arrived with missionary enthusiasm, bringing elaborate plans and first-rate educators. Not since the old colonial days had they had such an opportunity to practice their *mission civilisatrice*. They left with their ambitions unfulfilled, but with the Germans less nationalistic and less parochial.

The British brought a similar array of experts, but theirs seemed content with giving advice rather than being coercive. The British and German systems operated on similar social wavelengths—both institutionalized the system of tracking. Within two years, the British began returning the school system to the Germans.

In contrast, the Americans were just getting their second wind in 1947. The Americans had first concentrated on denazification, carefully removing Nazi party members from the schools and starting to reform the curriculum. They replaced Nazi books with those of the Weimar Republic, forgetting that the Weimar schools were bastions of ultranationalism. The universities were immediately reopened with University Planning Committees to supervise who taught what and to whom. Following the precedent established at Marburg University, applicants were required to fill out a *Fragebogen*; after admission, they had to take a special orientation course that concentrated on Germany's relations with the world since 1935. The Americans gave feminism a big boost by abolishing the Nazi 10 percent ceiling on enrollments for women. The first postwar class admitted at Marburg was almost 40 percent female. The Joint Chiefs of Staff directive of July 1947 strongly linked educational reform with economic and political recovery, but the low status the American army accorded its educational specialists belied that contention.

Ultimately, Western plans to change the structure of German education by making the schools workshops for democracy and social unification fell short of their goals. The occupation only lasted four years, too short a time for rewards to keep pace with expectations. The United States had more influence through its cultural exchange programs than through its curriculum revisions. In addition, the educational programs of the Western democratic powers all contained a basic contradiction. The philosophe Jean-Jacques Rousseau had advocated liberating people from the chains of the past by forcing them to be free. In practice, though, military government proved to be a poor tutor for democracy.

The Demise of Central Administration

The Policy of Pauperization Ends. The Potsdam agreement mandated that the German standard of living be maintained at the European average—in effect, cut back to the levels that existed in the depression year of 1932. Despite the enormous destruction of the war, only 15 to 20 percent of German industry was irreparably damaged. In 1944, Germany actually produced 40 percent more goods than in 1938. In March 1946, however, a joint economics council directive set Germany's annual steel production at 7.5 million tons (a significant reduction from its prewar figure of 19 million tons). It reduced the production of chemicals to 40 percent of 1936 output, set machine tools at 11.4 percent of the 1938 level, and dropped heavy electrical equipment to 30 percent of the 1938 capacity. Under this directive German manufacturing would, on average, be stabilized at half the productive levels achieved in 1938. Most importantly, the Germans were prohibited from manufacturing all armaments and war materials, including ball bearings, synthetic rubber, heavy tractors, and radio transmitting equipment. The Germans were also to discontinue all experimentation with nuclear energy. The directive left only a few industries without limitations—building materials, bicycles, china dishes, and glass bottles. Even this was practically meaningless because the Germans did not have sufficient hard currency to purchase raw materials, which, for the most part, had to be imported.

Having set the policy, the occupying powers were sharply divided over how it should be carried out. The Russians and French pushed for even further reductions, while the British and Americans had come to the conclusion that maintaining artificially low levels of production was against their own national interests. For one thing, they reasoned that their exports were already keeping the Germans alive; with millions of refugees fleeing to the West from the Russian zone, this economic dependency would only get worse. Overriding these economic concerns was the British and American fear that unless the Germans were allowed to return to prosperity they would once again seek a solution to their problems in extremist politics, which now could only mean Communism. Therefore, German economic prosperity was a fundamental necessity.

Furthermore, the Soviets were insisting that the $10 billion due them in reparations be directly satisfied with goods from current production, including production from the Western zones. If the Soviet demand were met, the West would, in fact, be subsidizing the Soviet Union. The British and Americans tried to ease the economic tensions by advocating the establishment of a central import and export agency that would treat Germany as a single economic unit, but the Soviets (and also the French) were strongly opposed. Stalin withstood all attempts to conclude a formal treaty of peace until his demands were satisfied.

James Byrnes, the U.S. secretary of state, believed that Soviet intransigence was prompted by fear of another invasion. He, therefore, proposed a treaty to guarantee German demilitarization for twenty-five years. Byrnes hoped that such an agreement would pave the way for the early evacuation of all Allied military forces. The Soviets toyed with the idea and even induced Byrnes to extend the guarantee to forty years. Nevertheless, Stalin knew that any agreement that might lead to a Soviet evacuation from Germany would jeopardize the collection of reparations. Furthermore, the experiences after World War I suggested that German disarmament could not be ensured without occupation.

The Suspension of Reparations Payments. The British and Americans became convinced that Stalin was deliberately promoting German economic chaos to further the advance of Communism. On 3 May 1946, the United States suspended all payments of reparations from its zone to the Soviets. Byrnes concluded that the failure of the Soviet leaders to support his guarantee treaty meant that they did not want the United States involved in any system to maintain European security and that only the "pressure of American power would restrict the freedom of action which the Soviet Union, as the predominant military power in Europe, might otherwise enjoy."[38] The suspension of reparations payments to the Soviet Union was Byrnes's way of showing that a common German policy was impossible.[39] Britain and the United States refused to consider the resumption of reparations payments until there was a general willingness to share resources.

Byrnes then went further. On 11 July, he said that the United States was willing to join "with any other occupying government or governments in Germany for the creation of our respective zones as an economic unit."[40] On 6 September, Byrnes made the new policy more explicit when he told the minister-presidents of Württemberg, Bavaria, and Hesse at Stuttgart that the United States no longer considered the agreement to limit German production to be binding. "Germany must be enabled to use her skills and her energies to increase her industrial production and to organize the most effective use of her raw materials," he said. "Germany is a part of Europe, and recovery in Europe . . . will be slow indeed if Germany with her great resources of iron and coal is turned into a poorhouse."[41] Byrnes also stated that Germany must be permitted to develop democratically responsible government in which the central administrative agencies would function under an appropriate federal constitution. This, he emphasized, would take place under the full protection of the United States. "Security forces," he added significantly, "will probably have to remain in Germany for a long period. I want no misunderstanding. We will not shirk our duty. We are not withdrawing. We are staying and will furnish our proportionate share of security forces."[42]

Great Britain responded immediately to the American initiative, and the merger of their two zones was finalized in December 1946. The French at first tried to maintain a position of "nonalignment," hoping that they could, with Soviet support, annex the Saar and achieve internationalization of the Ruhr. The pursuit of such a policy, however, left them in the uncomfortable position of standing on the sidelines while a strong Germany once again emerged. No longer was there any possibility that Germany would be broken up into some sort of loose federal state. Therefore, Paris began negotiations toward joining the French zone with the British and American sector. At the same time, French leaders found the prospect so objectionable that they tried to delay the inevitable as long as possible by holding out for large concessions.

In creating Bizonia, the British and Americans nevertheless tried to avoid the complete breakdown of the policy of joint administration. They therefore allowed the continuation of the present currency system. This was a double-headed arrangement in which regular German reichsmarks were allowed to circulate alongside the special occupation currency that the Allies had issued to transact their own affairs. Both monies were highly inflated. During the war, the number of banknotes in circulation had quadrupled without a corresponding increase in goods and services. The occupation money was similarly inflated, largely because the Soviets, on their own, kept printing as much as they wanted to satisfy their needs. It thus became a way of collecting reparations. Since the real worth of both currencies was unrelated to their fixed rate, an active black market flourished. Under the circumstances, it was impossible to program any rational economic development. The Allies had tried to maintain economic stability by continuing the rationing and wage and price controls established under the Nazis. Still the amount of goods was small in relation to the superabundance of currency, and official prices were too low to stimulate production. Without any reliable currency, the Germans resorted to barter. In many areas, American cigarettes became a form of legal tender. The Soviets were clearly more interested in maintaining the financial chaos of Germany than they were in promoting its recovery. They refused to agree to any new banking scheme because that might weaken their hand.

Therefore, the British and Americans decided to act alone. In February 1948, they announced their intention to establish a new bank of issue, the *Bank Deutscher Länder*, under the supervision of the Allied Banking Commission. Before putting the scheme into effect, they asked the Soviets to help conclude a new four-power agreement. The Soviets came to the negotiations with the intention of sabotaging them. Stalin regarded the proposed reform as part of a plot to divide Germany. At the conference, the Soviets insisted that they had the right to continue printing money without restriction, but it was clear that the Americans and British were prepared to enact the reform without them—an obvious prelude to establishing a separate West German government. On 20 March, the Soviets withdrew their representatives from the Allied Control Commission. General Clay had seen the stiffening Soviet attitude and warned Washington to prepare for some major Soviet move. The Anglo-American determination to carry out the currency reform in Bizonia prodded France to merge its zone with theirs. Without waiting for parliamentary approval for the full merger plan, the French negotiators agreed to accept the new currency reform in their zone. At the same time, they continued to demand last-minute tax benefits. The French were of two minds: realizing they could not go it alone, they wanted to join the merger, but be independent at the same time.

The *Währungsreform* (currency reform) was announced on 18 June to take effect two days later when the new banknotes would be released simultaneously in the British, French, and American zones. Stalin was ready. He denounced the Western powers for violating the Yalta and Potsdam accords and suspended their rights to have access to Berlin by land. For Stalin the blockade was more than just a ploy to force a return to the status quo ante. The currency reform provided him with an opportunity to win a stunning Cold War victory by removing the West from Berlin. He had long viewed this outpost as a threat to the security of the whole Soviet position in Germany.

The Berlin Blockade. Stalin was in a much better position than he had been the previous year to seek a showdown with his former allies. In February 1948, he had considerably strengthened his hold over Eastern Europe with the formation of a Communist-controlled government in Czechoslovakia. The country had rapidly been integrated into the Soviet bloc. Stalinist governments were also in firm control of all the important Eastern European states, excluding Greece and Yugoslavia. Stalin chose Berlin for the showdown because it was completely surrounded by Soviet-controlled territory. The Soviets had been interfering with Western access to the city since January 1948. On 1 April, the Soviets demanded that Allied railroad traffic obtain special prior authorization before passing through the Soviet zone. Next came a claim that the Western allies had forfeited all their rights in the city because they had disrupted the four-power government of Germany. Now, Stalin argued that in organizing a West German government, the West had violated the Yalta and the Potsdam accords, and therefore he was not bound to follow these agreements on the status of Berlin.

On 24 June, four days after the Western currency reform went into effect, the Soviets stopped all surface freight and passenger traffic into the city from the West; a week later, they officially withdrew from the Berlin Kommandatura, bringing four-power rule to an end. Stalin had good reason to expect that his Berlin coup would succeed. The Western powers had only token forces in the city and were hardly mobilized for the kind of military action needed to challenge the might of the Red Army. Furthermore, there was no written agreement confirming ground access to the city. Such a formal reinforcement of rights had not seemed necessary in 1945, when few assumed that the military arrangements for the occupation of Germany would form the basis for two separate states. The Western powers could argue that Soviet acceptance of their presence in Berlin implied that they had an easement into the city to exercise their rights there. For this reason, they considered Stalin's behavior unacceptable and a violation of the agreements of 1944 and 1945.

Washington vetoed a plan advanced by General Lucius Clay to send an armored column up the autobahn to reassert Western rights. On paper, the only right of access the West had was a provision for the use of specific air corridors, which

A Skymaster flies low over the Berlin rooftops on its final approach to Templehof airport. The C-54 was the workhorse of the U.S. Air Force during World War II; the U.S. built more C-54s than any other cargo transport. Some three hundred of them participated in the Berlin airlift, and the last flight of the blockade was made by a C-54.

had been committed to writing more for the purpose of air safety than for politics. Yet upon this legality, the United States decided to base its countermeasure to the blockade. Until now the feasibility of supplying Berlin by air had hardly been considered. Commander R. N. Waite of the Royal Air Force (RAF) quickly concocted a plan showing it could be done, and the Americans and British scraped together practically every transport plane at their disposal to put it into effect.

The airlift began on 25 June with a flight of C-47s and was improvised as it went along. At first, people viewed it as a holding operation to give the politicians time to negotiate a settlement, but the longer the airlift continued, the more supplies it could fly into the beleaguered city. With the arrival of C-54s in late July, ten tons of goods could be carried per plane. At its height, the airlift supplied Berlin with 8,000 tons of food, raw materials, and fuel daily. On average, a plane landed at Berlin's Templehof Airport every three to five minutes, twenty-four hours a day. In all, some 2.3 million tons of provisions arrived; the United States Air Force carried two-thirds, the RAF was responsible for most of the rest. When the blockade began, the Americans moved their B-29 strategic bombers to Britain. The planes, armed with atomic bombs, were within striking distance of Moscow. President Harry S Truman saw the Berlin crisis as Stalin's attempt to test his resolve. He believed that if he gave in, there would be no end of bullying. The Berlin Blockade also prompted an Allied counterblockade. The West kept a broad range of products from being exported to the Soviet zone: machinery, chemicals, rubber, textiles, steel, tools, spare parts, and electrical goods.[43] The ban kept the East German government from fulfilling its Two-Year Plan.

Throughout the ordeal, the morale of the Berliners remained extremely high. Political cabarets were especially popular, as indeed were all sorts of cultural events and activities that brought the people of West Berlin closer together. The crisis ended all-city government, however. In December 1948, separate elections were held in West Berlin, resulting in the triumph of Ernst Reuter. Heretofore the Soviets had prevented this Social Democrat from becoming mayor. East Berlin then held its own separate elections. In addition to having two mayors, the city also separated economically, with each part having its own public services.

Berlin became divided educationally as well. The school system had already been marked by ideological and political confrontation as Social Democrats and Communists fought to control the administration and curriculum. The Communists had an advantage because the Soviets had entrenched themselves in power as soon as they arrived in the city, months before the others. Although the Allied Kommandatura had final authority, the constant East-West squabbles resulted in frustration and delays. The Soviets challenged every Western proposal. Meanwhile, they had taken over Berlin University (since 1949 Humboldt University), which was located in their zone, and shut everybody else out. Their secret police routinely harassed students, arresting and expelling those they found objectionable.

The Berlin Blockade presented the perfect opportunity to bring this impossible situation to an end by creating a separate elementary and secondary school system for West Berlin. At the same time, General Clay pushed for the creation of a new university. The proposal reached his desk in April 1948, and he immediately gave it his most enthusiastic endorsement, insisting that the new institution be opened in time for the autumn term. The Free University of Berlin was to be a German university run by Germans. It held its first classes in November. In addition to liberating Berlin's higher education from the grip of Marxist-Leninism, the university's founders wanted to promote free inquiry in all fields and avoid the traditional authoritarianism of German universities. On the occasion of the university's inauguration on 4 December 1948, Ernst Reuter, mayor-elect of Berlin and chairman of the Preparatory Committee, said, "Universities should be centers of free activity, free creativity, and free thinking, not centers where politics in the narrow sense of the word are perpetrated."[44] Thus, he linked the freedom of the university with the aspirations of Berliners for the freedom of their city.

The Berlin airlift dramatically confirmed the Western presence in Berlin. Truman did not think the Soviets really wanted to push the crisis to the point of war, but he feared that "a trigger-happy Russian pilot or hothead Communist tank commander might create an incident that could ignite the powder keg."[45] The crisis ended in a stalemate. The Soviets lifted the blockade on 12 May 1949. Berlin was divided, but so was all Germany. On 23 May, the British, American, and French zones officially became the German Federal Republic.

The Soviets denounced the *Bundesrepublik* as a Germany of warmongers, armaments tycoons, and large estate owners and established their own "sovereign" state. They claimed that their German Democratic Republic (*Deutsche Democratische Republik* or GDR) was the only regime to honor the Potsdam agreement's call for an independent and democratic Germany. The West saw the GDR as an illegitimate puppet regime, established by fiat, not by free elections. Thus, each side claimed its creation was legitimate and the only true basis for a united Germany. Rhetoric aside, none of the victors genuinely desired reunification, at least not then. They did not want a sovereign, independent Germany; nor did they want a united Germany under the control of the other party. Division was the most feasible solution. The Berlin crisis changed the character of the Cold War by ending the active competition for a unified Germany. The airlift also showed that neither side was willing to wage war to obtain more than it already had. Truman summed up the significance of the airlift succinctly: "When we refused to be forced out of the city of Berlin, we demonstrated to the people of Europe that with their co-operation we would act, and act resolutely, when their freedom was threatened. Politically it brought the peoples of western Europe more closely to us."[46]

THE BONN REPUBLIC

Constitutional and Political Reconstruction

The Basic Law. The Weimar Republic had foundered because most Germans thought that their problems could be solved by those who wanted to destroy democracy. In 1948, the framers of the new *Grundgesetz* (Basic Law) could hardly create an instant respect for representative institutions, but they did try to correct past structural weaknesses. They were not alone in their desire. On 1 July 1948, the Western allies issued a directive requiring the Germans to draft a "democratic constitution," establishing a "federal type" government to "protect the rights of the participating states, provide adequate authority, and contain guarantees of individual rights and freedoms."[47] During the drafting of the constitution, the military governors constantly offered advice and assistance, and, not surprisingly, the final document reflected their concepts of democratic practice as well as the Germans' notions of self-government.

The constituent assembly resurrected the parliamentary republic, but deprived the president of the power to issue emergency decrees and to act as commander-in-chief of the armed forces. To minimize the possibility of a cult of personality, a special Federal Convention would elect the president "without debate." The convention would be divided equally between representatives from the lower house of the legislature and from the local state diets. The president would have the authority to "propose" the head of the government, but could not participate in the process of selecting a cabinet; and an appropriate minister had to endorse all official acts (appointments and dismissals, proclamations of treaties, and official pardons). The president was clearly expected to be a figurehead, while the real executive power was concentrated in a cabinet, which was responsible to, and had to enjoy the majority support of, the lower house of parliament. The head of the government was the chancellor (*Bundeskanzler*), who could only be overthrown by a positive vote of no confidence: that is, the chancellor could not be ousted by a simple vote of no confidence; a viable successor had to be elected instead. This provision was inserted to avoid interregnums and to prevent the sort of situation that had occurred in the early 1930s when the Nazis and Communists overturned the government with the sole purpose of creating as much confusion as possible.

The legislative power, in keeping with the desires of the Western allies to promote federalism, was vested in two chambers. The lower house, the *Bundestag*, was the more powerful. Its deputies directly represented the whole people and were "not bound by orders and instructions and are subject only to their conscience."[48] In financial matters, the lower chamber had paramount authority. The upper house, the *Bundesrat*, directly represented the Länder and had to approve any laws that affected the states' administrative, territorial, and financial interests. On other legislation, it possessed only a suspensive veto.

In its "Letter of Advice," the Allied Military Government of the Western powers demanded that the Germans establish "an independent judiciary to review legislation, to review the exercise of executive power, to resolve conflict between the federal government and the states or between the states, and to protect civil rights and individual freedoms."[49] The principle of judicial review, which the United States strongly endorsed, was alien to the German tradition.[50] It was also foreign to the legal practices of the British and French, but they agreed that such a check on executive and legislative authority could prevent the central government from riding roughshod over the rights of the states and individual liberties. Accordingly, the Germans established a federal constitutional court to rule on the substantive and procedural rights of individuals and groups. The court had the authority to arbitrate jurisdictional disputes between the federal and the state governments; the responsibility of interpreting, supervising, and enforcing constitutional norms; and the duty to protect the basic rights of free speech, press, assembly, and equality before the law, even against private individuals and groups that sought to deprive citizens of these rights.[51] The court met in Karlsruhe to avoid making a single city the seat of the German government.

Allied Approval. The West Germans accepted judicial review, but they had difficulty achieving the amount of functional decentralization that the Allies demanded. The French, British, and American military governors, meeting in Frankfurt on 16 February 1949 to review a draft of the proposed constitution, feared that excessive authority had been given to the central government, especially in the fields of public health, public welfare, labor, revenue raising, and tax collection. They also mistrusted its power over the press. The Allies believed that giving broad concurrent legislative powers to both the federal government and the Länder would unnecessarily weaken the authority of the individual states. In addition, they were concerned that the new civil service would perpetuate undemocratic traditions.[52] The Allies were not unanimous in their demands. While the British were willing to accept the Basic Law, provided the provisions about the civil service were changed, the Americans and French wanted specific reductions in the financial and legislative powers of the central government.

Social Democratic party leader Kurt Schumacher announced publicly that he would try to force the constitution's ratification without change. His party felt that centralization was essential to carry out the socialization of the German economy. General Clay thought Schumacher was merely trying to score political points with the electorate: "If he and his party could defy the occupying powers and get away with it, they could go to the polls triumphantly proclaiming their success as defenders of the German people against the Allies."[53] Neither the Germans, nor the Allies, really wanted to delay the establishment of constitutional government. A major difference over financial authority was resolved by giving the federal government the receipts from customs, most excise taxes, and the sales tax and giving the Länder the income from property, inheritance, and motor-vehicle taxes. The states could also keep the tax revenues from the sale of alcoholic beverages—a concession that the 1871 constitution had accorded some states. Both the federal government and the Länder were to share the revenues from income and corporation taxes. These financial provisions, comprising ten articles of the Basic Law, were almost a constitution in themselves. The Basic Law is probably the only constitution in the world that specifically recognizes the right to collect a tax on beer.

Reestablishment of Party Government

A Multiparty System. The Basic Law came into force on 23 May 1949, after being ratified by two-thirds of the Länder. The first elections were held the following 14 August. The voting system combined proportional representation with single-member districts; each German cast two ballots—one for a specific candidate and the other for a particular party list. This device was supposed to promote the development of large, nationally organized political parties and discourage the growth of splinter groups. The election law also stated that any party receiving less than five percent of the vote would not be represented in the Bundestag. For the first time in German history, the constitution described the role of parties: "The political parties participate in the forming of the political will of the people. They may be freely formed. Their internal organization must conform to democratic principles. They must publicly account for the sources of their funds."[54]

The 1949 balloting gave seats in the Bundestag to ten political parties. Three of these won four-fifths of the seats. The Christian Democratic Union (with its Bavarian affiliate the Christian Social Union) had 139 delegates; the Social Democratic party, 131 delegates; and the Free Democratic party, 52 delegates. In subsequent elections, as the strength of the smaller parties dwindled, Germany came closer to having a two-party system than any other continental European nation. The new parliament met in Bonn in September 1949 and elected Theodor Heuss, leader of the Free Democrats, as first bundespräsident. The new chief of state had distinguished himself in the days of the Weimar Republic as a journalist and lecturer at the Berlin Institute of Politics. He had served in the Reichstag and was a convinced democrat. His conception of the presidency as a largely ceremonial office outside the main political arena helped to confirm the intent of the constitution. As part of the agreement to elect Heuss to the presidency, the Free Democrats supported the formation of a cabinet by Konrad Adenauer, the leader of the Christian Democrats. With additional support from several minor parties, he squeezed into office by 201 to 200 votes.

Adenauer's Christian Democratic Union (CDU) was a heterogeneous collection of old Center party veterans, Rhineland industrialists, landowners, economic free traders, Weimar liberals, and conservatives. Although the Christian Democrats were predominantly Roman Catholic, Adenauer wisely fought the creation of a confessionalist party and chose a Protestant, Ludwig Erhard, to hold the second position in the party. Adenauer's political acumen was demonstrated by his ability to hold these disparate elements together and, in less than a decade, mold them into a solid majority party. (For example, in the 1957 elections, the CDU received 50.2 percent of the votes and 270 of the 497 deputies in the Bundestag.) The CDU stood for the "maintenance of a socially-responsible free enterprise economy."[55] Accordingly, it adhered to the long-standing welfare goals of socialism, but balanced these with an endorsement of private initiative. The Christian Democrats called for the elimination of the monopolistic practices of the past that had acted as a hindrance to the free play of market forces. They wanted to strengthen small and medium-size private businesses and agricultural enterprises. They believed in a sound fiscal system and in the protection of savings and private property. In some regions, like Bavaria, the party posed as the champion of Roman Catholicism. However, it gained more support in the large urban areas of the north with its appeal to middle-class fears of socialism.

Despite the great loyalty to democracy that the Social Democratic party (*Sozialdemokratische Partei Deutschlands* or *SPD*) had shown during the Weimar Republic, many Germans were leery of turning power over to a group of Marxists. The SPD therefore remained the main opposition party, relying chiefly on working-class support. At their reorganization convention in October 1945, the Social Democrats advocated state economic planning and public ownership of the basic means of production. However, the party gradually became more moderate as it began to compete with the CDU for middle-class votes. Gallant though its leader Kurt Schumacher was, he proved a hindrance to creating a broad-based party. In order to win more than its usual 30 percent of the vote, the SPD needed to purge itself of all its revolutionary ideology. Schumacher's death paved the way for the Godesberg Program of 1959. This program advocated "freedom of choice in consumption and in employment, free competition and free economic initiative," and it pledged to protect and assist privately owned means of production "except where this may interfere with the development of a just social order."[56] The Social Democrats recognized that most Germans were no longer content with doctrinaire solutions to problems, and that the successful recovery of Germany meant a strong endorsement of the market economy.

Profile: Konrad Adenauer (1876–1967)

Until 1945, when Konrad Adenauer presided over the formation of the Christian Democratic Union—one of the four interregional parties that the Allied military government permitted to exist—he was practically unknown outside his native Cologne where he had served as mayor from 1917 to 1933. During this long tenure, he had exercised almost unchallenged control over the city's administration, dominating its council and requiring complete obedience from his subordinates. He was forced from office in 1933 when the Nazis accused him of embezzling money from the city treasury and of having betrayed Germany to the French by intriguing for the establishment of a separate Rhenish Republic. The charge of separatism was not without merit.

A key to understanding Adenauer's personality and subsequent career as chancellor of Germany can be found in the special characteristics of Cologne in the late nineteenth century where he was born on 5 January 1876. His father was a clerk of the city's Superior Tribunal, and his family was devoutly Roman Catholic. This was the time when Bismarck was conducting his famous *Kulturkampf* (Conflict of Beliefs) to subordinate the Roman Catholic religion to state regimentation. Adenauer grew up determined to combat the influence of Prussia. He became a lawyer in order to establish a power base within the local Cologne hierarchy. In 1897, he obtained his first position as an assistant in the public prosecutor's office. He joined the regionally powerful Catholic Center party, an alliance that led to his appointment as an administrative assistant in the city's taxation department. In six years, he rose to become vice-mayor, and in October 1917 he was elected mayor for his first twelve-year term.

After the fall of the kaiser, Adenauer tried to discern where his interest lay. On the one hand, he was sympathetic to Rhineland separatism, but at the same time he wanted to wait until he could obtain a clearer idea of the viability of the Weimar government. At one time, he advocated a West German Republic within the bounds of the Reich. This unit would have its own police force and diplomatic representation abroad. German nationalists suspected him of being pro-French, since his goals seemed to coincide with those of Paris, but Adenauer simply did not want to have his authority diluted by service to any foreign authority even that of the government in Berlin. When the independence movement fizzled, Adenauer redirected his energies to his duties as mayor of Cologne. The lord-mayors of German cities traditionally exercised power like the old prince-bishops of the Holy Roman Empire. Adenauer, in addition to holding the highest executive position, was also the permanent chief of every municipal department and used his authority to interfere routinely whenever he saw fit. Later, as chancellor, when the editor of *Die Zeit* criticized him for approaching politics like the director of a volunteer fire department, he shot back, "Herr Fuengel is probably quite right, but I'm sure he has no idea what a difficult time you can have with a volunteer fire department."[57]

Although he had little appreciation of democratic niceties, Adenauer wanted nothing to do with the Nazis, whom he regarded as upstarts and louts. Their raucous brutality conflicted with his high sense of moral purpose. It therefore came as no surprise when they gave him the boot. He quit active politics altogether, but not before making a pro forma declaration of obedience to the new regime in order to save his pension. Years of retirement kept him out of trouble. The Gestapo arrested him in April 1944, held him for a time, released him, and then arrested him once more. His status as a victim gave him a cachet with the Allies, who in March 1945 installed him once again in the city hall at Cologne. His appointment lasted only until the following August, when the British, dissatisfied with his performance, imperiously fired him. Three months after this dismissal, however, he became head of the largest branch of the Christian Democratic Union and thus began his march to the chancellorship, the post to which he was elected in August 1949.

As chancellor, Adenauer retained his authoritarian style. He took complete advantage of the powers given the chancellor under the Basic Law to appoint and dismiss ministers and to determine policy, especially in foreign affairs and defense. In 1951, he issued new rules of governmental procedure that recognized the chancellor's paramount responsibility to establish and supervise overall principles that were "binding on federal ministers and are to be put into practice by them in their departments independently and on their own responsibility. In cases of doubt the federal chancellor's decision must be sought."[58] Because of his age (he was seventy-three in 1949), Adenauer was expected to remain active in politics only a short time. However, from the outset, *Der Alte* (the old man) acted with the energy and determination of an immortal. He became the longest serving chancellor in twentieth-century German history, remaining in office a bit over fourteen years, until October 1963. He managed this impressive tenure not only because of his domestic political skills, but also in large part because he wisely retained the active support of the United States. Once again, he was denounced for subservience to foreign interests. The Social Democratic leader Kurt Schumacher called him the "chancellor of the Allies." Adenauer reacted with fury. He had Schumacher condemned for violating the parliamentary rules of order and suspended from participation in the Bundestag for twenty sitting days. Fortunately, Adenauer's successors were men of a different sort. Although Adenauer had helped to establish the viability of postwar German parliamentary government, German democracy was as yet too fragile to survive many chancellors with his readiness to manipulate the law when it served his purpose.

Growth and Readjustment

The Economic Miracle. Germany's phenomenal recovery (the *Wirtschaftswunder*) began with the currency reforms of 1948. Under the new currency law, old reichsmarks were converted into new deutsche marks at a graduated rate of exchange: 1 for 1 up to a total of 60; for amounts above that, the rate was 100 of the old for 6.5 of the new. Thus, those who had their money in savings suffered the most, while those who had their assets in commodities survived much better. The general effect on economic activity, however, was astounding. Hoarding ended almost overnight as goods and specialty foods returned to the stores. The Germans went on a buying spree. Production, spurred by demand, increased rapidly. It doubled during the last half of the year and continued to rise steadily over the next decade. In 1950, the West German gross national product was 97.2 billion marks (about $24 billion); ten years later, it had almost tripled, to 277.7 billion marks. In 1950, the millions of refugees from East Germany were considered a drain on the economy and helped push the overall unemployment rate to 10.3 percent. In 1960, despite the addition of 2 to 3 million more escapees from the Soviet zone, unemployment had fallen to 1.2 percent and, the following year, to a minuscule 0.7 percent. Between 1954 and 1961, real earnings increased by 42 percent, and personal consumption by 48 percent. The number of privately owned automobiles soared.[59] Although prestige models built by Mercedes-Benz and Porsche became the ultimate status symbol, the lowly *Käfer* (beetle), produced by Volkswagen, was the choice of most German car owners; the Volkswagen bug became the country's single most important export, helping to give Germany a consistent 3 to 4 percent surplus in its balance of payments.[60] Although the German recovery owed a great deal to American economic aid—from 1945 to 1961 over $3.5 billion worth—the Germans themselves were primarily responsible for their economic miracle.

The Germans worked hard for modest wages. Their small business owners and industrialists reinvested a great deal of the profits. Trade union leaders, realizing that sacrifice was essential to build a strong economy, refrained from strikes. (Besides, it was difficult to radicalize the proletariat in a period of full employment.) Codetermination, or labor-management decision making, helped keep labor peace. In the 1950s, Germans usually worked a 48-hour week. This was not reduced to 40 hours until 1961. At the beginning of the 1950s, the average worker earned one mark (25 cents) an hour; ten years later, he or she received three times as much. The increase represented a similar advance in real income. Inflation, as revealed by the retail price index, hardly ever exceeded two percent in any given year.

A Social Market Economy. The Christian Democrats and the Social Democrats both agreed on the necessity for social security and welfare. The Germans had a long tradition of social legislation, which at the level of the central government began with Bismarck's welfare program in the 1880s. The Christian Democratic Union proclaimed its desire to create a *Sozial Marktwirtschaft*, which, according to Economics Minister Ludwig Erhard, was "a simple Christian act" necessary "to free our fellow Germans from need and misery and give them back a sense of security and dignity."[61] Erhard had no intention of creating a total welfare state, which he believed would increase the collectivization of everyday life and produce a " 'social serf' whose material security is guaranteed by the almighty state, while economic progress in freedom becomes a thing of the past."[62]

Erhard's philosophical *éminence grise* was Wilhelm Röpke, then professor at the Graduate Institute of International Studies in Geneva, who believed that the study of economics was more than a matter of developing a methodology from the natural sciences. Economics was essentially "a moral science and as such has to do with man as a spiritual and moral being."[63] A neoliberal, Röpke was constantly aware that his discipline might move too far in the direction of mechanics, statistics, and mathematics to the neglect of human values:

Prosperous Berliners stroll through Tauentzienstrasse, one of the central city's principal shopping districts. The ruined tower of the Kaiser Wilhelm Memorial Church (center) stands as a witness to the destruction of the war and provides a stark contrast to the modern architecture that surrounds it.

It is a serious misunderstanding to wish to defend the mathematical method with the argument that economics has to do with quantities. That is true, but it is also true of strategy, and yet battles are not mathematical problems to be entrusted to an electrical computer. The crucial things in economics are about as mathematically intractable as a love letter or a Christmas celebration. They reside in moral and spiritual forces, psychological reactions, opinions which are beyond the reach of curves and equations. What matters ultimately in economics is incalculable and unpredictable.[64]

Röpke's contribution to the reconstruction of the West German economy earned him the Bundesrepublik's highest decoration, the Grand Cross of Merit.

The Adenauer government was committed to the market economy, which meant eliminating the monopolistic practices of the past. The Western allies, particularly the United States, had insisted on the destruction of the entire cartel system that had been so closely associated with the Nazi war machine. Erhard, a convinced free trader, agreed. Over the opposition of the Federation of German Industries, he convinced parliament to pass a bill (enacted in 1957) outlawing restrictions on competition (*Gesetz gegen Wettbewerbsbeschränkungen*). "If you reject state controls in industry," he told the Bundestag, "you cannot at the same time accept the collective control of industry by cartels or even regard it as useful and necessary. If you see political, social, and economic dangers in collectivism, you cannot at the same time defend cartels, which are a special form of collectivism."[65] The new law, which was mandated by membership in the supranational European Coal and Steel Community, replaced the anticartel legislation of the Allies. Nevertheless, a relatively small group of managers and directors still controlled German industry. The Christian Democrats were reluctant to enforce the law because a substantial amount of their political and financial support came from these same industrialists and bankers. Besides, cartels could exist legally if they were held to be beneficial to the overall economy. By 1964, some 136 cartels had been accorded this privilege, with many others operating clandestinely. The deconcentration policy was thus slowly undermined. The Krupp Steel Works survived virtually intact, as did most of the other great coal and steel combines. The three great commercial banks—the Deutsche Bank, the Dresdner Bank, and the Commerzbank—eluded a proposed breakup into thirty-odd successor institutions and, in 1957, were reintegrated under their former names. Erhard continued to warn that cartels were an extravagance Germany could not afford: "Where all groups want to have special protection and more security, people will enjoy less and less freedom and will lose more and more of genuine security. There can be no doubt that the advantages some people are out to acquire can only be acquired at the expense of others."[66]

Germany was prosperous, however, and with one-fourth of total state expenditures going to social services, few felt threatened. The German concept of proper economic management assigned the government a primary role in establishing a secure economic base for society. Government was expected to establish long-term conditions for growth by creating the proper infrastructure and stimulating areas lacking in development; thus, for example, government should boost the output of energy and promote the development of microtechnology. Government was also expected to work for a proper social partnership between capital and labor and encourage responsible collective bargaining. Above all, government was responsible for monetary stabilization. It relied on the banking industry to help identify weakness and assist with rescue operations.[67] The Germans did not forget the crippling experiences of the Weimar Republic with its two nightmarish bouts of inflation that led to the collapse of German democracy. The German term for economic order (*Wirtschaftsordunug*) suggested a harmony between economics and law in which the achievement of a secure political system is a logical counterpart of a properly run economy.

"Hitler? Never Heard of Him!" Even achieving the highest standard of living in their history did not automatically make the Germans enthusiastic about democratic values. They did become politically less extreme, however. Above all, they preferred to get on with the business of life and not be reminded of their past transgressions. By 1953, the apparent end to the prosecution of war criminals was generally greeted with approval. Adenauer rationalized that if those who had supported Hitler were too roughly handled, a backlash would set in and would actually contribute to the growth of neo-Nazism. Already the "refugee party" was trying to broaden its political base by appealing to all manner of dispossessed. As the pressure declined, former Nazis found little difficulty returning to important positions in industry and government—some even turned up in Adenauer's own cabinet.[68] One of the chancellor's most controversial appointments was that of Dr. Hans Globke as his chief administrative assistant in the chancellery. Globke had officially participated in drafting the racial laws against the Jews and Gypsies. Adenauer took the attacks on Globke personally, however, and continued to stand by him.

The sons and daughters of those who had supported Hitler seemed the most sensitive about war guilt. Yet many Germans seemed embarrassingly ignorant about how much suffering their country had caused others. Instead, they tended to concentrate on the barbarities of others: the bombing of Dresden, the massacre in the Katyn Forest, the rape of Freudenstadt. War was war. Heinrich Grüber, dean of the Evangelical church in Berlin and himself a victim of the Nazis, insisted that the extermination of the Jews, although immoral, was for some reason "part of

God's plan." Grüber continued: "God demands our death daily. He is the Lord, He is the Master, all is in His keeping and ordering."[69] Rabbi Richard Rubenstein joined the theological debate, charging that Grüber had failed to recognize the incongruity of regarding Hitler as an instrument of God's will. "Stated with theological finesse," Rubenstein remarked bitterly, "it comes to pretty much the same thing as the vulgar thought that the Christ-killers got what was coming to them."[70]

The degree to which such attitudes really reflected the sentiments of the mass of the German people or affected the functioning of their institutions was a matter of debate. Dr. Paule Sethe claimed that the Bonn judicial system was "still dominated by the spirit of the twenties which had caused the downfall of the Weimar Republic and had paved the way for Hitler." He added that justice would be better served "if the judges had some of the stench of the Auschwitz crematoria in their nostrils."[71] On the other hand, Sybille Bedford, an English author, sensed a new German compassion and respect for justice. "It would be hard for a Bismarck today to re-introduce the death penalty," she wrote. "There is the respect of man for man, the tending of liberty and the decencies and the due process of law, and with it goes a love, an almost avid love, of normality and all its trimmings."[72] Chronology frequently dictated which attitude would prevail. When Adenauer retired in 1963, most people in West Germany had either been born after Hitler had come to power or were too young to have been directly involved in Nazi atrocities. Most of the leaders of the Third Reich had been born at least ten years before the beginning of World War I and would have been 60 or more years old if they had lived until 1963. Had he lived, Hitler would have been 74, Göring 70, and Goebbels 66. The aging, lower-level Nazis increasingly made fit subjects for gerontologists. The Federal Republic was getting what the Weimar Republic did not have: peace, prosperity, and time with which to heal social wounds and adapt to democracy.

Nevertheless, the Germans were still reluctant to confront their Nazi past. Most of the current crop of teachers had been nurtured by a system that considered it unprofessional to teach democratic values. Since it was embarrassing for those who had served National Socialism to deal with events after 1933, most history lessons ended with World War I. Had Adenauer felt the matter deserved high priority, little would have stopped him from instituting a reform of German education. Instead, the federal government argued it could not be held responsible for the sorry conditions since education had been entrusted to the Länder. Educational reform was associated with the American efforts at reeducation and was discredited. All the direct efforts to restructure the universities, build comprehensive schools, and alter the authoritarian nature of German pedagogy met with strong resistance. The Western allies discovered that the time was too short and their methods too imperfect to teach democracy to a class that had no desire to learn.[73]

The educational system continued to foster social inequality. Primary and vocational schools were free, but most Länder charged tuition for secondary education. An official publication noted, with an obvious sense of embarrassment, that "exemption from the payment of school fees of any kind, and whenever possible from payment for instructional material, is something that has already been achieved in a varying degree in some of the Länder."[74] Only about 20 percent of the children from elementary schools continued their education in the secondary schools, and most of these came from the middle and upper-middle classes. In the universities, students from working-class families were practically nonexistent.[75] The universities remained institutions of specialization, run by faculty senates, which intentionally kept the number of professors small. In 1970, Heidelberg, a typical case, had only 190 full professors for 11,500 students. The lack of adequate facilities was equally scandalous: "Anatomy exercises become a macabre farce when 20 to 40 scalpel armed medical students crowd around one cadaver."[76] The Germans spent only 2.79 percent of their gross national product on their school system, about the same amount they expended for cigarettes and cigars.

The new generations rejoiced in their growing affluence. "It is our misfortune," wrote a German journalist, "that those outside Germany often form a picture of it today from this type of uninhibited, narrow-minded *nouveaux riches* who cannot see beyond the fenders of their Mercedes 400."[77] The citizens of this *Wirtschafts-wunderland* sometimes showed an incredible lack of sensitivity. In the early 1960s, a manufacturer of women's fashions blithely called a new line of nylon hosiery the "Ouradour" line, apparently forgetting that Ouradour was the name of a French village in Haute Vienne where, on 10 June 1944, soldiers from the SS "das Reich" division massacred the entire population of 650 men, women, and children. When German tourists traveled to other European countries, they were often just as gauche. "I like your country," the visitor might say. "I was here during the war."

THE GERMAN DEMOCRATIC REPUBLIC

The Tightening of Soviet Control

A Posture of Independence. Stalin hailed the creation of the *Deutsche Demokratische Republik* as "a turning point in the history of Europe." A "peace-loving democratic Germany side by side with the existence of the peace-loving Soviet Union excludes the possibility of new wars in Europe, puts an end to bloodshed in Europe and makes impossible the enslaving of the European countries by the world imperialists."[78] In 1949, the Communist-controlled part of Germany officially became an independent state, but the Soviet Control Commission, backed by the Red Army, kept tight political control on the new government. Formal sovereignty was not accorded until after Stalin's death (1953), and even then the East Germans did not become masters in their own house.

At first, Soviet control was disguised under a posture of respect for the independent development of socialism. In December 1945, Anton Ackermann, one of the Moscow-trained leaders of the German Communist party, published an article entitled, "Is there a separate German road to Socialism?" Ackermann stated: "It was no less an authority than Lenin who emphasized that it would be a great mistake to exaggerate the general applicability of the Russian experience, or to extend it beyond more than a few features of our (i.e., the Russian) Revolution. In this sense we must unquestionably give our assent to the concept of a separate German road to Socialism." Ackermann noted some of the differences between his present-day Germany and Russia three decades earlier: Germany was more developed industrially, had a greater number of highly trained professionals, and a working class that represented a majority of the total population—a fact of great importance because "it will mitigate the domestic political struggle, reduce the burden of sacrifices, and hasten the evolution of Socialist democracy."[79]

The publication of Ackermann's theses encouraged many German Communists (and Social Democrats) to believe that Soviet political control was temporary and that Red Army occupation would soon end, leaving the natives free "from foreign tutelage to find their own road to socialism, in accordance with their own traditions and conditions."[80] But this theory was only a means of making the

German Communist party more acceptable to the Social Democrats whose support was deemed useful in stimulating a new national consciousness of unity. The Socialist Unity party accepted a separate road to socialism as part of its official program in order to mask Stalinization and blame the "Western imperialists" for promoting the division of Germany.

Before the establishment of the German Democratic Republic (GDR), the Soviets had already established a whole series of organizations befitting a people's republic. These included a single trade union for industrial workers, the Free German Trade Union Federation; a union for farmers, the Peasants Mutual Aid Union; an organization for women, the Democratic Women's Federation; an official youth group, the Free German Youth Movement; and a similar organization for intellectuals, the German Cultural Federation. These groups all were represented in the national legislature, which, like its Soviet counterpart, was a rubber stamp. After the founding of the GDR, the Soviet Military Administration gave way to a Soviet High Commissioner who like his predecessor still had the final authority.

The *Volkskammer*, the legislature, was purportedly the highest authority of the state; its members were elected by secret ballot according to proportional representation. However, like all Soviet-style governments, only one party exercised real authority. In East Germany, this meant the Socialist Unity party. Walter Ulbricht was its secretary-general; Wilhelm Pieck and Otto Grotewohl were its co-chairmen. Pieck was also state president and Grotewohl was prime minister. The GDR's most important political agency was the Ministry of State Security (the Stasi). This was responsible to the Politburo of the Socialist Unity party, not to the government. The Stasi had wide arbitrary powers to protect the state against its enemies both at home and abroad. The German Economic Commission (*Deutsche Wirtschafts Kommission*) directed the economy and ensured state control over industry and agriculture, banking and finance, foreign and domestic trade, transportation, labor, and energy. The commission, which issued directives to all governmental and administrative departments, planned the transformation of the East German economy into a Soviet-style system, integrated within the Eastern bloc. In 1949, a Two-Year Plan was inaugurated to boost heavy industry and increase productivity to 81 percent of the levels achieved in 1936. Building industrial socialism also meant the collectivization of agriculture and the regulation of the cultural life of the nation. As in the Soviet Union, socialist realism was the only standard of creativity. Ulbricht talked of the evolution of the new man and woman. The party expected writers, composers, and artists to extoll the heroes of socialist labor who raised productivity.

Resentment Turns to Protest. Until 1953, the Soviets continued to dismantle German factories, while the East Germans were obliged to pay about one-fourth of their total production to the Soviet Union as reparations. Special corporations were established to produce almost entirely for the Soviet account. Sovietization caused considerable malaise throughout the party cadres and provoked resentment among the general population. By 1951, between 11,000 and 17,000 people a month were leaving the GDR to live in West Germany. The following year, over 23,000 people left during September alone; in the first half of 1953, the monthly average climbed above 37,000. The East Germans, it was said, were voting with their feet. Such an enormous loss of labor power seriously threatened the viability of the German Communist regime, but Socialist Unity party leaders could offer no effective countermeasures. Their regime was not yet sufficiently strong to risk closing the frontier, and Ulbricht refused to admit that his hard line was wrong and inaugurate a program of reform. Still some concessions had to be made.

In June 1953, two months after Stalin's death, the regime called off the persecution of the Catholic and Evangelical churches. Some businesses and farms were restored to their former owners. At the same time, the regime promised to increase social insurance benefits and review the sentences of political offenders. Workers were told that, in the meantime, they were expected to produce more goods with no increase in wages. The reaction was immediate. On 16 June 1953, the workers in Berlin went out on strike. The authorities, eager to show that the East German proletariat could express itself freely, let the demonstration take place. The situation soon got out of hand. On 17 June, the strikers, with their ranks swelled by members of the "People's Police," attacked public buildings, set some on fire, and tore the Red Flag from the Brandenburg Gate. The local authorities, unable to handle the disturbance, called on the Soviet Union for help. But when Red Army tanks moved into East Berlin, the rioters began to attack the tanks with bricks and anything else they could find.

On the afternoon of 17 June, the Soviet commander in Berlin proclaimed a state of emergency and proceeded to crush the revolt by shooting and hanging the demonstrators. More than five hundred were killed. By nightfall order returned to the streets of Berlin, but the revolt had already spread to other cities—Magdeburg, Halle, Jena, Brandenburg, in all about three hundred towns and villages. The authorities blamed the rising on capitalist agents provocateurs.

The riots clearly demonstrated the weakness of the Communist regime, but lack of effective leadership prevented the masses from taking advantage of the weakness. Consequently, the Communist bosses, with full support of the Soviet authorities, were easily able to regain control. They emerged from the crisis more entrenched in power than before. Ironically, Stalinization in the GDR did not really reach its height until after Stalin's death. The ruthless suppression of any oppositionist tendencies was sweetened with a promise to increase the general standard of living and improve working conditions, but no real progress appeared for the next several years.

Communist party boss Ulbricht, who after 1954 had become the most important political leader in the GDR, proved to be the most durable of the Eastern satellite rulers. A prototypical ruthless, unimaginative bureaucrat, he systematically eliminated all rivals within the party. In 1960, when President Wilhelm Pieck died, Ulbricht, in a move reminiscent of Hitler's strategy in 1934, abolished the presidency and had himself appointed chairman of a newly created Council of State. The prime minister, Otto Grotewohl, who had already been neutralized with the creation of the SED in 1946, now became little more than an office boy. Resentment smoldered just under the surface awaiting another opportunity to plunge East Germany into chaos.

A Highly Controlled Economy

The Tempo of Socialism. East Germany had difficulty adjusting to the dismantling of its industry and the deportation of many of its most skilled workers. Under Operation Ossavakim, the Soviets deported the human and material resources of entire firms, including Karl Zeiss Optics at Jena, the Junkers Aircraft works at Dessau, and the Leuna Synthetic Petrol and Plastics company near Merseburg. The economy also was victimized by poor planning and the difficulty of adjusting to the economies of its Communist-bloc trading partners, although the Soviets

East German youths attack a pair of T-34/85s. Tanks like these participated in the Battle of Berlin in 1945; the T-34 was probably the best such weapon of World War II. It mounts an 85 mm gun, which is more than a match for these rock-throwers.

bore part of the costs of transition. In 1958, Ulbricht attempted to speed up socialism by pushing the collectivization of agriculture. Within five years, the total amount of arable land under direct state control was increased from 37 percent to 86 percent, or from 2,386,020 hectares to 5,456,143 hectares.[81] The same process was carried out in industry and business; by 1963, 90 percent was under government control.

Under Ulbricht's command, East Germany led the Soviet satellites in industrial capacity. During the 1950s, the production of brown coal rose from 137,050,000 to 214,783,000 metric tons; pig iron rose from 337,000 to 1,898,000 metric tons; crude steel from 1,257,000 to 3,615,000 metric tons; and the output of electrical energy from 19.47 to 37.25 million kilowatt hours. Most of the gains were registered in the last half of the decade.[82] The results were not so encouraging in agriculture, however. Wheat and oats production remained almost unchanged, sugar beets and corn increased only slightly, and production of rye and potatoes actually declined.[83] In 1961, food shortages prompted a reintroduction of rationing in certain commodities. Ulbricht tried to solve all problems with more controls; but no matter how dictatorial these became, it was impossible to achieve economic stability as long as great numbers of East Germans, often the most productive and best trained, continued to flee westward. Flight was simple: first, get to East Berlin, next take the subway or the elevated train from the Soviet sector into the Allied sector, and then fly from Berlin to the West. Finally, Ulbricht, secure of his hold over East Germany, obtained permission from the Soviets to close the border.

The Berlin Wall. Early Sunday morning, 13 August 1961, East German police and soldiers sealed off sixty-eight of the eighty crossing points into West Berlin.[84] There was no retaliation. The Western powers made only a written protest. In time, a wall of concrete replaced the hastily sprawled coils of barbed wire, lookout towers were erected, and guards were given orders to shoot anyone who tried to flee. The East German regime viewed such extreme measures as an absolute necessity, and from their perspective, the wall was a great success. The exodus of so

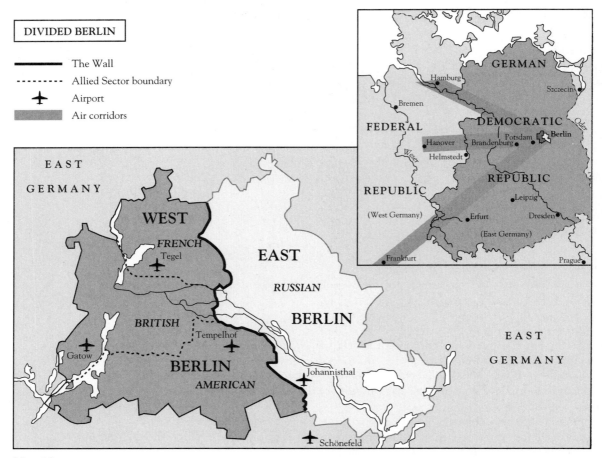

DIVIDED BERLIN

——————— The Wall
- - - - - - - Allied Sector boundary
✈ Airport
Air corridors

Map 16

much valuable laborpower virtually stopped, although every once in a while there would be news of a daring escape. In the West, the wall became a symbol of shame, but the East German regime appeared to become more viable. But the resignation of the East Germans was deceptive and proved temporary. The Communist regime had only bought time.

POSTSCRIPT   The problem of Germany remained the key to the security of Europe. The Soviets believed a weak but unified Germany was more in their interests than a divided Germany, but they were not prepared to ease their own rigorous standards of Stalinization. The Americans tried to calm Stalin's fears of a resurgent Germany with a security pact that guaranteed German disarmament for the next forty years. When this offer failed to reduce the tensions, the Americans assumed that Stalin had far-reaching and sinister intentions to extend his power westward. State Department adviser Robert Murphy thought the Soviets were seeking "not only to disarm Germany, but to render that country economically impotent."[85] His superior, Secretary of State James Byrnes, feared "that unless forced by world opinion to do so, the Soviet Union would not agree to a treaty of peace with Germany for years to come."[86] World opinion certainly seemed a curious weapon to consider using against a state that had the largest military force in Europe, but in time it did pay dividends. Nevertheless, any hopes that it would work in 1948 were quickly dispelled by the Berlin Blockade.

Both sides accused the other of causing the division of Germany, but neither appeared to have been disappointed when the division occurred. Ever since the end of World War I, many people had dreamed of dismantling the German colossus. Once it happened, only the West Germans seemed to take reunification seriously. The preamble of their constitution called upon the entire German people "to achieve in free self-determination the unity and freedom of Germany." In 1956, the Constitutional Court declared that this provision had "mainly political, but also legal significance, binding all national political organizations to strive with every means at their disposal for its fulfillment."[87] After his electoral victory in September 1953, Adenauer seemed to be setting a new foreign policy goal when he called for the liberation of "our 18 million brothers" who lived in East Germany,[88] but it is doubtful he really believed reunification was possible in the lifetime of most Germans. The accomplishment of such an objective seemed impossible without war; and furthermore the creation of the Bundesrepublik achieved Adenauer's goal of creating a Rhineland-dominated West German state purged of Prussian leadership.

The Bundesrepublik had to contend with the hegemony of the United States; the Democratic Republic had to accept the domination of the Soviets. Although West Germany, in particular, gradually became more independent, there was no question who had called the shots. World War II allowed the destiny of Germans to be decided by outsiders. Neither the United States nor the Soviet Union had wanted this conflict, which had extended their power, but neither showed any desire to give way. Their rivalries drowned out the wishes of the Germans themselves. But as friction between East and West diminished, and relations between East and West Germany improved, German unification, a dream that had never disappeared, moved closer to fulfillment.

ENDNOTES

1. Bernard Montgomery, *The Memoirs of Field-Marshal Montgomery* (New York: World Publishing Co., 1958), 339.
2. Lucius Clay, *Decision in Germany* (New York: Doubleday, 1950), 26.
3. In November 1945.
4. Georgi Zhukov, *The Memoirs of Marshal Zhukov* (New York: Delacorte Press, 1971), 662.
5. Furthermore, there were almost 5 million displaced persons; for the most part, these were people who had been forcibly brought to Germany to work for the Nazis.

6. *Documents on Germany under Occupation, 1945–1954* (London: Oxford University Press, 1955), 15.
7. Ibid., 22.
8. Montgomery, *Memoirs*, 356.
9. Hildegard Knef, *The Gift Horse* (New York: McGraw-Hill, 1970), 75.
10. Zhukov, *Memoirs*, 636.
11. Montgomery, *Memoirs*, 367.
12. Douglas Botting, *From the Ruins of the Reich: Germany, 1945–1949* (New York: New American Library, 1985), 252.
13. Georges Bidault, *Resistance* (London: Weidenfeld and Nelson, 1967), 83.
14. *International Herald Tribune*, 22 April 1968.
15. Ibid., 53.
16. Seated between Göring and Fritzsche were Rudolf Hess, former deputy führer who had flown to England in 1941; Joachim von Ribbentrop, the foreign minister; General Wilhelm Keitel, the army chief of staff; Alfred Rosenberg, the Nazi party ideologist; Hans Frank, the governor-general of Poland; Wilhelm Frick, the minister of interior; Julius Streicher, editor of *Der Stürmer* and gauleiter of Franconia; Walther Funk, economics minister; and Hjalmar Schacht, Funk's predecessor who had just been released from a Nazi jail and had no idea why he was there. In the second row, directly behind Göring, sat Admirals Karl Dönitz and Erich Raeder; then came Baldur von Schirach, Vienna gauleiter and one-time Hitler Youth leader; Fritz Sauckel, plenipotentiary for (Forced) Labor Allocation; Alfred Jodl, chief of operations for the Wehrmacht; Franz von Papen, Hitler's first vice-chancellor and the last Nazi ambassador to Turkey; Arthur Seyss-Inquart, reichscommissar for the occupied Netherlands and former chancellor of Austria; Albert Speer, minister of armaments and munitions; and Konstantin von Neurath, protector of Bohemia-Moravia and former foreign minister.
17. Bormann was tried and sentenced to death in absentia. In fact, he was already dead. Several hours after the Führer had committed suicide, Bormann had been killed while trying to leave Berlin. Supposedly, however, he had made it to South America on a Vatican passport. In December 1972, construction workers found some skeletal remains in Berlin's Tiergarten district. These were identified as Bormann's. On 11 April 1973, he was declared officially dead. *New York Times*, 12 April 1973, 2:4.
18. Robert Jackson, *The Nuremberg Case* (New York: Knopf, 1947), 35.
19. Gustav Mahler Gilbert, *Nuremberg Diary* (New York: New American Library, 1947), 46–50.
20. Ibid., 239.
21. Eugene Davidson, *The Trial of the Germans* (New York: Macmillan, 1966), 83.
22. Jackson, *Nuremberg Case*, 122.
23. Botting, *From the Ruins of the Reich*, 258–89.
24. *Documents on Germany*, 38.
25. Wolfgang Leonhard, *Child of the Revolution* (Chicago: Henry Regnery, 1958), 413.
26. Ibid., 414.
27. Martin McCauley, *The German Democratic Republic since 1945* (New York: St. Martin's Press, 1983), 10–17.
28. *Documents on Germany*, 124.
29. The SED received 4,658,483 to a combined total of 5,123,169 for its opponents. McCauley, *German Democratic Republic*, 31.
30. Leonhard, *Child of the Revolution*, 451.
31. *United States, Department of State, Potsdam Conference*, vol. 2 (Washington, D.C.: U.S. Government Printing Office), 1482.
32. Montgomery, *Memoirs*, 358.
33. *Survey of International Affairs: Four-Power Control in Germany and Austria, 1945–1946* (London: Oxford University Press), 188.

34. The Americans insisted especially on the establishment of an independent judiciary with powers of judicial review.

35. Clay, *Decision in Germany*, 98.

36. *Documents on Germany*, 17.

37. See James F. Tent, *Mission on the Rhine* (Chicago: University of Chicago Press, 1982).

38. James F. Byrnes, *Speaking Frankly* (New York: Harper, 1947), 176.

39. The action was aimed as much at the French as at the Soviets. De Gaulle had repeatedly vetoed plans for economic centralization. He objected to the creation of a unified transport administration, continued to insist on the annexation of the Saar, and advocated putting the Rhineland under French administration. He also demanded the internationalization of the Ruhr. Robert Murphy, the chief American political adviser, found it ironic "that Stalin, who always deplored French participation in the occupation of Germany, became the chief beneficiary of early French policy there." Robert Murphy, *Diplomat among Warriors* (Garden City, N.Y.: Doubleday, 1964), 287.

40. *Foreign Relations of the United States*, 1946, II, 897.

41. *Documents on Germany*, 156.

42. Ibid., 157.

43. Anthony Mann, *Comeback: Germany, 1945–1952* (London: MacMillan, 1980), 128–45.

44. James F. Tent, *The Free University of Berlin: A Political History* (Bloomington: Indiana University Press, 1988), 166–67.

45. Mann, *Comeback*, 131.

46. Harry S. Truman, *Memoirs*, vol. 2 (Garden City, N.Y.: Doubleday, 1956), 131.

47. *Documents on Germany*, 316.

48. *Grundgesetz*, Article 38.

49. Clay, *Decision in Germany*, 405–6.

50. The Italian constitution of 1948 contained a similar provision. See Chapter 19.

51. The court exercised this power in 1952 when it outlawed the neo-Nazi Socialist Reich party, and again, four years later, when it declared the Communist party disbanded and confiscated its assets. The court argued then that the minimum duty of any political party in a free society was to accept the paramount values of the constitution as binding and refrain from bringing that system into contempt. "Any party which consciously, continually, and systematically, undertakes a campaign of slander and mockery of these values and the order embodying them, is envisaging their impairment and even their destruction. It is unthinkable that such a party could constitutionally be called upon to cooperate in the formation of the will of the state in a free democracy." John J. Wuest and Manfred C. Vernon, eds., *Source Book in Major European Governments* (New York: World Publishing Co., 1966), 384.

52. They also disapproved of the inclusion of Berlin as one of the federal states because that was inconsistent with the legal position that Berlin was under quadripartite control by international agreement. Clay, *Decision in Germany*, 421–22.

53. Ibid., 431.

54. *Grundgesetz*, Article 21, para. 1.

55. Wuest and Vernon, *Source Book in Major European Governments*, 354.

56. Ibid., 356–57.

57. Rudolf Leonhardt, *This Germany: The Story since the Third Reich* (Baltimore: Penguin, 1968), 197.

58. Quoted in Richard Hiscocks, *The Adenauer Era* (New York: Lippincott, 1966), 91–92.

59. The number of automobiles per 1,000 people was 18.4 in 1938; 10.9 in 1950; 33.3 in 1955; 48.7 in 1957; 67.4 in 1959; 95.3 in 1961; and 112 in 1962. See the yearbooks of the *Statistisches Bundesamt* (Wiesbaden: Federal Statistical Office).

60. In 1969, Germany produced 145,000 passenger cars, second only to the United States. It also had one of the world's largest annual outputs of steel. In 1936, greater unified Germany produced 1,235,500 metric tons of crude steel: in 1956, West Germany (with only 53 percent of the former territory and 75 percent of the population) turned out 1,932,400 metric tons; in 1960, it produced 2,841,700 metric tons, an amount exceeded by only the United States and the Soviet Union. In 1960, West Germany's major customers were (in order) the Netherlands, France, the United States, Switzerland, Belgium-Luxembourg, Italy, Sweden, Austria, Great Britain, and Denmark. Trade with Eastern Europe, traditionally so important, had almost completely disappeared.

61. Ludwig Erhard, *The Economics of Success* (London: Thames and Hudson, 1963), 191.

62. Ibid., 184.

63. Wilhelm Röpke, *A Humane Economy* (London: Wolff, 1960), 247.

64. Ibid., 248.

65. Erhard, *Economics of Success*, 171.

66. Ibid., 177.

67. William E. Paterson and Gordon Smith, eds., *The West German Model: Perspectives on a Stable State* (London: Frank Cass, 1981), 41–43.

68. The East German regime was particularly adept at publishing lists and pictures of Nazi party members who were doing quite well in the Bundesrepublik. See, for example, *Grey Book: Expansionist Policy and Neo-Nazism in West Germany* (Dresden: 1967).

69. Richard L. Rubenstein, *After Auschwitz* (Indianapolis: Bobbs-Merrill, 1966), 54.

70. Ibid., 56.

71. T. H. Teters, *The New Germany and the Old Nazis* (New York: Random House, 1961), 167.

72. Sybille Bedford, *The Faces of Justice* (London: Collins, 1961), 152.

73. Tent, *Mission on the Rhine*, 312–18.

74. Helmut Arntz, *Facts about Germany* (Wiesbaden: Press and Information Office, 1966), 321.

75. By contrast, in East Germany at least two-thirds of the university student population came from the working class or peasantry.

76. *International Herald Tribune*, 2 April 1970.

77. Leonhardt, *This Germany*, 97.

78. *Documents of International Affairs, 1949–50*, 538.

79. Leonhard, *Child of the Revolution*, 440–41.

80. Ibid., 441.

81. *Handbuch der Deutsche Demokratischen Republik* (East Berlin: Staatsverlag, N.D.), 403. In 1952, only 3.3 percent of the East German land had been collectivized.

82. B. R. Mitchell, *European Historical Statistics* (New York: Columbia University Press, 1975), 366, 395, 402, 281.

83. Ibid., 270.

84. The Berlin crises are discussed in Chapter 21.

85. Murphy, *Diplomat among Warriors*, 302.

86. Byrnes, *Speaking Frankly*, 181.

87. Wuest and Vernon, *Source Book in Major European Governments*, 382.

88. Rudolf Augstein, *Konrad Adenauer* (London: Secker and Warburg, 1964), 28.

CHAPTER 19

PROSPERITY AND REFORM
IN WESTERN EUROPE

PREFACE   Clement Attlee, the leader of Britain's Labour party, wanted to build a truly equitable, socially just society on the ruins of the selfish capitalistic society of the past. This could only be done if the prevailing economic system were brought under greater public control. Nationalization was not an end in itself, however. "Controls were desirable not for their own sake, but because they were necessary to gain freedom from the economic power of the owners of capital." Attlee had no desire to take revenge on the rich; he wanted wealth distributed more equitably "because a society with gross inequalities of wealth and opportunity is fundamentally unhealthy."[1]

Attlee's theme could be heard in all the countries of Europe. People expected that recovery from the war would include social change as well as political reconstruction. They thought the years of struggle and destruction would have been in vain if they did not result in a better world. Now was the time to fulfill the lofty goals of the Atlantic Charter—freedom from want and freedom from fear. It was also the time to discard the old ways.

Nowhere was this longing for a better tomorrow more pronounced than in Great Britain. Discontent with the prewar record of the Tories—their bankrupt policy of appeasement, their failure to cure unemployment, their obsession with class and tradition—was widespread. Even the Conservatives recognized the popular mood and, like the Labour party, promised the people a public welfare system. The aspirations for a better life were reflected in the Beveridge Report, which inspired so much optimism that Prime Minister Churchill recognized that "bringing the magic of averages nearer to the rescue of the millions, constitutes an essential point of any post-war scheme of national betterment."[2] A government policy statement, issued in 1944, accepted full employment, based on increased productivity, as a fundamental responsibility of government.

The French National Council of the Resistance set essentially the same goals. In March 1944, it advocated the nationalization of key industries, a comprehensive system of sickness and accident insurance, a guaranteed standard of living, a program of family allowances, price supports for agricultural commodities, and recognition of the right of workers to participate in factory management. The French had grown up under governments that had not made changing society a high priority. The Resistance, though, had spawned a new generation of leaders who were dissatisfied with the record of the past. They believed that if society were to change, the state had to play a greater role in directing the economy and helping to make the labor force more productive.[3] Social security was a right, not a gift. Great economic progress could be achieved if traditional private entrepreneurship were bolstered by planning for the modernization and expansion of the nation's industrial structure.

Italian aspirations for a new society were expressed in their new constitution, which recognized the obligation of the state "to remove the obstacles of an economic order which . . . prevent the full development of the human personality." It recognized the right of the worker "to a compensation proportionate to the quantity and quality of his [sic] labor and in any case sufficient to assure him and his family a free and dignified existence."[4] It endorsed the right to work and to be socially secure, guaranteed the equality of women, and endorsed the right of workers to share in the management of business. At the same time the Italians endeavored to form a new social order, they also had to create a democratic system. Under Mussolini, respect for individual rights had been of no concern. Furthermore, the economy's problem was not too little central direction, but too much. Fascist controls had petrified the economy, wasted precious resources, and replaced cooperation with subservience to authority. These were poor foundations upon which to build a new society.

SOCIALIST BRITAIN

Labour Takes Charge

The Campaign. Perhaps Churchill's irritation came from physical exhaustion—throughout the war he rarely slept more than four hours a night—or from the increasing dislike he had for a "socialist" Eastern Europe, but in his first radio broadcast of the 1945 electoral campaign, he said cuttingly:

> I declare to you, from the bottom of my heart, that no Socialist system can be established without a political police . . . no Socialist Government conducting the entire life and industry of the country could afford to allow free, sharp, or violently-worded expressions of public discontent. They would have

Labour election posters promise a better and healthier tomorrow with full employment. Although Winston Churchill was the most popular man in Great Britain in 1945, it was not enough to ensure his party's victory. Many British voters had not forgotten the failings of the Tories during the 1930s.

to fall back on some form of Gestapo. . . . And this would nip opinion in the bud, it would stop criticism as it reared its head, and it would gather all the power to the supreme party and the party leaders, rising like stately pinnacles above their vast bureaucracies of civil servants, no longer servants and no longer civil.[5]

Churchill's "Gestapo" speech caused many to doubt that the man who had led his country to victory in war should preside over its fortunes in time of peace. Moreover, the Labour party appeared as the staunchest champion of the proposed Beveridge reforms, and this dedication to social welfare swept it triumphantly into office in the 5 July 1945 election. Labour increased its seats in the House of Commons by 154 to 393 seats, while the Conservatives dropped from 373 to 213. The already weakened Liberals were practically wiped out, winning only a scant 11 seats. The total vote was more evenly distributed,[6] but the Labour triumph was nevertheless genuine, a true national victory, won at the expense of all other parties and in all districts of the country. Now, for the first time in its history, the party had the power to implement its welfare policy and carry out its program of nationalization.

On 26 July 1945, shortly after the results of the election were certain, Winston Churchill drove to Buckingham Palace to offer his resignation to the king. Half an hour later, Clement R. Attlee arrived and was confirmed as the new prime minister. The leaders of the Labour party had little doubt that Attlee's competent, moderate style of leadership was best suited to maintain the unity of the party while carrying out the sweeping social and economic program that would further reform British capitalism by expanding the welfare and public sectors. Attlee's cabinet reflected his conservative nature; it was composed largely of bourgeois middle-aged professionals. Attlee chose the trade unionist leader Ernest Bevin to be his foreign secretary. The appointment of a true son of the working class to represent Britain abroad was wildly popular with the rank and file. Furthermore, Bevin, despite his lack of experience in foreign relations, turned out to be one of the best foreign secretaries of his age.

Labour took charge at one of the worst times in modern British history. The war had cost the lives of 388,000 persons, and German air raids had destroyed 6.5 percent of British real estate. The public debt had risen from $3 billion in 1938 to $13.5 billion by war's end. During the same period, exports had fallen by $312 million each year. Shipping revenues were down 75 percent; and income from overseas investments had slid by one-half. With the end of Lend-Lease, the British went scrambling to Washington for a $6 billion loan with which to begin reconstruction. They got $3.75 billion, but this was quickly spent,[7] and Britain seemed to face a bleak future.

The Program of Nationalization. The Labour government did not believe that the extension of social security alone was sufficient; it felt that the state also had to establish control over the country's most important resources and services. However, the program of nationalization was never total and was limited to essential public services and basic industries. The issue of nationalization had risen during the war, but Churchill had discouraged spending much time on postwar planning. He was not particularly keen on nationalization to begin with, and in any case, he believed that winning the war should be the first priority. In choosing industries for public control, the Labour party seemed to have been motivated more by the desire to improve efficiency and increase production than by ideology. Experience showed that many owners either did not want to or could not afford to modernize to make their companies more competitive. A good example was the coal industry, which had been plagued by poor organization and even worse labor relations. The average output per miner was one of the lowest in Europe, and the owners had made little effort to improve productivity by reinvesting their profits. Furthermore, the British people felt a moral duty toward those who earned their livelihood by such backbreaking, dangerous work. This sense of duty was reinforced by the fact that this resource upon which Britain's industrial revolution was based had not provided the miners a reward commensurate with their contribution. The Conservatives shared the sense of obligation toward the miners, but many would have preferred a policy of government subsidy rather than ownership.

Labour presented the Coal Industry Nationalization Bill to Parliament in December 1945. The Tories and Labour differed more over the details than on the principle of state ownership. The bill became law the following July. The act—a "bill" becomes an "act" when it passes Parliament—combined more than eight hundred private companies into the National Coal Board (NCB), which was under the Ministry of Fuel and Power. The NCB inherited an industry plagued by mismanagement, high unemployment, an aging work force, poor labor relations, and insufficient mechanization. Even with proper capitalization, the rundown mines of Yorkshire and Wales could not be made efficient, and many were closed down, while production at the modern collieries of Derbyshire and Nottinghamshire was increased to compensate for the weakness of the others.

The Ministry of Fuel and Power was also responsible for the nation's electricity under the Electricity Act, which passed in August 1947 with little controversy. The municipalities already owned most of the various power stations (362 systems out of 563), and the old system was hopelessly disordered: voltages differed from place to place, and rates fluctuated inequitably. London alone had seventy-five different standards. Former owners were compensated by averaging representative share quotations on the stock exchange over a previous two-year period. The Labour government completed its program to control the basic sources of industrial power by nationalizing the gas industry; but as in the case of the coal and electrical industries, the government's motivation was less socialist than the industry's need for reorganization and modernization.

Government control and supervision were already so strong in central banking that nationalization hardly constituted a radical departure. The Bank of England was private in name only. However, the Labour party leaders never felt safe until the institution was completely state owned. They feared, for example, that the bank's directors might pursue a deflationary policy that could obstruct an official commitment to full employment. Even Churchill did not see what the fuss was about, since the Exchequer already decided all major policy.

The public transportation industry was also heavily regulated: civil aviation had been a public monopoly for some time, and the railroads were practically so. The most controversial aspect of the government's Transport Bill concerned nationalization of long-distance trucking, which Labour believed was necessary to provide proper coordination with rail services. The act was roundly denounced by Conservative spokesman David Maxwell-Fife as "the greatest disservice which the Government had so far done to the trade and industry of the nation."[8] The measure made public functionaries of one million more people, almost six percent of the total work force. It transferred to state control sixty railways, with 52,000 miles of single track and 600,000 railway cars, and 2,100 miles of navigable canals. Also affected by the act were 200,000 licensed truckers who operated nearly 450,000 vehicles.

Clearly, Labour's bill to nationalize iron and steel was the government's most "socialistic" measure because it could hardly be argued that the industry was inefficient and needed government support. Neither could it be said that the industry was a basic public service, nor that it needed drastic reorganization. The workers had not demanded nationalization, nor had the industry been subject to much public control in the past. Churchill denounced the bill as a Labour government plot to establish a base for the ultimate penetration and paralysis of all forms of free enterprise. Ivor Thomas called it "dogma run mad." The steel industry fought it. The press was hostile. Labour insisted, however, that this industry, which was important for national security, should be in public hands. The bill became law on 15 February 1951.

The benefits of nationalization were not always readily apparent. The nationalized industries operated as separate corporations with a certain amount of local autonomy, but they remained under the final authority of an appropriate cabinet minister who was answerable to Parliament for their operation. A special agency had acquired the leading steel firms through stock purchase. That agency also supervised the firms' operation under their old names and with the same managers. Thus, the firms were not government departments, and their employees were not civil servants. This arrangement, intended to minimize disruption, was itself the source of much added confusion. Since it was often impossible to distinguish between overall state policy and day-to-day operations, differences frequently arose over prices and wages. Furthermore, the government had great difficulty raising enough capital for the fundamental reorganization of industry. Financing was handled in different ways. The Treasury subsidized the coal mines directly, while allowing the transport, electricity, and gas industries to raise their own capital by issuing public bonds.[9] Private investors, though, were not eager to put their money in the state enterprises (even though the government guaranteed the investment), and the bond issues were usually undersubscribed. This necessitated large-scale borrowing, which led to a steady increase in the public debt and distorted the British money market as the government provided over 40 percent of all capital to industry. Trying to improve the situation by funding the industries through direct taxation could have led to a depression.[10] Nationalization also failed to produce some of the social benefits it had promised. The transition from private ownership to public ownership did not make mining a more desirable job than before. The miners now had to deal with government bureaucrats who often were just as indifferent as the previous company owners. The Labour government's social welfare programs changed their lives more, especially the program of socialized medicine.

Regulating the Nation's Resources

The Welfare State. The establishment of universal socialized medicine came on the heels of a long effort to improve Britain's health, reaching back at least as far as the National Insurance Act of 1911, which provided medical care to a portion of the lower classes from obligatory contributions of employees, employers, and the government. That act, however, covered only the workers themselves and did not extend to their families. In 1926, a Royal Commission advocated a national health service bill supported entirely by public funds. Though the Labour party could not claim credit for that scheme, it nevertheless gave its enactment the highest priority. Attlee wanted all classes to be included, even the well-to-do, for he felt that there was something patronizing and undemocratic about recognized exemptions for the "top people."

Several months after the 1945 election, the minister of health, Aneurin Bevan, presented the first draft of a national health service, which embodied the intent "to make medical and dental attention free to all who cared to avail themselves of its provisions, without qualification or limitation."[11] The legislation proposed the establishment of nationwide medical executive councils that would solicit and organize the services of the country's doctors and dentists. Membership in the system was strictly voluntary, but practitioners who joined would receive a regular annual salary, plus a stipulated fee per patient, and they could still maintain a private practice for patients who had not registered for socialized medicine. The country's entire hospital system would be nationalized and administered by various regional boards under the overall authority of the Ministry of Health. Bevan estimated that the National Health Service would initially cost 152 million pounds ($612,560,000) a year, but he had no illusion that this amount could be raised by some insurance scheme. It would have to come directly from the public treasury.

The passage of the National Health Service Bill in September 1946 launched a two-year struggle for its acceptance. A British Medical Association (BMA) poll revealed that 54 percent of the doctors were against affiliation, with opposition particularly strong among general practitioners (10,024 against, 5,479 for). In January 1948, the BMA denounced the act as "grossly at variance with the essential principles of the profession," to which Bevan replied: "Parliament has spoken and the country now awaits the cooperation of the medical world." The doctors feared that they would become badly paid civil servants and, in a second more comprehensive plebiscite, voted against participation by an even greater margin: 40,814 to 4,735. Bevan now became more conciliatory. He quieted fears that the state would deny individuals the right to choose their own doctors or would interfere with the delicate relationship between physician and patient, and he repeatedly emphasized that adherence to the scheme would be voluntary. Gradually, the BMA, realizing that socialized medicine was inevitable anyway, came around and advised its members to cooperate. The comprehensive medical scheme began operation as scheduled, on 5 July 1948. Shortly afterwards, Bevan announced that over 90 percent of the British people had enrolled in the scheme. In time most of the doctors also decided to participate. The success of the National Health Service was vital for the reputation of the Attlee government. It was possibly the most popular feature of the British welfare state.[12]

Benefits were not restricted to the practice of curative medicine. Community care included prenatal and postnatal assistance, a meals-on-wheels program for the aged and infirm, and rehabilitation and training for the physically and mentally handicapped. The National Health Service also practiced preventive medicine, supervising the relationship between health and the environment and raising the physical fitness of the British people: The program gave Attlee a tremendous sense of personal achievement: "I feel cheered when I look at the children and babies and compare them with those of past times."[13] Although the minister of health was given the right, in 1949, to charge aliens for medical services, the authority was not exercised, and foreigners received the same free services as British citizens, a benefit that was later discontinued.

The Labour government also extended social services to provide cradle to grave protection. When the Tories complained about the cost, Attlee answered his critics by declaring that if Britain could not afford the expense, it would be an admission that "the sum total of the goods produced and the services rendered by the people of this country is not sufficient to provide for all our people at all times, in sickness, in health, in youth and in age, the very modest standard of life that is represented by the sums of money set out."[14] The prime minister was aware, though, that only by utilizing fully the human and natural resources of the United Kingdom could the benefits of the welfare state be guaranteed. He expected people to work for social security. Labour party leaders knew that until Britain's economic recovery was assured, the welfare system could not be fully implemented. Unfortunately, current economic conditions did not encourage optimism.

A Crippled Economy. The prospects for a substantial increase in British production at first seemed good. The markets of Western Europe were starved for consumer goods. Investment capital was cheap. Inflation was harnessed by wartime controls, and there was full employment. The expansion did not live up to expectations, however. Exports increased, but only by 20 percent instead of the anticipated 75 percent. A world shortage of raw materials drove up commodity prices, causing foreign loans to be depleted twice as fast. The reduction of incentives and a serious housing shortage cooled the ardor of the workers. By 1947, the country was in the throes of a major economic crisis.

As the year began, the severest winter in over half a century pummeled the United Kingdom. Blizzards and freezing temperatures blocked roads, isolated villages, and brought chaos to the transportation system. Neither railroads nor barges could supply British industry with enough coal. Electricity stations, given the highest priority, were reduced to two-week reserves, and the government drastically rationed power. Emmanuel Shinwell, the minister of fuel and power, suspended service to industrial consumers in London, the southeast, the Midlands, and the northwest. Residents were prohibited from heating their homes with electricity between 9:00 A.M. and noon and from 2:00 to 4:00 P.M. The service of the London public transit system was curtailed, the BBC's Third Program went off the air, and the greyhound tracks stopped racing. When Shinwell blamed the weather, a critic countered, "the crisis is not due to an act of God, but the inactivity of Emmanuel."

By March the worst was over. Nevertheless, in late April, industries were still guaranteed only half their usual quotas of solid fuel. The workers who had expected the Labour victory to bring immediate prosperity expressed their disillusionment through official and wildcat strikes, which lost 2.4 million working days. From January to June, walkouts in the still depressed coal industry reduced coal production by 559,000 tons. The effect was disastrous for Britain's balance of payments and accelerated the drain on its foreign credits. On 20 August, the government enacted exchange controls. Britain henceforth obtained hard currency through the direct sale of gold. More than at any other time, British leaders were embarrassed by their country's complete dependence on help from abroad. "I do not like being tied to money lenders at all," grumbled Foreign Secretary Ernest Bevin, but he admitted that without American aid "the British people must face a descending spiral of depression, for they could not by themselves solve the sterling-dollar problem of the world."[15] The pressure became so great that, in September 1949, the British pound was devalued from its prewar level of $4.08 to the pound to $2.80.

The government feared inflation could jeopardize Britain's position in foreign trade and finance and endanger its social welfare obligations. To stimulate exports and stabilize the economy, it proposed to retard demand. Taxes and restrictions on credit curtailed consumer spending. Price controls, ceilings on purchases of essential goods, and prolongation of stringent wartime rationing of basic foodstuffs helped quiet the demands for higher wages. The middle- and higher-income groups paid comparatively more taxes than the lower-income wage earners. The standard rate of income tax was 45 percent of the earnings left after deductions, to which was added a progressive surtax for incomes over 2,000 pounds. Those in the highest brackets could pay 95 percent of their earnings before exemptions and adjustments to the public treasury. Nevertheless, the bulk of the overall revenue continued to come from the lower-income taxpayers, who formed the largest group in society. The British were no strangers to such taxes. Before the war, the scale ranged from 27.5 to 75 percent of income. Most of the revenue from the postwar hikes went to industrial reconstruction and defense spending, not to an extension of social welfare. Escalating costs in the latter sector forced Labour to cut back on some of the intended services.

Britain recovered its prewar level of industrial production within three years after the German surrender. By 1950, production had risen another 25 percent.[16] Nevertheless, the increase was inferior to the gains made by Germany, France, and Italy during the same period. Furthermore, the Labour government's austerity program dampened its popularity and set the tone for the 1950 general election.

The Conservatives attacked the devaluation of the pound and the high level of public expenditures. They scored points by criticizing Labour's nationalization of the iron and steel industry and pledged to denationalize it if they won. Their campaign manifesto pledged, "This is the Road. We shall bring nationalization to a full stop here and now," and they promised to repeal the Steel Act and return the trucking industry to private ownership. By and large, however, the Tories accepted Labour's reforms, although they placed more emphasis on private enterprise as a basis for economic expansion. They too were committed to full employment, and they talked about increasing pensions and extending social services. Churchill was now seventy-five and fighting the thirteenth general election of his career. The results were close. The Labour party, with 46 percent of the vote, barely squeaked out a victory; it now had only a 7-vote majority, down from a once-proud 136. Such a slender margin meant another election would soon be held. Wrote Attlee, "It was not pleasant to have members coming from hospital at the risk of their lives to prevent a defeat in the House."[17]

The new campaign came in October 1951. Attlee fought strenuously—he was practically the only remaining minister from the old guard of 1945—but it was a tight race. Labour edged the Conservatives by almost one percent in the popular vote, but received fewer seats in the Commons.[18] On 26 October, Attlee resigned. Every important piece of legislation that he had submitted had been enacted, yet his party was still uncertain of its future. Its moderates wanted to consolidate their gains, while its radicals wanted to use these gains as a base for continuing the revolution. Both sides showed more skill in attacking each other than in providing leadership capable of reconciliation. When Attlee finally retired from active politics in 1955, he left behind a party unsure of its direction.

The End of Empire. The Labour government intended to couple its policy of austerity at home with one of retrenchment abroad. In 1945, the British had over five million men under arms, the largest army in their history. They had helped to develop the atomic bomb, and their world influence was formidable, with troops stationed in Germany, Italy, Greece, Turkey, Egypt, and their numerous colonial possessions in Africa and Asia. Britain had been the holder of the European balance of power for as long as anyone could remember and seemed likely to maintain this position as long as anyone could imagine. Indeed, shortly after coming to power, the Labour government decided to continue conscription, the first peacetime draft in British history. The costs were staggering. The government was outspending its income by over two billion pounds a year.

In August 1945, the United States discontinued Lend-Lease, the principal source of British military aid. The British tried to negotiate further credits, but the Truman administration was unsympathetic. John Maynard Keynes cabled home disgustedly that what was good enough for the ultraconservative directors of the Bank of England was apparently not good enough for the Americans: "We are negotiating in Washington, repeat Washington, fig leaves that pass muster with old ladies in Threadneedle Street wither in a harsher climate."[19] The Americans finally agreed to lend $4.4 billion, to which the Canadians added another $1.5 billion, but this was insufficient to enable Britain to build up its strength at home while also maintaining its traditional position in world affairs. Indeed, without serious economies, Britain appeared headed toward bankruptcy.

Some old-time imperialists might complain. Churchill had remarked only three years before that he had not become the king's first minister in order to preside over the liquidation of the British Empire, but the British people, in addition to their growing doubts about the righteousness of ruling over alien peoples, thought empire was too costly to preserve. Attlee felt that the sooner decolonization could proceed, the better. Accordingly, at the end of July 1945, he announced his intent to seek "an early realization of self-government for India." In the spring of 1946, an interim native government was established, and the drafting of a constitution began. The British had hoped that the transfer of power to the local leaders could be accomplished without destroying the unity of the country, but tensions between the Hindu majority and Muslim minority were already making this prospect extremely doubtful. Since the British had very few means of maintaining order, the only practical solution seemed to be partition.

Attlee said, in February 1947, that the British would definitely give up all power in India not later than June 1948, "either as a whole to some form of central government, or in some areas to provincial governments or in such other ways as might seem reasonable." He appointed Lord Louis Mountbatten, former supreme allied commander in South East Asia, to handle the responsibility. The new viceroy, fearing an all-out civil war was imminent, advanced the day of the British transfer of power to August 1947. There would be two states: Hindu India and Muslim Pakistan. Parliament approved the Independence Act in July. No sooner had the Union Jack been lowered over India than the subcontinent exploded into a ferocious religious and ethnic war that left at least a half million dead and another 12 million homeless. Many felt that the sudden departure of Mountbatten helped make the situation more inflammable. Indeed, the disaster might have been attenuated through a prolonged presence and additional deployment of British troops, but these were unavailable. Even if they had been, their use would no doubt have been regarded by Hindus and Muslims alike as evidence of British perfidy, producing an even greater catastrophe in the long run.

Indian independence marked the beginning of the end of British colonial domination throughout the world. Ceylon went free that same year; Burma followed in 1948. Britain also relinquished its mandate over Palestine. The British had the good sense to realize that the days of empire were over, and they wisely took steps to adjust to the new situation before it blew up in their faces. The rapidity of divestment was amazing. The duke of Windsor recalled a state visit he made to India in 1922 as prince of Wales: "British dominance in India was the product of two hundred years of war, work, and wisdom. Had anybody tried to persuade me as I left Karachi, with a regimental band on the quay crashing out 'God Save the King,' that all this would be lost in my lifetime, I would have put the man down as a lunatic."[20]

The Duration of Reconstruction

The Return of the Tories. The Conservatives remained in office until 1964, during which time they won two more national elections (1955 and 1959) and were led by four different prime ministers.[21] Such continuous tenure in office had not been achieved by one party since the great Whig ministries of the nineteenth century. The Tories returned to power as a rise in prices, brought on by Labour's policies and commodity shortages, threatened to produce serious inflation. In addition, the acceleration of the rearmament program, boosted by the Cold War, was necessitating a reordering of domestic priorities,[22] and the outflow of gold and dollar reserves had reached crisis proportions.

The Conservatives responded by doing the very thing for which they had taken Labour to task: they restricted credit, notably through an increase in the bank rate, and reduced foreign expenditures by imposing exchange controls and curtailing imports. Luck was on their side. The terms of trade—the prices manufacturers paid for foreign commodities—swung in Britain's favor, relieving pressure on the balance of payments. World food production expanded, finally enabling the government to abandon wartime rationing. The general level of production, which had dropped four percent during 1951 and 1952, rose six percent in 1953 and seven percent the year after. Except for denationalizing the iron, steel, and trucking industries, the Tories tampered very little with the Labour legislation. They even expanded social services, taking tremendous pride in their ability to fulfill a campaign promise to build 300,000 units of public housing a year. In 1953, the coronation of Queen Elizabeth II gave the Conservatives a psychological boost by holding out the prospect of a new Elizabethan age.

Churchill retired in the spring of 1955, when the economic condition of the country was better than it had been at any time since the war. His successor, Anthony Eden, immediately called for new elections and succeeded in increasing the Conservative majority in the Commons to 60 seats. However, the new prime minister soon ran into trouble when he ordered British intervention in the 1956 Israeli-Egyptian war. Even then, he might have survived this crisis had his health not been so precarious. His doctors advised him to retire from politics. Thus, after being Churchill's heir-apparent for a decade and a half, Eden held office just twenty months. Harold Macmillan, his successor, recalled the day Eden told him the news: "I can see him now on that sad winter afternoon, still looking so youthful, so gay, so debonair—the representative of all that was best of the youth that had served in the 1914–18 war. That band of men had faced the horrors of this fearful struggle with something of an Elizabethan gallantry. The survivors of that terrible holocaust had often felt under a special obligation, like men under a vow of duty."[23] Eden had symbolized the Conservative party at a time when Britannia neither ruled the waves, nor dominated world trade and finance; a time when surviving balance of payments crises and inflation was more important than maintaining imperial splendor; a time when foreign competition threatened domestic prosperity and any return to a policy of austerity was political suicide.

Continuity Amid Change. Nationalization did not prove to be the salvation of Britain's sick industries. During the economic boom of the 1950s, the real productive advances came almost entirely from the nonpublic sector. The low output of the mines continued to be a particular disappointment. Before World War I, British coal mines were capable of producing 287 million tons a year, a third of which was exported. Between 1919 and 1939, they averaged 200 million tons annually. They declined further during the war, but by 1947, the first year of nationalization, they had just about recovered their prewar level. Over the next several years, they showed a steady, but not spectacular, improvement. In 1950, the National Coal Board called for a capital investment of $1,778 million to ensure an annual production of 230–250 million tons. That same year, the British produced only 216 million tons, not enough to cover domestic needs and foreign obligations. They made up the shortages by buying coal from the United States. Five years later, production again had to be supplemented with foreign purchases.

While past mistakes and abuses were in part to blame, the greatest potential asset—the enthusiasm of the coal miners for nationalization—failed to materialize. Despite the improved productivity brought about by mechanization, British workers were poor competition for their German or American counterparts. Militancy rose in direct proportion to the miners' expectations of higher wages and better working conditions. Absenteeism rose to 11.5 percent of the workers in 1948. The unions rejected the recommendation of the joint committee on coal production to impose fines on the truants. Ultimately, the problems of the coal industry were not so much solved as transcended. Oil and natural gas offered other, more convenient sources of fuel. The Clean Air Act of 1956 also affected the situation. The legislation outlawed heavy smoke pollution and required new furnaces to be outfitted with special filters, thereby eliminating the burning of bituminous coal in many urban areas. During the 1960s, the famous London pea soupers (part water vapor, mostly chimney grit) gradually disappeared, and with them the demand for some 19 million tons of coal. In 1959, the Coal Board revised the goals it had set a decade earlier and lowered its intended productivity to 200 million tons a year. Later, a government report estimated that only 170 to 180 million tons would be required in the 1960s.

Of all the government programs, socialized medicine was the most popular, albeit one of the most expensive. By 1952–1953, its yearly cost had jumped to 518 million pounds (roughly $1.5 billion); forcing the government to charge patients for various medical services: half the cost of a set of dentures, a shilling for each prescription, five to ten shillings for elastic hosiery, two and a half pounds toward the price of a wig, and three pounds for orthopedic footwear. The 20 million pounds received from these new charges could not begin to cover the 76 million pounds increase in doctors' salaries that was granted in 1951 to prevent a threatened mass resignation of general practitioners from the National Health Service. By 1958, the National Health Service cost 710 million pounds (almost $2 billion), of which the Treasury paid 80 percent. Still, if one believed that medical care was a matter of right, not privilege, the British received their money's worth. Protected by the National Health Service, the average citizen did not face the enormous expense of catastrophic illness.

The Labour party had been particularly keen to abolish the great inequities of wealth. In particular, it went after inherited wealth, but without much success. In 1938–1939, about one-third of 1 percent of the people owned at least 21.6 percent of the country's personal wealth.[24] Two decades later, despite an increase in death duties in the upper brackets to as much as 75 percent, slightly over 1 percent still commanded 17 percent of the total personal wealth. Obviously, more than one generation was needed to promote social egalitarianism. Popular ingenuity in avoiding estate duties was limitless. A favorite ploy was to make the intended beneficiaries stockholders in a special company that would be subject only to corporate taxation. In sum, keeping great fortunes seemed easier than amassing them.

In general, though, the real wages of the average worker rose during the period by about 40 to 50 percent. Between 1952 and 1960, the number of private car registrations climbed from 187,616 to 805,017. In 1960, consumers were buying 63 percent more goods and services than they had ten years before, and a certain amount of complacency set in for which the British would ultimately suffer.

Profile: Clement Richard Attlee (1883–1967) and Charles-André-Marie-Joseph de Gaulle (1890–1970)

Attlee

Their styles of leadership and their personalities were completely different. Attlee always seemed so understated, de Gaulle so overblown. Attlee made every speech sound boring; de Gaulle made his sound exciting. Attlee was called "Clem the Clam"; de Gaulle was "le grand Charles." Did the British and French people get the leaders they deserved? Well yes—but with such men they probably did much better. Attlee and de Gaulle, each in his own way, epitomized the desires of the people. Both served them extremely well.

They were born in the last years of the nineteenth century to solid bourgeois parents who had relatively large families. Attlee had four brothers and three sisters; de Gaulle had two brothers and two sisters. In both households, patriotism and religion were inseparable, and respect for authority was considered a virtue. Yet both abandoned the safe and sane in their desire to serve their countries.

Attlee was born in the London suburb of Putney on 3 January 1883. As the son of a solicitor of "high standing" in the City of London, he was educated at public (private prep) schools, which gave him entry into the old boy network with its shared sentiments, accents, and jargon. After graduating from University College at Oxford, he studied law. He passed the bar examination in 1905 and went to work in his father's office. The Attlees were a politically conservative family who had long been defenders of established authority, a tradition Clement would break.[25]

Charles de Gaulle was born in Lille on 22 November 1890. His father was the headmaster of the Collège Stanislas, a Catholic school in town. Charles was educated in schools run by the Jesuits and, before his teens, had already decided that he would become a soldier. He had a great passion for the heroes of the past and a deep interest in military strategy, stimulated by his father's participation in the ill-fated defense of Sedan in 1870. He dreamed of the day when France would recover the lost territories of Alsace and Lorraine. In France, revenge and romance were often mortar for robust nationalism.

De Gaulle

In the conservative milieu of the Attlee family, the Christian duty to improve the lot of those less fortunate often took the form of acts of genteel charity. While trying to establish a career in the legal profession, Clement became involved with a boys' club on London's East Side. The experience of working in the city's worst slums forced him to reexamine the whole social and economic system that could produce such poverty. "I soon began to realize the curse of casual labour. I got to know what slum landlordism and sweating meant. . . . I learned also why there were rebels."[26] In 1907 he became the live-in manager of the Haileybury Boys' Club in the borough of Stepney. He joined a Fabian Society discussion group and in 1908 became a member of the Independent Labour party, a socialist group that advocated radical change, including the collective ownership of the means of production, distribution, and exchange. Impressed by their arguments, Attlee completely abandoned the practice of law and committed himself to finding a way to change society.

De Gaulle had fewer doubts about where he was headed. In 1909, he passed a special examination for admission to the national military school of Saint-Cyr. He finished the course three years later, in the top ten of a class of two hundred, emerging as a second lieutenant. His first posting as an officer was to the 33rd Infantry regiment at Arras, then commanded by a certain Colonel Philippe Pétain, who became a valuable mentor. The General Staff rated Pétain's unit as one of the most efficient in the army. When World War I began, it immediately saw action near Dinant. De Gaulle was then a full lieutenant and leader of a platoon. His service in the war was distinguished, if not brilliant. He was wounded three times and cited in dispatches three times before taken prisoner in 1916 during the early days of the Battle of Verdun. Despite five escape attempts, he returned home only after the Armistice.[27]

The German violation of Belgian neutrality shocked Attlee into joining the army two days after his country's declaration of war. He was thirty-one years old, one year over the official age limit. Nevertheless, he became an instructor in the Officer Training Corps and, from there, managed to transfer to a South Lancashire battalion. Commissioned a second lieutenant, he got his first chance to see combat in 1915 at Gallipoli, serving at Suvla Bay. His unit was evacuated with the big British retreat in December 1915 and sent to Mesopotamia where Attlee was wounded. He rose to the rank of major and later saw action in France. Discharged in January 1919, he returned to the East End.

De Gaulle returned from the war looking forward to a promising army career. In 1919, he was sent to Warsaw to advise the Fourth Polish Light Infantry division during the Russo-Polish War. After the conclusion of peace, he stayed on to teach tactics at the Polish war college, an experience that led to his subsequent appointment as a professor of military history at Saint-Cyr. Next came appointment to the General Staff of the army of the Rhine at Mainz (1924); then to the staff of Marshal Pétain, vice-president of the Superior War Council (1925–1927). This was followed by assignment to the General Staff of the French army in Beirut (1929–1931); and to the general-secretariat of the Superior National Defense Council (1932–1936).

Meanwhile, Attlee had gone into politics. The Labour party saw his well-to-do background, his army record, and his commitment to the poor as decided assets. It obtained his appointment as mayor of the district of Stepney and invited him to serve on the executive committee of the London Labour party. He was offered a five-year term as a city alderman and became a candidate for Parliament from Limehouse. In 1922, he entered the Commons. Attlee epitomized Labour's tendency to be a party run by middle-class politicians with a proletarian following. Less than one-fifth of Labour's parliamentary delegation were from the working class. In 1923, Attlee won reelection and, in 1924, became under secretary of state for war in the ill-fated Labour government of Ramsay MacDonald. During the period of Tory ascendency from 1924 to 1929, his standing within his own party increased. When MacDonald became prime minister again in 1929, Attlee became chancellor of the duchy of Lancaster and postmaster general. In 1931, however, he refused to join the National Government and broke with MacDonald. The Labour party was in shambles, and Attlee's chances for national leadership had apparently collapsed.

In contrast, de Gaulle's future seemed assured. He had found a powerful mentor in Marshal Pétain, who had been shepherding his career. De Gaulle had dedicated his book *The Edge of the Sword* (1932) to him. *The Edge of the Sword* was an intellectual discourse on the philosophy of leadership, containing a wealth of aphorisms about the qualities necessary for effective command: "Great warriors have always been conscious of the role and value of instinct." "Nothing heightens authority more than silence." "The man of action can do nothing without a strong dose of egotism, pride, endurance, and guile." In downplaying the use of the airplane and the tank, the study hardly challenged conventional military thinking. De Gaulle's next book was more controversial. In *The Army of the Future* (1934), he advocated creating a professionally trained army composed of independent, highly mechanized, armored units capable of engaging in rapid offensive action. Although this concept had already been developed by certain pioneer military thinkers during the 1920s, de Gaulle's lucid prose infused it with new meaning.[28] The High Command rejected these proposals, however, believing its current doctrine of defense to be less costly in money and lives. The ambitious de Gaulle never really seemed comfortable in the role of courtier, and by the time the book was published, he had broken with Pétain. His career apparently was now in limbo. When his term at the General Staff Strategic Center was over, de Gaulle was sent to cool his heels in Metz as commander of the 507th tank regiment. Meanwhile the army brass continued to rely on the Maginot Line to protect France against invasion.

Attlee had managed to survive the National Government debacle and hold on to his seat in Commons. He became deputy party leader in 1931; and four years later, when George Lansbury was forced out of office because of his pacifist views, Attlee was elected leader. During the late 1930s, Attlee supported collective security against Hitler and urged aid for Republican Spain, but was reluctant to agree to a massive program of rearmament.

At the same time, de Gaulle had found a new mentor in Paul Reynaud. Reynaud, a former minister of finance, was a leading advocate of the creation of an offensive army to support France's diplomatic commitments to the countries of Eastern Europe. Reynaud lacked sufficient influence, however, and a Chamber of Deputies' army committee rejected his ideas. The Battle of France in 1940 gave both men an opportunity to be vindicated. De Gaulle put his ideas into practice on the battlefield and earned promotion to the rank of brigadier general; Reynaud became the head of the government. Reynaud then recalled de Gaulle from the front to become his under secretary for war, a transfer that added to de Gaulle's prestige. In the aftermath of the defeat, de Gaulle fled to London, the only minister to do so. He refused to obey the orders of the new Pétain government to accept the Armistice, thereby becoming an outcast at odds with his fellow officers, most of whom chose obedience over exile.[29] De Gaulle's isolation increased his determination to establish his legitimacy, although his famous appeal for continued resistance, issued over the British Broadcasting System on 18 June 1940, had no authority behind it other than his own pretensions.

The war brought Attlee back into the government. In 1940, Prime Minister Winston Churchill chose Attlee to be one of his top aides. In 1942, Attlee became deputy prime minister with responsibility over domestic affairs. He was therefore involved in much of the planning for a new postwar society. Attlee was always more of a pragmatist than an ideologue. Churchill had once warned his ministers that they should "be careful not to raise false hopes, as was done [after World War I] by speeches about 'homes for heroes.' "[30] But Attlee wanted to transform British society and was not prepared to take these warnings seriously.

De Gaulle also set his own standards. He believed that truly great leaders could not be judged by the rules applied to others. In *The Edge of the Sword*, he had written approvingly of a comment that Admiral John Fisher once made about Sir John Jellicoe who had failed to destroy the German fleet after the Battle of Jutland. Fisher said that Jellicoe had "all the qualities of Nelson save one; he does not know how to disobey." De Gaulle certainly had such qualities; but when he became head of the provisional government in 1944, he was not willing to admit that others shared them as well.

Both Attlee and de Gaulle were solitary men with no close personal friends. Both possessed a sense of purpose and a strong commitment to ideals. In their careers, they had both taken risks, and were extremely lucky in having them pay off. Now, in power neither doubted that he was the man best qualified to preside over the regeneration of his country.

THE RISE AND FALL OF THE FOURTH FRENCH REPUBLIC

The Provisional Government of Charles de Gaulle

The Liberation. General Charles de Gaulle entered Paris at four o'clock on the afternoon of 25 August 1944. Earlier that day, General Philippe Leclerc, the commander of the Second Armored Division, had received the official surrender of Paris from the German commander, General Dietrich von Choltitz. De Gaulle had insisted that the capitulation be accepted in the name of the French, not the Allied, Supreme Command. De Gaulle's ultimate destination was the Hôtel de Ville, the city hall and the traditional birthplace of French republicanism, where a vast cheering crowd had assembled to greet him. Here also were the leaders of the Paris Liberation Committee. When de Gaulle finally arrived, the committee's leader Georges Bidault asked him to officially proclaim the reestablishment of the Republic before the mass of French citizens who were chanting the general's name in the square below. De Gaulle cut him short. "The Republic has never ceased to exist," he snapped. "Since I myself am the President of the Government of the Republic, why should I go and proclaim it?" But it would take more than pretensions to restore the greatness of France.

World War II had cost the lives of approximately 600,000 soldiers and civilians. Although the human losses were less than those of World War I, the material damage was more widespread and the demoralization much greater. Only ten out of ninety départements had been left undamaged. The infrastructure was particularly hard hit: telephone and telegraph systems had been demolished; railroads were paralyzed; and roads were blocked with rubble and marked with gaping holes. All the major bridges over the Seine, Loire, and Rhone had been blown up. No trains ran between Paris and Lyons or from Paris to Marseilles, Toulouse, Bordeaux, Nantes, Lille, and Nancy. The war had caused a tremendous decline in both industrial and agricultural productivity.[31] The cost of living had tripled between 1937 and 1944 and would increase even more the following year.[32]

Large areas of the country, although liberated, had yet to be pacified. The national gendarmerie was disorganized, making it difficult to ensure personal safety. Before order was restored, thousands of people were killed in a massive settling of accounts. Many of the victims had indeed collaborated with the Germans—the militiamen who handed over French Jews to the Gestapo or the active agents of Nazi propaganda—but many others perished because of old political rivalries and personal hatreds. The Communists went after members who had earlier defied party discipline by denouncing the Nazi-Soviet Non-Aggression Pact. Villagers found violent solutions to long-standing private feuds, social bitterness, and inter-family squabbles. In some towns, resistance groups made the rounds of apartment buildings, asking concierges to finger the collaborators in their buildings. Women who had, or were suspected of having, slept with German soldiers had their heads shaved and were sometimes—in a blend of outraged patriotism and sanctimonious prurience—marched naked through the streets.

De Gaulle realized that mere physical recovery was not alone sufficient. In a speech at the Palais de Chaillot on 12 September 1944, he stated that his goal was "to subordinate private interest to public advantage; to exploit the national resources of the nation and administer them to the general advantage; to abolish coalitions of interest once and for all; and finally, to permit each of France's sons and daughters to live, to work and to raise their children in security and dignity."[33] Thus, de Gaulle publicly committed himself to the economic and social goals of the Resistance Charter. He wrote that there must either "be an official and rapid move to institute a marked change in the conditions of the working people, and profound limitations upon financial privilege, or the embittered and suffering mass of workers would founder upon those disturbances which risked depriving France of what remained of her substance."[34]

The Trial of Marshal Pétain. The establishment of de Gaulle's position depended on the destruction of the legitimacy of the previous regime and of its leader, Marshal Philippe Pétain. The old marshal's trial began on Monday, 23 July 1945. The High Court, which exercised special authority over persons who had participated in the Vichy government, was comprised of magistrates who earlier had sworn allegiance to the man on whom they now presumed to sit in judgment. Pétain imperiously refused to recognize the court's competence and in his opening statement emphasized the legality of the Vichy government. "Power was entrusted to me lawfully and recognized by every country in the world from the Holy See to the U.S.S.R. I used this power as a shield to protect the French people, for whose sake I went so far as to sacrifice my personal prestige."[35] The irony of a man who had faithfully served his country all his life betraying his country when he was eighty-four years old was not lost on the French. Novelist Jules Roy, a reporter at Pétain's trial, offered this explanation:

> On the point of leaving this world, with every day that passed taking him one step nearer the shadows, he was suddenly offered a crown of light. . . . What octogenarian can resist a display of interest in himself, and why are Academy meetings so well attended if not because old men are afraid of solitude and boredom? All of a sudden the Marshal found himself a magus, kneeling before the star of a grandiose redemption.[36]

On 15 August, the court convicted Pétain of treason and sentenced him to death. De Gaulle allowed no appeal of Pétain's sentence, but he did commute it to life imprisonment. No such clemency was shown toward Pierre Laval, Pétain's unsavory subordinate. Laval knew too much about everybody's dirty linen. He had much to answer for, but his trial was a procedural monstrosity. The judges shouted at him, preventing him from presenting his defense. He was sentenced to death, but on the eve of his execution, he tried to poison himself. His stomach was pumped out, and he was hastily shot before he could cheat the firing squad. Few doubted that Laval got what he deserved—here was a man who said he welcomed a German victory—but the outrageous handling of his case brought no credit to his judges.

Other trials were held, but the justice coming from these special courts remained far from evenhanded. Economic collaboration was often treated more leniently than intellectual collaboration. It was said that a person who had helped the Germans build the Atlantic Wall need not fear arrest, but that an individual who had called the wall a good thing would go to jail. Often the big fish got away while their subordinates were left to suffer. For example, Admiral Jean-Pierre Esteva was sentenced to life imprisonment for permitting the German landings in Tunisia in 1942, although he was only following the orders of his superior, Marshal Alphonse Juin, who at the moment of Esteva's trial was the chief of staff of the Fourth Republic.[37]

Constitution Making. De Gaulle had returned, after four years of exile without official British or American recognition of his government.[38] Indeed, for almost a year and a half, he had no constitutionally recognized status in his own country. This limbo ended with the general election of 21 October 1945—the first such since 1936 and the first in which women voted. De Gaulle was unanimously elected president-premier of the Provisional Republic and, for the time being, set the legislative agenda. He divided his ministries among the three major parties, but took special care to keep the important posts of Interior, Foreign Affairs, and Defense out of the hands of the Communists who, with 160 delegates, could claim at last to be the first political party of France. The other two parties in this so-called Resistance Coalition were the newly created Popular Republican Movement (*Mouvement Populaire Républicain*, or MRP), a Catholic social action party, which won 152 seats; and the Socialists with 142 seats.[39]

The electorate clearly desired significant social and political change and had called for the establishment of a new republic. The three leading parties had all committed themselves to accepting the Resistance Charter as the basis of future legislation. What this meant in practice, however, was more difficult to ascertain. From the start, the coalition was beset by old rivalries and antipathies. The Communists had not changed their basic Leninist-Stalinist goals. They hoped tripartism would ensure them a permanent role in governing France and wanted to merge with the Socialists, the better to dominate them. The Socialists strongly opposed any such alliance as they had in the past. The MRP, although committed to social reform, was too distrustful of the anticlerical Socialists to develop any real association with them. The parties did agree on the need to restore the prerogatives of the legislative branch of government, but they ran into opposition from de Gaulle.

Although de Gaulle rejected government by executive decree, he opposed a system based on parliamentary supremacy. In his view, the old political parties had failed to provide adequate leadership: "Some among them could obtain the votes of an important fraction of the citizens, [but] not a single one was thought of as representing the public interest as a whole."[40] De Gaulle preferred a strong presidency that would directly represent the nation and stand above party politics. However, sensing his influence beginning to wear thin and perhaps hesitant to lead a France so weak that it would be overly subservient to the United States, he announced his retirement in a special meeting of the Council of Ministers on 20 January: "The exclusive regime of parties has reappeared. I disapprove of it. But aside from establishing by force a dictatorship which I do not desire and which could certainly end in disaster, I have not the means of preventing this experiment. I must therefore withdraw."[41] De Gaulle calculated that he would soon be recalled on his own terms.

Drafting an acceptable constitution was no easy task. The first attempt, submitted to the voters on 5 May 1946, was defeated by 10.6 to 9.5 million votes. The constitution, which had the support of the Communists and the Socialists, provided for a single-chamber legislature with a figurehead president. The MRP had opposed the constitution, fearing that a unicameral legislature would lead to a Communist dictatorship. Elections were held on 2 June to choose a second Constituent Assembly. The MRP, which received the largest number of seats with 169 (followed by the Communists with 153 and the Socialists with 127), was able to obtain a two-chamber legislature, but in actuality the differences were not significant. The lower house, or National Assembly, held the real power of governance with control over the premier and the cabinet. The upper house, or the Council of the Republic, could only examine and express its opinion on legislation before the Assembly. The president was essentially a figurehead. This second constitution was presented to the voters for ratification on 13 October.

De Gaulle, who had kept his silence during the first referendum, lambasted the second constitution with an appeal to legitimacy over legality: "The public powers have no validity, in fact or in law, unless they are in accord with the superior interests of the country and repose on the confident approval of the citizens." He advocated a strong executive, thereby foreshadowing changes that would be enacted in 1958. In 1946, however, his intervention failed. The voters accepted the second constitution by 9.2 to 8.2 million votes. Significantly, 31 percent of the eligible voters (8,468,000) did not bother to go to the polls. The French were clearly bored with constitution making and voted for a system that did not seem much of an improvement over the one they had lived under during the Third Republic. Institutionally, this was true, but the attitude of the French people had changed. In contrast to the previous period, they expected their government to contribute to the economic prosperity of the country and provide them with expanded social and welfare services.

The New Republic

Politics and Reorganization. France continued to be governed by an uneasy coalition of Socialists, Communists, and Popular Republicans, The "big three" did not agree on constitutional issues, however, and they had differing views on economics, religion, and foreign policy. Soon the strain became too great. The Communists controlled the economic ministries of Labor and Social Security, Industrial Production, and Reconstruction, but these posts failed to give them an effective power base from which to dominate the government. Therefore the Communists resorted to obstructionism. They opposed any political or economic association with the Western powers, and they voted against the policy to stabilize wages. In May 1947, Socialist Premier Paul Ramadier threw them out of the cabinet and replaced their ministers with Socialists and Popular Republicans. The Communists became a party of opposition.

Great labor unrest, increasing inflation, and growing political dissatisfaction from the Right added to the turmoil. The first clear proof of the Right's growing strength came with de Gaulle's reentry into politics. At Strasbourg, on 7 April, the second anniversary of the liberation of Alsace, the general delivered a spirited denunciation of the institutions and political parties of the Fourth Republic and announced the formation of the Rally of the French Republic (*Rassemblement du peuple français* or RPF). Its goals were to bring about a fundamental transformation of the political and social life of France and to act as a stout bulwark against Communism. In the municipal elections of October 1947, the RPF candidates and their allies won about 40 percent of the total vote, more than the MRP and Socialists combined. In 1951, the party won over 100 seats in the National Assembly. This proved to be the peak of its popularity, however. Although the Gaullists were united in protesting the current inertia of the Fourth Republic, some were clearly antiparliamentary, while others wanted to retain democracy and make it more progressive and modern. De Gaulle seemed committed to constitutionalism, but as he had made clear many times before, it must be a constitution that would strengthen the powers of the president.

The Gaullist successes had diminished the Communists' local support, and in November, they seized the initiative by launching a wave of strikes to paralyze the country. Organized through the Communist-led General Confederation of Labor, the demonstrations involved three million workers from all sectors of industry, particularly metallurgy, iron and steel, and coal. The strikes were also intended as a protest against the receipt of Marshall Plan aid and were thus a battle of the Cold War. In fact, Moscow had instructed the French Communists to incite the workers against their government and, if necessary, to sabotage trains carrying troops.

The government reacted as if it were facing an insurrection. The new premier, MRP leader Robert Schuman (November 1947–July 1948), enlarged his cabinet to include the Radicals and appointed the tough Jules Moch as minister of interior. Moch, a Socialist, quickly organized special detachments of the gendarmerie for rapid deployment to the major strike areas: the Paris region, Lyons, and Marseilles area, and the northern départements. He activated 80,000 reservists and recalled units from Germany. The government accompanied these hard-line measures with efforts to appease the strikers. Economic benefits were significantly increased. The carrot and stick policy worked, but the crisis had a lasting effect on French trade unionism. The Communist test of strength had failed to destroy the Fourth Republic and had weakened the unity of the General Confederation of Labor. Many non-Communist unions had opposed the strike; even many of the Communist-controlled unions boycotted the official demonstrations. Old-time syndicalists, who had never fully accepted affiliation with any political party, now thought it was time to become independent. Some organized a separate organization, the General Confederation of Labor of the Working Force; others, like the Federation of Teachers, declared their autonomy; and still more, tens of thousands, abandoned their union affiliation altogether. The divisions among the trade unions weakened their ability to effect social change.

The events of 1947 frightened those loyal to the institutions of the Fourth Republic. The MRP with its 166 seats, the Socialists with their 102, and the Radicals and their affiliates with 69 seats—altogether more than half of the seats in the National Assembly[42]—formed a political alliance to halt further disorder. This "Third Force" remained inherently unstable because its member parties were rarely able to agree on anything more basic than the defense of democracy. Moreover, the parties themselves were divided internally on major economic, social, and religious issues: the Socialist party was based upon "a more or less imaginary class concept," the Popular Republican Movement on "a religious ideal," and the Radical party "on historical memories."[43] Nevertheless, the Third Force managed to survive until 1951, when the Socialists, frustrated by the continual opposition of their coalition partners to economic reform, refused to accept any more cabinet portfolios. They went into opposition thereby leaving control of the government to the MRP, the Radicals, and various other rightist groups. For the remaining years of its life, the Fourth Republic was unable to produce a solid consensus on any significant issue.

The growing strength of powerful lobbies that spoke for the interests of business, farmers, labor, veterans, and others compounded the problem. For the most part, these groups chose to influence legislation by working behind the scenes within the prevailing political parties. However, the Defense of Shopkeepers and Artisans movement had a taste for more direct action. This group, founded by shopkeeper Pierre Poujade, served as a rallying point for discontented independent merchants who wanted to protest high taxes and denounce the stagnation of the parliamentary system. The movement drew most of its strength from the small towns and rural areas. In the elections of January 1956, the group, now transformed into the French Brotherhood Union (*Union et fraternité française*), entered candidates in almost every electoral district and managed to win over 2.5 million popular votes and 52 seats in the National Assembly. However, Poujadism was essentially negative. It appealed to the fears of the independent small business owners who were against the forces of change. Without effective leadership, the group soon degenerated into anti-Semitism and ultranationalism as its deputies scrambled for alliances with other right-wing parties. However, the contempt for the Fourth Republic upon which the forces of the French Right fed remained.

Economic Planning. In France, nationalization began with those companies that had actively collaborated with the Germans: the Renault Motor Car factories were seized on 4 October 1944, followed by the Berliet Engine Works and the Gnôme and Rhone airplane factory. The newspaper *Le Temps* was also nationalized.[44] In December, the Provisional Government took an important step to implement the promises of the Resistance Charter when it reorganized most of the coal industry as "the National Coal Industry of the Nord and Pas-de-Calais" and put it under the supervision of the Ministry of Mines. The government felt that an energy resource so important to French national security had to be under public control. In April 1946, the gas and electrical industries were handled the same way. That same year, the government nationalized the four major depository banks.[45] State domination of credit, it was argued, would lead to a more rational allocation of national resources and result in an inevitable rise in productivity. Many of the current problems were long-standing, however, and could not be solved by such expedients. In this respect, the Resistance Charter called for an intensification of production "in accordance with a Plan to be decided upon by the state, after consultation with all those concerned with this production."[46] The Provisional Government therefore created the Plan for Modernization and Equipment, with Jean Monnet as high commissioner. A Council of the Plan, formed on 3 January 1946, began a survey of French resources to be used in formulating a series of goals for the next four years.

Fears arose that France was headed toward a controlled economy, but planning was to be accomplished with the assistance, not the destruction, of private enterprise. The planners hoped to provide businesses with the means to chart a rational course on their own. These technocrats tried to take a middle ground between rigid control and complete laissez-faire, but they recognized that priorities could not be established without a certain amount of coercion. Not being true ideologues, however, they often found that the best way to get people to do what they desired was to bribe them. Doing so was fairly easy since the government controlled most of the total investment capital,[47] which was made available, at preferential interest rates, to those who agreed to follow the plan's established priorities. The government offered additional incentives through special depreciation allowances, tax reductions, and outright subsidies.[48] The state was also responsible for approximately one-third of total French investment spending, which went mostly to the nationalized industries and to basic industries in dire need of modernization: iron and steel, cement, electricity, coal, agricultural machinery, and transportation.

The government also tried to repeat Poincaré's "economic miracle" by fighting inflation psychologically. To gain people's confidence, solvency had first to be restored to government finances through a policy of austerity, an unpopular measure that politicians were reluctant to endorse. Direct taxation accounted for less than one-third of national revenues, scarcely enough to meet the mounting deficits, which were covered by advances from the Bank of France and by issuing interest-bearing Treasury bonds. The state also borrowed money from the deposits in state savings banks, paid for goods and services with credit, and relied upon money from abroad. Between 1947 and 1954, foreign loans, principally from the United States, offset between 20 and 50 percent of the French budget deficits. Aid made available to France under the Marshall Plan accounted for about 30 percent of total French investment.[49]

Inflation and the huge military expenditures, which cut a large slice out of the budget, undermined the success of the First Plan for Modernization and Equipment (1947–1953).[50] Furthermore, resources were very limited, and frequently the planners were unable to gather reliable data on the extent of war damage and the availability of materials.[51] Then too, the goals of the plan were frequently confused and unrealistic. For example, one goal was to exceed 1929 levels of production by 25 percent, but it was unclear whether the planners were referring to industrial production or to gross national product. The plan also failed to address the inequities that existed between different regions of France, such as between the underdeveloped southwest and the more advanced regions of Paris, Lyon, and the north. In addition, the sectors emphasized by the plan drained funds from other programs. For example, of the half a million new dwelling units promised by 1950, only 174,000 were actually built. However, in the targeted sectors, growth was significant.[52] The Second Plan (1954–1957) was more sophisticated than its predecessor and was more concerned with lowering production costs. At the same time, it hoped to expand overall production by 25 percent. The planners concentrated on increasing efficiency by promoting the restructuring of certain industries by regrouping and mergers. They fostered the reorganization of agricultural marketing and distribution and emphasized scientific and technological research. Their success was impressive. Goals in certain categories were even filled to excess: electrical equipment by 233 percent, textiles by 213 percent, and chemicals by 280 percent. For the first time, the planners had to face the problem of economic disequilibrium because of too much growth.

Such an embarrassment of riches seemed a good augury for stabilizing the political system of the Fourth Republic. The derisive clamor of the Communists and the Gaullists continued, but the defenders of the present constitutional system still managed to hold on to the reins of power. Nevertheless, their disagreements were becoming increasingly acute. The issue of German rearmament was particularly divisive, both among and within parties.[53] But colonial policy ultimately proved the most destructive. Throughout its entire life, the Fourth Republic was involved in an exhausting struggle with independence movements in Indochina and Algeria. France was no longer powerful enough to make reality conform to its confused ambitions. And in trying to hold on to everything, the French were ultimately left with nothing.

The French population had remained stable for many decades. In 1901, the nation had 38.9 million people (about 40.5 million including the separated départements of Alsace and Lorraine); in 1946, it contained 40.3 million people. Even allowing for the wartime losses, the fact remained that, for one reason or another, the French preferred small families. Since 1830, the French population had grown more slowly than that of any other major European country. From 1935 until World War II, the death rate consistently exceeded the birthrate. If this trend had continued, the French population by 1985 would have been only 30 million.

Why the French started having more babies at the end of World War II is difficult to answer. Perhaps the fighting, or an increase in the level of fecundity, or the 1939 program of family allowances produced the change. Certainly, the higher standard of living the French achieved after the war had little to do with it, for the birthrate rose before the recovery began. In 1945, births exceeded deaths by 13,000, a year later the difference jumped to 298,000, and by 1950 to 328,000. The celebration of marriages postponed because of the war, the return of prisoners of war and deportees, and the coming of age of the pre-Depression generation (least affected by the losses of World War I) would sustain the increase, but they did not start it.

In any case, a growing population required more housing, schools, and hospitals. The consumer-oriented parents of this new generation demanded these services as a matter of right and had less patience than their elders with a system that failed to provide them. People wanted to live for the present. The traditional belief in the value of saving disappeared and was replaced by an increased demand for durable goods. This change in the economic reflexes of the French, though difficult to quantify or depict in charts and graphs, was one of the most significant aspects of growth and development during the Fourth Republic.

The rising birthrate seemed to indicate that the dynamic France was winning out over the static France, a distinction usually based on regional differences. The northern area of the country, stretching from Paris to the Belgian frontier, drained population and resources from the rest of France. The steady growth of industrialization in this region contributed to the general decline of small farms, small-scale industry, and local handicrafts in such an alarming way that the planners would later turn their attention to the development of backward regions affected by this exodus of workers and talent. The French economy was both progressive and backward. For all its expansion, it remained an economy of small family businesses. Even in 1952 when production had returned to its prewar high, only 332 industrial companies employed more than 1,000 workers, and only 653 had between 500 and 1,000 workers; the number of large firms had actually declined since the Great Depression. As long as the marginally efficient French industries functioned within the confines of a protected domestic market and were so strongly rooted in class values, they were incapable of competing with foreign industries. Many small business owners and industrialists appeared more concerned with the preservation of social stability than with higher production.

Meanwhile, inflation continued to threaten those on fixed incomes. In 1958, the government decided to abolish any pensions that, due to the successive monetary depreciations, were worth less than the cost to the Treasury of printing and making out the checks. The decision provoked a protest by some World War I veterans who marched down the Avenue de l'Opéra and demonstrated in front of the Ministry of Finance. Their pensions had hardly permitted them to buy a package of cigarettes a month, but they felt humiliated to be told, in effect, that their service was now worth nothing.

Colonial Wars and the Death of the Fourth Republic

The Loss of Vietnam. The tremendous blow French national pride had suffered with the defeat in 1940 increased France's determination to maintain the integrity of its empire. The French believed the colonies were necessary to maintain their nation's world standing. After the surrender of the Japanese, the French repossessed Vietnam a piece at a time. In October 1945, they reinstalled themselves in Saigon; the following March, they did the same in Hanoi. Their reentry into the northern capital had been prepared by an agreement reached with the local Communist and nationalist leader Ho Chi Minh on 6 March 1946. This accord recognized the northern part of the country as a separate republic, possessing its own parliament and army and having control over local finances. France thereby appeared to be the first European state to come to terms with a native nationalist movement. For Ho Chi Minh's political organization, the Viet-Minh,[54] the pact was a first step toward a totally independent and unified Vietnam.

The local army commander, General Philippe Leclerc, was glad things had gone so well, and to emphasize his good intentions, he ordered his military vehicles to be painted with both French and Viet-Minh insignias. He deplored the Communist presence, but felt that problems had to be solved politically, rather than militarily. "France," he wrote, "will no longer be able to collar a coalescent mass of 24 million people possessed with a xenophobic and, possibly nationalist, ideology."[55] However, the French high commissioner, Admiral Thierry d'Argenlieu, thought differently. Profiting by indecision in Paris, he organized a separate state in South Vietnam, which also had its own government and army. In August 1946, while the French government was negotiating at Fontainebleau with Ho Chi Minh on the future status of Vietnam, he called together his own conference at Dalat to establish an Indochinese Federation comprised of Cochin China, Laos, and Cambodia. D'Argenlieu's action torpedoed the Fontainebleau talks. Foreign Minister Georges Bidault blamed the breakdown on Ho Chi Minh, thereby suggesting implausibly that the Communists were prepared to start an insurrection for what they hoped to get through negotiations. Such accusations were peripheral to the main issue, which was whether France had any real national interest in holding on to this bit of territory in Southeast Asia. The Paris government could not make up its mind, but there were others who could.

On 23 November 1946, following a series of confrontations between French and Viet-Minh troops in Haiphong, the French cruiser *Suffren* opened fire on the port, killing about six thousand persons. Four weeks later, the Vietnamese Communists retaliated by attacking Hanoi and declaring the start of a war of liberation. The opening years of the Vietnam conflict were inconclusive and unexciting, and initially most of the French people paid it scant attention. The Cold War in Europe and inflation were more immediate concerns. Since no conscripts were sent to Indochina, the fracas was dismissed as the concern of the professional soldiers and the Foreign Legion mercenaries who seemed more than able to handle a rabble enemy army. Moreover, d'Argenlieu had convinced many people that Ho Chi Minh had no real following in the country.

The fighting took on a new dimension when Mao Zedong's Communists came to power in China in 1949. Now the Viet-Minh were able to secure sufficient arms and supplies to push for control of the Tonkin delta. The French army, backed with aid from the United States, was able to stem their advance and maintain a stalemate. However, after five years with no end in sight, the French back home started to become restive. It seemed absurd to squander lives and resources on a country that would eventually be governed by Vietnamese, no matter which side won. Besides, Ho Chi Minh might be a revolutionary, but he came by it honestly. Had he not admitted, "It was not in Moscow that I learned what revolution was, but in Paris, in the capital of Liberty, Equality and Fraternity"?

Then, there was the problem of Bao Dai, the man whom the French government was trying to put forth as the emperor of a united Vietnam. Bao Dai had a well-earned reputation as a playboy more concerned with living it up on the Riviera than with the well-being of his subjects back home. On 28 August 1953, at a conference at Rambouillet, Vice-Premier Paul Reynaud demanded that the would-be ruler set a good example by stopping his gambling. To which Bao Dai replied meretriciously, "If you were to go into the Salles de Jeux [gambling rooms], you would meet more French colonels than Vietnamese."[56] The French Vietnamese policy clearly was in confusion. Even Vincent Auriol, the president of the Republic, had difficulty finding out who was in charge. Premier Joseph Laniel could not control his subordinates. His ministry was described as "manufactured, like his speeches, with scissors and paste." Although the government had recognized the right of Bao Dai to rule a completely independent Vietnam, it was impossible to achieve that goal without a military victory.

General Henri Navarre, the local French army commander in Vietnam, thought he could provide it. He would coax the head of the Viet-Minh army, General Vo Nguyen Giap, into a futile assault against Dien Bien Phu, the French base lying athwart the main enemy supply route to China, some two hundred air miles from Hanoi. Navarre was so confident of his superiority in men and matériel that he committed only nine out of the hundred battalions at his disposal to the operation. He intended to supply the 20,000-man garrison by air.

Giap accepted the challenge and slowly marshalled his forces. In four months, he had assembled an army of twenty-eight infantry battalions and had implanted over two hundred guns in the hills commanding the Dien Bien Phu valley. On 13 March 1954, the all-out attack began. The Communist artillery quickly made the tiny French airfield unserviceable, while Giap's shock troops cleared the French from their peripheral strong points and threw them back onto their main base in the village. Although the French fought heroically, they were soon cut off. After six weeks of constant siege, their position became hopeless.[57] Dien Bien Phu fell on 7 May. The French did not surrender; they were literally overwhelmed. Of the 13,000 prisoners, only 3,000 survived to return home. The defeat was not irreparable militarily, but it was catastrophic politically.

On 17 June 1954, Pierre Mendès-France of the Radical party became premier and swore to bring a satisfactory end to the war by 20 July or resign. He doubted he would succeed. A nine-power conference convened in Geneva and, three hours before the expiration of Mendès-France's deadline, reached an agreement. The premier's ploy proved to be one of his best trumps because it warned the Viet-Minh that if they allowed this opportunity to pass, Mendès-France's successor might be less willing to come to terms. Despite the loss of Dien Bien Phu, the French still had a formidable military presence in the country.

In the settlement, all the territory north of the 17th parallel was surrendered to the absolute control of the Viet-Minh. South Vietnam would remain with France, but was promised eventual independence. The division of the country was provisional, pending a general referendum to be held within two years. The French received the news that they had lost part of their colonial possessions without rejoicing, but nevertheless the agreement was popular. The National Assembly ratified it with an overwhelming vote of 471 to 14. The war had defied the efforts of eleven governments to bring it to a close. It had cost $8.5 billion (of which $6.8 billion came directly from the French budget); it had consumed the lives of 92,000 men of the expeditionary army (19,000 French, 43,000 Indochinese, and the rest Foreign Legionnaires) and wounded 114,000 more. It had never been popular with the French people, yet it had dragged on for eight and a half years and could conceivably have lasted longer.

Mendès-France was the most successful premier of the Fourth Republic. He sold the French on the need to join the security pact of the North Atlantic Treaty Organization. He set the plan in motion for Tunisian and Moroccan independence, and he convinced the French to support the Geneva accords on Vietnam by threatening to draft Frenchmen to fight there.

The loss of Vietnam was followed by the end of French control in its other overseas possessions: Morocco, Tunisia, and Equatorial Africa. But the colonial troubles of the Fourth Republic were far from over. Within six months after the end of the fighting in Vietnam, France was at war in Algeria.

The Algerian War. The series of terrorist attacks that broke the tranquillity of Algeria's major coastal cities at the end of October 1954 seemed at first to be no more than temporary disturbances. The assaults caused some loss of life, but did minimal damage to property and seemingly had little effect on the attitudes of the Muslim population. The attacks, however, had been well planned. As early as 1947, a group of young Muslim extremists had begun stockpiling arms and recruiting militants for an eventual uprising. Over the next seven years, the leaders of the intended rebellion held hundreds of secret meetings in Algiers, Cairo, Bern, and Geneva to crystallize their plans. In March 1954, they formed a special Revolutionary Committee to prepare for direct action. They divided Algeria into revolutionary districts, placing each under local commanders to handle military op-

An armored personnel carrier, mounting a thirty-caliber machine gun, patrols the frontier between Algeria and Tunis near the city of Tébessa. The French built an electric fence between the two countries to stop Muslim rebels from smuggling in supplies.

erations, and laid the groundwork for a political organization known as the Muslim National Liberation Front (*Front de Libération National* or *FLN*).

Even had the French been able to appreciate the dynamics of this truly determined liberation movement, they would not have considered Algerian independence negotiable. Few then regarded Algeria as a mere colony. Since 1871, when its representatives were allowed to sit in the National Assembly, Algeria had been constitutionally a direct part of metropolitan France. The country had been divided into départements administered by Paris-appointed prefects. Both in relative and in absolute terms, Algeria had the largest population of European settlers[58] of any French overseas possession; they comprised about 10 percent of the total population of nine million. The French presence was massive. The *colons*, or settlers, monopolized the local government; owned the best agricultural land (which they claimed, truthfully, to have been responsible for developing); controlled over nine-tenths of the country's industry; dominated the educational system; and had even turned the great mosque in Algiers into a Roman Catholic cathedral. French civil status was theoretically open to all Muslims who were willing to be Gallicized, but integration was a screen behind which the *colons* maintained their ascendancy. For example, they were able to frustrate the implementation of the 1947 Algerian Statute that had given the Muslims half the seats on a local legislature that was to assist the governor-general in implementing policy.

The *colons* now formed their own terrorist organizations to fight both the FLN and any French government that dared try to make concessions to the rebels. Some even formed a special committee of public safety to plot the overthrow of the Republic. Such subversive activity could flourish only because of the complicity of the local administration and, more importantly, the sympathy and support of the French army, which, after three years of fighting, seemed to have prevailed militarily. The weak and confused Paris government abdicated more of its powers to the military. In January 1957, following a series of FLN terrorist attacks in

Algiers, the government invested General Jacques Massu, the commander of the 10th Paratroop Division, with full police powers. Massu applied them with such violence that many people back home were alarmed and began to wonder if French civilization was only a sham.[59] The *colons* were threatening the Paris government with continued violence, and possibly civil war, if it made any concessions to the Algerian nationalists. The settlers regarded each cabinet crisis as an opportunity for their supporters to form a government.

Many French did not think that the retention of Algeria was worth the destruction of their own country. The old days when France ruled over an apathetic Muslim population were gone and would never return. Now keeping Algeria in the fold would require a permanent occupation force. The economic and political costs of such a policy were more than most cared to pay. In May 1958, a new ministry, headed by Pierre Pflimlin, advocated direct armistice negotiations with the FLN.

The *Algérie française* extremists believed the time had come to save the state by bringing the French army to power. On 13 May, the day the new government presented itself to the National Assembly for formal investiture, a crowd of eight thousand people, composed mostly of young men and students, and encouraged and supported by the paratroopers, attacked and occupied the building of the Government-General in Algiers. The riot's leaders urged General Massu to become the head of a newly formed Committee of Public Safety. One of its members, Léon Delbecque, declared that he would recognize no government's orders unless that government were headed by General de Gaulle. On 15 May, General Raoul Salan, the man to whom the Paris government had assigned the task of maintaining order, concluded a speech before a crowd assembled in the Algiers forum with the cry "Vive de Gaulle!" The French army had often played a political role in modern French history, but not since the Boulanger affair of the 1880s had army leaders taken such direct steps to overturn a regime. Many career officers were ready to support such a move. To them, the loss of Indochina had been an act of betrayal. They felt that any national liberation movement was bound to be Communist and had to be crushed. They also believed that the government of the Fourth Republic could not be relied upon to protect the security of France. "We centurions," reflected the paratroop hero in a best-selling novel, "are the last defenders of man's innocence against all those who want to enslave it in the name of original sin, against the Communists who refuse to have their children christened, never accept the conversion of an adult and are always ready to question it, but also against certain Christians who only talk of faults and forget about redemption."[60] Until this time, the prospect of de Gaulle's return to power had aroused little support, but now it seemed the perfect way to keep Algeria French.

The Return of de Gaulle. De Gaulle was hardly taken by surprise. Within six hours after Salan's pronunciamento, he replied that he was ready to assume the powers of the Republic. On 19 May, he held a press conference at the Hôtel Palais d'Orsay in Paris in which he expressed sympathy for the Algerian settlers' frustration with the Paris government. "How could such a population fail to revolt in the long run?" he asked. "It is absolutely normal and natural; and, then, it cries Vive de Gaulle as all Frenchmen do, in anguish and in hope." He praised the army for helping "to prevent this emotion from turning into disorder" and carefully tried to appease the principal groups that might oppose his resumption of power. Thus, his kindest words were for Guy Mollet, the leader of the Socialists, whose support he deemed absolutely crucial.

De Gaulle had made it plain that he would only come to power constitutionally, but he said that it was "obvious that this could not be done according to the rites and procedure that are so habitual that everyone is tired of them," and he proposed that the National Assembly directly invest him with full powers. Then, after making yet another declaration of his devotion to parliamentary democracy, he said he would return to his village of Colombey-les-deux-églises and "remain there at the disposal of the country."[61] The government began immediate discussions with de Gaulle, but while it was trying to establish a proper course of action, the rebels struck again.

On Saturday, 24 May, parachute units, acting under the orders of the Committee of Public Safety, seized the island of Corsica. The government had few resources on which it could rely: the army was Gaullist; the national gendarmerie and the Paris police were unreliable; and the labor unions were reluctant to call a general strike.[62] Moreover, the French people seemed indifferent. Parisians left the capital for their usual weekend in the country in greater numbers than before. Meanwhile, de Gaulle forestalled a Committee of Public Safety plan to seize power on the mainland by announcing that he had begun to form a government. Later, it was claimed that he had saved his country from civil war, but by then not very many French citizens were willing to die to save the Fourth Republic.

President René Coty, after persuading the current government to resign to avoid civil war, formally designated de Gaulle the new premier. On 1 June, de Gaulle presented himself to the National Assembly for confirmation of his powers. He read a short speech, asking for full powers to rule France for six months, during which he would reestablish order and restore unity. He made it clear, however, that he wanted to give France a new constitution, in which "the executive and the legislative branches must be separate and apart."[63] He was confirmed 327 to 224, with 37 abstentions.

During the twelve-year life of the Fourth Republic, governments were changed, on an average, about twice a year. The longest ministry, that of Guy Mollet (1956–1957), lasted sixteen months; the shortest, those of Robert Schuman (1948) and Henri Queuille (1950), were overthrown the same day they presented themselves to the National Assembly. An enormous amount of time—something over 300 days—was lost in negotiations to find a new government. The more the ministries changed, the more they remained the same. The ministers were interchangeable and constantly reappeared after a slight reshuffling of portfolios. This rapid turnover was almost identical to the experience of the Third Republic, especially the period between the wars. Article 51 of the 1946 constitution allowed for dissolution of the National Assembly and new elections if two cabinet crises—i.e., a formal vote of no confidence by an absolute majority of the deputies—occurred within a period of eighteen months. But the Council of Ministers, which exercised the power, was reluctant to take any steps that might increase the already existent divisions among the parties of the ruling coalition. Consequently, most governments left office before the specified constitutional provisions could be fulfilled: the governments either fell apart from internal feuding or resigned after losing a majority vote. Article 51 was used only once—in 1955, when the Radical Edgar Faure dissolved the National Assembly. Faure was subsequently thrown out of his own party for such audacity. The instability of the Fourth Republic was heightened because the country's two most powerful political forces—Communism and Gaullism—refused to accept the governmental system and were actively committed to its destruction.

The Fourth Republic ended, as had its three predecessors, with a savior assuming power. The French had a tradition of authoritarian, charismatic leaders. De Gaulle said he had no desire to save France by abolishing its basic liberties. Universal suffrage would continue as the source of all power, and the government would remain responsible to an elected assembly. "Why should I, at 67, begin a career as a dictator?" he asked.[64] His constitution, drafted by a specially appointed committee, perpetuated much of the parliamentary structure of the previous system. On paper, at least, the prime minister (the premier or president of the Council of Ministers under the Third and Fourth Republics) would continue to formulate and conduct state policy. However, the Fifth Republic differed significantly from its two immediate predecessors. The presidency was hardly the position of a figurehead. It was the focal point for the entire system, shifting the initiative of governance away from the legislature to the executive branch, which now had a commanding and independent advantage.

The French people endorsed the Fifth Republic constitution, on 28 September 1958, by a majority of nearly 80 percent. Remarkably, a substantial part of the working class and a large number of Communists voted for it. The parliamentary elections the following November were, by and large, a repeat performance. Most candidates, no matter what party, tried to get elected by professing loyalty to and faith in de Gaulle. The "Gaullist" party, the Union for the New Republic (*Union de la nouvelle république* or *UNR*), a hastily assembled collection of supporters and identifiers, emerged after the second round with 189 of the 467 seats in the assembly (over 40 percent). Leftist parties were the big losers. The Communists saw their strength dwindle from 145 in the previous legislature to a mere 10. The Socialists were down from 88 to 40. Even the middle-of-the-road Radicals, once the most prestigious of French parties, dropped from 55 to 13. With guaranteed support from other rightist parties, de Gaulle could rule as he chose. He appointed his own man, Michel Debré, to be prime minister and began to intervene actively in the business of government, all the while pretending he was above parties. "I am a man," he claimed, "who belongs to no one and who belongs to everyone."[65] He still freely identified himself with the French general will, but his skill as a politician stemmed from his ability to make his pretensions appear true or, as Georges Bidault put it, to make people believe that they owned "a piece of the True Cross of Lorraine."[66]

POSTWAR ITALY

Inauguration of a Republic

Constitutional Guarantees. Because of his close association with Fascism, King Victor Emmanuel III was not very popular. His strongest friends, the traditional ruling classes, who were similarly compromised, were currently in disarray and unable to give him their traditional support. The king hoped to protect his dynasty with a ruse. He would retire, not abdicate, and give his more popular son Umberto authority to act in his stead by naming him lieutenant-general of the realm.

The liberation brought a return of party government. The survival of any leader depended on the support he received from Italy's two major forces—the Marxists and the Catholics—and on the approval of the powerful Committee of National Liberation (CLN). In the year after the deliverance of Rome, on 4 June 1944, the moderate Labor Democrat Ivanoe Bonomi presided over the government. In June 1945, he was succeeded by Ferruccio Parri, a respected non-Communist leader of the northern armed resistance. Parri, a member of the small laic and republican Action party (*Partito d'azione*), became premier when the CLN deadlocked between the candidacies of Pietro Nenni (Socialist) and Alcide De Gasperi (Christian Democrat). Parri's government marked the furthest swing to the Left in postwar Italian politics. His vigorous attempt to purge the government and the bureaucracy of its Fascist elements was his undoing. In late autumn, the Conservatives succeeded in effecting his ouster, arguing that the purge should be halted so that the state could return to law and order. The government was also criticized for doing little to resolve the economic crisis or quiet Sicilian separatism. In December 1945, De Gasperi became premier, a post he held repeatedly until 1953. Christian Democrats, in fact, maintained a monopoly on the premiership until the early 1980s, but even then they continued to retain most of the cabinet posts.

Among the important items of business for these early governments was to prepare a referendum to decide the fate of the monarchy. Victor Emmanuel, fearful of the results, finally did abdicate, but the gesture came too late. The vote, held on 2 June 1946, showed that 54 percent of the electorate (12,717,923 to 10,719,284) favored scrapping the monarchy for a republic. The country had split along geographical lines: the south, including Rome, voted to retain the monarchy by 64 percent; in the more populous, industrially advanced north, the reverse was true. The vote was the first free election held in Italy since 1922. Some monarchists refused to accept its results and proposed rallying the south against the north. The new king, Umberto II, realized such a fight was useless and quietly went into exile. He had been his country's monarch for only thirty-four days.

At the same time the Italians sealed the fate of the monarchy, they also voted for a constituent assembly to draft a new Italian constitution. The results gave the newly formed Christian Democratic party (*Democrazia cristiana*) 35.2 percent of the vote and 207 seats in the assembly, the Socialists got 20.7 percent and 115 seats, and the Communists received 19 percent and 104 seats. The once powerful Liberals won only 6.8 percent and 41 seats.

The new constitution, which came into force in January 1948, was a curious blend of old and new. It guaranteed the inviolability of personal liberty, but perpetuated, in Article 13, preventive detention. The punitive legislation of the Fascist period was not automatically invalidated. People still could be charged with publishing falsehoods likely to disturb the public peace. They could be prohibited (until 1961) from moving from one locality to another unless they had a specific job offer. They could be ordered into exile without trial because they were believed to be a security risk. They could also be imprisoned on the ambiguous charge of *vilipendio*. Under the penal code, persons and institutions had honor that could be damaged by public criticism even when the attack was true. Thus, anyone could be jailed for speaking ill of the state, the armed forces, the police, the Catholic church, or a public official.[67]

The constitution recognized the rights of workers to join trade unions and engage in collective bargaining. However, the Fascist laws controlling labor migration still remained in force. A new law passed in 1949 reaffirmed the state's monopoly on regulating access to jobs. Thus, it was not unconstitutional to restrict a worker's employment to the area of his or her official residence. A worker who wanted to get a job elsewhere had to register in that area, but to register in another area, one had to have held a job elsewhere. The choice was to stay put or migrate illegally. In fact, the law was often violated, but workers who did so were usually paid much less than the going rate by their employers (who were also breaking the law). The legislation, rationalized as a means of controlling unemployment, was supported by powerful special interests. Industrialists favored it because they could hire labor at lower wages; the big agrarian groups liked it because it thwarted the emigration of cheap farm labor to the cities; the Communists welcomed it because they feared an influx of unintegrated workers; and municipal politicians approved it because the migration of unskilled labor to the cities would strain their social and educational systems. The prohibitions lasted until 1961.

Many articles of the 1937 Fascist Code of Public Security were still in force. During a state of emergency, provincial prefects had the authority to maintain order by whatever means they deemed necessary—even to the suspension of civil liberties. The recognition of the Lateran pacts as the law of the land likewise abridged freedom. Divorce was still illegal. The Roman Catholic clergy continued to enjoy special privileges. And criminal sanctions were applied to those who "either by word or deed" publicly offended or insulted the Sovereign Pontiff. Article 21 of the constitution officially recognized censorship. The article stated that everyone could freely "manifest his own thought by word, [and] by writing" as long as this was not "contrary to good morals." Thus, the publication, broadcasting, or performing of anything that violated this ambiguous standard was prohibited. An office to enforce this provision was established in the Ministry of Tourism and Spectacles. All scripts for movies, plays (until 1962), and radio and television shows had to be approved prior to public presentation.

Although the constitution guaranteed freedom of religion, Italy continued to be a virtual confessional state. Only Roman Catholics had the right to proselytize freely. Those who publicly questioned the validity of the 1929 Concordat could be prosecuted for offending the state religion. A 1931 Fascist law on public security was continually used to harass such Protestant evangelical denominations as the Church of Christ. Roman Catholic priests who were under ecclesiastical censure were still treated as second-class citizens and prevented from becoming state civil servants, schoolteachers, or municipal councillors. The Vatican, one of the principal defenders of state censorship, used Article 21 to frustrate any hostile social and political criticism.

Yet the constitution contained some attractive new features. A Constitutional Court was established that incorporated the American principle of judicial review. Under the old 1848 *Statuto*, the constitution could be amended by ordinary legislation, making it possible to use the democratic system to destroy the system. This was, in fact, what happened during the Fascist era. Now, such laws could be ruled unconstitutional, making a return to dictatorship more difficult. Another innovation recognized the country's diversity by creating nineteen federalized regions (later raised to 20) with limited powers of home rule. In addition, there were special grants of autonomy for the three frontier areas of Val d'Aosta, Trentino–Alto Adige, and Friuli–Venezia Giulia and for the two islands of Sicily and Sardinia. The move was intended to discourage local separatism. In Sicily, for example, there was a movement to become the forty-ninth state of the United States. Regionalization conferred on these units certain powers of finance and control over public services: the maintenance of schools, roads, health, and abandoned children. These powers were exercised through regional councils and assemblies that were established over the following two decades by statute.

The constitution established a parliamentary system with a bicameral legislature: the Chamber of Deputies and the Senate, to which the cabinet—the Council of Ministers—was legally responsible. The president, Italy's chief of state, appointed the prime minister, who then formed a government, provided it received the confidence of the legislature. In this multiparty system, ministries changed frequently: between 1945 and 1960, on an average of every nine months. Initially, however, there was no great instability because of the predominant position of the Christian Democratic party. Its leader, Alcide De Gasperi, served uninterrupted as prime minister from December 1945 to August 1953. His party continued to be the backbone of every government.

The Formation of Parties. Modern party government was an unknown commodity. Even before the Fascist period, political groups were not genuinely representative nor were they well organized. The groups in parliament had been formed mostly around individuals whose position was based on local influence rather than on any political program. Only the Socialists and the Popular party (*Partito popolare*) had really possessed permanent organization that provided a basis on which a postwar party structure could be built.

The Christian Democrats were the Popular party's reincarnation. De Gasperi, their leader, was one of the few members who had genuine professional experience. He had not only served under Don Sturzo before the Popolari were outlawed in 1924, but had also been a member of the Austro-Hungarian parliament before World War I. The Fascists arrested him in 1927, releasing him two years later after the Vatican intervened on his behalf. During most of the Fascist dictatorship, De Gasperi worked as a librarian in the Vatican. He felt that "governing a state creates an intimate tie with God our Father and . . . a responsibility which is immediate toward the people, but toward a people seen as a mediator of the divine will that governs us."[68] It was therefore natural for his party to look to the papacy for support. In many Italian towns and villages, the party headquarters was located next-door to the church.

During the 1920s, the papacy had sacrificed the Popolari to form an association with Mussolini. Now, however, with the Fascists in disgrace and the monarchists in disarray, there were no strong rightist parties around to challenge the parties of the Left. Present necessity dictated that the Christian Democrats receive papal endorsement. Nevertheless, Pius XII disagreed with many of the party's modernist positions, specifically, the establishment of public health services, free public education, and religious freedom. Pius usually made little distinction between Communists and Socialists and was disturbed to learn that the first postwar government of the Christian Democrats included representatives from both of these parties.

De Gasperi had formed his first cabinets with the anticlerical Socialists and Communists because government without them would have been difficult; together they controlled more seats in the Chamber than his own Christian Democrats. Besides, it was a time of national reconciliation, and the Marxists were likewise committed to social legislation and industrial reform. Still there was something ominous in their joint declaration of October 1946, "to achieve the concentration of all popular forces in the struggle against the conservative reactionary forces and [to work] for the conquest of power on the part of the working classes."[69]

The strength of the Christian Democratic party, as well as its weakness, derived from its diversity and its ability to maintain a certain amount of cohesion among its factions and their various social, regional, personal, and political interests. The right wing was a staunch champion of the rights and prerogatives of the papacy and the privileges of the rich and well-born, while the party's reformist wing was more socially conscious and committed to Christian charity and public service. De Gasperi spent most of his political life trying to steer a middle course between the extremists on the Left and the reactionaries on the Right inside as well as outside his own party. Many members of the traditional Italian Right had joined the Christian Democratic party in hopes of bringing about a conservative restoration. Committed, usually elderly, monarchists joined the Italian Democratic Party of Monarchical Unity (*Partito democratico italiano di unità monarchica*), while die-hard former Fascists joined the essentially Rome-based Italian Social Movement (*Movimento sociale italiano*).

The Communist party (*Partito comunista italiano*), led by Palmiro Togliatti, was the second most important party in Italy. The Communists showed a willingness to play by constitutional rules, but only insofar as doing so served their long-range purpose. Like other Marxist-Leninist parties, they subscribed to the rules of democratic centralism. No one could be sure whether they would maintain a pluralistic system should they actually come to power. The party won considerable popularity because many of its members had been willing to risk their lives in the armed struggle against Mussolini and the Germans. They also appeared to be one of the few parties that was sincerely committed to social change and to the improvement of the lot of the lower classes. Togliatti set his initial postwar strategy at a meeting at Salerno in March 1944.[70] He said that it was his intention to create a "new party" that would work with the Christian Democrats, the Socialists, and other parties to build a new society within the present system.

Operating under this new Popular Front strategy, the Communists helped draft the liberal democratic constitution and were even willing to support the inclusion of the 1929 Concordat. Their members served in all of De Gasperi's cabinets until they became too threatening and were thrown out in May 1947. Even during the Moscow-inspired protest riots against the Marshall Plan and against the inclusion of Italy in the western security alliance, the North Atlantic Treaty, Togliatti preferred to try to come to power through the ballot box. Had the Communists managed to pull it off, Togliatti would not have been the firm supporter of democracy as he pretended, although he would not have slavishly followed the lead of the Soviet Union. Stalin purportedly so distrusted Togliatti that he tried to entice him away from active leadership of the Italian Communist party by offering him the post of secretary-general of the Cominform in 1951. Togliatti's resignation would have cleared the way for the succession of Pietro Secchia, a man more willing to follow directives from Moscow. Whether the reports of Stalin's mistrust are true or not, Togliatti undoubtedly had his own ideas about a separate road to authoritarian socialism.

The Communists, unable to reenter a government coalition, much less gain power on their own, concentrated their energies on regional development and reform. The center of their local power base lay in the industrial centers of the north, the so-called Red Belt regions of Tuscany, Emilia-Romagna, and Umbria. For example, after 1946 they controlled the government of Bologna, making it a showpiece of urban reform. They rescued the historic district, adapting the old buildings to modern needs by installing nurseries, community centers, and public libraries in old palaces, monasteries, and churches. They built retirement homes and expanded health care, improved sanitation, and promoted traffic reform. As the Italians became more prosperous and political dogmatism lessened, the Communist party abandoned its commitment to the dictatorship of the proletariat and under a new liberal leader, Enrico Berlinguer (secretary of the party from 1972 until his death in 1984), seemingly endorsed democracy, even accepting that Italy should "in principle" remain a member of the North Atlantic Treaty Organization. These changes helped to calm many fears about Communist intentions, but did not bring the party any closer to national power.

The Communists managed to bring about this transformation of philosophy without destroying the unity of their party. The Socialists did not have it so easy.

From the time of the liberation, the Socialists could not agree on whether to be revolutionary or evolutionary, whether to work within the system or to overthrow it. The divisions, which were old ones dating back to the nineteenth century, resulted in constant confusion, bewilderment, and bemusement—all adding up to a loss of influence. The unity achieved in the Italian Socialist Party of Proletarian Unity (*Partito socialista di unità proletaria*) after the liberation did not last long. In 1947, the party's right—that is, nonviolent—wing formed its own faction, the Italian Workers' Socialist party (*Partito socialista dei lavoratori italiani*), in protest over the continued alliance with the Communists. Its leader, Giuseppe Saragat, believed that the mutual hatred of the proletariat and the middle class had contributed to the triumph of Fascism and was determined to prevent this from happening again. "We have seen," he said, "that always when the proletariat has linked to itself the workers of the middle classes by means of a truly democratic policy, there has been progress; and it is precisely when the proletariat has rebuffed them that there have been catastrophes."[71]

Further defections from the main party followed, resulting in the establishment of still more Socialist parties. The pro-Communist radicals who remained in the original party followed the leadership of Pietro Nenni, whose fellow traveler positions made it impossible for the Socialists to build an effective loyal opposition to the conservative Christian Democrats. A net result of the Socialists' ineffectiveness was the continued success of the Christian Democrats. Indeed, Saragat's moderates believed that the best way to achieve social justice and prevent a return of monopolistic capitalism was through continued cooperation with the Christian Democrats, even though this party contained many of the elements that had once supported Mussolini's dictatorship.

The failure of the Socialists to achieve unity was one of the most important negative factors of Italian politics in the postwar era, but support from the moderate wing was necessary for De Gasperi to remove the Communists from his cabinet in 1947, a move the Vatican and the United States welcomed. Indeed, some suggested that the Americans had threatened to withhold credits if this were not accomplished. In time, however, the virtual stranglehold the party had on the reins of power made its leaders increasingly more concerned with promoting special interests and less responsive to change and reform. Anti-Communism alone was not sufficient to create a dynamic ruling tradition or to develop an effective social conscience.

The Fragility of Centrist Government. The elections of April 1948—in which over one hundred parties ran candidates—produced a landslide victory for the Christian Democrats, who received 48.5 percent of the vote, giving them control of 305 of the 574 seats in the lower chamber. Despite Vatican threats that anyone who voted Communist was committing a mortal sin, the Communists came in second with a substantial 31 percent of the vote and 183 seats. The Vatican now tried to induce De Gasperi to form a one-party Roman Catholic government, but the prime minister refused and added representatives from the Liberal, Republican, and moderate Socialist parties to his cabinet. De Gasperi wisely attempted to avoid the acrimonious division between clericals and anticlericals that had so clouded the political atmosphere of the nineteenth century.

Under the Christian Democrats, the country was dominated by some of the groups that had earlier supported Mussolini: big business, landowners, and the Roman Catholic church. For the most part, organized labor was not under the thumb of the Christian Democrats, but because the working-class movements were so rent by schisms and factionalism, the conservatives were able to resist their demands for greater participation in political and economic decision making. The situation had parallels in the working of the Italian parliamentary system in the generation before World War I. For a decade and a half following the liberation, the Christian Democratic party became "the natural focus of opportunists and self-serving interests,"[72] behaving as if its anti-Communism excused an all-too-frequent association with financial and moral corruption. In betraying the public trust, it helped to bring parliamentary democracy into disrepute. De Gasperi spent much of his time trying to keep the Communists at bay in the legislature and the reactionaries at bay in his own party. Although he tried to maintain a reasonable independence from the church, his political strength depended critically on the influence the Vatican exercised over one-third of the Italian electorate.

Consequently, Roman Catholic influence grew steadily and was frequently decisive in determining who would advance in public service. The church was active in the censorship of the arts. It obtained state subsidies for parochial schools and carried religious instruction into the state schools. The semiofficial Catholic Action society constantly pushed for the formation of a rightist coalition of Christian Democrats, monarchists, and neo-Fascists. Its head, Luigi Gedda, threatened to form a new authoritarian church party despite De Gasperi's opposition.

The Christian Democrats' campaign rhetoric proclaimed the humanization of capitalism through social welfare. The role of government was to protect small businesses, small farmers, shopkeepers, and artisans and the poorer regions of the country. The party's left wing did take these things seriously, but many more party members were not particularly sensitive to the economic problems of underdogs. By 1953, the popularity of the Christian Democrats had slipped perceptibly. In preparation for the elections, the government passed a law reminiscent of the Acerbo Law of the Fascist period, which enabled a party with only a bare plurality of the votes to take two-thirds of the seats in parliament. The Christian Democrats failed to do so and thereby lost power in the Chamber of Deputies.[73] The 1953 election was a clear victory for the extremes. The monarchists and Fascists gained one-eighth of the seats in the Chamber; the Communists increased their strength, particularly in rural areas where dissatisfaction over the government's failure to enact an effective program of land reform ran high. When De Gasperi found he could not organize a strong government, he resigned and retired from politics. He died one year later.

The decline of centrist government initiated a period of increased political instability. For the next five years, a series of minority left-of-center ministries ruled Italy. They simply tried to hold their own against the political extremes.

The legislative immobility, together with a succession of political scandals, blighted the faith of Italians in centrist government. About 40 percent of them voted for extremist parties. "If only *he* were back, there would be order," people would say. They were referring to Mussolini. The Duce's widow, Donna Rachele, capitalizing on renewed sympathy for Fascism, opened a restaurant near Forlì in northern Italy. Featured on her menu were such delights as "spaghetti Blackshirt," "beefsteak Benito," and "Fascist Empire sponge cake." The government's fear of the extremists and unwillingness to push for further reform meant that Fascist civil and criminal law and Fascist civil and criminal trial procedure continued in force.

All in all, it is remarkable that representative institutions were as strong as they were, considering that most of the adult population had never known democratic government; that (as late as 1957) about 90 percent of the people had only five years or less of formal education; that most of the country south of Rome had hardly evolved from feudalism; and that practically all the political parties of post-war Italy officially embraced philosophies that, if carried to their logical extreme, would fundamentally deny the right of other organizations to function. Part of the answer lies in the caliber of the country's leaders; many of them were sensible men who sincerely wanted to build a new society on the discredited ruins of Fascism, even though the odds against them were great.

Although the legislators were ultimately accountable to the voters, the judges seemed accountable to no one. As a consequence, for the average Italian, justice was at best an abstract commodity. The courts sometimes took as long as three to six years to settle a routine case involving an automobile accident. More serious affairs could go through as many as four trials, with each court reaching a different verdict because each tried the case over from the beginning. Furthermore, the judiciary was so completely immersed in politics that rightist judges tended to impose their own conservative morals on the law while leftist judges viewed the courts as another element in the class struggle.[74] Frequently, basic civil liberties got lost in the shuffle. A certain police state mentality left over from the Fascist era still permeated the system. Arrests for sedition and disturbance of the peace were often made on the slightest suspicion. Because Italy had no bail, suspects in felony cases (whether they were accused of stealing a toy airplane or a Boeing 707) could be held in jail as long as four years before their case might come to trial. Yearly, thousands of individuals, including hundreds of motorists involved in automobile accidents, were routinely detained for questioning; sometimes they spent many months behind bars before being released without ever having been brought to trial. Only in 1972 were judges given discretionary authority to grant provisional liberty. Gaetano Salvemini, a distinguished historian and anti-Fascist, once remarked that if the police were to accuse him of raping the statue of the little Madonna on top of the Milan cathedral, he "would think first of escaping and only later of defending [himself] against the charge."[75]

The Economic Miracle

Foreign Aid and Reconstruction. The Fascist system had recklessly squandered national resources in a futile pursuit of glory: in 1935, the Italians attacked Ethiopia; from 1936 to 1939, they fought in Spain; then they conquered Albania; in 1940, they attacked France and Britain and then Greece. In 1941, they went marching into Yugoslavia. By 1943, the destruction that Mussolini had so freely brought to others had finally come home. For two years, it swept the entire length of the peninsula, leaving the Italians destitute and homeless. In addition, almost 450,000 people—30 percent of them civilians—had lost their lives. Over one-third of the nation's highways were destroyed or heavily damaged; 8,000 bridges were blown apart; 40 percent of the railroad stations were unusable; and 75 percent of the rolling stock was irreparable. The gross national product had tumbled to half of its level in 1938.

The war had been financed by lavish deficit spending, which expanded the amount of money in circulation by eighteen times and bloated the entire credit structure. At the time of the liberation, the Italian price index was twenty-five times its 1938 level. Yet prices continued to rise because money hoarded during the war reappeared, and the Allied military government put a new currency in circulation. Credit, unregulated by the government, expanded at a precipitous rate. Between July 1946 and September 1947, the Bank of Italy and other private banks loaned out some 590 billion lira (about $1.7 billion), more than the market could comfortably absorb. National production, though increasing, still remained below its prewar level. Only those fortunate workers whose wage scales were pegged to a cost of living index kept pace with inflation. Most Italians suffered terribly. The inflation also seriously affected Italy's foreign exchange. Between 1945 and May 1947, the lira depreciated from 100 to 906 to the dollar, while bad harvests drastically cut the supply and raised the cost of food. The ensuing discontent was a passport for the success of Communism.

The Allies could not afford the political risks of Italian pauperism, but as long as British and American troops directly held power in the north (which they did until December 1945), there was little danger of a Communist takeover. The military government controlled the allocation of raw materials and opposed any policy for the redistribution of wealth. The Americans defined "socialistic solutions" rather broadly and usually supported the Italian conservatives who opposed the imposition of controls and drastic reforms. The factories and plants, which had been commandeered and operated by special factory councils of the local resistance, were restored to their former owners. The National Liberation Committees were prevented from controlling local government.

De Gasperi wanted to revitalize the Italian economy, not revolutionize it. He favored market liberalization and eliminated most of the controls imposed by Mussolini on agriculture and industry. Nevertheless, the Christian Democrats wanted recovery to occur within the existing framework of the established business and industrial interests. This laissez-faire style of economics intensified the already serious inflation inherited from the Fascist era, endangering the Christian Democratic program of social progress. Matters could no longer be left to sort themselves out.

On 30 May 1947, De Gasperi transformed his committee on credit and saving into a sort of economic general staff. He appointed Professor Luigi Einaudi to be his deputy premier and ordered him to stabilize Italian finances. Einaudi was a staunch anti-Fascist and a liberal classical economist who preferred to curb inflation by the traditional methods of restricting credit and raising the discount rate. He ordered an increase in commercial bank reserves and forbade the Treasury to draw money from the state bank without specific legislation. The strategy exceeded expectations. Prices fell, foreign exchange stabilized, speculation declined, and savings increased. Italy began to invest in the raw materials and equipment necessary for industrial growth.

Unemployment, however, remained high, rising to almost two million in 1947. Einaudi held fast to his tight money policy, believing that a stable monetary system would automatically produce investment and growth. Indeed, Italy's recession proved temporary. In 1948, production began to rise and unemployment started to fall. The following year, Italians were producing more than they had before the war. The progress continued. Over the next two decades, the economy grew at more than five percent a year.[76] Einaudi was rewarded for his service by being elected the first president of Italy under the new constitution that went into effect in 1948. He served for seven years (1948–1955).

State Proprietorship. As long as inflation was kept in check, the Christian Democratic leaders saw no need to draft a general plan for the country's economic growth. Besides the state already exercised a commanding position in the economy. Most of the major Italian enterprises were already monopolies or semimonopolies in which the state had a direct financial interest. This situation dated from the Great Depression, when the Fascist government acquired vast amounts of stock in

Italian companies to save them from bankruptcy. In 1933, these holdings were organized into the Institute of Industrial Reconstruction (IIR), a conglomerate that ultimately administered a complex of 125 joint stock companies. After World War II, the institute included about one-quarter of Italy's industrial capital, divided into several main subsidiaries.

One subsidiary, *Finmare*, controlled most of Italy's shipping; *Fincantieri* accounted for four-fifths of its shipbuilding; *Finsider* controlled two-thirds of the country's iron and steel industry; *Fin-Meccanica* directed an assortment of engineering and mechanical companies, including automobile production (Alfa Romeo), electrical appliances, electronics, and optical instruments; *Stet* ran a complex of urban and interurban telephone services; and *Finelettrica* directed (until electricity was nationalized in 1962) one-fourth of the electrical power industry. The state also held the paramount interest in three of Italy's largest commercial banks (the Banca Commerciale, the Banco di Credito, and the Banca di Roma). In addition, it controlled radio and television broadcasting, the Italian Air Lines, and a potpourri of glass, paper, and plastics companies. By continuing the holding company pattern, the state demonstrated a desire to provide direction for economic development and expansion, albeit along rather different lines than French national planning.

Thus, in 1953, the state established another holding company, the National Association of Hydrocarbons (NAH), to administer its oil and natural gas interests. The holding company participated in every aspect of the industry from exploration and drilling to transportation, refining, and marketing. Subsidiaries of this company produced drilling equipment, developed atomic power, and operated a chain of motels. The government acquired control over the entire natural gas production of the Po valley and, under the direction of Enrico Mattei, built this monopoly into one of the most important elements of Italy's postwar industrial expansion. Mattei often acted on his own initiative; he negotiated an agreement with the Soviet Union to have Soviet oil transported by pipeline through Eastern Europe to Italy. Before his death in 1962, he had developed the NAH into one of the world's largest state hydrocarbon industries.

The IIR was a crucial element in promoting Italy's "economic miracle." Its enterprises operated within the framework of the market economy, but they possessed certain advantages not shared by private companies: the government would never allow any of its companies to default or go bankrupt, no matter how much money it lost (shipbuilding and the mechanical industries often had deficits), and state enterprises never had much difficulty obtaining investment capital. Government ownership of industry was a blend of corporatism and capitalism. The state rarely possessed all of the stock in the companies it controlled. The rest was held by private investors, who shared seats on the boards of directors with the government. Through such arrangements, the state could keep the politicians at arm's length while providing the necessary capital investment to create a modern economy. This government-fueled boom in investment encouraged others to put their money to work, including the Catholic church.

The modern wealth of the Vatican came from the assets it had received from the 1929 Concordat with Mussolini. Using this windfall wisely, the church amassed one of the greatest financial empires in Italy and gained control of hundreds of Italian industries. It directed one of the five main units of the State Institute for Industrial Reconstruction, *Finsider*, which rolled about two-thirds of Italian steel and also produced metal tubing, cement, and pig iron.[77] The church's principal investments were in real estate, however. Its *Società generale immobiliare (SGI)* was one of the largest hotel, office, and apartment building promoters in the world.[78] SGI's gross assets were worth around $50 million in 1955; twelve years later, their value had climbed to $170 million.[79]

Italian economic vitality was also evident in great private industrial firms like Fiat for automobiles, Pirelli for tires, Olivetti for office equipment, Beretta for armaments, Montecatini Edison for chemicals, and Snia Viscosa for textiles, to name just a few. In addition, Italy's tourist industry was Europe's largest, providing important seasonal employment for hundreds of thousands of people from Venetian gondoliers to Neapolitan waiters. Through these invisible exports, the Italians lived off their country's natural beauty and the art treasures in its museums. Yet, Italy's economic growth was due as much and perhaps even more to the country's exuberant "home industries." Many of these small-scale enterprises were owned by families who worked for themselves, usually with no more than seven employees.[80] These businesses, which turned out such products as knitted wear, jewelry, household goods, straw hats, machine tools, and precision equipment, worked long hours and kept costs low, enhancing their competitiveness. Moreover, their limited inventories and small outlays for equipment made them better able to take advantage of changes in the market than were larger, more established concerns. Only a small number of these small enterprises operated openly. Italy had one of the largest underground economies in Europe. The output from these under-the-table businesses, which avoided government control and taxation, probably added from 15 to 30 percent to the gross national product.

The popular view of the Italians as a people who spend long hours lounging around in idle chitchat belies the hard work that they performed to make their country one of Europe's industrial powerhouses. However, prosperity was not achieved by hard work alone. The Marshall Plan provided investment capital, but equally important was the boost offered by favorable terms of trade, especially low-cost raw materials, credit, and improved technology. While the standard of living of many Italians was now comparable to that of other Western European countries, Italy had one of the lowest per capita incomes.[81] Wealth was not distributed evenly. The greatest gains in industrial growth came in the area of the country that was already the most prosperous—north of the line traced by the Po River across the Lombardian plain from Piedmont to Venetia with particular concentration on the region around Milan. Italy's poorhouse continued to be the south, the old kingdom of Naples, the *mezzogiorno*, with the islands of Sicily and Sardinia.

The Problem of the South. The area south of Rome contained over one-third of the country's people and land area, but in 1950, it produced only one-fifth of the country's gross national product. The area had few natural resources. The sun had burned its soil; its roads were poor; and its people bore the weight of poverty, superstition, and violence. Its social structure had existed almost unchanged since the Middle Ages. The south was usually the last area to receive government aid, and private investors preferred to place their funds in already established markets where returns were surer and higher. Unification (the *Risorgimento*) had brought few benefits. Efforts to solve the problems of the south never seemed to get much farther than the discussion stage. The people who lived there were distinctly Mediterranean and had a dramatically different social culture and work ethic from that of the northerners. Centuries of foreign domination and exploitation had taught southerners to feel little obligation to serve the public interest or society as a whole; it was said that they put more emphasis on being clever than on being industrious.[82] They had a reputation of being warmhearted and compassionate, but

The more things change, the more they stay the same. Despite the economic miracle, life for many Italians went on much as it had before. Naples contained some of Europe's worst slums.

extremely reluctant to cooperate or compromise. Northerners generally regarded them as unfit for modern society and, indeed, somewhat barbaric. Nevertheless, after World War II, the politicians recognized that, unless something were done to bridge the gap between the two Italies, the prosperity of the entire country would suffer.

In 1950, the Christian Democratic government established the *Cassa per il mezzogiorno*, a credit institution with special authority to promote the social and economic growth of the south. Priority was given to the long-term improvement of agriculture with additional subsidies going to the development of water supplies, transportation, communications, industry, and tourism. The state hoped to entice private industry into the area by creating a modern infrastructure and by agreeing to advance up to 70 percent of the cost of land and equipment for the construction of new factories. The state-controlled Institute for Industrial Reconstruction was required to make three-fifths of its new investments in the south, and from 1950 to 1960, the Italian government spent about $6 billion on development in the area. The results were disappointing. The south was treated as a colony of the imperial industrial north. Frequently, the Christian Democrats used the Cassa per il mezzogiorno as a source of political patronage and dispensed its funds to likely supporters. On the positive side, though, the Cassa helped to reduce the traditional power of the landlords, but it encouraged thousands of young men to move elsewhere.

In 1960, the south had a per capita income of $297 a year, compared to $702 for the rest of the country. With the exception of certain regional complexes, such as the steel plants of Taranto and the petrochemical refineries at Gela, the south was hardly conducive to industrial development. Southern workers were largely unskilled and were ill equipped to work in the new, more highly automated factories, which required less, but more highly skilled, labor than the older plants. In addition, the region lacked the necessary infrastructure to support profitable industry; roads and other transportation facilities were still so poor, for example, that transportation costs were prohibitive. Energy was also a problem. The south lacked the hydroelectric power of the north, and with the discovery of new reserves of methane gas in the north, the energy gap between north and south widened. Agriculture was as backward as industry. It proved easier to break up large estates and decree the elimination of small, marginal farms than to develop the expertise to make the farms productive. Even when agriculture improved, greedy middlemen siphoned off the profits, leaving the producers as impoverished as before. Private industry, reluctant to follow the lead of the government, continued to invest in the more profitable north. Consequently, no matter how much the south improved, the rest of the country continued to grow at a faster rate.

One of the chief forces retarding the economic development of the south was local politics. For example, in western Sicily one of the strongest bulwarks against modernization was the *Mafia*, the criminal organization that sold protection against itself. This society, which developed in feudal times, owed its position and influence to its hold over the island's scarce resources. Its leaders would thus oppose the construction of aqueducts or dams because these projects might endanger the power they had over the peasants who depended on Mafia-controlled artesian wells. The *mafiosi* also ran a wide variety of rackets: they engaged in the recovery of stolen property; allocated monopolies to shopkeepers and artisans; managed the sale of plots in cemeteries; acted as middlemen for fishermen and farmers; and manufactured and sold devotional candles and religious relics. Among the items a Mafia enterprise exported to the United States in 1962 were "twenty suits of armour of Joan of Arc, twenty monastic gowns worn by St. Francis of Assisi, fifty rosaries alleged to have belonged to Bernadette, and . . . the wand carried by Moses when he led the children of Israel into the Promised Land."[83]

After the war, the Mafia took advantage of the power vacuum resulting from the political collapse of Fascism, and assumed direct control of the government in half the villages of Sicily. At first, many mafiosi were promoters of Sicilian separatism. When the central government granted Sicily local autonomy in May 1946, however, many mafiosi became supporters and allies of the Christian Democrats. Younger dons saw association with Italy's main political party as an avenue to new wealth and power. Extorting money from a factory owner or a construction company could be more profitable than terrorizing goat farmers. Owning real estate in Palermo brought more power than controlling olive trees in Corleone. The revenues from drug trafficking were astronomical compared to the sale of bogus religious relics. To these opportunists, the plan to develop the south was simply a means of increasing their wealth and influence, and their affiliation with the Christian Democrats made them virtually immune from prosecution.

But such corruption and terrorism were self-defeating. Sicilians abandoned their homeland in droves—in the decade between 1951 and 1961, some 400,000 left, more than 10 percent of the population. Most of these were young men who went north to find work, leaving behind their women and children and elderly parents. Capital from the mainland also disappeared as investors found the payment of protection a needless business expense. Thus, these sections of Sicily participated even less than other parts of the *mezzogiorno* in Italy's great economic miracle.[84]

POSTSCRIPT   Governments could no longer exist on promises alone. People expected them to provide more services and perform more duties than they had done in the past, chief among these being social security. During World War I, governments had become involved in all aspects of the nation's economy, but after the conflict was over, most states returned to the status quo ante. The result was unmitigated inflation and depression. After 1945, however, recovery would not be left to unpredictable market forces. Growth would be planned. Technocrats, nonelected officials, and experts with power exceeding those of elected officials would resolve economic problems once left to legislatures.

People took the rise of the public sector in stride. They had become used to wartime controls and welcomed the expanded welfare programs. In Britain, Aneurin Bevan hailed the success of the national health program: "Society becomes more wholesome, more serene, and spiritually healthier, if it knows that its citizens have at the back of their consciousness the knowledge that not only themselves, but all their fellows, have access when ill, to the best that medical skill can provide."[85] Yet the best in practice was often a far cry from what was first envisioned. The social services in all countries were overloaded. Furthermore, the benefits of economic growth all too often failed to be distributed equally throughout society. But despite such problems, great reforms all contributed to weakening the old society, making the economies more progressive, and making Europeans less class-conscious.

An immense change had, indeed, occurred. The average standard of living had risen dramatically. The boom created more opportunities for career advancement and, to that extent, broke down barriers to upward social mobility. Furthermore, benefits that were once considered radical were now taken for granted: free education and medical care, unemployment compensation, old-age pensions, family subsidies, and retirement income. During the 1950s, Western European peoples were better off than they ever had been; their rate of economic growth was historically unprecedented. Unemployment virtually disappeared, and income and the benefits of national productivity were more equitably distributed. Vast demographic changes had occurred as people flocked out of small towns and rural areas into the larger cities. By the decade of the 1960s, most Western Europeans had become more "middle class" in their outlook. Although all the major countries continued to have their share of have-nots, the postwar social revolution was based on the assumptions that all people should be guaranteed a minimum level of subsistence and that great differences in wealth were an insult to civilized society.

ENDNOTES

1. Clement R. Attlee, *As It Happened* (New York: Viking Press, 1954), 229.
2. Winston S. Churchill, *The Hinge of Fate* (Boston: Houghton, Mifflin, 1950), 959.

3. During the 1930s, the average output of French workers was consistently inferior to that of workers in most of the other major industrial nations. In 1938, the British worker outproduced the French worker by 22 percent, but American workers outproduced their French counterparts by more than four times.

4. "Constitution of the Italian Republic," Articles 3 and 36 in Norman Kogan, *The Government of Italy* (New York: Thomas Y. Crowell, 1964), 188–89, 193.

5. Winston S. Churchill, *Victory, War Speeches* (London: Cassell, 1946), 189.

6. In the popular vote, no party actually received a majority. Out of 25 million votes cast, Labour won 12 million, the Conservatives and their allies about 10 million, and the Liberals, as usual grossly underrepresented, 2.5 million.

7. The loan was advanced at a scant 2 percent interest. John Maynard Keynes, who negotiated the loan from Washington, managed to get an additional $1.25 billion from Canada. More from the United States would come later. From 1945 to 1950, Britain received slightly over $7 billion in Marshall Plan aid.

8. *Annual Register, 1946*, 101.

9. The practice was discontinued in 1955 when the Exchequer handled all such financing directly.

10. Roy Harrod, *The British Economy* (New York: McGraw-Hill, 1963), 106.

11. *Annual Register, 1946* (London: Longmans, 1946), 28.

12. Kenneth O. Morgan, *Labour in Power, 1951–1954* (Oxford: Clarendon Press, 1984), 151–63.

13. Attlee, *As It Happened*, 233.

14. *Hansard*, 418, col. 1900.

15. *Annual Register, 1947*, 78.

16. The production indexes, using 1937 as 100, were as follows: 94 in 1938; 90 in 1946; 98 in 1947; 109 in 1948; 116 in 1949; and 124 in 1950. *United Nations Statistical Yearbook, 1949–50* (New York: United Nations, 1950), 139.

17. Attlee, *As It Happened*, 290.

18. The Tories and their allies won 321 seats; Labour, 295; and the Liberals, 6.

19. *The Diaries of Sir Alexander Cadogan* (London: Cassell, 1971), 786.

20. *A King's Story, The Memoirs of the Duke of Windsor* (New York: G. P. Putnam's Sons, 1947), 180.

21. Winston Churchill served again from October 1951 to April 1955, Anthony Eden from April 1955 to January 1957, Harold Macmillan from January 1957 to October 1963, and Alex Douglas-Home from October 1963 to October 1964.

22. The Economic Survey for 1951 predicted defense spending would double within the next fiscal year, causing an adverse reduction in the exports of coal and metal products.

23. Harold Macmillan, *Riding the Storm* (New York: Harper and Row, 1971), 181.

24. The figures are based on the number and the capital value of estates over 100,000 pounds on which duty was paid.

25. See Trevor D. Burridge, *Clement Attlee: A Political Biography* (London: Jonathan Cape, 1985); and Kenneth Harris, *Attlee* (New York: Norton, 1982).

26. Attlee, *As It Happened*, 31.

27. See Brian Crozier, *De Gaulle* (London: Eyre Methuen, 1974).

28. Especially, Basil Liddell Hart, Jean-Baptiste Estienne, and Colonel J. F. C. Fuller.

29. General Eisenhower explained this predicament: "If de Gaulle was a loyal Frenchman, [the professional soldiers] had to regard themselves as cowards. Naturally, the officers did not choose to think of themselves in this light; rather they considered themselves as loyal Frenchmen carrying out the orders of constituted civilian authority, and it followed that they officially and personally regarded de Gaulle as a deserter." Dwight D. Eisenhower, *Crusade in Europe* (New York: Doubleday, 1948), 84.

30. Churchill, *The Hinge of Fate*, 958.

31. In 1944, production was about one-third of what it had been in 1937. The output of wheat had been 9,800 metric tons in 1938, but was only 4,210 metric tons in 1945. The output of potatoes was 17,310 metric tons in 1938; 6,060 in 1945. The

output of sugar beets was 7,980 metric tons in 1938; 4,470 in 1945. The output of wine was 60,300 hectoliters in 1938; 28,600 seven years later.

32. From an index of 311 in 1944 to 461 in 1945; 706 in 1946; 1,049 in 1947 and its all-time high 1,664 in 1948. Brian R. Mitchell, *European Historical Statistics, 1750– 1970* (New York: Columbia University Press, 1975), 253, 269, 280, 282, 745.

33. Charles de Gaulle, *War Memoirs, Salvation* (New York: Simon and Schuster, 1960), 8.

34. Ibid., 20.

35. Quoted by Jules Roy, *The Trial of Marshal Pétain* (New York, 1968), 18.

36. Ibid., 67–68.

37. In their first two years of operation, the special courts handled about 125,000 cases of collaboration; thereafter the number of trials diminished rapidly. Around 40,000 accused were found guilty of *indignité nationale* and deprived of their civil and political rights (sometimes the right to live in France) for varying periods. An equal number received prison sentences. Another 2,000 were condemned to death, but less than 800 sentences were carried out. Within five years after the end of the war, most of those still in jail received amnesties. The High Court sat for the last time in July 1949, and soon all trials ceased. They had become too unpopular; few people wanted to be reminded of the inglorious war years.

38. Roosevelt assumed that the British and Americans would administer France until a suitable government was found. In the meantime, he would allow de Gaulle's Committee for National Liberation to assume responsibility for maintaining public order in the areas of liberated France outside the battle zones, but French politics would have to serve Allied strategy. De Gaulle was not content with these arrangements. He had already prepared a list of candidates for every important post in the French government, including prefects in the départements; as the country was liberated, he had these men immediately installed in their assigned positions. In Paris, substitute ministers acted as stand-ins, pending the arrival of proper designates. Thus, de Gaulle hoped to frustrate any plans for an Allied military government. The strategy paid off. After the liberation of Paris, the Allies recognized the fait accompli and accorded de Gaulle the recognition they had previously denied him.

39. The Radical party, which had ruled the parliamentary destiny of France during the last years of the Third Republic, won only 29 seats.

40. De Gaulle, *War Memoirs, Salvation*, 271–72.

41. Ibid., 325.

42. The Communists controlled 182 delegates—the largest single representation.

43. Raymond Aron, "The Political 'System' of the Fourth Republic" in James Friguglietti and Emmet Kennedy, *The Shaping of Modern France* (New York: Macmillan, 1969), 528–29.

44. Its resources were later sold to its employees, and it reemerged as *Le Monde*.

45. These were the *Crédit Lyonnais*, the *Société Générale*, the *Banque Nationale pour le Commerce et l'Industrie*, and the *Comptoire Nationale d'Escompte de Paris*.

46. Alexander Werth, *France, 1940–1955* (New York: Henry Holt, 1956), 223.

47. The government controlled 77 percent of the capital in 1947, 65 percent in 1950, and 56 percent in 1958.

48. But the government continued to exercise restrictions on the allocation of resources in the building industry.

49. Total U.S. aid to France between 1945 and 1962 was $4.7 billion.

50. In 1949, military expenditures amounted to 19 percent of total state spending. By 1952, because of rearmament and the costs of fighting the Indochinese War, the military budget had climbed to 35 percent, or 1,290 billion francs ($3.7 billion).

51. No official statistical surveys of industry and agriculture had been made since the Great Depression. Businesses guarded production figures like peasants hoarding gold Napoleons.

52. By 1953, annual coal production had risen to 56.5 million tons, a 35 percent in-

crease since 1945 and 1.5 million tons above the previous all-time high set in 1929. The steel industry exceeded its 1929 production by 10 percent, and the output of electricity increased over two and a half times, while consumption more than tripled.

53. On the vote over the admission of Germany to the North Atlantic Treaty Organization, the Socialists split 86 for to 18 against, the MRP 16 to 54, the Radicals 61 to 28, the Conservatives 75 to 25, and the Gaullists 38 to 20. Only the Communists, in voting against, displayed complete unanimity.

54. The Viet-Minh had been founded in 1941 to resist the Japanese. Ten years later, it was transformed into the Fatherland Front, an organization that included the Workers' party and the North Vietnamese army.

55. Vincent Auriol, *Journal du Septennat,* vol. 1 (Paris: Armand Colin, 1970), 663.

56. Ibid., 7:406.

57. The only thing that might have saved the French was a massive air strike by the Americans. Secretary of State John Foster Dulles and the Joint Chiefs of Staff favored intervention, but President Eisenhower had no intention of letting himself be dragged into this war.

58. These were largely of French extraction blended with a sizable minority of Spanish, Italians, and other Mediterranean peoples who adopted or, like the Jewish natives, were accorded French citizenship. Very few of the settlers were descendants of the early landed colons who had arrived shortly after the conquest. Most were poor whites who lived in the large European cities. They were members of the lower-middle or laboring classes and strongly resisted any change in the system that allowed them to lord it over the indigenous Muslims.

59. The inquisitorial techniques of the French army were already being compared to those of the Gestapo. One of the victims, Henri Alleg, chillingly recalled one of his tormentors, a blond "youth with a sympathetic face, who could talk of the sessions of torture I had undergone as if they were a football match that he remembered and could congratulate me without spite as he would a champion athlete. A few days later I saw him, shriveled up and disfigured by hatred, hitting a Moslem who did not go fast enough down the staircase." Henri Alleg, *The Question* (New York: George Braziller, 1958), 104–5.

60. Jean Lartéguy, *The Centurions* (New York: Dutton, 1962), 370.

61. The text of the conference on 19 May is in *Major Addresses, Statements and Press Conferences of General Charles de Gaulle* (New York: French Embassy, n.d.), 1–6.

62. On 29 May, René Pleven told a meeting of the Council of Ministers: "Let's not waste words. We no longer have power. The Minister of Algeria can no longer cross the Mediterranean. The Minister of National Defense no longer has an army. The Minister of the Interior has no police." J. R. Tournoux, *Secrets d'état* (Paris: Plon, 1960), 361.

63. *Major Addresses, Statements and Press Conferences of General Charles de Gaulle,* 8.

64. Ibid., 6.

65. Ibid., 2.

66. Tournoux, *Secrets d'état,* 426.

67. "Only the weakest institutions," Wayland Kennet observed, "lay claim to respect by criminal sanctions." Wayland Kennet, *The Montesi Scandal* (New York: Doubleday, 1958), 247.

68. Shepard B. Clough and Salvatore Saladino, *A History of Modern Italy* (New York: Columbia University Press, 1968), 547.

69. Ibid., 544.

70. C. Grant Amyot, *The Italian Communist Party: The Crisis of the Popular Front Strategy* (New York: St. Martin's Press, 1981), 41–51.

71. Clough and Saladino, *A History of Modern Italy,* 547.

72. Kogan, *The Government of Italy,* 52–53.

73. Not the least disappointed at the results was the Eisenhower administration, which

had poured vast amounts of money into Italy to try to help De Gasperi's faction win.

74. Frederic Spotts and Theodor Wieser, *Italy: A Difficult Democracy* (Cambridge: Cambridge University Press, 1986), 158–66.

75. John Clarke Adams and Paolo Barile, *The Government of Republican Italy* (Boston: Houghton Mifflin, 1972), 219.

76. Using 1938 as the base year of 100, the index of industrial production had fallen to 29 in 1945. But in 1949, it was again 100; in 1950, it was 127; in 1954, 189. By the early 1960s, it had climbed to over 300; a decade later, it was over 500. Thus, in the quarter century after the war, it had risen a fantastic eighteen times. Mitchell, *European Historical Statistics*, 357–58.

77. It also held paramount interest in such diverse enterprises as the Bank of Rome, the General Insurance Company, the Industrial and Commercial Finance Company, the Italian Gas Company, the Vittorio Olcess Textile Company, and the Pantanella Flour and Spaghetti Company. Corrado Pallenberg, *Vatican Finances* (London: Owen, 1971), 105–16.

78. The SGI was responsible for the construction of Rome's famed Hotel Cavalieri Hilton; it financed the huge Paris headquarters of Pan American Air Lines at 90 Avenue des Champs Elysées; it constructed and owned the six-hundred-foot skyscraper that housed the stock exchange in Montreal, Canada; and it developed the five blocks of apartments and offices of the luxurious Watergate Hotel complex in Washington, D.C. Ibid., 102–5.

79. Nino Lo Bello, *The Vatican Empire* (New York: Trident, 1968), 907.

80. Two cities where the small business ethic has been practiced for generations are the Tuscan towns of Prato and Carrara. In Prato the main industry is textiles, produced in 15,000 different workshops, many comprising only family members. Carrara, the marble capital of the world, is loaded with artisans who render the models sent to them by artists throughout the world into large-scale sculptures. See Denis Mack Smith, *Italy* (Amsterdam: Time-Life Books, 1986), 59–65, 135–139.

81. In 1955: Italy: $464; the Netherlands: $892; France: $969; Germany: $975; and Britain: $1,152. Shepard Clough, *The Economic History of Modern Italy* (New York: Columbia, 1964), 289.

82. Adams and Barile, *The Government of Republican Italy*, 14–22.

83. Norman Lewis, *The Honoured Society* (London: Collins, 1964), 39–40.

84. Lewis, *The Honoured Society*, 205–6.

85. Aneurin Bevan, *In Place of Fear* (London: Heinemann, 1952), 100.

CHAPTER 20

THE COUNTRIES OF THE COMMUNIST BLOC

PREFACE   The war had disrupted Stalin's drive to create his personal brand of socialism and had exposed the Soviet people to alien influences. The German occupation had temporarily cut off most of European Russia from control by Moscow. The Nazi conquerors, although more adept in terrorizing the local populations than in exploiting discontent with Stalinist rule, did allow the formation of a Committee for the Liberation of the Peoples of Russia to work for the abolition of Communist controls and the emancipation of the Russian minorities. Established in September 1944 under the leadership of Colonel-General Andrei Vlasov, it had no influence on the course of German operations.[1] Nevertheless, it caused great alarm among Stalinist leaders.

Despite the government's efforts to keep contacts with the Allies at a minimum, the war gave many Soviet people an opportunity to see life outside their country and to discover that other European nations had a life-style superior to their own. Stalin warned his people to beware of the tinsel of Western society, but this did not assuage his fear that anyone tainted by outside influences was potentially disloyal. He had already banished certain national minorities whom he could not trust[2] and had ordered returning prisoners of war to be arrested and sent to work camps in the east to isolate them from the rest of the population.

Ideological purity had been one of the casualties of the war. To help maintain morale, the Communist leaders had returned tsarist heroes to the national pantheon; allowed the Russian Orthodox church to reestablish its patriarchate and resume the training of priests; encouraged Soviet writers to extol patriotism instead of Marxist-Leninism; and relaxed membership standards for the Communist party.[3] But as soon as the German armies were pushed from the soil of Russia, the campaign to return to rigid orthodoxy began. Only when the Soviets were firmly entrenched in Eastern Europe did the full winter of repression begin, as the Cold War became a necessary ingredient in Stalin's reassertion of control.

No flight of genius was needed to figure out that the defeat of Nazi Germany would leave the Soviet Union the dominant power in Eastern and Central Europe. When Winston Churchill visited Moscow in October 1944, he tried to uphold the interests of the West. The Soviet armies were then in Romania and Bulgaria. The British prime minister proposed that the Soviet Union "have ninety percent predominance in Romania, for [Britain] to have ninety percent of the say in Greece, and go fifty-fifty about Yugoslavia." Churchill wrote the figures on a sheet of paper, adding Bulgaria, which he gave 75 percent to the Soviets and 25 percent to all the other countries, and Hungary, which would be split fifty-fifty. The prime minister passed the paper to Stalin who, after a moment's reflection, put a large blue check on the document and shoved it back across the table to Churchill.[4]

But the Western powers were not fighting the kind of war that would ensure them political influence in Eastern Europe, nor had their foreign policy ever guaranteed the security of this area. Churchill vainly hoped that by juggling percentages he could induce Stalin to treat the interests of those nations with some measure of generosity. But Stalin was not inclined to tolerate independence. His aims went beyond mere military control. He wanted not only to establish Soviet suzerainty over the area but also to ensure that the political systems of Eastern Europe conformed to Moscow's standard. To this end, he intended to fill their governments with reliable native leaders even though such dedicated Stalinists were currently in short supply. Until more leaders could be developed, Stalin planned to work through controlled coalitions, a process that might take several years.

Communism had not been an important force in Eastern Europe before World War II. Béla Kun's government in Hungary had fallen in 1920 after less than a year in power; a Marxist insurrection in Bulgaria in 1923 had also failed miserably; and in Yugoslavia a conspiracy of junior army officers was easily suppressed in 1932. Communist cells had existed in various Eastern European universities, but nowhere, save in Czechoslovakia,[5] the area's most highly industrialized state, did anything like a mass party following exist. In a sense, however, the absence of strong, native Communist parties and leaders was a blessing in disguise for Stalin. He had no reason to fear competition and could more easily create subservient regimes once the non-Communist parties had been eliminated and proper machinery for control was in place. This process followed a distinct pattern.

THE SOVIET STATE IN THE AFTERMATH OF VICTORY

Rebuilding Communism

Bitter Spoils. The Soviet victory parade on 24 June 1945 had been carefully rehearsed and was performed with precision and élan despite the gray overcast sky and persistent drizzle. "Little streams of rain [trickled] from the peaks of the men's caps, but the unanimous spiritual uplift was so great that none bothered to notice it," wrote Marshal Georgi Zhukov, who took the salute from horseback in front of the Kremlin walls. The jubilation reached its peak when two hundred captured German battle standards were flung on the concrete pavement before Lenin's tomb. But, as Zhukov sadly recalled, so many had died in battle and were not alive "to see this happy day, the day of our triumph."[6]

The Soviet Union's losses were truly horrendous; they were even more appalling than those suffered a generation earlier on the killing grounds of the Marne and Champagne, which had previously set the standard for systematic slaughter. More Soviet soldiers died in the defense of Stalingrad than the Americans lost altogether. The siege of Leningrad took upwards of a million lives. The entire war resulted in the death of some 25 million, at least half of whom were civilians.[7] Seven million soldiers were killed in battle, the rest died as German prisoners. The fighting laid waste to 800,000 square miles of the country's most productive land, leaving 25 million people homeless. Overall, 30 percent of the national wealth was destroyed, but the percentage of steel and coal production lost was close to 60 percent. In the German-occupied areas, 1,209,000 of 2,567,000 residential buildings were destroyed, along with 32,850 large and medium-size industrial enterprises, 82,000 schools, and tens of thousands of hospitals, museums, and stores.[8] Stalin, fearing that other nations might try to exploit Soviet weakness, refused to release damage figures. In the Soviet view, such losses were more than enough justification for the acquisition (since 1939) of 262,000 square miles of new territories with their 22,162,000 inhabitants.

After four years of the bloodiest war in their history, the Soviet people deserved a rest, but Stalin asked them for new sacrifices. There could be no relaxation. Not only must the structures destroyed by the war be rebuilt, but, more importantly, the ideological laxity of the war years must be ended. Stalin took full credit for the salvation of his country and shunted most of the famous army commanders into obscurity, denigrating their achievements to enhance his own reputation. Nikita Khrushchev, Stalin's eventual successor, wrote that "he tried to inculcate in the people the version that all victories gained by the Soviet nation during the Great Patriotic War were due to the courage, daring, and genius of Stalin and to no one else."[9] The official Stalinist history of the war also largely ignored the contribution the Soviet Union's allies made to the defeat of Hitler.

At the war's end, Stalin was sixty-six years old and firmly set in his ways. He still delighted in humiliating his subordinates. Milovan Djilas of Yugoslavia remembered a Kremlin dinner where Stalin proposed that all the guests guess the outside temperature and drink the number of vodkas corresponding to the degrees they guessed wrong. Djilas was appalled and recalled those suppers held by Peter the Great, "at which they gorged and drank themselves into a stupor while ordaining the fate of Russia and the Russian people."[10] Two and a half years later, Djilas met the Communist dictator again and found him worse, ravaged now by "conspicuous signs of his senility." Despite his physical decline, Stalin fought hard to force the Soviet Union back into the orthodox path it had trod during the 1930s. Ever fearful of a threat to his authority, he governed in an atmosphere of suspicion, distrust, and tyrannical subjectivity. Anyone, no matter how high his position, could be apprehended on any charge and had absolutely no legal protection.Marshal Nikolai Bulganin once remarked, after coming home from an evening at the Kremlin, "You come to Stalin's table as a friend, but you never know if you'll go home by yourself or if you'll be given a ride to prison."[11]

A New Wave of Repression. Since the Great Terror, the composition of the Politburo had remained fairly stable; Stalin kept its members in line by playing them off against one another, giving none the chance to establish a power base from which to challenge his leadership. By the end of the war, however, two of its members—Andrei Zhdanov and Georgi Malenkov—had risen to special prominence. Malenkov held important positions in the government, notably on the State Committee of Defense, and Zhdanov had become the first secretary of the Leningrad party organization following Sergei Kirov's assassination. Zhdanov had been transferred to Moscow in 1945 and made a secretary of the Central Committee, thereby becoming the most important man in the party behind Stalin. Zhdanov, an ideological fanatic who had fashioned the cultural doctrine of socialist realism, was now assigned the task of purifying Soviet cultural life from the corrupt influences of cosmopolitanism.

The *Zhdanovschina*, a pejorative term for the new purge,[12] opened with an attack on creative artists, specifically novelists, dramatists, filmmakers, and composers. It then moved to the government bureaucracy, the party cadres, and the military hierarchies. But Zhdanov did not live to carry it through to its conclusion. On 31 August 1948, shortly after he had restored Stalinist orthodoxy to the Soviet Composers' Union, he died of a heart attack. Zhdanov was publicly mourned, the Ukrainian city of Mariupol was renamed in his honor, and the anniversary of his death was officially commemorated. But Stalin shed few tears at his passing. Months before, Stalin had replaced him as his top deputy with Malenkov. Stalin blamed Zhdanov for his failure to turn the Cominform into a major weapon of the Cold War and his failure to prevent the defection of Yugoslavia.[13] In domestic politics, he blamed him for not extending the Zhdanovschina into the biological sciences. Stalin now undertook to rectify this sin of omission.

Stalin considered himself the supreme authority in the field of genetics. In 1938, he had Trofim Lysenko, a Ukrainian agronomist and biologist, appointed president of the Academy of Agricultural Sciences. Lysenko was a strong opponent of those who accepted the chromosome theory of heredity. He explained genetic evolution as the inheritance of acquired characteristics and maintained that heritable change could be accomplished through alteration of the environment. Thus, he claimed that scientists could produce a better crop of winter wheat by subjecting grain to freezing temperatures. Such a contention complemented the ideological belief that human character could be changed and that a new and better Soviet citizen could be produced in a proper social environment.

In 1948, the quack geneticist received full backing from the party Central Committee and instituted a reign of terror among his colleagues in the academy. He ousted everyone who did not endorse his attack on cytogenetics in favor of natural selection. He conceived a grand plan to change the climate of Russia and increase agricultural productivity by planting oak seedlings in dense clusters as protection against the hot dry winds of Central Asia. This "Great Stalin Plan for the Transformation of Nature" was a great fiasco, but until Stalin's death in 1953, Lysenko remained an absolute dictator in the field of biology. The purge was not an isolated event. Not only did it retard and pervert the study of genetics, but it also had a profound effect on the fields of psychology and sociology. It also discouraged experimentation and development in the fields of computers and cybernetics, an omission that would cost the Soviets dearly a generation later.

Official endorsement of Lysenko's pseudoscientific beliefs came at a time when Stalin was aiming his purge more directly at the politicians. During the war, the Communist party had risen to a position of power and prestige that it had not enjoyed since the early 1930s before the great show trials. The party had been instrumental in organizing the successful resistance to Nazi aggression. Its agents were responsible for mobilizing civilian resistance and organizing partisan activity in the occupied areas. Party members joined the army in great numbers—70 percent of the Leningrad organization served at the front and 90 percent of the members from Odessa and Sevastopol. Three and a half million party members, or 60 percent of its total membership, had been in the armed forces.[14] The party's prestige was too high for Stalin's comfort. From 1947 to 1952, he called no sessions of the Central Committee, despite the statutory limit of four months. He ignored the party hierarchy and directed the affairs of state through the Secretariat of the Politburo. The secret police continued to be responsible to him alone.

The purge of the party, directed by Malenkov, began with an attack on the "Leningrad Center." By 1949, he had replaced the entire five-man Secretariat of the Leningrad City Committee and had appointed one of his protégés, Vasili Andrianov, to the position of chairman. Former Zhdanov supporters, such as Nikolai Voznesensky, were weeded out. Stalin opposed Voznesensky's wholesale price reforms and expelled him from the Politburo and stripped him of his post as chairman of State Planning. In Stalin's view, Voznesensky's concept of economic planning did not depend sufficiently on direction from the central administrative authority.[15] Nevertheless, he kept Voznesensky around, occasionally even inviting him to dinner at the Kremlin.[16] Eventually, Stalin tired of the game and ordered Voznesensky arrested and shot. Just as he had done during the Great Terror of the 1930s, Stalin took a personal interest in the investigation and preparation of treason cases. Evidence against the Leningrad organization was fabricated by Lavrenti Beria's deputy, Viktor Abakumov, the one-time head of the NKVD hit squad SMERSH. The verdicts had already been decided.

The purge spread from the party into the government bureaucracy and the armed forces. Stalin demoted and replaced Admiral Ivan Yumashev, the commander-in-chief of the navy; Marshal Nikolai Voronov, the commander of the artillery; Marshal Semyon Bogdanov, the commander of the armored corps; and General Iosif Shikin, the head of the Army Political Directorate. Air Marshal Aleksandr Novikov, denounced by Stalin's pilot son Vasili, was charged with accepting defective airplanes and thrown in prison. Marshal Zhukov was disgraced.[17] In 1949, Stalin separated the party from the government by forcing the members of the Politburo to resign their ministerial positions. Later the same year, he brought Nikita Khrushchev, party boss of the Ukraine, to Moscow to offset the growing influence of Malenkov and Beria. Khrushchev was named First Secretary of the Moscow Party Committee with a seat on the ruling Secretariat. But

Khrushchev realized that nobody, no matter what his position or how much he appeared to be in official favor, was safe. "Everything depended on what Stalin happened to be thinking when he glanced in your direction," he wrote.[18]

Stalin was convinced that Zionism threatened the Soviet Union. His anti-Semitism had recently been inflamed by the demonstrations that greeted Golda Meir when she visited Moscow as the new Israeli foreign secretary in October 1949. Stalin was shocked at the deference the Soviet Jews paid to this representative of a foreign power.[19] On his own initiative, he launched a campaign of "anticosmopolitanism." He ordered Jews purged from the party and the bureaucracy and had Jewish cultural institutions dissolved. He also instituted a quota system to limit Jewish personnel in universities, scientific institutes, and factories. Lazar Kaganovich, who was Jewish by ancestry, directed the campaign; its purpose, not unlike that of the Nazi Nuremberg Laws, was to destroy all Jewish influence in the state, especially in the arts, and to turn Jews into second-class citizens. Important Jewish figures were arrested and sent to detention camps.[20] Many never returned. Stalin directed his greatest fury against those Jews who had not become culturally Russian. He ordered the murder of the Yiddish actor Solomon Mikhoels. Stalin wanted Mikhoels dead because he was a leader of the Jewish Anti-Fascist Committee, which was suspect for having solicited donations from the United States. According to one version, Mikhoels was shot in Minsk during a performance of *King Lear*.[21] The actor's death was then explained as a traffic accident. There were other executions and arrests. Vyacheslav Molotov's Jewish wife was suspected of being connected with the Anti-Fascist League and arrested. Molotov was unhappy, but continued to serve Stalin.

Return to the Five-Year Plans. During the war, overall production had fallen by 23 percent with certain sectors more seriously affected: pig iron had dropped by 41 percent, oil by 38 percent, timber by 48 percent, cement by 66 percent, and sugar by 79 percent. Consumer goods were off 41 percent. Yet the economy began a slow recovery. In the Fourth Five-Year Plan, introduced on 18 March 1946, Stalin gave top priority to repairing the ravaged areas of the country and to rebuilding the country's heavy industry. He believed that only by tripling industrial production over prewar output could the Soviet Union protect itself against capitalist agression. Special emphasis was put on the production of strategic minerals, armaments, nuclear energy, heavy machinery, and transportation equipment. People were required to work a forty-eight hour week. In return, they could expect barely adequate housing and few consumer goods.[22]

The Fourth Plan envisaged a 28 percent increase over the 1940 level in industry, but set only a 7 percent goal in agriculture. Even this modest amount was too ambitious. The war had hit the agricultural sector the hardest. As in the 1930s, agricultural workers were asked to make superhuman sacrifices, but now labor was in even shorter supply. The peasantry had suffered high casualties during the war. Once the conflict was over, higher pay in industry discouraged many survivors from returning to the farms. Much of the Ukraine, the most productive agricultural region, had been a battlefield. Livestock had been slaughtered by the millions. The Germans had destroyed 2,890 tractor stations. As a result of this devastation, collectivization in the Ukraine had broken down, with the peasants appropriating many acres of kolkhoz land for their personal use. To make matters worse, 1946 was a year of drought and disastrous harvests. State planners had little sympathy for the privations suffered by the peasantry. They expected the peasants to fulfill their quotas no matter how unrealistic. Lacking consumer goods with which to encourage the peasants to produce, the regime resorted to force. The planners tried to bring more and more land under cultivation and increase the yield per acre. But to meet these goals, the obligatory deliveries had to be raised, killing incentive. When Khrushchev complained about the famine conditions in the countryside, Stalin accused him of "writing memoranda to prove that the Ukraine was unable to take care of itself."[23] Beneath Stalin's accusation lurked the basic animosity he, and many other Communist leaders, felt toward the peasantry. To Stalin, low productivity contained the seeds of counterrevolution. He preferred to believe his own propaganda about the well-fed peasants happy in their rustic utopia.

As a result of these policies, Soviet agriculture recovered slowly. By 1953, the year Stalin died, gross agricultural output was no higher than it had been in 1940 despite the extension of the Soviet frontiers. Livestock and wheat showed some improvement, but most cereals still lagged behind their earlier levels.[24] All aspects of agricultural production had become politicized. Disputes over whether to plant spring or winter wheat, or whether to plow deeply or not, were part of the struggle for power and were resolved on political, not agricultural, grounds. This politicization only worsened the already sorry state of Soviet agriculture.

City dwellers also suffered deprivations. Since 1940, the average amount of urban living space had declined from 54 square feet per capita to 48 square feet. The standard of living had dropped as well. By 1950, a Soviet laborer had to work almost 1 hour for a quart of milk, 4 hours for a dozen eggs, 22 hours for a pound of tea, 72 hours for a pair of women's shoes, and 376 hours for a man's wool suit. The currency devaluation of 1947 cut drastically into savings and income—currency was exchanged at the rate of 10 to 1, ordinary state bonds at two-thirds, and bank deposits at a third to a half. As a result, people had to work harder to maintain marginal comforts. Still, people no longer lived in canvas tents and the ruins of bombed-out buildings as millions had done at the end of the war.

A Fifth Five-Year Plan began to be drafted in January 1951, but its directives were not revealed publicly until August 1952. Capital and military goods, including a nuclear buildup, remained a top priority with consumer goods coming in last. The start of the Korean War in 1950 had made the production of tanks more important than tractors. The regime blithely pretended that it no longer had a grain problem.[25] In *Economic Problems of Socialism in the U.S.S.R.*, published in 1952, Stalin revealed that political enthusiasm could not transcend the laws of cause and effect, but gave little hope for any fundamental change. He emphasized that the Soviet system would remain committed to rigid socialist planning. Characteristically, Stalin wanted to have it both ways—rigid planning and increased production. He also liked to keep his subordinates guessing; that way, no matter what course of action he eventually chose, he could take the credit if it worked and blame others if it did not.

At the Nineteenth Party Congress in October 1952, the first in over thirteen years, Stalin announced his intention to replace the Politburo and Orgburo with a larger, more flexible "Presidium to the Central Committee of the Communist Party of the Soviet Union." This new group would have twenty-five members and eleven alternates and would include a larger percentage of government administrators as opposed to mere party functionaries. A secret inner bureau, its composition determined by Stalin, would dominate this new enlarged group. Stalin now had a framework in which he could play off the older elite by threatening to replace them with younger, less experienced but more trustworthy *apparatchiki*. The change seemed a prelude to a purge of the old guard. Vyacheslav Molotov and Anastas Mikoyan were already out of favor, and Klementi Voroshilov had to telephone Stalin before each meeting of the Politburo to see if he would be allowed to attend. Beria had to endure the humiliation of not having his associates re-elected to the Central Committee. Two new lieutenants, Malenkov and Khrushchev, played prominent parts in the congress's proceedings. Malenkov gave the main report of the Central Committee, usually the duty of an heir presumptive, while Khrushchev gave the report on the new party rules. Of the 125 members elected to the Central Committee, 79 were new faces. The congress endorsed the Fifth Five-Year Plan, published the previous month, and asserted the need for strict hierarchy in party ranks with added supervisory authority for the top echelons. The secret police were given greater authority over party members.

Stalin now proceeded with the next step, the so-called Doctors' Plot. In November 1952, a group of Kremlin doctors—six of whom were Jewish—were arrested on the charge that they had poisoned prominent Soviet officials, including Zhdanov. Five of the doctors were accused of working for the American intelligence through an international Jewish organization, the other three were supposedly British agents. Beria was berated for not having uncovered the plot sooner. *Pravda*, which publicized the arrests in January 1953, called for tighter discipline and greater vigilance. Building on his campaign of anti-Semitism and counter-espionage, Stalin was clearly setting the stage for a resumption of the Great Terror of the 1930s. How far this would have gone and how many lives it would have claimed will never be known. Stalin died from a cerebral hemorrhage on 5 March 1953 before the second bloodletting could get under way.

Stalin's Heirs

An Interregnum. Stalin's chief henchmen gathered at his dacha at Kuntsevo as soon as they were informed he had suffered a stroke. They arranged shifts for an around-the-clock vigil. Over the next three days, they witnessed the dictator's death agonies.[26] Voroshilov, Kaganovich, Malenkov, Bulganin, and Khrushchev appeared genuinely grieved, but none let his sorrow dispel his fears of the others. Since the Soviet system had no provisions for a formal succession of power, Malenkov and Beria formed an alliance of convenience—they had shared the day shift during the death watch. In the first government following Stalin's departure, they seized the most important posts. Malenkov took the chairmanship of the Council of Ministers and secretaryship of the Communist party, while Beria took the Ministry of State Security and the Ministry of Internal Affairs, now merged into a single organization. The members of Stalin's Presidium were reduced in numbers from twenty-five to ten, most of whom had been in the old Politburo.

The Malenkov-Beria affiliation could not maintain its cohesion—each man was too afraid of the other. The other members of the Presidium also distrusted anyone who held a top position in the party or the government. Malenkov tried to conduct business as usual, but he was hardly capable of filling Stalin's shoes. He lost his post as party senior secretary after only ten days. A five-man directorate replaced him. The most powerful member of this group was Khrushchev, who now became the prime mover in a plot against Beria. The conspirators, looking for a way to arrest the regime's chief policeman, finally decided to do it at a special session of the Presidium in June. They assembled a gendarmerie of eleven Soviet marshals and generals who, at a prearranged signal, entered the council chamber with guns drawn and arrested Beria. The indictment charged Beria with trying "to set the Ministry of Internal Affairs above the Party and Government in order to seize power and liquidate the Soviet worker-peasant system for the purpose of restoring capitalism and the domination of the bourgeoisie."[27] He was sentenced to death and shot. His associates were also liquidated. Subsequently, Beria's full-page picture was cut from the *Great Soviet Encyclopedia* and replaced by an article about whaling in the Bering Straits.

In February 1955, Bulganin replaced Malenkov, Beria's one-time ally, as premier. The campaign against Malenkov had begun two months earlier when his policy of producing more consumer goods at the expense of heavy industry was denounced as a threat to the national security. Khrushchev, with the support of the military leaders, had planned the attack.

The Rise of Khrushchev. The shakeup in the Kremlin gave Khrushchev the opportunity to become first among equals in the collective leadership. However, as important as he became, he was never able to establish a true one-man rule and could never really ignore the views of his colleagues. Khrushchev cloaked his ambition through a policy of de-Stalinization that had already begun shortly after the dictator's death with the termination of the "Doctors' Plot." Those who had not died under torture were released and exonerated. After the execution of Beria, the party reasserted its control over the secret police, taking away its status as a separate government ministry with power over a wide spectrum of economic activities. New laws forbade administrative arrest and disbanded slave labor camps. Coercion continued, but it became more indirect. Now nonconformists were more likely to be deprived of benefits, subjected to education or mass media persuasion, or exiled to mental health facilities than to find the secret police knocking on the door in the middle of the night. Khrushchev also advocated economic reforms, concentrating first on easing restrictions in agriculture. He tried to increase incentives by raising the prices the state paid the peasants for their quotas of food, reducing the taxes on produce from the collective farms' private plots, and allowing the kolkhozy to set their own work schedules. He also started to break up the great centralized administrative empires that had directed agricultural affairs from the remoteness of their Moscow headquarters. He embarked on dramatic projects, most notably one to reclaim 90 million acres of uncultivated land in Kazakhstan and southwestern Siberia, an area as large as all the farmland in Britain, France, and Spain. Khrushchev emphasized that this "virgin lands" scheme could achieve enormous gains at relatively low cost.

Khrushchev's driving force was even more in evidence in February 1956 at the Twentieth Congress of the Communist party when he delivered a scathing denunciation of Stalin and the "cult of the individual." The speech was remarkable for the vehemence of its attack against a man whom many had regarded as a god. Khrushchev tried to depict Stalin's reign of terror as an aberration of Leninism rather than its logical extension. Where Lenin tried to "induce people to follow him without using compulsion," Stalin violated "all existing norms of morality and of Soviet laws."[28] Further, Stalin had left the country unprepared to face the Germans in 1941, contributing to a series of defeats, though he later broadcast the lie that all victories came from his own "courage, daring and genius." Khrushchev also attacked Stalin for more recent sins: his fabrication of the Leningrad Affair, his responsibility for the break with Yugoslavia, his role in the trumped-up Doctors' Plot, and his disastrous agricultural policy. Khrushchev held up to ridicule the myth that all progress in the Soviet Union since Stalin took charge was due to his leadership.

De-Stalinization was not attractive to some members of the current leadership who feared it might pose a threat to their own existence.[29] While Khrushchev had the support of a few trusted associates, the initiative for the policy was undoubtedly his. His decision to destroy Stalin's reputation was a deliberate effort to strengthen the Soviet Union by getting rid of the shackles of the past. Among other things, he intended to replace the hard line in foreign policy with a policy of "peaceful coexistence" with the West. Improving relations with the United States and the countries of Western Europe would allow more resources to be diverted from military needs to improving the basic economy. It would also lead to more cooperative, less adversarial relations with the people of the Eastern bloc. Stalinism had petrified Soviet society making progress and improvement impossible. As long as the Soviet regime continued to make war against its own people, the country would remain backward and would fall progressively farther behind the nations of the European Community. Stalin had showed that the only way to preserve the Communist system was through naked force. Khrushchev thought that political relaxation would promote new levels of prosperity. But the sins of the past could not be purged by only a little reform. Once started, de-Stalinization proved difficult to stop. In time its own irreversible dynamic would ultimately consign Marxist-Leninism to the dustbin of history.

Khrushchev turned anti-Stalinism to his advantage by denouncing his rivals for violating the principles of collective leadership. Thus, the campaign became a means to weaken the power of the Stalinist old guard—Molotov, Kaganovich, and Malenkov. Khrushchev appealed for support to those in the party and the government who had fearsome and bitter memories of the sufferings caused by the Great Purge. His speech was intended to be secret and therefore only for domestic consumption among a privileged few. But, leaked to the world through the Italian Communist party, it had a significant effect on the political life of the Eastern European satellites and provoked crises in Poland and Hungary. The Stalinists in the Presidium and the Central Committee saw these crises as their chance to strike back, and in December 1956, they forced Khrushchev to abandon his efforts to decentralize the economy. But their victory was only temporary.

Khrushchev had been steadily building up personal alliances among the cadres, and he currently had the support of more than one-third of the membership of the Central Committee. The five members elected to the Presidium immediately after the Twentieth Party Congress were his supporters, as was the chairman of the new Committee for State Security, General Ivan Serov, and the general Soviet prosecutor, Roman Rudenko, formerly the Soviet prosecutor at the Nuremberg trials. Most of these men had served Khrushchev when he had been party boss of the Ukraine or first secretary of the Moscow party organization. With them behind him, Khrushchev was ready to counterattack.

On 17 February 1957, he took a step toward the decentralization of industry by pushing through the Central Committee a resolution to reorganize the State Economic Commission. The following May, at a meeting of the Supreme Soviet, he succeeded in abolishing ten National Republic and fifteen Union Republic ministries. This move gained him the support of Marshal Zhukov, who favored decentralizing the economy as a protection against aerial attack.[30] At the meeting of the Presidium in June 1957, Khrushchev's opponents voted seven to four to replace him with Molotov. Khrushchev boldly appealed the result directly to the Central Committee, which reversed the decision of the Presidium by a solid majority. The Central Committee, although nominally superior to the Presidium or the earlier Politburo had never before exercised its power. By supporting Khrushchev, it allowed him to purge the Presidium.

Khrushchev shunted Molotov off to Outer Mongolia as ambassador; he put Malenkov in charge of a hydroelectric station in Kazakhstan; he gave Bulganin the sinecure of chairman of the board of the state bank; and he entrusted Kaganovich with the production of cement in the Urals. Next, he reasserted the position of the Communist party in affairs of state. Emerging as spokesman for the party's liberal wing, Khrushchev advocated producing more consumer goods and presented his policy of peaceful coexistence as an alternative to the Leninist theory of the inevitability of war with the capitalist nations.

Dictatorship in Different Clothes. In February 1958, Khrushchev became both the chairman of the Council of Ministers and the first secretary of the Communist party. But the arrangement did not signal a return to the cult of personality. Although Khrushchev was able to dominate the party, he never succeeded in placing himself above it. Not only did circumstances oppose such a move, but the age of terror had died with Stalin. Khrushchev had a style of leadership that was dramatically different from that of his predecessors—some called him the first Western politician in Russian history.[31] Once he had fought hard for Stalin's General Line, now he was leaving it in ruins. He did not lose his taste for dictatorship, however. He was a pragmatist rather than a theoretician, an opportunist as well as a dreamer. He related well to people and enjoyed giving them practical advice on how things should be done. He had a vulgarity that both repelled and attracted. He once remarked that Stalin had known that the Soviet Union did not win World War II by itself, but had "admitted it only to himself in the toilet."[32] This common touch gave Khrushchev the ability to swap friendly stories with workers, but his bonhomie could be deceptive. For example, he could assure the peasants he was looking after their interests while preparing legislation to convert their collective farms into state farms and to deprive them of their family vegetable plots. Yet, despite his bullying, he was not bloodthirsty. His great shortcoming was his belief that he could bring great changes to the Soviet system without changing the basic nature of the totalitarian state. He, therefore, continued to rely on a command society and to enhance his place in it. He removed the old elements of the Communist party and even replaced most of the old district secretaries with his own men; he reorganized the entire Army High Command until almost every important military office was occupied by soldiers who had served with or under him at Stalingrad during October-December 1942.[33] He did not tolerate politically ambitious generals, including Marshal Zhukov whom he denounced for "Bonapartism" and removed from the Presidium in October 1957.[34] Khrushchev also had his erstwhile ally Bulganin dropped from the Presidium in September 1958. Bulganin had voted against Khrushchev on an important vote the previous year.

During this housecleaning, Khrushchev continued his efforts to alter the Stalinist economic system. The powers of the local economic administration were enhanced. Regional planning councils, or *sovnarkhozy*, were created and made directly responsible for industrial development within their area. Khrushchev scrapped the Sixth Five-Year Plan, adopted in 1956, which was intended to prepare the Soviet Union to surpass the industrial productivity of the United States, and put forth his own Seven-Year Plan at a special, early meeting of the Twenty-First Communist Party Congress in January 1959. In this plan, Khrushchev outlined an ambitious program to increase the supply of consumer goods in order, as he explained, to eradicate class distinctions and ensure the flowering of the spirit of true Communism. Khrushchev, now appearing as the party's leading theoretician, said that with "the victory of Socialism, the USSR [had] entered a new historical period of gradual passage from socialism to communism," and that the new plan would reflect this change by creating "the material and technological basis of Communism."[35] A significant reordering of economic priorities was essential. No longer would heavy industry, iron and steel, and capital goods automatically take precedence. Thus, Khrushchev pitted himself against one of the country's most powerful interest groups—the military-industrial complex or, as the Soviets called them, the "metal-eaters." Khrushchev believed that, with proper reorganization, productivity could be increased in the agricultural and light industrial sectors without seriously curtailing defense and capital goods expenditures. He hoped to accomplish this by increasing the enthusiasm of the Soviet people for work, among other things.

The masses, however, failed to respond, especially those in the rural areas. In the first five years after Stalin's death, the Soviet economy had shown gradual, if unspectacular, improvement. In 1958, wheat production reached a postwar high of 76.6 million metric tons. However, the next five years saw an overall slide of 42 percent. In 1963, the Soviets produced only 49.7 million metric tons,[36] and began to purchase grain from abroad. Khrushchev's boast that he would make the Soviet Union as productive as the United States now seemed a joke. His great virgin lands scheme had been a debacle. Initially, it had appeared to be a success, but after a few years the original nutrients in the soil were exhausted; since they were not replenished with adequate fertilizer, the yields began to tumble. Khrushchev had ignored previous cautions that the Asian steppes were too arid and saline to produce wheat. Now the warnings came back to haunt him. The virgin lands were becoming a dust bowl. The venture was also plagued by the usual Soviet mismanagement, administrative chaos, and decisions based on ideology rather than economics. The Asian steppes lacked the basic infrastructure to accommodate a new agricultural work force, which was mostly "volunteer" labor drawn from the Komsolmol youth organization and army recruits. Furthermore, Khrushchev's plan to make "Agriculture keep step with industry" did not find favor with Gosplan bureaucrats who were reluctant to restrict steel production and armaments so more funds could be allocated to agriculture. Tension with the West over the status of Berlin brought even greater demands for military expenditures.[37] Khrushchev had recognized the necessity of taking bold measures to cure the agricultural backwardness of the Soviet Union, but his policies succeeded only in increasing the polarization between the peasants and the workers who lived in the great industrial centers of the five-year plans. To add to his problems, Khrushchev also ran into trouble in his campaign of de-Stalinization.

The Thaw Was Too Good to Last. At the Twenty-Second Party Congress in 1961, Khrushchev continued his attack on Stalin's heritage. He revealed that Stalin was directly responsible for the assassination of Kirov in 1934 and that false documents supplied by the Nazis had led to Marshal Mikhail Tukhachevsky's execution. Khrushchev also renounced Stalin's thesis that the closer a society came to Communism, the more intense its class struggle became—a 1937 thesis that served to justify the Great Terror. Khrushchev openly attacked certain Soviet leaders, namely, Malenkov, Molotov, Voroshilov, and Kaganovich, for their participation in the crimes of the Stalinist era. The Congress voted to remove Stalin's embalmed body from Lenin's tomb on Red Square. During the debate D. A. Lazurkina, one of the delegates, claimed she had a visitation from Lenin. "Yesterday I consulted Ilyich as if he were alive in front of me, and he told me, 'It is unpleasant for me to lie next to Stalin, who brought so much misfortune to the Party.' "[38] (Stalin was reburied in a plot in front of the Kremlin wall.) The Congress also decided to replace one quarter of the membership of the Presidium and the Central Committee at all regular elections. This move was intended to winnow out the old leaders and prevent the return of a personality cult. Khrushchev also promised that the Soviet state would begin to wither away and be replaced by communal autonomy. As part of this withering away, the coercive state organs would disappear. Nevertheless, the Communist party would still direct the economy.[39] But Khrushchev's goals were contradictory. The Marxist-Leninist system and the authority of the party could not be preserved without centralization, coercion, and punition.

The decline of Stalinism promised an end to socialist realism and a lessening of state interference in the cultural life of the nation. The novelist Ilya Ehrenburg described the period as "the Thaw." And the poet Yevgeni Yevtushenko wrote that it was "a rough spring, a difficult spring with late frosts and cold winds, a spring which takes a step to the left, then a step to the right, then a step back, but which is certain, nevertheless, to go on and take two or three steps forward."[40] By 1961, Yevtushenko was widely regarded, both inside and outside his country, as the chief spokesman of the post-Stalinist generation of young writers. In that year he published *Babii Yar*, a poetic memorial to the thousands of Jews who were murdered by the Nazis in a ravine outside Kiev. The Soviet Union had never recognized that the Jews suffered more at the hands of the Germans than any other national group. In pointing out that the massacre site was marked by no special memorial—it was, in fact, currently being used as a garbage dump—Yevtushenko was actually criticizing the anti-Semitism that was still rampant in the Soviet Union.[41] Yevtushenko claimed Khrushchev had personally authorized the poem's publication.

One of the highlights of the thaw was the publication of *One Day in the Life of Ivan Denisovich*, the sensational novel by Aleksandr Solzhenitsyn, that first appeared in the November 1962 issue of the literary journal *Novy Mir*. The book's action takes place, with true classical unity, on a single day and in a single place in a Siberian concentration camp in January 1951. The hero-narrator, Ivan Denisovich Shukhov, is in the eighth year of a ten-year sentence for espionage. In 1942, Shukhov had been captured by the Germans, escaped, and rejoined the Soviet army. The authorities believed the Germans intentionally released him to betray his country. Shukhov confessed because he felt he had no other choice: "If he did not sign, he was as good as buried. But if he did, he'd still go on living a while, so he signed."[42] Shukhov's companions in prison have also been sentenced for crimes they did not commit. Thus, the prison becomes a microcosm for the entire Stalinist state. The book is filled with references to the forced collectivization of the peasants, the mass liquidation of the kulaks, the systematic persecution of the ethnic minorities and religious groups, the Great Purges of the 1930s, and the return to repression after World War II. Thus, Solzhenitsyn exposed the basic injustices of Soviet society in a way never before allowed in print. As with *Babii Yar*, the novel's publication was supposedly authorized by Khrushchev.

Khrushchev, however, was under tremendous pressure from colleagues who were ill at ease with such revisionism and feared its consequences. Khrushchev himself was having second thoughts. He saw that liberalization could ultimately undermine the power of the Communist party and his control over it. The official counterattack began on 1 December 1962, when Khrushchev and some of his cronies visited an art show sponsored by the Moscow section of the Artists Union. Most of the canvases were painted in the officially approved socialist realist style, but an adjoining room contained a special display of abstract art. When Khrushchev saw these paintings, he became furious and launched into an obviously premeditated tirade. He wanted to know how painters dared perpetrate such an outrage.

In the next several months, musicians and writers, as well as artists, came under attack. But the new hard line could not save Khrushchev from his own transgressions and contradictions, specifically, from his failed agricultural policy and setbacks in foreign affairs.

His virgin lands scheme had wasted precious resources to little effect. He had failed to resolve the conflicts over economic priorities—the "metal eaters" and militarists versus the decentralizers and consumer goods advocates. He had allowed relations with China to deteriorate and had embarked on an unpopular rapprochement with West Germany. The base of Soviet authority in Eastern Europe had considerably deteriorated. Many of the Soviet Union's problems transcended Khrushchev's personal responsibility, but his contradictory policies hardly helped. He had abandoned Stalin's collision course with the West in favor of peaceful coexistence, yet his last great adventure brought the country to the brink of war with the United States over the installation of missiles in Cuba. Khrushchev's restless energy could not compensate for his lack of coherence and efficiency. The world press liked to see him in action, banging his fists on tables and taking off his shoe at the United Nations, but his colleagues found these antics an embarrassment. Khrushchev knew that he would either have to carry out another purge of the Presidium or risk losing his position. He therefore planned a new plenary session of the Central Committee to launch a vast administrative and power reorganization. However, in October 1964, before the session could take place, his opponents toppled him from power. Leonid Brezhnev replaced Khrushchev as party first secretary, and Aleksei Kosygin became chairman of the Council of Ministries. These men, who came from the party apparatus, had benefited by the elimination of the Stalinist old guard; Khrushchev had brought them to prominence, appointing Brezhnev president of the Soviet Union and Kosygin head of the Gosplan.

On 17 October 1964, *Pravda* denounced Khrushchev for his "hare-brained schemes, half-baked conclusions and hasty decisions and actions, divorced from reality; bragging and bluster; attraction to rule by fiat; unwillingness to take into account what science and practical experience have already discovered." He, henceforth, became a nonperson and lived out the rest of his life in virtual isolation. He was not buried in Red Square, but nevertheless was interred in a prestigious Moscow cemetery that also holds the remains of Chekhov and Gogol.

COMMUNIST HEGEMONY IN EASTERN EUROPE

The Stalinization of Eastern Europe. The process had a textbook quality. In most countries it was carried out in three phases. The first began with the organization of a coalition of anti-Fascist parties. These groups ran the political gamut from Communist to socialist, from peasant to middle class. Most of the non-Communist groups respected political freedoms. The Communists also pretended to favor a representative democracy, while insinuating their members and supporters into positions of responsibility, particularly in the Ministry of Interior and armed forces. This initial phase could last anywhere from six months, as in Romania and Bulgaria, to more than three years, as in Czechoslovakia. Some countries, like Poland and East Germany omitted this phase. The second stage usually occurred when the Communists felt they were sufficiently well entrenched to go on the offensive, first against all political groups outside the coalition and then against the non-Communist parties within. In this phase, non-Communist parties ostensibly shared power with the Communists, but in fact their independence was in the process of extinction. Their leaders were in prison or had been transformed into obedient stooges. In the third or last phase, the Communists ruled alone, having completely destroyed opposition of every kind throughout the country.[43]

The Soviets assured subservience and uniformity through a series of institutions backed up by the presence of the Red Army, which had liberated most of Eastern Europe from the German yoke. The Communist Information Bureau, established in 1947 as a counter to the Marshall Plan, replaced the dissolved Comintern as an agency for controlling foreign Communist parties. Its new mission, foreshadowed in April 1945 by the French Communist leader, Jacques Duclos, in an article in *Cahiers du Communisme (Communist Notebooks)*, was to reorganize international Communism to prepare for a resumption of revolutionary militancy under a tightly centralized bureaucracy. The Soviet embassies provided most of the on-the-spot supervision; the ambassador usually acted in the capacity of a proconsul with the authority to use military force should that prove necessary. Educational, social, political, and economic systems became monotonously standardized. The constitutions followed the Soviet model.

The Soviets looked on Eastern Europe both as a security zone and as a storehouse of goods and services to be exploited for the benefit of the crippled Soviet economy. The Soviets insisted on uniformity. They established five-year plans, demanded the nationalization of basic industries, and insisted on the collectivization of agriculture. In 1949, they established the Council for Mutual Economic Assistance, or Comecon, to make sure that all the economies of the bloc were geared first to the needs of the Soviet Union and then to the demands of the area as a whole. Through a series of bilateral treaties, the Soviets bound the foreign trade of each satellite directly to the Soviet Union. The satellites were obliged to consult directly with their Soviet masters on all important questions. The Soviets insisted on frequent purges in the local Communist parties to ensure constant loyalty and prevent deviation from the party line. Opposition, real or imaginary, resulted in imprisonment or death.

Bulgaria

A Smooth Takeover. The process of Stalinization was most readily accomplished in Bulgaria where the people were traditionally friendly toward Russia and had never declared war on the Soviet Union. On 9 September 1944, the day after the Red Army entered the country, the Fatherland Front (a collection of left-wing elements including the Agrarian Union, Social Democrats, Communists, and some progressive republicans known as the Zveno) overthrew the pro-German Sofia government and began a thorough purge of the former ruling classes. Kimon Georgiev, a leader of the Zveno and a former premier (1934), headed the new government, but the Communists took the posts of vice-premier and minister of the interior (the department in charge of national police) and used them as a base from which they proceeded to capture power. Interior Minister Anton Uygov staffed the national gendarmerie with Communists and put party members into provincial and village administrations. These appointees then began harassing the non-Communist parties in the Fatherland Front. Opposition newspapers were closed, their leaders were arrested, and the lives of their party members were threatened.

Comintern-trained Georgi Dimitrov, one-time defendant at the Reichstag fire trial, directed the campaign from Moscow. As the Communists completed their control of the Fatherland Front, they intensified the attack on all opposition parties, breaking up their meetings and terrorizing their supporters. The Communists bluntly warned that all those who did not vote for Communist candidates in the elections of 18 November 1945 would experience another Saint Bartholomew's night, a reference to a bloody massacre of French Protestants in the sixteenth century. Dimitrov returned home to preside over the last stages of the takeover. He had not set foot in his country for twenty-two years.

When the national elections were held in 1945, the Fatherland Front claimed it captured 88 percent of the vote, making it appear that a vast majority of the voters clearly favored a Communist-dominated, Soviet-supported government. The British and Americans protested this rigged election as a gross violation of the Declaration of Liberated Europe and refused to recognize the validity of the results. Stalin, therefore, promised that he would "advise" the Bulgarian government to include two representatives of opposition parties. But nothing really changed. The West accused the Soviets of a lack of good faith, but withheld recognition only until a Bulgarian peace treaty was signed in February 1947.

The Creation of a One-Party Dictatorship. In December 1945, the Communists declared that the Fatherland Front was the real leader of the people since it ensured "the possibility of being masters of their own destiny." They insisted ominously that "vigilance of the people against its open and hidden enemies must increase."[44] All free political expression now disappeared. In September 1946, a referendum scrapped the monarchy in favor of a republic, and Georgiev was removed as premier. Most of the key leaders of the Socialist party and the Agrarian Union were placed under arrest.

The following month, on 27 October, elections were held for a National Constituent Assembly. The Fatherland Front won by a landslide, and Dimitrov at last emerged from behind the scenes to take charge himself. Political repression intensified. In June 1947, Nikola Petkov, head of the Agrarian Union, the most popular and best-known opposition leader in the country, was arrested and charged with conspiring with Bulgarian army officers to overthrow the government. His trial was conducted in a style reminiscent of the old Moscow purge trials, complete with Communist-controlled groups all over the country demanding his death. The Sofia Miners' Union said that capital punishment would inspire the miners to "harder work and greater achievement in the production field." The court obliged, and the sentence was carried out on 23 September.

By the end of 1947, all non-Communist parties had ceased to exist. Moscow-trained functionaries ran the government ministries. The new Bulgarian constitution mirrored the 1936 Soviet constitution. On 28 December 1947, a far-reaching program to control the entire economy began with the nationalization of all mines and industries and the collectivization of agriculture. By the end of the following year, the last year of the Bulgarian Two-Year Plan, very little private trade remained. The Bulgarian Communists proved so thoroughly Soviet in style that when Dimitrov died in July 1949, he was embalmed, like Lenin, and his corpse was put on public display in the old Sofia cathedral.[45]

Romania

A Tradition of Russophobia. The Communist takeover in Romania proved troublesome and took longer to accomplish than in Bulgaria. Part of the problem was the endemic suspicion and mistrust that the Romanian people had for anything Russian: ill feelings toward the Russians had existed since the formation of the

Romanian state in the nineteenth century.[46] The Romanians had already abandoned their ties with the Axis by the time the Red Army entered Bucharest in August 1944. A group of generals, headed by General Constantin Sănătescu, ran the government. Sănătescu had come to power as a result of a coup against the dictatorship of Marshal Ion Antonescu. King Michael announced the end of the war against the Allies and, on 25 August, declared war on Hitler. The Romanian army, which had already suffered about 500,000 casualties fighting the Soviet Union, now joined the Red Army in the assault against the Germans in Hungary and Slovakia. Thus, Romania helped the Soviets extend their control over Central Europe. In appreciation, Stalin gave King Michael the Soviet Union's highest decoration: the Order of Victory.

At the time of King Michael's coup, the Romanian Communist party, which had been officially outlawed since 1924, had perhaps 1,000 members; the number of hard-core Stalinists or "Muscovites" was considerably smaller and included a sizable number of non-Romanians. Nevertheless, the Soviets began imposing their authority on the country. Many areas were currently ruled by the Red Army either directly or through local appointees, and only in Wallachia and southern Transylvania was the old administration still functioning. In December, the Soviets denounced both the premier and the minister of interior for being soft on Fascism and forced their resignations. Both posts were then given to the elderly, more reliable General Nicolas Radescu.

Shortly after the Yalta Conference in February 1945, Stalin sent his chief hatchet man, Andrei Vyshinsky, Soviet deputy foreign minister, to Romania to pressure King Michael into replacing the present government with one totally controlled by the Communists. By this time, the Communists had infiltrated the other political parties, especially the Ploughman's Front. This agrarian party already had a number of crypto-Communists who talked "democracy" and "social and political reform" while pressing forward with their agenda of Stalinization.

A Stalinist Agenda. On 24 February 1945, a clash in Bucharest between Communist and non-Communist workers gave the Communists a pretext for occupying the headquarters of the Romanian army and disarming the local garrison. Vyshinsky forced King Michael to create the National Democratic Front, amalgamating the Communists and the left-wing Social Democrats with the Ploughman's Front and some liberals. Petru Groza of the Ploughman's Front, headed the new cabinet, which emerged on 6 March. The Communists took charge of the three crucial ministries of Interior, Justice, and Foreign Affairs. Only two of the cabinet posts were held by members of "bourgeois" parties. This coalition government lasted for the next two years.

During this time, the government enacted a major land reform and nationalized the National Bank of Romania, but the Soviets devoted most of their attention to gaining control of Romania's natural resources, particularly its petroleum, timber, and chemicals. They accomplished this through special agencies, or *Sovroms*, that had been created by economic and commercial treaties between Romania and the Soviet Union. At the same time, the "home" Communists, led by Party Secretary Gheorghe Gheorghiu-Dej, worked to gain uncontested control of the Romanian Communist party. Once the peace treaty was signed in February 1947, and the British and Americans had recognized the Romanian government, the Stalinists abandoned all restraints. They muzzled, then dissolved, the opposition parties, arresting their leaders and trying them for conspiracy. They fused the non-Communist parties of the National Democratic Front with the Communist party.

In November 1947, they forced the king to abdicate, and Romania became a People's Republic with a Soviet-style constitution. Stalin continued to push for the complete subordination of the Romanian economy to the demands of the Soviet Empire. He was clearly more interested in exploiting this former enemy state than in creating socialism.[47] But such organized looting would eventually backfire. The Romanian Communist leaders were in no position to object, but they were still nationalists and became increasingly uncomfortable in their role of servitude.

Poland

Free Soviet-Style Elections. Russia had been meddling in Polish affairs since the Poles came into existence. But Stalinization was, of course, a more recent form of intervention. It began with the Soviet invasion of eastern Poland on 17 September 1939 and continued with the subsequent partition of the country in accordance with the secret treaty with Hitler. This period lasted until June 1941, when the Germans launched Operation Barbarossa. During that year and a half, the Poles were given a taste of the meaning of Soviet tutelage: the Communists deported about 10 percent of the area's inhabitants and liquidated many of the old Polish elites, including the murder of thousands of army officers and other leaders in Katyn Forest.

In 1944, before the end of the war with Germany, the Soviets established their own Polish government in exile, the National Council of the Homeland, which was completely dominated by the Polish Communist Workers' party. On 22 July 1944, after the liberation of some Polish territory by the Red Army, the Polish Committee of National Liberation was set up and declared itself the unique representative of the will of the Polish people. At the end of the year, it became the provisional government and was immediately recognized by the Soviet Union. But because Roosevelt and Churchill at Yalta insisted upon broader representation, the council was expanded to include more non-Communists. Even so, the Polish Communists remained very much in charge, controlling the police and the armed forces. In March 1945, the Soviets arrested sixteen leaders of the Polish underground who had been loyal to the London government in exile. The men were taken into custody while attending a Soviet-sponsored conference to determine the composition of a government of national unity; they had been invited to the conference under a pledge of safe conduct. All sixteen were charged with subversion against the Red Army and sent to Moscow for trial. The British and Americans protested that such conduct violated the Declaration of Liberated Europe, but Stalin told the Western leaders to mind their own business, adding that he resented being dictated to.[48] He would later explain that the arrests were necessary because the Red Army was "forced to protect its units and its rear-lines against saboteurs and those who create disorder."[49]

The Process of Communization. The Soviets also began bringing the areas taken from Germany under Communist control. They had established a separate Ministry of Regained Territories, entrusted directly to the general secretary of the Polish Communist party, Wladyslaw Gomulka, who had spent the war years in the Polish underground. Thus, even before the complete Soviet takeover of Poland, there already existed a Communist state within the state. Moscow insisted that the usual pattern of Stalinization be followed. Non-Communist parties were harassed, especially those formerly associated with the London government in exile. Opponents were tried and imprisoned or executed. The socialist parties were fused with the Communists into a United Workers party.

Elections took place in January 1947, as a pro forma honoring of the promises in the Potsdam accords, but the results were shockingly fraudulent. Many of the campaign workers of the important Peasant party had already been put in jail before election day. The party was awarded only 28 seats, compared to the 394 accorded the Communist-Socialist coalition. Peasant party leader Stanislaw Mikolajczyk was denounced as an agent of Western imperialism. In October, fearing he would be arrested, he fled the country. The British and Americans protested, but without effect. The elections led to the adoption of a Soviet-style constitution.

Gomulka, although a willing actor in the creation of a one-party state, believed that the Polish Communists should be allowed to chart an independent road to socialism. He therefore opposed compulsory collectivization of agriculture and did not approve the Cominform's supervision of Polish domestic affairs. This stand brought him into direct opposition to the Stalinist group headed by Boleslaw Bierut and Edward Ochab. The Stalinists accused Gomulka of being a bourgeois reactionary and stripped him of his party and government posts and in 1951 put him under house arrest. By then the Polish Communist party had become a faithful replica of the Soviet party. Gomulka's fate was not unique; the purge of deviationist elements eventually encompassed many other comrades who also wanted independence from Soviet tutelage. The housecleaning was carried out by the Polish security police under the direction of the NKVD, but proved less bloody than similar purges in other Eastern European countries.

The government now headed by Bierut pushed for the complete integration of the Polish and Soviet economies. All nonparty organizations were either dissolved or were coopted by the new regime. Only the Catholic church retained any measure of independence. Consequently, the Stalinists launched a campaign of increasing intensity against the church and its institutions. The Stalinists nationalized the church's publishing houses, dissolved its youth groups, secularized its schools, seized the assets of its charitable organization, *Caritas,* and confiscated all its estates over fifty hectares without compensation.

In April 1950, the Polish Catholic church had signed an agreement with the Communist government; in this pact, the first of its kind, the church promised to respect the authority of the state in temporal matters in exchange for the preservation of its jurisdiction in spiritual matters, including recognition of the authority of the pope. The state soon began to violate this concordat, however. It restricted religious instruction, harassed priests, claimed the right to make church appointments, and demanded that all church dignitaries take an oath of loyalty to the Communist state. Those who refused were arrested including Stefan Cardinal Wyszynski who was confined to a monastery in 1953. Despite the persecution, the church remained, as in the past, a symbol of Polish independence. Support for Catholicism became a form of political protest against the regime.[50]

Hungary

A Losing Battle. In Hungary, the Soviets initially displayed a sense of moderation. Hungary became a republic again in 1946 and was directed by a non-Communist coalition until 1947, while the Communists marshalled their forces. Stalin's spearbearers, Ernö Gerö, Imre Nagy, and Matyas Rákosi, returned from Moscow to join forces with local Communist underground leaders, such as Laszlo Rajk and János Kádár. The Communists also augmented their political strength through an aggressive policy of recruitment—from a few thousand adherents, party membership soon reached 200,000—and through associations with other parties. Thus, they formed an alliance with the Social Democrats and tried to do the same with the agrarian Smallholders party.

The Smallholders had gained immense popularity because of their commitment to land reform, which had broken up the estates of the Magyar gentry and created hundreds of thousands of new peasant proprietors. Even in areas with working-class majorities, the gains of the Smallholders were impressive. In the Budapest municipal elections of 2 October 1945, they won 51 percent of the vote, demonstrating the proletariat's lack of confidence in the Communist–Social Democrat ticket. The chairman of the Allied Control Commission, Marshal Klimenti Voroshilov, became alarmed and summoned the leaders of the Smallholders party to a meeting in an attempt to limit the number of parliamentary seats the Smallholders would be allowed to win in the forthcoming national elections on 4 November 1945. Voroshilov first proposed 40 percent, but when the Smallholders protested, he raised it to 45 percent. Again the Smallholders refused. Voroshilov said his last offer was 47.5 percent. The Smallholders still found it unacceptable and refused any preelection deal, but promised vaguely to work with the other parties of the "Independence Front" to create a common policy.

The Smallholders won 57 percent of the total seats in parliament. The Communists and Social Democrats each got only 17 percent. But despite their majority, the Smallholders were pressured into forming a coalition ministry in which the Communists obtained the key Ministry of Interior with control of the police. The result was predictable.

The Extinction of the Opposition. The Communists gradually assumed control of the other main instrumentalities of power: the armed forces and the trade unions. They denounced the Smallholders party as a haven of Fascists and bourgeois reactionaries and vilified its general secretary, Béla Kovács. In February 1947, he was arrested and never seen alive again. Presumably, he was executed, but not before he had been forced to denounce his friend Premier Ferenc Nagy for espionage against the Soviet Union. The allegation was made public in May, when Nagy was on holiday in Switzerland. The Communists demanded Nagy's resignation and threatened to arrest his son unless he complied. Nagy agreed, but said he would do so only after the boy had joined him in Switzerland. Soviet Foreign Minister Molotov claimed he did not understand the concern of the British and Americans, since events in Hungary did not threaten any Allied interests.[51]

The Communists extended their attack against the Smallholders to include all other political groupings. At the start of 1948, the only non-Communist party still in existence was the Social Democratic party. Its independence ended in June, when it was forced to merge with the Communists into the newly named Hungarian Workers party. The attack on the political opposition was accompanied by an offensive against the Reformed Calvinist, Evangelical Lutheran, and Roman Catholic churches. The regime mobilized and pressured the faithful, confiscated church property, and closed down church schools. The police maintained a record of those who attended religious services. To show that nobody was safe, the regime arrested Joseph Cardinal Mindszenty, the primate of the Hungarian Catholic church. The regime charged him with conspiring to restore the landlord-capitalist order and the Habsburg regime. In February 1949, a people's court sentenced the cardinal to life imprisonment for treason and espionage. He had also been charged with currency violations.

The creation of a one-party state and Soviet domination of Hungary were now virtually complete. In April 1949, new parliamentary elections were held. No opposition candidates appeared on the ballot. The Communists now began an attack against all those within their ranks whom they felt were not sufficiently Stalinist. One of the first to be arrested was the foreign minister Laszlo Rajk.

Rajk's Communist credentials were impeccable, but he had two failings: he was a personal rival of Rákosi, and he had not been an émigré in Moscow during the war. The Stalinists accused Rajk and his associates of acting as agents of Tito of Yugoslavia and the Western imperialists. His trial in September 1949 was worthy of the great Stalinist show trials of the 1930s. The witnesses had been interrogated constantly to make sure they would follow the prosecution's script. Rajk and his codefendants all confessed. Rajk, à la Lev Kamenev, even declared in advance that he considered the sentence of the court to be a just one.[52] He was sentenced to death and hanged. Thus, Rajk fell victim to the very police state he had helped to create. On his orders, many of the leaders of the Smallholders and Social Democrats had been tortured and sent to the scaffold. In appearance, however, he was far from odious. Rajk was tall and handsome, almost courtly; he had a solid reputation based on his service in the Spanish Civil War and in the anti-Nazi underground. Rákosi, in contrast, was short and dumpy, with a bullet head that sat on his shoulders as if he had no neck; generally, he was coarse and rude, although he could be charming when he tried. He had spent the war in Moscow and owed his position to Stalin's favor. The two men were a study in contrasts, but contrasts in evil.

Czechoslovakia

A Tradition of Accommodation. The Czechs tried to ward off Soviet interference by voluntarily including Communists in the postwar government. Communism had a stronger popular following here than in any neighboring state. The National Front was composed entirely of parties in existence before 1938, namely, the Social Democrats, Communists, and the People's Catholic party. The Communists controlled the crucial Ministry of Interior, but the voluntary withdrawal of the Red Army in December 1945 left the local party without the military backup that had been critical for a takeover elsewhere.[53] But of all the Eastern countries, Czechoslovakia seemed to present the best chance for the Communist party to come to power legally. In the first postwar parliamentary elections, held by free and secret ballot in May 1946, the Communists managed to win an impressive 38 percent of the popular vote, receiving support from both working-class and agricultural districts. President Edvard Beneš therefore invited party leader Klement Gottwald to be premier. The Moscow-trained Gottwald formed a ministry with nine Communists and seventeen non-Communists.

Beneš, one of the principal architects of Czech democracy, apparently had been under no specific Communist pressure to appoint Gottwald, but did so in the hope of maintaining his country's independence within the Soviet orbit. He realized that Czechoslovakia's ultimate fate was directly related to the postwar relationship between the Soviet Union and the Western powers. If these two power blocs could cooperate, then Czech democracy could survive. He also hoped that the Communists "having already come so far on the way to real power [would] understand that they must impose some restraint on themselves, that while they need not retreat anywhere they must have the patience to choose the correct moment for continuing in a reasonable way along the evolutionary road."[54]

In 1943, Beneš had forestalled the creation of a Moscow-sponsored Czech exile government by going to Moscow to conclude a Soviet-Czechoslovak Friendship Treaty in which both states agreed "to maintain close and friendly co-operation after the re-establishment of peace and to regulate their actions according to the principles of mutual respect of their independence and sovereignty and non-interference in the internal affairs of the other signatory."[55] Throughout the negotiations, Beneš had been repeatedly assured that the Soviets were not interested in interfering in Czech affairs. He was therefore confident that his country would be allowed to exist as a bridge between the two superpowers. Soon, however, Stalin let the Czechs know their optimism was misplaced.

When the Czechoslovak government unanimously accepted the invitation of the United States to participate in the Marshall Plan for European Economic Recovery on 7 July 1947, Stalin informed Gottwald, who was in Moscow at the time with other Czech officials, that the real aim of the Marshall Plan was to "create a Western bloc and isolate the Soviet Union with loans." Stalin warned that he would regard Czechoslovak participation as a "proof to the people of the U.S.S.R. of the fact that [the Czechs] have allowed [themselves] to be used as an instrument against the U.S.S.R., something which neither the Soviet public nor the Soviet Government could tolerate."[56] The Soviet leader insisted that the invitation be rejected. The Czechs obediently complied.

The Coup in Prague. Henceforth, Stalin resolved to take no chances. As it no longer seemed likely that the Czech Communists would capture a majority of the votes in a free election, he approved the usual tactics of subversion, beginning with an attempt by the Communist Interior Minister, Vaclav Nosek, to purge the National Police Force. On 12 February 1948, the non-Communists in the cabinet demanded that this subversion cease, but Nosek, backed by Premier Gottwald, refused. On 21 February, twelve ministers from the Catholic, National Socialist, and Slovak Democratic parties resigned in protest; they anticipated that President Beneš would refuse to accept their resignations, thereby forcing the Communists to back down. But Beneš feared that if he intervened, the Communists would start an insurrection, providing the Soviets with an excuse to enter Czechoslovakia to restore order.

Meanwhile, on 19 February, Soviet Ambassador Valerian Zorin had arrived in Prague to arrange a *coup d'état*. Communist "Action Committees" and trade union militias were hastily organized, armed with new rifles, and let loose in the streets. They seized the Czech radio network and threatened a general strike unless Beneš formed a new government, giving the Communists an absolute majority of the posts. Beneš caved in. On 25 February, he appointed a Communist-controlled government with Gottwald retaining his post as premier. The only important post occupied by a non-Communist was the Foreign Ministry, which was given to Jan Masaryk, the son of the founder of the republic. Masaryk had decided to stay on in "the faint hope that he would be able to soften the impact of Communist ruthlessness for a short time, and perhaps aid others in leaving the country."[57] But within two weeks he was dead.

Shortly before sunrise on 10 March, his crumpled, pajama-clad body was found in the courtyard of Czernin Palace, thirty feet below a small bathroom window in the minister's third-floor apartment. Gottwald announced that Masaryk had taken his own life in a fit of despondency. In reality, one of Zorin's terrorist squads had murdered him. The assassins had suffocated him with bed pillows and thrown him feet first out the window.[58] The Communists feared that Masaryk would flee to the West, from which he could make radio appeals to his fellow Czechs. These events completely crushed Beneš, and he resigned the presidency, thereby allowing the Communist boss Gottwald to take his place.

To the West, the Communist coup in Czechoslovakia was especially shocking; it destroyed any lingering illusions that cooperation with the Soviet Union was possible. The Czechs had been a symbol of hope. They alone of all Eastern European peoples had managed to create a functioning democracy. Now, for the second time in less than a decade, their aspirations had been crushed under the heel of totalitarianism. But some people felt that the Czechs themselves were hardly blameless, that they had not fought hard enough to preserve the values they cherished. One of the harshest judgments came from the American ambassador in Prague, Laurence Steinhardt, who wrote bluntly that the Czechs "have never seemed able to exercise firmness, courage and noble traits in time of crisis but rather have chosen to bow to political storms which have ravaged about the country."[59] This unfair assessment revealed the degree of frustration that the West felt at being unable to prevent the consolidation of Communist power in Eastern Europe. No other state in Eastern Europe, except Yugoslavia where the circumstances were different, had been able to prevent a Soviet takeover.

Although the Prague coup seemed to establish Stalin's unquestioned control over Eastern Europe, at the very time it occurred, the independent-minded Yugoslavs were creating serious difficulties for the Soviet dictator. In fact, the Soviets had not ended the Eastern European peoples' longings to control their own destinies. Forcing a state to become Communist did not make it less nationalist. Independence could be smothered by fear, but forcing a people into submission did not make them loyal or reliable.

Yugoslavia

Apparent Compliance. At the end of the war, the Yugoslav Communist party, backed by its powerful army of Partisans, had established clear control of the National Liberation Front. It had replaced the monarchy with a republic and prevented the older ruling parties from participating in the national elections of 11 November 1945, thus gaining 96 percent of the vote and control of the country. But the Yugoslav Communists did not need such chicanery to win. As the driving force in the resistance against Nazi Germany, they were the closest the country had to a party of national unity, although no amount of popularity could overcome the state's basic ethnic differences. Although the Communist party leader Josip Tito admired the Communist system, he did not believe the Soviet Union had created its most perfect example. Furthermore, he had no particular respect for Soviet leaders, in whose company he often felt ill at ease. Once, coming home from a state dinner at the Kremlin, he remarked, "I don't know what the devil is wrong with these Russians that they drink so much—plain decadence."[60] Of course, it was not just the Soviet capacity to down large quantities of alcoholic beverages that made an eventual declaration of independence from "Big Brother" inevitable.

Still, the new Yugoslav constitution of January 1946 followed the Soviet model in creating a federal system of separate republics and autonomous regions, with a Council of Nationalities designed to give the major ethnic groups specific representation. The Communists established immediate control over the economy by nationalizing those enterprises that the Germans had confiscated during the war and by expropriating the businesses and industries of Nazi collaborators. Their sole ambition seemed to be to turn the country into a faithful replica of the Soviet Union. In 1947, Tito officially abolished the monarchy.

If the Soviets had any objection, it was that "the Yugoslavs were taking the Marxist socioeconomic model somewhat too seriously." Moscow, possibly fearing that the Yugoslavs would create the Communist utopia first, advised them to "relax a bit . . . be less virginal, less doctrinaire."[61] In a speech made three months after the end of the war, Tito proclaimed that the "most significant foreign policy event in the history of the new Yugoslavia" was "the signing of the Treaty of Mutual Assistance, Friendship and Economic and Cultural Cooperation" (11 April 1945) that established "indestructible links with the Soviet Union [for] the guarantee of our security and of great value for the development of our country."[62] But Tito left no doubt that the liberation of his country was essentially the work of the Partisans. In fact, serious friction between Yugoslavia and the Soviet leaders had arisen soon after Belgrade had been liberated in the autumn of 1944, when the Yugoslavs protested the raping and looting of civilians by Red Army soldiers in northeastern Yugoslavia, the only part of the country the Russians had occupied. The Russian commander Marshal Ivan Konev was not sympathetic. He angrily rejected the charge as an attempt to smear the honor of the glorious Red Army. Like most Soviet military leaders, he belittled others' contribution to the defeat of Nazi Germany. The Soviets also made much of their gifts of wheat to the Belgrade government even though the grain "was in fact wheat that the Germans had collected from Yugoslav peasants and had stored on Yugoslav territory"; the Soviets "looked upon that wheat, and much else besides, simply as their spoils of war."[63] The Yugoslavs were confused and annoyed by this insistence on eternal gratitude.

Profile: Josip Broz Tito (1892–1980)

Unlike other Eastern European Communist leaders, who had come back to their countries in the baggage trains of the Red Army, Tito had stayed in his country to fight. He was a genuine national hero, a modern-day version of those legendary Slavic warriors who had risked everything for the freedom of their people. He therefore possessed the stature to forge the strong national authority from which he could challenge Stalin by taking an audacious, independent line. He had been born Josip Broz, the seventh of fifteen children of a blacksmith in the rural village of Kumrovec in Croatia.[64] (His revolutionary name of Tito became firmly affixed only during World War II.) Josip remembered a childhood of constant scarcity. He had very few years of formal education—the Croatian peasants believed formal schooling was unnecessary. At the age of twelve, he began to work as a cowherd. At fifteen, he left his village to learn the trade of a locksmith. He became acquainted with machines and farm production, but only in metalworking was this knowledge more than superficial. Tito had an ear for languages, however. He spoke Serbo-Croatian, Slovenian, Russian, French, German, and English, but could not express himself fluently except in his own native dialect. This difficulty gave rise to rumors that he was not really Yugoslav, but Russian or even German.

Service in the Austro-Hungarian army led to his lifelong association with Communism. Captured by the Russians in the Brusilov offensive in 1916, he was freed two years later during the Revolution, when he joined the Bolsheviks. He returned home to work as a trade union agitator. Imprisoned in 1928 for revolutionary activities, he left for Moscow to work for the Comintern upon his release in 1934. Although he was introduced to the major works of Marx, Lenin, and Stalin, his knowledge of Communism was slight. In the party schools in Moscow, loyalty was more highly prized than social and economic theory. In 1937, in the midst of the Great Terror, Stalin named him head of the Yugoslav Communist party.

Party work gave Tito a mission. He had a strong romantic view of history and found personal meaning in the messianic struggle of the working class. He also believed that his success in helping the proletariat of his country fulfill its historical destiny entitled him to assume greater responsibilities. His real talents as a political organizer were revealed during World War II, although even his efforts could not eliminate the divisions that had plagued Yugoslavia before the war. Tito and his Partisan army not only had to fight the German invaders, but also had to contend with the Chetniks, a force used by King Alexander to support his royal dictatorship. The Chetnicks, led by General Draza Mihailović, had links to the Serbian government in exile. In 1943, however, after the Teheran Conference, Churchill halted further supply drops and missions to the Chetniks because he believed that the Partisans were more effective in fighting the Germans, and he also believed they would be easier to work with after the liberation.[65] By the autumn of 1944, before the Soviet army arrived, Tito's forces had taken advantage of the general German disengagement to liberate most of the country, even managing to help capture Belgrade. Thus, they were accustomed to making critical military and political decisions without considering what might be acceptable to Moscow. In September 1944, Tito went to Moscow where he obtained Stalin's promise to withdraw the Red Army from Yugoslavia as soon as the war with Germany was over. Tito treated the Soviet dictator with respect, but he had not come to Moscow to lick his boots. As the commander of a successful national army, Tito was accustomed to giving orders, not taking them.

Tito had led his forces with a mixture of courage and common sense; he combined a singleness of purpose with the flexibility necessary to achieve his goals.[66] He could be jovial, but also utterly ruthless. Later as chief of state, he developed a taste for a luxurious life-style, including splendid uniforms that he believed befit his position. Formerly, however, he had shared all the hazards and hardships of war with his Partisans who had responded to his leadership with a willingness to make great sacrifices. Probably for the first time since the founding of the Yugoslav state, many had been inspired to fight together for a common cause. Yugoslavia was a country in which a true sense of natural cohesion was always a scarce commodity. The state had come apart during World War II, and Tito put it back together. The unity lasted, at least as long as he remained alive. Having a common enemy in the Soviet Union helped.

An Aborted Satellite. The first *public* sign of Soviet-Yugoslav difficulties after the war came in the dispute over the Adriatic seaport of Trieste. The city had been given to Italy in 1920, but now its status had yet to be determined. Both Italy and Yugoslavia wanted it. The city proper was populated by Italians, but most of the inhabitants of the surrounding areas were Slavs. At first, Stalin supported Yugoslavia's claims, but he grew alarmed at Tito's determination to create a power base in the Balkans and changed his mind.[67] Stalin was also concerned with promoting the Italian Communist party. In February 1947, the Paris Peace Treaty created a free territory in which Trieste was put under the joint military government of the United States and Great Britain. Yugoslavia was allowed to govern the Istrian Peninsula. In the meantime, Tito had advanced plans to create a Balkan confederation with Yugoslavia, Albania, and Bulgaria. In December 1947, Stalin, fearing that this would upset the balance of power in Yugoslavia's favor, summoned Tito and Bulgarian leader Dimitrov to Moscow for discussions. But Tito pleaded ill health and sent Milovan Djilas instead. Stalin viewed Tito's insubordination as "not only heresy but the denial of the Soviet Union's 'sacred rights.' "[68] In the months that followed, tension with Moscow increased with an angry exchange of letters.[69] In that time, Stalin completed the takeover of Czechoslovakia, possibly as a warning to the Yugoslav Communists of what could happen should they become too independent.

In June 1948, Yugoslavia was expelled from the Cominform. The news was announced appropriately by the Czechoslovak Communist party newspaper, *Rude Pravo*. The article denounced the Yugoslavs for Bukharinist opportunism, petty bourgeois nationalism, Menshevism, Trotskyism, adventurism, Turkish terrorism, and, worst of all, the pursuit of "an unfriendly policy toward the Soviet Union." The formal resolution of banishment, which had been signed by representatives from all the Iron Curtain parties, plus the Communist parties of France and Italy, accused the Yugoslav Communists of serious violations of Marxist-Leninist doctrine, including the denial of the (Stalinist) dogma that the class struggle intensifies during the period of transition from capitalism to socialism. The Yugoslavs were lambasted for disregarding class differentiation among the peasantry, belittling "the role of the party in the political life of the country," having no "inner party democracy," and violating the doctrine "of the equality of the Communist Parties." Cutting through all this verbiage, the real issue was that "the Yugoslav leaders think that they can maintain Yugoslavia's independence and build socialism without the support of the Communist parties of other countries, without the support of the Peoples' Democracies, without the support of the Soviet Union."

Stalin once boasted to Khrushchev, "I will shake my little finger and there will be no more Tito."[70] The boast simply showed how little he understood the limitations of his country's power and the character of the man he believed he could crush so easily. As Djilas pointed out, the Soviets were caught in their own trap: they had committed themselves to the cult of the leader and were in no position to resist the cult of Tito, which "would serve to strengthen Yugoslavia's capacity for independent resistance."[71] The break with Moscow seemingly left the Yugoslavs isolated and exposed to Soviet intervention. However, the subversion that usually accompanied such a move was doomed to fail because of the personal stature of Tito and the tight-knit political organization over which he ruled. Many of Tito's supporters had been with him during the war and were ready to follow him in another struggle to maintain Yugoslav independence—if need be, against the Soviets.

Independence did not make the Yugoslavs any less Communist, however. Tito did not favor the development of representative government. Indeed, in the first two or three years after the liberation, his ideology was as doctrinaire as Stalin's. After the schism, however, Tito became more flexible and, by Stalin's definition, more heretical. Tito did not emphasize collectivization of agriculture and, in 1953, actually allowed peasants to withdraw from land cooperatives they had previously joined. The private farm sector increased significantly as a result. Yugoslav workers also had considerably more say in the running of factories than did workers in other Communist countries. Tito simultaneously increased his contacts with the countries of the West. Britain and the United States proved more than willing to give him aid—even military assistance—without question. Being able to play off the East and West obviously had its advantages.

Trying to Keep the Faith

Reform in Poland. Tito had dramatized Soviet relations with the Eastern bloc by denouncing the Stalinist leaders of the Eastern European satellites: "These men have their hands soaked in blood, have staged trials, given false information, sentenced innocent men to death." He was, in effect, saying that as long as such men remained in power, there could be no real rapprochement with the Soviet Union. The death of Stalin aroused hope that direct Soviet interference in the affairs of Eastern Europe would decline. Indeed, Moscow's New Course, which called for a certain amount of economic decentralization and an easing of the tension of the Cold War, seemed to promise better times. The program did not come soon enough to prevent the riots in East Berlin in June 1953 and the less serious demonstrations in Pilsen in Czechoslovakia, however. Elsewhere people wanted change but seemed content to wait for it. Khrushchev wanted to put relations among the Soviet-bloc states on a more rational and, he hoped, firmer basis. However, the promise of a new era raised expectations of greater independence. His speech at the Twentieth Party Congress in February 1956 seemed to indicate that the Soviets no longer regarded their system as the only model for Communism.

All the Eastern European satellites had demands, but only in Poland and Hungary did the situation become really dangerous. In Warsaw, almost as if on cue, the leading Polish Stalinist Boleslaw Bierut died in March 1956, opening the way for a reshuffling of forces within the government. Prime Minister Josef Cyrankiewicz said that the new policy would include improving living standards, restoring intraparty democracy, and developing the political initiative of individuals and of the masses. He recognized that economic grievances were widespread and that reforms were needed.

But the Poles were unwilling to wait. On 28 June 1956, in the city of Poznan, a peaceful demonstration by workers from the Stalin Engineering Works quickly turned into a political protest against the government. The government called out the troops and restored order within a day and a half, but the seeds of unrest continued to germinate. The government at first blamed the riots on agents of the imperialist powers—an explanation in perfect harmony with the views of the Soviet Union. Then, the party line began to take a more realistic turn. The regime now conceded that the Poznan workers had legitimate grievances and demands that had to be recognized. This about-face displeased the Soviets.

Marshals Bulganin and Zhukov arrived during the July meeting of the Polish Central Committee to put the matter straight. Bulganin dismissed the explanation that the disturbances were due to economic unrest and clung to the version that they were caused by agents provocateurs. The Polish leaders disagreed. They refused to launch a Soviet-style repression, proposing instead that further democratization was needed. In their view, the Poznan rising was a profound reflection of the country's political and social problems; it should be analyzed and evaluated and answered with far-reaching concessions and reforms. But before they could institute reforms, the Polish leaders had to ensure that the Soviets would not intervene (six Red Army divisions were currently stationed in the country). To do so, the Poles had to prove that they were in control of the situation. Although the reformers wanted to replace the Stalinist party chief Edward Ochab whose authority had been critically weakened, they feared this move might trigger a pro-Soviet coup.

The reformers tried to consolidate their position by calling for the return to power of a number of leaders who had been removed from government in the purges of the late 1940s and early 1950s. They especially wanted to bring back former First Secretary Wladyslaw Gomulka, who, they felt, could command the support of the party rank and file while at the same time not alarming the Soviets. For their part, the Soviets were watching for any signs that the Poles intended to defect from the Warsaw Pact. "In short," said Khrushchev, "it looked to us as though developments in Poland were rushing forward on the crest of a giant anti-Soviet wave. Meetings were being held all over the country, and we were afraid Poland might break away from us at any moment."[72] Khrushchev formally requested an invitation to attend the meeting of the Polish Central Committee, on 19 October, at which a new Politburo would be elected. The Poles recommended that he come later. He came anyway and brought with him Marshal Ivan Konev, the commander-in-chief of the Soviet ground forces and deputy minister of defense. As a precaution, Khrushchev ordered the Soviet troops stationed in Silesia to be moved closer to Warsaw. The Soviet leader had already reconciled himself to the appointment of Gomulka as first secretary, but he wanted to make sure that this would not involve a significant loss of Soviet authority. On 21 October 1956, the Polish Communist leaders elected Gomulka as party secretary, but allowed Ochab to retain a seat on the Politburo.

Gomulka began his rule by insisting on the dismissal of various pro-Soviet ministers, including Minister of Defense Marshal Konstantin Rokossovsky, a Soviet citizen of Polish birth. He also demanded that the Soviet units heading toward Warsaw be returned to their bases, but at the same time he assured the Soviet leaders that Poland would continue to be a firm partner in the Soviet alliance. Khrushchev, apparently convinced, ordered the Soviet units to halt. "We believed him when he said he realized we faced a common enemy, Western imperialism," he wrote.[73] Despite their desire for independence, the Poles still relied on the Soviet Union to guarantee the territorial integrity of their country, which included land taken from Germany. To dramatize the fact, Gomulka made Khrushchev an honorary citizen of Szczecin, the former German city of Stettin on the Oder. Khrushchev, who realized the implications of the honor, was only too willing to accept. Gomulka knew that he would have to act with extreme caution; any hint that Polish economic and political reforms could endanger Soviet security might result in Soviet intervention. Ironically, however, Gomulka had become popular precisely because of Soviet meddling.

In time, the Polish Communist system gradually became less dogmatic and more pragmatic. Contact with the West increased. The collectivization of agriculture was halted, and within less than a decade, private farmers held 85 percent of all arable lands and accounted for almost 90 percent of total production. Most industry remained nationalized, but private enterprise continued to exist and was actually encouraged. Despite official censorship, some freedom of expression was allowed. Yet, for all its liberalization, Poland remained a one-party dictatorship. Gomulka was a dedicated Communist, not, as some had hoped, a democrat in disguise. Khrushchev said he was glad the Polish crisis had not produced a showdown: "an armed clash between Soviet soldiers and Polish workers [would have] been a fierce one—and the most welcome one of all for the enemies of the Soviet Union, of Communism, and of Poland."[74] As the Soviets proved by their handling of the more volatile situation in Hungary, they would hardly have been squeamish about forcing a satellite back into obedience if they had thought it necessary.

Counterrevolution in Hungary. In June 1953, three months after Stalin's death, the new Kremlin rulers informed Hungarian party leader Matyas Rákosi and some of his lieutenants, including Ernö Gerö, that the days of a Stalinist-style leadership were over. Budapest already had a workers' strike, and the Kremlin leaders feared that without reform the country might soon be at the brink of chaos. They allowed Rákosi to remain as general-secretary, but they wanted the authority of the party to be separated from the state. Rákosi was forced to relinquish his post as prime minister in favor of his political rival, Imre Nagy. Nagy wanted to return the country to a rule of law, ending the police state and one-man rule.

Nagy also wanted to relax economic controls, which would allow the return of small-scale private enterprise and the disbanding of collective farms. In April 1955, however, the old hard-liners, led by Rákosi, forced Nagy to resign and moved to strip him of his party membership. Turning back the clock proved difficult, however. In July 1956, following Khrushchev's secret speech, Anastas Mikoyan engineered the election of Gerö as the new Hungarian party chief at a meeting of the Hungarian Central Committee. However, Gerö, once a Rákosi protégé, was not entirely acceptable to the party's "moderates," who favored more liberalization and the return of Imre Nagy. Consequently, Gerö had difficulty consolidating his position.

Meanwhile, dissatisfied Hungarian intellectuals were pressuring for democratization. Delegates to the Hungarian Writers' Union, which met in September, stressed the importance of artistic freedom and the necessity of concluding "a stubborn, protective alliance among ourselves to tell the truth."[75] Election of the union's new executive board resulted in the wholesale ouster of the old Stalinists. Journals and papers henceforth spoke openly of the necessity of breaking with the past. In its 6 October 1956 edition, the Communist party paper, *Szabad Nep (Free People)*, covered the reinterment of four victims of the purge trials of 1949 and wrote that the ceremony was also a remembrance of "the dark practices of tyranny, lawlessness, slander and defrauding of the people."[76] The editorial reflected a national mood. Over the next two weeks, the Writers' Union called for a democratically elected national leadership, the Journalists' Union insisted on new laws permitting a free press, and the students at the Technical College of Budapest demanded an end to compulsory Russian language courses and a reduction in the hours devoted to the study of Marxist-Leninism. Such agitation would not have been so successful had not the ruling party itself been so badly split. Few of its members actually considered abandoning Communism, but they did debate what form Communism should take. To many, the choice seemed to be between the hard line of Ernö Gerö and the liberalization of Imre Nagy.

Nagy had recently been reinstated in the party and restored to regular membership in the Hungarian Academy of Sciences. Tension was particularly high, and an editorial in *Szabad Nep* on 23 October warned college students to be "on guard under all circumstances lest their democratic and socialist unity be disrupted by some sort of provocation."[77] Already the Hungarian protest movement was taking a newer, more dangerous turn.

The news of Gomulka's success in Poland prompted a group of writers and university students to organize a sympathy demonstration in front of the Polish embassy in Budapest. On the afternoon of 23 October, some 50,000 people thronged the streets carrying Polish and Hungarian flags from which the Communist emblems had been removed and singing the "Internationale," the "Anthem of Kossuth," and the "Marseillaise." Toward evening, the bulk of the crowd had coalesced in the square before the House of Parliament, while others gathered in front of the broadcasting headquarters where Gerö was scheduled to address the nation at eight o'clock. His speech would be carried to those in the streets via

A Red Army major is one of the casualties of the bloody Budapest revolt in October 1956. However, the Soviets soon restored order with their T-34 tanks.

loudspeakers. Gerö had recently returned from the Crimea, where he had met with Khrushchev and Tito, and most of those in the crowd assumed he would announce significant concessions. But Gerö's address, actually a remote transcription from party headquarters, was just the opposite: We "condemn those who strive to spread the poison among our youth and who have taken advantage of the democratic freedom insured by our state to working people to carry out a demonstration of a nationalist character."[78] The speech, which lasted just over ten minutes, ended with an appeal to party unity. Gerö's intransigence inflamed an already nasty situation, and when units of the dreaded Hungarian Security Police (*Allamvédelmi Hatósag* or *AVH*) who were protecting the radio building opened fire on the crowd, Budapest erupted into civil war. People raided ammunition depots and police stations for weapons. They destroyed Soviet bookstores. They toppled the huge bronze statue of Stalin on Dozso Gyorgy Street. They seized and wrecked the newspaper offices of the Communist paper *Szabad Nep*. All over the city, members of the crowd clashed with the forces of order. Gerö proclaimed martial law and called upon the Soviets to support his tottering regime. On 24 October, between one and two o'clock in the morning, Soviet motorized units entered the city. At the same time, the Hungarian party Central Committee met and agreed to make Imre Nagy prime minister in an apparent effort to restore popular confidence in the national leadership. Later that day, Anastas Mikoyan and Mikhail Suslov arrived from Moscow, just in time for one of the most decisive events of the Hungarian revolt.

On 25 October, demonstrators in front of the House of Parliament were gunned down by troops of the hated AVH; many were killed or wounded (as were several members of a Soviet tank crew stationed in the center of the square). The crowd returned the fire. The skirmish convinced Mikoyan and Suslov that Gerö had no hope of bringing the situation under control; they replaced him with János Kádár, a former Stalinist loyalist whom Rákosi had imprisoned for being "an imperialist agent." From all appearances, the Soviets seemed inclined to be conciliatory. But the situation in Hungary was significantly different from Poland where the Gomulka government could count on solid support from the working class and the army. Hungary was becoming federalized; local provincial councils were taking charge of their own affairs and making demands on the Budapest government. The Hungarian Communist party had lost considerable authority and was on the verge of disintegration.

A new government that included non-Communists was organized on 27 October 1956. The next day, Nagy made a radio address to the Hungarian people. He said that his government supported "those new organs of democratic self-government which have sprung up at the people's initiative and [would] strive to find a place for them in the administrative machinery."[79] Appealing to the crowds to lay down their arms, he declared an amnesty for those who had participated in the fighting. He promised to begin negotiations with the Soviets for the withdrawal of their forces from Hungary. Over the next several days, the Nagy government began returning the country to the status that had existed before the Stalinist takeover. It ordered the reorganization of the armed forces, decreed the construction of a new unified democratic police force, and on 30 October proclaimed the restoration of the multiparty system to put "the country's Government on the basis of democratic cooperation between the coalition parties, reborn in 1945."[80] Also on 30 October, Cardinal Mindszenty was released in response to rebel demands that all persecuted religious leaders be rehabilitated. Mindszenty returned to Budapest prepared to take up where he had left off; he even formed a new Christian Democratic party. The narrow-minded cardinal had little appreciation of the current situation, however. Nor for that matter did Nagy himself. Nagy had hardly envisaged the rebirth of a true representative system when he and his fellow group of "Muscovites" returned home after World War II to carry out the Communist revolution. He might have been willing to change with the time, but the Soviets were not.

They viewed the collapse of Communist authority with the greatest alarm and were particularly concerned when Nagy announced on 1 November that he intended to withdraw Hungary from the Warsaw Treaty and proclaim it a neutral state. For Khrushchev, allowing Hungary to pull out of the Soviet bloc would have been political suicide. As a matter of fact, at the end of October, the Presidium had already unanimously resolved to crush the Nagy government, in order, as Khrushchev put it, to "help the working classes of Hungary in its struggle against the counter-revolution."[81] But before the Soviets ordered their troops into action, they took special pains to assure themselves of the support of other Communist countries.[82] Khrushchev personally obtained the concurrence of the leaders of Poland, Romania, Bulgaria, and Yugoslavia.[83]

The Red Army began its advance on Budapest before dawn on the morning of 4 November 1956. Up until the last moment, the Soviets had continued negotiations with the Nagy government, offering hope of a peaceful solution. A four-man Hungarian military delegation, including Minister of Defense General Pal Maléter, came to Soviet headquarters in Tokol for talks, lured there with a promise of safe conduct. The men were arrested shortly after they arrived. The Soviets had more difficulty with the Hungarian army and the armed freedom fighters of Budapest, but the issue was never in doubt. The Nagy government disappeared. Nagy sought asylum in the Yugoslav embassy. Later, guaranteed immunity from arrest, he left, but was kidnapped by the Soviets and taken to Romania. Cardinal Mindszenty sought refuge in the American embassy where he remained cooped up as a none-too-welcome guest for the next fifteen years.[84]

On the heels of the Red Army came members of the Soviet-sponsored Revolutionary Worker-Peasant Government led by party secretary János Kádár. Kádár promised to work for Hungarian national independence and sovereignty and to institute certain economic, administrative, and industrial reforms. Although the new regime was a front for Soviet rule, Hungary was, in fact, far more independent than before the revolt began. The Soviet Union gradually abandoned its exploitative trade practices over the Hungarian economy. And, in time, Kádár became more liberal; in the 1960s, his slogan would be "Those who are not against us are with us." But this was no comfort in 1956.

The Soviet repression resulted in about 25,000 casualties. About 20,000 Hungarians were arrested for political crimes, of whom 2,000 were executed, including Imre Nagy and Pal Maléter. During the revolt, about 200,000 Hungarians fled to Austria; most of these were young people, including many of Hungary's most talented and ambitious citizens. The revolt's strongest supporters and leading participants were often the very people whom the Communist regime had groomed to become the country's ruling elite. These cadres were old enough to recognize the brutality and hypocrisy of totalitarianism and still young enough not to be cynical. Few ever returned permanently to Hungary.

Khrushchev claimed that Soviet intervention was necessary to protect the Hungarian working class. "We, the Soviet Union, support the revolutionary forces of the world," he wrote. "We do so out of our international obligations. We wholeheartedly join in the struggle being waged by the working classes under the red banner emblazoned with the slogan, 'Proletarians of the world unite.' We are against the export of counterrevolution. That is why it would be unthinkable and unforgivable for us to refuse help to the working class of any country in its struggle against the forces of capitalism."[85] Although in practice the "Khrushchev Doctrine" was less bloodthirsty than the old Stalinism, it was extremely open-ended, and few Hungarians were willing to give it the benefit of the doubt.

Communist party leaders in the West almost universally sided with Khrushchev—at least at first. Their fear of the effects of de-Stalinization made them conveniently willing to ignore the crushing of a true working-class movement in Hungary. Nevertheless, the Hungarian October uprising had caused a split in the ranks of European leftists. It brought to an end many of the existing alliances between the Communists and socialists. It had forced Communists to reappraise their loyalty to the Soviet Union. Intellectuals, disgusted by the ossified Communist ideology, quit the party in droves. Communist sympathizers, or fellow travelers as they were called, almost ceased to exist.[86] The hard-liners in the party did not have an easy time retaining their influence. Reformists demanded changes that eventually led to the development of Eurocommunism in which Communist politicians seemingly accepted democracy and expressed their willingness to play the parliamentary game. After Hungary, Communists found it hazardous to be attached to the Soviet Union. Even as the Eurocommunist movement developed, the credibility of the Soviet Union continued to decline as its system became more economically backward and its hold over its satellites more tenuous.

POSTSCRIPT   As events in Yugoslavia had shown, Stalin had overestimated his power in Eastern Europe. His experience with Tito made him determined to take no further chances. He ordered a thorough purge of nationalist tendencies in Bulgaria, Poland, Hungary, Romania, and Czechoslovakia, placing their governments and Communist parties more firmly in the hands of trusted Muscovites. Traditional Soviet-style show trials followed, with most of the suspected "Titoists" being liquidated after summary hearings. The Soviet Union tried to strengthen its hold over the satellites by concluding bilateral treaties to enforce economic subservience. As a result, many local industries were put under direct Soviet management, and within five years Stalinization appeared complete. The Stalinization campaign impressed the British and American governments as primary evidence that Stalin was motivated by the desire to extend Soviet power westward rather than by a desire for security. After the coup in Prague, nothing that the Stalinist government could have done would have convinced the West that the Soviet dictator was not aiming at European, or even world, domination. Considering how the Soviets had institutionalized the expansion of their power, the assumption was not wholly unreasonable.

In "Stalin's Heirs," Yevtushenko wrote of the difficulty of de-Stalinization in a society shaped according to Stalin's will:

No, Stalin has not given up.
He thinks he can cheat death
We carried him from the mausoleum.
But how to remove Stalin's heirs from Stalin! . . .

They, the former henchmen,
hate this era of emptied prison camps
and auditoriums full of people listening to poets.[87]

Khrushchev was a different sort of dictator from his murderous predecessor. Khrushchev claimed he sincerely wanted to raise the standard of living of Soviet citizens because he believed that only this would ensure the survival of the Communist system. "It's time for us to realize that the teachings of Marx, Engels and Lenin cannot be hammered into people's heads only in the classroom and newspapers and at political rallies; agitation and propaganda on behalf of Soviet power must also be carried on in our restaurants and cafeterias. Our people must be able to use their wages to buy high-quality products manufactured under socialism if they are ultimately to accept our system and reject capitalism."[88] Although he talked about dismantling the coercive apparatus of the state, he seemed more sincere about using it to his own advantage.

The collective leadership that followed Khrushchev abandoned de-Stalinization, permitted the secret police to resume some of their earlier judicial prerogatives, scrapped Khrushchev's efforts at economic reorganization, and reaffirmed the need for central control. The satellite states were discouraged from taking an independent path to socialist development, and Soviet influence was pushed into areas of the world—Africa, India, Cuba, and Southeast Asia—that had formerly been considered outside the immediate Soviet sphere of interest. Khrushchev could not create a human face for Soviet Communism, although he did present a human side to his own extraordinary personality. But his successors failed to do even that. Brezhnev developed the doctrine that the Soviet Union had the right and duty to interfere in the internal policies of the satellite states to protect the socialist system. Perhaps he believed the relative ease with which Moscow's will had originally been imposed augered well for continued domination.

As future events showed, however, the Soviet Union would have neither the strength nor the will to maintain indefinite control over its rebellious satellites. Although for the time being Tito was the only Eastern European Communist leader who could chart an independent course for his country's affairs, his example gave the other Eastern European countries hope that, in the right circumstances, their own deliverance might be possible and even ordained.

ENDNOTES

1. Vlasov was a Soviet war hero who had become disgusted with the brutality and corruption of Stalinism. He wanted to organize fighting divisions from Russian prisoners of war, but the Germans were wary of arming men they might not be able to control. Vlasov ultimately surrendered to the Americans; they turned him over to the Russians, who hanged him.

2. The Volga Germans, the Crimean Tatars, some Caucasus Muslims (principally the Karachai, Balkars, Ingushi, and Chechens), and the Kalmyks were sent to Central Asia and Siberia. The deportees were rounded up by the NKVD with only several hours to get ready and loaded into cattle trucks bound for the uninhabited regions in the east. Nikita Khrushchev claimed the Ukrainians avoided a similar fate "only because there were too many of them and there was no place to which to deport them." Nikita Khrushchev, *Khrushchev Remembers: The Last Testament* (Boston: Little, Brown, 1974), 596.

3. From 1941 to 1945, the party increased its membership from 3.5 to almost 6 million, suffering a loss of discipline in the process.

4. "It was all settled in no more time than it takes to set down," Churchill observed. Winston S. Churchill, *Triumph and Tragedy* (Boston: Houghton Mifflin, 1953), 227.

5. In the years following the Great Depression, something like 10 percent of the Czech electorate voted Communist.

6. Georgi Zhukov, *The Memoirs of Marshal Zhukov* (New York: Delacorte Press, 1971), 654.

7. Ironically, some who survived owed their lives to the Great Terror. "If I hadn't been in a camp in 1941," recalled a former political prisoner, "I would have been called up, and a Russian soldier's chance of surviving till 1945 was practically nil .... I don't suppose you often hear people say, as I do, 'Thank God for Stalin and Yezhov,' though in fact, hundreds of thousands of people who were in camps right through the war were saved that way." Alexander Werth, *Russia: Hopes and Fears* (New York: Simon and Schuster, 1969), 85.

8.   A. M. Prokhorov, ed., *Great Soviet Encyclopedia*, vols. 7 and 21 (New York: Macmillan, 1975, 1978), 29, 141.

9.   Khrushchev, *Khrushchev Remembers*, 594.

10. Milovan Djilas, *Conversations with Stalin*, (New York: Harcourt, Brace and World, 1962), 151.

11. Khrushchev, *Khrushchev Remembers*, 258.

12. Literally, the bad rule or the bad regime of Zhdanov.

13. Werner G. Hahn, *Postwar Soviet Politics: The Fall of Zhdanov and the Defeat of Moderation, 1946–53* (Ithaca: Cornell University Press, 1982), 102.

14. *Information U.S.S.R.* (New York: Macmillan, 1962), 215.

15. Robert Conquest, *Power and Policy in the U.S.S.R.* (London: Macmillan, 1962), 109.

16. Khrushchev, *Khrushchev Remembers*, 251.

17. All resumed their careers after Stalin's death. Yumashev became the head of the Voroshilov Naval Academy, Voronov the president of the Artillery Academy, Bogdanov the head of the Soviet Tank Academy, Novikov the commander of Strategic Aviation, and Shikin an official of the Central Committee of the Communist party. Zhukov became deputy minister of defense.

18. Khrushchev, *Khrushchev Remembers*, 257–58.

19. Ronald Hingley, *Joseph Stalin: Man and Legend* (New York: McGraw-Hill, 1974), 406–7.

20. Stuart Kahan, *The Wolf of the Kremlin* (New York: William Morrow, 1987), 250–51.

21. Ibid., 251.

22. Warren Bartlett Walsh, *Russia and the Soviet Union* (Ann Arbor: University of Michigan Press, 1968), 538–39.

23. Khrushchev, *Khrushchev Remembers*, 234.

24. In 1953, there were 56.6 million cows, up from 47.8 million in 1940, 28.5 million pigs versus 22.5 million, and 94.3 million sheep versus 66.6 million. The number of horses was less in 1953, 15.3 million down from 17.7 million. When one adjusts for the addition of Latvia, Lithuania, and Estonia, these gains (or losses) seem less (or more) significant. Brian R. Mitchell, *European Historical Statistics* (New York: Columbia University Press, 1975), 316–17. In 1950, 31.8 million hectoliters of wheat were grown. In 1953 it was 41.3 million hectoliters, but these gains came at the expense of rye, barley, oats, and maize, all of which dropped on an average of more than 50 percent without compensating for the addition of the Baltic states. Ibid., 262, 273.

25. Timothy Dunmore, *Soviet Politics, 1945–53* (New York: St. Martin's Press, 1984), 86.

26. His daughter shared the grisly details as if the dictator's final agony somehow helped atone for the misery he had caused others. "The hemorrhaging had gradually spread to the rest of the brain. . . . His breathing became shorter and shorter. For the last twelve hours the lack of oxygen was acute. His face altered and became dark. His lips turned black and features grew unrecognizable. The last hours were nothing but a slow strangulation." Svetlana Alliluyeva, *Twenty Letters to a Friend* (New York: Harper and Row, 1967), 10.

27. Conquest, *Power and Policy*, 440.

28. Nathaniel Weyl, ed., *The Anatomy of Terror: Khrushchev's Revelations about Stalin's Regime* (Westport: Greenwood Press, 1956), 26.

29. On the other hand, some suggested that the Stalinists actually encouraged the policy because they hoped that a denunciation of the personality cult would thwart Khrushchev's own rise to the top.

30. The reorganization also increased the general's power. Of the eight central ministries that remained, all but two were now included in the Defense Department.

31. Edward Crankshaw, *Khrushchev: A Career* (New York: Viking, 1966), 214.

32. Khrushchev, *Khrushchev Remembers*, 225.

33. Alan Clark, *Barbarossa* (New York: William Morrow, 1965), 506.

34. Zhukov's disgrace was a singular act of ingratitude. During the leadership contro-

versy the previous June, Zhukov had performed a valuable service for Khrushchev by flying Khrushchev's Central Committee supporters in the provinces to Moscow by military aircraft.

35. Conquest, *Power and Policy*, 361.

36. Mitchell, *European Historical Statistics*, 273.

37. In the murky world of Soviet politics, two main explanations of the interaction of domestic affairs with foreign affairs have been advanced. According to one, Khrushchev provoked the Berlin crisis to divert attention to foreign affairs and thereby quiet his critics. If so, the tactic backfired, for the heavy industry lobby used the crisis to its own advantage. The other explanation contradicts the first, to wit: Khrushchev, realizing he had overreached himself, agreed to greater military expenditures and prompted the crisis as a pretext.

38. Comrade Lazurkina had been a survivor of a Stalinist prison and at the Twenty-Second Congress related that in spite of her arrest she had never lost faith in his leadership. Roy Medvedev, *Let History Judge* (New York: Columbia University Press, 1989), 524–25.

39. Roger Pethybridge, *A History of Postwar Russia* (New York: New American Library, 1966), 242–49.

40. Yevgeny Yevtushenko, *A Precocious Autobiography* (New York: Dutton, 1963), 100.

41. It was not exactly a trade-off, nor was it intended to be, but eventually the Soviet authorities did erect a commemorative statue at Babii Yar. The memorial made no reference to the fact that the victims had been Jews; in a later edition of his poem, Yevtushenko was forced to add that the Nazis killed Russians as well as Jews.

42. Alexander Solzhenitsyn, *One Day in the Life of Ivan Denisovich* (New York: Praeger, 1963), 19.

43. Hugh Seton-Watson, *The Pattern of the Communist Revolution* (London: Methuen, 1953), 248–56.

44. *Foreign Relations of the United States*, 1945, IV, 416.

45. In 1990, following the end of the Communist system, Dimitrov's remains were removed and cremated.

46. During the nineteenth century, Romania had an ongoing dispute with Russia over the ownership of Bessarabia, which Russia had acquired from the Turks in 1812. However, in 1859, the southern part was incorporated in the newly created Romania. Russia managed to get it back in 1878, but at the end of World War I, all Bessarabia became Romanian. The seesaw was not finished. The Red Army occupied Bessarabia in 1940. The Romanians again ruled it from 1941 to 1944. The Soviets "liberated" it at the end of World War II. Throughout all this, neither the Romanians nor the Russians bothered to consult the wishes of the local Moldavian peoples.

47. In part, this was a natural consequence of the war. It was difficult for the Soviets to forgive a nation that, among other things, had fought alongside the Germans in their offensive at Stalingrad.

48. *Stalin's Correspondence with Churchill and Attlee, 1941–1945* (New York: Capricorn Books, 1965), 331.

49. Ibid., 348.

50. Václav Benes and Norman Pounds, *Poland* (New York: Praeger, 1970), 282–90.

51. *Foreign Relations of the United States*, 1947, IV, 191.

52. David Irving, *Uprising* (London: Hodder and Stoughton, 1981), 70.

53. Stalin demanded and received Ruthenia, the eastern tail of Czechoslovakia—a bit of territory that had never been part of the historic Russian state. Its acquisition more than compensated for the withdrawal of the Red Army because it extended Soviet territory across the Carpathian Mountains and gave them a common frontier with Hungary.

54. Edvard Beneš, *Memoirs* (Boston: Houghton Mifflin, 1954), 285.

55. Ibid., 256.

56. *Foreign Relations of the United States*, 1947, III, 319.

57. Ibid., 1948, IV, 742.

58. Claire Sterling, *The Masaryk Case* (New York: Harper and Row, 1969).

59. The judgment became even more extreme: "From the American viewpoint, it seems despicable that, with the exception of a few students, not a single person from the President of the Republic down to the humblest citizen even uttered a public word in defense of their political liberties." *Foreign Relations of the United States*, 1948, IV, 752.

60. Milovan Djilas, *Conversations with Stalin* (New York: Harcourt, Brace and World, 1962), 115.

61. George Zaninovich, *The Development of Socialist Yugoslavia* (Baltimore: John Hopkins Press, 1968), 57.

62. Henry Christman, ed., *The Essential Tito* (New York: St. Martin's Press, 1970).

63. Djilas, *Conversations with Stalin*, 92.

64. For a sympathetic biography, see Phyllis Auty, *Tito: A Biography* (New York: McGraw-Hill, 1970).

65. Walter R. Roberts, *Tito, Mihailovic and the Allies, 1941–1945* (New Brunswick: Rutgers University Press, 1973) 187–253.

66. Fitzroy Maclean, *The Heretic: The Life and Times of Josip Broz-Tito* (New York: Harper, 1957), 194–98.

67. Tito was also intending to annex Albania.

68. *Documents on International Affairs, 1947–1948*, 348–87.

69. Ibid., 175.

70. Weyl, *The Anatomy of Terror*, 55.

71. Milovan Djilas, *Tito: The Story from the Inside* (New York: Harcourt Brace Jovanovich, 1980), 30.

72. Khrushchev, *Khrushchev Remembers*, 199–200.

73. Ibid., 205.

74. Ibid., 204.

75. Paul E. Zinner, ed., *National Communism and Popular Revolt in Eastern Europe* (New York: Columbia University, 1956), 383.

76. Ibid., 385.

77. Ibid., 396.

78. Ibid., 404.

79. Ibid., 430–31.

80. Ibid., 431.

81. Khrushchev, *Khrushchev Remembers*, 417.

82. The Red Chinese leader, Mao Zedong, had earlier advised the Soviets against military intervention in Poland and his representative Liu Shaoqi now told Khrushchev that it was not necessary to use armed force in Hungary. He said the Soviets should withdraw "and let the working class build itself up and deal with counterrevolution on its own." Ibid., 418. Khrushchev replied that the opposite might well be true, that the Hungarian working class, if left to its own devices, might take a fancy to counterrevolution. Later, he claimed that his argument changed Mao's mind.

83. Why Tito agreed is not clear since Hungarian independence would clearly have been in his interest. Possibly, he was opposed to any popular uprising against a Communist system, or perhaps he felt that since he could not change Soviet intentions, he should go along in the hope of obtaining some future Soviet concession. As it turned out, Khrushchev's visit to Tito was pro forma, because the Soviets had already finalized their military plans.

84. Irving, *Uprising*, 507–8, 539–41, 547.

85. Khrushchev, *Khrushchev Remembers*, 428.

86. Fernec Fehér and Agnes Heller, *Hungary 1956 Revisited* (London: Allen and Unwin, 1983), 42–49.

87. *The Poetry of Yevgeny Yevtushenko*, trans. George Reavy (London: Calder and Boyars, 1965), 165.

88. Khrushchev, *Khrushchev Remembers*, 147.

CHAPTER 21

THE BATTLES OF THE COLD WAR, 1949–1962

PREFACE Soviet puppet regimes had been installed in Bulgaria and Romania, the Communists were trying to foment rebellion in Iran, and it seemed likely that they intended to invade Turkey and seize the Black Sea straits. Harry Truman was nettled. On 5 January 1946, the American president warned his secretary of state, James Byrnes, that "unless Russia is faced with an iron fist and strong language, another war is in the making." The Russians, he insisted, only understood one language, "how many divisions have you?" Truman thought the time for compromise was over. "I'm tired of babying the Soviets,"[1] he said.

The power vacuum in Central Europe, caused by the defeat of Nazi Germany, invited a confrontation between the Americans and the Soviets. The Americans quickly replaced their wartime portrait of Stalin as kindly Uncle Joe with that of a power-hungry barbarian. The Soviet Union, once the noble ally in the fight against tyranny, had become a huge octopus with evil, thrashing tentacles reaching out to seize the world. The Americans saw their duty to keep this monster at bay. They were superbly equipped for such a task.

The United States emerged from World War II far more powerful than it had been when the war began. The war had been waged overseas, not on American soil, and American losses had not been crippling. Indeed, many Americans not directly affected by the war had a notion of battle, derived from Hollywood movies, as a relatively clean affair in which the good guys always finished first and most survived intact. The hellish nature of combat, especially as it had been waged on the Eastern Front, was beyond their comprehension. Roosevelt and his military chiefs made sure that the Americans fought a different kind of war. They saved lives by insisting on the maximum use of machines and firepower rather than masses of infantry divisions.

The Soviets, who had squandered human lives more freely, did not believe that the Americans appreciated their sacrifice, nor did they think the United States was willing to recognize their legitimate security interests. The Soviets thought American insistence on free elections in Eastern Europe was just a ploy to install anti-Soviet, anti-Communist governments in the region. The Soviets were determined to control what they had conquered and establish a huge strategic territorial barrier from the Baltic to the Black Sea to protect them against future attack.

Truman found the Soviet goals offensive. He thought it outrageous that at Potsdam the Americans "were faced with an accomplished fact and we were by circumstances almost forced to agree to Russian occupation of Eastern Poland and the occupation of that part of Germany east of the Oder River by Poland."[2] The failure of the postwar negotiations to change this situation only further frustrated the president. Clearly, the only way the Soviets could be budged from Eastern Europe was by military force. The Americans still believed in the self-determination of peoples, and they still wanted to make the world safe for democracy. Now they had to think in terms of new alliances and rearmament programs instead.

The ability of the United States and the Soviet Union to determine Europe's fate was in sharp contrast to the situation after World War I when neither state had played a major role in the continent's affairs. Moreover, their confrontation was not confined to Europe but encompassed the Far East, the Middle East, and the Western Hemisphere. Nevertheless, the focus of the Cold War was always in Europe. Here it began and here it would have to be resolved.

THE POLICY OF CONTAINMENT

A Military Equation

The North Atlantic Treaty Organization. The Stalinization of Eastern Europe prompted the governments of Britain, France, Belgium, the Netherlands, and Luxembourg to conclude a treaty for collective self-defense. The agreement, signed at Brussels in March 1948, specified that an attack on any one of the signatories would oblige the others to respond with "all the military and other aid and assistance in their power." Such a commitment was intended "to fortify and preserve the principles of democracy, personal freedom and political liberty, the constitutional traditions and the rule of law, which are [the] common heritage."[3] However, when the Brussels treaty was signed, the Western European countries had scant means of protecting themselves. Only the United States could guarantee their security, but there was, as yet, no indication of how this would be done.

The Soviet coup in Prague did induce the U.S. Senate to adopt a resolution, on 11 June 1948, to support regional defense pacts with military assistance "if such aid were shown to be in the interest of the United States." But this intent did not take more tangible form until after the start of the Berlin crisis, when the

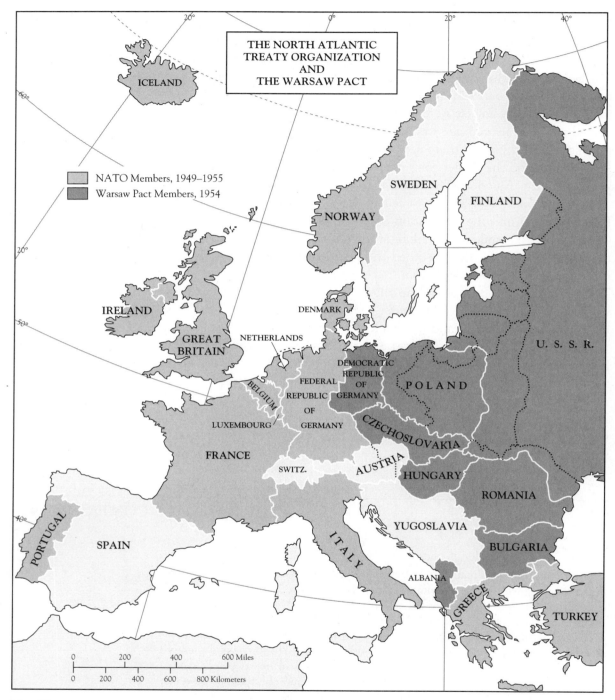

THE NORTH ATLANTIC TREATY ORGANIZATION AND THE WARSAW PACT

NATO Members, 1949–1955
Warsaw Pact Members, 1954

Map 17

North Atlantic Treaty was signed on 4 April 1949. The heart of this agreement was contained in Article 5: "The Parties agree that an armed attack against one or more of them in Europe or North America shall be considered an attack against them all" and will commit them "individually and in concert with the other Parties" to take such action deemed necessary, "including the use of armed force, to restore and maintain the security of the North Atlantic area."[4] The signatories—the five Brussels Pact countries, plus the United States, Canada, Denmark, Italy, Norway, Iceland, and Portugal[5]—also agreed to establish a permanent council to help "maintain and develop their individual and collective capacity to resist armed attack."

No more would the United States send troops to Europe only *after* the outbreak of war. Once the Senate ratified the treaty, the United States had a long-range commitment to preserve the status quo in time of peace and was bound to an extensive military aid program. The Truman administration, though, gave the impression that the American role would be restricted to strategic bombing and keeping sea lanes open, and that the bulk of any ground troops would come from the Europeans themselves. Like the British in an earlier time, the Americans appeared willing to fight to the last soldier of their allies. In fact, the European governments had grave doubts about the sincerity of the United States toward its new commitments. With the forces currently at their disposal, the North Atlantic Treaty Organization (NATO) partners could fight no more than a delaying action that would—they hoped—give the United States time to deploy its nuclear weaponry. But the atomic bomb suddenly seemed less a deterrent than before, when on 23 September 1949, the world learned that the Soviets had set off their first atomic explosion. The news acted as a tonic; Truman's $1.5 billion military aid program sailed through Congress.

Europeans were more apprehensive. Many believed that improved economic and social conditions alone would be sufficient to prevent the spread of Communism. Some feared that building strong defense forces would provoke the very war they were trying to prevent. Emanuel Shinwell, Labour's secretary of state for war, remarked that it was no use getting free dentures if you were going to get your head blown off. The Italian Communist leader Palmiro Togliatti, in his speech against ratification of the North Atlantic Treaty, warned, "The pact that you are about to sign will ensure that Italy will be a military objective and a theater of war if it breaks out, or as I should say, wherever it breaks out. Italy is one of those countries which will be 'a carpet of atom bombs,' as the American strategists so elegantly express it."[6] Fears that Stalin was planning to attack Western Europe did not seem so farfetched, and many Europeans were thinking that it was better to be Red than Dead.

The North Atlantic Alliance, according to Lord Ismay, the organization's first secretary-general, was created to keep the Russians out, the Americans in, and the Germans down. The NATO alliance developed gradually, concentrating first on standardization of weapons and equipment. The planners also worked to develop a strategic concept of integrated defense and to provide a program for the production and supply of armaments. Despite such activity, the NATO alliance would hardly have deterred a determined aggressor. It existed primarily as an alarm system to warn of the drastic consequences that could arise should its resolve be tested. Stalin, no doubt, concluded that challenging the status quo in Europe was too hazardous. In any event, he was soon forced to focus his attention on events in another part of the world, where the risks proved difficult to calculate.

The Korean War. At the end of the war in the Far East, the Allies agreed that all Japanese troops north of the 38th parallel in Korea would surrender to the Soviet Union and all those south of the 38th parallel would surrender to the United States. The line was established for military convenience and was not intended to be a final political frontier. However, like the zonal boundaries in Germany, the Korean demarcation line became permanent. The discussions over unification broke down in September 1947, and the United States turned the problem over to the United Nations (UN), which resolved that the Koreans themselves should decide the issue in a nationwide referendum. The Soviets refused to cooperate, so only the south voted. The results led to the creation of the Republic of Korea (ROK) in August 1948. One month later, the Soviets established a separate state in the north and began supplying it with tanks, aircraft, and heavy artillery—more apparently than would be required for defense. The Americans, in the meantime, withdrew most of their forces from the ROK as a signal that the peninsula was outside their sphere of interest. In January 1950, Secretary of State Dean Acheson said the U.S. Pacific Ocean defense perimeter ran along the Aleutians to Japan and south to the Ryukyu Islands. His statement proved to be an invitation for aggression.

On 25 June 1950, the North Koreans launched their armies across the 38th parallel. Stalin had not approved the move and apparently was as surprised as the Americans that it had occurred. President Truman was in the library of his home in Independence, Missouri, when Secretary of State Acheson called to inform him of the attack. Truman returned to Washington the next day. As he contemplated what action to take, he made several assumptions: He assumed that the Communist bloc was monolithic and that Stalin had ordered the North Koreans to act. He thought of earlier examples of aggression against Manchuria, Ethiopia, and Austria, and he remembered "how each time that the democracies failed to act it had encouraged the aggressors to keep going ahead." He believed that if "the Communists were permitted to force their way into the Republic of Korea without opposition from the free world, no small nation would have the courage to resist threats and aggression by stronger Communist neighbors. If this was allowed to go unchallenged it would mean a third World War, just as similar incidents had brought on the Second World War."[7] Truman feared the Communists might strike next in Yugoslavia or Germany. He ordered the U.S. Eighth Army hastily flown to South Korea to keep the peninsula from falling into Communist hands. Then he requested a special session of the United Nations Security Council to endorse an American-sponsored resolution declaring North Korea guilty of a breach of peace and recommending that the UN members give South Korea all aid necessary to repel the attackers and reestablish peace and security. Fortunately, the Soviet Union did not attend,[8] and the motion passed unanimously (9 to 0 with Yugoslavia abstaining). The Americans established a unified UN command under the direction of General Douglas MacArthur. Forty-eight states responded with some form of assistance. Truman viewed this as a test of American world leadership; he had not bothered to consult Congress for proper authorization for his action. The Cold War had begun to distort the American Constitution.

The Korean War lasted over three years. The North Koreans almost won the day. Within two months, they had captured all of Korea except the southeast corner around Pusan. Their failure to break the American perimeter allowed MacArthur to launch a daring counterstroke. In September, his amphibious landing at the western port of Inchon, two hundred miles behind the North Korean front lines, brought about the complete disintegration of the North Korean army and put American troops at the 38th parallel. It was one of the most spectacular military operations of modern times and encouraged Truman to turn it into a major Cold War victory by liberating the whole of Korea. MacArthur assured him that the Americans had nothing to fear from the Red Chinese who might view American forces on the Manchurian frontier as a threat to their security. On 27 September, a Joint Chiefs of Staff instruction gave him authorization to go on.[9] American forces reached the Yalu River at the end of October.

On 26 November, however, the Chinese Communists counterattacked with an army of 300,000 men. They found the American forces badly divided, vulnerable, and incapable of supporting each other. MacArthur had divided his forces in the face of an obvious Chinese threat, a mistake in military preparedness for which he rightly deserved criticism. By January 1951, the Chinese had pushed the American forces some sixty miles south of the 38th parallel. The Americans held and eventually recovered some lost ground, but they never managed to push the battle lines much beyond the 38th parallel. Americans, who had grown up believing that they had never lost a war, were outraged, but the frustration must have been just as intense in the Kremlin. Stalin could hardly rejoice at Mao Zedong's entry into the war, which would give the Chinese a sphere of influence in the Korean Peninsula. Nor could he welcome the increased strain put on the Communist system by the need to supply the military and economic needs of the North Koreans. The Soviets in turn required more goods and services from their Eastern European satellites. The reactions of the Eastern Europeans to the pressure for increased production ranged from apathy to various forms of resistance including absenteeism and occasional strikes. The mounting resentment would soon have more dramatic expression in Poland and Hungary. Equally alarming to the Soviets was the effect the war had on the NATO alliance.

The war pushed the United States into a massive program of rearmament. From 1950 to 1953, American defense spending almost quadrupled, rising from $11.9 billion to $43.6 billion. Similar dramatic increases occurred in all the other NATO countries. The NATO members also considerably enhanced and unified their command and organization. This consolidation of the alliance made it easier to reintegrate the Federal Republic of Germany into Western European security affairs, virtually ending the occupation. In December 1950, General Dwight D. Eisenhower became supreme commander of all the alliance forces in Europe, from Norway to the Mediterranean and from Turkey to the Atlantic Ocean. The American presence in Europe was now overwhelming. American foreign policy, in effect, determined the defense policies of all the NATO members, with the ultimate weapon, the atomic bomb, subject only to American control. In fact, the separate nuclear capacities of the superpowers bound them together in a special power relationship outside any alliance system and crystallized the lines of demarcation between East and West in what became known as a balance of terror. However, the determination of the United States and its allies, acting together under the banners of the UN to halt the aggression of the North Koreans, undoubtedly had a chilling effect on other regional adventurers who might contemplate trying the same thing.

Nuclear Politics

The Posture of Liberation. The Soviets exploded their first atomic bomb on 29 August 1949. That was sooner than the Washington experts had expected. President Truman could not believe that "those asiatics" had been capable of building something so complicated. He was alarmed, but, so he claimed, not panicked. He at once ordered the secretaries of state and defense and the chairman of the Atomic Energy Commission (AEC) to prepare a technical, military, and political analysis "as to whether and in what manner the United States should undertake the development and possible production of 'super' atomic weapons."[10] Such weapons would have a thousand times the power of the device dropped on Hiroshima.

Research on the thermonuclear process had been under way since 1942, but had not received a high priority. Some scientists doubted that a weapon of this magnitude could be built. The AEC gave the task of examining the possibility to the General Advisory Committee (GAC), headed by Robert Oppenheimer. Its discussions were held in strict secrecy; the American people were never informed, much less consulted. The GAC recommended that research and development of fissionable weapons be accelerated, but it did not favor making the development of a superbomb a high priority. Its objections were technical, political, ecological, and moral. The committee pointed out that a single such bomb could devastate a vast area, threaten the environment with radioactive fallout, and become a weapon of genocide. The committee saw a "unique opportunity of providing by example some limitations on the totality of war and thus limiting the fear and arousing the hopes of mankind."[11] The GAC conclusions, minus some technical data, were released to the public and sent to President Truman for the final decision. Truman rejected the advice. In doing so, he relied strongly on the arguments of Edward Teller and Teller's associates who maintained that developing the superbomb could assure the United States of its paramount position in the struggle against world Communism. Teller argued that the Soviets would, in time, build their own superbomb anyway, leaving the United States at a great disadvantage.[12]

As a companion piece to the study of nuclear feasibility, Truman had also requested a broad foreign policy statement from his diplomatic and military chiefs. Shepherded by Dean Acheson, this State-Defense study team produced a special brief for the necessity of active American participation in world affairs. The study argued that the United States had to develop a military posture in excess of that required to protect the western hemisphere and essential lines of communication with its allies. More specifically, the United States should develop and stockpile all types of improved weapons, conventional as well as atomic, and augment the military and economic assistance it provided to its allies and to other countries in which it had special interests. The experts insisted on maintaining the policy of containment, but not the balance of power as it currently existed. Thus, the United States, while increasing its will and means to resist Communist aggression and subversion, "should take dynamic steps to reduce the power and influence of the Kremlin inside the Soviet Union and other areas under its control. The objective would be the establishment of friendly regimes not under Kremlin domination. Such action is essential to engage the Kremlin's attention, keep it off balance and force an increased expenditure of Soviet resources in counteraction."[13]

Truman never specifically endorsed these recommendations (rearmament actually occurred in response to the demands of the Korean War), but much of the study became an accepted part of American foreign policy, if only, at times, rhetorically. For example, Acheson's successor, John Foster Dulles, talked a great deal about replacing the policy of containment with a policy of liberation, but his words were largely for domestic consumption. The United States remained basically a proponent of the status quo. Americans hoped that the Soviet system would eventually collapse under its own contradictions and weaknesses, which the State-Defense study identified as "universal suspicion, fear, and denunciation"; Soviet survival and power depended "on intricately devised mechanisms of coercion." In a brilliant analysis, which at the time seemed to be wishful thinking, the report characterized the Soviet monolith as a system with no natural cohesion "held together by the iron curtain around it and the iron bars within it." Therefore, relationships within the Soviet bloc were bound to be fragile. Nationalism remained the most potent emotional-political force and was all the more dangerous to the survival of the Soviet system because the Communist leaders demanded that their satellites "accept not only the imperial authority of Moscow but that they believe in and proclaim the ideological primacy and infallibility of the Kremlin." The report concluded: "In short, Soviet ideas and practices run counter to the best and potentially the strongest instincts of men, and deny their most fundamental aspirations."[14] And the Soviet regime, if faced with the determination of the free world to defend itself, would "become convinced of the falsity of its assumptions" and allow workable agreements to be formulated. At the very least, the Soviets could be induced "to coexistence on tolerable terms with the non-Soviet world."[15]

The New Arms Race. Superbomb weaponry added a new dimension to the strategy of power politics. It was no longer possible, as in the past, to redress a balance of power through war without the risk of mutual annihilation. The Americans exploded their first hydrogen bomb on 8 May 1951; the Soviets had their first successful firing on 12 August 1953. Throughout the 1950s and into the 1960s, both countries built up their arsenals far beyond any rational equation of self-defense, stockpiling thousands of warheads with the collective capacity to destroy the enemy many times over. In neither country did the public have any influence in stopping the kilotonnage race.

During this period of nuclear expansion, the Soviet Union made various attempts to break out of its encirclement. Some sort of revisionism seemed justified by the vast increase in its military strength. This certainly would have been a valid assumption half a century earlier, but now anticipated gains could not overcome the risks. The territorial status quo, established in Europe after the 1948 Berlin crisis, therefore remained fixed as the two superpowers engaged in a will-o'-the-wisp arms race of horrendous proportions. The buildup emphasized technology and invention: the development of better delivery systems and smaller, more powerful warheads. Each side feared that the other might produce a weapon of destruction so powerful and diabolical that nothing could deter its use.

Hitler had prompted people to think of foreign policy in terms of blueprints and time tables: a remilitarized Rhineland, then an annexed Austria, next a destroyed Czechoslovakia, an invaded Poland, and a conquered France. The superpowers, therefore, tended to regard each move made by their adversary as part of a plan to master the universe. In this atmosphere, correct judgments were hard to come by, and both parties frequently ignored or downplayed their adversary's weakness. For example, the U.S. Secretary of State John Foster Dulles (1953–1959) consistently exaggerated the menace of the Communists whom he felt were malevolently hostile to the values of the free world. Since he believed that any sort of accommodation with them was impossible, he had little incentive to take many positive steps toward easing the tensions of the Cold War.

Dulles's intransigence worried many Europeans who feared they were being forced to accept annihilation without representation. Antinuclear movements developed in all the countries of Western Europe. Some were hardly even-handed. They denounced the threat of the United States, but not that of the Soviet Union. However, many people were genuinely afraid that the nuclear umbrella could become a shroud. The situation became more complex with nuclear proliferation. Britain joined the "nuclear club" in 1952; France followed in 1960. China exploded its first bomb four years later. It seemed that almost every country that wanted a bomb might eventually have one. These weapons might even fall into the hands of terrorist groups who could use them to hold nations hostage. A horrible picture emerged of bombs being smuggled in suitcases into great metropolitan areas and detonated by remote control. What did deterrence mean when the threat of the nuclear winter was worldwide and so pervasive? Nobody could be safe again, especially the Europeans who were in the trenches of the Cold War.

Some small efforts were made to defuse the situation. Partly to deflect criticism that the United States only thought of nuclear energy in terms of destruction, in the early 1950s, President Dwight D. Eisenhower launched his "atoms for peace program," which emphasized beneficial civilian uses of atomic energy. In 1952, the United Nations established its first disarmament commission to coordinate plans for the reduction of conventional and nuclear weaponry. However, unless the superpowers themselves were able to reach agreement, the problem proved insoluble.

TOWARD PEACEFUL COEXISTENCE

De-Stalinization

A Collective Leadership. Protecting vested interests seemed to be as important as ensuring national security as the military and industrial leaders formed an alliance to push for greater defense expenditures. They routinely overestimated the strength of their adversaries. Washington operated under the assumption that Soviet power was monolithic despite its economic problems and the growing restiveness in Eastern Europe and among the Soviet Union's non-Russian peoples. During the transitional period that followed Stalin's death, Soviet foreign policy appeared less forceful and less abrasive and even somewhat conciliatory. In a speech before the Supreme Soviet on 8 August 1953, Prime Minister Georgi Malenkov claimed that there were no outstanding disputes that could not be solved by mutual agreement: "We stand, as we have always stood, for the peaceful coexistence of the two [Communist and capitalist] systems. We hold that there are no objective reasons for clashes between the United States of America and the Soviet Union. The security of the two states and the world, and the development of trade between the United States of America and the Soviet Union, can be ensured on the basis of normal relations between the two countries."[16] The Kremlin's collective leadership still ruled in an atmosphere of insecurity and suspicion and remained apprehensive of the strength of the West; nevertheless, they believed that a more reasonable, less threatening foreign policy might forestall the rearmament of Germany and enable them to divert resources from military to consumer goods, thereby strengthening their system at home and improving their ties with the satellites. Washington dismissed the Soviet overtures as a ploy to make the West lower its guard.

Nevertheless, at the Conference of Foreign Ministers held in Berlin from 25 January to 18 February 1954, the Soviet Union and the Western powers made an attempt—the first in five years—to reach an agreement on European security. Neither side as yet seemed willing to alter the existing status quo. Vyacheslav Molotov proposed that all foreign troops be withdrawn from Germany so that it could become a neutral state. Reunification would follow, accompanied by a general European security treaty open to all European states that promised to settle their disputes by peaceful means. He said that in the event of aggression, an attack against one state would be considered an attack against all, and "each one of the parties, in the exercise of the right of individual or collective self-defense, shall assist the state or states which had been so attacked by all the means at its disposal."[17] Molotov's use of the language of the North Atlantic Treaty was a neat touch in a scheme that seemed designed to destroy NATO. Furthermore, the West did not think much of the Soviet Union's proposal to withdraw its troops from Europe, provided the United States did the same. The Soviet armies would only cross the Bug River, the border between the Soviet Union and Europe, while the American armies would withdraw across the Atlantic Ocean. The West refused to discuss the matter. Again the Soviets appeared to have deliberately courted Western intransigence to give them an excuse to reassert their power.

At Moscow in November 1954, the Soviets opened their own conference on European security at which they revealed a plan to create their own military alliance to counter NATO. The agreement, eventually called the Warsaw Pact, would give the Soviets a perfect excuse to maintain their armies in Eastern Europe where they could intervene in their satellites' domestic affairs when necessary. Nevertheless, by 1954, Soviet foreign policy was outwardly less Stalinist. Though Molotov continued as foreign minister, Nikita Khrushchev, the first secretary of the Central Committee of the Communist party and the new *primus inter pares* of the ruling circle, actually conducted foreign policy. In style at least, Khrushchev was a refreshing departure from previous Soviet leaders. Despite a certain ruthlessness, he enjoyed socializing—he was seen so frequently at official receptions with a bottomless glass in his hand that it was rumored he had a "drinking problem"—and he professed a seemingly genuine desire to reduce international tensions. Where Stalin had insisted that the solution of the Austrian problem had to wait for an agreement over Germany, Khrushchev was willing to pull Soviet troops out of Austria in exchange for Austrian neutrality. There was a good bit of method to his decision. A neutral Austria flanking an already neutral Switzerland created a huge neck of neutral territory that blocked north-south NATO communications. In a most remarkable move, Khrushchev also sought to improve relations with Yugoslavia.

Efforts at Conciliation. Stalin was hardly entombed, when, on 29 April 1953, the Kremlin sounded out Belgrade on the prospect of normalizing relations. The Soviets encouraged their satellites to follow suit. On 10 October 1954, the Soviets signed a barter agreement with Yugoslavia under which the Soviets would trade their manufactured articles for an equal value of Yugoslav raw materials. At a meeting of the ruling Presidium in March 1955, the unimaginative Molotov openly criticized the new policy, objecting to any attempt to reestablish relations with a country whose policies were so anti-Soviet and so far removed from Communism. Khrushchev pressed ahead anyway, and at the end of May, accompanied by Defense Minister Nikolai Bulganin, he paid Tito a personal visit. Molotov was excluded from the official Soviet delegation. Khrushchev did not want any hint of Stalinism to mar this major ideological turnaround. In essence, Khrushchev was giving up on the Stalinist claims to impose ideological purity on the peoples of Eastern Europe. By tacitly admitting that there was a separate path to socialism, he was ending the pretense of a Soviet monolith. Thus, Khrushchev's visit was a kind of apology for previous Soviet excesses.

Tito, however, did not seem impressed. He met his guests at the Belgrade airport, but refused to smile. Khrushchev appealed to the "ties of an age-old fraternal friendship and joint struggle against the . . . fascist invaders, in the years of the Second World War." He said that he sincerely regretted the Soviet-Yugoslav parting of the ways, which he blamed on "enemies of the people, the contemptible agents of imperialism who fraudulently wormed their way into the ranks of our Party." He promised to "take all the necessary steps in order to remove all the obstacles to make the relations between our states completely normal."[18] Throughout the visit, Tito remained exceedingly formal. He suspected that Khrushchev was primarily interested in weakening the associations that Yugoslavia had made with the countries of the West.

On 28 February 1953, Tito had concluded a Treaty of Friendship and Assistance with Greece and Turkey to safeguard the peace and security of the Balkans. The agreement had called for the formulation of plans for the common defense and increased technical, economic, and cultural cooperation. It also invited the other states of the region to join under the same conditions and rights. Moscow viewed this treaty, which linked Yugoslavia with two members of the North Atlantic Alliance, with special alarm. Tito denied any intention of formally seeking admission to NATO, but four months later he declared that he was willing to cooperate with the Western allies in creating a system of collective security. Since Yugoslavia was already receiving American military aid, the Soviets surmised that Tito was deliberately trying to undermine the Soviet position in Europe. In August 1954, the Balkan treaty became a formal defensive alliance, obliging each of the signatories to come to each other's aid should any one be attacked. The Stalin-Tito feud had cost the Soviets dearly and obviously would not be laid to rest with one trip to Belgrade.

Khrushchev also inaugurated a new foreign policy toward the nonaligned countries of Asia. At the end of 1954, he, again in the company of Marshal Bulganin, visited India, Burma, and Afghanistan. Everywhere they went, the two leaders professed devotion to the doctrine of peaceful coexistence and respect for the sovereignty of nations. They offered to provide each country with economic assistance and to engage in scientific, technical, and cultural exchange programs. Such assistance and cooperation were to be the cornerstone of their policy to gain influence among the underdeveloped nations. With the failures of the Stalinist period and the uncertain power relationships among the succeeding Soviet leaders, the Soviet Union was in need of new directions. Although Khrushchev constantly preached peaceful coexistence, ironically his foreign policy became more adventuresome as his position became more secure. Indeed, he resurrected the practices of the past, complete with the old Soviet world view, and seemed to have no great desire to end the Cold War. Whether this shift reflected Khrushchev's own views or his fears that he might be replaced should he show too much flexibility is not certain. Khrushchev, more than any previous Soviet leader, was a proponent of peaceful coexistence, but as long as the Americans were determined to maintain and strengthen their nuclear superiority, the Soviet Union could not afford to relax lest this be taken as a sign of weakness. For this reason, the Soviets refused to consider German reunification before all foreign troops were withdrawn from Europe. They knew this condition was unacceptable to the United States. But even had the Americans agreed to disband NATO and disengage from European affairs, the Soviets would certainly not have agreed to dismantle their East German satellite regime. Agreeing on disarmament was just as difficult. Both the Soviet Union and the United States favored an end to the arms race and the conversion of atomic energy to peaceful uses, but they were stymied by their inability to devise a workable system of inspection and control.

At the summit conference in Geneva attended by the Soviet Union, France, Britain, and the United States (18–23 July 1955), President Eisenhower proposed an "Open Skies" plan, whereby the United States and the Soviet Union would have the right to photograph each other's territory and would exchange blueprints of military installations. This scheme, Eisenhower explained, would "convince the world that we are providing as between ourselves against the possibility of great surprise attack, thus lessening danger and relaxing tension."[19] Earlier over dessert at their first official dinner, Eisenhower had told Khrushchev that they should control the threat of thermonuclear weapons. Their countries had enough bombs to wipe out the entire northern hemisphere from fallout alone. Khrushchev agreed: "We get your dust, you get our dust, the winds blow and nobody's safe."[20]

However, the Soviets found the Open Skies plan of dubious reciprocal benefit. They already had access to general information on American military installations by subscribing to various U.S. newspapers and publications, whereas if they allowed the Americans unrestricted access to Soviet installations, the Americans would have the opportunity to gather information they could not get from any other source. Besides, the Soviets viewed the American bases in Europe and the Middle East—not those in the United States—as the real threat to their security. They therefore rejected all proposals to inspect or monitor their military establishments, claiming this would be a grave violation of national sovereignty—a point that was hard to refute. Nor did the Americans seem particularly anxious to lessen East-West tensions. Eisenhower continued to call for free elections in Germany and Eastern Europe, a matter the Soviets did not consider open for discussion. Secretary of State Dulles went even further—he advocated the liberation of Eastern Europe.

However, the atmosphere at the Geneva Summit Conference was noticeably free of name calling and bullying. Both Khrushchev and Eisenhower were plainly eager to make good impressions and privately had complimentary things to say about each other. (Khrushchev, though, thought Secretary of State Dulles "a cur.") British Prime Minister Harold Macmillan, however, considered Khrushchev fat and ugly with pig eyes, while to French Foreign Minister Antoine Pinay he was coarse with "fat paws."[21] The British and French, though, had to watch the "Big Two" from positions of inferiority. The sessions were detailed and extensive, but produced no solutions to the problems of disarmament and European security. Yet, even without detente, the superpowers had at least tacitly agreed to avoid the threat of a nuclear showdown.

The Suez Crisis

Egyptian Resentment of the West. The British were committed to decolonization; and the French, after their defeats in Indo-China and the decline in their control over North Africa, had no other choice. But the transfer of authority from Europeans to local native leaders brought great confusion and instability. Most of the new Third World leaders had been inadequately prepared for self-government by the colonial powers; now they tried to establish their identities by stridently denouncing Western neocolonialism and making a great virtue of not taking sides in the Cold War. Many tried to play off one side against the other, a game that was not devoid of risks.

Egypt, with its Suez Canal, had long been an area of special British interest. Under a 1936 treaty, Britain was allowed to keep a force of 10,000 men near the canal, but in 1954, under pressure from the Egyptian government of Gamal Abdel Nasser, the British agreed to remove them. Nasser had come to power as a result of a military coup on 23 July 1952, which had overthrown King Farouq, a ruler long associated with corruption, indifference, and subservience to the interests of the West. The new Egyptian regime's abrogation of the canal-forces treaty was a bitter draught for the British government, which had constantly maintained that British military presence at Suez was essential for the security of the canal. Prime

Minister Anthony Eden, trying to put the agreement in the best possible light, said that "Britain would be more likely to be able to influence Egyptian policy when [this] main cause of Egyptian antipathy to Britain was removed."[22] The British, still a paramount power in the Middle East, wanted to remain on good terms with Egypt as part of their policy to keep the peace between the Israelis and the Arabs.

On 14 May 1948, the United Nations had proclaimed the existence of the state of Israel, bringing to an end the old British League of Nations mandate in Palestine. The General Assembly recommended the creation of a Jewish state and an Arab state, but the Arabs refused to recognize the existence of the Jewish state. The day after Israel came into existence, Egypt, Iraq, Jordan, Lebanon, and Syria invaded its territory. During the ensuing Israeli "War of Independence," Israel took some of the land that had been previously allotted to the Arabs, but lost some it had received—some territory across the Jordan River and the Gaza Strip. The fighting ceased in January 1949. In May 1950, France, Britain, and the United States issued the Tripartite Declaration in which they pledged to take immediate action, both inside and outside the United Nations, should Israel or any of the Arab states try to violate the current frontiers or change the armistice lines.

The Egyptians proved most troublesome. In violation of the 1949 accords and international law, they refused to allow Israeli ships to use the Suez Canal and mounted coastal artillery at the southern tip of the Sinai Peninsula to prevent Israeli ships from passing through the Straits of Tiran. Thus, the Egyptians had effectively blocked Israeli maritime contacts with Africa and the Far East. Constant border clashes occurred and seemed part of an organized plan. In 1955, following a series of raids and counterraids across the demarcation line in the Gaza Strip, Israel attacked an Egyptian military outpost in the Sinai desert.

Nasser was determined to avenge the affront. The attack also gave him an opportunity to attempt the all-out destruction of the state of Israel, a feat that would earn him the highest esteem from his own people and the Arab world in general. First, he concentrated on building up his army, making the British, French, and Americans extremely nervous in the process. The United States refused to sell additional weapons to Egypt, but the Soviets took this opportunity to extend their influence into an area from which they had been heretofore excluded. They allowed Egypt to buy large amounts of military hardware through Czechoslovakia, including tanks, armored troop carriers, artillery pieces, combat aircraft, destroyers, torpedo boats, and submarines. Nasser paid for this hardware by mortgaging future Egyptian cotton crops and cutting down on investment in his country's economic development. Alarmed at the rise of Soviet influence in Egypt, the Americans offered Nasser financial assistance to build a high dam at Aswan on the Upper Nile. Washington hoped that with proper handling Nasser could become a force for Middle Eastern stability. However, while accepting aid from the West, Nasser continued to cultivate the Communist powers. On 16 May 1956, he ostentatiously recognized Red China, for example. The Americans began to have second thoughts and, in July 1956, withdrew their offer to help Nasser finance the dam. They were confident that the Soviet Union, troubled by the unrest in Poland and Hungary, would be unable to take advantage of the situation.

Nasser responded, not with an appeal to Moscow, but by announcing, on 26 July, that he would nationalize the Suez Canal and use its tolls to finance the building of the dam. The shock wave hit Paris and London especially hard. The security and prosperity of Western Europe depended upon Middle Eastern petroleum that came through the Suez Canal. Nobody believed the Egyptians were capable of running the canal by themselves, but that was not the point. Prime Minister Eden wanted Nasser gone. He believed him no better than Hitler and was determined not to allow him "to have his thumb on [Britain's] windpipe." He insisted he would protect Britain's essential interests even if this meant going to war and even if the British had to act alone.[23] Eden already knew that he could count on French support to bring Nasser into line. The French feared that if Nasser were not curbed, the Algerian rebels would seek his backing in their struggle for independence from France. The French were also suffering from the same Munich complex as the British. This notion that Nasser was another Hitler who must be stopped before it was too late provided French leaders with a certain moral justification and a faith that their decisions would receive public support.[24] Eden also believed that the Americans "did not exclude the use of force if all other methods failed."[25] The British and the French military began drawing up contingency plans for an invasion of Egypt at the end of July 1956, determining what units would be involved. At the same time, the British and French fleets were mobilized for service in the Mediterranean, measures described as "precautionary."[26]

In August, representatives of the countries who were major users of the Suez waterway met in London. They endorsed an American plan to establish a special international organization to operate, maintain, and develop the canal. Nasser, however, immediately denounced the scheme as a derogation of national sovereignty "provocative to the people of Egypt." Such a summary rejection convinced Britain and France that the time had come for sterner measures. The British were convinced that a failure to preserve the balance of power in the Middle East would end their status as a world power. But the United States, upon whom both counted for support, was reluctant to engage in force. Washington felt that keeping the canal open was more important than punishing Nasser. Eisenhower, in his press conference of 11 September, flatly opposed intervention: "We established the United Nations to abolish aggression, and I am not going to be a party to aggression."

Eden tried to cover all bases, all the while continuing his military buildup and clandestine maneuvers to depose Nasser. At the same time, the French strengthened their ties with Israel. They had no difficulty obtaining the Israelis' agreement to cooperate in an Anglo-French war against Egypt. Israeli Prime Minister David Ben Gurion was looking for an opportunity to launch a preemptive strike to curb Egypt's growing military power. He also wanted certain strategic bases in the Sinai Peninsula, including Sharm el-Sheik, which would unblock the entrance to the Gulf of Aqaba and open the Israeli port of Eilat. Nevertheless, Moshe Dayan, chief of staff of the Israeli army, was doubtful whether Israel without the support of the British and French "would have launched her campaign; and if she had, its character, both military and political, would have been different."[27]

In London, on 21 September, the users of the canal brought forth another plan: they would create an association to manage the canal, hire pilots, and organize navigation. This idea had no more chance of being approved by Nasser than the others. The French suspected that it was a deliberate American ploy to forestall any Anglo-French move against Egypt. Time was on Nasser's side. He was now a hero to his own people and the most significant leader in the Arab world. The Egyptians had demonstrated that they could run the canal and maintain free passage without outside help. The United Nations Security Council discussed the Suez crisis in October. The British and French introduced a resolution that called upon the Egyptian government to recognize the rights of the canal users to operate the canal, but opposed any solution that left control of the waterway in Egyptian hands. On 13 October 1956, the Soviet Union obligingly vetoed the Anglo-French resolution.

Resort to Arms. On 22 October, representatives of Britain, France, and Israel met at a secluded villa in the Paris suburb of Sèvres. The delegations were headed by British Foreign Secretary Selwin Lloyd, French Premier Guy Mollet, and Israeli Prime Minister Ben Gurion. The basic plan to attack Egypt had already been drafted two months before: code-named Operation Musketeer, it called for an Anglo-French airborne operation against Alexandria, followed by an infantry advance on Cairo. The attack had initially been scheduled to begin on 13 September, but Eden's elaborate efforts to tranquilize the Americans by waiting for the Security Council meeting had led to one delay after another. The plan became "Musketeer Revised," essentially the same plan as before with the initial objective changed from Alexandria to Port Said. At the Sèvres meeting, the British insisted on having a proper pretext before beginning the attack.

The British wanted the Israelis to attack first so that they could claim Anglo-French intervention was necessary to prevent the conflict from spreading. The French agreed. According to General André Beaufre, the operation's deputy commander, the French and British would become a United Nations "advanced guard and might lead with equal certainty to the political results at which we aim."[28] This last reference was to the overthrow of Nasser, now the operation's principal aim. The political objective of getting rid of the Egyptian leader confused the operation, however. What was the main military objective now—securing the canal or occupying Cairo?

The meeting broke up without agreement, but later the Israelis agreed to strike first, provided they were required to hold out alone for no more than thirty-six hours. France had been actively supplying the Israeli armed forces with new military hardware since August. The Israeli high command felt confident they could mobilize the army in three days and advance rapidly into the Sinai to defeat the Egyptian army; this offensive would be followed by double thrusts, one north to the Gaza Strip, one south to the Gulf of Aqaba. The Israelis calculated that the Soviet Union was too involved with affairs in Hungary to give Egypt much support and that the Americans would be distracted by the presidential election campaign.

The attack began on the evening of 29 October. Before dawn of the following day, the Israelis had swept halfway to Ismailia. Soviet Premier Bulganin warned, "there are countries now which need not have sent a navy or air force to the coasts of Britain, but could have used other means, such as rocket technique. We are filled with determination to use force to crush the aggressors and to restore peace in the [Middle] East."[29] But nobody really believed the Soviets would begin a world war over Egypt, a country not vital to their national security. The Americans warned the Israelis and the Egyptians to stop all military action and withdraw their forces to a distance of ten miles from the canal.

Eden tried unsuccessfully to convince Eisenhower that the Americans should join the British and French in taking immediate, decisive action to stop hostilities. The prime minister did not think that the American refusal to participate meant opposition to the British and French taking action by themselves. The British, without previously informing the Americans, demanded "temporary" Anglo-French occupation of Port Said, Ismailia, and Suez, which would have placed the canal in British and French hands. However, the real aim all along had been, in Eden's words, to "knock Nasser off his perch."[30] Therefore the British never intended for the Egyptians to take the twelve-hour ultimatum seriously. In any case, its terms would only have applied to Egypt since Israeli forces were not yet within ten miles of the canal. Nasser rejected the British demand, and on the evening of 31 October, the Anglo-French bombardment of the Egyptian Air Force began.

World reaction was instantaneous and almost universally hostile. Britain and France vetoed Security Council consideration of the attack, but the General Assembly, by a vote of 64 to 5, the largest majority in UN history, passed a resolution for a cease-fire. The French and British responded that they would stop their "police action" only if the UN organized a special task force (acceptable to both Israel and Egypt) to keep the peace. The operation against Port Said was launched on 5 November as scheduled. But, by now, the goal of ousting Nasser had been scaled down to simply holding the canal until the arrival of the United Nations Special Force. But the intended advance along the canal to Ismailia and Suez never took place. Israel and Egypt accepted a cease-fire, and the British had to follow suit. Eden realized that he had run out of excuses.[31] The United States had applied tremendous pressure to force the British to suspend operations. Heavy trading against the pound had weakened the British economy. Eden was in poor health, still weak after a recent gallbladder operation. Pleading ill health, he resigned as prime minister.

General Beaufre, a key participant in the Suez affair, believed it was a major turning point: "Before Suez, European prestige was still intact in the eyes of the Third World and the victor nations of 1945 had maintained their solidarity. After Suez, prestige and solidarity had vanished. This was the end of the empire, the end of an epoch."[32] Eden again tried to justify his actions with historical comparisons: "I thought and think that failure to act would have brought the worst of consequences, just as I think the world would have suffered less if Hitler had been resisted in the Rhine, in Austria or in Czechoslovakia rather than in Poland."[33] Eden had not come to grips with the serious damage British and French prestige had suffered nor with the loss of their position in the Mediterranean. Far from humiliating Nasser, much less removing him from power, the Suez crisis had made him a hero. His nationalization of the Suez Canal epitomized the longings of the Arab world for emancipation from Western tutelage. The Egyptian army had made a very poor showing on the battlefield, but Nasser had no difficulty transforming military defeat into political victory. He captured the imagination of the Middle Eastern world with his call for Arab nationalism, thereby confirming his own legitimacy and leadership.[34] Nasserism became a powerful expression of pan-Arab sentiment that lasted long after his sudden death from a heart attack in 1970. Since then other leaders have tried to take his place by echoing his appeal to Arab nationalism.

Israel did succeed in opening the Gulf of Aqaba, but the crisis did not add perceptibly to Israeli security. The British and French attack on Egypt and its consequences accelerated the decline of these two nations as world powers, thereby continuing a process that had begun with World War I. The crisis was a stunning example of their inability to take any significant action, whether good or bad, without the approval of the United States. The Americans now became the paramount power in the Middle East. They felt they had no other choice if they were to keep the Soviets at bay. As for the Soviets, the Hungarian uprising had prevented them from turning the situation to their advantage, an indication of the dangers of being overextended in a part of the world that was not crucial to their national security. The Soviets wanted to protect Eastern Europe against possible defection as much as the United States wanted to protect the Middle East from Soviet intervention. Consequently, the Soviet reaction to the Suez crisis, like that of the United States toward events in Hungary, was more remarkable for words than deeds.[35] Both superpowers had learned how to pull their punches. Consequently, the 1956 crisis brought no alteration in the East-West balance. By now the politics of the Cold War seemed almost predictable.

Until 1957, the Americans had the capacity to attack the Soviet Union directly without the Soviets being able to strike at the United States. That immunity came to an end with the launching of the first Soviet space satellite—*Sputnik*. This new development heightened European fears that the two superpowers might be deterred from striking at each other's homelands and confine their attacks to the other's positions in Europe instead. Indeed, NATO strategy emphasized the use of short-range, or tactical, nuclear weapons to compensate for the numerical superiority of the Soviet armed forces. At the same time, some Europeans doubted whether the Americans would really defend Europe at all. In frustration, the European people took to the streets. Protesters in Western European countries marched on American military bases where atomic weapons were stockpiled and on facilities where nuclear research was carried out. In Eastern Europe, the Soviets encouraged antinuclear demonstrations against the policies of the Western powers, especially against the buildup of an American nuclear arsenal in West Germany. Despite the protest, the likelihood of a slowdown in the arms race remained remote as long as so many security issues between East and West remained unresolved.

The Emergence of a Third Force

Western European Integration and the German Problem. Superpower control of European affairs had been the dominant factor in European politics since the end of World War II. Thus, the Geneva summit of 1955, like previous such meetings on European security, was mainly a Soviet-American duet. The British and French were on stage; they even had a few lines from time to time (both sponsored their own disarmament plans), but clearly they filled the roles of choristers. On occasion, the Soviets were outright condescending, secretly rejoicing that French and British political influence was waning in those areas in which the Soviet Union was trying to advance. The Americans, although less overtly obnoxious, also kept their own counsel. Neither superpower treated the European states as sovereign entities entitled to make their own decisions without outside interference. The United States allowed much more freedom of action than did the Soviets, but the Suez crisis clearly showed that there were limits to how much the Americans would tolerate. Both the Soviets and the Americans formed their spheres of interest into alliances and bound them together militarily, politically, and economically. But whereas Soviet rule in Eastern Europe led to economic backwardness, rebellion, and smoldering ethnic hatred, American tutelage of Western Europe resulted in the creation of a secure and sophisticated community on the way to becoming a third superpower.

Although the "European Movement" had many intellectual ancestors, its true parentage was the most fundamental of imperatives—necessity. The dramatic events of the Cold War boosted unification in the form of the Marshall Plan, which required Western European nations to promote integration across national boundaries. The Berlin crisis and the Soviet rape of Czechoslovakia in 1948 hastened the formation of a Western European military alliance in NATO. There were attempts to bring about a similar political association. A Council of Europe convened in Strasbourg in 1949 to establish "a closer unity" among the states of Western Europe.[36] However, no one was willing to give this body supranational powers despite the belief that such an organization could help prevent Germany from once again threatening the peace of Europe.

The necessity of containing the ambitions of the Germans was as urgent as containing the ambitions of the Soviets. Germany was obviously not going to become a pastoral state, and with the remarkable prospects for European recovery offered by the Marshall Plan, it showed every indication of once again becoming an economic powerhouse. Such a state would be impossible to keep in a position of international inferiority, especially considering its strategic geographic position, which it could use to exploit the divisions of the Cold War to its advantage. The process toward German independence had already begun.

On 22 November 1949, Chancellor Konrad Adenauer achieved the first tangible recognition of sovereignty for the Federal Republic with the Petersberg agreement, which allowed West Germany to "reestablish consular and commercial relations with those countries where such relations appear advantageous."[37] The Allies also agreed to stop dismantling the equipment in a number of chemical factories and steel plants and recognized Germany's right to rebuild its commercial fleet. The price for these concessions was Germany's agreement to allow a special international authority to regulate the industrial production of the Ruhr valley. Adenauer accepted willingly. He hoped that the internationalization of the resources of the Ruhr would enable him to further his policy of reconciliation with France; the latter, in turn, was a means through which Germany could once again return to a position of prominence in European affairs.

The French, however, saw German cooperation as a means of enhancing their security. They realized that it was preferable to integrate an independent Germany within the Western alliance than to perpetuate the kind of control that had so poisoned relations between the two countries after World War I. On 9 May 1950, French Foreign Minister Robert Schuman formally proposed the creation of the European Coal and Steel Community in which France and Germany would place those industries under a common authority, thereby integrating the iron ore deposits of Lorraine with the adjacent coal reserves of the Saar and Ruhr. The economic advantages were secondary to the political benefits—Germany would be deprived of control over vital national resources as a guarantee against future aggression. The treaty included the Netherlands, Belgium, Luxembourg, and Italy as well as Germany and France and cleared the way for similar integration in military affairs.

The United States guaranteed the security of Western Europe, but it had never intended to do the job by itself. The Americans believed that the Europeans, including the West Germans, had to demonstrate a commitment to their own security. The Americans regarded the Federal Republic as the first line of defense against Soviet aggression. Therefore, it seemed logical, especially after the Berlin Blockade, that Germany should be included in NATO, which had been created in April 1949 to protect all the signatories against a Soviet attack.[38] The Americans hoped to ease the anxieties of the French by allowing German militarization to occur only within an international framework.[39]

Questions still remained about how far the Bonn government could be trusted. Even in Germany itself, some people had doubts about remilitarization. The Social Democrats were vehemently against it. University students and other young people clearly expressed their attitude with the slogan *"ohne mich"* (freely translated, "count me out"). Leaders of the Evangelical church, like Pastor Martin Niemöller, denounced it and launched a popular campaign against it. Adenauer himself had once opposed an armed Germany, which he had associated with Prussianism, but now his ideas had changed. He believed that German armament was a necessary ingredient in the restoration of German sovereignty, and he proposed that a German contingent be integrated into a general Western European defense force. The creation of a German army within the framework of a general Western alliance would lead to the end of Allied occupation.

Meanwhile the French were working to limit the possible damage and proposed the Pleven Plan of the European Defense Community. This scheme was a sort of military equivalent to the Schuman Plan. The nations of West Europe would pool their armies and operate under a common military budget and joint command. Thus, German contingents would be outnumbered by the more numerous units from the other countries. Germany would have no need to develop a separate ministry of defense or a general staff. Many of the features of the Pleven Plan found their way into the text of the final treaty, signed on 26 May 1952.

The Fate of the European Defense Community. The Federal Republic agreed to integrate its armed forces into the European Defense Community in exchange for the full recognition of sovereignty including the abolition of the Allied High Commission. Under this agreement, the British, French, and Americans would continue to station armed forces in the Federal Republic and would retain their prerogatives in Berlin. They also reserved the right to intervene in German affairs to preserve the democratic system and would retain their interest in German reunification. The agreement cleared the Bundestag without difficulty. On 30 August 1954, however, the French National Assembly rejected it by a vote of 319 to 264, with 43 abstentions. The parliamentary divisions say much about the political chaos in the last days of the Fourth Republic. The Gaullists and the Communists were united in opposition, the Catholic Popular Republicans were in favor, and the Socialists and the Radicals were badly split. Many French still believed that German aggression was more plausible than Soviet aggression. They criticized the British for not committing more of their troops to the European army. Some opponents feared that France, with a large part of its military strength absorbed in the European Defense Community, would be unable to defend its interests in the rest of the world.

German rearmament therefore had to be achieved in other ways. The United States paved the way for the creation of a German ministry of defense by allowing the Federal Republic to assume responsibility for all questions concerning the Allied occupying forces in a Commission for the Federal Government. Meanwhile British Prime Minister Eden cleared the path for a European army by giving the Western European Union (WEU), created in 1948, power to regulate the size of the national armed forces. In 1955, the Federal Republic established a formal Ministry of Defense and conferred commissions on the first officers of the new German army. Germany (and Italy) then became official members of the WEU. Ironically, the union allowed Germany more independence in the development of its military establishment than would have been permitted under the defunct European Defense Community. The Federal Republic also joined NATO in 1955. The creation of a supranational authority to curb Germany's control over its warmaking potential was followed by the general economic integration of Western Europe.[40]

The Treaty of Rome. On 1 January 1958, France, Italy, the German Federal Republic, Belgium, Luxembourg, and the Netherlands, joined hands in the European Economic Community (EEC or Common Market).[41] The action followed the ratification of the Treaty of Rome the previous year. According to this arrangement, goods produced in the member countries could travel freely within all the member countries without tariffs or other taxes and duties. A common level of protection against nonmember countries would be set by averaging the preexisting tariffs of the member states. The agreement also provided for the free movement of workers and gave business firms the right to provide unrestricted services anywhere in the Community. Restrictions on the movement of capital would also end.[42] In Article 119, the Treaty of Rome laid down the principle of "equal remuneration for equal work as between men and women workers." The provision sprang from the desire to avoid giving a competitive advantage to member states that practiced wage discrimination, but it had social implications. Members were to be in full compliance with the provisions of the treaty after a transition period of twelve years.[43]

The organization had a full set of institutions, including a permanent bureaucracy. Its executive and chief decision-making body was the Council, which consisted of the six foreign ministers of the member countries and represented their individual political interests.[44] The Council was assisted by the Commission, which was divided into several branches according to function; each major branch was headed by a commissioner who prepared policy recommendations for presentation to the Council.[45] The Commission was composed of career functionaries who formulated objective policy for the whole Community. The Community's legislature was the Assembly, later to be known as the European Parliament; its members, appointed by the member states in approximate ratio to the strength of the country's political parties, rendered advice on proposals submitted to it by the Council. The judicial arm of the Common Market was the European Court of Justice, which ensured compliance with the treaties, acted on complaints of member states, and settled disputes between institutions. The Common Market organizations were scattered among several cities to distribute the political and economic benefits. The Council was in Brussels, the Assembly in Strasbourg, and the Court of Justice in Kirchberg, just north of Luxembourg City.[46] Together the states of the Community had a population of 170 million. Many of the architects of the Community hoped it would be the first step in the creation of a European political union, a United States of Europe.

The United States favored the organization of the Common Market for several reasons. For one thing, the Americans believed it would continue the work of the sixteen-nation Organization for European Economic Cooperation developed out of the Marshall Plan. The Americans thought that pooling the collective energies of the European countries, establishing common institutions, and harmonizing their social policies would be an effective way to confront Soviet power. Furthermore, the economic strength of the Common Market, added to the unified military force created by NATO, would eventually enable the Europeans to assume a larger role in guaranteeing their own security. In this sense, it was a proper substitute for the stillborn European Defense Community and could provide a way for an independent, economically strong Germany, without a taste for nationalist adventurism, to regain its place in the council of nations. For this reason, the Common Market also had the support of the French, who were looking for ways to harness German power. The Germans themselves were delighted by this opportunity to return to respectability. They did not feel that they had sacrificed their dream of unification, since unification was hardly practical at the moment.[47]

The timing was propitious for European cooperation. Moderate parties were in office, and all states endorsed liberal market economies. Furthermore, the Suez crisis of 1956 with its threat of cutting off Europe's access to Middle Eastern oil had prompted the feeling that the individual European states were no longer capable of protecting their prosperity by unilateral action. They also realized that if they were ever to move away from the tutelage of the superpowers, they would have to act as a unit.

European federalism had scant appeal in Great Britain, however. Winston Churchill had once talked about creating a United States of Europe, but he was careful to exclude his own country. The British were reluctant to consider themselves Europeans, whom they traditionally had distrusted, and preferred instead to base their security on the United States and their own nuclear capability. Nor did the British want to undertake any commitments that might imply a loss of their own sovereignty. They felt that they could cooperate with the members of the Community without sacrificing any freedom of action. According to the British, their associations with the Commonwealth prevented their participation in the Community. As a result of their aloofness, they played no part in the development of the Common Market and thus had no opportunity to influence it.

The Common Market, like any such organization, had the effect of both expanding and restricting trade. That the forces of growth were more important than those of constriction was due in large part to the economic development that had already occurred before the organization came into existence. Businesses rushed to take advantage of the new prosperity. In the first decade of the Common Market, trade among its members quadrupled, while trade between the Common Market and the rest of the world only doubled. France, which in 1958 had returned to economic stability and peace under the leadership of Charles de Gaulle, was able to reduce the deficits in its foreign exchange. Germany became one of the world's major trading nations; its exports almost equaled the total exports of the other five countries combined.[48] Eastern Europe, once a major customer of the Common Market countries, now received an insignificant two percent of their exports.[49] Eastern Europe's exports to France and Germany, formerly its best customers, also temporarily declined. In time, however, the Common Market countries would expand their exports to Eastern Europe because what the West had to sell could no longer be furnished by the Soviet Union. This gave Western Europe added political leverage.

Showdown of the Superpowers

Berlin Revisited. In June 1957, Khrushchev pried the Stalinist hard-liners from the Presidium, but his power was still not secure. He felt under constant pressure to maintain the initiative at all costs, particularly in foreign affairs. Now the inclusion of the Federal Republic in NATO raised the specter of German militarism. Furthermore, Khrushchev had few domestic triumphs to which he could point. Although industrial productivity had shown some improvement, agriculture, the sector in which he claimed particular expertise, was in a sorry state. On the other hand, the Soviets had made progress in armaments. By 1958, they had developed long-range bombers capable of striking the United States. They had fired an experimental intercontinental ballistic missile (ICBM) a distance of 4,500 miles and, on 4 October 1957, had launched an artificial satellite (*Sputnik*) into orbit around the earth. Soon they might be able to hit targets throughout the world at will. The Americans had started worrying about a "missile gap."

Under a traditional balance-of-power system, the increased military strength of the Soviet Union—its new nuclear capacity combined with its existing advantage in ground forces—would have entitled it to demand certain concessions. Khrushchev thought this should still be the case. On 10 November 1958 in Moscow, Khrushchev told a group of visiting Polish party officials that the time had come "for the signatories of the Potsdam Agreement to discard the remnants of the occupation regime in Berlin and thereby make it possible to create a normal situation in the capital of the German Democratic Republic."[50] Two and a half weeks later, he followed these words with an ultimatum: if the West had not reached a suitable agreement with Moscow on the status of Berlin within six months (i.e., by 27 May 1959), the Soviets would hand over control over access to the city to the East German government. If the Western powers challenged this arrangement by force, they would face Soviet guns.

Khrushchev probably never expected these extreme demands to be met—however much he may have desired to force the Western powers out of Berlin, it is doubtful that he actually believed he could do it. In fact, his immediate goals were quite different: he hoped that, in the aftermath of the Hungarian revolt, a bold flourish in foreign affairs would confirm the basic dynamics of the Soviet system; more specifically, he wanted to foment a Berlin crisis, which he could then use as a lever to prevent the United States from supplying the new West German army with tactical nuclear weapons. On 10 November 1958, he gave the impression he believed this had already occurred: "The German militarists—with the blessing of the Western Powers, and primarily the United States are receiving nuclear weapons. The Federal Republic already has American rockets which can be fitted with nuclear warheads."[51] The Soviets apparently feared a preemptive strike from the Germans more than they feared an attack from the Americans.

The Soviets had strongly endorsed the Rapacki Plan, which the Polish Foreign Minister Adam Rapacki had revealed in a speech to the United Nations General Assembly in October 1957. This scheme called for an atom-free zone in Central Europe, chiefly in the two Germanies and in Poland. The United States had rejected the scheme because it provided "no method for balanced and equitable limitations of military capabilities and would perpetuate the basic cause of tension in Europe by accepting the continuation of the division of Germany."[52] Now Khrushchev was going to try to convince the Americans to change their mind.

The Americans regarded the current status of Berlin as a matter that was not subject to compromise. They therefore decided to call the Soviet's bluff, ignoring the fact that the Soviets had more troops in the area. But relative troop strength was no longer very important. Khrushchev himself had said that nations could no longer calculate "the alignment of forces on the basis of who has the most men." That might have been possible in the age of fists or bayonets, but "when the machine gun appeared, the side with more troops no longer necessarily had the advantage. And now with the atomic bomb, the number of troops on each side makes practically no difference to the alignment of real power and the outcome of a war. The more troops on a side, the more bomb fodder."[53] The Soviets proposed a conference of heads of state to discuss the Berlin issue, while at the same time making threats about the dire consequences of nuclear war if the Berlin crisis were not resolved. But such propaganda did little to weaken the NATO alliance.

Khrushchev, realizing that his belligerent attitude had not accomplished much, became conciliatory. In March 1959, he said that the deadline he set for the solution of the Berlin situation was no longer fixed, and he publicly acknowledged the rights of the Western allies to maintain troops in the city. The crisis had passed—until the next time. Meanwhile, behind the bluster, the Soviets had been working to put their relations with the United States on a more rational basis.

Deputy Premier Anastas Mikoyan had first tested the waters in an "informal" trip to the United States the previous January. His efforts resulted in a cultural exchange: the Soviets agreed to send an exhibit to the trade show to be held at New York's Colosseum; the Americans agreed to mount an exhibit at the Sokolniky Park fair scheduled for Moscow the following July.[54]

The spring of 1959 also brought an exchange of American industrialists and Soviet engineers who looked into various aspects of each other's economies, particularly shipbuilding. In June 1959, Eisenhower invited Khrushchev to visit the United States. Khrushchev arrived in Washington on 15 September. He stayed in the United States almost two weeks and covered a lot of territory: he had lunch with some movie stars at the Twentieth Century Fox studios in Hollywood; talked with American labor leaders in the Mark Hopkins Hotel in San Francisco; inspected a stand of hybrid corn on an Iowa farm; and had a *tête-à-tête* with Eisenhower at the president's retreat at Camp David. The Camp David meeting came just before Khrushchev returned home, and the intimate atmosphere seemed to inspire the two leaders to a new cordiality.[55] Journalists were soon talking about the "Spirit of Camp David." The sharp about-face was typical of the Khrushchev years: he conducted a spasmodic foreign policy that alternated between periods of crisis and detente. Such ambivalence flowed naturally from the state of siege in which Khrushchev constantly felt himself. Relations with China were worsening, and Khrushchev feared the ambitions of Mao Zedong: Mao is "a nationalist . . . bursting with an impatient desire to rule the world."[56] For his part, Mao was openly critical of Khrushchev's foreign policy; peaceful coexistence, he said, was a bourgeois pacifist notion. Khrushchev could hope to quiet these Chinese slanders only by achieving some dramatic success.

The Camp David meeting set the stage for a summit meeting in Paris that finally began on 16 May 1960 after prolonged disagreements over the agenda. But no sooner had the leaders of the United States, the Soviet Union, Britain, and France seated themselves at the conference table than Khrushchev launched a broadside. He demanded that the United States condemn its spy plane flights that had violated Soviet airspace and that those guilty of such actions be punished. Khrushchev was referring to the capture two weeks before of Gary Powers, the pilot of a U-2 plane that had crashed some 1,200 miles within the Soviet Union. The Soviets had removed the plane's aerial photography equipment intact. Eisenhower had first lied about the flight because he believed the equipment and the pilot could have not survived the crash.[57] Khrushchev gave him a chance to put the blame on his subordinates, but Eisenhower candidly admitted he knew about the flights and assumed full personal responsibility. He gave Khrushchev no satisfaction except to say that there would be no more U-2 flights. He now accused Khrushchev of coming "all the way from Moscow to Paris with the sole intention of sabotaging this meeting on which so much of the hopes of the world have rested."[58]

Khrushchev, in a press conference two days later, declared that the Soviet Union would "not tolerate insults, we have our pride and our dignity. We represent a mighty socialist state." He promised that in the future not only would such planes be shot down, *but* the bases from which they flew would be attacked. Khrushchev was under tremendous pressure from the hard-liners at home. Had he not complained so much publicly, they might have accused him of not taking Soviet security seriously. Some believe he was not serious about negotiating at Paris and that he used the U-2 incident to break up the summit. More likely, he had hoped to make some progress toward a limited test ban treaty and toward a resolution of

The Berlin Wall winds around the Brandenburg gate, now cut off from the West. The Soviets began sealing off their zone from those of West Berlin on 13 August 1961, gradually replacing the early temporary cinder block and barbed wire barrier with a more substantial structure of concrete sections. The entire area east of the boundary, including "Checkpoint Charlie," was off-limits. Anyone caught there without permission could be shot.

the German problem that would keep nuclear weapons out of the hands of the "revanchist" West German military. This scenario would explain why he gave Eisenhower an opportunity to deny that he had sent the U-2 into Soviet airspace. The U-2 incident had forced Khrushchev to show how tough he was and to come home with a diplomatic success. But, when it became clear that Eisenhower was not prepared to make significant concessions, Khrushchev chose to save face by torpedoing the summit.[59] Khrushchev made a blustery speech in which he again promised "to conclude a peace treaty with the German Democratic Republic, to draw a line under the Second World War and thereby to deprive the Western powers of the right to have occupation troops in West Berlin."[60] Then he left Paris and flew to East Berlin, where he repeated his threats. Perhaps the history of European affairs would have taken a different turn if Eisenhower, in that tense encounter in Paris, had given Khrushchev more help in repairing his already damaged reputation.

The U-2 incident and the failed summit were the latest in a long string of Soviet defeats. In his years at the helm, Khrushchev had achieved no notable success in foreign affairs. His German policy had failed. So had his efforts to significantly increase Soviet influence in the Third World. He had had no success in making the United Nations more responsible to the Soviet will.[61] He had also failed to head off a rupture with Communist China. When he traveled abroad, he often reacted with incredible cloddishness when he was subjected to criticism of the sort he was unaccustomed to hearing at home. In New York at the Fifteenth Session of the United Nations General Assembly, he responded to an unfavorable speech by delegates from the Philippines by taking off his shoe and pounding it on the desk. He was probably sincere in wanting to find some common security agreement with the West, but as long as the U.S. policy of encirclement continued, he felt his country would always negotiate at a disadvantage. As recent trouble in the satellites had indicated, the Communist bloc seemed threatened more by erosion from within than from the West.

Khrushchev certainly knew he could not force the Western powers out of Berlin short of an atomic war, but he was not averse to provoking another crisis there to strengthen the Soviet position. At a meeting in Vienna, on 3–4 June 1961, with the newly elected American president, John F. Kennedy, Khrushchev warned that if the Americans were not willing to resolve the German question by negotiation, the Soviets would conclude a unilateral agreement with the Democratic Republic. When Khrushchev returned home, he issued an ultimatum, informing the signatories of the Potsdam agreement that they had until the end of the year to reach a settlement. In the meantime, on 13 August 1961, the Soviets, after secret preparations, sent their troops into position along the city's border, sealing off West Berlin from East Berlin. The Allies protested but accepted the change without armed resistance. The situation, however, remained tense for the next several months. General Lucius Clay, the hero of the 1948 blockade, was sent to the city, and the American garrison was reinforced with 15,000 troops, sent to Berlin via the autobahn. On 21 August, the Soviet Union announced its intention to resume nuclear testing, which had been discontinued since November 1958; over the next two months, there were some fifty explosions, culminating on 30 October with a blast of 57 megatons (Soviet propaganda claimed it was 100 megatons!).

The third 1961 Berlin crisis could be counted a Soviet success. As on previous occasions, the Soviets took the initiative and decided how far they wanted to push. This time they discovered that although the West reiterated its intention to remain in Berlin, it would not actively oppose alteration of the city's four-power status. Henceforth, any negotiations on Germany would have to proceed from the assumption that the division of the country was permanent. On 13 August 1961, to drive this point home, the East Germans began to seal off their border with the West by stringing serpentine barbed wire around their section of Berlin. Two days later, they began installing the first slabs of concrete. Khrushchev had feared Western reprisals and had made his approval of the construction of the more permanent structure conditional on the West doing nothing.[62]

The Berlin crisis strengthened Khrushchev's hand in dealing with his foreign and domestic enemies. At the Twenty-Second Communist Party Congress in October and November 1961, he lambasted the leaders of the Albanian Communist party for perpetuating the Stalinist cult of the individual and deliberately slandering the Soviet Union. The real issue was not Soviet-Albanian relations. Khrushchev was actually attacking the Albanians' main supporters, the Red Chinese. In his closing remarks, he said sarcastically that if "the Chinese comrades wish to make efforts towards normalizing the relations between the Albanian Party of Labor and the fraternal parties, there is hardly anyone who can communicate to the solution of this problem more than the Communist Party of China."[63] The Sino-Soviet schism had now become public, but how this split would affect the overall conduct of Soviet foreign policy was not yet clear. The Soviet leaders seemed to have given up hope that they could prevent the Chinese from developing an independent nuclear capacity, or that they could control West German rearmament, but they still had a strong desire to achieve a position in the world commensurate with their military strength.

The Cuban Missile Crisis. Although Khrushchev boasted that the Soviet Union possessed "indisputable superiority in rocketry and nuclear arms,"[64] he realized that the Soviet atomic arsenal was quantitatively inferior to that of the United States. His efforts to overcome this deficiency led Khrushchev into one of the most desperate gambles of the Cold War: his attempt to install medium-range and intermediate-range ballistic missiles on the island of Cuba.

American Central Intelligence chief John A. McCone had already warned President Kennedy that the Soviets might try to install such weapons in Cuba. McCone reasoned that the attempt would be made so the Soviets could "greatly improve their bargaining position vis-à-vis the United States, for whatever use they cared to make of it."[65] But Kennedy and his advisers simply did not believe that the Kremlin would deliberately commit such a reckless act. The Americans assumed that the Soviets would behave rationally and, that before they embarked on a specific course of action, they would have examined their options and considered the consequences that might follow. However, the fact that the Soviets were capable of doing such cost-benefit analysis did not mean that they would necessarily arrive at the same supposedly logical conclusions as the experts in Washington. There were simply too many unknowns—the exact relationship between Khrushchev and his Politburo colleagues being one of the most important. As for Khrushchev himself, he seemed determined to teach the Americans a lesson no matter what the cost:

> The Americans had surrounded our country with military bases and threatened us with nuclear weapons, and now they would learn just what it feels like to have enemy missiles pointing at you; we'd be doing nothing more than giving them a little of their own medicine. And it was high time America learned what it feels like to have her own land and her own people threatened. We Soviets have suffered three wars over the last century; World War I, the Civil War, and World War II. America has never had to fight a war on her own soil, at least not in the past fifty years. She has sent troops abroad to fight in the two world wars and made a fortune as a result. America has shed a few drops of her own blood while making billions by bleeding the rest of the world dry.[66]

The Cuban missile crisis lasted thirteen days—from Monday, 15 October 1961, when aerial photographs taken by U-2 spy planes revealed the presence of the missile sites, to Sunday, 28 October, when Khrushchev agreed to dismantle the weapons and return them to the Soviet Union. Kennedy had recently read *The Guns of August* by Barbara Tuchman and was impressed that the major European powers in 1914 seemed to have tumbled into war "through stupidity, individual idiosyncrasies, misunderstandings, and personal complexes of inferiority and grandeur."[67] He therefore took special pains to be in constant contact with Khrushchev and to leave him in no doubt that the United States was totally committed to eliminating Soviet missiles from Cuba. He underlined American determination by proclaiming a naval blockade of Cuba, and when this failed to effect a withdrawal, he warned Khrushchev that either the Soviets would have to remove the missiles or the United States would do it for them. Faced with American determination to regard the presence of Soviet missiles in Cuba as a *casus belli*, Khrushchev backed down. As a trade-off of sorts, Kennedy promised to respect the sovereignty of Cuba and to close a couple of (marginal) air bases in Turkey.

Throughout the crisis, the American president made a conscious effort not to behave arrogantly; he made it clear that the U.S. objective was only the removal of the missiles, not the humiliation of Khrushchev. Kennedy did not believe that the Soviet Union would regard the Cuban adventure as vital to its own security: "Thus, if hostilities were to come, it would be either because our national interests collided which, because of their united interests and our purposely limited objec-

The Soviets display their military strength at the forty-fifth anniversary of the Bolshevik revolution on 7 November 1962. A "Scud" moves past party leaders assembled on the reviewing stand of Lenin's tomb in Red Square. This intermediate-range missile could travel 175 miles and carry a nuclear, chemical, or conventional warhead. It was designed to strike at cities and major enemy control centers.

tives, seemed unlikely—or because of our failure or their failure to understand the other's objectives."[68]

Khrushchev later explained the whole missile business as a Soviet effort to prevent the Americans from sponsoring another attempt to invade Cuba as they had in April 1961 at the Bay of Pigs: "We had no other way of helping them meet the American threat, except to install our missiles on the island, so as to confront the aggressive forces of the United States with a dilemma: if you invade Cuba, you'll have to face a nuclear attack against your own cities. Our intention was to install the missiles not to wage war against the U.S. but to prevent the U.S. from invading Cuba and thus starting a war."[69] But if the Soviets had merely wanted to protect the regime of Fidel Castro, they could have done so with less risk by sending a contingent of troops to Cuba to act as a deterrent in the same way American troops guaranteed Berlin from outside attack. The installation of offensive weapons ninety miles from Florida, with a range capable of destroying "New York, Chicago, and the other huge industrial cities, not to mention a little village like Washington,"[70] would openly invite the very attack the Soviets said they were trying to avoid. In fact, some analysts assumed that the missiles were sent to Cuba for that very reason. According to this scenario, the American bombing of Cuba would cause such confusion at home and arouse such animosity abroad that it would wreck the NATO alliance and allow the Soviets to move with impunity against Berlin or some other area of the world. However, if this hypothesis were true, why did Khrushchev withdraw the missiles before an American attack? It has also been suggested that the Soviets installed the missiles to use as bargaining chips to get the United States to dismantle its atomic bases in Turkey, Italy, and England. If so, the quid pro quo would not have resulted in any significant increase in Soviet security; the bulk of the Americans' missile strike force was not located in these overseas bases, although the Americans did remove their Jupiter missiles from Turkey a few months after the crisis. Perhaps Khrushchev was once again only testing American intentions; President Kennedy thought so. But why choose Cuba, a place thousands of miles from the Soviet Union? If the United States showed itself ready to stand firm in Berlin, how much more willing would it be to do so when the threat was only ninety miles off its shores?

POSTSCRIPT   The Cold War was more about geography than ideology. Stalin had drawn the Eastern European frontiers to maximize the influence of the Soviet Union. Much of this effort was aimed at recovering the territories lost in World War I; hence, the Soviets reintegrated the Baltic states, regained chunks of the Ukraine and Belorussia from Poland, and obtained Bessarabia from Romania. But the Soviets also took additional pieces of territory to increase their strategic advantage. They carved out an enclave around Königsberg, renamed Kaliningrad, in order to obtain another port on the Baltic and to interpose themselves between Lithuania and Poland. (This new acquisition, which was not contiguous with a Soviet-Russian ethnic base, was sure to be the source of future troubles.) They chopped off the Ruthenian tail of Czechoslovakia to put themselves on the other side of the Carpathian Mountains and give them a common frontier with Hungary. They extended their Moldavian territory to the mouth of the Danube, a truly international waterway that flows through or along a dozen states. All in all, these additions increased Soviet influence.

By the 1950s, however, the Soviets were finding it increasingly difficult to maintain the kind of political control these changes facilitated. A series of adventures outside Europe added to their sense of vulnerability. The two superpowers came closest to blows in the Cuban missile crisis, which ironically led to a period of relaxation in their relations. The following year, the United States and the Soviet Union concluded a treaty banning the testing of nuclear weapons in the atmosphere and in the oceans. They also installed a special telegraph circuit—a hot line—between their capitals to allow their leaders instant communication in the event of a future crisis. These fail-safe procedures, which were passed along to the Soviets, had been developed by the United States. The Cold War was not over, but there was a new realization that no crisis was worth escalating into actual warfare.

The skirmishes of the Cold War resulted in no great victories, only occasional tactical advantages. By the late 1960s, both sides, although not yet willing to change their basic goals and beliefs, had recognized that the old ways were too costly and too dangerous. The new Kremlin leaders had grown up in Stalin's era, but they proved more flexible and significantly less bloodthirsty than he. Still, contradictions remained. The Soviets no longer wantonly plundered the resources of their satellites, but they refused to relinquish their control, even though it was becoming ever more costly. The Soviets also had to cope with the effects of such crises as Berlin, Korea, and Cuba, which had strengthened the resolve of the Western alliance and endangered the very security the Soviets were trying to protect.

Clearly, a relaxation of tension with the West was in the Soviets' best interests, considering the backwardness of their economy, their bureaucratic bungling, inadequate mechanization, and woeful lack of incentives. Soviet farmers, for example, were about one-tenth as productive as their

American counterparts; as a result, the country was plagued with chronic shortages. Increasingly, the Soviet Union had to rely on food purchases from abroad, paid for by increased sales of gold. The Soviets also needed technical assistance and investment capital to modernize their ailing industry. Shifting scarce resources from arms and munitions to more productive ventures would help them close the widening gap with the more highly productive countries of the West.

At the beginning of the Cold War, an extension of Soviet power into Western Europe seemed not only possible but imminent. By the mid-1960s, it was the least likely scenario. Nevertheless, American calculations were still based on such an eventuality, while the Soviets still feared an American preemptive strike against them. Almost by habit, as well as by vested interest, the two cold warriors followed their old paths of rivalry; each country was reluctant to give way lest the other take advantage of the show of weakness. Yet ironically, as mentioned earlier, this balance of the superpowers created one of the longest periods of peace in European history. Not since 1945 had any European state fought another. These decades of peace permitted the less-than-superpower European states, at least those in the West, to develop their economic and political strength to the stage where they could determine their own destinies free from outside domination.

ENDNOTES

1. Harry S Truman, *Memoirs*, vol. 1 (Garden City, N.Y.: Doubleday, 1955), 552.
2. Ibid., 551–52.
3. *Command Papers, Cmd.* 7599 (London: H.M.S.O., 1948).
4. *Documents on International Affairs, 1949–1950,* 258.
5. Turkey and Greece joined in 1952, and West Germany in May 1955.
6. *Documents on International Affairs, 1949–1950,* 256.
7. Truman, *Memoirs,* 2:333.
8. Stalin had temporarily withdrawn his representatives in a protest against the refusal to give the Red Chinese a seat on the Security Council following Mao Zedong's victory the previous year over the Nationalists of Jiang Jieshi (Chiang Kai-shek).
9. Acheson, *Present at the Creation* (New York: Norton, 1969), 453.
10. Truman, *Memoirs,* 2:309.
11. "The GAC Report of October 30, 1949," in Herbert F. York, *The Advisors, Oppenheimer, Teller, and the Superbomb* (San Francisco: W. H. Freeman, 1976), 152–59.
12. Ibid., 65–74.
13. NSC-68, "A Report by the Secretaries of State and Defense on 'United States Objectives and Programs for National Security April 7, 1950,'" reprinted in *Naval War College Review* (May-June 1975):51–108.
14. Ibid., 62–63.
15. Ibid., 57–58.
16. *Documents on International Affairs, 1953,* 30.
17. *Documents on International Affairs, 1954,* 32.
18. *Documents on International Affairs, 1955,* 265–66.

19. Ibid. 40.
20. Michel R. Beschloss, *Mayday: Eisenhower, Khrushchev and the U-2 Affair* (New York: Harper and Row, 1986), 102.
21. Ibid., 93–4.
22. *Annual Register 1954*, 35.
23. Anthon Eden, *Full Circle* (Boston: Houghton Mifflin, 1960), 475. Eden wrote: "Some say Nasser is no Hitler or Mussolini. Allowing for a difference in scale, I am not so sure. He has followed Hitler's pattern, even to concentration camps and the propagation of *Mein Kampf* among his officers. He had understood and used the Goebbels pattern of propaganda in all its lying ruthlessness." Ibid., 481.
24. William Roger Louis and Roger Owen, eds., *Suez 1956: The Crisis and its Consequences* (Oxford: Clarendon Press, 1989), 134–38.
25. Eden, *Full Cycle*, 488.
26. Donald Neff, *Warriors at Suez* (New York: Simon and Schuster, 1981), 289.
27. Moshe Dayan *Diary of the Sinai Campaign, 1956* (London: Sphere Books, 1967), 11.
28. André Beaufre, *The Suez Expedition, 1956* (New York: Frederick Praeger, 1969), 74.
29. Eden, *Full Circle* 620.
30. Selwyn I. Troen nd Moshe Shemesh, eds., *The Suez-Sinai Crisis 1956: Retrospective and Reappraisal* (New York: Columbia University Press, 1990), 17–18.
31. Eden, *Full Circle*, 24.
32. Beaufre, *Suez Expedition*, 14.
33. Eden, *Full Circle*, 65.
34. Troen and Shemesh *Suez-Sinai Crisis*, 150–60.
35. Louis and Owen, *Suez 1956*, 233–53.
36. Richard Vaughn, *PostWar Integration in Europe: Documents of Modern History* (New York: St. Martin's Press, 1976), 43. The states were Belgium, Denmark, France, Ireland, Italy, Luxembourg, Netherlands, Norway, Sweden, and Great Britain.
37. *Documents on Germany under Occupation, 1945–1954* (London: Oxford University Press, 1955), 440.
38. See the discussion of NATO earlier in this chapter.
39. In the Petersberg protocol (1950). *Documents on Germany under Occupation*, 445.
40. See Arnold J. Zurcher, *The Struggle to Unite Europe, 1940–1958* (New York: New York University Press, 1958).
41. The European Atomic Energy Community (Euratom) was created at the same time to engage in a common program of scientific research for the peaceful use of atomic energy. However, this organization remained fairly weak because several nations, especially France, refused to provide it with adequate funding. Later Euratom and the Common Market were consolidated into the European Community.
42. Carl H. Fulda, "The Legal Structure of the European Community," in *France and the European Community*, ed. by Sidney N. Fisher (Columbus: Ohio State University Press, 1964), 21–34.
43. See Finn B. Jensen, *The Common Market: Economic Integration of Europe* (Philadelphia: Lippincott, 1965); Katharin Savage, *The Story of the Common Market* (New York: Walck, 1970); John Paxton *The Developing Common Market: The Structure of the EEC in Theory and Practice* (London: Macmillan, 1976); and Steven J. Warnecke, *The European Community* (New York: Council for European Studies, 1978).
44. Sometimes when less important decisions were taken, the foreign ministers might be replaced by the ministers of agriculture, finance, or other branches of government if their expertise was deemed necessary.
45. Over time these senior posts became the fiefs of certain countries. Thus, the commissioner of agriculture was traditionally from the Netherlands, the director-general was French, and so forth.
46. See Anthony J. C. Kerr, *The Common Market and How it Works* (New York: Perga-

mon Press, 1986), Chapter 3.

47. William Diebold, Jr., "The Process of European Integration," in Lawrence B. Krause, ed., *The Common Market: Progress and Controversy* (Englewood Cliffs, N.J.: Prentice-Hall, 1964), 34–39.

48. Brian R. Mitchell, *European Historical Statistics* (New York: Columbia University Press, 1975), 498.

49. John P. de Gara, *Trade Relations between the Common Market and the Eastern Bloc* (Bruges: De Tempel, 1964), 36.

50. Nikita Khrushchev, *For Victory in Peaceful Competition with Capitalism* (New York: Dutton, 1960), 738.

51. Ibid., 736.

52. *Survey of International Affairs,* 1956–58, 564.

53. In remarks to Chinese Communist leader Mao Zedong. Nikita Khrushchev, *Khrushchev Remembers: The Last Testament* (Boston: Little, Brown 1974), 470.

54. Khrushchev came to see the capitalists' display but, as he stated later, was not terribly impressed: "The Americans wanted to impress Russians with a lot of fancy gadgets." Ibid., 366.

55. However, the nastier, more disgusting (but characteristic) aspects of the Cold War seemed hardly to have changed. From Khrushchev's stay at Camp David, the American Central Intelligence Agency (CIA) obtained a specimen of the Soviet leader's feces from which they hoped to ascertain the state of his general health.

56. Khrushchev, *Khrushchev Remembers,* 474.

57. The Soviets interrogated Gary Powers for two months, then put him on trial in August 1960. The televised trial was the greatest show trial of the Cold War. The court sentenced Powers to ten years deprivation of liberty. In February 1962, he was exchanged for Soviet master spy Rudolf Abel.

58. *Documents of International Affairs 1960,* 31.

59. Beschloss, *Mayday,* 374–82.

60. Ibid., 36.

61. Khrushchev had wanted to change the office of secretary-general into an executive troika that would include one representative from the West, one from the Soviet Union, and one from the uncommitted nations.

62. Peter Wyden, *Wall: The Inside Story of Divided Berlin* (New York: Simon and Schuster, 1989), 85–90.

63. Nikita Khrushchev, *Khrushchev Speaks* (Ann Arbor University of Michigan Press, 1963), 433.

64. Ibid., 426.

65. Elie Abel, *The Missile Crisis* (New York: Bantam 1966), 13.

66. Khrushchev, *Khrushchev Remembers,* 494.

67. Robert Kennedy, *Thirteen Days* (New York: W.W. Norton, 1971), 40.

68. Ibid., 103–4.

69. Khrushchev, *Khrushchev Remembers,* 511.

70. Khrushchev, Ibid., 496.

PART SEVEN

SOCIETY AND CULTURE, 1945–1990

CHAPTER 22

THE URBAN ASCENDENCY

PREFACE   Despite the massive destruction of people and property, World War I had spared most of Europe's cities, at least those not in the direct path of battle. Cannons had pounded Paris and Antwerp; zeppelins had bombed London and towns along the southeastern English coast; gunboats had opened up on Belgrade; and bombers had struck western Germany. Nevertheless, the technology of the Great War was not sufficiently developed to enable warring nations to hit targets very remote from the battlefield. Besides, the belligerents felt a certain reluctance to pursue strictly civilian targets. None of these restrictions applied to World War II, which left very few cities of strategic value intact.

The Germans were certainly not squeamish about leveling enemy cities. Paris was spared because Wehrmacht commander, Dietrich von Choltitz, refused to carry out the Führer's order to destroy it,[1] and Rome was saved by becoming an open city. But others, including Warsaw, London, Rotterdam, Valenciennes, Coventry, Milan, Leningrad, Kiev, and Stalingrad—the list goes on—were not so fortunate. Neither were cities in Germany itself. The Allies repeatedly struck Berlin, Cologne, and Hamburg. In the last year of the war, the British and Americans bombed Germany with practically every plane that could get off the ground. One-third of Germany's buildings were completely destroyed, another 44 percent partially so. In Cologne, 66 percent of the city was demolished and 93 percent of Düsseldorf was seriously damaged.[2] Dresden was gutted in one great terror raid. Fire storms and bombings alone killed 500,000 Germans.[3] The center of Berlin was in complete ruins. Bombs and shells had wrecked or flattened one-fifth of the city's 250,000 buildings and damaged another 150,000. Vital public services, including power plants, transportation, and police and fire protection had ceased functioning. Untreated sewage sluiced through the city's waterways. Almost all of Berlin's bridges that had not already been bombed had been blown up in the last days of the fighting. Streets and roads were choked with rubble. Dead bodies floated in the lakes and

674

canals and were hidden under the debris. The restoration of gas utilities throughout Berlin had a macabre by-product: the suicide rate suddenly increased in those districts.[4]

By 1945, all Europeans from Belfast to the Urals showed at least some signs of neurosis. When the guns fell silent, they were left to clean away the fragments of buildings, bury the bodies, restore public services, and provide temporary shelter for the homeless. The cities became places of refuge for thousands of displaced persons. Refugees reasoned that no matter how miserable life was in the cities, it was still safer than in the country-side. The great migration continued even after order had been restored. Urban life meant prosperity and escape from boredom. By the 1980s, more than 80 percent of the people of Western Europe and 60 percent of those in Eastern Europe lived in urban areas.[5] Cities had long played an impor-tant role in European life, but never before had they been so prominent; never before had their values and problems so shaped the life of European nations.

CITY DYNAMICS

Town Planning and Reconstruction

The Experience of Western Europe. Repairing the damage of war was a task beyond the resources of private enterprise. People everywhere expected govern-ment would assume a major role in recovery and development. Nevertheless, urban planning took different forms in the various Western European countries. In Bel-gium, France, and Italy, which already had strong traditions of urban physical design, engineers and architects played a dominant role. But in Great Britain, the Netherlands, and Denmark, where planning had often been less specialized and more liberal, land-use policies continued to depend more upon private interests. Yet even in these countries, central control increased as land became scarcer.

The Netherlands had a long history of town planning. By the end of the nine-teenth century the Dutch had managed to devise a national spatial policy that provided for the needs of a steadily growing population by encouraging develop-ment through economic incentives. In 1958, with Amsterdam's population ap-proaching a million, the government forbade further expansion inside the city's municipal boundaries and concentrated on developing separate residential districts north and south of the city. At the same time, it took steps to preserve a green belt between its major cities by limiting new construction in other areas of the country.

In Italy, planning was less rational, and urban growth was more chaotic. Squat-ters frequently took over vacant lands that had been designated for parks or in-dustrial areas and threw up makeshift dwellings that lacked the normal amenities of sanitation, electricity, and heat. Approximately 800,000 such people lived on the outskirts of Rome in "houses" built without the necessary permits on land that the inhabitants did not own; frequently, the squatter settlements were near already established public housing.[6] The authorities occasionally tried to tear down these shanty towns, but as soon as the bulldozers left, the squatters rebuilt their villages.

Le Corbusier's Swiss
Pavilion at the Cité
Universitaire (1930–
1932) shows off the
architect's severe
functional style; it
incorporates his
characteristic slab
structure on stilts. Le
Corbusier believed that
the massive simplicity of
an American grain
elevator was functional
architecture at its best.

Some of these houses had a certain air of permanence despite having been put together one room and one floor at a time. The residents even demanded, and sometimes received, proper city services including a bus stop.

The French tried to avoid unregulated growth by creating new towns, or satellite cities, filled with apartments and located outside many of the large urban areas. In France, three-fourths of urban dwellers would ultimately live in apartment houses.[7] To create this new housing, the government established planning offices in eight designated metropolitan areas and asked Le Corbusier (Edouard Jeanneret), one of the country's most famous architects, to help develop a standard housing formula. No town planner had thought more about the relation of people to their environment. "Le Corbu" saw the city as an architectural landscape, a vital element of human geography, a dimensional truth that reflected human activity at its moment of use.[8] He wanted his creations to provide more than clean, healthy housing: set within a rational infrastructure, they would organize work and provide the necessary amenities for free time. He proposed the linear city (*la ville radieuse*) as a proper balance between the workplace and the home, with human activity organized around a geometric grid.

In 1946, he began the construction of the *unité d'habitation* at Marseilles. This was a reinforced concrete block of 337 units, built on a slab supported above the ground on pilings or *pilotis*. Le Corbusier created a proper social mix by including apartments of various sizes, from one-room studios to large duplexes for families. Every other floor contained large interior streets, and the sixth and seventh levels enclosed a vast shopping mall. The major center of public activity, however, was the roof, which featured an artificial mountain range, a gymnasium, two solariums, a 1,000-foot cinder track, a swimming pool, a day nursery, a kindergarten, and an open air theater. It was one of the great roofs of the world. Le Corbusier elevated social activities far above street level to remove recreation from the "fungus" that had eaten up the pavements of Paris. He found it illogical that "one entire superficie of a town should be unused and reserved for a flirtation between the tiles and the stars."[9]

In the Marseilles project, Le Corbusier tried to apply the same concept to apartment living that he had attempted in a workers' housing development he had designed after World War I for the town of Pessac, near Bordeaux. In this earlier project, he had also wanted to replace "the brutality, squalor, and stupidity [of the typical town] with machines for living in." Trouble was, not many French seemed to appreciate living in Le Corbusier's cubist, architectural masterpieces. At Pessac, they had modified the houses to make them more cozy. They had replaced the horizontal windows with cottage windows, tacked on additional rooms, and hung the family wash on the roof terraces. They had also decorated the stark exteriors with plaster swans, flower boxes, and fake stone veneers.[10] In Marseilles, the residents preferred to shop and take their recreation closer to the ground so the space provided for such activities went largely unused. People called the Marseilles project the *"maison du fada"* (the nut house). Le Corbusier was offended and never designed another such building in France. His later apartments at Nantes, Briey-en-Forêt, and Firminy followed conventional designs. The French government also grew tired of such visionary planning. The costs of trying to control the whole range of urban activity were too high. After 1955, the government embarked on a policy of liberalization with greater opportunities for the private sector.

The Germans favored new urban construction, but they also wanted to save and restore as much of their ruined real estate as possible. Their passion to preserve the fronts of bombed-out buildings gave their cities a curious appearance—starkly modern facades frequently stood alongside German empire baroque. Much of the first building after the war was of inferior quality, however, due to the necessity to provide immediate housing for the millions of refugees who poured into the urban regions around Hamburg and in the Ruhr, the Rhineland, and the south. Later, spatial planning and design became more important, but this new emphasis led to a constant tug of war between private developers and public authorities who wanted to use planning as an element in the creation of a modern progressive society.[11]

Communist Development. The Communists associated cities with capitalist exploitation and therefore believed they had a duty to make radical changes in the urban environment in order to create a new society. Soviet leaders were also committed to changing their essentially agrarian country into an industrial powerhouse. In 1931, they officially decreed that urban society was the basis of modern Communism and announced that town planning should be dedicated to the dynamics of the work ethic. In the Soviet view, people lived in cities for the purpose of building socialism. In general, the Soviets preferred to transform their older cities by expanding into new districts away from the historical centers. Certain cities, however, had to be completely rebuilt. At Stalingrad, for example, new apartment complexes resembling rectangular boxes were built to house the workers near fortresslike factories laid out along a geometric grid. Cities like Stalingrad, which had suffered extensive damage during the war, were fairly easy to repair because there was no imperative to preserve important architectural monuments. However, the older towns with their historical and cultural treasures were another matter.

The war had brought a new reverence for the artifacts of the past despite their tsarist associations. Restoring the classical architecture of Leningrad, the city of the Revolution and the thousand-day siege, became high priority. As part of this commitment, the Communists allowed many of the city's old prerevolutionary street names to be revived, including that of the main thoroughfare, which again became the Nevskii Prospekt. At the same time, however, Leningrad had to accommodate a new influx of people. During the war, the city had lost about 2 million of its inhabitants, leaving it with a population of 639,000. By September 1945, the population had skyrocketed to double its size in 1940. Most of the recent migrants came from the rural areas of the Ukraine, Byelorussia, and the Tatar Republic and had few work skills suited to an urban environment.

The Leningrad experience was not unique. All the major Soviet cities experienced similar population growth. By the 1980s, the Soviet Union had 297 cities with more than 100,000 inhabitants, and about 75 percent of all Soviets lived in cities with more than 2,000 inhabitants.[12] Soviet planners estimated that by the middle of the twenty-first century that number would rise to 95 percent. Most of the increased population was housed in great superblocks that sprawled endlessly into the suburbs. Since very few Soviets possessed private motor cars, the residents of these apartment blocks became prisoners of public transportation. The complexes were occupied mostly by younger families, while older couples, pensioners, government officials, and students lived in the older residential districts. Only they could enjoy the old walking character of urban life.

Profile: Moscow and Paris

Paris

Both the Soviets and the French regarded their respective capital cities as the center of the world, the focus of their centralized state, and the heart of their civilization and art. Decisions affecting the world had been made in both Paris and Moscow. Each city had begun modestly and had grown outward in ever-widening circles, relentlessly pushing beyond a series of defensive walls. When these were torn down, they were replaced by boulevards, then by belts of housing, and finally by more boulevards and more housing.

Moscow, the center of the world's last great empire, was little damaged by the war. Therefore, the Soviets could simply continue the great plan for the city's transformation that had been developed in 1935. Already the center of the city had been transformed by the construction of new buildings—the most conspicuous being the Stalinist wedding-cake skyscrapers with their tall spires—and broad highways. The width of Gorki Street, Moscow's main thoroughfare, was more than tripled from its original forty feet. Moscow was to be the Soviet Union's model city, and its development was carefully controlled. Postwar planners limited its population to 5 million persons, a maximum they intended to enforce through the use of internal passports that allowed settlement only by special permission.[13] But these plans proved unrealistic. By 1965, the city's population exceeded 7 million people. The surrounding regions with their semi-isolated suburban subcommunities added another 28 million. The 1971 plan predicted that the population of the metropolitan area would grow to over 50 million by the year 2000. At the end of the 1980s, Moscow's population already approached 9 million people.[14]

In its headlong rush to create a new world metropolis, the Soviet government launched a massive housing program, extending the city's official limits and pushing the subway farther into the suburbs. Although the large expenditures on public utilities and apartments drained investment capital from other parts of the economy, the quality of the new construction was frequently shoddy. The social costs were also very high. The minimum size of each habitation cluster was 50,000 people. The huge apartment buildings, which were often built without connecting streets or integrated neighborhood services, remained isolated units, giving their residents no sense of neighborhood.

On average, people spent between two and four hours a day commuting to and from work. Shopping for food might add another two hours. Understandably, people placed an enormous premium on weekend leisure activities: theater, movies, sports, or watching television. Realizing this, the regime tried to encourage people to participate in social activities around their workplace. Women, especially, took advantage of these services as a relief from the demands placed upon them at home.[15] In their collectives, they could nurture friendships and enjoy some relaxation.[16] Moscow had a conspicuous absence of public restaurants, cafés, or marketplaces where friends could meet to chat and retreat from an overbearing political system. Shops were drab and lacked merchandise. The displays in the windows were frequently just an indication of what the store would sell if it had any goods to sell. Soviet planners did not consider shopping to be a valuable social or recreational activity.

The drabness of Moscow life resulted in high rates of public intoxication. To handle the drunkenness, the regime created a special police squad to round up the drunks and take them to one of the city's twelve sobering-up stations where they would be detained forty-eight hours. There was never a shortage of people to arrest. The special squads handled over 140,000 cases a year. They plucked tipsy Muscovites off the streets and responded to calls from shops, subway stations, factories and offices, and private homes. A person who was arrested three times in one year could be sentenced to a labor camp. Yet, alcohol was very expensive. A bottle of vodka in a state liquor store cost two-days wages, but black marketeers got twice that amount. Muscovites also drank home brew, hair tonic, eau de cologne, aftershave lotion, and medicinal alcohol.

Paris was more charitable to its drunks. The police seldom bothered them as long as they did not block traffic. Many drunks had the good sense to stay out of the way and sleep it off on side streets. Paris was also more tolerant toward its *clochards*. The Nazis had had no patience with such derelicts and cleared them off the streets. After the occupation, the bums came back, much to the delight of the Parisians who considered them part of the landscape. Paris contained all the activities, vices, and services appropriate to a great international metropolis: boutiques, world-class restaurants, fashion houses, five-star hotels, street vendors, and Gypsy children who picked your pocket. The city took in half of all the money tourists spent in France.

But Paris was also a working town, the center of activity for government and industry; it provided a livelihood for at least a quarter of the nation's population. Ever since World War I, the Paris region had been the country's largest industrial area—a preeminence that had caused many of its districts to become blighted with inadequate sanitation and pollution. Indeed, Paris was the center of just about every French economic activity except mining and truffle gathering. After Tokyo, New York, and London, it was the largest metropolitan area in the world. In 1964, the number of departements in the Paris region increased from three to eight; the city constituted an entire departement by itself. The nearer and outer suburbs beyond the city proper included 279 towns, over half with populations exceeding 10,000 people. At the end of the 1980s, Paris itself had 8.5 million inhabitants,[17] but most of the recent growth was in the areas of low-cost housing in the suburbs. Surrounding the city was a drab industrial belt of chemical plants, steel mills, textile plants, and automobile factories, the so-called Red suburbs, where the workers lived in public housing and traditionally voted Communist.

In Paris itself, the working class lived in the older sections around the Hôtel de Ville and to the east of the Latin Quarter, while the rich monopolized the districts in the western part of town near the Bois du Boulogne. Central Paris, the historic and artistic Paris of legend and lovers, covered only two percent or roughly eight square miles of the entire metropolitan area. This Paris retained much of its old character; in many areas it was still the Paris of Baron Haussmann, the great city planner of Napoleon III in the mid-nineteenth century. Here the old facades were preserved although many of the quarters were giving way to offices, luxury apartments, and condos.

More songs have probably been written about Paris than about any other city. Paris was, by legend, the city where everyone fell in love. Indeed, the city had a charm all its own. It was an easy city to navigate. Its public transportation was convenient and highly efficient, but it was still a place where people walked. It offered a cultural and social richness—day or night, at any season of the year— that few other metropolises could emulate. The weekly activity publication, *Pariscop*, contained almost 150 pages of activities: places to eat, sporting events, theaters and movie houses, music halls, clubs, and cabarets appealing to every sort of taste and perversion, from poetry readings and troubadours to the most explicit forms of pornography. Paris gave its inhabitants every reason to spend their discretionary income. Parisians were clearly not bored. Yet Paris had a divorce rate double that of the rest of the country.

The Material Ethic

For Love of a Car. A sense of alienation and a feeling of entrapment were not exclusive to Communist societies. In the so-called capitalist West, however, the pangs of desperation were alleviated by material opportunity. In the twenty years following World War II, Western Europe experienced its greatest period of sustained material growth. People expected their governments to ensure the continuation of this prosperity and to provide the consumer goods and comfortable lifestyle to which they had grown accustomed. They wanted protection against unemployment, poverty, and disease. Keynesian economics seemed to provide the perfect mechanism for balancing central direction with market forces.

In virtually all Western European countries, people with steady jobs were told that they had a right to a private automobile. The automobile industry, led by the British, Germans, and French, had consolidated itself into a few leading companies that were able to produce cars for a mass market. After World War II, these companies concentrated on small-car production. The idea of attracting lower-income buyers was not new; it dated back to the Austin Seven in Great Britain, the Fiat Topolino (Little Mouse) in Italy, and the Volkswagen in Germany in the 1930s. In 1947, the French state-owned Renault Company launched its popular 4 CV (750 cc), a four-seater with a rear engine and rear-wheel drive. At first, all these cars were colored desert-sand yellow from supplies of paint confiscated from Rommel's Afrika Korps. By 1950, the factories were turning out approximately 400 cars a day, with 20 percent of the sales going overseas. The Renault factory then employed 50,000 workers. The success of the 4 CV was followed, in 1956, with that of the more stylish Dauphine, which sold for $1,600, about $400 less than its nearest competitor. Soon most of the other major European car manufacturers were trying to duplicate Renault's success.

The reconstruction of the German motor car industry was aided by massive assistance from the United States. The Volkswagen Company, under Heinz Nordhoff, captured the popular car market while Opel, under the direction of General Motors, went after middle-income buyers. Nordhoff reputedly had a Nazi past that

The Mercedes-Benz was the status symbol par excellence throughout Germany and the rest of Europe. On this assembly line at the Daimler Benz factory at Stuttgart, several lines of 250 series cars pass a final inspection.

the British authorities were willing to overlook. Fiat, the largest company in Italy, had been badly damaged by the war but, within five years, had again risen to prominence with the moderately priced four-cylinder 1400, which featured unitary body construction and synchromeshed gears. Great Britain's entry in the mass auto market was the Morris Minor, unveiled in 1950. Over one million units were produced in its first decade of production. It continued to be produced for another ten years with virtually no modifications.[18] The European motor car industry, initially protected by import controls, enjoyed twenty years of continuous expansion. West German production rose from 219,000 private cars a year to 3,380,000; French production went from 257,000 to 2,168,000 units; the British from 523,000 to 1,729,000 units; and the Italian from 100,000 to 1,477,000.[19] Production increased in Eastern Europe as well, but on a much smaller scale than in the West.[20]

In Western Europe, new housing developments were always linked by roadway as well as rail to the great urban centers; in contrast, Eastern European countries rarely built more than train and subway connections. Almost all Western European countries constructed superhighways, the most famous being the German autobahns. These roadways, which had been started by the Nazis to make it easier to move their armies, were greatly expanded by the Federal Republic. The autobahns had no speed limits. The average cruising speed was around 125 kilometers or 78 miles per hour, but the fastest "flyers" usually drove their high-powered Mercedes-Benzes, Porsches, or BMWs at speeds in excess of 220 kilometers or 138 miles. The Germans claimed that the fastest drivers were the best drivers, but Germany, along with France, had the highest automobile death rate in Europe.

Greater mobility brought greater headaches in the form of monumental traffic jams, especially in older cities that had been built for the horse and buggy and for pedestrians. The supply of parking places could not keep up with the demand, and drivers left their cars anywhere there was room: on the grass in public parks, on sidewalks, and at the corners of intersections. Constabularies and police departments struck back with the "Denver boot," a bright orange clamp that attached to a wheel and immobilized the vehicle. To get the boot removed, the scofflaw had to pay a hefty fine on the spot. Many European cities also adopted bans against horn blowing. In Paris, where honking had been considered a constitutional right, the policy of prohibition proved a surprising success.

All urban planners tried to accommodate the design of their historical city centers to the invasion of vehicular traffic. Traffic was rerouted, certain streets became one way, boulevards were widened, and sidewalks were narrowed. Overpasses and underpasses were built. In Paris, an east-west freeway reduced the width of the Seine River. Cities tried to encourage people to use public transportation by making constant improvements and keeping the cost of commuting low. Meanwhile private developers built shopping malls away from the center of town. These vast multi-unit commercial centers came complete with their own free or low-cost parking facilities. Europeans liked these concentrated supermarkets, whether in or outside the towns. Here, they could buy everything from light bulbs to salami, from wines and spirits to Valencia oranges, from peanut butter to *paté de foie gras*. Having to go to five separate stores to get meat, milk, bread, beer, and vegetables no longer seemed quaint to those caught in the daily grind. Reducing the time spent on basic chores increased time for leisure and relaxation. It no longer seemed so important to know the butcher personally.

The Entertainment Center. As expectations for more material possessions increased, so did the demands for greater convenience. Within a generation after the end of the war, many Western Europeans had a more comfortable life-style than that enjoyed by ancien-régime monarchs whose drafty palaces lacked central heat, indoor plumbing, and electric lights. Most modern households did not have servants to do the dirty work, but they did have an abundance of helpful appliances. The most important of these was undoubtedly the television set. It did not clean the house, but it helped take one's mind off a dirty one.

In 1950, only Britain and the Soviet Union had national television, but by the end of the decade all the other European countries had established their own broadcasting systems. By 1970, Western Europe had 75 million sets, the Soviet Union another 30 million.[21] These quantities would double over the next twenty years until more Europeans owned television sets than had previously owned radios. The increased concentration of people in urban areas, where they could easily be reached by the relatively short-range television signals, made this explosion in viewership feasible. (Even the practicality of cable television, which appeared later, required a concentration of viewers.) Furthermore, since Europeans now spent relatively fewer hours at their jobs, they had more free time to lounge around.

The power of the electronic eye alarmed many intellectuals who lamented that cultural standards were declining. Dubious that television would ever live up to its high aesthetic promise, they blamed it for promoting indifference and apathy and predicted it would create a generation of illiterates. Nevertheless, the masses loved it and watched it three to four hours a day.

Television broadcasting in the Soviet Union was a state monopoly that presented the state's point of view. Lenin had said that it was the duty of the press to propagandize, agitate, and organize. Television continued this tradition and became a participant in the development of socialism, an assistant that would help the party accomplish its task. Soviet leaders admitted this propagandistic purpose quite openly and somewhat self-righteously. Consequently, Soviet television presented a consistently positive image of society and made no attempt to separate information from ideology. Domestic achievements were always presented in the most favorable light with heavy emphasis on the fulfillment of production quotas and lavish praise for exemplary workers whose pictures were on display in their factories. In a sense, television became the nation's "honor board." No matter what the program, viewers were reminded that they were working to build Communism and were encouraged to be more productive.[22] Soviet television was also expected to point up the contradictions inherent in the capitalistic system and therefore concentrated on strikes, labor violence, class conflict, social decadence, and crime. The principal source of this news was TASS (Telegraph Agency of the Soviet Union), founded in 1925, which got its information largely from Western television broadcasts. The State Committee for Radio and Television in Moscow approved all programming for 123 regional centers; its director was a government minister.

Sporting events were televised to instill pride in the Soviet system, which took the credit for the achievements of the athletes. Similarly, broadcasts of opera, ballet, and symphony orchestra performances were intended to promote cultural pride. Educational programs taught people, especially children, about the sacrifices of earlier generations. Soviet television favored documentaries and dramas that depicted the heroic struggles of World War II. Television not only attempted to make higher education available to those who did not go to the university, but also offered programs on literature, science, and the arts aimed at university students. Broadcasting to regional audiences was frequently a daunting task, considering that the Soviet Union included 129 ethnic groups, and 89 languages. This difficulty was somewhat offset by the general knowledge of the Russian language, a compulsory subject in all the nation's schools. Soviet television also broadcast Russian language classes as well as instruction in other languages, particularly French, Spanish, English, and German.

The regime wanted to give all Soviet citizens access to five channels through satellite and cable hookups, but most could receive only one channel. Moscow, the center of state broadcasting, had four channels, which carried national events, regional news, educational programs, films, and concerts. Most Soviet citizens could afford a black and white set although its cost—between 200 and 300 rubles—was equivalent to two months' salary. Color television, which had been available in the Soviet Union since 1967, cost twice that amount. Only one in twenty television owners had color.

In France, television broadcasting was also a state monopoly that operated on three channels through the ORTF (Office for French Radio and Television Transmission). The politicians of the Fourth Republic generally practiced a hands-off policy, allowing commentators a certain latitude and independence in presenting material unfavorable to the government. This policy changed with the advent of Charles de Gaulle. The general, who faced a hostile press, wanted to avoid as much additional grief as possible. Criticism dried up; those who persisted were fired or reassigned. Not until de Gaulle left office was the ORTF allowed to reestablish its own identity. News programs and political commentary formed only a small part of French television's offerings, however. Viewing fare ran the gamut from the sublime to the ridiculous, from grand opera to the silliest of game shows. Through it all, the French broadcasters retained a strong compulsion to educate.

One of the most prominent shows in the 1970s was "Screen Dossier," which featured a movie about some historical person or event followed by a high-level discussion of its meaning and relevance. The experts tried to outshine each other with brilliant analyses. For example, a film about Admiral Horatio Nelson, starring Laurence Olivier, drew commentary from historians, naval experts, and the great-grand-nephew of the commander of Napoleon's fleet, Admiral Pierre de Villeneuve, who refused to acknowledge that his famous ancestor had committed suicide. The ORTF also presented dramatizations of French novels. By initiating this type of programming, it managed to keep foreign imports down to less than 20 percent of the total. French television also included a hefty diet of boxing, soccer, bicycling, horse racing, and road racing. In addition, it had a *"Soirée poli-cière"* that showed cops and robbers movies.

At first, there was no commercial advertising. Then ads were presented in one chunk at the beginning of the viewing evening, just after the children's programs. Often this parade of thirty-second time bites was the most entertaining fifteen minutes of the evening. Pressure mounted to make French television more commercial. In the early 1970s, ORTF officials, facing persistent difficulties in balancing their budgets, allowed brand names to be introduced into programs. Sporting events were named after products, and private charities were allowed to solicit donations.[23] Some thought that the time had come to privatize the networks completely. This did not happen, but the state did loosen its control, permitting the number of channels to double, including the addition of an all-movie channel.

The Italian television industry, which was part of the state-owned RAI (Italian Radio-Television) company, also concentrated its commercials in a lively segment before the evening's main entertainment, but there the similarity ended. The Italian television corporation took elaborate precautions to avoid political domination by any one faction. Each news program had as many as six anchors, each representing one of the major political parties. Another way the company's directors protected themselves against the slings and arrows of controversy was to take refuge in the past. Italian television was strong on historical drama and culture. Its programming was generally of high quality, with many of its feature films being produced by the country's leading film directors—Vittorio da Sica, Federico Fellini, and Roberto Rossellini. Multipart dramatizations of novels were especially favored. Even then, the RAI had to take care lest a political or religious leader infer an insult from the dramatization of a novel or a past event. Nevertheless, Italian television managed to present rather hard-hitting historical drama. It successfully showed the seamy side of the pontificate of Alexander VI including his incestuous relationship with his daughter Lucrezia. However, one of Italy's most popular programs was also one of its most tasteless. In April 1987, the television impresario Umberto Smolia launched "Colpo grosso" ("Big Hit"). The format was an update of the traditional striptease in which, for extra points, a contestant could join the act. Viewership of the program surpassed 5 million a night.

The Dutch tried to avoid political arguments over programming by conceding regular television time to any group that had an established membership of more than 100,000 members. These groups included advocates of homosexual rights, abortion and sterilization, group marriage, and nuclear disarmament. The Dutch bragged that their television was the freest and most open in the world. Hilversum, a city twenty miles east of Amsterdam, not only was home to the Dutch broadcasting company, but became the headquarters for the largest associations. The conservatives, the Roman Catholic church, the Protestant church, and the socialists divided the lion's share of programming time. If others felt that their views were not adequately represented, they could try to form their own group. Despite their diversity, the major interest groups could not afford to be too heavy-handed if they wanted to attract an audience. Accordingly, they kept their opinion programs down to a minimum and tried to steer clear of controversy elsewhere. One way of doing so was to buy foreign programs—for example, "Bonanza," "Dallas," and "Falcon Crest" from the United States—all of which were presented in their original versions with Dutch subtitles.

In Germany, the regional governments, the Länder, were responsible for licensing television stations. As a result, various regional stations were established with the most powerful located in major urban areas, like Hamburg, Cologne, and Munich, where the viewing audiences were the largest. These giants determined the bulk of the programming. Sports, news programs, and detective shows were popular fare, but other offerings also attracted viewers. "Tutti-Frutti," a spin-off of "Colpo grosso," added wacky filmstrips and, like its parent version, was immensely popular.[24] Such bawdiness was a far cry from German television's origins in 1935, when it was required to imprint the image of the Führer in the hearts of the German people. The quality of much German programming was rather low. People debated whether "Sesame Street" was a desirable program for German children, but stations had no hesitancy about buying other American programs for their viewers. "Dallas" was hugely popular here as well.

The British had begun regular transmissions of high-definition television back in 1936, but had yet to develop an audience. Consequently, only 10,000 people watched the coronation of George VI in May 1937. Sales for the limited number of television sets were slow, and the government was reluctant to finance a program of expansion. Despite the lack of additional subsidies, the BBC directors were determined not to raise monies through commercial sponsorship. At the same time, they realized that if this new medium were ever to attract a wide audience, it would have to make concessions to the tastes of the British people. Hence, the last program to be televised before the BBC went out of business on 1 September 1939 for the duration of World War II was a Mickey Mouse cartoon.[25]

The BBC resumed broadcasting in June 1946 and remained the only source of television programming in the British Isles until 1955 when commercial television broke the government monopoly. Lord Reith, the BBC's founding father, likened this intrusion to an assault by "smallpox, bubonic plague, and the Black Death."[26] Nevertheless, the competition proved to be a blessing. Under a new director, Hugh Greene, BBC television became less stodgy and academic. The number of channels expanded, as did the variety of programming. Vulgarity, which was certainly not alien to British audiences, came into its own. Comedians like Benny Hill made a career of chasing scantily clad females. In the famous "Steptoe and Son," a junk dealer constantly bickered with his family, especially his son; in "Till Death Do Us Part," the inspiration for American television's "All in the Family," the balding middle-aged cockney Alf Garnett ranted and raved against every ethnic, social, or religious group he hated—and he hated them all. Whenever the queen's name was mentioned, he became a superpatriot. The British loved it and made Alf Garnett a national hero.

When the BBC was at the top of its form, it set an enviable standard of excellence. Its dramatic adaptations of novels, historical series, and cultural programs established its reputation at home and abroad. The U.S. Public Broadcasting System benefited from the availability of such programs as "Upstairs, Downstairs," "Elizabeth R," "Civilization," "The Ascent of Man," "The Fall of Eagles," and "The Flame Trees of Thicka." Even the Roman Empire soap opera "I Claudius" traveled extremely well. Amplifying its original mission to educate, the BBC produced some riveting documentaries. "The War Game," which dealt with the aftermath of an atomic attack on Britain, chillingly understated its grisly effects. Another documentary, chronicling the effects of smoking, lampooned the romanticized ads of the tobacco companies by showing Marlboro country to be inhabited by a lot of wheezing cowboys on their last legs from cancer and emphysema.[27]

The medium of television was a natural for a highly literate people such as the British. They kept their programming remarkably free of political and commercial pressure. The BBC was thus able to criticize British politicians mercilessly often with a great deal of insight and black humor. A popular program of political satire once had a feature showing a puppet version of Prime Minister Margaret Thatcher at the hairdressers. "Make it a style that's universally popular," she tells the barber, whereupon he promptly cuts off her head. On 5 October 1969, the BBC received the gratitude of millions when it first presented "Monty Python's Flying Circus," showcasing the most zany bunch of comic geniuses to come along since the Marx Brothers.

If television could make stars out of people playing fictitious characters, it could also make heroes out of performers who played themselves. Nowhere was this truer than in the realm of professional sports.

Modern Sports

Urban Nationalism. Modern European sports enthusiasts marked their year with playing seasons just as medieval peasants marked theirs with religious festivals. The sporting year began in the fall with soccer. It then proceeded through the winter with hockey and into the spring and summer with bicycling and tennis. Between times, there were skiing events, motorcar grand prix, horse racing, boxing, and basketball—one of the very few sports the Europeans adopted from the United States. Modern commercial sports were vastly different from the old upper-class competitions played for fun in English public schools.

Soccer, already established as a solid team sport before the war, was far and away the most popular. This game, like rugby and field hockey, began its modern development in Britain during the last half of the nineteenth century.[28] Reportedly, it was spread abroad by railroad construction crews who played it in their time off. In any case, working-class players took over from the aristocrats, formed their own clubs, and held regular matches in front of paying audiences. Increased professionalization, bigger purses, better communications, and improved organization spread the competition nationally and internationally. The World Cup competition drew greater radio, television, and live audiences than any other sporting event.

The attraction of soccer lay in its simplicity. It did not require a great deal of money to play, equipment was minimal, and a flat playing surface was all that was necessary to get started. In time, vast stadiums were built, such as Berlin's 35,000-seat Grunewald Arena, which was finished before World War I. Soccer action was fast paced, continuous, constantly changing, and ever-fluid. All players, with the exception of the goalkeeper, were expected to attack or defend whichever was necessary, whenever necessary. Fortunes changed frequently and instantaneously, and a player was constantly required to balance his own egocentrism with the necessity of playing as a member of a team. Thus, the player had to be both aggressive and cooperative, individualistic but helpful. Timing and setting up scoring opportunities were paramount.

The age of television turned the game into great theater and the soccer players into superheroes. The teams had their own battle colors, legends, superstitions, groupies, and sacred victories.[29] They retained strong local and regional ties. In Britain, many of the most dedicated fans came from the industrial Midlands and the lower-class districts of London and Glasgow. When match day arrived, they

Belgian police confront angry soccer fans at Heysel stadium in Brussels, 29 May 1985. Moments later, the rioting spread to the stands. In the melee scores of people were trampled to death.

eagerly anticipated "the peaks of high tension and emotional drama that the game will bring, breaking their steady routine with surging moments of almost unbearable excitement."[30] The teams enhanced the reputation of the urban areas they represented. Bringing home a silver cup was tangible proof of the superiority of both the team and its region. Pep rallies were held to confirm this loyalty. Since soccer was so territorial, it was only natural that teams might perform less well on the turf of their opponents. Visitors coming to watch a match on home turf were often regarded as invaders. This hostility could lead to verbal insults and even violence.

The amount of hooliganism attached to soccer appeared to increase after the 1960s, especially in Great Britain. Fans attacked each other, the referees, players, and police officers. Following a match, the visitors' dressing room might be besieged. Postmatch demonstrations resulted in dented cars, broken shop windows, vandalized buses and trains, and even burned buildings. In 1985, incidents of violence were particularly numerous. Following a rampage at Luton in March, Prime Minister Thatcher called a special cabinet meeting to discuss emergency measures. An apprehensive sports minister, Neil McFarlane, canceled the annual Scotland versus England match at Wembley because he feared things might get out of hand. On 11 May, the Leeds fans ran wild on Birmingham City's field, injuring ninety-six police officers. One boy died after a wall collapsed on him. But the worst was yet to come.

On 29 May at the European Cup Finals in the Heysel stadium in Brussels, supporters of Turin's Juventus, a club owned by Fiat's boss Gianni Agnelli, began throwing pieces of crumbling masonry at the Belgian police. Then, a group of drunken Liverpool "Reds" fans charged Juventus's fans who retreated in panic. In the melee, a barrier collapsed. Thirty-eight people were killed. The riot was witnessed by hundreds of millions of people watching on television. (The game continued—Juventus beat Liverpool on a penalty kick.) The British Football Association conducted an investigation and banned all British teams from participation in matches on the Continent for one year. The Thatcher government enacted legislation prohibiting alcohol sales at English playing fields and outlawing special football trains and buses.[31]

Everybody had an opinion about what had gone wrong. Some believed that soccer violence was society in microcosm, a protest against inadequate living conditions and too few job opportunities. Others found explanations in the changing nature of the soccer crowds, especially those who stood in "the terraces." The spectators here were mostly white, young, working-class high school dropouts who were used to asserting tribal territoriality. With the disappearance of the old class solidarity and the erosion of traditional values, devotion to football provided the young with "a kind of surrogate community," giving them a way to demonstrate hardness and machismo and an opportunity for "mixing it up."[32] In a sense, this fierce pride and aggressive behavior were part of a larger context in which people viewed sports as an expression of national pride. In their first half century, the Olympiads had been more reflective of national rivalries and hostility than of international peace and harmony. The years after World War II were hardly an exception.

Olympic Nationalism. The Olympiads were halted for World War II as they had been for the world conflict a quarter of a century before. When the games resumed in 1948, the Cold War had begun and would continue to influence competition for the next generation and a half. The 1956 Melbourne games were held shortly after the Soviet Union had crushed the rebellion in Hungary. Anticipating trouble, Avery Brundage, the president of the International Olympic Committee, reminded people that the games were "contests between individuals and not between nations."[33] It did no good. A semifinal water polo match between the Soviet and Hungarian teams set off a riot in the stands as well as in the pool. But the worst violence ever to besmirch the games occurred in 1972 in Munich when eight Palestinian terrorists of the Black September group invaded the Olympic village and took nine Israeli athletes hostage. The gunmen demanded the release of two hundred Arabs being held in Israeli jails. The Israeli government refused and told the German government to do the best it could. In a final shootout at Furstenfeld-bruck airport, German sharpshooters managed to kill five of the terrorists but not before the terrorists had killed all their hostages. With this drama in progress, the Olympic games continued as before. When the full extent of the massacre became known, the games were called off—for one day. Any illusion that the Olympic games could insulate themselves from the imperfections of the world at large had been shattered forever. In certain quarters, using the games for specific political purposes even became respectable.

In early 1980, the United States decided to boycott the games in Moscow in protest against the Soviet invasion of Afghanistan the previous December. The action was part of a series of measures the Carter administration took against the Soviets, including an embargo on grain and on all sporting goods and Olympic-related products. President Jimmy Carter solicited international support for the policy, and ultimately sixty-one other countries also decided not to send teams. The games took place anyway, with eighty-five countries present.[34] The boycott proved mainly symbolic, hardly an adequate basis upon which to conduct foreign policy. It certainly did not persuade the Soviets to change their policy toward Afghanistan. The main damage was suffered by the 6,000 athletes who were deprived of the chance to display their all-too-transitory skills. Four years later, the Soviets had an opportunity to return the favor by refusing to participate in the Los Angeles games. Most of the Eastern bloc countries followed suit. The absence of the Soviets weakened the quality of the competition, but gave the United States the opportunity to dominate the games in a way it had not been able to do in years. Never was American nationalism more on display or so blatant as in the television coverage of the events by the jingoistic commentators of the American Broadcasting Company.[35] The American athletes, especially the good-looking, fair-haired members of the gymnastics team, were hailed as heroes, shining examples of all that was good and noble about the United States. In a way, such adulation was in the Olympic tradition, but American pride was so narrowly focused that no other country could relate to it.

CHANGING ATTITUDES AND VALUES

A New Feminism

Guarantees—Written and Practical. Modern wars cannot be waged without the participation of women even though most of the fighting is done by men. Recognition that women's efforts were indispensable for success in World War I made it difficult to deny the "weaker sex" the same legal rights as men. Only France, Italy, Belgium, Switzerland, and Hungary refused.[36] This omission was finally rectified after World War II when women in these countries were finally granted equal social and economic rights.

The Italian constitution promised women equal pay for equal work and equal eligibility for public office. It protected them against working at night, hard or dangerous jobs, and termination of employment because of marriage or pregnancy. By law, women had the right to retain their maiden names, have an equal say in where the family lived, and determine how the children were to be educated. A woman could have her own bank account and could travel abroad without her husband's permission. If a woman worked for a firm employing more than thirty-five people, she could insist that the firm provide free nursery care for her minor children. Italy eliminated all the restrictions of the Fascist and pre-Fascist eras and replaced them with one of the most progressive packages of legal protection enjoyed by women in Europe.

Similarly, the 1946 French constitution guaranteed women legal, economic, and social equality as did the Basic Law (1949) of West Germany. And in the Soviet Union, much of the antifeminist legislation of the Stalin years was revoked after the dictator's death in 1953, as the Communist regime returned to the official liberalization of earlier times. The Soviet Union pretended that because socialism promoted the emancipation of everyone regardless of class, race, or sex, no separate women's issue had existed. This theme was echoed in the Soviet satellites, all of which drafted constitutions that insisted the sexes enjoyed the same rights and privileges.

The International Labor Office (ILO) of the United Nations boosted the cause of women's rights by drafting two pieces of model legislation that were designed to end discrimination against women in the workplace: the Equal Remuneration Convention (1951) and the Employment and Occupation Convention (1958). All the countries of Europe, except the United Kingdom, officially ratified these provisions. The British passed a more comprehensive Equal Pay Act and Sex Discrimination Act (1975), protecting women against discrimination in pay and working conditions and guaranteeing them equal educational opportunities and equal retirement compensation. The law also forbade discrimination in the provision of goods and services including housing. Other countries also showed their determination to go beyond the ILO provisions. In 1981, the French created a special Ministry for Women's Rights to help train women for technically advanced jobs and to promote women's cultural activities, including the sponsorship of literary competitions. The ministry also helped prepare new legislation on women's issues. In 1986, it became part of the Ministry for Social Security and Employment. Other countries had comparable commissions and councils that were entrusted with the task of promoting and monitoring women's rights. The Austrians had a Government Committee for Women's Affairs (1969); the Finns had a Council for Equality (1972); the Danes had an Equal Status Council (1975); the Dutch a Woman's Emancipation Council (1981) and a Woman's Arbitration Body; the Swedes an Equal Opportunities Research Commission (1983) and an Equal Opportunities Ombudsman; and the West Germans a Central Office for the Equality of Women (1979) and a Department of Women's Affairs (1986), which was part of the Federal Ministry of Youth, Family Affairs, Women and Health.[37]

Although women had more options and received more protection than before, the kind of egalitarian society promised by the postwar constitutions was a long way off. Many of the constitutional guarantees lacked proper legislative codification; and even where laws had been passed, many of them were not enforced. Women's groups therefore devoted less of their time to calling for new rights than to trying to obtain those already accorded. The struggle was not without hope. Women were better trained and educated than ever before; they were entering the labor force in greater numbers; and they were no longer willing to remain passive.

Women under Communism. Despite the laws on equality, Soviet men still considered women biologically inferior; women were loved, but not respected. Yet women comprised a greater percentage of the labor force than did men (50.9 percent in 1986) and also edged men in enrollment in higher education and in many of the professions. Sixty percent of the doctors were women and 72 percent of the schoolteachers. Nevertheless, equality eluded them. Ironically and importantly, the high female participation in medicine, education, and elsewhere did little to raise the status of women. It simply lowered the status of those professions. Women were conspicuous by their absence in leadership or managerial positions. The majority of Soviet women, old and young alike, continued to be employed in low-paying, manual labor jobs. They were especially numerous as street sweepers, window washers, painters, and hod-carriers. They accounted for more than one-third of the road construction crews. Educated women usually filled jobs beneath their skill levels and earned only 70 percent as much as their male counterparts. In industry, only two percent of the women earned the same as the men who performed the same job.

The full weight of child raising also fell on their shoulders. Stalin had preached the cult of motherhood, but had done little to relieve women's burdens by providing adequate child care facilities or a sufficient supply of relevant consumer goods. In addition to completing a full work schedule, women were expected to wait in long lines for the family's food. About the only thing that men waited in line for was vodka. The Soviet Union had serious shortages of baby care products and feminine hygiene and beauty products. If a woman wanted to make herself more attractive, she had to do so without basic cosmetics. When Estée Lauder opened a shop in Moscow at the end of the 1980s, it had to impose a four-item limit to control the demand despite the high prices of its products. At Lauder's a basic cosmetic budget could easily equal one-third of a woman's average monthly wage. Christian Dior's Moscow outlet also priced its products beyond the range of most Soviet consumers. In October 1990, the first Russian language edition of the *Ladies Home Journal* appeared in Moscow. Its 10,000 copies were quickly snapped up despite the fact that the seven-ruble cost was more than a day's pay for an average Russian woman. The magazine described a world beyond the reach of most of its readers. Upon reading the articles, including those on how to make the perfect dessert, how to look like fashion models, and why husbands should do more around the house, some Russian women were divided as to whether they should laugh or cry.[38] Small wonder that the Soviet Union, especially the Russian Republic, became a nation of one-child families. The social impact of this trend is still unclear.

Half of Soviet marriages ended in divorce. Women complained that men were rude and incapable of sustaining warm relationships. The grounds most frequently cited for divorce were adultery, poor fathering, and alcoholism. Many couples had married in order to obtain an apartment, and the apartment became the chief item in the property settlement. Frequently, the couple continued to live in the same apartment after the divorce because the former husband had no place else to go. The result was anger and often violence.

In the other nations of the Communist bloc, women also formed a high percentage of the active labor force. In the 1980s, they were 45 percent of the work force in Hungary, 46 percent in Czechoslovakia, 45 percent in Romania and Poland, and more than 47 percent in Bulgaria. As in the Soviet Union, women remained concentrated in the lower-paying jobs in the service sector. In Romania, the only woman in the ruling politburo was Elena Ceausescu, wife of the president. On the whole, Czech women were better educated than men, but they filled three-fourths of the lower-status jobs, mainly positions in retailing, the service sector, and health services. In Poland, the development of feminist sentiment had been complicated by the prominent position of the Catholic church, which regarded women primarily as wives and mothers. The Polish birth rate was high, and abortions, although legal, were performed less frequently than in any other country in Eastern Europe. In Hungary, feminism exercised an influence not found in other Eastern European countries, but it remained an urban phenomenon, concentrated mostly among the artistic and intellectual elite whose members found it difficult to organize into a national movement. Women in Communist countries were expected to follow the direction of the government. Their primary goal was to encourage the other members of their sex to fulfill the state's economic goals. In East Germany, Hungary, and Romania where the birth rate was low, women's societies were also required to encourage the production of more babies.

Female Rights in the Western Democracies. Nobody had given women their rights until they demanded them. However, women in the Western democracies had greater opportunities to organize and assert their strength than the women in Eastern Europe. In the early days of the feminist movement, solidarity among women often meant hostility to men. Following the lead of Simone de Beauvoir, women argued that they had to change the culture in which they lived. In her monumental work *The Second Sex*, de Beauvoir argued that women would never shed their second-class status until they became economically independent. "It is through gainful employment that women have traversed most of the distance that separated her from the male; and nothing else can guarantee her liberty in practice."[39] But economic equality was only part of the solution.

Western European women already had entered the labor force in increasing numbers, but as in Eastern Europe, many were concentrated in low-paying, low-status jobs; women accounted for a smaller number of the high-paying jobs in individual occupational groups than did men.[40] In France, 45 percent of the women were in "female professions" such as nursing and secretarial work. French women were also likely to work fewer hours per week than men and were usually the first to be let go during a recession. In Britain, women made up over 80 percent of the part-time work force and over three-fourths of those employed in food services, cleaning, and hairdressing. In Ireland, 93 percent of all typists were women, as were 61 percent of all textile workers. In Sweden, 78 percent of primary schoolteachers and 53 percent of the secondary schoolteachers were women. In Spain, employers could still dismiss pregnant women. Western European women, on average, earned between 65 percent (Germany) and 86 percent (Denmark) of the pay received by men.

In the 1960s and 1970s, the number of women's organizations grew dramatically. Many of these had their own newsletters and meeting places, coffee houses, and shelters. Some of these organizations had originated in the late nineteenth century. For example, Britain's National Council of Women dated from 1895; Italy's *Unione Femminile Nazionale* (National Female Union) had been founded in Milan in 1899; and the *Nederlandse Vereniging voor Vrouwenbelangen* (Netherlands Association for Women's Interests) had been established in 1894. These "traditional" groups wanted to remove the barriers to full female participation in the life of the nation while giving protection to working women and their children. However, most of the Western European women's organizations that came into existence after World War II were more narrowly focused. The *Parti Feministe Unifié* (United Feminist party) of Belgium wanted to ban the production of all nuclear and chemical weapons. The French *Ligue de Droit des Femmes* (Women's Rights League) campaigned for the elimination of physical and mental abuse of women, giving particular support to women who were trying to regain their children who had been kidnapped by Algerian fathers. The *Associazione Nazionale Donne Elettrici* (National League of Women Voters) campaigned for electoral reform and encouraged Italian women to exercise their right of suffrage. The Movement for the Ordination of Women pushed for the admission of women to the Anglican priesthood. Other European women's groups created facilities and support groups for lesbian women, divorced women, housewives, and working women. Sweden's *Alla Kvinnors Hus* provided sanctuary for women and children who were victims of physical or sexual abuse.

Such groups discovered that government authorities were extremely reluctant to become involved in domestic relations between a husband and his family no matter how violent. Women also found it difficult to persuade a traditionally male-dominated society to accept women in nontraditional roles. Many men still believed that the only true woman's job was that of housewife and mother, and they resented the competition that women presented when they succeeded in entering business and the professions. Women who did get their feet in the door found it difficult to advance into the upper echelons. In Italy, women still suffered from a rigid caste system within the family that rising affluence, ironically, did much to reinforce. When it was no longer necessary to have two incomes to make ends meet, many women quit work and returned to the home where their prestige was much greater. However, this phenomenon did not occur in France where motherhood did not have the same hallowed cachet. French working women got more support from the trade unions, which were generally willing to support women's causes. Moreover, Frenchwomen had impressive historical forebears: warriors like Joan of Arc (canonized in 1920) and Jeanne Hachette; painters like Berthe Morrisot, Elizabeth Vigée-Lebrun, and Rosa Bonheur; writers like Georges Sand, Marie-Madeleine de La Fayette, and Colette; and scientists like Marie Curie, Irène Joliet-Curie, and Emilie du Chatelet.[41] With such role models, Frenchwomen could confidently avoid feeling guilty for not devoting their talents to the so-called domestic pleasures, but many Frenchmen no doubt shared the sentiments of Voltaire, the lover of Madame du Chatelet, whom he praised by saying that "she was a great man whose only fault was in being a woman."[42] Moreover, other European women probably did not consider their French sisters as liberated as they seemed to be. In May 1991, France obtained the first woman premier in its history when President François Mitterrand appointed Edith Cresson to the post. Cresson's combative style did not seem very ladylike and earned her a certain amount of gratuitous criticism.

Until Cresson's appointment, the only major European nation with a female head of government had been Great Britain.[43] Many had served in lesser posts, however, as cabinet ministers, regional administrators, or legislators in national and provincial assemblies. Among the minor powers, Portugal had a female prime minister in Maria des Pintassilgo, who formed a two-week caretaker government in July 1979. Of longer duration was the election of Mary Robinson as president of Ireland in November 1990. Robinson, a Socialist and leading constitutional lawyer, campaigned on a platform of pluralism and women's rights. Government and business, however, continued to be dominated by an "old-boy" network, a group of chums whose bonding had been accomplished in their formative years when females were regarded as members of another race.

British women who might have challenged this exclusive male-club mentality tended to avoid political and social causes and devoted many hours to genteel charity instead. Consequently, women continued to be discriminated against in university enrollments and were less likely than their sisters on the Continent to enter a profession. Some women left the country to make careers elsewhere. But British women did not want to make a fuss; they put their class before their sex.

In Germany, however, the reduced numbers of men because of the war heightened women's prestige. Men still held a majority of the important positions in business and politics, but women were elected to national and state offices in increasing numbers. They were more prominent in the service sector than in the professions and suffered because of their popular image as *Hausfrau*, but they also held important positions in labor, industry, and education. German women were often obliged to do double duty. Working outside the home did not give them an excuse to neglect their wifely and motherly duties. Demanding husbands had little sympathy if dinner was not ready on time or if their shirts were not properly ironed. Some attributed the demands put on women to lingering authoritarian patterns in German society, possibly reinforced by traditional religious practices.[44] In any case, the superwoman work ethic continued to flourish.[45]

An Americanized Exterior

A Manner of Speaking. American English is a hungry language. It gobbles up foreign words and expressions with great voracity, creating an enormous linguistic resource in the process. The Americans are also generous in their linguistic exports, and therein lies the problem. Throughout Europe, defenders of linguistic purity mobilized in a grim stand against the back-across-the-ocean invasion. The French were especially alarmed and tried to rally their troops to defend the barricades. Already before the war, some words had crept in such as *pullover, knockout, cocktail, self-service, lunch, poker,* and *slapstick.* Now the struggle seemed to grow more desperate. The new arrivals included *hamburger, bulldozer, briefing, pipeline, timing, ketchup, motel, blockbuster, landing,* and *poster.* Those who tried to head off the onslaught proposed French equivalents. They wanted to call blue jeans *les salopettes;* the happy hunting ground would become *le pays de la chasse perpetuelle,* and a pie fight would be *une débâcle à patisserie*. But the contest was lost from the beginning. Borrowed words were here to stay. Not surprisingly, the most successful intruders were the words with the greatest cultural influence such as sports terms or words related to food, fashions, business, politics, and entertainment. The words entered the French language unchanged except in pronunciation, appearing in the masculine gender. Some Americanisms were modified slightly, but hardly enough to make a difference. A *bartender* became *un barman*; an *escalator*, once an *escalier roulant*, became an *escalateur*; a supermarket was a *supermarché*, and *picnic* survived as *piquenique*. There were *les holdups par les gangsters* and *le eye-liner avec eye-shadow*. Some nouns emerged in an abbreviated form: *un pull* for *a pullover*, *un trench* for *a trench coat*, and *le foot* for *football* (soccer). Curiously, however, *jogging* became *le footing*; and wrestling was *le catch* from the old-fashioned English phrase catch-as-catch-can.

Even linguistic purists had to recognize that some of their translations were conceptually inadequate. The *weekend*, an Anglicanism, was different from *la fin de semaine*, the latter referring more to location than to the leisurely interlude between work weeks; and a *fauteuil* was less comfortable as a seat than a *lounge chair*. Furthermore, the defenders of the French language could not overcome the growing tendency of the French to equate Americanisms with sophistication, just as the English upper classes often used French expressions to be snooty.

Articles and letters to the editor appeared in the European press, complaining that American speech was bastardizing the language. The perceived damage was usually worse than the reality, if indeed any damage had been done at all. Moreover, European peoples who butchered their native tongues hardly needed help from the Americans. Slang was practiced generously in all countries, and elegance had nothing to do with it. But mounting watch on the linguistic beaches facing westward across the Atlantic seemed more worthwhile than building linguistic barricades against the forces of Babel at home. European youths listened to American popular music and mouthed the words of songs in American English. American speech patterns began to permeate foreign consciences. The British often used American expressions because they were class neutral and frequently more direct. At one time Europeans had tried to speak English with an Oxonian accent, but that was now being challenged by the accent of the American Midwest.

In England, some people maintained that language *was* the clearest form of class delineation.[46] One word was thus deemed better than another. For example, to *have one's bath* was considered Upper Class or U, while to *take a bath* was non–Upper Class (non-U). *Stays* were U, *corsets* were non-U; *jam* was U, *preserves* were non-U; *rich* was U, *wealthy* was non-U. Non-U speakers ate *dinner* at noon and took their *evening meal* at night, while U speakers had *lunch* in the middle of the day and *dinner* at night. Many non-U usages were Americanisms. A U father of an eleven year old remarked, "I tell my son he can go anywhere but to the toilet. To the lavatory, the loo, what-have-you. But the toilet—it grates on my ears."[47] Professor Alan Ross of the University of Birmingham maintained that the modern phenomenon of verbal distinctness came about with the creation of the new-rich class in the 1960s; old-line aristocrats lapsed into determined anachronism to set themselves off from the upstarts.

Fast Foods and Fashion. A restaurant in Wiesbaden advertised its pizza as "real American" and insisted that it tasted better. Most of this "junk food" might have been a caloric and cholesterol horror, but it was a boon to the timesavers and pinchpennies and frequently was quite palatable. American food culture was not just displayed on a few streets in a few locations, it was everywhere: McDonald's, Burger King, Colonel Sanders, Wendy's, Pizza Hut. The menus were reassuringly familiar, and the terminology was practically identical. Fries and Coke were fries and Coke in any land. So was a cheeseburger—hamburger *mit käse*, or *avec fromage*, or *con formaggio* did not make the grade.[48] Although the American impact on Europe was frequently overestimated, this was not the case in the imperialism of such proletarian bill of fare. Even Iron Curtain countries were not immune.

After fourteen years of negotiations, McDonalds opened its first *Big Mak* in Moscow, finally raising the golden arches on Pushkin Square in February 1990. The emporium had a seating capacity of 700, making it one of the largest hamburger joints in the world. Its 605 employees could serve 15,000 customers a day. Twenty-seven thousand people had filled out applications to work there. The $50 million deal had been closed by McDonald's Canadian subsidiary, which agreed to purchase all the restaurant's raw materials from Soviet producers in exchange for control of its own distribution plant, located just outside Moscow. Here, McDonald's had its own bakery, dairy, meat processing plant, and microbiology laboratory. It practiced quality control on its waiters, training them to look each customer in the eye and smile. The Muscovites loved the friendly service—so rare in their own native businesses—and stood in line as long as forty-five minutes to get served. By Soviet standards, the wait was short. A Big Mak, french fries, and milkshake initially cost 5.5 rubles, roughly half an average day's pay. The customers took their plastic forks and Styrofoam plates home as souvenirs.[49] That was a good thing too, for everywhere else in Europe the American fast-food craze had left litter in its wake—cast-off hamburger wrappers and red and white decorated boxes with the picture of an elderly, goateed gentleman in a string tie, the perpetrator of an American culinary delight known as "finger lickin' good." Everybody knew, of course, that Styrofoam coffee cups did not cause litter, people did.

Fast-food restaurants were merely one aspect of a food merchandising onslaught that included a wide range of products that found their way down European gullets.[50] The product that best expressed the American style and philosophy of eating was breakfast cereal. Although corn flakes and other cereals had already been established in Europe after World War I, these were now joined by an array of breakfast foods with designer names like "Captain Crunch" and "Frosted Mini-wheats." In the meantime, Europeans had developed their own, less spectacular versions. The British had created *Wheatabix*, which received the endorsement "By-appointment-to-Her-Majesty-the-Queen." The cereal was a kind of wheat cake that turned soggy as soon as the milk hit it, creating an instant mush. The British pretended that they designed it that way.

Such products adapted themselves well to the urban rushing-off-to-the-job environment. In families where eating in a hurry, often alone, was not a necessity, breakfast could be more in keeping with local culture: kippers and fried bread for the British, "bouncers" egg and ham on bread for the Dutch, a boiled egg and *wurst* on pumpernickel for the Germans. The French still had croissants and the Italians polenta (cornmeal mush). However, even these so-called traditional breakfasts were not eaten every morning—they were expensive and took too long to prepare.

American-style convenience foods, based on improved food technology and mass production, affected other aspects of the European diet. Tomato ketchup and baked beans did not exert the same kind of social influence on the European food culture as fast-food restaurants and packaged breakfasts, but they were immensely popular items nevertheless. The war of the colas—Pepsi versus Coke—was fought out on European battlefields with the persistence of the dynastic wars of bygone years. That the popularity of such sugary fizz-water might have contributed to a diminished consumption of alcohol was possible but not proven, especially not in France where alcoholism still killed more people than in all the other Western European nations combined.

The faster-paced urban societies of Europe also found sustenance in other American exports. High fashion was still associated with the great *couturiers* of Paris and Rome, but leisure and sports attire was becoming increasingly Americanized, especially among the young. It was frequently impossible, even in Moscow, to tell nationality from attire. Jeans, T-shirts, and sweat suits all became internationalized. The keen observer might be able to pick out national characteristics from the shoes, but not from the ankles up. European youths adored pullovers with American university logos. American informality of dress was not only comfortable, but it conveyed a sort of proletarian chic.

The Sexual Revolution

Contraception and Abortion. After World War II, Europeans entered the greatest period of sexual transformation in their history.[51] This change was variously ascribed to the trauma of two world wars, the weakening of religious ties, the drive for equality by women, the availability of contraception and abortion, and the ease with which people could terminate their marriages. Many countries had recognized adultery, cruelty, and desertion as legitimate grounds for divorce before World War II. Now, they recognized divorce by mutual consent.[52]

By the 1960s, people had the time, money, and desire to practice as well as accept new forms of sexual behavior. They were also more willing to talk about it publicly. Orgasms, masturbation, and homosexuality were discussed freely in the press and on television. Women no longer regarded sex as a painful duty, but as a natural right. Not having "good sex" was dysfunctional. Women demanded an end to all restraints that controlled their sexuality and fertility. Through protests and political lobbying, they won a great deal of control over their own bodies. Contraception was legalized and often subsidized through public health services.[53] In any case, it was readily available in all Western European countries save Ireland. In Eastern Europe, contraception, though legal, was constrained by the inadequate supplies and low quality of contraceptive devices. Condoms, when available, were generally of such poor quality that they broke during use. In the Soviet Union, more than half of the women had no reliable form of birth control. Some even believed that contraception was dangerous for one's health. Consequently, for every 100 live births, there were 106 abortions—the highest rate in the world. Abortion was clearly the Soviet Union's standard form of birth control—an estimated 50 million were performed in the 1970s and 1980s. An average woman underwent between five and six abortions; some had as many as twenty-five.

In 1920, the Soviet Union had become the first European country to legalize abortion, only to see it prohibited again under Stalin in 1936. The prohibition lasted until the dictator's death in 1953. The 1938 Swedish law legalizing abortion was the first of its kind in Western Europe. This measure was liberalized in 1975 to grant a free abortion on request up to the eighteenth week of pregnancy. After that, obtaining an abortion was less routine, but in general any Swedish woman could get an abortion unless the abortion presented a danger to *her* life. By the 1980s, most of the countries of Western Europe had laws permitting abortion.

The British abortion law dated from 1967. Denmark adopted one in 1973, West Germany and France in 1974, Italy in 1975, Finland and Austria in 1978, Norway in 1979, and Spain in 1985. Many countries imposed restrictions, however. In Britain, abortion was available with the approval of two doctors, provided that the pregnancy presented a threat to the woman's physical or mental health. In the Netherlands, the abortion had to be performed in a special licensed hospital. In France, a woman had first to receive special counseling and then wait a week. In Germany, the waiting period was three days. Luxembourg permitted abortion in cases of rape or if the fetus was malformed or presented a danger to the woman's health. Doctors in Britain, Austria, and Italy could refuse to perform an abortion on grounds of personal conscience. Under a 1985 Spanish law, abortion was permitted in the first trimester if the pregnancy resulted from a rape, and in the first twenty-two weeks if the fetus was malformed.[54] Abortion was still listed as a crime in the Swiss penal code, but the practice was permitted if the woman's life were in danger. Enforcement of the code was left to the cantons' discretion. Geneva once enjoyed a reputation as one of the abortion centers of Europe. French women unable to obtain abortions in their own country flocked there in great numbers for "routine" D and Cs (dilation and curettage). Abortion was prohibited only in Belgium and Ireland. In September 1983, in a national referendum, Irish voters approved adding the ban to the constitution. Consequently, many women went to other countries to terminate their pregnancies.

The number of legal abortions in France in 1986 was 166,797; 88,540 were performed in the German Federal Republic in 1987; 174,652 in the United Kingdom in 1987; and 84,540 in Hungary in 1987. In 1984 in Italy, 228,377 abortions were performed, most of them in the industrial north. Hospitals could not keep up with the demand. Many more unauthorized abortions, through shame or ignorance, were reputedly undertaken in rural areas.[55] In Romania, the Ceausescu regime allowed abortions only for women over forty years old and for those with four or more children. Women who wanted to travel outside the country were checked before they left and after they returned to ensure they did not have an abortion while abroad.

Pornography. By reputation, France was the country of the dirty postcard par excellence. There Americans and British could buy all those books that had been banned in their own countries—from the unexpurgated edition of D. H. Lawrence's *Lady Chatterley's Lover* to Henry Miller's *Tropic of Cancer* and collections of dirty limericks. However, the French market was not as open as most people believed. Charles de Gaulle began a crackdown on hard-core pornography. The distinction of being the first European country to remove *all* restrictions on explicit materials therefore went to Denmark.

In 1969, the Danes permitted the publication of all pornographic material and allowed it to be distributed to anyone over the age of sixteen. Copenhagen's porno merchants celebrated the law with a "Sex 69" fair. Porn shops, "film centers," and a wide variety of magazines grew like mushrooms. "Private clubs" catered to various pornographic tastes. Tourists came to Denmark by the thousands, some on charter flights. But the Danish pornography boom did not last long. The craze ran its course, the tourists had their fill and left, and at the end of the summer season, over 80 percent of the smut shops closed. Knud Thestrup, the Danish minister of justice who had introduced the bill abolishing the indecency statutes, had predicted the novelty would soon wear off.[56] The Danes felt vindicated. Their society was freer and studies showed it had suffered no ill effects. Incidents of rape and exhibitionism remained about the same, but child molestation had decreased.

Other countries followed the Danish example. The end of restrictive legislation in Germany produced a new class of porno-entrepreneurs like Beate Uhse who opened a sex shop, the first in an empire of such boutiques that spread throughout Germany. Uhse became one of her country's most successful businesswomen and a national celebrity. She was featured in articles and appeared on television talk shows. Her face became as familiar as that of a movie star.[57] The marketing of pornography was so prevalent in European cities that few natives paid much attention to it. London had Soho, where peep shows nestled side-by-side with the ethnic restaurants for which the area was once best known. In Paris, those who found the show at the vaunted Folies-Bergère or the Lido too tame could visit the famous Crazy Horse Saloon, a topless bar. Other night clubs featured acts that were even more revealing. Public advertising also began to feature nudity. Nude beaches appeared in many countries. Every age and every society of modern Europe has in some way commercialized sex. Nevertheless, few periods since the decline of the Roman Empire have been more openly "permissive" than the postwar era.

The accelerated breakdown of conventional morality and the increased mobility of populations led to a wide spread of sexually transmitted diseases. Syphilis became epidemic in 1944 and 1945, but the use of penicillin, which had been discovered in 1939, gave the authorities the means to bring the disease under control. Postwar treatment was initially so effective that optimists predicted that syphilis would soon entirely disappear. This was not the case as its revival in the 1960s showed, but the concern over the increased incidence of this once-dread disease were soon directed at a "new" ailment that was both noncurable and deadly.

The AIDS Pandemic. Acquired immune deficiency syndrome, or AIDS, first began to spread in an observable way in 1981. The virus had probably been existent before then, although its current, deadly form may have been a recent mutation. The disease was carried in blood and semen and spread chiefly in urban areas.[58] Hemophiliacs, recipients of blood transfusions, and heroin addicts were all high risk, but most of the early cases of AIDS were contracted by homosexuals and by those with multiple sex partners. As such, the disease became a matter of instant shame. Some moralists even considered it evidence of God's judgment. People with common sense, though, realized that such a disease has no regard for sexual preference, and they looked to science to find the cause and develop a cure.

In Europe, AIDS was first detected in Copenhagen, one of Europe's most sexually tolerant cities. All of the Danish victims had direct or indirect links to infected persons in New York, Los Angeles, and San Francisco.[59] Soon, instances of AIDS were discovered in France, England, West Germany, Spain, Portugal, Belgium, Switzerland, and Portugal. All of the victims had connections with infected people in either the United States or Africa. The Africans, suffering from a different strain, spread the disease mostly through heterosexual contact. Modern aerial transportation and the increased movement of peoples rapidly escalated the disease into a pandemic. The world was not only smaller, it had become more socially and sexually permissive. It also used more hypodermic needles and gave more blood transfusions.[60]

In June 1983, Dr. Luc Montagnier, director of the Pasteur Institute in Paris, confirmed that his research team had isolated the AIDS virus. The initial discovery had been made the previous January by Françoise Barre. (The technology enabling her to do so had only become available as recently as 1978.) The Pasteur Institute's breakthrough did not take the scientific world by storm. Indeed, the National Cancer Institute (NCI) at Bethesda, Maryland, where similar work was in progress, was positively hostile. The NCI's leading retrovirologist, Dr. Robert Gallo, even insinuated that the French results had been contaminated. The NCI's reluctance to credit the work of French "amateurs" was a disturbing example of scientific nationalism that cost precious time in fighting the epidemic.[61] French researchers even had difficulty getting their articles published in American journals.

Finally, in April 1984, the NCI announced its own discovery of the virus. The French protested this slap in the face without success. Their work continued to be slighted. In 1985, the Pasteur Institute filed a lawsuit against the NCI demanding a share in the royalties that the NCI had received from its patent of an AIDS blood test. Montagnier had strong evidence that Gallo had used French research samples to make his discovery, but the French were suing for more than the money, which would be theirs from a patent on the blood test. They wanted full credit for their accomplishment.[62] The matter was settled out of court in March 1987, when President Ronald Reagan and Premier Jacques Chirac signed an agreement recognizing Montagnier and Gallo as co-discoverers. The incident was probably the first time heads of government helped to resolve a question of who should take credit for discovering a virus. The virus was named human immunodeficiency virus, or HIV.

During the first half of the 1980s, European health officials viewed AIDS as an American problem because the United States continued to be the most heavily infected part of the world, with two-thirds of its cases occurring in New York City. In time, however, the steady increase of AIDS cases in Europe changed their attitude. From 1984 to 1988, the number of reported instances in Europe jumped from 880 to 20,000. France had about one-third of the total; over half of the cases were concentrated in the Paris region. French medical demographers believed these figures were too conservative and estimated that as many as a quarter of a million people were HIV positive. The French also led Europe in treatment of the disease. While their antiviral drug HPA-23 was not a cure, AIDS sufferers from around the world flocked to Paris, feeling they had nothing to lose. This migration included American movie star Rock Hudson, whose affliction helped to increase public awareness of AIDS. American patients were gratified that the French viewed AIDS as just another disease like leukemia, not a moral judgment.[63] Cases of AIDS also rose dramatically in Italy where most of the infections—about 70 percent—involved drug users, the opposite of northern Europe where AIDS continued to be a disease primarily affecting homosexuals.[64]

Communist bloc countries considered AIDS a capitalist disease, something to be expected from a decadent society. The Soviets even asserted that the virus had been developed in the biological warfare laboratories of the CIA. They maintained that the Soviet Union had no AIDS cases because it was virtually free of drug abuse and had only 70,000 homosexuals, all of whom were registered with the Ministry of Health. By the end of the 1980s, however, the Soviets had come to their senses. They either refused to reveal or did not know the precise number of confirmed cases of AIDS, but they were plainly worried. *Pravda* estimated that 15 million Soviet people would be infected with AIDS by the year 2000.[65] Soviet authorities now concentrated on finding solutions, but the backward nature of Soviet health services made this extremely difficult. The system had problems handling even rudimentary infectious diseases. Encouraging safe sex was difficult when the economy could not even produce enough condoms. Moreover, there was a chronic shortage of diagnostic kits. In 1986, the Ministry of Health set a goal of establishing 1,000 diagnostic testing centers throughout the Soviet Union to perform 1.5 million tests a month.[66] However, announcing goals was one thing, achieving them another. In the meantime, the Soviets concentrated on screening Africans and other foreigners, deporting anyone who tested positive.

One of the primary ways AIDS was transmitted was through intravenous injections. In the West, most such transmittals occurred through the use of "dirty" needles by drug users; in the Soviet Union, the contamination happened in hospitals. In 1988, a group of mothers and children contracted the disease in a Ukrainian hospital where unsterilized syringes were reused. There was insufficient alcohol to clean the needles because people would drink it. Romania experienced an even worse scandal, which came to light only after the death of President Nicolae Ceausescu in December 1989. Tests carried out on children in pediatric hospitals showed that one-third of them had AIDS. They most likely had contracted the disease through the reuse of dirty needles and through the traditional Romanian practice of injecting minute quantities of adult blood into children to make them stronger. The Ceausescu regime had ordered the testing stopped, pretending that AIDS existed only in capitalist countries.[67]

AIDS was also present elsewhere in Eastern Europe.[68] East Germany admitted to having 4,000 victims, the highest number in Eastern Europe and, in January 1990, signed an agreement with West Germany for AIDS assistance. Yugoslavia was reported to have more AIDS cases than Romania. The fall of the repressive dictatorships brought a more honest attitude toward the disease, but the desperate state of health care and the greater freedoms encouraged its spread. Condoms remained in short supply, as did lifesaving syringes, diagnostic testing, and treatment facilities. Poland simply denied AIDS patients entrance to hospitals. Sexual promiscuity, a heightened use of illicit drugs, and increasing contacts with foreigners put these societies at high risk. In 1990, the World Health Organization detected a shifting pattern of HIV transmission away from Europe and North America to Africa, parts of the Caribbean, and Latin America. It was a small consolation.

POSTSCRIPT   After World War II, Europe's cities defined the strength, values, and identity of their respective nations as never before. They called the tune in art, music, and sports and provided the arena for the further emancipation of women, which proved to be a necessity for continued national prosperity. No modern society could exist without the active participation of its female population. French Premier Edith Cresson said that it was easier to do without men. "I say, in general, that you can replace men everywhere except in private life," she quipped.[69]

Women became more prominent in the European work force because they were increasingly holding down jobs that had been male monopolies. In addition, the nature of work itself was changing. Women gained ground in the sectors that used new technology: banking, insurance, biotechnology, and information management. Even if women did not achieve executive positions in proportion to their numbers, they did account for a significant minority of supervisory positions. Women now enjoyed the same property and inheritance rights as men. They had similar educational opportunities and could file for divorce. Along with these practical gains, women began to demand an end to the gender prejudices inherent in their languages and argued that their cultures should be studied from a woman's perspective.[70] They also wanted to serve in the armed forces in combat roles.

Men, though, continued to dominate, especially in professional team sports. Thanks to the increased coverage provided by modern electronics, the playing field became sacred turf. Jet transportation enabled teams to maintain a widely dispersed schedule, and satellite transmissions and instant play-by-play transformed the weekly game into something resembling a historical force. For television viewers, professional sports satisfied the search for identity and enabled the most determined layabout to participate vicariously in the great cult of youth. Sports promoters presented the matches as theater, creating a sort of urban nationalism that transcended class.

The most significant change in the way people entertained themselves, however, was in their new attitudes toward morality. Saint Augustine believed that marriage was the only place for sex and that its only purpose was procreation. But now the more respected prophets were those like Havelock Ellis and Sigmund Freud who wrote that sex was natural and desirable, pleasurable for men and women alike. The old strict moral codes crumbled before this new attitude. The great sexual revolution after 1945 led to the widespread liberalization of the laws on divorce and abortion and to a freer attitude toward sexual mores. However, the sudden intrusion of the deadly AIDS virus again made people cautious. In 1990, the World Health Organization predicted that between 8 and 10 million people worldwide would contract the fatal disease during the following decade. The greatest relative increase would occur in women and children.[71]

The last chapter on the bitter AIDS discovery controversy has yet to be written. In the 1987 agreement, the Pasteur Institute agreed to split the revenues coming from the invention of the blood test with American researchers. However, in December 1991, following the disclosure that the U.S. Department of Health and Human Services had withheld crucial data supporting the French claim to prior discovery, the Pasteur Institute, backed by the French government, demanded that the earlier agreement be renegotiated.[72] There were few scientists who were by then reluctant to accord the French the credit they deserved. However, many people were more inclined to reserve their highest accolades for those who would eventually produce a cure for the disease.

ENDNOTES

1. See Larry Collins and Dominique Lapierre, *Is Paris Burning?* (New York: Simon and Schuster, 1965).
2. *Survey of International Affairs: Four-Power Control in Germany and Austria* (1956), 7–11.
3. By comparison, German air raids killed 58,000 British civilians.
4. John McGinnis, *Military Government Journal* (Amherst, Mass.: University of Massachusetts Press, 1974), 304.
5. In 1986, the percentage of the population living in cities of more than 2,000 people was 91.4 in Spain; 88.5 in the Netherlands, 87.8 in the United Kingdom, 80 in the German Federal Republic; 76.8 in the German Democratic Republic; 74.7 in

Czechoslovakia; 73.4 in France; 65.8 in the Soviet Union; 65.2 in Bulgaria; 60.7 in Poland; and 50.5 in Romania. United Nations, *1968 Demographic Yearbook* (New York: United Nations, 1968), 199–302.

6. Leonardo Benevolo, *The History of the City* (Cambridge, Mass: MIT Press, 1980), 967–1008.

7. In contrast, the British preferred row houses to huge apartment complexes, and about three-fourths of their new buildings took this form.

8. See Carlo Cresti, *Le Corbusier* (London: Hamlyn, 1969) and Maurice Besset, *Who Was Le Corbusier?* (Geneva: Skira, 1968).

9. Le Corbusier, *Towards a New Architecture* (London: John Rodker, 1931), 60–61.

10. In 1980, the Bâtiments de France assumed the authority to approve all future construction projects at Pessac in the hope of eventually restoring the district to its original condition, but many of the houses' owners put up a stiff resistance. Fiona Gleizes, "For Living, It's Hard to Beat a House," *Newsweek,* 8 March 1990, 28.

11. See David H. McKay, *Planning and Politics in Western Europe* (New York: St. Martin's Press, 1982).

12. United Nations, *1988 Demographic Yearbook,* 302, 330–33.

13. B. Michael Frolic, "Moscow: The Socialist Alternative," in H. Wentworth Eldredge, *World Capitals: Toward Guided Urbanization* (New York: Doubleday, 1975), 309–15.

14. The population of Leningrad, the Soviet Union's second largest city, was about 4.5 million. United Nations, *1988 Demographic Yearbook,* 330–33.

15. Francine du Plessix Gray, *Soviet Women: Walking the Tightrope* (New York: Doubleday, 1989), 183.

16. Ibid., 185–86.

17. United Nations, *1988 Demographic Yearbook,* 322.

18. Marco Ruiz, ed., *One Hundred Years of the Automobile, 1886–1986* (New York: Gallery Books, 1985), 78–86.

19. Brian R. Mitchell, *European Historical Statistics, 1750–1970* (New York: University of Columbia Press, 1975), 469.

20. Private car production in the Soviet Union rose from less than 500 to 294,000 with most of these cars intended for official use; Czech production went from 24,500 to 132,400; East German from 7,200 to 12,100; and Polish from less than 100 to 47,000. Ibid., 469.

21. The Soviets were second only to the United States in overall number.

22. Jean Philippe Rapp and Roger Burkhardt, "Heroes, Workers and the Party Line" (Geneva: Swiss Television, 1979). Distributed by the Corporation for Public Broadcasting, David Fanning, Executive Producer.

23. Ruth Thomas, *Broadcasting and Democracy in France* (Philadelphia: Temple University Press, 1976), 117.

24. It gave rise to yet another version that debuted on Spanish television in 1991.

25. The BBC ceased broadcasting because the television antenna was a perfect direction finder for German aircraft. Asa Briggs, *The BBC: The First Fifty Years* (London: Oxford University Press, 1985), 155–71.

26. Timothy Green, *The Universal Eye: The World of Television* (New York: Stein and Day, 1972), 83.

27. The British also had an independent television network that tried to be less intellectual, more informal, and more regional than the BBC. It too had its share of great successes, chief among these being the action serials "The Avengers," "The Saint," and "The Prisoner."

28. The basic rules established in 1862 have never changed, namely, that the ball must be moved with the feet and may not be aimed at another player. Joan M. Chandler, *Television and National Sport: The United States and Britain* (Chicago: University of Illinois Press, 1988), 132–52.

29. Desmond Morris, *The Soccer Tribe* (London: Jonathan Cape, 1981), 114.

30. Ibid., 234.

31. H. V. Hodson, *The Annual Register, 1985* (London: Longman, 1985), 456–57.

32. Richard Holt, *Sport and the British: A Modern History* (New York: Oxford University Press, 1990), 337–39.

33. Richard Espy, *The Politics of the Olympic Games* (Berkeley: University of California Press, 1981), 40.

34. Ibid., 188–97.

35. Randy Roberts and James S. Olson, *Winning Is the Only Thing: Sports in America since 1945* (Baltimore: Johns Hopkins University Press, 1989), 207.

36. Some countries had already accorded women the right to vote before the war. Finland had done so in 1906, Norway in 1907, and Denmark in 1915.

37. See the appropriate national entries in *Women's Movements of the World*, edited by Sally Shreir (Burnt Mill, Harlow, Essex: Longman, 1988).

38. Thom Shanker, "Sorry, Natasha, U.S. magazine is dreamland," *Chicago Tribune*, October 7, 1990, 1, 18.

39. Simone de Beauvoir, *The Second Sex* (New York: Alfred Knopf, 1976), 679.

40. By the 1980s, women comprised over 49 percent of the active work force in Sweden, 45 percent in Norway, 43 percent in Great Britain, 40 percent in Belgium, 38 percent in West Germany, 37 percent in France, 36 percent in Italy, and 33 percent in Luxembourg and the Netherlands.

41. Madame du Chatelet, the author of the physics text *Institutions de physique* (1740), possessed a confidence in her abilities that spoke directly to women of all ages: "It may be that there are metaphysicians and philosophers whose learning is greater than mine, although I have not met them. Yet, they are but frail humans, too, and have their faults; so, when I add the sum total of my graces, I confess that I am inferior to no one." Margaret Alic, *Hypathia's Heritage: A History of Women in Science from Antiquity through the Nineteenth Century* (Boston: Beacon Press, 1986), 147.

42. Alic, *Hypathia's Heritage*, 139.

43. In Norway, though, Gro Harlem Bruntland had served twice as prime minister.

44. Uta Ranke-Heinemann in her book *Eunuchs for the Kingdom of Heaven: Women, Sexuality, and the Catholic Church* (New York: Doubleday, 1991) attacked the Roman Catholic church for its sexism in vilifying women as the cause of men's passions and lust. Ranke-Heinemann felt that in emphasizing theological gymnastics, the church had failed to teach men and women to be more humane and kinder to each other. The German Catholic church took the book in stride. *Chicago Tribune*, 3 March 1991, Books, 7.

45. See Shari Steiner, *The Female Factor: A Study of Women in Five Western European Societies* (New York: Putnam, 1977).

46. Alan Ross, "U and Non-U," in Nancy Mitford, ed., *Noblesse Oblige* (New York: Harpers, 1956), 56–58.

47. *International Herald Tribune*, 20 November 1969.

48. In all fairness, the all-meat patty, as well as the sausage known in the United States as the hot dog, originally came from Germany. But the Americans knew a good thing and turned these items into true foods for the international market. The cheeseburger seems to be an American refinement.

49. Thomas Moore, "For the Leninists It's Mac in the U.S.S.R.," *U.S. News and World Report*, 12 February 1990, 11; Ann Blackman, "Moscow's Big Mak Attack," *Time*, 5 February 1990, 51.

50. Magnus Pyke, "The Influence of American Foods and Food Technology in Europe," in C. W. E. Bigsby, *Superculture: American Popular Culture and Europe* (Bowling Green, Ohio: Bowling Green University Press, 1975), 83–95.

51. Alfred Kinsey's works, published after World War II, were highly influential in Europe. *Sexual Behavior in the Human Male* (New York: W. B. Saunders, 1948) and *Sexual Behavior in the Human Female* (New York: W. B. Saunders, 1953).

52. Germany and Switzerland recognized the irretrievable breakdown of a marriage. In Ireland, a popular referendum in June 1986 on a proposal to legalize divorce was defeated with 63.5 percent against the measure.

53. Certain fundamentalist Protestant churches and the Roman Catholic church staunchly opposed all "artificial" contraception. The Catholic church regarded the "rhythm method" as the only acceptable form of birth control.

54. The law was bitterly opposed by the Spanish bishops who threatened to excommunicate anyone who received or assisted an abortion.

55. United Nations, *1988 Demographic Yearbook*, 393–94.

56. Jan Sjöby, "Denmark and Pitfalls of Pornography," *International Herald Tribune*, 30 August 1979.

57. Steiner, *The Female Factor*, 210–11.

58. The term AIDS unfortunately is not very adaptable phonetically outside the English language. The French, though, had their own analogous acronym in SIDA (*Syndrome d'Immuno-Déficience Acquise*).

59. Mirko D. Grmek, *History of AIDS: Emergence and Origin of a Modern Pandemic* (Princeton, N.J.: Princeton University Press, 1990), 21–22.

60. Ibid., 109.

61. Randy Shilts, *And the Band Played On: Politics, People, and the AIDS Epidemic* (New York: Penguin Books, 1988), 372.

62. Ibid., 592.

63. Ibid., 562.

64. Grmek, *History of AIDS*, 194.

65. Jerome E. Groopman, "Red Scare, AIDS in the U.S.S.R.," *The New Republic*, 17 April 1989, 25.

66. Ibid., 27.

67. See Eloise Salholz, "Watching the Babies Die," *Newsweek*, 19 February 1990, 63; and Andrew Purvis, "Rumania's Other Tragedy," *Time*, 19 February 1990, 74.

68. "A sneak attack of Eastern Europe," *U.S. News and World Report*, 19 February 1990, 11.

69. Sharon Waxman, "For Cresson, honeymoon is over," *Chicago Tribune*, 20 July 1991.

70. Bonnie S. Anderson and Judith P. Zinsser, *A History of Their Own: Women in Europe*, vol. 2 (New York: Harper and Row, 1988), 426–29.

71. Anne-Christine d'Adesky, "WHO predicts dramatic rise in global AIDS toll: Women and children newly affected," *UN Chronicle* (December 1990), 66–68.

72. *Chicago Tribune*, 31 December 1991, Section 1, 1 and 12.

CHAPTER 23

HIGH BROW, LOW BROW

PREFACE   Popular culture and elite culture had been rivals since, at least, the beginning of the twentieth century. After World War II, however, the contest seemed to gather intensity, although it was hardly a fight to the death. The two could coexist, albeit with a certain amount of snobbishness from one and spite from the other. Cultural elites who prided themselves on their refined taste and looked down their noses at those who preferred more basic forms of entertainment could always point to history to justify their attitudes. Indeed, great works of art, practically by definition, proved more durable than those of lesser quality, which were produced for a mass market and maximum revenues. Elites could also count on governmental support. Those aspects of culture deemed to be of the highest quality and worthy of preservation had always enjoyed a certain amount of official favoritism.

In music, government subsidies favored the works of the great masters, allowing them to be performed in appropriate surroundings. This was especially true of grand opera. More than most other forms of musical creativity, opera became a matter of national pride. Opera houses were cultural basilicas, places of reverence and worship as well as centers for entertainment.[1] World War II, unfortunately, had not been kind to these great edifices. Practically all of Germany's more than fifty opera houses were either partially or totally destroyed. The casualty list included the prestigious Berlin Staatsoper and the Munich Bayerische Staatsoper. Italy's opera houses, the most numerous in Europe after Germany, had also experienced extensive material damage, including the severe bombing of La Scala in Milan, the nation's best-loved opera house. In Austria, another world-famous building, the Staatsoper, had suffered even worse damage from an attack in 1945 that left only the vestibule and the loggia standing.

When the fighting stopped, nations and cities frequently gave the highest priority to the reconstruction of their opera houses and concert halls,

705

often in a form as close to the original as possible. In Vienna, private homes had to wait while the opera-loving Viennese rebuilt the Staatsoper.[2]

Despite all the special attention lavished on opera and other high-brow forms of musical entertainment, these never won a truly mass audience. Popular entertainment was to be found elsewhere. Young audiences, in particular, liked the music from the United States, with its Afro-American cultural roots. They turned its musicians into folk heroes, made many of them multimillionaires, and accorded them the status of poets, prophets, and social revolutionaries. The most significant musical export was rock and roll, which, thanks to the speed of communications and the physical presence of the American military, arrived in Europe as fast as it did at home. The Europeans assimilated rock and roll so well that they were soon contributing to its development. In Britain popular musicians gave the genre a new life of titanic proportions.

The presence of the United States was also felt in the world of the visual arts. European painters and sculptors had crossed the Atlantic after World War I, and the fusion of their energy and talent with that of the Americans had produced a true international art style. Much of this new modern art was confusing and controversial and left spectators and traditionalists perplexed and bewildered. Giorgio de Chirico, the principal founder of metaphysical painting, remarked with great disillusionment, "No one enjoys modern art, neither those who do it, nor those who buy it. They are all afraid to tell the truth."[3] But such a statement could hardly be taken seriously considering that modern art encompassed many more diverse styles than the art of almost any previous age.

THE VISUAL IMAGE

Post-Modernism

The Nonobjective Renaissance. Abstract expressionism, the artistic style that held sway after 1945, seemed ideally suited to the confusion and anxiety of the age of mutually assured destruction. Actually, however, the style first developed in Europe prior to World War I and gradually spread throughout the world.[4] Eventually, New York City became the center for abstract expressionism, but many of its most famous practitioners were European expatriates. Although these painters came from diverse backgrounds and were fiercely individualistic, they shared common nonobjective roots. They were determined to create a new art that was resistant to and independent of the restraints of a materialistic society.[5] Many were in their forties when World War II ended.

Arshile Gorky, a Turkish-Armenian who came to the United States in 1920 when he was sixteen, created a series of biomorphic paintings, splashed with bold contrasting colors, in which all the abstract objects seem to be in the process of transforming themselves into something more alarming. His close friend Willem de Kooning, born in Rotterdam in 1904, was equally nonobjective, but painted with more dynamic brush strokes that he slashed across the canvas in jagged, architectural lines, aggressively conveying the power of the haphazard—a form of dramatic creativity that had first appeared in the surrealist automatic painting of the 1920s. This form of artistic spontaneity with its revolt against academic conformity influenced Wyoming-born Jackson Pollock, who created the drip technique.[6] Pollock stood on a stepladder or a chair and poured paint from a bucket onto a canvas or board. He used commercial pigments applied directly from a can. Pollock would also fling or splash his colors without predetermined patterns. The physical process itself was thus part of the artistic result and became known as action painting.

This form of creativity, largely divorced from geometric traditions, showed that abstract expressionism was not so much a style as an artistic concept. If its practitioners had anything in common, it was their strong individuality. Still, despite its amorphous internationalism, some practitioners of abstract expressionism were influenced by more traditional antecedents.

In France, for example, many abstract artists preferred a more Cartesian and less free-spirited approach. Pierre Soulages imposed formalistic black strips on a colorful background to produce depth and perspective in the restrained manner of oriental calligraphy. Roger Bissière, who created the geometric abstract school, blended strong lyrical color with the cubist tradition of Cézanne. Meanwhile Jean Bazaine drew on a wide range of periods and cultures, claiming not only Cézanne and Rembrandt but also Paolo Uccello, Van Eyck, and Vermeer as his artistic forebears. In addition, he said he was influenced by African art, Hindu, Chinese, and primitive Greek sculpture, and the religious aspect of medieval art.[7] Bazaine was looking for something beyond painting and trying to express a universal truth. In his abstract landscapes, he attempted to give greater dimension to the external world.[8] For him, unlike Pollock, abstract painting was a matter of precision, an eternal quest for the essential. Sometimes he repainted his canvases as much as fifty times "to get an effect which seemed to [him] to express a truth, or a more accurate and more profound aspect of reality."[9] His fellow countryman, Alfred Manessier, agreed. Manessier saw abstract painting as the means by which he would achieve "a higher sense of reality and take account of what was essential in himself."[10] In his paintings, a flowing geometry of irregular shapes moved through a sea of color.

In general, though, the abstract expressionist revolution seemed to float freely in time. Although its European roots were obvious, encompassing the whole expressive tradition of modern art from Cézanne onwards, it leapfrogged so rapidly across national boundaries that any predominant tendencies soon got jet lag. Creative techniques also varied. Some artists painted conventionally to gain better control of gesture and texture; the so-called color-field painters pushed a wide variety of materials to their limits to form powerful images with the force of randomness. Consequently, abstractionism cannot be appreciated by relying on comfortable generalizations, but only by concentrating on the specific output of individual painters.

Art and Popular Culture. Not all artists wanted to divorce creativity from the recognizable—far from it. For every artist who wanted to retreat into a purer, abstract world, at least as many wanted their art to represent the figurative world around them. Their goal was to produce a graphic depiction of the real world of machines, science, and consumerism. They wanted an art that embraced the garish and the smelly city environment of popular taste—an art that was the essence of modern society. In their view, art should reflect modern urban culture, not a pastoral wilderness. Necessarily, their art built upon the banal and the vulgar.

Nonobjective art was inaccessible; it was foreign and distant from most viewers. In art museums, spectators passed quickly through the rooms where it hung. They found it dull. Popular art, on the other hand, spoke directly to many people. It was the art of the billboard, the poster, the comic strip, and sometimes the obscene graffiti on the walls of buildings. It appeared in cigarette, clothing, and perfume advertisements, enlivened newspapers, and flashed across television screens.

In 1956, the Whitechapel Art Gallery in London hosted an exhibition called "This is Tomorrow." The show featured the works of the Independent Group, young artists who were fascinated by the new popular urban culture epitomized by postwar America. The exhibit proposed to introduce viewers into a series of modern environments; its tone was set by the entrance display, a collage by Richard Hamilton entitled *Just What is it that Makes Today's Homes so Different, so Appealing?* The collage consisted of a series of images that included all the artifacts of modern society: a television set, a tape recorder, a vacuum cleaner, a canned ham, a suite of boxy furniture with a black lacquer cocktail table, a Ford logo on a dark lampshade. A stripper, clad only in pasties and a bow around her waist, reclined on the sofa with a lampshade on her head. In the left foreground was a body builder in posing strap carrying a huge lollipop labeled "tootsie pop." A picture of the cover of a "young romance" comic book hung on the wall; a movie theater could be seen through the window. There was a picture of the moon on the ceiling.

The collage's creator was demonstrating the intellectual parameters of pop art, whose qualities he described as transcendent, witty, sexy, youthful, and glamorous.[11] Hamilton was touting and satirizing the extravagant pleasures of American consumerism in a postausterity Britain. Other practitioners of the style hardly needed Hamilton to tell them how to tout the new economy of abundance.

The Swede Claus Oldenburg, who spent many of his early years in the United States with his diplomat father, carried the artistic lampoon of postwar commercialism to absurd heights with great canvas-filled, sculptural creations of everyday food items: an eleven-foot-long ice cream cone (*Floor Cone*), a huge piece of cake (*Floor Cake*), and a giant hamburger (*Floor Burger*). "I am for U.S. Government Inspected Art, Grade A art, Regular Price art, Yellow Ripe art, Extra Fancy art, Ready-to-eat art, Fully cleaned art, Spend less art, Eat better art, Ham art, pork art, chicken art, tomato art, banana art, apple art, turkey art, cake art, cookie art," he wrote.[12] Oldenburg carried his architectural-scale concepts into the construction of a monumental *Clothespin*, a *Giant Ice Bag* (with a mechanism inside to make it move), a *Lipstick (Ascending) on Caterpillar Tracks*, a *Baseball Bat*, and a *Giant 3-Way Plug*.[13] Equally arresting were certain projects that never were realized—the *Good Humor Bar* proposed for Park Avenue in New York City, *Scissors in Motion* intended to replace the Washington Monument, and the two toilet balls designed to float on the Thames River near the Houses of Parliament. He also proposed a new facade for the Chicago Museum of Contemporary Art in the shape of a geometric mouse. Oldenburg's surrealistic concept of the menace of everyday objects both glorified and mocked the mechanistic society that had given them birth.

Pop art had a dual nationality—Britain and the United States—and a dual ancestry—the urban consumer society and the world of Dada.[14] In the postwar era, everyday objects were made in such quantity that they no longer possessed any distinction independent of their utility. If in a disposable society everything seemed to collapse in a welter of cultural egalitarianism, then perhaps the disposable had to be taken more seriously.

Roy Lichtenstein found the inspiration for his art in the comic strip. He cribbed from the pages of actual war and romance comics, enlarging them to monumental proportions. His famous triptych, entitled *As I Opened Fire*, was taken from "Wingmate of Doom" in the Detective Comics book *All-American Men of War* series. A fighter plane is shooting off its 50-caliber guns, with each succeeding section being a close-up of the preceding panel. The title proceeds: (1) "As I opened fire, I knew why Tex hadn't buzzed me . . . if he had . . . (BRAT!); (2) The enemy would have been warned (BRATATATATA!); (3) That my ship was below them . . . (BRATATATA)." Each panel measured 5 feet 8 inches by 4 feet 8 inches.

One critic wrote that Lichtenstein was searching for a modern paradisiacal mythology, "an imaginary folk culture, a coherent world of stereotyped action that seemed at once to echo and second the apparently sophisticated world of avant-garde gestures."[15] If true, his pretension was disturbing. Few pop artists deserved to be taken that seriously. Merely blowing up images found in a comic book failed to make a case that Lichtenstein's achievement was very significant. Nor could the works of other artists. Jasper Johns, for example, put sculp-metal over an ordinary flashlight and mounted it on a piece of wood. Jeff Koons copied a vinyl, inflatable rabbit in stainless steel. And Andy Warhol created thirty-two red and white polymer paintings of *Campbell's Soup Cans*; the paintings differed only in the flavors that gave them their titles: *Onion, Scotch Broth, Pepper Pot, Chicken Gumbo*, and so on. The pictures, which individually measured 20 by 16 inches, were arranged in four rows of eight paintings. Warhol, arguably one of the most pretentious and least talented artists of the modern age, explained that he painted because he wanted to be a machine. "I think it would be terrific if everybody was alike," he said.[16] Warhol achieved the ultimate in pop art when he began simply signing the labels of the soup cans themselves, thereby creating a work of art from his name alone.

The Spectator as Participant

The New Tendency. In much post–World War II art, the viewer was given a central place in the aesthetic process. The artists of this genre thought it their duty to involve the spectators by provoking their optical and tactile reactions. The separate status of the object was thereby weakened for the object had no independent value without the active role of the spectator.

Spectator involvement had already been solicited by Alexander Calder, whose form of kinetic art, called the "mobile," was intended to encourage viewer participation. However, the beginning of a coherent movement came with the artists of the *Nouvelle tendance*. According to Karl Gerstner, the New Tendency aimed to establish reciprocity between the viewer and the artist. "What we are trying to achieve," he explained, "is for your joy before the work of art to be no longer that of an admirer but of a partner." Gerstner said that art was a means of "procuring visual sensations" bringing out the active participation of the viewer.[17] If artistic standards needed any further shove into the chasm of chaos, this was it. Artists who worked this vein wanted to move art out of the museums and the galleries into a larger optical environment. They wanted to create a pictorial experience on an urban scale, sometimes static, sometimes kinetic, but mostly ephemeral.

Nicolas Uriburu used water for his canvas. In 1968, he dumped thirty kilograms of fluorescent sodium into the Grand Canal of Venice, turning the water green

Bulgarian-born Christo Javacheff has wrapped the Pont Neuf with 430,000 square feet of silky sandstone-colored cloth, held in place with seven miles of cable. The project, completed on 7 October 1985 after two weeks' work, cost $2.1 million and involved a team of divers, mountain climbers, tree cutters, and other technicians. Christo got the idea for projects like this in Sofia, where the Communist regime used him and other art students to embellish the landscape to impress Western visitors passing through the country on the Orient Express.

over a three-kilometer length. Uriburu said he was probing the relationship between the durable and the fleeting. He was so pleased with the green canal that he later repeated the exercise first in New York's East River and then in the Seine River at Paris, giving the conception a certain rakish internationalism.

The Bulgarian Christo Javacheff pursued another form of artistic expression by inventing the technique of *empaquetage*. Christo wanted to wrap anything that was technically capable of being wrapped. Some of his packaging projects included the Art Museum at Bern and the trees along the Champs Élysées in Paris. He also hung a curtain across a valley in Rifle, Colorado, and covered a million square feet of a craggy inlet near Sydney, Australia, with a blanket of polypropylene plastic. The eighty-foot cliffs of Little Bay took almost a month to "wrap." A team of sixty volunteers sewed the fabric together and tacked it to the rock with staples fired from ramset guns. The artist explained that containing an object exposed "its commonness in a beautiful and relaxed manner."[18] Spectators had to pay twenty cents to see the result. Christo said he was trying to return objects and institutions to a state of nothingness. From 1985 to 1991, he worked on a $26 million project to open 1,340 twenty-foot blue umbrellas along a twelve-mile stretch of land in Japan and 1,760 similar yellow umbrellas along eighteen miles of California hills. When all the umbrellas were unfurled, Christo announced enigmatically, "The project mirrors the people around it."[19]

Other examples of unmarketable eccentric action or conceptual art involved such projects as tracing various lines and designs on a piece of land, ploughing a pattern in a field with a tractor, piling up masses of earth in temporary sculptural forms, and creating a pattern in the sand by running back and forth at low tide. Roland Balandi wanted to enclose the Arc de Triomphe in Paris with a plastic dome where artificial snow would continually swirl about.

Yves Klein, a former judo instructor and merchant seaman, hit upon another sort of happening in his *Anthropometries*. These were monochromatic paintings using nude women as brushes. The first such creation was produced before a roomful of spectators at the Galérie Internationale d'Art Contemporaine in Paris on 9 March 1960. While an orchestra played Klein's "Monotone Symphony," consisting naturally of one note, two blue-splotched women flopped around on a canvas stretched out on the floor. Klein had patented the intense cobalt blue color as "Klein International Blue"; he was so fond of it that he created a whole series of paintings using it alone.

Anything Goes and Usually Does. Avant-garde art was collapsing under the presumption that anything new should be taken seriously. Museums and galleries seemed game for virtually any concept. Hence, Walter de Maria, claiming that a concept could be "just as strong in ideas as real sensations,"[20] filled three rooms in a Munich gallery with a layer of dirt two feet deep. Joseph Beuys, an artist from Düsseldorf, filled an open space with an assortment of large objects. Included were an operating table, a battery with wires and canisters, a stretcher, and a Red Cross blanket, which was hung on the wall. The clutter was supposed to suggest a concentration camp. Lygia Clark expressed her concept of the pleasures and traumas of life in the uterus by creating a series of tentlike pouches, or stages, through which visitors were invited to crawl. Clark was nonchalant about her objects, most of which were disposable. What mattered was the concept behind them: "What remained of importance was only the act."[21] The work appeared at the Venice Biennial. Keith Arnatt painted pictures on which were written words like "OOF" or "KEITH ARNATT IS AN ARTIST," while Robert Barry hung a sign on an outside door that read: "For the exhibition, the gallery will be closed."[22] The latter was a great stroke of Dada, showing that conceptual art not only did not need gallery space for its venue, but need not be art at all.

Inanity reached its apogee with the mercifully short-lived "movement" known as body art. Here the artist's own body became the exposition space, both the subject and object of the art work. The artist might spit water from his mouth like a fountain or wrap himself in thongs and rope like a trussed chicken. The occasions would be preserved with photographs. Body art in its most gruesome incarnation involved self-mutilation, like the slashing of shoulders and arms with razor blades to re-create pagan rituals. In 1969, at the age of twenty-nine, Austrian artist Rudolf Schwarzkogler literally killed himself for his art. To critic Robert Hughes, the gesture had an emblematic value: "Having nothing to say, and nowhere to go but further out, he lopped himself and called it art."[23]

Most artists who challenged the conventional standards of art desired more destruction and absurdity for its own sake. Even the Dadists did not believe that anti-art devices formed an adequate basis on which a sound art could be built. Marcel Duchamp was astonished when latter-day pop artists talked about the significance of his ready-mades: "I threw the bottlerack and the urinal into their faces as a challenge and now they admire them for their aesthetic beauty," he wrote in surprise.[24] Shortly before his death in 1968 at the age of eighty-one, Duchamp complained that the artists of this postwar generation were too integrated into society. "In my day," he reflected, "artists wanted to be outcasts, pariahs."[25] Duchamp's indictment was a bitter condemnation of an age when each new artistic monstrosity could be peddled to some collector as an investment.

MUSIC: CLASSICAL AND POPULAR

Musical Theater

The Production of Grand Opera. With the reconstruction of Europe's great opera houses came the reestablishment of their traditional repertoire. Europe's leading houses were museums where the great works of the great composers of the past, predominantly those of the nineteenth century, were on constant display. Both economics and audience preference limited the performance of works by contemporary composers. Rumor had it that a composer had to be dead or almost dead to have a work performed at the Paris Opera. On the other hand, the Hamburg Opera, one of the oldest in Europe, felt an express obligation to mount the works of living composers. And La Scala, while still emphasizing the "oldies," sometimes included as many as four contemporary works in its almost year-long season. But no opera house could afford to neglect the tried and true. Simply put, modern works did not sell tickets.

Opera houses were more willing to take chances in the staging of operas than in the choice of the operas themselves. One of the great revolutions in stagecraft came at Bayreuth, the home of the Wagnerian musical dramas. Production resumed in 1951 under the direction of Richard Wagner's grandsons Wieland and Wolfgang. Together they completely changed the nature of Bayreuth productions. They junked all the exaggerated neoromantic naturalism with its lavish, realistic sets, heavy props, and overblown stage effects complete with fire-belching dragons and Rhinemaidens swimming around while suspended on cables. In its place, they adopted streamlined, stylized sets based on a geometric use of space. In this, they were following in the footsteps of the great Swiss *metteur en scène*, Adolphe Appia, who stripped his sets to their bare essentials in an attempt to transcend external reality. Appia set the mood not with painted flats, but through the skillful use of light. He used economy and simplicity to emphasize the dramatic vision created by the music. Wieland Wagner claimed that he used the stylistic elements of modern art to render the operas as timeless "archetypal musical theater."[26]

This concept was carried beyond Bayreuth by Günther Schneider-Siemssen, the chief set designer at the Vienna Staatsoper. In addition to his home turf, Schneider-Siemssen productions appeared in Stuttgart, Cologne, Frankfurt, Düsseldorf, Munich, Geneva, Zurich, Sofia, London, Buenos Aires, Moscow, and New York. In his textbook, *The Stage as Cosmic Space*, he explained that to create a scene on stage was to point toward a cosmic, existential nexus, which was the essence of all great cultures.[27] Schneider-Siemssen's sets had an ethereal quality in which gravity apparently disappeared. He believed that the stage designer's task was to portray spiritual and religious striving, to create a theater of the future that would influence all the arts.[28]

Rudolf Bing, the Viennese impresario, who became general-manager of the Metropolitan Opera in New York, once described his function as preserving the great works of the past in excellent modern frames.[29] But the packaging did not have to follow the stylistic dictates of directors like Schneider-Siemssen. Franco Zeffirelli used a more traditional approach. Zeffirelli sought to give authenticity to his productions, at least those definable historically, by imitating the decor appropriate to the period in which the action occurred. Thus, he tried to make the inside of a church or a palace look as realistic as possible by piling detail upon detail.

Stage designers who followed no specific concept, let alone any ideology, tried to bring out the qualities of the work in accordance with their personal artistic image. They were thus able to draw upon whatever styles—realist, surrealist, impressionist, expressionist—they thought would highlight the specific work to be performed. For example, Jean-Pierre Ponelle constructed an entire town for Rossini's *Barber of Seville*. He made the town fit in perspective with the opera's main playing areas—the town square, the barber shop, and Doctor Bartolo's house—by putting the latter on a turntable stage. In this way, he integrated each element into a definite landscape with its own social conditions, climate, and mores.[30]

If the leading designers took their talents from one opera house to another, so did the singers. In fact, the ease of travel and the publicity obtained through radio and television helped the star system, already present in Europe's prestigious houses before the war, to become more firmly entrenched. Because many great singers tended to become associated with certain parts, the leading roles in the large opera houses came to be rotated among a pool of relatively few singers. Getting the talents of one of these singers could often make the difference between a routine performance and a great success. Singers with international reputations usually did not sign long-term contracts with one house, but kept themselves free to shuttle around. Thus, in the course of a year, Placido Domingo might sing at Covent Garden, La Scala, the Met, Chicago, San Francisco, Sydney, and places in between. In the large houses, casting became less nationalistic. It was not unusual to do an *Aida*, say, with an American tenor, a Polish soprano, an Italian baritone, a German mezzo-soprano, and a Bulgarian bass. This conglomeration of nationalities often forced the opera houses to present the operas in their original language rather than the language of the country where they were being performed, as had often been the custom in the nineteenth century.

American singers, as if to counterbalance the European operatic migration to the United States, routinely appeared in all the leading opera houses of Europe. Europe had more opera houses than the United States and gave singers a greater opportunity to gain experience. James McCracken, for example, started out singing small parts at the Metropolitan Opera, then migrated to Zurich where he improved his talent with larger roles. Ultimately, he came back home when the Met mounted a new production of *Otello* to showcase his talents. Nevertheless, he also continued to sing in Europe.

The Return of Naturalism. Styles in opera composition roughly paralleled the artistic or literary movements of the time. Following the great periods of classicism and romanticism, opera had developed in more abstract directions: impressionism, symbolism, and expressionism. Composers such as Claude Debussy (*Pelléas and Mélisande*, 1902), Richard Strauss (*Electra*, 1909), and Béla Bartók (*Duke Bluebeard's Castle*, 1918) depicted character and situation through allusion and relied on the music to reveal the inner emotions of the characters. Russian composers like Nikolai Rimsky-Korsakov (*The Golden Cockerel*, 1909), Igor Stravinsky (*The Nightingale*, 1914) and Sergei Prokofiev (*The Love of Three Oranges*, 1921) composed works of fantasy and escape in which exotic color, satire, and fantasy were interwoven. In all these operas, the characters stood apart from society. Of course, such themes never completely dominated opera composition. Many composers, including Gustave Charpentier (*Louise*, 1900), Giacomo Puccini (*Madame Butterfly*, 1904), and Italo Montemezzi (*The Love of Three Kings*, 1913), had always held fast to the realistic and melodramatic tradition. However, fantasy and exaggeration became less popular after World War I. Modern audiences wanted characters they could identify with, individuals whose dilemmas reflected their own. The return to dramatic naturalism dominated opera production for the next two generations and became the mainstay of opera production after World War II.

In Great Britain, naturalism was most strongly associated with the works of Benjamin Britten, who did more than any other composer since Henry Purcell (*Dido and Aeneas*, 1689) to stimulate the development of English national opera. In restoring his country's confidence in musical drama, Britten was able to establish a distinctive tradition in his own right. His *Peter Grimes*, performed at the reopening of the Sadler's Wells Theater in June 1945, was a psychological drama about an English fisherman who is wrongly suspected of killing two of his apprentices. To escape his fears and rage, he drowns himself. In this work, Britten combined set arias with the composite character of the crowd, using lyrical orchestral passages to heighten the mood. The opera incorporates many different musical elements—sea chanteys, dance-hall tunes, church music. *Peter Grimes* was an instant success and propelled its creator into the first rank of contemporary opera composers. It was translated into eight languages and was soon performed throughout the world.

Peter Grimes marked the beginning of a period of great productivity for its composer. Over the next eighteen years, Britten wrote sixteen stage works, eight of which were full-length operas. The most famous of these was his adaptation of Herman Melville's novel, *Billy Budd*, which appeared in 1951. *Billy Budd*, recognized as one of Britten's greatest works, again had as its theme the psychological anguish of a hero victimized by an unjust accusation. Billy Budd, the main character, is menaced by the villainous Claggert until he unintentionally kills his tormentor, an act for which he is court-martialed and hanged. The opera, written only for male voices, consists mostly of recitatives; its dramatically powerful themes are often briefly expressed so the audience will not be distracted from the mood of impending violence and doom. The three main characters are all strongly developed: Billy Budd's goodness is contrasted with Claggert's villainy. Captain Vere has noble, but flawed, intentions that force him to perform a duty alien to his humanity. The work quickly found a solid place in the British repertory.

Italian opera fell on lean times for several decades after World War I—most of the great composers of the post-Verdian generation were approaching the end of their careers—and not until the appearance of Gian-Carlo Menotti did someone arrive to carry on the tradition. Though born in Italy and influenced by the Italian operatic tradition, Menotti emigrated to the United States in 1927, when he was sixteen. He is probably best-known for his television opera *Amahl and the Night Visitors* (1951), which had its premiere on the NBC Television Opera Theatre and was shown every Christmas for many years thereafter. His short opera *The Medium* (1946) was made into a film that won prizes at both the Venice and Cannes film festivals in 1951. His other works include *Amelia Goes to the Ball* (1937), *The Saint of Bleeker Street* (1954), *The Last Savage* (1963), and *Help! Help! the Globolinks* (1968). All of these were in the Italian operatic tradition of tonal melody, in which the human voice is given preeminence. Menotti's rhythms were natural and easily remembered and were supported by a light and open orchestration. He also invariably wrote about ideas: "I haven't written one single opera," he said, "that doesn't have some sort of philosophical idea or social statement behind it."[31]

This was especially true of his first full-length, and possibly greatest, opera, *The Consul* (1950). The opera includes fully developed arias, duets, trios, and ensembles, but the composer believed its real strength was its recitatives, which sustained the work's dramatic development. Written in the *verismo* tradition, the opera takes political oppression as its theme. Set in some authoritarian country, the plot concerns the efforts of Magda, the wife of a political suspect, to obtain a visa to leave the country and join her husband in exile. Her failure leads to her suicide. Menotti wrote the libretto for *The Consul* himself, as he did for all his works (typically, it was in English), because he was more comfortable matching the music with his own poetry. The results are extraordinarily powerful, as in Magda's aria:

> *To this we've come:*
> *that men withhold the world from men;*
> *no ship nor shore from him who drowns at sea,*
> *no home nor grave for him who dies on land.*[32]

By choosing a contemporary theme, Menotti hoped to make the work more accessible to the public. *The Consul* premiered on Broadway at the Ethel Barrymore Theater on 15 March 1950. It was greeted with tremendous acclaim and ran for a solid eight months. It then went on a tour that included performances in leading European cities. At La Scala in Milan, it became a victim of the Cold War. At the first performance, somebody shouted "Down with the Americans," and throughout the rest of the performance people blew whistles.[33] The Communists denounced it as blatant anti-Soviet propaganda. However, despite the controversy and criticism, *The Consul* remains one of the most significant operatic works of the post–World War II era.

The Soviet Imperative. In the Soviet Union, composers and directors had to adjust their creative styles to the demands of the state. For example, naturalistic set designs might reproduce the past, but had to reflect more than a desire for authenticity. Socialist realism dictated that realistic sets be socially realistic sets. That is, they had to release the works from their historical period so that they could speak with the voice of the present. The past could only be presented in a manner that reflected positively on the Communist society of the present. Contemporary operas were expected to depict the triumph of Communism. Their characters could be ordinary peasants or heroes fighting the forces of Fascism.

During World War II, the regime had encouraged Soviet composers to write music that would raise morale and reinforce traditional Russian patriotism. This new mandated usefulness made the composers respectable once again. (Sergei Prokofiev, for one, responded with his great epic *War and Peace*.) But the honeymoon ended in 1947.

The regime launched a vicious attack on Vano Muradeli's opera *The Great Friendship*, which the Bolshoi Theater had mounted to commemorate the thirtieth anniversary of the 1917 Bolshevik Revolution. *The Great Friendship* concerned the warm association between the Georgian and Russian peoples. The censors, however, judged the treatment of the subject false, artificial, and symptomatic of the general heresy currently existing among Soviet composers. They called the music weak, confused, and cacophonous and castigated the opera for having no memorable arias. They damned its ear-splitting sounds: "Occasional lines and scenes, making a pretense of melodiousness, are suddenly interrupted by discordant noises, alien to a normal human ear, which produces a depressing effect on the listener."[34] Dimitri Shostakovich, Prokofiev, and Aram Khachaturian were also singled out as composers who had become infatuated with "confused, neuro-pathological combinations" that transformed music "into a chaotic agglomeration of sounds." The organizational committee of the Union of Soviet Composers was denounced for being a "hotbed of formalistic distortions."[35]

From 17 to 26 February 1948, Stalin's deputy Andrei Zhdanov chaired the meetings of the Moscow Composers Union. He denounced its members for formalistic and antidemocratic tendencies and ordered them to come forward one by one to confess their sins. Muradeli praised Zhdanov for encouraging the Soviet composers to fight unswervingly "for the great ideals of building up Communist society in our country." Shostakovich said he was effusively grateful to the party for its criticism and solemnly swore to "try again and again to create symphonic works close to the spirit of the people from the standpoint of ideological subject matter, musical language and form." Prokofiev, who was in poor health and did not attend, made his genuflection in writing. He tried to explain that, in recent years, he had used atonal music only sporadically and without much sympathy, "mainly for the sake of contrast, in order to bring tonal passages to the fore." He said that his fear of creating immobility on the stage had led him to use recitative more than cantilena in his operas, but he promised that his forthcoming *Tale of a Real Man* would include "trios, duets, and contrapuntally developed choruses, for which I will make use of some interesting Northern Russian folk songs [as well as] lucid melody, and as far as possible, a simple harmonic language."[36] The musicians' meeting closed by giving thanks to Stalin for his personal suggestions on the creation of Soviet classical opera. The composers pledged to concentrate on producing realistic music that would reflect the struggles of the Soviet people.

Prokofiev immediately came forth with *A Tale of a Real Man*, a patriotic drama about a World War II pilot who loses both of his legs fighting the Germans. An old commissar in the hospital urges him to conquer his subsequent depression by becoming a real Soviet man. The pilot gets outfitted with wooden legs, climbs back into the cockpit, and returns to the fray. Presumed lost on his last mission, he nevertheless makes it back and is reunited with his fiancée, who loves him despite his handicap. The two embrace and look forward to their new life together. The music was perhaps the most traditional of the composer's works, featuring some popular-style melodies, even a waltz and a rumba; nevertheless, it was deemed not melodious enough. The authorities condemned it as modernistic and antimelodic trickery and denounced its treatment of the Soviet people as a gross distortion. Though already in rehearsal, the work was summarily withdrawn. It was not performed publicly until 1960.

Censorship also continued to dog the path of Shostakovich, who also tried to make his peace with the regime. He even acted as a cultural ambassador abroad and joined the government in its attacks on the musical avant-garde. Even after the death of Stalin, he remained cautious, composing within the general guidelines of socialist realism. In 1959, he wrote *Moscow, the Cherry Trees*, a musical comedy about the current housing shortage. He also revised his *Lady Macbeth of the Mtzensk District*, which had been damned in 1936 as "fidgety, screaming, neurotic ... coarse, primitive, and vulgar."[37] It was difficult to tell how political or honest the revision was because doing musical penance was not as pressing in the Khrushchev era as it had been under Stalin. However, the new version, renamed

Katerina Izmaylova, did soften the earlier work's dissonant edge in an attempt to deliver it from its "eccentricities."

At the same time the Soviets were forcing conformity on their own composers, they continued to attack those of Western Europe and the United States with increasing ferocity. Tikhon Khrennikov, the newly appointed leader of the Composers Union, claimed he was unable to name a single Western composer who was not infected with "formalistic diseases, subjectivism and mysticism, and lack of ideological principles." The most odious of these reactionaries was Igor Stravinsky, with Paul Hindemith, Ernst Krenek, Alban Berg, Benjamin Britten, Max Brand, and Gian-Carlo Menotti not far behind. Khrennikov stigmatized their works as a "reversion to the primitive savage cultures of prehistoric society; eroticism is glorified along with psychopathology, sexual perversion, amorality and the shamelessness of the contemporary bourgeois heroes of the Twentieth Century."[38] Only after Stalin's death was this harsh judgment abandoned. In the 1960s, Stravinsky was finally allowed to visit his homeland where he was treated to performances of his works.

The Blockbuster Musical. In 1990, Peter Hoffmann, one of Germany's most famous Wagnerian tenors, decided to take a vacation from the opera stage. He signed a two-year contract to portray the title role in the Hamburg production of Andrew Lloyd Webber's *Phantom of the Opera*. Hoffmann, having sung a full range of music from classical to rock and roll, wanted to perform one of the most significant roles written for the contemporary stage. His defection highlighted what many people had known for some time—that Andrew Lloyd Webber was a remarkable musical talent. Lloyd Webber became a superstar in an age when that description was rarely applied to composers; he was a throwback to the sacred monsters of the nineteenth century. Lloyd Webber's musical antecedents were diverse; he drew as much from the great American musical dramas of Victor Herbert, Jerome Kern, and Irving Berlin as from the grand opera lyricism of Giacomo Puccini.

At a time when the New York and London musical stages were languishing in nonharmonic doldrums and grand opera was becoming more allegorical, thematically more moral and philosophical, Lloyd Webber brought modern musical theater back to life with a string of successes including *Jesus Christ Super Star* (1971), *Evita* (1976), *Cats* (1981), *Starlight Express* (1984), *The Phantom of the Opera* (1986), and *Aspects of Love* (1989). Although he was often accused of being superficial and facile, he wrote music people enjoyed hearing and wanted to hear again. If his orchestrations did not quite measure up to the sophistication of the masters, his tunes were eminently hummable and spoke to the desires of a latter-day romantic age as much the music of the great composers of the past did to theirs. His stories were basic, and he had no social or political ax to grind. His shows had an international appeal. *The Phantom of the Opera* with its great themes of profane and happily-ever-after love enchanted audiences simultaneously in London, New York, Los Angeles, Hamburg, Tokyo, Toronto, Stockholm, Vienna, and Chicago. Moreover, *Phantom*, like other Lloyd Webber hits, created an entire industry. Its spin-offs included cast albums, books, souvenir programs, T-shirts, coffee mugs, pins, posters, bathroom towels, and Phantom masks.

Lloyd Webber's success, though not surpassed, was at least duplicated by the French composer Claude-Michel Schönberg, who gave the world the two megahits of *Les Misérables* (1980) and *Miss Saigon* (1990). These musicals, also written in a traditional operatic style, shared a common organizational link with *Phantom* in that all three were produced by British impresario Cameron Mackintosh. (He had also been responsible for the "now and forever" mounting of *Cats*, which in 1991 entered its second decade of continuous performances at the New London Theater.) In the age of the celebrity, these shows were virtually star-proof because they depended more on their comfortably melodious scores and energetic staging than on the personalities singing them.

When American composer Leonard Bernstein saw *Miss Saigon* on Broadway, he realized after five minutes that he was not going to hear any musical talent in the score, so he "just sat back and watched the lighting cues and had a wonderful time."[39] What he saw, among other stage effects and overblown production numbers, was a helicopter drop from the fly space and hover over the set to reenact the flight of the Americans from the embassy at Saigon during the Vietnam War. Rarely had musicals created such joy in going to the theater. As Mackintosh acknowledged, "You can remind people of your existence, but you cannot persuade. Word of mouth does that. In a long run, that is what any show depends on."[40]

In the six years after its London premiere in September 1986, *Les Misérables* was performed 12,200 times in twenty-three worldwide productions; its performances were seen by 19.2 million people.[41] The story, following Victor Hugo's novel, is set in France in 1830—a period that might not seem to have much historical relevance for modern audiences. Yet when they left the theater after hearing the last rousing chorus of the musical's revolutionary theme, many were ready to return to Louis Philippe's Paris—at least on the stage—to hear the rousing chorus about revolution and the rights of the people to be free:

> *Do you hear the people sing?*
> *Say, do you hear the distant drums?*
> *It is the future that they bring*
> *When tomorrow comes.*[42]

The Rock Mania

The New World Influence. The Americanization of European musical tastes had begun in the years immediately prior to World War I when Tin Pan Alley songs were imported into British music halls. In 1912, the American Ragtime Octette did a turn around the continent. The new beat influenced such serious composers as Claude Debussy ("Golliwog's Cakewalk") and Darius Milhaud ("The Cow on the Roof") as well as Igor Stravinsky. Following World War I, American jazz carved out a permanent place in European culture. One branch developed into the commercial, sweet variety known as swing; the other, much prized by connoisseurs, remained raucous and more directly attached to its black African roots. The French called this version *le jazz hot*.

The American musical presence in Europe was boosted by the actual physical presence of American soldiers in both world wars. After 1945, the Americans not only stayed around as occupation troops, but their Armed Forces Radio Network beamed American popular music all over Europe, reducing the normal waiting period for cultural transmission to zero. Any European with a radio could now hear American popular music as soon as it appeared in the United States. American popular singers became as popular as movie stars. In the early 1950s, balladeers such as Frank Sinatra, Johnny Ray, and Frankie Laine seemed to epitomize the relaxed, comfortable American life-style that most of Europe's youth wanted to emulate.

Europeans, plagued by class traditions, were slow to develop the American rock and roll teenage subculture, but this changed as increasing economic independence gave young people the means to indulge their musical tastes without worrying what others thought. They listened to American rock and roll singers like Elvis Presley, Chuck Berry, and Little Richard—all three of whom burst on the musical scene around 1954–1955. In 1955, Bill Haley's "Shake, Rattle, and Roll" made the British record charts. The spirit of revolt and overt sexuality that came with such songs was irresistible. In England, Teddy Boys and Rockers—lower-class and lower-middle-class youth groups, who developed their own exaggerated masculine subculture of violence and vandalism[43]—were particularly addicted to loud pulsating music. Youths in other European cities followed suit. Hamburg, Germany, became a sort of proving ground where would-be emulators could play loud, fast, raw music.[44] The groups that came here were often more remarkable for their frenzy and noise than their talent. However, among the groups playing a gig in one of Hamburg's nightclubs was an unknown combo from Liverpool, England, which called itself the Beatles.

The Rise of the Groups. In 1961, Brian Epstein, a Liverpool record store owner, went to hear the Beatles playing in a Liverpool dive called the Cavern. The place was located in a cellar. Epstein found them "ill-presented, unkempt . . . with untidy hair."[45] Still, he liked their hard rock and rhythm and blues "Mersey Sound" and became their manager.[46] He was determined to make them bigger than Elvis.

Epstein first worked on elevating their social status. He got them to cut out their smart-alecky stage repartee, curb their drinking, and limit their smoking. He had them appear in public wearing conservative narrow-lapel mohair jackets with their hair in bangs—not too long, not too short—always properly washed and combed. Frequently, they wore ties and black nylon socks. All this upgrading carried the risk that the Beatles would lose some of their lower-class fans who identified with the scruffy, working-class look. Epstein, though, created something more universally appealing and decidedly more commercial.[47] Establishing the collective identity of a group constituted a break with the solo performer acts of the 1950s.

The Beatles' music was not only upbeat and melodic, it was written largely by themselves. Their song "I Want to Hold Your Hand" (1964), which quickly climbed to the top of the charts, was hailed as the most popular rock song since Elvis's "All Shook Up." The Beatles sang it to instant success in New York in February 1964 when they appeared on the "Ed Sullivan Show," the TV vaudeville hour that launched their American career. For foreign rock stars, success in the United States was essential in the climb to superstardom.

Almost singlehandedly, the Beatles launched a second pop explosion—the last the rock and roll craze produced. According to true believers, the advent of the Beatles brought about a significant shift in people's "sexual behavior and even helped change their political beliefs."[48] The Beatles' fans regarded them as demigods and copied their hair style, manner of speech, and dress. They lined the walls of their rooms with Beatles' pictures. Every detail of the Beatles' personal lives became a matter of international concern. Drummer Ringo Starr's tonsillectomy in December 1964 set off a worldwide vigil. In 1985, Queen Elizabeth II gave each member of the group an M.B.E. (Member of the British Empire).

In August 1966, with Beatlemania at its height, guitarist John Lennon told a reporter from the *London Evening Standard* that Christianity would eventually end. Lennon claimed that the Beatles were "more popular than Jesus," adding that, although Jesus was right, the religious leader's "disciples were thick and ordinary." Lennon confessed, "It's them twisting it that ruins it for me."[49] The British took the remarks in stride, after all Lennon had not said the Beatles were better than

Protected by New York police officers, **the Beatles make a hasty exit** from Carnegie Hall to avoid getting crushed by enthusiastic admirers. The Liverpool quartet just played to two sold-out houses in a pair of Lincoln's Day concerts on 12 February 1964.

Jesus, only that they were more popular, which to some sounded plausible. In the United States, however, the words hit hard. Many Americans were indignant at such blasphemy. In the South, they threw Beatles' records on bonfires; many radio stations stopped playing their music. There were even threats of violence. The Beatles were scheduled to begin an American tour. Something had to be done to calm the furor.

Lennon was pressured into making an apology of sorts. He did so in Chicago. "I wasn't saying whatever they're saying I was saying. I'm sorry I said it really. I never meant it to be a lousy antireligious thing. I apologize if that will make you happy."[50] The tour could now proceed. It was a great success, but it was the last the Beatles ever made. Afterwards, they satisfied their screaming fans with performances in a recording studio. Their popularity did not diminish. The release of their album *Sgt. Pepper's Lonely Hearts Club Band* in 1967 prompted one reviewer to hail it as a major factor in bringing Western civilization closer to unification than it had been "since the Congress of Vienna in 1815."[51]

Many of the rock groups that followed the Beatles were more outrageous. They had more loose ends, were more raucous and disrespectful, and were certainly nastier and more petulant. They were also degenerate, sexy, and antisocial. The

Rolling Stones, who presumed to replace the Beatles as trendsetters, cast themselves in the role of outlaws, leaving their hair uncombed and dressing as if they had just sauntered in off the mean streets.[52] They were arrogant and lewd, but they fulfilled their fans' fantasies about glamour, success, and fame. One critic wrote: "More than the Beatles, whose personal appeal derived in large part from their talent as songmakers, the people would gladly pay to see the Rolling Stones just stand around and look like pop stars."[53] From their debut at the Crawdaddy Club in Richmond, England, in February 1963, they grew into an international cult. Their loud, persistent songs often with explicit lyrics were sometimes banned. Where the Beatles wanted to hold your hand, the Stones proposed "Let's Spend the Night Together" (1967). The Beatles projected a certain mellow boyish bonhomie, the Stones a high-decibel wickedness. Members of the group had brushes with the law: they smoked pot, were into various other controlled substances, and had wild parties with nude women. It was said they practiced Satanism. All this added to their mystique and popularity.

The Rolling Stones style was much copied, especially in the United States, but it reached its height in the British youth culture of the 1960s. The fans apparently cared more about the Stones' message of a liberated life-style and their doctrine of liberation from social and sexual frustration than they did about the quality of the group's musicianship. Still, despite all their antics, the Stones sometimes seemed sincere about creating good music.

That could not be said about many other practitioners of rock, especially these groups that played a new form known as punk rock, a genre that took musical self-indulgence to its raucous, uncompromising limits. Typical was a group known as the Sex Pistols who debuted in 1975. The ensemble was completely manufactured. Lead singer John Lydon (a.k.a. Jonny Rotten) had been recruited primarily for his ability to sneer and posture. He had little musical experience before he joined. As part of his performance, Rotten would throw empty beer bottles at the audience, blow his nose, and make obscene gestures. During the performance, other members of the quartet might spit in the air, vomit, or become even more vulgar. Sometimes they wore safety pins through their cheeks. The music of the Sex Pistols was repetitive, tribal, electronic, and ear-shattering, but their showmanship carried the day. Sex Pistol performances were hectic, outrageous, and vulgar.[54] They touted their drug and alcohol abuse and their sexual prowess. They intended to be ugly, and their songs reflected it.

Nevertheless, the group seemed to be capable of creating the true sense of community that many rock fans craved, while being its lowest common denominator. In Britain, punk rock spoke for those who felt they had no stake in the present society. Many of its fans were unemployed and cared nothing for their country's traditions.

One of the Sex Pistols' ditties, "God Save the Queen," called Elizabeth II a moron. The song was released during the Silver Jubilee of her reign. Another, "Anarchy in the U.K.," extolled nihilism: "I'm an antichrist, Don't know what I want, But I know how to get it, I want to destroy."[55] These songs appeared in *Never Mind the Bollocks, Here's the Sex Pistols,* an album that was briefly banned from display in Britain. The record company that released it subsequently canceled its contract with the group because some executives thought the Sex Pistols were preaching anarchy.[56] The group lasted less than five years, destroyed by its own excesses. Rotten feared he was being turned into something chic and quit. Lead bassist John Ritchie (a.k.a. Sid Vicious) died of an overdose of heroin after he had murdered his girl friend. The story of their relationship became the subject of the Alex Cox film *Sid and Nancy* (1986).

The Sex Pistols' squalid values represented the darkest side of rock culture, an exercise in outrageous media hype and little else. The group guitarist Steve Jones confessed that their antisocial posture was a sham. He said he only joined the group to meet girls and get drunk. "I was really a football hooligan. I went to matches and bashed people. Punk was the perfect way to do what I wanted to do—cause trouble—and get paid for it."[57]

Outside Britain, the boom and blast school of musicality also had aficionados. The amount of money rock music generated, the number of careers it supported, the hefty amount of taxes and revenues it produced appeared to make it worthy of respect. The rock movement produced a succession of talented musicians and frauds. Every time the style appeared exhausted and about to fade, another singer or group would come along to give it a new vitality and perhaps take the movement into yet another, although not necessarily a better, direction.

POSTSCRIPT Art and music are dialectical: one movement contains the seeds of its own transformation or, at least, the means through which new schools can be developed and different techniques can be tested and formed. The period after World War II was one of significant cultural creativity, although whether it surpassed the great golden or silver ages of yesteryear was debatable.

In the visual arts, the modern synthesis, coming on the heels of the great artistic outpourings of the past, had yet to run its course and, considering its variety, was conceivably impossible to exhaust, much less objectively evaluate. The resultant frustration may have encouraged the very lack of standards that carried artistic expression to the point of absurdity. That many conscientious, talented artists were still at work encouraged people to ask questions about the fundamental nature of artistic creation and the basic definition of an artist. While some had a sneaking suspicion that much work being passed off as art was really a product of adolescent self-indulgence or even fraud, the fact remained that no matter how outlandish some new form of artistic expression might be, a museum or gallery would take it seriously and afford it space.

Art, though, like music evolves. It does not necessarily progress or improve. So the fight over what constitutes art continues. The traditionalists held that art was about values that were communicated by beauty and that there was no such thing as ugly art. Nor was art created for itself. Art, they maintained, was not a suicide pact that people had to follow even when it went over a cliff. Others said that art was the fulfillment of a human need, something that made people think and feel at the same time. It was something that took them someplace they had not been before even if it involved that great leap into space.

ENDNOTES

1. Milan's La Scala, for example, reinforced the religious identity by opening its season on 7 December, the feast day of Saint Ambrose, the city's patron saint.

2. Joseph Wechsberg, *The Opera* (London: Weidenfeld and Nicolson, 1972), 245.

3. Cima Star, "Modern Art: It's Awful," *International Tribune*, 16 June 1970.

4. H. W. Janson, *History of Art* (Englewood Cliffs, N.J.: Prentice-Hall, 1986), 695–715.

5. Norbert Lynton, *The Story of Modern Art* (Ithaca, N.Y.: Cornell University Press, 1980), 226–46; Charles Harrison, "Abstract Expressionism," in Tony Richardson and Nikos Stangos, ed., *Concepts of Modern Art* (New York: Harper and Row, 1974), 168–201.

6. Pollock said there was no such thing as "American painting" any more than there could be American physics or American mathematics. The basic problems of contemporary artistic creation were universal. Jean-Clarence Lambert, *La peinture abstraite* (Lausanne: Editions Rencontre, 1967), 71.

7. Jean Bazaine interview, L'Oeil, *The Selective Eye* (New York: Random House, 1955), 50.

8. Lambert, *La peinture abstraite*, 149–50.

9. *The Selective Eye*, 50.

10. Lambert, *La peinture abstraite*, 178–79.

11. Edward Lucie-Smith, *Late Modern: The Visual Arts since 1945* (New York: Praeger, 1969), 135.

12. Kirk Varnedoe and Adam Gopnik, *High and Low: Modern Culture and Popular Art* (New York: Museum of Modern Art, 1990), 351.

13. Ellen H. Johnson, *Modern Art and the Object: A Century of Changing Attitudes* (New York: Harper and Row, 1976), 156–65.

14. H. Harvard Arnason, *Modern Art* (New York: Harry Abrams, n.d.), 575–601.

15. Varnedoe and Gopnik, *High and Low*, 212.

16. Richardson and Stangos, *Concepts of Modern Art*, 231.

17. Gerstner gave his description in 1964. Frank Popper, *Art—Action and Participation* (New York: New York University Press, 1975), 15.

18. *Time*, 14 November 1969, 50.

19. *Time*, 21 October 1991, 99.

20. *Time*, 22 November 1968, 75.

21. Ibid., 77.

22. Ibid., 18 December 1972, 112.

23. Robert Hughes, "The Decline and Fall of the Avant-Garde," *Time*, 18 December 1972, 111–12.

24. Edward Lucie-Smith, "Pop Art" in Richardson and Stangos, *Concepts of Modern Art*, 226.

25. *Time*, 24 September 1973, 102.

26. Stanley Sadie, ed., *The New Grove Dictionary of Music and Musicians*, vol. 13 (London: Macmillan, 1980), 636.

27. Günther Schneider-Siemssen, *Die Bühne als kosmischer Raum* (Vienna: Bergland Verlag, 1976).

28. Rudolf Hartmann, ed., *Opera* (New York: William Morrow, 1977), 55.

29. Wechsberg, *The Opera*, 250.

30. Hartmann, *Opera*, 129.

31. Joel Honig, "The Menotti Theorem," *Opera News* (June 1991), 15.

32. Gian-Carlo Menotti, *The Consul* (New York: G. Shirmer, 1950), act II, scene 2.

33. John Gruen, *Menotti: A Biography* (New York: Macmillan, 1978), 99–102.

34. Nicolas Slonimsky, *Music since 1900* (New York: Coleman-Ross, 1949), 684.

35. Ibid., 684.

36. David Ewen, *Encyclopedia of the Opera* (New York: Hill and Wang, 1955), 494.

37. Sadie, *The New Grove Dictionary of Music*, 19:265.

38. Ibid., 695.

39. David Patrick Sterns, "Bernstein's Last Hurrah," *Connoisseur* (September 1991), 106.

40. William A. Henry, "They Just Keep Rolling Along," *Time*, 2 September 1991, 73.
41. Ibid., 73.
42. Alain Boubil and James Fenton, *Les Misérables* (London: Alain Boubil Music, Ltd.: 1985).
43. The Teds adopted exaggerated Edwardian dress; the Rockers donned black leather motorcycle costumes to fit their favorite mode of transportation.
44. Jim Miller, *The Rolling Stone Illustrated History of Rock and Roll* (New York: Random House, 1980), 170.
45. Ray Coleman, *The Man Who Made the Beatles: An Intimate Biography of Brian Epstein* (New York: McGraw-Hill, 1989), xi.
46. David Dalton and Lenny Kaye, *Rock 100* (New York: Grosset and Dunlap, 1977), 89–94.
47. Ibid., 100–102.
48. Miller, *Rolling Stone Illustrated History*, 181.
49. Dalton and Kaye, *Rock 100*, 281.
50. Ibid., 283.
51. Miller, *Rolling Stone Illustrated History*, 183.
52. See Tim Dowley, *The Rolling Stones* (New York: Hippocrene Books, 1983).
53. Lloyd Grossman, *A Social History of Rock Music from the Greasers to Glitter Rock* (New York: David McKay, 1976), 49.
54. Miller, *Rolling Stone Illustrated History*, 451–62.
55. "The Sex Pistols Are Here," *Time*, 16 January 1978, 62.
56. "The Sex Pistols," *Stereo* (February 1978), 132.
57. Irwin Stambler, ed., *Encyclopedia of Pop Rock and Song* (New York: St. Martin's Press, 1989), 609.

PART EIGHT

THE REUNIFICATION OF EUROPE, 1962–1991

CHAPTER 24

A TIME FOR DETENTE, 1962–1985

PREFACE   The Europeans were increasingly reluctant to follow the superpowers wherever they might lead. They were naturally uneasy that their foreign policy was being fashioned in Washington and Moscow. Eastern Europeans had learned they must accept a subservient place in the Warsaw Pact bloc or risk Soviet intervention. The countries in the West had come to expect more freedom of action, but within the North Atlantic Treaty Organization (NATO), they were still very much junior partners. They never felt that the Americans took their advice seriously. President John F. Kennedy seemed an exception, however. He appeared to be a different kind of cold warrior, more sympathetic and more willing to listen than his predecessors. Relatively young, friendly, and handsome, he made nice speeches and liked to show off his pretty wife. Many European politicians tried to develop their own Kennedy-like style while ordinary people kept a picture of him in their homes.

Kennedy's recklessness during the Cuban missile crisis of October 1962 helped jar the Europeans back to reality. Nikita Khrushchev touched off the confrontation by trying to put medium-range weapons close to American soil, but Kennedy's reaction was disturbingly reckless. Without consulting his allies or trying to persuade Khrushchev to retreat through quiet, diplomatic channels, he provocatively threatened the Soviets with nuclear war via television. Although the governments of the NATO countries supported his action, Europeans nevertheless believed that Kennedy was risking war to show his voters how tough he could be. They asked how all this posturing might affect their own security. Cynics among them suspected that Khrushchev and Kennedy were accomplices in a gigantic theatrical presentation.

The crisis begged many questions. Was the crisis worth the risk? Had a few missiles on the island of Cuba really changed the current balance of power? Was not the United States ringing the Soviet Union with even more menacing weapons? Could not the confrontation in the Caribbean have produced an explosion in Europe? Would the Soviets react by making another move against Berlin? Some Europeans feared the worst and made a run on food stores. Newspapers expressed greater concerns. The *Manchester Weekly Guardian* was shocked that the Americans would even consider dropping an atomic bomb.[1] André Fontaine of *Le Monde* observed darkly that "never since the last war ended has any confrontation between the Big Two so closely grazed the brink of catastrophe."[2] In the end, most Western Europeans still believed in the worth of the Atlantic alliance, but some were more than willing to call down a plague on both superpower houses.

The crisis led to a renewed arms race. The Soviets felt they had to erase the humiliation by building up their nuclear arsenal, especially in intercontinental ballistic missiles. The Americans pushed the development of Polaris missiles, which were fired from submarines, and other, land-based missiles. They began a new round of talks with their partners in NATO to facilitate the new strategy, especially the British on whose land the new weapons would primarily be based. They also beefed up their military presence throughout the rest of the alliance countries. Western European opposition leaders responded by calling for more independence in national defense policy. Antinuclear protests increased. Although the British agreed to equip their submarines with the new Polaris missiles, they refused to have these units integrated totally within NATO.[3] French president Charles de Gaulle went a step further. He removed his military forces entirely from the NATO command.

The Soviets, recovering from the desultory Khrushchev era, convinced themselves that their ideology was triumphant. With optimistic boldness, they pushed their influence into parts of the world heretofore considered off-limits—Ethiopia, Angola, and Latin America—and reinforced the centralization of their own government. However, their Achilles heel continued to be Eastern Europe where the threat of defection was constantly present. In 1968, it was the turn of Czechoslovakia. The Kremlin, however, did not want a repeat of its ruthless crushing of the Hungarians in 1956 and handled the Czechoslovaks with relative restraint. The Soviet leaders wanted to keep the lid on the satellites, but they tried to do so by stimulating a greater willingness to cooperate. They also hoped to gain access to Western technology, which was essential to invigorate their flagging economy. Finally, although the Soviet leaders were slow to realize it, the Soviet Union no longer had the resources to project its will as it had done in the past.

The United States also encountered limitations on its power, for which, in a sense, it had only itself to blame. Massive expenditures on weapons of war had diverted resources from problems at home. The Americans had enhanced their influence in Europe, but in doing so, they had also helped those they once nurtured to grow sturdy. The creation of the European Community was an American success story, but offspring do not remain children forever and often grow up to challenge their parents. The Cold War had outlived its usefulness as a means of boosting Western integration. If the Europeans wanted to increase their prosperity, if the Soviets and the Americans wanted to survive as great powers, they would have to end their rivalries in Europe. But old habits were hard to break.

THE INTEGRATION OF WESTERN EUROPE

The Politics of Grandeur

The End of the War in Algeria. Before France could again become the paramount power in Western Europe, the Algerian war had to end. But ending it was a dangerous task because those who had helped return Charles de Gaulle to power expected him to do everything possible to keep Algeria part of France. De Gaulle, though, came to realize that the Algerian affair could destroy French unity; and he therefore made secret contact with the Algerian rebel leaders to explore ways to bring the conflict to an end—hopefully with a maximum amount of respect for French rights. It was a difficult juggling act.

The National Liberation Front leaders were stubborn; they wanted France to withdraw from Algeria unconditionally. The *colons*, or Algerian settlers, were equally intransigent. They wanted to maintain their power and position, and when they got wind of the behind-the-scenes negotiations, they took to the streets in protest. In January 1960, a group of extremists seized control of downtown Algiers and had to be dispersed by military force. When de Gaulle pushed ahead, opening up formal talks with the rebel leadership at the resort city of Evian-les-Bains on Lake Geneva, the opposition went underground. They formed a Secret Army Organization (*Organization de l'armée secrète* or *OAS*) and began a campaign of terror, bringing the war home. In Paris, bombs exploded at the place Vendôme, the stock exchange, and even in the Palais-Bourbon, home of the French National Assembly. In April 1961, a cabal of generals, led by Maurice Challe and Raoul Salan, took control of Algiers and tried to rally the colonial garrisons and the Foreign Legion for an invasion of France itself. The government was clearly worried. De Gaulle went on television to forbid all French citizens to obey the rebels' orders. For the first time in history, a president of France ordered soldiers to disobey commands of their superior officers. The revolt collapsed after three days. Many professional soldiers were sympathetic to the mutineers, but had no intention of jeopardizing their careers for a venture that lacked a reasonable chance of success. Conscripts, who made up the bulk of troop strength in Algeria, were not eager to join a war against their own government. De Gaulle emerged shaken, but triumphant. More than ever, he was determined to bring the war to an end.

Most of the French people were sick of the bloodshed that threatened the lives of their sons and drained the country of its other vital resources. In March 1962, 90 percent of the voters endorsed the Evian accords in a referendum that recognized the sovereignty of Algeria. Although the treaty contained safeguards for the property and personal security of those colons who chose to remain in Algeria, the French settlers left the country in droves. Almost 800,000 came to France, a country they little knew, and whose inhabitants they feared would treat them with hostility. Their suspicions were exaggerated. Within a generation, the pieds-noirs were largely assimilated into French society.

De Gaulle's Grand Design. At the same time de Gaulle ended the war in Algeria, he took vigorous steps to end the inflation that had plagued the country since the end of World War II and that was fueled by a dramatic increase in demand. De Gaulle's financial experts carried out a policy of austerity. They devalued the franc by 17.5 percent in order to attract foreign investment and boost exports. Then, they increased taxes and reduced government expenditures. They also ended certain subsidies to nationalized industries, ordering them to balance receipts with expenses. These measures helped change the traditionally protectionist nature of the French economy; protectionist policies had been adopted in the first place because French goods and services (aside from certain luxury products) were poor competitors on the world market. The planners realized that the economy had to be globalized if the country were to hold its own with its partners in the Common Market and with the major industrial powers in the rest of the world.[4] As a vital element in this process, the French franc had to become convertible.

De Gaulle created the "new franc," a hard currency achieved by moving the decimal point two notches to the left, thereby converting 500 old francs to 5 new francs. But there was more substance to the new franc than that. The new unit was a symbol of de Gaulle's determination to achieve monetary stability and to avoid another round of inflation that would cause further devaluation. The government therefore began to balance its budget and improve efficiency. Creating a hard currency was part of de Gaulle's plan to make Paris the principal money market of the European Community. Managing the French economy was his way of restoring France to its place as a great power, able to counterbalance the increasing importance of Germany and determine the destiny of Europe.

The policy got off to a good start. French goods became less expensive; increased sales abroad boosted foreign reserves; and production continued to rise.[5] In 1963, France adopted a stabilization plan aimed at controlling prices and wages and at reducing the budget deficits. The government then tried to stimulate the economy by trying to funnel private savings into capital investment and to increase the international competitiveness of French companies by making them larger. De Gaulle realized that even though the world was getting smaller and nations were becoming more interdependent, French industry had to develop economies of scale.

De Gaulle also wanted to free himself from the day-to-day management of politics and establish an independent base from which he could dominate the political process. Under the 1958 constitution, a college of 80,000 electors chosen by the local units of government elected the president. De Gaulle wanted this procedure changed so he could be elected by direct popular vote, thereby giving him a true national constituency. In 1962, he presented this proposal to the French electorate, which adopted it by a 62 percent majority. Later that year, the Gaullist Union for the New Republic swept the parliamentary elections, giving him control of the legislature. He replaced the premier, Michel Debré, whom he did not consider a very effective manager of domestic affairs, with Georges Pompidou, whom he was grooming as his successor. Now de Gaulle could concentrate his efforts almost exclusively on trying to increase French influence abroad. "France cannot be France without grandeur," he had written in his memoirs.[6] He wanted to steer a middle course between the superpowers, with France holding the balance of power among the states of Western Europe and in the Third World.

It was essential that France not lose ground to Germany. France had an edge militarily because it possessed the atomic bomb, but this alone was not enough. De Gaulle wanted Germany's support in creating a European Political Union, a new organization that would have its own parliamentary assembly and would preside over the reform of NATO. De Gaulle could no longer tolerate NATO in its American-dominated form. He artfully concealed his intention to use the new arrangement as a springboard for world leadership by convincing Konrad Adenauer that the union was a means through which Germany could enhance its own international status. But convincing other European leaders proved much harder, and the scheme never got off the ground. This failure prompted de Gaulle to diminish British influence in European affairs in order to establish a bilateral arrangement with West Germany.

A Franco-German treaty was signed in Paris on 22 January 1963.[7] The agreement obliged the two nations to consult on all foreign policy questions concerning the other members of the European Community and the states of Eastern Europe. They also agreed to hold mutual discussions on anything involving NATO, carry on joint research in the development of armaments, and harmonize their military strategy and tactics. The treaty did not mention nuclear weapons—Adenauer was not interested in acquiring them. De Gaulle wanted German technical know-how, but did not want to share French results. He hoped that Europe would one day be able to defend itself rather than having to rely on the United States, a country he doubted had any long-range commitment to European security.

The treaty was the high-water mark in his attempt to bolster French influence through an association with Germany. It was also the last foreign policy association of de Gaulle and Adenauer. The German chancellor retired later that year and was replaced by Ludwig Erhard, a man who did not hold an association with France in such high regard. De Gaulle, however, continued to pursue the policy of independence by developing his own country's nuclear deterrence.[8] The French could not possibly match the nuclear capacity of the United States, so their *force de frappe* (strike force) was intended to be more diplomatic than military and was aimed primarily at reinforcing French influence in European and world affairs. Ironically, though, it would also ensure that the Americans would not abandon Europe, since the use of French nuclear weapons automatically would involve the United States.

In 1965, de Gaulle, now seventy-five years old, ran for reelection as president of France. Expecting an easy victory against his two challengers, he was dismayed when he received only 44 percent of the vote and was forced into a runoff election with François Mitterrand. Mitterrand had the support of most of the parties of the Left, including the Communists. In the second round, de Gaulle won by 55 percent, hardly a landslide considering who he was. Nevertheless, he did not feel that he should significantly alter his policy of national greatness. In 1966, in a further display of independence, he withdrew his country from the military structure of the NATO alliance. France remained part of the NATO political structure, however. (As a result, NATO headquarters was moved from Paris to Brussels.) De Gaulle, who did not view Soviet westward expansion as a realistic eventuality, felt the American troop presence in his country provided less protection than his *force de frappe*. Besides, France could still enjoy American nuclear protection. Thus, in all but an extreme emergency, the Europeans themselves would maintain the European balance of power. However, the decision to go it alone so strained French resources that it threatened social stability at home. In playing to the world, de Gaulle had neglected the mounting discontent of his own people.

The Events of May 1968. The end of the Gaullist era began with a student protest at the University of Nanterre in the Paris suburbs. The leaders, radicalized by the war in Vietnam and abuses in the educational system, put forth a vague leftist program that called for the support of "democratic" forces in the United States and in the Federal Republic of Germany. Some radicals, hoping to bring down the bourgeois system, raised abstract, philosophical questions about the validity of hierarchical institutions as a valid basis for modern French society. The students arrogated to themselves the right to use force against those who did not agree with their lofty pretensions of social reform. The protest spread to Paris proper where the demonstrators were joined by young workers. Many of these workers were not yet members of unions and felt threatened by the high rate of unemployment in their age group, which made their jobs insecure; they found radical politics appealing. Demonstrations on the Left Bank on 3 May 1968 led the police to occupy the Sorbonne, the seat of the science and letters faculty of the University of Paris. The police beat the demonstrators with billy clubs and made arrests willy-nilly. Soon the Latin Quarter looked like a war zone. Police cars were stoned, autos were overturned, pavements were torn up, and trees were cut down. Fourteen barricades were thrown up on the avenue Gay-Lussac. The smell of tear gas hung over the area like a pall. On 13 May, a crowd estimated at 650,000 people, which included the leaders of the opposition, like Socialists Mitterrand and Guy Mollet, converged on the place Denfert-Rochereau and demanded de Gaulle's resignation. At the same time, students occupied important university buildings, and de Gaulle's opponents in the National Assembly tried to introduce a motion of censure. Despite the unrest, de Gaulle left for Bucharest to visit Romanian president Nicolae Ceausescu to pursue his East/West policy of mediation. The revolt continued.

A wave of strikes swept the city. At one time, between 9 and 10 million workers, out of a total labor force of 17 million, stopped work. Unlike the students, the striking workers had bread-and-butter grievances. They were protesting the Gaullist policy of austerity and stabilization that had reduced their standard of living. They wanted an increase in the minimum wage and an improvement in benefits. The gap between skilled and unskilled labor had become larger, and many young workers sensed that they were bearing the brunt of an austerity policy that was benefiting chiefly the bankers and the technocrats. The protest extended to other classes of workers as well. Wildcat strikes brought services to a standstill. Trains did not run, and airplanes did not fly. Customs officers abandoned their posts.[9] Gasoline scarcities developed. The post offices were closed. The workers seized control of the Renault factory while the students "liberated" the Sorbonne and declared it under permanent occupation.[10]

De Gaulle hastily returned from Romania. On 24 May, he tried to restore calm by making a television address to the nation as he had done during the Algerian war. The appeal did not work, and the disorder continued. But time was on his side. The demonstrators had difficulty agreeing on a common program of reform. Paris was a mess. Trash and broken glass littered the streets, making it hard for people to go about their daily tasks. There were wanton acts of vandalism. A crowd of students attacked the stock exchange and, crying "down with the temple of capitalism," set it on fire. Automobiles were smashed as symbols of the consumer society. A great deal of the destruction occurred in the more modest sections of the city and had the greatest effect on people of lesser means. Cafés remained shuttered, bakeries and food stores stayed closed. Sympathy rapidly turned to disgust.

Many young workers now discovered they had little in common with the students, many of whom came from the comfortable middle classes and were, in fact, the offspring of the government ministers, company presidents, diplomats, and industrialists of the French elite. The unfocused kind of revolution that the silver-spoon students advocated offered uncertain rewards for unanswered questions. The skilled workers, who were already enjoying the benefits of modern materialism—cars, electric appliances, and electronic gadgets—never really joined the protest. Farmers, whose standard of living had increased since the end of the war, also remained aloof. The Communist party, under great pressure to throw in its lot with the militants, had actually found much in Gaullism with which it could agree, especially the policy to weaken the American-led alliance. They did not want a revolution under such tenuous circumstances. The younger workers booed the party union officers when they tried to restore order in the factories, but the leadership finally succeeded in regaining control over its followers.

On 30 May, de Gaulle made another address on the radio. This time he was better received. De Gaulle dissolved the National Assembly and ordered new elections. He transformed the prefects into commissioners of the Republic, ordering them to take extraordinary steps to maintain order.[11] This was the de Gaulle of old, successfully beating back the forces of anarchy. The police threw the students out of the Sorbonne, cleaners swept the trash from the streets, glaziers repaired the broken windows, and sidewalk cafés brought out the chairs and reopened for business.

France paid dearly for the affair of May. The franc had been put under so much pressure that the government contemplated another devaluation. It was the end of French pretensions to become the premier capital market of Europe. The myth of Gallic superiority and de Gaulle's grand design lay in ruins. The general, faced with a precipitous decline in his domestic popularity, no longer had a popular base on which to build his claim to international leadership. De Gaulle's moral prestige had always been based on an unshakable claim to represent the French general will, and he was not content to serve out the remaining four years of his presidential term in limbo. Looking for a way to recover his popular support, he proposed another change in the constitution. The referendum had two parts: one would increase regional autonomy; the other would make the Senate more representative of the country's social and economic needs. Although neither proposition seemed to have much popular support, de Gaulle made the vote a matter of confidence. The referendum failed—by 47 to 53 percent—and de Gaulle gave up the presidency, leaving office without a formal letter of resignation.

He retired to his home at Colombey-les-Deux-Églises, where he died in November 1970. He was buried in the local village cemetery, and his grave soon became a pilgrimage site. Whatever his arrogance, his special sense of purpose, his resemblance to a latter-day monarch, he had restored the unity of France on at least two occasions. But the country he loved so much lacked the desire to measure up to his costly ideal of greatness. The European Community was becoming too strong to allow one nation to entertain such ambitions.

The Strength of the Common Market

Britain Tries to Join. The growing strength of the Common Market produced a policy change in Great Britain. The British first proposed establishing a free-trade zone in which the Western European states would abolish tariffs among themselves. When the French vetoed the plan, the British proceeded to create the European Free Trade Association (EFTA) of non-Common Market countries— the so-called Outer Seven—in conjunction with Austria, Sweden, Portugal, Switzerland, Norway, and Denmark. The EFTA, supposedly an alternative to the Common Market, was really an attempt to match the Common Market's economic power. In the first decade of the EFTA, trade between its members jumped by two and a half times, but the British did not share in this increase. The British boom, begun in the early 1950s, was slowing down, and the country's balance of payments was in deficit. The British were, therefore, forced to recognize that their decision not to join the Common Market had been a mistake. At the same time, the Kennedy administration, believing that European economic unity was a vital ingredient of the Western alliance, put pressure on the British to join.

In 1961, the Conservative government of Harold Macmillan (1957–1963) began formal negotiations for membership. This move was prompted more by a lack of faith in Britain's power to halt its own decline than by any great enthusiasm to join forces with the rest of Europe. Furthermore, for Britain to abandon its special relationships with the countries of the Commonwealth seemed a betrayal of its history. The paucity of domestic support for the move reflected this ambivalence. Politicians in both major parties feared a loss of their nation's sovereignty. Certain economic interest groups, like the farmers, feared the new competition would mean a loss of revenue and lead to higher costs. Some private citizens feared they would be inundated with nasty influences from abroad.[12] The Labour party put forth a series of conditions. The government worked to gain special protection for British agriculture and to demonstrate to the voters that it was not going to make too many concessions. However, the question of whether Britain would be allowed to join the Common Market was not a matter for British voters to decide.

On 14 January 1963, President de Gaulle announced that his country could no longer support British membership. De Gaulle feared that Britain's traditional ties with the United States would prevent the British from establishing a closer relationship with Europe, but more importantly, he suspected that British membership might weaken his leadership of Europe. The European Community had definitely enhanced the French political presence. By depicting Britain as a Trojan horse for the interests of the Americans, de Gaulle found allies in other Common Market countries. He wanted a consortium approach to European integration, a Europe of separate parts in which each nation's sovereignty would be reaffirmed, not diminished. British membership would detract from his consortium arrangement with Germany, so he publicly torpedoed British membership the week before the signing of the Franco-German treaty.

The French leader's insistence on more national integrity clashed with the notion of integration that the economic planners in other Common Market countries desired. Most of them favored a federated Europe—a concept advanced by Germany's Walter Hallstein, chairman of the European Community Commission. These planners wanted a European parliament with the authority to approve the Community's budget, while de Gaulle opposed reaching decisions by majority vote. To make his point, de Gaulle ordered the French representatives on the Common Market Council home from Brussels.[13] He insisted on the right of veto, and only when this was accorded—in the Luxembourg Agreement of 1967—did he end the French boycott. As long as de Gaulle's policy prevailed, the institutions of the European Community could not neutralize the power of its member states.

De Gaulle won another point in 1967, when he again dashed British hopes of joining the Common Market.[14] The general wanted to promote the modernization of the French economy, so it could keep pace with the other members of the Common Market, and to protect it against undesirable political and cultural consequences of American investment. His singular determination to fashion Europe in his own image fanned European fears of French domination. Other Community members did not regard the entry of Britain or the American presence in Europe as a liability. Jean Monnet, the founding father of the Common Market, believed that the absence of the British would fetter Europe's civilizing mission: "The British have a better understanding than the continentals of institutions and how to use them. Continentals tend to believe that problems are solved by men . . . but without institutions they reach no great and enduring decisions. This the British have long understood."[15] Such support encouraged the British to try a third time—but only after de Gaulle had left office.

The Conservative government of Edward Heath (1970–1974) began negotiations for the final attempt in July 1970. Under the Treaty of Accession, signed in Brussels on 22 January 1972, Britain abandoned its special economic ties with the Commonwealth and with the United States and accepted a diminished role for sterling. It had to meet all requirements for membership within three years.[16] The French gave the arrangement their blessing. President Georges Pompidou (1969–1974) supported British entry as a balance against a strong Germany. The British Labour party, however, in another of its reversals, took a firm stand against membership and fought it to the end without success.

Denmark and Ireland entered the Common Market at the same time as the British in 1973, thereby creating the Community of Nine. (In a referendum, Norway decided to stay out.) The European Community now had a combined population of 257 million people; it was responsible for 26 percent of the world's exports and over 27 percent of its imports. Further increases would occur in 1981 when Greece became a member—some say merely to prevent the Turks from also joining—and in 1986 when Spain and Portugal joined. By that time, Austria and Norway had displayed interest in becoming members, as had Switzerland and Sweden, to say nothing of Yugoslavia and Turkey.

The Community in Operation. Agriculture was the glue that held the Common Market together, but finding a common policy proved to be the organization's most controversial and structurally most difficult task.[17] The Community contained some of the best farmland in the world. With a vast diversity of soils and climates, stretching from the Arctic to the Mediterranean seas, from the Atlantic Ocean to the Aegean, the region produced an enormous variety of crops and livestock, most of which enjoyed a certain amount of protection against foreign competition. The reasons for this were both political and emotional. National legislatures had deferred to farming interests, endorsing, sincerely or otherwise, an agrarian romanticism in which farmers were depicted as the soul of the nation. This protectionism was supposed to end with the Common Market, but the practice continued, becoming even more complicated.

For example, the Germans wanted to continue their industrial expansion without alarming the French. So, they agreed to guarantee French wheat at a price adequate to meet its costs of production.[18] They also protected their own farmers who might be hurt by this policy; and, for good measure, they protected the small family farms because they believed them to be historically and socially important. Such props inflated costs and stimulated overproduction, resulting in huge surpluses. As a result, the wealthier farmers got wealthier, while the marginal farmers, whom the policy was designed to benefit, fell farther behind. Most of the German farms remained small and inefficient, the so-called dwarf-farms. Moreover, the consumers did not receive any economic benefits. In fact, they were hurt twice: they paid higher taxes and had to pay high fixed prices for farm products.

Common Market import duties were based on a variable price structure. When the world market price was low, tariffs would be adjusted accordingly. Often, when it was to its advantage, the Common Market found ways to exclude foreign imports altogether. For example, the Common Market prohibited imports of American beef by claiming that it contained too many hormones that were harmful to peoples' health. On the other hand, the Common Market saw nothing wrong with dumping its surpluses on the world market at prices 20 to 50 percent below market price to beat down the competition. Thus, the Common Market countries protected all sorts of products for all sorts of political, economic, moral, and social reasons. The results were sometimes impressive, like the great "wine lakes" and "butter mountains" that appeared in the 1970s. But, by committing such large resources to the agricultural sector, member states deprived the more dynamic industrial and urban sectors of the investment needed for further growth.

In trying to even out advantages and disadvantages between countries, member states collected "compensatory amounts" on goods crossing national frontiers. They thereby collected customs in disguise, making a mockery of economic unity. Agricultural policy, for example, protected from the mechanics of the free market, tried to reconcile the irreconcilable. The pricing needs and demands of the food-importing countries, like Great Britain and West Germany, constantly conflicted with the pricing needs and supplies of the food-exporting countries, like France. Food-importing countries were not enthusiastic about favoring the agricultural sector, whose expenses drained as much as 75 percent of the European Community budget, but bringing about significant change was difficult. Unable to rearrange this fundamental priority, the British compensated by successfully obtaining, in the 1982 Fontainebleau agreement, a rebate on their budget contributions.

Planners responded to the overstimulation of agriculture by pushing for greater modernization of the farming sector and for more functionalism, or product specialization. For example, they wanted Britain and Ireland to concentrate on the production of beef, France to produce wheat, and Italy to grow fruit and vegetables. But, not surprisingly, such plans lacked the support of the producers they were designed to eliminate—producers who frequently possessed the political power to protect their special position. Dramatic rural protests became a feature of agricultural politics in the Common Market. Since the decisions taken in Brussels influenced the income of all Common Market farmers, the farmers used whatever leverage they had to get special treatment. One tactic was to dump their produce in a village square, block the roads with their tractors, mobilize their lobbyists, and call in the media. Consequently, eliminating, or even controlling, price guarantees to producers was extremely difficult.[19] In 1987, the Commission sought to cut the farm subsidies, but at the same time moved to raise tariffs. This helped to reduce the dumping of surplus goods on the world market, but those who did not benefit from the scheme fought to have it changed. As a result, the Common Market was unable to take a clear position on protectionism or free trade with nations outside the Community.

However, pressure to remove all internal barriers to trade continued. In July 1987, the Common Market adopted the Single Act of European Union. This law, which was based on a study entitled "Completing the Internal Market," advocated eliminating all exchange controls and restrictions on the movement of labor and capital to achieve a completely integrated market by 1992. All countries would then have a standard "value-added tax."[20] Monetary compensation would no longer be paid on agricultural goods. State aid to industry would be controlled to prevent certain industries from gaining a competitive edge. The Single European Act also reversed de Gaulle's policy of unanimity by providing for majority voting by the European Community Council and envisaged an expanded role for the European parliament. This push for integration came at a time when European business had become more integrated and more multinational through mergers and takeovers. It was also determined to compete with the United States and Japan for a greater share of the world market.

A Community-funded study, the Cecchini report, indicated that a single European market would raise gross national productivity by at least six percent and lead to greater expenditure on research and development. Consumers would benefit from lower prices and a greater variety of goods. Governments would save money from the elimination of border formalities and lower expenditures on regulation. While few people believed that the task would be finished by the time targeted for its completion, the progress achieved was surprising. Long-term movements of capital were freed, and short-term movements were liberalized. Telecommunications were targeted for deregulation. An additional boost to integration occurred in October 1990, when Great Britain, traditionally reluctant to yield more of its economic sovereignty to the Community, announced that it would tie the pound to the other European currencies. In joining the system, Britain pledged to adjust its economic policies and interest rates to ensure that its currency stayed within a certain range of the nine currencies already in the system. (Only Portugal and Greece now remained outside.) Under current arrangements, central banks had to intervene if currencies drifted outside the prescribed limits. The announcement was greeted with a surge of stock prices on the London exchange. The Confederation of British Industry was pleased because the stabilization of the pound against the other European currencies would result in more predictable export prices for British businesses. However, the British government still refused to consider a single currency, a long-time goal of European Community planners.

Other steps toward complete integration proved equally thorny. Still to be resolved were problems concerning the standardization of labor relations, the harmonization of corporate taxation, the reduction of variations in indirect taxes among members, the elimination of visas, the creation of an internal energy market, the formulation of an environmental protection policy, the creation of a single market for banking and securities, and—most importantly—the establishment of a single central bank and a single currency. Further integration along these lines came close to the marrow of statehood, especially since the pretensions of the Common Market went beyond mere economics.

Article 119 of the Treaty of Rome, concerning equal pay for equal work, was economic in origin, but it took the Community into the controversial world of sex discrimination. The European Court of Justice ruled that Article 119 committed the members of the European Community "to ensure social progress and seek the constant improvement of the living and working conditions of their peoples."[21] Enforcement, though, depended on the national courts and legislatures, a difficult proposition considering the enormous differences in attitudes and customs in the various Common Market countries.[22] For example, Great Britain's tradition-based, common-law political system posed an inherent obstacle to the application of this fundamental right. British law respected the right of the individual to do all that was not prohibited, but "fundamental rights" could not be used to strike down the acts of Parliament.[23] Therefore, European Community law could not have a direct effect, even though it was treaty law. The negative consequences of this were largely moral. Unless a state specifically decided to enact the European Court's rulings, there could be no real compliance, especially on social, as opposed to economic, matters. The court was still feeling its way in this new domain of international jurisprudence.[24] In many countries, the rights of women did not receive the highest priority. The Community, therefore, refrained from legislating social progress and from trying to force the least progressive members to bring about change. Furthermore, as memories of World War II grew dimmer and with them the likelihood that Germany might again disrupt the peace, the Common Market nations became more reluctant to surrender further national sovereignty to a group of experts meeting in Brussels or legislating in Strasbourg. Thus, de Gaulle's fear that supranationalism would deprive France of its sovereignty proved exaggerated, but on that issue he fashioned his own policy of greatness.

The Reign in Spain

The Twilight of the Franco Regime. The government of General Francisco Franco was based on the fundamental political principle that might makes right. But this did not mean that he could do entirely as he chose. The support he received from the aristocracy, the landowners, and the Catholic church was conditional on his respecting their traditional rights, something he had little difficulty doing. However, it was his military victory in the Spanish Civil War in 1939 that had established his legitimacy and confirmed his position as Caudillo "by the grace of God." Franco remained the supreme commander of the armed forces, the chief of the government of the Spanish state, and the chief of the Movement—that is, of the state's only legal political organization. Theoretically, he could pass any law or issue any decree he chose and had no constitutional limitations on his power save God and history. He ruled both as president and prime minister until 1973, two years before his death, when ill health forced him to hand over the active affairs of state to others. Even before that, however, Franco had already allowed his ministers a good deal of initiative. As long as he thought they were carrying out the overall goals of his regime, he interfered little in the running of their departments. Franco believed that his destiny was to re-create the greatness of Spain's monarchical past and, in the process, destroy the evils of democracy and separatism. The other states of Western Europe regarded Franco's Spain as a pariah.

In 1947, as the first step to restoring the Spanish monarchy, he promulgated the Law of Succession, which set out the job description for the future monarch: male, Spanish, Catholic, at least thirty years old, and willing to uphold the fundamental laws of the regime and the Movement.[25] Franco, in tandem with the enactment of the Law of Succession, established a Council of the Realm as a special prop for the consolidation of authoritarianism. The council had power to declare war and rule on all laws passed by the Cortes, the national legislature, which had only advisory powers. Not until 1969 did Franco announce a specific candidate for king in the person of the thirty-one-year-old Juan Carlos, the grandson of Alfonso XIII, Spain's last reigning monarch who had gone into exile in 1931. In doing this, Franco skipped over Juan Carlos's father Don Juan, the legitimate heir, because Don Juan favored a limited monarchy instead of one-man rule. Despite his antipathy toward the regime, however, Don Juan favored a restoration and allowed his son to be educated in Spain to further that prospect.

As the Cold War heated up, the Atlantic community states began to soften their harsh attitude toward Franco's dictatorship. In 1948, France opened its Spanish frontier. Spain was considered for Marshall Plan aid. This came to nothing, but in 1949 the regime managed to negotiate a $25 million loan from the Chase National Bank; the following year, the U.S. Congress approved a $62.5 million loan. Spain was not invited to join NATO, but in 1953, it signed the Pact of Madrid, granting the United States the right to construct three air bases and one naval base and lease them for ten years in exchange for military and economic aid.[26] The Americans reserved the right to use these facilities to launch a nuclear attack on the Soviet Union. Not all Spaniards were as enthusiastic as Franco about the Madrid agreement because they feared the incorporation of Spain into the American and European security zone might involve the country in a war between the superpowers. In 1955, Spain received some consolation when it became a member of the United Nations.

Increased interaction with the West began to modify the restrictive nature of the regime, although this was not immediately apparent. Freedom of the press and association were still severely restricted. The police had wide discretionary powers to arrest and detain suspected enemies. Officials had the authority to restrict privileges and might take away driver's licenses or passports or have dissidents discharged from their employment. If politics seemed business as usual, such was not the case in economics. Within a generation after World War II, Spain had moved from a primarily agricultural economy toward an advanced industrialized society. Improvement was slow at first. The Franco regime wanted to make the economy self-sufficient in the autarkic manner of Fascist Italy. This entailed high tariffs, trade quotas, price regulation, and special protection and subsidies to a whole host of industries. In the 1950s, however, a new class of technocrats, many associated with the Catholic movement *Opus Dei* (Work of God), began pressuring for the modernization of the Spanish economy as a necessary prelude for integration into the Western Europe markets. Opus Dei, an order recognized by the Vatican in 1943 as a secular institute, had originally concentrated on spreading Catholicism throughout state institutions, especially the universities. In 1952, it opened the University of Navarre at Pamplona, the only Spanish secular institution of higher learning devoted mainly to Catholic principles. The organization's members were also prominent in business and finance. Some of them strongly supported the antiliberal economics of the Franco regime, but another, ultimately more important, group wanted to bring about reform through rapid capitalistic growth. They hoped to neutralize politics through prosperity.[27] Although essentially favoring the interests of the upper-middle class, the reformers believed that employers had to recognize the rights of the working class if they wanted to increase productivity. Many of Franco's ministers were members of Opus Dei.

In 1957, the technocrats of Opus Dei succeeded in centralizing all the ministries dealing with economic policy into the single Office of Economic Coordination and Planning. The timing was fortuitous as that was the year the Treaty of Rome was signed. Spain then began to dismantle the apparatus of autarky. The country's balance of payments was stabilized. Controls were dropped, foreign investment was encouraged. Slowly, Spain was converted to a market economy. The results were palpable. During the 1940s and 1950s, Spain's industrial productivity grew at a respectable 7 percent per year; in the 1960s, the growth rate rose to 11 percent. This gain of 50 percent over the previous decade was especially impressive because it came when the overall levels of industrial productivity were greatly superior to those at the beginning of the period. By 1969, Spanish industrial production was 5.69 times higher than in 1949.[28] By comparison, agriculture remained backward. Its gains were very modest compared to those in industry.[29]

The rehabilitation of the Franco regime and the foreign loans that came as a result provided real benefits for the Spanish economy. Spain needed the loans because it could not earn enough foreign capital from its exports to pay for foreign capital goods. In addition, Spain received foreign exchange from the money its nationals working abroad sent home. In 1973, a quarter of a million Spaniards were working in Germany, and twice that number were in France, many of them in unskilled or manual labor jobs. Spain further relied on tourism, which during the 1970s brought in $3 billion a year.[30] The devaluation of the peseta in 1959 made Spain one of the cheapest vacation spots in Europe.

The Spanish technocrats borrowed their concept of planning from the French. In their desire to expand private investment, however, they were more willing to ignore the social costs and worried less about the development of the public sector. Taxes fell heavier on those with lower incomes than on the very wealthy who traditionally were unaccustomed to paying their fair share. As a result, Spain still had a large underclass for whom poverty continued to be a way of life. The amount of begging and the malnutrition, especially in backward areas, were startling. Emigration from rural to urban areas created the surplus population necessary for the expansion of the industrial and service sectors. Nevertheless, unsolved social problems led to growing resentment of the Franco regime. Workers' strikes and student protests broke out in many areas, but the Basque national resistance was the most serious form of radicalism. In December 1973, Basque extremists managed to kill the president of the government, Luis Carrero Blanco, a strong advocate of authoritarianism. The assassins blew Carrero Blanco's car with him in it four stories high to the roof of a Jesuit monastery. The army went on alert, but no attempt at a coup followed the assassination. Until his death, the Caudillo enjoyed such popularity, or encouraged such apathy, that at no point was he in any real danger of being toppled.

Reconstructing Spanish Democracy. General Franco hoped that his designated successor would preserve the character of his regime after the general had been laid to rest in his tomb in the Valley of the Fallen. As long as Franco lived, Juan Carlos was in a difficult position. The regime's hard-liners did not trust him; the leftists thought him a stooge. For many moderates, however, Juan Carlos represented the best hope for a transition to a peaceful and more liberal Spain. The prince guarded his counsel so carefully it was difficult to predict what he might do when he came into his inheritance. He said as little as possible, studiously avoiding involvement in the affairs of state while the Caudillo lived. Remarkably, Franco made no direct attempt to indoctrinate him, no doubt hoping that Juan Carlos would do the right thing when the time came.

The time came on 20 November 1975. Even before Franco breathed his last, however, his regime was no longer the one he had originally created. The country was more prosperous than it had ever been in its history. Much of this progress had taken place despite Franco's efforts or desires. It simply happened without much opposition. Franco's authoritarianism, no matter how objectionable, did provide a stable environment for steady economic growth. The Spanish people seemed content to wait patiently until the Caudillo died before making comparable changes in their political system. The Civil War had been so traumatic that few wanted to resolve their differences again in a bloody manner. Franco's long reign gave them the opportunity to outlive their extremism. That Franco had fought so hard to extinguish democracy made the successful transformation to Western-style parliamentary institutions the more remarkable. Much of the credit for this transition was due to the thirty-seven-year-old king.

Juan Carlos knew that the survival of the monarchy and the future well-being of his country depended on the successful dismantling of the Franco state. In doing this, Juan Carlos proved a skilled politician. At first, he treaded very carefully, trying not to antagonize those who feared he would go too far, but reassuring those who feared he would not go far enough. He was lucky in that he did not face any strong competition. The elimination of Carrero Blanco had removed one possible source of opposition; Franco's failure to nominate a new president of the Council of the Realm had removed another.

The king tried to run his first government with men who had Francoist credentials, but were personally loyal to him. He appointed Torcuato Fernández Miranda to head the Council of the Realm and the Cortes. Fernández Miranda was flexible and could be relied upon to help neutralize the rightist opposition. He also retained Carlos Arias Navarro, Carrero Blanco's successor, as prime minister. Although Juan Carlos made it clear to the ministers of his first government that his aim was the complete democratization of the Spanish political system, the government could not agree on a program of political reform. There was much squabbling and not much progress.[31] Meanwhile unrest and public protest increased in Madrid, Barcelona, the Basque country, and elsewhere. The Communist and Socialist opposition formed an alliance in the *Coordinacion Democrática* (Democratic Coordination) to which the Christian Democrats, the Carlists, and the trade unions added their strength. The Francoist forces were calling for a crackdown. In July 1976, the king dismissed Arias and replaced him with Adolfo Suárez González.

Suárez continued the process of democratization with great success. He turned the Franco apparatus against itself and, within a year, had dismantled it beyond recognition. In July 1976, using the very legal instruments Franco had created, he suppressed the police state Tribunal of Public Order. In November, he and Fernández Miranda persuaded the Francoist Cortes, which had been only a rubber stamp, to vote itself out of existence by passing the Law of Political Reform, which called for the election of a new bicameral Cortes by universal suffrage. In February 1977, the Law of Political Associations legalized all political parties except the Communist party. (Two months later, the Communists achieved legal status, after promising to accept the monarchy and respect the state's political institutions.) In March, labor unions were legalized, thereby destroying the old Francoist labor syndicates. As fears spread that the army was plotting to seize power, Juan Carlos worked to keep it loyal. He had a great institutional advantage. The officers could not act against him as a politician without challenging his authority as the chief of the Spanish state and commander-in-chief of the armed forces. Such treason would have destroyed everything they had sworn to uphold.

In June, Spain held free elections for the first time since 1936. The campaign lasted a month; 18 million people, almost 80 percent of the entire electorate, came to the polls. The voters overwhelmingly rejected the parties of the extremes. Of the 350 seats in the *Congreso* (Congress), the lower house in the new Cortes, the right-wing neo-Francoist party *Alianza Popular* (Popular Alliance) won only 16 (five percent of the popular vote); the Communist party (*Partido Comunista Español*), despite its professed willingness to play by democratic rules, got only 20 seats (nine percent of the popular vote). The big winners were the moderate coalition *Union de Centro Democrático* (Union for the Democratic Center), led by Suárez, with 165 seats (34.3 percent of the popular vote) and the *Partido Socialista Obrero Española* (Socialist Workers' party), led by Felipe González Márquez, which captured 118 seats (28.5 percent of the popular vote). These two parties also dominated the upper chamber, the *Senado*. The Christian Democratic party of José Mariá Gil Robles, a prominent politician of the Second Republic, had been practically wiped out. The Spanish people, having rejected the parties of the center to their misfortune in 1936, had now embraced them with a vengeance.

Since 1975, Spain had been so concerned with political reorganization that economic problems were often ignored. The country's heavy industries needed further rationalization; unemployment was on the rise, and an increase in the world price of oil cut into foreign exchange. In 1977, the inflation rate reached more than 24 percent. A proposed policy of austerity was unpopular and shook people's faith in the Suárez government. Nevertheless, the workers and left-wing parties agreed to make sacrifices in exchange for a promise of social reform, including a more equitable tax structure.

Meanwhile, a committee of the Congreso worked to draft a new constitution. The process, wending its way through many amendments, compromises, and alterations in committees, took fifteen months to complete. The final document, which passed both houses of the Cortes in October 1978, created a parliamentary monarchy based on liberty, justice, equality, and political pluralism. The drafters were determined not to repeat some of the mistakes of the 1931 constitution. Therefore, although the constitution did not establish a state religion, it did promise to maintain relations with the Catholic church and other religions. Similarly, although education was to be free and public, the constitution promised that the state would aid private schools, i.e., mostly Catholic schools. While the constitution affirmed the unity of the Spanish state, it recognized the right to autonomy of the various nationalities, including the right of these ethnic minorities to teach their local language and fly their own flag. The provision did not go far enough for the Basques but went too far for the neo-Francoist Popular Alliance. Nevertheless, almost 88 percent of the Spanish people gave the constitution their approval.[32]

The first elections held under this constitution on 1 March 1979 changed the distribution of power very little; both the Democratic Union and the Socialist Workers' party picked up three seats at the expense of the smaller parties, including the Communists who had aggressively campaigned as a party of Western democracy. The Spanish Right suffered a further loss and was not even represented in most of the country. Yet Franco's legacy persisted. Some senior officers of the Spanish army harbored strong desires for the old days. Largely out of touch with the rest of the country and lacking any real support among the general population, they nevertheless continued to conspire against the democratic regime. The Suárez government's failure to improve the economy and deal with a mounting wave of Basque terrorism—Basque gunmen liked to kill Castilian police officers—led to an attempted coup in Madrid. The rebels wanted to dissolve the Cortes and create a new military government of national unity. They made their move on 23 February 1981, when the Congreso had assembled to vote on the investiture of a new prime minister. (Suárez, buffeted by dissension in his own party and in the Cortes, had just resigned.) The conspirators believed that the king secretly welcomed such a move and would accede to their fait accompli.

Two hundred members of the Guardia Civil, led by Lieutenant-Colonel Antonio Tejero Molina, burst into the Congreso with guns at the ready. It was 6:20 P.M. One of the police officers fired some shots into the ceiling prompting the deputies to dive for cover. Tejero announced he would obey no one save Lieutenant-General Jaime Milans del Bosch, captain-general of Valencia and the conspiracy's leader. Milans telephoned the country's other military leaders, telling them he was acting "in the name of the king." Juan Carlos, however, began calling the same generals, telling them that his name was being used in vain and ordering them to support the legitimate government. He was not always successful. General Alfonso Armanda Comyn tried to exploit the coup by intriguing to get himself named head of the government in the style of General de Gaulle. In the end, though, most of the generals obeyed their commander-in-chief. That same night the king addressed the nation on television. He declared that he would not tolerate any subversion of the constitution.

The coup collapsed, but it had been a close call. Had the king not acted decisively, the conspirators might have succeeded in undoing the democratic achievements of the past four years. It was one of Juan Carlos's finest hours. His strong stand for democracy kept the army in line and convinced many hidebound republicans that the monarchy had some value after all. Juan Carlos was determined to avoid the blunder of his grandfather, Alfonso XIII, who in 1923 violated the constitution by turning the government over to a dictator. The king feared, however, that the democratic system that he had helped create might not survive if it constantly had to depend on such extraordinary efforts. The day after the coup, he advised the leaders of the Cortes to promote concord and unity and recommended against taking revenge on the armed forces.[33] Only a small proportion of those involved in the coup were actually brought to justice. Thirty-three were tried, most of whom received relatively light sentences. The chief conspirators Milans, Tejero, and Armanda received the maximum—thirty years. The fledgling Spanish democracy, although badly shaken, had successfully survived its first major threat.

Leopoldo Calvo Sotelo, who succeeded Suárez, took steps to restore confidence by intensifying the war against terrorism. He also negotiated the entrance of Spain into the NATO alliance. In doing this, the government hoped to find a new role for the military besides meddling in domestic politics. Still, some feared that the 1981 coup would not be the last time the army would try to seize power. The Socialists, who had increased their strength throughout the country, were especially apprehensive that the military might try to prevent them from ever assuming power.

The Socialist secretary-general Felipe González had worked hard to make his party respectable. He had eliminated Marxist ideology as a central component of the party's philosophy and had excluded the party's left-wingers from all positions of importance. He had also abandoned the nationalization of industry as a political objective. Now González put pragmatism ahead of ideology and concentrated on fighting unemployment, protecting democracy, and achieving administrative reform. His popularity was phenomenal; he was the only Spanish leader who was affectionately referred to by his first name. He believed that refashioning socialism was the best insurance against Communism and a revival of Francoism.

The Socialist Workers' party swept the elections of October 1982 with 48 percent of the popular vote, capturing 210 of the 350 seats in the Congreso. This was an increase of 120 over the January 1979 balloting. The Communists practically disappeared, dropping from 20 to 5 seats. The Union for the Democratic Center fell catastrophically from 168 seats to a scant 13. Many of the Democratic Union's former supporters had voted Socialist. The rightist Popular Alliance led by Manuel Fraga Iribarne became the second largest party. Fraga had been the minister of information and tourism in the Franco government. The elections gave Spain a virtual two-party system. The Spanish army pledged to respect the election results.

González downplayed his lopsided victory. At the age of forty, he was the youngest government leader in Europe. He had epitomized the aspirations of the Spanish for the consolidation of the democratic system and their desire to integrate their country with the rest of Western Europe. Yet, Spain had a 16 percent unemployment rate and a 12 percent inflation rate and also faced a significant threat in the form of Basque terrorism. Furthermore, a significant part of the electorate had voted for an opposition party whose roots lay in the former authoritarian system. Nevertheless, the Socialist victory showed that the Spanish people's hope for a new beginning outweighed their longing for the past. The Socialists dominated Spanish politics for the rest of the decade. They became a centrist party, a party of moderation, the kind of political organization that Spaniards had previously ignored at their peril.

Privatization of the British Welfare State

The Faltering Consensus. In the nineteenth century, the British created a liberal democracy by extending the right to vote, but after World War I, political liberalization was no longer enough. People now had greater demands. They expected government help in raising their standard of living. All major political parties adopted the rhetoric of compassion, beginning with the promise to veterans that Britain would be made a fit place for heroes to live in. Even people who felt no moral obligation to share their privileges with others nevertheless recognized that some welfare legislation was necessary to maintain constitutional and institutional stability. The Conservative governments of the 1920s and 1930s could point to some successes in expanding the public sector, but generally they dragged their feet on making any real economic and social changes.

During World War II, the promises were taken more seriously. Both major parties agreed that the inequities of the present system could not be corrected without more state intervention. They agreed that the British people should have proper medical assistance, subsidized housing, and improved education. They agreed to provide care for disadvantaged children, the mentally and physically disabled, and the elderly. They also accepted the principles of Keynesian economics, in particular, that the state has a major role to play in guaranteeing a stable economy with full employment and a steady rate of growth. Accordingly, they believed the government should keep a tight rein over the country's monetary system and expected it to manipulate prices, income levels, and foreign exchange. They also favored, or at least accepted, the direct ownership of certain industries, including coal, steel, transportation, and public utilities.

Although the Conservative and Labour parties disagreed on the reasons for nationalization—the former finding its worth primarily in economic development, the latter believing it was necessary to promote economic equality—both advocated developing national priorities and solving problems through the tripartite cooperation of government, labor, and industry. The "beer and sandwiches" approach extended from the national level down to local units and assumed that all decisions must be reached through compromise.[34] Although the communality of Conservative-Labour belief was more often fiction than fact, the areas of consensus seemed more important than those of disagreement. The Conservatives did not attack the welfare state directly, although they disagreed vehemently with the Labour party over how it was to be financed, how the growing power of the trade unions should be treated, and how wealth should be distributed.[35] Much of the Conservatives' later criticism of Labour, whether justified or not, stemmed from the relatively poor performance of the British economy compared to other European countries.

West Germany and France grew at a rate of between 3 and 5 percent per year, while Britain squeezed out a bare 2 percent. Some people warned that the country would fall behind Italy or even Portugal and blamed the welfare state for a multitude of sins: failure to shake British industry out of its hidebound ways, failure to make labor more productive, and failure to promote class harmony. None of this was new. Before World War II, people had complained about worsening labor relations, the rise of class hatred, and the declining productivity of industry. Only now the stakes were higher. The existence of the welfare state depended on a healthy, growing economy. In many ways, growth was more important to Labour than to the Conservatives because Labour's constituents were traditionally those less well off.

By the 1970s, social security benefits were taken for granted. People were used to the improved health care resulting from the National Health Service, and they expected the state to subsidize their housing and guarantee their well-being. The cost of such benefits, however, was rising. One answer was to reduce benefits—a politically risky proposition. Failing that, the answer was to increase revenues. Monies could be obtained in various ways. The government could levy taxes on property, goods, or income; it could borrow, or it could promote a policy of inflation, which would enable it to pay its bills with depreciated currency. But each option entailed social and economic costs even assuming the government made an effort to be fair. In any case, the cost of living would rise, which would inevitably precipitate a demand for higher wages. From the 1960s through the 1980s, the Conservative and Labour governments struggled fitfully to raise revenues to maintain services, increase the standard of living, ensure full employment, and improve productivity.

Harold Macmillan did not live up to his 1959 election promises to increase British productivity. His government sponsored a host of studies and reiterated a heightened commitment to planning, and in 1962 it urged employers to hold the line on pay increases at two percent to aid the economy. Under pressure, however, it allowed as much as three times that amount for civil servants and workers in nationalized industries. People complained that the moratorium was unfair. Meanwhile domestic production remained about the same. Disenchantment with the Conservatives' performance resulted in Labour and Liberal party victories in the 1962 by-elections. The improvement in the British standard of living in the previous decade had contributed to high expectations about continuing prosperity that the Conservatives seemed incapable of sustaining. In 1961, the index of industrial production had risen about 1 percent over the previous year; in 1962, it was up just over 3 percent; and in 1963, it remained about the same as in the previous year.[36] From 1963 to 1964, the index of industrial production shot up by more than 13 percent, but the increase came too late to restore Macmillan's popularity. Thanks to de Gaulle, he had also failed to bring his country into the Common Market. And, in March 1963, his administration was faced with a major sex scandal. Secretary of state for war, John Profumo, had an affair with a call girl who also shared her attractions with a naval attaché from the Soviet embassy. Profumo at first lied about his involvement, then had to admit he had "misled" his colleagues. Macmillan was an innocent party, but his position as leader was shaken nevertheless. In October, following a prostate operation, he announced his resignation and turned over the leadership of his party to Sir Alec Douglas-Home, a lackluster crossover from the House of Lords.[37] Douglas-Home had little time to put his own stamp on British politics before he was faced with a general election.

The Conservatives promised more public housing. Labour promised a reduction in medical costs, an improvement in education, and an increase in insurance benefits. The programs would be paid for out of revenues from higher productivity—a familiar promise. Labour won—its first government (1964–1970) since Attlee's victory in 1945—controlling the Commons with a slim majority of four seats.[38] Harold Wilson, the new prime minister, sought to turn Britain around. His goals were to reverse the deficit in the balance of payments, increase industrial productivity, and stabilize prices. The government produced a "National Plan" to control and stimulate growth primarily through technological modernization. The results were disappointing. Only in 1968 did the index of industrial productivity reach 6 percent; for the rest of Labour's term in office, the index hovered around 2 to 3 percent growth per year. From 1966 to 1967, there was no growth at all.[39]

In 1970, the Conservatives again took charge under their new leader Edward Heath. Heath, like his predecessors, promised more than he delivered. He wanted to reduce expenditures, cut taxes, stimulate investment, and expand productivity. But as before, inflationary wage demands and the loss of working days through stoppages and strikes squandered human and material resources and further weakened the country's industrial base. Furthermore, a war in the Middle East in 1973 led to a significant rise in the price of oil, which greatly affected all European economies. Everything suddenly became more expensive; at least, everything that was dependent on petroleum, plastics, transportation, and fertilizers. The consumer price index skyrocketed, pushing the inflation rate into double digits. Between 1974 and 1978, prices doubled, especially in the public sector. The value of the pound began to tumble, pushing up the cost of imports. Heath could not control inflation in time for the 1974 elections. Although the Conservatives outpolled Labour, they fell three seats short of a plurality. Labour, still led by Harold Wilson, formed the first minority government since 1929. By calling another election eight months later, however, Wilson was able to gain a majority of three seats, small but adequate. He resigned in 1976 and was replaced by James Callaghan (1976–1979), the former foreign secretary and the first prime minister since the war who had never been to a university. Callaghan always thought himself less bright than he actually was.

Britain was still plagued by inflation, but Callaghan was reluctant to shrink the money supply and begin a program of austerity for fear of jeopardizing the jobs of his working-class constituents. But if inflation were to be brought under control, a higher rate of unemployment seemed inevitable. Labour bit the bullet and, in July 1976, adopted a tighter monetary policy, slashing public spending by one million pounds. It also applied for a loan from the International Monetary Fund. Still the cost of living continued to rise. In October, the government trimmed another 2.5 million pounds. Unemployment rose to 1.5 million people. The situation was reminiscent of the early 1930s when Ramsay MacDonald had tightened the nation's belt in order to get credits from New York bankers. Prime Minister Callaghan placed the blame on Keynesian manipulation of the economy. He said that the inflation had been caused by boosting public spending to increase employment. Indeed, previous administrations, including those of the Tories, had tried to maintain a high standard of living through increased spending.

In a 1976 speech, Callaghan told the Labour Party Conference that the nation could no longer afford a policy of cutting taxes and engaging in deficit spending.[40] His task seemed impossible. He tried to hold the line on wages, knowing the country could not afford such inflationary increases. One way of doing this was through high levels of unemployment, a practice he found intolerable.[41] The government tried to limit public employees to a five percent increase. It intended to enforce these guidelines against private corporations by refusing to order goods from companies that violated them. The Trade Union Congress opposed the policy.

The floodgates opened in the winter of 1978 when the Ford Motor Company, which had had a very profitable year, decided to give its workers a pay increase of 17 percent. This prompted the road transport workers to demand 25 percent and, when they did not get it, to go on strike. Shop stewards in other industries came out in favor of secondary picketing, which encouraged workers in businesses totally unconnected to the original dispute to show their solidarity by also downing their tools. Consequently, workers from garbage collectors and gravediggers to nursery school attendants also stopped work. The disruption of services, the nondelivery of goods, and the loss of purchasing power damaged the economy further. Industrial output fell by one-third. This "winter of discontent" helped return the Conservatives to power in the general elections of March 1979. Ironically, the Labour party did not lose support; its national vote was actually higher than it had been five years earlier. Rather the Conservatives, who had abstained in 1974, returned to vote in great numbers. They feared more labor unrest and welcomed the lower taxes that their party promised. Callaghan, on leaving office, felt that it was a miracle that he had stayed as long as he had.[42]

Britain had lagged behind the other industrial powers of Europe since the beginning of the century, but the British could not agree on whether the reasons for the "decline" were technical or psychological or both. British industry suffered from a lack of investment, especially in new manufacturing techniques. Moreover the products the British tried to sell failed to claim their share of either the world market or the domestic market. The reasons were sometimes easy to see. For centuries, the British had been claiming "British is best" when in fact it was not. British products were often poorly designed, badly marketed, late in delivery, and inadequately serviced. Some products, such as the British motorcycle, clung to old-fashioned technology. The Japanese had created a bike that could be started by pushing a button on the handlebars, but the British models still used the old kick starter that took several hard pumps to produce an ignition. As a result, the British motorcycle industry went into recession. Even British souvenirs—T-shirts, horse brasses, china ashtrays—frequently came from abroad. Britain was no longer the workshop of the world and had not been for decades. The British themselves frequently preferred foreign goods to those produced at home.

Also blamed for the British malaise was the class-ridden educational system that failed to train a properly skilled work force. Universities and secondary schools often put a premium on the liberal arts to the neglect of science, engineering, and technology. Futhermore, business executives had lower social prestige than in more aggressive societies. Many of the technicians and entrepreneurs that Britain did produce left the country to find work in the Commonwealth countries or the United States. American and Canadian universities are full of examples of this "brain drain." Some critics preferred to blame the welfare state itself for Britain's faults, blaming it for inflation, the lack of resources, the fall in the standard of service, and the decline in self-reliance. They accused the welfare state of diminishing Britain's creative vitality by subsidizing unproductive industries and by overregulating and overtaxing. In their view, the welfare state stripped resources from the more vital private sector, did not respond to individual needs, and failed to involve people in decisions that affected their lives.[43] Many of the arguments were ideological and emotional, and many tended to overlook the achievements of the welfare state.[44] But whatever its faults, most commentators agreed that the British people would have to work harder and produce more if their benefits were to increase.

Thatcherism. Margaret Thatcher, the new prime minister (1979–1990), thought she had the answer. Thatcher, the first woman to become the head of government in British history (unless one counts the Tudor and Stuart queens), had strong opinions about what was wrong with the country. Labour leader James Callaghan had already rejected the Keynesian concept of managing demand, but this was only the beginning of a solution. Thatcher wanted to blast the state out of its command position over economic affairs and restore the free market. She was prepared to take on the establishment, specifically, the civil servants and government planners whom she derided for telling the British people what they should eat, how they should be housed, and under what conditions they should work. Thatcher wanted a decisive break with what she saw as an all powerful paternalistic government that turned its citizens into dependent beneficiaries.[45] Her strong, aggressive personality, which would have been accepted as normal in a man, seemed unfeminine in a woman. Tory backbencher Julian Critchley quipped that Thatcher had an urge to hit British institutions with her handbag. Despite such sexism, her impact was enormous. And she soon established a base of popular support that transcended her base in her own party.

Thatcher believed that all those who worked for their money should be allowed to accumulate wealth by keeping a larger share of it. She therefore began by cutting income taxes. The 1979 budget clipped the highest rate from 98 percent to 60 percent, and the basic rate from 33 to 30 percent.[46] It exempted the first 5,000 pounds of investment income from tax altogether. More cuts followed. In the 1988 budget, the upper rate dropped to 40 percent, the basic rate to 25 percent. The new taxation policy increased the gap between high- and low-wage earners, but also made it possible for more Britons to buy their own homes, accelerating a trend that had begun in the early 1970s. The Thatcher government chose a "salami-

Prime Minister Thatcher celebrates the victory of her party in the elections of 1983. The Conservatives won 397 of the 650 seats in the Commons. This solid majority convinced many of them that they no longer need pay lip service to the welfare state.

slicer" style of reform. It began by selling public housing units to tenants, eventually privatizing whole rows of public housing. It then reduced subsidies to public housing. Next it tried to stimulate private housing development by relaxing rent controls on new buildings and on new tenancies.[47] Owner occupation increased from 50 to over 64 percent.

Privatization was the cornerstone of the government's policy to reverse collectivization and revitalize the national economy. Thatcher proceeded to assault state-owned industries, which, she thought, were inefficient in meeting public demand and in encouraging working-class productivity. The problem, as she saw it, lay in the *fact* of public ownership itself. Costs would never be reduced and efficiency would never be achieved as long as industries lacked the discipline of the marketplace, and the government paid for their losses. Allowing the market to work would reduce inflation, make labor more productive, and stimulate the kind of investment that would make the country's industry more competitive. In practice, privatization led to the sale of such public services as British Telecommunications, British Gas, British Airways, British Airports Authority, British Petroleum, and ten water companies. In addition, the government got rid of Rolls Royce, Jaguar, Sealink, Vickers Shipbuilding, National Bus Company, British Rail Hotels, and Royal Ordinance, to name a few of the more prominent.[48] Most of these divestitures were accomplished either by offering shares on the open market or through private sales. In a few cases, such as British Steel, joint ventures were worked out between the government and the private sector. Critics of privatization countered that most of the privatized industries were already operating at a profit and thus were already performing well while less efficient industries remained state property. In response, the government pointed to the benefits the taxpayers received from reduced government spending and from the billions of additional pounds pumped into the public treasury. It took pride in the growing number of households that owned shares of stocks.

In 1979, only seven percent of British citizens held shares; in 1988, that number had almost trebled. Of the 600,000 workers transferred from the public to the private sector between 1979 and 1986, over half became shareholders, many in the enterprises where they worked. For example, in 1983, the employees of British Airways agreed to accept minimal wage increases for two years in exchange for a profit-sharing plan that would give them shares in the company's stock. The government gave tax breaks to those who participated in such programs.[49] The government hoped this grass-roots capitalism would weaken the trade unions. Whatever the reasoning, many of the initial employee-shareholders did benefit when the value of their investments increased as the economy improved. Instead of focusing on preventing unemployment, the government emphasized removing obstacles to growth. To this end, the Tories curbed the power of the trade unions and facilitated the free exchange of goods and services and the movement of capital. The main weapon of control over the economy that was still in the state arsenal was the power to regulate interest rates.

From 1973 to 1979, the British economy continued to plod along, growing at an annual rate of 1.5 percent; but from 1983 to 1989, the rate of growth jumped to 3.5 percent per year. The Conservatives believed that this improvement vindicated their policy, even though overall output was only slightly more than it had been twenty years earlier.[50] Although inflation declined, it did not go away, and it still exceeded that of Italy and France. Moreover, unemployment had emerged on a scale unseen since the Great Depression. By January 1986, 14 percent of the labor force, or 3.4 million people, were out of work—an enormous rate for a society that had been taught that employment was a fundamental right.[51] The impact was felt all over Britain. At the same time, the number of British households living below the poverty line increased,[52] and the gap between the rich and the poor widened.

Prime Minister Thatcher was so confident that she was steering the right course that she planned to denationalize large public utilities, in particular water and electricity. The government also wanted to trim government expenditures for the social security program. While full benefits for the most needy would be retained, benefits for others would be drastically reduced. Thatcher believed that handouts discouraged self-reliance and independence and lowered people's incentive to find work. She instituted a means test for receiving social security benefits and achieved additional savings by changing the way benefits were calculated. The unemployed had to show evidence they were actively looking for employment in order to continue receiving benefits. Eventually, under Thatcher's plan, the national government would transfer the responsibility of paying room and board allowances to local authorities. She also talked about cutting child allowances and streamlining the popular National Health Service as well as raising the fees for its services. Thatcher thought the private health care sector should be enlarged. Altogether, she planned so many alterations in welfare services that many suspected that the Conservative government intended more than mere reformation. Ironically, a majority of the British people did not agree with much of what Thatcher was doing. They favored more welfare, not less, and preferred an expansion of public spending to a cut in taxes. Yet such opinions were not sufficiently focused to threaten the Conservatives' parliamentary majority.

Part of the reason for the Tories' success was the inability of the Labour opposition to heal its divisions and mount an effective challenge. The presence of radical groups within the Labour party, such as the faction called the Militant Tendency, made it difficult for the party to agree on a course of action. Moreover, the party's left wing wanted further nationalizations and advocated unilateral nuclear disarmament. Tony Benn, the leader of this radical faction, was an avowed Marxist who believed that the capitalists were trying to overthrow the democratic system. He attempted to become the deputy leader of the party in 1981, failing by a whisker. Throughout the rest of the decade, Labour continued to suffer from ideological confusion.

Thatcher's popularity received a great boost in April 1982, when Argentina seized the Falkland Islands. By grabbing these islands, which had been British for the last 150 years, the generals who ran Argentina hoped to gain a quick foreign policy success that would redeem their declining popularity. Thatcher rallied the country to defend the Falklanders' right of self-determination. During the month or more required to assemble and transport a military force 8,000 miles to the South Atlantic, Thatcher tried negotiations. When these failed to remove the Argentines, she ordered a counterinvasion. The attack began on 21 May, with the establishment of a bridgehead at San Carlos Bay on East Falkland Island. Three and a half weeks later, on 14 June, the British forced the surrender of the main Argentine army. There were only 255 British casualties. The British greeted the victory with great ebullience. When Thatcher heard the news of the Argentine defeat, she appeared at the door of the prime minister's residence at 10 Downing Street and shouted, "Rejoice! Rejoice!" She had reason to be happy. Her handling of the crisis made her one of the most popular leaders of the postwar era. The crisis also helped her divert attention from the social stress caused by her domestic policies.

A trace of magnanimity toward the losers surfaced in a proposal that the Lord's Prayer be recited in Spanish as well as English at the commemorative service in St. Paul's Cathedral. The suggestion was rejected.[53] The British were smug and self-righteous about their victory, but this did not mean that the Argentine generals, who had cynically provoked the war, were any less disreputable, although they were hardly on a par with Hitler. Throughout the affair, Thatcher had mirrored the Churchillian spirit to remain resolute in pursuit of justice. She saw the war, not as a rivalry between two states, but as a test of the resolve of Western democratic nations to stand up to the aggression of dictators. The Falklands' conflict was her fight for a new international order. It was her way of saying that Britain was on the road to recovery from its period of socialist decline.[54] The ability of Britain to mount such a venture, however, was due more to the added revenues it was getting from the sale of North Sea oil, which came pouring forth almost at the moment she entered office, than to Thatcher's messianic determination to refashion British politics. The North Sea windfall also enabled Britain to reduce its budget deficit and mobilize capital for long-term investment.

Thatcher's popularity began to slide after the 1987 elections. Those elections gave her party a one-hundred–seat edge over Labour in the House of Commons, but the economy turned sour, inflation rose into the double digits, investment slowed, and productivity began to decline. Thatcher reacted by pushing up interest rates, to as much as 15 percent, and by reforming the local tax structure. She instituted a "poll tax," substituting the current property tax with a flat rate on every adult. This new means of getting revenue hit the poorer classes especially hard and produced weeks of public demonstrations, culminating in a particularly bloody riot in Trafalgar Square in March 1990. The Tories began losing by-elections to Labour. Thatcher's loss of popularity also extended to within her own party. Many of her colleagues tired of her tirades; they resented her confrontational style and her zest to solve nonexistent problems. Since the last election, almost her entire cabinet had either resigned or been fired. In November 1990, with the Labour party leading ten points or more in the polls, former Defense Minister Richard Heseltine challenged her for party leadership, forcing her into a second round of balloting. However, before this took place, Thatcher resigned. She clearly had become the problem that threatened to split the party. Her replacement was the modest, low-key John Major. Shortly after taking office, he began to talk about a "social market" economy and a more "caring" government. Clearly, the British people wanted their government to provide more, not fewer, public services.

Toward German Reunification

A Search for National Identity. The defeat of Germany in 1945 dealt a serious blow to the country's sense of national identity. The Nazi regime was so linked with the spirit of the people that discrediting one affected the other. Love of country in all its political or nonpolitical manifestations was now suspect. Political leadership passed into the hands of the Allies, who determined the shape and character of the disunited country. The eventual solidification of Germany into two sections, each with its own government, seemed to spell the end of German unity. Although the Western powers were locked in a cold war with the Soviet Union, both sides accepted partition as the best way to guarantee the stability of Europe. Whatever reconstruction the German Federal Republic and the German Democratic Republic (GDR) would achieve would have to be accomplished at the bidding and the expense of Germany's former enemies.

Of the two Germanies, the eastern regime had the most difficulty establishing its own legitimacy and integrity. The Soviets hailed the GDR as the true Germany, a classless state of peasants and workers separated from the imperialistic and capitalistic Federal Republic. Yet the Soviets were not above sacrificing their satellite if it served their interests. At Geneva in 1955, the Soviet Union tried to prevent the Federal Republic from joining any Western military alliance by proposing the reunification of Germany as a neutral state through free elections. Britain, France, and the United States did not take the bait. But the Soviet overtures showed the GDR leaders the fragility of their tenure. Until the 1970s, the only countries that had exchanged ambassadors with East Germany were those of the Communist bloc and some newly emergent nations. This was largely due to the Hallstein Doctrine, the West German threat to break diplomatic relations with nations that recognized the GDR. East Germany tried to become a more viable state by creating a cult of economic progress, but promised improvements failed to materialize. Its consumer goods and industrial productivity lagged a generation behind those of the West. The Communist leaders' boast that they had ended exploitation fell on deaf ears. While the regime continued to preach that only under socialism did science and technology serve human needs, East German workers continued to devise ways to flee to the West. The GDR clung to its close association with the Soviet Union. It hailed the policy of detente pursued by Leonid Brezhnev as the correct course of action. But the relaxation of tensions between East and West presented real problems. East Germany had constructed its ideology around continued tension with the other Germany. This proved to be a very weak reed.

The West Germans also had problems of identity, but the Allies permitted them a longer leash. Spared the subservience that was mandatory in the East, the Federal Republic was able to develop a viable parliamentary system. The Cold War also enabled the Federal Republic to assert its independence rather rapidly, even though that independence was firmly tied to the Western alliance. The most tangible proof of West German sovereignty was its inclusion in the NATO alliance in 1955 and the rebuilding of its army. These came as a direct result of the Western need to develop an additional bulwark against Soviet expansionism. Thus, at a time when the East Germans were coming increasingly under the control of the Soviets, the West Germans were able to win more freedom. The reemergence of West Germany as a major power was also due to its *Wirtschaftswunder* (economic miracle), which gave real substance to the West German sense of identity and self-confidence. One of the proudest symbols of that ascendancy was the Mercedes-Benz, an artifact that combined elegant design with authoritative style. The West Germans reveled in their materialism; such pride had not been seen since the boom years of the German Reich prior to World War I. The preamble of the West German constitution claimed West Germany would carry the torch of German freedom and unity through free self-determination,[55] and the country's great industrial expansion suggested this might be more than an optimistic dream. A new generation, unsullied by Hitlerism, had developed the confidence to exercise power without guilt to make their nation once again the arbiter of Europe.

Eastern Politics. Konrad Adenauer had apparently failed to appreciate the threat that de Gaulle's European union presented to the NATO alliance. But unlike de Gaulle, Adenauer was not unduly alarmed at American dominance, which he regarded as necessary to protect Germany against aggression and guarantee the integrity of West Berlin. Furthermore, the 1954 agreements, which underscored the responsibility of the Big Three in German reunification, limited Germany's options. The bilateral cooperation between Germany and France, upon which de Gaulle counted to make his independent Europe a reality, did not survive Adenauer's retirement. The Germans saw no reason to undertake an uncertain association with France, especially since de Gaulle was not inclined to commit his country's nuclear capacity to the common defense of Europe. Even had de Gaulle been willing, the *force de frappe* was hardly in the same league with the striking power of the United States. German military cooperation with the United States therefore expanded.

The government of Ludwig Erhard (1963–1966) was under considerable pressure from "German Gaullists" to become more independent of the United States. The chancellor's determination to remain on good terms with both France *and* the United States prompted de Gaulle, on the eve of his withdrawal from NATO, to link French support for German reunification to support for his defense policy. The scheme to separate Bonn from Washington backfired. The Erhard government remained a staunch member of NATO, believing that the eventual reunification of Germany could only be achieved through the Atlantic alliance, with an undiluted American presence. The Germans concluded that de Gaulle's nuclear defense policy would result in their subservience to France. They figured that the American nuclear umbrella came with fewer strings. Besides, German leadership in the Common Market provided a secure base from which Germany could assert an increasingly active role in foreign policy. They also believed German industrial strength would prove especially valuable in dealing with the economically backward states of the Soviet bloc. Accordingly, the Germans began changing their strategy on reunification.

One flaw in these calculations was the chancellor himself. Erhard lacked the stature of his predecessor. He had been an able economics minister, but in becoming chancellor, he had risen to his level of incompetence. He was always more at home with numbers than with people, and his enforcement of a secondary policy like the Hallstein Doctrine was pathetic. Even before his fall, Erhard had damaged the cohesion of his own party.

The new government was a Grand Coalition of Christian Democrats and Socialists (1966–1969), led by Kurt Georg Kiesinger of the CDU as chancellor and Social Democrat Willy Brandt as foreign minister. These leaders recognized that German reunification need not be a prerequisite for the normalization of relations with the East. In its new *Ostpolitik* (Eastern policy), the West German government acknowledged that the Federal Republic did not have an exclusive right to represent all Germans and abandoned the Hallstein Doctrine. The concession paved the way for the inclusion of both Germanies in the United Nations. (East Germany established diplomatic relations with other Western European states, the United States, and most other major powers.) Two important events in 1968 allowed the West Germans greater freedom of action. De Gaulle, faced with the riots in Paris, began concentrating more on domestic affairs. The Soviets sent troops to Prague, Czechoslovakia, in a desperate effort to hold their crumbling satellite empire together. The West Germans, freed of French competition, decided they would not try to exploit Soviet insecurities.

In 1969, Willy Brandt formed his own government supported by votes from the small Free Democratic party. In the five years (1969–1974) he remained chancellor, he helped change the face of West German relations with the Soviet bloc countries. In Moscow on 12 August 1970, he signed an agreement with the Soviet Union in which both countries promised to respect "without restriction" the territorial integrity of *all* European states, including the present frontier between West and East Germany and the Oder-Neisse line between East Germany and Poland.

Four months later, the Brandt government drove the point home by signing a similar accord in Warsaw. Again the Federal Republic recognized the Oder-Neisse boundary between Poland and the GDR. During the visit, Brandt made an important symbolic gesture. He placed a wreath on the Polish war memorial and dropped to his knees in prayer. The Catholic Poles were genuinely touched.

The Ostpolitik bore further fruit. In September 1971, the Soviets officially recognized the independent status of West Berlin in a Four-Power treaty. In December 1972, the Federal Republic and the GDR extended de facto recognition to each other, with an exchange of permanent representatives (not ambassadors).[56] In June 1973, West Germany and Czechoslovakia signed an agreement in which the 1938 Munich Agreement, which had been concluded under the threat of force, was declared null and void. The treaty also included a mutual renunciation of force, respect for the inviolability of frontiers, and a pledge to settle all disputes peacefully. Taken together, the agreements signed between 1970 and 1973 amounted to a collective Locarno in which the Germans showed they had no desire to change the territorial status quo established at the end of World War II. By undoing the past insofar as it was possible, they hoped to clear the way for the eventual reunification of their country.

The foreign policy of Willy Brandt and Konrad Adenauer stood in dramatic contrast. Under Adenauer, the Federal Republic considered itself the only legitimate German state and the only one capable of representing Germany's interests. Adenauer dramatized the foreign menace to help spur his country's recovery and revitalize its sense of purpose. He felt that Germany's final borders could be established only by an eventual peace treaty. He believed that reunification had to come before detente. Brandt, however, recognized that confrontation was no longer necessary for a Germany that was economically one of the world's strongest states as well as one of the most secure. Thus Germany could afford to be more conciliatory. Brandt's doctrine of "two states of one nation" indicated that henceforth the Federal Republic's relations with the GDR would be characterized by mutual exchange and cooperation. Accordingly, Brandt agreed to respect the inviolability of East Germany's frontiers. He believed that detente would pave the way for reunification, but he and his colleagues were also aware that if the Soviet Union opposed reunification, then reunification would not take place. They also knew that other Europeans did not want the two Germanies to become one Germany. Although a generation had passed since the war, memories of German aggression and atrocities were still vivid, and many Europeans still believed the Germans were not to be trusted. A popular joke went: "What do you get if the Germans unite? Out of the way." Therefore it only seemed reasonable that the Germans should make the best of partition.

Helmut Schmidt, the Social Democratic leader who followed Brandt as chancellor (1974–1982), believed that West Germany had to gain Soviet acceptance of the Federal Republic's right to help improve the living standards of Germans living under Communism.[57] Schmidt recognized Germany's strategic position in the defense of the democratic West, but at the same time, he was determined to continue and strengthen the Ostpolitik. His negotiations with the Soviets focused on two principal areas: economic exchange and the status of Berlin. Clearly, the Germans wanted to be free of the tutelage of the superpowers; but, as Schmidt recognized, this was not likely as long as the Europeans could not achieve proper integration or agree on common objectives. Schmidt was less obvious and possibly more sincere than de Gaulle in advocating European independence (he certainly was less exclusionary when it came to Great Britain), but the idea of fortress Europe was a strong component in his thoughts. The Europeans, he believed, had "a right to protect and defend [themselves] against any attempt to force foreign rule or dictatorial social and governmental forms." The chance that the Europeans could defend themselves successfully would increase if, through its own unification process, Western Europe were to develop into a great power.[58] Naturally, a re-unified Germany would be expected to play a significant role in that amalgam.

Building Socialism in the GDR. The Stalinist regime of Walter Ulbricht had become rancid. The long-time political boss of the East German Communist party had weathered many changes and threats. He had survived demands for his resignation during the Berlin riots of 1953; maintained rigidity in the face of de-Stalinization and the denunciation of the cult of personality; and secured the GDR's borders by fostering the erection of the Berlin Wall in 1961. But Ulbricht's insistence on full freedom of action for his country in its foreign relations clashed with the broader interests of the Soviet Union for detente and led to his ouster as party chief in May 1971.[59] (Ulbricht remained as head of state, however, until his death in 1976.) His place was taken by Erich Honecker, a man created in Ulbricht's image but without his force or determination. Honecker emphasized economic improvement over ideological purity. He concentrated on raising national income and on such projects as expanding public housing and producing more consumer goods. Honecker's accession to power coincided with the new Ostpolitik of the Federal Republic, which had produced the first "basic treaty" between the two countries. The agreement prompted Honecker to suggest a new formula for separate socialist nationhood: "There are not two states of a single nation," he explained, "but instead two nations in states of different social orders."[60] Because East Germany was the heir to everything progressive, it was a legitimate historical German entity.

On 7 October 1979, at the official commemoration of the thirtieth anniversary of the founding of the GDR, Honecker hailed the triumph of socialism in East Germany as a turning point in the history of the German people and of Europe:

> The course and results of the socialist revolution on German soil once again confirm the correctness and triumphant nature of the ideas of Marxism-Leninism. It has become perfectly clear that our workers' and farmers' state is the guardian of the revolutionary traditions of the German working class and the humanistic heritage of the German people.[61]

However, the state's increased contacts with the West were producing greater indebtedness. A marked deterioration in the terms of trade, especially the increase in the world price of oil, made its balance of payments worse. The Soviet Union, the main supplier of raw materials to East Germany, raised its prices, thereby adding to the trade deficit. Naturally, East German consumers bore the cost of such adversity. Growth in retail trade slowed, and the supply of consumer goods fell. Demands for political liberalization began to be heard, spurred on by the protest movements in the other Eastern European countries, especially Poland. Honecker tried to avoid a crisis that might endanger his position, but the regime over which he presided was in deep trouble and would soon lose its ability to survive.[62]

DISCORD IN THE EASTERN BLOC

The Degeneration of Soviet Power

The Brezhnev Succession. Nikita Khrushchev had a buccaneer's spirit. While talking peaceful coexistence, he threatened war. Part of his daring undoubtedly came from his frustration at having his country encircled with enemy military bases. To this was added the humiliation he suffered from the U-2 spy plane flights. Only in 1960, after ten years of trying, were the Soviets finally able to shoot one of these intruders down. Perhaps a more prudent man would have tempered his frustration with caution, but that was not Khrushchev's style. He provoked two crises at Berlin and followed these with an attempt to place missiles on the island of Cuba. The risks were too great for his Kremlin colleagues. In October 1964, they forced him to resign.

Leonid Brezhnev, his successor (1964–1982) and former protégé, was more cautious. He wanted to stabilize his country's foreign relations, while carrying out a massive arms buildup that would make the Soviet Union invulnerable to attack. The experiences of World War II influenced Brezhnev, as they had Khrushchev, and he was determined that the Soviet Union would not be caught off guard again. He wanted to be able to conduct foreign policy from a position of nuclear parity with the United States. At the same time, however, he realized that the next war would have no winners. His goal, set out at the Twenty-third Congress of the Communist party in 1966, was to safeguard the earth from another world war by practicing peaceful coexistence with states that had different social systems.[63] Yet while Brezhnev wanted to participate in building a new world order, the Soviets also wanted to retain what they had, especially their sphere of influence in Eastern Europe, and, if possible, to transform themselves from a continental to a global power.

The policy of de-Stalinization, which discontinued Soviet economic exploitation of the satellites and loosened its political control over them, did not mean that the Communist leaders were ready to allow the satellites to chart their own course in politics and economics. The events of the 1950s had showed that Eastern Europe could no longer be considered an unqualified asset, but it was still vital as the outer defense perimeter of the Soviet Union. Even so, the Soviets had to ask themselves if the advantages outweighed the liabilities. The Eastern European peoples were undergoing a nationalistic renaissance and could hardly be considered reliable allies. Furthermore, their economies were a mess and needed constant assistance from the Soviet Union. Accordingly, Brezhnev tried to establish more business-like relations with the satellites. He was prepared to tolerate some latitude and diversity, but he insisted that the states remain members of the Warsaw Pact and that their policies not threaten Soviet strategic interests. However, it was difficult to determine how much local autonomy was compatible with Soviet hegemony.

The Soviets still feared a rearmed Germany. For this reason, Stalin's offer to accept reunification (with the proviso that the country be neutralized) may not have been insincere. Brezhnev tried to strengthen Soviet ties with the GDR. At the same time, he pursued improved relations with the Federal Republic. The Soviets had also tried to exploit de Gaulle's dissatisfaction with NATO and his growing differences with West Germany by expressing concern about German militarization. But trying to maintain close relations with both Germany and France has always been historically difficult. Being on friendly terms with one has usually resulted in alienating the other. Brezhnev's timing was particularly bad. The Federal Republic, like the other nations of Western Europe, had yet to get over its outrage at the Soviet invasion of Czechoslovakia in August 1968.

The Prague Spring. While other Eastern European satellites had sought to extricate themselves from the crushing pressure of Soviet tutelage, the Czechoslovaks seemed content to remain an obedient satellite. During the 1960s, however, many people inside and outside the Czechoslovak Communist party concluded that an independent road to socialism was necessary if the country were to develop economically. When Klement Gottwald died in March 1953, his body was embalmed and put on display in a Prague mausoleum in the manner of Lenin and Stalin, but the hope of burying his system with him seemed forlorn. Antonín Novotný, an unfaltering Stalinist, became his successor.

The new secretary-general proceeded to consolidate his hold on power with a wave of arrests and persecutions. In the aftermath of Stalin's death, the Soviets were urging the Hungarian and Polish party leaders to relax their police states to calm popular discontent, but left the Czechoslovaks practically alone. Khrushchev apparently had more confidence in Novotný than in Hungary's Matyas Rákosi or Poland's Boleslaw Bierut. Indeed, considering Czechoslovak quiescence during the events of 1956, the trust did not seem misplaced. While the Polish and Hungarian Communists were purging themselves of Stalinists, the Czechoslovak party continued with basically the same faces. In 1957, Novotný also assumed the Czechoslovak presidency. Although some opposed his growing personal power, the dissidents, many of them intellectuals, presented no threat to the regime. Indeed, Novotný felt so secure that he set about eliminating the last vestiges of capitalism by abolishing private farms and single-proprietor businesses. Members of the old middle class were dismissed from their jobs and forced to take unskilled or manual labor jobs. In 1960, the party boasted that Czechoslovakia had achieved the highest level of socialism outside the Soviet Union. The new constitution contained an article pledging cooperation with the Soviet Union and the other countries of the Eastern bloc.[64]

De-Stalinization in the Soviet Union troubled the Czechoslovak hard-liners, however, and they resorted to a series of cosmetic changes. They sent the corpse of Gottwald to the crematorium, dismantled Stalin's monument in Prague, and rehabilitated some prominent Communist victims of earlier purges. Novotný found scapegoats for previous excesses and mistakes in Gottwald and his henchmen. Emulating Khrushchev, Novotný removed the Stalinists from the party hierarchy and the government and replaced them with younger men. But this new leadership was not as dependable as Novotný thought. Many had lost their early reverence for the Soviet system as the proper model for socialist development. They wanted to reform the Communist system, but believed this was impossible under Novotný. Furthermore, the Slovaks wanted an end to Czech centralization. The Czechoslovak Communist party appeared to be breaking down into its national units as an anti-Novotný coalition formed in the party Central Committee.

The party secretary of Slovakia, Alexander Dubček, led the rebellion against Novotný at the Central Committee meeting in November 1967. Novotný called upon the Soviets for support. Brezhnev came to Prague in December, but remained noncommittal. During his visit, the Soviet leader consulted with Dubček. Brezhnev's apparent lack of support for Novotný emboldened the reformers, and they pushed for Novotný's ouster. On 5 January 1968, Dubček became first secretary of the Communist party, although Novotný retained his post as Czechoslovak president. The forty-six-year-old Dubček was a compromise candidate, a Slovak with good Communist credentials. He seemed to be a typical *apparatchik*.[65] Between the wars, he had lived in the Soviet Union where he attended primary and secondary schools; he had stayed there again from 1955 to 1958 and studied at a higher political school in Moscow. Novotný had found him reliable and had selected him to be the first secretary of the Slovak party in 1963.

Shortly after becoming first secretary, Dubček went to Moscow for consultations, the tenor of which can be gathered from one of his speeches published soon after his return. Dubček insisted that he did not intend to change the general nature of Czechoslovak internal and foreign policy, but he did promise reform: the adoption of new methods and a rapid advance in science and technology. He also pledged to develop socialist democracy.[66] The "new direction" sounded like the old Communist double-talk, but Dubček did not intend to conduct business as usual, and he had more than enough support to carry out his plans. Demands for real change came from many quarters and from all parts of the country in countless meetings and rallies. On 22 March, Novotný was forced to relinquish the post of president. A mass resignation of his supporters from their leadership positions followed.[67] General Ludvik Svoboda, who had helped deliver the country to Communism in 1948, became the new president, the perfect man to forestall possible Soviet interference.

The reform continued on many levels. While Dubček and his associates tried to create Communism "with a human face" by bringing about change within the party, others tried to force the pace of reform while ignoring the party. Already by March the mass media were publishing information and news with little restriction, but without official approval. Radio and television followed suit. As millions of people expressed support for the reform process, demands arose for an investigation into the death of Tomás G. Masaryk, the foreign minister who had been murdered after the 1948 Communist takeover. On 5 April 1968, the Czechoslovak Communist party adopted an Action Program that reiterated the party's right to maintain its leadership role as a guarantor of progress, but acknowledged that freedom of expression, "a broad scope for social initiative, a frank exchange of views, and the democratization of the whole social and political system have literally become a necessity if socialist society is to remain dynamic."[68] The program promised to guarantee freedom of speech and curb the authority of the secret police. It also advocated a greater role for free enterprise in the economy. In May, the Dubček government officially abolished censorship. But could the party continue in power if Czechoslovakia adopted real democracy? The Czechoslovak Communist party momentarily enjoyed great popularity, but it could no longer control the pace of democratization. The Soviets knew that it would only be a question of time before Czechoslovakia would dismantle its Communist system.

Shortly after Novotný's ouster as president, Brezhnev, supported by Wladyslaw Gomulka of Poland and Ulbricht of East Germany, warned of unpleasant consequences if the Czechoslovaks were to continue on their current path of reform. Relations with Czechoslovakia grew noticeably worse. In May, Dubček again went to Moscow to try to reassure the Kremlin leaders that his reforms presented no threat to Soviet security and were compatible with socialism. Even while he spoke, however, other Warsaw Pact countries were carrying out military maneuvers in southern Poland just across the Czech border, and the Soviets were increasing their military force in Czechoslovakia to about 30,000 troops. The Kremlin feared it might lose control of all Eastern Europe. On the night of 20–21 August, units of the Red Army crossed into Czechoslovakia. The Soviet troops were supported by forces from Poland, the GDR, Hungary, and Bulgaria. The 500,000-man army made it the largest military action since the end of World War II. Of the Eastern bloc countries, only Romania condemned the action and refused to participate. The Romanians had no sympathy for Dubček's policies of liberalization, but they understandably opposed foreign intervention in another nation's domestic affairs.

The Soviets tried to make their aggression more palatable by claiming that the Czechoslovak Communist party had invited them in to give fraternal assistance to the Czechoslovak people. Unfortunately for this ploy, the Soviets could not find any Communist leader who would admit he made such a request. They therefore asserted that they had a right to intervene to preserve socialism in Eastern Europe whenever they thought it was necessary. The "Brezhnev Doctrine" was the high-water mark of Soviet pretensions of control over the satellites. It stated that every Communist party was "responsible not only to its own people but also to all socialist countries and to the entire Communist movement."[69] The policy stipulated that each socialist country maintained its independence only because it was part of the socialist commonwealth backed by the power of the Soviet Union. In essence, the doctrine was a throwback to the Stalinist practice of maintaining "friendly" governments in Eastern Europe for the strategic needs of the Soviet Union.

The Czechoslovaks met the invasion with passive resistance. They even tried to talk to the Soviet soldiers and convince them to respect their rights, but to no avail. The Soviets arrested Dubček and his associates, but found it impossible to put together a coherent government to run the country.[70] President Svoboda went to Moscow to negotiate, but insisted that Dubček and the other imprisoned leaders be allowed to participate in the talks. The Soviets reluctantly agreed. They managed to convince Svoboda to accept their fifteen-point protocol, however. This program effectively destroyed the reform movement and removed its leaders from positions of power. The process of "normalization" led to the ouster of Dubček. Gustáv Husák replaced him on 17 April 1969. Husák was also a Slovak, but he was more willing to give the Kremlin what it wanted and presided over the wholesale dismissal of reformers from the government, the party, the trade unions, the universities, and the mass media.[71] The Husák regime jailed many reformers for being counterrevolutionaries,[72] but it did not carry out a bloodletting as had occurred in Hungary in 1956. Dubček was treated relatively leniently, for example. He was first appointed ambassador to Turkey and then received a minor post in the State Forestry Service in Bratislava. The Hungarian uprising and the Prague Spring also differed in another respect. In 1956, the Hungarian leaders had clearly forsaken Communism; in 1968, the Czechoslovak government was trying to put a human face on it. The Soviets, however, considered both movements dangerous because both aimed at independence from Moscow.

Restricting the Use of Force. By the end of the 1960s, the Soviets had been able to overcome their ten-year inferiority in intercontinental ballistic missiles and had actually surpassed the United States in overall number of missiles. Not only had the Soviets increased their strategic rocket forces, thereby adopting the American policy of deterring aggression through the threat of massive retaliation, but they had also achieved an across-the-board increase in their conventional military strength. They thus had the capability of conducting their rivalry with the United States on a global scale. This new position of strength, which was roughly comparable to American military power, assured that the Soviets could enter any serious Strategic Arms Limitations Talks (SALT) without being disadvantaged. After numerous delays, such negotiations finally got underway at Helsinki on 17 November 1969. Despite the international tensions that existed as a result of the war in Vietnam and the conflict in the Middle East, the superpowers finally produced an agreement on 26 May 1972.

One of the things that helped convince the Soviets that it was in their interest to sign an agreement at this time was the triangular policy of National Security Affairs Adviser Henry Kissinger who hoped to gain leverage against the Soviets by using the Red Chinese. Kissinger had secretly gone to China in July 1971 to talk directly with Zhou Enlai. This diplomacy cleared the way for the admission of the People's Republic of China to the United Nations—Taiwan unceremoniously lost its Security Council seat—and its diplomatic recognition by the United States. President Richard M. Nixon cemented the deal in a historic visit to Beijing in February 1972. The Communist Chinese were obviously more afraid of the ambitions of the Soviets than they were of the Americans. Periodic military skirmishes had erupted on their northern border, and the Soviets had built an air base in Mongolia.

The first SALT agreement prohibited deployment of antiballistic systems, set limits on strategic delivery systems, and defined technical issues related to such things as radar and testing; it also included provisions for monitoring the treaty through electronic and other surveillance. The United States recognized what it heretofore was reluctant to do: that the Soviet Union had a right to full nuclear parity. The SALT treaty was followed with a general agreement that tried to reduce tensions further. In Moscow on 22 June 1973, President Nixon and Chairman Brezhnev pledged to "refrain from the threat or use of force against the other Party, against the allies of the other Party, and against other countries, in circumstances which may endanger international peace and security."[73] They also promised to cooperate in a wide range of activities, including trade, health, and science.[74] The Soviet-American summit did not so much remove basic problems, as underscore the obsolescence of the policy of confrontation. Nevertheless, some viewed the Soviet move as only a ploy to lull Europe into a more sympathetic attitude toward the Soviet Union in order to erode American influence. Critics also believed that the Soviets were using detente to convince the American public, already undergoing a new mood of isolationism because of the loss of the Vietnam War, that they should reduce their military commitment to Europe. At the very least, it seemed clear that the Soviets wanted international acceptance of the territorial changes that had been made in Europe after World War II.

In July 1975, thirty-five nations met in Helsinki, Finland, for the grand conference on European Security and Cooperation. Over two years of negotiations had been needed to produce the Final Document that was signed on 1 August. The ceremony took seventeen minutes. The Helsinki accord was one of intent rather than actual commitment, but it resolved many issues stemming from World War II—at least on paper. The Soviets specifically recognized the inviolability of all current European frontiers, while the Western democracies insisted on a clause in which the signatories promised to respect "fundamental freedoms, including freedom of thought, conscience, religion, or belief." The signatories also pledged to accord each other most-favored-nation treatment in trade and to facilitate "the freer and wider dissemination of information of all kinds." They pledged to cooperate in the fields of science, technology, and the environment, to facilitate wider travel, and to ease restrictions on movements of citizens, especially families, from one state to another. Finally, they expressed a desire "to search for peaceful solutions to all outstanding differences."[75] The agreement had a little in it for everyone and was comfortably void of sanctions. Although the agreement was a symbol that the two superpowers were becoming less confrontational in Europe, their interests continued to clash in other parts of the world: the Middle East, Africa, and Southeast Asia.

American president Jimmy Carter (1977–1981) took the moral high ground in a campaign of human rights throughout the world—a latter-day example of Wilson's desire to make the world safe for democracy. Nevertheless, Carter signed a second SALT treaty with the Soviets at a summit meeting in Vienna on 18 June

1979. SALT II set a limit of 2,250 on strategic delivery systems and cruise missiles whose range exceeded 600 kilometers. It also allowed the Soviets a 308 to 0 advantage in silo-based intercontinental ballistic missiles. The American Senate was reluctant to ratify the arrangement. A majority of the senators feared that the president had conceded too many advantages to the Soviets, thereby increasing the likelihood of a Soviet first strike. Detente received a further blow when the Soviets invaded Afghanistan in December 1979 to secure Communist rule against local Afghani freedom fighters or *Mujahideen;* the invasion marked the beginning of a bloody eight-year war. In January 1980, Carter effectively withdrew the SALT treaty from consideration. The administration took further action by suspending American participation in the Olympic games set for Moscow in the summer of 1980 and canceling American grain sales to the Soviet Union. Increased expenditure on armaments accompanied the breakdown of detente. Throughout the years of Carter's administration, more and more money was allocated for high-tech weaponry, including smart bombs, cruise missiles, and stealth technology.

A Brief Return of the Cold War. Ronald Reagan, who succeeded Carter in 1981, was also an ideologue but in a different way. Reagan believed that the United States was a chosen nation, the only country in the world whose entire system was based on the words "we the people." Reagan made hatred of the Communist Soviet Union a main feature of his campaign for the presidency in 1980; upon his accession to office in January 1981, it became clear that this was not just campaign rhetoric. The new president had an abiding hostility toward the Soviet Union, which he called the "evil empire." To show he meant business, he continued the arms buildup of his predecessor. Reagan liked big weapons systems, the most impressive of which was the Strategic Defense Initiative. Dubbed "Star Wars," it was envisioned as a vast, movable, stratospheric Maginot Line composed of laser beams that would shoot down all enemy missiles targeted on the United States, giving the country absolute immunity from attack. The possibility of developing advanced technology with such precision seemed remote. Progress in armaments' development had made it feasible for missiles to intercept and shoot down other incoming missiles, although not with the infallible precision necessary to make the United States invulnerable to attack. The Reagan administration believed otherwise.[76] The president was so confident that this new technology would end a superpower showdown that he offered to share it with other nations.

The Soviets, already lagging behind the United States in the sophistication of their weaponry, feared that Star Wars or even a system approaching Star Wars could prompt the United States into carrying out a first strike. They did not believe that the Americans were simply interested in bargaining from strength, and it seemed preposterous that the United States would actually give away the Star Wars secret. The Soviets feared that Reagan was actually preparing the United States to fight a nuclear war it would win. In May 1981, Yuri Andropov, the chairman of the Soviet secret police, made a secret speech to the Politburo in which he revealed that the KGB was cooperating with Soviet military intelligence to ascertain the exact timing of such an operation. For example, KGB operators in London were monitoring the number of lighted windows and automobile traffic at all government buildings and military installations outside the usual working hours to report any deviation from the norm. In 1982, when Andropov at the age of sixty-eight succeeded Brezhnev as head of the Communist party (1982–1984), fear of nuclear attack reached its height. Andropov claimed that the Reagan administration had imperial ambitions, and he doubted "whether Washington has

A visibly ailing **Leonid Brezhnev inaugurates a memorial building complex in Kiev** on 9 May 1981. He is accompanied by Soviet Defense Minister Dimitri Ustinov and the First Secretary of the Ukrainian Party, Vladimir Shcherbitsky. The gerontocrats' hold over the destiny of the Soviet Union was approaching its end.

any brakes at all preventing it from crossing the mark before which any sober-minded person must stop."[77] In November 1981, the KGB center in Moscow believed that American armed forces had been put on alert as a prelude to the countdown of an attack. The Soviet fears, of course, proved to have been exaggerated. Though unknown in the West, the crisis was one of the last great nuclear alarms of the postwar period.

When Andropov died in February 1984, he was succeeded by the colorless, stolid, and if anything more conservative Konstantin Chernenko, who was seventy-three. Brezhnev (who was seventy-six when he died), Andropov, and Chernenko all came from a class of leaders whose careers had profited from the purges of the 1930s.[78] This gerontocracy no longer represented many of the post-Stalinist leaders who were uncomfortable with straitjacket ideological formulas. The younger generation believed the security of the country depended on its ability to modernize its economy, even if this meant introducing the incentives of the marketplace. Such a policy had not been seen since the New Economic Policy of the 1920s. This pressure for reform would grow in strength and eventually lead the country away from Communist-dominated government.

The Restive Satellites

The Frailty of Allegiance. The Soviets maintained control of their satellites through their domination of government and party leaders. The Soviet ambassadors acted as the regime's proconsuls and could call on the Red Army to back up their authority if necessary. However, tight Soviet control had led to economic backwardness and popular hostility born of dark memories of lives broken and families destroyed. The Communist path had all too often led to a graveyard. All the satellites suffered from the same deficiencies and scarcities that plagued the Soviet economy: shoddy and insufficient consumer goods, declining worker productivity, low rates of growth, wasted resources, and environmental pollution. While the market economies of Western Europe flourished, the economies of Eastern Europe were plagued by gross mismanagement, antiquated equipment, and bloated bureaucracies. Pricing structures bore little relationship to actual costs or customer demand. Restrictive and hostile to change and innovation, Eastern European industry used technology reminiscent of an earlier age. Khrushchev had talked about allowing the satellite states to develop their own socialist systems, but whenever the Soviet Union was faced with divergence, it endeavored to bring the irregulars back into line. The Brezhnev Doctrine was merely the latest example.

Western European Communism seemed to present an alternative, however. "Eurocommunists" contended that political power was dependent on the free will of the electorate in a multiparty system with a mixed economy. Detente and the policy of Ostpolitik had made strict orthodoxy passé.

Communist rule was especially fragile in Poland where five attempts to shake loose from Soviet domination were made between 1956 and 1981. Each crisis had been preceded by predictable complaints and predictable demands: the expansion of political freedom, the end of central economic planning, and independence from the Soviet Union. The 1956 crisis, which had brought Gomulka to power, had, at first, expanded freedom of speech and halted the persecution of the Roman Catholic church, but under Soviet pressure and with Gomulka's own preference for authoritarianism, repression had returned. Gomulka hardly enhanced his popularity by announcing price increases (as much as 20 percent) on a range of basic commodities. At the same time, he tried to boost production by offering new incentives. Many Poles viewed this program as a trick to induce them to work harder for fewer benefits. Gomulka launched his austerity program just before Christmas on 12 December 1970. Two days later, shipyard workers in Gdansk (formerly Danzig), Gdynia, and Sopot went on strike to protest the price increases. The strike led to clashes with the police and an attempt to burn down the regional Communist party headquarters. The violence spread to other cities throughout Poland. In an attempt to restore order, the Communist party, at a special Central Committee meeting on 20 December 1970, deposed Gomulka and replaced him with Edward Gierek. Gierek immediately promised the Poles a higher standard of living and a greater degree of worker participation in running the factories. The new party chief did not rescind the decrees of the previous week, but did promise a two-year freeze on prices.[79] The turmoil, however, continued through the rest of the decade, an indication that the Communist party leadership was incapable of changing its basic authoritarian style or providing the Polish people with a decent standard of living.

The new leadership's answer was to take advantage of the current mood of detente to borrow as much money as it could from the West to invest in the development of Polish industry. Much of the money, however, was used to buy off the workers with higher wages rather than to improve capital equipment. Although it guaranteed worker satisfaction in the short run, such a policy of bribery was bound to backfire. If Poland were to be considered a good capital risk, it would eventually have to repay the loans. But without fundamental economic changes that would enable it to produce goods the West wanted in exchange, repaying the loans would prove difficult. The Poles tried to meet their foreign obligations by exporting agricultural products, but this put a heavy strain on their own domestic market.

Although Poland had some of the best farmland in northern Europe, and the regime had backed away from the policy of collectivization begun after World War II, food production did not keep pace with demand. Farming techniques had changed little from those employed half a century earlier. Mechanized equipment was scarce, and the government was not eager to remedy the situation because doing so might enhance the position of the private farmers. Therefore, the more efficient private sector was frequently deprived of fertilizers and other supplies necessary for increased output. Agricultural exports, especially in meat, caused domestic shortages. In June 1976, the government raised the price of food to reflect the limited supply. Immediately, workers in Warsaw and Radom went out on strike. The authorities backed down and rescinded the increases. Aware of their growing power, workers and intellectuals began to organize. Their petitions demanded respect for the rule of law and civil rights. In October 1978, the election of Karol Wojtyla as pope (John Paul II), the first Pole to be so honored, gave a tremendous boost to the aspirations of the Polish Catholic church to bring an end to Communism. But the most persistent irritant proved to be the high cost of food; it constantly stoked the fires of discontent. In July 1980, the regime raised the price of meat by as much as 60 percent. Gierek went on nationwide television to try to explain the necessity for such hikes.

The lesson in economics fell on deaf ears. This time the workers did not have to take to the streets. Instead, they used their recently organized committees to negotiate wage increases to match the price increases. Such collective bargaining was heretofore unheard of in a Communist state. The regime opportunistically tried to limit the damage by satisfying those workers with the most muscle at the expense of the weaker groups. This divide-and-conquer policy did not work. The Lenin shipyards at the Baltic port of Gdansk, the locus of previous strife, went out on strike. In addition to their grievances over pay and benefits, the workers demanded the democratization of Polish society, the lifting of restrictions on the Catholic church, and an end to the Communist monopoly of the trade unions. The Gdansk shipbuilders, led by Lech Walesa, demanded the legal recognition of Solidarity, an independent federation of trade unions that would act as the workers' main collective bargaining unit. The protest was too strong for the government and the seriously divided Communist party.

In the Gdansk Agreement of 31 August 1980, the government recognized the legitimacy of Solidarity, thereby becoming the first Communist state to recognize an independent trade union. The workers had the support of dissident intellectuals and the Catholic church, which had traditionally played a strong political role in protecting Polish nationalism. Standing behind the claim of the Catholic church to be the moral guardian of the Polish people was Pope John Paul II who intended to use his influence to defend the Polish Catholic church's prerogatives by encouraging more political activism. The Soviets feared the Gdansk Agreement could lead to Polish defection from the Warsaw Pact and the end of their control in

Thirty-seven-year-old electronics technician **Lech Walesa inspires fellow workers** at the Lenin shipyards in Gdansk in May 1980. The discontent of the shipbuilders led to the establishment of the first independent trade union movement in the Communist bloc.

Eastern Europe. They considered military intervention, but were not eager to take such action. They knew that intervention would end detente and any hope of future arms control agreements, both of which were essential to allow the Soviet Union to shift its resources from armaments production to economic development. Furthermore, at a Warsaw Pact meeting in December 1980, all of the other satellite countries opted for a political solution, preferring to let the Polish leadership re-establish order by itself. The satellites decided that the best way to bring Solidarity to heel was for the Polish army itself to mount a coup.

Moscow found a candidate in General Wojciech Jaruzelski, a Politburo member and currently a minister of the government without portfolio. In the fall of 1981, the Soviet leaders pressured the Polish Communist party to make Jaruzelski its leader. On 13 December, Jaruzelski proclaimed martial law, and the following year, he ordered 6,000 members of Solidarity, including Walesa, placed under arrest. Despite the crackdown, Jaruzelski ruled with a certain amount of moderation, at least by Communist standards. He tried to co-opt Solidarity's campaign for more worker participation in the management of factories by creating new, non-Solidarity trade unions to handle complaints. These new groups remained under party control. He allowed non-Communist candidates in parliamentary elections, and once he had lifted martial law and released the Solidarity leaders, he tolerated a certain amount of freedom of speech. The policy of "normalization" offended Polish Communist hard-liners, who unsuccessfully tried to have him removed. But no amount of official moderation could restore credibility to the Polish Communist regime.

Jaruzelski's motives were the subject of controversy. Some regarded him as a dedicated Communist ideologue who willingly served the interests of his foreign masters; others saw him as a hero who acted in the best interests of his country in helping to prevent a Soviet takeover. The sharp division reflected the nature of survival in a Soviet satellite. In a broader sense, it posed the dilemma of how to judge collaboration. Jaruzelski's supporters said that the general had prevented a war that would have drowned the Poles in a sea of blood; others claimed that he had declared war on his own people. Michael Jagiello, the first ranking Communist official to resign in protest over the imposition of martial law, said that Jaruzelski was an example of a patriotic Pole who found himself tragically trapped in the Communist system. In Jagiello's view, Jaruzelski's greatest political error was that he kept his illusions too long: "He failed to recognize the collapse of socialism until his last years." His actions were well-intentioned, but misguided.[80]

The Spread of Reform. The Soviet Union had further cause for alarm. Crushing the Prague Spring in 1968 in Czechoslovakia did not stop the steady erosion of faith in the Communist system. The regime of Gustáv Husák, who succeeded Alexander Dubček, had restored stability, but tension lay just under the surface. In January 1977, three hundred Czech intellectuals circulated a petition, "Charter 77," which condemned the current wave of political repression. The protest was quickly and brutally suppressed, but its drafters were not exterminated.[81] Even after Husák's purge of the party, no one wanted to go back to the Stalinist tactics of the past. Many Czech citizens, deprived of an open forum in which to vent their opposition, turned to religious activity as a means of keeping the protest alive. Thus the Czechoslovak Catholic church served the same purpose as its Polish counterpart in providing an avenue through which people could express their opposition to Communism.

In Hungary, the government of János Kádár rebuilt the Communist party after Soviet tanks invaded the country in 1956 following Hungary's withdrawal from the Warsaw Pact. Kádár was a politician who wanted to survive, and to do so he tried to build up a constituency in his own country independent of close Soviet direction. He launched a middle-of-the-road economic program, called "the New Economic Mechanism," which featured a departure from rigid central control. Henceforth, factory managers would be allowed to set their own wages, contract for their own supplies—even from abroad—and set their own standards of efficiency with the intent of turning a profit. Individual enterprises were therefore able to reduce waste and adjust their output to the demands of the market.

In agriculture, the New Economic Mechanism heralded the end of the policy of collectivization. Individual farmers could now set their own quotas and manage their own time and labor. As a consequence, agricultural production increased so much that the Hungarians were able not only to feed their own people but also to produce a surplus for export. The quality and variety of produce also expanded. At the same time, the New Economic Mechanism created problems for a system that, by its nature, seemed impervious to change. Resources flowed into the new sectors, leaving the old industries to wallow in inefficiency. The older leaders who feared that any movement away from centralized control would weaken their influence began to fret. Moreover, the increased imports of Western goods added to Hungary's foreign debt. Unable to pay its bills, the government launched a policy of austerity, which increased the cost of living and stunted economic growth.

In Romania and Bulgaria, popular resentment of the current regimes was less marked. Bulgaria was perhaps the most servile and docile of all the Soviet satellites. The Bulgarians, whose pattern of trustworthiness was set by Georgi Dimitrov, the first postwar leader of the Bulgarian Communist party, identified strongly with the Bolshevik revolutionary tradition and political example. For this support, Moscow rewarded them with extensive political backing and economic assistance. Dimitrov's successors (Vulko Chervenkov in 1949 and Todor Zhivkov in 1954) continued his loyal policies, even to the extent of accepting the Soviet view that bilateral relations with Moscow were the best way to deal with regional Balkan problems. (Bulgaria had once entertained the idea of conducting an independent regional diplomacy with its neighbors, Yugoslavia, Greece, Romania, and Turkey, with which it had much in common economically.) Under Soviet tutelage, Bulgaria had completely collectivized its agriculture, but allowed some decentralization of its industry. Although it extended invitations to foreign capitalists to invest in Bulgarian enterprises, there was no comparable relaxation of political control.[82]

Zhivkov increasingly consolidated his position, and at his direction, the new 1971 constitution recognized the Communist party as the leading force in the society and the state. A state council became the chief organ of power with both executive and legislative authority. Zhivkov became its chairman and was thus well placed when the 1975 Helsinki accords and Eurocommunism began to offer a promise of liberalization. As compensation for such tight political control, Bulgaria undertook a program of economic expansion in the early 1980s, known as the New Economic Model (NEM). The intent was to institute technological changes to make Bulgaria more competitive with the nations of the West while, at the same time, increasing the supply of consumer goods. The latter was deemed essential to prevent the Bulgarian people from catching the Polish virus. By decentralizing industry, the NEM aimed to make the economy more self-sufficient and competitive. But the great improvement did not occur. The quality of Bulgarian goods did not improve, and Bulgaria's trade balance worsened as the country became more dependent on imported energy. In addition, after years of strict central control, Bulgarian economic planners and factory managers simply did not have the expertise to achieve new levels of productivity. Living standards remained depressed, the bureaucracy continued to be indolent and corrupt, and the leadership grew increasingly remote and isolated from the population. In the mid-1980s, a noticeable cooling of relations between the leaders of the Bulgarian Communist party and the Kremlin put their continued tenure increasingly in doubt.

In Romania, the dictatorship of Nicolae Ceausescu seemed unshakable. Both Ceausescu and his predecessor Gheorghe Gheorghiu-Dej, who died in 1965, held fast to the Communist system, tolerating no criticism from their people and no show of disrespect for the Soviet Union. Such protestations of loyalty convinced the Soviets to withdraw their troops from the country in 1958. They also had tolerated a removal of the "Muscovites" from the government, thereby allowing the Romanians to nationalize their party in much the same way as Tito had done in Yugoslavia. Without the immediate threat of Soviet intervention, the Romanians were able to embark on their own program of industrial development and even direct their own foreign policy to a certain extent.

In the late 1950s, the Romanians began an independent program of industrialization, thereby flouting the Soviet mutual economic assistance program under which Romania was to concentrate on expanding its agricultural sector and export primary products to the satellite countries to the north. During the time of the Sino-Soviet split, the Romanians continued to maintain relations with Beijing, insisting that Moscow respect the independence of other Communist parties and not interfere in their internal affairs. They thus opposed the Soviet intervention in Czechoslovakia and the Warsaw Pact intervention in Poland. The Romanians proceeded to expand relations with the West, paying special attention to the United States from which they hoped to secure huge development loans. The Soviets did not believe these deviations from the satellite norm posed a threat to the continuation of Soviet power in Eastern Europe and therefore tolerated them. Indeed, a stern political dictatorship free of the contagion of reformist tendencies was a positive asset, counterbalancing the unpleasant examples of Poland, Hungary, and Czechoslovakia. Furthermore, the country was not as strategically important as the satellites that protected the Soviet Union from a direct assault by NATO forces.

Ceausescu tightened his hold on the countryside, completing the process of collectivization by obliterating farming villages and relocating their inhabitants to high-rise apartment complexes. He deemed it necessary to destroy all attachment to the land in order to carry out his crash program of industrial development. He also enhanced his central control with a policy of cadre rotation that prevented upper-echelon bureaucrats from establishing a power base in the administration by moving them to a new position after two or three years. He also passed out important state positions to members of his family, including his wife Elena. In 1974, after he became president and commander-in-chief of the Romanian armed forces, he appointed her the first deputy prime minister and president of the Romanian Academy. In all, Ceausescu found important jobs for an estimated forty members of his tightly run clan.[83] The dictator's reliance on members of his own family was prompted by his fear of his own people, a paranoia that rivaled Stalin's.

Repression was also a hallmark of the regime. Owning an unregistered typewriter was illegal. Contact with foreigners was strictly limited—it was permitted only in the presence of at least two officials—and citizens were required to report any such contact they had or suspected others of having. Critics of the regime often disappeared without a trace. Protests and strikes, of which there were few, were suppressed with summary executions. The secret police were everywhere, moving about quite openly; their agents, dressed in black leather jackets, watched suspects with little subtlety. They infiltrated every department of government. Many of these men were orphans who were specially recruited because their primary allegiance would be to the regime, not to their families. In exchange for their loyalty, they were rewarded with a high standard of living. Few others in the state could match the secret police in data processing and high-tech communications.

The Ceausescu regime retained and expanded its power by rekindling old ethnic hatreds. Ceausescu targeted the two million Hungarians who lived mostly in Transylvania and the more widely dispersed, but less numerous, Jews. Anti-Semitism needed little encouragement. During the war, the Romanians had actively participated in the killing process. As a result, the Jewish population had dropped from 800,000 to a little over 400,000. The decline continued after 1945, and by the early 1980s, only 35,000 Jews remained in Romania. The Ceausescu regime depicted the Romanian Jews as seditious and traitorous, but also established ties with Israel, the only satellite state to do so.

At a time when other Eastern European satellites were going through a period of liberalization, repression continued full tilt in Romania. Political control absorbed a tremendous portion of the state's time and resources. Improving the general standard of living was of secondary concern. As a result, the Romanians were among Europe's poorest peoples. Shortages of consumer goods were the norm; food was frequently scarce. Despite sizable oil reserves, there were shortages of energy. Ceausescu's compulsion to liquidate a foreign debt of $10 billion led him to sell petroleum and food abroad. Working conditions were among the most miserable in the Eastern bloc, being little better than in the nineteenth century; industrial pollution was menacingly bad, and wages were low. Romania's iron-fisted regime of dynastic socialism was without incentives; it was a system in which the most routine aspects of life were subject to regulation and control—from the temperature of private apartments (a chilly 59°F) to the number of children a woman was required to produce before she was forty-five years old (four). From all external indications, the Ceausescu system was a great success, but hatred and resentment smoldered just below the surface, waiting for an opportunity to claim a terrible vengeance.

POSTSCRIPT　The Cold War divided Europe into two broad zones of confrontation, but it also led to the resolution of age-old conflicts. The nations in Western Europe, which had been at each others' throats for centuries, abandoned their mercantilistic barriers and sought unity in formal cooperation. The states of the European Community used their combined economic power to emerge as a third international force. The nations in the Warsaw Pact, still fettered by rigid economic centralism and Communist exploitation, grew relatively weaker and in many respects more divided. In Western Europe, where greater political independence was possible, the movement for integration was strong, while the supposedly monolithic Soviet bloc was alive with ethnic and political tensions.

The momentary collapse of authoritarianism in Czechoslovakia in 1968, a feat heretofore believed impossible in a Communist country, was a foretaste of what would happen in Spain in the next decade after Franco's death. The Spanish, however, did not have to worry about foreign intervention. They could transform their system with the support and encouragement of outside powers. Their rapid progress toward democracy after so many years as a dictatorship was until then unique in Western European history.

The Soviets' efforts to bring reluctant satellites back into the fold showed how crucial they considered the control of Eastern Europe to be to their own security. Czechoslovakia was important strategically because it guarded the border with West Germany. Poland guaranteed the Soviet Union's lines of communication to East Germany. But the Soviets also feared the influence that Eastern European movements would have within their own country. Letting go might provoke demands for reform in the Ukraine, in the Baltic states, and among other nationalities that resented Muscovite control over their affairs. The ethnic diversity and nationalistic yearnings of the Soviet minorities had always been a major historical concern. To tolerate self-determination in one part of the empire might open dangerous floodgates elsewhere. Maintaining control of such restive peoples was an increasingly difficult task, however, and would become more costly and dangerous as time went on. Eventually, the Soviet Union might have to choose which it would keep and which it would let go. In the meantime, the best way to minimize the damage was through a relaxation of tensions with the West.

Detente would reduce the need for a powerful and costly military establishment, allowing resources to be put to better use elsewhere. But as long as the nations of the Atlantic community feared Soviet expansionism, there could be no hope for real accommodation. The strategy of NATO, largely set by the United States, was geared to the unlikely assumption that the Soviets, given the opportunity, would send their armies all the way to the English Channel. In historical terms, such expansionism was not farfetched.

Russian power had grown steadily since the eighteenth century, creating the empire that the Soviets inherited and managed to extend. That much of this power was in the process of dissolution hardly seemed possible. The Soviet Union was the last great empire of Europe, and its power and unity seemed capable of enduring for centuries. The Soviets paradoxically assumed the right to guarantee their satellites a socialist form of government, but nevertheless took a pledge of noninterference in their affairs. The promise of noninterference eventually turned out to be genuine as the Soviets, like so many imperial masters before them, came to realize the impossibility of dictating the passions of the peoples over whom they ruled.

ENDNOTES

1. *Atlas*, November 1962, 405.
2. Ibid., 406.

3. The British insisted that they would control these weapons during a non-NATO crisis.

4. See François Caron, *An Economic History of Modern France* (New York: Columbia University Press, 1979), 205–19.

5. In 1958, the index of industrial production was 191; in 1959, 193; in 1960, 208; in 1962, 220; and in 1963, 233. It rose steadily throughout the rest of the decade until 1969 when it was 341. Brian R. Mitchell, *European Historical Statistics* (New York: Columbia University, 1975), 358.

6. Charles de Gaulle, *Mémoires de guerre* (Paris: Plon, 1954), vol. 1, 5.

7. The signing was accomplished in the immediate aftermath of de Gaulle's vetoing of Britain's entry into the Common Market, an action he had taken without prior consultation with Adenauer.

8. See especially Wilfrid L. Kohl, *French Nuclear Diplomacy* (Princeton: Princeton University Press, 1971), 123–77.

9. It was rumored that wealthy people, prohibited by the currency restrictions from transferring large amounts of capital abroad, took advantage of the open frontiers by loading up the trunks of their cars with banknotes and driving unchallenged into Switzerland.

10. Eyewitness accounts appeared in Claude Durand, dir., *Le livre noir des journées de mai* (Paris: Éditions du Seuil, 1986).

11. France-Soir, *Les journées de mai* (Paris: Librarie Hachette, 1969).

12. The push to join the Common Market came during the same period that Britain was enacting the Immigration Act of 1962 to limit the amount of colored immigration from the multiracial nations of the Commonwealth.

13. The Rome Treaty, which gave the Common Market Council certain powers to make decisions binding on the member states, provided for no power of enforcement.

14. The effort this time was made by the Labour government of Harold Wilson. Earlier the Labour party had been opposed to joining the Common Market.

15. Jean Monnet, *Memoirs* (Garden City, N.Y.: Doubleday and Company, 1978), 451.

16. On 17 February, the British Parliament passed the necessary enabling legislation to bring British law into accord with that of the European Community. The British officially joined on 1 January 1973.

17. G. N. Minshull, *The New Europe: An Economic Geography of the EEC* (New York: Holmes and Meier, 1985), 103–28.

18. Peter Coffey, *Main Economic Policy Areas of the EEC—Towards 1992* (Boston: Kluwer Academic Publishers, 1988), Part 2.

19. Guy de Bassompierre, *Changing the Guard in Brussels: An Insider's View of the EC Presidency* (New York: Praeger, 1988), 43–44.

20. The value-added tax is a tax that governments add to a product at each step of the productive chain. It must be paid whenever any improvements are added to the value of a product. It has been a great revenue enhancer, and its cost is naturally passed on to the consumer. Without standardization, producers in some countries could gain a competitive edge over those elsewhere.

21. The ruling involved the case of a female flight attendant of Sabena Airlines who was forced to retire because she had reached the age of forty, a restriction not applied to men. *Columbia Journal of Transnational Law*, 21 (1983): 640.

22. See Christopher McCridden, ed., *Women, Employment and European Equality Law* (London: Eclipse, 1987).

23. Peter Oliver, "Enforcing Community Rights in the English Courts," *Modern Law Review* 50 (1987): 881–907.

24. Stephen Wiseman, "Sex Discrimination: Some Recent Decisions of the European Court of Justice," *Columbia Journal of Transnational Law* 21 (1983): 621–40.

25. Stanley G. Payne, *The Franco Regime, 1936–1975* (Madison: University of Wisconsin Press, 1987), 372.

26. These were Moron Air Base near Seville, Torrejon Air Base near Madrid, Zaragoza

Air Base near Zaragoza, and Rota Naval Station near Rota. *Military Travel Guide* (Washington, D.C.: Raisor, 1985), 130.

27. Raymond Carr and Juan Pablo Fusi Aizpurua, *Spain: Dictatorship to Democracy* (London: Allen and Unwin, 1981), 29–31.

28. Mitchell, *European Historical Statistics,* 357–58.

29. Between 1939 and 1969, the annual production of wheat increased by 61 percent, that of barley 1.8 percent, potatoes by 37 percent, olives by 52 percent, and citrus fruits by 1.93 percent. The output of a crop like sugar beets, though, increased 5.91 percent. Ibid., 264, 274, 286, 287.

30. Carr and Aizpurua, *Spain,* 57–58.

31. David Gilmour, *The Transformation of Spain: From Franco to the Constitutional Monarchy* (London: Quartet Books, 1985), 139–44.

32. Ibid., 195–201.

33. Paul Preston, *The Triumph of Democracy in Spain* (London: Methuen, 1986), 203–4.

34. Stephen P. Savage and Lynton Robins, eds., *Public Policy under Thatcher* (New York: St. Martin's Press, 1990), 2–4.

35. Peter Jenkins, *Mrs. Thatcher's Revolution* (Cambridge, Mass.: Harvard University Press, 1988), 3–6.

36. Mitchell, *European Historical Statistics,* 358.

37. Douglas-Home had renounced his family title as the fourteenth earl of Home. No member of the House of Lords had been allowed to head a British government since the marquess of Salisbury in 1886–1902. In 1963, when Douglas-Home stood for election to the Commons as prime minister, he technically was a member of neither house.

38. Alfred F. Havighurst, *Britain in Transition in the Twentieth Century* (Chicago: University of Chicago Press, 1979), 506–7.

39. Mitchell, *European Historical Statistics,* 358.

40. Kenneth Harris, *Thatcher* (Boston: Little, Brown, 1988), 66.

41. James Callaghan, *Time and Chance* (London: Collins, 1987), 417–18.

42. Ibid., 563–64.

43. Paul Wilding, "The debate about the welfare state," in Bill Jones, ed., *Political Issues in Britain* (Manchester: Manchester University Press, 1989), 185–92.

44. Although their views were more curious than cogent, the Marxists thought the welfare state was a gigantic ploy to keep the workers subservient by pandering to their basic needs. Radical feminists believed the welfare state contributed to the subordination of women.

45. Denis Kavanagh, *Thatcherism and British Politics* (Oxford: Oxford University Press, 1987), 252.

46. The 98 percent rate amounted to 83 percent on earned income and another 15 percent on investment income.

47. "Margaret Thatcher's Ten Years, A Singular Prime Minister," *The Economist,* 29 April 1989, 20–21.

48. Savage and Robins, *Public Policy under Thatcher,* 34–41.

49. Jones, *Political Issues in Britain,* 141–43.

50. Savage and Robins, *Public Policy under Thatcher,* 43–44.

51. Jones, *Political Issues in Britain,* 160–66.

52. Jenkins, *Mrs. Thatcher's Revolution,* 373.

53. *The Annual Register* (1982), 7–18.

54. Harris, *Thatcher,* 134–39.

55. John J. Wuest and Manfred C. Vernon, *New Source Book in Major European Governments* (Cleveland: World Publishing Company, 1966), 291.

56. Helga Haftendorn, *Security and Detente: Conflicting Priorities in German Foreign Policy* (New York: Praeger, 1985), 225–30.

57. Helmut Schmidt, *Men and Powers: A Political Retrospective* (New York: Random House, 1989), 19.

58. Ibid., 386.
59. Ulbricht, for example, wanted full recognition of East German sovereignty with ex-clusive control of the access routes leading into West Berlin, something the Soviets, let alone the other responsible powers, were not prepared to yield.
60. Harold James, *A German Identity, 1770–1990* (New York: Routledge, 1989), 173.
61. Heinz Heitzer, *D.D.R.: An Historical Outline* (Dresden: Berlag Zeit im Bild, 1981), 244.
62. Mike Dennis, *German Democratic Republic: Politics, Economics and Society* (London: Pinter, 1988), 41.
63. Jonathan Steel, *Soviet Power: The Kremlin's Foreign Policy—Brezhnev to Andropov* (New York: Simon and Schuster, 1983), 23.
64. Hans Renner, *A History of Czechoslovakia since 1945* (London: Routledge, 1989), 25–33.
65. H. Gordon Skilling, *Czechoslovakia's Interrupted Revolution* (Princeton: Princeton University Press, 1976), 185.
66. The speech appeared in *Rudé právo* on 2 February 1968. Robin A. Remington, ed., *Winter in Prague: Documents of Czechoslovak Communism in Crisis* (Cambridge, Mass.: M.I.T. Press, 1969), 40.
67. Novotný's final fall from power was triggered by the defection to the West of Major General Jan Sejna. Sejna, a personal friend of Novotný, had been chief of the sec-retariat of the Ministry of Defense and therefore knew the highest secrets of the Czech military and the Warsaw Pact. His flight to the waiting arms of the U.S. Central Intelligence Agency hopelessly compromised Novotný and his clique.
68. Remington, *Winter in Prague*, 16.
69. The Brezhnev Doctrine was printed in *Pravda* on 26 September 1968. Alvin Z. Rubenstein, *Soviet Foreign Policy since World War II: Imperial and Global* (Boston: Little, Brown, 1985), 95.
70. Philip Windsor, *Czechoslovakia, 1968: Reform, Repression, and Resistance* (New York: Columbia University Press, 1969), 102–30.
71. Jirí Pelican, *Socialist Opposition in Eastern Europe: The Czechoslovak Example* (New York: St. Martin's Press, 1976), 35–44.
72. Vladimir Kusin, *From Dubček to Charter 77: A Study of Normalization in Czechoslo-vakia, 1968–1978* (New York: St. Martin's Press, 1978), 109–18.
73. *Annual Register of World Events* (1973), 524.
74. By way of implementation, it was subsequently agreed to pool information on can-cer research and to make joint preparations for a rendezvous in orbit of American and Soviet space ships in 1975.
75. *New York Times*, 30 July 1965, 8.
76. The president's first introduction to the concept apparently came from a Hollywood thriller of the 1940s in which enemy planes were knocked out of the sky with an electrical beam.
77. Oleg Gordievsky, "Inside the KGB: A Double Agent's Tale," *Time*, 22 October 1990, 82.
78. Brezhnev's increasing senility toward the end of his rule occasioned many jokes and anecdotes. The leader's speech, for example, was so slurred and his diction was so poor that he had difficulty pronouncing the name of the country: Union of Soviet Socialist Republics. "Socialist" in Russian is *Sotsailisticheskikh*. Brezhnev would re-duce the seven syllables to three so it sounded like *sososkikh*—the Russian word for sausage.
79. Leslie Holmes, *Politics in the Communist World* (Oxford: Clarendon Press, 1986), 303–5.
80. *Chicago Tribune*, 23 September 1990, 26.
81. Janusz Bugajski, *Czechoslovakia: Charter 77's Decade of Dissent* (New York: Praeger, 1987), 8–51.

82. R. J. Crampton, *A Short History of Modern Bulgaria* (Cambridge: Cambridge University Press, 1987), 173–209.

83. One of his brothers, Ilie, became an army general and deputy defense minister; another brother, Nicolae Andruta, became a police general and deputy minister of the interior; a third brother, Ion, was head of state economic planning; and a fourth, Florea, was an editor of the Communist newspaper, *Scinteia*. Ceausescu also took care of his in-laws, making one brother-in-law a party secretary in charge of agriculture and putting another in charge of trade unions. Ceausescu's youngest son, reputedly the regime's crown prince, became party secretary in Sibiu province in southern Transylvania, headquarters of a powerful military and security garrison.

CHAPTER 25

THE COLLAPSE OF THE SOVIET EMPIRE

PREFACE   German and Soviet expansionism threatened the independence of the other European states through much of the twentieth century. The collapse of the Nazi empire in the defeat of World War II left a power vacuum into which the Soviet Union expanded. However, the Soviet Union did not seem content to establish its authority only in Eastern Europe. The Western European states, buttressed by the might and insistence of the United States, formed the Atlantic Alliance to keep such power contained.

The European equilibrium changed from a multilateral system into a bipolar system, an arrangement long believed to be inherently unstable. Indeed, the point was proved in the Cuban missile crisis, the most serious of a series of confrontations between the superpowers. However, weapons of mass destruction had shown their limited nature as much as they had shown their gargantuan possibilities. Assertions to the contrary, both the U.S.A. and the U.S.S.R. knew that nuclear wars were not winnable. The showdown over Cuba was a sobering experience. Afterwards, relations between the two states became more restrained, each side having learned that there was a point beyond which it dared not push.

Yet behind its powerful facade, the Communist world was coming apart. The Soviet state, which had been expected to last for many more generations, collapsed in only three years. Such a peacetime transformation was unprecedented in European history. The forces of nationalism and ethnic hatred, long kept in check by the Soviet Holy Alliance, burst forth with sudden vigor. In Eastern Europe a dangerous multipolar world emerged with more opportunities, more crises, and more bloodshed. The new countries that took shape had little prior experience in running their own affairs. Ending the Cold War had been such an article of faith in the chancelleries of Western Europe that few politicians had considered the dangers that might arise once that goal was achieved. A new era began just as Europe had become successful in ironing out the uncertainties of the old.

THE DAY OF THE DEMOCRATIC REVOLUTION

A Radical in Office

The secretary-general of the Communist party of the Soviet Union, Konstantin Chernenko, died on 10 March 1985. His successor, Mikhail Sergeievich Gorbachev, was the youngest man on the Politburo. After being ruled by a gerontocracy for the past decade, the party and the Soviet Union now had a comparatively youthful, energetic leader. Gorbachev was fifty-four years old, nineteen years younger than his predecessor. The difference was more than just one of age. Gorbachev, and the men he subsequently brought to power with him, came from a new generation in Soviet politics. This group had risen to prominence after the purges of the Stalin era and had been too young to fight in World War II. Consequently, they were the country's first intact generation since World War I. Unlike their elders, they were ready to confront the country's shortcomings and were confident they could overcome its problems. Gorbachev himself was a convinced Communist who believed his "second revolution" could be achieved within the broad parameters of the present system. He still thought the Soviet system was basically superior to that of capitalism.

Until he became secretary-general, Gorbachev gave every indication that he was a faithful, dependable disciple of the regime. Hardworking, with a strong desire to please his superiors, he advanced steadily through the local party hierarchy in his home district of Stavropol, some 750 miles south of Moscow. He became first secretary in April 1970 when he was thirty-nine. His success in increasing agricultural output brought him to the attention of certain members of the Politburo.

Mikhail Gorbachev addresses the top officers of the Kremlin on 2 November 1987. After he had been first secretary of the Communist Party for two years, he began a revolution from above by telling the officials that Communism must be radically reformed in order for it to survive.

Thanks to them, he was brought to Moscow and elevated to the post of secretary of the party Central Committee in 1978. This appointment came toward the end of the Brezhnev period. Now known as the "years of crisis," this time of intense economic and political decline was probably the most corrupt of the postwar era. Gorbachev was put in charge of Soviet agriculture, a sector of the economy that was almost impervious to improvement. It was a hazardous assignment; Soviet agriculture had long been the graveyard of political careers. However, the fortuitous death of Leonid Brezhnev in 1982 opened new opportunities including membership in the ruling Politburo. Two years and two secretaries-general later, Gorbachev became its chief.

That Gorbachev's rule was not going to be business as usual became obvious at the early meetings he held with the managers of the country's factories and farms. At these sessions, he revealed things about the nation's lamentable state that had rarely been discussed in public before. Gorbachev described an economy where tens of thousands of factories produced goods nobody wanted, many enterprises stood idle, and thousands of collective farms were on the brink of collapse.[1] He wanted to introduce changes immediately without waiting until the older leaders had retired or died off.

Perestroika and Glasnost

Gorbachev was determined to make his policy of *glasnost* (openness) and *perestroika* (restructuring) irreversible. At the Communist party conference, which took place in Moscow from 28 June to 1 July 1988—the first such held since 1941—Gorbachev proposed a radical reform of the whole political system beginning with the demolition of the centralized, bureaucratic monolith that had led to the ossification of government and the alienation of the workers. He proposed infusing the system with democracy by creating a new representative body, the Congress of People's Deputies, that would elect the country's legislature, the Supreme Soviet. The Soviet would, in turn, elect the chairman (the chief of state), who would nominate the prime minister. Secret elections by competitive ballot would be held with the candidates chosen through a "lively and free expression of the will of the electorate."[2] Gorbachev also favored decentralizing power to give more responsibility to the local managers. Individual enterprise would be encouraged, and the economy would give more scope to private ownership.

The floor debate when Gorbachev's proposals were presented publicly for the first time was remarkable for its frankness and openness. Never during the past sixty years had Soviet citizens had such an opportunity to express their opinions openly. The conference voted to accept Gorbachev's proposals, but the vote was not unanimous. They became law at the end of the year with Gorbachev himself being elected as the new chairman of the Supreme Soviet.

Gorbachev next proposed a constitutional amendment (December 1988) to break the Communist party's exclusive hold over the electoral system. Henceforth, various other organizations could nominate candidates, who could have their own campaign organizations and present their own platforms. Moreover, candidates were required to actually live in the areas they represented. The first parliamentary elections under this new law (March 1989) saw a frenzied array of 3,000 candidates fighting for 1,500 offices. In some districts, as many as a dozen candidates vied for each seat, although in others only a single candidate emerged. The Communist party ran candidates in all the districts, but experienced a great electoral defeat. Thirty-eight regional or district Communist party secretaries throughout the country lost their positions. The party was voted out of office in Leningrad and Kiev. In Moscow, Boris Yeltsin, the onetime local Communist party chief, ran on an antiparty program and received 89.4 percent of the votes. Also victorious was Andrei Sakharov, the human rights activist and hydrogen bomb developer, who had been freed from internal exile in Gorki in 1986 at Gorbachev's orders and allowed to return to Moscow. The elections also showed the strength of nationalist candidates, especially those in the Baltic states.

Ironically, Gorbachev, who had created this electoral democracy, was now confronted with a collection of deputies who advocated everything from the breakup of the Soviet Union to curbs on the powers of the presidency.[3] In fact, the Soviet people, in the first real elections the country had held since the balloting for the Constituent Assembly in 1918, had again delivered a significant snub to the Communist party. Gorbachev tried to put the best possible face on the results. He said that the Communist party members who failed to be elected were conservatives who did not favor his campaign of liberalization. He denied that he was presiding over the dismantling of Communism, but claimed instead that his policies were putting its ideals into practice. To be a Communist, he maintained, meant "first of all to be consistently democratic and to put universal human values above everything else."[4] But he took no chances and strengthened his hand in his own party.

By January 1990, he had gotten rid of all twenty-five members of the Politburo and the Secretariat who had held office since the time of Brezhnev except himself and Eduard Shevardnadze, the foreign secretary. Bringing the party under his control was an essential element of perestroika, since Gorbachev wanted to transform the Communist party into the most progressive political force in the state. It was a daunting, and ultimately impossible, task, however. The party was more conservative than revolutionary and had long ago ceased to be a force for change. It was the party of the permanent ruling class, and its leaders were primarily concerned with holding on to their power and their perquisites. Still reeling from the trauma of Stalinism, they had learned to protect themselves against the danger of making decisions and, in doing so, had gradually lost control of the bureaucratic Soviet state.[5] Gorbachev wanted to streamline the party apparatus to make it more efficient in order to save it. However, the party was not part of the solution, but was itself the problem. Thus, the success of perestroika depended not on the rejuvenation of the Communist party, but on its removal from any significant role in the affairs of state. Gorbachev played a game of contradictions. He established his independence from the Communist party, but at the same time tried to hold it together under his control. By trying to turn it into a democratic organization, Gorbachev hastened its decline.

In February 1990, he convinced the Central Committee to change Article 6 of the Constitution, which Brezhnev had inserted in 1977. The article stated: "The leading and guiding force of Soviet society and the nucleus of its political system, of all state organizations and public organizations is the Communist Party of the Soviet Union." In removing Article 6, Gorbachev was ending all pretensions of one-party rule. He argued that the party should at last recognize that its political leadership could come only through free elections. The Soviet Constitution was amended accordingly.[6] In March 1990, Gorbachev also transformed the Soviet political system into a presidential form of government—a development that had no precedent in the previous political institutions of the country. The new powers gave the president the right to nominate the premier and other members of the cabinet, all of whom were accountable to him. The president could also suspend legislation, dissolve the legislature, and, in time of declared emergency, rule by decree. For example, he had the right to institute emergency decrees "to stabilize the country's socio-political life" for a period of eighteen months. He presided over a new council of federation composed of the presidents of the fifteen union republics. In effect, this council became the supreme decision-making body of the state. Gorbachev argued that such powers were needed to ensure that swift executive action could be taken. Although the president was to be elected by universal, popular suffrage, an exception was made for Gorbachev himself. He took office after securing a majority of the votes in the Congress of People's Deputies. Many feared that he was preparing for a return to dictatorship.

Meanwhile support for Communism was rapidly declining. Between January and September 1990, 1.5 million members quit the party. Those who stayed became engaged in bitter disputes over the organization's future. One faction, the Democratic Platform, wanted to abandon Leninism completely and become a general parliamentary party with no pretensions of being the vanguard of the proletariat. Another faction, the Marxist Platform, wanted to retain the party's revolutionary elitism and base its strength on the industrial working class. The Communist party also began to fragment into its ethnic components, which broke down further into independent and pro-Moscow factions. The Twenty-eighth Party Congress, which met in Moscow from 2 to 13 July 1990 and reelected Gorbachev as party leader, reiterated the principle of democratic centralism. That is, members could express their opinions on issues until the Central Committee had made a decision, then all would support it and conform to it. The party would act like any other parliamentary party in its external relationships, but would continue to be a vanguard party in its organizations in the workplace, the armed forces, and the homes. By now much of this resolve was romantic fantasy. Even if the Communist party could remain an important political organization, the authority of the central government had become so tenuous and the prevailing economic, social crisis, and ethnic problems so enormous that the country's very existence was in doubt.

The Nationality Question

In a wide arc, from the Baltic states in the northwest, through Belorussia to Moldavia in the south, and east to Georgia and across to Tadzhikistan, the Soviet Union was coming apart, collapsing into more than a dozen independent states. Lenin had believed that nationalism would disappear under Communism, but in reality, only the tight grip of Moscow and the Communist party had created a Pax Sovietica that kept nationalist and ethnic forces under control. When the force from the center disappeared, old passions and hatreds flared anew, culminating in demands for independence. The inability of perestroika to produce any improvement in the economy also convinced local leaders that they would have a better chance of recovery without the presence of Moscow.

In 1988, in the Caucasus, the national passions of the Armenians and the Azeris turned against each other. At issue was control of the district of Nagorno-Karabakh whose population of Christian Armenians had been included within the Muslim republic of Azerbaijan in 1921. Now the Armenians wanted to annex the district. The result was cross-border raids, "pacification" of villages, and riots that claimed the lives of hundreds of people and left thousands homeless. Moscow opposed any change in the borders and sent helicopters, artillery, and armored vehicles to the area to restore order. Using military force against civilians to quell internal unrest eroded army morale. Some officers openly protested the government's policy.[7] The ethnic violence accelerated both Armenian and Azeri demands for independence. No longer interested in preserving the Soviet Union, the Armenian government adopted a goal of independence within five years; it announced it would begin by recruiting its own "popular militia" and conducting its own foreign policy. In September 1989, the Azeris became the first Soviet people to declare their independence amid rumors that their country would merge with Iran. In January 1990, the Azerbaijan capital of Baku erupted in violence with a pogrom against the Armenians. The Soviets rushed in troops to keep the peace. But after two years, with no solution to the war in sight, Moscow ordered all the forces withdrawn to let the Azeris and the Armenians fight it out amongst themselves.

Christian Armenians were also harassed in other Muslim republics, where the new religious toleration that accompanied glasnost had led to a new assertiveness. In some Muslim republics, protesters called for Islam to be made the only official religion. Religious particularism went hand in hand with a new insistence on the primacy of the local culture, including the revival of the Arabic script instead of the Cyrillic alphabet forced upon them by Stalin in 1939.

The desire to retain their cultural integrity was also a primary factor in the drive of the Baltic republics for freedom from Moscow. Latvia, Lithuania, and Estonia had never really accepted their forceful incorporation into the Soviet Union in 1940. At the Communist party conference in June 1988, the non-Russian delegates from the Baltic states demanded greater political, economic, and cultural autonomy. Their demands were followed by the formation of People's Fronts in the three republics to continue to agitate for freedom. In November 1988, the Supreme Soviet of Estonia adopted a "Declaration of Sovereignty," which included the right to veto laws passed by the central government. Moscow promptly ruled the declaration null and void, but that hardly ended the matter. During 1990, all three Baltic states declared their independence. The Lithuanians began the process on 11 March; the Estonians followed suit with a more insistent declaration on 30 March, and the Latvians added their voice on 4 May.

Gorbachev answered the Lithuanian fait accompli by reinforcing the 30,000-man Soviet garrison and imposing an economic blockade on the country. He commanded the 1,500 Lithuanian soldiers who had deserted from the Soviet army to return to their units and ordered the Lithuanian people to turn in all firearms. Lithuanian president Vytautas Landsbergis, leader of the Sajudis nationalist movement, urged the deserters to seek sanctuary in churches and declared the Soviet decrees an unlawful interference in Lithuania's internal affairs. The Lithuanians were gambling that Gorbachev would not risk the end of perestroika by ordering a full-scale invasion to crush the revolt.

At one time, President Landsbergis, a former professor of music at Vilnius State Conservatory, had been more at home in front of a piano than on the barricades. Now he was his country's symbol of resistance. Landsbergis saw the crisis as a clear-cut question of whether the country belonged to the Lithuanians or the Russians. First, however, he had to determine how successfully Lithuania could withstand Soviet pressure. The country had fewer than 4 million people, 20 percent of whom were non-Lithuanians. Although Lithuania could produce enough food to feed itself, it was almost totally dependent on the Soviet Union for energy and raw materials. In short, the Soviets had the power to close down the Lithuanian economy and throw most of its people out of work. The Lithuanians decided to moderate their demands. On 29 June, they "suspended" their vote of independence. The Soviets then ended the blockade, and the two sides sat down to resolve their differences through discussions.

The declarations of sovereignty in the Baltic countries encouraged other independence movements. On 29 May 1990, Boris Yeltsin was elected the chairman of the Russian Supreme Soviet, thereby becoming the de facto president of the Russian republic. Shortly after coming to power, he asserted that his republic had the right to control its own natural resources, establish its own separate citizenship, proclaim the primacy of its legislation over that of the Soviet Union, and conduct its own foreign policy. The Russian republic operated from a greater position of strength than the Baltic states. It included slightly over half of the Soviet population and produced almost two-thirds of the Soviet Union's electricity, three-fourths of its natural gas, 90 percent of its oil, 55 percent of its coal, and 58 percent of its steel. The Russian district of Siberia supplied three and a half times more raw materials than the rest of the country combined. No matter what became of the Soviet Union, the Russian republic would remain a great power with the ability to dominate its neighbors. The separatist stance of the Russian federation put Yeltsin on a collision course with Gorbachev for leadership of the second revolution.

The Ukraine, the next most important republic, took similar moves toward sovereignty, aiming for control of its own economy and foreign affairs. The Ukraine, with a population of 52 million, roughly equivalent to that of France, inaugurated a system of coupons for the purchase of certain commodities, a first step in the creation of a Ukrainian currency. In addition, it declared itself a nuclear-free zone. Elsewhere Belorussia enacted measures to control exports to other republics. The Moldavian parliament declared its independence from the Soviet Union, renamed itself Moldovia, adopted its own flag, and declared Moldavian the official language. Many suspected that Moldavia wanted to reunite with Romania from which it was separated in 1940. This fear prompted the ethnic Russians who lived in a region of the Dniester River valley near the Moldavian capital of Kishinev to declare their independence from Moldavia, while the Gagauz minority of 150,000 people also demanded self-rule. The Moldavians who insisted on their own right of self-determination refused to recognize it for others.

Independence movements were also in progress in all of the other republics including Georgia, Kazakhstan, Turkmenistan, Uzbekistan, and Tadzhikistan. In the predominantly Muslim Central Asian republics, where ethnic and religious tensions took precedence over nationalist sentiments, Islamic fundamentalists insisted their religion should be the only state religion and that women again take the veil. The autonomy movement even spread to districts within republics and to cities. The Russian republic was also beset with demands for separatism, mostly from distinct ethnic groups such as the Chuvash, Buryat, Tatar, Karelian, and Bashkir peoples. In addition, the predominantly Muslim Chechen-Irgusk region proclaimed its "equality and independence," while the city of Nizhni-Novgorod petitioned for its own special status.

Gorbachev hoped that declarations of sovereignty did not necessarily mean a desire to sever all ties with the Soviet Union. Assuming that the independence-minded republics would recognize the economic advantages of maintaining some type of union, he tried to design a federation that would satisfy most local sensibilities. In June 1991, the Kremlin and nine constituent republics negotiated a new treaty of union that would turn the Soviet Union into a confederation. The treaty ended control by the central government, transferring to the republics the power to tax, control natural resources, and run the police. The initial phase would begin with the adherence of the Russian and Kazakhstan republics on 20 August 1991. But two days before the ceremony, a group of anti-perestroika Communists, calling themselves the Committee for the State of Emergency, arrested Gorbachev and seized control of the central government.

The Coup That Failed

The attempt to bring back the country's authoritarian past began on 18 August. It lasted three days. Gennadi Yanayev, the coup's acting president, tried to convince the Soviet people that the takeover was essential to restore order. The situation was out of control, he said, the country was disintegrating, the economic situation had gone from bad to disastrous, and nobody was in charge. Yanayev declared that the eight-member Committee for the State of Emergency stood for genuine democratic reforms. In the meantime, it prohibited all political opposition and claimed the power to rule by decree.

Gorbachev had been warned that a coup might be afoot, but he had dismissed the warnings. President George Bush and other American officials had given him information that a revolt was brewing, but Gorbachev did not lend it credence because he was "deeply convinced that only a paranoiac, a madman, [could] attempt a coup."[8] He was in his Crimean retreat at Foros working on the speech he would make at the treaty signing, when a special detachment of the KGB surrounded the house and held him incommunicado. The next morning, the world learned what had happened, when TASS announced the formation of the Committee for the State of Emergency.

The committee ordered army units to enter Moscow to seize vital areas, but it did not undertake a mass arrest of all potential opposition leaders. The coup leaders also failed to gain control of the communications network. Even if they had, their success would not have been assured. Even the ruthless Bolsheviks had accomplished their takeover only after several years of bitter fighting. Lenin knew that a revolution without a bloodbath was no revolution. The men of the Committee for the State of Emergency were not cast in the same mold—to their credit. But even had they been, the country had changed dramatically from the days of the Bolshevik coup. By now, the Soviet people had had their fill of murder carried out in the name of the working class. Perestroika had given them hope, making it difficult to turn back the clock. The plotters knew they lacked widespread support and were so eager to establish their legitimacy that they pretended that Gorbachev was merely undergoing treatment for physical exhaustion. In his first press conference, Yanayev said that he hoped that as soon as Gorbachev felt better he would resume his office and work with the committee. The plotters promised to continue his policies until then.

Many officials in the government decided to see which way the wind was blowing before committing themselves, but some with a clearer appreciation of what was at stake immediately denounced the coup as unconstitutional. On 19 August, Anatoli Sobchak, the mayor of Leningrad, called on the people of his city to come to the defense of the legitimate government. As a result, thousands flocked to the square in front of the Winter Palace to prevent army units from entering the center of the city. In Moscow, just after noon on the same day, Boris Yeltsin climbed on an armored truck parked outside the Russian republic headquarters and called for a general strike against this illegal seizure of power. His dramatic gesture prompted tens of thousands of people to converge on the square in front of the Russian parliament building to protect it from hostile army units. Many of the soldiers sent into Moscow by the coup leaders began to defect. People started to throw up barricades. Pizza Hut delivered 260 pizzas, 20 cases of Pepsi, and gallons of hot coffee to Yeltsin and his associates inside the Russian parliament building. By now, it was plain that the coup leaders could only persist in the takeover at

Clutching the text of his speech, **Boris Yeltsin denounces the August coup leaders** from atop a tank in front of the Russian parliament building. Yeltsin was the first freely elected president of the Russian Republic. He now takes charge of the democratic revolution, thereby eclipsing Gorbachev's power.

the expense of considerable bloodshed, and the military leaders were clearly reluctant to storm the Russian parliament building. With no means of enforcing their decrees, the coup started to come apart. The leaders began running for cover; some went into hiding; others committed suicide. Many officials, who had earlier been hesitant to choose sides, suddenly decided that they had supported the legitimate government all along.[9]

On 21 August, four of the conspirators went to see Gorbachev in the Crimea to seek his forgiveness but were promptly arrested. Gorbachev returned to Moscow early in the morning of 22 August. But although he was restored to his position, the authority he had once had was gone. The man of the hour was Yeltsin. His assertiveness and determination, his strong voice for reform, had determined the fate of the country. His influence soared. He did not forget the help that Pizza Hut had provided, however, and called the Moscow restaurant to thank it for its support.

Gorbachev, who had tried to reform the Communist party and make it the spearhead for reform, now watched it vanish as a political entity. Without fanfare he resigned his post of secretary-general. Throughout the Soviet Union, local republican leaders used the coup as an excuse to wipe away the last remnants of the Communist party. It was banned, its headquarters and offices sealed, its property confiscated, and its special commissaries and stores closed. Many of its apparatchiks found themselves without work. (On the other hand, some of the old party bosses managed to hold on by only slightly changing their stripes.) As a symbol of the new order, local governments began to topple the statues of Communist heroes. In Moscow, 10,000 people crammed the square in front of the KGB headquarters to watch construction cranes pull down the fourteen-ton statue of Feliks Dzerzhinsky, the founder of the Cheka. Afterwards, people scrawled the word "fascist" on the empty pedestal and smeared a swastika on the KGB building itself.[10] Throughout the country, statues of Lenin were removed from public squares and parks. Leningrad returned to its tsarist name of St. Petersburg.[11] There were discussions of whether Lenin's body should be removed from its tomb on Red Square.

The Continuing Crisis

The end of the Soviet Union as a centralized political force brought with it the end of the command economy upon which that unity was conditioned. In supporting perestroika, people were in effect betting on the chance of improvement, not on present strength. The inefficiency of management and labor and the prevalence of antiquated techniques—the very problems that had led to perestroika in the first place—resulted in a steady decline in productivity and increased shortages of goods. Under Stalin, economic development had been secondary to political control. The Gosplan had destroyed local economic integrity in order to disperse the industrial processes, thereby making it impossible for any factory to survive on its own. As a result, only a minority of the republics were self-sufficient in energy or in food production. All of them had to rely on the others for the goods and services necessary to complete the manufacturing process. For example, practically all of the country's locomotives were assembled in the Ukraine, but 800 different factories throughout the rest of the Soviet Union made their component parts. Distribution of resources and products depended on priorities established in Moscow.

The ongoing crisis of leadership and the battle of the republics over the control of their vital resources removed this coherence without putting anything better in its place. Despite his intent to carry out radical reforms, Gorbachev was reluctant to abandon central planning in favor of a true free market. His hesitation was not unique. After decades of expecting Big Brother to mind the store, the average Soviet had difficulty adapting to the idea of individual initiative. Private property was considered anti-people. Furthermore, the transition to privatization risked throwing millions of people out of work, an unthinkable social consequence. Even with minimal side effects, a free economy, with its mortgages, securities, fixed rates, and market surveys, was alien turf.

A 500-Day Plan, that had been presented to the Supreme Soviet in September 1990, proposed privatizing 80 percent of the economy. State enterprises would be turned into joint-stock companies; farmers would be allowed to withdraw from the collective farms, and prices would be set by the marketplace. Gorbachev, however, beset by doubts about how to carry out the transformation, dragged his feet. His compromise solution called for the transformation of the economy in four stages. Such gradualism condemned the economy to a series of half-measures that did little to halt the steady decline in output.[12]

The Soviet economy was in its worst condition since 1945. Along with the shortages of food and basic commodities, the quality of health care was declining, and housing was scarce. Beggars in large numbers began appearing on city streets. The crisis stemmed in large part from mismanagement, incompetence, and outright hoarding rather than an absence of resources. For example, the farms had the capacity to produce enough food to supply the entire country, but primitive storage facilities and inadequate methods of harvesting and distributing the crops led to a threat of scarcity. Potatoes were frequently stored in closed containers, the sprouted with the unsprouted, and sometimes were enclosed with onions—a system that guaranteed almost instant spoilage. In 1990, soldiers, factory workers, and students were sent into the fields to help harvest potatoes. Yet despite the added labor, much of the crop rotted in the fields. A bumper crop of wheat was harvested that year, but the surpluses did not reach the city markets because the regions, especially in the south and east, withheld their produce to barter for other goods. Many shipments did not reach Moscow because of deliberate sabotage. Communist party officials ordered huge quantities to be sent to remote warehouses in order to discredit perestroika.[13]

Some areas auctioned off their agricultural produce to the highest bidder. Furthermore, the republics were not above using food as an instrument of blackmail. The Ukraine, for example, threatened to stop sending grain to Russia unless Russia continued to sell it oil at a subsidized price.[14] A wide range of products, including meat, tobacco, and tea, disappeared from state stores. Of course, the Soviet economy had always been conspicuous for its shortages, especially in consumer goods. As a result, people had accumulated huge cash savings, estimated at hundreds of billions of rubles. The increased scarcities posed a huge inflationary threat as all the reserve currency now chased after fewer and fewer goods. Blackmarketing flourished. Gangsters emerged to provide "protection" for the owners of the cooperative enterprises and joint private ventures that were allowed to exist.

Clearly, the Soviet Union's new commitment to human rights and economic freedom could not be sustained without some improvement in the standard of living of its people. The threat of dictatorship had been temporarily removed, and Communism totally discredited with the collapse of the coup in August 1991. But the danger that this country without a democratic tradition would seek some sort of authoritarian solution and the threat of economic and financial upheaval were still present. Even if the republics managed to keep the wolf from the door, the conversion to a new economic order could not take place without rising unemployment and inflation. The old system, with all its faults, did manage to provide certain minimum goods and services at subsidized prices. For the new regime not to do at least that would be catastrophic.

Yet, under the new reforms, the basic relationship between the citizen and the state had been transformed. Instead of being viewed as a ward of the state with an obligation to serve a collective need, the citizen was now guaranteed rights as an individual. This transformation from a corporate structure in which rights were defined within the group to one in which they were to conform to individual needs and desires brought an emancipation heretofore unknown in the Soviet Union or in tsarist Russia. At the same time, however, it removed the state's obligation to provide people with birth-to-death protection.

Yeltsin's determination to create a market economy in Russia regardless of what the other republics might do made the role of President Gorbachev increasingly irrelevant. Yeltsin had fought for the triumph of the reform movement during the August coup, but with the economic situation worsening, the Russian leaders had to consider whether the democracy they had saved could be preserved. The debate in the halls of parliament was over whether to grant Boris Yeltsin the power to rule by decree to save the country from economic collapse.

REFORM IN EASTERN EUROPE

The Independence of the Satellites

Stalin had kept the satellites in line by the direct use of force; his decisions were backed by the power of the Red Army. His successors continued the policy, but allowed the states of Eastern Europe more leeway to make their own decisions as long as they did not threaten the integrity of the socialist system and the security of the Soviet Union. Brezhnev elevated Soviet hegemony into a doctrine in which

Moscow arrogated to itself the right to determine acceptable limits, to guarantee, as it were, the satellites a Communist form of government. However, when Gorbachev began his reforms, the people in the satellites tried to figure out how they could use the new policies to their own advantage. At first, it was not clear how far the reform process might go; nor was there even any assurance it would continue. Gorbachev himself seemed tentative. His desire to maintain a socialist order, albeit a reformed one, still held ominous implications for the peoples of the Soviet bloc countries who remembered the thaws of the past that had never endured. Of particular concern was the 1985 renewal of the Warsaw Treaty for another thirty years. By reinforcing the obligation of its members to cooperate closely in international affairs, the pact reaffirmed the leadership of Moscow and gave a certain amount of support to hard-line governments.

In Poland, the authorities enacted a new penal code that established summary court procedures denying the accused the right to legal counsel. The Czechoslovak Communist party confirmed the old ideological line, including the state's limited freedom within the Soviet orbit. In Hungary, conservatives in the ruling party seemed resistant to any changes that would endanger their long-held privileges. In Romania, Nicolae Ceausescu further consolidated his position; and in Bulgaria, Todor Zivikov enacted measures against the country's restive young people who were not engaged in "socially useful work."

In all the Eastern European countries, the economy was sluggish, the goals of central planning were in jeopardy, and trade deficits were rising. Leaders put on a brave front, but offered no new solutions. They enjoined the people to work harder and make greater sacrifices. As the Gorbachev reforms gained greater momentum in the Soviet Union, however, the clamor for change became more vocal. In 1987, Poland's Solidarity movement presented its alternative to a government recovery program by calling for a mixed economy, expansion of private enterprise, and self-government for the workers. In Hungary, populists, journalists, democrats within the Communist party, and intellectuals called for more pluralism in the government and in public life. Romania saw public demonstrations of protest. The Bulgarian Communists tried to ward off expressions of discontent by pursuing their own version of perestroika, but without much conviction or success.

In 1988, Gorbachev repudiated the Brezhnev doctrine. He declared that the Soviet Union would no longer use force to keep the present Eastern European governments in power. His pronouncement was a sentence of death to the Communist regimes of Eastern Europe. Within a year, they had all disappeared.

The ax dropped first in Poland in January 1989. After a year of strikes and pressure from Solidarity and other forces, the Polish United Workers' party was forced to end its monopoly on power and accept political and trade union pluralism. Now the opposition could run candidates in the parliamentary elections in June; however, the party managed to obtain a guarantee that it and its allies would automatically receive 299 seats of the 460 in the Sejm. The newly created 100-seat Senate would be freely elected, however. Without their guaranteed allotment, the Communists would have been virtually eliminated as a political force. Solidarity won 80 percent of the popular vote and 160 of the 161 allocated free seats in the Sejm and 92 of the seats in the Senate. When Lech Walesa, the head of Solidarity, persuaded the Communists' allies to desert and join his parliamentary group, he assured that the non-Communists would control the government. In September, for the first time since the end of World War II, a non-Communist prime minister became head of the government. Shortly afterwards, the Communists abandoned Marxist-Leninism and declared their intent to change into a new social democratic party. The end of Communism led to a profusion of new political parties. In a short time, over 250 had emerged.

The new Polish government proposed a rapid transition to a market economy, which led to a dramatic increase in unemployment. More than a third of the 4,500 state factories headed toward bankruptcy. Many of the small, marginal farms were also going out of business. The number of homeless increased dramatically.[15] To complicate matters, the Polish Catholic bishops began pushing for the abolition of the separation of church and state, leaving many Poles wondering if they had rid themselves of Communism only to fall into the arms of clericalism.[16]

In Hungary, the Communist Social Workers' party also lost its direction. Reformers gradually gained control and in October 1989 voted it out of existence. It reemerged as the Hungarian Socialist party. The rapid change caught the opposition by surprise, thereby depriving the Hungarian people of any sense they had participated directly in the transformation.

The end of Communism did not come as easily in Czechoslovakia where the party still felt strong enough to resist democratization. Nevertheless, with the retreat of Communism elsewhere in Eastern Europe, holding the line against the mounting opposition became increasingly difficult. The ruthless suppression of a student demonstration in Prague in November 1989 led to mass demonstrations in the capital and other major cities. The protests were followed by a general strike accompanied by demands for the abolition of the one-party state. In December, with the election of Václav Havel, the head of the democratic Civic Forum, as president, the rule of the Communist party came to an end. Czechoslovakia established a pluralistic political system with a market economy. President Havel was a great admirer of Thomas Jefferson and was determined that the Jeffersonian spirit would take root in his own country. But what that country would be was

Playwright Václav Havel flashes a victory sign from the balcony of the Prague Castle to the thousands of well-wishers who, on 29 December 1989, hail his election as president of Czechoslovakia. His occupancy of the castle signalled that Communist power was finally at an end, but Havel preferred to go on living at his top-floor apartment in one of the city's rundown districts.

still not certain because the Slovaks began to talk about establishing their own independent state.

In most of Eastern Europe, the end of Communism was achieved peacefully with virtually no loss of life. Romania proved the exception. At the beginning of 1989, the Ceausescu dictatorship still seemed firmly entrenched. Thus far, the most serious protest had been mounted by six retired Communist party officials who wrote an open letter criticizing the president for violating the constitution. The letter writers were put under house arrest. In November 1989, the Communist party confirmed its monopoly on power at its annual congress and rejected the reform movements taking place elsewhere as models to be followed at home. The regime continued to harass political opponents and subjected some of them to violence.

In December, the regime ordered Lázló Tökés, an activist Protestant clergyman and an ethnic Hungarian living in the city of Timisoara (Transylvania), to move to another part of the country. Tökés refused and continued to defend the religious and ethnic rights of his people. When the police attempted to arrest him, local Hungarians and Romanians intervened. On 16 December, the security forces fired on the demonstrators, killing hundreds, perhaps even thousands. Ceausescu was not concerned. He believed the situation had been brought under control and left the country on a state visit to Iran. The protest continued, however.

Ceausescu returned on 20 December and put the western part of the country under a state of emergency. On 21 December, he staged a progovernment rally in Bucharest. But the move backfired. The crowd turned against Ceausescu, and the army refused to intervene. Some military units even joined the demonstrators and attacked Communist party headquarters. Army officers, intellectuals, and anti-Ceausescu Communist officials hastily formed a National Salvation Front and declared the president deposed. Ceausescu and his wife fled the capital, but were soon captured. After a secret trial, they were found guilty of genocide and corruption, sentenced to death, and immediately shot. The National Salvation Front now took steps to dismantle Ceausescu's repressive regime, bringing the hated secret police, the Securitate, under the control of the army. Abortion was legalized, the village destruction program was halted, and the way was prepared for free, multiparty elections.

The year 1989 was one of the most significant in the history of Europe; it ended forty years in which Eastern Europe had been subjected to authoritarianism and isolated from the rest of Europe. It has been compared in importance to 1848, another year in which Europe was swept by revolution. After the overthrow of the French monarchy in February 1848, the revolutionary fervor spread to Italy, Austria, Germany, and Poland. People demonstrated against their rulers, demanding an end to the reactionary regimes that had run European affairs since the collapse of the Napoleonic empire. As in 1989, the 1848 uprisings were led by men who had little previous governmental experience and who fanned the flames of nationalism.

However, the differences between 1848 and 1989 were just as apparent as their similarities. In the nineteenth century, democracy had few champions, and the forces of authority and reaction were still strong and willing to fight to survive. Consequently, the "Springtime of Nations" collapsed in a bloody repression. In contrast, in 1989, the protest movements of Eastern Europe were backed by strong popular support and had the tacit blessing of the only empire that had it within its power to destroy them. The restraint of Gorbachev plus the determination of the reformers ensured that change would occur and would remain largely peaceful.

The Suicide of Yugoslavia

Tito had created a federal system in order to diminish Yugoslavia's ethnic and religious hatreds and rivalries. His association of equals helped to minimize the power of Serbia and keep the lid on regional nationalism. He bolstered the socialist economy with massive loans from the West. His successors were not as capable at holding things together, nor were they necessarily eager to do so. They were more interested in reasserting their own regional identities than they were in furthering proletarian internationalism. With the monumental changes taking place in the other countries of Eastern Europe and the Soviet Union, Yugoslavians were ready to abandon Communism. Shortly after the fall of Ceausescu in Romania, Ante Markovic, the president of the Federal Executive Council, instituted a program that favored the privatization of state-owned enterprises and the reintroduction of political pluralism. The democratization movement continued. By March 1990, the Communist party, the League of Communists of Yugoslavia, had virtually ceased to function; many of its component ethnic parts simply reorganized themselves as social democratic parties. These, together with a hundred other parties, many with specific ethnic constituencies, began demanding significant changes in the overall organization of the state. By year's end, control of most of the component republics had passed to local nationalists. No longer compelled to stay together to protect itself against the Soviet threat, Yugoslavia had begun to break apart.

In December 1990, the Slovenes revised their constitution to create Slovenia as an independent, sovereign, and autonomous state. They warned that they would withdraw from the federation within six months if they could not reach an accommodation with the central government. When such efforts failed, the Slovenes declared their independence on 25 June 1991. The same day, Croatia followed suit. Yugoslavia, the state put together at the Paris Peace Conference in 1919–1920 as the Kingdom of the Serbs, Croats, and Slovenes, was ending for good. This was not the first time Yugoslavia had come apart. During World War II, a separate Fascist state had been established in Croatia, and the Nazis had partitioned the rest. However, Tito had managed to put the country back together and create a central government that lasted until his death in 1981. Since then, the political dynamic was centrifugal. In 1991, it again became bloody.

The Croatian declaration of independence was answered by action from the Serb-dominated Yugoslav national army. The military intervention was occasioned by a rebellion among the 600,000 Serbs who lived in enclaves and villages in the eastern part of Croatia. These Serbs were irate that the Roman Catholic Croatians had reduced their status from equal citizens to that of a national minority and had begun an intensive policy of cultural transformation that ranged from changing street names to mandating the use of the Latin alphabet and the Croatian language.[17] The Serbs remembered the massacres of their people under the Croatian Fascist regime during World War II. Serbian intervention was motivated by more than the desire to protect the Serbs in Croatia from harm, however. The breakup of Yugoslavia was destroying a Serbian dream of a Greater Serbia that went back at least a century.

The war was particularly nasty, as the Yugoslav forces were not always careful in their choice of targets. Civilians frequently came under fire. The Yugoslav army attacked the city of Vukovar with such frenzy that Serbian and Croatian property was destroyed without distinction. The army also ruthlessly shelled the old medieval port of Dubrovnik, the "Pearl of the Adriatic" and one of Europe's richest cultural treasures, in an apparent attempt to destroy Croatia's multimillion dollar tourist industry. The city had no military value.

The struggle between the Croats and the Serbs was the first full-scale European war since 1945, and the parties defied all efforts of the European Community to arrange a permanent cease-fire. No sooner were truces arranged than they were broken; by the end of 1991, there had been at least fifteen. The nations of the European Community condemned the killing and Serbia's obvious attempt to expand its boundaries at the expense of its breakaway neighbor; but outside of adopting economic sanctions, which proved ineffectual, they made no effort to intervene themselves. Times had changed since 1914 when the affairs of the Balkans could touch off a general war. Now none of the Great Powers had rivalries in Eastern Europe. The European Community tried to mediate the crisis without success— Yugoslavia had been a powder keg of superannuated xenophobia for centuries, an artifical concoction of disparate cultures. Spurred by Germany, the EC countries recognized the independence of Slovenia and Croatia on 15 January 1992. This action encouraged nearby Bosnia-Herzegovina to also declare independence and solicit similar recognition. Shortly afterwards, Macedonia followed suit. Yugoslavia now consisted of just two republics, Serbia and Montenegro, with less than 40 percent of its former territory and only 10.5 million of its nearly 24 million people.

Hope that self-determination would restore peace proved short-lived. Within days after the Bosnian declaration, Serbian troops invaded the country, purportedly to protect the Serbian minority. However, the Serbs in Bosnia, unlike those in Croatia, were not being threatened. Bosnia's Muslims (44 percent), Serbs (31 percent), and Croats (17 percent) had lived in relative harmony. The only justification for the Serbian action was a grab for more territory. Slobodan Milosevic, the fiery nationalist leader of the Serbs, also wanted to divert attention from his failure to reform the economy after the collapse of Communism. The country had an inflation rate of 500 percent a year and unemployment of 750,000.

In playing the nationalist card, Milosevic plunged his country deeper into debt, prolonged the solution of the country's real problems, and cut it off from the international community. The government in Belgrade proclaimed a new federal republic in an attempt to lay claim to the assets of former Yugoslavia: membership in the United Nations, the World Bank, and the International Monetary Fund, and ownership of the diplomatic establishment, including all of its embassies and consulates. In fact, though, as long as the aggression continued, the new state remained a pariah and could expect no help from abroad.

Even were hostilities to end, the future remained bleak. None of the new states was economically viable, and few of their products were able to compete on the world market. The prospect of restoring a measure of cooperation amongst them seemed unlikely. The nations of the EC did not like to see such chaos and ruin in the heart of Europe, but none of them wanted to intervene actively. They encouraged the United Nations to send its "blue berets," but such forces were not equipped to separate armies fighting in the field. The other nations believed that those who started the bloodshed had to end it. Unless the war spread to other states, the combatants would be allowed to continue to kill each other until they came to their senses or collapsed from exhaustion.

THE REUNIFICATION OF THE GERMAN STATE

The Revolt in East Germany

Erich Honecker's regime pretended that the reforms being carried out in the Soviet Union would have little effect on the way it conducted its own affairs, and it repressed dissent with its habitual heavy-handedness. On 17 January 1988, a protest organized by a small group of critics and dissidents at a ceremony commemorating the slain Communist leaders Karl Liebknecht and Rosa Luxembourg resulted in the arrest of a hundred demonstrators. The government's action touched off a wave of public meetings and church services in favor of the detainees, prompting the authorities not only to release them all, but even to allow some to emigrate to the West. The move was uncharacteristically generous.

Although many East Germans hoped Gorbachev's reforms would lead to change, the German Democratic Republic persisted in its hard-line policies. Later in 1988, it even forbade the distribution of the Soviet journal *Sputnik*, deeming it to be too liberal. The only deference paid to glasnost was the easing of travel restrictions to the West and some talk of formulating a new process for appealing administrative decisions. These sops did nothing to assuage popular dissatisfaction. In August 1989, the full extent of the discontent became clear when Hungary, Poland, and Czechoslovakia decided to open up their frontiers with East Germany.

Within three days after the announcements, 15,000 East Germans had fled their country to seek asylum in the West German embassies in Prague, Warsaw, and Budapest. In September, the Iron Curtain came down as the three countries allowed the escapees to continue their flight to West Germany. The exodus increased and soon involved 225,000 people—out of a population of 16 million. Most of those leaving were between the ages of twenty and forty, and many were skilled workers. They left behind a critical shortage of trained personnel. On 7 October, Gorbachev made a state visit to East Germany. His visit encouraged East Berliners to take advantage of the official celebrations to mount their own demonstrations. The crowds clashed with the police as the situation began to get out of control. On 18 October, Honecker was forced to resign his party and state posts.

Egon Krenz, his successor, promised more openness and tried to make up for lost time by embarking on a program of economic and political reform. But it was too late. During the second week of November, the country was shaken by a series of protests that brought close to one million demonstrators into the streets of the country's major cities. The most important occurred in Leipzig where open protests had been going on for weeks. One demonstration had drawn half a million people. These popular protest movements led to the mass resignation of the East German government and the Communist Politburo. On 9 November, the Central Committee of the Communist party agreed to permit free travel to the West, thereby ending the era of the Wall. In Berlin, people from both sides came with hammers to tear down the Cold War's most hated symbol.

Krenz had prevented bloodshed by forbidding the use of firearms to crush the demonstrations. But he still thought that the East German state could be saved if all the political and social forces in the country could reach a consensus. Krenz claimed that the East German people had no interest in giving up their socialist society for capitalism.[18] He believed that no responsible leaders really wanted German unification at this time. He promised free, secret elections, but set no date.

In December, the Communist party held an emergency congress and changed its name to the Party of Democratic Socialism, apparently gambling that by committing itself to change it could retain its influence. Many of the delegates at this conclave denounced the party's past corruption and wrongdoings. But the change of heart was insufficient to keep the party together. Within a few weeks, membership dropped from 2.3 million to 1.6 million and continued to fall. A group of reformers, led by Hans Modrow, took charge, but their days as leaders were over. Now the protests were accompanied by demands for reunification. In January 1990,

The first legal anti-government demonstration in East Germany, in November 1989, brings one million Berliners into the streets to demand radical change. The protesters want an end to "cosmetic solutions," to state controls, and to repression.

Modrow went to Moscow to persuade Gorbachev to allow the creation of a united, but neutral Germany. Gorbachev was hesitant, but agreed. The West Germans did not. Meanwhile, the Soviet Union, Britain, the United States, and France opened a series of talks on how they could control the unification process, which was now accepted as inevitable. Out of the talks came the "two plus four" scheme in which the four victorious nations of World War II would join with East and West Germany to arrange the merger.

In March 1990, East Germans went to the polls in their first free, democratic elections to vote on how to proceed toward unification. Forty-eight percent voted for the Alliance for Germany, which advocated rapid unification. The Socialists who favored a more gradual transition came in second with 21 percent, while the former Communist party was third with only 16 percent. The new government, headed by Christian Democratic leader Lothar de Maizière, began immediate negotiations to join the two Germanies economically. On 1 July, East Germany officially agreed to surrender its economic and monetary sovereignty to Bonn.

The Triumph of Ostpolitik

The drive for German unification was a testament to the undiminished strength of nationalism, but its immediate impulse came from the people of East Germany who were disgusted with the abuses and inefficiency of four decades of Communist rule. They had not only been cut off from the rest of their country, in many cases from members of their families, but also from the great material prosperity that

Map 18

the West German people enjoyed. With the opening of the Berlin Wall on 9 November 1989, the flight of people rose to an unstanchable 2,000 per day, and the East German regime quickly lost any remaining viability. At the same time, the flood of refugees put a tremendous strain on the resources of the Federal Republic. These newcomers from the East were no longer welcomed with open arms.

The government of Chancellor Helmut Kohl was ideologically committed to unification as all the previous West German governments had been. The imperative could be found in the country's Basic Law. But West German politicians would have preferred for unification to be accomplished gradually. The present crisis, prompted by the popular revolution in East Germany, mandated that the process be accelerated. Otherwise, the Federal Republic would founder under the crush of millions of wound-be settlers. Unification could induce this feared horde to stay where it was. Furthermore, if the citizens of East Germany could not be persuaded to work in the regions where they lived, the East German economy would never become viable. Finally, a commitment to immediate unification paid Kohl great political dividends.

The chancellor suddenly saw his lackluster image transformed into that of a great German statesman. The timing was particularly fortuitous, coming when his Christian Democratic party was losing ground to the rival Social Democrats. When Kohl had gone to Berlin in November 1989 to help celebrate the opening of the Wall, he had been repeatedly booed. The experience profoundly disturbed him. To his credit, Kohl recognized the uniqueness of this moment in history. He cast off his previous doubts and threw himself into the struggle for unification with single-minded determination. Almost overnight he built up a Christian Democratic party as a force in East German politics, enabling it to score an upset victory in the March 1990 elections. Kohl even crisscrossed the border to campaign directly in East Germany. At a rally in Erfurt at the end of February, he declared, "We are one Germany! We are one people!"[19] Soon he was being touted as the chancellor of the German Fatherland. His opponents now criticized his blitzkrieg tactics for their recklessness and presumption.

Kohl's refusal to renounce all claims to the territories east of the Oder-Neisse frontier, lands once German but now part of Poland, earned him more critics. Although the Federal Republic had already recognized the loss of these lands in its 1970 treaty with Poland and in the 1975 Helsinki accords, which affirmed the inviolability of frontiers, Kohl maintained that only a united Germany could make the final decision. But such legalisms did not impress the international community. Poland, in particular, feared that without a specific guarantee a united Germany would seek to revise the eastern frontiers. Kohl backed down. He claimed he had been misunderstood and had the Bundestag and the East German parliament pass resolutions stating that a united Germany would unconditionally guarantee the inviolability of the border with Poland. The matter was finally laid to rest in five specific paragraphs of Article I of the Treaty on the Final Settlement with Respect to Germany, which included the obligation of Germany and Poland to confirm their existing border with a treaty that had the force of international law. Germany further pledged that it had "no territorial claims whatsoever against any other states and shall not assert any in the future." The four victorious powers of World War II added their own guarantees.[20]

Throughout the process, the Soviets showed a great willingness to compromise, which was all the more remarkable considering that they had lost 26 million people during World War II. At the beginning of 1990, Gorbachev had opposed reunification. When it appeared inevitable, he tried to weaken German sovereignty by postponing a decision on German military alliances. Eventually, the Soviets dropped even this qualifier. However, in the "two plus four" treaty, initialed in Moscow on 12 September 1990, Germany had to renounce the manufacture and possession of nuclear, biological, and chemical weapons and agree to reduce its armed forces to 370,000 troops. In exchange, Germany would be considered fully sovereign, have complete control over Berlin, and be free to join alliances as it saw fit, even NATO. The Soviets agreed to withdraw all of their troops by 1994.

The united German government promised to ease their repatriation through special subsidies, including building new barracks for them in the Soviet Union. The united German government also pledged to give the Soviet Union general economic aid.

After forty-five years, the division of Germany officially ended on 3 October 1990. It was celebrated with ceremonies and festivities throughout the country. In Berlin at the stroke of midnight, a German flag, seventy-two yards square and carried by fourteen schoolchildren from both the East and West, was hoisted on the 132-foot flagpole in front of the Reichstag building, while fireworks thundered overhead. Next came a performance of Beethoven's Ninth Symphony, culminating, appropriately, in the "Ode to Joy."

Taking Charge

Kohl ended 1990 as the chancellor of 78 million united Germans, his position cemented by a Christian Democratic electoral triumph that had reduced the Social Democrats to their weakest position since the days of Konrad Adenauer. Part of the reason for the Christian Democrats' success was the rosy picture Kohl painted of the cost of unification. He promised that East Germany could become "a flowering garden" in five years without raising taxes. Kohl believed the hard work the task ahead would entail would restore the moral strength of the German people, which during the years of affluence had been covered over with "a layer of butter and kiwi and shrimp."[21]

But East Germany was a basket case. It was West Germany's Albania, with much of the land having no value. Some areas were so polluted with deadly chemicals and nuclear by-products that many residents were sick with cancer or had already died from the disease. Six thousand miles of rivers had been contaminated with raw sewage and chemical wastes that had killed all life. Forty-four percent of the forests had been damaged by acid rain. Toxic dump sites were everywhere. If West German environmental standards were applied to the factories of the East,

Germans celebrate the reunification of their country at Berlin's Brandenburg gate, 3 October 1990.

discharged so much radioactive steam into the air that they should have been shut down completely. The German Environment Ministry estimated that pollution in the East caused $18 billion worth of damage a year.[22] Moreover, as the Soviet forces began their repatriation, they left virtual junk heaps in the areas they had controlled. The hulks of broken-down motor vehicles and trashed weapons of war littered the landscape. The terrain they had used for artillery practice was permeated with unexploded shells. The soldiers stripped the buildings, taking the plumbing, woodwork, and anything else in scarce supply in their own country.

The first stage of German unification had taken place on 1 July 1990 when East Germany became a member of the Western economic community. The shock was instantaneous. Although East Germany had been an industrial powerhouse in the Communist bloc, its state-owned enterprises were highly inefficient compared to those in the West. Unable to compete, East German factories began to close in great numbers. Unemployment, which stood at 272,000 in July 1990, had almost quadrupled by the end of the year. An estimated 20 percent of the industrial workers and 50 percent of the agricultural workers were likely to lose their jobs.

The end of Communist domination also meant unemployment for thousands of party members and bureaucrats. The entire diplomatic corps, for example, was fired. These jobs, like those in other government departments, were filled with skilled non-Communists from the West. Even those East Germans who managed to retain their jobs often were not competitive by Western standards. Under Communism, they had not been required to work as hard or display the same initiative as workers in the West. Many West Germans looked down their noses at the "lazy Osties" and complained that all they wanted to do was live on handouts and sit around and drink coffee.

The East was clearly going to be a drain on the resources of the more prosperous West for some time to come. Kohl's promise not to raise taxes to pay for the transition proved to be election politics. Estimates of the cost of bringing the East up to the standard of living of the West ran as high as $2 trillion or more. The German government hoped that much of this money would come from private sources and set up a special department to try to sell former East German state property to potential investors.

Despite its immediate problems, Germany's economic power would be awesome once reunification was achieved. Many of Germany's neighbors feared that strength. Yet their fear seemed baseless since the development of German democracy and the firm integration of the country into the European Community had apparently solved the age-old problem of what to do with an aggressive, expansionist Germany. Chancellor Kohl believed that his country should flex its economic and political muscles only within the framework of a larger democratic union of states. Nevertheless, the union of the two medium-sized German states did create a new European superpower, which would no longer be content to defer to the leadership of the British and the French and, most likely, would again become the chief arbiter of European affairs.

WESTERN UNITY, EASTERN DIVISION

The Reinforcement of the European Community

The Americans believed they could continue to play a major role in the new Europe. But their influence was gradually declining. The high deficit spending of the Reagan years left the United States with a weakened economy and a soft dollar compared to the German mark, the Dutch guilder, or the Swiss franc. Following the collapse of Soviet power, the NATO alliance, through which American power had most directly affected the affairs of Europe, searched for a new mission. Thwarting an invasion from the east had been its sole raison d'être. Now that this threat had disappeared, the French thought it opportune to push for the creation of a new European military force outside the framework of the NATO alliance. The French had wanted such an independent military since the presidency of Charles de Gaulle and proposed to begin by raising the strength of an already existing Franco-German brigade to the size of a corps. The Germans seemed willing to cooperate in creating such a force, but the scheme alarmed the Americans.

At a meeting of the NATO powers in Rome, on 7 November 1991, President George Bush told the other members that if they wanted to go their own way on defense, they should come right out and say so. "Our premise is that the American role in the defense and affairs of Europe will not be made superfluous by European Union," he remarked in closed session. "If our premise is wrong, if, my friends, your ultimate aim is to provide independently for your own defense, the time to tell us is today."[23] Washington policymakers clearly could no longer chart the course of the Western alliance with full expectation of European compliance. Nevertheless, European leaders were not yet ready to sacrifice the stability and certainty of the NATO alliance system for something more indefinite. They agreed that the presence of the United States was vital to the security of Europe, but at the same time, they favored less reliance on nuclear weapons and more emphasis on multinational allied forces. They clearly wanted to assume more responsibility for their own security. Autonomy in matters of defense was a natural complement to the strength they had achieved from economic and political integration.

On 10 and 11 December 1991, the twelve countries of the European Community (EC) furthered the process of integration in a meeting at Maastricht in the southern Netherlands. On the first day of deliberations, the delegates adopted a broad financial arrangement directed toward monetary union. The scheme, first spelled out two years earlier by Jacques Delors, the president of the European Commission, envisaged a three-stage development for a common European currency. The Maastricht meeting created a timetable for these stages: in 1994, the EC would establish a European Monetary Institute as a prelude to establishing a central European bank; in 1997, it would inaugurate the European currency unit, or ecu, providing seven of the twelve EC members met certain stringent economic standards;[24] in 1999, it would adopt the ecu automatically even if fewer than a majority of states met the criteria. These measures seemed irreversible. The EC members expected that in time the ecu would be one of the world's strongest currencies.[25] Furthermore, a common currency, in Delors's view, would be a first step toward complete economic unity and would lead to coordinated policies on inflation, interest and exchange rates, and national budgets.

Despite the anticipated advantages of a common currency, the British reserved the right to opt out of any single-currency arrangement. They also received an "out" on social and political matters. Prime Minister John Major insisted that his country must be sovereign in defense and national security matters and must have the right to set its own policies on such things as vacations, maternity leave, and equality between men and women in the workplace. The British had even opposed describing the community as "federal"—known in Britain as the F-word.

The driving forces for European unity at the Maastricht meeting had been French president François Mitterrand and German chancellor Kohl. Both agreed on the need for a common defense policy and greater harmonization of domestic policies. Their goal was to raise the EC to the status of a world power. Kohl was a convinced European who wanted to increase the power of the 518-member European Parliament as a way of bolstering Germany's democratic system and aiding its reunification. Despite his efforts, however, the Maastricht delegates hardly changed the powers of the European Parliament. They gave the assembly the right to monitor the EC budget, but not the right to initiate legislation. The conference did agree to expand joint action in the areas of industrial affairs, health, education, trade, environment, energy, culture, consumer protection, and tourism. The member nations also agreed to coordinate their judicial and immigration policies and to improve cooperation on police matters by forming a new international police force known as Europol. The richer members specifically promised to provide more aid to their poorer associates—Spain, Portugal, Greece, and Ireland. At the same time, the delegates reaffirmed national sovereignty by deciding that a common foreign and security policy could only be adopted by unanimous vote. Once adopted, however, the policy could be applied by a two-thirds majority.

The Americans approved of the Maastricht agreement. Beginning with the Marshall Plan, they had consistently supported the cause of European unity even though their own influence had suffered as a result. The adoption of a new European currency posed further risks to that influence. Foreign banks, for example, might decide to hold a greater proportion of ecus than dollars, thereby undermining the power of the dollar in international finance. Furthermore, the agricultural policy of the EC, which hurt the sale of American farm products, now seemed less likely to be changed.[26] Already, Washington had been trying to persuade the Europeans to modify their protectionist policies in talks held the past year under the auspices of the General Agreement on Tariffs and Trade (GATT). In addition to being anxious about economic repercussions, the Americans feared that Germany presented a challenge to their political leadership of the Western alliance.

Chancellor Kohl felt that Germany need no longer be constrained by the ugly record of its past. The nation's firm commitment to democracy and European unity gave it the right to play a leading role in European affairs. A week after the Maastricht meeting, Kohl announced that Germany would recognize the independence of the secessionist republics of Croatia and Slovenia. At the same time, the Bundesbank, which was independent from the government but usually followed government policy, raised the prime lending rate to eight percent. Kohl argued that in recognizing Croatia and Slovenia, Germany was simply acknowledging the obvious fact that Yugoslavia was already dead. Recognition might even help end the fighting. Meanwhile Helmut Schlesinger, the president of the German central bank, justified the increase in the lending rate as essential to holding the German rate of inflation at its current four percent. These explanations were not convincing outside Germany.

Germany's recognition of Croatia raised the specter of a revived Teutonic bloc in Eastern Europe where German investment was already significant. People recalled that Nazi Germany had once been allied to the Fascist Ustashi, which had ruled Croatia during World War II. Additionally, Germany's decision to promote an increase in the value of the mark put German needs first. The Germans had made their decisions unilaterally and expected their EC partners to adjust as best they could. In fact, despite their fears that recognition of Croatia and Slovenia might encourage the Serbs to more determined resistance, the other members of the EC did "ratify" the German action. They stipulated, though, that Croatia and Slovenia must commit themselves to respect human and minority rights, agree to settle all future border questions peacefully, and establish a democratic government.[27] Recognition took place as promised on 15 January 1992.[28] On the monetary issue, the other EC states also had to adjust to Germany's fait accompli by raising their own prime rates. Increasing the prime rate presented a real hardship for Britain and France as both these countries had planned to stimulate their own economic expansion with a cheap money policy. Germany's action also destroyed what remained of the Bretton Woods arrangement under which industrial nations were to coordinate the value of their currency with each other.

Kohl reacted to complaints that his country was becoming overbearing by remarking that Germany had no reason "to be ashamed" of its actions since it had "great concern [for] the fate of others." He pointed to the efforts the Germans had made to support the reforms in Eastern Europe and to the cooperative position Germany had taken during the process of reunification.[29] Many Europeans, however, could not rid themselves of the suspicion that the Germans were seeking European hegemony under a new guise; that is, that Germany intended to dominate the new European superstate, though now its weapons would be economic power and market strength rather than armies and the threat of war.

The Commonwealth of Independent States

The dissolution of the Soviet Union had moved the political weight of Europe westward and enhanced Germany's position. The age-old rivalry between Germany and Russia, which had contributed to the outbreak of both world wars, was being redefined in a new geopolitical arrangement. But while Western European nations had submerged their old rivalries in the common pursuit of greater material prosperity, Eastern European nations were entering a new period of deprivation and turmoil. Nowhere was this more evident than in the republics of the Soviet Union whose people, accustomed to being told what to do, headed toward an uncertain future along the newly charted path of democracy and free enterprise.

Following the collapse of the ill-fated August coup, the last hurrah of Soviet centralism, the Soviet Union rapidly unraveled. On 29 August, the Congress of People's Deputies suspended the activities of the Communist party and froze its bank accounts, giving the coup de grace to one of the country's greatest cohesive forces. The republics rapidly usurped the powers of the Kremlin. Gorbachev recognized the demise of the central authority, but he still hoped to preserve a semblance of unity by holding the remains of the once-centralized country together with a new economic union. At the beginning of September, Gorbachev convinced the leaders of ten republics to agree to transfer authority to an emergency State Council that would run the country until a new union government could be fashioned. This new council officially recognized the independence of Latvia, Lithuania, and Estonia, on 6 September, and began negotiations to withdraw the 200,000 or more Soviet troops stationed in the Baltics. The other republics agreed to maintain the Soviet Union's collective defense with a single central control over the nuclear arsenal. The council began working on a plan for economic union.

Meanwhile, the disintegration of central authority continued. Many of the Soviet republics wanted to maintain some sort of economic ties with the other republics, but they also wanted to control their own resources and run their own governments. They could not have it both ways. Secessionist fever accelerated. The Russian republic had assumed control of the Soviet money supply and had begun regulating trade in gold, diamonds, and foreign currency. Yeltsin had taken over the old Soviet Finance Ministry and consolidated the Russian and Soviet budgets. The Russian republic had even assumed responsibility for paying the sal-

Map 19

aries of the remaining Soviet officials, including that of Gorbachev. Yeltsin prepared to absorb the KGB's domestic and foreign intelligence operations into the bureaucracy of the Russian republic.

In November, the Ukraine refused to join any new confederation and scheduled a referendum on sovereignty for 1 December. The Ukrainian leaders expected 70 percent of the people to vote for independence. They made preparations to issue the republic's own currency and went ahead with plans to create their own armed forces. When Leonid Kravchuk, the Ukrainian leader, met with Russian officials, he spoke in Ukrainian and had his words translated into Russian even though he was fluent in Russian.[30] At one time, Kravchuk had been a loyal Kremlin-centered Communist who worked to eradicate Ukrainian nationalism, but he had quickly trimmed his sails in the aftermath of the August coup. "A man cannot keep the same views all his life," he glibly explained.[31] The Ukrainians voted for independence by an astounding majority of 90 percent. Kravchuk stated categorically that he would not take part in any new union treaty, and he even disavowed his previous commitment to economic union, suspending all further payments to the Soviet budget. Yeltsin stated that if Ukraine would not sign, neither would he.[32]

Gorbachev protested. He insisted on his right to overrule any attempt by a republic to nationalize the Soviet armed forces, but the threat sounded hollow. In any case, Yeltsin ignored the threat and arranged to meet with Kravchuk and Stanislav Shushkevich, the leader of the Belorussian parliament, to discuss the formation of a new Slavic union. The meeting took place at a country estate near the city of Brest on 7 and 8 December 1991. The talks produced the Commonwealth of Independent States, a loosely knit organization that would coordinate the economic, political, and military affairs of its sovereign members. It had no enforcement powers. The three leaders agreed to respect each other's territorial integrity and to guarantee equal rights and freedom to their citizens. They also pledged to sign cooperative agreements on a wide range of political and economic issues from education to foreign policy. The commonwealth would have its capital at Minsk in Belarus (Belorussia), not at Moscow. Its nuclear weapons would remain under joint control "without distribution or division."[33]

In the course of the meeting, the three leaders wrote the obituary of the Soviet Union: "The Union of Soviet Socialist Republics, as a subject of international law and a geopolitical reality, is ceasing its existence."[34] Yeltsin, to show the irrelevancy of the Gorbachev government, dialed the White House to inform President Bush about the meeting before Shushkevich phoned the Kremlin to tell Gorbachev. The leaders of the other republics were then also informed and told that they could join the commonwealth, if they wished.

Nursultan Nazarbayev, president of Kazakhstan, suspected that the Slavic presidents were trying to create a union along religious, ethnic, and cultural lines and was hesitant to join. He argued that Gorbachev's economic union plan should be given a chance to work.[35] However, 40 percent of the people in his Muslim country were ethnic Russians. The Kazakhs themselves were actually a minority among the state's 16 million citizens. Under the circumstances, joining the new commonwealth was probably the least divisive choice. Nazarbayev, therefore, changed his mind and even insisted that Kazakhstan be considered a founding member. The membership of Kazakhstan persuaded the other Central Asian republics—Uzbekistan, Turkmenistan, Tadzhikstan, and Kirghizia—to suppress their fear of Slavic hegemony and also join. In fact, any of these states would have had difficulty surviving economically without some sort of association with another power.

The new commonwealth members considered the disposition of the old Soviet Union's nuclear arsenal, consisting of an estimated 27,000 to 30,000 warheads, at a meeting in Alma-Ata, the capital of Kazakhstan, on 21 December 1991.[36] Moldova and Azerbaijan, both commonwealth members, also sent delegates. Other items on the agenda included economic cooperation, human rights, and the future of Gorbachev. Gorbachev had strongly opposed the commonwealth structure and had even suggested that the way Yeltsin had handled its creation raised questions about his moral standards.[37] Even at this late hour, Gorbachev still believed he had a role to play in forming a new union and insisted that he wanted to "stay the course." "I feel that the capital I've accumulated should be fully used for the freedom of my country and international relations," he added.[38] Although Gorbachev was now the head of a nonexistent state, Yeltsin wanted to obtain his formal resignation as soon as possible because he still could cause mischief. He might, for example, convoke a meeting of the Supreme Soviet even though it would not have a quorum without the representatives from Russia and Ukraine.

Gorbachev announced his decision to "discontinue" his activities as president of the Soviet Union on 25 December 1991. He was regretful and bitter at being forced from office, but in his speech he focused on his accomplishments during the six years and nine months he had held office. He took pride in having inaugurated a multitier economy, ended the Cold War and the arms race, and halted Soviet interference in other nations' internal affairs. He took credit for eliminating the totalitarian system and replacing it with freedom of the press, freedom of worship, representative legislatures, and a multiparty system. He hoped to be remembered for these reforms:

I consider it vitally important to preserve the democratic achievements which have been attained in the last few years. We have paid with all our history and tragic experience for these democratic achievements, and they are not to be abandoned, whatever the circumstances, and whatever the pretexts. Otherwise, all our hopes for the best will be buried. I am telling you all this honestly and straightforwardly because this is my moral duty.[39]

The Legacy

Yeltsin's government now braced for the protests that were expected to erupt after the elimination of most price supports and the consequent rise in the cost of food on 2 January 1992. Yeltsin believed that an abrupt move to a market economy, rather than the gradual approach Gorbachev had advocated, was necessary to change people's behavior. He hoped that market forces would eventually produce deep changes in the structure of the economy. Few people had any idea what economic competition meant or how to exchange goods and services without central direction. State planning had eliminated any rational connection between the costs of production and prices. Yeltsin and his advisers anticipated that a rise in prices would bring a rush of goods into the market. If producers had to pay real costs for their materials, capital, and labor, they would learn the lessons of supply and demand. Higher prices would encourage greater production.

As soon as the Russian government lifted the controls, prices skyrocketed. The average cost of basic commodities rose 300 to 500 percent. But the supply of staple goods did not always increase as anticipated. People waited in long lines to buy bread and gasoline. The crisis also caused the value of money to decline.[40] To meet expenses, the government tripled the amount of currency in circulation, issuing bills in new denominations of 200, 500, and 1,000 rubles. Consequently, producers of durable goods and agricultural products traded for other commodities rather than selling their goods for almost worthless paper. However primitive, reversion to a barter system may have been a necessary phase in the transition from a planned economy to a market economy. It enabled people to learn about the value of commodities and to master the rudiments of a price system. Under the old regime, money did not necessarily ensure the ability to purchase goods. Sometimes personal connections were needed. Small wonder that the old party and managerial elites were opposed to the new system and tried to sabotage it. This resistance from the old guard was the true reason Gorbachev's reforms could not have succeeded.

Yeltsin knew this and, convinced he was pursuing the right course, proceeded with plans to denationalize large parts of the Russian economy. He promised to sell to the private sector a whole range of enterprises, including thousands of stores, cafés, construction firms, food processing plants, and other light industry. Yeltsin wanted to commercialize small trade as a prelude to privatization. He hoped to attract extensive foreign investment and expertise to help run the large state enterprises, many of which would also, in time, be privatized. Agriculture would undergo major changes as well. Government subsidies to state and collective farms would end. Land would be sold to individuals and families, and the government's role would be restricted to technical assistance and credit.

Two weeks after the reforms went into effect, some 5,000 people demonstrated in Red Square, demanding a return to Communism. Photographs of the crowd indicate that the demonstrators and, hence, the dissatisfied populace were mostly middle-aged or older. Shortly afterwards, Yeltsin spoke to the Russian parliament and exhorted its members not to lose their nerve. The president said that the

Russian people had not lost hope and accused entrenched bureaucrats of standing in the way of change. He charged that those state organizations that still had a monopoly over the production and distribution of certain goods were purposely forcing up prices.[41] He also blamed "criminal elements." Yeltsin concluded by preaching patience, promising that the benefits of his program would become evident in the next six to eight months. "The legacy we received [from 74 years of Communism] is simply depressing—it's as though an enemy had occupied and managed our land."[42] Yeltsin knew, however, that Russia would have to have help from the West for his reforms to succeed. In making a plea for that assistance, he warned: "If the reform in Russia goes under, that means there will be a Cold War [which could] turn into a hot war. There is again going to be an arms race."[43]

The confusion afoot in Russia also appeared in the other republics. Many of their leaders thought Yeltsin was proceeding too fast. The leaders of some states, especially those bordering Russia, felt they had no choice but to go along with Yeltsin and allow their prices to increase. Otherwise they might be faced with hordes of Russians descending upon them to buy up goods at cheap subsidized rates that no longer existed in the Russian republic. The republics' leaders foundered in indecision and lack of planning. There were no blueprints for dismantling totalitarian systems. In charting a course toward the new, they constantly had to confront the old. They argued over fundamentals and tried to make up for years of isolation from the rest of the world. The worth of democracy was on trial. If it could not satisfy the basic needs of the people, democracy might fail. Such a breakdown had already occurred in the republics of Central Asia and in Georgia. Indeed, rival groups had pushed Georgia to the brink of civil war.

Zviad Gamsakhurdia, the president of Georgia, had been elected with 87 percent of the vote in the country's first free elections. He once had been an outspoken advocate of human rights and a strong nationalist who was imprisoned for his opposition to the Kremlin. In power, however, he had become increasingly dictatorial and arbitrary, closing down the opposition press and imprisoning his political opponents. Dissatisfaction with his rule increased and led to demands for his resignation. He refused and his opponents sought to topple him by force.

In December 1991, armed units of the so-called Military Council laid siege to his Government House headquarters in Tbilisi. After sixteen days of fighting, Gamsakhurdia fled the country for Armenia. But he remained in exile only ten days. Returning to western Georgia, he called for a crusade against the Tbilisi regime and began recruiting an army. The Russian government expressed hope that the Georgian people would be able to find a peaceful solution to their problems, but realized it could do little to mediate the crisis.[44] Georgia had declined to join in the new Commonwealth of Independent States, and Moscow was anxious to withdraw its remaining troops from the country as soon as possible. With their own transition problems, the Russians could not afford to sort out the turbulent affairs of the Transcaucasus. The leaders of the Georgian Military Council had set a dangerous precedent in overthrowing a legally elected government, especially since they were hardly the democrats they pretended to be.

Adjustment was also extremely difficult in the three Baltic states, which, although sovereign, still remained tied to Russia by a common currency and a common market. Their industries were dependent on the supply of raw materials that Russia made available to them at less than the world-market price. It would take many years before these ties of half a century could really be severed. In January 1992, Estonia declared a three-month state of emergency in the face of mounting fuel and food shortages. Its parliament voted 53–37 to establish a joint government-parliamentary commission to assume wide powers over production and

Throughout the Soviet Union, people toppled the statues of the great Communist heroes. Here, a statue of Lenin, which used to stand in the main square of Riga, lies on its back before being carted off to the scrap heap. For the Latvians, the monument's demise in August 1991 is more than the symbolic end of the Communist system; it is also a strong statement of their desire to become independent.

distribution. The elimination of price controls was postponed. Estonia still depended on Russia for 90 percent of its trade.[45]

While the commonwealth republics tried to create new political and economic institutions, they also engaged in the frequently bitter task of dividing up the tangible assets and liabilities of the old Soviet Union. They had to decide how to apportion the massive $80 billion foreign debt and how to divide their common cultural,[46] scientific, administrative, and military property. The states had already agreed to unified control of the Strategic Deterrent Force—that is, nuclear weapons and rockets. Yeltsin currently possessed the Soviet Union's nuclear codes.[47] The republics also recognized that each republic had control over its local property and natural resources. But conventional military hardware and diplomatic property had to be apportioned.[48] At first, both the Russians and the Ukrainians claimed the entire Black Sea fleet, but eventually, they agreed to divide it. Even then, deciding how the division should be carried out and settling a whole host of other claims proved to be a long and arduous task.

EPILOGUE   The statues that the Communist system erected to its heroes expressed its aspirations for a perfect society. In truth, however, many of the "heroes" represented were tyrants and murderers. Thus, it is not surprising that people celebrated the end of Communist rule by toppling the statues. Throughout the country, these monuments were desecrated and consigned literally to the scrap heap of history.[49]

Gorbachev, to his credit, had realized that a modern society could not be built upon a culture of cynicism and resentment. He interpreted perestroika as an effort to "break the back of the totalitarian monster" that repressed people intellectually and forced them "to conform with stereotypes."[50] Yet, in attempting to reform Communism, he hastened its end and left in its place mass confusion and a renewed, frequently aggressive nationalism. In his role as tsar-liberator, Gorbachev inaugurated the mightiest peacetime revolution of the twentieth century. The nations that emerged out of the debris of the Soviet Union began the laborious task of transforming the political, social, and economic institutions of their civilization. They had to reallocate power, define new property rights, and create different human values. None of them had any real experience with free institutions. They had always played by the rules of democratic centralism, which taught them that there was only one right way to do something and that all those who thought otherwise were enemies and saboteurs. Pluralism was an alien concept. There was a similar lack of comprehension when it came to a free market system. People looked to the state to set their priorities and provide them with protection. Profit was a political rather than an economic concept. Communism had also repressed religious and ethnic identity in favor of class identity. The collapse of central government released the pent-up forces of nationalism, frequently in their most intolerant and aggressive forms. Harmonizing the forces of disintegration and reintegration would take many years, understanding them would take many more. Progress could not be assured, but the age of mutually assured destruction seemed over. The United States and the remnants of the Soviet Union began to scale down their nuclear arsenals, removing land- and sea-based delivery systems. Their missiles were no longer targeted at each other's cities and bases.

The downfall of the Soviet empire was one of the great defining moments in history, ranking in importance with the two great political eras inaugurated by World War I and World War II. After both conflicts, Europe had sought to regain its stability in the face of political and economic collapse. Now, the great powers enjoyed a harmony that had not been present in such degree at any previous time in the twentieth century. When Boris Yeltsin spoke to the United Nations Security Council on 31 January 1992, thereby making his debut as the head of an independent Russia, he said: "Russia considers the United States and the West not as mere partners, but rather as allies. It is a basic prerequisite for, I would say, a revolution in peaceful cooperation among civilized nations."[51] It is fair to say that none of his listeners ever expected to hear a Russian leader utter such words during their lifetime. Yet the period in which they lived had taught them not to take too much for granted. They knew that revolutions, like Janus, wear two faces and that such upheavals have as often spawned betrayal as rejuvenation.

ENDNOTES

1. Vincent J. Schodolski and Charles M. Madigan, "The Gorbachev story," *Chicago Tribune*, 11 March 1990, section 1, 1.
2. Alan J. Day, ed., *The Annual Register, 1988* (London: Longman, 1988), 105.
3. Vincent J. Schodolski, "Soviet reforms sowed political whirlwind," *Chicago Tribune*, 24 March 1991, section 4, 4.
4. Gorbachev interview, *Time*, 4 June 1990, 31.
5. Gyula Józsa, "The Heart of Gorbachev's Reform Package: Rebuilding the Party Apparatus," *The Soviet Union, 1988–1989: Perestroika in Crisis?* (Boulder: Westview Press, 1990), 23–29.
6. *Annual Register, 1990*, 105–6.
7. *Chicago Tribune*, 19 May 1991, section 1, 18.
8. *Chicago Tribune*, 13 November 1991, section 1, 4. See also Mikhail Gorbachev, *The August Coup: The Truth and the Lessons* (New York: HarperCollins, 1991).
9. See *Time*, September 1991, 20–55 and *U.S. News and World Report*, 20 August 1991, 128–41.
10. *Chicago Tribune*, 23 August 1991, section 1, 5.
11. Approved by the Executive Council of the Russian republic, the change took effect on 1 October 1991.
12. However, the Supreme Soviet of the Russian Republic adopted the 500-Day Plan by 213 to 2. *Time*, 24 September 1990, 58–60.
13. *Chicago Tribune*, 24 November 1991, section 7, 2.
14. *Chicago Tribune*, 2 September 1991, section 1, 4.
15. Joseph A. Reaves, "Growing legions of homeless roam Poland," *Chicago Tribune*, 23 September 1991, section 1, 2.
16. James L. Graff, "Power to the Pulpit," *Time*, 20 May 1991, 40.
17. The Serbs were, of course, Eastern Orthodox in religion, spoke their own language, and used the Cyrillic alphabet.
18. Interview with Egon Krenz, *Time*, 11 December 1989, 47.
19. James O. Jackson, "Waiting for the Magic Words," *Time*, 5 March 1990, 29.
20. *Annual Register, 1990*, 566.
21. Interview with Helmut Kohl, *Time*, 25 June 1990, 38.
22. Ray Moseley, "E. Germans fear ecological crisis," *Chicago Tribune*, 4 February 1990, section 1, 23.
23. Ray Moseley, "French plan for army irks president," *Chicago Tribune*, 7 November 1991, section 1, 16.
24. For example, total government debt had to be below 60 percent, and budget deficits could not surpass 3 percent of gross national product. Only France and Luxembourg met those standards at the time of the Maastricht meeting.
25. *New York Times*, 10 December 1991, A1 and A6.
26. *New York Times*, 12 December 1991, A8.
27. *Time*, 30 December 1991, 29.
28. Recognition by the EC was buttressed by recognition by many of the other European states: Poland, Hungary, Bulgaria, Austria, Norway, Estonia, Latvia, Lithuania, Switzerland, and Sweden.
29. *Chicago Tribune*, 11 January 1992, section 1, 3.
30. *Wall Street Journal*, 25 November 1991, A14.
31. *Time*, 23 December 1991, 22.
32. Calling the independent republic "Ukraine," meaning "on the edge (of Russia)," instead of "the Ukraine" makes sense only to speakers of English because the Ukrainian language, like the Russian language, does not have articles. The Ukrainians distinguish between a province and a sovereign state in the prepositional phrase "in the Ukraine," but they still retained the form used in the days of nonindepend-

ence. Apparently, they were less concerned with establishing political correctness than Ukrainian groups outside the country that advocated the change.

33. There would be three nuclear buttons, each controlled by a member of the commonwealth. All would have to be pushed simultaneously to launch rockets. However, Yeltsin moved swiftly to bring all these weapons under his own command so that only he and the chief of staff of the Russian military had the power to effect a launch.

34. *Time*, 23 December 1991, 30.

35. Nazarbayev, like Kravchuk, had been the Communist party leader in his republic and only left the party after the August coup.

36. Yeltsin flew here directly from meetings in Brussels with NATO officials. One of the matters discussed in Brussels was the possibility of eventual Russian membership in NATO, a prospect that British Foreign Secretary Douglas Hurd said was "a long way off." *Chicago Tribune*, 21 December 1991, section 1, 3.

37. Interview with Mikhail Gorbachev, *Time*, 23 December 1991, 26.

38. Ibid., 26, 27.

39. The complete text of Gorbachev's address appeared in the *New York Times*, 26 December 1991, A6.

40. The average Russian worker earned 432 rubles a month in 1991. This was worth $758 at the official rate of exchange, but only $4 on the open market. *Los Angeles Times*, 4 January 1992, A3.

41. *Chicago Tribune*, 17 January 1992, section 1, 5.

42. *Los Angeles Times*, 30 December 1991, A8.

43. *Chicago Tribune*, 2 February 1992, section 1, 1.

44. *Chicago Tribune*, 17 January 1992, section 1, 4.

45. Ibid., section 1, 4.

46. The opening of the Winter Olympic Games in Albertville, France, on 8 February 1992 raised the immediate problem of how the commonwealth republics would enter their athletes. They decided to have the athletes represent their individual republics but participate as a united team. The athletes marched together at the opening ceremony, entering the stadium to the strains of Beethoven's "Ode to Joy." When a team member won a gold medal, the Olympic flag was hoisted and the Olympic anthem played.

47. Russia had been designated the recipient by Belarus (Belorussia), Kazakhstan, and Ukraine, the other republics possessing such weapons.

48. *Time*, 13 January 1992, 25–26.

49. Place-names also fell victim to the new mood of emancipation, changing too fast for mapmakers to keep pace. Leningrad again became St. Petersburg, Gorky was back to Nizhi-Novgorod, and Sverdlovsk returned to Yekaterinburg (named after Peter the Great's wife). Cities named for former party secretary generals were renamed: Brezhnev, Andropov, and Chernenko became Naberezhnye Chelny, Rybinsk, and Sharypovo, respectively. The names of lesser Communist officials and other heroes also disappeared. *Time*, 27 January 1992, 36.

50. Mikhail Gorbachev, "My Final Hours," *Time*, 11 May 1992, 42–43

51. *Chicago Tribune*, 1 February 1992, section 1, 1.

A NOTE ON BIBLIOGRAPHY

This book has been written using a combination of sources: document collections, newspaper accounts, memoirs, biographies, monographs and other special studies, general histories, and annuals. Full citation of these works has been given in the endnotes, which serve as a guide for further reading. The literature on the history of Europe in the twentieth century is so vast that any list of materials could only scratch the surface. Nonetheless, the following standard reference books, which contain extensive bibliographies, should provide a reasonably representative selection. These bibliographies contain sub-divisions of author, title, and subject.

Derek Howard Aldcroft and Richard Roger, *Bibliography of European economic and social history* (Manchester, England: Manchester University Press, 1984).

American Historical Association, *Guide to historical literature* (New York: Macmillan, 1961).

Gwyn M. Bayliss, *Bibliographic guide to the two World Wars: An annotated survey of English-language reference materials* (London: Bowker, 1977).

Dieter K. Buse and Juergen C. Doerr, *German Nationalism: A bibliographic approach* (New York: Garland, 1985).

Frances Chambers, *France* (Oxford, England: Clio Press, 1980).

Council of Foreign Relations, *Foreign affairs bibliography: A selected and annotated list of books on international relations 1919–* (New York: Harper, 1933–).

Alfred George Enser, *A subject bibliography of the First World War* (London: André Deutsch, 1979).

Alfred George Enser, *A subject bibliography of the Second World War* (Boulder, Colorado: Westview Press, 1977).

Stephen M. Horak, *Russia, the USSR, and Eastern Europe: A bibliographic guide to English language publications* (Littleton, Colorado: Libraries Unlimited, 1982).

Paul Louis Horecky, *East Central Europe: A guide to basic publications* (Chicago: University of Chicago Press, 1969).

Clara M. Lovett, *Contemporary Italy* (Washington, D.C.: Library of Congress, 1985).

Royal Historical Society, *Annual bibliography of British and Irish history* (Hassocks, England: Harvester Press, 1986–).

Albert John Walford, *Walford's Guide to reference material* (London: Library Association, 1982).

The Bibliographic Index, a cumulative bibliography of bibliographies (New York: The H. H. Wilson Company, 1937–1992) regularly examines about 2,800 periodicals and lists those works which contain the most extensive bibliographies. See also Theodore Besterman, *A world bibliography of bibliographies* (Lausanne: Societas Bibliographica, 1939–66) and its supplement, Alice F. Toomey, *A world bibliography of bibliographies, 1964–1974* (Totowa, N.J.: Rowman and Littlefield, 1977).

INDEX

Fourteen Points, 67–68, 73, 79, 101
France
  agriculture in, 214
  AIDS in, 698–99, 699
  and Algerian War, 583–85, 728–29
  and allied intervention in Soviet
    civil war, 118
  and appeasement, 392, 395–97, 398,
    399
  army in, 163
  automobile industry in, 356, 357
  aviation in, 356
  at Casablanca Conference, 452–54
  colonial empire of, 82, 83
  Communists in, 284, 515, 577–78,
    732
  demand for reparations, 89
  democracy in, 279–86
  economy in, 162–65, 278, 285–86,
    578–80, 729, 732, 743–44
  and encouragement of Rhenish
    separatist movements, 179
  and European Community, 732–33,
    795–96
  Fifth Republic in, 587
  foreign refugees in, 360
  and foreign trade, 662
  and Fourth Republic in, 573–87
  General Confederation of Labor in,
    161, 577, 578
  and Geneva Protocol, 192
  and German remilitarization of
    Rhineland, 381–83
  and German repudication of war
    guilt clause, 193–94
  Great Depression in, 208, 213–14,
    215, 279–80, 358
  Hitler's diplomacy with, 374–75
  industry in, 286, 577–78
  and Italian colonial ambitions, 377
  labor movement in, 577–78, 731–32
  and Locarno Agreement, 181–83
  and loss of Vietnam, 581–83
  and Maginot Line, 382–83
  nationalization of, 578–80
  National Liberation front in, 728
  negotiations with Stalin, 400, 401
  and nuclear weapons, 649
  and occupation of Germany, 129,
    193–94, 525, 527, 532, 533,
    536, 537, 538
  and partitioning of Ottoman Empire,
    99
  and payment of reparations, 175–77
  Popular Republican Movement in,
    575–76, 577
  population in, 580–81
  and protest of May 1968, 731–32
  provisional government of, 573–77
  and recognition of Federal Republic
    of Germany, 660

  relations with Belgium, 173
  relations with Czechoslovakia, 174
  relations with Great Britain, 163,
    180
  relations with Hungary, 174
  relations with Poland, 173–74
  relations with Romania, 174
  relations with West Germany, 730,
    751–52
  relations with Yugoslavia, 174
  resistance movement in, 465, 467
  and Rhineland controversy, 87
  and Ruhr occupation, 178–79
  and Saar dispute, 87–88
  sexual revolution in, 696, 697
  socialists in, 284–86, 575–76, 577,
    578
  and Soviet expansion, 410–11
  and Spanish Civil War, 386, 387,
    388
  and Suez Crisis, 654–55, 656–57
  television broadcasting in, 683–84
  Third Republic in, 62–64, 419–20
  and Turkish revolution, 183–85
  urban planning in, 675, 676–77,
    678–80
  and Versailles Treaty, 80, 170–73,
    176–77, 178
  Vichy government in, 432–33, 438–
    39
  and Washington Conference, 190–92
  wine industry in, 214
  women in, 689–93
  in World War I, 10–14, 16, 19–20,
    20–22, 23, 31, 51–52, 59–60,
    62–63, 65–66, 68, 69–70, 141
  post World War I, 173–75, 180, 204
  in World War II, 416–20, 431, 438,
    493, 574
Francisme, 281
Franco, Francisco, 301, 360, 384–85,
  387, 388, 737–39
Franco-Prussian War (1870–1871), 3
Franco-Russian Alliance (1894), 3
Frank, Hans, 125, 431, 433
  war crimes trial of, 528–29
Frankfurt
  French occupation of, post World
    War I, 173
  Treaty of, 3
Franklin-Bouillon, Henri, 184
Franz Josef (Austria), 7, 50
Free Democratic party, in West
  Germany, 543
Freedom or Death, 6
Free French movement, 452–54
Free German Youth Movement, 551
Free University of Berlin, 540
Freikorps, 124–25, 126, 172, 224
French, John, 12, 18, 154
French Action, 280

French Brotherhood Union, 578
French Committee of National
  Liberation, 454
French National Committee, 453
French National Council of the
  Resistance, 560
French Solidarity, 281
French War College, 5
Freud, Sigmund, 319, 701
Frick, Wilhelm, 229
  war crimes trial of, 529
Friendship and Assistance with Greece
  and Turkey, Treaty of (1953), 652
Friendship and Cooperation, Treaty of
  (1927), 134
Fritsch, Werner von, 384
Fritzsche, Hans, war crimes trial of,
  528, 529
Friuli-Venezia Giulia, 589
Front Fighters, 136
Frottage, 321
Fumage, 321
Functionalism, 337
Funk, Walter, 240
Furtwängler, Wilhelm, 323
Futurism, 319, 332–35

G
Gabcik, Josef, 465
Gabo, Naum, 338
Gagauz, 779
Galicia, 15, 20, 88, 384
Galliéni, Joseph, 13
Gallipoli, 24, 184
Gallo, Robert, 698, 699
Gamelin, Maurice, 411
Gamsakhurdia, Zviad, 801–2
Garat, Joseph, 282
Garbai, Alexander, 97
Garnett, Alf, 685
Gas industry, nationalization of, in
  France, 579
Gasparri, Pietro, 151, 152
Gauguin, Paul, 329
Gaullist Union for the New Republic,
  729
Gaza Strip, 654, 656
Gdansk Agreement (1980), 763–64
Gedda, Luigi, 593
General Agreement on Tariffs and
  Trade (GATT), 796
General Association of Wheat
  Growers, 214
General Confederation of French
  Production, 284–85
General Confederation of Industry, 143
General Confederation of Labor, in
  France, 161, 284–85, 286, 577,
  578
General Electric Company, 190
Generalitat, in Spain, 299

PHOTO CREDITS